Fodor's 2000

New England

W9-CBD-789

Fodor's Travel Publications, Inc. • New York, Toronto, London, Sydney, Auckland
www.fodors.com/newengland

CONTENTS

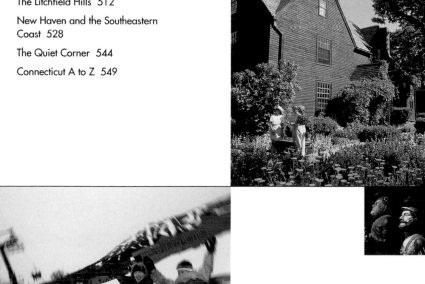

3

MAPS

Circled letters in text correspond to letters on the photographs. For more information on the sights pictured, turn to the indicated page number Ⓐ on each photograph.

DESTINATION
NEW ENGLAND

If New England didn't exist, Currier & Ives might have had to invent it. Its immaculate village greens, brilliant white clapboard churches, covered bridges, and lighthouses are national emblems, along with the seasons themselves: the Green Mountains in autumn oranges, the White Mountains mounded with snow, Cape Cod polka-dotted with beach-plum blossoms. But New England is much more than a colossal picture postcard: The historic sites witnessed events chronicled in classrooms across the country, the antiques shops and discount malls are legendary, and urban pleasures flourish, from lively restaurants to the performing arts. New England is a pleasure trove—if you know where to look.

Maine's rugged splendor sets it apart from its more pastoral neighbors. The state is vast—New England's Big Sky Country. Lush pine and spruce forests extend from a few miles inland all the way to the

MAINE

Canadian border, a ragged carpet of dark green punctuated by sparkling ponds and lakes where vacationers get cozy in rustic summer homes and generations of children have gobbled s'mores at camp. The streams that connect some of these clear blue waters, among them the celebrated Allagash River, attract canoeists from far and wide. But for most travelers Maine's coast is its big draw. You can pick blueberries (they are a major commercial crop on the northern end of the coast) or just enjoy the pristine quality of light at places like Ⓐ**Acadia National Park** and Ⓑ**Pemaquid Point Light.**

B 65

C 77

Photographers and painters have long been drawn by the light, beginning with the great 19th-century landscapist Winslow Homer, who first made a name for himself as a combat artist in the Civil War. (As in lovely ©**Castine**, you'll see many a monument to this conflict throughout the state: In the Battle of Gettysburg the 20th Maine Infantry Regiment held a strategic knoll called Little Round Top and helped determine the course of American history.) Lobster pots and buoys, monuments to another key coastal pleasure, stand at the ready up and down the shore at ⑩**Boothbay Harbor** and beyond. They're a constant reminder of what's cooking for dinner: sweet, sea-tangy lobster at sardine prices.

D 63

MAINE

Many states front the ocean, but none has a bond to the sea as powerful as Maine's. Long before Europeans came, Native Americans harvested the sea off the rocky shores. Vikings probably made landfall here, long enough for some murderous brawls with the natives. In 1607 colonists at Popham built the *Virginia,* the first European ship launched in the Americas. The sturdy sailing vessel took them back to England when things didn't work out. Today commercial fishing is in steep decline, but the maritime museums in Bath and several other towns as well as elaborate sea captains' homes up and down the coast recall Maine's seafaring glory days. As you travel along the sawtooth coast, skirting myriad inlets and venturing onto adjacent promontories, the sea remains a presence.

Sea views greet you at every turn, and you are never far from bracing salt breezes. Even the signage—on tackle shops, boatyards, seafood restaurants—is perpetually nautical. In summer, sailors turn out by the score to compete in regattas and schooner races, windjammers give romantic travelers a feel for the ships of Maine's past, and lighthouses, most of them unromantically run by computer, have their Kodak moments.

(One of the prettiest is Ⓔ**Portland Head Light**, dating from 1791; it's also the state's oldest.) Offshore, ferries and excursion boats—Maine's everyday transport—will take you to any number of rock-bound landfalls. On much-loved Ⓕ**Monhegan Island**, wildflowers carpet the meadows and an artist's colony has taken root, with accompanying restaurants and stores. You may not find the pirate gold that legend says is buried there, but you'll discover another slice of quintessential Maine, and that's good enough.

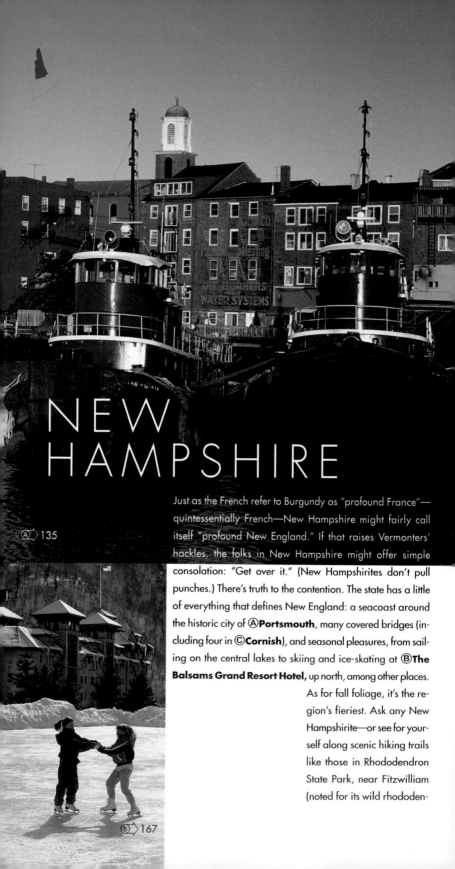

NEW
HAMPSHIRE

(A)>135

Just as the French refer to Burgundy as "profound France"—quintessentially French—New Hampshire might fairly call itself "profound New England." If that raises Vermonters' hackles, the folks in New Hampshire might offer simple consolation: "Get over it." (New Hampshirites don't pull punches.) There's truth to the contention. The state has a little of everything that defines New England: a seacoast around the historic city of (A)**Portsmouth**, many covered bridges (including four in (C)**Cornish**), and seasonal pleasures, from sailing on the central lakes to skiing and ice-skating at (B)**The Balsams Grand Resort Hotel,** up north, among other places. As for fall foliage, it's the region's fieriest. Ask any New Hampshirite—or see for yourself along scenic hiking trails like those in Rhododendron State Park, near Fitzwilliam (noted for its wild rhododen-

(B)>167

© 165

drons), and in the 770,000-acre White Mountain National Forest, way up north. It's positively soul-stirring to walk the section of the Maine-to-Georgia Appalachian Trail that passes through the forest and over the rocky, wind-pummeled summit of Mt. Washington, the Northeast's highest peak. But if you're not up to the exertion, not to worry: Driving up the ⒟**Mt. Washington Auto Road** yields equally stunning views. With most of New Hampshire's population in the industrial south, most of the state is gloriously rustic.

NEW
HAMPSHIRE

Artist Maxfield Parrish came to the west-central wilderness early in the 20th century to paint the Technicolor sunsets over the Connecticut River. Country life here, among other factors, charmed Robert Frost away from England, where he had spent a few years becoming a famous poet, to "live cheap and get Yankier

Ⓔ 168

and Yankier" on a farm near tiny Franconia. Succeeding, he attained a fierce streak of independence summed up by the state motto: Live Free or Die. The same spirit makes itself felt in many ways, not the least in the absence of a state sales tax, which is instrumental in parting shoppers from their money in the outlet stores of North Conway and antiques stores far and wide. You may also detect a certain brasher-than-usual gonzo attitude among the snowboarders flipping and flying at modern winter sports venues such as Ⓔ**Attitash Bear Peak**. Maybe it's the architecture

Ⓕ 154

Ⓗ 169

that forges the local character: Towns like Ⓖ**Walpole** and Hanover, home of Dartmouth College, are paragons of simple grace, devoid of affectation and flamboyance, yet as moving as any Gothic cathedral. Or perhaps it's all that wilderness that sets the tone in the state: Wouldn't life in a place like the ruggedly beautiful Ⓕ**Presidential Range** in the White Mountains cleanse a person of pretense? Hard weather builds character as well, and New Hampshire has its share: It was the weather station atop Mt. Washington, the king of the Presidentials, that recorded the highest winds

Ⓖ 184

ever measured on earth (231 miles per hour) as well as some of the most precipitous temperature drops. Ride the venerable Ⓗ**Mt. Washington Cog Railway** to the summit in summer, or tramp up Tuckerman's Ravine. Afterward repair to one of the charming inns around Jackson or to the bright, graceful veranda of the Ⓘ**Mount Washington Hotel**, sit back, and let New Hampshire nourish your soul.

Ⓘ 169

VERMONT

Having spent many years of his life in New Hampshire, Robert Frost is spending eternity in Vermont, buried in a lovely old churchyard in Bennington, in the southern part of the state. Even while alive he might not have noticed when he had crossed the border. "Anything I can say about New Hampshire," he wrote, "will serve almost as well about Vermont." Today, both contemporary residents and visiting New England observers might differ, however. Over the past few decades, many parts of Vermont have absorbed waves of middle-class urban refugees bent on taking up residence year-round. Along with these well-dressed masses, yearning to be stress-free, has come a touch of semiprecious gentrification. Vermont chic exists in the form of Range Rovers and top-of-the-line cold-weather gear. Whether this is good or bad is up to the beholder, and for millions of beholders, including closet Vermontophiles from New Hampshire, it is just fine. Some of the happy visitors come to ski at world-famous resorts such as Stowe, Sugarbush, Killington, Mount Snow, and the defiantly retro Ⓐ**Mad River Glen**, where expert skiers hone their skills on natural snow and steep, narrow trails that make few concessions to the intermediates to whom almost every other U.S. ski area kowtows. Other visitors drink in the charm of picture-book villages like Ⓑ**Newfane**. Still others stop along superscenic country roads like Ⓒ**Route 100**, to learn about maple syrup in local sugar shacks, or wet their lines in trout streams like the Battenkill. If that's your fancy, make a pilgrimage to one of angling's shrines—the American Museum of Fly Fishing in Manchester, home to Bing Crosby's rod and reel.

Ⓑ 220

Ⓒ 205

VERMONT

Some Vermontophiles maintain, only half jokingly, that all of Vermont should be made into a national park. Chuckle at the notion if you like, but you have to commend what's behind it: the desire to preserve a national treasure, all 9,609 square miles of it, for future generations. Since the national park designation is not even remotely in the cards, Vermont tries hard to preserve itself. Billboards are banned, and laws attempt to ensure that new buildings blend harmoniously into their surroundings. Artisans open their studios to show just how long and hard they labor to craft items such as hand-woven rugs and mouth-blown glass. (Ⓓ**Simon Pearce** in Quechee is famous for his beautiful work, made in a renovated mill.) New businesses, ranging from inns and innovative restaurants to bagel shops and travel agencies, are shoehorned into vintage barns, mills, and clapboard houses. And you will never see a highrise go up near a gazebo like the one on the green of Ⓔ**Craftsbury Common**, in the heart of the Northeast Kingdom, Vermont's most rural corner. Here and around Ⓕ**South Woodstock**, the farms are picture-perfect, and the mixed coniferous forests traversed by the celebrated

Ⓓ 225

Ⓔ 250

Long Trail through the Green Mountains seem more like sacred groves than ordinary woods. The bits of industry that do exist trade on Vermont's distinctive character: You will find cheese and Ben & Jerry's ice cream among them. Every carton of Chunky Monkey and Bovinity Divinity shipped into stores around the country and every round of cheese that goes out from the (G)**Cabot Creamery** in Cabot spreads the Vermont message a little farther. If not "America's Dairyland," like Wisconsin, it's at least New England's. There is even a cow on the official state seal, although cows no longer outnumber people.

(G) 263

Massachusetts, and arguably America, began on Cape Cod: The Pilgrims landed at what is now Provincetown before moving on to nearby Ply-

MASSACHUSETTS

mouth a few decades shy of 400 years ago. So it's fitting that Cape Cod is now one of America's favorite travel destinations. Sun, sand, and sparkling sea are the lures, of course, not any deep homing instinct that leads us back to ancestral ground. But it's an interesting notion, isn't it? To think that thousands of us keep returning, year after year, to the place where the first seeds of the United States were sown. There may be no other pocket of New England, not even coastal Maine, that relies more heavily on visitors than does Cape Cod. If people stopped coming, the Cape would revert to the marshlands

that still protect its inland acres from hurricanes and fearsome nor'easters. Owners of antiques shops and galleries like those packed into vintage clapboard houses in Brewster and Provincetown would soon fold up. The bunting would no longer flutter on the porches of landmarks like the Ⓐ**Brewster Store**. Boats would stand empty at the P'town docks, and 6 miles offshore, on the Ⓑ**Stellwagen Bank**, giant whales would spend their summer feeding and frolicking in tourist-free solitude. That will never be. Full of salty, windswept beauty, the Cape—and the neighboring islands of Nantucket and Martha's Vineyard—are irresistible, and those who love them return every year like swallows to Capistrano, to trek out to lovingly maintained lighthouses like the one at Nantucket's Ⓒ**Brant Point Light** and to body-surf, rock-hunt, look for eagles, and walk, endlessly, at beaches like Provincetown's Ⓓ**Herring Cove Beach**—some of the most glorious expanses of sand on earth.

Ⓑ 350

Ⓒ 368

Ⓓ 348

MASSACHUSETTS

Ⓔ 321

Ⓕ 414

Throw three darts at a map of Vermont or New Hampshire and visit the points that they hit. Chances are, these places will be beautiful and eat up rolls of film. Chances are, also, that they will resemble each other in topography, architecture, and speech patterns. Try the same exercise with a map of Massachusetts—the most cosmopolitan and diverse corner of New England—and you may think you've ended up in three different states (or three centuries). In museum villages like Ⓔ**Plimoth Plantation** in Plymouth, costumed interpreters demonstrate the Pilgrim fathers' sturdy determination to make a go of it against all odds in the New World; Ⓖ**Old Sturbridge Village** in Sturbridge, in the center of the state, documents the changes of early America confronting the Industrial Revolution. In the gently rolling Berkshire Hills to the west, at a lovely Lenox estate known as Ⓕ**Tanglewood**, magnificent hedges and spreading trees date from the late 19th century, as does some of the music that's the big draw in summer, supplied by Seiji Ozawa and the Boston Symphony Orchestra. Boston takes

Ⓖ 401

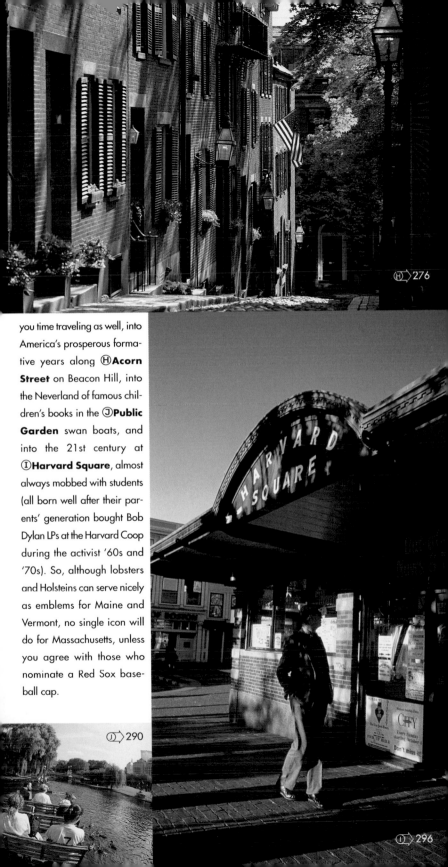

you time traveling as well, into America's prosperous formative years along Ⓗ**Acorn Street** on Beacon Hill, into the Neverland of famous children's books in the Ⓙ**Public Garden** swan boats, and into the 21st century at Ⓘ**Harvard Square**, almost always mobbed with students (all born well after their parents' generation bought Bob Dylan LPs at the Harvard Coop during the activist '60s and '70s). So, although lobsters and Holsteins can serve nicely as emblems for Maine and Vermont, no single icon will do for Massachusetts, unless you agree with those who nominate a Red Sox baseball cap.

Ⓗ▷276

Ⓙ▷290

Ⓘ▷296

RHODE ISLAND

Years ago a former governor of Texas named Pat Neff, having shed the burdens of office and, with them, the need to care about whatever bubbled out of his mouth, proclaimed, "Texas could wear Rhode Island as a watch fob." (One wonders whether the governor had designs on Massachusetts as a tie clip.) Yet for the smallest state in the Union, Rhode Island is long on diversions.

About a fifth of the National Historic Landmarks in the United States sit within Rhode Island's compact borders, some near the handsome Riverwalk in Ⓐ**Providence**, the state capital and the home of Brown University. If you visit the 1786 mansion of John Brown, one of the school's founding fathers, contemplate the source of the family wealth: the China trade and the slave trade. Many other

landmarks are in Newport, including a number of marble-and-gilt "cottages" like ⒷⒸ**The Breakers**, where a Texas oilman with a jumbo ego might wish to spend his summer. Cornelius Vanderbilt II, who created the mansion, spent his Augusts clinking champagne flutes with his buddies in their own ballrooms, rallying on the grass tennis courts of the Newport Casino, and letting sea breezes put pretense behind him on the waters of Narragansett Bay, much like the Wall Street titans who summer in Rhode Island today.

Ⓐ 542

CONNECTICUT

New England's most distinctive border with the rest of America is in Connecticut. While you don't notice much change as you move from Massachusetts or Vermont into upstate New York, the regional feeling is very striking when you come into the area from New York's Westchester County, immediately north of the Bronx. The stone walls of nearby towns as well as those farther afield like Ⓐ**Stonington** take on a special poignancy here, as if they are barriers to the encroachment of the glitz and bustle from points south. With the state's many highways, it's all too

Ⓑ 489

easy to shoot past such bits of New England charm. Those who pause are rewarded along the coast by reminders of the area's seafaring past, such as the Ⓑ**Maritime Aquarium** in Norwalk, and in ©Ⓓ**Mystic Seaport**, aboard the *Joseph Conrad* ship and in its Wendell Building, where 17 figureheads are on display. Inland and northward on up to the border with Massachusetts, all across the state, picturesque small towns such as Ridgefield, Litchfield, and Salisbury, each a study in white clapboards and green shutters, can hold their own with any on the New England scene; Woodstock's Ⓔ**Roseland Cottage,** a rosy example of the Gothic Revival style, epitomizes New England grace. Home to many a bedroom community of commuters who earn their big bucks in Manhattan, much of Connecticut is wealthy as well. (Local wags call the annual Greenwich–Darien high school football game the "BMW Bowl.") As you leave Connecticut through the lovely towns of Fairfield County, treat yourself to a gawking tour of the local streets. It's a nice place to visit, and you may want to live there, if you don't already. Come to think of it, the same could be said of New England as a whole.

Ⓔ 547

GREAT ITINERARIES

Highlights of New England

14 to 19 days

In a nation where distances can often be daunting, New England packs its highlights into a remarkably compact area. Understanding Yankeedom might take a lifetime—but it's possible to get a good appreciation for the six-state region in a 2- to 2½-week drive.

HARTFORD

1 day. The Mark Twain House resembles a Mississippi steamboat beached in a Victorian neighborhood. Downtown, visit Connecticut's ornate State Capitol and the Wadsworth Atheneum, which houses fine Impressionist and Hudson River School paintings.
☞ *Hartford and the Connecticut River Valley in Chapter 6.*

LOWER CONNECTICUT RIVER VALLEY, BLOCK ISLAND SOUND

1 or 2 days. Here centuries-old towns such as Essex and Chester coexist with a well-preserved natural environment. In Rhode Island, sandy beaches dot the coast in Watch Hill, Charlestown, and Narragansett.
☞ *Hartford and the Connecticut River Valley in Chapter 6, South County in Chapter 5.*

NEWPORT

1 day. Despite its Colonial downtown and seaside parks, to most people New-

port means mansions—the most opulent, cost-be-damned enclave of private homes ever built in the United States. Turn-of-the-century "cottages" such as The Breakers and Marble House are beyond duplication today.
☞ *Newport County in Chapter 5.*

PROVIDENCE
1 day. Rhode Island's capital holds treasures in places such as Benefit Street, with its Federal-era homes, and the Museum of Art at the Rhode Island School of Design. Savor a knockout Italian meal on Federal Hill and visit Waterplace Park.
☞ *Providence in Chapter 5.*

CAPE COD
2 or 3 days. Meander along Massachusetts' arm-shape peninsula and explore Cape Cod National Seashore. Provincetown, at the Cape's tip, is Bohemian, gay, and touristy, a Portuguese fishing village on a Colonial foundation. In season, you can whale-watch here.
☞ *Cape Cod in Chapter 4.*

PLYMOUTH
1 day. "America's home-town" is where 102 weary settlers landed in 1620. You can climb aboard the replica *Mayflower II,* then spend time at Plimoth Plantation, staffed by costumed "Pilgrims."
☞ *Boston in Chapter 4.*

BOSTON
2 or 3 days. In Boston, the famous buildings are not merely civic landmarks but national icons. From the Boston Common, the Freedom Trail extends to encompass foundation stones of American liberty such as Old North Church and the Paul Revere House. Walk the gaslit streets of Beacon Hill, too. On your second day, explore the Museum of Fine Arts and the grand boulevards and shops of Back Bay. Another day, visit the Cambridge campus of Harvard University and its museums.
☞ *Boston in Chapter 4.*

SALEM AND NEWBURYPORT
1 or 2 days. In Salem, many sites, including the Peabody and Essex Museum, recall the dark days of the 1690s witch hysteria and the fortunes amassed in the China trade. Newburyport's Colonial and Federal homes testify to Yankee enterprise on the seas.
☞ *The North Shore in Chapter 4.*

MANCHESTER AND CONCORD
1 day. Manchester, New Hampshire's largest city, holds the Amoskeag Textile Mills, a reminder of New England's industrial past. Smaller Concord is the state capital. Near the State House is the fine Museum of New Hampshire History, housing one of the locally built stagecoaches that carried Concord's name throughout the West.
☞ *Western and Central New Hampshire in Chapter 2.*

GREEN MOUNTAINS AND MONTPELIER
1 or 2 days. Route 100 travels through the heart of the Green Mountains, whose rounded peaks assert a modest grandeur. Vermont's vest-pocket capital, Montpelier, has the gold-dome Vermont State House and the quirky Vermont Museum.
☞ *Central Vermont and Northern Vermont in Chapter 3.*

WHITE MOUNTAINS
1 day. U.S. 302 threads through New Hampshire's White Mountains, passing beneath brooding Mt. Washington and through Crawford Notch. In Bretton Woods the Mt. Washington Cog Railway still chugs to the summit, and the Mount Washington Hotel recalls the glory days of White Mountain resorts.
☞ *The White Mountains in Chapter 2.*

PORTLAND
1 day. Maine's maritime capital shows off its restored waterfront at the Old Port Exchange. Nearby, two lighthouses on Cape Elizabeth, Two Lights and Portland Head, stand vigil.
☞ *Portland to Pemaquid Point in Chapter 1.*

Fall Foliage Tour
7 to 12 days

In fall, New England's dense forests explode into reds, oranges, yellows, and purples. Like autumn itself, this itinerary works its way south from northern Vermont into Connecticut. Nature's schedule varies from year to year; as a rule, this trip is best begun around the third week of September. Book accommodations well in advance.

NORTHWESTERN VERMONT
1 or 2 days. In Burlington the elms will be turning color on the University of Vermont campus. A ferry ride across Lake Champlain affords great views of Vermont's Green Mountains and New York's Adirondacks. After visiting the resort town of Stowe, continue beneath the cliffs of Smugglers' Notch. The north country's palette unfolds in Newport, where the blue waters of Lake Memphremagog reflect the foliage.
☞ *Northern Vermont in Chapter 3.*

NORTHEAST KINGDOM
1 day. After a side trip along Lake Willoughby, explore St. Johnsbury, where the St. Johnsbury Athenaeum and Fairbanks Museum reveal Victorian tastes in art and natural-history collecting. In Peacham, stock up for a picnic at the Peacham Store.
☞ *Northern Vermont in Chapter 3.*

WHITE MOUNTAINS AND LAKES REGION
1 or 2 days. In New Hampshire, I–93 narrows as it winds through craggy Franconia Notch. Watch for the Old Man of the Mountain, a natural rock profile. The sinuous Kancamagus Highway passes through the mountains to Conway. In

Center Harbor in the Lakes Region, you can ride the M/S *Mount Washington* for views of the Lake Winnipesaukee shoreline, or ascend to Moultonborough's Castle in the Clouds for a falcon's-eye look at the colors.
☞ *The White Mountains and Lakes Region in Chapter 2.*

MT. MONADNOCK REGION

1 or 2 days. In Concord stop at the Museum of New Hampshire History and the State House. Several trails climb Mt. Monadnock, near Jaffrey Center, and colorful vistas extend as far as Boston.
☞ *Western and Central New Hampshire in Chapter 2.*

THE BERKSHIRES

1 or 2 days. The scenery around Lenox, Stockbridge, and Great Barrington has long attracted the talented and the wealthy. You can visit the homes of novelist Edith Wharton (the Mount, in Lenox), sculptor Daniel Chester French (Chesterwood, in Stockbridge), and diplomat Joseph Choate (Naumkeag, in Stockbridge).
☞ *The Berkshires in Chapter 4.*

THE LITCHFIELD HILLS

1 or 2 days. This area of Connecticut combines the feel of up-country New England with exclusive exurban polish. The wooded shores of Lake Waramaug harbor country inns and wineries in New Preston and other pretty towns. Litchfield has a village green that could be the template for anyone's idealized New England town center.
☞ *The Litchfield Hills in Chapter 6.*

THE MOHAWK TRAIL

1 day. In Shelburne Falls, Massachusetts, the Bridge of Flowers displays the last of autumn's blossoms. Follow the Mohawk Trail as it ascends into the Berkshire Hills—and stop to take in the view at the hairpin turn just east of North Adams. In Williamstown the Sterling and Francine Clark Art Institute houses a collection of Impressionist works.
☞ *The Pioneer Valley and the Berkshires in Chapter 4.*

Newport
Lake Memphremagog
5
Lake Willoughby
100
100C
46 mi
15
65 mi
5
St. Johnsbury
Lake Champlain
Smugglers' Notch
Burlington
108
Stowe
100
89
36 mi
Peacham
93
Montpelier
75 mi
Franconia Notch
KANCAMAGUS HWY
112
Conway
White Mountains
16
39 mi
25
Center Harbor
104
Moultonborough
Lake Winnipesaukee
MAINE
93
Kennebunkport
9
85 mi
NEW HAMPSHIRE
40 mi
202
202
Concord
Portsmouth
1
47 mi
Odiorne Point State Park
Hampton Beach
1A
Manchester
Newburyport
Parker River NWR
VERMONT
Mt. Monadnock
Jaffrey Center
1A
Rockport
133
Williamstown
127
Gloucester
North Adams
MOHAWK TRAIL
2
2
202
22 mi
MASSACHUSETTS
Salem
65 mi
7
Berkshires
72 mi
Shelburne Falls
1A
ATLANTIC OCEAN
Boston
93
3
Lenox
Stockbridge
Great Barrington
Provincetown
6
78 mi
Plymouth
7
Litchfield Hills
3
125 mi
6
Cape Cod
45
Litchfield
RHODE ISLAND
202
New Preston
Providence
New Bedford
Lake Waramaug
Hartford
Narragansett Bay
24
114
195
6
6
CONNECTICUT
138
Newport
New London
Groton
1
66 mi
1
Mystic
Watch Hill
Long Island Sound

Portland
1
Cape Elizabeth
Brunswick
Bath
Freeport
1

The Seacoast
8 to 14 days

Every New England state except Vermont borders on salt water. For history buffs this means there are plenty of vivid links to the days when the sea was the region's lifeblood; for water-sports enthusiasts, it's a guarantee of fun on beaches from the sandy shores of Long Island Sound to the bracing waters of down east Maine. A journey along the coast also brings the promise of fresh seafood, incomparable sunrises, and a quality of light that has entranced artists from Winslow Homer to Edward Hopper.

re-created Pilgrim village. ☞ *Boston and Cape Cod in Chapter 4.*

BOSTON, THE NORTH SHORE
2 days. To savor Boston's centuries-old ties to the sea, take a half-day stroll by Faneuil Hall and Quincy Market or a boat tour of the harbor. In Salem, America's early shipping fortunes are chronicled in the Peabody and Essex Museum and the Salem Maritime National Historic Site. Spend a day exploring more of the North Shore, including the old fishing port of Gloucester and Rockport, one possible place to buy that seascape painted in oils. Newburyport, with its Federal-era shipowners'

Cape Elizabeth, with its Portland Head and Two Lights lighthouses.
☞ *The Coast in Chapter 2 and York County Coast and Portland to Pemaquid Point in Chapter 1.*

Campobello Island

DOWN EAST
2 or 3 days. Beyond Portland ranges the ragged, island-strewn coast that Mainers call Down East. On your first day, travel to Camden or Castine. Some highlights are the retail mecca Freeport, home of L. L. Bean; Brunswick, with the museums of Bowdoin College; and Bath, with the Maine Maritime Museum and Shipyard. Perhaps you'll think about cruising on one of the schooners that sail out of Rockland. In Camden and Castine, exquisite inns occupy homes built from inland Maine's gold, timber. On your second day, visit the spectacular rocky coast of Acadia National Park, near the resort town of Bar Harbor. If you have another day, drive the desolately beautiful stretch of Maine's granite coast to the New Brunswick border, where President Franklin Roosevelt's "beloved island," Campobello, and Roosevelt Campobello International Park lie across an international bridge.
☞ *Portland to Pemaquid Point, Penobscot Bay, Mount Desert Island, and Way Down East in Chapter 1.*

Castine
Camden
Rockland
Bar Harbor
Acadia National Park

SOUTHEASTERN CONNECTICUT, NEWPORT
1 to 3 days. Begin in New London, home of the U.S. Coast Guard Academy, and stop at Groton to tour the *Nautilus* at the Submarine Force Museum. In Mystic the days of wooden ships and whaling adventures live on at Mystic Seaport museum. In Rhode Island, savor the Victorian resort of Watch Hill and the Block Island Sound beaches. See the extravagant summer mansions in Newport. ☞ *New Haven and the Southeastern Coast in Chapter 6, South County and Newport County in Chapter 5.*

MASSACHUSETTS' SOUTH SHORE AND CAPE COD
2 to 4 days. New Bedford was once a major whaling center; exhibits at the New Bedford Whaling Museum capture this vanished world. Cape Cod can be nearly all things to all visitors, with quiet Colonial villages and lively resorts, gentle bay-side wavelets and crashing surf. In Plymouth visit the *Mayflower II* and Plimoth Plantation, the

homes, is home to the Parker River National Wildlife Refuge, beloved by birders and beach-walkers.
☞ *Boston and the North Shore in Chapter 4.*

NEW HAMPSHIRE AND SOUTHERN MAINE
1 or 2 days. New Hampshire fronts the Atlantic for a scant 18 miles, but its coastal landmarks range from honky-tonk Hampton Beach to quiet Odiorne Point State Park in Rye and pretty Portsmouth, whose Georgian and Federal mansions once sheltered the cream of pre-Revolutionary society. Visit a few at Strawbery Banke Museum and elsewhere. Between here and Portland, Maine's largest city and the site of a waterfront revival, you will find oceanside resorts such as Kennebunkport. Near Portland is

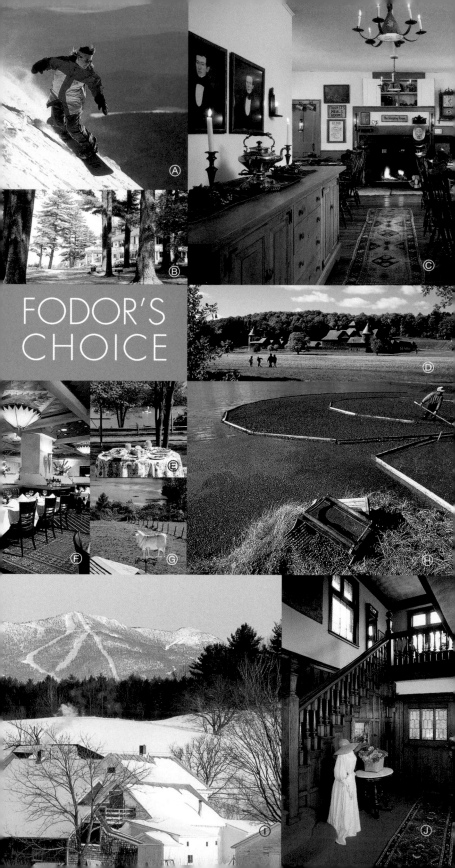

FODOR'S
CHOICE

Even with so many special places in New England, Fodor's writers and editors have their favorites. Here are a few that stand out.

FLAVORS

ⓖ Golden Lamb Buttery, Brooklyn, CT. This is Connecticut's most unusual—and magical—dining experience. *$$$$* ☞ p. 545

Go Fish, Mystic, CT. This big, bright, colorful restaurant serves up the bounty of the sea. *$$–$$$* ☞ p. 541

White Barn Inn, Kennebunkport, ME. One of Maine's best restaurants, it combines fine dining with unblemished service in a rustic setting. *$$$$* ☞ p. 48

Round Pond Lobstermen's Co-op, Round Pond, ME. For lobster-in-the-rough, you can't beat this dockside takeout. *$* ☞ p. 65

Blantyre, Lenox, MA. If you choose to dine on the imaginative French cuisine here, set aside several hours and dress up. *$$$$* ☞ p. 412

Chillingsworth, Brewster, MA. The chefs at this cozy spot prepare luscious French fare. *$$$$* ☞ p. 339

ⓔ Biba, Boston, MA. The city's favorite place to see and be seen serves gutsy fare from five continents. *$$$–$$$$* ☞ p. 298

The Balsams Grand Resort Hotel, Dixville Notch, NH. The summer buffet lunch is heaped upon a 100-ft-long table; dinners might include salmon with caviar. *$$–$$$* ☞ p. 167

Al Forno, Providence, RI. The Italian dishes here make the most of the region's fresh produce. *$$$* ☞ p. 433

COMFORTS

Boulders Inn, New Preston, CT. This idyllic inn on Lake Waramaug has panoramic views. *$$$$* ☞ p. 513

ⓙ Manor House, Norfolk, CT. Twenty stained-glass windows by Louis Tiffany are a unique feature. *$$$–$$$$* ☞ p. 520

Lodge at Moosehead Lake, Greenville, ME. This lumber baron's mansion is as luxurious as it gets in the North Woods. *$$$$* ☞ p. 113

ⓕ Ullikana, Bar Harbor, ME. Within this Tudor mansion is a riot of color and art. Water views and gourmet breakfasts make it a real treat. *$$–$$$$* ☞ p. 84

Charlotte Inn, Edgartown, MA. Rooms in one of the region's finest inns are smartly furnished. *$$$$* ☞ p. 360

Ritz-Carlton, Boston, MA. A perennial favorite stands for understatement combined with luxury. *$$$$* ☞ p. 308

ⓒ Historic Merrell Inn, South Lee, MA. Built as a stagecoach stopover around 1794, this inn has an unfussy style. *$$–$$$* ☞ p. 417

ⓑ Manor on Golden Pond, Holderness, NH. The rooms in this English-style manor are filled with luxurious touches. *$$$$* ☞ p. 148

Snowvillage Inn, Snowville, NH. Rooms in this book-filled inn near North Conway are named after authors; the nicest, with 12 windows, is a tribute to Robert Frost. *$$–$$$$* ☞ p. 160

Weekapaug Inn, Weekapaug, RI. This retreat is on a peninsula surrounded by the tidal waters of Quonochontaug Pond. *$$$$* ☞ p. 444

West Mountain Inn, Arlington, VT. A former 1840s farmhouse anchors a llama ranch with 150 acres of glorious views. *$$$$* ☞ p. 210

ⓓ Inn at Shelburne Farms, Shelburne, VT. This Tudor-style inn sits on the edge of Lake Champlain. *$$–$$$$* ☞ p. 256

SKI RESORTS

ⓐ Sugarloaf/USA, ME. At 2,820 ft, Sugarloaf/USA's vertical drop is greater than that of any other New England ski peak except Killington. ☞ p. 109

Sunday River, ME. Good snowmaking and reliable grooming ensure great snow from November to May. ☞ p. 105

Attitash Bear Peak, NH. There's always something innovative happening here—from demo days to race camps. ☞ p. 168

Jay Peak, VT. It gets the most natural snow of any Vermont ski area. ☞ p. 260

Mad River Glen, VT. The apt motto at this area owned by a skiers cooperative is "Ski It If You Can." ☞ p. 241

ⓘ Smugglers' Notch, VT. Morse Mountain at Smugglers' is tops for beginners. ☞ p. 252

Sugarbush, VT. Sugarbush is an overall great place to ski; nearly everyone will feel comfortable. ☞ p. 241

MEMORABLE SIGHTS

Long Island Sound from Stonington, CT. Wander past the historic buildings and climb up into the Old Lighthouse Museum for a spectacular view. ☞ p. 542

Sunrise from Cadillac Mountain, Mt. Desert Island, ME. From the summit you have a 360° view of the ocean, islands, woods, and lakes. ☞ p. 86

ⓗ Cranberry harvest time, Cape Cod and Nantucket, MA. Cape Cod's Rail Trail passes salt marshes, cranberry bogs, and ponds. On Nantucket, visit lovely Milestone Bog. ☞ p. 372

Cobblestone streets and antique houses, Nantucket, MA. Settled in the mid-17th century, Nantucket has a pristine town center. ☞ p. 367

Early October views, Kancamagus Highway, NH. The White Mountain vistas on this 34-mi drive burst into color each fall. ☞ p. 158

Bellevue Avenue, Newport, RI. Mansions with pillars and marble preside over gardens and lawns that roll to the ocean. ☞ p. 464

The Appalachian Gap, Route 17, VT. Views from this mountain pass near Bristol are a just reward for the challenging drive. ☞ p. 238

1 MAINE

At its extremes Maine measures 300 miles by 200 miles; all the other states in New England could fit within its perimeters. The Kennebunks hold classic townscapes, rocky shorelines, sandy beaches, and quaint downtown districts. Portland has the state's best selection of restaurants, shops, and cultural offerings, and Freeport is a mecca for outlet shoppers. North of Portland, sandy beaches give way to rocky coast. Acadia National Park is one of Maine's treasures. Outdoors enthusiasts head to inland Maine's lakes and mountains and the vast North Woods.

Revised and
updated by
Hilary M.
Nangle

ON THE MAINE–NEW HAMPSHIRE BORDER is a sign that plainly announces the philosophy of the region: WELCOME TO MAINE: THE WAY LIFE SHOULD BE. Local folk say too many cars are on the road when you can't make it through the traffic signal on the first try. Romantics luxuriate upon the feeling of a down comforter on an old, yellowed pine bed or in the sensation of the wind and salt spray on their faces while cruising in a historic windjammer. Families love the unspoiled beaches and safe inlets dotting the shoreline and the clear inland lakes. Hikers and campers are revived by the exalting and exhausting climb to the top of Mt. Katahdin, and adventure seekers get their thrills rafting the Kennebec or Penobscot river.

There is an expansiveness to Maine, a sense of distance between places that hardly exists elsewhere in New England, and along with the sheer size and spread of the place there is a tremendous variety of terrain. People speak of "coastal" Maine and "inland" Maine, as though the state could be summed up under the twin emblems of lobsters and pine trees. Yet the topography and character in this state are a good deal more complicated.

Even the coast is several places in one. Portland may be Maine's largest city, but its attitude is decidedly more big town than small city. South of this rapidly gentrifying city, Ogunquit, Kennebunkport, Old Orchard Beach (sometimes called the Québec Riviera because of its popularity with French Canadians), and other resort towns predominate along a reasonably smooth shoreline. North of Portland and Casco Bay, secondary roads turn south off U.S. 1 onto so many oddly chiseled peninsulas that it's possible to drive for days without retracing your route. Slow down to explore the museums, galleries, and shops in the larger towns and the antiques and curio shops and harborside lobster shacks in the smaller fishing villages on the peninsulas. Freeport is an entity unto itself, a place where a bewildering assortment of off-price, name-brand outlets has sprung up around the famous outfitter L. L. Bean.

Inland Maine likewise defies characterization. For one thing, a lot of it is virtually uninhabited. This is the land Henry David Thoreau wrote about in *The Maine Woods* more than 150 years ago; aside from having been logged over several times, much of it hasn't changed since Thoreau and his Native American guides passed through. Ownership of vast portions of northern Maine by forest-products corporations has kept out subdivision and development; many of the roads here are private, open to travel only by permit.

Wealthy summer visitors, or "sports," came to Maine beginning in the late 1800s to hunt, fish, and play in the clean air and clean water. The state's more than 6,000 lakes and more than 3,000 mi of rivers and streams still attract such people, and more and more families, for the same reasons. Sporting camps still thrive around Greenville, Rangeley, and in the Great North Woods.

Logging in the north created the culture of the mill towns, the Rumfords, Skowhegans, Millinockets, and Bangors that lie at the end of the old river drives. The logs arrive by truck today, but Maine's harvested wilderness still feeds the mills and the nation's hunger for paper.

Our hunger for potatoes has given rise to an entirely different Maine culture, in one of the most isolated agricultural regions of the country. Northeastern Aroostook County is where the Maine potatoes come from. This place is also changing. In what was once called the Potato Empire, farmers are as pressed between high costs and low prices as any of their counterparts in the Midwest, and a growing national preference for Idaho baking potatoes to small, round Maine boiling potatoes has only compounded Aroostook's troubles.

If you come to Maine seeking an untouched fishing village with locals gathered around a potbellied stove in the general store, you'll likely come away sadly disappointed; that innocent age has passed in all but the most remote villages. Tourism has supplanted fishing, logging, and potato farming as Maine's number one industry; most areas are well equipped to receive the annual onslaught of visitors. But whether you are stepping outside a motel room for an evening walk or watching a boat rock at its anchor, you can sense the infinity of the natural world. Wilderness is always nearby, growing to the edges of the most urbanized spots.

Pleasures and Pastimes

Boating
Maine's long coastline is justifiably famous: All visitors should get on the water, whether on a mail boat headed for Monhegan Island for the day or on a windjammer for a relaxing weeklong vacation. Windjammers, traditional two- or three-masted tall ships, sail past long, craggy fingers of land that jut into a sea dotted with more than 2,000 islands. Sail among these islands and you'll see hidden coves, lighthouses, boat-filled harbors, and quiet fishing villages. Most windjammers depart from Rockland, Rockport, or Camden, all ports on Penobscot Bay. Boating trips, including whale-watching, run in season, mid- to late May through September or mid-October.

Dining
Lobster and Maine are synonymous. As a general rule, the closer you are to a working harbor, the fresher your lobster will be. Aficionados eschew ordering lobster in restaurants, preferring to eat them "in the rough" at classic lobster pounds, where you select your dinner out of a pool and enjoy it at a waterside picnic table. Shrimp, scallops, clams, mussels, and crab are also caught in the cold waters off Maine. Restaurants in Portland and in resort towns prepare shellfish in creative combinations with lobster, haddock, salmon, and swordfish. Blueberries are grown commercially in Maine, and Maine cooks use them generously in pancakes, muffins, jams, pies, and cobblers. Full country breakfasts of fruit, eggs, breakfast meats, pancakes, and muffins are commonly served at inns and bed-and-breakfasts.

Hiking
From seaside rambles to backwoods hikes, Maine has a walk for everyone. This state's beaches are mostly hard packed and good for walking. Many coastal communities, such as York, Ogunquit, and Bar Harbor, have shoreside paths for people who want to keep sand out of their shoes yet enjoy the sound of the crashing surf and the cliff-top views of inlets and coves. Those who like to walk in the woods will not be disappointed: Ninety percent of the state is forested land. Acadia National Park has more than 150 mi of hiking trails, and within Baxter State Park are the northern end of the Appalachian Trail and Mt. Katahdin. At nearly 1 mi high, Katahdin is the tallest mountain in the state.

Lodging
The beach communities in the south beckon visitors with their weathered look. Stately digs can be found in the classic inns of Kennebunkport. Bed-and-breakfasts and Victorian inns furnished with lace, chintz, and mahogany have joined the family-oriented motels of Ogunquit, Booth-

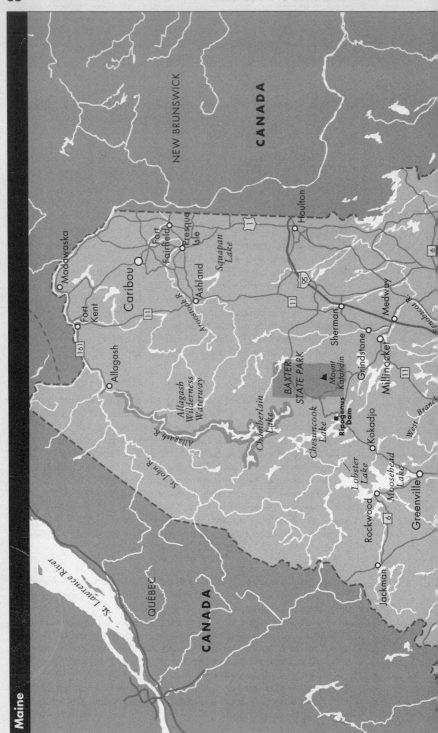

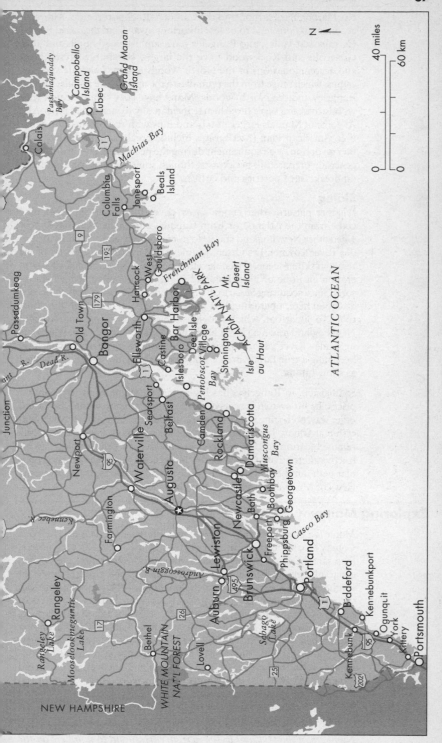

N

40 miles

60 km

Passamaquoddy Bay

Campobello Island

Grand Manan Island

Lubec

Calais

Machias Bay

1

Columbia Falls

Jonesport

Beals Island

9

193

Frenchman Bay

Passadumkeag

Old Town

179

West Gouldsboro

Hancock

Ellsworth

Bar Harbor

ACADIA NAT'L PARK

Mt. Desert Island

Bangor

11

Castine

Islesboro

Deer Isle

Stonington

Isle au Haut

Dead R.

R.

ant

Searsport

Belfast

Penobscot Bay

Junction

Newport

95

Waterville

Camden

Rockland

Kennebec R.

Augusta

Damariscotta

Muscongus Bay

Farmington

Newcastle

Bath

Boothbay

Georgetown

ATLANTIC OCEAN

Rangeley Lake

Rangeley

Mooselookmeguntic Lake

17

Androscoggin R.

Lewiston

Auburn

Brunswick

495

Freeport

Phippsburg

Casco Bay

Portland

Bethel

26

Sebago Lake

Biddeford

Kennebunkport

WHITE MOUNTAIN NAT'L FOREST

Lovell

25

Kennebunk

Ogunquit

York

Kittery

95

1

202

Portsmouth

NEW HAMPSHIRE

bay Harbor, Bar Harbor, and the Camden–Rockport region. Although accommodations tend to be less luxurious away from the coast, Bethel, Carrabassett Valley, and Rangeley have sophisticated hotels and inns. Greenville and Rockwood have the largest selection of restaurants and accommodations in the North Woods region. Lakeside sporting camps, which range from the primitive to the upscale, are popular around Rangeley and the North Woods. Many have cozy cabins heated with woodstoves and serve three hearty meals a day (American Plan, or AP). At some of Maine's larger hotels and inns with restaurants, the Modified American Plan (MAP; rates include breakfast and dinner) is either an option or a requirement during the peak summer season. B&Bs generally prepare full breakfasts, though some serve only a Continental breakfast of pastries and coffee.

Skiing

Weather patterns that create snow cover for Maine ski areas may come from the Atlantic or from Canada, and Maine may have snow when other New England states do not—and vice versa. Thanks to Sunday River's owner, Les Otten, Maine is moving to the forefront of the regional skiing scene. Otten developed Sunday River from a small operation into one of New England's largest and best-managed ski resorts. Since acquiring Sugarloaf/USA in 1996, he's focused much-needed attention here, upgrading lifts and snowmaking. It's worth the effort to get to Sugarloaf, which provides the only above-tree-line skiing in New England and also has a lively base village. Mt. Abram, which sits in Sunday River's shadow, has also blossomed under new ownership, becoming a true family area with reliable skiing day and night as well as snow tubing.

Saddleback, in Rangeley, has big-mountain skiing at little-mountain prices. Its lift system is sorely out of date, but many would have it no other way, preferring its down-home, wilderness atmosphere. New ownership at Squaw Mountain in Greenville is making improvements. Its remote location ensures few crowds, and its low prices make it an attractive alternative to other big mountains. Shawnee Peak remains popular with families and for night skiing; by day the resort has awesome views of Mt. Washington in New Hampshire.

Exploring Maine

Maine is a large state that offers many different experiences. The York County Coast, in the southern portion of the state, has easy access, long sand beaches, historic homes, and good restaurants. The coastal geography changes in Portland, the economic and cultural center of southern Maine. From there north, long fingers of land jut into the sea, sheltering fishing villages. Penobscot Bay is famed for its sailing, rockbound coast, and numerous islands. Mount Desert Island lures crowds of people to Acadia National Park, which is filled with jaw-dropping natural beauty. Way down east, beyond Acadia, the tempo changes; fast food joints and trinket shops all but disappear, replaced by family-style restaurants and artisans' shops. Inland, the western lakes and mountains provide an entirely different experience. Summer camps, ski areas, and small villages populate this region. People head to Maine's North Woods to escape the crowds and to enjoy the great outdoors by hiking, rafting, camping, or canoeing.

Numbers in the text and in the margin correspond to numbers on the maps: Southern Maine Coast, Portland, Penobscot Bay, Mount Desert Island, Way Down East, Western Maine, and the North Woods.

Great Itineraries

You can spend days exploring just the coast of Maine, as these itineraries indicate, so plan ahead and decide whether you want to ski and dogsled in the western mountains, raft or canoe in the North Woods, or simply meander up the coast, stopping at museums and historic sites, shopping for local arts and crafts, and exploring coastal villages and lobster shacks. Trying to see everything in one visit is complicated by the lack of east–west roads in the state and heavy traffic on popular routes, such as U.S. 1 and U.S. 302. Build extra time into your schedule and relax. You'll get there eventually, and in the meantime, enjoy the view.

IF YOU HAVE 2 DAYS

A two-day exploration of the southern coast provides a good introduction to different aspects of the Maine coast. Begin in **Ogunquit** ③ with a morning walk along the Marginal Way. Then head north to **Kennebunkport** ⑥, allowing at least two hours to wander through the shops and historic homes around Dock Square. Relax on the beach for an hour or so before heading to ⊞ **Portland** ⑧–⑬. If you thrive on arts and entertainment, spend the night here. Otherwise, continue north to ⊞ **Freeport** ⑯, where you can shop all night at L. L. Bean. On day two, head north, stopping in **Bath** ⑱ to tour the Maine Maritime Museum, and finish up with a lobster dinner on **Pemaquid Point** ㉑.

IF YOU HAVE 4 DAYS

A four-day tour of midcoast Maine up to Acadia National Park is one of New England's classic trips. From New Harbor on **Pemaquid Point** ㉑, take the boat to ⊞ **Monhegan Island** ㉓ for a day of walking the trails and exploring the artists' studios and galleries. The next day, continue northeast to **Rockland** ㉔ and ⊞ **Camden** ㉕. On day three, visit the Farnsworth Museum in Rockland, hike or drive to the top of Mt. Battie in Camden, and meander around Camden's boat-filled harbor. Or, bypass midcoast Maine in favor of ⊞ **Mount Desert Island** ㉝–㊶ and Acadia National Park. To avoid sluggish traffic on U.S. 1, from Freeport, stay on I–95 to Augusta and the Maine Turnpike; then take Route 3 to Belfast and pick up U.S. 1 north there.

IF YOU HAVE 8 DAYS

An eight-day trip allows time to see a good portion of the coast. Spend two days wandering through gentrified towns and weather-beaten fishing villages from ⊞ **Kittery** ① to ⊞ **Portland** ⑧–⑬. On your third day explore Portland and environs, including a boat ride to **Eagle Island** ⑮ or one of the other Casco Bay islands and a visit to Portland Head Light and Two Lights in Cape Elizabeth. Continue working your way up the coast, letting your interests dictate your stops: outlet stores in **Freeport** ⑯, Maine Maritime Museum in ⊞ **Bath** ⑱, antiques shops in **Wiscasset** ⑲, fishing villages and a much-photographed lighthouse on **Pemaquid Point** ㉑. Allow at least one day in the **Rockland** ㉔ and ⊞ **Camden** ㉕ region before taking the leisurely route to **Bar Harbor** ㉝ via the **Blue Hill** ㉙ peninsula and ⊞ **Deer Isle Village** ㉚. Finish up with two days on ⊞ **Mt. Desert Island** ㉝–㊶.

When to Tour Maine

From July to September is the choice time for a vacation in Maine. The weather is warmest in July and August, though September is less crowded. In warm weather, the arteries along the coast and lakeside communities inland are clogged with out-of-state license plates, campgrounds are filled to capacity, and hotel rates are high. Midweek is less busy, and lodging rates are often lower then than on weekends.

Fall foliage can be brilliant in Maine and is made even more so by its reflection in inland lakes or streams or off the ocean. Late September is peak season in the north country, while in southern Maine the prime viewing dates are usually from October 5 to 10. In September and October the days are sunny and the nights crisp.

In winter, the coastal towns almost completely close down. If the sidewalks could be rolled up, they probably would be. Maine's largest ski areas usually open in mid-November and, thanks to excellent snowmaking facilities, provide good skiing often into April.

Springtime is mud season here, as in most other rural areas of New England. Mud season is followed by spring flowers and the start of wildflowers in meadows along the roadsides.

YORK COUNTY COAST

Maine's southernmost coastal towns, most of them in York County, won't give you the rugged, wind-bitten "down-east" experience, but they are easily reached from the south, and most have the sand beaches that all but vanish beyond Portland.

These towns are highly popular in summer, an all-too-brief period. Crowds converge and gobble up rooms and dinner reservations at prime restaurants. You'll have to work a little harder to find solitude and vestiges of the "real" Maine here. Still, even day-trippers who come for a few fleeting hours to southern Maine will appreciate the magical warmth of the sand along this coast.

North of Kittery, the Maine coast has long stretches of hard-packed white-sand beach, closely crowded by nearly unbroken ranks of beach cottages, motels, and oceanfront restaurants. The summer colonies of York Beach and Wells Beach have the crowds and ticky-tacky shorefront overdevelopment. Ogunquit is more upscale and offers much to do, from shopping to taking a cliff-side walk. Farther inland, York's historic district is on the National Register of Historic Places.

More than any other region south of Portland, the Kennebunks—and especially Kennebunkport—provide the complete Maine-coast experience: classic townscapes where white clapboard houses rise from manicured lawns and gardens; rocky shorelines punctuated by sandy beaches; quaint downtown districts packed with gift shops, ice cream stands, and tourists; harbors where lobster boats bob alongside yachts; lobster pounds and well-appointed dining rooms.

These towns are best explored on a leisurely holiday of two days— more if you require a fix of solid beach time. U.S. 1 travels along the coast. Inland, the Maine Turnpike (I–95) is the fastest route if you want to skip some towns.

Kittery

❶ *55 mi north of Boston, 5 mi north of Portsmouth, New Hampshire.*

Kittery, which lacks a large sand beach of its own, hosts a complex of factory outlets that makes it more popular, or at least better known with visitors, than the summer beach communities.

As an alternative to shopping, drive north of the outlets and go east on Route 103 for a peek at the hidden Kittery most people miss. Along this winding stretch are two forts, both open in summer. **Ft. Foster** (1872), off Route 103, was an active military installation until 1949. **Ft. McClary** (1690) was staffed during five wars. There are also hiking and biking trails and, best of all, great views of the water.

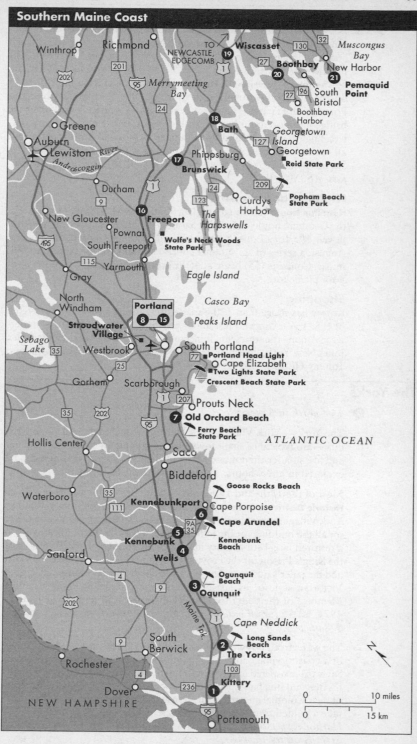

Winthrop
Richmond
TO
NEWCASTLE
EDGECOMB
19 **Wiscasset**
130
32
Muscongus Bay
201
27 **Boothbay**
20
New Harbor
95
Merrymeeting Bay
27 96 South Bristol
21 **Pemaquid Point**
24
Boothbay Harbor
Greene
18 **Bath**
Georgetown Island
127
Georgetown
Auburn
Lewiston
River
17 Phippsburg
Reid State Park
Androscoggin
Brunswick
209
Popham Beach State Park
Durham
1
24
9
123
Curdys Harbor
16
The Harpswells
New Gloucester
Freeport
Pownal
Wolfe's Neck Woods State Park
South Freeport
115
Eagle Island
Gray
Yarmouth
North Windham
Casco Bay
Portland
Stroudwater Village
8 **15**
Peaks Island
Sebago Lake
35
Westbrook
South Portland
Portland Head Light
77
Cape Elizabeth
25
Two Lights State Park
Gorham
Scarborough
Crescent Beach State Park
35
202
1
207
Prouts Neck
95
7 **Old Orchard Beach**
Ferry Beach State Park
Hollis Center
Saco
ATLANTIC OCEAN
Biddeford
Waterboro
Goose Rocks Beach
35
Kennebunkport
111
Cape Porpoise
6
9A
35
Cape Arundel
5
Kennebunk
Kennebunk Beach
Sanford
4 **Wells**
4
Ogunquit Beach
9
3 **Ogunquit**
202
Maine Tpk.
1
Cape Neddick
South Berwick
2
Long Sands Beach
9
The Yorks
Rochester
103
4
1 **Kittery**
236
Dover
NEW HAMPSHIRE
95
Portsmouth

0   10 miles
0   15 km

Dining and Lodging

$–$$$ ✕ **Warren's Lobster House.** A local institution, this waterfront restaurant specializes in lobster and seafood but also serves steak and chicken and has a huge salad bar. In season, you can dine outdoors overlooking the water. ⊠ *U.S. 1 and Water St.,* ☎ *207/439–1630. AE, MC, V.*

$$$ ☷ **The Inn at Portsmouth Harbor.** This brick Victorian built in 1889 on the old Kittery town green overlooks the Piscataqua River and Portsmouth Harbor. The convenient location is an easy walk over the bridge into Portsmouth or a quick drive up U.S. 1 to the Kittery outlets. English antiques and Victorian watercolors decorate the inn, and all rooms have cable TV as well as phones with voice mail. ⊠ *6 Water St., 03904,* ☎ *207/439–4040,* ℻ *207/438–9286. 6 rooms. Full breakfast. AE, MC, V.*

Nightlife and the Arts

Hamilton House (⊠ Vaughan's La., South Berwick, ☎ 603/436–3205), the Georgian home featured in Sarah Orne Jewett's historical romance novel, *The Tory Lover,* presents "Sundays in the Garden" in July and August, a series of six summer concerts ranging from classical to folk music. Concerts ($5) begin at 4; the grounds are open from noon until 5 for picnicking.

Shopping

Kittery has more than 120 outlet stores. Along a several-mile stretch of U.S. 1 you can find just about anything, from hardware to underwear. Among the stores you'll encounter are Crate & Barrel, Eddie Bauer, Jones New York, Esprit, Waterford/Wedgwood, Lenox, Ralph Lauren, Tommy Hilfiger, DKNY, and J. Crew.

The Yorks

❷ *4 mi north of Kittery.*

The Yorks—York Village, York Harbor, York Beach, and Cape Neddick—are typical of small-town coastal communities in New England and are smaller than most. Many of their nooks and crannies can be explored in a few hours. The beaches are the big attraction here.

Most of the 18th- and 19th-century buildings within the **York Village Historic District** are clustered along York Street and Lindsay Road in York Village; some charge admission. You can buy an admission ticket for all the buildings at the **Jefferds Tavern** (⊠ U.S. 1A at Lindsay Rd.), a restored late-18th-century inn. The **Old York Gaol** (1720) was once the King's Prison for the Province of Maine; inside are dungeons, cells, and the jailer's quarters. The 1731 **Elizabeth Perkins House** reflects the Victorian style of its last occupants, the prominent Perkins family. Members of the Old York Historical Society lead tours. ☎ 207/363–4974. ☷ *$6 for all buildings.* ☉ *Mid-June–mid-Oct., Tues.–Sat. 10–5, Sun. 1–5.*

The waterfront **Sayward-Wheeler House** (1718) mirrors the fortunes of a coastal village in the transition from trade to tourism. Jonathan Sayward prospered in the West Indies trade in the 18th century; by 1860 his descendants had opened the house to the public to share the story of their Colonial ancestors. The house reflects both these eras. You must take a guided tour to see the house. ⊠ *79 Barrell La. extension, York Harbor,* ☎ *603/436–3205.* ☷ *$4.* ☉ *June–mid-Oct., weekends noon–5; tours on the hr, 11–4.*

If you drive down Nubble Road from U.S. 1A and go to the end of Cape Neddick, you can park and gaze out at the **Nubble Light** (1879), which sits on a tiny island just offshore. The keeper's house is a tidy Victorian cottage with gingerbread woodwork and a red roof.

U.S. 1A runs right behind **Long Sands Beach,** a 1½-mi stretch of sand in York Beach that has roadside parking and a bathhouse. **Short Sands Beach** in York Beach has a bathhouse and is convenient to restaurants and shops.

Dining and Lodging

$$$ ✕ **Cape Neddick Inn.** The American bistro-style menu at this restaurant and art gallery changes with the seasons. Past offerings have included entrées such as sage-roasted quail and poached Atlantic salmon on lobster succotash. ✉ *U.S. 1, Cape Neddick,* ☎ *207/363–2899. D, MC, V. Closed Mon. and mid-Oct.–May. No lunch.*

$–$$$ ✕ **Cafe Shelton.** This perky restaurant decorated in blue and white sits across from Short Sands Beach. Lunch fare includes soups, sandwiches, and salads. Dinner is more elaborate, with entrées such as Grand Marnier salmon and lobster ravioli sharing the menu with linguine and meatballs. A children's menu is available. ✉ *1 Ocean Ave., York Beach,* ☎ *207/363–0708. MC, V.*

$$–$$$ ✕🏠 **York Harbor Inn.** A mid-17th-century fishing cabin with dark
★ timbers and a fieldstone fireplace forms the heart of this inn, to which various wings and outbuildings have been added over the years. The rooms are furnished with antiques and country pieces; many have decks overlooking the water, and a few have whirlpool tubs or fireplaces. Room in the Harbor Cliffs next door, acquired in 1998, have the intimate appeal of a classic Maine cottage. The dining room (no lunch off-season) has great ocean views. For dinner, start with Maine crab cakes, a classic Caesar salad, or a creamy seafood chowder, and then try the lobster-stuffed chicken breast or the angel-hair pasta with shrimp and scallops. The Cellar Pub ($) offers soups, salads, burgers, and sandwiches. ✉ *Box 573, U.S. 1A, York Harbor 03911,* ☎ *207/ 363–5119 or 800/343–3869,* ℻ *207/363–7151. 25 rooms, 15 suites. Restaurant, pub. Continental breakfast. AE, DC, MC, V.*

$$–$$$ 🏠 **Cutty Sark Motel.** The rooms are standard motel fare, but you can't beat the oceanfront location, right on the edge of Long Sands Beach. Every room has an ocean view. ✉ *58 Long Beach Ave., York Beach 03910,* ☎ *207/363–5131 or 800/543–5131,* ℻ *207/351–1335. 42 rooms. Refrigerators. Continental breakfast. D, MC, V.*

$$–$$$ 🏠 **Union Bluff.** This fortresslike modern white structure, with balconies across the front and turrets on the ends, sits right across from Short Sands Beach with views to forever. The best rooms are in the front of the inn, but many on the north side, which cost less, also have ocean views. The front rooms in the adjacent motel have ocean views, but the motel has fewer services. ✉ *Box 1860, 8 Beach St., York Beach 03910,* ☎ *207/363–1333 or 800/833–0721,* ℻ *207/363–1381. 36 rooms, 4 suites in inn; 21 rooms in motel. Restaurant, pub. AE, D, MC, V.*

$–$$ 🏠 **Edward's Harborside.** This turn-of-the-century B&B sits on the harbor's edge and is just a two-minute walk from the beach. Rooms are spacious, with big windows to take in the water views. One room has a whirlpool tub. ✉ *Box 866, Stage Neck Rd., York Harbor 03911,* ☎ *207/363–3037. 4 rooms share 2 baths, 3 suites. Dock. Continental breakfast. MC, V.*

Outdoor Activities and Sports

Capt. Tom Farnon (✉ Rte. 103, Town Dock #2, York Harbor, ☎ 207/ 363–3234) takes passengers on lobstering trips, weekdays 10–2.

Ogunquit

❸ *10 mi north of the Yorks, 39 mi southwest of Portland.*

Probably more than any other south-coast community, Ogunquit combines coastal ambience, style, and good eating. The village became a resort in the 1880s and gained fame as an artists' colony. A mini Provincetown, Ogunquit has a gay population that swells in summer; many inns and small clubs cater to a primarily gay and lesbian clientele. Families love the protected beach area and friendly environment. Shore Road, which takes you into downtown, passes the 100-ft **Bald Head Cliff,** with views up and down the coast. On a stormy day the surf can be quite wild here.

Perkins Cove, a neck of land connected to the mainland by Oarweed Road and a pedestrian drawbridge, has a jumble of sea-beaten fish houses. These have largely been transformed by the tide of tourism to shops and restaurants. When you've had your fill of browsing and jostling the crowds at
★ Perkins Cove, stroll out along the **Marginal Way,** a mile-long footpath that hugs the shore of a rocky promontory known as Israel's Head. Benches along the route give walkers an opportunity to stop and appreciate the open sea vistas, flowering bushes, and million-dollar homes.

The **Ogunquit Museum of American Art,** in a low-lying concrete building overlooking the ocean, is set amid a 3-acre sculpture garden. Inside are works by Henry Strater, Marsden Hartley, Winslow Homer, Edward Hopper, Gaston Lachaise, Marguerite Zorach, and Louise Nevelson. The huge windows of the sculpture court command a view of cliffs and ocean. ⊠ *183 Shore Rd.,* ☎ *207/646–4909.* ☞ *$4.* ☉ *July–Sept., Mon.–Sat. 10:30–5, Sun. 2–5.*

Ogunquit Beach, a 3-mi-wide stretch of sand at the mouth of the Ogunquit River, has snack bars, a boardwalk, rest rooms, and, at the Beach Street entrance, changing areas. Families gravitate to the ends; gay visitors camp at the beach's middle. The less-crowded section to the north is accessible by footbridge and has portable rest rooms, all-day paid parking, and trolley service.

Dining and Lodging

$$$$ ✕ **Arrows.** Elegant simplicity is the hallmark of this 18th-century farmhouse, 2 mi up a back road. Grilled salmon and radicchio with marinated fennel and baked polenta and Chinese-style duck glazed with molasses are typical entrées on the daily-changing menu. The Maine crabmeat mousse and lobster risotto appetizers and desserts like strawberry shortcake with Chantilly cream and steamed chocolate pudding are also beautifully executed. ⊠ *Berwick Rd.,* ☎ *207/361–1100. Reservations essential. MC, V. Closed Mon. and Dec.–late Apr. No lunch.*

$$$–$$$$ ✕ **Hurricane.** Don't let the weather-beaten exterior deter you—this small
★ seafood bar and grill with spectacular views of the crashing surf turns out first-rate dishes. Start with lobster chowder, a chilled fresh-shrimp spring roll, or the house salad (assorted greens with pistachio nuts and roasted shallots). Entrées may include lobster cioppino, rack of lamb, and fire-roasted veal chop. Save room for the classic crème brûlée. ⊠ *Oarweed La., Perkins Cove,* ☎ *207/646–6348. AE, D, DC, MC, V. Closed late Dec.–mid-Jan.*

$–$$ ✕ **The Impastable Dream.** If it's good pasta you crave, you'll find it in abundance at this cozy restaurant. Dining rooms are bright and decorated with stenciling and floral linens. Favorites include Greek pasta (with feta cheese, spinach, and black olives) and lobster ravioli. The food is reasonably priced and plentiful; a children's menu is offered from 5 to 6:30. ⊠ *105 Shore Rd.,* ☎ *207/646–3011. Reservations not accepted. AE, D, MC, V. Closed Jan. and midweek off-season. No lunch.*

$$$$ 🖭 **Cliff House.** Elsie Jane Weare opened the Cliff House in 1872. Her granddaughter Kathryn now presides over this sprawling oceanfront resort comprising three buildings atop Bald Head Cliff. Every room has a view of the water, which makes up for the unremarkable decor. This place has a loyal following, so reserve well in advance. ⊠ *Box 2274, Shore Rd., 03907,* ☎ *207/361–1000,* ℻ *207/361–2122. 162 rooms. Restaurant, 1 indoor and 1 outdoor pool, hot tub, sauna, 2 tennis courts, exercise room. AE, D. Closed mid-Dec.–late Mar.*

$$–$$$ 🖭 **The Rockmere.** Midway along Ogunquit's Marginal Way, this shingle-style Victorian cottage is an ideal retreat from the hustle and bustle of Perkins Cove. All the rooms have corner locations and are large and airy, and all but one have ocean views. You'll find it easy to laze the day away on the wraparound porch or in the gardens. ⊠ *Box 278, 40 Stearns Rd., 03907,* ☎ *207/646–2985. 8 rooms. Continental breakfast. AE, D, MC, V.*

Nightlife and the Arts

Much of the nightlife in Ogunquit revolves around the precincts of Ogunquit Square and Perkins Cove, where people stroll, often enjoying an after-dinner ice cream cone or espresso. Ogunquit is popular with gay and lesbian visitors, and its club scene reflects this.

The **Club** (⊠ 13 Main St., ☎ 207/646–6655) is Ogunquit's main gay disco. **Jonathan's Restaurant** (⊠ 7 Bourne La., ☎ 207/646–4777) has live entertainment, usually blues, in season. The **Ogunquit Playhouse** (⊠ U.S. 1, ☎ 207/646–5511), one of America's oldest summer theaters, mounts plays and musicals with name entertainment from late June to Labor Day.

Outdoor Activities and Sports

Finestkind (⊠ Perkins Cove, ☎ 207/646–5227) operates cocktail cruises, lobstering trips, and cruises to Nubble Light.

Wells

4 *5 mi north of Ogunquit, 35 mi southwest of Portland.*

This family-oriented beach community consists of several densely populated miles of shoreline interspersed with trailers and summer and year-round homes.

The **Wells Reserve** sprawls over 1,600 acres of meadows, orchards, fields, and salt marshes, as well as two estuaries and 9 mi of seashore. This nature preserve has extensive trails through its diverse habitats. The visitor center screens an introductory slide show and holds five rooms of exhibits. In winter, cross-country skiing is permitted. ⊠ *342 Laudholm Farm Rd.,* ☎ *207/646–1555.* 🖾 *$2 July–Aug. and weekends Sept.– mid-Oct.* ◔ *Grounds daily 8–5. Visitor center May–Dec., Mon.–Sat. 10–4, Sun. noon–4; weekends only in winter.*

Rachel Carson National Wildlife Refuge (⊠ Rte. 9, ☎ 207/646–9226) has a mile-long loop nature trail through a salt marsh. The trail borders the Little River and a white-pine forest where migrating birds and waterfowl of many varieties are regularly spotted.

☾ A must for motor fanatics and youngsters, the **Wells Auto Museum** has 70 vintage cars, antique coin games, and a restored Model T you can ride in. ⊠ *U.S. 1,* ☎ *207/646–9064.* 🖾 *$3.50.* ◔ *Mid-June–Labor Day, daily 10–5; Labor Day–Columbus Day, weekends 10–5.*

Dining and Lodging

$–$$ ✕ **Billy's Chowder House.** Visitors and locals head to this simple restaurant in a salt marsh for the generous lobster rolls, haddock sandwiches, and chowders. ✉ *216 Mile Rd.,* ☎ *207/646–7558. AE, D, MC, V. Closed mid-Dec.–mid-Jan.*

$–$$ ✕⌂ **Grey Gull.** A century-old Victorian inn, the Grey Gull has views of the open sea and rocks on which seals like to sun themselves. The unpretentious rooms, most with ocean views, have shared or private baths. The restaurant ($$–$$$) serves excellent seafood dishes like soft-shell crabs almandine and regional fare such as Yankee pot roast or chicken breast rolled in walnuts and baked with maple syrup. Breakfast is popular here in summer: Blueberry pancakes or eggs McGull served on crab cakes with hollandaise sauce are good choices. ✉ *475 Webhannet Dr., at Moody Point,* ☎ *207/646–7501,* FAX *207/646–0938. 8 rooms, 6 with bath. Restaurant. Continental breakfast; MAP available. AE, D, MC, V.*

Shopping

Kenneth & Ida Manko (✉ Seabreeze Dr., ☎ 207/646–2595) sells folk art, rustic furniture, paintings, and 19th-century weather vanes. From U.S. 1 head east on Eldridge Road for a half mile, and then turn left on Seabreeze Drive. **Douglas N. Harding Rare Books** (✉ 2152 Post Rd./U.S. 1, ☎ 207/646–8785) has many old books, maps, and prints. **R. Jorgensen** (✉ 502 Post Rd./U.S. 1, ☎ 207/646–9444) stocks 18th- and 19th-century formal and country antiques from the British Isles, Europe, and the United States.

The **Lighthouse Depot** (✉ U.S. 1, ☎ 207/646–0608) calls itself the world's largest lighthouse gift store.

Kennebunk

❺ *5 mi north of Wells, 30 mi southwest of Portland.*

Handsome white clapboard homes with shutters lend Kennebunk, a shipbuilding center in the first half of the 19th century, a look that's quintessential New England. The historic town is a fine place for a stroll. The cornerstone of the **Brick Store Museum,** a block-long preservation of early 19th-century commercial buildings, is **William Lord's Brick Store.** Built as a dry-goods store in 1825 in the Federal style, the building has an open-work balustrade across the roof line, granite lintels over the windows, and paired chimneys. Walking tours of Kennebunk's National Historic Register District depart from the museum on Friday at 1 and Wednesday at 10 from June to October. ✉ *117 Main St.,* ☎ *207/985–4802.* 🖼 *$5.* ⊙ *Tues.–Sat. 10–4:30.*

The **Taylor-Barry House** house, owned by the Brick Store Museum (☞ above), is an early 19th-century sea captain's home that's open for tours. ✉ *24 Summer St.,* ☎ *207/985–4802.* 🖼 *$4.* ⊙ *July–Oct., Tues.–Fri. 1–4:30.*

Kennebunk Beach has three parts: **Gooch's Beach, Mother's Beach,** and **Kennebunk Beach.** Beach Road, with its cottages and old Victorian boardinghouses, runs right behind them. Gooch's and Kennebunk attract teenagers; Mother's Beach, which has a small playground and tidal puddles for splashing, is popular with families. For parking permits (a fee is charged in summer), go to the **Kennebunk Town Office** (✉ 1 Summer St., ☎ 207/985–2102).

The **Wedding Cake House** (✉ 104 Summer St./Rte. 35) has long been a local landmark. The legend behind this confection in fancy wood fretwork is that its builder, a sea captain, was forced to set sail in the middle of his wedding, and the house was his bride's consolation for the lack of wedding cake. The home, built in 1826, is not open to the public, but the attached carriage house holds a gallery and studio.

Lodging

$ ⚍ **St. Anthony's Franciscan Monastery Guest House.** Individuals and families in search of a quiet, contemplative retreat may want to choose one of the simple, unadorned, motel-style rooms in a former dormitory on the grounds of a riverside monastery. The guest house is private yet within walking distance of Dock Square and the beach. The landscaped grounds, open to the public, have trails and shrines. The monks live in a Tudor mansion on the property, where Mass is said daily in an attached chapel. This place is not recommended for those uncomfortable with Christian symbolism, although no religious participation is required. ⊠ *28 Beach Ave., Kennebunk 04043,* ☏ *207/ 967–2011. 60 rooms. No credit cards. Closed Oct.–May.*

Shopping

J. J. Keating (⊠ 70 Portland Rd./U.S. 1, ☏ 207/985–2097) deals in antiques, reproductions, and estate furnishings. **Marlow's Artisans Gallery** (⊠ 39 Main St., ☏ 207/985–2931) carries a large and eclectic collection of crafts.

Kennebunkport

❻ *10 mi northeast of Ogunquit.*

When George Bush was president, Kennebunkport was his summer White House. But long before Bush came into the public eye, visitors were coming to Kennebunkport to soak up the salt air, seafood, and sunshine. This is a picture-perfect town with manicured lawns, elaborate flower beds, freshly painted homes, and a small-town wholesomeness. People flock to Kennebunkport mostly in summer; some come in early December when the **Christmas Prelude** is celebrated on two weekends. Santa arrives by fishing boat and the Christmas trees are lighted as carolers stroll the sidewalks.

Route 35 merges with Route 9 in Kennebunk and takes you right into Kennebunkport's **Dock Square,** the busy town center. Boutiques, T-shirt shops, a Christmas store, a decoy shop, and restaurants encircle the square. Although many businesses close in winter, the best bargains often are had in December. Walk onto the drawbridge to admire the tidal Kennebunk River.

The very grand **Nott House,** known also as White Columns, is an imposing Greek Revival mansion with Doric columns that rise the height of the house. It is a gathering place for village walking tours; call for schedule. ⊠ *8 Maine St.,* ☏ *207/967–2751.* ▣ *$3.* ⊙ *Mid-June–mid-Oct., Tues.–Fri. 1–4.*

Ocean Avenue follows the Kennebunk River from Dock Square to the sea and winds around the peninsula of **Cape Arundel.** Parson's Way, a small and tranquil stretch of rocky shoreline, is open to all. As you round Cape Arundel, look to the right for the entrance to George Bush's summer home at Walker's Point.

★ ☾ The **Seashore Trolley Museum** displays streetcars built from 1872 to 1972 and includes trolleys from major metropolitan areas and world capitals—Boston to Budapest, New York to Nagasaki, and San Francisco to Sydney, Australia—all beautifully restored. Best of all, you can take a trolley ride for nearly 4 mi over the tracks of the former Atlantic Shoreline trolley line, with a stop along the way at the museum restoration shop, where trolleys are transformed from junk into gems. Both guided and self-guided tours are available. ⊠ *Log Cabin Rd.,* ☎ *207/ 967–2800.* ☞ *$7.* ⊙ *Late May–mid-Oct., daily 10–5; reduced hrs in spring and fall.*

Goose Rocks, a few minutes' drive north of town, is the largest beach in the Kennebunk area and the favorite of families with small children. You can pick up a parking permit ($5 a day, $15 a week), at the Kennebunkport Town Office (⊠ 6 Elm St., ☎ 207/967–4244) or the police department (⊠ 1 Main St./Rte. 9, ☎ 207/967–2454).

Dining and Lodging

$$$–$$$$ ✕ **Seascapes.** The emphasis is on seafood at this pretty harborfront restaurant where the view takes center stage. You can begin with pan-fried oysters or lobster spring rolls, then move on to roasted lobster or try the Mediterranean-inspired saddle of lamb. ⊠ *Pier Rd., Cape Porpoise Harbor, Cape Porpoise,* ☎ *207/967–8500. AE, D, MC, V. Closed mid-Oct.–mid-May.*

$$$–$$$$ ✕ **Windows on the Water.** This restaurant overlooks Dock Square and the working harbor of Kennebunkport. Lobster ravioli and rack of lamb are two noteworthy entrées. The special five-course dinner for two, including wine, tax, and gratuity (total: $87), is a good value if you have a healthy appetite. ⊠ *12 Chase Hill Rd.,* ☎ *207/967–3313. Reservations essential. AE, D, DC, MC, V.*

$–$$$ ✕ **Alisson's.** A year-round favorite, this restaurant in the heart of Dock Square serves reliable salads, burgers, sandwiches, and dinner fare. ⊠ *5 Dock Square,* ☎ *207/967–4841,* 🅵🅰🆇 *207/967–2532. AE, D, MC, V.*

$–$$ ✕ **Cape Porpoise Lobster Co., Inc.** You can watch the surf crash over distant ledges near the Goat Island lighthouse and see lobster boats returning with their day's catch at this oceanfront lobster shack. Seating is on the deck or inside. The fare includes lobster, clams, and fried foods. ⊠ *15 Pier Rd., Cape Porpoise,* ☎ *207/967–4268 or 800/967–4268. MC, V. Closed early Nov.–late Mar.*

$$$–$$$$ ✕🏠 **White Barn Inn.** For a romantic overnight stay or a superb meal,
★ you need look no further than the exclusive White Barn Inn, known for its attentive service. The meticulously appointed rooms have luxurious baths and are decorated with a blend of hand-painted pieces and period furniture; some rooms have fireplaces and whirlpool baths. Regional New England fare is served at the rustic but elegant dining room ($$$$; jacket required), one of the region's best. The fixed-price menu, which changes weekly, might include steamed Maine lobster nestled on fresh fettuccine with carrots, ginger, and snow peas. ⊠ *Box 560C, 37 Beach St., 04046,* ☎ *207/967–2321,* 🅵🅰🆇 *207/967–1100. 16 rooms, 9 suites. Restaurant, pool, bicycles. Continental breakfast. AE, MC, V.*

$$$ ✕🏠 **Cape Arundel Inn.** This shingle-style inn commands a magnificent ocean view that takes in the Bush estate at Walker Point. The spacious rooms are furnished with country-style furniture and antiques, and most have sitting areas with ocean views. You can relax on the front porch, furnished with antique white wicker, or in front of the living-room fireplace. In the candlelighted dining room ($$$–$$$$), open to the public for dinner, every table has a view of the surf. The entrées include seafood, lamb, duckling, and steak. ⊠ *Ocean Ave., 04046,* ☎ *207/ 967–2125,* 🅵🅰🆇 *207/967–1199. 13 rooms, 1 apartment. Restaurant. AE, D, MC, V. Closed early Dec.–early May.*

$$$$ 🏠 **Captain Lord Mansion.** Of all the mansions in Kennebunkport's historic district that have been converted to inns, the 1812 Captain Lord Mansion is the most stately and sumptuously appointed. The three-story Federal inn is topped with a widow's walk, from which you can peer out over the town and harbor, just three blocks away. Distinctive architecture, including a suspended elliptical staircase and gas fireplaces

in 15 rooms, and decorating of near museum quality make for a formal but not stuffy atmosphere. Five rooms have whirlpool tubs. The most extravagant suite has fireplaces in the bathroom and the sleeping area, a double whirlpool, a hydro-massage body spa, a TV/VCR and stereo system, exercise equipment, and a king-size canopy bed. ⊠ *Box 800, Pleasant and Green Sts., 04046,* ☎ *207/967–3141,* FAX *207/ 967–3172. 16 rooms, 1 suite. Full breakfast. D, MC, V.*

$$$–$$$$ ⛶ **Maine Stay Inn and Cottages.** On a quiet residential street a short walk from Dock Square is the circa 1860 Maine Stay Inn. Three of the accommodations in the Italianate main house have fireplaces. Families often stay in the cottages behind the inn; some have fireplaces, whirlpools, and kitchens. ⊠ *Box 500A, 34 Maine St., 04046,* ☎ *207/ 967–2117 or 800/950–2117,* FAX *207/967–8757. 4 rooms, 2 suites, 11 rooms in cottages. Full breakfast. AE, MC, V.*

$$$–$$$$ ⛶ **The Seaside.** This handsome seaside property has been in the hands of the Severance family for 12 generations. The modern motel units, all with cable TVs and sliding-glass doors that open onto private decks or patios (half with ocean views), are appropriate for families; so are the cottages, which have from one to four bedrooms. The four bedrooms in the 1756 inn, furnished with antiques, are more suitable for adults. ⊠ *80 Beach Ave., 04046,* ☎ *207/967–4461,* FAX *207/967– 1135. 26 rooms, 10 cottages. Beach, playground, laundry service. Continental breakfast. AE, MC, V. Inn rooms closed Labor Day– June; cottages closed Nov.–Apr.*

$$$ ⛶ **Bufflehead Cove.** On the Kennebunk River at the end of a winding dirt road, this gray-shingle B&B amid quiet country fields and apple trees is only five minutes from Dock Square. Rooms in the main house have white wicker and flowers handpainted on the walls. The Hideaway Suite, with a two-sided gas fireplace, king-size bed, and large whirlpool tub, overlooks the river. The Garden Studio has a fireplace and the most privacy. ⊠ *Box 499, 18 Bufflehead Cove Rd., 04046,* ☎ FAX *207/967–3879. 2 rooms, 3 suites, 1 cottage. Dock. D, MC, V.*

Outdoor Activities and Sports

Cape-Able Bike Shop (⊠ Townhouse Corners, ☎ 207/967–4382) rents bicycles. **Chick's Marina** (⊠ 75 Ocean Ave., ☎ 207/967–2782) conducts sightseeing and fishing cruises for up to six people. **First Chance** (⊠ Arundel Wharf, Lower Village, ☎ 207/967–5912) guarantees whale sightings in season. **Venture Inn Charters** (⊠ Performance Marine, near the Rte. 9 bridge, ☎ 207/967–0005 or 800/853–5002) operates full- and half-day deep-sea fishing trips.

Old Orchard Beach

➐ *15 mi north of Kennebunkport, 18 mi south of Portland.*

Old Orchard Beach, a few miles north of Biddeford on Route 9, is a 7-mi strip of sand beach with an amusement park that's like a small Coney Island. Despite the summertime crowds and fried-food odors, the atmosphere can be captivating. During the 1940s and '50s, in the heyday of the Big Band era, the pier had a dance hall where stars of the era performed. Fire claimed the end of the pier, but booths with games and candy concessions still line both sides. In summer the town sponsors fireworks (usually on Thursday night). The many places to stay run the gamut from cheap motels to cottage colonies to full-service seasonal hotels. The area is popular from July 4 to Labor Day with people from Québec. You won't find free parking anywhere in town, but there are ample lots.

A world away in atmosphere from the beach scene is **Ocean Park** (☎ 207/934–9068), on the southwestern edge of town. This vacation community was founded in 1881 as a summer assembly, following the example of Chautauqua, New York. Today the community still has a wide range of cultural offerings, including movies, concerts, workshops, and religious services. Most are presented in the Temple, which is on the National Register of Historic Places.

Ⓒ **Palace Playland** (⊠ 1 Old Orchard St., ☎ 207/934–2001), open from Memorial Day to Labor Day, has rides, booths, and a roller coaster

Ⓒ that drops almost 50 ft. **Funtown/Splashtown** (⊠ U.S. 1, Saco, ☎ 207/284–5139 or 800/878–2900) has more than 30 rides and amusements, including miniature golf, waterslides, a wave pool, and Excalibur, a new wooden roller coaster.

Lodging

$$$$ 🏠 **Black Point Inn.** Toward the top of the peninsula that juts into the ocean at Prouts Neck, 12 mi south of Portland and about 10 mi north of Old Orchard Beach by road, stands a stylish, tastefully updated old-time resort with views up and down the Maine coast. Mahogany bedsteads, Martha Washington bedspreads, and white-ruffle priscilla curtains decorate the rooms. The extensive grounds contain beaches, trails, a bird sanctuary, and sports facilities. New this year are three dining rooms: one formal, one casual, and one for family dining. ⊠ *510 Black Point Rd., Scarborough 04074,* ☎ *207/883–4126 or 800/258–0003,* FAX *207/883–9976. 68 rooms, 12 suites. Restaurant, bar, 1 indoor and 1 outdoor pool, hot tub, golf, 14 tennis courts, croquet, volleyball, boating, bicycles. MAP. AE, D, MC, V. Closed mid-Nov.–Apr.*

Outdoor Activities and Sports

Bird-watchers can check out the shorebirds that congregate at the **Biddeford Pool East Sanctuary** (⊠ Rte. 9, Biddeford). The **Maine Audubon Society** (⊠ Rte. 9, Scarborough, ☎ 207/781–2330; 207/883–5100 from mid-June to Labor Day) operates guided canoe trips and rents canoes in Scarborough Marsh, the largest salt marsh in Maine. Programs at Maine Audubon's Falmouth headquarters (north of Portland) include nature walks and a discovery room for children.

York County Coast A to Z

Arriving and Departing

BY CAR

U.S. 1 from Kittery is the shopper's route north; other roads hug the coastline. Interstate 95 is usually faster for travelers headed to towns north of Ogunquit. The exit numbers can be confusing: As you go north from Portsmouth, Exits 1–3 lead to Kittery and Exit 4 leads to the Yorks. After the tollbooth in York, the Maine Turnpike begins, and the numbers start over again, with Exit 2 for Wells and Ogunquit and Exit 3 (and Route 35) for Kennebunk and Kennebunkport. Route 9 goes from Kennebunkport to Cape Porpoise and Goose Rocks.

BY PLANE

The closest airport is the Portland International Jetport (☞ Arriving and Departing *in* Maine A to Z, *below*), 35 mi northeast of Kennebunk.

Getting Around

BY CAR

Parking is tight in Kennebunkport in peak season. Possibilities include the municipal lot next to the Congregational Church ($2 an hour from May to October), the Consolidated School on School Street (free from late June to Labor Day), and, except on Sunday morning, St. Martha's Church (free year-round) on North Street.

Trolleys ($1–$3) serve several areas. A trolley circulates among the Yorks from June to Labor Day. Eight trolleys serve the major tourist areas and beaches of Ogunquit, including four that connect with Wells from mid-May to mid-October. The trolley from Dock Square in Kennebunkport to Kennebunk Beach runs from late June to Labor Day.

Contacts and Resources

EMERGENCIES

Maine State Police (⊠ Gray, ☎ 207/793–4500 or 800/482–0730). **Kennebunk Walk-in Clinic** (⊠ U.S. 1 N, ☎ 207/985–6027). **York Hospital** (⊠ 15 Hospital Dr., ☎ 207/351–2157) also operates Tel-A-Nurse (☎ 800/283–7234). **Southern Maine Medical Center** (⊠ Rte. 111, Biddeford, ☎ 207/283–7000; 207/283–7100 for emergency room).

VISITOR INFORMATION

Maine Tourism Association Visitor Information Center (⊠ U.S. 1 and I–95, Kittery 03904, ☎ 207/439–1319). **Kennebunk-Kennebunkport Chamber of Commerce** (⊠ 17 Western Ave., Kennebunk 04043, ☎ 207/967–0857). **Kittery-Eliot Chamber of Commerce** (⊠ 191 State Rd., Kittery 03904, ☎ 207/384–3338). **Ogunquit Chamber of Commerce** (⊠ Box 2289, U.S. 1, Ogunquit 03907, ☎ 207/646–2939). **Old Orchard Beach Chamber of Commerce** (⊠ Box 600, 1st St., Old Orchard Beach 04064, ☎ 207/934–2500 or 800/365–9386). **Wells Chamber of Commerce** (⊠ Box 356, Wells 04090, ☎ 207/646–2451). The **Yorks Chamber of Commerce** (⊠ 571 U.S. 1, York 03903, ☎ 207/363–4422).

PORTLAND TO PEMAQUID POINT

Maine's largest city, Portland, is small enough to be explored in a day or two. It holds some pleasant surprises, including the Old Port Exchange, among the finest urban renovation projects on the East Coast. Freeport, north of Portland, was made famous by its L. L. Bean store, whose success led to the opening of scores of other clothing stores and outlets. Brunswick is best known for Bowdoin College. Bath has been a shipbuilding center since 1607; the Maine Maritime Museum preserves its history. Wiscasset contains many antiques shops and galleries.

The Boothbays—the coastal areas of Boothbay Harbor, East Boothbay, Linekin Neck, Southport Island, and the inland town of Boothbay—attract hordes of vacationing families and flotillas of pleasure craft. The Pemaquid peninsula juts into the Atlantic south of Damariscotta and just east of the Boothbays. Near Pemaquid Beach you can view the objects unearthed at the Colonial Pemaquid Restoration.

This south–mid-coast area provides an overview of Maine: a little bit of city, a little more coastline, and a nice dollop of history and architecture.

Portland

105 mi northeast of Boston, 320 mi northeast of New York City, 215 mi southwest of St. Stephen, New Brunswick.

Portland's role as a cultural and economic center for the region has given the gentrifying city of 65,000 a variety of attractions. Its restored Old Port Exchange balances modern commercial enterprise and salty waterfront character in an area bustling with restaurants, shops, and galleries. Water tours of the harbor and excursions to the Calendar Islands depart from the piers of Commercial Street. Downtown Portland, in a funk for years, is now a burgeoning arts district connected to the Old Port by a revitalized Congress Street, where L. L. Bean operates a factory store.

Portland's first home was built on the peninsula now known as Munjoy Hill in 1632. The British burned the city in 1775, when residents refused to surrender arms, but it was rebuilt and became a major trading center. Much of Portland was destroyed on July 4 in the Great Fire of 1866, when a boy threw a celebration firecracker into a pile of wood shavings; 1,500 buildings burned to the ground. Poet Henry Wadsworth Longfellow said at the time that his city reminded him of the ruins of Pompeii. The Great Fire started not far from where people now wander the streets of the Old Port Exchange.

Congress Street runs the length of the peninsular city from alongside the Western Promenade in the southwest to the Eastern Promenade on Munjoy Hill in the northeast, passing through the small downtown area. A few blocks southeast of downtown, the bustling Old Port Exchange sprawls along the waterfront. Below Munjoy Hill is India Street, where the Great Fire of 1866 started.

8 One of the notable homes on Congress Street is the **Neal Dow Memorial,** a brick mansion built in 1829 in the late Federal style by General Neal Dow, an abolitionist and prohibitionist. The library has fine ornamental ironwork, and the furnishings include the family china, silver, and portraits. Don't miss the grandfather clocks. ✉ *714 Congress St.,* ☎ *207/773–7773.* ▱ *Free.* ⊙ *Tours weekdays 11–4.*

★ **9** For well more than a century, the tower of the Morse-Libby House, better known as the **Victoria Mansion,** has been a landmark visible from Casco Bay and Portland's harbor. A National Historic Landmark, the Italianate-style villa, built between 1858 and 1860, is widely regarded as the most sumptuously ornamented dwelling of its period remaining in the country. The lavish exterior is understated compared to the interior, which has colorful frescoed walls and ceilings, ornate marble mantelpieces, gilded gas chandeliers, stained-glass windows, and a freestanding mahogany staircase. ✉ *109 Danforth St.,* ☎ *207/772–4841.* ▱ *$5.* ⊙ *May–Oct., Tues.–Sat. 10–4, Sun. 1–5.*

10 Touching is okay at the **Children's Museum of Maine,** where kids can pretend they are fishing for lobster or are shopkeepers or computer experts. Camera Obscura, an exhibit about optics, charges a separate admission fee ($3). ✉ *142 Free St.,* ☎ *207/828–1234.* ▱ *$5, $6 for combination ticket.* ⊙ *Summer and school vacations, Mon.–Sat. 10–5, Sun. noon–5; during school yr, Wed.–Sat. 10–5, Sun. noon–5.*

★ **11** The **Portland Museum of Art** has a strong collection of seascapes and landscapes by Winslow Homer, John Marin, Andrew Wyeth, Marsden Hartley, and other painters. Homer's *Pulling the Dory* and *Weatherbeaten,* two quintessential Maine-coast images, are here. The Joan Whitney Payson Collection includes works by Monet, Picasso, and Renoir. Harry N. Cobb, an associate of I. M. Pei, designed the strikingly modern Charles Shipman Payson building. An exhibition about surrealism will be a summer 2000 highlight. ✉ *7 Congress Sq.,* ☎ *207/ 775–6148, 800/639–4067 for recorded information.* ▱ *$6; free Fri. evenings 5–9.* ⊙ *Columbus Day–Memorial Day, Tues.–Wed. and weekends 10–5, Thurs.–Fri. 10–9; Memorial Day–Columbus Day, Mon.–Wed. and weekends 10–5, Thurs.–Fri. 10–9.*

12 The **Wadsworth Longfellow House,** the boyhood home of the poet and the first brick house in Portland, is worth a stop. The late-Colonial-style structure, built in 1785, sits back from the street and has a small portico over its entrance and four chimneys surmounting the hip roof. Most of the furnishings are original to the house. Christmas is celebrated with special tours of the house that highlight a particular

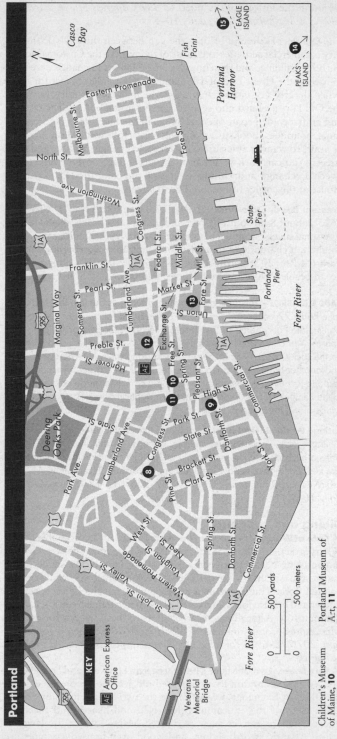

Portland

KEY

AE American Express Office

Children's Museum of Maine, **10**

Eagle Island, **15**

Neal Dow Memorial, **8**

Old Port Exchange, **13**

Peaks Island, **14**

Portland Museum of Art, **11**

Victoria Mansion, **9**

Wadsworth Longfellow House, **12**

period in the history of the poet. ⊠ *489 Congress St.,* ☎ *207/879–0427.* ▭ *$4.* ⊙ *June–Oct., daily 10–4.*

★ ⑬   The **Old Port Exchange** bridges the gap between the city's 19th-century commercial activities and those of today. Like the Customs House, the brick buildings and warehouses of the Old Port Exchange were built following the Great Fire of 1866 and were intended to last for ages. When the city's economy slumped in the mid-20th century, however, the Old Port declined and seemed slated for demolition. Then artists and craftspeople began opening shops in the late 1960s, and restaurants, boutiques, bookstores, and gift shops followed. Allow a couple of hours to wander at leisure on Market, Exchange, Middle, and Fore streets. You can park your car at the city garage on Fore Street (between Exchange and Union streets) or opposite the U.S. Customs House at the corner of Fore and Pearl streets.

Crescent Beach State Park (⊠ Rte. 77, Cape Elizabeth, ☎ 207/767–3625), about 8 mi south of Portland, has a sand beach, picnic tables, a seasonal snack bar, and a bathhouse. Popular with families with young children, it charges a nominal fee for admittance. **Scarborough Beach Park** (⊠ Rte. 207, Scarborough, ☎ 207/283–0067) is a long, sandy ocean beach with primitive facilities; admission is charged in season.

OFF THE   **CAPE ELIZABETH –** This upscale Portland suburb juts out into the Atlantic.
BEATEN PATH   Take Route 77 south and east from Portland and follow signs to Two Lights State Park, home to Two Lights, one of the Cape's three lighthouses. You can wander through old World War II bunkers and picnic on the rocky coast. Stay on Two Lights Road to the end, where you'll find another lighthouse, privately owned, and the Lobster Shack, a seafood-in-the-rough restaurant where you can dine inside or out. Return to the center of Cape Elizabeth and turn right on Shore Road, which winds along the coast to Portland.

Historic **Portland Head Light,** about 2 mi from town center in Fort Williams Park, was commissioned by George Washington in 1791. Besides a harbor view, the park has walking paths and picnic facilities. The keeper's house is now the **Museum at Portland Head Light.** *Museum:* ⊠ *1000 Shore Rd.,* ☎ *207/799–2661.* ▭ *$2.* ⊙ *June–Oct., daily 10–4.*

Dining and Lodging

$$–$$$ ✕ **Café at Wharf Street & the Wine Bar.** Tucked away on cobblestoned Wharf Street, an alley that runs parallel to Fore Street between Moulton and Union, this place is really two finds in one. The small, informal restaurant has a partially exposed kitchen, brick walls, and a painted floor. The menu changes seasonally, but the house specialty, lobster and brie ravioli with roasted grapes and caramelized onion sauce, is a mainstay. After dinner, head upstairs to the Wine Bar for dessert, wine, espresso, and drinks. ⊠ *38 Wharf St.,* ☎ *207/773–6667 for restaurant, 207/772–6976 for wine bar. Reservations essential. AE, MC, V. No lunch.*

$$–$$$ ✕ **Fore Street.** Two of Maine's best chefs, Sam Hayward and Dana Street,
★   opened this restaurant in a renovated old warehouse on the edge of the Old Port Exchange. Every table in the two-level main dining room has a view of the enormous brick oven and hearth and the open kitchen, where entrées such as roasted Maine lobster, applewood-grilled Atlantic swordfish loin, and wood-oven-braised cassoulet are prepared. ⊠ *288 Fore St.,* ☎ *207/775–2717. AE, MC, V. No lunch.*

$$–$$$ ✕ **Street and Co.** You enter through the kitchen, with all its wonder-
★ ful aromas, and dine, amid dried herbs and shelves of staples, on one
of a dozen copper-topped tables (so your waiter can place a skillet of
steaming seafood directly in front of you). In one dining room is a beer
and wine bar. Fish and seafood are the specialties here, and you won't
find any better or fresher. The entrées include lobster diavolo for two,
scallops in Pernod and cream, and sole Française. A vegetarian dish is
the only alternative to seafood. ✉ *33 Wharf St.,* ☎ *207/775–0887.
AE, MC, V. No lunch.*

$$ ✕ **Aubergine.** This bistro and wine bar has staked out a prime down-
town location, across the street from L. L. Bean and down the street
from the Portland Museum of Art. The atmosphere is casual and the
food is very good. The menu changes daily but might include appe-
tizers such as Swiss onion soup with fresh tarragon or fried Pemaquid
oysters, and entrées like spiced duck breast with fennel sauce or crispy
salmon with spinach and Pernod. Wines by the glass are chosen to com-
plement the dishes. ✉ *555 Congress St.,* ☎ *207/874–0680. Closed Sun.
night and Mon. No lunch. MC, V.*

$$ ✕ **Katahdin.** Painted tables, flea-market decor, mismatched dinnerware,
and a log-pile bar provide a fun and unpretentious setting for dining
on large portions of home-cooked New England fare. Try the chicken
potpie, fried trout, crab cakes, or the nightly blue-plate special, and
save room for the fruit cobbler. ✉ *106 High St.,* ☎ *207/774–1740.
D, MC, V. Closed Sun. No lunch.*

$–$$ ✕ **Portland Public Market.** The more than 20 locally owned businesses
inside this new market specialize in fresh foods, organic produce, and
imported specialty foods, including fresh-baked goods, soups and
chowders, smoked seafood, rotisserie chicken, aged cheeses, and German meats. At Hanson Bros. Seafood Café, you can choose a fresh Maine
lobster roll, a blackened swordfish wrap, or a Wolfe's Neck burger,
made with free-range Black Angus beef from a Freeport farm. A skywalk connects the market to the third floor of a parking garage on Elm
Street; parking is free if you have a vendor stamp your ticket. Most
merchants accept a number of credit cards. ✉ *25 Preble St.,* ☎ *207/
228–2000.* ☉ *Daily 7–7.*

$$$$ ✕🏠 **Inn by the Sea.** On greater Portland's most prime real estate, this
all-suites inn is set back from the shoreline and has views of the ocean—
Crescent Beach and Kettle Cove in particular. The dining room ($$–
$$$$), open to nonguests, serves fine seafood and regional dishes. The
cottage-style architecture throughout is typical New England. ✉ *40
Bowery Beach Rd., Cape Elizabeth 04107 (7 mi south of Portland),*
☎ *207/799–3134 or 800/888–4287,* ℻ *207/799–4779. 25 suites, 18
cottage condominiums. Restaurant, pool, tennis court, croquet, bicy-
cles. AE, D, MC, V.*

$$$$ 🏠 **Portland Regency Hotel.** The only major hotel in the center of the
Old Port Exchange, the Regency building was Portland's armory in the
late 19th century. Rooms have four-poster beds, tall standing mirrors,
floral curtains, and love seats. ✉ *20 Milk St., 04101,* ☎ *207/774–4200
or 800/727–3436,* ℻ *207/775–2150. 87 rooms, 8 suites. Restaurant,
massage, sauna, steam room, health club, nightclub, meeting rooms.
AE, D, DC, MC, V.*

$$$ 🏠 **Inn on Carleton.** After a day of exploring Portland's museums and
shops, you'll find a quiet retreat at this elegant brick town house on
the city's Western Promenade. Built in 1869, it is furnished throughout with period antiques as well as artwork by contemporary Maine
artists. The entryway features a restored trompe l'oeil painting by
Charles Schumacher, and more of his work has been uncovered in the
back dining room. ✉ *46 Carleton St., 04102,* ☎ *207/775–1910 or 800/
639–1779,* ℻ *207/761–0956. 6 rooms. Full breakfast. D, MC, V.*

Nightlife and the Arts

NIGHTLIFE

Asylum (⊠ 121 Center St., ☎ 207/772–8274) has live entertainment and dancing. **Brian Boru** (⊠ 57 Center St., ☎ 207/780–1506) is an Irish pub with occasional entertainment and an outside deck. **Comedy Connection** (⊠ 6 Custom House Wharf, ☎ 207/774–5554) hosts stand-up comedians from Wednesday to Sunday.

Gritty McDuff's—Portland's Original Brew Pub (⊠ 396 Fore St., ☎ 207/772–2739) brews fine ales and serves British pub fare and seafood dishes. **Stone Coast Brewery** (⊠ 14 York St., ☎ 207/773–2337) is a brew pub with entertainment. The **Wine Bar** (⊠ 38 Wharf St., ☎ 207/772–6976) has comfortable chairs, couches, and a fireplace. A dozen of the 250 wines by the bottle can be ordered by the glass. Espresso, light meals, and desserts are served.

THE ARTS

Portland Performing Arts Center (⊠ 25A Forest Ave., ☎ 207/761–0591) presents music, dance, and theater performances. **Cumberland County Civic Center** (⊠ 1 Civic Center Sq., ☎ 207/775–3458) hosts concerts, sporting events, and family shows.

Portland City Hall's Merrill Auditorium (⊠ 20 Myrtle St., ☎ 207/874–8200) is home to the Portland Symphony Orchestra and Portland Concert Association and the site of numerous theatrical and musical events. **Portland Symphony Orchestra** (⊠ 30 Myrtle St., ☎ 207/773–8191) concerts take place from October to August. **Mad Horse Theatre Company** (⊠ 92 Oak St., ☎ 207/797–3338) performs classic, contemporary, and original works. **Portland Stage Company** (⊠ 25A Forest Ave., ☎ 207/774–0465) mounts productions year-round at the Portland Performing Arts Center.

Outdoor Activities and Sports

BALLOON RIDES

Balloon Rides (⊠ 17 Freeman St., ☎ 207/772–4730) operates scenic flights over southern Maine.

BASEBALL

The Class AA **Portland Sea Dogs** (☎ 207/879–9500), a farm team of the Florida Marlins, play at Hadlock Field (⊠ 271 Park Ave.). Tickets cost from $4 to $6.

BOAT TRIPS

For tours of the harbor, Casco Bay, and the nearby islands, try **Bay View Cruises** (⊠ Fisherman's Wharf, ☎ 207/761–0496), **Casco Bay Lines** (⊠ Maine State Pier, ☎ 207/774–7871), **Eagle Tours** (⊠ Long Wharf, ☎ 207/774–6498), **Old Port Mariner Fleet** (⊠ Long Wharf, ☎ 207/775–0727, 207/642–3270, or 800/437–3270), or **Palawan Sailing** (⊠ Old Port, ☎ 207/774–2163).

HOCKEY

The **Portland Pirates,** the farm team of the Washington Capitals, play home games at the Cumberland County Civic Center (⊠ 85 Free St., ☎ 207/828–4665). Tickets cost from $8 to $13.

Shopping

ART AND ANTIQUES

Abacus (⊠ 44 Exchange St., ☎ 207/772–4880) has unusual gift items in glass, wood, and textiles, plus fine modern jewelry. **F. O. Bailey Antiquarians** (⊠ 141 Middle St., ☎ 207/774–1479), Portland's largest retail showroom, carries antique and reproduction furniture and jewelry, paintings, rugs, and china.

Greenhut Galleries (✉ 146 Middle St., ☎ 207/772–2693) carries contemporary Maine art. The **Pine Tree Shop & Bayview Gallery** (✉ 75 Market St., ☎ 207/773–3007 or 800/244–3007) has original art and prints by prominent Maine painters. **Stein Glass Gallery** (✉ 195 Middle St., ☎ 207/772–9072) specializes in decorative and utilitarian contemporary glass.

BOOKS

Carlson and Turner (✉ 241 Congress St., ☎ 207/773–4200) is an antiquarian book dealer with an estimated 50,000 titles.

MALL

Maine Mall (✉ 364 Maine Mall Rd., South Portland, ☎ 207/774–0303), 5 mi south of Portland, has 145 stores, including Sears, Filene's, JCPenney, and Macy's.

Casco Bay Islands

The islands of Casco Bay are also known as the Calendar Islands because an early explorer mistakenly thought there was one for each day of the year (in reality there are only 140). The brightly painted ferries of Casco Bay Lines (☞ Getting Around *in* Portland to Pemaquid Point, *below*) are the islands' lifeline. There is frequent service to the most populated ones, including Peaks, Long, Little Diamond, and Great Diamond.

⑭ **Peaks Island,** nearest to Portland, is the most developed of the Calendar Islands, but you can still commune with the wind and the sea, explore an old fort, and ramble along the alternately rocky and sandy shore. The trip to the island by boat is particularly enjoyable at or near sunset. Order a lobster sandwich or cold beer on the outdoor deck of **Jones' Landing** restaurant, steps from the dock. A circle trip without stops takes about 90 minutes. On the far side of the island you can stop on the rugged shoreline and have lunch. A small museum with Civil War artifacts, open in summer, is maintained in the **Fifth Maine Regiment** building. When the Civil War broke out in 1861, Maine was asked to raise only a single regiment to fight, but the state raised 10 and sent the 5th Maine Regiment into the war's first battle at Bull Run.

⑮ The 17-acre **Eagle Island,** owned by the state and open to the public for day trips in summer, was the home of Admiral Robert E. Peary, the American explorer of the North Pole. Peary built a stone-and-wood house on the island as a summer retreat in 1904 but made it his permanent residence. With Peary's stuffed Arctic birds, the quartz he brought home and set into the fieldstone fireplace, and other objects, the house remains as it was when Peary lived here. The *Kristy K.* and *Fish Hawk* depart from Long Wharf and make four-hour narrated tours; there are also tours of Portland Head Light and seal-watching cruises. ✉ *Long Wharf,* ☎ *207/774–6498.* ▣ *$8–$15, depending on tour.* ☉ *Departures late May–Labor Day, daily beginning 10 AM.*

Chebeague Island measures about 5 mi long and is less than 2 mi across at its widest. Service to the island is via **Casco Bay Lines** (☎ 207/774–7871) from Portland or the **Chebeague Transportation Company** (☎ 207/846–3700) from the dock on Cousins Island, north of Portland and accessible by car. You can stay overnight at the **Chebeague Island Inn** (☎ 207/846–5155), open from mid-May to mid-October, or the Chebeague Orchard B&B (☎ 207/846–9488).

Outdoor Activities and Sports

Maine Island Kayak Co. (✉ 70 Luther St., Peaks Island, ☎ 800/796–2373) provides sea-kayaking instruction and conducts expeditions and tours along the Maine coast.

Freeport

16 *17 mi northeast of Portland, 10 mi southwest of Brunswick.*

Freeport, on U.S. 1, has charming back streets lined with historic buildings and old clapboard houses, and there's a small harbor on the Harraseeket River. Most people, however, come here to shop—L. L. Bean is the store that put Freeport on the map.

Wolfe's Neck Woods State Park has 5 mi of hiking trails along Casco Bay, the Harraseeket River, and a fringe salt marsh. Naturalists lead walks. The park has picnic tables and grills but no camping. ⊠ *Wolfe's Neck Rd. (follow Bow St. opposite L. L. Bean off U.S. 1),* ☎ *207/865–4465.* ⊟ *$2 Memorial Day–Labor Day, $1 off-season.*

Bradbury Mountain State Park has moderate trails to the top of Bradbury Mountain, which has views of the sea. A picnic area and shelter, a ball field, a playground, and 41 campsites are among the facilities. ⊠ *Rte. 9, Pownal (5 mi from Freeport-Durham exit off I–95),* ☎ *207/688–4712.* ⊟ *$2 Memorial Day–Labor Day, $1 off-season.*

☾ At the **Desert of Maine,** a 40-acre desert, a safari coach tours the sand dunes and you can walk nature trails, hunt for gemstones, and watch sand artists at work. Poor agricultural practices in the late 18th century combined with massive land clearing and overgrazing uncovered this desert, which was actually formed by a glacier during the last Ice Age. ⊠ *95 Desert Rd. (Exit 19 off I–95),* ☎ *207/865–6962.* ⊟ *$6.75.* ⊙ *Early May–mid-Oct.*

Dining and Lodging

$–$$ ✕ **Harraseeket Lunch & Lobster Co.** Seafood baskets and lobster dinners are what this bare-bones place beside the town landing in South Freeport is all about. You can eat outside on picnic tables in good weather. ⊠ *On the pier, end of Main St., South Freeport,* ☎ *207/865–4888. Reservations not accepted. No credit cards. Closed mid-Oct.–Apr.*

$$$$ ✕⊞ **Harraseeket Inn.** Despite modern appointments such as elevators, whirlpool baths, and an indoor pool, this 1850 Greek Revival home and newer section provide an old-fashioned country-inn experience. Afternoon tea is served in the mahogany drawing room, and guest rooms have reproductions of Federal canopy beds. The formal dining room, which serves excellent contemporary New England–influenced cuisine, is a simply decorated space with picture windows facing a garden courtyard. The casual Broad Arrow Tavern, with an open kitchen and a wood-fired oven and grill, serves heartier fare. ⊠ *162 Main St., 04032,* ☎ *207/865–9377 or 800/342–6423,* ℻ *207/865–1684. 82 rooms, 2 suites. Restaurant, bar, indoor pool, hot tubs, croquet. Full breakfast. AE, D, DC, MC, V.*

$$–$$$ ⊞ **Isaac Randall House.** On a 5-acre lot outside town, this circa-1829 inn is a quiet retreat. Victorian antiques and country pieces fill the rooms. A red caboose in the backyard has been turned into a room that's ideal for families. ⊠ *10 Independence Dr., 04032,* ☎ *207/865–9295 or 800/865–9295,* ℻ *207/865–9003. 11 rooms, 1 suite. Playground. AE, D, MC, V.*

Outdoor Activities and Sports

Atlantic Seal Cruises (⊠ South Freeport, ☎ 207/865–6112) operates day trips to Eagle Island and evening seal and osprey watches. L. L. Bean's year-round **Outdoor Discovery Schools** (⊠ Freeport, ☎ 888/552–3261) include half- and one-day classes, as well as longer trips, that teach canoeing, kayaking, fly-fishing, and other sports. Classes are for all skill levels; it's best to sign up several months in advance if possible.

Shopping

The *Freeport Visitors Guide* (☎ 207/865–1212; 800/865–1994 for a copy) lists the more than 100 shops and factory outlet stores that can be found on Main Street, Bow Street, and elsewhere. **Cuddledown of Maine** (✉ 237 U.S. 1, ☎ 207/865–1713) has a selection of down comforters, pillows, and luxurious bedding. Head upstairs for discounted merchandise. **Thos. Moser Cabinetmakers** (✉ 149 Main St., ☎ 207/ 865–4519) carries high-quality handmade furniture with clean, classic lines.

Founded in 1912 as a mail-order merchandiser of products for hunters, guides, and fisherfolk, **L. L. Bean** (✉ 95 Main St./U.S. 1, ☎ 800/341– 4341) attracts 3½ million shoppers a year to its giant store (open 24 hours a day) in the heart of Freeport's shopping district. You can still find the original hunting boots, along with cotton, wool, and silk sweaters; camping and ski equipment; comforters; and hundreds of other items for the home, car, boat, or campsite. Across from the main store, a Bean factory outlet has seconds and discontinued merchandise at discount prices. **L. L. Bean Kids** (✉ 8 Nathan Nye St., ☎ 800/341–4341) specializes in children's merchandise and has a climbing wall and other kid-appealing activities.

Harrington House Museum Store (✉ 45 Main St., ☎ 207/865–0477) is a restored 19th-century merchant's home owned by the Freeport Historical Society; all the period reproductions that furnish the rooms are for sale. You can also buy books, rugs, jewelry, crafts, Shaker items, toys, and kitchen utensils.

Brunswick

⑰ *10 mi north of Freeport.*

Lovely brick and clapboard homes and structures are the highlights of the town's **Federal Street Historic District**, which includes Federal Street and Park Row and the stately campus of Bowdoin College. Pleasant Street, in the center of town, is the business district. Harriet Beecher Stowe wrote *Uncle Tom's Cabin* while living in Brunswick.

The 110-acre campus of **Bowdoin College** (✉ Maine, Bath, and College Sts., off east end of Pleasant St.) holds an enclave of distinguished architecture, gardens, and grassy quadrangles, along with several museums (☞ *below*). Campus tours (☎ 207/725–3000) depart daily except Sunday from the admissions office in Chamberlain Hall. Among the historic buildings are Massachusetts Hall, a stout, sober, hip-roofed brick structure dating from 1802 that once housed the entire college. Nathaniel Hawthorne and the poet Henry Wadsworth Longfellow attended the college.

Bowdoin's Hubbard Hall, an imposing 1902 neo-Gothic building, is home to Maine's only gargoyle and the **Peary–MacMillan Arctic Museum.** The museum contains photographs, navigational instruments, and artifacts from the first successful expedition to the North Pole, in 1909, by two of Bowdoin's most famous alumni, Admiral Robert E. Peary and Donald B. MacMillan. ☎ *207/725–3416.* ✇ *Free.* ⊘ *Tues.– Sat. 10–5, Sun. 2–5.*

The **Bowdoin College Museum of Art,** in a splendid Renaissance Revival–style building designed by Charles F. McKim in 1894, has collections that encompass Assyrian and classical art and works by Dutch, Italian, French, and Flemish old masters; a superb gathering of Colonial and Federal paintings, notably Gilbert Stuart portraits of Madison and Jefferson; and a Winslow Homer Gallery of engravings, etchings, and memorabilia (open in summer only). The museum's collection also includes 19th- and 20th-century American painting and sculpture, with works by Mary Cassatt, Andrew Wyeth, and Robert Rauschenberg. ⊠ *Walker Art Bldg.,* ☎ *207/725–3275.* 🎟 *Free.* ⊙ *Tues.– Sat. 10–5, Sun. 2–5.*

The **General Joshua L. Chamberlain Museum** displays memorabilia and documents the life of Maine's most celebrated Civil War hero. The general, who played an instrumental role in the Union army's victory at Gettysburg, was elected governor in 1867. From 1871 to 1883 he served as president of Bowdoin College. ⊠ *226 Main St.,* ☎ *207/729–6606.* 🎟 *$3.* ⊙ *Tues.–Sat. 10–4.*

OFF THE BEATEN PATH

THE HARPSWELLS – A side trip from Bath or Brunswick on Route 123 or Route 24 takes you to the peninsulas and islands known collectively as the Harpswells. Small coves along Harpswell Neck shelter the boats of lobstermen, and summer cottages are tucked away amid the birch and spruce trees. Along Route 123, signs with blue herons mark the studios and galleries of the Harpswell Craft Guild. For lunch, follow the signs off Route 123 to **Dolphin Marina** (⊠ End of Basin Point Rd., off Ash Point Rd.) and try the delicious fish stew and a blueberry muffin.

Dining and Lodging

$$ ✕ **The Great Impasta.** You can match your favorite pasta and sauce to create your own dish at this storefront restaurant, which is a good choice for lunch, tea, or dinner. The seafood lasagna is tasty, too. ⊠ *42 Maine St.,* ☎ *207/729–5858. Reservations not accepted. D, DC, MC, V.*

$ ✕ **Fat Boy Drive-In.** Put your lights on for service at this old-fashioned drive-in restaurant renowned for its BLTs made with Canadian bacon, frappes (try the blueberry), and onion rings. ⊠ *Bath Rd.,* ☎ *207/729– 9431. No credit cards. Closed mid-Oct.–mid-Mar.*

$$$ 🏨 **Captain Daniel Stone Inn.** This Federal inn overlooks the Androscoggin River. No two rooms are furnished identically, but all contain executive-style comforts and many have whirlpool baths, queen-size beds, and pullout sofas. A guest parlor, a breakfast room, and excellent service in the Narcissa Stone Restaurant (no lunch on Saturday) make this an upscale escape from college-town funkiness. ⊠ *10 Water St., 04011,* ☎ 🖷 *207/725–9898. 30 rooms, 4 suites. Restaurant. Continental breakfast. AE, DC, MC, V.*

$$–$$$ 🏨 **Captain's Watch Bed and Breakfast and Sail Charter.** Built in 1862 and originally known as the Union Hotel, the Captain's Watch is the oldest surviving hotel on the Maine coast. Although much smaller than originally built, this National Historic Register property retains its distinctive octagonal cupola and a homey, old-fashioned feel. Two guest rooms share access to the cupola. Others have less inspired but still pleasant water views. Guests can arrange to go on a day sail aboard the inn's 37-foot sloop, *Symbion.* ⊠ *2476 Cundy's Harbor Rd., Cundy's Harbor 04011,* ☎ *207/725–0979. 4 rooms, 1 suite. Full breakfast. MC, V.*

$–$$$ 🏨 **Harpswell Inn.** Spacious lawns and neatly pruned shrubs surround the stately white clapboard Harpswell Inn, built in 1761. The three-story inn was the center of a shipbuilding operation on Lookout Point, and the living room faces Middle Bay and Birch Island. Half the rooms have water views, as do the three carriage-house suites, one with a whirlpool. The inn is no-smoking. ⊠ *141 Lookout Point Rd., South Harpswell 04079,* ☎ *207/833–5509 or 800/843–5509. 9 rooms, 7 with bath, 1 with half bath; 3 suites. Full breakfast. MC, V.*

Nightlife and the Arts

Bowdoin Summer Music Festival (☎ 207/725–3322 for information; 207/725–3895 for tickets) is a six-week concert series featuring performances by students, faculty, and prestigious guest artists. **Maine State Music Theater** (✉ Pickard Theater, Bowdoin College, ☎ 207/725–8769) stages musicals from mid-June to August. **Theater Project of Brunswick** (✉ 14 School St., ☎ 207/729–8584) performs semiprofessional, children's, and community theater.

Outdoor Activities and Sports

H2Outfitters (☎ 207/833–5257) provides sea-kayaking instruction and rentals and conducts day or overnight trips. **Logan's Marina** (✉ Off Rte. 24, Bailey Island, ☎ 207/833–2810) rents small power boats.

Shopping

ICON Contemporary Art (✉ 19 Mason St., ☎ 207/725–8157) specializes in modern art. **O'Farrell Gallery** (✉ 58 Maine St., ☎ 207/729–8228) represents artists such as Neil Welliver, Marguerite Robichaux, and Sheila Geoffrion. **Wyler Craft Gallery** (✉ 150 Maine St., ☎ 207/729–1321) carries an intriguing selection of crafts, jewelry, and clothing.

Tontine Fine Candies (✉ Tontine Mall, 149 Maine St., ☎ 207/729–4462) has chocolates and other goodies. A **farmers' market** takes place on Tuesday and Friday from May to October, on the town mall between Maine Street and Park Row.

Bath

⓲ *11 mi northeast of Brunswick, 38 mi northeast of Portland.*

Bath has been a shipbuilding center since 1607, so it's appropriate that a museum here explores the state's rich maritime heritage. These days the Bath Iron Works turns out guided-missile frigates for the U.S. Navy and merchant container ships. It's a good idea to avoid Bath and U.S. 1 on weekdays between 3:15 and 4:30 PM, when BIW's major shift change occurs. The massive exodus can tie up traffic for miles.

★ The **Maine Maritime Museum and Shipyard** contains ship models, journals, photographs, and other artifacts and displays. The 142-ft Grand Banks fishing schooner *Sherman Zwicker,* one of the last of its kind, is on display when in port. You can watch boatbuilders wield their tools on classic Maine boats at the restored Percy & Small Shipyard and Boat Shop. The outdoor shipyard is open from May to November; during these months the *Linekin II* sails the scenic Kennebec River. During the off-season, the Maritime History Building has indoor exhibits, videos, and activities. ✉ *243 Washington St.,* ☎ *207/443–1316.* ⊠ *$7.75.* ☉ *Daily 9:30–5.*

The **Chocolate Church Arts Center** (☞ Nightlife and the Arts, *below*) offers guided walking tours of private homes and historic buildings from mid-June to mid-September. Call for schedule and fees.

Reid State Park (☎ 207/371–2303), on Georgetown Island, off Route 127, has 1½ mi of sand on three beaches. Facilities include bathhouses, picnic tables, fireplaces, and snack bar. Parking lots fill by 11 AM on summer Sundays and holidays; admission is charged.

OFF THE BEATEN PATH

POPHAM – Follow Route 209 south from Bath to Popham, the site of the short-lived 1607 Popham Colony, where the *Virginia,* the first European ship built in the New World, was launched. Benedict Arnold set off from Popham on his ill-fated march against the British in Québec. Granite-walled **Ft. Popham** (✉ Phippsburg, ☎ 207/389–1335) was built in

1607. **Popham State Park,** at the end of Route 209, has a good sand beach, a marsh area, bathhouses, and picnic tables; admission is charged.

Dining and Lodging

$$$–$$$$ ✕ **Robinhood Free Meetinghouse.** Chef Michael Gagne, one of Maine's
★   best, finally has a restaurant that complements his classic and creative multi-ethnic cuisine. The 1855 Greek Revival–style meetinghouse has large-pane windows and is decorated simply: cream-color walls, pine floorboards, cherry Shaker-style chairs, white table linens. You might begin with the artichoke strudel; veal saltimbocca and confit of duck are two entrées. Finish up with Gagne's signature Obsession in Three Chocolates. Jazz and theme nights take place in the off-season. ⊠ *Robinhood Rd., Georgetown,* ☎ *207/371–2188. AE, D, MC, V. Closed some weeknights mid-Oct.–mid-May. No lunch.*

$$–$$$ ✕ **Kristina's Restaurant & Bakery.** This restaurant in a frame house with a front deck prepares some of the finest pies, pastries, and cakes on the coast. The satisfying new American cuisine served for dinner usually includes fresh seafood and grilled meats. All meals can be packed to go. ⊠ *160 Centre St.,* ☎ *207/442–8577. D, MC, V. Closed Jan. No dinner Sun. Call ahead in winter.*

$$–$$$ ⊡ **The Inn at Bath.** Filled with antiques, this handsome 1810 Greek Revival inn in the town's historic district makes a convenient and comfortable base for exploring Bath on foot. Five rooms have wood-burning fireplaces, and two of these also have two-person whirlpool tubs. ⊠ *969 Washington St., 04530,* ☎ *207/443–4294,* F̱A̱X̱ *207/443–4295. 9 rooms. Full breakfast. AE, D, MC, V.*

$$–$$$ ⊡ **The 1774 Inn.** On the National Register of Historic Places, the 1774 Inn is a pre-Revolutionary mansion. Architecture buffs will savor the interior detailing and antiques lovers will appreciate the magnificent pieces in the house. The inn, on a bend in the Kennebec River, has large corner guest rooms, two with fireplaces, two with river views. ⊠ *44 Parker Head Rd., Phippsburg Center 04562,* ☎ *207/389–1774. 4 rooms. Full breakfast. No credit cards.*

Nightlife and the Arts

Chocolate Church Arts Center (⊠ 804 Washington St., ☎ 207/442–8455) hosts folk, jazz, and classical concerts, theater productions, and performances for children. The gallery presents exhibits of works in various media by Maine artists.

Shopping

The **Montsweag Flea Market** (⊠ U.S. 1 between Bath and Wiscasset, ☎ 207/443–2809) is a roadside attraction with trash and treasures. It takes place on weekends from May to October and also on Wednesday (for antiques) and Friday during the summer. **West Island Gallery** (⊠ 27 Centre St., ☎ 207/443–9625) carries contemporary Maine art, quality crafts, and clothing.

Wiscasset

⑲ *10 mi northeast of Bath, 46 mi northeast of Portland.*

Settled in 1663 on the banks of the Sheepscot River, Wiscasset fittingly bills itself as Maine's Prettiest Village. Stroll through town and you'll pass by elegant sea captains' homes (many now antiques shops or galleries), old cemeteries, churches, and public buildings.

The **Nickels-Sortwell House,** maintained by the Society for the Preservation of New England Antiquities, is an outstanding example of Federal architecture. ⊠ *Main St.,* ☎ *207/882–6218.* ☑ *$4.* ☉ *June–Sept., Wed.–Sun. 11–5; tours on the hr, 11–4.*

The 1807 **Castle Tucker,** one of the properties maintained by the Society for the Preservation of New England Antiquities, is known for its extravagant architecture, Victorian decor, and freestanding elliptical staircase. ⊠ *Lee and High Sts.,* ☎ *207/882–7364.* ☑ *$4.* ☉ *July–Aug., Thurs.–Sat. noon–5; tours on the hr, noon–4.*

The **Musical Wonder House** contains a vast collection of antique music boxes from around the world. ⊠ *18 High St.,* ☎ *207/882–7163.* ☑ *1/2-hr presentation on main floor $6.50; 1-hr presentation $12; 3-hr tour of entire house $30 or $50 for 2 people.* ☉ *Memorial Day–late Oct., daily 10–6; last tour usually at 4; call ahead for 3-hr tours.*

 The restored 1930s coaches of the **Maine Coast Railroad** travel from Wiscasset to Bath and Newcastle. ⊠ *Water St.,* ☎ *207/882–8000 or 800/795–5404.* ☑ *$10.* ☉ *Late June–early Sept., daily; late May–late June and early Sept.–mid-Oct., weekends only; call for schedule.*

Dining and Lodging

$–$$ ✕ **Sarah's.** Locals and visitors alike rely on this popular family restaurant for breakfast (weekends only), lunch, and dinner. The dining room and the deck have views over the Sheepscot River. Soups, pizzas, Mexican-style foods, hearty sandwiches, and fresh-baked goodies are on the menu. ⊠ *U.S. 1 and Water St.,* ☎ *207/882–7504. AE, D, MC, V.*

$$–$$$$ ✕▣ **Squire Tarbox.** The Federal-style Squire Tarbox is equal parts inn, restaurant, and working goat farm. Its country setting toward the end of Westport Island, midway between Bath and Wiscasset, is far removed from the rushing traffic of U.S. 1, yet area attractions are easily accessible. Rooms are simply furnished with antiques and country pieces; four have fireplaces. The menu at the dining room ($$$; reservations essential) changes nightly but always includes a vegetarian entrée and a sampling of the inn's own goat cheese. ⊠ *Box 1181, Rte. 144, Westport 04578,* ☎ *207/882–7693,* FAX *207/882–7107. 11 rooms. Restaurant. Full breakfast; MAP available. AE, D, MC, V. Closed late Oct.–mid-May.*

Shopping

The Wiscasset area rivals Searsport (☞ Penobscot Bay, *below*) as a destination for antiquing. Shops line Wiscasset's main and side streets and extend over the bridge into Edgecomb.

The **Butterstamp Workshop** (⊠ Middle St., ☎ 207/882–7825) carries handcrafted folk-art designs from antique molds. The **Maine Art Gallery** (⊠ Warren St., ☎ 207/882–7511) carries the works of local artists. **Treats** (⊠ Main St., ☎ 207/882–6192) is a good place to pick up fancy foods for a picnic at Waterfront Park. The **Wiscasset Bay Gallery** (⊠ Main St., ☎ 207/882–7682) specializes in the works of 19th- and 20th-century American and European artists.

Boothbay

㉑ *10 mi southeast of Wiscasset, 60 mi northeast of Portland, 50 mi southwest of Camden.*

When Portlanders want a break from what they know as city life, many come north to the Boothbay region, which comprises Boothbay proper, East Boothbay, and Boothbay Harbor. This part of the shoreline is a craggy stretch of inlets where pleasure craft anchor alongside trawlers and lobster boats. Commercial Street, Wharf Street, the By-Way, and Townsend Avenue are filled with shops, galleries, and ice cream parlors. Excursion boats (☞ Outdoor Activities and Sports, *below*) leave from the piers off Commercial Street. From the harbor, you can catch a boat to Monhegan Island.

Ⓒ At the **Boothbay Railway Village,** about a mile north of Boothbay, you can ride 1½ mi on a narrow-gauge steam train through a re-creation of a century-old New England village. Among the 24 buildings is a museum with more than 50 antique automobiles and trucks. ⊠ *Rte. 27,* ☎ *207/633–4727.* ☞ *$7.* ☉ *Early June–Columbus Day, daily 9:30– 5; special Halloween schedule.*

Ⓒ The **Department of Marine Resources Aquarium** has a shark you can pet, touch tanks, and rare blue and multiclawed lobsters. ⊠ *McKown Point Rd., West Boothbay Harbor,* ☎ *207/633–9559.* ☞ *$2.50.* ☉ *Memorial Day–Columbus Day, daily 10–5.*

Dining and Lodging

$$–$$$ ✕ **Christopher's Boathouse.** You can't beat the harbor view or the food at this restaurant in a renovated boathouse where you can watch the chefs at work. The lobster and mango bisque with hot and spicy lobster wontons is noteworthy. Some main-course options are lobster succotash and Asian-spiced tuna steak with Caribbean salsa; finish off with the raspberry almond flan. ⊠ *25 Union St., Boothbay Harbor,* ☎ *207/633–6565. MC, V. Mid-Oct.–mid-May; call in advance.*

$ ✕ **Lobstermen's Coop.** Crustacean lovers and landlubbers will find something to like at this dockside working lobster pound. Lobster, steamers, hot dogs, hamburgers, sandwiches, and desserts are on the menu. Eat indoors or outside and watch the lobstermen at work. ⊠ *Atlantic Ave., Boothbay Harbor,* ☎ *207/633–4900. Closed mid-Oct.–mid-May.*

$$$$ ✕🏨 **Spruce Point Inn.** Escape the hubbub of Boothbay Harbor at this sprawling resort, which is a short shuttle ride to town yet a world away. Guest rooms are in the main inn, family cottages, and condominiums. Most rooms are comfortable but not fancy and have ocean views. Lobster cioppino made with local shellfish and served over cappellini is the signature dish at the dining room ($$$–$$$$), which has an unparalleled view of the outer harbor and open ocean. ⊠ *Box 237, Atlantic Ave., Boothbay Harbor 04538,* ☎ *207/633–4152 or 800/553– 0289,* 🖷 *207/633–7138. 37 rooms, 26 suites, 7 family cottages, 4 condominiums. Lounge, freshwater pool, saltwater pool, 2 tennis courts, health club, spa, dock. MAP. MC, V. Closed mid-Oct.–mid-May.*

$$–$$$ 🏨 **Admiral's Quarters Inn.** This renovated 1830 sea captain's house is ideally situated for those wanting to explore Boothbay Harbor by foot, a good thing since in-town parking is limited and expensive. The rooms have private decks, many overlooking the harbor, and on rainy days you can relax by the woodstove in the solarium. ⊠ *71 Commercial St., Boothbay Harbor 04538,* ☎ *207/633–2474,* 🖷 *207/633–5904. 2 rooms, 4 suites. Full breakfast. D, MC, V. Closed mid-Dec.–mid-Feb.*

Outdoor Activities and Sports

Balmy Day Cruises (☎ 207/633–2284 or 800/298–2284) operates day boat trips to Monhegan Island and tours of the harbor and nearby lighthouses. **Cap'n Fish's Boat Trips** (⊠ Pier 1 for departures, ☎ 207/633– 3244 or 800/636–3244) operates sightseeing cruises throughout the region, including puffin-watching cruises, lobster-hauling and whale-watching rides, and trips to Damariscove Harbor, Pemaquid Point, and up the Kennebec River to Bath.

Shopping

BOOTHBAY HARBOR

Gleason Fine Art (⊠ 15 Oak St., ☎ 207/633–6849) carries fine art— regional and national, early 19th century and contemporary. **House of**

Logan (✉ 32 Townsend Ave., ☎ 207/633–2293) stocks upscale casual and fancy attire for men and women. Beautiful housewares and attractive children's clothes can be found at the **Village Store & Children's Shop** (✉ 34 Townsend Ave., ☎ 207/633–2293).

EDGECOMB

Edgecomb Potters (✉ Rte. 27, ☎ 207/882–6802) sells high-end glazed porcelain pottery and other crafts at rather high prices; some discontinued items or seconds are discounted. These potters have an excellent reputation. There's a store in Freeport if you miss this one. **Sheepscot River Pottery** (✉ U.S. 1, ☎ 207/882–9410) has original hand-painted pottery as well as a large collection of American-made crafts, including jewelry, kitchenware, furniture, and home accessories.

Pemaquid Point

㉑ *8 mi southeast of Wiscasset.*

A detour off U.S. 1 via Routes 130 and 32 leads to the Pemaquid Peninsula and a satisfying microcosm of coastal Maine. Art galleries, country stores, antiques and crafts shops, and lobster shacks dot the country roads that meander to the tip of the point, where you'll find a much-photographed lighthouse perched on an unforgiving rock ledge, as well as a pleasant beach. Exploring here reaps many rewards, including views of salt ponds, the ocean, and boat-clogged harbors. The twin towns of Damariscotta and Newcastle anchor the region, but small fishing villages such as Pemaquid, New Harbor, and Round Pond give the peninsula its purely Maine flavor.

At what is now the **Colonial Pemaquid Restoration,** on a small peninsula jutting into the Pemaquid River, English mariners established a fishing and trading settlement in the early 17th century. The excavations at **Ft. William Henry,** begun in the mid-1960s, have turned up thousands of artifacts from the Colonial settlement, including the remains of an old customs house, a tavern, a jail, a forge, and homes. Some items are from even earlier Native American settlements. The state operates a museum displaying many of the artifacts. ✉ *Off Rte. 130, New Harbor,* ☎ *207/677–2423.* ▣ *$2.* ☉ *Memorial Day–Labor Day, daily 9:30–5.*

★ Route 130 terminates at the **Pemaquid Point Light,** which looks as though it sprouted from the ragged, tilted chunk of granite that it commands. The former lighthouse-keeper's cottage is now the **Fishermen's Museum,** with photographs, models, and artifacts that explore commercial fishing in Maine. Here, too, is the **Pemaquid Art Gallery,** which mounts exhibitions from July to Labor Day. ✉ *Museum: Rte. 130,* ☎ *207/677–2494.* ▣ *Donation requested.* ☉ *Memorial Day–Columbus Day, Mon.–Sat. 10–5, Sun. 11–5.*

Pemaquid Beach Park (✉ Off Rte. 130, New Harbor, ☎ 207/677–2754) has a good sand beach, a snack bar, changing facilities, and picnic tables overlooking John's Bay; admission is charged.

Dining and Lodging

$ ✕ **Round Pond Lobstermen's Co-op.** Lobster doesn't get much rougher,
★ any fresher, or any cheaper than that served at this no-frills dockside takeout. The best deal is the dinner special: a 1-pound lobster, steamers, and corn-on-the-cob, with a bag of chips. Regulars often bring beer, wine, bread, and/or salads. Settle in at a picnic table and breathe in the fresh salt air while you drink in the view over dreamy Round Pond Harbor. ✉ *Round Pond Harbor, off Rte. 32, Round Pond,* ☎ *207/ 529–5725. MC, V.*

$$–$$$$ ✕🏠 **Newcastle Inn.** This classic country inn with a riverside location and an excellent dining room attracts guests year-round. All the rooms are filled with country pieces and antiques; some rooms have fireplaces and whirlpool baths. Guests spread out in the cozy pub, comfortable living room, and sunporch overlooking the river. Breakfast is served on the back deck in fine weather. The four-course dinners ($$$$) at the inn, which is open to the public by reservation, emphasize Pemaquid oysters, lobster, Atlantic salmon, and other Maine seafood. ⊠ *60 River Rd., Newcastle 04553, ☎ 207/563–5685 or 800/832–8669, FAX 207/563–6877. 14 rooms, 2 suites. 2 dining rooms, pub, TV room. Full breakfast. AE, MC, V.*

$$ 🏠 **Briar Rose.** Round Pond is a sleepy harborside village with an old-fashioned country store, two lobster co-ops, a nice restaurant, and a handful of antiques and crafts shops. The mansard-roof Briar Rose commands a ship captain's view over it all. Antiques and whimsies decorate the airy rooms. ⊠ *Box 27, Rte. 32, Round Pond 04556, ☎ 207/529–5478. 2 rooms, 1 suite. Full breakfast. No credit cards.*

$$ 🏠 **Mill Pond Inn.** A quiet residential street holds this circa-1780 inn, which is on a mill pond across the street from Damariscotta Lake. Loons, otters, and bald eagles reside on the lake, and you can arrange a trip with the owner, a Registered Maine Guide, on the inn's 17-ft antique lapstrake boat. The rooms are warm and inviting and there's a pub for guests, though you may find it hard to tear yourself away from the hammocks-for-two overlooking the pond. ⊠ *50 Main St., off Rte. 215 N, Nobleboro 04555, ☎ 207/563–8014. 5 rooms, 1 suite. Horseshoes, boating, bicycles. Full breakfast. No credit cards.*

Nightlife and the Arts

Round Top Center for the Arts (⊠ Business Rte. 1, Damariscotta, ☎ 207/563–1507) has a gallery with rotating exhibits and a performance hall where classical, folk, operatic, and jazz concerts are regularly held.

Shopping

Of the villages on and near the Pemaquid Peninsula, downtown Damariscotta offers boutiques, a book shop, clothing stores, and galleries. New Harbor and Round Pond have crafts and antiques shops as well as artisans' studios.

You never know what you'll find at **Reny's** (⊠ Rte. 1A, Damariscotta, ☎ 207/563–5757)—perhaps merchandise from L. L. Bean or a designer coat. This bargain chain has outlets in many Maine towns, but this is its hometown, and there are outlets on both sides of the street: one for clothes, the other for everything else. **Granite Hill Store** (⊠ Backshore Rd., Round Pond, ☎ 207/529–5864) has penny candy, kitchen goodies, baskets, and cards on the first floor, antiques and books on the second, and an ice cream window on the side. The **Roserie at Bayfields** (⊠ Rte. 32, Waldoboro, ☎ 207/832–6330) specializes in practical roses for tough places in your yard. The gardens here have sweeping views over the Medomak River.

Portland to Pemaquid Point A to Z

Arriving and Departing

See Arriving and Departing *in* Maine A to Z, *below.*

Getting Around

BY BUS

Greater Portland's **Metro** (☎ 207/774–0351) runs seven bus routes in Portland, South Portland, and Westbrook. The fare is $1; exact change ($1 bills accepted) is required. Buses run from 5:30 AM to 11:45 PM.

BY CAR

Congress Street leads from I–295 into the heart of Portland; the Gateway Garage on High Street, off Congress, is a convenient place to leave your car while exploring downtown. North of Portland, I–95 takes you to Exit 20 and U.S. 1, Freeport's Main Street, which continues on to Brunswick and Bath. East of Wiscasset you can take Route 27 south to the Boothbays, where Route 96 is a good choice for further exploration.

BY FERRY

Casco Bay Lines (☎ 207/774–7871) provides ferry service from Portland to the islands of Casco Bay.

Contacts and Resources

CAR RENTAL

See Contacts and Resources *in* Maine A to Z, *below.*

EMERGENCIES

Maine Medical Center (✉ 22 Bramhall St., Portland, ☎ 207/871–0111). **Mid Coast Hospital** (✉ 1356 Washington St., Bath, ☎ 207/443–5524; ✉ 58 Baribeau Dr., Brunswick, ☎ 207/729–0181). **Miles Memorial Hospital** (✉ Bristol Rd., Damariscotta, ☎ 207/563–1234). **St. Andrews Hospital** (✉ 3 St. Andrews La., Boothbay Harbor, ☎ 207/633–2121).

VISITOR INFORMATION

Boothbay Harbor Region Chamber of Commerce (✉ Box 356, Boothbay Harbor 04538, ☎ 207/633–2353). **Chamber of Commerce of the Bath/Brunswick Region** (✉ 45 Front St., Bath 04530, ☎ 207/443–9751; ✉ 59 Pleasant St., Brunswick 04011, ☎ 207/725–8797). **Convention and Visitors Bureau of Greater Portland** (✉ 305 Commercial St. 04101, ☎ 207/772–5800 or 877/833–1374). **Damariscotta Region Chamber of Commerce** (✉ Box 13, Damariscotta 04543, ☎ 207/563–8340). **Freeport Merchants Association** (✉ Box 452, Freeport 04032, ☎ 207/865–1212 or 877/865–1212). **Greater Portland Chamber of Commerce** (✉ 145 Middle St., Portland 04101, ☎ 207/772–2811). **Maine Tourism Association** (✉ U.S. 1, Exit 17 off I–95, Yarmouth 04347, ☎ 207/846–0833).

PENOBSCOT BAY

Purists hold that the Maine coast begins at Penobscot Bay, where the vistas over the water are wider and bluer; the shore a jumble of broken granite boulders, cobblestones, and gravel punctuated by small sand beaches; and the water numbingly cold. Port Clyde in the southwest and Stonington in the southeast are the outer limits of Maine's largest bay, 35 mi apart across the bay waters but separated by a drive of almost 100 mi on scenic but slow two-lane highways. From Pemaquid Point at the western extremity of Muscongus Bay to Port Clyde at its eastern extent, it's less than 15 mi across the water, but it's 50 mi for the motorist, who must return north to U.S. 1 to reach the far shore.

Rockland, the largest town on the bay, is Maine's major lobster distribution center and the port of departure for trips to Vinalhaven, North Haven, and Matinicus islands. The Camden Hills, looming green over Camden's fashionable waterfront, turn bluer and fainter as you head toward Castine, the small town across the bay. In between Camden and Castine are Belfast and the antiques and flea-market mecca of Searsport. Deer Isle is connected to the mainland by a slender, high-arching bridge, but Isle au Haut, accessible from Deer Isle's fishing town of Stonington, can be reached by passenger ferry only: More than half of this steep, wooded island is wilderness, the most remote section of Acadia National Park.

The most promising shopping areas are Main Street in Rockland, Main and Bay View streets in Camden, Main Street in Blue Hill, and Main Street in Stonington. Antiques shops are clustered in Searsport and scattered around the outskirts of villages, in farmhouses and barns. Yard sales abound in summer.

Tenants Harbor

㉒ *13 mi south of Thomaston.*

Tenants Harbor is a quintessential Maine fishing town, its harbor dominated by lobster boats, its shores rocky and slippery, its center a scattering of clapboard houses, a church, a general store. The fictional Dunnet Landing of Sarah Orne Jewett's classic book *The Country of the Pointed Firs* is based on this region.

The keeper's house at the **Marshall Point Lighthouse** has been turned into a museum containing memorabilia from the town of St. George (a few miles north of Tenants Harbor). The setting has inspired Jamie Wyeth and other artists. You can stroll the grounds and watch the boats go in and out of Port Clyde. ⊠ *Marshall Point Rd., Port Clyde,* ☎ *207/372–6450.* ⊡ *Free.* ☉ *June–Sept., weekdays 1–5 and Sat. 10–5.*

Dining and Lodging

$$–$$$ ✕🏠 **East Wind Inn & Meeting House.** Overlooking the harbor and the islands, the East Wind has unadorned but comfortable rooms, suites, and apartments in three buildings; some accommodations have fireplaces. The inn is open to the public for dinner, breakfast, and Sunday brunch. Dinner options include prime rib, boiled lobster, and baked stuffed haddock. ⊠ *Mechanic St., 04860,* ☎ *207/372–6366 or 800/ 241–8439,* 𝔽𝔸𝕏 *207/372–6320. 23 rooms, 9 with bath; 3 suites; 4 apartments. Restaurant. AE, D, MC, V. Closed Dec.–Apr. No lunch.*

Shopping

Gallery-by-the-Sea (⊠ Port Clyde Village, Port Clyde, ☎ 207/372–8631) carries works by a dozen local artists including Leo Brooks, Lawrence Goldsmith, and Emily Muir.

Monhegan Island

★ **㉓** *East of Pemaquid Point, 10 mi south of Port Clyde.*

Remote Monhegan Island, with its high cliffs fronting the open sea, was known to Basque, Portuguese, and Breton fishermen well before Columbus "discovered" America. About a century ago Monhegan was discovered again by some of America's finest painters, including Rockwell Kent, Robert Henri, A. J. Hammond, and Edward Hopper, who sailed out to paint its meadows, savage cliffs, wild ocean views, and fishermen's shacks. Tourists followed, and today three excursion boats dock here. The village bustles with activity in summer, but you can escape the crowds on the island's 17 miles of hiking trails, which lead from the village to the lighthouse, through the woods and to the cliffs. Those who choose to overnight here have a quieter experience, since lodging is limited. Day visitors should bring a picnic lunch, as restaurants can have long waits at lunchtime.

Port Clyde, a fishing village at the end of Route 131, is the point of departure for the *Laura B.* (☎ 207/372–8848 for schedules), the mail boat that serves Monhegan Island. The *Balmy Days* (☎ 207/633–2284 or 800/298–2284) sails from Boothbay Harbor to Monhegan on daily trips in summer. **Hardy Boat Cruises** (☎ 207/677–2026 or 800/ 278–3346) leaves daily from Shaw's Wharf in New Harbor.

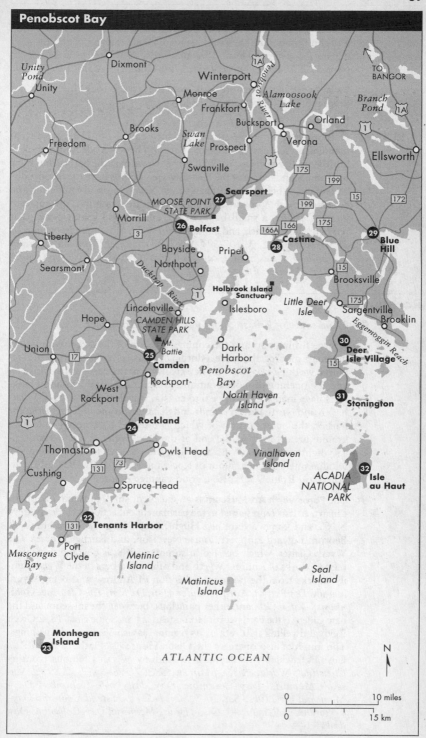

The **Monhegan Museum,** in an 1824 lighthouse and an adjacent, newly built assistant-keeper's house, has wonderful views of Manana Island and the Camden Hills in the distance. Inside, artworks and displays depict island life and local flora and birds. ⊠ *White Head Rd.,* ☎ *no phone.* 🎟 *Donations accepted.* ⊘ *July–mid-Sept., daily 11:30–3:30.*

Swim Beach, a five-minute walk from the ferry, is rocky but rarely has more than a few sun worshipers.

Lodging

$$$–$$$$ 🏨 **Island Inn.** This three-story inn, which dates from 1807, has a commanding presence on Monhegan's harbor. The waterside rooms, though mostly small, are the nicest, with sunset views over the harbor and stark Manana Island. Some of the meadow-view rooms have the distinct disadvantage of being over kitchen vents. New owners are updating and redecorating the property, which includes the main inn, the adjacent Pierce Cottage, a small bakery-café, and a good dining room that serves breakfast, lunch, and dinner. ⊠ *Box 128, Monhegan Island 04852,* ☎ *207/596–0371,* 𝖥𝖠𝖷 *207/594–5517. 29 rooms, 12 with bath; 4 suites in 2 buildings. Restaurant, café. Full breakfast. MC, V. Closed Columbus Day–Memorial Day.*

Rockland

㉔ *27 mi south of Belfast, 53 mi northeast of Brunswick.*

A large fishing port and the commercial hub of the coast, with working boats moored alongside a flotilla of cruise schooners, Rockland retains a working-class flavor. The expansion of the Farnsworth Museum and the opening of more boutiques, restaurants, and bed-and-breakfasts have increased its appeal to coastal travelers. Day trips to Vinalhaven and North Haven islands and distant Matinicus depart from the harbor, the outer portion of which is bisected by a nearly mile-long granite breakwater. At the end of the breakwater is a late-19th-century lighthouse, one of the best places in the area to watch the many windjammers sail in and out of Rockland Harbor. Owl's Head Lighthouse, off Route 73, is also a good vantage point.

★   The **Farnsworth Art Museum** is an excellent small museum of American art. Artists represented in the permanent collection include Andrew, N. C., and Jamie Wyeth; Fitz Hugh Lane; George Bellows; Frank W. Benson; Edward Hopper; Louise Nevelson; and Fairfield Porter. The **Wyeth Center,** which opened in summer 1998, is devoted to Maine-related works of Andrew Wyeth and other members of the Wyeth family. Works from the personal collection of Andrew and Betsy Wyeth include *The Patriot, Adrift, Maiden Hair, Dr. Syn, The Clearing, Geraniums, Watch Cap,* and other paintings. Between the museum and the new gallery is the **Farnsworth Homestead,** a handsome circa-1852 Greek Revival dwelling that retains its original lavish Victorian furnishings. The museum also operates the **Olson House** (⊠ Hathorn Point Rd., Cushing), which was depicted in Andrew Wyeth's famous painting *Christina's World.* ⊠ *356 Main St.,* ☎ *207/596–6457.* 🎟 *$9.* ⊘ *Museum Memorial Day–Columbus Day, daily 9–5; Columbus Day–Memorial Day, Tues.–Sat. 10–5, Sun. 1–5. Homestead Memorial Day–Columbus Day, daily 9–5. Olson House Memorial Day–Columbus Day, daily 11–4.*

☙   The **Shore Village Museum** displays many lighthouse and Coast Guard artifacts and has exhibits of maritime and Civil War memorabilia. ⊠ *104 Limerock St.,* ☎ *207/594–0311.* 🎟 *Donation suggested.* ⊘ *June–mid-Oct., daily 10–4; rest of yr "by chance and appointment."*

Owls Head Transportation Museum displays antique aircraft, cars, and engines and stages weekend air shows. ⊠ *Rte. 73, Owls Head (2 mi south of Rockland),* ☎ *207/594–4418.* 🖾 *$6.* ☉ *Apr.–Oct., daily 10– 5; Nov.–Mar., daily 10–4.*

Montpelier: General Henry Knox Museum was built in 1930 as a replica of the late-18th-century mansion of Major General Henry Knox, a general in the Revolutionary War and secretary of war in Washington's Cabinet. Antiques and Knox family possessions fill the interior. Architectural features of note include an oval room and a double staircase. ⊠ *U.S. 1 and Rte. 131, Thomaston,* ☎ *207/354–8062.* 🖾 *$5.* ☉ *Early June–early Oct., Tues.–Sat. 10–4, Sun. 1–4.*

The **Maine Watercraft Museum** displays more than 125 antique and classic small craft both in and out of the water. ⊠ *4 Knox St. Landing, Thomaston,* ☎ *207/354–0444.* 🖾 *$4.* ☉ *Memorial Day–Sept., Wed.–Sun. 10–5.*

OFF THE BEATEN PATH	**VINALHAVEN** – You can take the ferry from Rockland to this island for a pleasant day of bicycling or walking. A number of parks are within walking distance of the ferry dock, including Armbrust Hill, the site of an abandoned quarry, and Lane's Island Preserve, a 40-acre site of moors, granite shoreline, tide pools, and beach. You can learn about the island's quarrying history at the Historical Society Museum on High Street and even take a dip in the cool, clear waters of two quarries. Lawson's is 1 mi out on the North Haven Road; Booth Quarry is 1½ mi out East Main Street. Neither has changing facilities, so go prepared. For ferry information, call Maine State Ferry Service (☎ 207/596–2202).

Dining and Lodging

$$ ✕ **Café Miranda.** Expect to wait for a table at this cozy bistro, where the daily-changing menu reflects fresh, seasonal ingredients and the chef's creative renditions of both new American and traditional home-style foods. You can make a meal from the 20 or so appetizers, many roasted in the brick oven. The two dozen entrées may include crispy pan-fried soft-shell crabs with red bean ragout and yellow jasmine rice. If you sit at the small counter, you can watch the chef prepare your meal. ⊠ *15 Oak St.,* ☎ *207/594–2304. MC, V. Closed Sun.–Mon. No lunch.*

$$ ✕ **Jessica's Bistro.** Jessica's occupies four cozy rooms in a Victorian ★ home on a hill at the southern end of Rockland. Billed as a European bistro, the restaurant lives up to its Continental label with creative entrées that include veal Zurich, paella, and pork Portofino; other specialties of the Swiss chef are risottos, pastas, and focaccia. ⊠ *2 S. Main St. (Rte. 73),* ☎ *207/596–0770. D, MC, V. Closed Tues. in winter.*

$–$$ ✕ **Waterworks.** This restaurant in a brick building off Main Street serves light pub fare, including soups and home-style suppers like turkey and meat loaf. Maine microbrewery beers are on tap, and the selection of single-malt Scotches is excellent. A wall of water decorates the small dining room, and a stone fireplace dominates the pub. A children's menu is available. ⊠ *Lindsey St.,* ☎ *207/596–2753. AE, D, MC, V.*

$$$$ 🏨 **Samoset Resort.** On the Rockland-Rockport town line next to the breakwater, this sprawling oceanside resort has excellent golf and fitness facilities. Most of the spacious rooms, decorated in soothing blue and rose tones, have views of Penobscot Bay over the fairways; all have patios or decks. ⊠ *220 Warrenton St., Rockport,* ☎ *207/594–2511; 800/341–1650 outside ME;* FAX *207/594–0722. 132 rooms, 18 suites. Restaurant, 1 indoor and 1 outdoor pool, 18-hole golf course, 2 tennis courts, exercise room, racquetball, children's programs. AE, D, DC, MC, V.*

$$-$$$ ⚐ **Limerock Inn.** You can walk to the Farnsworth and the Shore Vil-
★   lage museums from this magnificent Queen Anne–style Victorian on
a quiet residential street. The meticulously decorated rooms include
Island Cottage, with a whirlpool tub and doors that open onto a private deck overlooking the backyard garden, and Grand Manan, which
has a fireplace, a whirlpool tub, and a four-poster king-size bed. ⊠ 96
Limerock St., 04841, ☎ *207/594–2257 or 800/546–3762,* FAX *207/594–
1846. 8 rooms. Croquet, bicycles. Full breakfast. MC, V.*

Outdoor Activities and Sports

BOAT TRIPS

Bay Island Yacht Charters (⊠ 120 Tillison Ave., ☎ 207/236–2776 or
800/421–2492) operates bareboats and charters. **North End Shipyard
Schooners** (☎ 800/648–4544) operates three- and six-day cruises on the
schooners *American Eagle, Isaac H. Evans,* and *Heritage.* **Three Cheers**
(⊠ Rockland Landing, Marina Park Dr., ☎ 207/594–0900) operates lob-
ster-fishing and lighthouse cruises. **Vessels of Windjammer Wharf** (☎
207/236–3520 or 800/999–7352) organizes three- and six-day cruises
on the *Pauline,* a 12-passenger motor yacht, and the *Stephen Taber,* a
windjammer. *Victory Chimes* is a 132-ft, three-masted schooner, the largest
in Maine's windjammer fleet, that takes three- and six-day trips.

TOURS

Coastal Explorer Tours (☎ 207/594–7568) operates specialty tours for
lighthouse viewing, boat building, photography, and other interests.
Downeast Air Inc. (☎ 207/594–2171 or 800/594–2171) offers scenic
flights and lighthouse tours.

Shopping

Rockland's Main Street has experienced a quiet change in the wake of
the expansion of the Farnsworth Art Museum. Galleries are clustered
around the museums, and boutiques and antiques and specialty stores
are sprouting up along both the main and side streets. **Between the Muse**
(⊠ 8 Elm St., ☎ 207/596–6868) specializes in modern art and has a
sculpture garden. **Caldbeck Gallery** (⊠ 12 Elm St., ☎ 207/596–5935)
features contemporary Maine works by artists such as William Thon.
Maine authors frequently sign books at the **Personal Bookstore** (⊠ 78
Main St., Thomaston, ☎ 207/354–8058 or 800/391–8058). The **Reading Corner** (⊠ 408 Main St., ☎ 207/596–6651) carries many cookbooks, children's books, and Maine-related titles, and has good
newspaper and magazine selections. **Thomaston Books & Prints** (⊠ 105
Main St., Thomaston, ☎ 207/354–0001) sells Maine-themed photo-
graphic, lithographic, and limited-edition prints as well as books.

Camden

㉕ *8 mi north of Rockland, 19 mi south of Belfast.*

"Where the mountains meet the sea," Camden's longtime publicity slo-
gan, is an apt description, as you will discover when you step out of
your car and look up from the harbor. The town is famous not only
for geography but for its large fleet of windjammers—relics and replicas from the age of sail. At just about any hour during warm months
you're likely to see at least one windjammer tied up in the harbor. The
best shopping in the region can be found in the busy downtown. The
district's compact size makes it perfect for exploring on foot: Shops,
restaurants, and galleries line Main Street (U.S. 1) and Bayview, as well
as side streets and alleys around the harbor.

If you're accustomed to the Rockies or the Alps, you may not be impressed with heights of not much more than 1,000 ft, yet the hills in
Camden Hills State Park are lovely landmarks for miles along the low,

rolling reaches of the Maine coast. The 5,500-acre park contains 20 mi of trails, including the easy Nature Trail up Mt. Battie. Hike or drive to the top for a magnificent view over Camden and island-studded Penobscot Bay. The 112-site camping area, open from mid-May to mid-October, has flush toilets and hot showers. The entrance is 2 mi north of Camden. ⊠ *U.S. 1,* ☎ *207/236–3109.* ☞ *Trails and auto road up Mt. Battie $2.* ☉ *Daily dawn–dusk.*

Merry Spring Gardens is a 66-acre retreat with herb, rose, rhododendron, hosta, and children's gardens as well as woodland trails. ⊠ *Off U.S. 1 on the Conway Rd.,* ☎ *207/236–2239.* ☞ *Free.* ☉ *Daily dawn–dusk.*

Ⓒ **Kelmscott Farm** is a rare-breed animal farm (sheep, pigs, horses, poultry, goats, and cows) with displays, a nature trail, children's activities, a picnic area, heirloom gardens, and frequent special events. ⊠ *Rte. 52, Lincolnville,* ☎ *207/763–4088.* ☞ *$5.* ☉ *May–Nov., Tues.–Sun., 10–5; Nov.–May.Tues.–Sun., 10–3.*

Dining and Lodging

$$–$$$ ✕ **Waterfront Restaurant.** A ringside seat on Camden Harbor can be had here; the best view is from the outdoor deck, open in warm weather. The fare is primarily seafood: boiled lobster, scallops, bouillabaisse, seafood risotto. Lunchtime highlights include lobster and crabmeat rolls. ⊠ *Bay View St.,* ☎ *207/236–3747. Reservations not accepted. MC, V.*

$$$ ✕🛏 **Whitehall Inn.** One of Camden's best-known inns, just north of town, is an 1843 white clapboard sea captain's home with a wide porch and a turn-of-the-century wing. The Millay Room, off the lobby, preserves memorabilia of the poet Edna St. Vincent Millay, who grew up in the area. The sparsely furnished rooms have dark-wood bedsteads, white bedspreads, and claw-foot tubs. The dining room, which serves traditional and creative American cuisine, is open to the public for dinner. ⊠ *Box 558, 52 High St., 04843,* ☎ *207/236–3391 or 800/789–6565,* 🖷 *207/236–4427. 44 rooms, 40 with bath. Restaurant, tennis court, shuffleboard. MAP. AE, MC, V. Closed mid-Oct.–mid-May.*

$$–$$$ ✕🛏 **Youngtown Inn.** Inside this white Federal farmhouse are a French-inspired country retreat and a well-respected French restaurant ($$$). The country location guarantees quiet, and the inn is a short walk to the Fernald Neck Preserve on Lake Megunticook. Simple, airy rooms open to decks with views of the rolling countryside. Two have fireplaces. The restaurant, open to the public for dinner, serves entrées such as lobster ravioli and pan-seared breast of pheasant with foie gras mousse. ⊠ *Rte. 52 at Youngtown Rd., Lincolnville 04849,* ☎ *207/763–4290 or 800/291–8438,* 🖷 *207/763–4078. 6 rooms, 1 suite. Full breakfast. AE, MC, V.*

$$$$ 🛏 **Inn at Ocean's Edge.** Perched on the ocean's edge, this shingle-style ★ inn looks as if it has been here for decades. In actuality, it's brand-new and built with modern-day comforts in mind. Every room has a king-size bed, an ocean view, a fireplace, and a whirlpool for two, and all have TVs, VCRs, and individually controlled heat and air-conditioning. The Lincolnville setting is private, yet minutes from Camden. ⊠ *U.S. 1, Lincolnville; mailing address: Box 704, Camden 04843,* ☎ *207/236–0945,* 🖷 *207/236–0609. 14 rooms, 1 suite. Exercise room, meeting room. Full breakfast. AE, MC, V.*

$$$–$$$$ 🛏 **Victorian Inn.** It's less than 10 minutes from downtown Camden, but ★ with a quiet waterside location well off U.S. 1, the Victorian Inn feels a world away. Most rooms and the wraparound porch have magnificent views over island-studded Penobscot Bay. Romantic touches include canopy and brass beds, braided rugs, white wicker furniture, and floral

wallpapers. Six guest rooms have fireplaces, and there are four more in common rooms, including the glass-enclosed breakfast room in the turret, where a full breakfast is served. ⊠ *Sea View Dr., Lincolnville; mailing address: Box 1385, Camden 04843,* ☎ *207/236–3785 or 800/382–9817,* FAX *207/236–0017. 5 rooms, 2 suites. Full breakfast. AE, MC, V.*

$$
★ 🎝 **Camden Maine Stay.** This 1802 clapboard inn within walking distance of shops and restaurants is on the National Register of Historic Places. The grounds are classic and inviting, from the colorful flowers lining the granite walk in summer to the snow-laden bushes in winter. The equally fresh and colorful rooms contain many pieces of Eastlake furniture; six have fireplaces. ⊠ *22 High St., 04842,* ☎ *207/236–9636,* FAX *207/236–0621. 5 rooms, 3 suites. Full breakfast. AE, MC, V.*

Nightlife and the Arts

Bay Chamber Concerts (⊠ Rockport Opera House, 6 Central St., Rockport, ☎ 207/236–2823 or 888/707–2770) presents chamber music on Thursday and Friday night during July and August; concerts are given once a month from September to May. **Gilbert's Public House** (⊠ 12 Bay View St., ☎ 207/236–4320) has dancing and live entertainment. **Sea Dog Tavern & Brewery** (⊠ 43 Mechanic St., ☎ 207/236–6863), a popular brew pub in a converted woolen mill, has live entertainment in season. The **Whale's Tooth Pub** (⊠ U.S. 1, Lincolnville Beach, ☎ 207/236–3747) has low-key entertainment on weekends.

Outdoor Activities and Sports

Maine Sport (⊠ U.S. 1, Rockport, ☎ 207/236–8797 or 800/722–0826), the best sports outfitter north of Freeport, rents bikes, camping and fishing gear, canoes, kayaks, cross-country skis, ice skates, and snowshoes. It also conducts skiing and kayaking clinics and trips.

The *Betselma* (⊠ Camden Public Landing, ☎ 207/236–4446) offers one- and two-hour powerboat trips.

Windjammers create a stir whenever they sail into Camden harbor, and a voyage around the bay on one of them, whether for an afternoon or a week, is unforgettable. The season for the excursions is from June to September. Excursion boats also provide an opportunity for getting afloat on the waters of Penobscot Bay. Eggemoggin Reach is a famous cruising ground for yachts, as are the coves and inlets around Deer Isle and the Penobscot Bay waters between Castine and Camden.

The **Maine Windjammer Association** (⊠ Box 1144, Blue Hill 04614, ☎ 800/807–9463) represents the Camden-based windjammers *Angelique, Grace Bailey, J & E Riggin, Lewis R. French, Mary Day, Mercantile, Nathaniel Bowditch, Roseway,* and *Timberwind,* which sail on cruises that last from three to eight days.

Shopping

Shops and galleries line Camden's Bay View and Main streets and the alleys that lead to the harbor. **Maine Coast Artists** (⊠ 162 Russell Ave., Rockport, ☎ 207/236–2875) specializes in contemporary Maine art. **Maine's Massachusetts House Galleries** (⊠ U.S. 1, Lincolnville, ☎ 207/789–5705) display regional art, including bronzes, carvings, sculptures, and landscapes and seascapes in pencil, oil, and watercolor. The **Owl and Turtle Bookshop** (⊠ 8 Bay View St., ☎ 207/236–4769) sells books, CDs, cassettes, and cards. The two-story shop has rooms devoted to marine and children's books. The **Pine Tree Shop & Bayview Gallery** (⊠ 33 Bay View St., ☎ 207/236–4534) specializes in original art, prints, and posters, almost all with Maine themes. The **Windsor Chairmakers** (⊠ U.S. 1, Lincolnville, ☎ 207/789–5188 or 800/789–5188) sells custom-made, handcrafted beds, chests, china cabinets, dining tables, highboys, and chairs.

Skiing and Snow Sports

CAMDEN SNOW BOWL

The Maine coast isn't known for skiing, but this small, lively park has downhill skiing as well as magnificent views over Penobscot Bay. ✉ Box 1207, Hosmer Pond Rd., 04843, ☎ 207/236–3438.

Downhill. In a Currier & Ives setting the park has a 950-ft-vertical mountain, a small lodge with cafeteria, a ski school, and ski and toboggan rentals. Camden Snow Bowl has 11 trails accessed by one double chair and two T-bars. It also has night skiing.

Other activities. Camden Snow Bowl has a small lake that is cleared for ice-skating, a snow-tubing park, and a 400-ft toboggan run that shoots sledders out onto the lake.

CROSS-COUNTRY SKIING

There are 16 km (10 mi) of cross-country skiing trails at **Camden Hills State Park** (✉ U.S. 1 ☎ 207/236–9849). **Tanglewood 4-H Camp** (✉ U.S. 1 ☎ 207/789–5868), about 5 mi away in Lincolnville, has 20 km (12½ mi) of trails.

En Route   Queen Anne cottages with freshly painted porches and exquisite architectural details dot the community of **Bayside,** a section of Northport off U.S. 1 on the way to Belfast. Some of these homes line the main one-lane thoroughfare, George Street; others are on bluffs with water views around town greens complete with flagpoles and swings; and yet others are on the shore.

Belfast

26   *27 mi north of Rockland, 46 mi east of Augusta.*

Like many other Maine towns, Belfast has ridden the tides of affluence and depression. A shipbuilding center in the 1800s and home to many sea captains, the city fell on hard times, only to be rescued by the chicken-processing industry. In the 1980s, that moved south. This time it's high tech, namely credit-card giant MBNA, that has helped rescue the city economically. The upswing in the economy promises well for visitors, who'll find an old-fashioned redbrick Victorian downtown and a lively waterfront, as well as affordable lodging and dining. The houses on Church Street are a veritable glossary of 19th-century architectural styles; pick up a map with a walking tour at the visitor center at the foot of Main Street.

A ride on the **Belfast & Moosehead Lake Railroad** (✉ One Depot Sq., Unity, ☎ 207/948–5500 or 800/392–5500), which operates from mid-June to December ($14), is especially enjoyable in the fall after the leaves begin to change colors. During the run between Belfast and Waldo Station, the notorious Waldo Station Gang "robs" the train. The railroad's timetable coordinates with a **cruise boat;** a discount applies if you travel on both.

Moose Point State Park (✉ U.S. 1 between Belfast and Searsport, ☎ 207/548–2882) is ideal for easy hikes and picnics overlooking Penobscot Bay.

Dining and Lodging

$$ ✗ **90 Main.** Young chef-owner Sheila Costello is at the helm of this family-run restaurant. Using Pemaquid oysters, Maine blueberries, organic vegetables grown on a nearby farm, and other local ingredients, Costello creates flavorful dishes that delight the senses. The chalkboard of specials includes a macrobiotic option, or you can start with the smoked seafood and pâté sampler or the spinach salad with sautéed chicken, sweet peppers, hazelnuts, and a warm raspberry vinaigrette.

Entrées include rib-eye steak and seafood linguine. The adjacent deli and bakery sells sandwiches and delicious homemade breads and treats. ✉ *90 Main St.,* ☎ *207/338–1106. AE, MC, V.*

$–$$ ▨ **Jeweled Turret Inn.** Turrets, columns, and gables embellish this inn, originally built in 1898 as the home of a local attorney. The magnificent woodwork is oak, maple, fir, and pine, and elegant Victorian pieces furnish the rooms. The inn is named for the jewel-like stained-glass windows in the stairway turret; the gem theme continues in the den, where the ornate rock fireplace is said to include rocks from every state in the Union. ✉ *40 Pearl St., 04915,* ☎ *207/338–2304 or 800/696–2304. 7 rooms. Full breakfast. MC, V.*

$–$$ ▨ **The White House.** New owners have poured their hearts and purses into renovating this fine example of Greek Revival architecture, an 1840–1842 landmark by architect Calvin Ryder. An eight-sided cupola tops the house; inside are ornate plaster ceiling medallions, rare Italian marble fireplaces, an elliptical flying staircase, and intricate moldings. Crystal chandeliers, Asian rugs, and antiques and reproduction pieces elegantly decorate the spacious rooms. Two guest rooms have whirlpool tubs. You can relax in the English garden, in the gazebo, or under the enormous copper beech tree. ✉ *1 Church St., 04915,* ☎ *207/338–1901 or 888/290–1901,* ℻ *207/338–5161. 4 rooms, 2 suites. Full breakfast. D, MC, V.*

Searsport

㉗ *11 mi north of Belfast, 57 mi east of Augusta.*

Searsport, Maine's second-largest deepwater port (after Portland), bills itself as the antiques capital of Maine. The town's stretch of U.S. 1 has many antiques shops and a large weekend flea market in summer. A former shipbuilding center, Searsport also holds homes built by the many sea captains who made their homes here; some are now bed-and-breakfasts.

★   The fine holdings within the nine historic and four modern buildings of the **Penobscot Marine Museum** provide fascinating documentation of the region's seafaring way of life. These buildings, including a church (still active) and a sea captain's house, have not been moved but remain where they were built in town. Included are display photos of 284 sea captains, artifacts of the whaling industry (lots of scrimshaw), navigational instruments, treasures collected by seafarers around the globe, an outstanding collection of marine art, and models of famous ships. Plan to spend about two hours here. ✉ *U.S. 1 at Church St.,* ☎ *207/548–2529.* 🎟 *$6.* ☉ *Memorial Day–late-Oct., Mon.–Sat. 10–5, Sun. noon–5.*

Dining and Lodging

$$$ ✕ **The Rhumb Line.** The upscale restaurant in this 18th-century sea captain's home delivers fine dining, although the service and decor need some fine-tuning. The waitstaff are formally attired but perform unevenly, and the light pine chairs don't seem the best choice with the Asian rugs and gleaming hardwood floors. If you can ignore these drawbacks, the artfully presented food does shine. Pepper-glazed pork tenderloin, barbecued duck with potato pancakes, and horseradish-crusted salmon are typical entrées. ✉ *U.S. 1,* ☎ *207/548–2600. MC, V. No lunch.*

$–$$ ▨ **Homeport Inn.** This 1861 inn, a former sea captain's home, provides an opulent Victorian environment that might put you in the mood to rummage through the nearby antiques and treasure shops. The back rooms downstairs have private decks and views of the bay. Families often stay in the two-bedroom housekeeping cottage. ✉ *U.S. 1,* ☎ *207/548–2259 or 800/742–5814. 10 rooms, 7 with bath; 1 2-bedroom cottage. Full breakfast. AE, D, MC, V.*

Shopping

Along U.S. 1 you'll see several dozen shops and, in season, outdoor flea markets. More than 70 dealers show their wares in the two-story **Searsport Antique Mall** (⊠ 149 E. Main St./ U.S. 1, ☎ 207/548–2640); look for everything from linens and silver to turn-of-the-century oak. **Pumpkin Patch Antiques** (⊠ 15 W. Main St./U.S. 1, ☎ 207/548–6047) displays such items as quilts, nautical items, and painted and wood furniture from about 20 dealers. It's open April through Thanksgiving or by appointment.

Castine

28 *30 mi southeast of Searsport.*

The French, the British, the Dutch, and the Americans fought over Castine from the 17th century to the War of 1812. Present-day Castine's many attributes include its lively harborfront, Federal and Greek Revival houses, and town common; there are two museums and the ruins of a British fort to explore. For a nice stroll, park your car at the landing and walk up Main Street past the two inns and on toward the white Trinitarian Federated Church, which has a tapering spire.

Among the white clapboard buildings that ring the town common are the Ives House (once the summer home of the poet Robert Lowell), the Abbott School, and the Unitarian Church, capped by a whimsical belfry.

Castine's **Soldiers and Sailors Monument** (⊠ Castine town common), typical of many town memorials that honor the state's participation in the Civil War, was dedicated in May 1887 to the veterans of that conflict.

Dining and Lodging

$$ ★ ✕▥ **Castine Inn.** Amy and Tom Gutrow have taken this well-respected inn and infused it with youthful, contemporary flair. Upholstered easy chairs and fine prints and paintings are typical of the furnishings in this inn's airy rooms. The third floor has the best views: the harbor over the formal gardens on one side, the village on the other. The dining room ($$$), decorated with a wraparound mural of Castine and its harbor, is open to the public for breakfast and dinner; the creative menu features local ingredients and entrées such as Kalamata-olive-crusted salmon with a yellow-pepper–grapefruit sauce. There's a snug, English-style pub off the lobby. ⊠ *Box 41, Main St., 04421,* ☎ *207/326–4365,* ℻ *207/326–4570. 15 rooms, 4 suites. Restaurant, pub, sauna. Full breakfast. MC, V. Restaurant hrs limited mid-Oct.–mid-Dec. Inn closed mid-Dec.–Apr.*

Shopping

Chris Murray Waterfowl Carver (⊠ Upper Main St., ☎ 207/326–9033) sells award-winning wildfowl carvings. **H.O.M.E.** (⊠ U.S. 1, Orland, ☎ 207/469–7961) is a cooperative crafts village with a crafts and pottery shop, weaving shop, flea market, market stand, and woodworking shop. **McGrath-Dunham Gallery** (⊠ Main St., ☎ 207/326–9938) carries fine art.

Blue Hill

29 *19 mi east of Castine.*

Blue Hill has a dramatic perch over the harbor. It is renowned for its pottery and has good shops and galleries.

Dining and Lodging

$$–$$$ ✕ **Jonathan's.** The downstairs room at nautically themed Jonathan's has captain's chairs, linen tablecloths, and local art; in the post-and-

beam upstairs, there's wood everywhere, plus high-back chairs and candles with hurricane globes. Fresh fish and meat entrées are always on the menu. The lengthy wine list has French, Italian, Californian, and Maine-produced vintages. ⊠ *Main St.,* ☎ *207/374–5226. MC, V.*

$$$–$$$$ ✕⊞ **Blue Hill Inn.** Rambling and antiques-filled, this inn is a com-
★ forting place to relax after exploring nearby shops and galleries; four rooms have fireplaces. The multicourse, candlelighted dinners at the renowned dining room ($$$; reservations essential) are prepared with organically raised produce and herbs, local meats, and seafood. An hors d'oeuvres hour in the garden, or by the living-room fireplace, precedes dinner. ⊠ *Box 403, Union St./Rte. 177, 04614,* ☎ *207/374–2844 or 800/826–7415,* FAX *207/374–2829. 11 rooms, 1 apartment. Restaurant. MAP. D, MC, V. Closed Dec.–Apr. and midweek in Nov.*

$ ⊞ **Bucks Harbor Inn.** The spirit and decor are those of a traditional B&B (shared baths, friendly hosts, nothing too fancy), but owners Peter and Anne Eberling, unlike many other innkeepers, welcome children. Breezes off the water cool the large corner rooms. A full cooked-to-order breakfast is served on the porch. ⊠ *Box 268, Rte. 176, South Brooksville 04617,* ☎ *207/326–8660,* FAX *207/326–0730. 6 rooms without bath. Full breakfast. MC, V.*

Nightlife and the Arts

Kneisel Hall Chamber Music Festival (⊠ Kneisel Hall, Rte. 15, ☎ 207/374–2811) has concerts on Sunday and Friday in summer. **Left Bank Bakery and Café** (⊠ Rte. 172, ☎ 207/374–2201) presents musical talent from across the nation. **Surry Opera Co.** (⊠ Morgan Bay Rd., Surry, ☎ 207/667–2629) stages operas throughout the area in summer.

Outdoor Activities and Sports

Holbrook Island Sanctuary (⊠ Off Cape Rosier Rd., Brooksville, ☎ 207/326–4012) has a gravelly beach with a splendid view, a picnic area, and hiking trails. The **Phoenix Centre** (⊠ Rte. 175, Blue Hill Falls, ☎ 207/374–2113) operates sea-kayaking tours of Blue Hill Bay and Eggemoggin Reach.

Shopping

Big Chicken Barn (⊠ U.S. 1, Ellsworth, ☎ 207/374–2715) has three floors filled with books, antiques, and collectibles. **Handworks Gallery** (⊠ Main St., ☎ 207/374–5613) carries unusual crafts, jewelry, and clothing. **Leighton Gallery** (⊠ Parker Point Rd., ☎ 207/374–5001) shows oil paintings, lithographs, watercolors, and other contemporary art in the gallery, and sculpture in its garden. **North Country Textiles** (⊠ Main St., ☎ 207/374–2715) specializes in fine woven shawls, place mats, throws, baby blankets, and pillows in subtle patterns and color schemes. **Old Cove Antiques** (⊠ Rte. 15, Sargentville, ☎ 207/359–2031) has folk art, quilts, and hooked rugs.

Rackliffe Pottery (⊠ Rte. 172, ☎ 207/374–2297) is famous for its vivid blue pottery, including plates, tea and coffee sets, pitchers, casseroles, and canisters. **Rowantrees Pottery** (⊠ Union St., ☎ 207/374–5535) has an extensive selection of styles and patterns in dinnerware, tea sets, vases, and decorative items.

En Route Scenic Route 15 south from Blue Hill passes through Brooksville and on through the graceful suspension bridge that crosses Eggemoggin Reach to Deer Isle. The turnout and picnic area at **Caterpillar Hill,** 1 mi south of the junction of Routes 15 and 175, commands a fabulous view of Penobscot Bay, hundreds of dark green islands, and the Camden Hills across the bay. From this perspective the hills look like a faraway mountain range, although they are less than 25 mi away.

Deer Isle Village

① *16 mi south of Blue Hill.*

In Deer Isle Village, thick woods give way to tidal coves. Stacks of lobster traps populate the backyards of shingled houses, and dirt roads lead to summer cottages.

Haystack Mountain School of Crafts attracts internationally renowned glassblowers, potters, sculptors, jewelers, blacksmiths, printmakers, and weavers to its summer institute. You can attend evening lectures or visit artists' studios (by appointment only). ⊠ *South of Deer Isle Village on Rte. 15, turn left at Gulf gas station and follow signs for 6 mi,* ☎ *207/348–2306.* ⊠ *Free.* ☉ *June–Sept.*

Dining and Lodging

$$$$ ✕⚏ **Goose Cove Lodge.** This heavily wooded property at the end of a back road has a fine stretch of ocean frontage, a sandy beach, and a long sandbar that leads to a nature preserve. Cottages and suites are in secluded woodlands and on the shore. Some are attached, some have a single large room, and still others have one or two bedrooms. All but three units have fireplaces. Dinner at the restaurant (reservations essential) is always superb and includes at least one vegetarian entrée; complimentary hors d'oeuvres precede the meal. On Friday night, there's a lobster feast on the inn's private beach. ⊠ *Box 40, Goose Cove Rd., Sunset 04683,* ☎ *207/348–2508 or 800/728–1963,* ℻ *207/348–2624. 2 rooms, 9 suites, 13 cottages. 2 restaurants, hiking, volleyball, beach, boating. MAP. AE, D, MC, V. All but 4 units closed mid-Oct.–mid-May.*

$$$ ✕⚏ **Pilgrim's Inn.** A deep-red, four-story gambrel-roof house, the Pil-
★ grim's Inn dates from about 1793 and overlooks a mill pond and harbor in Deer Isle Village. The library has wing chairs and Oriental rugs; a downstairs taproom has a huge brick fireplace and pine furniture. Guest rooms have English fabrics and carefully selected antiques. The dining room (reservations essential; no lunch) is in the attached barn, a rustic yet elegant space with farm implements, French oil lamps, and tiny windows. The five-course menu changes nightly but might include rack of lamb or fresh seafood. ⊠ *Rte. 15A, 04627,* ☎ *207/348–6615,* ℻ *207/348–7769. 13 rooms, 10 with bath; 2 seaside cottages. Restaurant, bicycles. Full breakfast; MAP available. MC, V. Closed mid-Oct.–mid-May.*

Shopping

Blue Heron Gallery & Studio (⊠ Church St., ☎ 207/348–6051) sells the work of the Haystack Mountain School of Crafts faculty. **Harbor Farm** (⊠ Rte. 15, Little Deer Isle, ☎ 207/348–7737) carries wonderful products for the home, such as pottery, artworks, furniture, dinnerware, linens, and folk art. **Old Deer Isle Parish House Antiques** (⊠ Rte. 15, ☎ 207/348–9964) is a place for poking around in jumbles of old kitchenware, glassware, books, and linens. **Turtle Gallery** (⊠ Rte. 15, ☎ 207/348–9977) shows contemporary painting and sculpture.

Stonington

③ *7 mi south of Deer Isle.*

Stonington is an emphatically ungentrified community that tolerates summer visitors but makes no effort to cater to them. Main Street holds gift shops and galleries, but this is a working port town—the principal activity is at the waterfront, where fishing boats arrive with the day's catch. At night, the town can be rowdy. The high, sloped island that rises beyond the archipelago known as Merchants Row is Isle au Haut (☞ Isle au Haut, *below*), accessible by mail boat from Stonington, which contains a remote section of Acadia National Park.

Dining and Lodging

$$–$$$ ✕ **The Cafe Atlantic.** Whether you want ice cream, lobster, or a nice meal, you'll find it at this harborfront eatery. Country linens and antiques decorate the restaurant, which serves fresh seafood as well as chicken and steak. For lobster-in-the-rough, head to the deck overhanging the water. For a quick snack, visit the ice cream window. ⊠ *Main St.,* ☎ *207/367–6373. AE, D, MC, V.*

$$–$$$ 🏠 **Inn on the Harbor.** From the front, this inn composed of four 100-year-old Victorian buildings is as plain and unadorned as Stonington itself. But out back it opens up, with an expansive deck over the harbor. Many guests take breakfast here in the morning. Rooms on the harbor side have views, and some have fireplaces and private decks. Those on the street side lack the views and can be noisy at night. ⊠ *Box 69, Main St., 04681,* ☎ *207/367–2420 or 800/942–2420,* ℻ *207/367–5165. 13 rooms, 1 suite. Espresso bar. Continental breakfast. AE, D, MC, V.*

Shopping

Dockside Books & Gifts (⊠ W. Main St., ☎ 207/367–2652) stocks an eclectic selection of books, crafts, and gifts in a harborfront shop. **Eastern Bay Gallery** (⊠ Main St., ☎ 207/367–5006) carries contemporary Maine crafts; summer exhibits highlight the works of specific artists.

Isle au Haut

㉜ *14 mi south of Stonington.*

Isle au Haut thrusts its steeply ridged back out of the sea south of Stonington. Accessible only by **passenger mail boat** (☎ 207/367–5193 or 207/367–6516), the island is worth visiting for the ferry ride itself, a half-hour cruise amid the tiny islands of Merchants Row, where you might see terns, guillemots, and harbor seals.

More than half the island is part of **Acadia National Park:** 17½ mi of trails extend through quiet spruce and birch woods, along beaches and seaside cliffs, and over the spine of the central mountain ridge. (For more information on the park, *see* Bar Harbor *and* Acadia National Park, *below.*) From mid-June to mid-September, the mail boat docks at **Duck Harbor** within the park. The small campground here, with five Adirondack-type lean-tos, is open from mid-May to mid-October and fills up quickly. Reservations, which are essential, can be made after April 1 by writing to Acadia National Park (⊠ Box 177, Bar Harbor 04609).

Lodging

$$$$ 🏠 **The Keeper's House.** Thick spruce forest surrounds this converted lighthouse-keeper's house on a rock ledge. There is no electricity, but every guest receives a flashlight upon registering; guests dine by candlelight on seafood or chicken and read in the evening by kerosene lantern. Trails link the inn with Acadia National Park's Isle au Haut trail network, and you can walk to the village. The spacious rooms contain simple, painted-wood furniture and local crafts. A separate cottage, the Oil House, has no indoor plumbing. Access to the island is via the mail boat from Stonington. ⊠ *Box 26, Lighthouse Rd., 04645,* ☎ *207/367–2261. 4 rooms share 2 baths, 1 cottage. Dock, bicycles. AP. No credit cards. BYOB. Closed Nov.–Apr.*

Penobscot Bay A to Z

Arriving and Departing
See Arriving and Departing *in* Maine A to Z, *below.*

Getting Around

BY CAR

U.S. 1 follows the west coast of Penobscot Bay, linking Rockland, Rockport, Camden, Belfast, and Searsport. On the east side of the bay, Route 175 (south from U.S. 1) takes you to Route 166A (for Castine) and Route 15 (for Blue Hill, Deer Isle, and Stonington). A car is essential for exploring the bay area.

Contacts and Resources

B&B RESERVATION AGENCY

Camden Accommodations (☎ 207/236–6090 or 800/236–1920, FAX 207/236–6091) provides assistance for reservations in and around Camden.

BOAT TRIPS AND TOURS

See Outdoor Activities and Sports *in* Rockland *and* Camden, *above.*

The **Maine Windjammer Association** (⊠ Box 1144, Blue Hill 04614, ☎ 800/807–9463) represents 12 windjammers.

EMERGENCIES

Blue Hill Memorial Hospital (⊠ Water St., Blue Hill, ☎ 207/374–2836). **Island Medical Center** (⊠ Airport Rd., Stonington, ☎ 207/367–2311). **Penobscot Bay Medical Center** (⊠ U.S. 1, Rockport, ☎ 207/596–8000). **Waldo County General Hospital** (⊠ 56 Northport Ave., Belfast, ☎ 207/338–2500).

VISITOR INFORMATION

Belfast Area Chamber of Commerce (⊠ Box 58, 1 Main St., Belfast 04915, ☎ 207/338–5900). **Blue Hill Chamber of Commerce** (⊠ Box 520, Blue Hill 04614, ☎ no phone). **Castine Town Office** (⊠ Emerson Hall, Court St., Castine 04421, ☎ 207/326–4502). **Deer Isle–Stonington Chamber of Commerce** (⊠ Box 459, Stonington 04681, ☎ 207/348–6124). **Rockland–Thomaston Area Chamber of Commerce** (⊠ Harbor Park, Box 508, Rockland 04841, ☎ 207/596–0376 or 800/562–2529). **Rockport-Camden-Lincolnville Chamber of Commerce** (⊠ Public Land ing, Box 919, Camden 04843, ☎ 207/236–4404 or 800/223–5459). **Waldo County Regional Chamber of Commerce** (⊠ School St., Unity 04988, ☎ 207/948–5050 or 800/870–9934).

MOUNT DESERT ISLAND

Acadia is the informal name for the area east of Penobscot Bay that includes Mount Desert Island (pronounced "dessert") as well as Blue Hill Bay and Frenchman Bay. Mount Desert, 13 mi across, is Maine's largest island, and it encompasses most of Acadia National Park, an astonishingly beautiful preserve with rocky cliffs, crashing surf, and serene mountains and ponds. Maine's number one tourist attraction, it draws more than 4 million visitors a year. The 40,000 acres of woods and mountains, lake and shore, footpaths, carriage roads, and hiking trails that make up the park extend to other islands and some of the mainland. Outside the park, on Mount Desert's eastern shore, Bar Harbor has become a busy tourist town. Less commercial and congested are the smaller island towns, such as Southwest Harbor and Northeast Harbor, and the outlying islands.

Bar Harbor

③ *160 mi northeast of Portland, 22 mi southeast of Ellsworth on Rte. 3.*

An upper-class resort town in the 19th century, Bar Harbor now serves visitors to Acadia National Park with inns, motels, and restaurants. Most of its grand mansions were destroyed in a fire that devastated the island in 1947, but many surviving estates have been converted into inns and restaurants. Motels abound, yet the town retains the beauty of a commanding location on Frenchman Bay. Shops, restaurants, and hotels are clustered along Main, Mt. Desert, and Cottage streets.

The **Bar Harbor Historical Society Museum** displays photographs of Bar Harbor from the days when it catered to the very rich. Other exhibits document the fire of 1947. ⊠ *33 Ledgelawn Ave.,* ☎ *207/288–3807 or 207/288–0000.* ☞ *Free.* ☉ *June–Oct., Mon.–Sat. 1–4 or by appointment.*

☾ The small **Natural History Museum** at the College of the Atlantic has wildlife exhibits, a hands-on discovery room, interpretive programs, and a self-guided nature trail. ⊠ *Rte. 3,* ☎ *207/288–5015.* ☞ *$2.50.* ☉ *Mid-June–Labor Day, Mon.–Sat. 10–5; Labor Day–Columbus Day, Thurs.–Mon. 10–4.*

☾ The **Acadia Zoo** has pastures, streams, and woods that shelter about 45 species of wild and domestic animals, including reindeer, wolves, monkeys, and a moose. A barn has been converted into a rain-forest habitat for monkeys, birds, reptiles, and other Amazon creatures. ⊠ *Rte. 3, Trenton, north of Bar Harbor,* ☎ *207/667–3244.* ☞ *$6.* ☉ *May–Dec., daily 9:30–dusk.*

On Frenchman Bay but off Mount Desert Island, the 55-acre **Lamoine State Park** (⊠ Rte. 184, Lamoine, ☎ 207/667–4778) has a boat-launching ramp, a fishing pier, a children's playground, and a 61-site campground that's open from mid-May to mid-October.

Dining and Lodging

$$$ ✕ **The Burning Tree.** Fresh is the key word at this casual restaurant just outside town. The menu emphasizes seafood and organic produce and chicken; some typical items are pan-sautéed monkfish, Cajun lobster, crab au gratin, and chicken pot roast. There are always two or three vegetarian choices. Local contemporary art adorns the walls in the two dining rooms and porch. ⊠ *Rte. 3, Otter Creek,* ☎ *207/288–9331. MC, V. Closed Tues. and mid-Oct.–late May.*

$$$ ✕ **George's.** Candles, flowers, and linens grace the tables, and art fills
★   the walls of the four small dining rooms in this old house. The menu's Mediterranean influences can be tasted in the phyllo-wrapped lobster; the lamb and wild-game entrées are superb. The prix-fixe menu includes an appetizer, an entrée, and dessert. Jazz musicians perform nightly in peak season. ⊠ *7 Stephen's La.,* ☎ *207/288–4505. AE, D, DC, MC, V. Closed Nov.–mid-June. No lunch.*

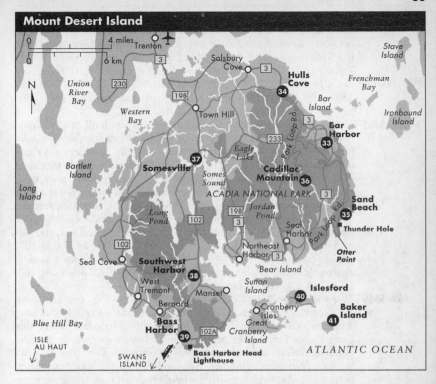

Mount Desert Island

$$$ ✕ **Porcupine Grill.** This restaurant, named for a cluster of islets in Frenchman Bay, has a menu that changes regularly but might include starters such as pan-roasted mussels or citrus barbecued quail and main courses like grilled lobster, twin Portobello fillets, or filet mignon. Soft green walls, antique furnishings, and Villeroy & Boch porcelain create an ambience that complements the cuisine. ⊠ *123 Cottage St.,* ☎ *207/288–3884. AE, MC, V. Closed Sun. and Mar.–Apr.; closed weekdays Oct.–Feb. and May–June. No lunch.*

$$–$$$ ✕ **Café This Way.** Jazz, unmatched tables and chairs, and a few couches provide a relaxing background for the creative, internationally inspired menu at this restaurant tucked in a back street in Bar Harbor. You might begin with crab cakes with tequila-lime sauce and then move on to cashew-crusted chicken over sautéed greens with sesame-ginger aioli or perhaps butternut squash ravioli with roasted red peppers, broccoli, and a rosemary maple cream sauce. Save room for the homemade desserts. ⊠ *14½ Desert St.,* ☎ *207/288–4483. MC, V.*

$–$$$ ✕ **Galyn's.** The upstairs dining rooms at this casual restaurant have a
★ limited view of the harbor, but most people come for the well-crafted dishes and affordable prices. The dinner menu lists fish, chicken, lobster, seafood, beef, and vegetarian dishes. Sandwiches, salads, and entrées like quiche, jambalaya, ribs, and stir-fries are served at lunch. ⊠ *17 Main St.,* ☎ *207/288–9706. AE, D, MC, V.*

$$$–$$$$ ✕⊞ **Bar Harbor Inn.** The roots of this genteel inn date from the 1880s. Rooms are spread out over three buildings on nicely landscaped waterfront property, just a short walk to town. The main inn was completely renovated in 1998. Most rooms have balconies, hot tubs, fireplaces, and great views. The two-level suites are a good choice for families. Rooms in the Oceanfront Lodge offer private decks or patios overlooking the ocean, while those in the Newport Lodge, behind it, are more simply furnished and smaller. The formal waterfront Reading Room serves mostly Continental fare but has some Maine specialties like lobster pie and a scrumptious Indian pudding. The more casual Terrace Grill is an outdoor restaurant on the waterfront. ⊠ *Newport Dr., 04609,* ☏ *207/288–3351 or 800/248–3351,* FAX *207/288–5296. 153 rooms. 2 restaurants, no-smoking rooms, exercise room, pool, business services. Continental breakfast. AE, D, DC, MC, V.*

$$$–$$$$ 🏨 **Balance Rock Inn.** This grand summer cottage built in 1903 commands a prime, secluded location on the water but is only two blocks from downtown. The atmosphere is a bit stuffy, but service is thorough and thoughtful. Rooms are spacious and meticulously furnished with reproduction pieces—four-poster and canopy beds in guest rooms, crystal chandeliers and a grand piano in common rooms. Some rooms have fireplaces, saunas, steam rooms, whirlpool tubs, or private porches, and most have views of the pool and well-tended gardens on the front lawn and to the water beyond. From the bar on the veranda, you can watch the activity in the harbor. ⊠ *21 Albert Meadow, 04609,* ☏ *207/ 288–2610 or 800/753–0494,* FAX *207/288–5534. 13 rooms, 1 suite, 3 apartments. Bar, pool, exercise room, concierge. Full breakfast. AE, D, MC, V. Closed late Oct.–early May.*

$$$–$$$$ 🏨 **Inn at Canoe Point.** Seclusion and privacy are the main attributes
★ of this snug, 100-year-old Tudor-style house on the water at Hulls Cove, 2 mi from Bar Harbor and ¼ mi from Acadia National Park's Hulls Cove Visitor Center. The Master Suite, a large room with a gas fireplace, has French doors that open onto a waterside deck. The inn's living room has huge windows that look out on the water, a granite fireplace, and a waterfront deck where breakfast is served on summer mornings. ⊠ *Box 216, Rte. 3, 04609,* ☏ *207/288–9511,* FAX *207/ 288–2870. 3 rooms, 2 suites. Full breakfast. D, MC, V.*

$$–$$$$ 🏨 **Ullikana.** Inside the stucco-and-timber walls of this traditional
★ Tudor cottage, the riotous decor juxtaposes antiques with contemporary country pieces, vibrant color with French country wallpapers, and abstract art with folk creations. The combination not only works—it shines. Rooms are large, most have at least a glimpse of the water, many have fireplaces, and some have decks. Breakfast is an elaborate multicourse affair. The owners have refurbished the Yellow House across the drive, with an additional six rooms decorated in traditional Old Bar Harbor style. Ullikana is a short walk to downtown shops, yet it's a private location with pretty gardens. ⊠ *16 The Field, 04609,* ☏ *207/ 288–9552,* FAX *207/288–3682. 16 rooms. Full breakfast. MC, V. Closed Nov.–May.*

$–$$ 🏨 **Bass Cottage in the Field.** What a bargain! Anna Jean Turner began welcoming guests to this former summer estate when she came here as a young girl in 1928. She continues to operate the inn with the help of her niece. Behind Bar Harbor's Main Street and a short walk from the Shore Path, Bass Cottage is a step back in time in both decor and price. The rooms could use a face-lift, but most likely you'll spend your time on the glassed-in wraparound porch, which is furnished with antique white wicker. ⊠ *In the Field, 04609,* ☏ *207/288–3705,* FAX *207/ 288–2005. 10 rooms, 6 with baths. No credit cards. Closed mid-Oct.– late May.*

Nightlife and the Arts

For dancing, try **Carmen Verandah** (⊠ 119 Main St., upstairs, ☏ 207/ 288–2766). **Geddy's Pub** (⊠ 19 Main St., ☏ 207/288–5077) has live entertainment early in the evening followed by a DJ spinning discs. At the **Lompoc Cafe & Brewpub** (⊠ 30 Rodick St., ☏ 207/288–9513) you can relax in a garden setting and play a game of bocce. You can sink into an easy chair with a pizza and a beer and watch a flick at **Reel Pizza Cinerama** (✉ 33B Kennebec Pl., ☎ 207/288–3811).

Arcady Music Festival (☎ 207/288–3151) schedules concerts (primarily classical) at locations around Mount Desert Island and at some off-island sites, year-round. **Bar Harbor Music Festival** (✉ 59 Cottage St., ☎ 207/288–5744) arranges recitals, jazz, chamber music, string-orchestra, and pop concerts by young professionals from July to early August.

Outdoor Activities and Sports
BICYCLING
Acadia Bike & Canoe (✉ 48 Cottage St., ☎ 207/288–9605) and **Bar Harbor Bicycle Shop** (✉ 141 Cottage St., ☎ 207/288–3886) rent bicycles.

BOATING AND WHALE-WATCHING
For canoe rentals try **Acadia Bike & Canoe** (☞ Bicycling, *above*). For guided kayak tours, try **National Park Kayak Tours** (✉ 39 Cottage St., ☎ 207/288–0342) or **Coastal Kayaking Tours** (✉ 48 Cottage St., ☎ 207/288–9605).

Acadian Whale Watcher (✉ Golden Anchor Pier, West St., ☎ 207/288–9794 or 800/421–3307) runs 3½-hour whale-watching cruises from June to mid-October. **Downeast Windjammer & Lighthouse Cruises** (✉ Bar Harbor Inn Pier, ☎ 207/288–4585) offers 1½- to 2-hour tours aboard the four-masted schooner *Margaret Todd* and the historic 1911 fishing schooner *Sylvia W. Beal* between mid-May and October. **Whale Watcher Inc.** (✉ 1 West St., ☎ 207/288–3322 or 800/508–1499) operates the windjammer *Bay Lady,* the nature-sightseeing cruise vessel *Acadian,* and the 300-passenger *Atlantis* in summer.

Shopping
Bar Harbor in summer is prime territory for browsing for gifts, T-shirts, and novelty items. For bargains, head for the outlets that line Route 3 in Ellsworth, which have good discounts on shoes, sportswear, cookware, and more.

Ben and Bill's Chocolate Emporium (✉ 66 Main St., ☎ 207/288–3281) is a chocolate lover's nirvana, and the adventurous can try lobster ice cream here. **Birdsnest Gallery** (✉ 12 Mt. Desert St., ☎ 207/288–4054) sells fine art, paintings, and sculpture. The **Eclipse Gallery** (✉ 12 Mt. Desert St., ☎ 207/288–9048) carries handblown glass, ceramics, art photography, and wood furniture. **Island Artisans** (✉ 99 Main St., ☎ 207/288–4214) is a crafts cooperative. The **Lone Moose–Fine Crafts** (✉ 78 West St., ☎ 207/288–4229) has art glass and works in clay, pottery, wood, and fiberglass.

Acadia National Park

4 mi northwest of Bar Harbor (to Hulls Cove).

There is no one Acadia. The park holds some of the most spectacular and varied scenery on the eastern seaboard: a rugged coastline of surf-pounded granite and an interior graced by sculpted mountains, quiet ponds, and lush deciduous forests. Cadillac Mountain, the highest point of land on the eastern coast, dominates the park. Although it's
★ rugged, **Acadia National Park** is also a land of graceful stone bridges, horse-drawn carriages, and the elegant Jordan Point Tea House. The 27-mi Park Loop Road provides an excellent introduction, yet to truly appreciate the park you must get off the main road and experience it by walking or taking a carriage ride on the carriage trails, by hiking or perhaps sea kayaking. If you get off the beaten path, you'll find places in the park that you can have practically to yourself, despite the millions of visitors who descend in summer.

③④ The popular **Hulls Cove** approach to Acadia National Park, northwest of Bar Harbor on Route 3, brings you to the start of the **Park Loop Road.** Even though it is often clogged with traffic in summer, the road provides the best introduction to the park. You can drive it in an hour, but allow at least half a day or more to explore the many sites along the route. At the start of the loop, the **visitor center** shows a free 15-minute orientation film. Also available at the center are the *Acadia Beaver Log* (the park's free newspaper detailing guided hikes and other ranger-led programs), books, maps of hiking trails and carriage roads, the schedule for naturalist-led tours, and cassettes for drive-it-yourself tours. Traveling south on the Park Loop Road, you'll reach a small ticket booth where you pay the $10-per-vehicle entrance fee, good for seven consecutive days. Take the next left to the parking area for Sand Beach. ⊠ *Visitor center, Park Loop Rd. off Rte. 3,* ☎ *207/288–3338.* ⊙ *Park daily. Visitor center late June–Aug., daily 8–6; mid-Apr.–mid-June and Sept.–Oct., daily 8–4:30.*

③⑤ **Sand Beach** is a small stretch of pink sand backed by the mountains of Acadia and the odd lump of rock known as the Beehive. The **Ocean Trail,** which runs alongside the Park Loop Road from Sand Beach to the Otter Point parking area, is an easily accessible walk with some of the most spectacular scenery in Maine: huge slabs of pink granite heaped at the ocean's edge, ocean views unobstructed to the horizon, and **Thunder Hole,** a natural seaside cave into which the ocean rushes and roars.

★ ③⑥ **Cadillac Mountain,** at 1,532 ft, is the highest point on the eastern seaboard. From the smooth, bald summit you have an awesome 360-degree view of the ocean, islands, jagged coastline, and woods and lakes of Acadia and its surroundings. You can drive or hike to the summit.

The Sieur de Monts Spring exit off the Park Loop offers two enticing sites. The **Abbé Museum** holds a treasure trove of Maine's Native American history, including arrowheads, moccasins, tools, jewelry, and a well-documented collection of baskets. A new museum, planned for downtown Bar Harbor, will open in 2000 or 2001. ⊠ *Sieur de Mont Spring exit from Rte. 3 or Acadia National Park Loop Rd.,* ☎ *207/ 288–3519.* ☞ *$2.* ⊙ *July–Aug., daily 9–5; mid-May–June and Sept.–mid-Oct., daily 10–4.*

The **Wild Gardens of Acadia** present a miniature view of the plants that grow on Mt. Desert Island. ⊠ *Rte. 3 at the Sieur de Mont Spring exit,* ☎ *207/288–3400.* ☞ *Free.* ⊙ *Paths 24 hrs.*

Dining and Lodging

$$–$$$ ✕ **Jordan Pond House.** The restaurant's setting overlooking Jordan Pond is magnificent and serene, but the loudspeaker blaring out the names of parties to be seated is jarring. Come for tea and the oversize popovers with homemade strawberry jam and ice cream, a century-old tradition. If you choose to sit on the terrace or lawn, be forewarned that bees are more than a nuisance. The menu offers lunch and dinner items, including lobster stew, but these get mixed reviews. ⊠ *Park Loop Rd.,* ☎ *207/276–3316. AE, D, MC, V. Closed late Oct.–mid-May.*

$ ⚠ **Blackwoods and Seawall.** These two campgrounds with a total of 530 campsites fill up quickly during the summer. Space at Seawall is allocated on a first-come, first-served basis, starting at 8 AM. Between mid-June and mid-September, reserve a Blackwoods site within five months of a visit. No reservations are required in the off-season. *Blackwoods:* ⊠ *Rte. 3, Northeast Harbor,* ☎ *800/365–2267.* ⊙ *Year-round. Seawall:* ⊠ *Rte. 102A, Northeast Harbor,* ☎ *207/244–3600. Closed late Sept.–late May.*

Outdoor Activities and Sports

BIKING

The carriage roads that wind through the woods and fields of Acadia National Park are ideal for biking (☞ Bar Harbor for rentals) and jogging when the ground is dry and for cross-country skiing in winter. The Hulls Cove visitor center has maps.

CARRIAGE RIDES

Wildwood Stables (✉ Park Loop Rd., near Jordan Pond House, ☎ 207/276–3622) gives romantic tours in horse-drawn carriages on the 51-mi network of carriage roads designed and built by philanthropist John D. Rockefeller, Jr. There are three two-hour trips and three one-hour trips daily, including a "tea-and-popover ride" that stops at Jordan Pond House (☞ Dining and Lodging, *above*) and a sunset ride to the summit of Day Mountain.

HIKING

Acadia National Park maintains nearly 200 mi of foot and carriage paths, from easy strolls along flatlands to rigorous climbs that involve ladders and handholds on rock faces. Among the more rewarding hikes are the Precipice Trail to Champlain Mountain, the Great Head Loop, the Gorham Mountain Trail, and the path around Eagle Lake. The Hulls Cove visitor center has trail guides and maps and will help you match a trail with your interests and abilities.

Around Acadia

On completing the 27-mi Park Loop Road, you can continue an auto tour of the island by heading west on Route 233 for the villages on Somes Sound, a true fjord—the only one on the East Coast—which **③** almost bisects Mount Desert Island. **Somesville,** the oldest settlement on the island (1621), is a carefully preserved New England village of white clapboard houses and churches, neat green lawns, and bits of blue water visible behind them.

③ **Southwest Harbor,** south from Somesville on Route 102, combines the salty character of a working port with the refinements of a summer resort community. From the town's Main Street (Route 102), turn left onto Clark Point Road to reach the harbor.

⊙ **Mount Desert Oceanarium** has exhibits in two locations on the fishing and sea life of the Gulf of Maine, a live-seal program, a lobster hatchery, and hands-on exhibits such as a touch tank. ✉ *Clark Point Rd., Southwest Harbor,* ☎ *207/244–7330;* ✉ *Rte. 3, Thomas Bay, Bar Harbor,* ☎ *207/288–5005.* ▣ *Call for admission fees (combination tickets available for both sites).* ⊙ *Mid-May–mid-Oct., Mon.–Sat. 9–5.*

Wendell Gilley Museum of Bird Carving showcases bird carvings by Gilley, presents carving demonstrations and workshops and natural-history programs, and exhibits wildlife art. ✉ *4 Herrick Rd., Southwest Harbor,* ☎ *207/244–7555.* ▣ *$3.25.* ⊙ *July–Aug., Tues.–Sun. 10–5; June and Sept.–Oct., Tues.–Sun. 10–4; May and Nov.–Dec., Fri.–Sun. 10–4.*

③ In **Bass Harbor,** 4 mi south of Southwest Harbor (follow Route 102A when Route 102 forks), visit the **Bass Harbor Head lighthouse,** which clings to a cliff at the eastern entrance to Blue Hill Bay. It was built in 1858. The tiny lobstering village has cottages for rent, inns, a restaurant, and a gift shop. Also here is the **Maine State Ferry Service**'s car-and-passenger ferry (☎ 207/244–3254) to Swans Island. The ferry has six daily runs June to mid-October, fewer the rest of the year.

Dining and Lodging

$–$$ ✕ **Beal's Lobster Pier.** You can watch lobstermen bringing in their catch at this working lobster pound, where you can order lobster at one take-out window, fried foods, burgers, and dessert at another. ✉ *End of Clark Point Rd., Southwest Harbor,* ☎ *207/244–3202 or 207/ 244–7178 or 800/245–7178. Closed mid-Oct.–mid-May.*

$–$$ ✕ **Keenan's.** Come early, and don't be put off by the exterior of this shack housing a casual restaurant; the food is considered among the best on the island. Specialties are seafood gumbo, shrimp étouffée, and baby back ribs. Children can order burgers. ✉ *Corner of Rte. 102A and Flatiron Rd., Bass Harbor,* ☎ *207/244–3403. Reservations not accepted. No credit cards. No lunch.*

$$–$$$$ ✕🔲 **Claremont Hotel.** Built in 1884 and operated continuously as an inn, the Claremont calls up memories of the long, leisurely vacations of days gone by. The yellow clapboard structure commands a view of Somes Sound. Croquet is played on the lawn, and cocktails and lunch are served at the Boat House in summer. The cottages have not been updated as much as the inn's rooms; some guests complain about the facilities in them. The old-style dining room ($$$), open to the public for breakfast and dinner, has picture windows overlooking the sound. The menu changes weekly and always includes fresh fish and at least one vegetarian entrée; reservations are essential, and a jacket is required for dinner. ✉ *off Clark Point Rd., Box 137, Southwest Harbor 04679,* ☎ *207/244–5036 or 800/244–5036,* FAX *207/244–3512. 29 rooms, 1 suite, 13 cottages. Restaurant, tennis court, croquet, dock, boating, bicycles. Full breakfast; MAP available. No credit cards. Hotel and restaurant closed mid-Oct.–mid-June; cottages closed Nov.–mid-May.*

$$ 🔲 **Island House.** This sweet B&B on the quiet side of the island has four simple and bright rooms in the main house. The carriage-house suite comes complete with a sleeping loft and a kitchenette. ✉ *Box 1006, 121 Clark Point Rd., Southwest Harbor 04679,* ☎ *207/244–5180. 4 rooms, 1 suite. Full breakfast. MC, V.*

$–$$ 🔲 **The Moorings Inn & Cottages.** Nothing is fancy here except the jaw-dropping view of Somes Sound. The roots of the Maine House date back to the late 18th century; the cottages and a small motel are more recent. Rooms in the Maine House are decorated with antiques and country charm; the motel rooms lack the atmosphere but have sliding glass doors onto decks. The homey cottage rooms offer the most privacy and have cooking facilities. Lookout Front has a fireplace, screened porch, and king-size bed. ✉ *Box 744, 135 Shore Rd., Manset 04679,* ☎ *207/244–5523, 207/244–3210, or 800/596–5523. 13 rooms, 5 cottages, 1 apartment. Dock. Continental breakfast. No credit cards. Closed late Oct.–late Apr.*

Nightlife and the Arts

A lively boating crowd frequents the lounge at the **Moorings Restaurant** (✉ Shore Rd., Manset, ☎ 207/244–7070), which is accessible by boat and car. The lounge stays open until after midnight from mid-May to October.

Outdoor Activities and Sports

BICYCLING

Southwest Cycle (✉ Main St., Southwest Harbor, ☎ 207/244–5856) rents bicycles.

BOATING

Manset Yacht Service (✉ Shore Rd., Manset, ☎ 207/244–4040) rents power boats and sailboats. **National Park Canoe Rentals** (✉ Pretty Marsh Rd., Somesville, at the head of Long Pond, ☎ 207/244–5854) rents canoes.

The *Rachel B. Jackson* (⊠ Manset Town Wharf, Manset, ☎ 207/244–7813), a Maine-built windjammer, takes passengers on 2½-hour sails around Somes Sound and the Cranberry Isles.

Shopping
E. L. Higgins (⊠ Bernard Rd., off Rte. 102, Bernard, ☎ 207/244–3983) carries antique wicker as well as antique furniture and glassware. **Marianne Clark Fine Antiques** (⊠ Main St., Southwest Harbor, ☎ 207/244–9247) has formal and country furniture, American paintings, and accessories from the 18th and 19th centuries. **Port in a Storm Bookstore** (⊠ Main St., Somesville, ☎ 207/244–4114) is a book lover's nirvana.

Excursions to the Cranberry Isles

Off the southeast shore of Mount Desert Island at the entrance to Somes Sound, the five Cranberry Isles—Great Cranberry, Islesford (or Little Cranberry), Baker Island, Sutton Island, and Bear Island—escape the hubbub that engulfs Acadia National Park in summer. Great Cranberry and Islesford are served by the **Beal & Bunker passenger ferry** (☎ 207/244–3575) from Northeast Harbor and by **Cranberry Cove Boating Company** (☎ 207/244–5882) from Southwest Harbor. Baker Island is reached by the summer cruise boats of the **Islesford Ferry Company** (☎ 207/276–3717) from Northeast Harbor; Sutton and Bear islands are privately owned.

40 **Islesford** comes closest to having a village: a collection of houses, a church, a fishermen's co-op, a market, and a post office near the ferry dock.

The **Islesford Historical Museum,** run by Acadia National Park, has displays of tools, documents relating to the island's history, and books and manuscripts of the poet Rachel Field (1894–1942), who summered on Sutton Island. ⊠ *Isleford,* ☎ *207/288–3338.* 🎟 *Free.* ☉ *Mid-June–late Sept., daily 10:30–noon and 12:30–4:30.*

41 The 123-acre **Baker Island,** the most remote of the Cranberry Isles, looks almost black from a distance because of its thick spruce forest. The Islesford Ferry cruise boat from Northeast Harbor conducts a 4½-hour narrated tour, during which you are likely to see ospreys nesting on a sea stack off Sutton Island, harbor seals basking on ledges, and cormorants flying low over the water. Because Baker Island has no natural harbor, the boat ties up offshore, and you take a fishing dory to get to shore.

Mount Desert Island A to Z

Arriving and Departing
See Arriving and Departing *in* Maine A to Z, *below.*

Getting Around
BY CAR

North of Bar Harbor, the scenic 27-mi Park Loop Road leaves Route 3 to circle the eastern quarter of Mount Desert Island, with one-way traffic from Sieur de Monts Spring to Seal Harbor and two-way traffic between Seal Harbor and Hulls Cove. Route 102, which serves the western half of Mount Desert, is reached from Route 3 just after it enters the island or from Route 233 west from Bar Harbor. All these island roads pass through the precincts of Acadia National Park.

Contacts and Resources
CAR RENTAL

Avis (⊠ Bangor International Airport, 299 Godfrey Blvd., ☎ 207/947–8383 or 800/331–1212). **Budget** (⊠ Hancock County Airport, Rte. 3, Trenton, ☎ 207/667–1200 or 800/527–0700). **Hertz** (⊠ Bangor International Airport, 299 Godfrey Blvd., ☎ 207/942–5519 or 800/

654–3131). **Thrifty** (✉ Bangor International Airport, 357 Odlin Rd., ☎ 207/942–6400 or 800/367–2277).

EMERGENCIES
Mount Desert Island Hospital (✉ 10 Wayman La., Bar Harbor, ☎ 207/ 288–5081). **Maine Coast Memorial Hospital** (✉ 50 Union St., Ellsworth, ☎ 207/667–5311). **Southwest Harbor Medical Center** (✉ Herrick Rd., Southwest Harbor, ☎ 207/244–5513).

GUIDED TOURS
Bar Harbor Taxi and Tours (☎ 207/288–4020) conducts half-day historic and scenic tours of the area. **National Park Tours** (☎ 207/288–3327) operates a 2½-hour bus tour of Acadia National Park, narrated by a naturalist. The bus departs twice daily, from May to October, across from Testa's Restaurant at Bayside Landing on Main Street in Bar Harbor.

Acadia Air (☎ 207/667–5534), on Route 3 in Trenton, between Ellsworth and Bar Harbor at Hancock County Airport, rents aircraft and flies seven aerial sightseeing routes, from spring to fall.

VISITOR INFORMATION
Acadia National Park (✉ Box 177, Bar Harbor 04609, ☎ 207/288–3338). **Bar Harbor Chamber of Commerce** (✉ 93 Cottage St., Box 158, Bar Harbor 04609, ☎ 207/288–3393, 207/288–5103, or 800/288–5103). **Southwest Harbor/Tremont Chamber of Commerce** (✉ Box 1143, Main St., Southwest Harbor 04679, ☎ 207/244–9264 or 207/423–9264).

WAY DOWN EAST

East of Ellsworth on U.S. 1 is a different Maine, a place pretty much off the beaten path that seduces with a rugged, simple beauty. Red-hued blueberry barrens dot the landscape, and scraggly jack pines hug the highly accessible shoreline. The quiet pleasures here include hiking, birding, and going on whale-watching and puffin cruises. Many artists live in the region; you can often purchase works directly from them.

Hancock

42 *9 mi east of Ellsworth.*

As you approach the small town of Hancock and the summer colony of cottages at Hancock Point, stunning views await, especially at sunset, over Frenchman Bay toward Mt. Desert.

Dining and Lodging
$$$ ✕🖬 **Le Domaine.** Owner-chef Nicole L. Purslow whips up classic haute cuisine, the perfect accompaniments to which can be found amid the more than 40,000 bottles of French wine in the restaurant's cellar. Le Domaine is known primarily for its food, but its small French-country-style guest rooms are also inviting. Ask for a room in the rear, overlooking the lawns and gardens and away from the noise of U.S. 1. ✉ *HC 77, Box 496, U.S. 1, 04640,* ☎ *207/422–3395 or 800/554–8498,* 🖷 *207/422–2316. 7 rooms. Restaurant, hiking. Full breakfast; MAP available. AE, D, MC, V. Closed late Oct.–mid-May.*

$$–$$$ ✕🖬 **Crocker House Inn.** Set amid tall fir trees, this century-old shingle-style cottage is a mere 200 yards from the water and holds comfortable rooms decorated with antiques and country furnishings. The accommodations in the Carriage House, which also has a TV room and a hot tub, are best for families. The inn's dining room draws Maine residents from as far away as Bar Harbor for meals that might include poached salmon or rack of lamb. ✉ *HC 77, Box 171, Hancock Point Rd., 04640,* ☎ *207/422–6806,* 🖷 *207/422–3105. 11*

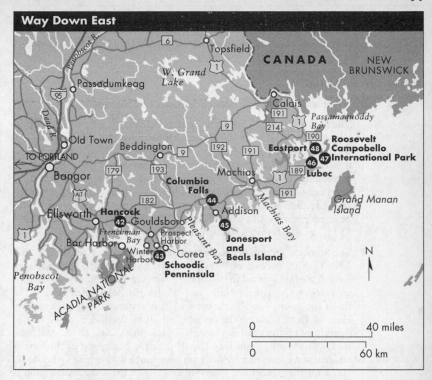

Way Down East

rooms. *Restaurant, hot tub, bicycles. Full breakfast; MAP available. AE, D, MC, V.*

$$ ⊡ **Island View Inn.** Noted Maine architect John Calvin Stevens is rumored to have designed this waterfront shingle-style cottage, which has a wraparound porch and views of Frenchman's Bay and Cadillac Mountain. All the rooms have decks, but the nicest (and quietest) accommodations are in the rear. ⊠ *HC 32, Box 24, U.S. 1, Sullivan Harbor, 04664,* ☎ *207/422–3031. 6 rooms. Beach, boating. Full breakfast. D, MC, V. Closed mid-Oct.–late May.*

$$ ⊡ **Sullivan Harbor Farm.** Antiques and country pieces decorate this simple bed-and-breakfast in an 1829 farmhouse built by Captain James Urann, a shipbuilder who launched his boats across the road. The house, set well back from the road, has nice views of Frenchman Bay and Mount Desert Island. You can relax on the pretty grounds or take a canoe or kayak to the cove across the way. Even if you don't stay here, stop by to purchase some of the award-winning salmon cold-smoked here in the traditional Scottish manner. ⊠ *Box 96, U.S. 1, 04664,* ☎ *207/422–3735 or 800/ 422–4014,* 𝖥𝖠𝖷 *207/422–8229. 4 rooms, 3 with bath; 2 cottages available by week. Boating. Full breakfast. D, MC, V. Closed late Oct.–May.*

Nightlife and the Arts

Pierre Monteux School for Conductors (⊠ Off U.S. 1, ☎ 207/422–3931) presents orchestral and chamber concerts from mid-June through July. The **Monteux Opera Festival** (⊠ Off U.S. 1, ☎ 207/422–3931) stages works in the Forest Studio of the Pierre Monteux Memorial Foundation from mid-July to mid-August.

Shopping

Hog Bay Pottery (⊠ Rte. 200, Franklin, ☎ 207/565–2282) sells pottery by Charles Grosjean and handwoven rugs by Susanne Grosjean. **Spring Woods Gallery** (⊠ Rte. 200, Sullivan, ☎ 207/422–3006) carries contemporary art by Paul and Ann Breeden and other artists, as well as Native American pottery, jewelry, and instruments. The sculpture garden is a delight. **Sugar Hill Gallery** (⊠ U.S. 1, ☎ 207/422–8207) offers high-quality Maine crafts.

Schoodic Peninsula

ⓙ *23 mi southeast of Hancock; 32 mi east of Ellsworth.*

The landscape of the Schoodic Peninsula makes it easy to understand why the overflow from Bar Harbor's wealthy summer population settled in Winter Harbor: the views over Frenchman's Bay to Mount Desert, the craggy coastline, and the towering evergreens. A drive through the community of Grindstone Neck shows what Bar Harbor might have been like before the Great Fire of 1947. Artists and craftspeople have opened galleries in and around Winter Harbor, to which no visit would be complete without a stop at **Gerrish's Store** (⊠ Main St. ☎ 207/963–5575), an old-fashioned ice cream counter.

★ The Schoodic section of **Acadia National Park** (⊠ Off Rte. 186, ☎ 207/288–3338), 2 mi east of Winter Harbor, has a scenic 6½-mi one-way loop that edges around the tip of the peninsula and yields views of Winter Harbor, Grindstone Neck, and Winter Harbor Lighthouse. At the tip of the point, you'll get a sense of how unforgiving the sea can be: Huge slabs of pink granite lie jumbled along the shore, thrashed unmercifully by the crashing surf, and jack pines cling to life amid the rocks. The Fraser Point Day-Use Area at the beginning of the loop is an ideal place for a picnic. Work off your lunch with a hike up Schoodic Head for the panoramic views up and down the coast. Admission is free, but there is no visitor center here.

Prospect Harbor, on Route 186 northeast of Winter Harbor, is a small fishing village nearly untouched by tourism. There's little to do in **Corea,** at the tip of Route 195, other than watch the fishermen at work, pick your way over stone beaches, or gaze out to sea—and that's what makes it so special.

Dining and Lodging

$$$ ✕ **Kitchen Garden.** This restaurant just off U.S. 1 in an old Cape-style house is a wonderful surprise. The six-course, fixed-price menu emphasizes organic foods, home-grown produce, and Jamaican specialties. Bring your own wine or beer. ⊠ *335 Village Rd., Steuben,* ☎ *207/546–2708. Reservations essential. No credit cards. Closed Mon.–Tues. June–Nov., and Sun.–Thurs. in winter.*

$$–$$$ ✕ **Fisherman's Inn.** The wide-ranging menu at the two pine-panel dining rooms here includes straightforward seafood, Italian, and beef dishes. Service can be frightfully slow. ⊠ *7 Newman St., Winter Harbor,* ☎ *207/963–5585. AE, D, MC, V. Closed Nov.–Mar.*

$–$$ ✕ **West Bay Lobsters in the Rough.** Lobsters, steamers, corn-on-the-cob, coleslaw, baked beans, and homemade blueberry pie are among the offerings here. Eat at picnic tables or picnic on nearby Schoodic Point. ⊠ *Rte. 186, Prospect Harbor,* ☎ *207/963–7021. AE, D, DC, MC, V. Closed Nov.–May.*

$$$ ▥ **Oceanside Meadows.** Inspired by the ocean out the front door; fields,
★   woods, and a salt marsh out back; and moose, eagles and other wildlife, the owners have created an environmental center here with lectures, musical performances, and other events held weekly in the barn. Rooms, furnished with antiques, country pieces, and family treasures, are spread out among two white clapboard buildings, and many have ocean views. Breakfast is an extravagant multicourse affair. In the off-

season, the inn is open by special arrangement. ✉ *Box 90, Rte. 195/ Corea Rd., Prospect Harbor 04669*, ☎ *207/963–5557*, ℻ *207/963– 5928. 13 rooms, 1 suite. No-smoking rooms, croquet, horseshoes, hiking, beach. Full breakfast. MC, V. Closed Nov.–Apr.*

$$ 🏠 **Black Duck.** This small bed-and-breakfast has comfortable public areas and guest rooms. Two tiny cottages perch on the harbor. ✉ *Crowley Island Rd., Corea 04624*, ☎ *207/963–2689*, ℻ *207/963–7495. 4 rooms, 2 with bath; 2 cottages. MC, V.*

$ 🏠 **The Pines.** The rooms may be small and undistinguished, but this motel's location, right at the beginning of the Schoodic Point Loop, makes it a good value. Six units have kitchenettes. ✉ *Rte. 186, 04693*, ☎ *207/963–2296. 3 rooms, 4 cottages, 2 cabins. Snack bar. MC, V.*

Outdoor Activities and Sports
Moose Look Guide Service (✉ Rte. 186, Gouldsboro, ☎ 207/963–7720) provides kayak tours and rentals, rowboat and canoe rentals, and bike rentals and conducts guided fishing trips.

Shopping
The wines sold at the **Bartlett Maine Estate Winery** (✉ off Rte. 1, Gouldsboro, ☎ 207/546–2408) are produced from locally grown apples, pears, blueberries, and other fruit. The **Harbor Shop** (✉ Newman St., Winter Harbor, ☎ 207/963–4117) has handmade gifts by American artisans. **Lee Art Glass Studio** (✉ Main St., Winter Harbor, ☎ 207/ 963–7004) carries fused-glass tableware and other items. Whimsical and serious metal sculptures can be found at **McDavid Sculpture** (✉ 177 Main St., Winter Harbor, ☎ 207/963–5990). **Pyramid Glass** (✉ Rte. 186, South Gouldsboro, ☎ 207/963–2027) sells stained-glass artwork and mosaics. **U.S. Bells** (✉ Rte. 186, Prospect Harbor, ☎ 207/ 963–7184) carries hand-cast bronze wind and door bells.

Columbia Falls

④④ *41 mi east of Ellsworth, 78 mi west of Calais.*

Columbia Falls, founded in the late 18th century, is a small, pretty village on the Pleasant River.

★ Judge Thomas Ruggles, a wealthy lumber dealer, store owner, postmaster, and Justice of the Court of Sessions, built **Ruggles House** in 1818. The house's distinctive Federal architecture, flying staircase, Palladian window, and woodwork—supposedly crafted over a period of three years by one man with a penknife—are worth making the ¼-mi detour off U.S. 1. ✉ *Main St.,* ☎ *no phone.* 🎫 *Donation requested.* ☉ *June 1– Oct. 15, weekdays 9:30–4:30, Sun. 11–4:30.*

Lodging
$ 🏠 **Pleasant Bay Inn and Llama Keep.** This Cape-style inn takes advantage of its riverfront location. You can stroll the nature paths on the property, which winds around a peninsula and out to Pleasant Bay, and you can even take a llama with you for company. The rooms, all with water views, are decorated with antiques and have country touches. ✉ *Box 222, West Side Rd., Addison 04606*, ☎ *207/483–4490. 3 rooms, 1 with bath. Full breakfast. MC, V.*

Shopping
Columbia Falls Pottery (✉ Main St., ☎ 207/483–4075) stocks stoneware and a sampling of Maine foods.

Jonesport and Beals Island

④⑤ *12 mi south of Columbia Falls, 20 mi southwest of Machias.*

Jonesport and Beals Island, two fishing communities joined by a bridge over the harbor, are less polished than the towns on the Schoodic Peninsula (☞ *above*). The birding here is superb.

Norton of Jonesport (☎ 207/497–5933) takes passengers on day trips to Machias Seal Island, where there's a large puffin colony.

Great Wass Island Preserve (☎ 207/729–5181) a 1,540-acre nature conservancy at the tip of Beals Island, protects rare plants, stunted pines, and raised peat bogs. Trails lead through the woods and emerge onto the undeveloped, raw coast, where you can make your way along the rocks and boulders before retreating into the forest. To get to the preserve from Jonesport, cross the bridge over Moosabec Reach to Beals Island. Go through Beals to Great Wass Island. Follow the road, which eventually becomes unpaved, to Black Duck Cove, about 3 mi from Beals, where there is a parking area on the left. Admission is free.

Dining and Lodging

$$ ✕ **Seafarer's Wife and Old Salt Room.** These two restaurants share a central kitchen. Allow at least a couple of hours to dine at the Seafarer's Wife, where a five-course meal (hors d'oeuvres, soup, salad, entrée, and dessert) is presented at a leisurely pace in a candlelighted dining room. The casual Old Salt Room, open for lunch and dinner, specializes in fresh fish and seafood. Bring your own wine—neither restaurant has a liquor license. ⊠ *Rte. 187, Jonesport,* ☎ *207/497–2365. MC, V. No lunch at the Seafarer's Wife.*

$$ ✕🏠 **Harbor House.** The first floor of this three-story waterfront building houses an antiques shop and a lobster-in-the-rough restaurant ($–$$; closed late October–April). You can eat on the porch overlooking the water or on picnic tables on the lawn. Upstairs, two rooms face the water. ⊠ *Box 468, Sawyer Sq., Jonesport 04649,* ☎ *207/497–5417,* 🖷 *207/497–3211. 2 rooms. Restaurant, no-smoking rooms. Full breakfast. MC, V.*

$ 🏠 **Raspberry Shores.** This comfortably furnished Victorian sits on Main Street, but its backyard slopes down to a small beach on Jonesport Harbor. Rooms in the back of the house share the view, but the nicest room is in the turret and right on the road, which can be noisy. ⊠ *Box 217, Rte. 187, Jonesport 04649,* ☎ *207/497–2463. 3 rooms without bath. Beach. Full breakfast. MC, V. Closed Nov.–Apr.*

Lubec

④⑥ *28 mi east of Machias.*

Lubec is the first town in the United States to see the sunrise. Once a thriving shipbuilding and sardine packing site, it now attracts residents and visitors with its rural beauty.

★ **Quoddy Head State Park,** the easternmost point of land in the United States, is marked by candy-striped West Quoddy Head Light. The mystical, magical, 2-mi path along the cliffs here yields magnificent views of Canada's Grand Manan island. Whales can often be sighted offshore. The 483-acre park has a picnic area. ⊠ *S. Lubec Rd. off Rte. 189,* ☎ *no phone.* 🚻 *$1 donation requested.* ◔ *Memorial Day–mid-Oct., daily 8 AM–sunset; Apr.–early May and mid-Oct.–Dec., weekends 9 AM–sunset.*

④⑦ **Roosevelt Campobello International Park,** a joint project of the American and Canadian governments, has hiking trails and history. It can be reached by land only by crossing the International Bridge from Lubec. Stop at the information booth for an update on tides—specifically, when you will be able to walk out to East Quoddy Head Lighthouse—as well as details on walking and hiking trails. Keep in mind that once you've crossed the bridge, you're in the Atlantic time zone. Neatly manicured, preening itself in the bay, Campobello Island has always had a special appeal to the wealthy and the famous. It was here that the Roosevelt family spent its summers. The 34-room **Roosevelt Cottage,** which is open for touring, was presented to Eleanor and Franklin as a wedding gift. ⊠ *Rte. 774, Welshpool, Campobello Island, New Brunswick, Canada,* ☎ *506/752–2922.* ⊡ *Free.* ☉ *House mid-May–mid-Oct., daily 10–6; grounds daily.*

Dining and Lodging

$–$$　✕⊞ **Home Port Inn.** The grandest accommodations in Lubec are in this 1880 Colonial atop a hill. The spacious rooms, some with water views, are furnished with antiques and family pieces. The large living room has a fireplace and a television, and there are two sitting areas. The dining room ($$), the best in town, is open to the public for dinner. The menu emphasizes seafood. ⊠ *45 Main St., 04652,* ☎ *207/733–2077 or 800/457–2077. 7 rooms. Restaurant. Continental breakfast. D, MC, V. Closed mid-Oct.–late-May.*

$–$$　⊞ **Peacock House.** Four generations of the Peacock family lived in this 1860 Victorian before it was converted into an inn. The Maine hospitality of owners Chet and Veda Childs comes with a southern accent. A few of the simply furnished rooms have water views through lace-curtained windows; rooms on the first floor have air-conditioning. ⊠ *27 Summer St., 04652,* ☎ ℻ *207/733–2403. 5 rooms. Full breakfast. MC, V. Closed mid-Oct.–mid-May.*

$　⊞ **Bayviews.** This unfussy waterfront B&B welcomes families and musicians; there are pianos in the living room and one guest room. Some rooms have water views. ⊠ *6 Monument St., 04652,* ☎ *207/733–2181. 4 rooms, 1 with bath; 1 suite. Continental breakfast. No credit cards. Closed Oct.–June.*

Outdoor Activities and Sports

East Coast Charters (⊠ Peacock Canning, 72 Water St., ☎ 800/853–3999) operates whale-watching trips and sea-kayaking tours.

En Route　The road to Eastport leads through the Pleasant Point Indian Reservation, where the **Waponahki Museum and Resource Center** explains the culture of the Passamaquoddy, or "People of the Dawn." Tools, baskets, beaded artifacts, historic photos, and arts and crafts are displayed. ⊠ *Rte. 190, Perry,* ☎ *207/853–4001.* ⊡ *Free.* ☉ *Weekdays 8:30–11 and noon–4.*

Eastport

48　*39 mi from Lubec, 102 mi east of Ellsworth.*

The town of Eastport is actually a small island, connected to the mainland by a granite causeway. In the late 19th century, 14 sardine canneries operated in Eastport. The decline of that industry in the 20th century has left the city economically depressed, though a new port facility, growing aquaculture, and an increase in tourism bode well for the future. From the waterfront, you can take a ferry to Deer Island and Campobello.

The **National Historic Waterfront District** extends from the Customs House, down Water Street to Bank Square and the Peavey Library. Pick up a walking map at the **Chamber of Commerce** (⊠ 78 Water St., ☎ 207/853–4644) and wander through streets lined with historic homes and buildings. You can also take the waterfront walkway to watch the fishing boats and freighters. The tides fluctuate as much as 28 ft, which explains the ladders and steep gangways necessary to access boats.

Raye's Mustard Mill is the only remaining mill in the U.S. producing stone-ground mustard. Historically, this mill served the sardine-packing industry. You can purchase mustards made on the premises at the mill's Pantry Store; local crafts are also for sale. ⊠ *85 Washington St.,* ☎ *207/853–4451 or 800/853–1903.* ⊡ *Free.* ⊘ *Jan.–Mar., weekdays 8–5; Apr.–Dec., daily 10–5. Tours on the hr Memorial Day–Labor Day; rest of year subject to guide availability.*

The short hike to **Shakford Head** (⊠ Behind Washington County Technical College on Deep Cove Rd.) affords views over Passamaquoddy Bay to Campobello. From here you can see the pens for Eastport's growing salmon-farming industry as well as the construction site of the new port facility.

Cobscook Bay State Park is one of Maine's prettiest and least- crowded parks. More than 200 species of birds, including the American bald eagle, have been identified in and around the park, which has picnic grounds, a playground, a nature trail, and campsites ($12–$16) with showers. ⊠ *RR1 off Rte. 1, Dennysville,* ☎ *207/726–4412.* ⊡ *$1.* ⊘ *Mid-May–mid-Oct.*

Dining and Lodging

$$–$$$ ✕ **Eastport Lobster and Fish.** Fish and seafood don't come much fresher than they do at this restaurant, where the lobsters weigh as much as 2½ pounds. You can eat in the dining room, the downstairs pub, or out on the dock. Service can be frustratingly slow. ⊠ *167 Water St.,* ☎ *207/853–9669. MC, V. Call ahead Oct.–mid-May.*

$–$$ ✕ **La Sardina Loca.** Bright lights and Christmas decorations are among the festive touches at the easternmost Mexican restaurant in the United States. ⊠ *28 Water St.,* ☎ *207/853–2739. MC, V. Closed Mon. No lunch.*

$$ ☷ **Motel East.** Rooms at this waterfront motel are spacious; many have kitchenettes, and most have private balconies overlooking the water. ⊠ *23A Water St., 04631,* ☎ FAX *207/853–4747. 14 rooms, 1 cottage. AE, D, DC, MC, V.*

$–$$ ☷ **Brewer House.** In 1827, Captain John Nehemiah Marks Brewer built an ornate Greek Revival house across from one of his shipyards. Now a B&B, the house, which is on the National Register of Historic Places, is distinguished by details like carved Grecian moldings, Ionic pilasters, marble fireplaces, silver doorknobs, and an elliptical staircase. ⊠ *Box 94, U.S. 1, Robbinston 04671,* ☎ *207/454–2385 or 800/821–2028. 4 rooms, 2 with bath; 1 apartment. Full breakfast. MC, V.*

$ ☷ **Weston House.** A Federal-style home built in 1810, the antiques-
★   filled Weston House overlooks Eastport and Passamaquoddy Bay from a prime in-town location. An elegant multicourse breakfast is served in the formal dining room. The family room, with a fireplace and a TV, is a casual place to plan the day's activities. Naturalist John J. Audubon stayed here in 1833. Dinner is available by advance reservation. ⊠ *26 Boynton St., 04631,* ☎ *207/853–2907 or 800/853–2907,* FAX *207/856–0981. 5 rooms share 2½ baths. Full breakfast. No credit cards.*

Outdoor Activities and Sports

East Coast Ferries, Ltd. (☎ 506/747–2159) provides ferry service between Eastport and Deer Island and Deer Island and Campobello from late June to mid-September. **Harris Whale Watching** (⊠ Harris Point Rd., Eastport, ☎ 207/853–2940 or 207/853–4303) operates three-hour tours. **Tidal Trails** (⊠ Water St., ☎ 207/853–7373) operates boat charters, natural-history tours, and guided bird-watching, canoeing, sea-kayaking, and saltwater-fishing trips.

Shopping

Dog Island Pottery (✉ 224 Water St., ☎ 207/853–4775) stocks stoneware pottery and local crafts. The **Eastport Gallery** (✉ 69 Water St., ☎ 207/853–4166) displays works by area artists. **Jim's Smoked Salmon** (✉ 37 Washington St., ☎ 207/853–4831) sells Atlantic salmon, mussels, and roe hot-smoked in apple wood. **Joe's Basket Shop** (✉ Rte. 190, Pleasant Point, ☎ 207/853–2840) sells fancy and course (work) baskets and jewelry made by the Passamaquoddy.

Way Down East A to Z

Arriving and Departing

See Arriving and Departing *in* Maine A to Z, *below.*

Getting Around

BY CAR

U.S. 1 is the primary coastal route, with smaller roads leading to the towns on the long fingers of land in this region. Route 182 is a pleasant inland route; Route 186 loops through the Schoodic Peninsula. The most direct route to Lubec is Route 189, but Route 191, between East Machias and West Lubec, is a scenic coastal drive.

BY FERRY

East Coast Ferries, Ltd. (☎ 506/747–2159) provides ferry service between Eastport and Deer Island and Deer Island and Campobello from late June to mid-September.

Contacts and Resources

GUIDED TOURS

Quoddy Air (✉ Eastport Municipal Airport, County Rd., Eastport, ☎ 207/853–0997) operates scenic flights. **Scenic Island Tours** (✉ 37 Washington St., Eastport, ☎ 207/853–2840) offers guided tours of Eastport in a 1947 Dodge Woody bus that once transported workers to sardine factories. Picnic lunches featuring smoked salmon are available.

VISITOR INFORMATION

Eastport Area Chamber of Commerce (✉ Box 254, 78 Water St., 04631, ☎ 207/853–4644). **Lubec Area Chamber of Commerce** (✉ Box 123, 04652, ☎ 207/733–4522). **Machias Bay Area Chamber of Commerce** (✉ Box 606, 378 Main St., 04654, ☎ 207/255–4402). **Quoddy Coastal Tourism Association of New Brunswick and Maine** (✉ Box 1171, St. Andrews, New Brunswick, Canada E0G 2X0, ☎ 800/377–9748). **Schoodic Peninsula Chamber of Commerce** (✉ Box 381, Winter Harbor 04693, ☎ no phone).

WESTERN LAKES AND MOUNTAINS

Less than 20 mi northwest of Portland and the coast, the sparsely populated lake and mountain areas of western Maine stretch north along the New Hampshire border to Québec. In winter this is ski country; in summer the woods and waters draw vacationers.

The Sebago–Long Lake region has antiques stores and lake cruises on a 42-mi waterway. Kezar Lake, tucked away in a fold of the White Mountains, has long been a hideaway of the wealthy. Children's summer camps dot the region. Bethel, in the Androscoggin River valley, is a classic New England town, its town common lined with historic homes. The far more rural Rangeley Lake area brings long stretches of pine, beech, spruce, and sky—and stylish inns and bed-and-breakfasts with easy access to golf, boating, fishing, and hiking.

Sebago Lake

49 *17 mi northwest of Portland.*

Sebago Lake, which provides all the drinking water for Greater Portland, is Maine's best-known lake after Moosehead (☞ The North Woods, *below*). Many camps and year-round homes surround Sebago, which is popular with water-sports enthusiasts. At the north end of the lake, the **Songo Lock** (☎ 207/693–6231), which permits the passage of watercraft from Sebago Lake to Long Lake, is the one surviving lock of the Cumberland and Oxford Canal. Built of wood and masonry, the original lock dates from 1830 and was expanded in 1911; today it sees heavy traffic in summer.

The 1,300-acre **Sebago Lake State Park** on the north shore of the lake provides opportunities for swimming, picnicking, camping (250 sites), boating, and fishing (salmon and togue). ⊠ *11 Park Access Rd., Casco,* ☎ *207/693–6615 May–mid-Oct.; 207/693–6231 at other times.* ⊠ *$2.50.* ⊙ *Daily 9–8.*

The **Jones Museum of Glass & Ceramics** houses more than 7,000 objects of glass, pottery, stoneware, and porcelain from around the world. Also on the premises are a research library and gift shop. ⊠ *35 Douglas Mountain Rd. off Rte. 107,* ☎ *207/787–3370.* ⊠ *$5.* ⊙ *Mid-May–mid-Nov., Mon.–Sat. 10–5, Sun. 1–5.*

OFF THE
BEATEN PATH   **SABBATHDAY LAKE SHAKER MUSEUM** – Established in the late 18th century, this is the last active Shaker community in the United States. Members continue to farm crops and herbs, and you can see the meetinghouse of 1794—a paradigm of Shaker design—and the ministry shop with 14 rooms of Shaker furniture, folk art, tools, farm implements, and crafts from the 18th to early 20th centuries. There is also a small gift shop, but don't expect to find furniture or other large Shaker items. On the busy road out front, a farmer usually has summer and fall vegetables for sale. In autumn, he sells cider, apples, and pumpkins. On Sunday, the Shaker day of prayer, the community is closed to visitors. ⊠ *Rte. 26, New Gloucester (20 mi north of Portland, 12 mi east of Naples),* ☎ *207/926–4597.* ⊠ *Tour $5, extended tour $6.50.* ⊙ *Memorial Day–Columbus Day, Mon.–Sat. 10–4:30.*

Naples

50 *16 mi northwest of North Windham, 32 mi northwest of Portland.*

Naples swells with seasonal residents and visitors in summer. The town occupies an enviable location between Long Lake and Sebago Lake.

The **Naples Historical Society Museum** has a jailhouse, a bandstand, a 1938 Dodge fire truck, a coach, and information about the Cumberland and Oxford Canal and the Sebago–Long Lake steamboats. ⊠ *Village Green, U.S. 302,* ☎ *207/693–4297.* ⊠ *Free.* ⊙ *July–Aug., Fri. 10–3; call for additional hrs.*

☾ ***Songo River Queen II,*** a 92-ft stern-wheeler, takes passengers on hour-long cruises on Long Lake and longer voyages down the Songo River and through Songo Lock. ⊠ *U.S. 302, Naples Causeway,* ☎ *207/693–6861.* ⊠ *Long Lake cruise $7, Songo River ride $10.* ⊙ *July–Labor Day, daily at 9:45, 1, 2:30, 3:45, 7; call for schedule of reduced spring and fall hrs.*

Western Maine

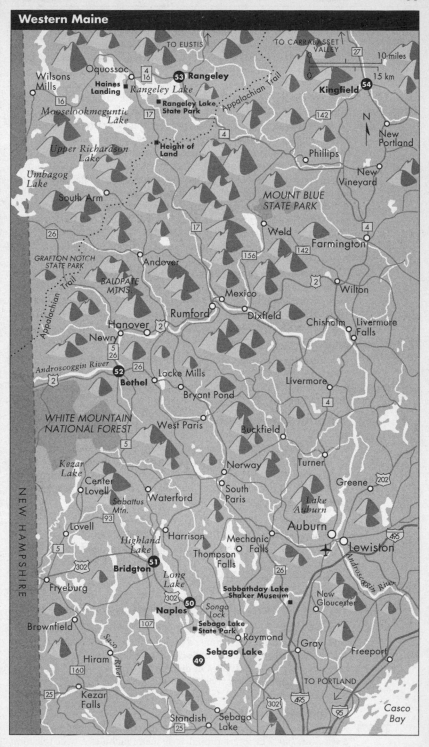

TO EUSTIS

TO CARRABASSET VALLEY

27

0 10 miles

0 15 km

Wilsons Mills

Oquossoc

4 16

53 Rangeley

Haines Landing

Rangeley Lake

Appalachian Trail

Kingfield 54

16

Rangeley Lake State Park

New Portland

Mooselookmeguntic Lake

17

142

N

Upper Richardson Lake

4

Phillips

Umbagog Lake

Height of Land

New Vineyard

South Arm

MOUNT BLUE STATE PARK

26

Weld

4

GRAFTON NOTCH STATE PARK

Andover

17

156

142

Farmington

Appalachian Trail

BALDPATE MTNS.

Mexico

2

Wilton

Rumford

Dixfield

Chisholm

Livermore Falls

Hanover

2

Newry

5 26

Androscoggin River

26

Locke Mills

Livermore

52

Bethel

Bryant Pond

4

WHITE MOUNTAIN NATIONAL FOREST

West Paris

Buckfield

5

Kezar Lake

Norway

Turner

Greene

202

Center Lovell

Sabattus Mtn.

Waterford

South Paris

Lake Auburn

93

Lovell

Harrison

Mechanic Falls

Auburn

5

Highland Lake

Thompson Falls

495

Lewiston

Bridgton

51

26

Androscoggin River

Fryeburg

302

Long Lake

Sabbathday Lake Shaker Museum

New Gloucester

Naples

50

Songo Lock

Brownfield

107

Sebago Lake State Park

Raymond

Gray

Freeport

Saco River

Hiram

160

49

Sebago Lake

TO PORTLAND

25

Kezar Falls

302

495

95

Casco Bay

Standish

25

Sebago Lake

NEW HAMPSHIRE

Dining and Lodging

$$$$ ✕ **Bistro du Lac.** This casual restuarant inside a big red farmhouse across from Sebago Lake has a perhaps-too-ambitious country-French menu. Though entrées like salmon with caramelized leeks and rack of lamb don't quite live up to their potential, the food is good and the prix-fixe menu ($47) fairly reasonable. Sunday brunch is also served. ⊠ *U.S. 302 and Rte. 85, Raymond,* ☎ *207/655–4100. MC, V. Closed Tues.– Wed. No lunch.*

$$$$ ⊞ **Migis Lodge.** The lodge's pine-panel cottages, scattered among 100 shorefront acres, have fieldstone fireplaces and are handsomely furnished with braided rugs and handmade quilts. A warm, woodsy feeling pervades the main inn. The deck has views (marvelous at sunset) of Sebago Lake. Though you may be tempted just to gaze out on the lake, the lodge provides plenty of outdoor and indoor activities, all of which are included in the room rate. Guests gather in the main dining room for three fancy meals daily. ⊠ *Box 40, Migis Lodge Rd., off U.S. 302, South Casco 04077,* ☎ *207/655–4524,* FAX *207/655–2054. 29 cottages, 6 rooms. Dining room, tennis court, exercise room, beach, boating, waterskiing, fishing, playground. AP. No credit cards.*

$$–$$$ ⊞ **Augustus Bove House.** Built as the Hotel Naples in the 1820s, this rambling brick B&B sits across from the Naples Causeway and has views down Long Lake. Rooms are furnished with antiques and a television. ⊠ *Box 501, R.R. 1, U.S. 302, 04055,* ☎ *207/693–6365. 10 rooms, 7 with bath; 1 suite. Hot tub. Full breakfast. AE, D, MC, V.*

Nightlife and the Arts

Deertrees Theater and Cultural Center (⊠ Deertrees Rd. off Rte. 117, Harrison, ☎ 207/583–6747) hosts musicals, dramas, dance performances, shows for children, concerts, and other events from late June through Labor Day.

Outdoor Activities and Sports

U.S. 302 cuts through Naples, and in the center at the Naples Causeway are rental craft for fishing or cruising. Sebago, Long, and Rangeley lakes are popular areas for sailing and motorboating. For rentals, try **Mardon Marine** (⊠ U.S. 302, ☎ 207/693–6264), **Naples Marina** (⊠ U.S. 302 and Rte. 114, ☎ 207/693–6254; motorboats only), or **Sun Sports Plus** (⊠ U.S. 302, ☎ 207/693–3867).

Shopping

The **Shops of South Casco Village** (⊠ U.S. 302, South Casco, ☎ 207/ 655–5060) include a gift shop, an antiques shop, and an art gallery with a sculpture garden.

Bridgton

⑤ *8 mi north of Naples, 16 mi east of Fryeburg, 30 mi south of Bethel.*

In and around the drab town of Bridgton, between Long and Highland Lakes, are antiques shops, a museum, and the Shawnee Peak ski resort. The **Bridgton Historical Society Museum** is in a former fire station that was built in 1902. On display are artifacts of the area's history and materials on the local narrow-gauge railroad. ⊠ *Gibbs Ave.,* ☎ *207/647–3699.* ⌸ *$2.* ☉ *July–Aug., Tues.–Fri. 10–4.*

Dining and Lodging

$$–$$$ ✕ **Tom's Homestead.** An 1821 house holds two quiet dining rooms and a spacious bar. The international-style menu includes a wide selection of choices, from Louisiana frog legs Provençale to Wiener schnitzel. ⊠ *U.S. 302,* ☎ *207/647–5726. AE, D, MC, V. Closed Mon.*

$–$$$ ✕ **Black Horse Tavern.** A Cape Cod cottage more than 200 years old houses this country-style restaurant with a shiny bar, horse blankets, and stirrups for decor. On the menu are steaks, seafood, soups, salads, and burgers. ✉ *8 Portland St.,* ☎ *207/647–5300. Reservations not accepted. D, MC, V.*

$$$$ ✕⌑ **Quisisana.** Music lovers may think they've found heaven on earth at this delightful resort on Kezar Lake, about 14 mi northwest of Bridgton. After dinner, the staff, students, and graduates of some of the finest music schools in the country perform at the music hall—everything from Broadway tunes to concert piano pieces. White cottages have pine interiors and cheerful decor. One night you might have a typical New England dinner of clam chowder, lobster, and blueberry pie; the next night the choice might be saddle of lamb with a black-olive tapenade or salmon-and-leek roulade with a roasted-red-pepper sauce. All meals and activities are included in the rates (except for a nominal fee for the use of the motorboats). For most of the resort's season, a one-week stay beginning Saturday is required. ✉ *Pleasant Point Rd., Center Lovell 04016,* ☎ *207/925–3500,* FAX *207/925–1004 in season. 11 rooms in 2 lodges, 32 cottages. Restaurant, 3 tennis courts, windsurfing, boating, waterskiing. AP. Closed Sept.–mid-June.*

$$ ⌑ **Bear Mountain Inn.** After swimming at the private beach on Bear Lake or hiking up Bear Mountain (across the street), it's nice to return to this rambling farmhouse inn, which the owner has meticulously decorated in a woodsy theme. A country breakfast with an emphasis on organic ingredients is served in the dining room, which has a fieldstone fireplace and views over the lake. ✉ *Rte. 35, South Waterford 04081,* ☎ *207/583–4404. 9 rooms, 5 with bath; 1 suite; 1 cottage. Badminton, croquet, horseshoes, volleyball, beach, boating, fishing, ice-skating, cross-country skiing, snowmobiling. Full breakfast. MC, V.*

$$ ⌑ **Bridgton House.** It's an easy walk from this white clapboard cottage to village shops and restaurants or to Highland Lake. When the weather's nice, breakfast is served on the fine wraparound porch. The rooms in the back of the house are quieter than those on the U.S. 302 side of the house. ✉ *2 Main St./U.S. 302, 04009,* ☎ *207/647–0979. 6 rooms, 3 with bath. Full breakfast. No credit cards. Closed Nov.–Apr.*

$–$$ ⌑ **Waterford Inne.** This gold-painted house on a hilltop provides a good home base for trips to lakes, ski trails, and antiques shops. The bedrooms have lots of nooks and crannies. The Nantucket, with a whale motif, and the Chesapeake, with a private porch and a fireplace, are the nicest. A converted woodshed holds five additional rooms, and though they have less character than the rooms in the inn, four have sunny decks. ✉ *Box 149, Chadbourne Rd., Waterford 04088,* ☎ FAX *207/583–4037. 9 rooms, 6 with bath; 1 suite. Badminton, ice-skating, cross-country skiing. Full breakfast. AE. Closed Apr.*

Outdoor Activities and Sports

Two scenic canoeing routes on the Saco River (near Fryeburg) are the gentle stretch from Swan's Falls to East Brownfield (19 mi) and from East Brownfield to Hiram (14 mi). For rentals, try **Canal Bridge Canoes** (✉ U.S. 302, Fryeburg Village, ☎ 207/935–2605) or **Saco River Canoe and Kayak** (✉ Rte. 5, Fryeburg, ☎ 207/935–2369). **Sporthaus** (✉ 61 Main St., Bridgton, ☎ 207/647–5100) rents bicycles, canoes, sailboats, sailboards, skis, and snowshoes.

Shopping

Craftworks (✉ Main St., ☎ 207/647–5436) carries American crafts, Maine foods, women's clothing, and gifts. The **Maine Theme** (✉ Main St., ☎ 207/647–2161) specializes in handcrafted wares from throughout New England.

Skiing and Snow Sports

SHAWNEE PEAK

On the New Hampshire border, Shawnee Peak draws many skiers from the North Conway, New Hampshire, area (18 mi away) and from Portland (45 mi). Popular with families, this facility is being upgraded. There's also snowshoeing. ⊠ *Box 734, U.S. 302, 04009,* ☎ *207/647–8444.*

Downhill. Shawnee Peak has a 1,300-ft vertical and perhaps the most night-skiing terrain in New England. Most of the 36 runs are pleasant cruisers for intermediates, with some beginner slopes, a few pitches suitable for advanced skiers, and a few gladed runs. Lifts include one quad, one double, and two triple chairs and one surface lift.

Child care. The area's nursery takes children from age 6 months to 6 years. The SKIwee program is for children between ages 4 and 6; those between 7 and 12 also have a program. Children under 6 ski free when accompanied by a parent. The Youth Ski League has instruction for aspiring racers.

En Route   From Bridgton, the most scenic route to Bethel is along U.S. 302 west, across Moose Pond to Knight's Hill Road, turning north to Lovell and Route 5, which will take you on to Bethel. It's a drive that lets you admire the jagged crests of the White Mountains outlined against the sky to the west and the rolling hills that alternate with brooding forests at roadside. At Center Lovell you can barely glimpse the secluded Kezar Lake to the west, the retreat of wealthy and very private people; Sabattus Mountain, which rises behind Center Lovell, has a public hiking trail and stupendous views of the Presidential Range from the summit.

Bethel

❺❷ *66 mi north of Portland, 22 mi east of Gorham, NH.*

Bethel is pure New England, a town with white clapboard houses and white-steeple churches and a mountain vista at the end of every street. The architecture here is something to behold. In winter this is ski country: Bethel is midway between Sunday River in Newry and Mt. Abram in Locke Mills. Sunday River (☞ Skiing and Snow Sports, *below*) has plenty of action in summer, too.

A stroll in Bethel should begin at the **Moses Mason House and Museum,** a Federal home of 1813. The museum, on the town common across from the Bethel Inn and Country Club, has nine period rooms and a front hall and stairway wall decorated with murals by Rufus Porter. You can pick up materials here for a walking tour of Bethel Hill Village, most of which is on the National Register of Historic Places. ⊠ *14 Broad St.,* ☎ *207/824–2908.* 🖭 *$2.* ☉ *July–Labor Day, Tues.–Sun. 1–4; Labor Day–June, by appointment.*

The **Major Gideon Hastings House** on Broad Street has a columned-front portico typical of the Greek Revival style. The severe white **West Parish Congregational Church** (1847), with an unadorned triangular pediment and a steeple supported on open columns, is on Church Street, around the common from the Major Gideon Hastings House. The campus of **Gould Academy** (⊠ Church St., ☎ 207/824–7777), a preparatory school, opened its doors in 1835; the dominant style of the school buildings is Georgian.

White Mountain National Forest straddles New Hampshire and Maine. Although the highest peaks are on the New Hampshire side, the Maine section has magnificent rugged terrain, camping and picnic areas, and hiking opportunities from hour-long nature loops to a 5½-hour scramble up Speckled Mountain. ⊠ *Evans Notch Visitation Center, 18 Mayville Rd., 04217,* ☎ *207/824–2134.* ⊑ *Parking $3.* ☉ *Center daily 8–4:30 in summer; closed Wed. in winter.*

At **Grafton Notch State Park** (⊠ Rte. 26, 14 mi north of Bethel, ☎ 207/824–2912) you can take an easy nature walk to Mother Walker Falls or Moose Cave and see the spectacular Screw Auger Falls, or you can hike to the summit of Old Speck Mountain, the state's third-highest peak. If you have the stamina and the equipment, you can pick up the Appalachian Trail here, hike over Saddleback Mountain, and continue on to Katahdin. The **Maine Appalachian Trail Club** (⊠ Box 283, Augusta 04330) publishes a map and trail guide.

Dining and Lodging

$$–$$$$ ✕⊞ **Bethel Inn and Country Club.** Bethel's grandest accommodation is a full-service resort that includes 36 km (22 mi) of cross-country ski trails. Although not very large, the rooms in the main inn, sparsely furnished with Colonial reproductions, are the most desirable: The choice rooms have fireplaces and face the mountains that rise over the golf course. All 40 two-bedroom condos on the fairway face the mountains; they are clean, even a bit sterile. A formal dining room ($$–$$$; reservations essential) serves elaborate dinners of roast duck, prime rib, lobster, and swordfish. The room rates include a full breakfast and dinner. ⊠ *Box 49, Village Common, 04217,* ☎ *207/824–2175 or 800/654–0125,* ℻ *207/824–2233. 48 rooms, 9 suites, 40 condo units. Restaurant, bar, pool, 18-hole golf course, tennis court, health club, cross-country skiing, conference center. MAP. AE, D, DC, MC, V.*

$$ ✕⊞ **Victoria Inn.** It's hard to miss this turreted inn, with its beige-, mauve-, and teal-painted exterior and massive attached carriage house topped with a cupola. Inside, Victorian details include ceiling rosettes, stained-glass windows, elaborate fireplace mantels, and gleaming oak trim. Guest rooms vary in size and decor; most are furnished with antiques. The one-bedroom-with-loft units in the carriage house are perfect for families. The restaurant, open to the public for dinner ($$–$$$), has three rooms, one with a wraparound mural of Italian scenes. Chef Eric Botka's menu lists entrées such as beef tenderloin au poivre and rack of lamb. A children's menu is available. ⊠ *Box 249, 32 Main St., 04217,* ☎ *207/824–8060 or 888/774–1235,* ℻ *207/824–3926. 15 rooms. Restaurant. Full breakfast. MC, V. Restaurant closed Mon.–Tues.*

$$–$$$$ ⊞ **Jordan Grand Resort Hotel.** A hit with Sunday River skiers, this condominium hotel provides ski-in, ski-out access to the Jordan Bowl trails. Most units have kitchenettes, and there's a heated outdoor pool to relax in after a day on the slopes. ⊠ *Box 450, 1 Grand Circle, off Skiway Rd. and off U.S. 2, Newry 04217,* ☎ *207/824–5000 or 800/543–2754,* ℻ *207/824–5399. 195 condominiums. Two restaurants, pool, tennis court, health club, baby-sitting, meeting rooms. AE, D, MC, V.*

$$$ ⊞ **Sunday River Inn.** This modern chalet on the Sunday River ski area access road has private rooms for families and dorm rooms (bring your sleeping bag) for groups and students, all within easy access of the slopes. A hearty breakfast and dinner are served buffet-style, and a stone hearth dominates the comfortable living room. The inn operates an excellent ski-touring center. ⊠ *19 Skiway Rd., Newry 04261,* ☎ *207/824–2410,* ℻ *207/824–3181. 3 rooms with bath, 12 rooms share 2 baths, 5 dorms share 2 baths, 4 rooms in separate building share 2 baths. Hot tub, sauna, cross-country skiing. MAP. AE, MC, V. Closed Apr.–late-Nov.*

$$ ⊞ **Chapman Inn.** New owners are renovating and updating this circa-1865 Colonial inn on Bethel's town green. Inn rooms are comfortably furnished with antiques and country pieces, and there are dorm accommodations in the barn. Guests have use of a game room and a kitchen. The huge country-style breakfast will fuel skiers and others

for an active morning. ⌧ *Box 1067, Bethel Common, 04217,* ☎ *207/ 824–2657 or 877/359–1398,* ⅸ *207/824–7152. 7 rooms, 5 with bath; 1 efficiency; 24-bed dormitory. Saunas, hot tub, ice-skating, coin laundry. Full breakfast. AE, D, MC, V.*

$$ ✕⌕ **Sudbury Inn.** Value and location are the chief attributes of this white clapboard inn, whose guest rooms and dining room have country charm. Prime rib, sirloin au poivre, broiled haddock, lasagna, and other standards are on the menu. The pub, which offers a large selection of microbrews and weekend entertainment, is a popular hangout. The huge breakfast includes omelets, eggs Benedict, pancakes, and homemade granola. ⌧ *Box 369, 151 Main St., 04217,* ☎ *207/824–2174 or 800/395–7837,* ⅸ *207/824–2329. 10 rooms, 7 suites. Restaurant, pub. Full breakfast. AE, MC, V.*

Nightlife and the Arts

Sunday River nightlife is spread out between the mountain and downtown Bethel. For a quiet evening, head to the piano bar at the **Bethel Inn** (⌧ The Common, ☎ 207/824–2175). At the mountain, try the **Bumps Pub** (⌧ Whitecap Lodge, ☎ 207/824–5269) for après-ski and evening entertainment—Tuesday night is comedy night, ski movies are shown on Wednesday, and bands play on weekends and holidays. **Sunday River Brewing Company** (⌧ U.S. 2, ☎ 207/824–4253) has pub fare and live entertainment—usually progressive rock bands—on weekends. The **Sudbury Inn** (⌧ 151 Main St., ☎ 207/824–2174) is popular for après-ski and has music that tends toward the blues.

Outdoor Activities and Sports

Mahoosuc Guide Service (⌧ Bear River Rd., Newry, ☎ 207/824– 2073) leads day and multiday dog-sledding expeditions on the Maine– New Hampshire border. Lifts at **Sunday River Mountain Bike Park** (⌧ Sunday River Rd., Newry, ☎ 207/824–3000) bring cyclists to the trails. **Telemark Inn & Llama Treks** (⌧ King's Hwy., Mason Township, ☎ 207/836–2703) operates one- to six-day llama-supported hiking trips in the White Mountain National Forest.

Shopping

Bonnema Potters (⌧ 146 Lower Main St., ☎ 207/824–2821) sells plates, lamps, tiles, and vases in colorful modern designs. The **Lyons' Den** (⌧ U.S. 2, Hanover, ☎ 207/364–8634), a great barn of a place near Bethel, stocks antique glass, china, tools, prints, rugs, hand-wrought iron, and some furniture. **Mt. Mann Jewelers** (⌧ 57 Maine St. Pl., ☎ 207/824–3030) carries contemporary jewelry with unusual gems.

Skiing and Snow Sports

MT. ABRAM

This ski area has a rustic Maine feeling and is known for its snow grooming, home-style cooking, and family atmosphere. Skiers here prefer the low-key attitude and wallet-friendly rates. Night skiing and snow tubing are available. Many skiers stay in the reasonably priced condominiums on the mountain road. ⌧ *Box 120, Rte. 26, Locke Mills 04255,* ☎ *207/875–5003.*

Downhill. The mountain reaches just over 1,000 vertical ft. The majority of the terrain is intermediate, with fall-line steep runs and two areas for beginning and novice skiers. The area has two double chairlifts and three T-bars. Plans for the 1999–2000 season include a new base lodge and the replacement of one of the T-bars with a chairlift. In addition to learn-to-ski classes, there are improvement clinics for all ability levels and age groups. Facilities include two base lodges, a children's terrain garden, a halfpipe for snowboarders, a snowboard park, and a snow-tubing park.

Child care. The Mt. Abram's Day Care Center takes children from age 6 months to 6 years. Children between 3 and 6 who are enrolled in the center can take lessons on weekends and during vacation weeks. For juniors from 6 to 16 there are individual classes plus a series of 10 two-hour lessons on weekends.

SUNDAY RIVER

In the 1980s, Sunday River was a sleepy little ski area with minimal facilities. Today it is among the best-managed ski areas in the East and the flagship of the owner Les Otten's American Skiing Company empire. Spread throughout the valley are three base areas, two condominium hotels, trailside condominiums, town houses, and a ski dorm. Sunday River is home to the Maine Handicapped Skiing program, which provides lessons and services for skiers with disabilities. In summer, Sunday River's Adventure Park attracts families with its water slides, climbing wall, BMX park, and in-line skating park, as well as hiking and mountain biking. ⊠ *Sunday River Rd. off U.S. 2, Newry, mailing address: Box 450, Bethel 04217, ☎ 207/824–3000; 207/824–5200 for snow conditions; 800/543–2754 for reservations.*

Downhill. White Heat has gained fame as the steepest, longest, widest lift-served trail in the East; but skiers of all abilities will find plenty of suitable terrain, from a 5-km (3-mi) beginner run to steep glades and in-your-face bumps. The area has 126 trails, the majority of them in the intermediate range. Expert and advanced runs are grouped from the peaks, and most beginner slopes are near the base. Trails spreading down from eight peaks have a total vertical descent of 2,340 ft and are served by nine quads, four triples, and two double chairlifts and three surface lifts.

Other activities. Within the housing complexes are indoor pools, outdoor heated pools, saunas, and hot tubs. Sunday River also has a snowboard park. The Entertainment Center at White Cap has a lighted halfpipe, a lighted ice-skating rink, a tubing area, a teen center, and a nightclub with live music.

Child care. Sunday River operates three licensed day-care centers for children from ages 6 weeks to 6 years. Coaching for children from ages 3 to 18 is available in the Children's Center at the South Ridge base area.

En Route   The routes north from Bethel to the Rangeley district are all scenic, particularly in the autumn when the maples are aflame with color. In the town of Newry, make a short detour to the **Artist's Bridge** (turn off Route 26 onto Sunday River Road and drive about 3 mi), the most painted and photographed of Maine's eight covered bridges. Route 26 continues on to **Grafton Notch State Park,** about 12 mi from Bethel. Here you can hike to stunning gorges and waterfalls and into the Baldpate Mountains. Past the park, Route 26 continues to Errol, New Hampshire, where Route 16 will return you east around the north shore of Mooselookmeguntic Lake, through Oquossoc, and into Rangeley. A more direct route (if marginally less scenic) from Bethel to Rangeley still allows a stop in Newry. Follow U.S. 2 north and east from Bethel to the twin towns of Rumford and Mexico, where Route 17 continues north to Oquossoc, about an hour's drive. When you've driven for about 20 minutes beyond Rumford, the signs of civilization all but vanish and you pass through what seems like untouched territory—though the lumber companies have long since tackled the virgin forests—and sporting camps and cottages are tucked away here and there. The high point of this route is **Height of Land,** about 30 mi north of Rumford, with its unforgettable views of range after range of mountains and the island-studded blue mass of Mooselookmeguntic Lake directly below.

Turnouts on both sides of the highway allow you to pull over for a long look. **Haines Landing** on Mooselookmeguntic Lake lies 7 mi west of Rangeley. Here you can stand at 1,400 ft above sea level and face the same magnificent scenery you admired at 2,400 ft from Height of Land on Route 17. Boat and canoe rentals are available at Mooselookmeguntic House.

Rangeley

① *67 mi north of Bethel.*

Rangeley, north of Rangeley Lake on Route 4/16, has lured fisherfolk, hunters, and winter-sports enthusiasts for a century to its more than 40 lakes and ponds and 450 square mi of woodlands. Equally popular in summer or winter, Rangeley has a rough, wilderness feel to it. Lodgings are in the woods, around the lake, and along the golf course.

On the south shore of Rangeley Lake, **Rangeley Lake State Park** (✉ Off Rte. 17, ☎ 207/864–3858) has superb lakeside scenery, swimming, picnic tables, a boat ramp, showers, and 50 campsites.

The **Wilhelm Reich Museum** interprets the life and work of controversial physician-scientist Wilhelm Reich, who believed that a force called orgone energy was the source of neurosis. The Orgone Energy Observatory, designed for Reich in 1948, exhibits biographical materials, inventions, and the equipment used in his experiments. Also on view are Reich's library, personal memorabilia, and artwork. Trails lace the 175-acre grounds, and the observatory deck has magnificent views of the countryside. ✉ *Dodge Pond Rd.,* ☎ *207/864–3443.* ✉ *$3.* ☉ *July–Aug., Tues.–Sun. 1–5; Sept., Sun. 1–5.*

OFF THE   **SANDY RIVER & RANGELEY LAKES RAILROAD** – You can ride a mile
BEATEN PATH through the woods along a narrow-gauge railroad on a century-old train
             drawn by a replica of the *Sandy River No. 4* locomotive. ✉ *Bridge Hill
             Rd., Phillips (20 mi southeast of Rangeley),* ☎ *207/639–3352.* ✉ *$3.*
             ☉ *June–Oct., 1st and 3rd Sun. each month; rides at 11, 1, and 3.*

Dining and Lodging

$$–$$$ ✕ **Gingerbread House.** A big fieldstone fireplace, well-spaced tables, and an antique marble soda fountain, all with views to the woods beyond, make for a comfortable atmosphere at this gingerbread-trim house, which is open for breakfast, lunch, and dinner. The ambitious dinner menu doesn't quite deliver, but the portions are huge. ✉ *Rtes. 17 and 4, Oquossoc,* ☎ *207/864–3602. Reservations essential on summer weekends. AE, D, DC, MC, V. Closed Mon.–Tues. No dinner Sun.*

$–$$ ✕ **Porter House Restaurant.** This popular restaurant, seemingly in the middle of nowhere, draws diners from Rangeley, Kingfield, and Canada with its good service, excellent food, and casual atmosphere. Of the 1908 farmhouse's four dining rooms, the front one downstairs, which has a fireplace, is the most intimate and elegant. The broad Continental-style menu includes entrées for diners with light appetites. On the heavier side are porterhouse steak and roast duckling. Try the boneless lamb loin and lobster Brittany casserole if they're on the menu. ✉ *Rte. 27, Eustis, 20 mi north of Rangeley,* ☎ *207/246–7932. Reservations essential on weekends. AE, D, MC, V.*

$$ ✕⛶ **Country Club Inn.** Built in the 1920s on the Mingo Springs Golf Course, this retreat enjoys a secluded hilltop location and sweeping lake and mountain views. The inn's baronial living room has a cathedral ceiling, a fieldstone fireplace at each end, and game trophies. The rooms downstairs in the main building and in the motel-style wing added in the 1950s are cheerfully if minimally decorated. The glassed-in din-

ing room—open to nonguests by reservation only—has linen-draped tables set well apart. The menu includes roast duck, veal, fresh fish, and filet mignon. ⊠ *Box 680, Mingo Loop Rd., 04970,* ☎ *207/864–3831. 19 rooms. Restaurant, pool. Full breakfast; MAP available. AE, MC, V. Closed Apr.–mid-May and mid-Oct.–late-Dec.*

$$$$ 🏨 **Grant's Kennebago Camps.** People rough it in comfort at this traditional Maine sporting camp on Kennebago Lake. "Sports" and families have been coming here for more than 85 years, lured by the fresh water, mountain views, excellent fly-fishing, and hearty home-cooked meals. The wilderness setting, between the Kennebago Mountains, is nothing less than spectacular. The cabins, whose screened porches overlook the lake, have woodstoves and are finished in knotty pine. Meals (included in the price) are served in the cheerful waterfront dining room. Motorboats, canoes, sailboats, Windsurfers, and mountain bikes are available. Float-plane rides and fly-fishing instruction can be arranged. ⊠ *Box 786, off Rte. 16, 04970,* ☎ *207/864–3608 in summer; 207/282–5264 in winter; 800/633–4815. 19 cabins. Dining room, lake, hiking, boating, fishing, mountain bikes, baby-sitting, playground. AP. MC, V. Closed Oct.–late May.*

$$–$$$ 🏨 **Hunter Cove on Rangeley Lake.** These lakeside cabins, which sleep from two to six people, provide all the comforts of home in a rustic setting. The interiors are unfinished knotty pine and include kitchens, full baths, and comfortable, if plain, living rooms. Cabin No. 1 has a fieldstone fireplace, and others have wood-burning stoves. Cabins No. 5 and No. 8 have hot tubs. Summer guests can take advantage of a sand swimming beach, boat rentals, and a nearby golf course. In winter, snowmobile right to your door or ski nearby (cross-country and downhill). ⊠ *Mingo Loop Rd.,* ☎ *207/864–3383. 8 cabins. Beach, boating. AE.*

$$ 🏨 **Rangeley Inn and Motor Lodge.** From Main Street you see only the three-story, blue inn building (circa 1907), but behind it is a newer motel wing with views of Haley Pond, a lawn, and a garden. Some of the inn's sizable rooms have iron-and-brass beds and subdued wallpaper, some have claw-foot tubs, and others have whirlpool tubs. The motel units contain Queen Anne reproduction furniture and velvet chairs. ⊠ *Box 160, 51 Main St., 04970,* ☎ *207/864–3341 or 800/666–3687,* FAX *207/864–3634. 36 inn rooms, 15 motel rooms, 2 cabins. Restaurant, bar, meeting room. MAP available. AE, D, MC, V.*

Nightlife and the Arts

Rangeley Friends of the Arts (⊠ Box 333, 04970, ☎ no phone) sponsors musical theater, fiddlers' contests, rock and jazz, classical, and other summer fare, mostly at Lakeside Park.

Outdoor Activities and Sports

BOATING

Rangeley and Mooselookmeguntic lakes are good for canoeing, sailing, and motorboating. For rentals, call **Oquossoc Cove Marina** (⊠ Oquossoc, ☎ 207/864–3463), **Dockside Sports Center** (⊠ Town Cove, ☎ 207/864–2424), or **River's Edge Sports** (⊠ Rte. 4, Oquossoc, ☎ 207/864–5582).

FISHING

Fishing for brook trout and salmon is at its best in May, June, and September; the Rangeley area is especially popular with fly-fishers. Nonresident anglers over the age of 12 must have a fishing license. The **Department of Inland Fisheries and Wildlife** (⊠ 284 State St., Augusta 04333, ☎ 207/287–2871) can provide further information.

If you'd like a fishing guide, try **Clayton (Cy) Eastlack** (☎ 207/864–3416) or **Westwind Charters and Guide Service** (☎ 207/864–5437).

SNOWMOBILING

This is a popular mode of winter transportation in the Rangeley area, with more than 100 mi of maintained trails linking lakes and towns to wilderness camps. The **Maine Snowmobile Association** (☞ Contacts and Resources *in* Maine A to Z, *below*) has information about Maine's nearly 8,000-mi Interconnecting Trail System.

Skiing and Snow Sports

SADDLEBACK SKI AND SUMMER LAKE PRESERVE

A down-home atmosphere prevails at Saddleback, where the quiet and the absence of crowds, even on holiday weekends, draw return visitors—many of them families. The base area has the feeling of a small community. ⊠ *Box 490, Saddleback Rd. off Rte. 4, 04970,* ☎ *207/864–5671; 207/864–3380 for snow conditions; 207/864–5364 for reservations.*

Downhill. The expert terrain is short and concentrated at the top of the mountain; an upper lift makes the trails easily accessible. The middle of the mountain is mainly intermediate, with a few meandering easy trails; the beginner or novice slopes are toward the bottom. Two double chairlifts and three T-bars carry skiers to the 41 trails on the 1,830 ft of vertical.

Cross-country. Forty km (25 mi) of groomed cross-country trails spread out from the base area and circle Saddleback Lake and several ponds and rivers.

Child care. The nursery takes children from age 6 weeks to 8 years. There are ski classes and programs for kids of different levels and ages.

Kingfield

54 *33 mi east of Rangeley, 15 mi west of Phillips, 21 mi north of Farmington.*

In the shadows of Mt. Abraham and Sugarloaf Mountain, Kingfield has everything a "real" New England town should have: a general store, historic inns, and a white clapboard church. Don't ignore Sugarloaf/USA in summer: The ski resort has an 18-hole golf course and six tennis courts for public use in warmer months.

The **Stanley Museum** houses a collection of original Stanley Steamer cars built by the Stanley twins, Kingfield's most famous natives. ⊠ *School St.,* ☎ *207/265–2729.* ⌑ *$2.* ☉ *May–Oct., Tues.–Sun. 1–4; Nov.–Apr. by appointment.*

Nowetah's American Indian Museum displays an extensive collection of baskets as well as artifacts from native peoples of North and South America. This small museum is part of a store. ⊠ *Rte. 27, New Portland,* ☎ *207/628–4981.* ⌑ *Free.* ☉ *Daily 10–5.*

Dining and Lodging

$$$–$$$$ ✕☐ **Sugarloaf Inn Resort.** This lodge provides ski-on access to Sugarloaf/USA, a complete health club, and rooms that range from king-size on the fourth floor to dorm-style (bunk beds) on the ground floor. A greenhouse section of the Seasons Restaurant ($$–$$$) affords views of the slopes; "ski-in" lunches are served here. At breakfast the sunlight pours into the dining room, and at dinner you can watch the snow-grooming machines prepare your favorite run. ⊠ *Box 5000, R.R. 1, Sugarloaf Access Rd., Carrabassett Valley 04947,* ☎ *207/237–6814 or 800/843–5623,* FAX *207/237–3773. 38 rooms, 4 dorm-style rooms. Restaurant, health club, meeting rooms. AE, D, MC, V.*

$ ✕🅔 **One and Three Stanley Avenue.** These sister properties, a gourmet restaurant and a simple B&B, are in adjacent Victorian houses. The quiet neighborhood is a few minutes' walk from downtown Kingfield and about a 20-minute drive from Sugarloaf/USA. Both are decorated with period furnishings. The restaurant specializes in creative Continental fare and emphasizes fresh Maine ingredients. ⊠ *Box 169, 3 Stanley Ave., 04947,* ☎ *207/265–5541. 6 rooms, 3 with bath. Full breakfast. MC, V. Restaurant closed May–Nov.*

$$$$ 🅗 **Grand Summit.** A six-story brick structure at the base of the lifts on Sugarloaf, this hotel combines New England ambience with European-style service. Oak and redwood paneling in the main rooms is enhanced by contemporary furnishings. Valet parking, ski tuning, lockers, and mountain guides are available through the concierge. The Double Diamond Pub has a lively après-ski scene. ⊠ *R.R. 1, Box 2299, Carrabassett Valley 04947,* ☎ *207/237–2222 or 800/527–9879,* FAX *207/ 237–2874. 100 rooms, 19 suites. Restaurant, pub, hot tub, massage, sauna, spa. AE, D, DC, MC, V.*

Nightlife and the Arts

At Sugarloaf, nightlife is concentrated at the mountain's base village. Monday is blues night at the **Bag & Kettle** (☎ 207/237–2451), which is the best choice for pizza and burgers. In the base village you'll find **Gepetto's** (☎ 207/237–2953), a popular après-ski hangout that serves American-style food. A microbrewery on the access road called the **Sugarloaf Brewing Company** (☎ 207/237–2211) pulls in revelers who come for après-ski brewskies. **Widowmaker Lounge** (☎ 207/237–6845) frequently presents live entertainment in the base lodge.

Outdoor Activities and Sports

T.A.D. Dog Sled Services (⊠ Rte. 27, Carrabassett Valley, ☎ 207/246–4461) conducts short 1½-mi rides near Sugarloaf/USA. Sleds accommodate up to two adults and two children.

Skiing and Snow Sports

SUGARLOAF/USA

Abundant natural snow, a huge mountain, and the only above-tree-line skiing in the East have made Sugarloaf one of Maine's best-known ski areas. Improvements by the American Skiing Company have resulted in increased snowmaking, new lifts, and new trails. Sugarloaf skiers like the nontrendy Maine atmosphere and the base village, which has restaurants and shops. Two slopeside hotels and hundreds of slopeside condominiums provide ski-in/ski-out access. Once you are here, a car is unnecessary—a shuttle connects all mountain operations. Summer is much quieter than winter, but you can bike, hike, golf, and fish. ⊠ *R.R. 1, Box 5000, Sugarloaf Access Rd., Carrabassett Valley 01947,* ☎ *207/ 237–2000; 207/237–6808 for snow conditions; or 800/843–5623.*

Downhill. With a vertical of 2,820 ft, Sugarloaf is taller than any other New England ski peak except Killington in Vermont. The advanced terrain begins with the steep snowfields on top, wide open and treeless. Coming down the face of the mountain, there are black-diamond runs everywhere, often blending into easier terrain. Many intermediate trails can be found down the front face, and a couple more come off the summit. Easier runs are predominantly toward the bottom, with a few long, winding runs that twist and turn from higher elevations. Serving the resort's 126 trails are two high-speed quad, two quad, one triple, and eight double chairlifts and one T-bar.

Cross-country. The Sugarloaf Ski Outdoor Center has 95 km (62 mi) of cross-country trails that loop and wind through the valley. Trails connect to the resort.

Other Activities. Snowboarders will find two snowboard parks and a halfpipe, the largest in the Northeast. The **Sugarloaf Sports and Fitness Club** (☎ 207/237–6946) has an indoor pool, six indoor and outdoor hot tubs, racquetball courts, full fitness and spa facilities, and a beauty salon. Use of club facilities is included in all lodging packages. Snowshoeing and ice skating are available at the Outdoor Center.

Child care. A nursery takes children from age 6 weeks to 6 years. Children's ski programs begin at age 3. A night nursery is open on Thursday and Saturday from 6 to 10 PM by reservation. Instruction is provided on a half-day or full-day basis for children from ages 4 to 14. Nightly children's activities are free. The teen club, Avalanche, is in the base lodge.

Western Lakes and Mountains A to Z

Arriving and Departing
See Arriving and Departing *in* Maine A to Z, *below.*

Getting Around
BY CAR
A car is essential to tour the western lakes and mountains. To travel from town to town in the order described in this section, take U.S. 302 to Route 26 to U.S. 2 to Route 17 to Route 4/16 to Route 142.

BY PLANE
Mountain Air Service (✉ Rangeley, ☎ 207/864–5307) provides air access to remote areas, scenic flights, and charter fishing trips. **Naples Flying Service** (✉ Naples Causeway, Naples, ☎ 207/693–6591) operates sightseeing flights over the lakes in summer.

Contacts and Resources
EMERGENCIES
Bethel Area Health Center (✉ Railroad St., Bethel, ☎ 207/824–2193). **Mt. Abram Regional Health Center** (✉ Depot St., Kingfield, ☎ 207/265–4555). **Northern Cumberland Memorial Hospital** (✉ S. High St., Bridgton, ☎ 207/647–8841). **Rangeley Regional Health Center** (✉ Main St., Rangeley, ☎ 207/864–3303).

RESERVATION SERVICES
Condominium lodging at Shawnee Peak is available through the **Bridgton Group** (☎ 207/647–2591). Bethel's **Chamber of Commerce** (☎ 207/824–3585 or 800/442–5826) has a reservations service. For reservations at Sugarloaf/USA, contact **Sugarloaf Area Reservations Service** (☎ 800/843–2732).

VISITOR INFORMATION
Bethel Area Chamber of Commerce (✉ Box 439, 30 Cross St., Bethel 04217, ☎ 207/824–2282 or 800/442–5526). **Bridgton–Lakes Region Chamber of Commerce** (✉ Box 236, U.S. 302, Bridgton 04009, ☎ 207/647–3472). **Greater Windham Chamber of Commerce** (✉ Box 1015, U.S. 302, Windham 04062, ☎ 207/882–8265). **Naples Business Association** (✉ Box 412, Naples 04055, ☎ 888/627–5379). **Rangeley Lakes Region Chamber of Commerce** (✉ Box 317, Main St., Rangeley 04970, ☎ 207/864–5571 or 800/685–2537). **Sugarloaf Area Chamber of Commerce** (✉ R.R.1, Box 2151, Kingfield 04947, ☎ 207/235–2100).

THE NORTH WOODS

Maine's North Woods, the vast area in the north-central section of the state, is best experienced by canoe or raft, hiking trail, or on a fishing trip. Some great theaters for these activities are Moosehead Lake, Baxter State Park, and the Allagash Wilderness Waterway—as well as the summer resort town of Greenville, dramatically situated Rockwood, and the no-frills outposts that connect them. For outfitters, *see* Contacts and Resources *in* North Woods A to Z, *below*.

Rockwood

⑤ *180 mi north of Portland, 91 mi northwest of Bangor.*

Rockwood, on Moosehead Lake's western shore, is a good starting point for a wilderness trip or a family vacation on the lake. Moosehead Lake, Maine's largest, supplies more in the way of rustic camps, restaurants, guides, and outfitters than any other northern locale. Its 420 mi of shorefront, three-quarters of which is owned by paper manufacturers, is virtually uninhabited. Though it doesn't possess many amenities, Rockwood has the most striking location of any town on Moosehead: The dark mass of **Mt. Kineo,** a sheer cliff that rises 789 ft above the lake and 1,789 ft above sea level, looms just across the narrows (you get an excellent view just north of town on Route 6/15).

East Outlet of the Kennebec River, a popular Class II and III white-water run for canoeists and white-water rafters, is about 10 mi from Rockwood on Route 6/15 south. You'll come to a bridge with a dam to the left. The outlet ends at the Harris Station Dam at Indian Pond, headwaters of the Kennebec.

OFF THE
BEATEN PATH

KINEO – Once a thriving summer resort, the original Mount Kineo Hotel (built in 1830 and torn down in the 1940s) was accessed primarily by steamship. An effort to renovate the remaining buildings in the early 1990s failed, but Kineo still makes a pleasant day trip from Rockwood. You can rent a motorboat in Rockwood and make the journey across the lake in about 15 minutes. There's a small marina on the shore, in the shadow of Mt. Kineo, and a half dozen buildings dot the land. Some are for sale and others are being restored, but there is no real town here. A tavern sells cold libations to drink there or take with you. A walkway laces the perimeter of the mountain.

Lodging

$$$$ ☷ **Attean Lake Lodge.** The Holden family has owned and operated this island lodge about an hour west of Rockwood since 1900. The 18 log cabins, which sleep from two to six people, provide a secluded environment. The tastefully decorated central lodge has a library and games. ☒ *Box 457, off Rte. 201, Birch Island, Jackman 04945,* ☏ *207/ 668–3792,* ℻ *207/668–4016. 18 cabins. Beach, boating, recreation room, library. AP. AE, MC, V. Closed Oct.–May.*

$–$$ ☷ **The Birches.** This family-oriented resort supplies the full north-country experience: Moosehead Lake, birch woods, log cabins, and boats. The century-old main lodge has four guest rooms, a lobby with a trout pond, and a living room dominated by a fieldstone fireplace. The 15 cottages have wood-burning stoves or fireplaces and sleep from 2 to 15 people. The dining room (closed in December and April) overlooking the lake is open to the public for breakfast and dinner; the fare at dinner is pasta, seafood, and steak. ☒ *Box 41, off Rte. 6/15, on Moosehead Lake, 04478,* ☏ *207/534–7305 or 800/825–9453,* ℻ *207/534– 8835. 4 lodge rooms share bath, 15 cottages. Dining room, hot tub, sauna, boating. AE, D, MC, V.*

$ ☷ **Rockwood Cottages.** These eight white cottages on Moosehead Lake, off Route 15 and convenient to the center of Rockwood, have screened porches and fully equipped kitchens and sleep from two to seven people. There is a one-week minimum stay in July and August.

The North Woods

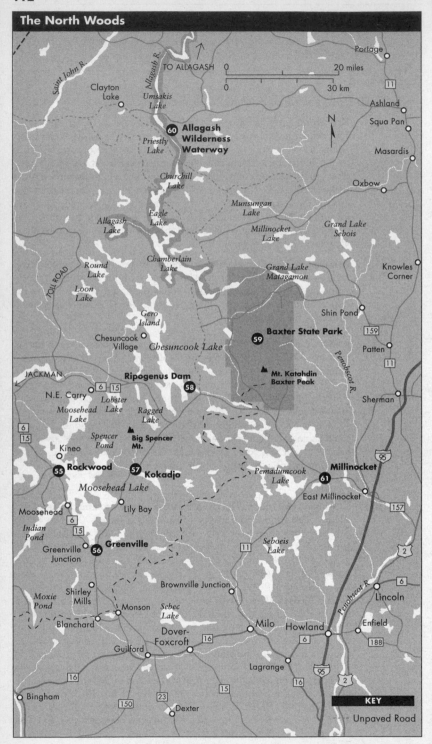

KEY
Unpaved Road

✉ *Box 176, Rte. 15, 04478,* ☎ FAX *207/534–7725. 8 cottages. Sauna, dock, boating. D, MC, V. Closed Dec.–Apr.*

Outdoor Activities and Sports

Mt. Kineo Cabins (✉ Rte. 6/15, ☎ 207/534–7744) rents canoes and larger boats on Moosehead Lake for the trip to Kineo. Rent a boat or take a shuttle operated by **Rockwood Cottages** (☎ 207/534–7725) or **Old Mill Campground** (☎ 207/534–7333) and hike one of the trails to the summit of Mt. Kineo for a picnic lunch and panoramic views. The **Birches** (☎ 207/534–7305) operates a moose cruise.

Greenville

56 *20 mi south of Rockwood, 160 mi northeast of Portland.*

Greenville has a smattering of shops, restaurants, and hotels. The largest town on Moosehead Lake, it is home to the Big Squaw Mountain Resort (☞ Skiing and Snow Sports, *below*), a ski area that in summer runs a recreation program for children and has two tennis courts, hiking, and lawn games.

Moosehead Marine Museum has exhibits on the local logging industry and the steamship era on Moosehead Lake, plus photographs of the Mount Kineo Hotel. ✉ *Main St.,* ☎ *207/695–2716.* 🎟 *Free.* ☉ *Late May–early Oct., daily 10–4.*

★ The Moosehead Marine Museum offers three-hour and six-hour trips on Moosehead Lake aboard the *Katahdin,* a 1914 steamship (now diesel). The 115-ft *Katahdin,* fondly called *The Kate,* carried passengers to Kineo until 1942 and then was used in the logging industry until 1975. ✉ *Main St. (boarding is on the shoreline by the museum),* ☎ *207/695–2716.* 🎟 *$9–$24.* ☉ *Late May–Columbus Day.*

Lily Bay State Park (✉ Lily Bay Rd., ☎ 207/695–2700), 8 mi northeast of Greenville, has a good swimming beach, two boat-launching ramps, and a 93-site campground.

Dining and Lodging

$–$$ ✕ **Kelly's Landing.** This family-oriented restaurant on the Moosehead shorefront has indoor and outdoor seating, excellent views, and a dock for boaters. The fare includes sandwiches, burgers, lasagna, seafood dinners, and prime rib. ✉ *Rte. 6/15, Greenville Junction,* ☎ *207/695–4438. MC, V.*

$$$–$$$$ ✕🏨 **Greenville Inn.** Built more than a century ago, this rambling structure is a block from town on a rise over Moosehead Lake. The ornate cherry and mahogany paneling, Oriental rugs, and leaded glass create an aura of masculine ease. Cottages have mountain and lake views, and some have decks. The restaurant ($$$; reservations essential; no lunch) has water views. The menu, revised daily, reflects the owners' Austrian background: shrimp with mustard-dill sauce, salmon marinated in olive oil and basil, a veal cutlet with a mushroom cream sauce. ✉ *Box 1194, Norris St., 04441,* ☎ *207/695–2206 or 888/695–6000,* FAX *207/695–0335. 4 rooms and 1 suite in main inn, 1 suite in carriage house, 6 cottages. Restaurant. Full breakfast. D, MC, V.*

$$$$ 🏨 **Lodge at Moosehead Lake.** This mansion overlooking Moosehead
★ Lake is about as close as things get to luxury in the North Woods. All rooms have whirlpool baths, fireplaces, and hand-carved four-poster beds; most have lake views. The restaurant, where breakfast is served, has a spectacular view of the water. ✉ *Lily Bay Rd., 04441,* ☎ *207/695–4400,* FAX *207/695–2281. 5 rooms, 3 suites. Restaurant. D, MC, V. Closed late Oct.–mid-Jan.; mid-Mar.–mid-May; mid-Jan.–mid-Mar., Tues.–Wed.*

$–$$ ⊡ **Devlin House.** You get nearly the same sweeping views over Moosehead Lake at this small bed-and-breakfast as you do from the more exclusive and expensive Lodge at Moosehead Lake (☞ *above*). Rooms have king-size beds. ⊠ *Box 1102, Lily Bay Rd., 04441,* ☎ *207/695–2229. 3 rooms. Full breakfast. Open year-round, but call ahead in winter.*

$ ⊡ **Chalet Moosehead.** Fifty yards off Route 6/15 and right on Moosehead Lake, this accommodation holds efficiencies (with two double beds, a living room, and a kitchenette), motel rooms, and cabins, all with picture windows to capture the view. The attractive grounds include a private beach and dock. ⊠ *Box 327, Rte. 6/15, Greenville Junction 04442,* ☎ *207/695–2950 or 800/290–3645. 8 efficiencies, 7 motel rooms, 2 cabins. Horseshoes, beach, dock, boating. AE, D, MC, V.*

Outdoor Activities and Sports

Kineo Kayak Guide Service (☎ 207/474–3945 or 207/695–2896) offers guided kayak tours and moose safaris throughout the Moosehead Lake and Kennebec Valley area. **Moose Country Safaris and Dogsled Trips** (☎ 207/876–4907) leads moose safaris, dogsled trips, and canoe and kayak trips.

FISHING

Togue, landlocked salmon, and brook and lake trout lure thousands of anglers to the region from ice-out in mid-May until September; the hardiest return in winter to ice-fish. For up-to-date **information** on water levels, call ☎ 207/695–3756 or 800/322–9844.

RAFTING

The Kennebec and Dead rivers and the West Branch of the Penobscot River offer thrilling white-water rafting (guides are strongly recommended). These rivers are dam-controlled, so trips run rain or shine daily from May to October (day and multiday trips are conducted). Most guided raft trips on the Kennebec and Dead rivers leave from the Forks, southwest of Moosehead Lake, on Route 201; Penobscot River trips leave from either Greenville or Millinocket. Many rafting outfitters operate resort facilities in their base towns. **Raft Maine** (☎ 800/723–8633) has lodging and rafting packages and information about outfitters.

Shopping

Indian Hill Trading Post (⊠ Rte. 6/15, ☎ 207/695–2104) stocks just about anything you might need for a North Woods vacation, including sporting and camping equipment, canoes, and fishing licenses; there's even an adjacent grocery store. You enter **Moosehead Traders** (⊠ Moosehead Center Mall, Rte. 6/15, ☎ 207/695–3806) through an antler archway; inside are books, clothing, and antiques and artifacts.

Skiing and Snow Sports

BIG SQUAW MOUNTAIN RESORT

The management is modernizing this remote but pretty resort overlooking Moosehead Lake. The emphasis is on affordable family skiing—prices are downright cheap compared with those at other in-state areas. New snowmaking, new grooming equipment, and a new attitude make this a wonderful place for skiers longing to escape crowds. ⊠ *Box D, Rte. 6/15, 04441,* ☎ *207/695–1000.*

Downhill. Trails are laid out according to difficulty, with the easy slopes toward the bottom, intermediate trails weaving from midpoint, and steeper runs high up off the 1,750-vertical-ft peak. The 22 trails are served by one triple and one double chairlift and two surface lifts.

Child care. The nursery takes children from infants through age 6. The ski school has daily lessons and racing classes for children of all ages.

Kokadjo

57 *22 mi northeast of Greenville.*

Kokadjo, population "not many," has a sign that reads "Keep Maine green. This is God's country. Why set it on fire and make it look like hell?" This is the last outpost before you enter the North Woods. As you leave Kokadjo, bear left at the fork and follow signs to Baxter State Park. A drive of 5 mi along this road (now dirt) brings you to the Bowater/Great Northern Paper Company's Sias Hill checkpoint, where from June to November you must sign in and pay a user fee ($8 per car for nonresidents, valid for 24 hours) to travel the next 40 mi. Access is through a forest where you're likely to encounter logging trucks (which have the right of way), logging equipment, and work in progress. At the bottom of the hill after you pass the checkpoint, look to your right—there's a good chance you'll spot a moose.

Lodging

$$ ☒ **Northern Pride Lodge.** North Woods–quaint with basic creature comforts is the best way to describe this lakefront lodge decorated with Victorian-era antiques and fishing and hunting trophies. Rooms are small, but the big porch is likely where you'll be spending much of your time. A huge country breakfast is served to all guests; lunch and dinner are available, too. The restaurant is open to the public for dinner. ☒ *HC 76, Box 588, Greenville Rd., 04441,* ☎ *207/695–2890. 5 rooms without bath. Restaurant. Full breakfast; MAP and AP available. MC, V.*

Ripogenus Dam

58 *20 mi northeast of Kokadjo, 25 mins southeast of Chesuncook Village by floatplane.*

Ripogenus Dam and the granite-walled Ripogenus Gorge are on Ripogenus Lake, east of Chesuncook Lake. The gorge is the jumping-off point for the famous 12-mi West Branch of the Penobscot River whitewater rafting trip and the most popular put-in point for Allagash canoe trips. The Penobscot River drops more than 70 ft per mile through the gorge, giving rafters a hold-on-for-your-life ride. The best spot to watch the Penobscot rafters is from Pray's Big Eddy Wilderness Campground, overlooking the rock-choked **Crib Works Rapid** (a Class V rapid). To get here, follow the main road northeast and turn left on Telos Road; the campground is about 10 yards after the bridge.

En Route From the Pray's Big Eddy Wilderness Campground, take the main road (here called the Golden Road for the amount of money it took the Great Northern Paper Company to build it) southeast toward Millinocket. The road soon becomes paved. After you drive over the one-lane Abol Bridge and pass through the Bowater/Great Northern Paper Company's Debsconeag checkpoint, bear left to reach Togue Pond Gatehouse, the southern entrance to Baxter State Park.

Baxter State Park

★ **59** *24 mi northwest of Millinocket.*

Few places in Maine are as remote or as beautiful as Baxter State Park and the Allagash Wilderness Waterway (☞ *below*). Baxter, a gift from Governor Percival Baxter, is the jewel in the crown of northern Maine, a 204,733-acre wilderness area that surrounds **Katahdin**, Maine's highest mountain (5,267 ft at Baxter Peak) and the terminus of the Appalachian Trail. There are 46 mountain peaks and ridges, 18 of which exceed an elevation of 3,000 ft. Day-use parking areas fill quickly in season; it's best to arrive early, before 8 AM. The park is intersected by about 175 mi of trails. No pets, domestic animals, oversize vehicles, or motorcycles are allowed in the park, and there are no pay phones or gas stations. The one visitor center is at Togue Pond, for which Millinocket is the nearest gateway. ✉ *mailing address: Baxter State Park Authority, 64 Balsam Dr., Millinocket 04462,* ☎ *207/723–5140.* 🖾 *$8 per vehicle; free to Maine residents. Office closed mid-Oct.–mid-May.*

OFF THE
BEATEN PATH

LUMBERMAN'S MUSEUM – This museum comprises 10 buildings filled with exhibits depicting the history of logging, including models, dioramas, and equipment. ✉ *Shin Pond Rd./Rte. 159, Patten (22 mi southeast of Baxter State Park),* ☎ *207/528–2650.* 🖾 *$2.50.* ☉ *Memorial Day–Sept., Tues.–Sat. 9–4, Sun. 11–4.*

Camping

$ ⛺ **Baxter State Park.** Camping spaces at the 10 campgrounds here can only be reserved by mail (phone reservations not accepted). Reservations can be made beginning January 1—some sites are fully booked for midsummer weekends soon after that. The state also maintains primitive backcountry sites that are available without charge on a first-come, first-served basis. ✉ *Baxter State Park Authority, 64 Balsam Dr., Millinocket 04462,* ☎ *207/723–5140. Closed mid-Oct.–mid-May.*

Outdoor Activities and Sports
Katahdin, in Baxter State Park (☞ *above*), draws thousands of hikers every year for the daylong climb to the summit and the stunning views of woods, mountains, and lakes from the hair-raising Knife Edge Trail along its ridge. The crowds can be formidable on clear summer days, so if you crave solitude, tackle one of the 45 other mountains in the park, all of which are accessible from a 150-mi network of trails. South Turner can be climbed in a morning (if you're fit)—it has a great view of Katahdin across the valley. On the way you'll pass Sandy Stream Pond, where moose are often seen at dusk. The Owl, the Brothers, and Doubletop Mountain are good day hikes.

Allagash Wilderness Waterway

⑥⓪ *22 mi north of Ripogenus Dam.*

The Allagash is a spectacular 92-mi corridor of lakes and rivers that cuts across 170,000 acres of wilderness, beginning at the northwest corner of Baxter and running north to the town of Allagash, 10 mi from the Canadian border. For information, contact the **Allagash Wilderness Waterway** (✉ 106 Hogan Rd., Bangor 04401, ☎ 207/941–4014).

Outdoor Activities and Sports
The Allagash rapids are ranked Class I and Class II (very easy and easy), but that doesn't mean the river is a piece of cake; river conditions vary greatly with the depth and volume of water, and even a Class I rapid can hang your canoe up on a rock, capsize you, or spin you around. On the lakes, strong winds can halt your progress for days. The Allagash should not be undertaken lightly or without planning; the complete 92-mi course requires 7 to 10 days. The canoeing season along the Allagash is from mid-May to October, although it's wise to remember that the black-fly season ends about July 1. The best bet for a novice is to go with a guide; a good outfitter (☞ Contacts and Resources *in* North Woods A to Z, *below*) will help plan your route and provide your craft and transportation.

The Mt. Everest of Maine canoe trips is the 110-mi route on the St. John River from Baker Lake to Allagash Village, with a swift current all the way and two stretches of Class III rapids. The best time to canoe the St. John is between mid-May and mid-June, when the river level is high.

Those with their own canoe who want to go it alone can take Telos Road north from Ripogenus Dam, putting in at Chamberlain Thoroughfare Bridge at the southern tip of Chamberlain Lake, or at Allagash Lake, Churchill Dam, Bissonnette Bridge, or Umsaskis Bridge. One popular and easy route follows the Upper West Branch of the Penobscot River from Lobster Lake (just east of Moosehead Lake) to Chesuncook Lake. From Chesuncook Village you can paddle to Ripogenus Dam in a day.

The Aroostook River from Little Munsungan Lake to Fort Fairfield (100 mi) is best run in late spring. More challenging routes include the Passadumkeag River from Grand Falls to Passadumkeag (25 mi with Class I–III rapids); the East Branch of the Penobscot River from Matagamon Wilderness Campground to Grindstone (38 mi with Class I–III rapids); and the West Branch of the Pleasant River from Katahdin Iron Works to Brownville Junction (10 mi with Class II–III rapids).

Millinocket

61 *90 mi northwest of Greenville, 19 mi southeast of Baxter State Park, 70 mi north of Bangor.*

Millinocket, with a population of 7,000, is a gateway to Baxter State Park (☞ *above*).

OFF THE
BEATEN PATH

KATAHDIN IRON WORKS – For a worthwhile day trip from Millinocket, take Route 11 west to a trailhead 5 mi north of Brownville Junction. Drive the gravel road 6 mi to Katahdin Iron Works, the site of a mining operation that employed nearly 200 workers in the mid-1800s; a deteriorated kiln, a stone furnace, and a charcoal-storage building are all that remain. From here, a hiking trail leads over fairly rugged terrain to **Gulf Hagas,** with natural chasms, cliffs, a 3-mi gorge, waterfalls, pools, exotic flora, and rock formations.

Dining and Lodging

$–$$ ✕ **Scootic Inn and Penobscot Room.** This informal restaurant and lounge has a varied menu of steak, seafood, pizza, and sandwiches. The large-screen TV is usually tuned to sports. ⊠ *70 Penobscot Ave.,* ☎ *207/723–4566. AE, D, MC, V.*

$ 🏨 **Atrium Motel.** Off Route 157 next to a shopping center, this motor inn has a large central atrium with facilities that make up for its unappealing location and standard motel furnishings. ⊠ *740 Central St., 04462,* ☎ FAX *207/723–4555. 72 rooms, 10 suites. Indoor pool, hot tub, health club. Continental breakfast. AE, D, DC, MC, V.*

$ 🏨 **Big Moose Inn.** There's nothing fancy about this old-fashioned inn and the cabins and campsites nestled between Ambejesus and Millinocket lakes, just 8 mi from the entrance to Baxter State Park. The inn has a big stone and brick fireplace decorated with a moose trophy and snowshoes; inn rooms are comfortably furnished with country pieces. The popular dining room ($$), open for dinner Wednesday through Saturday, emphasizes seafood. Canoes and a store are other amenities. ⊠ *Box 98, Baxter State Park Rd., 04462,* ☎ *207/723–8391,* FAX *207/723–8199. 11 rooms share 3 baths, 11 cabins, 44 campsites. Restaurant, boating. Continental breakfast. MC, V. Closed mid-Oct.–May.*

Outdoor Activities and Sports

Kathadin Area Guide Service (⊠ 74 Water St., ☎ 207/723–9522 or

800/548–4355) outfits fishing, snowmobiling, canoeing, and camping expeditions. **Penobscot River Outfitters** (☎ 800/794–5267) rents canoes and offers a shuttle service. **New England Outdoor Center** (☎ 207/723–5438 or 800/766–7238) rents snowmobiles and offers guided trips.

North Woods A to Z

Arriving and Departing

Bangor International Airport (☞ Arriving and Departing *in* Maine A to Z, *below*) is the closest airport.

Getting Around

BY CAR

A car is essential to negotiate this vast region but may not be useful to someone spending a vacation entirely at a wilderness camp. Public roads are scarce in the north country, but lumber companies maintain private roads that are often open to the public (sometimes by permit only). When driving on a logging road, always give lumber company trucks the right of way. Be aware that loggers often take the middle of the road and will neither move over nor slow down for you.

I–95 offers the quickest access to the North Woods. U.S. 201 (Exit 36 off I–95) is the major route to Jackman and to Québec. Route 15 connects Jackman to Greenville and Bangor. The Golden Road is a private, paper company–operated road that links Greenville to Millinocket.

BY PLANE

Charter flights, usually by seaplane, from Bangor, Greenville, or Millinocket to smaller towns and remote lake and forest areas can be arranged with the following flying services, which will transport you and your gear and help you find a guide: **Currier's Flying Service** (✉ Greenville Junction, ☎ 207/695–2778), **Folsom's Air Service** (✉ Greenville, ☎ 207/695–2821), **Katahdin Air Service** (✉ Millinocket, ☎ 207/723–8378), **Scotty's Flying Service** (✉ Shin Pond, ☎ 207/528–2626).

Contacts and Resources

CAMPING

Reservations for state park campsites (excluding Baxter State Park) can be made through the **Bureau of Parks and Lands** (☞ Contacts and Resources *in* Maine A to Z, *below*). **Maine Sporting Camp Association** (☎ 800/305–3057) publishes a list of its members, with details on the facilities available at each camp.

The **Bureau of Parks and Lands** (✉ State House Station 22, Augusta 04333, ☎ 207/287–3821) will tell you if you need a camping permit and where to obtain one. The **Maine Forest Service, Department of Conservation** (✉ State House Station 22, Augusta 04333, ☎ 207/287–2791) will direct you to the nearest ranger station, where you can get a fire permit (✉ Greenville Ranger Station, Box 1107, Lakeview St., Greenville 04441, ☎ 207/695–3721). The **Maine Campground Owners Association** (✉ 655 Main St., Lewiston 04240, ☎ 207/782–5874) publishes a helpful annual directory of its members; 18 are in the Katahdin-Moosehead area, and 25 are in the Kennebec and Moose River valleys. **Maine Tourism Association** (✉ Box 2300, 325B Water St., Hallowell 04347, ☎ 207/623–0363; 800/533–9595 outside ME) publishes a listing of private campsites and cottage rentals. **North Maine Woods** (✉ Box 421, Ashland 04732, ☎ 207/435–6213) maintains 500 primitive campsites on commercial forest land and takes reservations for 20 of them; early reservations are recommended.

CANOEING

Most canoe rental operations will arrange transportation, help plan your route, and provide a guide. Transport to wilderness lakes can be arranged through the flying services listed under Getting Around by Plane, *above*.

The **Bureau of Parks and Lands** (☞ Camping, *above*)) provides information on independent Allagash canoeing and camping. The following outfitters serve the area:

Allagash Canoe Trips (✉ Box 713, Greenville 04441, ☎ 207/695–3668) operates guided trips on the Allagash Waterway, plus the Moose, Penobscot, and St. John rivers. **Allagash Wilderness Outfitters/Frost Pond Camps** (✉ Box 620, Greenville 04441, ☎ 207/695–2821) provides equipment, transportation, and information for canoe trips on the Allagash and the Penobscot rivers. **Mahoosuc Guide Service** (✉ Bear River Rd., Newry 04261, ☎ 207/824–2073) conducts guided trips on the Penobscot, Allagash, and Moose rivers. **North Country Outfitters** (✉ Box 41, Rockwood 04478, ☎ 207/534–2242 or 207/534–7305) operates a white-water canoeing and kayaking school, rents equipment, and sponsors guided canoe trips on the Allagash Waterway and the Moose, Penobscot, and St. John rivers. **North Woods Ways** (✉ R.R. 2, Box 159-A, Guilford 04443, ☎ 207/997–3723) organizes wilderness canoeing trips on the Allagash, as well as on the Penobscot and St. John rivers. **Willard Jalbert Camps** (✉ 6 Winchester St., Presque Isle 04769, ☎ 207/764–0494) has been sponsoring guided Allagash trips since the late 1800s.

EMERGENCIES

Charles A. Dean Memorial Hospital (✉ Pritham Ave., Greenville, ☎ 207/695–2223 or 800/260–4000). **Mayo Regional Hospital** (✉ 75 W. Main St., Dover-Foxcroft, ☎ 207/564–8401). **Millinocket Regional Hospital** (✉ 200 Somerset St., Millinocket, ☎ 207/723–5161).

GUIDES

Fishing guides are available through most wilderness camps, sporting goods stores, and canoe outfitters. For assistance in finding a guide, contact North Maine Woods (☞ Visitor Information, *below*). A few well-established guides are **Gilpatrick's Guide Service** (✉ Box 461, Skowhegan 04976, ☎ 207/453–6959), **Maine Guide Fly Shop and Guide Service** (✉ Box 1202, Main St., Greenville 04441, ☎ 207/695–2266), and **Professional Guide Service** (✉ Box 346, Sheridan 04775, ☎ 207/435–8044).

HORSEBACK RIDING

Northern Maine Riding Adventures (✉ 64 Garland Line Rd., Dover-Foxcroft 04426, ☎ 207/564–3451), owned by registered Maine guides Judy Cross-Strehlke and Bob Strehlke, conducts one-day, two-day, and weeklong pack trips (10 people maximum) through parts of Piscataquis County. A popular two-day trip explores the Whitecap–Barren Mountain Range, near Katahdin Iron Works (☞ Millinocket, *above*).

RAFTING

Raft Maine (☎ 800/723–8633) is an association of white-water outfitters licensed to lead trips down the Kennebec and Dead rivers and the West Branch of the Penobscot River. Rafting season begins May 1 and continues through mid-October.

VISITOR INFORMATION

Baxter State Park Authority (✉ 64 Balsam Dr., Millinocket 04462, ☎ 207/723–5140). **Katahdin Area Chamber of Commerce** (✉ 1029 Central St., Millinocket 04462, ☎ 207/723–4443). **Moosehead Lake Re-

gion Chamber of Commerce (⊠ Box 581, Rtes. 6 and 15, Greenville 04441, ☎ 207/695–2702). **North Maine Woods** (⊠ Box 421, Ashland 04732, ☎ 207/435–6213 for maps; a canoeing guide for the St. John River; and lists of outfitters, camps, and campsites).

MAINE A TO Z

Arriving and Departing

By Bus

Concord Trailways (☎ 800/639–3317) provides service between Boston and Bangor (via Portland); a coastal route connects towns between Brunswick and Searsport. **Vermont Transit** (☎ 207/772–6587) connects towns in southwestern Maine with cities in New England and throughout the United States. Vermont Transit is a subsidiary of **Greyhound** (☎ 800/231–2222).

By Car

Interstate 95 is the fastest route to and through the state from coastal New Hampshire and points south, turning inland at Brunswick and going on to Bangor and the Canadian border. U.S. 1, more leisurely and scenic, is the principal coastal highway from New Hampshire to Canada. U.S. 302 is the primary access to the Sebago Lake region, while Route 26 leads to the western mountains and Route 27 leads to the Rangeley and Sugarloaf regions. U.S. 201 is the fastest route to Québec and Route 9 is the inland route from Bangor to Calais.

By Ferry

Bay Ferries (☎ 888/249–7245) operates the Cat, a high-speed car-ferry service on a catamaran, between Yarmouth, Nova Scotia, and Bar Harbor from mid-May to mid-October. The crossing takes 2½ hours, and the Cat has everything from a casino to sightseeing decks. **Prince of Fundy Cruises** (☎ 800/341–7540; 800/482–0955 in Maine) operates a car ferry from May to October between Portland and Yarmouth, Nova Scotia.

By Plane

Portland International Jetport (⊠ Westbrook St. off Rte. 9, ☎ 207/774–7301) is served by Business Express, Continental, Delta, United, and US Airways. **Bangor International Airport** (⊠ Godfrey Blvd., Exit 47 off I–95, ☎ 207/947–0384) is served by American, Business Express, Continental, Delta, Northwest Airlink, and US Airways. **Hancock County Airport** (⊠ Rte. 3, ☎ 207/667–7329), in Trenton, 8 mi northwest of Bar Harbor, is served by Continental Connection/Colgan Air. **Knox County Regional Airport** (⊠ Off Rte. 73, ☎ 207/594–4131), in Owls Head, 3 mi south of Rockland, has flights to Boston and Bar Harbor on Continental Connection/Colgan Air.

See Air Travel *in* Smart Travel Tips A to Z for airline phone numbers.

Getting Around

By Car

The maximum speed limit is 65 mph, unless otherwise posted, on I–95 and the Maine Turnpike. Local municipalities post speed limits on roads within their jurisdictions. It is a state law to stop for pedestrians. Drivers can make right turns on red if no sign prohibits such turns. Note that Maine law requires drivers to turn on their lights when windshield wipers are operating.

In many areas a car is the only practical means of travel. The *Maine Map and Travel Guide,* available for a small fee from the Maine Tourism Association, is useful for driving throughout the state; it has directories, mileage charts, and enlarged maps of city areas. DeLorme's *Maine Atlas & Gazetteer,* sold at local bookstores, includes enlarged, detailed maps of every part of the state.

By Ferry
Maine State Ferry Service (☎ 207/596–2202 or 800/491–4883) provides service from Rockland, Lincolnville, and Bass Harbor to islands in Penobscot and Blue Hill bays.

By Plane
Regional flying services, operating from regional and municipal airports (☞ Arriving and Departing, *above*), provide access to remote lakes and wilderness areas as well as to Penobscot Bay islands.

Contacts and Resources

Antiques
For a directory of members of the **Maine Antique Dealer Association,** send a self-addressed, stamped envelope to MADA (✉ Box 604, North Turner 04266). You can send $3 to receive a copy of the **Maine Antique Dealer Directory** (✉ R.R. 3, Box 1290, Winslow 04901).

Camping
Reservations for state park campsites (excluding Baxter State Park) can be made from January until August 23 through the **Bureau of Parks and Lands** (☎ 207/287–3824; 800/332–1501 in ME). Make reservations as far ahead as possible (at least seven days in advance), because sites go quickly. The **Maine Campground Owners Association** (✉ 655 Main St., Lewiston 04240, ☎ 207/782–5874, FAX 207/782–4497) has a statewide listing of private campgrounds.

Car Rental
Alamo (✉ Rear 9 Johnson St., ☎ 207/775–0855; 800/327–9633 in Portland). **Avis** (✉ Portland International Jetport, ☎ 207/874–7501 or 800/331–1212). **Budget** (✉ Portland International Jetport, ☎ 207/772 6789 or 800/527–0700). **Hertz** (✉ 1049 Westbrook St., Portland International Jetport, ☎ 207/774–4544 or 800/654–3131). **Thrifty** (✉ 1000 Westbrook St., Portland International Jetport, ☎ 207/772–4628 or 800/367–2277).

Fishing
For information about fishing and licenses, contact the **Department of Inland Fisheries and Wildlife** (☎ 207/287–8000).

Kayaking
Maine Island Kayak Co. (✉ 70 Luther St., Peaks Island, ☎ 800/796–2373) provides sea-kayaking instruction and conducts tours along the Maine coast.

Rafting
Raft Maine (✉ Box 3, Bethel 04217, ☎ 800/723–8633) provides information on whitewater rafting on the Kennebec, Penobscot, and Dead rivers.

Skiing
For information on alpine skiing, contact **Ski Maine** (✉ Box 7566, Portland 04112, ☎ 207/622–6983, 207/761–3774 or 888/624–6345 for ski conditions). For information on cross-country skiing, contact the **Maine Nordic Ski Council** (✉ Box 645, Bethel 04217, ☎ 800/754–9263).

Snowmobiling
The **Maine Snowmobile Association** (✉ Box 77, Augusta 04332, ☎ 207/622–6983 or 207/626–5717 for trail conditions) offers an excellent state-wide trail map of about 8,000 mi of trails.

Visitor Information

Maine Innkeepers Association (✉ 305 Commercial St., Portland 04101, ☎ 207/773–7670). **Maine Publicity Bureau** (✉ Box 2300, 325B Water St., Hallowell 04347, ☎ 207/623–0363; 800/533–9595 outside ME).

The **Maine Publicity Bureau** operates wlcome centers on U.S. 2 in Bethel and U.S. 302 in Fryeburg. **State of Maine Visitor Information Centers** are located on I–95 in Hampden, I–95 and U.S. 1 in Kittery, and on U.S. 1 in Yarmouth, off Exit 17 of I–95.

2 NEW HAMPSHIRE

New Hampshire's coast has a small stretch of towns with sandy beaches and ocean vistas. It's also home to the engaging city of Portsmouth. The Lakes Region is primarily a summer and fall haven for fishing, swimming, and boating. The White Mountains attract visitors who come to gaze on Mt. Washington, the tallest peak in the East, to ski and snowboard, to hike, and to shop at North Conway's outlet stores. Western and central New Hampshire have a string of cities along I–93 and a large unspoiled area of small towns, each with its own historic district and town green.

Revised and
updated by
Paula J.
Flanders

CRUSTY, INDEPENDENT NEW HAMPSHIRE is often defined more by what it is not than by what it is. It lacks the folksy charm of neighboring Vermont, nor does it have the miles of awe-inspiring rocky coast of Maine, its neighbor on its other side. And New Hampshire's politics generally range only from conservative to moderate, unlike the decidedly more liberal Massachusetts.

Whether in spite of or because of its differences, New Hampshire has been welcoming visitors for centuries. The first hiker to reach the top of Mt. Washington was Darby Field, in 1642. The first summer home appeared on one of the state's many lakes in 1763. Ralph Waldo Emerson, Henry David Thoreau, Nathaniel Hawthorne, and Louisa May Alcott all visited and wrote about the state, sparking a strong literary tradition that continues today. Filmmaker Ken Burns, writer J. D. Salinger, and poet Donald Hall all make their homes here.

New Hampshire's independent spirit nourishes other branches of the arts as well. Portsmouth has several theater groups, both cutting-edge and mainstream. New Hampshire's oldest professional theater, Tamworth's Barnstormers, claims the son of a president (Francis Cleveland) as founder. Throughout the state, a large number of stores display the work of local artisans. On back roads and in small towns, you can find makers of fine furniture and museum-quality pewter, glassblowers and potters, weavers and woodworkers. The League of New Hampshire Craftsmen operates eight stores around the state and runs the nation's oldest crafts fair each year during the first week of August.

But it was the mountain peaks, clear air, and sparkling lakes that attracted most of New Hampshire's early visitors, the same things that first attract people today. You can ski, snowboard, hike, and fish, or explore on snowmobiles, sailboats, and mountain bikes. Rock climbing and snowshoeing are popular, too. The diversity of the state's natural resources makes it a popular spot with everyone from avid adventurers to young families looking for easy access to nature.

New Hampshire natives had—and still have—no objection to others' enjoying the natural beauty of the state as long as they left some of their money behind when they returned home. The state has long resisted taxes on items other states take for granted, like sales and income, so the tourism adds much-needed revenue to the state coffers.

Taxes are only one hotly debated topic in the politically minded Granite State. New Hampshire was the first colony to declare itself independent from Great Britain, the first to adopt a state constitution, and the first to require that constitution to be referred to the people for approval. From the start, New Hampshire residents were independent-minded folk who took their hard-won freedoms seriously. Twenty years after the Revolutionary War's Battle of Bennington, New Hampshire native General John Stark, who led the troops to that crucial victory, wrote a letter to be read at the reunion he was too ill to attend. In it, he reminded his men, "Live free or die; death is not the worst of evils." The first half of that sentiment is now the state's motto, appearing even on its license plates. Nothing symbolizes those freedoms more than voting, and residents relish their role as host of the nation's earliest presidential primary.

With several of its cities consistently rated among the most livable in the nation, New Hampshire has seen considerable growth over the past decade or two. Even as growth has leveled in the rest of New England,

New Hampshire's population continues its upward trend, a trend fueled mainly by outsiders choosing to make their homes here.

Much of this population boom is located in the southern section of the state, so longtime residents worry that New Hampshire will soon take on two distinct personalities: one driven by the new cities of the south, such as Nashua, Derry, and Londonderry, and the other by the small towns and villages that make up the northern tier of the state. Only time will tell how New Hampshire will cope. But while the influx of newcomers has brought inevitable change, the independent nature of the people and the state's natural beauty continue to be embraced by newcomers and locals alike.

Pleasures and Pastimes

Beaches and Lakes

New Hampshire makes the most of its 18-mi coastline with several good beaches, among them Hampton Beach and Wallis Sands in Rye. Those who prefer warm lake waters to the bracing Atlantic can choose among some of the finest lakes in New England, such as Lake Winnipesaukee, Lake Sunapee, and Newfound Lake.

Biking

A safe, scenic route along New Hampshire's seacoast is the bike path along Route 1A, for which you can park at Odiorne Point and follow the road 14 mi south to Seabrook. Some bikers begin at Prescott Park and take Route 1B into New Castle, but beware of the traffic. Another pretty route is from Newington Town Hall to the Great Bay Estuary. The volume of traffic on the major coastal roads makes cycling dangerous for people unfamiliar with the area: Avoid U.S. 1 and 4 and Route 101. You'll find excellent routes in the White Mountains detailed in the mountain-bike guide map "The White Mountain Ride Guide," sold at area sports and book shops. There's also a bike path in Franconia Notch State Park at the Lafayette Campground and a mountain-biking center, Great Glen Trails, at the base of Mt. Washington. Many ski areas permit summer mountain biking on some trails.

Dining

New Hampshire is home to some of the best seafood in the country, not just lobster but also salmon pie, steamed mussels, fried clams, and seared tuna steaks. Each region has its share of country-French dining rooms and nouveau American kitchens, but the best advice is to eat where the locals do. That can be anywhere from a greasy-spoon diner to an out-of-the-way inn whose chef creates everything—including the butter—from scratch. Restaurants around the lakes and along the seacoast are busy in summer, so always make reservations.

Fishing

Lake trout and salmon swim in Lake Winnipesaukee, trout and bass in smaller lakes, and trout in streams all around the Lakes Region. Alton Bay has an "Ice Out" salmon derby in spring. In winter, ice fishers fish on all the lakes from huts known as "ice bobs." In the Sunapee region, you can fish for brook, rainbow, and lake trout; smallmouth bass; pickerel; and horned pout. The Monadnock region has more than 200 lakes and ponds, most with good fishing for rainbow trout, brown trout, smallmouth and largemouth bass, northern pike, white perch, golden trout, pickerel, and horned pout.

Lodging

In the mid-19th century, wealthy Bostonians would pack up and move to their grand summer homes in the countryside for two- or three-month stretches. Many of these homes have been restored and converted into

New Hampshire

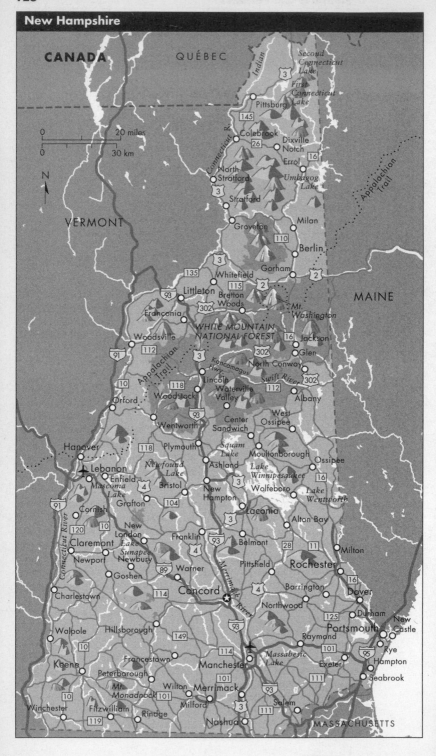

CANADA   QUÉBEC

VERMONT

MAINE

MASSACHUSETTS

Second Connecticut Lake
First Connecticut Lake
Indian R.
Pittsburg
145
Colebrook
26
3
Dixville Notch
Errol
16
North Stratford
Umbagog Lake
3
Stratford
Milan
Groveton
110
Berlin
3
Gorham
135
Whitefield
2
2
115
Littleton
Bretton Woods
93
Franconia
302
Mt. Washington
WHITE MOUNTAIN NATIONAL FOREST
Woodsville
16
Jackson
91
112
302
Glen
3
North Conway
Kancamagus Hwy.
Lincoln
Swift River
302
10
118
Waterville Valley
112
Albany
Orford
Woodstock
93
Wentworth
Center Sandwich
West Ossipee
118
Plymouth
Squam Lake
Moultonborough
Ossipee
Hanover
Newfound Lake
Ashland
Lake Winnipesaukee
16
Lebanon
Enfield
Bristol
New Hampton
Wolfeboro
Lake Wentworth
Mascoma Lake
4
Grafton
3
91
Cornish
104
Laconia
Alton Bay
120
10
New London
Franklin
3
Claremont
Lake Sunapee
Belmont
28
11
Milton
Newport
Newbury
4
89
Goshen
Warner
Pittsfield
Rochester
16
Charlestown
114
Concord
4
Barrington
Dover
Northwood
125
Durham
93
Raymond
Portsmouth
New Castle
Walpole
Hillsborough
149
101
Rye
Francestown
114
Massabesic Lake
Exeter
95
Hampton
Keene
10
Manchester
111
Seabrook
Peterborough
101
Merrimack
Wilton
Mt. Monadnock
101
Milford
93
Salem
10
Winchester
Fitzwilliam
Rindge
3
111
Nashua
119

Connecticut River
Appalachian Trail
Connecticut R.
Merrimack River

0   20 miles
0   30 km
N

country inns. The smallest have only a couple of rooms; typically, they're done in period style. The largest contain 30 or more rooms, with private baths, fireplaces, and even hot tubs. A few of the grand old resorts still stand, with their world-class cooking staffs and tradition of top-notch service. In Manchester and Concord, as well as along major highways, chain hotels and motels dominate the lodging scene.

National and State Parks and Forests

Parklands vary widely, even within a region. The White Mountain National Forest covers 770,000 acres in northern New Hampshire. Major recreation parks are at Franconia Notch, Crawford Notch, and Mt. Sunapee. Rhododendron State Park, in Fitzwilliam in the Monadnock Region, has a singular collection of wild rhododendrons. Mt. Washington Park is on top of the highest mountain in the Northeast. Twenty-three state recreation areas offer camping, picnicking, hiking, boating, fishing, swimming, biking, and winter sports.

Shopping

Outside the state's outlet meccas of North Conway and Tilton, shopping revolves around antiques and local crafts, which are plentiful and generally high in quality. In the southern end of the Lakes Region and in Hampton Beach, shops and boutiques are all geared to summer tourists—the wares tend toward T-shirts and tacky trinkets. Many close from late October to mid-April. Summertime fairs, such as the one operated by the League of New Hampshire Craftsmen at Mt. Sunapee State Park, offer another way to see some of the state's best arts and crafts. Signs on roads throughout the state mark the locations of antiques shops, galleries, and open studios.

The densest clusters of antiques shops are along U.S. 4, between Route 125 and Concord; along Route 119, from Fitzwilliam to Hinsdale; along Route 101, from Marlborough to Wilton; and in the towns of North Conway, North Hampton, Hopkinton, Hollis, and Amherst. In the Lakes Region, most shops are along the eastern side of Winnipesaukee, near Wolfeboro and around Ossipee. Particularly in the Monadnock region, stores in barns and homes along back roads are "open by chance or by appointment." And don't ignore the summer flea markets and yard sales—deals are just waiting to happen.

Skiing and Snow Sports

Scandinavian settlers who came to New Hampshire's high, handsome, rugged peaks in the late 1800s brought their skis with them. Skiing got its modern start in the Granite State in the 1920s with the cutting of trails on Cannon Mountain; you can now ski or snowboard at nearly 20 areas, from the old, established slopes (Cannon, Cranmore, Wildcat) to more contemporary ones (Attitash, Loon, Waterville Valley). Promotional packages assembled by the ski areas allow you to sample different resorts. There's Ski 93 (referring to resorts along I-93), Ski the Mt. Washington Valley, and more.

Exploring New Hampshire

New Hampshire can be divided into four regions. The main attraction of the coast is historic Portsmouth. Inland a bit is Exeter, home of the eponymous prep school. The Lakes Region, in the east-central part of New Hampshire, has good restaurants, hiking trails, antiques shops, and, of course, water sports. People go to the White Mountains in the state's north to hike, ski, and photograph vistas and vibrant foliage. Western New Hampshire is the unspoiled heart of the state, although that beauty is bounded by the central corridor of fast-growing cities and towns along I-93.

Numbers in the text and in the margin correspond to numbers on the maps: New Hampshire Coast, New Hampshire Lakes, The White Mountains, Dartmouth–Lake Sunapee, and Monadnock Region and Central New Hampshire.

Great Itineraries

Some people come to New Hampshire to pursue a favorite sport: hiking or skiing the mountains, fishing or boating on the lakes, biking the back roads. Others prefer to drive, wandering through scenic towns and stopping to visit museums or shop for local treasures. Although New Hampshire is a small state, roads have to go around lakes and mountains, making distances longer than they appear. You can get a taste of the coast, lake, and mountain areas of the state in three to five days or so; a little more than a week gives you time to do a good loop of a number of areas around the state.

IF YOU HAVE 3 DAYS

Drive along Route 1A to see the coastline or take a boat tour of the Isles of Shoals before exploring ⊞ **Portsmouth** ⑧. On the next day, visit Lake Winnipesaukee. ⊞ **Wolfeboro** ㉑, on the eastern edge of the lake, makes a good overnight stop. On the following day, drive across the scenic Kancamagus Highway from Conway to **Lincoln** ㉕ to see the granite ledges and mountain streams for which the White Mountains are famous. Interstate 93 will take you to Route 101, on which you can return to Portsmouth or head straight south to Massachusetts.

IF YOU HAVE 5 DAYS

After visiting ⊞ **Portsmouth** ⑧ and ⊞ **Wolfeboro** ㉑, explore Squam and Ossipee lakes and the charming towns that surround them: **Moultonborough** ⑲, **Center Harbor** ⑯, and **Tamworth** ⑳. Spend your third night in the White Mountain town of ⊞ **Jackson** ㉘, which is equally beautiful in the winter, when cross-country skiing is popular, and in the summer, when hiking is the main activity. After crossing the Kancamagus Highway to **Lincoln** ㉕, tour the western part of the White Mountain National Forest by following Route 112 to Route 118. Take Route 25A and then follow Route 10 south through the upper Connecticut River valley. ⊞ **Hanover** ㊷, home of Dartmouth College, is a good overnight stop. Interstate 89 will bring you back to I–93 via **Newbury** ㊵ and the Lake Sunapee region.

IF YOU HAVE 8 DAYS

If you spend two nights in ⊞ **Portsmouth** ⑧, you'll have time to visit Strawbery Banke Museum and soak up more of the city's restaurant and cultural scene. After exploring ⊞ **Wolfeboro** ㉑ and ⊞ **Jackson** ㉘, continue north on Route 16 through Pinkham Notch to Mt. Washington, where you can hike or drive to the top. Return via U.S. 302 and U.S. 3 to ⊞ **Franconia** ㉞ and Franconia Notch State Park. Drive along Route 112 to Route 118 and take Route 25A; follow Route 10 south through the upper Connecticut River valley, where the scenery is straight out of Currier & Ives. Stop by ⊞ **Hanover** ㊷ and the Shaker Community at **Enfield** ㊶; then take either Route 12A along the Connecticut River or Route 10 south to ⊞ **Keene** ㊻. Route 119 East leads to Rhododendron State Park in **Fitzwilliam** ㊼. Continue east along Route 101 to return to the coast.

When to Tour New Hampshire

New Hampshire is a year-round destination. In summer, people flock to seaside beaches, mountain hiking trails, and lake boat ramps. In the cities, festivals bring music and theater to the forefront. Fall brings leaf-peepers, especially to the White Mountains and along the Kancamagus Highway. Skiers take to the slopes in winter, when Christmas lights and carnivals brighten the long, dark nights. April's mud season, the black fly season in late May, and unpredictable weather keep visitor numbers low in spring, but the season has its joys, not the least of which is the appearance of New Hampshire's state flower, the purple lilac, from mid-May to early June.

THE COAST

The first VIP to vacation on the New Hampshire coast was George Washington, in 1789. By all accounts he had a good time, though a bizarre fishing accident left him with a nasty black eye. Accompanied as he was by 14 generals (all in full dress uniform), he probably didn't walk barefoot along the area's sandy beaches or picnic at Odiorne Point, though he may have visited the homes of John Paul Jones and John Langdon, both of which still stand.

A visit to the coast can take an afternoon or several days. This section begins with Exeter, the first state capital; follows the coast to Portsmouth; and circles inland along the rivers to Newington and Durham.

Exeter

❶ *8 mi north of the Massachusetts border, 11 mi southwest of Portsmouth, 47 mi southeast of Concord.*

Exeter's first settlers built their homes in 1638 around the falls where the freshwater Exeter River meets the salty Squamscott. During the Revolutionary War, Exeter was the state capital, and it was here that the first state constitution and the first Declaration of Independence from Great Britain were put to paper. Phillips Exeter Academy, which opened in 1783, is still one of the nation's most- esteemed prep schools.

The **American Independence Museum,** adjacent to Phillips Exeter Academy in the Ladd-Gilman House, celebrates the birth of our nation. The story of the Revolution unfolds during each guided tour, on which you'll see drafts of the U.S. Constitution and the first Purple Heart. ⊠ *1 Governor's La.,* ☎ *603/772–2622.* ⊠ *$4.* ☉ *May–Oct., Wed.– Sun. noon–5 (last tour at 4).*

Dining and Lodging

$$ ✕ **Vincent's String Bridge Cafe.** Vincent's creates veal scallopini, chicken marsala, and other Italian dishes in the heart of town. Many specials, like the shrimp in a garlic sherry sauce, incorporate fresh local ingredients. For lunch, try soup or a salad with a loaf of bread still warm from the oven. ⊠ *69 Water St.,* ☎ *603/778–8219. AE, D, MC, V.*

$ ✕ **Loaf and Ladle.** Hearty chowders, soups, and stews and huge sandwiches on homemade bread are served cafeteria-style at this understated eatery. Check the blackboard for the ever-changing rotation of chef's specials, breads, and desserts, and don't miss the fresh salad bar. Overlooking the river, the café is handy to the shops, galleries, and historic houses along Water Street. ⊠ *9 Water St.,* ☎ *603/778–8955. Reservations not accepted. AE, D, DC, MC, V.*

$$–$$$ ✕🏨 **Exeter Inn.** This brick Georgian-style inn on the campus of Phillips Exeter Academy has been the choice of visiting parents for the past half century. It is furnished with antique and reproduction pieces and possesses every modern amenity. Among the specialties at the Terrace Restaurant are a fillet of salmon wrapped in a pastry crust and stuffed with wild mushrooms and onions, and a napoleon of grilled vegetables with layers of Boursin cheese. On Sunday, the line forms early for a brunch with more than 40 options. ⊠ *90 Front St., 03833,* ☎ *603/*

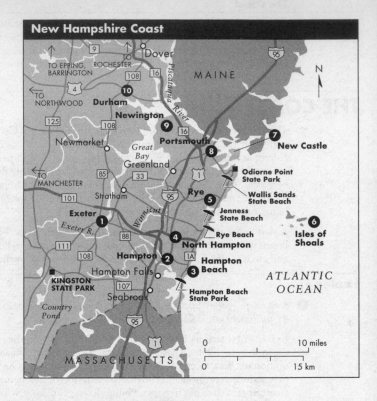

New Hampshire Coast

772–5901 or 800/782–8444, FAX 603/778–8757. 47 rooms. Restaurant, meeting rooms. AE, D, DC, MC, V.

$$–$$$$ ☒ **Inn by the Bandstand.** Common rooms in this 1809 Federal town house, which is listed on the National Register of Historic Places, are decorated in period style. Seven guest rooms have working fireplaces; some have whirlpool baths, too. After a day of sightseeing, you can relax with a glass of the complimentary sherry found in each room. ☒ 4 Front St., 03833, ☎ 603/772–6352, FAX 603/778–0212. 7 rooms, 2 suites. Continental breakfast. AE, D, MC, V.

$ △ **Exeter Elms Family Campground.** This campground has 200 sites (some riverfront), a swimming pool, a playground, canoes for rent, and a recreation program. ☒ 188 Court St., 03833, ☎ 603/778–7631. MC, V. Closed mid-Sept.–mid-May.

Shopping

The shop of the **Exeter League of New Hampshire Craftsmen** (☒ 61 Water St., ☎ 603/778–8282) carries original jewelry, woodworking, and pottery. **A Picture's Worth a Thousand Words** (☒ 65 Water St., ☎ 603/778–1991) stocks antique and contemporary prints, old maps, town histories, and rare books. **Starlight Express** (☒ 103 Water St., ☎ 603/ 772–9477) sells clocks with elaborate hand-painted faces, picture frames, candles, and other accessories for the house. **Water Street Artisans** (☒ 20 Water St., ☎ 603/778–6178) carries fine crafts.

Hampton

② 5 mi east of Exeter, 12 mi south of Portsmouth.

One of New Hampshire's first towns, Hampton was settled in 1638. Its name in the 17th century was Winnacunnet, which means "beautiful place of pines." The center of the early town was **Meeting House Green,** where 42 stones represent the founding families.

Tuck Museum, across from Meeting House Green, contains displays on the town's early history. ✉ *40 Park Ave.,* ☎ *603/929–0781; 603/ 926–2543 for appointments.* 🎟 *Free.* ☉ *June–Sept., Wed.–Fri. and Sun. 1–4 PM; and by appointment.*

At **Applecrest Farm Orchards,** you can pick your own apples and berries or buy fresh fruit pies and cookies from the bakery. Fall brings cider pressing, hay rides, pumpkins, and music on weekends. In winter you can follow a cross-country ski trail through the orchard. ✉ *Rte. 88, Hampton Falls,* ☎ *603/926–3721.* ☉ *Daily 8 AM–dusk.*

The **Raspberry Farm** has pick-your-own raspberries, strawberries, blueberries, blackberries, and other berries. The shop sells fresh- baked goods, jams, and sauces. ✉ *3 mi inland on Rte. 84, Hampton Falls,* ☎ *603/926–6604.* ☉ *Early June–late Oct., weekdays noon–5, weekends 9–5. Call for picking conditions.*

☾ At the **Seabrook Science & Nature Center,** adjacent to the Seabrook Station nuclear power plant 4 mi south of Hampton, you can tour exhibits on the science of power, see control-room operators in training, walk through a replica of a cooling tunnel, pedal a bike to create electricity, and use interactive computer games that further explain nuclear power. The center maintains the ¾-mi Owascoag nature trail, a touch pool for kids, and several large aquariums of local sea life. ✉ *Lafayette Rd., Seabrook,* ☎ *800/338–7482.* 🎟 *Free.* ☉ *Weekdays 10–4.*

Lodging

$$ 🏨 **Hampton Falls Inn.** Intricate Burmese wall hangings and leather furniture decorate the lobby of this modern motel only a few minutes from Hampton Beach. The rooms are typical of those in chain motels, but many have a view of the neighboring farm; all have microwave ovens. An enclosed porch by the indoor pool looks out over the woods and fields. ✉ *11 Lafayette Rd./U.S. 1, 03844,* ☎ *603/926–9545,* 🖷 *603/ 926–4155. 33 rooms, 15 suites. Restaurant (no dinner), refrigerators, indoor pool, meeting rooms. AE, D, DC, MC, V.*

$$ 🏨 **Victoria Inn.** Built as a carriage house in 1875, this romantic bed-and-breakfast is done in the style Victorians loved best: wicker, chandeliers, and lace. One room is completely lilac; the honeymoon suite has white eyelet coverlets and a private sunroom. Innkeepers Nickie Fuller and Jason Bolduc have named one room in honor of President Franklin Pierce, who for years summered in the home next door. ✉ *430 High St. (½ mi from Hampton Beach), 03842,* ☎ *603/929–1437. 6 rooms, 3 with bath. Full breakfast. MC, V.*

$ 🏨 **Curtis Field House.** This Cape-style B&B decorated with Federal-era antiques and some reproductions occupies 10 acres between Exeter and Hampton and is only 1½ mi from I–95. Guest rooms have four-poster beds, comfortable chairs, and private baths. Relaxing on the sundeck with a good book and enjoying the fragrant gardens are favorite pastimes at this quiet property that's a short drive from Portsmouth and the beaches. ✉ *735 Exeter Rd., 03842,* ☎ *603/929– 0082. 3 rooms. Full breakfast. No credit cards. Closed Nov.–May.*

$ ⛺ **Tidewater Campground.** This camping area has 200 sites, a large playground, a pool, a game room, and a basketball court. ✉ *160 Lafayette Rd., 03842,* ☎ *603/926–5474. MC, V. Closed mid-Oct.–mid-May.*

Nightlife and the Arts

From July to September, the **Hampton Playhouse** (✉ 357 Winnacunnet Rd./Rte. 101E, ☎ 603/926–3073) brings familiar Hollywood movie and New York theater actors to the coast. Performances are held in the evening except on Monday, with matinees on Wednesday and

Friday; children's shows take place on Saturday at 11 and 2. Schedules and tickets are available at the box office or at the Chamber of
Commerce Seashell on Ocean Boulevard in Hampton Beach.

Shopping

Antiques shops line U.S. 1 (Lafayette Rd.) in Hampton and neighboring Hampton Falls. The more than 50 dealers at **Antiques at Hampton Falls** (☎ 603/926–1971) have all types of antiques and collectibles.
Antiques New Hampshire (☎ 603/926–9603) is a group shop with 35
dealers. **Antiques One** (☎ 603/926–5332) carries everything but furniture, including books and maps. The **Barn at Hampton Falls** (☎ 603/
926–9003) is known for American and European furniture.

Hampton Beach

❸ *2 mi east of Hampton, 14 mi south of Portsmouth.*

An estimated 150,000 people visit Hampton Beach on the Fourth of
July, and it draws plenty of people until late September, when things
close up. If you like fried dough, loud music, arcade games, palm readers, parasailing, and bronzed bodies, don't miss it. The 3-mi boardwalk, where kids can play games and see how saltwater taffy is made,
looks as if it was snatched out of the 1940s. Free outdoor concerts are
held on many evenings in summer, and once a week there's a fireworks
display. Talent shows and karaoke performances take place in the
Seashell Stage, right on the beach.

Each summer locals hold a children's festival in August and celebrate
the end of the season with a huge seafood feast on the weekend after
Labor Day. For a quieter time, stop by for a sunrise stroll, when only
seagulls and the odd jogger interrupt the serenity.

Dining and Lodging

$$–$$$$ ✕ **Ron's Landing at Rocky Bend.** Nestled in among the souvenir shops
and motels is this casually elegant restaurant that prepares fresh
seafood, pasta, beef, and veal dishes. Specialties include smoked Vir-
ginia oysters and filet mignon topped with fresh horseradish sauce and
served with Alaskan king crab legs. In summer, dine on the second-
floor screened porch, which has a sweeping view of the Atlantic. ⊠
379 Ocean Blvd., ☎ *603/929–2122. AE, D, DC, MC, V.*

$$$–$$$$ ✕🏨 **Ashworth by the Sea.** This family-owned hotel was built across
the street from Hampton Beach in 1912; most rooms have private decks,
and the furnishings vary from period to contemporary. The beachside
rooms have breathtaking ocean views. The others look out onto the
pool or the quiet street. The Ashworth Dining Room ($$–$$$) serves
steaks, poultry, and fresh seafood—including seven variations on lob-
ster. ⊠ *295 Ocean Blvd., 03842,* ☎ *603/926–6762 or 800/345–6736,*
FAX *603/926–2002. 105 rooms. 3 restaurants, in-room data ports, pool,
gift shop. AE, D, DC, MC, V.*

$$–$$$ 🏨 **Oceanside Inn.** The square front and simple awnings of this ocean-
front inn look much the same as those on all the other buildings lin-
ing Ocean Boulevard. Inside, though, is a hidden treasure. Carefully
selected antiques and collectibles, individually decorated rooms, a cozy
living room and library with a fireplace, and a second-floor veranda
for watching the waves give the Oceanside the feel of a late-19th-cen-
tury home. Should the resort's crush of people and noise begin to
overwhelm, you'll appreciate the soundproofing that makes this inn
seem like a calm port in a storm. ⊠ *365 Ocean Blvd., 03842,* ☎ *603/
926–3542,* FAX *603/926–3549. 10 rooms. Refrigerators, in-room safes.
Full breakfast. AE, D, MC, V. Closed mid-Oct.–mid-May.*

Nightlife and the Arts

The **Hampton Beach Casino Ballroom** (✉ 169 Ocean Beach Blvd., ☎ 603/926–4541; 603/929–4201 for event hot line) books name entertainment from April to October. Tina Turner, the Monkees, Jay Leno, and Loretta Lynn have all played here. Note that this is a performance venue, not a gambling casino.

North Hampton

4 *3 mi north of Hampton, 11 mi southwest of Portsmouth.*

Factory outlets along U.S. 1 coexist in North Hampton with mansions lining the ocean along Route 1A.

Fuller Gardens, a turn-of-the-century estate garden designed in the Colonial Revival style by Arthur Shurtleff, has a 1930s addition by the Olmsted brothers. It blooms all summer long and has 2,000 rosebushes of every shade and type. Other plantings include a hosta display garden and a serenity-inspiring Japanese garden. ✉ *10 Willow Ave.,* ☎ *603/964–5414.* ⊠ *$4.50.* ⊙ *Early May–mid-Oct., daily 10–6.*

Shopping

The **North Hampton Factory Outlet Center** (✉ Lafayette Rd./U.S. 1, ☎ 603/964–9050) has tax-free goods and discounts on brand names like Famous Footwear and American Tourister. Among the center's stores are the Paper Factory, the Sports Outpost, and Bass.

En Route On Route 1A as it winds through North Hampton and Rye sits a group of mansions known as **Millionaires' Row.** Because of the way the road curves, the drive south along this route is even more breathtaking than the drive north.

Rye

5 *5 mi north of North Hampton, 6 mi south of Portsmouth.*

In 1623 the first European settlers landed at Odiorne Point in what is now Rye, making it the birthplace of New Hampshire. The main reasons for visiting the area are a lovely state park, oceanfront beaches, and the view from Route 1A.

★ ☾ **Odiorne Point State Park** and the **Seacoast Science Center** encompass more than 350 acres of protected land. You can pick up an interpretive brochure on any of the nature trails or simply stroll and enjoy the vistas of the nearby Isles of Shoals. The tidal pools, considered the best in New England, shelter crabs, periwinkles, and sea anemones. The science center conducts guided nature walks and interpretive programs, has exhibits on the area's natural history, and traces the social history of Odiorne Point back to the Ice Age. Kids love the tide-pool touch tank and the 1,000-gallon Gulf of Maine deepwater aquarium. ✉ *Rte. 1A north of Wallis Sands State Beach,* ☎ *603/436–8043.* ⊠ *Science Center $1; park in summer, fall, and on weekends $2.50.* ⊙ *Daily 10–5.*

Good for swimming and sunning, **Jenness State Beach,** on Route 1A, is a favorite with locals. The facilities include a bathhouse, lifeguards, and parking. **Wallis Sands State Beach,** on Route 1A, is a swimmers' beach with bright white sand and a bathhouse. Parking is ample and costs $8 on weekends, $5 weekdays.

Lodging

$$ ☷ **Rock Ledge Manor.** Built out on a point, this mid-19th-century summer house with a wraparound porch was part of a resort colony and predates the houses along Millionaires' Row. All rooms have water views. Owners Stan and Sandi Smith serve breakfast in the *sunny dining room overlooking the Atlantic. This no-smoking B&B has a two-night minimum on weekends and holidays. ⊠ 1413 Ocean Blvd./Rte. 1A, 03870, ☎ 603/431–1413. 2 rooms with bath, 2 rooms with half bath and shared shower. Full breakfast. No credit cards.*

Isles of Shoals

❻ *10 mi off the coast.*

The Isles of Shoals are nine small islands (eight at high tide). Many, like Hog Island, Smuttynose, and Star Island, retain the earthy names given them by the transient fishers who visited in the early 17th century. A colorful history of piracy, murder, and ghosts surrounds the archipelago, long populated by an independent lot who, according to one writer, hadn't the sense to winter on the mainland. Not all the islands lie within the New Hampshire border: After an ownership dispute between Maine and New Hampshire, they were divvied up between the two states (five went to Maine, four to New Hampshire).

Celia Thaxter, a native islander, romanticized these islands with her poetry in *Among the Isles of Shoals* (1873) and celebrated her garden in *An Island Garden* (1894; now reissued with the original illustrations by Childe Hassam, who loved the island). In the late 19th century, **Appledore Island** became an offshore retreat for her coterie of writers, musicians, and artists. The island is now used by the Marine Laboratory of Cornell University. **Star Island** contains a nondenominational conference center and is open to those on guided tours. For information about visiting the Isles of Shoals, *see* Guided Tours *in* The Coast A to Z, *below.*

New Castle

❼ *5 mi north of Rye, 1 mi south of Portsmouth.*

Though it consists of a single square mile of land, the small island of New Castle was once known as Great Island. The narrow roads lined with pre-Revolutionary houses make the island, which is accessible from the mainland by car, perfect for a stroll.

Wentworth by the Sea, the last of the great seaside resorts, is impossible to miss as you approach New Castle on Route 1B. Empty these days, it was the site of the signing of the Russo-Japanese Treaty in 1905, a fact that attracts many Japanese tourists. Because the current owners and the town have been unable to come to agreement on a restoration and redevelopment plan, this grand old hotel may be torn down.

Ft. Constitution was originally Ft. William and Mary, a British stronghold overlooking Portsmouth Harbor. Rebel patriots raided the fort in 1774 in one of revolutionary America's first overt acts of defiance against King George III. The rebels later used the captured munitions against the British at the Battle of Bunker Hill. Panels throughout the fort explain its history. ⊠ *Rte. 1B at the Coast Guard Station,* ☎ *no phone.* ☒ *$2.50.* ☉ *Mid-June–Labor Day, daily 9–5; Labor Day–mid-June, weekends 9–5.*

Lodging

$$ ⊞ **Great Islander Bed & Breakfast.** This charming 1740 Colonial faces New Castle's Main Street and has a view of the water from the deck by the lap pool in back. Wide pine floors and exposed beams recall the pre-Revolutionary era. Antiques, quilts, and reproduction floral-patterned wallpapers decorate the rooms of this no-smoking B&B. ⊠ *Box 135, 62 Main St., 03854-0135,* ☎ *603/436–8536. 3 rooms, 1 with bath. Fans, lap pool. Continental breakfast. MC, V.*

Portsmouth

★ ❽ *1 mi north of New Castle, 45 mi southeast of Concord.*

Originally settled in 1623 as Strawbery Banke, Portsmouth became a prosperous port before the Revolutionary War. The cultural epicenter of the coast, it contains some notable museums (including the collection of buildings that make up Strawbery Banke), restaurants of every stripe, plus theaters, music venues, and art galleries. Most of these attractions are in and around Market Square in the heart of the city.

The **Portsmouth Trail** passes many pre–Revolutionary War homes in the historic district. The trail breaks the city into three sections that can be explored separately or together. The walking trail can be enjoyed year-round; six houses along the way are open to visitors in summer and fall. Purchase a tour map at the information kiosk on Market Square, the Chamber of Commerce, or any of the houses.

The yellow, hip-roof **John Paul Jones House** was a boardinghouse when Jones lived here while supervising the outfitting of two ships for the Continental Navy. The 1758 structure, the headquarters of the **Portsmouth Historical Society,** contains costumes, glass, guns, portraits, and documents of the late 18th century. ⊠ *43 Middle St.,* ☎ *603/436–8420.* ▦ *$5.* ☉ *Memorial Day–mid-Oct., Mon.–Sat. 10–4, Sun. noon–4.*

Lining the hall staircase of the 1716 **Warner House** are the oldest-known wall murals still in place in the country. ⊠ *150 Daniel St.,* ☎ *603/436– 5909.* ▦ *$5.* ☉ *June–mid-Oct., Mon.–Sat. 10–4, Sun. 1–4.*

The **Moffatt-Ladd House,** built in 1763, tells the story of Portsmouth's merchant class through portraits, letters, and fine furnishings. ⊠ *154 Market St.,* ☎ *603/436–8221.* ▦ *$5.* ☉ *June–mid-Oct., Mon.–Sat. 10– 4, Sun. 2–5.*

★ The first English settlers named the area around what's now called Portsmouth for the abundant wild strawberries they found along the shore of the Piscataqua River. The city's largest museum, **Strawbery Banke Museum,** now uses the name: This 10-acre outdoor museum with period gardens, exhibits, and craftspeople holds 46 buildings that date from 1695 to 1820. Ten furnished homes represent 300 years of history in one continuously occupied neighborhood. The **Drisco House,** built in 1795, was first used as a dry-goods store, and half the house still depicts this history; the living room and kitchen, on the other hand, are decorated just as they were in the 1950s. The **Shapiro House** has been restored to reflect the life of the Russian Jewish immigrant family who lived in the home in the early 1900s. Perhaps the most opulent house is the 1860 **Goodwin Mansion,** former home of Governor Ichabod Goodwin. It is decorated in plush Victorian style. ⊠ *Marcy St.,* ☎ *603/433– 1100 or 603/433–1106.* ▦ *$12 pass for 2 consecutive days.* ☉ *Mid-Apr.–Oct., daily 10–5; 1st 2 weekends in Dec., 4:30–9:30.*

Picnicking is popular in **Prescott Park,** on the waterfront between Strawbery Banke Museum and the Piscataqua River. A large formal garden with fountains is perfect for whiling away an afternoon. The park also contains **Point of Graves,** Portsmouth's oldest burial ground, and two warehouses that date from the early 17th century. The **Sheafe Museum** was the warehouse where John Paul Jones outfitted the USS *Ranger,* one of the U.S. Navy's earliest ships. The Strawbery Banke Museum (☞ *above*) gives boatbuilding demonstrations here. ⊠ *Marcy St.,* ☎ *603/431–1101.* ☉ *Call for hrs and events.*

Ⓒ Nineteen hands-on exhibits at the **Children's Museum of Portsmouth** explore lobstering, sound and music, computers, space travel, and other subjects. Some programs require reservations. ⊠ *280 Marcy St.,* ☎ *603/436–3853.* ⊡ *$4.* ⊙ *Tues.–Sat. 10–5, Sun. 1–5; also Mon. 10–5 in summer and during school vacations.*

The **Wentworth-Coolidge Mansion,** a National Historic Landmark, was originally the residence of Benning Wentworth, New Hampshire's first Royal Governor (1753–1770). Notable among the period furnishings in the house is the carved pine mantelpiece in the council chamber. Wentworth's imported lilac trees, believed to be the oldest in North America, bloom each May. Lectures and exhibits are presented in the visitor center. ⊠ *Little Harbor Rd., near South Street Cemetery,* ☎ *603/436–6607.* ⊡ *$2.50.* ⊙ *June–Oct., Tues.–Sat. 10–3, Sun. 1–5.*

Docked at the **Port of Portsmouth Maritime Museum** in Albacore Park is the USS *Albacore,* built here in 1953. You can board this prototype submarine, which was a floating laboratory assigned to test a new hull design, dive brakes, and sonar systems for the navy. The nearby **Memorial Garden** and its reflecting pool are dedicated to those who lost their lives in submarine service. ⊠ *600 Market St.,* ☎ *603/436–3680.* ⊡ *$4.* ⊙ *May–Columbus Day, daily 9:30–5:30; Columbus Day–Apr., Thurs.–Mon. 9:30–4.*

The **Redhook Ale Brewery,** visible from the Spaulding Turnpike, conducts tours that end with a beer tasting. If you don't have time to tour, you can stop in the Cataqua Public House to sample the fresh ales and have a bite to eat. ⊠ *Pease International Tradeport, 35 Corporate Dr.,* ☎ *603/430–8600.* ⊡ *$1.* ⊙ *Call for tour times.*

Dining and Lodging

$$$ ✕ **Dunfey's Aboard the *John Wanamaker.*** Portsmouth's floating restaurant, aboard a restored tugboat, prepares delicacies like shiitake-encrusted halibut with wild-mushroom ravioli and Black Angus beef with garlic mashed potatoes. You can watch the river from the bar, enjoy the bistro-like atmosphere of the main dining room, or relax in the romantic Captain's Room. The upper-level deck is a favorite on starry summer nights for light meals, a glass of wine, or dessert and cappuccino. ⊠ *1 Harbour Pl.,* ☎ *603/433–3111. Reservations essential on weekends. AE, MC, V.*

$$–$$$ ✕ **Blue Mermaid World Grill.** The chefs at Blue Mermaid prepare hot Jamaican-style dishes on a wood-burning grill. Specialties include smoked-scallop chowder and grilled Maine lobster with mango butter. In summer you can eat on a deck that overlooks the 13 historic houses collectively known as the Hill. Entertainers perform (outdoors in summer) on Friday and Saturday. ⊠ *409 Hanover St.,* ☎ *603/427–2583. AE, D, DC, MC, V.*

$$–$$$ ✕ **Library at the Rockingham House.** This Portsmouth landmark was a luxury hotel, but most of the building has been converted to condominiums. The restaurant retains the original atmosphere, though, with hand-carved mahogany paneling and bookcases on every wall. The food also seems to belong in a social club of another century: Don't miss the grilled rack of lamb with a port wine and rosemary *demi-glace* (sauce) or the filet mignon with béarnaise sauce. The waitstaff presents the check between the pages of a vintage best-seller. ⊠ *401 State St.,* ☎ *603/431–5202. Reservations essential. AE, DC, MC, V.*

$$–$$$ ✕ **Muddy River Smokehouse.** Red-check tablecloths and wall murals of trees and meadows make this restaurant look like an outdoor summer barbecue joint—even when the weather turns cold. Roll up your sleeves and dig into platters of ribs, homemade corn bread, and molasses baked beans. Chicken, steak, and other dishes are on the menu, but the signature dish is hickory-smoked St. Louis ribs. ⊠ *21 Congress St.,* ☎ *603/430–9582. AE, MC, V.*

$$–$$$ ✕ **Porto Bello Ristorante Italiano.** This family-run restaurant has
★ brought the tastes of Naples to downtown Portsmouth. In the second-
story dining room overlooking the harbor, you can savor daily antipasto
specials ranging from grilled calamari to stuffed baby eggplant. Pastas include spinach gnocchi and homemade ravioli. A house specialty
is veal *carciofi*—a 6-ounce cutlet served with artichokes. The tastes are
so pure and the ingredients so fresh that you won't have trouble fin-
ishing four courses. ✉ *67 Bow St., 2nd floor,* ☎ *603/431–2989. Reservations essential. AE, D, MC, V. Closed Mon.–Tues.*

$$$ ✕⊞ **Sheraton Harborside Portsmouth Hotel.** Portsmouth's only lux-
ury hotel, this five-story redbrick building is within easy walking dis-
tance of shops and attractions. Suites have full kitchens and living rooms.
The main restaurant, Harbor's Edge ($$$–$$$$), serves fresh seafood
and American cuisine. The Krewe Orleans restaurant and bar dishes
up Cajun specialties. ✉ *250 Market St., 03801,* ☎ *603/431–2300 or
800/325–3535,* FAX *603/433–5649. 181 rooms, 24 suites. 2 restau-
rants, bar, indoor pool, sauna, exercise room, nightclub, meeting
rooms. AE, D, DC, MC, V.*

$$$–$$$$ ⊞ **Sise Inn.** Each room at this Queen Anne town house in Portsmouth's
★ historic district is decorated in Victorian style, with special fabrics, an-
tiques, and reproductions of antiques. Some rooms have whirlpool baths.
The no-smoking inn is close to the Market Square shopping area and
within walking distance of the theater district and several restaurants.
✉ *40 Court St., 03801,* ☎ FAX *603/433–1200 or* ☎ *800/267–0525.
26 rooms, 8 suites. In-room VCRs, meeting rooms. Continental break-
fast. AE, DC, MC, V.*

$$ ⊞ **Martin Hill Inn.** Two buildings downtown hold a charming inn
that's within walking distance of the historic district and the water-
front. Extensive perennial gardens enhance the B&B. The quiet rooms,
comfortably furnished with antiques, are decorated in formal Colonial or country-Victorian style. The Greenhouse suite has a private solarium facing the water garden. The inn is no-smoking. ✉ *404 Islington
St.,* ☎ *603/436–2287. 4 rooms, 3 suites. Full breakfast. MC, V.*

Nightlife and the Arts

NIGHTLIFE

The **Portsmouth Gas Light Co.** (✉ 64 Market St., ☎ 603/430–9122)
is a popular brick-oven pizzeria and restaurant by day. On summer nights,
the management opens up the back courtyard, brings in local rock bands,
and serves a special punch in plastic sand pails. By midnight, the three-
story parking garage next door has become a makeshift auditorium.
People come from as far away as Boston and Portland to hang out at
the **Press Room** (✉ 77 Daniel St., ☎ 603/431–5186), which showcases
folk, jazz, blues, and bluegrass performers.

THE ARTS

The **Prescott Park Arts Festival** (✉ 105 Marcy St., ☎ 603/436–2848)
presents theater, dance, and musical events outdoors during June, July,
and August.

Beloved for its acoustics, the 1878 **Music Hall** (✉ 28 Chestnut St., ☎
603/436–2400, film line 603/436–9900) brings the best touring events
to the seacoast—from classical and pop concerts to dance and theater.
The hall also hosts an ongoing art-house film series. The **Player's Ring**
(✉ 105 Marcy St., ☎ 603/436–8123) highlights original plays and performances by local theater groups from September through May. The
Pontine Movement Theater (✉ 135 McDonough St., ☎ 603/436–
6660) presents dance performances in a renovated warehouse. The **Seacoast Repertory Theatre** (✉ 125 Bow St., ☎ 603/433–4472 or 800/

639–7650) offers a year-round schedule of musicals, classic dramas, and works by up-and-coming playwrights.

Outdoor Activities and Sports

Portsmouth doesn't have any beaches, but the **Seacoast Trolley** departs from Market Square on the hour, servicing a continuous loop between Portsmouth sights and area beaches (☞ Odiorne Point State Park *and* Wallis Sands State Beach *in* Rye, *above*). You can get a schedule for the trolley, which operates from mid-June to Labor Day, at the information kiosk in Market Square. The **Urban Forestry Center** (✉ 45 Elwyn Rd., ☎ 603/431–6774) has gardens and marked trails appropriate for short hikes on its 180 acres.

Shopping

Market Square, in the center of town, has gift and clothing boutiques, book and card shops, and exquisite crafts stores.

Kumminz Gallery (✉ 65 Daniel St., ☎ 603/433–6488) carries pottery, jewelry, and fiber art by New Hampshire artisans. The **Museum Shop at the Dunaway Store** (✉ 66 Marcy St., ☎ 603/433–1114) stocks quilts, crafts, candy, gifts, postcards, reproduction and contemporary furniture, and books about the area's history. **N. W. Barrett** (✉ 53 Market St., ☎ 603/431–4262) specializes in leather, jewelry, pottery, and fiber and other art and crafts and sells furniture, including affordable steam-bent oak pieces and one-of-a-kind lamps and rocking chairs. **Pierce Gallery** (✉ 105 Market St., ☎ 603/436–1988) has prints and paintings of the Maine and New Hampshire coasts. The **Portsmouth Bookshop** (✉ 1 Islington St., ☎ 603/433–4406) carries old and rare books and maps. At **Salamandra Glass Studios** (✉ 7 Commercial Alley, ☎ 603/436–1038), you'll find hand-blown glass vases, bowls, and other items. **Tulips** (✉ 19 Market St., ☎ 603/431–9445) specializes in wood crafts and quilts.

Newington

9 *2 mi northwest of Portsmouth.*

With the closing of Pease Air Force Base and the conversion of that space to public lands and private industry, Newington is undergoing a transformation. The region's only malls are here, and from the highway this seems like simply a commercial town. But the original town center, hidden away from the traffic and the malls, retains an old-time New England feel.

Great Bay National Wildlife Refuge preserves one of Newington's greatest assets: its shoreline on the Great Bay Estuary (☞ Off the Beaten Path, *below*). Although not all of the refuge's 1,000 acres are open to the public, two trails for hiking, cross-country skiing, and snowshoeing loop through a section that is home to eagles in winter and herons, white-tail deer, and harbor seals year-round. ✉ *336 Nimble Hill Rd.,* ☎ *603/431–7511.* ▣ *Free.* ☉ *Daily, dawn–dusk.*

Dining

$–$$$ ✕ **Newick's Seafood Restaurant.** Newick's might serve the best lobster roll on the New England coast, but regulars cherish the onion rings, too. This oversize shack serves seafood and atmosphere in heaping portions. Picture windows allow terrific views over Great Bay. ✉ *431 Dover Point Rd., Dover,* ☎ *603/742–3205. AE, D, MC, V.*

Shopping

Country Curtains (✉ Old Beane Farm, 2299 Woodbury Ave., ☎ 603/431–2315) sells curtains, bedding, furniture, and folk art from the catalog company of the same name. The huge and generic **Fox Run Mall**

(✉ Fox Run Rd., ☎ 603/431–5911) houses Filene's, Macy's, JC Penney, Sears, and 100 other stores.

OFF THE
BEATEN PATH

GREAT BAY ESTUARY – Great blue herons, ospreys, and snowy egrets, all of which are especially conspicuous during their spring and fall migrations, can be found among the 4,471 acres of tidal waters, mud flats, and about 48 mi of inland shoreline that compose the Great Bay Estuary. New Hampshire's largest concentration of winter eagles also lives here. Access to the estuary can be tricky and parking is limited, but the Fish and Game Department's **Sandy Point Discovery Center** (✉ Depot Rd. off Rte. 101, Greenland, ☎ 603/778–0015) distributes maps and information and has trails for walking. Nearby towns have recreation areas along the bay. Hikers will find trails at Adam's Point (in Durham) and Great Bay National Wildlife Refuge (☞ Newington, *above*). Canoeists can put in at Chapman's Landing (✉ Rte. 108, Stratham) on the Squamscott River.

Durham

⑩ *7 mi northwest of Newington, 9 mi northwest of Portsmouth.*

Settled in 1635 and home of General John Sullivan, a Revolutionary War hero and three-time New Hampshire governor, Durham was where Sullivan and his band of rebel patriots stored the gunpowder they captured from Ft. William and Mary (☞ New Castle, *above*). Easy access to Great Bay via the Oyster River made Durham a center of maritime activity in the 19th century. Among the lures today are the water, farms that welcome visitors, and the University of New Hampshire, which occupies much of the town's center.

The **Art Gallery** at the University of New Hampshire occasionally exhibits items from a permanent collection of about 1,100 pieces but generally uses its space to host traveling exhibits of contemporary and historic art. Noted items in the collection include 19th-century Japanese woodblock prints and American landscape paintings. ✉ *Paul Creative Arts Center, 30 College Rd.,* ☎ *603/862–3712.* ⌨ *Free.* ☉ *Sept.– May, Mon.–Wed. 10–4, Thurs. 10–8, weekends 1–5.*

Emery Farm sells fruits and vegetables in summer (including pick-your-own raspberries, strawberries, and blueberries), pumpkins in fall, and Christmas trees in December. The farm shop carries breads and pies, as well as local crafts. Children can pet the resident goats, sheep, and other furry critters. ✉ *U.S. 4,* ☎ *603/742–8495.* ☉ *May–Dec., call for hrs.*

Several dozen American bison roam the **Little Bay Buffalo Farm.** The on-site Drowned Valley Trading Post sells bison-related gifts and top-quality bison meat. ✉ *50 Langley Rd.,* ☎ *603/868–3300.* ☉ *Trading Post daily 10–5, observation area daily 9–dusk.*

Dining and Lodging

$$$–$$$$ ✕▥ **Three Chimneys Inn.** This stately yellow Georgian house on more than 3 acres has graced a hill overlooking the Oyster River since 1649. Rooms in the house and the barn, mostly named after plants from the extensive gardens, are decorated with Georgian- and Federal period antiques and reproductions, canopy or four-poster beds with Edwardian bed drapes, and Oriental rugs. Specialties in the Maples dining room include New England mussel salad and roast leg of farm-raised duckling stuffed with veal and pine nuts. The ffrost-Sawyer Tavern serves simpler fare in a cozy setting. The inn is no-smoking. ✉ *17 Newmarket Rd., 03824,* ☎ *603/868–7800 or 888/399–9777,* ℻ *603/868–2964. 25 rooms. 2 restaurants, in-room data ports, meeting rooms. Full breakfast. AE, D, MC, V.*

$$–$$$ ✕ New England Conference Center and Hotel. In a lush wooded area on the campus of the University of New Hampshire, this hotel is large enough to be a full-service conference center but quiet enough to feel like a retreat. The Woods restaurant specializes in American regional cuisine and is a favorite place for Sunday brunch. ⊠ *15 Strafford Ave., 03824,* ☎ *603/862–2801 or 800/590–4334,* FAX *603/862–4897. 115 rooms. 2 restaurants, bar, meeting rooms. AE, DC, MC, V.*

$ Hickory Pond Inn. The rooms at this no-smoking inn have fresh, flowered wallpaper and individualized color schemes. The common areas, spiffy as well, include a charming breakfast room and a reading nook with a woodstove. ⊠ *1 Stagecoach Rd., 03824,* ☎ *603/659–2227 or 800/658–0065,* FAX *603/659–7910. 16 rooms, 14 with bath. 9-hole golf course. Continental breakfast. AE, MC, V.*

Nightlife and the Arts
The **Celebrity Series** (☎ 603/862–3227) at the University of New Hampshire brings music, theater, and dance to Durham. The **UNH Department of Theater and Dance** (☎ 603/862–2919) produces a variety of shows. The University of New Hampshire's **Whittemore Center** (☎ 603/862–4000) hosts everything from Boston Pops concerts to home shows.

Outdoor Activities and Sports
Take a picnic to **Wagon Hill Farm** (⊠ U.S. 4 across from Emery Farm, ☎ no phone), overlooking the Oyster River. The old farm wagon, sitting by itself on the top of a hill, is one of the most photographed spots in New England. Park next to the farmhouse and follow walking trails to the wagon and through the woods to the picnic area by the water. Sledding and cross-country skiing are popular winter activities.

Shopping
Durham's stores tend to cater to college students, but some interesting shops are nearby. **Calef's Country Store** (⊠ Rte. 9, Barrington, ☎ 603/664–2231 or 800/462–2118) stocks gifts and farm products. **Salmon Falls Pottery & Stoneware** (⊠ Oak St. Engine House, Dover, ☎ 603/749–1467 or 800/621–2030) produces handmade, salt-glaze stoneware using a method that was favored by early American potters. Potters are on hand should you want to place a special order or watch them work. **Tuttle's Red Barn** (⊠ Dover Point Rd., Dover, ☎ 603/742–4313) carries jams, pickles, and other farm products.

The Coast A to Z

Arriving and Departing
BY BUS
C&J (☎ 603/431–2424), **Concord Trailways** (☎ 800/639–3317) and **Vermont Transit** (☎ 603/436–0163 or 800/451–3292) provide bus service to New Hampshire's coast from other regions.

BY CAR
The main route to New Hampshire's coast from other states is I–95, which travels from the border with Maine to the border with Massachusetts.

BY PLANE
Manchester Airport (☞ Arriving and Departing *in* New Hampshire A to Z, *below*) is a one-hour drive from the coastal region.

Getting Around
BY BUS
Coast (☎ 603/862–2328) provides limited access to towns in New Hampshire's coastal section.

BY CAR

Coastal Route 1A has views of water, beaches, and summer estates. The more convenient U.S. 1 travels inland. Route 1B tours the island of New Castle. The Spaulding Turnpike (Route 16) and U.S. 4 connect Portsmouth with Dover, Durham, and Rochester. Route 108 links Durham and Exeter. The quick route along the coast is I–95.

Contacts and Resources

EMERGENCIES

New Hampshire State Police (☎ 603/679–3333 or 800/852–3411). **Portsmouth Regional Hospital** (⊠ 333 Borthwick Ave., Portsmouth, ☎ 603/436–5110 or 603/433–4042). **Exeter Hospital** (⊠ 10 Buzzell Ave., Exeter, ☎ 603/778–7311).

FISHING

For information about fishing and licenses, call the **New Hampshire Fish and Game Office** (☎ 603/868–1095).

Between April and October, deep-sea fishermen head out for cod, mackerel, and bluefish. There are rentals and charters aplenty, offering half- and full-day cruises, as well as some night fishing at the Hampton, Portsmouth, Rye, and Seabrook piers. Try **Al Gauron Deep Sea Fishing** (⊠ Hampton Beach, ☎ 603/926–2469), **Atlantic Fishing Fleet** (⊠ Rye Harbor, ☎ 603/964–5220 or 800/942–5364), **Eastman Fishing & Marine** (⊠ Seabrook, ☎ 603/474–3461), and **Smith & Gilmore** (⊠ Hampton Beach, ☎ 603/926–3503).

GUIDED TOURS

Clip-clop your way through Colonial Portsmouth and Strawbery Banke with **Portsmouth Livery Company** (☎ 603/427–0044), which gives narrated horse-and-carriage tours. Look for carriages in Market Square.

The **Isles of Shoals Steamship Company** (⊠ Barker Wharf, 315 Market St., Portsmouth, ☎ 603/431–5500 or 800/441–4620) runs island cruises, river trips, and whale-watching expeditions from May to October. Trips on Great Bay may include foliage excursions and tours of the Little Bay Buffalo Farm in Durham. Captains Matt Brewster and John Hodges host these voyages aboard the M/V *Thomas Laighton,* a replica of a Victorian steamship. Breakfast, lunch, and light snacks are available on board, or you can bring your own. Some trips include a stopover and historic walking tour on Star Island.

New Hampshire Seacoast Cruises (⊠ Rte. 1A, Rye, ☎ 603/964–5545 or 800/964–5545) conducts naturalist-led whale-watching tours and Isles of Shoals cruises aboard the M/V *Granite State* from June to Labor Day out of Rye Harbor State Marina. From May to October, **Portsmouth Harbor Cruises** (⊠ Ceres Street Dock, Portsmouth, ☎ 603/436–8084 or 800/776–0915) operates tours of Portsmouth Harbor, trips to the Isles of Shoals, foliage trips on the Cocheco River, and sunset cruises aboard the M/V *Heritage.*

HIKING

An excellent 1-mi trail reaches the summit of **Blue Job Mountain** (⊠ Crown Point Rd. off Rte. 202A, 1 mi from Rochester), where a fire tower has a good view. The **New Hampshire Division of Parks and Recreation** (☎ 603/271–3254) maintains the Rockingham Recreation Trail, which wends 27 mi from Newfields to Manchester and is open to hikers, bikers, snowmobilers, and cross-country skiers.

24-HOUR PHARMACY

Rite Aid (800 Islington St., Portsmouth, ☎ 603/436–2214).

VISITOR INFORMATION

Exeter Area Chamber of Commerce (⊠ 120 Water St., Exeter 03833, ☎ 603/772–2411). **Greater Dover Chamber of Commerce** (⊠ 299 Central Ave., Dover 03820, ☎ 603/742–2218). **Greater Portsmouth Chamber of Commerce** (⊠ 500 Market St. Ext., Portsmouth 03801, ☎ 603/436–1118). **Hampton Beach Area Chamber of Commerce** (⊠ 836 Lafayette Rd., Hampton 03842, ☎ 603/926–8718).

LAKES REGION

Lake Winnipesaukee, a Native American name for "Smile of the Great Spirit," is the largest of the dozens of lakes scattered across the eastern half of central New Hampshire. With 283 mi of shoreline, it's the largest in the state. Some claim Winnipesaukee has an island for each day of the year, but the total actually falls a tad short: 274.

Unlike Winnipesaukee, which hums with activity all summer long, the more secluded Squam Lake has a dearth of public-access points. Its tranquillity no doubt attracted the producers of *On Golden Pond*; several scenes of the Oscar-winning film were shot here. Nearby Lake Wentworth is named for the first Royal Governor of the state, who, in building his country manor here, established North America's first summer resort.

Well-preserved Colonial and 19th-century villages are among the region's many landmarks, and you'll find hiking trails, good antiques shops, dozens of good restaurants, several golf courses, and myriad water-oriented activities. This section begins with Alton Bay, at Lake Winnipesaukee's southernmost tip, and the area's towns are presented clockwise around the lakes, starting on Route 11.

Alton Bay

⓫ *35 mi northeast of Concord, 41 mi northwest of Portsmouth.*

Neither quiet nor secluded, Lake Winnipesaukee's southern shore is alive with visitors from the moment the first flower blooms until the last maple has shed its leaves. Two mountain ridges hold 7 mi of Winnipesaukee in Alton Bay, the name of both the inlet and the town at its tip. The lake's cruise boats dock here. There's a dance pavilion, along with miniature golf, a public beach, and a Victorian-style bandstand.

Mt. Major, 5 mi north of Alton Bay on Route 11, has a 2½-mi trail with views of Lake Winnipesaukee. At the top is a four-sided stone shelter built in 1925.

Dining

$$$$ ✕ **Crystal Quail.** The tiny (12-seat) Crystal Quail, inside an 18th-century farmhouse, is worth the drive even if you don't like quail. The prix-fixe menu might include saffron-garlic soup, a house pâté, quenelle-stuffed sole, or duck in crisp potato shreds. ⊠ *Pitman Rd., Center Barnstead (12 mi south of Alton Bay),* ☎ *603/269–4151. Reservations essential. No credit cards. BYOB. Closed Mon.–Tues. No lunch.*

Gilford

⓬ *18 mi northwest of Alton Bay, 30 mi northeast of Concord.*

One of the larger public beaches on Lake Winnipesaukee is in Gilford, a resort community. When it was incorporated in 1812, the town asked its oldest resident to name it. A veteran of the Battle of the Guilford Courthouse, in North Carolina, he borrowed that town's name—though apparently he didn't know how to spell it. Quiet and peaceful,

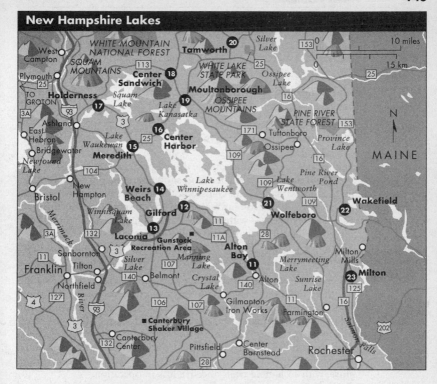

Gilford remains decidedly uncommercial. The **New Hampshire Music Festival** (⊠ 88 Belknap Mountain Rd., ☎ 603/524–1000) presents award-winning orchestras from early July to mid-August.

The **Gunstock Recreation Area** has an Olympic-size pool, a children's playground, hiking trails, mountain-bike rentals and trails, horses, paddleboats, and a campground. A major downhill-skiing center (☞ Skiing and Snow Sports, *below*), it once claimed the longest rope tow lift in the country—an advantage that helped local downhill skier and Olympic silver medalist Penny Pitou perfect her craft. ⊠ *Rte. 11A,* ☎ *603/293–4341 or 800/486–7862.*

Ellacoya State Beach, on Route 11, covers just 600 ft along the southwestern shore of Lake Winnipesaukee, with views of the Ossipee and Sandwich mountain ranges.

Lodging

$$–$$$ 🏨 **B. Mae's Resort Inn.** All the rooms in this resort and conference center are large; some are suites with kitchens. Close to Gunstock ski area and within walking distance of Lake Winnipesaukee, B. Mae's is popular with skiers in winter and boaters in summer. ⊠ *Rtes. 11 and 11B, 03246,* ☎ *603/293–7526 or 800/458–3877,* FAX *603/293–4340. 58 rooms, 24 suites. 2 restaurants, bar, 1 indoor and 1 outdoor pool, hot tub, exercise room, recreation room. AE, D, DC, MC, V.*

$–$$$ 🏨 **Gunstock Country Inn.** This country-style resort and motor inn is about a minute's drive from the Gunstock Recreation Area (☞ *above*). The rooms, of various sizes and furnished with American antiques, have views of the mountains and Lake Winnipesaukee. ⊠ *580 Cherry Valley Rd./Rte. 11A, 03246,* ☎ *603/293–2021 or 800/654–0180,* FAX *603/293–2050. 25 rooms. Restaurant, indoor pool, health club. AE, MC, V.*

$ ⚠ **Gunstock Campground.** The campground at the Gunstock Recreation Area (☞ *above*) has a pool and 300 tent and trailer sites. ✉ *Box 1307, Rte. 11A, Laconia 03247,* ☎ *603/293–4341 or 800/486–7862. AE, D, MC, V.*

Shopping

Pepi Herrmann Crystal (✉ 3 Waterford Pl., ☎ 603/528–1020) sells hand-cut crystal chandeliers and stemware. You can take a tour and watch the artists at work.

Skiing and Snow Sports

GUNSTOCK

High above Lake Winnipesaukee, this all-purpose area that dates from the 1930s attracts some skiers and snowboarders for overnight stays and others for day skiing. Gunstock allows patrons to return lift tickets for a cash refund for any reason—weather, snow conditions, health, equipment problems—within an hour and 15 minutes of purchase. Thrill Hill, a tubing park, has 10 runs, multipassenger tubes, and lift service. ✉ *Rte. 11A, 03246,* ☎ *603/293–4341 or 800/486–7862; mailing address:* ✉ *Box 1307, Laconia 03247.*

Downhill. Clever trail cutting along with grooming and surface sculpting three times daily have made this otherwise pedestrian mountain good for intermediates. That's how most of the 44 trails are rated, with a few more challenging runs and designated sections for slow skiers and learners. Lower Ramrod trail is set up for snowboarding. Gunstock, which has one quad, two triple, and two double chairlifts and two surface tows, has the largest night-skiing facility in New Hampshire, with 15 lighted trails and five lifts in operation.

Cross-country. Gunstock has 50 km (30 mi) of cross-country trails. Fifteen kilometers (9 mi) are for advanced skiers, and there are backcountry trails as well.

Child care. The nursery takes children ages 6 months and up; the ski school teaches the SKIwee system to children from age 3 to 12.

Laconia

⑬ *4 mi southwest of Gilford, 26 mi north of Concord.*

When the railroad reached Laconia—then called Meredith Bridge—in 1848, the formerly sleepy community became a manufacturing and trading center. Laconia borders both Winnisquam and Winnipesaukee lakes and is easily accessible from I–93, making it the commercial hub of the Lakes Region. The town's **Belknap Mill** (✉ Mill Plaza, ☎ 603/524–8813), the oldest unaltered, brick-built textile mill in the United States (1823), contains a knitting museum devoted to the textile industry and a year-round cultural center that sponsors concerts, exhibits, a lecture series, and workshops. Area beaches include **Bartlett Beach** (✉ Winnisquam Ave.) and **Opechee Park** (✉ N. Main St.).

Dining and Lodging

$$–$$$ ✕ **Le Chalet Rouge.** This yellow house with a modestly decorated dining room recalls a country-French bistro. To start, try the house pâté, escargots, or steamed mussels. The steak au poivre is tender and well spiced, and the duckling is prepared with seasonal sauces: rhubarb in spring, raspberry in summer, orange in fall, creamy mustard in winter. ✉ *385 W. Main St., Tilton (10 mi west of Laconia),* ☎ *603/286–4035. Reservations essential. MC, V.*

$ ✕▥ **Hickory Stick Farm.** The 200-year-old Cape-style inn has two
★ large, old-fashioned rooms with cannonball beds, stenciled wallpaper, and lace curtains. Breakfast, served on the sunporch, might include

French toast stuffed with peaches and cream cheese. Roast duckling with herb stuffing and orange-sherry sauce is the specialty of the restaurant ($$–$$$; no lunch). Also consider the prime rib, rack of lamb, or vegetarian lasagna. ⊠ *60 Bean Hill Rd., Belmont (4 mi south of Laconia) 03220,* ☎ *603/524–3333. 2 rooms. Restaurant. Full breakfast. AE, D, MC, V. Closed Mon. Call for winter restaurant hrs.*

$$ ⊡ **Ferry Point House.** Built in the 1800s as a summer retreat for the Pillsbury family of baking fame, this red Victorian farmhouse has superb views of Lake Winnisquam. White wicker furniture and hanging baskets of flowers decorate the 60-ft veranda, and the gazebo by the water's edge may make you want to spend your whole vacation lounging and listening for loons. A paddleboat and a rowboat await those eager to get in the water. The pretty rooms have Oriental-style rugs and Victorian furniture. ⊠ *100 Lower Bay Rd., Sanbornton 03269,* ☎ *603/524–0087,* FAX *603/524–0959. 6 rooms. Beach, boating, fishing. Full breakfast. No credit cards. Closed Nov.–Apr.*

Shopping

The **Belknap Mall** (⊠ U.S. 3, ☎ 603/524–5651) has boutiques, crafts stores, and a New Hampshire state liquor store. The **Bending Birch** (⊠ 569 Main St., ☎ 603/524–7589) sells local crafts, including Laconia pottery, birdhouses made in Meredith, and lap robes in New Hampshire's official tartan. The 54 stores at the **Lakes Region Factory Stores** (⊠ 120 Laconia Rd., Tilton, ☎ 603/286–7880) center include Brooks Brothers, Eddie Bauer, and Black & Decker.

OFF THE **CANTERBURY SHAKER VILLAGE –** This outdoor museum and National His-
BEATEN PATH toric Landmark provides insight into the world of the Shakers. A religious community founded in 1792, the Canterbury village flourished in the 1800s and practiced equality of the sexes and races, common ownership, celibacy, and pacifism. Members lived here until 1992. Shakers invented household items such as the clothespin and the flat broom and were known for the simplicity and integrity of their designs, especially furniture. Ninety-minute tours pass through some of the 694-acre property's 24 restored buildings, and crafts demonstrations take place daily. The Creamery Restaurant serves lunch daily and candlelight dinners on Friday and Saturday. A large shop sells fine Shaker reproductions. ⊠ *288 Shaker Rd., 7 mi from Exit 18 off I–93, Canterbury,* ☎ *603/783–9511 or 800/982–9511.* ⊡ *$10 for 2 consecutive days.* ☉ *May–Oct., daily 10–5; Apr. and Nov.–Dec., weekends 10–5; Fri.–Sat. 6:45 dinner and tour (reservations essential).*

Weirs Beach

⑭ *7½ mi north of Laconia, 33½ mi north of Concord.*

Weirs Beach is Lake Winnipesaukee's center for arcade activity. Anyone who loves souvenir shops, fireworks, water slides, and hordes of children will feel right at home. Several cruise boats (☞ Guided Tours *in* Lakes Region A to Z, *below*) depart from the town dock.

The period cars of the **Winnipesaukee Scenic Railroad** carry passengers along the lake's shore on one- or two-hour rides; boarding is at Weirs Beach or Meredith. ⊠ *U.S. 3, Meredith,* ☎ *603/279–5253 or 603/745–2135.* ⊡ *1-hr trip $7.50, 2-hr trip $8.50.* ☉ *July–mid-Sept., daily; weekends only Memorial Day–late June and late Sept.–mid-Oct. Call for hrs and for special Santa trains in Dec.*

○ A giant **Water Slide** (⊠ U.S. 3, ☎ 603/366–5161) overlooks the lake. For an aquatic experience, visit **Surf Coaster** (⊠ U.S. 3, ☎ 603/366–

4991), which has seven slides, a wave pool, and a large area for young children. Day or night you can work your way through the miniature golf course, 20 lanes of bowling, and more than 500 games at **Funspot** (⊠ Rte. 11B, at U.S. 3, ☎ 603/366–4377).

Nightlife and the Arts

Moonlight dinner-and-dance cruises take place on the **M/S Mount Washington** (☎ 603/366–5531 or 888/843–6686) from Tuesday to Saturday, with two bands and a different menu each night.

Outdoor Activities and Sports

Thurston's Marina (⊠ U.S. 3 at the bridge, ☎ 603/366–4811 or 800/834–4812) rents pontoon boats, power boats, and personal watercraft.

Meredith

⑮ *6 mi north of Weirs Beach, 42 mi north of Concord.*

Meredith, on U.S. 3 at the western end of Lake Winnipesaukee, has a fine collection of crafts shops and art galleries. An information center
☺ is across from the Town Docks. At **Annalee's Doll Museum,** you can view a collection of the famous poseable felt dolls and learn about the woman who created them. Annalee Davis Thorndike began making the dolls after her graduation from high school in 1933. Her dolls caught on with collectors, and the Meredith Company has grown into an empire. ⊠ *Hemlock Dr. off Rte. 104,* ☎ *603/279–3333.* 🎫 *Free.* ☾ *Memorial Day–Labor Day, call for hours.*

Wellington State Beach (⊠ Off Rte. 3A, Bristol, 12 mi west of Meredith), on the western shore of Newfound Lake, is one of the most beautiful area beaches. You can swim or picnic along the ½-mi shoreline or take the scenic walking trail.

Lodging

$$ 🏨 **Nutmeg Inn.** A sea captain dismantled his ship to provide the timber for this 1763 Cape-style house. Although the house has been updated over the years, the wide-board floors, wall paneling, and five fireplaces are original. All the rooms, two of which have fireplaces, are named after spices and are decorated accordingly. The no-smoking inn is on a rural side street off Route 104, the main link between I–93 and Lake Winnipesaukee. ⊠ *80 Pease Rd., 03253,* ☎ *603/279–8811,* ℻ *603/279–7703. 8 rooms. Pool, exercise room, billiards. Full breakfast. MC, V. Closed Nov., Mar.–Apr., and weekdays Dec.–Feb.*

$ ⛺ **Clearwater Campground.** This wooded tent and RV campground on Lake Pemigewasset has 153 shady sites, a large sandy beach, a recreation building, a playground, basketball and volleyball courts, and boat rentals and slips. ⊠ *26 Campground Rd., off Rte. 104, 03253,* ☎ *603/279–7761. Closed mid-Oct.–mid-May.*

$ ⛺ **Meredith Woods.** An indoor heated pool, a hot tub, and a game room are among the amenities at this year-round campground, whose patrons have full use of the waterfront facilities across the road at Clearwater Campground (☞ *above*). ⊠ *26 Campground Rd./Rte. 104, 03253,* ☎ *603/279–5449 or 800/848–0328. 101 sites for RVs and tents.*

Nightlife and the Arts

The **Lakes Region Summer Theatre** (⊠ Interlakes Auditorium, Rte. 25, ☎ 603/279–9933) presents Broadway musicals.

Outdoor Activities and Sports

BOATING

Meredith Marina and Boating Center (⊠ Bay Shore Dr., ☎ 603/279–7921) rents power boats. **Wild Meadow Canoes & Kayaks** (⊠ Rte. 25

between Center Harbor and Meredith, ☎ 603/253–7536 or 800/427–7536) rents canoes and kayaks.

GOLF

Waukewan Golf Course (⊠ Off U.S. 3 and Rte. 25, ☎ 603/279–6661) is an 18-hole, par-71 course. The greens fee ranges from $22 to $28; an optional cart costs $22.

Shopping

About 170 dealers operate out of the three-floor **Burlwood Antique Center** (⊠ U.S. 3, ☎ 603/279–6387), which is open daily from May to October. The **Meredith League of New Hampshire Craftsmen** (⊠ U.S. 3, ½ mi north of Rte. 104, ☎ 603/279–7920) sells the works of area artisans. **Mill Falls Marketplace** (⊠ U.S. 3, ☎ 603/279–7006), on the bay in Meredith, contains nearly two dozen shops with clothing, gifts, and books. The **Old Print Barn** (⊠ Winona Rd.; look for LANE on the mailbox, ☎ 603/279–6479), the largest print gallery in northern New England, carries rare prints from around the world.

Center Harbor

⑯ *6 mi northeast of Meredith, 45 mi northwest of Concord.*

In the middle of three bays at the northern end of Winnipesaukee, the town of Center Harbor also borders Lakes Squam, Waukewan, and Winona. This prime location makes it popular in summer, especially with boaters who spend summer weekends on the water.

Dining and Lodging

$$–$$$ ✕🏠 **Red Hill Inn.** The large bay window in the common room of this rambling inn overlooks Squam Lake. Rooms are furnished with Victorian pieces and country furniture. Twenty rooms have fireplaces, some have claw-foot tubs, and 10 have two-person whirlpool baths. For dinner, try the Vermont goat cheese bruschetta, followed by the rack of lamb encrusted in fresh rosemary and garlic. ⊠ *R.D. 1, Box 99M, Rte. 25B, 03226, ☎ 603/279–7001 or 800/573–3445, FAX 603/279–7003. 18 rooms, 8 suites. Restaurant, pub, pool, outdoor hot tub, cross-country skiing. Full breakfast. AE, D, DC, MC, V.*

Outdoor Activities and Sports

Red Hill, a hiking trail on Bean Road off Route 25, northeast of Center Harbor, really does turn red in autumn. The reward at the end of the trail in any season is a view of Squam Lake and the mountains.

Shopping

Keepsake Quilting & Country Pleasures (⊠ Senter's Marketplace, Rte. 25B, ☎ 603/253–4026), reputedly America's largest quilt shop, contains 5,000 bolts of fabric, hundreds of quilting books, and countless supplies.

Holderness

⑰ *15 mi northwest of Center Harbor, 10 mi north of Meredith, 44 mi north of Concord.*

Routes 25B and 25 lead to the town of Holderness, perched between Squam and Little Squam lakes. *On Golden Pond,* starring Katharine Hepburn and Henry Fonda, was filmed on Squam, whose quiet beauty attracts nature lovers.

ⓒ The several trails at the 200-acre **Science Center of New Hampshire** include a ¾-mi path that passes by black bears, bobcats, otters, and other native wildlife in trailside enclosures. Educational events at the center include the "Up Close to Animals" series in July and August, at which you can study species like the red-shouldered hawk. The Children's Activity Center has interactive exhibits. ⊠ *Rtes. 113 and 25,* ☎ *603/968–7194.* 🎫 *$8.* ⊙ *May–Oct., daily 9:30–4:30.*

Dining and Lodging

$$$$ ✕🛏 **Manor on Golden Pond.** Built in 1903, this dignified inn with a
★ British-manor ambience has well-groomed grounds and a private dock with canoes, paddle boats, and a boathouse. You can stay in the main inn, the cottages, or, during summer and fall, the carriage house. Sixteen rooms have wood-burning fireplaces; eight have two-person whirlpool baths. Five-course prix-fixe dinners (reservations required) may include rack of lamb, filet mignon, and apple pie. The inn is no-smoking. ⊠ *U.S. 3 and Shepard Hill Rd., 03245,* ☎ *603/968–3348 or 800/ 545–2141,* 𝖥𝖠𝖷 *603/968–2116. 21 rooms, 4 cottages. Restaurant, pub, pool, tennis court, beach, boating. Full breakfast. AE, MC, V.*

$$–$$$ 🛏 **Glynn House Inn.** Innkeepers Karol and Betsy Paterman restored the elegance of this three-story 1890s Queen Anne–style home but added modern touches like whirlpool baths. The two-level honeymoon suite, with a large whirlpool tub and fireplace downstairs and a four-poster bed and skylights above, is a favorite. Breakfast, served in the oval dining room, always includes fresh-baked strudel. The inn is no-smoking. ⊠ *Box 719, 43 Highland St., Ashland 03217,* ☎ *603/968–3775 or 800/637–9599,* 𝖥𝖠𝖷 *603/968–3129. 9 rooms, 4 suites. In-room VCRs. Full breakfast. MC, V.*

$$ 🛏 **Inn on Golden Pond.** This informal country home, built in 1879 and set on 50 wooded acres, is just across the road from Squam Lake. Rooms have a traditional country decor of hardwood floors, braided rugs, easy chairs, and calico-print bedspreads and curtains; the quietest rooms are in the rear on the third floor. The homemade jam at breakfast is made from rhubarb grown on the property. ⊠ *Box 680, U.S. 3, 03245,* ☎ *603/968–7269,* 𝖥𝖠𝖷 *603/968–9226. 7 rooms, 1 suite. Hiking. Full breakfast. AE, MC, V.*

$–$$ ⚱ **Yogi Bear's Jellystone Park.** Geared toward families, this camping resort has wooded, open riverfront sites as well as basic and deluxe cabins. It also has a pool, a hot tub, planned activities, miniature golf, a basketball court, river swimming, canoe and kayak rentals, and daily movies. Among the many special events are country-western-jamboree weekends and Yogi Olympics. ⊠ *R.R. 1, Box 396, Rte. 132N, Ashland 03217,* ☎ *603/968–9000. 261 sites, 33 cabins.*

$ ⚱ **Squam Lakes Camp Resort and Marina.** The 119 sites at this campground have full hookups, and there's cable TV, a heated pool, a hot tub, lake frontage, a playground, restaurant, and hiking trails. ⊠ *R.F.D. 1, Box 42, U.S. 3, Ashland 03217,* ☎ *603/968–7227.*

Outdoor Activities and Sports

White Mountain Country Club (⊠ N. Ashland Rd., Ashland, ☎ 603/ 536–2227) has an 18-hole, par-71 golf course. The greens fee ranges from $26 to $32; an optional cart costs $22.

Center Sandwich

★ ⑱ *12 mi northeast of Holderness, 56 mi northeast of Concord.*

With Squam Lake to the west and the Sandwich Mountains to the north, Center Sandwich claims one of the prettiest settings of any town in the Lakes Region. So appealing are the town and its views that John Greenleaf Whittier used the Bearcamp River as the inspiration for his poem "Sunset on the Bearcamp." The town attracts artisans—crafts shops abound. The village center holds charming 18th- and 19th-century buildings.

The **Historical Society Museum** traces the history of Center Sandwich largely through the faces of its inhabitants. Works by mid-19th-century portraitist and town son Albert Gallatin Hoit hang alongside a local photographer's exhibit portraying the town's mothers and daughters. The museum houses a replica country store and furniture and items belonging to or made by people from Center Sandwich. ⊠ *4 Maple St.*, ☎ *603/284–6269.* ⊑ *Free.* ☉ *June–Sept., Tues.–Sat. 11–5.*

Dining

$–$$$ ⊞ **Corner House Inn.** The restaurant, in a converted barn decorated with local arts and crafts, serves standard American fare. Before you get to the white-chocolate cheesecake with key-lime filling, try the chef's lobster-and-mushroom bisque or tasty crab cakes. On Thursday, storytellers perform in the glow of the woodstove. ⊠ *Rtes. 109 and 113,* ☎ *603/284–6219. AE, D, MC, V. Closed Mon. Nov.–May.*

Shopping

Ayottes' Designery (⊠ Rte. 113, ☎ 603/284–6915), open from Tuesday to Saturday between 10 and 5, sells weaving supplies, hand-dyed yarns, rugs, wall hangings, and place mats. **Sandwich Home Industries** (⊠ Rte. 109, ☎ 603/284–6831) presents crafts demonstrations in July and August and sells home furnishings and accessories from mid-May to October.

Moultonborough

⑲ *5 mi south of Center Sandwich, 48 mi northeast of Concord.*

Moultonborough claims 6½ mi of shoreline on Lake Kanasatka, a large chunk of Lake Winnipesaukee, and even a small piece of Squam. The highly browsable store, which is part of the **Old Country Store and Museum** (⊠ Moultonborough Corner, ☎ 603/476–5750), has been selling maple products, aged cheeses, penny candy, and other items since 1781. Much of the equipment used in the store is antique, and the museum displays antique farming and forging tools.

Construction of the **Castle in the Clouds,** the town's best-known attraction, began in 1911 and continued for three years. The odd, elaborate stone mansion, which was built without nails, has 16 rooms, eight bathrooms, and doors made of lead. Owner Thomas Gustave Plant spent $7 million, the bulk of his fortune, on this project and died penniless in 1946. A tour includes the mansion and the Castle Springs Microbrewery on the property. ⊠ *Rte. 171,* ☎ *603/476–2352 or 800/729–2468.* ⊑ *$10 with tour, $4 without tour.* ☉ *Mid-June–mid-Oct., daily 9–5; mid-May–mid-June, weekends 10–4.*

The **Loon Center** at the Frederick and Paula Anna Markus Wildlife Sanctuary is the headquarters of the Loon Preservation Committee, an Audubon Society project. The loon, one of New Hampshire's most popular birds, is threatened by lake traffic, poor water quality, and habitat loss. The center presents changing exhibits about the black-and-white birds, whose calls haunt New Hampshire lakes. Two nature trails wind through the 200-acre property; vantage points on the Loon Nest Trail overlook the spot resident loons sometimes occupy in June. ⊠ *Lees Mills Rd. (follow signs from Rte. 25 to Blake Rd. to Lees Mills Rd.),* ☎ *603/476–5666.* ⊑ *Free.* ☉ *July 4–Columbus Day, daily 9–5; rest of yr, Mon.–Sat. 9–5.*

Dining

$$–$$$ ✕ **The Woodshed.** Farm implements and antiques hang on the walls of this former barn, built in 1860. Make your way through the raw bar or try the New England section of the menu, which includes clam chowder, tender sea scallops, and Indian pudding for dessert. Another favorite is the Denver chocolate pudding, a dense pudding-cake served

warm with vanilla ice cream. ⊠ *Lee's Mill Rd.,* ☎ *603/476–2311. AE, D, DC, MC, V. Closed Mon.*

Tamworth

    ⑳   *11 mi northeast of Moultonborough, 59 mi northeast of Concord.*

President Grover Cleveland summered here. His son, Francis, returned to stay and founded the Barnstormers Theater. Tamworth has a clutch of villages within its borders. At one of them—Chocorua—the view through the birches of Chocorua Lake has been so often photographed that you may feel as if you've been here before. The tiny South Tamworth post office looks like a children's playhouse.

Dining and Lodging

$$$ ✕▥ **Tamworth Inn.** Every room at this inn 1½ mi from Hemenway State
★   Forest has 19th-century American pieces and handmade quilts. Among the menu highlights in the dining room (closed on Sunday and Monday in summer, and from Sunday to Tuesday in winter) are the lobster-stuffed ravioli and the grilled pork loin chop with pomegranate and pear demi-glace. The profiterole Tamworth is big enough for two. Sunday brunch is a summer favorite. ⊠ *Main St., 03886,* ☎ *603/323–7721 or 800/642–7352,* 𝔽𝔸𝕏 *603/323–2026. 16 rooms. Restaurant, pub, pool. Full breakfast; MAP available. MC, V.*

Nightlife and the Arts

The **Arts Council of Tamworth** (☎ 603/323–8104) produces concerts—soloists, string quartets, revues, children's programs—from September to June and an arts show on the last weekend in July. **Barnstormers** (⊠ Main St., ☎ 603/323–8500), New Hampshire's oldest professional theater, performs in July and August. The box office opens in June; before June, call the Tamworth Inn (☞ *above*) for information.

Outdoor Activities and Sports

The 72-acre stand of native pitch pine at **White Lake State Park** (⊠ Rte. 16, ☎ 603/323–7350) is a National Natural Landmark. The park has hiking trails, a sandy beach, trout fishing, canoe rentals, two separate camping areas, a picnic area, and swimming.

Shopping

The many theme rooms—a Christmas room, a bride's room, a children's room, among them—at the **Country Handcrafters & Chocorua Dam Ice Cream Shop** (⊠ Rte. 16, Chocorua, ☎ 603/323–8745) contain handcrafted items. When you're done shopping, try the ice cream, coffee, or tea and scones.

En Route   Route 16 between Ossipee and West Ossipee passes Lake Ossipee, known for fine fishing and swimming. Among these hamlets you'll find several antiques shops and galleries. Local craftspeople create much of the jewelry, turned wooden bowls, pewter goblets, and glassware sold at **Tramway Artisans** (⊠ Rte. 16, West Ossipee, ☎ 603/539–5700).

Wolfeboro

    ㉑   *28 mi south of Tamworth, 41 mi northwest of Portsmouth.*

Wolfeforo has been a resort since Royal Governor John Wentworth built his summer home on the shores of Lake Wentworth in 1763. The town borders both that lake and Lake Winnipesaukee, but the modern center of town is on the shore of Winnipesaukee. The Chamber of Commerce estimates that the population increases tenfold each June, as throngs of visitors descend upon the lake. Unlike the atmosphere in

Weirs Beach, however, the tone here is relaxed and sedate, comfortable for all ages. Wolfeboro has managed to control development and maintain a small-town feel while still offering plenty of shopping and entertainment options.

Uniforms, vehicles, and other artifacts at the **Wright Museum** illustrate the contributions of those on the home front to America's World War II effort. ⊠ *77 Center St.,* ☎ *603/569–1212.* ⌷ *$5.* ☉ *May–Oct., daily 10–4; Nov.–Apr., weekends 10–4.*

The artisans at the **Hampshire Pewter Company** (⊠ 43 Mill St., ☎ 603/ 569–4944 or 800/639–7704) use 17th-century techniques to make pewter tableware and accessories. Their Christmas ornaments are popular with collectors. Free tours are conducted at 10, 11, 1, 2, and 3 between Memorial Day and Labor Day and at 10, 11, 2, and 3 from Labor Day to Columbus Day. The gift shops on Mill Street and Main Street are open year-round.

Wentworth State Beach (⊠ Rte. 109, ☎ 603/569–3699) has good swimming and picnicking areas and a bathhouse.

Dining and Lodging

$$–$$$ ✕ **The Bittersweet.** This converted barn with an eclectic display of old quilts, pottery, sheet music, and china has the feel of a cozy crafts shop, but it's really a restaurant that locals love for the nightly specials that range from a popular lobster pie to steak Diane. The upper level has antique tables and chairs and dining by candlelight. The lower-level lounge, decorated with Victorian wicker furniture, serves lighter fare. ⊠ *Rte. 28,* ☎ *603/569–3636. AE, D, MC, V.*

$$ ✕⛉ **Wolfeboro Inn.** Built 200 years ago, this white clapboard house has 19th- and 20th-century additions with views of the waterfront of Wolfeboro Bay. The rooms have polished cherry and pine furnishings, armoires (to hide the TVs), stenciled borders, and country quilts. More than 70 brands of beer are available at Wolfe's Tavern, where fireplaces make cool evenings cozy. The main dining room ($$–$$$) serves fresh seafood and a popular slow-roasted prime rib. ⊠ *Box 1270, 90 N. Main St., 03894,* ☎ *603/569–3016 or 800/451–2389,* FAX *603/569–5375. 41 rooms, 3 suites, 1 1-bedroom apartment. 2 restaurants, bar, beach, boating, meeting rooms. Continental breakfast. AE, MC, V.*

Outdoor Activities and Sports

BOATING

Winnipesaukee Kayak Company (⊠ 17 Bay St., ☎ 603/569–9926) gives kayak lessons and leads group excursions on the lake.

GOLF

Kingswood Golf Course (⊠ Rte. 28, ☎ 603/569–3569) has an 18-hole, par-72 course. The greens fee ranges from $35 to $48 and in the summer includes an optional cart. At other times, a cart costs $25.

HIKING

A few miles north of town on Route 109 is the trailhead to **Abenaki Tower.** A short (¼-mi) hike to the 100-ft post-and-beam tower, followed by a more rigorous climb to the top, rewards you with a vast view of Lake Winnipesaukee and the Ossipee mountain range.

WATER SPORTS

Look for water-skiing regulations at every marina. Scuba divers can explore a 130-ft-long cruise ship that sank in 30 ft of water off Glendale in 1895. **Dive Winnipesaukee Corp.** (⊠ 4 N. Main St., ☎ 603/569–2120) runs charters out to this and other wrecks and offers rentals, repairs, scuba sales, and lessons in waterskiing and windsurfing.

Wakefield

㉒ *18 mi east of Wolfeboro, 26 mi southeast of Tamworth, 40 mi north of Portsmouth.*

East of Winnipesaukee, several laid-back villages combine to form Wakefield, a town with 10 lakes. Wakefield's registered historic district, on Wakefield Road near the Maine border, has a church, houses, and an inn that look just as they did in the 18th century.

Ⓒ The **Museum of Childhood** displays a one-room schoolhouse, a child's room and a kitchen from 1890, model trains, antique sleds, teddy bears, 3,000 dolls, and 44 furnished dollhouses. Special events are scheduled for most Fridays. ✉ *Wakefield Corner, off Rte. 16,* ☎ *603/522–8073.* ✆ *$3.* ☉ *Memorial Day–Labor Day, Mon. and Wed.–Sat. 11–4, Sun. 1–4.*

Lodging

$–$$ ☐ **Wakefield Inn.** The restoration of this 1804 stagecoach inn, a high-
★   light of Wakefield's historic district, has been handled with an eye for detail. The dining-room windows retain the original panes and shutters, but the centerpiece of the building is the freestanding spiral staircase, which rises three stories. The large rooms, named for famous guests or past owners, have wide-board pine floors, big sofas, and handmade quilts. The 2-mi Wakefield Heritage Trail runs from the inn to the center of town. In late fall and early spring, you can learn how to quilt as part of the weekend Quilting Package. ✉ *2723 Wakefield Rd., 03872,* ☎ *603/522–8272 or 800/245–0841. 7 rooms. Full breakfast. MC, V.*

Milton

㉓ *15½ mi south of Wakefield, 25 mi north of Portsmouth.*

Milton stretches alongside the Salmon Falls River, Town House Pond, Milton Pond, and Northeast Pond, all of which flow together to create a seemingly endless body of water.

The **New Hampshire Farm Museum** houses more than 60,000 artifacts recalling New Hampshire farm life from 1700 to the early 1900s. Take a guided tour through the Jones Farmhouse and then explore the Grand Barn—filled with vehicles, farm implements, and tools—the gardens, and the nature trails at your leisure. Special events demonstrating farm-related crafts take place throughout the season. ✉ *Rte. 125 (White Mountain Hwy.),* ☎ *603/652–7840.* ✆ *$5.* ☉ *Mid-May–mid-Oct., Wed.–Sun. 10–4.*

Lakes Region A to Z

Arriving and Departing

BY BUS
Concord Trailways (☎ 800/639–3317) stops daily in Tilton, Laconia, Meredith, Center Harbor, Moultonborough, and Conway.

BY CAR
Most people driving into this region arrive via I–93 to U.S. 3 in the west or by the Spaulding Turnpike (Route 16) to Route 11 in the east.

BY PLANE
Manchester Airport (☞ Arriving and Departing *in* New Hampshire A to Z, *below*) is about an hour's drive from the Lakes Region.

Getting Around

BY BUS

See Arriving and Departing, *above.*

BY CAR

On the western side of the Lakes Region, I–93 is the principal north–south artery. Exit 20 leads to U.S. 3 and Route 11 and the southwestern side of Lake Winnipesaukee. Take Exit 23 to Route 104 to Route 25 and the northwestern corner of the region. From the coast, the Spaulding Turnpike (Route 16) heads to the White Mountains, with roads leading to the lakeside towns.

BY PLANE

Moultonborough Airport (⌧ Rte. 25, Moultonborough, ☎ 603/476–8801) operates chartered flights and tours.

Contacts and Resources

BOATING

The **Lakes Region Association** (☎ 603/744–8664 or 800/925–2537) provides boating advice.

EMERGENCIES

Lakes Region General Hospital (⌧ 80 Highland St., Laconia, ☎ 603/524–3211).

FISHING

The **New Hampshire Fish and Game** office (☎ 603/744–5470) has information about fishing and licenses.

GUIDED TOURS

The 230-ft **M/S Mount Washington** (☎ 603/366–5531) makes 2½-hour scenic cruises of Lake Winnipesaukee between mid-May and mid-October from Weirs Beach, Wolfeboro, Alton Bay, and Center Harbor. Evening cruises include live music and a buffet dinner.

The **M/V Sophie C.** (☎ 603/366–2628) has been the area's floating post office for more than a century. The boat departs Weirs Beach with mail and passengers daily except Sunday from mid-June until the Saturday following Labor Day; call for stops.

Sky Bright (⌧ Laconia Airport, Rte. 11, ☎ 603/528–6818) operates airplane and helicopter tours and instruction on aerial photography.

From Memorial Day to late October, **Golden Pond Boat Tour** (⌧ Manor on Golden Pond, U.S. 3, Holderness, ☎ 603/279–4405) visits filming sites of the movie *On Golden Pond* on Squam Lake, aboard the *Lady of the Manor,* a 28-ft pontoon craft.

From May to late October, **Squam Lake Tours** (☎ 603/968–7577) takes up to 48 passengers on a two-hour pontoon tour of "Golden Pond." The company also operates guided fishing trips and private charters.

HIKING

Contact the Alexandria headquarters of the **Appalachian Mountain Club** (☎ 603/744–8011) or the **Laconia Office of the U.S. Forest Service** (☎ 603/528–8721) for trail advice and information.

VISITOR INFORMATION

Greater Laconia Chamber of Commerce (⌧ 11 Veterans Sq., Laconia 03246-3485, ☎ 603/524–5531 or 800/531–2347). **Lakes Region Association** (⌧ Box 589, Center Harbor 03226, ☎ 603/253–8555 or 800/925–2537). **Squam Lakes Area Chamber of Commerce** (⌧ Box 65, Ashland 03217, ☎ 603/968–4494). **Wolfeboro Chamber of Commerce** (⌧ Box 547-WT7, Railroad Ave., Wolfeboro 03894, ☎ 603/569–2200 or 800/516–5324).

THE WHITE MOUNTAINS

Sailors approaching East Coast harbors frequently mistake the pale peaks of the White Mountains—the highest range in the northeastern United States—for clouds. It was 1642 when explorer Darby Field could no longer contain his curiosity about one mountain in particular. He set off from his Exeter homestead and became the first man to climb what would eventually be called Mt. Washington, the king of the Presidential Range. More than a mile high, Mt. Washington must have presented Field with formidable obstacles—its peak claims the highest wind velocity ever recorded and it may see snow every month of the year.

More than 350 years after Field's climb, curiosity about the mountains has not abated. People come by the tens of thousands to hike and climb in spring and summer, to photograph the vistas and the vibrant foliage in autumn, and to ski in winter. In this four-season vacation hub, many resorts (some of which have been in business since the mid-1800s) are destinations in themselves, with golf, tennis, swimming, hiking, cross-country skiing, and renowned restaurants.

Roughly 770,000 acres of forested mountains, valleys, and notches (deep mountain passes) in the White Mountains make up the White Mountain National Forest. Long popular with hikers, campers, and skiers, and easily accessible to Bostonians and New Yorkers, it is one of the most heavily used for recreation of the nation's protected forests. The forest includes the Presidential Range of the White Mountains: These peaks, like Mt. Washington, are all named after early presidents. Notorious for its foul weather, Mt. Washington is, nonetheless, a favorite with hikers. An auto road and a railway also lead to the top. The mountain scenery of Franconia Notch, Crawford Notch, and Pinkham Notch also fall within the forest's boundaries. Crawford and Franconia Notches are doubly protected since they are state parks as well.

This section begins in Waterville Valley, off I–93; continues to Lincoln, across the Kancamagus Highway to North Conway; and circles north on Route 16 and U.S. 302 back to the northern reaches of I–93. There is some backtracking involved because of the mountains.

Waterville Valley

24 *63 mi north of Concord.*

In 1835, visitors began arriving in Waterville Valley, a 10-mi-long cul-de-sac cut by one of New England's Mad Rivers and circled by mountains. They have come in increasing numbers ever since. First a summer resort, then more of a ski area, and now a year-round resort, Waterville Valley retains a small-town feel. There are inns, lodges, and condominiums; restaurants, cafés, and taverns; shops, conference facilities, a grocery store, and a post office. Hiking and mountain biking are the popular summer sports.

In winter, those who don't ski can ice-skate, snowboard, or snowshoe, or amuse themselves in the **White Mountain Athletic Club** (✉ Rte. 49, ☎ 603/236–8303), a fitness center that has tennis, racquetball, and squash courts; a 25-meter indoor pool, a jogging track, exercise equipment, whirlpools, saunas, steam rooms, and a games room. The club is open to guests at many area lodgings.

Dining and Lodging

$–$$ ✕ **Chile Peppers.** Southwest-inspired Chile Peppers caters to skiers with fajitas, tacos, enchiladas, and other Tex-Mex staples. The food here may not be authentic Mexican, but it's well priced and filling. If

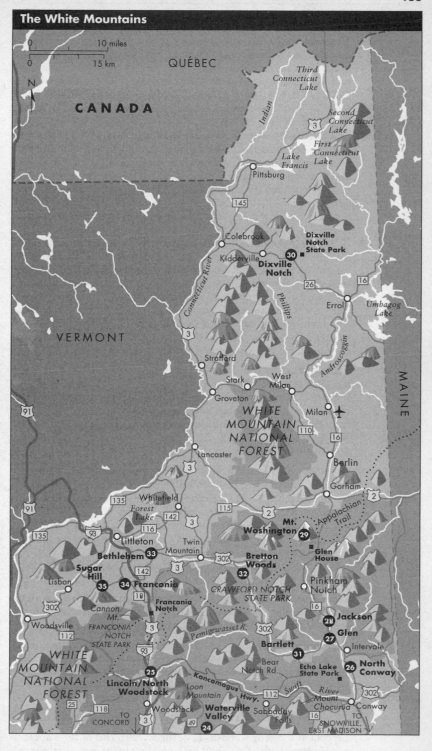

The White Mountains

0 — 10 miles
0 — 15 km

N

QUÉBEC

CANADA

VERMONT

MAINE

Third Connecticut Lake

Second Connecticut Lake

First Connecticut Lake

Lake Francis

Indian

3

Pittsburg

145

Connecticut River

Colebrook

Kidderville

Dixville Notch

30

Dixville Notch State Park

Phillips

26

16

Errol

Umbagog Lake

3

Stratford

Stark

West Milan

Groveton

Androscoggin

WHITE MOUNTAIN NATIONAL FOREST

Milan

Berlin

110

16

2

Gorham

91

Lancaster

3

Whitefield

135

142

3

115

2

Mt. Washington

29

Appalachian Trail

Forest Lake

116

91

93

Littleton

Twin Mountain

302

Bretton Woods

Glen House

Bethlehem

33

3

32

Pinkham Notch

135

142

Lisbon

Sugar Hill

35

34 **Franconia**

19

CRAWFORD NOTCH STATE PARK

16

28 **Jackson**

302

Franconia Notch

27 **Glen**

Cannon Mt.

FRANCONIA NOTCH STATE PARK

93

Pemigewasset R.

302

Bartlett

31

Intervale

Woodsville

112

Bear Notch Rd.

Echo Lake State Park

26 **North Conway**

WHITE MOUNTAIN NATIONAL FOREST

25

Lincoln/North Woodstock

25

Kancamagus Hwy.

Loon Mountain

112

Swift

River

Mount Chocorua

302

Conway

118

TO CONCORD

3

Woodstock

Waterville Valley

49

24

Sabbaday Falls

16

TO SNOWVILLE, EAST MADISON

you're solely into Tex, the lineup includes ribs, steak, seafood, and chicken. ⊠ *Town Square,* ☎ *603/236–4646. AE, DC, MC, V.*

$$–$$$$ 🏨 **Golden Eagle Lodge.** Waterville's premier condominium property recalls the grand hotels of an earlier era. The full-service complex, which opened in 1989, has a two-story lobby and a very capable front-desk staff. Guests have access to the White Mountain Athletic Club (☞ *above*). ⊠ *Snow's Brook Rd., 03215,* ☎ *603/236–4600 or 888/703–2453,* FAX *603/236–4947. 139 suites. Kitchenettes, indoor pool, sauna, recreation room. AE, D, DC, MC, V.*

$–$$$$ 🏨 **Black Bear Lodge.** This family-oriented all-suites hotel has one- and two-bedroom units with full kitchens. Each unit is individually owned and decorated. Children's movies are shown at night in season, and there's bus service to the slopes. Guests can use the White Mountain Athletic Club (☞ *above*). ⊠ *Box 357, Village Rd., 03215,* ☎ *603/ 236–4501 or 800/349–2327,* FAX *603/236–4114. 107 suites. Indoor- outdoor pool, hot tub, sauna, steam room, exercise room, recreation room. AE, D, DC, MC, V.*

$–$$ 🏨 **Snowy Owl Inn.** The fourth-floor bunk-bed lofts at this inn are ideal for families; first-floor rooms, some with whirlpool tubs, are suitable for couples seeking a quiet getaway. The atrium lobby, where guests are treated to afternoon wine and cheese, contains a three-story fieldstone fireplace and many prints and watercolors of snowy owls. Four restau- rants are within walking distance. Guests have access to the White Mountain Athletic Club (☞ *above*). ⊠ *Box 407, Village Rd., 03215,* ☎ *603/236–8383 or 800/766–9969,* FAX *603/236–4890. 84 rooms. In- door pool, hot tub. Continental breakfast. AE, D, DC, MC, V.*

Skiing and Snow Sports

WATERVILLE VALLEY

Former U.S. ski-team star Tom Corcoran designed this family-ori- ented resort. The lodgings and various amenities are about a mile from the slopes, but a shuttle makes a car unnecessary. ⊠ *Box 540, Rte. 49, 03215,* ☎ *603/236–8311; 603/236–4144 for snow conditions; 800/468–2553 for lodging.*

Downhill. Mt. Tecumseh, a short shuttle ride from the Town Square and accommodations, has been laid out with great care. This ski area has hosted more World Cup races than any other in the East, so most advanced skiers will be adequately challenged. Most of the 52 trails are intermediate: straight down the fall line, wide, and agreeably long. A 7-acre tree-skiing area adds variety. Snowmaking coverage of 100% ensures good skiing even when nature doesn't cooperate. The lifts serving the 2,020 ft of vertical rise include two high-speed detachable quad, two triple, three double, and four surface lifts.

Cross-country. The Waterville Valley cross-country network, with the ski center in the Town Square, has 101 km (63 mi) of trails. About two- thirds of the trails are groomed; the rest are backcountry.

Child care. The nursery takes children from age 6 months to 4 years. There are SKIwee lessons and other instruction for children ages 3 to 12. The Kinderpark, a children's slope, has a slow-running lift.

Lincoln/North Woodstock

㉕ *26 mi northwest of Waterville Valley, 65 mi north of Concord.*

Lincoln and North Woodstock, at the western end of the Kancama- gus Highway and at Exit 32 off I–93, combine to make one of the state's liveliest ski-resort areas. Festivals, like the New Hampshire Scottish High- land Games in mid-September, keep Lincoln swarming with people year- round, while North Woodstock maintains more of a village feel.

A ride on the **Hobo Railroad** yields scenic views of the Pemigewasset River and the White Mountain National Forest. The narrated excursions take 1 hour and 20 minutes. ⊠ *Rte. 112, Lincoln,* ☎ *603/745–2135.* ⊡ *$8.* ⊙ *June–Labor Day, daily 11, 1, 3 (sometimes 5), and 7 (dinner train); May and Sept.–Oct., weekends 11, 1, 3 (sometimes 5), and 7 (dinner train).*

Ⓒ In summer and fall at **Loon Mountain,** a popular ski resort, you can ride New Hampshire's longest gondola to the summit for a panoramic view of the White Mountain National Forest. Daily activities at the summit include lumberjack shows, storytelling by a mountain man, and nature tours. You can also take self-guided walks to glacial caves. Other recreational opportunities include a popular wildlife theater show, archery, horseback riding, mountain biking, and in-line skating. ⊠ *Kancamagus Hwy., Lincoln,* ☎ *603/745–8111.* ⊡ *Gondola $9.50, separate fees for other activities.* ⊙ *Daily.*

Ⓒ At the **Whale's Tale Water Park,** you can float on an inner tube along a gentle river, careen down water slides, or body-surf in the large wave pool. ⊠ *U.S. 3, North Lincoln,* ☎ *603/745–8810.* ⊡ *$16.50.* ⊙ *Mid-June–Labor Day, daily 10–6; call for early and late-season hrs.*

Dining and Lodging

$$$ ✕⊞ **Indian Head Resort.** Views across the 180 acres of this resort motel near the Loon and Cannon Mountain ski areas are of Indian Head Rock Profile and the Franconia Mountains. Groomed cross-country ski trails and a mountain-bike trail from the resort connect to the Franconia Notch trail system. The Profile Room restaurant ($$–$$$) serves a nice selection of standard American dishes. ⊠ *U.S. 3, North Lincoln 03251,* ☎ *603/745–8000 or 800/343–8000,* FAX *603/745–8414. 98 rooms, 40 cottages. Restaurant, 1 indoor and 1 outdoor pool, indoor and outdoor hot tubs, lake, sauna, tennis court, fishing, biking, ice-skating, cross-country skiing, recreation room. AE, D, DC, MC, V.*

$–$$ ✕⊞ **Woodstock Inn.** The inn's 21 rooms, spread over three buildings, are named after local geographic features. The romantic Ellsworth room comes with a whirlpool tub, a king-size canopy bed, and complimentary champagne. The Notchview, great for families, has two double beds; a ladder leads to a cozy tower with a daybed. The restaurants include the elegant Clement Room Grill; Woodstock Station ($), where everything from meat loaf to fajitas is prepared; and the Woodstock Inn Brewery. ⊠ *Box 118, U.S. 3, North Woodstock 03262,* ☎ *603/745–3951 or 800/321–3985,* FAX *603/745–3701. 21 rooms, 13 with bath. 2 restaurants, bar, refrigerators, outdoor hot tub. Full breakfast. AE, D, MC, V.*

$$–$$$$ ⊞ **Mountain Club on Loon.** This first-rate slopeside resort hotel has an assortment of accommodations: suites that sleep as many as eight, studios with Murphy beds, and 117 units with kitchens. All rooms are within walking distance of the lifts, and condominiums are on-slope and nearby. Entertainers perform in the lounge on most winter weekends. ⊠ *Rte. 112, Kancamagus Hwy., Lincoln 03251,* ☎ *603/745–2244 or 800/229–7829,* FAX *603/745–2317. 234 rooms. Restaurant, bar, indoor pool, massage, sauna, aerobics, health club, racquetball, squash. AE, D, MC, V.*

$$ ⊞ **Mill House Inn.** This country inn–style hotel on the western edge of the Kancamagus Highway offers free transportation to Loon Mountain during ski season. Nearby are shopping, restaurants, a cinema, and the North Country Center for the Performing Arts. ⊠ *Box 696, Rte. 112, Lincoln 03251,* ☎ *603/745–6261 or 800/654–6183,* FAX *603/745–6896. 74 rooms, 21 suites. Restaurant, 1 indoor and 1 outdoor pool, indoor and outdoor hot tubs, sauna, tennis court, exercise room, nightclub. AE, D, DC, MC, V.*

Nightlife and the Arts

The **North Country Center for the Performing Arts** (⊠ Mill at Loon Mountain, Kancamagus Hwy., ☎ 603/745–6032) presents theater for children and adults and art exhibitions from July to September. Skiers head to the **Granite Bar** at the Mountain Club at the Loon Mountain resort (⊠ Kancamagus Hwy., ☎ 603/745–8111). You can dance at the **Loon Saloon** ⊠ Kancamagus Hwy., ☎ 603/745–8111) at the ski area. **Thunderbird Lounge** (⊠ Indian Head Resort, U.S. 3, North Lincoln, ☎ 603/745–8000) has nightly entertainment year-round and a large dance floor. The **Timbermill Pub** (⊠ Mill at Loon Mountain, Kancamagus Hwy., ☎ 603/745–3603) hosts bands on weekends.

Outdoor Activities and Sports

At **Lost River Reservation** (⊠ Rte. 112, North Woodstock, ☎ 603/745–8031), open from mid-May to mid-October, you can hike along the river gorge and view geological wonders like the Guillotine Rock and the Lemon Squeezer.

Shopping

CRAFTS

The **Curious Cow** (⊠ Main St., North Woodstock, ☎ 603/745–9230) is a multidealer shop selling country crafts. The **Russell Crag Gallery of Fine Crafts** (⊠ 110 Main St., North Woodstock, ☎ 603/745–8664) carries pottery, jewelry, and other items by New Hampshire artisans. **Sunburst Fashions** (⊠ 108 Main St., North Woodstock, ☎ 603/745–8745) stocks handcrafted gemstone jewelry and imported gift items.

MALL

Millfront Marketplace, Mill at Loon Mountain (⊠ I–93 and the Kancamagus Hwy., Lincoln, ☎ 603/745–6261), a former paper factory, contains restaurants, boutiques, a bookstore, and a post office.

Skiing and Snow Sports

LOON MOUNTAIN

A modern resort on the Kancamagus Highway and the Pemigewasset River, Loon Mountain opened in the 1960s and underwent serious development in the 1980s. In the base lodge and around the mountain are many food-service and lounge facilities. At night, you can try lift-serviced tubing on the lower slopes. ⊠ *Kancamagus Hwy., Lincoln 03251,* ☎ *603/745–8111; 603/745–8100 for snow conditions; 800/227–4191 for lodging.*

Downhill. Wide, straight, and consistent intermediate trails prevail at Loon. Beginner trails and slopes are set apart. Most- advanced runs are grouped on the North Peak section farther from the main mountain. Snowboarders have a halfpipe and their own snowboard park, and an alpine garden with bumps and jumps provides thrills for skiers. The vertical is 2,100 ft; a four-passenger gondola, one high-speed detachable quad, two triple and three double chairlifts, and one surface lift serve the 43 trails and slopes.

Cross-country. The touring center at Loon Mountain has 35 km (22 mi) of cross-country trails.

Child care. The day-care center takes children as young as 6 weeks old. The ski school runs several programs for children of different age groups. Children 5 and under ski free.

Kancamagus Highway

34½ mi between Lincoln and Conway.

Interstate 93 is the fastest way to the White Mountains, but it's hardly

★ the most appealing. The section of Route 112 known as the **Kancamagus Highway** passes through classic mountain vistas with some of the state's most unspoiled scenery. This stretch, punctuated by scenic overlooks and picnic areas, erupts into fiery color each fall, when photosnapping drivers can really slow things down. Prepare yourself for a leisurely pace. There are also campgrounds off the highway. In bad weather, check with the Saco Ranger Station (☎ 603/447–5448) for road conditions.

Outdoor Activities and Sports

A couple of short hiking trails off the highway yield great rewards for relatively little effort. The **Lincoln Woods Trail** starts from the large parking lot of the Lincoln Woods Visitor Center, 4 mi east of Lincoln. You can purchase the recreation pass ($5 per vehicle, good for seven consecutive days) needed to park in any of the White Mountain National Forest lots or overlooks here; stopping to take photos or to use the rest rooms at the visitor center is permitted without a pass. The trail crosses a suspension bridge over the Pemigewasset River and follows an old railroad bed for 3 mi along the river. The parking and picnic area for **Sabbaday Falls,** about 20 mi east of Lincoln, is the trailhead for an easy ½-mi trail to the falls, a multilevel cascade that plunges through two potholes and a flume.

North Conway

26 *72 mi northeast of Concord, 42 mi east of Lincoln.*

North Conway is a shopper's paradise, with more than 150 outlet stores ranging from Anne Klein to Joan & David. Most of them stretch along Route 16. Before the arrival of the outlets, the town was popular with skiers and hikers, who still come for the inspiring scenery, ski resorts, and access to White Mountain National Forest.

The **Conway Scenic Railroad** operates trips of varying durations in vintage coaches pulled by steam or diesel engines. The dome observation coach on the 5½-hour trip through Crawford Notch offers views of some of the finest scenery in the Northeast. Lunch is served aboard the dining car on the Valley Train to Conway or Bartlett. The 1874 Victorian train station has displays of railroad artifacts, lanterns, and old tickets and timetables. ⊠ *Rte. 16 and U.S. 302 (38 Norcross Circle),* ☎ *603/356–5251 or 800/232–5251.* ⊡ *$8.50–$52, depending on trip.* ☺ *Mid-May–late Oct., daily 9–6; Apr.–mid-May and Nov.–late Dec., weekends 10–3. Call for departure times. Reserve early during foliage season for Crawford Notch or Valley dining car.*

At **Echo Lake State Park,** you needn't be a rock climber to glimpse views from the 1,000-ft **White Horse** and **Cathedral** ledges. From the top you'll see the entire valley, in which Echo Lake shines like a diamond. An unmarked trailhead another ⁷⁄₁₀-mi on West Side Road leads to **Diana's Baths,** a spectacular series of waterfalls. ⊠ *Off U.S 302,* ☎ *603/356–2672.* ⊡ *$2.50.* ☺ *Mid-June–mid-Oct., daily dawn–dusk.*

The **Hartmann Model Railroad Museum** houses 14 operating layouts (from G to Z scales), about 2,000 engines, and more than 5,000 cars and coaches. A café, a crafts store, a hobby shop, and an outdoor ride-on train are also on site. ⊠ *U.S. 302 and Town Hall Rd., Intervale,* ☎ *603/356–9922 or 603/356–9933.* ⊡ *$5.* ☺ *Daily 10–5.*

Dining and Lodging

$–$$$ ✕ **Delaney's Hole in the Wall.** Perfect after a long day of shopping or skiing, this casual restaurant has an eclectic decor of sports and other memorabilia that includes autographed baseballs. An early photo of skiing at Tuckerman's Ravine hangs over the fireplace. The menu is varied as well, with entrées ranging from a spicy chicken and roasted red pepper quesadilla to medallions of sirloin fillet with steamed broccoli, sautéed baby shrimp, and hollandaise sauce. ⊠ ¼ *mi north of North Conway on Rte. 16,* ☎ *603/356–7776. D, MC, V.*

$$$–$$$$ ✕🖾 **Darby Field Inn.** After a day of outdoor activity in the adjacent White Mountain National Forest, you can warm yourself by the fieldstone fireplace in the Darby Inn's living room or by the woodstove in the bar. Most rooms in this unpretentious 1826 converted farmhouse have mountain views. The menu at the restaurant ($$$) usually includes roast duckling with a raspberry Chambord sauce, rack of lamb with a burgundy sauce, and daily specials like Jamaican jerk pork with a mango puree. For dessert try the dark-chocolate pâté with white-chocolate sauce or the famous Darby cream pie. ⊠ *Box D, Bald Hill Rd., Conway 03818,* ☎ *603/447–2181 or 800/426–4147,* 🖾🗙 *603/447–5726. 12 rooms, 3 suites. Restaurant, bar, pool, outdoor hot tub, cross-country skiing. MAP available; required during foliage season and Christmas wk. AE, MC, V. Closed Apr.*

$$–$$$$ ✕🖾 **Eastern Slope Inn Resort.** This National Historic Site on 40 acres in the heart of North Conway near Mt. Cranmore has been an operating inn for more than a century. The restaurant ($$–$$$) serves creative American fare in a glassed-in courtyard and has weekly entertainment. ⊠ *2760 Main St., 03860,* ☎ *603/356–6321 or 800/862–1600,* 🖾🗙 *603/356–8732. 145 rooms. Restaurant, pub, indoor pool, hot tub, sauna, tennis courts, recreation room. AE, D, MC, V.*

$$–$$$$ ✕🖾 **Snowville Inn.** Journalist Frank Simonds built the main gam-
         ★ brel-roof house in 1916. To complement the inn's tome-jammed bookshelves, guest rooms are named for famous authors. The nicest of the rooms, with 12 windows that look out over the Presidential Range, is a tribute to native son Robert Frost. Two additional buildings—the carriage house and the chimney house—also have libraries. Menu highlights in the candlelighted dining room ($$$; reservations essential) include roasted rack of lamb with herbes de Provence. Among the dessert treats are a cranberry walnut tart and a chocolate truffle cake. ⊠ *Box 68, Stuart Rd. (5 mi southeast of Conway), Snowville 03849,* ☎ *603/447–2818 or 800/447–4345,* 🖾🗙 *603/447–5268. 18 rooms. Restaurant, sauna, cross-country skiing. Full breakfast; MAP available. AE, D, DC, MC, V.*

$$$ ✕🖾 **Hale's White Mountain Hotel and Resort.** The rooms at this hotel at the base of Whitehorse Ledge have mountain views. Proximity to the White Mountain National Forest and Echo Lake State Park makes you feel farther away from civilization (and the nearby outlet malls) than you actually are. Dinner at the Ledges restaurant might include farm-raised White Mountain venison in a cranberry currant sauce or beef Wellington. ⊠ *Box 1828, West Side Rd., 03860,* ☎ 🖾🗙 *603/356–7100 or* ☎ *800/533–6301. 80 rooms, 13 suites. Restaurant, bar, pool, hot tub, saunas, 9-hole golf course, tennis court, health club, hiking, cross-country skiing. MAP available. AE, D, MC, V.*

$$–$$$$ 🖾 **Best Western Red Jacket Mountain View.** The Red Jacket's location atop Sunset Hill provides guests with panoramic views of the Mount Washington Valley. Many of the spacious guest rooms have balconies or decks for enjoying the view. Cozy public rooms have deep chairs and plants, and the 40-acre grounds are neatly landscaped with walking trails and gardens. ⊠ *Box 2000, Rte. 16, 03860,* ☎ *603/356–5411 or 800/752–2538,* 🖾🗙 *603/356–3842. 152 rooms, 12 town houses. 2 restaurants, refrigerators, 1 indoor and 1 outdoor pool, sauna, 2 tennis courts, sleigh rides, recreation room, playground, meeting rooms. AE, D, DC, MC, V.*

$$$ 🏨 **Purity Spring Resort.** In the late 1800s, Purity Spring was a farm and sawmill on a private lake. Since 1944 it's been a four-season resort with two Colonial inns, lakeside cottages, and a ski lodge. The King Pine Ski Area (☞ *below*) is right on the property. East Madison is 15 mi south of North Conway. ⊠ *HC 63 Box 40, Rte. 153, East Madison 03849,* ☎ *603/367–8896 or 800/373–3754,* FAX *603/367–8664. 72 rooms, 68 with bath. Restaurant, indoor pool, lake, hot tub, tennis court, hiking, volleyball, fishing. AP, MAP. AE, D, MC, V.*

$–$$ 🏨 **Cranmore Inn.** This authentic country inn opened in 1863, and many of its furnishings date from the mid-1800s. Some rooms have kitchens. A mere ⅓ mi from the base of Mt. Cranmore, the inn is within easy walking distance of North Conway Village. ⊠ *Kearsarge St., 03860,* ☎ *603/356–5502 or 800/526–5502. 18 rooms. Pool. Full breakfast. AE, MC, V.*

Nightlife and the Arts

The **Best Western Red Jacket Mountain View** (⊠ Rte. 16, ☎ 603/356–5411) has weekend and holiday entertainment. **Horsefeather's** (⊠ Main St., ☎ 603/356–6862) hops on weekends. **Mt. Washington Valley Theater Company** (⊠ Eastern Slope Playhouse, Main St., ☎ 603/356–5776) presents musicals and summer theater from mid-June to Labor Day. The Resort Players, a local group, gives pre- and postseason performances.

Outdoor Activities and Sports

Snowvillage Inn (☞ Dining and Lodging, *above*) conducts a llama trek up Foss Mountain. Your picnic will include champagne and fine food. Reservations are essential.

Shopping

ANTIQUES

The **Antiques & Collectibles Barn** (⊠ 3425 Main St., ☎ 603/356–7118), 1½ mi north of the village, is a 35-dealer colony with everything from furniture and jewelry to coins and other collectibles. **North Country Fair Jewelers** (⊠ Main and Seavy Sts., ☎ 603/356–5819) carries diamonds, antique and estate jewelry, silver, watches, coins, and accessories. **Richard M. Plusch Fine Antiques** (⊠ Rte. 16/U.S. 302, ☎ 603/356–3333) deals in period furniture and accessories, including glass, sterling silver, Oriental porcelains, rugs, and paintings. **Sleigh Mill Antiques** (⊠ off Rte. 153, Snowville, ☎ 603/447–6791), an old sleigh and carriage mill 6 mi south of Conway, specializes in 19th-century oil lighting and early gas and electric lamps.

CRAFTS

The **Basket & Handcrafters Outlet** (⊠ Kearsarge St., ☎ 603/356–5332) sells gift baskets, dried-flower arrangements, and country furniture. **Handcrafters Barn** (⊠ Main St., ☎ 603/356–8996) stocks the work of 350 area artists and artisans. **League of New Hampshire Craftsmen** (⊠ 2526 Main St., ☎ 603/356–2441) carries the works of the area's best artisans. **Zeb's General Store** (⊠ Main St., ☎ 603/356–9294 or 800/676–9294) looks like an old-fashioned country store but sells up-to-the-minute food items, crafts, and other products, all made in New England.

FACTORY OUTLETS

More than 150 factory outlets—including Timberland, Pfaltzgraff, London Fog, Anne Klein, and Reebok—can be found around Route 16. The **Mount Washington Valley Chamber of Commerce** (☎ 603/356–3171) has guides to the outlets.

SPORTSWEAR

Popular stores for skiwear include **Chuck Roast** (⊠ Rte. 16, ☎ 603/

356–5589), **Joe Jones** (✉ 2709 Main St., Conway, ☎ 603/356–9411), and **Tuckerman's Outfitters** (✉ Norcross Circle, ☎ 603/356–3121).

Skiing and Snow Sports

KING PINE SKI AREA AT PURITY SPRING RESORT

King Pine, a little more than 9 mi south of Conway, has been a family-run ski area for more than 100 years. Some ski-and-stay packages include free skiing for midweek resort guests. Among the facilities and activities are an indoor pool and fitness complex, ice-skating, and dogsledding. ✉ *Rte. 153, East Madison 03849,* ☎ *603/367–8896; 800/ 367–8897; 800/373–3754 for ski information.*

Downhill. King Pine's gentle slopes make it an ideal area for those learning to ski. Because most of the terrain is geared to beginner and intermediate skiers, experts won't be challenged here except for a brief pitch on the Pitch Pine trail. Sixteen trails are serviced by two triple chairs and a double chair. There's tubing on Saturday and Sunday afternoons, and night skiing and tubing on Friday and Saturday.

Cross-country. King Pine has 15 km (9 mi) of cross-country skiing.

Child care. Children up to 6 years old are welcome (from 8:30 to 4) at the nursery on the second floor of the base lodge. Children ages 4 and up can take lessons.

MT. CRANMORE

This ski area on the outskirts of North Conway opened in 1938. Two glades, one for beginners and intermediates, one for intermediates and experts, have opened more skiable terrain. The fitness center has an indoor climbing wall, tennis courts, exercise equipment, and a pool. ✉ *Box 1640, Snowmobile Rd., 03860,* ☎ *603/356–5543; 603/356– 8516 for snow conditions; 800/786–6754 for lodging.*

Downhill. The mountain's 38 trails are well laid out and fun to ski. Most runs are naturally formed intermediates that weave in and out of glades. Beginners have several slopes and routes from the summit, but experts must be content with a few short but steep pitches. In addition to the trails, snowboarders have a terrain park and a halfpipe. One high-speed quad, one triple, and three double chairlifts carry skiers to the top. There are also two surface lifts. Night skiing is an option from Thursday to Saturday and during holiday periods. Other activities are outdoor skating, snowshoeing, and, on Fridays and Saturdays until 9 and Sundays until 4, tubing.

Child care. The nursery takes children 6 months to 5 years. There's instruction for children from age 3 to 12.

CROSS-COUNTRY

Sixty-four kilometers (40 miles) of groomed cross-country trails weave through North Conway and the countryside along the **Mt. Washington Valley Ski Touring Association Network** (✉ Rte. 16, Intervale, ☎ 603/356–9920 or 800/282–5220).

Glen

㉗ *6 mi north of North Conway, 78 mi northeast of Concord.*

Glen is hardly more than a crossroads between North Conway and Jackson, but its central location has made it the home of a few noteworthy attractions and dining and lodging options.

☺ That cluster of fluorescent buildings on Route 16 is **Story Land,** a children's theme park with life-size storybook and nursery-rhyme characters. The 16 rides and four shows include a flume ride, a

Victorian-theme river-raft ride, a farm-family variety show, and a simulated voyage to the moon. ⊠ *Rte. 16,* ☎ *603/383–4186.* 🎫 *$17.* ☉ *Mid-June–Labor Day, daily 9–6; Labor Day–Columbus Day, weekends 10–5.*

A trip to **Heritage New Hampshire,** next door to Story Land, is as close as you may ever come to experiencing time travel. Theatrical sets, sound effects, and animation usher you aboard the *Reliance* and carry you from a village in 1634 England over tossing seas to the New World. You will saunter along Portsmouth's streets in the late 1700s and hear a speech by George Washington, then continue through other exhibits to the present day. ⊠ *Rte. 16,* ☎ *603/383–9776.* 🎫 *$10.* ☉ *Mid-June–mid-Oct., daily 9–5.*

Dining and Lodging

$–$$$ ✗ **Red Parka Pub.** Practically an institution, the Red Parka Pub has been in downtown Glen for more than two decades. The menu has everything a family could want, from an all-you-can-eat salad bar to scallop pie. The barbecued ribs are local favorites. ⊠ *U.S. 302,* ☎ *603/ 383–4344. Reservations not accepted. AE, D, MC, V.*

$$ ✗🏨 **Bernerhof Inn.** This Old World–style hotel is right at home in its alpine setting. The rooms have hardwood floors with hooked rugs, antiques, and reproductions. The fanciest six rooms have brass beds and spa-size bathtubs; one suite has a Finnish sauna. The menu at the Prince Palace restaurant ($$$) includes Swiss specialties like fondue and Wiener schnitzel, along with new American and classic French dishes. The Black Bear pub ($) pours many microbrewery beers. Ask the hosts about A Taste of the Mountains cooking school. ⊠ *Box 240, U.S. 302, 03838,* ☎ *603/383–9132 or 800/548–8007,* 🗚 *603/383–0809. 9 rooms. Restaurant, pub. Full breakfast. AE, D, MC, V.*

$$–$$$ 🏨 **Best Western Storybook Resort Inn.** On a hillside near Attitash Bear Peak, this motor inn with large rooms is well suited to families. Copperfield's Restaurant has gingerbread, sticky buns, omelets, and a children's menu. ⊠ *Box 129, intersection of U.S 302 and Rte. 16, Glen Junction 03838,* ☎ *603/383–6800,* 🗚 *603/383–4678. 78 rooms. Restaurant, bar, refrigerators, 1 indoor and 1 outdoor pool, indoor and outdoor hot tubs, sauna, tennis court, playground. AE, DC, MC, V.*

Nightlife and the Arts

The **Bernerhof Inn** (☞ Dining, *above*) is the setting for an evening of fondue and soft music by the fireside. **Red Parka Pub** (☞ Dining, *above*) is a hangout for barbecue and steak lovers. During ski season, the crowd swells to capacity in the Pub Downstairs when musical entertainers perform on Sunday afternoons and Thursday evenings.

Jackson

★ ㉘ *4 mi north of Glen, 82 mi northeast of Concord.*

The village of Jackson on Route 16 has retained its storybook New England character. Art and antiques shopping, tennis, golf, fishing, and hiking to waterfalls are among the draws. When the snow falls, Jackson becomes the state's cross-country skiing capital. The village's proximity to four downhill areas makes it popular with alpine skiers, too.

Dining and Lodging

$$$–$$$$ ✗🏨 **Christmas Farm Inn.** Despite its winter-inspired name, this 200-year-old village inn is an all-season retreat. Rooms in the main inn and the saltbox next door, five with whirlpool baths, are done in Laura Ashley and Ralph Lauren prints. The suites, in the cottages, log cabin, and dairy barn, have beam ceilings, fireplaces, and rustic Colonial furnishings. Some standbys in the restaurant ($$–$$$) include chicken Dijon with

artichoke hearts and shiitake mushrooms, grilled swordfish with citrus salsa, and New York sirloin; soups and desserts vary nightly. ⊠ *Box CC, Rte. 16B, 03846,* ☎ *603/383–4313 or 800/443–5837,* ℻ *603/383–6495. 34 rooms. Restaurant, pub, pool, sauna, hot tub, volleyball, cross-country skiing, recreation room. MAP. AE, MC, V.*

$$$–$$$$ ✕⊞ **Inn at Thorn Hill.** Architect Stanford White designed this 1895 Victorian house, which is a few steps from cross-country trails and Jackson Village. Romantic touches include rose-motif papers and antiques like a blue-velvet fainting couch. The restaurant (reservations essential; closed mid-week in April) serves new American dishes like the roasted pork tenderloin marinated with cider and chiles and the brook trout stuffed with herb-roasted tomatoes. Leave room for the Sacher torte or the cranberry sorbet. The inn is no-smoking. ⊠ *Box A, Thorn Hill Rd., 03846,* ☎ *603/383–4242 or 800/289–8990,* ℻ *603/383–8062. 11 rooms, 8 suites. Restaurant, pub, pool, hot tub, cross-country skiing. MAP. AE, D, MC, V.*
★

$$$–$$$$ ✕⊞ **Wentworth.** This resort built in 1869 retains a Victorian look with individually decorated rooms accented with antiques. All rooms have TVs and telephones; some have working fireplaces and two-person whirlpool tubs. The dining room ($$$) serves a five-course, candlelight dinner with a menu that changes seasonally. Try the pan-seared red snapper with Himalayan red rice. ⊠ *Rte. 16A, 03846,* ☎ *603/383–9700 or 800/637–0013,* ℻ *603/383–4265. 60 rooms in summer, 52 in winter. Restaurant, bar, pool, tennis court, ice-skating, cross-country skiing, sleigh rides, billiards. MAP. AE, D, DC, MC, V.*

$$–$$$$ ✕⊞ **Ellis River House.** Most of the period-decorated rooms in this romantic country inn on the Ellis River have fireplaces, and some have two-person whirlpool baths or private balconies. In winter, a snow bridge across the river connects you with the Ellis River Trail and Jackson's renowned cross-country trail system. The elegant dining room (reservations required; $$–$$$) serves nightly specials as well as standards like boneless breast of duck. The inn is no-smoking. ⊠ *Box 656, Rte. 16, 03846,* ☎ *603/383–9339 or 800/233–8309,* ℻ *603/383–4142. 17 rooms, 3 suites, 1 cottage. Restaurant, pub, pool, hot tub, sauna. Full breakfast. AE, D, DC, MC, V.*
★

$$–$$$$ ⊞ **Inn at Jackson.** The builders of this 1902 Victorian followed a design by Stanford White. The inn has spacious rooms—six with fireplaces—with oversize windows and an airy feel. Other than an imposing grand staircase in the front foyer, the house is unpretentious, with hardwood floors, braided rugs, a smattering of antiques, and mountain views. The hearty breakfast may fill you up for the entire day. ⊠ *Box 807, Thornhill Rd., 03846,* ☎ *603/383–4321 or 800/289–8600,* ℻ *603/383–4085. 14 rooms. Hot tub, cross-country skiing. Full breakfast. AE, D, DC, MC, V.*

$$–$$$$ ⊞ **Nordic Village Resort.** The light wood and white walls of these deluxe condos near several ski areas are as Scandinavian as the snowy views. The Club House has pools and a spa, and there is a nightly bonfire at Nordic Falls. Larger units have fireplaces, full kitchens, and whirlpool baths. ⊠ *Rte. 16, Jackson 03846,* ☎ *603/383–9101 or 800/472–5207,* ℻ *603/383–9823. 140 condominiums. 1 indoor and 2 outdoor pools, hot tub, steam room, ice-skating, cross-country skiing, hiking, sleigh rides. D, MC, V.*

$$–$$$ ⊞ **Eagle Mountain House.** This country estate, which dates from 1879, is close to downhill ski slopes and even closer to cross-country trails, which begin on the property. The public rooms of this showplace have a tycoon-roughing-it feel, and the bedrooms are large and furnished with period pieces. On a warm day, you can nurse a drink in a rocking chair on the wraparound deck. ⊠ *Carter Notch Rd., 03846,* ☎ *603/383–9111 or 800/966–5779,* ℻ *603/383–0854. 93 rooms. Restau-*

rant, pool, hot tub, sauna, 9-hole golf course, 2 tennis courts, health club, playground. AE, D, DC, MC, V.

$$–$$$ ⚅ **Wildcat Inn & Tavern.** After a day of skiing, you can collapse on a comfy sofa by the fire in this small 19th-century tavern in the center of Jackson Village. The fragrance of home-baking permeates into suite-style guest rooms, which are full of interesting furniture and knickknacks. The tavern, where bands often perform, attracts many skiers. In summer, dining is available in the landscaped garden. ✉ *Rte. 16A, 03846,* ☎ *603/383–4245 or 800/228–4245,* FAX *603/383–6456. 6 rooms, 4 with bath; 7 suites; 1 cottage. Restaurant, bar. Full breakfast; MAP available. AE, MC, V.*

Outdoor Activities and Sports

Nestlenook Farm (✉ Dinsmore Rd., ☎ 603/383–0845) maintains an outdoor ice-skating rink with rentals, music, and a bonfire. Going snow-shoeing or taking a sleigh ride are other winter options; in summer you can fly-fish or ride in a horse-drawn carriage.

Skiing and Snow Sports

BLACK MOUNTAIN

The atmosphere at Black Mountain is fun, friendly, and informal—perfect for families and singles who want a low-key skiing holiday. The Family Passport, which allows two adults and two juniors to ski at discounted rates, is a good value. Midweek rates here are usually the lowest in Mt. Washington Valley. ✉ *Box B, Rte. 16B, 03846,* ☎ *603/383–4490 or 800/698–4490.*

Downhill. The 38 trails and two glades on the 1,100-vertical-ft mountain are evenly divided among beginner, intermediate, and expert. There are a triple and a double chairlift and two surface tows. Most of the skiing is user-friendly, particularly for beginners—although recent expansion has added trails geared toward experts—and the southern exposure keeps skiers warm. In addition to trails, snowboarders can use two terrain parks and the halfpipe.

Child care. The nursery takes children from age 6 months to 5 years. Children from 3 to 12 can take classes at the ski school.

JACKSON SKI TOURING FOUNDATION

Rated as one of the top four cross-country skiing areas in the country and by far the largest in New Hampshire, Jackson offers 158 km (98 mi) of trails. Ninety-six kilometers (60 mi) are track groomed, 85 km (53 mi) are skate groomed, and there are 63 km (38½ mi) of marked backcountry trails. ✉ *Main St., 03846,* ☎ *800/927–6697.*

Mt. Washington

★ ㉙ *15 mi north of Jackson, 91 mi north of Concord.*

In summer, you can drive to the top of Mt. Washington, the highest mountain (6,288 ft) in the northeastern United States and the spot where weather observers have recorded 231-mph winds, the strongest in the world. But you'll have to endure the **Mt. Washington Auto Road** to get here. This toll road opened in 1861 and is said to be the nation's first manufactured tourist attraction. Closed in inclement weather, the road begins at **Glen House,** a gift shop and rest stop 15 mi north of Glen on Route 16. Allow two hours round-trip and check your brakes first. Cars with automatic transmissions that can't shift down into first gear aren't allowed on the road. A better option is to hop into one of the vans at Glen House for a 1½-hour guided tour (two hours if you purchase your ticket before 9:30 AM). In winter, the tours go to just above tree line and you have the option of cross-country skiing or snowshoeing down. (You can also take the Mt. Washington Cog Railway to the summit; ☞ Bretton Woods, *below*.) Up top, visit the **Sherman Adams Summit Building**, which contains a museum of memorabilia from each of the three hotels that have stood on this spot and a display of native plant life and alpine flowers. Stand in the glassed-in viewing area to hear the roar of that record-breaking wind. ☎ *603/466–3988.* 🖃 *$15 per car and driver plus $6 for each adult passenger; van fare $20.* ⊘ *Daily (weather permitting).*

Although not a town per se, scenic **Pinkham Notch** covers the eastern side of Mt. Washington and includes several ravines, including Tuckerman's Ravine, famous for spring skiing. It is one of the most eastern notches in the White Mountains. The **Appalachian Mountain Club** (☞ Hiking *in* The White Mountains A to Z, *below*) maintains a visitor center here on Route 16 that provides information to hikers and travelers and has guided walks.

Great Glen Trails Outdoor Center (☞ Skiing and Snow Sports, *below*) has an extensive trail network for hiking and mountain biking, as well as programs in mountain biking, canoeing, kayaking, and fly-fishing.

Skiing and Snow Sports

WILDCAT

Glade skiers head to Wildcat, which has official glade trails with 28 acres of tree skiing. Wildcat's runs include some stunning double-black-diamond trails. Skiers who can hold a wedge should check out the 4-km-long (3-mi-long) Polecat. Experts can zip down the Lynx. On a clear day, the views of Mt. Washington and Tuckerman's Ravine are superb. The trails are classic New England—narrow and winding. 🖃 *Rte. 16, Pinkham Notch, Jackson 03846,* ☎ *603/466–3326; 800/643–4521 for snow conditions; 800/255–6439 for lodging.*

Downhill. Wildcat's expert runs deserve their designations and then some. Intermediates have mid-mountain-to-base trails, and beginners will find gentle terrain and a broad teaching slope. Snowboarders have several terrain parks and the run of the mountain. The 44 runs, with a 2,100-ft vertical drop, are served by a two-passenger gondola, one detachable quad, one double and three triple chairlifts.

Child care. The child-care center takes children ages 6 months and up. All-day SKIwee instruction is offered to children from age 5 to 12. Ski instruction for children takes place on a separate slope.

GREAT GLEN TRAILS OUTDOOR CENTER

There are 40 km (24 mi) of cross-country trails here and access to more than 1,100 acres of backcountry. You can even ski the lower half of the Mt. Washington Auto Road. Trees shelter most of the trails, so Mt. Washington's famous weather shouldn't be a concern. Evenings of cross-country skiing and snowshoeing by moonlight are scheduled throughout the winter. 🖃 *Box 300, Rte. 16, Pinkham Notch (Mailing: Box 300, Gorham 03581),* ☎ *603/466–2333.*

Dixville Notch

 60 mi north of Mt. Washington, 166 mi north of Concord.

Not everyone likes to venture this far north, but if you want to really get away from it all, Dixville Notch is the place to go. Just 12 mi from the Canadian border, this tiny community is known for two things. It's the home of the Balsams Grand Resort Hotel, one of the oldest and most celebrated resorts in New Hampshire. And Dixville Notch and Harts Location are the first election districts in the nation to vote in the presidential elections. Long before the sun rises on election day, the 30 or so Dixville Notch voters gather in the little meeting room beside the hotel bar to cast their ballots and make national news.

One of the favorite pastimes for visitors in this area is watching for moose, those large, ungainly, yet elusive members of the deer family. Although you may catch sight of one or more yourself, **Northern Forest Moose Tours** (☎ 603/752–6060) offers bus tours of the region that have a 97% success rate for spotting moose.

Dining and Lodging

$$$$ ✕🗈 **The Balsams Grand Resort Hotel.** At this resort founded in 1866,
★ you will find many nice touches: valet parking, dancing and entertainment, cooking demonstrations, wine tastings, and organized activities (many included in the cost). Families particularly enjoy late-night games of broomball. The Tower Suite, with its 20-ft conical ceiling, is in a Victorian-style turret and offers 360-degree views. Rooms vary in size but are generally spacious and comfortably furnished; all have views of the 15,000-acre estate and the mountains beyond. In the dining room ($$–$$$; jacket and tie), the summer buffet lunch is heaped upon a 100-ft-long table. Given the awesome amount of food, it's amazing that anyone has room left for the stunning dinners. A starter might be chilled strawberry soup spiked with Grand Marnier, followed by poached salmon with golden caviar sauce and chocolate hazelnut cake. ✉ *Rte. 26, 03576,* ☎ *603/255–3400 or 800/255–0600; 800/255–0800 in NH;* 𝕱𝕬𝕏 *603/255–4221. 202 rooms. Restaurant, pool, 18-hole and 9-hole golf courses, driving range, 6 tennis courts, hiking, boating, fishing, mountain bikes, ice-skating, cross-country skiing, downhill skiing, children's programs. MAP in winter, AP in summer. AE, D, MC, V. Closed late Mar.–mid-May and mid-Oct.–mid-Dec.*

$$$ 🗈 **The Glen.** This rustic lodge with stick furniture, fieldstone, and cedar is on First Connecticut Lake, surrounded by log cabins, seven of which are right on the water. The cabins come equipped with efficiency kitchens and minirefrigerators—not that you'll need either, because rates include meals in the lodge restaurant. ✉ *77 Glen Rd., 1 mi off U.S. 3, Pittsburg 03592,* ☎ *603/538–6500 or 800/445–4536. 8 rooms, 10 cabins. Restaurant, dock. AP. No credit cards. Closed mid-Oct.–mid-May.*

Outdoor Activities and Sports

Dixville Notch State Park (✉ Rte. 26, ☎ 603/823–9959), the northernmost notch in the White Mountains, has picnic areas, a waterfall, and many hiking trails.

Skiing and Snow Sports

THE BALSAMS WILDERNESS
Skiing was originally provided as an amenity for hotel guests at the Balsams, but the area has become popular with day-trippers as well. ✉ *Rte. 26, 03576,* ☎ *603/255–3400 or 800/255–0600; 800/255–0800 in NH; 603/255–3951 for snow conditions;* 𝕱𝕬𝕏 *603/255–4221.*

Downhill. Slopes with names like Sanguinary, Umbagog, and Magalloway may sound tough, but they're only moderately difficult, leaning toward intermediate. There are 12 trails and four glades from the top of the 1,000-ft vertical for every skill level. One double chairlift and two T-bars carry skiers up the mountain. There is a halfpipe for snowboarders.

Cross-country. Balsams has 86 km (53 mi) of cross-country skiing, tracked and groomed for skating (a cross-country technique). Natural-history markers annotate some trails; you can also try telemark and backcountry skiing, and 30 km (19 mi) of snowshoeing trails.

Child care. The nursery takes children up to age 6 at no charge to hotel guests. Lessons are for children 3 and up.

OFF THE
BEATEN PATH

PITTSBURG – Just north of the White Mountains, Pittsburg contains the four Connecticut Lakes and the springs that form the Connecticut River. The entire northern tip of the state—a chunk of about 250 square mi—lies within the town's borders, the result of a dispute between the United States and Canada. The two countries could not decide on a border, so the inhabitants of this region declared themselves independent of both countries in 1832 and wrote a constitution providing for an assembly, a council, courts, and a militia. They named their nation the Indian Stream Republic, after the river that passes through the territory—the capital of which was Pittsburg. In 1835 the feisty, 40-man Indian Stream militia invaded Canada—with only limited success. The Indian Stream war ended more by common consent than surrender; in 1842 the Webster-Ashburton Treaty fixed the international boundary. Indian Stream was incorporated as Pittsburg, making it the largest township in New Hampshire. Canoeing, fishing, and taking photos are favorite pastimes up here; the pristine wilderness teems with moose. Contact the **North Country Chamber of Commerce** (☞ Visitor Information *in* The White Mountains A to Z, *below*) for information about the region.

Bartlett

③① *7 mi southwest of Glen, 85 mi north of Concord.*

Bear Mountain to the south, Mt. Parker to the north, Mt. Cardigan to the west, and the Saco River to the east combine to create an unforgettable setting for the village of Bartlett, incorporated in 1790. Lovely Bear Notch Road in Bartlett has the only midpoint access to the Kancamagus Highway (closed winter).

☾ **Attitash Bear Peak** (⊠ U.S. 302, ☎ 603/374–2368; ☞ Skiing and Snow Sports, *below*) has a dry alpine slide, a water slide, a children's area, and a driving range. A chairlift whisks passengers to the White Mountain Observation Tower, which delivers 270-degree views of the Whites.

Dining and Lodging

$$$–$$$$ ✕🏨 **Grand Summit Hotel & Conference Center.** The gables and curves of this resort hotel at the base of Attitash Bear Peak (☞ *above*) mimic the mountain's peaks and slopes. The luxurious contemporary-style rooms have kitchenettes, VCRs, and stereo systems. Entrées in the Alpine Garden restaurant include pan-roasted chicken with garlic potato cakes and lobster spring rolls. ⊠ *Box 429, U.S. 302, 03812,* ☎ *603/ 374–1900 or 800/554–1900,* 🖷 *603/374–3040. 143 rooms. Restaurant, bar, café, heated pool, hot tubs, sauna, steam room, exercise room, gift shop. AE, D, MC, V.*

$$$–$$$$ 🏨 **Attitash Mountain Village.** The style at this condo-motel complex—across the street from the mountain via a tunnel—is alpine contemporary, and the staff is young and enthusiastic. The many amenities include indoor and outdoor pools and whirlpools. Units, some with fireplaces and kitchens, accommodate from 2 to 14 people. The restaurant has unobstructed views of the mountain. ⊠ *Rte. 302, 03812-0358,* ☎ *603/374–6501 or 800/862–1600,* 🖷 *603/374–6509. 300 rooms. Restaurant, pub, indoor pool, sauna, recreation room. AE, D, MC, V.*

Skiing and Snow Sports

ATTITASH BEAR PEAK

This high-profile resort, which hosts many special events and ski races, continues to expand. Lodging at the base of the mountain is in condiniums and motel-style units, away from the hustle of North Conway. Attitash has a computerized lift-ticket system that in essence allows skiers to pay by the run. Skiers can share the ticket, which is good for two years. ⊠ *U.S. 302, 03812,* ☎ *603/374–2368; 603/374–0946; 800/223–7669 for snow conditions; 800/223–7669 for lodging.*

Downhill. Enhanced with massive snowmaking (97%), the trails now number 60 on two peaks, both with full-service base lodges. The bulk of the skiing and boarding is geared to intermediates and experts, with some steep pitches, glades, and good use of terrain. Beginners have a share of good terrain on the lower mountain and some runs from the top. Serving the 30 km (18 mi) of trails and the 1,750-ft vertical drop are two high-speed quads, one fixed-grip quad, three triples, four double chairlifts, and two surface tows.

Cross-country. Bear Notch Ski Touring Center (☎ 603/374–2277) has more than 70 km (43 mi) of cross-country trails, with more than 60 km (37 mi) skate groomed and tracked. Backcountry skiing is unlimited. Guests staying at the Grand Summit Hotel (☞ Dining and Lodging, *above*) can connect to the trail system from the hotel door.

Child care. Attitots Clubhouse takes children from age 6 months to 5 years. Other programs accommodate children up to 16 years of age.

En Route   Scenic U.S. 302 winds through the steep, wooded mountains on either side of spectacular Crawford Notch, north of Bartlett, and passes through **Crawford Notch State Park** (⊠ U.S. 302, Harts Location, ☎ 603/374–2272), where you can stop for a picnic and a short hike to Arethusa Falls or the Silver and Flume cascades.

Bretton Woods

③② *20 mi northwest of Bartlett, 95 mi north of Concord.*

Early in this century, as many as 50 private trains a day brought the rich and famous from New York and Philadelphia to the Mount Washington Hotel, the jewel of Bretton Woods. The hotel was the site of a famous World Monetary Fund conference in 1944 that greatly affected the post–World War II economy. The area is also known for its cog railway and for skiing.

In 1858, when Sylvester Marsh asked the state legislature for permission to build a steam railway up Mt. Washington, one legislator responded that he'd have better luck building a railroad to the moon.
★ Despite such doubters, the **Mt. Washington Cog Railway** opened in 1869 and has since provided a thrilling alternative to driving or climbing to the top. Allow three hours round-trip. ⊠ *U.S. 302, 6 mi northeast of Bretton Woods,* ☎ *603/846–5404; 800/922–8825 outside NH.* ☑ *$39 round-trip.* ◎ *Mid-June–mid-Oct., daily 8–5, weather permitting; May–mid-June and mid-Oct.–early Nov., limited schedule.*

Dining and Lodging

$$$$ ✕🏨 **Mount Washington Hotel.** The 1902 construction of this leviathan
★   was one of the most ambitious projects of its day. It quickly became one of the nation's favorite grand resorts, most notable for its 900-ft-long veranda, which affords a full view of the Presidential Range. With its stately public rooms and large, Victorian-style bedrooms and suites, the hotel retains a turn-of-the-century formality; jacket and tie are required in the dining room. The regional cuisine highlights seasonal dishes such as lemon lobster ravioli with shrimp and scallops and roast pork with onions, mushrooms, and berry marmalade. This 2,600-acre property has an extensive recreation center. The hotel remains open in the 1999–2000 winter season for the first time in its long history,

making it a winter playground as well as a summer one. ⊠ *U.S. 302, 03575,* ☎ *603/278–1000 or 800/258–0330,* FAX *603/278–8838. 200 rooms. 2 restaurants, indoor-outdoor pool, outdoor pool, sauna, 2 18-hole golf courses, driving range, 12 tennis courts, hiking, horseback riding, bicycles, cross-country skiing, sleigh rides, children's programs. MAP. AE, MC, V.*

$$–$$$ ✕⛉ **Bretton Arms Country Inn.** Built in 1896, this restored inn predates the Mount Washington Hotel (☞ *above*) across the way. Reservations are required in the dining room ($$$) and should be made on arrival. Guests are invited to use the facilities of the Mount Washington Hotel. ⊠ *U.S. 302, 03575,* ☎ *603/278–1000 or 800/258–0330,* FAX *603/ 278–8838. 31 rooms, 3 suites. Restaurant, lounge. AE, D, MC, V.*

$–$$$ ⛉ **Bretton Woods Motor Inn.** Rooms here have contemporary furnishings, a balcony or patio, and mountain views. The Continental cuisine at Darby's Restaurant is served around a circular fireplace. The bar is a hangout for skiers. The motor inn, across from the Mount Washington Hotel, shares the hotel's facilities. ⊠ *U.S. 302, 03575,* ☎ *603/ 278–1000 or 800/258–0330,* FAX *603/278–8838. 50 rooms. Restaurant, bar, indoor pool, sauna, recreation room. AE, D, MC, V.*

$ ⚠ **Dry River Campground.** This rustic campground in Crawford Notch State Park has 30 tent sites and is a popular base for hiking the White Mountain National Forest. ⊠ *U.S. 302, Harts Location; mailing address: Box 177, Twin Mountain 03595,* ☎ *603/374–2272. Closed mid-Dec.–mid-May.*

Skiing and Snow Sports

BRETTON WOODS

This area has a three-level, open-space base lodge, a convenient drop-off area, easy parking, and an uncrowded setting. On-mountain town houses are available as part of reasonably priced packages. The views of Mt. Washington alone are worth the visit; the scenery is especially beautiful from the Top o' Quad restaurant. ⊠ *U.S. 302, 03575,* ☎ *603/ 278–3300, 800/232–2972 for information, 800/258–0330 for lodging.*

Downhill. The skiing on the 33 trails is novice and intermediate, with steeper pitches near the top of the 1,500-ft vertical and glade skiing to satisfy expert skiers. Skiers and snowboarders can try a terrain park with jumps and halfpipes. The Accelerator halfpipe is for snowboarders only. One detachable quad, one triple, and two double chairlifts service the trails. The area has night skiing and snowboarding on Friday, Saturday, and holidays. A limited lift-ticket policy helps keep lines short.

Cross-country. The large, full-service cross-country ski center at Bretton Woods has 95 km (59 mi) of groomed and double-track trails and also rents snowshoes. Half the trails are in the White Mountain National Forest.

Child care. The nursery takes children from age 2 months to 5 years. The ski school has an all-day program for children ages 4 to 12, using progressive instructional techniques. There's also a snowboarding program for children 8 to 12. Rates include lifts, lessons, equipment, lunch, and supervised play.

Bethlehem

㉝   *25 mi west of Bretton Woods, 84 mi north of Concord.*

In the days before antihistamines, hay-fever sufferers came by the busload to the town of Bethlehem, elevation 1,462 ft, whose crisp air has a blissfully low pollen count.

Lodging

$$$–$$$$ **Adair.** In 1927 attorney Frank Hogan built this three-story Geor-
★ gian Revival home as a wedding present for his daughter, Dorothy Adair.
Walking paths on this luxurious country inn's 200 acres wind through
gardens and offer magnificent mountain views. The rooms, which
have garden or mountain views, are decorated with period antiques
and antique reproductions. One suite has a large two-person hot tub,
a fireplace, a balcony, and a king-size sleigh bed. The inn is no-smok-
ing and has a two-night minimum on weekends, three on holiday
weekends. ⊠ *80 Guider La., 03574,* ☎ *603/444–2600 or 888/444–
2600,* 𝔽𝕏 *603/444–4823. 7 rooms, 2 suites, 1 cottage. Tennis court,
billiards. Full breakfast. AE, MC, V.*

Outdoor Activities and Sports

The Society for the Protection of New Hampshire Forests owns two
properties in Bethlehem open to visitors. **Bretzfelder Park** (⊠ Prospect
St., ☎ 603/444–6228), a 77-acre nature and wildlife park, has a pic-
nic shelter, hiking, and cross-country ski trails. The **Rocks Estate** (⊠
113 Glessner Rd., ☎ 603/444–6228) is a working Christmas-tree farm
with walking trails, historic buildings, and educational programs.

Franconia

㉞   *8 mi south of Bethlehem, 74 mi north of Concord.*

Travelers first came to Franconia because the notch of the same name
provided a north–south route through the mountains. The town, which
is north of the notch, and the scenic notch itself are well worth a look.
Famous literary visitors to the area have included Washington Irving,
Henry Wadsworth Longfellow, and Nathaniel Hawthorne, who wrote
a short story about the Old Man of the Mountain. I–93 is called the
Franconia Notch Parkway as it passes through the notch.

The **Frost Place,** Robert Frost's home from 1915 to 1920, is where the
poet wrote one of his most-remembered poems, "Stopping by Woods
on a Snowy Evening." Two rooms contain memorabilia and signed edi-
tions of his books. Outside, you can follow short trails marked with lines
from Frost's poetry. Occasional poetry readings take place here. ⊠
Ridge Rd. (off Rte. 116; follow signs), ☎ *603/823–5510.* 🖭 *$3.* ☉ *Memo-
rial Day–June, weekends 1–5; July–Columbus Day, Wed.–Mon. 1–5.*

Franconia Notch State Park, south of Franconia, contains a few of New
Hampshire's best-loved attractions. A multiuse recreational path runs
parallel to the Franconia Notch Parkway. **Cannon Mountain Aerial
Tramway** will lift you 2,022 ft for one more sweeping mountain vista.
It's a five-minute ride to the top, where marked hiking trails lead to
the observation platform. ⊠ *Cannon Mountain ski area, Exit 3 off Fran-
conia Notch Pkwy.,* ☎ *603/823–8800.* 🖭 *Tramway $9.* ☉ *Tramway
Memorial Day–3rd weekend in Oct., daily 9–4:30.*

The **New England Ski Museum,** north of Cannon Mountain at the foot
of the tramway, has photographs and old trophies, skis and bindings,
boots, and ski apparel dating from the late 1800s. A gift shop stocks
ski-related books, posters, videos, and gift items. ⊠ *Franconia Notch
Pkwy., Exit 2,* ☎ *603/823–7177.* 🖭 *Free.* ☉ *Dec.–Mar., Thurs.–Tues.
noon–5; Memorial Day–Columbus Day, daily noon–5.*

It would be a shame to come to the White Mountains and leave with-
out seeing the granite profile of the **Old Man of the Mountain,** the icon
of New Hampshire. Nathaniel Hawthorne wrote about it, New Hamp-
shire resident Daniel Webster bragged about it, and P. T. Barnum
wanted to buy it. The two best places to view the giant stone face are

the highway parking area on the Franconia Notch Parkway or along the shores of Profile Lake.

The **Flume** is an 800-ft-long natural chasm with narrow walls that give the gorge's running water an eerie echo. The route through the flume has been built up with a series of boardwalks and stairways. The visitor center has exhibits on the region's history. ⊠ *Franconia Notch Pkwy., Exit 2,* ☎ *603/745–8391.* ⌨ *$7.* ⊙ *May–Oct., daily 9–5.*

Dining and Lodging

$$ ✕⌷ **Franconia Inn.** This resort has recreations for all seasons. You can golf next door at Sunset Hill's nine-hole course, play tennis, ride horseback, swim in the pool or sit in the hot tub, order your lunch to go for a day of hiking—even try soaring from the inn's airstrip. The inn has a cross-country ski center, too (☞ Skiing and Snow Sports, *below*). Rooms have designer chintzes, canopy beds, and country furnishings; some have whirlpool baths or fireplaces. At meals ($$–$$$), children choose from a separate menu. Among the fare for adults are the medallions of veal with apple-mustard sauce and the filet mignon with green-chili butter and Madeira sauce. ⊠ *1300 Easton Rd., 03580,* ☎ *603/ 823–5542 or 800/473–5299,* ☏ *603/823–8078. 34 rooms. Restaurant, pool, hot tub, 4 tennis courts, croquet, horseback riding, bicycles, ice-skating, cross-country skiing, sleigh rides. Full breakfast; MAP available. AE, MC, V. Closed Apr.–mid-May.*

$$ ⌷ **Horse and Hound Inn.** Off the beaten path yet convenient to the Cannon Mountain tram, this inn is on 8 acres surrounded by the White Mountain National Forest. Antiques and assorted collectibles provide a cheery atmosphere, and on the grounds are 65 km (39 mi) of cross-country ski trails. Pets are welcome ($8.50 per stay). ⊠ *205 Wells Rd., 03580,* ☎ *603/823–5501 or 800/450–5501. 10 rooms, 8 with bath. Restaurant, bar, cross-country skiing. Full breakfast. AE, D, DC, MC, V. Closed Apr. and Nov.*

$ ⚲ **Lafayette Campground.** This campground has hiking and biking trails, 97 tent sites, showers, a camp store, a bike trail, and easy access to the Appalachian Trail. ⊠ *Franconia Notch State Park, 03580,* ☎ *603/823–9513 for information; 603/271–3628 for reservations. No pets. MC, V.*

Nightlife and the Arts

Hillwinds (⊠ Main St., ☎ 603/823–5551) has live entertainment on weekends.

Shopping

The **Franconia Marketplace** (⊠ Main St., ☎ 603/823–5368) sells only products made in Franconia. Stores in the complex include the Grateful Bread Quality Bakery and Tiffany Workshop, which stocks clothing and crystal jewelry.

Skiing and Snow Sports

CANNON MOUNTAIN

Nowhere is the granite of the Granite State more pronounced than here. One of the first ski areas in the United States, Cannon, which is owned and run by the state, gives strong attention to skier services, family programs, snowmaking, and grooming. The New England Ski Museum (☞ *above*) is adjacent to the base of the tramway. ⊠ *Franconia Notch State Park, Franconia Notch Pkwy., Exit 3, 03580,* ☎ *603/823–8800; 603/823–7771 for snow conditions; 800/237–9007 for lodging.*

Downhill. The quality of this mountain's skiing is reflected in the narrow, steep pitches off the peak of the 2,146 ft of vertical rise. Some trails marked intermediate may seem more difficult because of the side-hill slant of the slopes (rather than the steepness). Under a new fall of snow, Cannon's 42 trails have challenges not often found at modern ski areas. For additional fun, try the two glade-skiing trails, Turnpike and Banshee. There is a 70-passenger tramway to the top, one quad, one triple, and two double chairlifts, and one surface lift.

Cross-country. Nordic skiing is available on a 13-km (8-mi) multiuse recreational path through Franconia Notch State Park.

Child care. Cannon's Peabody Base Lodge takes children ages 1 year and older. All-day and half-day SKIwee programs are available for children from age 4 to 12, and season-long instruction can be arranged.

FRANCONIA VILLAGE CROSS-COUNTRY SKI CENTER
This ski center at the Franconia Inn (☞ Dining and Lodging, *above*) has 65 km (39 mi) of groomed trails and 40 km (24 mi) of backcountry trails. One popular trail leads to Bridal Veil Falls, a great spot for a picnic lunch. There are horse-drawn sleigh rides and ice-skating on a lighted rink as well. ⊠ *1300 Easton Rd., 03580,* ☎ *603/823–5542 or 800/473–5299,* FAX *603/823–8078.*

Sugar Hill

③⑤ *4 mi west of Franconia, 11 mi south of Bethlehem, 77 mi north of Concord.*

Sugar Hill, a town of 500 people, is deservedly famous for the spectacular sunsets and views of the Franconia Mountains, best seen from Sunset Hill, where a row of grand hotels and summer "cottages" once stood. Quiet country charm and good-quality bed-and-breakfasts and small inns make Sugar Hill an ideal spot for a romantic getaway.

The surprisingly well done **Sugar Hill Historical Museum** has permanent and changing exhibits that focus on the history of the area from settlement through the resort era. ⊠ *Rte. 117,* ☎ *603/823–5336.* 🖾 *$2.* ☉ *July–mid-Oct., Thurs. and weekends 1–4.*

Dining and Lodging

$ ✕ **Polly's Pancake Parlor** This local institution, originally a carriage shed built in 1830, was converted to a tea room during the depression, when the Dexters began serving "all you can eat" pancakes, waffles, and French toast for 50¢. The prices have gone up some, but the descendants of the Dexters continue to serve pancakes and waffles made from grains ground on the property, their own country sausage, and local maple syrup. ⊠ *Rte. 117,* ☎ *603/823–5575. MC, V. No dinner.*

$$–$$$$ ✕🖾 **Sugar Hill Inn.** The old carriage on the lawn and wicker chairs on the wraparound porch set a nostalgic mood before you even enter this converted 1789 farmhouse. Many rooms have hand-stenciled walls, views of the Franconia Mountains, and rippled antique windowpanes; all contain antiques. The late film star Bette Davis visited friends in this house before she bought her own farm nearby—the room with the best view is named after her. The restaurant ($$$; reservations required) serves meat, fish, and poultry dishes and delicious desserts. There are 10 rooms in the inn and 6 (some with fireplaces) in three country cottages. The inn is no-smoking. ⊠ *Rte. 117, 03585,* ☎ *603/823–5621 or 800/548–4748,* FAX *603/823–5639. 16 rooms. Restaurant, pub, cross-country skiing. Full breakfast; MAP available (required during foliage season). AE, MC, V.*

$$–$$$ 🖾 **Hilltop.** Staying with innkeepers Mike and Meri Hern is just like dropping by Grandma's—they even welcome pets. The rooms in their 1895 country farmhouse are done in a quirky mix of antiques with handmade quilts, Victorian ceiling fans, piles of pillows, and big, fluffy towels. The TV room has hundreds of movies on tape. Rockers on the porch

are perfect for watching the sun set behind the mountains. The large country breakfast includes homemade jams, pancakes made with homegrown berries, soufflés, and smoked ham, bacon, or salmon. The no-smoking inn has a two-night minimum during foliage season, summer weekends, and on holidays. ⊠ *Rte. 117, 03585,* ☎ *603/823–5695 or 800/770–5695,* FAX *603/823–5518. 3 rooms, 3 suites, 1 2-bedroom cottage. Restaurant, bar, library. Full breakfast. D, MC, V.*

$$–$$$ 🖼 **Foxglove.** Extensive gardens with hammocks for relaxing are just one of the sybaritic delights at this rambling turn-of-the-century home next to Lover's Lane. The delicious breakfast is different each day, as is the china on which it is served. Common areas are decorated in country-French style with antiques. Guest rooms are thoughtfully furnished, each in a different motif. The Serengeti Room has animal- print linens, a chandelier with carnival glass shades, and black and brass fixtures in the bath. The inn is no-smoking. ⊠ *Rte. 117, 03585,* ☎ *603/823–8840,* FAX *603/823–5755. 6 rooms. Full breakfast.*

The White Mountains A to Z

Arriving and Departing

BY BUS

Concord Trailways (☎ 800/639–3317) stops in Chocorua, Conway, Franconia, Glen, and Jackson.

BY CAR

Access to the White Mountains is from I–93 via the Kancamagus Highway or U.S. 302. From the seacoast, Route 16 is the popular choice.

BY PLANE

Manchester Airport (☞ Arriving and Departing *in* New Hampshire A to Z, *below*) is about an hour's drive from the White Mountains region.

Getting Around

BY BUS

See Arriving and Departing, *above.*

BY CAR

I–93 and U.S. 3 bisect the White Mountain National Forest, running north from Massachusetts to Québec. The Kancamagus Highway (Route 112), the east–west thoroughfare through the White Mountain National Forest, is a scenic drive. U.S. 302, a longer, more leisurely east–west path, connects I–93 to North Conway.

BY PLANE

Charters and private planes land at **Franconia Airport & Soaring Center** (⊠ Easton Rd., Franconia, ☎ 603/823–8881) and **Mt. Washington Regional Airport** (⊠ Airport Rd., Whitefield, ☎ 603/837–9532).

Contacts and Resources

CAMPING

White Mountain National Forest (⊠ U.S. Forest Service, 719 N. Main St., Laconia 03246, ☎ 603/528–8721; 877/444–6777 for campground reservations) has 20 campgrounds with more than 900 campsites spread across the region; only some take reservations. All sites are subject to a 14-day limit.

CANOEING, KAYAKING, AND RAFTING

River outfitter **Saco Bound Canoe & Kayak** (⊠ Box 119, Center Conway 03813, ☎ 603/447–2177) leads gentle canoeing expeditions, guided kayak trips, and white-water rafting on seven rivers and provides lessons, equipment, and transportation.

EMERGENCIES

Memorial Hospital (✉ 3073 White Mountain Hwy., North Conway, ☎ 603/356–5461).

FISHING

For trout and salmon fishing, try the Connecticut Lakes, though any clear stream in the White Mountains will do. Many are stocked, and there are 650 mi of them in the national forest alone. Conway Lake is the largest of the area's 45 lakes and ponds; it's noted for smallmouth bass and—early and late in the season—good salmon fishing. The **New Hampshire Fish and Game Office** (☎ 603/788–3164) has up-to-date information on fishing conditions.

The **North Country Angler** (✉ 3643 White Mountain Hwy., Intervale, ☎ 603/356–6000) schedules intensive guided fly-fishing weekends.

HIKING

With 86 major mountains in the area, the hiking possibilities are endless. Innkeepers can usually point you toward the better nearby trails; some inns schedule guided day-trips for guests. The **White Mountain National Forest** (☞ Visitor Information, *below*) has hiking information and information about parking passes ($5) required in the national forest. These are available at visitor centers; if you can't buy one in advance, you can park and you'll probably find an envelope with information on your windshield.

The **Appalachian Mountain Club** (✉ Box 298, Gorham 03581, ☎ 603/466–2721; 603/466–2725 for trail information; 603/466–2727 for reservations or a free guide to huts and lodges) headquarters at Pinkham Notch offers lectures, workshops, slide shows, and outdoor skills instruction from June to October. Accommodations include a 100-bunk main lodge, a 24-bed hostel in Crawford Notch, and two rustic cabins. The club's eight trailside huts provide meals and dorm-style lodging, June through October, on several trails in the Whites.

New England Hiking Holidays (✉ Box 1648, North Conway 03860, ☎ 603/356–9696 or 800/869–0949) conducts scheduled guided hiking tours with lodging in country inns for two to eight nights.

LODGING RESERVATION SERVICES

Country Inns in the White Mountains (☎ 603/356–9460). **Jackson Chamber of Commerce Reservation Service** (☎ 800/866–3334).

VISITOR INFORMATION

Jackson Chamber of Commerce (Box 304, Jackson 03846, ☎ 603/383–9356 or 800/866–3334). **Mt. Washington Valley Chamber of Commerce** (☎ 603/356–3171 or 800/367–3364). **Mt. Washington Valley Hot Line** (☎ 877/948–6867). **North Country Chamber of Commerce** (✉ Box 1, Colebrook 03576, ☎ 603/237–8939 or 800/698–8939). **White Mountain Attractions Association** (✉ Kancamagus Hwy., North Woodstock 03251, ☎ 603/745–8720 or 800/346–3687). **White Mountain National Forest** (✉ U.S. Forest Service, 719 N. Main St., Laconia 03246, ☎ 603/528–8721; 877/444–6777 for campground reservations).

WESTERN AND CENTRAL NEW HAMPSHIRE

Here is the unspoiled heart of New Hampshire. The beaches on the state's coast attract sun worshipers, and the resort towns to the north keep the skiers and hikers beating a well-worn path up I–93, but western and central New Hampshire have managed to keep the water slides and the outlet malls at bay. In the center of New Hampshire you'll see one pristine town green after another. Each village has its own historical society and tiny museum filled with odd bits of memorabilia.

Two other lures in this area are the shining waters of Lake Sunapee and the looming presence of Mt. Monadnock. When you're done climbing and swimming and visiting the past, look for the wares and small studios of area artists. The region has long been an informal artists' colony where people come to write, paint, and weave in solitude.

The towns in this region, beginning with Concord, are described in counterclockwise order. From Concord, take I–89 through the Lake Sunapee region to Hanover, follow the Connecticut River south to Keene, and then meander through the Monadnock region to Manchester.

Concord

③⑥ *40 mi north of the Massachusetts border via I–93, 20 mi north of Manchester, 45 mi northwest of Portsmouth.*

New Hampshire's capital (population 38,000) is a quiet, conservative town that tends to the state's business but little else. The residents joke that the sidewalks roll up promptly at 6. The **Concord on Foot** walking trail winds through the historic district. Maps are available from the **Chamber of Commerce** (✉ 244 N. Main St.) or stores along the trail. The **Pierce Manse** is the Greek Revival home in which Franklin Pierce lived before moving to Washington to become the 14th U.S. president. ✉ *14 Penacook St.,* ☎ *603/224–9620 or 603/224–7668.* 💲 *$3.* ☉ *Mid-June–Labor Day, weekdays 11–3.*

At the gilt-domed neoclassical **State House,** New Hampshire's legislature still meets in its original chambers. The building dates to 1819 and is the oldest in the United States in continuous use as a state capitol. ✉ *107 N. Main St.,* ☎ *603/271–2154.* ☉ *Weekdays 8–4:30; guided tours by reservation.*

Among the artifacts at the **Museum of New Hampshire History** is an original Concord Coach. During the 19th century, when more than 3,000 coaches were built in Concord, this was about as technologically perfect a vehicle as you could find—many say it's the coach that won the West. Other exhibits provide an overview of New Hampshire's history, from the Abenaki to the settlers of Portsmouth up to current residents. ✉ *6 Eagle Sq.,* ☎ *603/226–3189.* 💲 *$5.* ☉ *Jan.–June and mid-Oct.–Nov., Tues.–Wed. and Sat. 9:30–5, Thurs.–Fri. 9:30–8:30, Sun. noon–5; Dec. and July–mid-Oct., Mon.–Wed. and Sat. 9:30–5, Thurs.–Fri. 9:30–8:30, Sun. noon–5.*

ᗌ The high-tech **Christa McAuliffe Planetarium** presents shows on the solar system, constellations, and space exploration that incorporate computer graphics, sound, and special effects in the 40-ft dome theater. Children love seeing the tornado tubes, magnetic marbles, and other hands-on exhibits. Outside, explore the scale-model planet walk and the human sundial. The planetarium was named for the Concord teacher and first civilian in space, who was killed in the *Challenger* space-shuttle explosion in 1986. ✉ *New Hampshire Technical Institute campus, 3 Institute Dr.,* ☎ *603/271–7827.* 💲 *Exhibit area free, shows $6.* ☉ *Tues.–Thurs. 9–5, Fri. 9–7, weekends 10–5. Call for show times and reservations.*

Guided tours of the late-Victorian **Kimball-Jenkins Estate** focus on the craftsmanship of the mansion—including the woodwork, tilework, and frescoed ceilings—and stories of more than 200 years of life in Concord. The formal gardens are the perfect spot for a summer picnic. ✉ *266 N. Main St.,* ☎ *603/225–3932.* 💲 *$4.* ☉ *June–Oct. Call for hrs.*

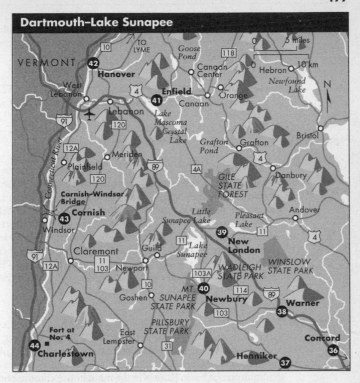

Dartmouth–Lake Sunapee

Dining and Lodging

$–$$$ ✕ **Hermanos Cocina Mexicana.** The food at this popular two-level restau-
★ rant is standard Mexican but with fresher ingredients and more sub-
tle sauces than might be expected. Everything on the menu is available
à la carte, so you can mix and match to build a meal. ✉ *11 Hills Ave.,*
☎ *603/224–5669. Reservations not accepted. D, MC, V.*

$$–$$$ ✕▥ **Centennial Inn.** Built in 1896 for widows of Civil War veterans,
this brick-and-stone building is set back from busy Pleasant Street. Much
of the original woodwork has been preserved. Each room is decorated
with antiques and reproduction pieces, and all have ceiling fans and
VCRs. In the Franklin Pierce dining room, try the shredded-duck pizza
and the roast medallions of venison. ✉ *96 Pleasant St., 03301,* ☎ *603/*
225–7102 or 800/360–4839, ☞ *603/225–5031. 27 rooms, 5 suites.*
Restaurant, bar, in-room data ports. AE, D, DC, MC, V.

Nightlife and the Arts

The **Capitol Center for the Arts** (✉ 46 S. Main St., ☎ 603/225–1111)
has been restored to reflect its Roaring '20s origins. It hosts touring
Broadway shows, dance companies, and musical acts. The lounge at
Hermanos Cocina Mexicana (☞ Dining and Lodging, *above*) has live
jazz on Sunday and Wednesday nights.

Outdoor Activities and Sports

Hannah's Paddles, Inc. (✉ 15 Hannah Dustin Dr., ☎ 603/753–6695)
rents canoes for use on the Merrimack River.

Shopping

CRAFTS

Capitol Craftsman and Romance Jewelers (✉ 16 N. Main St., ☎ 603/
224–6166 or 603/228–5683), which share adjoining shops, sell fine
jewelry and handicrafts. The **Den of Antiquity** (✉ 2 Capital Plaza, ☎
603/225–4505) carries handcrafted country gifts and accessories. The

League of New Hampshire Craftsmen (⊠ 36 N. Main St., ☎ 603/228–8171) exhibits crafts in many media. **Mark Knipe Goldsmiths** (⊠ 2 Capitol Plaza, Main St., ☎ 603/224–2920) sets antique stones in rings, earrings, and pendants.

MALLS

Steeplegate Mall (⊠ 270 Loudon Rd., ☎ 603/224–1523) has more than 70 stores, including chain department stores and some smaller crafts shops.

Henniker

③⑦ *17 mi west of Concord.*

Governor Wentworth, the first Royal Governor of New Hampshire, named this town in honor of his friend John Henniker, a London merchant and member of the British Parliament (residents delight in their town's status as "the only Henniker in the world"). Once a mill town producing bicycle rims and other light-industrial items, Henniker reinvented itself after the factories were damaged, first by spring floods in 1936 and then by the hurricane and flood of 1938. New England College was established in the following decade. One of the area's covered bridges can be found on campus.

Dining and Lodging

$$–$$$$ ✗⌸ **Colby Hill Inn.** The cookie jar is always full in this Colonial farmhouse, where guests are greeted by Delilah, the inn dog. There is no shortage of relaxing activities: You can curl up with a book by the parlor fireplace, stroll through the gardens and 5 acres of meadow, or play badminton out back. Rooms in the main house contain antiques, Colonial reproductions, and frills like lace curtains. In the carriage-house rooms, plain country furnishings, stenciled walls, and exposed beams are the norm. The dining menu ($$$–$$$$) is excellent: Try the chicken Colby Hill (breast of chicken stuffed with lobster, leeks, and Boursin) or the crab crepes. ⊠ *Box 779, 3 The Oaks, 03242,* ☎ *603/428–3281,* ℻ *603/428–9218. 16 rooms. Restaurant, in-room data ports, pool, ice-skating, recreation room. Full breakfast. AE, D, DC, MC, V.*

$–$$ ✗⌸ **Meeting House Inn & Restaurant.** The owners of this 200-year-old farmhouse at the base of Pats Peak, who tout the complex as a lovers' getaway, start guests' days off with breakfast in bed. The old barn has become a restaurant ($$–$$$) that specializes in leisurely, romantic dining. Items like lobster pepito are served in a heart-shape puff pastry, and the chocolate-raspberry frozen mousse is also heart-shape. ⊠ *Rte. 114/Flanders Rd., 03242,* ☎ *603/428–3228,* ℻ *603/428–6334. 6 rooms. Restaurant, hot tub, sauna. Full breakfast. AE, D, MC, V.*

Shopping

The **Fiber Studio** (⊠ 9 Foster Hill Rd., ☎ 603/428–7830) sells beads, hand-spun natural-fiber yarns, spinning equipment, and looms.

Skiing and Snow Sports

PATS PEAK

Convenient for Bostonians who can make a quick trip up I–93, Pats Peak is geared to families. Base facilities are rustic, and friendly personal attention is the rule. ⊠ *Rte. 114, 03242,* ☎ *603/428–3245; 800/742–7287 for snow conditions.*

Downhill. Despite Pats Peak's size of only 710 vertical ft, the 20 trails and slopes have something for everyone. New skiers and snowboarders can take advantage of a wide slope and several short trails; intermediates have wider trails from the top; and advanced skiers have a couple of real thrillers. Night skiing and snowboarding take place in

January and February. One triple and two double chairlifts, one T-bar, and three surface lifts serve the runs. Pats Peak also has afternoon snow-tubing on weekends and holiday periods.

Child care. The nursery takes children from age 6 months to 5 years. Special nursery ski programs operate on weekends and during vacations for children from 4 to 12; all-day lessons for self-sufficient skiers in this age range are scheduled throughout the season.

Warner

③⑧ *18 mi north of Henniker, 22 mi northwest of Concord.*

Three New Hampshire governors were born in this quiet agricultural town just off I–89. Buildings dating from the late 1700s and early 1800s and a charming library give the town's main street a welcoming feel.

Mount Kearsarge Indian Museum, Education, and Cultural Center gives guided tours of the extensive collection of Native American artistry, including moose-hair embroidery, quillwork, and basketry. Signs on the self-guided Medicine Woods trail identify plants and explain how Native Americans used them as foods, medicines, and dyes. ⊠ *Kearsarge Mountain Rd., 03278,* ☎ *603/456–2600.* ☞ *$6.* ⊙ *May–Oct., Mon.–Sat. 10–5, Sun. noon–5; Nov.–Dec., Sat. 10–5, Sun. noon–5.*

A scenic auto road at **Rollins State Park** (⊠ off Rte. 103) snakes nearly 3,000 ft up the southern slope of Mt. Kearsarge, where you can then tackle on foot the ½-mi trail to the summit.

New London

③⑨ *12 mi northwest of Warner, 10 mi west of Andover, 34 mi northwest of Concord.*

New London, the home of Colby-Sawyer College (1837), is a good base for exploring the Lake Sunapee region. A worthwhile stop is 10,000-year-old **Cricenti's Bog,** off Business Route 11 (Business Route 11 goes right through town; Route 11 goes around town). A short trail, maintained by the local conservation commission, shows off the shaggy mosses and fragile ecosystem of this ancient pond.

Dining and Lodging

$–$$ ✕ **Peter Christian's Tavern.** Exposed beams, wooden tables, a smattering of antiques, and half shutters on the windows make Peter Christian's a cool oasis in summer and a cozy haven in winter. Tavern fare like beef stew and shepherd's pie has been updated for this century. ⊠ *186 Main St., 03257,* ☎ *603/526–4042. AE, D, MC, V.*

$$–$$$ ✕⊡ **Inn at Pleasant Lake.** This family-run property is aptly named for its location and ambience. The original farmhouse dates from 1790, and that early country look has been maintained by keeping frills to a minimum. Five acres of woods, fields, and gardens surround the inn. Candlelight and classical music accompany the restaurant's five-course prix-fixe dinner. ⊠ *Box 1030, 125 Pleasant St., 03257,* ☎ *603/526–6271 or 800/626–4907,* ℻ *603/525–4111. 12 rooms. Restaurant. Full breakfast. MC, V.*

$$–$$$ ✕⊡ **New London Inn.** The two porches of this rambling 1792 country inn overlook Main Street. Rooms have a Victorian decor; those in the front of the house overlook the pretty campus of Colby-Sawyer College. The nouvelle-inspired menu in the restaurant starts with items like butternut squash with a sun-dried cranberry pesto and includes entrées such as grilled cilantro shrimp with a saffron risotto. The inn is no-smoking. ⊠ *Box 8, 140 Main St., 03257,* ☎ *603/526–2791 or 800/526–2791,* ℻ *603/526–2749. 28 rooms. Restaurant. Full breakfast. AE, MC, V.*

$$ 🏠 **Follansbee Inn.** Built in 1840, this quintessential country inn on the shore of Kezar Lake is a perfect fit in the 19th-century village of North Sutton, about 4 mi south of New London. The common rooms and bedrooms are loaded with collectibles and antiques. You can ice-fish on the lake and ski across it in winter and swim or boat from the inn's pier in summer. A 3-mi walking trail circles the lake. The inn is no-smoking. ⊠ *Rte. 114, North Sutton 03260,* ☎ *603/927–4221 or 800/ 626–4221. 23 rooms, 11 with bath; 1 cottage. Lake, hiking, boating, fishing, ice-skating, cross-country skiing. Full breakfast. MC, V.*

$ 🏕 **Otter Lake Camping Area.** The 28 sites on Otter Lake have plenty of shade, and there are numerous activities. Facilities include a beach, boating, fishing, a playground, and canoe and paddleboat rentals. ⊠ *55 Otterville Rd., 03257,* ☎ *603/763–5600.*

Nightlife and the Arts

The **New London Playhouse** (⊠ 209 Main St., ☎ 603/526–6710) presents Broadway-style and children's plays every summer in New Hampshire's oldest continuously operating theater.

Outdoor Activities and Sports

Pleasant Lake, off Route 11, has salmon, brook trout, and bass.

Shopping

Artisan's Workshop (⊠ Peter Christian's Tavern, 186 Main St., ☎ 603/ 526–4227) carries jewelry, hand-blown glass, and other local handicrafts.

Skiing and Snow Sports

NORSK CROSS COUNTRY SKI CENTER

The 75 km (46½ mi) of scenic cross-country ski trails here are also perfect for hiking in the warmer months. ⊠ *Rte. 11,* ☎ *603/526–4685 or 800/426–6775.*

Newbury

❹⓪ *10 mi south of New London, on the edge of Mt. Sunapee State Park; 38 mi northwest of Concord.*

Mt. Sunapee, which rises to an elevation of nearly 3,000 ft, and sparkling Lake Sunapee are the region's outdoor recreation centers. **Mt. Sunapee State Park** has 130 acres of hiking and picnic areas, a beach, and a bathhouse. You can rent canoes at the beach. In winter the mountain becomes a downhill ski area and host to national ski competitions. In summer the park holds the League of New Hampshire Craftsmen's Fair, a Fourth of July flea market, and the Gem and Mineral Festival. ⊠ *Rte. 103,* ☎ *603/763–2356.* 🎫 *$2.50.* ☉ *Daily dawn–dusk.*

The narrated cruises aboard **M/V Mt. Sunapee II** (⊠ Sunapee Harbor, ☎ 603/763–4030) provide a closer look at Lake Sunapee.

Lodging

$ 🏕 **Crow's Nest Campground.** This year-round campground on the Sugar River has 100 sites, some on the river. The facilities include a recreation hall, a swimming pool, a children's wading pool, miniature golf in summer, and a warm-up room with fireplace for winter use. River swimming and fishing are summer pastimes; you can skate or sled in the winter, and area snowmobile trails connect to the campground. ⊠ *Rte. 10, Newport 03773,* ☎ *603/863–6170.*

Outdoor Activities and Sports

Lake Sunapee has brook and lake trout, salmon, smallmouth bass, and pickerel.

Shopping

Dorr Mill Store (⊠ Rte. 11/103, Guild, ☎ 603/863–1197), the yarn and fabric center of the Sunapee area, has a huge selection of fiber.

Skiing and Snow Sports

MOUNT SUNAPEE

Although the resort is state-owned, the operation of Mount Sunapee is now leased to Vermont's Okemo Mountain resort, known for its family-friendly atmosphere. The lease agreement brought a necessary influx of capital to update aging lifts, snowmaking, and other facilities. ⊠ *Mt. Sunapee State Park, Rte. 103, 03772,* ☎ *603/763–2356; 800/ 552–1234 for snow conditions; 800/258–3530 for lodging.*

Downhill. This mountain is 1,510 vertical ft, the highest in southern New Hampshire, and has 41 trails, mostly intermediate, with a couple of steep pitches. A nice beginner's section is beyond the base facilities, well away from other trails. Black-diamond slopes now number nine—including Goosebumps, a double-black diamond—so experts have some challenges. A new halfpipe expands the options for snowboarders. Two base lodges and a summit lodge supply the essentials. One high-speed detachable quad, one fixed-grip quad, one triple, and three double chairlifts and two surface lifts transport skiers.

Child Care. The Duckling Nursery takes children from ages 1 to 5. The Little Indians children's program gives ages 3 and 4 a taste of skiing, and SKIwee lessons are available for kids ages 5 to 12.

Enfield

④ *35 mi north of Newbury, 55 mi northwest of Concord.*

In 1782, two Shaker brothers from Mount Lebanon, New York, arrived at a community on the northeastern side of Mascoma Lake. Eventually, they formed Enfield, the ninth of 18 Shaker communities in this country, and moved it to the lake's southern shore, where they erected more than 200 buildings.

The **Enfield Shaker Museum** preserves the legacy of the Enfield Shakers. A self-guided walking tour takes you through 13 of the buildings that remain. The museum preserves and explains Shaker artifacts, and skilled craftspeople demonstrate Shaker techniques. Numerous special events take place each year. ⊠ *2 Lower Shaker Village Rd.,* ☎ *603/ 632–4346.* ▦ *$5.* ◉ *Memorial Day–mid-Oct., Mon.–Sat. 10–5, Sun. noon–5; mid-Oct.–Memorial Day, Sat. 10–4, Sun. noon–4.*

Dining and Lodging

$$–$$$ ✗▦ **The Shaker Inn.** Built between 1837 and 1841, the Great Stone Dwelling is the largest main dwelling ever built by a Shaker community. Adjacent to the Enfield Shaker Museum (☞ *above*), it is now an inn, and the guest rooms in the original Shaker sleeping chambers have reproduction Shaker furniture and are decorated with the simplicity and style for which the religious community was known. The dining room serves Shaker-inspired cuisine such as pumpkin ravioli and maple-glazed baked ham. ⊠ *447 Rte. 4A, 03748,* ☎ *603/632–7810 or 888/707–4257. 24 rooms. Restaurant. AE, D, MC, V.*

Outdoor Activities and Sports

Anglers can try for rainbow trout, pickerel, and horned pout in **Lake Mascoma.**

Hanover

42 *12 mi west of Enfield via Rte. 120 from Lebanon, 60 mi northwest of Concord.*

Eleazer Wheelock founded Hanover's Dartmouth College in 1769 to educate the Abenaki "and other youth." When he arrived, the town consisted of about 20 families. The college and the town grew symbiotically, with Dartmouth becoming the northernmost Ivy League school. Today Hanover is still synonymous with Dartmouth, but the town is also a respected medical center and the cultural center for the upper Connecticut River valley.

Robert Frost spent part of a brooding freshman semester at Ivy League **Dartmouth College** before giving up college altogether. The buildings that cluster around the green include the **Baker Memorial Library,** which houses literary treasures including 17th-century editions of Shakespeare's works. If the towering arcade at the entrance to the **Hopkins Center** (☎ 603/ 646–2422) appears familiar, it's probably because it resembles the project that architect Wallace K. Harrison completed just after designing it: New York City's Metropolitan Opera House at Lincoln Center. The complex includes a 900-seat theater for film and music, a 400-seat theater for plays, and a black-box theater for new plays. The Dartmouth Symphony Orchestra performs here, as does the Big Apple Circus (in summer). In addition to African, Peruvian, Oceanic, Asian, European, and American art, the **Hood Museum of Art** owns the Picasso painting *Guitar on a Table,* silver by Paul Revere, and a set of Assyrian reliefs from the 9th century BC. Rivaling the collection is the museum's architecture: a series of austere redbrick buildings with copper roofs arranged around a courtyard. Free guided tours are given on some weekend afternoons. ⊠ *Museum: Wheelock St.,* ☎ *603/646–2808.* ☜ *Free.* ☉ *Tues. and Thurs.–Sat. 10–5, Wed. 10–9, Sun. noon–5.*

Dining and Lodging

$$$$ ✕🏨 **Hanover Inn.** Owned and operated by Dartmouth College, this
★ Georgian brick house rises four white-trimmed stories. The building was converted to a tavern in 1780 and has been open ever since. Rooms have Colonial reproductions, Audubon prints, and large sitting areas. The formal Daniel Webster Room ($$$–$$$$) serves regional American dishes like stuffed rabbit with prunes, cognac, and kale. The contemporary Zins wine bar ($–$$$) prepares lighter meals. ⊠ *Box 151, The Green, 03755,* ☎ *603/643–4300 or 800/443–7024,* ℻ *603/ 646–3744. 92 rooms. 2 restaurants. AE, D, DC, MC, V.*

$$–$$$$ 🏨 **Trumbull House.** This white Colonial-style house sits on 16 acres on the outskirts of Hanover. The sunny guest rooms are furnished with king- or queen-size beds, window seats, writing desks, and other comfortable touches. Breakfast is served in the formal dining room or in front of the fireplace in the living room. The inn is no-smoking. ⊠ *40 Etna Rd., 03755,* ☎ *603/643–2370 or 800/651–5141. 5 rooms. Pond. Full breakfast. AE, D, DC, MC, V.*

Outdoor Activities and Sports

The Connecticut River is generally considered safe after June 15, but canoeists should always exercise caution. This river is not for beginners. **Ledyard Canoe Club of Dartmouth** (☎ 603/643–6709) provides canoe and kayak rentals and classes.

Shopping

Goldsmith Paul Gross of **Designer Gold** (⊠ 3 Lebanon St., ☎ 603/643– 3864) designs settings for gemstones—all one-of-a-kind or limited-edition. He also carries some silver jewelry by other artisans.

West Lebanon, south of Hanover on the Vermont border, has a busy commercial section. The owners of the **Mouse Menagerie of Fine Crafts** (⊠ Rte. 12A, West Lebanon, ☎ 603/298–7090) have created a collector's series of toy mice and also sell furniture, wind chimes, and other gifts. The **Powerhouse Mall** (⊠ Rte. 12A, 1 mi north of Exit 20 off I–89, West Lebanon, ☎ 603/298–5236), a former power station, comprises three buildings of specialty stores, boutiques, and restaurants.

Cornish

➃ *18 mi south of Hanover on Rte. 12A, 70 mi northwest of Concord.*

Today Cornish is best known for its four covered bridges, but at the turn of the century the village was known primarily as the home of the country's then most popular novelist, Winston Churchill (no relation to the British prime minister). His novel *Richard Carvell* sold more than a million copies. Churchill was such a celebrity that he hosted Teddy Roosevelt during the president's 1902 visit. At that time Cornish was an enclave of artistic talent. Painter Maxfield Parrish lived and worked here, and sculptor Augustus Saint-Gaudens set up his studio and created the heroic bronzes for which he is known.

The 460-ft **Cornish-Windsor Bridge,** built in 1866, is the longest covered bridge in the United States. It spans the Connecticut River, connecting New Hampshire with Vermont.

★ The **Saint-Gaudens National Historic Site,** 1½ mi north of the Cornish-Windsor covered bridge, contains sculptor Augustus Saint-Gaudens's (1848–1907) house, studio, gallery, and 150 acres of grounds and gardens. Scattered throughout are full-size casts of his works. The property has two hiking trails, the longer of which is the 2½-mi Blow-Me-Down Trail. ⊠ *Off Rte. 12A,* ☎ *603/675–2175.* ☞ *$4.* ☺ *Buildings Memorial Day weekend–Oct., daily 9–4:30; grounds daily dawn–dusk.*

Dining and Lodging

$$$–$$$$ ✕⊞ **Home Hill Inn.** This restored 1800 mansion set back from the river on 25 acres of meadow and woods is a tranquil place best suited to adults. The owners have given the inn a French influence with 19th-century antiques and collectibles. Rooms in the main house have canopy or four-poster beds, and four have fireplaces; a suite in the guest house can be a romantic hideaway. Golf is on a nine-hole, par-3 executive course. The dining room serves classic and Mediterranean French cuisine like braised pheasant with apple and bacon sauerkraut or fresh, oven-poached turbot with sea urchin roe. ⊠ *River Rd., Plainfield 03781,* ☎ *603/675–6165. 6 rooms, 2 suites, 1 seasonal cottage. Pool, 9-hole golf course, tennis court, cross-country skiing. Continental breakfast. AE, D, MC, V.*

$$ ⊞ **Chase House Bed & Breakfast Inn.** Innkeepers Barbara Lewis and
★ Ted Doyle love sharing the history of this 1775 Federal house. It was the birthplace of Salmon P. Chase, who was Abraham Lincoln's secretary of the treasury, chief justice of the Supreme Court, and a founder of the Republican Party. Careful restoration with Colonial furnishings and Waverly fabrics has recaptured 19th-century elegance. Ask for a room with a canopy bed or one with a view of the Connecticut River valley and Mt. Ascutney. The inn is no-smoking. ⊠ *R.R. 2, Box 909, Rte. 12A (1½ mi south of Cornish-Windsor covered bridge), 03745,* ☎ *603/675–5391 or 800/401–9455,* ☒ *603/675–5010. 5 rooms, 3 suites. Exercise room, boating, snowshoeing. Full breakfast. MC, V. Closed Nov.*

Nightlife and the Arts

The beautifully restored 19th-century **Claremont Opera House** (⊠ Tremont Sq., Claremont, ☎ 603/542–4433) hosts plays and musicals from September to May.

Outdoor Activities and Sports

Northstar Canoe Livery (⊠ Rte. 12A, Balloch's Crossing, ☎ 603/542–5802) rents canoes for half- or full-day trips on the Connecticut River.

Charlestown

44 *20 mi south of Cornish, 32 mi north of Keene.*

Charlestown has the state's largest historic district: 63 homes of Federal, Greek Revival, and Gothic Revival architecture are clustered about the center of town; 10 of them were built before 1800. Several merchants on Main Street distribute brochures that contain an interesting walking tour of the district.

The **Fort at No. 4,** 1½ mi north of Charlestown, was in 1747 an outpost on the lonely periphery of Colonial civilization. That year fewer than 50 militia men at the fort withstood an attack by 400 French soldiers that changed the course of New England history by ensuring that northern New England remained under British rule. Costumed interpreters at the only living-history museum from the era of the French and Indian War cook dinner over an open hearth and demonstrate weaving, gardening, and candlemaking. Each year the museum holds full reenactments of militia musters and battles of the French and Indian War. ⊠ *Rte. 11/Springfield Rd.,* ☎ *603/826–5700.* ⊠ *$6.* ☉ *Late May–mid-Oct., Wed.–Mon. 10–4 (weekends only 1st 2 wks of Sept.).*

On a bright, breezy day you might want to detour to the **Morningside Flight Park** (⊠ Rte. 12/11, ☎ 603/542–4416), not necessarily to take hang-gliding lessons, although you could. You can watch the bright colors of the gliders as they swoop over the school's 450-ft peak.

Walpole

45 *12 mi south of Charlestown, 20 mi north of Keene.*

Walpole possesses one of the state's perfect town greens. This one is surrounded by homes built about 1790, when the townsfolk constructed a canal around the Great Falls of the Connecticut River and brought commerce and wealth to the area. The town now has 3,200 inhabitants, more than a dozen of whom are millionaires.

OFF THE BEATEN PATH

SUGARHOUSES – Maple-sugar season—a harbinger of spring—occurs about the first week in March when days become warmer but nights are still frigid. A drive along maple-lined back roads reveals thousands of taps and buckets catching the fresh but labored flow of unrefined sap. Plumes of smoke rise from nearby sugarhouses where sugaring off, the process of boiling down this precious liquid, takes place. Many sugarhouses are open to the public; after a tour and demonstration, you can sample the syrup with traditional unsweetened doughnuts and maybe a pickle—or taste hot syrup over fresh snow, a favorite confection. Open to the public in this area of the state are **Bacon's Sugar House** (⊠ 243 Dublin Rd., Jaffrey, ☎ 603/532–8836); **Bascom Maple Farm** (⊠ Mt. Kingsbury, off Rte. 123A, Alstead, ☎ 603/835–6361), which serves maple pecan pie and maple milk shakes; and **Stuart & John's Sugar House & Pancake Restaurant** (⊠ Rtes. 12 and 63, Westmoreland, ☎ 603/399–4486), which offers a tour and pancake breakfast.

Keene

46 *20 mi southeast of Walpole, 53 mi west of Manchester.*

Keene is the largest city in the southwest corner of the state and the proud locus of the widest main street in America. Each year, on the Saturday before Halloween, locals use that street to hold a Pumpkin Festival, where they seek to retain their place in the record books for the most carved, lighted jack-o-lanterns—13,500 in 1997. **Keene State College,** hub of the local arts community, is on the tree-lined main street. The college's **Redfern Arts Center on Brickyard Pond** (☎ 603/358–2171) has three theaters and eight art studios. The **Thorne-Sagendorph Art Gallery** (☎ 603/358–2720) houses George Ridci's *Landscape* and presents traveling exhibitions. The **Putnam Art Lecture Hall** (☎ 603/358–2160) shows art films and international films.

Dining and Lodging

$–$$$ ✕ **Mangos Cafe on Main.** Paintings of fruits and vegetables on the wall and fruit-motif tablecloths adorn this restaurant, which serves vegetarian dishes—such as the grilled eggplant sandwich or the mixed grilled vegetables with a side of spicy pepper jelly—along with non-veggie fare like New Zealand rack of lamb and grilled Atlantic salmon. ✉ *81 Main St.,* ☎ *603/358–5440. D, MC, V.*

$–$$ ✕ **One Seventy Six Main.** This restaurant in the heart of Keene has a relaxed atmosphere and a menu that runs the gamut from steak fajitas to blackened catfish. The bar stocks an equally wide selection of domestic and imported beers, with 16 on tap. ✉ *176 Main St.,* ☎ *603/357–3100. AE, D, MC, V.*

$$$–$$$$ ✕🏠 **Chesterfield Inn.** Surrounded by gardens, the Chesterfield sits above
★ Route 9, the main Brattleboro–Keene road. The spacious rooms, decorated with armoires, fine antiques, and period-style fabrics, have telephones in the bathroom and refrigerators. The views from the dining room are of the gardens and the Vermont hills. Crab cakes with *rémoulade* (a seasoned sauce made with mayonnaise) and salmon with a mustard-mango glaze are among the menu highlights. ✉ *Box 155, Rte. 9, Chesterfield 03443,* ☎ *603/256–3211 or 800/365–5515,* 䕏 *603/256–6131. 13 rooms, 2 suites. Restaurant. Full breakfast. AE, D, DC, MC, V.*

$$ 🏠 **Carriage Barn.** Antiques and wide pine floors lend this inn across from Keene State College a cozy charm. An expansive buffet is served each morning in the breakfast room, but many guests savor a second cup of coffee in the summerhouse under the lilacs. ✉ *358 Main St., 03431,* ☎ *603/357–3812. 4 rooms. Continental breakfast. MC, V.*

$ ⚠ **Swanzey Lake Camping Area.** This 82-site campground for tents and RVs has a sandy beach, a dock, a ball field, a recreation area, and boat rentals. ✉ *88 E. Shore Rd.; mailing address: Box 115, W. Swanzey 03469,* ☎ *603/352–9880. Closed Nov.–Apr.*

Nightlife and the Arts

The **Apple Hill Chamber Players** (✉ E. Sullivan, ☎ 603/847–3371) produce summer concert series. The **Colonial Theatre** (✉ 95 Main St., ☎ 603/352–2033) opened in 1924 as a vaudeville stage. Recently refurbished, it now hosts folk and jazz concerts and has the largest movie screen in town. The **Redfern Arts Center at Brickyard Pond** (✉ 229 Main St., ☎ 603/358–2171) has year-round music, theater, and dance performances.

Outdoor Activities and Sports

The Monadnock region has more than 200 lakes and ponds, most of which offer good fishing. Rainbow trout, smallmouth and largemouth bass, and some northern pike swim in **Spofford Lake** in Chesterfield. **Goose Pond** in West Canaan, just north of Keene, holds smallmouth bass and white perch.

Monadnock Region and Central New Hampshire

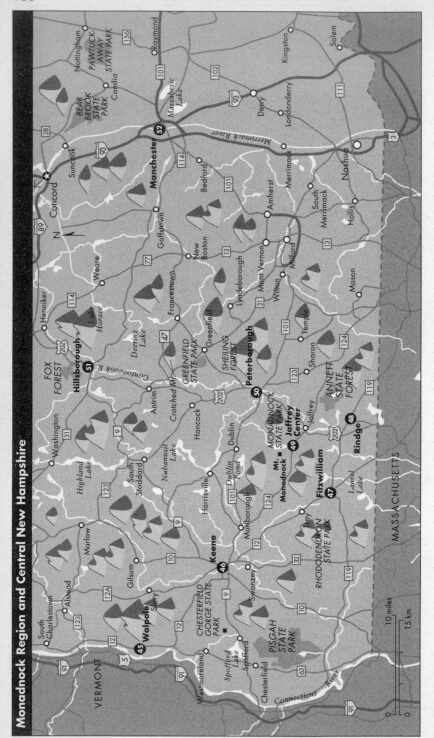

Shopping

ANTIQUES

The more than 240 dealers at **Antiques at Colony Mill** (⊠ 222 West St., ☎ 603/358–6343) sell everything from furniture to dolls.

BOOKS

The extraordinary collection of used books at the **Homestead Bookshop** (⊠ Rtes. 101 and 124, Marlborough, ☎ 603/876–4213) includes biographies, cookbooks, and town histories.

MARKETPLACE

Colony Mill Marketplace (⊠ 222 West St., ☎ 603/357–1240), an old mill building, holds 30-plus stores and boutiques such as Country Artisans (☎ 603/352–6980), which showcases the stoneware, textiles, prints, and glassware of regional artists; the Toadstool Bookshop (☎ 603/352–8815), which carries many children's and regional travel and history books; and Ye Goodie Shoppe (☎ 603/352–0326), whose specialty is handmade chocolates and confections.

Fitzwilliam

47 *12 mi southeast of Keene, 50 mi southwest of Manchester.*

A well-preserved historic district of Colonial and Federal houses has made the town of Fitzwilliam, on Route 119, the subject of thousands of postcards—particularly views of its landscape in winter, when a fine white snow settles on the oval common. Town business is still conducted in the 1817 meeting house. The **Amos J. Blake House,** maintained by the Fitzwilliam Historical Society, contains a museum with period antiques and artifacts and the law office of its namesake. ⊠ *Village Green,* ☎ *603/585–7742.* ☞ *Free.* ☉ *Late May–mid-Oct., weekends 1–4 or by appointment.*

More than 16 acres of wild rhododendrons burst into bloom in mid-July at **Rhododendron State Park.** This is the largest concentration of *Rhododendron maximum* north of the Allegheny Mountains. Bring a picnic lunch and sit in a nearby pine grove, or follow the marked footpaths through the flowers. ⊠ *Off Rte. 12, 2½ mi northwest of the town common,* ☎ *603/532–8862.* ☞ *$2.50 weekends and holidays; free at other times.* ☉ *Daily 8–sunset.*

Lodging

$$$–$$$$ ☒ **Inn at East Hill Farm.** At this 1830 farmhouse resort at the base of Mt. Monadnock, children are not only allowed but expected. In fact, if you don't have kids, you might be happier elsewhere. Children collect the eggs for the next day's breakfast, milk the cows, feed the animals, and participate in arts and crafts, storytelling, hiking, and games. Three meals, all served family-style, are included in the room rate. The innkeepers schedule weekly sleigh rides or hay rides and can whip up a picnic lunch for families who want to spend the day away from the resort. ⊠ *Monadnock St., Troy 03465,* ☎ *603/242–6495 or 800/242–6495,* 𝔽𝔸𝕏 *603/242–7709. 65 rooms. Restaurant, 1 indoor and 2 outdoor pools, indoor and outdoor whirlpools, wading pool, sauna, tennis court, horseback riding, boating, water-skiing, fishing, cross-country skiing, baby-sitting. AP, D, MC, V.*

$$ ☒ **Amos Parker House.** The garden of this old Colonial B&B is the
★ town's most stunning, complete with lily ponds, Asian stone benches, and Dutch waterstones that create a gently burbling waterfall effect. Two rooms have garden views; three have wood-burning fireplaces. In winter, breakfast is served in an elegant setting in front of a roaring fire. ⊠ *Box 202, Rte. 119, 03447,* ☎ *603/585–6540. 4 rooms. Full breakfast. No credit cards.*

$-$$ ☒ **Hannah Davis House.** This 1820 Federal house just off the village
★   green has retained its elegance. The original beehive oven still sits in
      the kitchen, and one suite has two Count Rumford fireplaces. Your
      host has the scoop on area antiquing. ☒ *186 Rte. 119W, 03447,* ☎
      603/585–3344. 6 rooms. Full breakfast. D, MC, V.

Outdoor Activities and Sports
You can find rainbow and golden trout, pickerel, and horned pout in
Laurel Lake. Rainbow and brown trout line the **Ashuelot River.**

Rindge

48 *8 mi east of Fitzwilliam on Rte. 119, 42 mi southeast of Manchester.*

The small town of Rindge sits on a hill overlooking the Monadnock
region. Most diversions center on outdoor activities in this scenic setting. **Cathedral of the Pines** is an outdoor memorial to American men
and women, both civilian and military, who have sacrificed their lives
in service to their country. There's an inspiring view of Mt. Monadnock and Mt. Kearsarge from the **Altar of the Nation,** which is composed of rock from every U.S. state and territory. All faiths are welcome
to hold services here; organ meditations take place at midday from Tuesday to Thursday in July and August. The **Memorial Bell Tower,** with
a carillon of bells from around the world, is built of native stone; Norman Rockwell designed the bronze tablets over the four arches. Flower
gardens, an indoor chapel, and a museum of military memorabilia share
the hilltop. ☒ *75 Cathedral Entrance Rd., off Rte. 119,* ☎ *603/899–
3300.* ⊠ *Free.* ☉ *May–Oct., daily 9–5.*

Lodging
$$-$$$ ☒ **Woodbound Inn.** This rustic inn was built as a farmhouse in 1819
      and became an inn in 1892. A favorite with families and people who
      fish, it occupies 200 acres on the shores of Contoocook Lake. Ac-
      commodations are basic and range from traditional rooms in the main
      inn to modern hotel-style rooms in the Edgewood building to cabins
      by the water. ☒ *62 Woodbound Rd., 03461,* ☎ *603/532–8341 or 800/
      688–7770,* FAX *603/532–8341 ext. 213. 35 rooms, 31 with bath, 4 rooms
      share bath, 11 cottages. Restaurant, bar, lake, 9-hole golf course, ten-
      nis court, croquet, hiking, horseshoes, shuffleboard, volleyball, fish-
      ing, ice-skating, cross-country skiing, tobogganing, recreation room.
      Full breakfast; MAP available. AE, MC, V.*

$ ☒ **Cathedral House Bed and Breakfast.** This 1850s farmhouse on the
      edge of the Cathedral of the Pines was the home of the memorial's
      founders. Innkeepers Don and Shirley Mahoney are well versed in area
      history. Rooms have high ceilings, flowered wallpapers, quilts, and well-
      stocked cookie jars, all of which help create the feeling that you've just
      arrived at Grandmother's house. ☒ *63 Cathedral Entrance Rd., 03461,*
      ☎ *603/899–6790. 5 rooms, 1 with bath. Full breakfast. MC, V.*

Jaffrey Center

49 *7 mi north of Rindge, 46 mi west of Manchester.*

Novelist Willa Cather came to the historic village of Jaffrey Center in
1919 and stayed in the Shattuck Inn, which now stands empty on Old
Meeting House Road. She pitched a tent not far from here in which she
wrote several chapters of *My Antonia*. She returned nearly every summer thereafter until her death and was buried in the Old Burying Ground.
Amos Fortune Forum, near the Old Burying Ground, brings nationally
known speakers to the 1773 meeting house on summer evenings.

The chief draw at **Monadnock State Park** is Mt. **Monadnock**. The oft-quoted statistic about the mountain is that it's the most-climbed mountain in America—second in the world to Japan's Mt. Fuji. Whether this is true or not, locals agree that it's never lonely at the top. Some days more than 400 people crowd its bald peak. Monadnock rises to 3,165 ft, and on a clear day the hazy Boston skyline is visible from its summit. The park maintains picnic grounds and some tent campsites and sells a trail map for $2. Five trailheads branch into more than two dozen trails of varying difficulty that wend their way to the top. Some are considerably shorter than others, but you should allow between three and four hours for any round-trip hike. A visitor center has exhibits documenting the mountain's history. ⊠ 2½ mi north of Jaffrey Center off Rte. 124, 03452, ☎ 603/532–8862. ☞ $2.50.

Lodging

$–$$$ ⌖ **Benjamin Prescott Inn.** The working dairy farm surrounding this 1853 Colonial farmhouse makes guests feel as though they are miles out in the country rather than just minutes from Jaffrey Center. Stenciling, quilts handmade by innkeeper Jan Miller, and wide pine floors add to the country feel. A full breakfast of Welsh miner's cakes, baked French toast with fruit, and Jaffrey maple syrup prepares you for a day of antiquing or climbing Mt. Monadnock. ⊠ Rte. 124, 03452, ☎ 603/532–6637. 10 rooms, 3 suites. Full breakfast. AE, MC, V.

Outdoor Activities and Sports

Gilmore Pond in Jaffrey has several types of trout.

Shopping

Sharon Arts Center (⊠ Rte. 123, Sharon, ☎ 603/924–7256) has a gallery that exhibits locally made pottery, fabric, and woodwork and also houses a school with classes in everything from photography to paper marbling.

Peterborough

⑤⓪ 8 mi north of Jaffrey Center, 40 mi west of Manchester.

The nation's first free public library opened in Peterborough in 1833. The town, which was the first in the region to be incorporated (1760), is still a commercial and cultural hub. The **MacDowell Colony** (⊠ 100 High St., ☎ 603/924–3886) was founded by the composer Edward MacDowell in 1907 as an artists' retreat. Willa Cather wrote part of Death Comes for the Archbishop here. Thornton Wilder was in residence when he wrote Our Town; Peterborough's resemblance to the play's Grover's Corners is no coincidence. Only a small portion of the colony is open to visitors.

In **Miller State Park** (⊠ Rte. 101, ☎ 603/924–3672), 3 mi east of town, an auto road takes you almost 2,300 ft up Mt. Pack Monadnock.

Dining and Lodging

$$–$$$ ✕ **Latacarta.** The innovative menu at Latacarta, where the dining room overlooks a waterfall, relies heavily on fresh, organic products. Start with gyoza, pan-grilled Japanese dumplings filled with vegetables and tofu, and then try the fresh Atlantic salmon or the hormone-free teppanyaki beef served with a sauce made from saki and apples. Dessert might be a mocha custard or wonderful hot pear crunch. ⊠ Noone Falls, U.S. 202, ☎ 603/924–6878. AE, D, MC, V. Closed Mon. No lunch weekends.

$$–$$$$ ✕⌖ **Hancock Inn.** Dating from 1789, this Federal inn is the pride of the well-preserved town for which it's named. Common areas possess the warmth of a tavern, with fireplaces, big wing chairs, couches, dark wood paneling, and Rufus Porter murals. Rooms, done in traditional

Colonial style, have antique four-poster beds. One suite has the original domed ceiling from the inn's 1800s ballroom. Updated Yankee fare is served by candlelight in the dining room; the specialty is Shaker cranberry pot roast. ⊠ *Box 96, 33 Main St., Hancock 03449,* ☎ *603/525–3318,* ℻ *603/525–9301. 11 rooms, 4 suites. Restaurant, bar. Full breakfast. AE, D, DC, MC, V.*

$$ ✕▥ **Inn at Crotched Mountain.** This 1822 Colonial inn has nine fireplaces, four of which are in private rooms. The other five spread cheer in several common areas. The inn, whose rooms are furnished with early Colonial reproductions, is a particularly romantic place to stay when snow is falling on Crotched Mountain. The restaurant's multicultural menu includes Eastern specialties such as Indonesian charbroiled swordfish with a sauce of ginger, green pepper, onion, and lemon; cranberry-port pot roast is one of the regional entrées. ⊠ *Mountain Rd., Francestown 03043,* ☎ *603/588–6840. 13 rooms. Restaurant, bar, pool, tennis court, cross-country skiing. Full breakfast; MAP required weekends. No credit cards.*

$ ✕▥ **Birchwood Inn.** Thoreau slept here, probably on his way to climb Monadnock or to visit Jaffrey or Peterborough. Country furniture and handmade quilts outfit the bedrooms of this no-smoking inn, as they did in 1775 when the house was new and no one dreamed it would someday be listed on the National Register of Historic Places. Allow time to linger in the dining room ($$; reservations essential; BYOB; no lunch; closed Sunday and Monday), where Rufus Porter murals cover the walls and she-crab soup, roast duckling, and fresh-fruit cobblers are among the specialties. ⊠ *Box 197, Rte. 45, Temple 03084,* ☎ *603/ 878–3285,* ℻ *603/878–2159. 7 rooms, 5 with bath. Restaurant. Full breakfast. No credit cards.*

$ ▥ **Apple Gate Bed and Breakfast.** With 90 acres of apple orchards across the street, this B&B is appropriately named. The four rooms and even the yellow labrador, Macintosh, are named for types of apples. Some rooms are small, but Laura Ashley prints and stenciling make them cheery and cozy. The house dates from 1832, and the original beams and fireplace still grace the dining room. A music and reading room has a piano and a television with VCR tucked in the corner. From June to October, there's a two-night minimum on weekends. ⊠ *199 Upland Farm Rd., 03458,* ☎ *603/924–6543. 4 rooms. Full breakfast. MC, V.*

Nightlife and the Arts

Monadnock Music (☎ 603/924–7610 or 800/868–9613) produces a summer series of concerts from mid-July to late August, with solo recitals, chamber music, and orchestra and opera performances by renowned musicians. The concerts, at locations throughout the region, usually take place in the evening at 8 and on Sunday at 4; many are free. The **Peterborough Players** (⊠ Stearns Farm, off Middle Hancock Rd., ☎ 603/924–7585) have performed for more than 60 seasons. Plays are staged in a converted barn. The **Temple Town Band** (☎ 603/924–3478) was founded in 1799. Members range from teenagers to septuagenarians. The band plays a selection of patriotic songs, traditional marches, and show tunes at the Jaffrey Bandstand, the Sharon Arts Center, and local festivals and events.

Outdoor Activities and Sports

Several types of trout swim in **Dublin Pond,** near Dublin.

Shopping

Artek Creations (375 Jaffrey Rd., ☎ 603/924–0003) sells museum reproductions of jewelry, bookends, boxes, and other ornamental objects. The corporate headquarters and retail outlet of **Eastern Mountain Sports** (⊠ 1 Vose Farm Rd., ☎ 603/924–7231) sells everything from tents to skis to hiking boots, gives hiking and camping classes, and conducts kayaking and canoeing demonstrations. **Harrisville Designs** (⊠ Mill Alley, Harrisville, ☎ 603/827–3333) sells hand-spun and hand-dyed yarn sheared from local sheep, as well as looms for the serious weaver. The shop also hosts classes in knitting and weaving. **North Gallery at Tewksbury's** (⊠ Rte. 101, ☎ 603/924–3224) stocks thrown pots, sconces, candlestick holders, and woodworkings.

Hillsborough

⑤ *20 mi north of Peterborough, 25 mi west of Manchester.*

The four villages that make up Hillsborough include the historic district, Hillsborough Center, where 18th-century houses surround the town green. Many houses are still occupied by descendants of the original settlers who founded the town in 1769.

President Franklin Pierce was born in Hillsborough and lived here until he married. The **Pierce Homestead,** operated by the Hillsborough Historical Society, welcomes visitors for guided tours. The house is decorated much as it was during Pierce's life. ⊠ *Rte. 31,* ☎ *603/478–3165.* ☜ *$2.50.* ☉ *June and Sept.–Columbus Day, Sat. 10–4, Sun. 1–4; July–Aug., Mon.–Sat. 10–4, Sun. 1–4.*

Lodging

$–$$ 🛏 **Inn at Maplewood Farm.** The white-clapboard 1794 farmhouse on the side of Peaked Hill beside a quiet country road may make you feel as if you've been transported back in time. The rooms, three with fireplaces, have antiques and quilts but contain modern bathrooms. The luxurious Garden suite has a queen-size canopy bed, a fireplace, a skylight over the bathtub, and a sitting area. All rooms have vintage radios so that you can listen to the old-time radio shows broadcast nightly on the inn's transmitter. The inn is no-smoking. ⊠ *Box 1478, 447 Center Rd., 03244,* ☎ *603/464–4242,* FAX *603/464–5401. 2 rooms, 2 suites. Guest kitchen with refrigerator and coffeemaker. Continental breakfast. AE, D, DC, MC, V. Closed Nov.–May.*

Outdoor Activities and Sports

Fox State Forest (Center Rd., ☎ 603/464–3453) has 20 mi of hiking trails and an observation tower.

Shopping

At **Gibson Pewter** (⊠ 18 East Washington Rd., ☎ 603/464–3410), the father-and-son team of Raymond and Jonathan Gibson create and sell museum-quality, lead-free pewter in contemporary and traditional designs. You are welcome to watch them work. **William Thomas, Master Cabinetmaker** (⊠ 217 Saw Mill Rd., ☎ 603/478–3488), a founding member of the New Hampshire Furniture Masters Association, creates well-crafted wood furniture.

Manchester

⑤② *25 mi east of Hillsborough, 23 mi north of the Massachusetts border.*

Manchester, with just over 100,000 residents, is New Hampshire's largest city. The town grew around the power of the Amoskeag Falls on the Merrimack River, which fueled small textile mills through the 1700s. Today Manchester is mainly a banking and business center. The state's major airport is here, though, so you may want to spend a day visiting its museums or walking through the former mill yards.

By 1828, a group of investors from Boston had bought the rights to the Merrimack's water power and built on its eastern bank the

Amoskeag Textile Mills, which became a testament to New England's manufacturing power. In 1906, the mills employed 17,000 people and churned out more than 4 million yards of cloth per week. The enterprise formed the entire economic base of Manchester; when it closed in 1936, the town was devastated. As part of an economic recovery plan, the mill buildings have been converted into warehouses, classrooms, restaurants, and office space. You can wander among these huge blood-red buildings; contact the **Manchester Historic Association** (✉ 129 Amherst St., ☎ 603/622–7531) for a map.

The **Currier Gallery of Art,** in a 1929 Beaux Arts Italianate building, has a permanent collection of European and American paintings, sculpture, and decorative arts from the 13th to the 20th century, including works by Monet, Picasso, Edward Hopper, and Georgia O'Keeffe. Also part of the museum is the Frank Lloyd Wright–designed **Zimmerman House,** built in 1950. Wright called this sparse, utterly functional living space "Usonian." The house is New England's only Wright-designed residence open to the public. ✉ *201 Myrtle Way,* ☎ *603/669–6144, 603/626–4158 for Zimmerman House tours.* ☞ *$5; free Sat. 10–1; Zimmerman House $7 (reservations required).* ☉ *Sun.–Mon. and Wed.– Thurs. 11–5, Fri. 11–9, Sat. 10–5; call for tour times.*

☞ Salmon, shad, and river herring "climb" the **Amoskeag Fishways** fish ladder near the Amoskeag Dam during the migration period, from May to June. The visitor center has an underwater viewing window, year-round interactive exhibits and programs, and a hydroelectric-station viewing area. ✉ *Fletcher St.,* ☎ *603/626–3474.* ☉ *Call for hrs.*

Dining and Lodging

$$$–$$$$ ✕🛏 **Bedford Village Inn.** This luxurious Federal-style inn, just minutes from Manchester, was once a working farm and still shows horsenuzzle marks on its old beams. Gone, however, are the hayloft and the old milking room, which have been converted into lavish suites containing king-size beds, whirlpool baths, and three telephones. The tavern has seven intimate dining rooms, each with original wide pine floors and huge fireplaces. The menu, which often includes New England favorites like lobster and Atlantic salmon with a chardonnay beurre blanc, changes every two weeks. ✉ *2 Village Inn La., Bedford 03110,* ☎ *603/472–2001 or 800/852–1166,* ⅏ *603/472–2379. 12 suites, 2 apartments. Restaurant, meeting rooms. AE, DC, MC, V.*

Nightlife and the Arts

American Stage Festival (✉ 14 Court St., Nashua, ☎ 603/886–7000) is the state's largest professional theater. The season, with shows presented at two locations, runs from March through October and includes five Broadway plays, one new work, and a children's-theater series.

Shopping

Bell Hill Antiques (✉ Rte. 101 at Bell Hill Rd., Bedford, ☎ 603/472–5580) sells country furniture, glass, and china. The enormous **Mall of New Hampshire** (✉ 1500 S. Willow St., ☎ 603/669–0433) has every conceivable store and is anchored by Sears and Filene's.

Western and Central New Hampshire A to Z

Arriving and Departing

BY BUS

Concord Trailways (☎ 800/639–3317) runs from Concord to Boston. **Vermont Transit** (☎ 603/351–1331 or 800/552–8737) links the cities of western New Hampshire with major cities in the eastern United States.

BY CAR

Most people who travel up from Massachusetts do so on I–93, which passes through Manchester and Concord before cutting a path through the White Mountains. I–89 connects Concord, in the Merrimack Valley, with Vermont. Route 12 runs north–south along the Connecticut River. Farther south, Route 101 connects Keene and Manchester, then continues to the seacoast.

BY PLANE

Manchester Airport (☞ Arriving and Departing *in* New Hampshire A to Z, *below*) is the main airport in western and central New Hampshire. Colgan Air offers flights to Rutland, Vermont, and Newark, New Jersey, from **Keene Airport** (⊠ Rte. 32 off Rte. 12, North Swanzey, ☎ 603/357–9835). **Lebanon Municipal Airport** (5 Airpark Rd., West Lebanon, ☎ 603/298–8878), near Dartmouth College, is served by US Airways. *See* Air Travel *in* Smart Travel Tips A to Z for airline phone numbers.

Getting Around

BY BUS

Advance Transit (☎ 802/295–1824) stops in Enfield and Hanover. **Keene City Express** (☎ 603/352–8494) buses run from 9 AM to 4 PM. **Manchester Transit Authority** (☎ 603/623–8801) has hourly local bus service around town and to Bedford from 6 AM to 6 PM.

BY CAR

On the western border of the state, Routes 12 and 12A are picturesque but slow-moving. U.S. 4 crosses the region, winding between Lebanon and the seacoast. Other pretty drives include Routes 101, 202, and 11.

Contacts and Resources

BIKING

Eastern Mountain Sports (☞ Shopping *in* Peterborough, *above*) and the **Greater Keene Chamber of Commerce** (⊠ 8 Central Sq., Keene 03431, ☎ 603/352–1303) have information about local bike routes.

EMERGENCIES

Cheshire Medical Center (⊠ 580 Court St., Keene, ☎ 603/352–4111). **Concord Hospital** (⊠ 250 Pleasant St., Concord, ☎ 603/225–2711). **Dartmouth Hitchcock Medical Center** (⊠ 1 Medical Center Dr., Lebanon, ☎ 603/650–5000). **Elliot Hospital** (⊠ 1 Elliot Way, Manchester, ☎ 603/669–5300 or 800/235–5468). **Monadnock Community Hospital** (⊠ 452 Old Street Rd., Peterborough, ☎ 603/924–7191). **Southern New Hampshire Medical Center** (⊠ 8 Prospect St., Nashua, ☎ 603577–2000).

Monadnock Mutual Aid (☎ 603/352–1100) responds to any emergency, from a medical problem to a car fire.

FISIIING

For word on what's biting where, contact the **Department of Fish and Game** (☎ 603/352–9669) in Keene.

LODGING RESERVATION SERVICE

The **Sunapee Area Lodging and Information Service** (☎ 603/763–2495 or 800/258–3530) can help with reservations.

24-HOUR PHARMACY

Brooks Pharmacy (⊠ 53 Daniel Webster Hwy., Manchester, ☎ 603/623–1135). **CVS Pharmacy** (⊠ 271 Mammouth Rd., Manchester, ☎ 603/623–3995).

VISITOR INFORMATION

Concord Chamber of Commerce (⊠ 244 N. Main St., Concord 03301, ☎ 603/224–2508). **Hanover Chamber of Commerce** (⊠ Box A-105, Hanover 03755, ☎ 603/643–3115). **Keene Chamber of Commerce** (⊠

48 Central Sq., Keene 03431, ☎ 603/352–1303). **Lake Sunapee Business Association** (✉ Box 400, Sunapee 03782, ☎ 603/763–2495; 800/258–3530 in New England). **Manchester Chamber of Commerce** (✉ 889 Elm St., Manchester 03101, ☎ 603/666–6600). **Monadnock Travel Council** (✉ 8 Central Sq., Keene 03431, ☎ 603/355–8155). **Peterborough Chamber of Commerce** (✉ Box 401, Peterborough 03458, ☎ 603/924–7234). **Southern New Hampshire Visitor & Convention Bureau** (✉ 1 Airport Rd., Suite 198, Manchester 03103, ☎ 603/645–9889).

NEW HAMPSHIRE A TO Z

Arriving and Departing

By Bus

C&J (☎ 603/431–2424) serves the seacoast area of New Hampshire. **Concord Trailways** (☎ 603/228–3300) links the capital with other parts of the state. **Vermont Transit** (☎ 603/228–3300 or 800/451–3292) links the cities of western New Hampshire with major cities in the eastern United States.

By Car

Interstate 93 is the principal north–south route through Manchester, Concord, and central New Hampshire. To the west, I–91 traces the Vermont–New Hampshire border. To the east, I–95, which is a toll road, passes through the coastal area of southern New Hampshire on its way from Massachusetts to Maine. Interstate 89 travels from Concord to Montpelier and Burlington, Vermont.

By Plane

Manchester Airport (✉ 1 Airport Rd., Manchester 03103, ☎ 603/624–6539), the state's largest airport, has scheduled flights by Continental, Delta, United, and US Airways. **Lebanon Municipal Airport** (✉ 5 Airpark Rd., West Lebanon, ☎ 603/298–8878) has commuter flights by US Air Express, Delta Business Express, and Northwest. *See* Air Travel *in* Smart Travel Tips A to Z for airline phone numbers.

Getting Around

By Bus

See Arriving and Departing, *above,* and the A to Z sections of the New Hampshire regions covered in this chapter.

By Car

The official state map, available free from the New Hampshire Office of Travel and Tourism Development (☞ Visitor Information, *below*), has directories for each of the tourist areas.

Speed limits on interstate highways are generally 65 mph, except in heavily settled areas, where 55 mph is the norm. On state routes, speed limits vary considerably. On any given stretch, the limit may be anywhere from 25 mph to 55 mph, so watch the signs carefully. Right turns are permitted on red lights unless otherwise indicated.

By Plane

Small local airports that handle charters and private planes are **Berlin Airport** (✉ Rte. 16, Milan, ☎ 603/449–7383), **Concord Airport** (✉ 71 Airport Rd., Concord, ☎ 603/229–1760), **Laconia Airport** (✉ Rte. 11, Laconia, ☎ 603/524–5003), **Nashua Municipal Airport** (✉ Borie Field, Nashua, ☎ 603/882–0661), and, in Rochester, **Skyhaven Airport** (✉ 238 Rochester Hill Rd., ☎ 603/332–0005).

Contacts and Resources

Biking

Bike & Hike New Hampshire's Lakes (☎ 603/968–3775), **Bike the Whites** (☎ 800/933–3902), **Great Outdoors Hiking & Biking Tours** (☎ 603/356–3271 or 800/525–9100), **Monadnock Bicycle Touring** (☎ 603/827–3925), **New England Hiking Holidays** (☎ 603/356–9696 or 800/869–0949), and **Sunapee Inns Hike & Bike Tours** (☎ 800/662–6005) organize bike tours.

Bird-Watching

Audubon Society of New Hampshire (✉ 3 Silk Farm Rd., Concord 03301, ☎ 603/224–9909) schedules monthly field trips throughout the state and a fall bird-watching tour to Star Isle and other parts of the Isles of Shoals.

Camping

New Hampshire Campground Owners Association (✉ Box 320, Twin Mountain 03595, ☎ 603/846–5511 or 800/822–6764, FAX 603/846–2151) publishes a guide to private, state, and national-forest campgrounds.

Emergencies

Ambulance, fire, police (☎ 911).

Fishing

For information about fishing and licenses, call the **New Hampshire Fish and Game Office** (☎ 603/271–3421).

Foliage and Snow Hot Lines

A fall **foliage hot line** (☎ 800/258–3608) is updated twice weekly from mid-September through October. Two **snow hot lines** (☎ 800/258–3608 for information on New Hampshire alpine ski conditions; ☎ 800/262–6660 for cross-country ski conditions) provide updates on snow conditions at ski centers.

Visitor Information

New Hampshire Office of Travel and Tourism Development (✉ Box 1856, Concord 03302, ☎ 603/271–2343; 800/386–4664 for a free vacation packet). **Events** (☎ 800/258–3608 or 800/262–6660). **New Hampshire Parks Department** (☎ 603/271–3556). **New Hampshire State Council on the Arts** (✉ 40 N. Main St., Concord 03301, ☎ 603/271–2789).

3 VERMONT

Southern Vermont has manicured landscapes, immaculate villages, and summer theaters, as well as a surprisingly large chunk of wilderness in the Green Mountain National Forest. Central Vermont offers the state's largest ski resort, Killington, along with the rolling farmland vistas of the lower Lake Champlain valley. Up north, Vermont attractions include the state's largest city, cosmopolitan and collegiate Burlington; the nation's smallest state capital, Montpelier; the legendary slopes of Stowe; and the leafy back roads of the Northeast Kingdom.

Revised and updated by Kay and Bill Scheller

EVERYWHERE YOU LOOK AROUND VERMONT, the evidence is clear: This is not the state it was 30 years ago. That may be true for the rest of New England as well, but the contrasts between the present and recent past seem all the more sharply drawn in the Green Mountain State, if only because an aura of timelessness has always been at the heart of the Vermont image. Vermont was where all the quirks and virtues outsiders associate with upcountry New England were supposed to reside. It was where the Yankees were Yankee-est and where there were more cows than people.

Not that you should be alarmed, if you haven't been here in a while; Vermont hasn't become southern California, or even, for that matter, southern New Hampshire. This is still the most rural state in the Union (meaning that it has the smallest percentage of citizens living in statistically defined metropolitan areas), and it still turns out most of New England's milk, even though there are, finally, more people than cows. It's still a place where cars occasionally have to stop while a dairy farmer walks his herd across a secondary road; and up in Essex County, in what George Aiken dubbed the Northeast Kingdom, there are townships with zero population. And the kind of scrupulous, straightforward, plainspoken politics practiced by Governor (later Senator) Aiken for 50 years has not become outmoded in a state that still turns out on town-meeting day.

How has Vermont changed? In strictly physical terms, the most obvious transformations have taken place in and around the two major cities, Burlington and Rutland, and near the larger ski resorts, such as Stowe, Killington, Stratton, and Mt. Snow. Burlington's Church Street, once a paradigm of all the sleepy redbrick shopping thoroughfares in northern New England, is now a pedestrian mall with chic bistros; outside the city, suburban development has supplanted farms in towns where someone's trip to Burlington might once have been an item in a weekly newspaper. As for the ski areas, it's no longer enough simply to boast the latest in chairlift technology. Slopeside hotels and condos have boomed, especially in the southern part of the state, making ski areas into big-time resort destinations. And once-sleepy Manchester has become one of New England's factory-outlet meccas.

But the real metamorphosis in the Green Mountains has to do more with style, with the personality of the place, than with development. The past couple of decades have seen a tremendous influx of outsiders—not only skiers and "leaf peepers" but people who have come to stay year-round—and many of them are determined either to freshen the local scene with their own idiosyncrasies or to make Vermont even more like Vermont than they found it. On the one hand, this translates into the fact that Vermont is the only state represented in Washington by an independent socialist congressman; on the other, it means that sheep farming has been reintroduced to the state, largely to provide a high-quality product for the hand-weaving industry.

This ties in with another local phenomenon, one best described as Made in Vermont. Once upon a time, maple syrup and sharp cheddar cheese were the products that carried Vermont's name to the world. The market niche that they created has since been widened by Vermonters—a great many of them refugees from more hectic arenas of commerce—offering a dizzying variety of goods with the ineffable cachet of Vermont manufacture. There are Vermont wood toys, Vermont apple wines, Vermont chocolates, even Vermont gin. All of it is marketed with the tacit suggestion that it was made by Yankee elves in a shed out back on a bright autumn morning.

Vermont

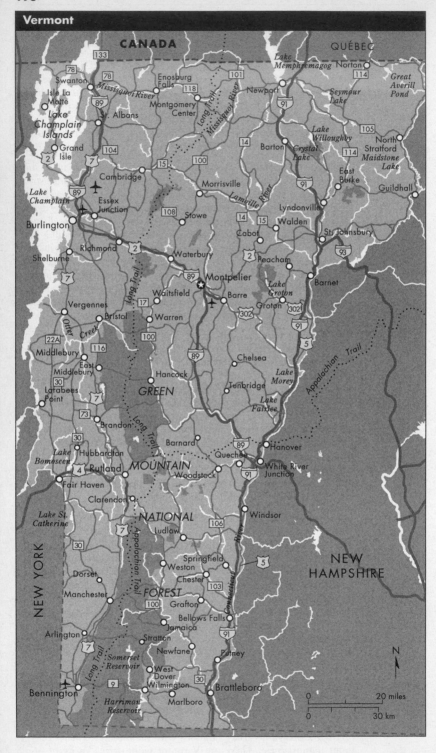

CANADA   QUÉBEC

Lake Memphremagog

Norton

133

78 Swanton   Enosburg Falls   101   114   Great Averill Pond

Isle La Motte   78   Mississquoi River   118   Montgomery Center   Newport   91   Seymour Lake

89   St. Albans   14   Barton   Lake Willoughby   105

Lake Champlain Islands   104   15   100   Crystal Lake   114   North Stratford Maidstone Lake

Grand Isle   2   7   Cambridge   Morrisville   Lambville River   East Burke   Guildhall

89   108   Stowe   14   15   Lyndonville

Lake Champlain   Essex Junction   Walden   St. Johnsbury

Burlington   Richmond   2   Waterbury   Cabot   93

Shelburne   7   Montpelier   2   Peacham   Barnet

Vergennes   Waitsfield   Barre   Lake Groton   Groton   302

Bristol   17   Warren   302   91

Otter Creek   22A   116   100   5

Middlebury   Chelsea   Appalachian Trail

East Middlebury   Hancock   Lake Morey

30   7   GREEN   Tunbridge   Lake Fairlee

Larabees Point   73   Brandon   Barnard   89   Hanover

30   Hubbardton   Quechee   White River Junction

Lake Bomoseen   Rutland   MOUNTAIN   Woodstock   91

Fair Haven   4   Clarendon   NATIONAL   Windsor

Lake St. Catherine   30   7   Ludlow   106

Springfield   5   NEW HAMPSHIRE

Dorset   Weston   Chester   103

Manchester   FOREST   100   Grafton

Arlington   7   Bellows Falls   91   Jamaica

Stratton   Newfane   Putney

Somerset Reservoir   West Dover   30

Bennington   9   Wilmington   Brattleboro

Harriman Reservoir   Marlboro

N

0   20 miles
0   30 km

NEW YORK

The most successful Made in Vermont product is Ben & Jerry's ice cream. Neither Ben nor Jerry comes from old Green Mountain stock, but their product has benefited immensely from the magical reputation of the place where it is made. Along the way, the company (which started in Burlington under the most modest circumstances in 1979) has become the largest single purchaser of Vermont milk.

Pleasures and Pastimes

Biking

Vermont is great bicycle-touring country, especially the often deserted roads of the Northeast Kingdom. Many companies lead weekend tours and weeklong trips throughout the state. If you'd like to go it on your own, most chambers of commerce have brochures highlighting good cycling routes in their area, including *Vermont Life* magazine's "Bicycle Vermont" map and guide, and many bookstores sell *25 Bicycle Tours in Vermont* by John Freidin.

Dining

Over the past few years, Vermont chefs have been working hard to live up to two distinct responsibilities. One is the need to honor the home-and-hearth traditions of Yankee cooking, the realm of pot roast and Indian pudding, sticky buns and homemade corn relish. But as travelers and residents have become more sophisticated, there has been a demand for the ethnic cuisines, lighter adaptations of classics, and new American treatments of seasonal ingredients that now characterize urban menus.

The more ambitious restaurants and inn kitchens have not only managed to balance these two gastronomic imperatives but have often succeeded in combining them. The trick is to take an innovative hand with Vermont game and local produce, introduce fresh herbs and other seasonings, and change menus to suit the season. Look for imaginative approaches to native New England foods like fiddlehead ferns (available only for a short time in the spring), maple syrup (Vermont is the largest U.S. producer), dairy products (especially cheese), native fruits and berries that are often transformed into jams and jellies, "new Vermont" products such as salsa and salad dressings, and venison, quail, pheasant, and other game.

Your chances of finding a table for dinner vary with the season: Many restaurants have lengthy waits during peak seasons (when it's always a good idea to make a reservation) and then shut down during the slow months of April and November. Some of the best dining is found at country inns.

Fishing

Central Vermont is the heart of the state's warm-water lake and pond fishing. Harriman and Somerset reservoirs have both warm- and cold-water species; Harriman has a greater variety. Lake Dunmore produced the state-record rainbow trout; Lakes Bomoseen and St. Catherine are good for rainbows and largemouth bass. In the east, Lakes Fairlee and Morey hold bass, perch, and chain pickerel, while the lower part of the Connecticut River contains smallmouth bass, walleye, and perch; shad are returning via the fish ladders at Vernon and Bellows Falls.

In northern Vermont, rainbow and brown trout inhabit the Missisquoi, Lamoille, Winooski, and Willoughby rivers, and there's warm-water fishing at many smaller lakes and ponds. Lakes Seymour, Willoughby, and Memphremagog and Great Averill Pond in the Northeast Kingdom are good for salmon and lake trout. The Dog River near Montpelier has one of the best wild populations of brown trout in the state.

Good news is that landlocked Atlantic salmon are returning to the Clyde River following removal of a controversial dam.

Lake Champlain, stocked annually with salmon and lake trout, has become the state's ice-fishing capital; walleye, bass, pike, and channel catfish are also taken. Ice fishing is also popular on Lake Memphremagog.

Lodging

Vermont's largest hotels are in Burlington and near the major ski resorts. There's a dearth of inns and bed-and-breakfasts in Burlington, though chain hotels provide dependable accommodations. Elsewhere you'll find a range of inns, B&Bs, and small motels. The many lovely and sometimes quite luxurious inns and B&Bs provide what many people consider the quintessential Vermont lodging experience. Rates are highest during foliage season, from late September to mid-October, and lowest in late spring and November, when many properties close. Many of the larger hotels offer package rates. Some quiet, romantic inns discourage bringing children.

National Forests

The two sections of the 355,000-acre Green Mountain National Forest (GMNF) are central and southern Vermont's primary stronghold of woodland and high mountain terrain. Like all national forests, it contains sections on which timber leases are sometimes granted, but it's possible to travel through much of this preserve without seeing significant evidence of human intrusion. In addition to the paved public highways that traverse the GMNF, many of the occasional logging roads are maintained for public use, and although unpaved, these are kept in good condition during snow-free times of the year.

The Forest Service maintains a number of picnic areas and primitive campgrounds; complete information is available from the Forest Supervisor (☞ Contacts and Resources *in* Vermont A to Z, *below*). Fishing, subject to state laws and seasonal closings and limits, is allowed throughout the GMNF. Canoeing, cross-country skiing, and hiking are also popular; the Appalachian and Long trails run the length of the forest. Snowmobiles and other forms of motorized transportation, such as all-terrain vehicles, are permitted on marked trails, except within roadless areas designated as wilderness.

Skiing

The Green Mountains run through the middle of Vermont like a bumpy spine, visible from almost every point in the state; generous accumulations of snow make the mountains an ideal site for skiing. Increased snowmaking capacity and improved, high-tech computerized equipment at many areas virtually assure a good day on the slopes. Vermont has 26 alpine ski resorts with nearly 1,000 trails and some 5,000 acres of skiable terrain. Combined, the resorts operate nearly 200 lifts and have the capacity to carry some 215,000 skiers per hour. Though grooming is sophisticated at all Vermont areas, conditions usually run to a typically Eastern hard pack, with powder a rare luxury and ice a bugbear after January thaw. The best advice for skiing in Vermont is to keep your skis well tuned.

Route 100 is also known as "Skier's Highway," passing by 13 of the state's ski areas. Vermont's major resorts are Stowe, Jay Peak, Sugarbush, Killington, Okemo, Mt. Snow, and Stratton. Midsize, less hectic areas to consider include Ascutney, Bromley, Smugglers' Notch, Pico, Mad River Glen, and Burke Mountain. At press time, Bolton Valley Ski Resort—long a favorite because of its proximity to Burlington and ample intermediate terrain—was scheduled to reopen for the 1999–

2000 season under a new owner. For information, call the **Vermont Ski Area Association** at ☎ 802/223–2439.

Exploring Vermont

Vermont can be divided into three regions. The southern part of the state, flanked by Bennington on the west and Brattleboro on the east, played an important role in Vermont's Revolutionary War–era drive to independence (yes, there was once a Republic of Vermont) and its eventual statehood. The central part is characterized by rugged mountains and the gently rolling dairy lands near Lake Champlain. Northern Vermont is the site of the state's capital, Montpelier, and its largest city, Burlington, yet it is also home to Vermont's most rural area, the Northeast Kingdom.

Numbers in the text correspond to numbers in the margin and on the Southern Vermont, Central Vermont, and Northern Vermont maps.

Great Itineraries

There are many ways to take advantage of Vermont's beauty—skiing or hiking its mountains, biking or driving its back roads, fishing or sailing its waters, shopping for local products, visiting its museums and sights, or simply finding the perfect inn and never leaving the front porch. Distances in Vermont are relatively short, yet the mountains and many back roads will slow a traveler's pace. You can see a representative north–south section of Vermont in a few days; if you have up to a week you can hit the highlights around the state.

IF YOU HAVE 3 DAYS

Spend a few hours in historic **Bennington** ⑤ in the southern part of Vermont; then travel north to see Hildene and stay in ⛳ **Manchester** ⑦. On your second day take Route 100 through Weston and travel north through the Green Mountains to Route 125, where you turn west to explore ⛳ **Middlebury** ㉔. On day three, enter the Champlain Valley, which has views of the Adirondack Mountains to the west. Stop at Shelburne Farms and carry on to **Burlington** ㉞; catch the sunset from the waterfront and take a walk on Church Street.

IF YOU HAVE 5 TO 7 DAYS

You can make several side trips off Route 100 and also visit the Northeast Kingdom on a trip this length. Visit **Bennington** ⑤ and ⛳ **Manchester** ⑦ on day one. Spend your second day walking around the small towns of **Chester** ⑪ and ⛳ **Grafton** ⑫. On day three head north to explore **Woodstock** ⑲ and ⛳ **Quechee** ⑱, stopping at either the Billings Farm Museum and Marsh-Billings National Park or the Vermont Institute of Natural Science. Head leisurely on your fourth day toward ⛳ **Middlebury** ㉔, along one of Vermont's most inspiring mountain drives, Route 125 west of Route 100. Between Hancock and Middlebury, you'll pass nature trails and the picnic spot at Texas Falls Recreation Area, then traverse a moderately steep mountain pass. Spend day five in ⛳ **Burlington** ㉞. On day six head east to **Waterbury** ㉙ and then north to ⛳ **Stowe** ㉚ and Mount Mansfield for a full day. Begin your last day with a few hours in **Montpelier** ㉘ on your way to **Peacham** ㊴, **St. Johnsbury** ㊳, ⛳ **Lake Willoughby** ㊱, and the serenity and back roads of the Northeast Kingdom. Especially noteworthy are U.S. 5, Route 5A, and Route 14.

When to Tour Vermont

The number of visitors and the rates for lodging reach their peaks along with the color of the leaves during foliage season, from late September to mid-October. But if you have never seen a kaleidoscope of autumn colors, it is worth braving the slow-moving traffic and paying the extra money. In summer the state is lush and green. Winter, of course, is high season at Vermont's ski resorts. Rates are lowest in late spring and November, although many properties close during these times.

SOUTHERN VERMONT

The Vermont tradition of independence and rebellion began in southern Vermont. Many towns founded in the early 18th century as frontier outposts or fortifications were later important as trading centers. In the western region the Green Mountain Boys fought off both the British and the claims of land-hungry New Yorkers—some say their descendants are still fighting. In the 19th century, as many towns turned to manufacturing, the farmers here retreated to hillier regions and, as the modern ski and summer-home booms got under way, retreated even farther.

The first thing you'll notice upon entering the state is the conspicuous lack of billboards along the highways and roads. The foresight back in the 1960s to prohibit them has made for a refreshing absence of aggressive visual clutter that allows unencumbered views of working farmland, fresh-as-paint villages, and quiet back roads—but does not hide the reality of abandoned dairy barns, bustling ski resorts, and strip-mall sprawl.

The towns are listed in counterclockwise order, beginning in the east, south of the junction of I–91 and Route 9 in Brattleboro, and following the southern boundary of the state toward Bennington, then north up to Manchester and Weston and south back to Newfane.

Brattleboro

❶ *60 mi south of White River Junction.*

Its downtown bustling with activity, Brattleboro, with about 13,000 inhabitants, is the center of commerce for southeastern Vermont. This town at the confluence of the West and Connecticut rivers originated as a frontier scouting post and became a thriving industrial center and resort town in the 1800s. More recently, the area has become a home to political activists and a raft of earnest counterculturists.

A former railroad station, the **Brattleboro Museum and Art Center** has replaced locomotives with art and historical exhibits. The museum's organs were made in Brattleboro between 1853 and 1961, when the city was home to the Estey Organ Company, one of the world's largest organ manufacturers. ⊠ *Vernon and Main Sts.,* ☎ *802/257–0124.* 🖙 *$3.* ☉ *Mid-May–early Nov., Tues.–Sun. noon–6.*

Larkin G. Mead, Jr., a Brattleboro resident, stirred 19th-century America's imagination with an 8-ft snow angel he built at the intersection of Routes 30 and 5. **Brooks Memorial Library** has a replica of the angel as well as exhibits of Vermont art. ⊠ *224 Main St.,* ☎ *802/254–5290.* ☉ *Labor Day–Memorial Day, Mon.–Wed. 9–9, Thurs.–Fri. 9–6, Sat. 9–5; Memorial Day–Labor Day, Sat. 9–noon.*

Dining and Lodging

$$$ ✕ **Peter Havens.** In a town better known for tofu than toniness, this chic little bistro knows just what to do with a filet mignon—serve it with Roquefort walnut butter, of course. Look for the house-cured gravlax made with lemon vodka and fresh seasonal seafood, which even includes a spring fling with soft-shelled crabs. The wine list is superb. ⊠ *32 Elliot St.,* ☎ *802/257–3333. MC, V. Closed Mon. No lunch.*

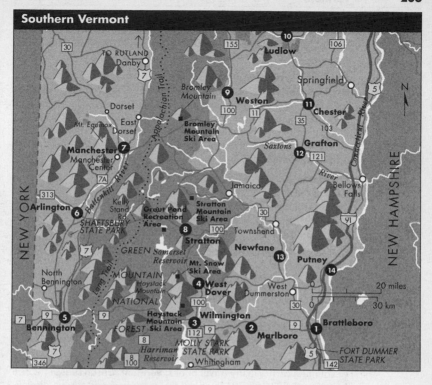

Southern Vermont

$ ✕ **Common Ground.** The political posters and concert fliers that line the staircase at Common Ground attest to Vermont's strong progressive element. The stairs lead to loftlike, rough-hewn dining rooms. Owned cooperatively by the staff, this mostly organic vegetarian restaurant serves cashew burgers, veggie stir-fries, curries, hot soup and stew, and the humble bowl of brown rice. All the desserts, including a chocolate cake with peanut butter frosting, are made without white sugar. ⊠ *25 Eliot St.,* ☎ *802/257–0855. No credit cards. Closed Mon.–Wed.*

$ ✕ **Sarkis Market.** Gail Sarkis's Lebanese grandmother gave her many of the recipes she uses to create Middle Eastern delicacies such as falafel, stuffed grape leaves, hummus, and *kibbe*—a layered meatloaf stuffed with ground lamb, pine nuts, and onions. Undecided about what to order? Go for the combination plate and finish with a wedge of homemade baklava. Bring your own bottle of wine. ⊠ *50 Eliot St.,* ☎ *802/ 258–4906. AE, MC, V. Closed Sun. except during Oct.*

$–$$ ✕🏠 **Latchis Hotel.** The current generation of Latchises run this 1938 downtown Art Deco landmark. Front rooms overlook busy—and often noisy—Main Street. All the rooms have coffeemakers and are furnished comfortably, if not in high style; the suites are a bargain. Muffins arrive outside your door in the morning, and you can catch a movie under the zodiac ceiling of the adjoining Latchis Theater. The Latchis Grille (closed on Monday and Tuesday in winter; no lunch on weekdays) serves pub food as well as more creative fare like chicken and watercress roulade and is home to the Windham Brewery, which brews rich ales and lagers. ⊠ *50 Main St., 05301,* ☎ *802/254–6300,* 🖷 *802/ 254–6304. 30 rooms. Restaurant. Continental breakfast. AE, MC, V.*

$$–$$$ 🏠 **40 Putney Road.** Joan Broderick welcomes guests to her antiques-filled French château–style estate with a glass of port and a smile and leaves handmade chocolates on the pillow at night. In warm weather, breakfast is served on the patio of the formally landscaped grounds,

which lead to the shores of the West River. Rooms have antiques, phones, and a TV/VCR; the suite has a gas fireplace and sleeps four. ⊠ *40 Putney Rd., 05301,* ☎ *802/254–6268 or 800/941–2413,* ℻ *802/258–2673. 3 rooms, 1 suite. Full breakfast. AE, D, MC, V.*

Nightlife and the Arts

Common Ground (⊠ 25 Elliot St., ☎ 802/257–0855) often presents folk music or performance art on weekends, especially during Sunday brunch. **Mole's Eye Cafe** (⊠ 4 High St., ☎ 802/257–0771) hosts musical performers: acoustic or folk on Wednesday, open mike on Thursday, danceable R&B or blues on weekends. There's a cover charge on Friday and Saturday.

Outdoor Activities and Sports

CANOEING

Connecticut River Safari (⊠ U.S. 5, ☎ 802/257–5008) has guided and self-guided tours as well as canoe rentals.

SKATING

Nelson Withington Skating Rink (⊠ Memorial Park, 4 Guilford St., ☎ 802/257–2311) rents skates.

STATE PARK

The hiking trails at **Fort Dummer State Park** (⊠ S. Main St., 2 mi south of Brattleboro, ☎ 802/254–2610) afford views of the Connecticut River valley; campsites are available.

Shopping

The **Book Cellar** (⊠ 120 Main St., ☎ 802/254–6026), with two floors of volumes, carries many travel books. **Vermont Artisan Design** (⊠ 106 Main St., ☎ 802/257–7044), one of the state's best crafts shops, displays contemporary ceramics, glass, wood, clothing, jewelry, and furniture.

Marlboro

❷ *10 mi west of Brattleboro.*

Tiny Marlboro draws musicians and audiences from around the world each summer to the Marlboro Music Festival, founded by Rudolf Serkin and joined for many years by Pablo Casals. **Marlboro College,** high on a hill off Route 9, is the center of musical activity. The college's white-frame buildings have outstanding views of the valley below, and the campus is studded with apple trees.

The **Southern Vermont Natural History Museum** opened its doors in 1997 when a privately held wildlife collection with more than 500 birds in 80 small dioramas was donated to the newly formed museum. One of New England's largest collections of mounted birds, it also holds specimens of three extinct birds as well as a complete collection of mammals native to the Northeast. ⊠ *Rte. 9,* ☎ *802/464–0048.* 🎟 *$2.* ☺ *Memorial Day–Oct., daily 9–5; call for hrs rest of yr.*

Nightlife and the Arts

The **Marlboro Music Festival** (⊠ Marlboro Music Center, Marlboro College, ☎ 802/254–2394; 215/569–4690 Sept.–June) presents chamber music in weekend concerts in July and August. The **New England Bach Festival** (☎ 802/257–4523), with a chorus under the direction of Blanche Moyse, is held at Marlboro College in October.

Wilmington

❸ *8 mi west of Marlboro.*

Wilmington is the shopping and dining center for the Mt. Snow ski area (☞ West Dover, *below*) to the north. Main Street has a cohesive assemblage of 18th- and 19th-century buildings, many of them listed on the National Register of Historic Places. For a great stroll, pick up a self-guided tour map from the **Chamber of Commerce** (⊠ Rte. 9, W. Main St., ☎ 802/464–8092).

North River Winery, which occupies a converted farmhouse and barn, produces fruit wines such as Green Mountain Apple and Vermont Pear. ⊠ *Rte. 112, 6 mi south of Wilmington,* ☎ *802/368–7557.* ☞ *Free.* ☉ *Daily 10–5; tours late May–Dec.*

OFF THE BEATEN PATH	**SCENIC TOUR –** To begin a scenic (though well-traveled) 35-mi circular tour with panoramic views of the region's mountains, farmland, and abundant cow population, drive west on Route 9 to the intersection with Route 8. Turn south and continue to the junction with Route 100; follow Route 100 through Whitingham (the birthplace of the Mormon prophet Brigham Young), and stay with the road as it turns north again and takes you back to Route 9.

Lodging

$$–$$$$ 🛏 **Trail's End.** A cozy and congenial four-season lodge set on 10 acres, Trail's End is 4 mi from Mt. Snow. The inn's centerpiece is its cathedral-ceiling living room with catwalk loft seating and a 21-ft fieldstone fireplace. Guest rooms are comfortable, if simple, though two suites have fireplaces, whirlpool tubs, cable TV, refrigerators, and microwaves; four other rooms also have fireplaces. Breakfast is served at immense round pine tables; dinner is prepared during the holiday season only. There's a stocked trout pond on site and cross-country ski trails are nearby. ⊠ *5 Trail's End La., 05363,* ☎ *802/464–2727 or 800/859–2585,* FAX *802/464–5532. 15 rooms. Pool, pond, tennis court. Full breakfast. AE, D, MC, V.*

$$–$$$$ 🛏 **White House of Wilmington.** The grand staircase in this Federal-style mansion leads to rooms with antique bathrooms and brass wall sconces. The newer section has more contemporary plumbing; some rooms have fireplaces, whirlpool tubs, and lofts. The leather wing chairs of the public rooms suggest formality, but the atmosphere is casual and comfortable. Although it's a 10-minute drive to Mt. Snow/Haystack, the White House is primarily a cross-country ski touring center, with a rental shop and 12 km (7 mi) of groomed trails. ⊠ *178 Rte. 9 E, 05363,* ☎ *802/464–2135 or 800/541–2135,* FAX *802/464–5222. 23 rooms. Restaurant, bar, 1 indoor and 1 outdoor pool, sauna, cross-country skiing. Full breakfast; MAP available. AE, D, DC, MC, V.*

Nightlife and the Arts

The standard fare on weekends at **Poncho's Wreck** (⊠ S. Main St., ☎ 802/464–9320) is acoustic jazz or mellow rock. **Sitzmark** (⊠ Rte. 100, ☎ 802/464–3384) hosts rock bands on weekends.

Outdoor Activities and Sports

SLEIGH RIDES

Adams Farm (⊠ 15 Higley Hill Rd., ☎ 802/464–3762) has three double-traverse sleighs drawn by Belgian draft horses. Rides include a narrated tour and hot chocolate. A petting farm is open during the summer.

STATE PARK

Molly Stark State Park (⊠ Rte. 9, east of Wilmington, ☎ 802/464–5460) has campsites and a hiking trail that leads to a vista from a fire tower on Mt. Olga.

WATER SPORTS

Lake Whitingham (Harriman Reservoir) is the largest lake in the state; there are boat launch areas at Wards Cove, Whitingham, Mountain Mills, and the Ox Bow. **Green Mountain Flagship Company** (⊠ Rte. 9, about 2 mi west of Wilmington, ☎ 802/464–2975) runs a cruise boat on Lake Whitingham and rents canoes, kayaks, surfbikes, and sailboats from May to late October.

Shopping

Quaigh Design Centre (⊠ Rte. 9, West Main St., ☎ 802/464–2780) sells New England crafts, artwork from New England and Britain, and Scottish woolens and tartans. **Wilmington Flea Market** (⊠ Rtes. 9 and 100 S, ☎ 802/464–3345) sells antiques on weekends from Memorial Day to mid-October.

West Dover

❹ *6 mi north of Wilmington.*

The Congregational church in small West Dover, a classic New England town, dates back to the 1700s. The year-round population of about 1,000 swells on winter weekends as skiers flock to Mt. Snow/Haystack Ski Resort. The many condos, lodges, and inns at the base of the mountain accommodate them.

Dining and Lodging

$$$–$$$$ ✕ **Doveberry Inn.** Rack of venison with a caper-and-fresh-tomato *demi-glace* (sauce) served over polenta, wood-grilled veal chop with wild mushrooms, and pan-seared salmon with herbed risotto are among the northern Italian dishes served in the Doveberry's intimate, candlelighted dining rooms. ⊠ *Rte. 100,* ☎ *802/464–5652 or 800/722–3204. AE, MC, V. Closed Tues. No lunch.*

$$–$$$$ ✕🏠 **Deerhill Inn and Restaurant.** The west-facing windows at this En-
★ glish-style country inn have views of the valley below and the ski slopes across the way. A huge fireplace dominates the living room, and English hand-painted yellow wallpaper, a garden-scene mural, and collections of antique plates accent the dining rooms. One guest room has an Asian bedroom set, several have hand-painted murals on the wall, and many have fireplaces. The four balcony rooms are the largest; they have great views. Longtime Deerhill Valley residents Linda and Michael Anelli enjoy sharing their wealth of information about the area with guests. In the restaurant ($$$–$$$$; closed Wednesday), Michael prepares upscale comfort food that might include fresh fish, a veal medallion with wild mushrooms in a lemon cream sauce, or a black-pepper sirloin steak. ⊠ *Box 136, Valley View Rd., 05356,* ☎ *802/464–3100 or 800/993–3379,* 🅵🅰🆇 *802/464–5474. 13 rooms, 2 suites. Restaurant, pool. Full breakfast; MAP available. AE, MC, V.*

Nightlife and the Arts

Deacon's Den Tavern (⊠ Rte. 100, ☎ 802/464–9361) books bands on weekends from Thanksgiving through Easter. The **Snow Barn** (⊠ Near the base of Mt. Snow, ☎ 802/464–1100, ext. 4693) presents entertainers several days a week.

Skiing and Snow Sports

MT. SNOW/HAYSTACK SKI RESORT

Mt. Snow, established in the 1950s, was purchased in 1996 by the American Skiing Company, which also owns Sugarbush, Killington, and Pico. Recent developments have included the 1998 opening of the year-round Grand Summit Hotel and Conference Center; the inauguration of the Learn to Ski and Ride Center at the Perfect Turn Discovery Center, complete with its own expanded terrain, triple chairlift and building; and increased snowmaking capability. Two new terrain parks are the Carnival mini-park for kids and the Inferno for advanced snowboarders. One lift ticket lets you ski at Mt. Snow and Haystack.

Haystack—the southernmost ski area in Vermont—is much smaller than Mt. Snow but has a more personal atmosphere. A modern base lodge is close to the lifts. A free shuttle connects the two ski areas. ⊠ *400 Mountain Rd., Mt. Snow 05356,* ☎ *802/464–3333; 800/245–7669 for lodging; 802/464–2151 for snow conditions.*

Downhill. Mt. Snow is a remarkably well formed mountain. Most of the trails down its 1,700-ft vertical summit are intermediate, wide, and sunny. Most of the beginner slopes are toward the bottom; most of the expert terrain is on the North Face, where there's excellent fall-line skiing. Of the 134 trails, about two-thirds are intermediate. The trails are served by three high-speed quads, one regular quad, 10 triple chairs, six double chairs, and two Magic Carpets (similar to an escalator). The ski school's Perfect Turn instruction program is designed to help advanced and expert skiers.

Most of the 44 trails at Haystack are pleasantly wide with bumps and rolls and straight fall lines—good cruising, intermediate runs. The Witches, with three double-black-diamond trails—is very steep but short. A beginner section, safely tucked below the main-mountain trails, provides a haven for lessons and slow skiing. Three triple and two double chairlifts and one T-bar service Haystack's 1,400 vertical ft.

Child care. Mt. Snow's lively, well-organized child care center (reservations necessary) takes children from ages 6 weeks to 6 years. The center has age-appropriate toys and balances indoor play—including arts and crafts—with trips outdoors. The Pre-ski program is for 3-year-olds, and a Perfect Kids program for ages 4–12 teaches skiing and snowboarding.

CROSS-COUNTRY SKIING

Four cross-country-trail areas within 4 mi of Mt. Snow/Haystack provide more than 150 km (90 mi) of varied terrain. The **Hermitage** (⊠ Coldbrook Rd., Wilmington, ☎ 802/464–3511) and the **White House of Wilmington** (⊠ Rtes. 9 and 100, ☎ 802/464–2135; ☞ Wilmington, *above*) both have 50 km (30 mi) of groomed trails. **Timber Creek** (⊠ Rte. 100, north of the Mt. Snow entrance, ☎ 802/464–0999) is appealingly small with 16 km (10 mi) of thoughtfully groomed trails. **Sitzmark** (⊠ East Dover Rd., Wilmington, ☎ 802/464–3384) has 40 km (24 mi) of trails, with 12 km (7 mi) of them machine tracked.

Bennington

 21 mi west of Wilmington.

Bennington, college town and commercial focus of Vermont's southwest corner, lies at the edge of the Green Mountain National Forest. It has retained much of the industrial character it developed in the 19th century, when paper mills, grist mills, and potteries formed the city's economic base. It was in Bennington, at the Catamount Tavern, that Ethan Allen organized the Green Mountain Boys, who helped capture Ft. Ticonderoga in 1775. Here also, in 1777, American general John Stark urged his militia to attack the British-paid Hessian troops across the New York border: "There are the redcoats; they will be ours or tonight Molly Stark sleeps a widow!"

A brochure available at the chamber of commerce (☞ Visitor Information *in* Southern Vermont A to Z, *below*) describes an interesting self-guided walking tour of **Old Bennington,** a National Register Historic District west of downtown. Impressive white-column Greek Revival and sturdy brick Federal homes stand around the village green. In the graveyard of the **Old First Church,** at Church Street and Monument Avenue, the tombstone of the poet Robert Frost proclaims, "I had a lover's quarrel with the world."

The **Bennington Battle Monument,** a 306-ft stone obelisk with an elevator to the top, commemorates General Stark's victory over the British, who attempted to capture Bennington's stockpile of supplies. The battle, which took place near Walloomsac Heights in New York State, helped bring about the surrender two months later of the British commander "Gentleman Johnny" Burgoyne. ⊠ *15 Monument Ave.,* ☎ *802/447–0550.* ⚏ *$1.50.* ☉ *Mid-Apr.–late Oct., daily 9–5.*

The **Bennington Museum**'s rich collections include vestiges of rural life, a good percentage of which are packed into towering glass cases. The decorative arts are well represented; one room is devoted to early Bennington pottery. Two rooms cover the history of American glass and contain fine Tiffany specimens. The museum displays the largest public collection of the work of Grandma Moses, who lived and painted in the area. Among the 30 paintings and assorted memorabilia is her only self-portrait and the famous painted caboose window. Also here are the only surviving automobile of Bennington's Martin company, a 1925 Wasp, and the Bennington Flag, one of the oldest versions of the Stars and Stripes in existence. ⊠ *W. Main St./Rte. 9,* ☎ *802/447–1571.* ⚏ *$6.* ☉ *Nov.–May, daily 9–5; June–Oct., daily 9–6.*

Built in 1865 and home to two Vermont governors, the **Park-McCullough House** is a 35-room classic French Empire–style mansion furnished with period pieces. Several restored flower gardens grace the landscaped grounds, and a stable houses a collection of antique carriages. A summer concert series and special events are held on the grounds each season. ⊠ *Corner of Park and West Sts., North Bennington,* ☎ *802/442–5441.* ⚏ *$5.* ☉ *Late May–late Oct., Thurs.–Mon. 10–4; last tour at 3. Call for Victorian Christmas dates.*

Contemporary stone sculpture and white-frame neo-Colonial dorms surrounded by acres of cornfields punctuate the green meadows of **Bennington College**'s placid campus. The small liberal arts college, one of the most expensive to attend in the country, is noted for its progressive program in the arts. ⊠ *Rte. 67A, off U.S. 7; look for stone entrance gate,* ☎ *800/833–6845 for tour information.*

Dining and Lodging

$ ✗ **Blue Benn Diner.** Breakfast is served all day in this authentic diner, where the eats include turkey hash and breakfast burritos with scrambled eggs, sausage, and chilies. Pancakes of all imaginable varieties are also prepared. The menu lists many vegetarian selections. Lines may be long, especially on weekends. ⊠ *U.S. 7N,* ☎ *802/442–5140. No credit cards. No dinner Sat.–Tues.*

$$–$$$ ▦ **South Shire Inn.** Canopy beds in lushly carpeted rooms, ornate plaster moldings, and a dark mahogany fireplace in the South Shire's library re-create the grandeur of the Victorian past; fireplaces and hot tubs in some rooms add warmth. Four freshly renovated rooms in the Carriage House have whirlpool baths. The furnishings are antique except for the reproduction beds. The South Shire is in a quiet residential neighborhood within walking distance of the bus depot and downtown stores. Breakfast is served in the burgundy-and-white dining room. ⊠ *124 Elm St., 05201,* ☎ *802/447–3839,* ℻ *802/442–3547. 9 rooms. Full breakfast. AE, MC, V.*

$$ ★ ⚷ **Molly Stark Inn.** This gem of a B&B may make you so comfortable that you'll feel like you're staying with an old friend. Tidy blue-plaid wallpaper, gleaming hardwood floors, antique furnishings, and a wood-burning stove in a brick alcove of the sitting room add country charm to this 1860 Queen Anne Victorian. Molly's Room, at the back of the building, gets less noise from Route 9 and has a whirlpool bath; the attic suite is the most spacious. A secluded cottage with a 16-ft ceiling, a king-size brass bed, and a two-person whirlpool bath surrounded by windows with views of the woods is the perfect spot for a romantic retreat. The innkeeper's genuine hospitality and quirky charisma delight guests, as does the full country breakfast, made with mostly local ingredients, which has been known to include puffed-apple pancakes and freshly baked cinnamon buns. ⊠ *1067 E. Main St./Rte. 9, 05201,* ☎ *802/442–9631 or 800/356–3076,* ℻ *802/442–5224. 7 rooms. Full breakfast. AE, D, MC, V.*

Nightlife and the Arts

Oldcastle Theatre Co. (⊠ Bennington Center for the Arts, Rte. 9 and Gypsy La., ☎ 802/447–0564) performs from May to October.

Outdoor Activities and Sports

Cutting Edge (⊠ 160 Benmont Ave., ☎ 802/442–8664) rents and repairs bicycles and also sells and rents snowboards and cross-country skis. It has one of Vermont's few skateboarding parks, open daily from noon to 6.

HIKING

About 4 mi east of Bennington, the **Long Trail** crosses Route 9 and runs south to the summit of Harmon Hill. Allot two or three hours for this hike.

STATE PARKS

Lake Shaftsbury State Park (⊠ Rte. 7A, 10½ mi north of Bennington, ☎ 802/375–9978) is one of a few parks in Vermont with group camping; it has a swimming beach, nature trails, boat and canoe rentals, and a snack bar. **Woodford State Park** (⊠ Rte. 9, 10 mi east of Bennington, ☎ 802/447–7169) has an activities center on Adams Reservoir, campsites, a playground, boat and canoe rentals, and marked nature trails.

Shopping

The **Apple Barn and Country Bake Shop** (⊠ U.S. 7S, ☎ 802/447–7780) sells home-baked goodies, fresh cider, Vermont cheeses, and maple syrup. The showroom at the **Bennington Potters Yard** (⊠ 324 County St., ☎ 802/447–7531 or 800/205–8033) stocks first-quality pottery and antiques in addition to seconds from the famed Bennington Potters. Prepare to get dusty digging for an almost-perfect piece of this utilitarian stoneware at a modest discount. On the free tour you can follow the clay through production and hear about the Potters Yard, in business for five decades. Tours begin at 10 and 2, daily. **Hawkins House Craftsmarket** (⊠ U.S. 7, 262 North St., ☎ 802/447–0488) showcases jewelry, woodenware, glass, pottery, rugs, and clothing from more than 450 Vermont craftspeople.

Arlington

❻ *15 mi north of Bennington.*

Don't be surprised to see familiar-looking (if considerably aged) faces among the roughly 2,200 people of Arlington. The illustrator Norman Rockwell lived here from 1939 to 1953, and many of the models for his portraits of small-town life were his neighbors. Settled first in 1763, Arlington was called Tory Hollow for its Loyalist sympathies—even though a number of the Green Mountain Boys lived here, too. Smaller than Bennington and more down-to-earth than upper-crust Manchester to the north, Arlington exudes a certain Rockwellian folksiness. Dorothy Canfield Fisher, a novelist popular in the 1930s and 1940s, also lived here.

There are no original paintings at the **Norman Rockwell Exhibition,** but the exhibition rooms are crammed with reproductions of the illustrator's works, arranged in every way conceivable: chronologically, by subject matter, and juxtaposed with photos of the models—several of whom work here. ✉ *Rte. 7A/Main St.,* ☎ *802/375–6423.* 🎟 *$2.* ⊙ *May–Oct., daily 9–5; Nov.–Dec. and Feb.–Apr., daily 10–4.*

Dining and Lodging

$$$$ ✕🏨 **West Mountain Inn.** A former farmhouse built in the 1840s, this
★   romantic inn has a front lawn with a spectacular view of the countryside. Its 150 acres include a llama farm. Rooms 2, 3, and 4 overlook the lawn; the three small nooks of Room 11 resemble railroad sleeper berths and are perfect for kids. A children's room, brightly painted with life-size Disney characters, is stocked with games, stuffed animals, and a TV with VCR. A low-beamed candlelighted dining room ($$$) is the setting for six-course prix-fixe dinners featuring updated Continental cuisine. Aunt Min's Swedish rye and other toothsome breads, as well as desserts, are all made on the premises. Try to get a table by the window. ✉ *River Rd., off Rte. 313, 05250,* ☎ *802/375–6516,* 🏠 *802/ 375–6553. 18 rooms, 6 suites. Restaurant, bar, hiking, cross-country skiing, meeting rooms. MAP or B&B rates available. AE, D, MC, V.*

$$–$$$ ✕🏨 **Arlington Inn.** The Greek Revival columns at the entrance to a home
★   built by a railroad magnate in 1848 lend it an imposing presence, but the atmosphere is hardly forbidding. The inn's charm is created by linens that coordinate with the Victorian-style wallpaper, claw-foot tubs in some bathrooms, and the house's original moldings and wainscoting. The carriage house, built a century ago, contains country-French and Queen Anne furnishings. Some rooms have TVs and phones. The restaurant serves French and Continental dishes and game, such as antelope from Texas. Polished wood floors, rose walls, and soft candlelight complement the food. ✉ *Rte. 7A, 05250,* ☎ *802/375–6532 or 800/443–9442,* 🏠 *802/375–6534. 16 rooms, 4 suites. Restaurant, bar, tennis court. Full breakfast. AE, D, DC, MC, V.*

$$–$$$ 🏨 **Hill Farm Inn.** This homey inn has the feel of the country farmhouse it used to be. The surrounding farmland, deeded to the Hill family by King George in 1775, is protected from development by the Vermont Land Trust. The fireplace in the informal living room, the sturdy antiques, and the spinning wheel in the upstairs hallway all convey a relaxed, friendly atmosphere. Room 7 has a beamed cathedral ceiling, and from its porch you can see Mt. Equinox. The rooms in the 1790 guest house are very private; the one- and two-bedroom cottages are charming. ✉ *Box 2015, Hill Farm Rd., off Rte. 7A, 05250,* ☎ *802/ 375–2269 or 800/882–2545,* 🏠 *802/375–9918. 11 rooms, 6 with bath; 2 suites; 4 cabins in summer. Full breakfast. AE, D, MC, V.*

Outdoor Activities and Sports

Battenkill Canoe, Ltd. (✉ Rte. 7A, ☎ 802/362–2800 or 800/421–5268) has rentals and day trips on the Battenkill and inn-to-inn tours.

Shopping

The shops at **Candle Mill Village** (✉ Old Mill Rd., between U.S. 7 and Rte. 7A, East Arlington, ☎ 802/375–6068 or 800/772–3759) specialize in community cookbooks from around the country, music boxes, and candles. The mill itself was built in the 1760s by Remember Baker, a cohort of Ethan Allen and one of the Green Mountain Boys. The nearby waterfall makes a pleasant backdrop for a picnic.

Equinox Valley Nursery (⊠ Rte. 7A, between Arlington and Manchester, ☎ 802/362–2610) is known for its perennials (more than 1,000 varieties) and materials for water gardens. The nursery has 17 greenhouses and a conservatory, sells 150 varieties of herbs, and carries many Vermont-made products in the large gift shop.

Manchester

★ ❼ *9 mi north of Arlington.*

Manchester, where Ira Allen proposed financing Vermont's participation in the American Revolution by confiscating Tory estates, has been a popular summer retreat since the mid-19th century. Manchester Village's tree-shaded marble sidewalks and stately old homes reflect the luxurious resort lifestyle of a century ago. Manchester Center's upscale factory outlets appeal to the affluent 20th-century ski crowd drawn by nearby Bromley and Stratton mountains. Warning: Shoppers come in droves at times, giving the place the feel of a crowded mall on the weekend before Christmas. If you're coming here from Arlington, take pretty Route 7A, which passes directly by a number of sights.

★ **Hildene,** the summer home of Abraham Lincoln's son and onetime Pullman company chairman Robert Todd Lincoln, is a beautifully preserved 412-acre estate. The 24-room mansion, with its Georgian Revival symmetry, welcoming central hallway, and grand curved staircase, is unusual in that its rooms are not roped off. When the 1,000-pipe Aeolian organ is played, the music reverberates as though from the mansion's very bones. Tours include a short film on the owner's life and a walk through the elaborate formal gardens. When snow conditions permit, you can cross-country ski on the property, which has views of nearby mountains. In December, the house is decorated for special holiday tours that include horse-drawn sleigh rides. ⊠ *Rte. 7A,* ☎ *802/362–1788.* ⌸ *$7.* ☉ *Mid-May–Oct., daily 9:30–5:30 (last tour at 4); Dec. tour hrs vary.*

The **American Museum of Fly Fishing,** which houses the largest collection of fly-fishing equipment in the world, displays more than 1,500 rods, 800 reels, 30,000 flies, and the tackle of famous people such as Winslow Homer, Bing Crosby, and Jimmy Carter. Its library of 2,500 books is open by appointment. ⊠ *Rte. 7A at Seminary Ave.,* ☎ *802/362–3300.* ⌸ *$3.* ☉ *Daily 10–4.*

The 10-room **Southern Vermont Art Center** is set on 375 acres dotted with contemporary sculpture. A popular retreat for local patrons of the arts, the nonprofit educational center has a permanent collection of 19th- and 20-century American art and presents changing exhibits. The graceful Georgian mansion is the frequent site of concerts, performances, and films. A botany trail passes by a 300-year-old maple tree. In summer a restaurant opens for business. ⊠ *West Rd.,* ☎ *802/ 362–1405.* ⌸ *$3, $2 in winter.* ☉ *Mid-May–late Oct., Tues.–Sat. 10–5, Sun. noon–5; Dec.–early Apr., Mon.–Sat. 10–5.*

You may want to keep your eye on the temperature gauge of your car as you drive the 5-mi toll road to the top of 3,825-ft **Mt. Equinox.** Along the way you'll see the Battenkill trout stream and the surrounding Vermont countryside. Picnic tables line the drive, and there's an outstanding view down both sides of the mountain from a notch known as the Saddle. The **Equinox Mountain Inn** (☎ 802/362–1113 or 800/ 868–6843) is perched on top of the mountain. ⊠ *Off Rte. 7A, south of Manchester,* ☎ *802/362–1114.* ⌸ *$6 for car and driver, $2 each additional adult.* ☉ *May–Oct., daily 8 AM–10 PM.*

Dining and Lodging

$$$$ ✕ **Chantecleer.** Intimate dining rooms have been created in a former dairy barn that has a large fieldstone fireplace. The menu reflects the chef's Swiss background: The appetizers include *Bündnerfleisch* (air-dried Swiss beef) and frogs' legs in garlic butter; among the entrées are rack of lamb, whole Dover sole filleted tableside, and veal chops. The restaurant is 5 mi north of Manchester. ⊠ *Rte. 7A, East Dorset,* ☎ *802/362–1616. Reservations essential. AE, DC, MC, V. Closed Mon.–Tues. in winter, Tues. in summer. No lunch.*

$$–$$$ ✕ **Bistro Henry's.** This airy restaurant on the outskirts of town attracts a devoted clientele for authentic Mediterranean fare. Recently on the menu were merlot-braised lamb shank with balsamic-glazed onions and garlic mashed potatoes; eggplant, mushroom, and fontina terrine Provençal; and crispy sweetbreads in Armagnac cream. The outstanding wine list is extensive. ⊠ *Rte. 11/30,* ☎ *802/362–4982. AE, DC, MC, V. Closed Mon. No lunch.*

$$ ✕ **Quality Restaurant.** Gentrification has reached the down-home neighborhood place that was the model for Norman Rockwell's *War News* painting. Quality has Provençal wallpaper and polished wood booths, and the sturdy New England standbys of grilled meat loaf and hot roast beef or turkey sandwiches have been joined by grilled lamb chops, sautéed scallops with a vegetable medley tossed with pesto and served on fettuccine, and grilled swordfish with lemon butter. The breakfasts are popular. ⊠ *Main St.,* ☎ *802/362–9839. AE, DC, MC, V.*

$$$$ ✕▦ **Barrows House.** Jim and Linda McGinniss's 200-year-old Federal-★ style inn is a longtime favorite with those who wish to escape the commercial hustle of Manchester (Bromley is about 8 mi away). The deep-red woodwork and library theme of the pub room make it an intimate venue for dining on country fare that might include Chesapeake crab cakes. The greenhouse room, with terra-cotta and deep-blue hues, is a pleasant summer eating spot. The rooms, spread among nine buildings on 12 acres, afford great privacy. ⊠ *Box 98, Rte. 30, Dorset (6 mi north of Manchester), 05251,* ☎ *802/867–4455 or 800/639–1620,* ℻ *802/867–0132. 18 rooms, 10 suites. Restaurant, pool, sauna, 2 tennis courts, bicycles, cross-country skiing. Full breakfast; MAP available. AE, D, DC, MC, V.*

$$$$ ✕▦ **The Equinox.** This grand white-column resort was a fixture even before Abe Lincoln's family began summering here; it's worth a look around even if you don't stay here. The spacious, sunny rooms are furnished with reproductions of antiques. In the Marsh Tavern, richly upholstered settees, stuffed armchairs, and several fireplaces create a plush traditional ambience. The food is equally pleasing: Devonshire shepherd's pie and a woodland supper of roast duck, venison sausage, and wild mushrooms are popular. The Colonnade, where men are requested to wear jackets, is elegant. Among the many facilities here is a school for falconry. The resort is often the site of large conferences. ⊠ *Skyline Dr., off Rte. 7A, Manchester Village 05254,* ☎ *802/362–4700 or 800/362–4747,* ℻ *802/362–1595. 119 rooms, 36 suites, 10 3-bedroom town houses. 2 restaurants, bar, 1 indoor and 1 outdoor pool, sauna, steam room, 18-hole golf course, 3 tennis courts, croquet, health club, horseback riding, fishing, mountain bikes, ice-skating, cross-country skiing. AE, D, DC, MC, V.*

$$$$ ✕▦ **Reluctant Panther.** The large bedrooms here have goose-down duvets and Pierre Deux linens and are styled with antique, country, and contemporary furnishings. All have fireplaces, and the suites have double sunken whirlpool baths. The best views are from Rooms B and D. In Wildflowers restaurant ($$$–$$$$; reservations essential; closed Tuesday and Wednesday; from November through May, open Friday and

Saturday only), a huge fieldstone fireplace dominates the larger of the two dining rooms. The menu, which changes daily, might include rack of venison with an herbed cornmeal crust or grilled veal chop with a ragout of shiitake and wild mushrooms. ⊠ *Box 678, West Rd., 05254,* ☎ *802/362–2568 or 800/822–2331,* FAX *802/362–2586. 14 rooms, 6 suites. Restaurant, bar, meeting room. MAP. AE, MC, V.*

$$$–$$$$ ⊡ **Lake St. Catherine Inn.** If you're lucky enough to have good friends with a big, rambling house on a lake, you've got an idea of what this inn has to offer. Hosts Pat and Ray Endlich have thought of everything—snug lounges and dining overlooking the water, a lakeside deck, and plenty of watercraft. The lake is a favorite among anglers, and Ray will be happy to cook your catch. Accommodations are simple and comfortable, and the food hearty and satisfying. Reserve early: the inn, 25 mi northwest of Manchester via Route 30, has a loyal following. ⊠ *Cones Point Rd., Poultney 05764,* ☎ *802/247–6411 or 800/626–5724 outside VT. 35 rooms, 1 housekeeping cottage. Lake, boating, fishing. MAP. No credit cards. Closed Nov.–Apr.*

$$–$$$$ ⊡ **1811 House.** The atmosphere of an English country home can be
★ experienced without crossing the Atlantic. The pub-style bar serves 63 single-malt Scotches and is decorated with horse brasses, Waterford crystal is used in the dining room, and 3 acres of lawn are landscaped in the English floral style. Rooms contain period antiques; six have fireplaces, and many have four-poster beds. Bathrooms are old-fashioned but serviceable, particularly the Robinson Room's marble-enclosed tub. ⊠ *Box 39, Rte. 7A, 05254,* ☎ *802/362–1811 or 800/432–1811,* FAX *802/362–2443. 14 rooms. Bar. Full breakfast. AE, D, MC, V.*

$$–$$$$ ⊡ **Inn at Ormsby Hill.** During the Revolutionary War, this 1774 Fed-
★ eral-style building provided refuge from the British for Ethan Allen, and it later served the same purpose for slaves heading north on the Underground Railroad. When renovating, the owners created interesting public spaces and romantic bedrooms. Furnished with antiques and canopied or four-poster beds, the rooms have fireplaces that can be viewed from the bed or the two-person whirlpool tub. Some have mountain views. Breakfasts in the conservatory—entrées may include baked, stuffed French toast with an apricot brandy sauce—are sumptuous. An optional buffet supper is served Friday night. ⊠ *1842 Main St./Rte. 7A, 05255,* ☎ *802/362–1163 or 800/670–2841,* FAX *802/362–5176. 10 rooms. Full breakfast. D, MC, V.*

$–$$ ⊡ **Aspen Motel.** A rare find in this area, the immaculate, family-owned Aspen is set well back from the highway and is moderately priced. The spacious, tastefully decorated rooms have Colonial-style furnishings, and all have cable TV and in-room coffee; some have refrigerators. The social room has a fireplace. ⊠ *Rte. 7A N, 05255,* ☎ *802/362–2450,* FAX *802/362–1348. 24 rooms, 2 2-bedroom suites. Pool, playground. AE, D, MC, V.*

Nightlife and the Arts

The two pre–Revolutionary War barns of the **Dorset Playhouse** (⊠ Off town green, ☎ 802/867–5777) host a community group in winter and a resident professional troupe in summer. The **Marsh Tavern** (☎ 802/362–4700) at the Equinox (☞ Dining and Lodging, *above*) has cabaret music and jazz from Wednesday to Sunday in summer and on weekends in winter. **Mulligan's** (⊠ Rte. 7A, ☎ 802/362–3663), which serves American cuisine, is a popular hangout in Manchester Village, especially for après-ski; DJs program the music on weekends.

Outdoor Activities and Sports

BIKING

The 20-mi Dorset–Manchester trail runs from Manchester Village north on West Street to Route 30, turns west at the Dorset village green onto West Road, and heads back south to Manchester. **Battenkill Sports** (✉ Exit 4 off U.S. 7, at Rte. 11/30, ☎ 802/362–2734 or 800/340–2734) rents and repairs bikes and provides maps and route suggestions.

FISHING

Battenkill Anglers (☎ 802/362–3184) teaches the art and science of fly-fishing. It has both private and group lessons. The **Orvis Co.** (✉ Rte. 7A, Manchester Center, ☎ 800/235–9763) hosts a nationally known fly-fishing school on the Battenkill, the state's most famous trout stream, with three-day courses given weekly between April and October.

HIKING

One of the most popular segments of the **Long Trail** starts at Route 11/30 west of Peru Notch and goes to the top of Bromley Mountain. The round-trip trek takes about four hours.

The **Mountain Goat** (✉ Rte. 7A south of Rte. 11/30, ☎ 802/362–5159) sells hiking, backpacking, and climbing equipment and rents snowshoes and cross-country and telemark skis. The shop also conducts rock- and ice-climbing clinics.

STATE PARK

Emerald Lake State Park (✉ Rte. 7, East Dorset, ☎ 802/362–1655), 9 mi north of Manchester, has campsites, a marked nature trail, an on-site naturalist, boat and canoe rentals, and a snack bar.

Shopping

ART AND ANTIQUES

Carriage Trade (✉ Rte. 7A north of Manchester Center, ☎ 802/362–1125) contains room after room of Early American antiques and has a fine collection of ceramics. **Danby Antiques Center** (✉ ⅛ mi off U.S. 7, Danby, ☎ 802/293–5990), 13 mi north of Manchester, has 11 rooms and a barn filled with furniture and accessories, folk art, textiles, and stoneware. **Gallery North Star** (✉ Rte. 7A, ☎ 802/362–4541) shows oils, watercolors, lithographs, and sculptures by Vermont artists. **Tilting at Windmills Gallery** (✉ Rte. 11/30, ☎ 802/362–3022) exhibits the works of well-known artists like Douglas Flackman of the Hudson River School.

BOOKS

Northshire Bookstore (✉ Main St., ☎ 802/362–2200 or 800/437–3700), a community bookstore for more than 20 years, carries many travel and children's books and sponsors readings year-round.

CLOTHING

Orvis Sporting Gifts (✉ Union St., ☎ 802/362–6455), a discount outlet that carries discontinued items from the popular outdoor clothing and home furnishings mail-order company, is housed in what was Orvis's shop in the 1800s. Anne Klein, Liz Claiborne, Donna Karan, Levi Strauss, Giorgio Armani, and Jones New York are among the shops on Route 11/30 and U.S. 7 South—a center for **designer outlet stores.**

FISHING GEAR

Orvis Retail Store (✉ Rte. 7A, ☎ 802/362–3750), an outdoor specialty store that is one of the largest suppliers of fishing gear in the Northeast, also carries clothing, gifts, and hunting supplies.

MALLS AND MARKETPLACES

Manchester Commons (✉ U.S. 7 and Rte. 11/30, ☎ 802/362–3736 or 800/955–7467), the largest and spiffiest of three large factory-direct minimalls, has such big-city names as Joan and David, Baccarat, Coach, Ralph Lauren, Calvin Klein, and Cole-Haan. **Manchester Square** (✉ Rte. 11/30 and Richville Rd.) has stores such as Giorgio Armani, Emporio Armani, Tommy Hilfiger, Brooks Brothers, Levis, and Escada.

Skiing and Snow Sports

BROMLEY MOUNTAIN

The first trails at Bromley were cut in 1936. Many families appreciate the resort's convivial atmosphere. The area has a comfortable red-clapboard base lodge, built when the ski area first opened more than 60 years ago and recently expanded. The resort has a large ski shop and a condominium village adjacent to the slopes. A reduced-price, two-day lift pass is available, as is a snowboard park–only lift ticket. Kids 6 and under ski free when accompanied by an adult. Eighty-four percent of the area is covered by snowmaking. ⊠ *Box 1130, Rte. 11, Manchester Center 05255,* ☎ *802/824–5522 for snow conditions; 802/865–4786; 800/865–4786 for lodging.*

Downhill. Most ski areas are laid out to face the north or east, but Bromley faces south, making it one of the warmer spots to ski in New England. Its 41 trails are equally divided into beginner, intermediate, and advanced terrain; the last is serviced by the Blue Ribbon quad chair on the east side. The vertical drop is 1,334 ft. Four double chairlifts, two quad lifts, a J-bar, and two surface lifts for beginners provide transportation. The high-speed quad lift takes skiers from the base to the summit in just six minutes.

Child care. Bromley is one of the region's best places to bring children. Besides a nursery for children from ages 6 weeks to 6 years, ski instruction is provided for children from ages 3 to 14.

CROSS-COUNTRY

With 26 km (16 mi) of marked trails, the **Meadowbrook Inn** (⊠ Landgrove, ☎ 802/824–6444 or 800/498–6445) offers an idyllic setting for cross-country skiing and snowshoeing. The inn, which has eight guest rooms and a restaurant, has rental gear and provides lessons.

Stratton

8 *18 mi southeast of Manchester.*

Stratton, home to the famous Stratton Mountain Resort, has a self-contained town center with shops, restaurants, and lodgings clustered at the base of the slopes. There's plenty of activity year-round between skiing and summer sports.

Dining and Lodging

$$$$ ★ ✕🖫 **Windham Hill Inn.** Antiques, throw blankets, and canopy beds decorate the rooms at this exquisite retreat. Most have fireplaces or Vermont Castings stoves, and several have large soaking tubs. The barn-loft rooms are the newest and most luxurious. The Marion Goodfellow room has its own private cupola with a 360-degree view of the 160-acre grounds, and a floor-to-ceiling bay window is the signature of the Meadowlook room. The restaurant serves nouveau French fare such as grilled mustardseed-encrusted lamb loin with a rosemary merlot sauce. Sports equipment is provided free of charge. ⊠ *311 Lawrence Dr., West Townshend (10 mi east of Stratton Mountain) 05359,* ☎ *802/874–4080 or 800/944–4080,* 🖷 *802/874–4702. 21 rooms. Restaurant, bar, pool, pond, tennis court, hiking, ice-skating, cross-country skiing. MAP. AE, D, MC, V. Closed during Christmas holidays.*

$$–$$$$ ✕🖫 **Stratton Mountain Inn and Village Lodge.** The complex includes a 120-room inn—the largest on the mountain—and a 91-room lodge of studio units equipped with microwaves, refrigerators, and small wet bars. The lodge is the only slopeside ski-in, ski-out hotel at Stratton. Ski packages that include lift tickets bring down room rates. ⊠ *Stratton Mountain Rd., 05155,* ☎ *802/297–2500 or 800/777–1700,* 🖷 *802/*

297–1778. 211 rooms. 2 restaurants, pool, hot tub, sauna, golf course, tennis courts. AE, D, DC, MC, V.

Nightlife and the Arts

Haig's Black Angus Steak House (⊠ River Rd., ☎ 802/297–1300 or 800/897–5894) in Bondville, 5 mi from Stratton, has a dance club with a DJ or a band on weekends and holidays. There's also a diverting indoor simulated golf course. Popular **Mulligan's** (⊠ Mountain Rd., ☎ 802/297–9293) serves American cuisine. Bands or DJs provide entertainment in the late afternoon and on weekends. The **Red Fox Inn** (⊠ Winhall Hollow Rd., ☎ 802/297–2488) in Bondville hosts musicians in the tavern on weekends.

Outdoor Activities and Sports

Summertime facilities at **Stratton Mountain** (☞ Skiing and Snow Sports, *below*) include 15 outdoor tennis courts, 27 holes of golf, horseback riding, mountain biking and hiking accessed by a gondola to the summit, and instructional programs in tennis and golf. The area also hosts summer entertainment and family activities, including a skating park and climbing wall.

Skiing and Snow Sports

STRATTON MOUNTAIN

Owned by Intrawest, the company that runs Whistler/Blackcomb and Mont Tremblant, Stratton has a new master plan that includes the only high-speed six-passenger lift in New England and an expanded village with additional lodging. Since its creation in 1961, Stratton has undergone physical transformations and upgrades, yet the area's sophisticated character has been retained. It has been the special province of well-to-do families and, more recently, young professionals from the New York–southern Connecticut corridor. Since the mid-'80s, an entire village, with a covered parking structure for 700 cars, has arisen at the base of the mountain: Adjacent to the base lodge are a condo-hotel, restaurants, and about 25 shops lining a pedestrian mall. Stratton is 4 mi up its own access road off Route 30 in Bondville, about 30 minutes from Manchester's popular shopping zone. ⊠ *R.R. 1, Box 145, Stratton Mountain 05155, ☎ 802/297–2200 or 800/843–6867; 802/297–4211 for snow conditions; 800/787–2886 for lodging.*

Downhill. Stratton's skiing is in three sectors. The first is the lower mountain directly in front of the base lodge-village-condo complex; several lifts reach mid-mountain from this entry point, and practically all skiing is beginner or low-intermediate. Above that, the upper mountain, with a vertical drop of 2,000 ft, has a high-speed, 12-passenger gondola, Starship XII. Down the face are the expert trails, and on either side are intermediate cruising runs with a smattering of wide beginner slopes. The third sector, the Sun Bowl, is off to one side with two quad chairlifts and two expert trails, a full base lodge, and plenty of intermediate terrain. Stratton hosts the U.S. Open Snowboarding championships; its snowboard park has a 380-ft halfpipe. A Ski Learning Park with 10 trails and five lifts has its own Park Packages available for novice skiers. In all, Stratton has 90 slopes and trails served by the gondola; a six-passenger lift; four quad, one triple, and three double chairlifts; and two surface lifts.

Cross-country. The Stratton area has more than 30 km (18 mi) of cross-country skiing and two Nordic centers: Sun Bowl and Country Club.

Other activities. The area's sports center contains two indoor tennis courts, three racquetball courts, a 25-meter indoor swimming pool, a hot tub, a steam room, a fitness facility with Nautilus equipment, and a restaurant.

Child care. The day-care center takes children from ages 6 weeks to 6 years for indoor activities and outdoor excursions. There is a ski school for children ages 4 to 12. A junior racing program and special instruction groups are geared toward more experienced young skiers.

Weston

⑨ *20 mi northeast of Manchester.*

Although perhaps best known for the Vermont Country Store, Weston is famed as one of the first Vermont towns to have discovered its own intrinsic loveliness—and marketability. With its summer theater, pretty town green, and Victorian bandstand, as well as an assortment of shops offering variety without modern sprawl, the little village really lives up to its vaunted image.

The **Mill Museum,** down the road from the Vermont Country Store, has numerous hands-on displays depicting the engineering and mechanics of one of the town's mills. The many old tools on view kept towns like Weston running smoothly. ✉ *Rte. 100,* ☎ *802/824–3119.* 🎫 *Donations accepted.* ☉ *Late May–early Sept., daily 11–4; early Sept.–mid-Oct., weekends 11–4.*

Nightlife and the Arts

The members of the **Weston Playhouse** (✉ Village Green, off Rte. 100, ☎ 802/824–5288), the oldest professional theater in Vermont, have produced Broadway plays, musicals, and other works since 1937. Their season runs from late June to mid-October.

Shopping

The **Vermont Country Store** (✉ Rte. 100, ☎ 802/824–3184) sets aside one room of its old-fashioned emporium for Vermont Common Crackers and bins of fudge and other candy. For years the retail store and its mail-order catalog have carried nearly forgotten items like Lilac Vegetal aftershave, Monkey Brand black tooth powder, Flexible Flyer sleds, and tiny wax bottles of colored syrup, but there are also plenty of practical items such as sturdy outdoor clothing and even a manual typewriter. Nostalgia-evoking implements dangle from the store's walls and ceiling. (There's another store on Route 103 in Rockingham.) **Weston Bowl Mill** (✉ Rte. 100, ☎ 802/824–6219) stocks finely crafted wood products at mill prices.

En Route   From Weston you can head south on Route 100 through Jamaica and then down Route 30 through Townshend to Newfane, all pretty hamlets typical of small-town Vermont. South of Townshend, near the Townshend Dam on Route 30, is the state's longest single-span covered bridge, now closed to traffic.

Ludlow

⑩ *9 mi northeast of Weston.*

Ludlow, a former mill town, relies on the popularity of Okemo Mountain Ski Resort to fill its shops and restaurants. A beautiful, often-photographed historic church sits on the town green. Calvin Coolidge went to school at Ludlow's Black River Academy.

Lodging

$$$–$$$$ 🏨 **Okemo Mountain Lodge.** Most rooms in this three-story brown-clapboard building have balconies and fireplaces, and the one-bedroom condominiums clustered around the base of the ski lifts are close to restaurants and shops. All have equipped kitchens, fireplaces, decks, and TVs with VCRs. Okemo Mountain Lodging Service also operates the Kettle Brook, Winterplace, and Solitude slopeside condominiums. Ski-and-stay packages are available. ⊠ *77 Okemo Ridge Rd., off Rte. 103, 05149,* ☎ *802/228–5571, 802/228–4041, or 800/786–5366,* 🖷 *802/228–2079. 76 rooms, 84 condos. Restaurant, bar. AE, MC, V.*

Outdoor Activities and Sports

Cavendish Trail Horse Rides (⊠ Twenty Mile Stream Rd., Proctorsville, ☎ 802/226–7821) operates horse-drawn sleigh rides in snowy weather and wagon rides at other times, and guided trail rides from mid-May to mid-October.

Skiing and Snow Sports

OKEMO MOUNTAIN RESORT

An ideal ski area for families with children, Okemo has evolved into a major resort. The main attraction is a long, broad, gentle slope with two beginner lifts just above the base lodge. All the facilities at the bottom of the mountain are close together, so family members can regroup easily during the ski day. The Solitude Village Area has a triple chairlift, two new trails, and lodging. The resort offers numerous ski and skateboarding packages. ⊠ *Rte. 100; mailing address: 77 Okemo Ridge Rd., 05149,* ☎ *802/228–4041; 800/786–5366 for lodging; 802/ 228–5222 for snow conditions.*

Downhill. Above the broad beginner's slope at the base, the upper part of Okemo has a varied network of trails: long, winding, easy trails for beginners; straight fall-line runs for experts; and curving, cruising slopes for intermediates. The 98 trails are served by an efficient lift system of seven quads, three triple chairlifts, and three surface lifts; 95% are covered by snowmaking. From the summit to the base lodge, the vertical drop is 2,150 ft, the highest in southern Vermont. Okemo has a self-contained snowboarding area serviced by a surface lift; the mile-long park is home to the Pipe, a massive 420-ft by 40-ft halfpipe. There's also a snowboard park for beginners.

Cross-country. The **Okemo Valley Nordic Center** (⊠ Fox La., ☎ 802/ 228–8871) has 26 km (16 mi) of trails, all groomed.

Child care. The area's nursery, for children from ages 6 weeks to 8 years, has many indoor activities and supervised outings. Children ages 3 to 4 can get a one-hour introduction to skiing; there's a SKIwee Snow-Star program for kids ages 4–7. Nursery reservations are required. Okemo also offers a Kids' Night Out evening child-care program on Saturdays during the regular season and certain holiday weeks.

Chester

⓫ *11 mi east of Weston.*

Gingerbread Victorians frame Chester's town green. The local pharmacy on Main Street has been in continuous operation since the 1860s. The **stone village** on North Street on the outskirts of town, two rows of buildings constructed from quarried stone, was built by two brothers and is said to have been used during the Civil War as a station on the Underground Railroad. The **National Survey Charthouse** (⊠ Main St., ☎ 802/875–2121) is a map-lover's paradise. The store is good for a rainy-day browse even if maps aren't your passion.

In Chester's restored 1872 train station you can board the *Green Mountain Flyer* for a 26-mi, two-hour round-trip to Bellows Falls, on the Connecticut River at the eastern edge of the state. The journey, in superbly restored cars that date from the golden age of railroading, travels through scenic countryside past covered bridges and along the Brockway Mills gorge. A six-hour tour takes place in the fall. ⊠ *Rte.*

103, ☎ 802/463–3069 or 800/707–3530. ⛴ 2-hr trip $12. ☉ Mid-June–mid-Sept., Tues.–Sun.; mid- Sept.–mid-Oct., daily. Train departs at 11, 12:10, 2, 3:10; also, special fall sunset trips. Call to confirm.

Dining and Lodging

$ ✗ **Raspberries and Thyme.** Breakfast specials, homemade soups, a large selection of salads, homemade desserts, and a menu listing more than 40 sandwiches make this one of the area's most popular spots for casual dining. ⊠ *On the Green,* ☎ *802/875–4486. AE, D, MC, V. No dinner Tues.*

$$–$$$ ✗⊞ **Fullerton Inn.** In 1998 Robin and Jerry Szawerda purchased the Inn at Long Last, completely redecorated the common areas and guest rooms, and then brought in the furniture and sign from their restaurant next door—Ye Old Bradford Tavern. The inn now serves breakfast and dinner daily except Wednesday, offering morning delicacies such as lobster omelets and nightly entrées like roast duck and trout Provençal. The rooms, with country quilts and lace curtains, vary in size and amenities. Some favorites are the bright corner rooms and numbers 8 and 10, which share a private porch. A shuttle bus to local attractions and ski areas stops in front of the inn. ⊠ *40 Common St., on the Green, 05143,* ☎ *802/875–2444,* ℻ *802/875–6414. 20 rooms, 2 suites. Restaurant. AE, D, MC, V.*

Outdoor Activities and Sports

A 26-mi driving or biking loop out of Chester follows the Williams River along Route 103 to Pleasant Valley Road north of Bellows Falls. At Saxtons River, turn west onto Route 121 and follow along the river to connect with Route 35. When the two routes separate, follow Route 35 north back to Chester.

Grafton

★ ⑫ *8 mi south of Chester.*

Like many Vermont villages its size, Grafton enjoyed its heyday as an agricultural community well before the Civil War, when its citizens grazed some 10,000 sheep and spun their wool into sturdy yarn for locally woven fabric. Unlike most other out-of-the-way country towns, though, Grafton was born again, following a long decline, by preservationists determined to revitalize not only its centerpiece, the Old Tavern, but many of the other commercial and residential structures in the village center as well. Beginning in 1963, the Windham Foundation—Vermont's second-largest private foundation—commenced the rehabilitation of Grafton. The town's **Historical Society** documents the town's renewal. ⊠ *Townshend Rd.,* ☎ *802/843–2255 for visitor center information.* ⛫ *$1. ☉ June–late Sept., weekends 1:30–4; late Sept.–Oct., daily 1:30–4.*

Dining and Lodging

$$$–$$$$ ✗⊞ **Old Tavern at Grafton.** White-column porches on both stories wrap around the main building of this commanding inn, which dates from 1801. The main building holds 14 rooms; the rest are dispersed among other buildings in town. Two dining rooms ($$$), one with formal Georgian furniture and oil portraits, the other with rustic paneling and low beams, serve inspired New England fare such as grilled choice sirloin steeped in McNeil's stout and a blend of spices. The Phelps Barn Bar is a popular hangout. ⊠ *Rte. 35, 05146,* ☎ *802/843–2231 or 800/ 843–1801,* ℻ *802/843–2245. 62 rooms, 3 suites. Restaurant, bar, pond, tennis court, paddle tennis, mountain biking, ice-skating, cross-country skiing, recreation room. Full breakfast. MC, V. Closed Apr.*

Shopping

Gallery North Star (⊠ Townshend Rd., ☎ 802/843–2465) exhibits the oils, watercolors, lithographs, and sculptures of Vermont artists.

Newfane

⑬ *15 mi south of Grafton.*

With a village green surrounded by pristine white buildings, Newfane is sometimes described as the quintessential New England small town. The 1839 First Congregational Church and the Windham County Court House, with 17 green-shuttered windows and a rounded cupola, are often open. The building with the four-pointed spire is Union Hall, built in 1832.

Dining and Lodging

$$–$$$ ✕▥ **Four Columns.** The majestic white columns of this Greek Revival mansion, built 150 years ago for a homesick southern bride, are more intimidating than the Colonial-style rooms inside. Rooms are decorated with a mix of antiques and turn-of-the-century reproductions. The third-floor room in the old section is the most private. The suites have cathedral ceilings, double whirlpool baths, and gas fireplaces. In the classy restaurant ($$$; closed Tuesdays and part of April), chef Greg Parks has introduced new American dishes like roasted young chicken with herbs served in a chardonnay and mushroom sauce. ⊠ *Box 278, West St., 05345,* ☎ *802/365–7713 or 800/787–6633,* ℻ *802/365–0022. 15 rooms. Restaurant, hiking. Continental breakfast; MAP in foliage season. AE, D, DC, MC, V.*

Shopping

The **Newfane Country Store** (⊠ Rte. 30, ☎ 802/365–7916) carries many quilts (which can also be custom ordered), homemade fudge, and other Vermont foods, gifts, and crafts. Collectibles dealers from across the state sell their wares at the **Newfane Flea Market** (⊠ Rte. 30, ☎ 802/365–7771), held every weekend during summer and fall.

Outdoor Activities and Sports

Townshend State Park (⊠ 3 mi north of Rte. 30, between Newfane and Townshend, ☎ 802/365–7500), the largest in southern Vermont, is popular for the swimming at Townshend Dam and the stiff hiking trail to the top of Bald Mountain. Campsites are available.

Putney

⑭ *7 mi east of Newfane, 9 mi north of Brattleboro.*

Putney, a Connecticut River valley town just upriver from Brattleboro, was a prime destination for many of the converts to alternative rural lifestyles who swarmed into Vermont during the late 1960s and early '70s. Those who remained maintain a tradition of progressive schools, artisanship, and organic farming.

☉ **Harlow's Sugar House** (⊠ U.S. 5, ☎ 802/387–5852), 2 mi north of Putney, has a working cider mill and sugar house, as well as berry picking in summer and apple picking in autumn. You can buy the fruits of these labors in the gift shop.

Tours are given of the **Green Mountain Spinnery,** a factory-shop where you can purchase yarn, knitting accessories, and patterns. ⊠ *Depot Rd. at Exit 4 off I–91,* ☎ *802/387–4528 or 800/321–9665.* ▦ *Tours $2.* ☉ *Tours of yarn factory at 1:30 on the 1st and 3rd Tues. of each month.*

Dining and Lodging

$$–$$$ ✕🔲 **Putney Inn.** The main building of this inn dates from the 1790s. The building was later part of a seminary—the present-day pub was the chapel. Two fireplaces dominate the lobby, and the guest rooms have Queen Anne mahogany reproductions. The exterior of the adjacent building is not terribly appealing, but the spacious, modern rooms are 100 yards from the banks of the Connecticut River. Regionally inspired cuisine—seafood, New England potpies, a wild-game mixed grill, and burgers with Vermont cheddar—contains innovative flourishes. Locally raised meat is butchered on the premises. ✉ *Depot Rd., 05346,* ☎ *802/387–5517 or 800/653–5517,* 𝖥𝖠𝖷 *802/387–5211. 25 rooms. Full breakfast. AE, D, MC, V.*

$$ 🔲 **Hickory Ridge House Bed and Breakfast.** This gracious 1808 Federal mansion, listed on the National Register of Historic Places, has Palladian windows, a parlor with a Rumford fireplace, and large, comfortable guest rooms filled with antiques and country furnishings. Four rooms have wood-burning fireplaces, and one has a gas fireplace stove. A two-bedroom cottage, with a full kitchen and fireplace, can be rented as a unit, or the rooms can be rented separately. A two-night minimum stay is required on some weekends and holidays. ✉ *R.D. 3, Box 1410, Hickory Ridge Rd., 05346,* ☎ *802/387–5709 or 800/380–9218,* 𝖥𝖠𝖷 *802/387–4051. 6 rooms, 1 cottage. Hiking, cross-country skiing. Full breakfast. MC, V.*

Shopping

Allen Bros. (✉ U.S. 5 north of Putney, ☎ 802/722–3395) bakes apple pies, makes cider doughnuts, and sells Vermont foods and products.

Southern Vermont A to Z

Arriving and Departing

See Vermont A to Z, *below.*

Getting Around

BY BUS

Vermont Transit (☎ 802/864–6811; 800/451–3292; 800/642–3133 in VT) links Bennington, Manchester, Brattleboro, and Bellows Falls.

BY CAR

In the south the principal east–west highway is Route 9, the Molly Stark Trail, from Brattleboro to Bennington. The most important north–south roads are U.S. 7; the more scenic Route 7A; Route 100, which runs through the state's center; I–91; and U.S. 5, which runs along the state's eastern border. Route 30 from Brattleboro to Manchester is a scenic drive.

Contacts and Resources

EMERGENCIES

Brattleboro Memorial Hospital (✉ 9 Belmont Ave., ☎ 802/257–0341).

VISITOR INFORMATION

Bennington Area Chamber of Commerce (✉ Veterans Memorial Dr., Bennington 05201, ☎ 802/447–3311). **Brattleboro Chamber of Commerce** (✉ 180 Main St., Brattleboro 05301, ☎ 802/254–4565). **Chamber of Commerce, Manchester and the Mountains** (✉ 2 Main St., Manchester 05255, ☎ 802/362–2100). **Mt. Snow Valley Chamber of Commerce** (✉ Box 3, W. Main St., Wilmington 05363, ☎ 802/464–8092).

CENTRAL VERMONT

Central Vermont's economy once centered on the mills and railroad yards of Rutland and the marble quarries that honeycomb nearby towns. Vermont's "second city" is still a busy commercial hub, but today, as in much of the rest of the state, it's tourism that drives the economic engine. The center of the dynamo is the massive ski-and-stay infrastructure around Killington, the East's largest downhill resort. There's a lot more to central Vermont than high-speed chairlifts and slopeside condos, however. The protected (except for occasional logging) lands of the Green Mountain National Forest surround the spine of Vermont's central range; off to the west, the rolling dairylands of the southern Lake Champlain valley are one of the truly undiscovered corners of the state. To the east, in the Connecticut River valley, are towns as diverse as Calvin Coolidge's Plymouth, a Yankee Brigadoon; and busy, polished-to-perfection Woodstock, where upscale shops are just a short walk from America's newest national park.

The coverage of towns begins with Windsor, on U.S. 5 near I–91 at the eastern edge of the state; winds westward toward U.S. 7; then continues north before heading up and over the spine of the Green Mountains.

Windsor

15 *50 mi north of Brattleboro, 42 mi east of Rutland.*

Windsor justly bills itself as the birthplace of Vermont. An interpretive exhibit on Vermont's constitution, the first in the United States to prohibit slavery and establish a system of public schools, is housed in the **Old Constitution House.** The site, where in 1777 grant holders declared Vermont an independent republic, contains 18th- and 19th-century furnishings, American paintings and prints, and Vermont-made tools, toys, and kitchenware. ⊠ *N. Main St.,* ☎ *802/828–3211.* ☞ *$1.* ☉ *Mid-May–mid-Oct., Wed.–Sun.; call for hrs.*

The firm of Robbins & Lawrence became famous for applying the "American system" (the use of interchangeable parts) to the manufacture of rifles. Although the company no longer exists, the **American Precision Museum** extols the Yankee ingenuity that created a major machine-tool industry here in the 19th century. The museum contains the largest collection of historically significant machine tools in the country and presents changing exhibits. ⊠ *196 Main St.,* ☎ *802/674–6628.* ☞ *$5.* ☉ *Memorial Day–Oct., weekdays 9–5, weekends 10–4.*

The mission of the **Vermont State Craft Center,** in the restored 1846 Windsor House, is to advance the appreciation of Vermont crafts through education and exhibition. The center presents crafts exhibitions and operates a small museum. ⊠ *54 Main St.,* ☎ *802/674–6729.* ☉ *Mon.–Thurs. 10–5, Fri.–Sat. 9–6, Sun. 11–5.*

A British-style pale ale, an American amber ale, and a dark porter are among the beers produced at **Catamount Brewery,** one of Vermont's most popular microbreweries. You can sample beer at the company store and at the conclusion of the tour. ⊠ *Windsor Industrial Park, U.S. 5S, Exit 9 off I–91,* ☎ *802/674–6700 or 800/540–2248.* ☞ *Free.* ☉ *Mon.–Sat. 10–6, tours at 11, 1, and 3; Sun. 1–5, tours at 1 and 3.*

At 460 ft, the **covered bridge** off U.S. 5, which spans the Connecticut River between Windsor and Cornish, New Hampshire, is the longest in the state.

Dining and Lodging

$$ ✕ **Windsor Station.** This converted main-line railroad station serves such main-line entrées as chicken Kiev, filet mignon, and prime rib. The booths, with their curtained brass railings, were created from the high-back railroad benches of the depot. Breakfast and lunch are served in the deli across the street every day except Sunday. ⊠ *Depot Ave.,* ☎ *802/674–2052. AE, MC, V. Closed Mon.*

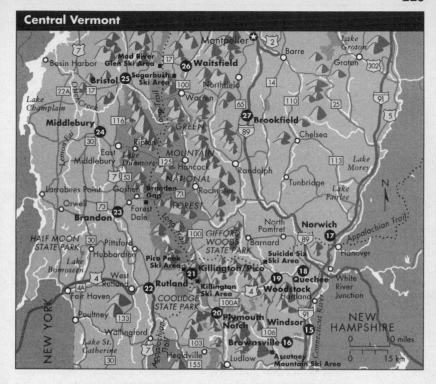

Central Vermont

$$–$$$ ×🏠 **Juniper Hill Inn.** An expanse of green lawn with Adirondack chairs and a garden of perennials sweeps up to the portico of this Greek Revival mansion, built at the turn of the century and now on the National Register of Historic Places. The central living room, with its hardwood floors, oak paneling, Oriental carpets, and thickly upholstered furniture, has a stately feel. The bedrooms are furnished with antiques; 11 have fireplaces. The four-course dinners ($$$) served in the candlelighted dining room may include herb-crusted rack of lamb or sautéed scallops with glazed garlic and champagne sauce. The inn is 7 mi from Mt. Ascutney. ✉ *Box 79, Juniper Hill Rd., 05089,* ☎ *802/ 674–5273 or 800/359–2541,* 🖷 *802/674–2041. 16 rooms. Restaurant, pool, hiking. Full breakfast. D, MC, V.*

Brownsville

🔟 *5 mi west of Windsor.*

Brownsville, a small village at the foot of Ascutney Mountain, has everything a village needs: country store, post office, town hall, and historic grange building. The Ascutney Mountain ski area is a self-contained four-season resort.

Dining and Lodging

$$–$$$$ ×🏠 **Ascutney Mountain Resort Hotel.** One of the big attractions of this five-building resort hotel–condo complex is the lift outside the main door. The comfortable, well-maintained suites come in different configurations and sizes—some with kitchens, fireplaces, and decks. Slopeside multilevel condos have three bedrooms, three baths, and private entrances. The Ascutney Harvest Inn ($$), which serves Continental and traditional cuisine, is within the complex. ✉ *Box 699, Hotel Rd., off Rte. 44, 05037,* ☎ *802/484–7711 or 800/243–0011,* 🖷 *802/484–*

3117. 240 *suites and condos. 3 restaurants, 2 bars, pool, health club, racquetball, ice-skating, billiards. AE, MC, V.*

$–$$ ⬚ **Mill Brook.** This Victorian farmhouse, built in 1880, is directly across from the Ascutney ski slopes. Making après-ski idleness easy are the four sitting rooms, decorated with antiques and contemporary furnishings. The honeymoon suite has a separate dressing room with a claw-foot bathtub; the other suites are perfect for families. ⊠ *Box 410, Rte. 44, 05037,* ☎ *802/484–7283. 2 rooms, 3 suites. Hot tub. Full breakfast. AE, MC, V.*

Nightlife and the Arts

Crow's Nest Club (⊠ Ascutney Mountain Resort Hotel, Rte. 33, ☎ 802/484–7711) has entertainment on weekends. **Destiny** (⊠ U.S. 5, Windsor, ☎ 802/674–6671) hosts rock bands most days and has a DJ on Sunday.

Skiing and Snow Sports

ASCUTNEY MOUNTAIN RESORT

The Plausteiner family, whose patriarch, John, was instrumental in operations at Mt. Snow, in Vermont, and White Face Mountain, in Lake Placid, New York, purchased this resort in the mid-1990s and in 1998 launched a five-year expansion that will include new lifts and trails. The five buildings of the resort village include hotel suites and condominium units spread throughout. ⊠ *Rte. 44, off I–91,* ☎ *802/484–7711; 800/ 243–0011 for lodging; mailing address: Box 699, Brownsville 05037.*

Downhill. Forty-six trails with varying terrain are covered by nearly 90% snowmaking. Like a stereotypical ski mountain cutout, this one reaches a wide peak and gently slopes to the bottom. Beginner and novice skiers stay toward the base, while intermediates enjoy the band that wraps the midsection. For experts, tougher black-diamond runs top the mountain. One disadvantage to Ascutney, however, is that there is no easy way down from the summit, so novice skiers should not make the trip. Trails are serviced by one double and three triple chairs. Ascutney is popular with families because it offers some of the least expensive junior lift tickets in the region.

Cross-country. The resort has 32 km (19 mi) of groomed cross-country trails; lessons, clinics, and rentals are provided.

Other activities. Ascutney Mountain Resort Hotel (☞ Dining and Lodging, *above*) has a sports-and-fitness center with full-size indoor and outdoor pools, racquetball, aerobics facilities and classes, weight training, and massage, as well as ice-skating on the pond.

Child care. Day care is available for children from ages 6 months to 10 years, with learn-to-ski options and rental equipment for toddlers and up. There are half- and full-day instruction programs for children from ages 3 to 12; a Mini-Olympians program for ages 4 to 7; and a Young Olympians program for children from ages 8 to 12. Evening baby-sitting is available.

Norwich

⑰ *6 mi north of White River Junction, 22 mi north of Brownsville.*

Norwich is home to an excellent science museum. The town is across the river from Hanover, New Hampshire, and Dartmouth College. **King Arthur Flour Baker's Store** (⊠ U.S. 5, ☎ 802/649–3361), a retail outlet for all things baking oriented, sells tools and hard-to-find grains and specialty flours. The company, which has been in business since 1790, displays historic photographs of flour being delivered by horse cart.

★ ⓒ Numerous hands-on exhibits at the **Montshire Museum of Science** explore space, nature, and technology; there are also living habitats, aquariums, and many children's programs. A maze of trails winds through 100 acres of pristine woodland. An ideal destination for a rainy day, this is one of the finest museums in New England. ⊠ *Montshire Rd., Box 770,* ☎ *802/649–2200.* ⌨ *$5.* ⊙ *Daily 10–5.*

Quechee

⑱ *6 mi west of White River Junction, 11 mi south of Norwich.*

Quechee is perched astride the Ottauquechee River. Quechee Gorge, 165 ft deep, is impressive, though overrun by tourists. You can see the mile-long gorge, carved by a glacier, from U.S. 4, but many people picnic nearby or scramble down one of several descents for a closer look. More than a decade ago Simon Pearce set up **Simon Pearce,** an eponymous glassblowing factory in an old mill by a waterfall here, using the water power to drive his furnace. The glass studio produces exquisite wares and houses a pottery workshop, a shop, and a restaurant (☞ Dining and Lodging, *below*); you can watch the artisans at work. ⊠ *The Mill, Main St.,* ☎ *802/295–2711 or 800/774–5277.* ⊙ *Store daily 9–9; workshop weekdays 9–9, weekends 9–5.*

Dining and Lodging

$$$ ✕ **Simon Pearce.** Candlelight, sparkling glassware from the studio downstairs, contemporary dinnerware, exposed brick, and large windows that overlook the roaring Ottauquechee River create an ideal setting for contemporary American cuisine. Sesame-crusted tuna with noodle cakes and wasabi and roast duck with mango chutney sauce are specialties of the house; the wine cellar holds several hundred vintages. ⊠ *Main St.,* ☎ *802/295–1470. AE, D, DC, MC, V.*

$$–$$$ ✕⊡ **Parker House.** The peach-and-blue rooms of this 1857 Victorian mansion are named for former residents: Emily has a marble fireplace, Walter is the smallest room, and Joseph has a view of the Ottauquechee River. All rooms on the third floor are air-conditioned. The elegant dining room ($$$) prepares sophisticated American comfort cuisine such as loin of venison with a port and balsamic vinegar sauce, and Maine crab cakes with a hint of wasabi. In warm weather, you can dine on the terrace, which has a spectacular river view. Guests have access to the Quechee Country Club's first-rate golf course, tennis courts, indoor and outdoor pool, and cross-country and downhill skiing. ⊠ *Box 0780, 16 Main St., 05059,* ☎ *802/295–6077,* ⅁⅄ *802/296–6696. 7 rooms. Full breakfast; MAP available. AE, MC, V.*

$$–$$$ ⊡ **Quechee Bed and Breakfast.** Dried herbs hang from the beams in
★ the living room of this B&B, where a wood settee sits before a floor-to-ceiling fireplace that was part of the original 1795 structure. Ask for one of the rooms in the back—they're away from busy U.S. 4 and overlook the Ottauquechee River. A small, 200-year-old post-and-beam cottage that sleeps two to four perches on a cliff over the river. The inn is within walking distance of Quechee Gorge. ⊠ *Box 80, U.S. 4 at Waterman Hill, 05059,* ☎ *802/295–1776 or 800/628–8610. 8 rooms. Full breakfast. MC, V.*

Outdoor Activities and Sports

The **Vermont Fly Fishing School/Wilderness Trails** (⊠ Quechee Inn, Clubhouse Rd., ☎ 802/295–7620 or 800/235–3133) leads workshops, rents fishing gear and mountain bikes, and arranges canoe and kayak trips. In winter, the company conducts cross-country and snowshoe treks.

POLO

Quechee Polo Club (✉ Dewey's Mill Rd., ½ mi north of U.S. 4, ☎ 802/295–7152) draws hundreds of spectators on summer Saturdays to its matches near the Quechee Gorge. Admission is $3 per person or $6 per carload.

Shopping

The 40 dealers at the **Hartland Antiques Center** (✉ U.S. 4, ☎ 802/457–4745) stock furniture, paper items, china, glass, and collectibles. More than 350 dealers sell their wares at the **Quechee Gorge Village** (✉ U.S. 4, ☎ 802/295–1550 or 800/438–5565), an antiques and crafts mall in an immense reconstructed barn that also holds a country store and the Farina Family Diner. A merry-go-round and a small-scale working railroad operate when weather permits. **Scotland by the Yard** (U.S. 4, ☎ 802/295–5351 or 800/295–5351) is the place to shop for all things Scottish, from kilts to Harris tweed jackets and tartan ties.

Woodstock

★ ⑲ *4 mi east of Quechee.*

Perfectly preserved Federal houses surround Woodstock's tree-lined village green, and streams flow around the town center, which is anchored by a covered bridge. The town owes much of its pristine appearance to the Rockefeller family's interest in historic preservation and land conservation.

The town's history of conservationism dates from the 19th century: Woodstock native George Perkins Marsh, a congressman and diplomat, wrote the pioneering book *Man and Nature* in 1864, and was closely involved in the creation of the Smithsonian Institution in Washington, D.C. The **Billings Farm and Museum,** on the grounds of Marsh's boyhood home, was founded by Frederick Billings in 1870 as a model of conservation. Billings, a lawyer and businessman, put into practice Marsh's ideas about the long-term effects of farming and grazing. Exhibits in the reconstructed Queen Anne farmhouse, school, general store, workshop, and former Marsh homestead demonstrate the lives and skills of early Vermont settlers. Splitting logs doesn't seem nearly so quaint when you've watched the effort that goes into it. ✉ *Rte. 12, ½ mi north of Woodstock,* ☎ *802/457–2355.* ⚅ *$7.* ☉ *May–late Oct., daily 10–5; Nov.–Dec., weekends 10–4.*

The 500-acre **Marsh-Billings-Rockefeller National Park,** which opened in 1998, is Vermont's only national park and the nation's first to focus on conservation and stewardship of natural resources. The park encompasses the forest lands planned by Frederick Billings according to the principles of George Perkins Marsh, as well as Billings's mansion, gardens, and carriage roads. The entire property was the gift of Laurance S. Rockefeller, who lived here with his late wife Mary, Frederick Billings's granddaughter. It is adjacent to the Billings Farm and Museum. ✉ *Rte. 12,* ☎ *802/457–3368.* ⚅ *Free.* ☉ *Memorial Day–Oct., daily for guided tours only; call for schedules.*

Period furnishings of the Woodstock Historical Society fill the white clapboard **Dana House,** built circa 1807. Exhibits include the town charter, furniture, maps, and locally minted silver. The converted barn houses the Woodstock Works exhibit, an economic portrait of the town. ✉ *26 Elm St.,* ☎ *802/457–1822.* ⚅ *$1.* ☉ *May–late Oct., Mon.–Sat. 10–5, Sun. noon–4; tours by appointment in winter.*

The Raptor Center of the **Vermont Institute of Natural Science** (VINS) houses 23 species of birds of prey, among them bald eagles, peregrine falcons, and 3-ounce saw-whet owls. There are also ravens, turkey vultures, and snowy owls. All the caged birds have been found injured and unable to survive in the wild. This nonprofit, environmental research and education center is on a 77-acre nature preserve with walking trails. ⊠ *Church Hill Rd.,* ☎ *802/457–2779.* ⬚ *$6.* ⊙ *May–Oct., daily 10–4; Nov.–Apr., Mon.–Sat. 10–4.*

Dining and Lodging

$$$–$$$$ ✕ **Prince and the Pauper.** Modern French and American fare with a
★ Vermont accent is the focus of this romantic restaurant in a candle-lighted Colonial setting. The grilled duck breast might have an Asian five-spice sauce; homemade lamb and pork sausage in puff pastry comes with a honey-mustard sauce. A less-expensive bistro menu is available in the lounge. ⊠ *24 Elm St.,* ☎ *802/457–1818. AE, D, MC, V. No lunch.*

$–$$$ ✕ **Bentley's.** Antique silk-fringed lamp shades, long lace curtains, and a life-size carving of a kneeling, winged knight lend a whimsical Victorian air to the proceedings here. Burgers, chili, and homemade soups are served; the entrées include roasted Maple Leaf Farm duckling with a sweet mango sauce or maple-mustard chicken coated with chopped pecans. A Sunday jazz brunch is presented from Thanksgiving through April, and there's dancing Saturday nights. ⊠ *3 Elm St.,* ☎ *802/457–3232. AE, DC, MC, V.*

$–$$ ✕ **Pane & Salute.** Authentic regional Italian breads are the specialty, but this bakery has a whole lot more to offer. You can try homemade pizzas and soups, sandwich specials, and, in season, pasta entrées such as penne with spinach, pine nuts, raisins, and Parmesan. Add a glass of Chianti and *mangia bene*. The bakery serves breakfast and lunch daily in summer, and dinner Friday and Saturday; call for winter hours. ⊠ *61 Central St.,* ☎ *802/457–4882. Reservations not accepted. MC, V. No dinner Mon.–Thurs. and Sun.*

$$$$ ✕⬚ **Kedron Valley Inn.** Many rooms have a fireplace or a Franklin stove, two have decks, another has a veranda, and a fourth has a terrace overlooking the stream that runs through the inn's 15 acres. Exposed-log walls make the motel units in back more rustic than the rooms in the main inn, but they're decorated similarly, with country antiques and reproductions. The chef creates French masterpieces like fillet of Norwegian salmon stuffed with herb seafood mousse in puff pastry, and shrimp, scallops, and lobster with wild mushrooms sautéed in shallots and white wine and served with a Fra Angelico cream sauce. A terrace with views of the grounds is open in summer. ⊠ *Rte. 106, 05071,* ☎ *802/457–1473 or 800/836–1193,* FAX *802/457–4469. 26 rooms. Restaurant, bar, pond, beach. MAP. AE, D, MC, V. Closed Apr. and 10 days before Thanksgiving.*

$$$–$$$$ ✕⬚ **Jackson House Inn.** When the Florins purchased this 1890 Victorian inn in 1996, they kept the European antiques, Oriental rugs, and French-cut crystal, as well as the formal parlor and cozy library. They added two wings: one for suites with gas fireplaces, Anichini linens, down duvets, and thermal massage tubs; the other, overlooking the inn's manicured grounds, to house the cathedral-ceiling restaurant, whose focal point is a granite, open-hearth fireplace. They also brought in executive chef Brendan Nolan, previously of Aujourd'hui at Boston's Four Seasons Hotel, to oversee a menu featuring new American cuisine. The result is an elegant, full-service inn with a first-class dining room. ⊠ *37 Old Rte. 4 W, 05091,* ☎ *802/457–2065 or 800/448–1890,* FAX *802/457–9290. 11 rooms, 6 suites. Restaurant, spa. Full breakfast. AE, MC, V.*

$$$–$$$$ ✕⬚ **Woodstock Inn and Resort.** Resort entrepreneur Laurance Rockefeller, long a Woodstock resident, made this a flagship property of his Rockresorts chain. Country formality might sound like an oxymoron,

but it best describes the relaxed yet polished atmosphere here. The lobbies and lounges hold a grand piano, decorative quilts, a monumental fieldstone fireplace, and bowls of shiny Vermont apples. Guest rooms are spacious, serene, and set well back from Woodstock's often noisy main drag. The dinner fare is nouvelle New England; the menu might list entrées like salmon steak with avocado beurre blanc, beef Wellington, and prime rib. The resort owns Suicide Six (☞ Skiing and Snow Sports, *below*). ⊠ *On the Green, U.S. 4, 05091,* ☎ *802/457–1100 or 800/448–7900,* FAX *802/457–6699. 144 rooms. 2 restaurants, bar, 1 indoor and 1 outdoor pool, saunas, 2 18-hole golf courses, 12 tennis courts, croquet, health club, racquetball, squash, cross-country and downhill skiing, meeting rooms. AE, MC, V.*

$$$$ 🏨 **Twin Farms.** At the center of this exclusive 300-acre resort stands
★   the 1795 farmhouse where writers Sinclair Lewis and Dorothy Thompson lived. Not that Lewis and Thompson would recognize the place: It's been transformed into Vermont's most sumptuous—and most expensive—resort. Twin Farms' rooms and cottages are fantasy environments, drawing their inspiration from Moorish, Scandinavian, Japanese, and Adirondack design. There are fireplaces throughout, along with museum-quality artworks. Chef Neil Wigglesworth prepares rich contemporary cuisine that emphasizes local ingredients. You can help yourself at the open bar. ⊠ *Stage Rd., off Rte. 12, 8 mi north of Woodstock,* ☎ *802/234–9999 or 800/894–6327,* FAX *802/234–9990. Mailing address: Box 115, Barnard 05031. 6 rooms, 8 cottages. 2 bars, dining room, Japanese baths, exercise room, boating, bicycles, ice-skating, cross-country and downhill skiing, recreation room, meeting rooms. AP. AE, MC, V.*

$$–$$$ 🏨 **The Woodstocker.** A short stroll from the covered bridge and the village green, this 1830s B&B offers the welcome and comfort that you would expect from a friend's living room. Big leather couches and an indoor hot tub add to the casual atmosphere. The large, light-filled rooms are furnished with a hodgepodge of antiques and reproductions. The suites have kitchens. ⊠ *61 River St./U.S 4, 05091,* ☎ *802/457–3896,* FAX *802/457–3897. 7 rooms, 2 suites. Full breakfast. MC, V.*

$–$$$ 🏨 **Shire Motel.** Some rooms in this immaculate, in-town motel have decks overlooking the Ottauquechee River and the Billings Farm. All have four-poster beds, wing chairs, color TVs, and telephones. Complimentary coffee is served each morning. ⊠ *46 Pleasant St., 05091,* ☎ *802/457–2211,* FAX *802/457–5836. 33 rooms. Refrigerators. AE, D, MC, V.*

$$ 🏨 **Winslow House.** This farmhouse built in 1872 once overlooked a
★   dairy farm that reached down to the Ottauquechee River. An unpretentious place, Winslow House has only four guest rooms and a small common area, but the two upstairs quarters are uncommonly spacious and have separate sitting rooms: Mahogany furnishings dominate Room 3, and the English oak bed, armoire, and Mission desk in Room 4 are a cut above what most small bed-and-breakfasts offer. Rooms have phones and TVs. ⊠ *38 U.S. 4, 05091,* ☎ *802/457–1820,* FAX *802/457–1820. 4 rooms. Refrigerators. Full breakfast. D, DC, MC, V.*

Outdoor Activities and Sports

BIKING

Cyclery Plus (⊠ 36 U.S. 4 W, West Woodstock, ☎ 802/457–3377), which rents, sells, and services equipment, has a free touring map of local rides.

GOLF

Robert Trent Jones, Sr., designed the 18-hole, par-69 course at **Woodstock Country Club** (⊠ South St., ☎ 802/457–6674), which is run by the Woodstock Inn. Greens fees are $32–$75; cart rentals are $36.

HORSEBACK RIDING

Kedron Valley Stables (✉ Rte. 106, South Woodstock, ☎ 802/457–2734 or 800/225–6301) gives lessons and conducts guided trail rides and excursions in a sleigh and a wagon.

RECREATION AREA

Suicide Six (☎ 802/457–6656 for fitness center; ☞ Skiing and Snow Sports, *below*) has outdoor tennis courts, lighted paddle courts, croquet, and an 18-hole golf course that are open in the summer.

STATE PARK

Coolidge State Park (✉ Rte. 100A, 2 mi north of Rte. 100, ☎ 802/672–3612) abuts Coolidge State Forest and has campsites (log lean-tos from the 1930s).

Shopping

The **Marketplace at Bridgewater Mills** (✉ U.S. 4, west of Woodstock, ☎ 802/672–3332) houses shops and attractions in a three-story converted woolen mill. There's an antiques and crafts center, a bookstore, Miranda Thomas pottery, and Charles Shackleton furniture. Sample Vermont stocks gourmet foods and gifts from all over the state. **North Wind Artisans' Gallery** (✉ 81 Central St., ☎ 802/457–4587) carries contemporary—mostly Vermont-made—crafts with sleek, jazzy designs. The **Village Butcher** (✉ Elm St., ☎ 802/457–2756) is an emporium of Vermont comestibles. **Who Is Sylvia?** (✉ 26 Central St., ☎ 802/457–1110), in the old firehouse, sells vintage clothing and antique linens, lace, and jewelry.

Skiing and Snow Sports

SUICIDE SIX

The site of the first ski tow in the United States (1934), this resort is owned and operated by the Woodstock Inn and Resort (☞ Dining and Lodging, *above*). The inn's package plans are remarkably inexpensive, considering the high quality of the accommodations. ✉ *Pomfret Rd., 05091,* ☎ *802/457–6661; 800/448–7900 for lodging; 802/457–6666 for snow conditions.*

Downhill. Despite Suicide Six's short vertical of only 650 ft, the skiing is challenging: There are steep runs down the mountain's face, intermediate trails that wind around the hill, and glade skiing. Beginner terrain is mostly toward the bottom. Two double chairlifts and one surface lift service the 22 trails and slopes.

Cross-country. The **Woodstock Ski Touring Center** (☎ 802/457–2114), headquartered at the Woodstock Country Club (✉ Rte. 106), has 60 km (37 mi) of trails. Equipment and lessons are available.

Other Activities. The resort has a snowboard area with a halfpipe. The **Woodstock Health and Fitness Center** (☎ 802/457–6656) has an indoor lap pool; indoor tennis, squash, and racquetball courts; whirlpool, steam, sauna, and massage rooms; and exercise and aerobics rooms.

Child care. The ski area has no nursery, but baby-sitting can be arranged through the Woodstock Inn if you're a guest. Lessons for children are given by the ski-school staff, and there's a children's ski-and-play park for those from ages 3 to 7.

Plymouth Notch

㉚ *14 mi southwest of Woodstock.*

U.S. president Calvin Coolidge was born and buried in Plymouth Notch, a town that shares his character: low-key and quiet. The perfectly preserved 19th-century buildings of the **Plymouth Notch Historic**

District look more like a large farm than a town; in addition to the homestead there's the general store once run by Coolidge's father, a visitor center, a cheese factory, and a one-room schoolhouse. Coolidge's grave is in the cemetery across Route 100A. The Aldrich House, which mounts changing historical exhibits, is open on some weekdays during the off-season. ⊠ *Rte. 100A, 6 mi south of U.S. 4, east of Rte. 100,* ☎ *802/672–3773.* ⌨ *$5.* ☉ *Late May–mid-Oct., daily 9:30–5.*

Killington/Pico

㉑ *11 mi (Pico) and 15 mi (Killington) east of Rutland.*

The intersection of U.S. 4 and Route 100 is the heart of central Vermont's ski country, with the Killington, Pico, and Okemo (☞ Ludlow *in* Southern Vermont, *above*) resorts nearby. Strip development characterizes the Killington access road, but the views from the top of the mountain are worth the drive.

Dining and Lodging

$$$$ ✕ **Hemingway's.** With a national reputation reinforced by major ★ awards and a loyal clientele, Hemingway's is as good as dining gets in central Vermont. You can tuck into the celebrated cream of garlic soup and a seasonal kaleidoscope of dishes based on native game, fresh seafood, and prime meats. Recent offerings on the prix-fixe menu have included autumn vegetable strudel with hazelnuts, Arctic char with flageolet beans, and Vermont venison with pumpkin sage pudding and parsnip crisps. Desserts are spectacular, as is the five-course wine tasting menu ($75), which matches each dish with an appropriate glass of wine. Request seating in either the formal, vaulted dining room or the intimate wine cellar. ⊠ *U.S. 4, Killington,* ☎ *802/422–3886. AE, MC, V. Closed most Mon. and Tues., and early Nov. and mid-Apr.–mid-May. No lunch.*

$$$–$$$$ ✕▦ **Inn at Long Trail.** This 1938 lodge is ¼ mi from the Pico ski slopes and even closer to the Appalachian and Long trails. The unusual decor—including massive indoor boulders—has nature as a prevailing theme. Irish music, darts, and Guinness always on tap are all part of the Irish hospitality, which is extended particularly to end-to-end hikers (who get a substantial break in the rates). Meals in the restaurant, open from Thursday to Sunday during peak season, might include roast duckling or mushroom and risotto strudel. The pub has live music Thursday and Saturday nights in winter and during foliage season. ⊠ *Box 267, U.S. 4, Killington 05751,* ☎ *802/775–7181 or 800/325–2540,* ℻ *802/747–7034. 22 rooms, 5 suites. Restaurant, pub. Full breakfast; MAP on winter and foliage weekends. AE, MC, V. Inn and restaurant closed mid-Apr.–mid-June; call for exact dates.*

$$$ ▦ **Cortina Inn.** This large lodge and mini-resort is comfortable and its location prime. About two-thirds of the rooms have private balconies, though the views from them aren't spectacular. Horseback riding, sleigh rides, ice-skating, and guided snowmobile, fly-fishing, and mountain biking tours are among the off-the-slopes activities. A breakfast buffet is served daily. ⊠ *U.S. 4, Mendon 05751,* ☎ *802/773–3333 or 800/451–6108,* ℻ *802/775–6948. 97 rooms. Restaurant, bar, indoor pool, hot tub, sauna, 8 tennis courts, health club. Full breakfast. AE, D, DC, MC, V.*

$$–$$$ ▦ **Summit Lodge.** Three miles from Killington Peak, this rustic two-story country lodge caters to a varied crowd of ski enthusiasts, who are warmly met by the lodge's mascots—a pair of Saint Bernards. Country decor and antiques blend with modern conveniences to create a relaxed atmosphere. Dining is formal at one of the restaurants and informal at the other. ⊠ *Killington Rd., Killington 05751,* ☎ *802/422–3535 or 800/635–6343,* ℻ *802/422–3536. 45 rooms, 2 suites. 2*

restaurants, bar, pool, pond, hot tub, massage, sauna, ice-skating, nightclub, recreation room. Full breakfast. AE, DC, MC, V.

Nightlife and the Arts

The pub at the **Inn at Long Trail** (☞ Dining and Lodging, *above*) hosts Irish music on weekends. The **Pickle Barrel** (⌧ Killington Rd., ☎ 802/422–3035), a favorite with the après-ski crowd, presents up-and-coming acts and can get pretty rowdy. The **Wobbly Barn** (⌧ Killington Rd., ☎ 802/422–3392), with dancing to blues and rock, is open during ski season.

Outdoor Activities and Sports

Cortina Inn (☞ Dining and Lodging, *above*) has an ice-skating rink with rentals and offers sleigh rides; you can also skate on Summit Pond. **Gifford Woods State Park**'s Kent Pond (⌧ Rte. 100, ½ mi north of U.S. 4, ☎ 802/775–5354) is a terrific fishing hole. Campsites are available.

Skiing and Snow Sports

KILLINGTON

"Megamountain," "Beast of the East," and plain "huge" are apt descriptions of Killington. The American Skiing Company operates Killington and its neighbor Pico—and over the past three years has spent $60 million to improve lifts, snowmaking capabilities, and lodging options. A project is under way to join Pico and Killington by interconnecting trails and lifts. The mountain has also developed numerous snowboarding parks. Lines on weekends (especially holiday weekends) can be downright dreadful—the resort has the longest ski season in the East and some of the best package plans. The area has been top rated for après-ski activities by several national ski magazines. With a single telephone call, skiers can select the price, date, and type of ski week they want; choose accommodations; book air or railroad transportation; and arrange for rental equipment and ski lessons. Ticket holders can also ski at Pico. ⌧ *400 Killington Rd., 05751,* ☎ *802/422–3333; 800/621–6867 for lodging; 802/422–3261 for snow conditions.*

Downhill. It would probably take several weeks to test all 205 trails on the six mountains of the Killington complex, even though everything interconnects. About 72% of the 1,200 acres of skiing terrain can be covered with machine-made snow. Transporting skiers to the peaks of this complex are three gondolas plus 12 quads (including six high-speed express quads), six triples, and five double chairlifts, as well as eight surface lifts (including a Magic Carpet). Several of the lifts reach the area's highest elevation, at 4,241 ft off Killington Peak, and a vertical drop of 3,150 ft to the base of the gondola. You can ride the Skyeship, the world's fastest and first heated eight-passenger lift, complete with piped-in music. The Skyeship base station has a rotisserie, food court, and a coffee bar. The skiing includes everything from Outer Limits, one of the steepest and most challenging trails anywhere in the country, to the 16-km-long (10-mi-long), super-gentle Juggernaut Trail. In the Fusion Zones, underbrush and low branches have been cleared away to provide tree skiing.

Child care. Nursery care is available for children from 6 weeks to 6 years old. There's a one-hour instruction program for youngsters from ages 3 to 8; those from 6 to 12 can join an all-day program.

PICO SKI RESORT

Although it's only 5 mi down the road from Killington, Pico has long been a favorite among people looking for uncrowded, wide-open cruiser skiing. When modern lifts were installed and a village square was constructed at the base, some feared a change in atmosphere might occur, but the condo-hotel, restaurants, and shops have not altered the essential nature of the area. Watch for big changes as the American Skiing Company brings Pico up to par with its other major resorts, Sugarbush and Killington. ⊠ *2 Sherburne Pass, Rutland 05701,* ☎ *802/422–3333; 800/621–6867 for lodging; 802/422–3261 for snow conditions.*

Downhill. Many of the 42 trails are advanced to expert, with two intermediate bail-out trails for the timid. The rest of the mountain's 2,000 ft of vertical terrain is mostly intermediate or easier. The mountain has nine lifts including two high-speed quads, two triples, and three double chairs, and has 85% snowmaking coverage. Snowboarders are welcome and have their own area, Triple Slope. For instruction of any kind, head to the Alpine Learning Center.

Other activities. A **sports center** (☎ 802/773–1786) at the base of the mountain has fitness facilities, a 75-ft pool, whirlpool tub, saunas, and a massage room.

Child care. Pico's nursery takes children from ages 6 months to 6 years and provides indoor activities and outdoor play. The ski school has full- and half-day instruction programs for children from ages 3 to 12.

CROSS-COUNTRY SKIING

Mountain Meadows (⊠ Thundering Brook Rd., Killington, ☎ 802/775–7077) has 57 km (34½ mi) of groomed trails and 10 km (6 mi) of marked outlying trails. You can also access 500 acres of backcountry skiing. **Mountain Top Inn and Resort** (☞ Rutland, *below*; ☎ 802/483–6089 or 800–445-2100) is mammoth, with 120 km (72 mi) of trails, 80 km (49 mi) of which are groomed.

Rutland

㉒ *15 mi west of Killington, 32 mi south of Middlebury, 31 mi west of Woodstock, 47 mi west of White River Junction.*

On and around U.S. 7 in Rutland are strips of shopping centers and a seemingly endless row of traffic lights, although the mansions of the marble magnates who made the town famous still command whatever attention can be safely diverted from the traffic. Rutland's compact downtown, one of only a handful of urban centers in Vermont, has experienced a modest revival and is worth an hour's stroll. The area's traditional economic ties to railroading and marble, the latter an industry that became part of such illustrious structures as the central research building of the New York Public Library in New York City, have been rapidly eclipsed by the growth of the Pico and Killington ski areas to the east.

The **Chaffee Center for the Visual Arts** (⊠ 16 S. Main St., ☎ 802/775–0356) exhibits and sells the output of more than 200 Vermont artists who work in various media. It's closed Tuesday.

OFF THE
BEATEN PATH

VERMONT MARBLE EXHIBIT – The highlight of the Rutland area is this exhibit and store 4 mi north of town. A sculptor-in-residence transforms stone into finished works of art or commerce (you can choose first-hand the marble for a custom-built kitchen counter). The gallery illustrates the many industrial and artistic applications of marble—there's a hall of presidents and a replica of Leonardo da Vinci's *Last Supper* in marble—and depicts the industry's history via exhibits and a video. Factory seconds and foreign and domestic marble items are for sale. ⊠ *62 Main St., Proctor (follow signs off Rte. 3),* ☎ *802/459–2300 or 800/427–1396.* ☞ *$5.* ⊙ *Memorial Day–Oct., daily 9–5:30.*

Dining and Lodging

$$–$$$ ✕ **Royal's 121 Hearthside.** Long a local favorite for a big night out, the institution built by the late Ernie Royal still turns out the best prime rib in town, accompanied by tasty hot popovers. Also look for rack of lamb with strawberry-mint sauce and pan-roasted salmon with dill hollandaise. ⊠ *37 N. Main St.,* ☎ *802/775–0856. AE, MC, V.*

$$ ✕ **The Palms.** This restaurant has been in the Sabataso family since it opened its doors on Palm Sunday, 1933; it was the first in the state to serve pizza. The menu is primarily southern Italian, with specialties such as fried mozzarella; antipasto Neapolitan (with provolone, pepperoni, mild peppers, anchovies, and house dressing); and the chef's personal creation, veal à la Palms—veal scallops topped with mushrooms, two kinds of cheese, and a special tomato sauce. The dessert choices are fairly pedestrian. ⊠ *36 Strongs St.,* ☎ *802/773–2367. AE, DC, MC, V. Closed Sun. in summer. No lunch.*

$-$$ ✕ **Back Home Café.** Wood booths, black-and-white linoleum tile, and exposed brick lend this second-story café the feel of a New York City hole-in-the-wall. Dinner might be chicken breast stuffed with roasted red peppers and goat cheese or tortellini Alfredo primavera. Soup-and-entrée lunch specials can cost less than $5. The large bar in the back of the restaurant is occasionally the site of weekend entertainment. ⊠ *21 Center St.,* ☎ *802/775–9313. AE, MC, V.*

$$$$ ✕⊞ **Mountain Top Inn and Resort.** Just minutes from Rutland, one of the state's three or four most spectacular family resorts occupies 500 lofty acres overlooking secluded Chittenden Reservoir and the Green Mountain National Forest. The Mountain Top is essentially an outdoorperson's inn, with an equestrian center, swimming and canoeing, fishing, trap and skeet shooting, and a golf school with a 5-hole pitch-and-putt course and driving range. Winter brings cross-country skiing on more than 70 mi of trails, sleigh rides, and skating. The dinner menu ($$$) runs to satisfying, uncomplicated American fare such as rack of lamb and roast pork tenderloin and unadventurous French fare such as sole meunière. A tip: Opt for the somewhat more expensive deluxe rooms, which are larger and have spectacular views. ⊠ *195 Mountaintop Rd., Chittenden 05737,* ☎ *802/483–2311 or 800/445–2100,* FAX *802/ 483–6373. 35 rooms, 6 cottages, 12 chalets. Restaurant, pool, driving range, horseback riding, beach, boating, fishing, cross-country skiing. MAP available. AE, MC, V. Closed Nov. and Apr.*

$$–$$$ ⊞ **Inn at Rutland.** One alternative to Rutland's chain motel and hotel accommodations is this renovated Victorian mansion. The ornate oak staircase lined with heavy embossed gold and leather wainscoting leads to rooms that blend modern bathrooms with late-19th-century touches such as elaborate ceiling moldings and frosted glass. The two large common rooms, one with a fireplace, have views of surrounding mountains and valleys. ⊠ *70 N. Main St., 05701,* ☎ *802/773–0575 or 800/808–0575,* FAX *802/775–3506. 12 rooms. Mountain bikes. Full breakfast fall and winter; Continental breakfast spring and summer. AE, D, DC, MC, V.*

$$ ⊞ **Comfort Inn.** Rooms at this chain hotel are a cut above the standard, with upholstered wing chairs and blond-wood furnishings. This place is popular with bus tours in foliage season. ⊠ *19 Allen St., 05701,* ☎ *802/775–2200 or 800/432–6788,* FAX *802/775–2694. 104 rooms. Restaurant, indoor pool, hot tub, sauna. Continental breakfast. AE, D, DC, MC, V.*

Nightlife and the Arts

Crossroads Arts Council (⊠ 39 E. Center St., ☎ 802/775–5413) presents music, opera, dance, jazz, and theater.

Outdoor Activities and Sports

Half Moon State Park's principal attraction is Half Moon Pond (⊠ Town Rd., 3½ mi off Rte. 30, west of Hubbardton, ☎ 802/273–2848). The park has nature trails, campsites, and boat and canoe rentals.

Shopping

An anthropologist opened **East Meets West** (⊠ U.S. 7 at Sangamon Rd., Pittsford, ☎ 802/443–2242 or 800/443–2242), which carries carvings, masks, statues, textiles, pottery, baskets, and other crafts of native peoples from around the world. **Tuttle Antiquarian Books** (⊠ 28 S. Main St., ☎ 802/773–8229) has a large collection of books on Asia. The store stocks rare and out-of-print books, genealogies, local histories, and miniature books.

Brandon

㉓ *15 mi north of Rutland.*

Straddling busy U.S. 7, Brandon nevertheless has broad side streets lined with gracious Victorian houses, lodging at the landmark Brandon Inn or at smaller B&Bs, and ready access to the mountain scenery and recreation of nearby Brandon Gap.

The **Stephen A. Douglas Birthplace** commemorates the "Little Giant" (he stood only 5 ft, 2 in tall), best known for his debates with Abraham Lincoln in 1858. Douglas, who became a U.S. representative and senator from Illinois, was born here on April 23, 1813. His boyhood home and a monument to his memory are just north of the village, next to the Baptist church. ⊠ *U.S. 7.* ☑ *Free.* ☉ *June–Labor Day, Thurs. 2–5, or by appointment (call the Nelsons at 802/247–6569 or the Martins at 802/247–6332).*

Maple syrup is Vermont's signature product, and the **New England Maple Museum and Gift Shop** explains the history and process of turning maple sap into syrup with murals, exhibits, and a slide show. ⊠ *U.S. 7, Pittsford (9 mi south of Brandon),* ☎ *802/483–9414.* ☑ *$1.25.* ☉ *May–Oct., daily 8:30–5:30; Nov.–Dec. and Mar.–Apr., daily 10–4.*

Dining and Lodging

$$ ✕☷ **Blueberry Hill Inn.** If you're looking for total peace and quiet, this is the place. In the Green Mountain National Forest and 5½ mi off a mountain pass on a dirt road, Blueberry Hill is an idyllic spot with lush gardens, a stream, an apple orchard, and a pond with a wood-fired sauna on its bank. Many rooms have views of the surrounding mountains; all are furnished with antiques, quilts, and hot-water bottles to warm winter beds. Three rooms have lofts (good for families), and the Moosalamoo Room is in a private cottage. The restaurant menu has listed dishes such as garlic fish soup with mussels and venison fillet with cherry sauce. Tony Clark, innkeeper for more than 20 years, often joins guests for cocktails (bring your own liquor). Blueberry Hill's ski-touring center focuses on mountain biking in the summer. Hikers can take advantage of the 50 mi of marked trails. ⊠ *Rte. 32, Goshen 05733,* ☎ *802/247–6735 or 800/448–0707,* ☒ *802/247–3983. 12 rooms. Restaurant, sauna, hiking, volleyball, mountain biking, cross-country skiing. MAP; B&B plan available. MC, V.*

$$–$$$$ ☷ **Lilac Inn.** The bridal suite at this Greek Revival mansion, which bills itself as a romantic retreat, is one of the most elegant inn rooms in Vermont, with a pewter canopy bed, whirlpool bath for two, and fireplace. The other rooms, all uniquely furnished and with claw-foot tubs and hand-held European shower heads, are also charming. A full breakfast is served on the patio or in the bright, gleaming dining room, both of which overlook the lovely gardens with 15 varieties of lilacs. Own-

ers Michael and Melanie Shane host musical and cultural events in the ballroom. The inn is home to three cats. ⊠ *53 Park St./Rte. 73, 05733,* ☎ *802/247–5463 or 800/221–0720, FAX 802/247–5499. 9 rooms. Full breakfast. Restaurant. AE, D, MC, V. Restaurant closed Nov.–Apr.*

Outdoor Activities and Sports

Moosalamoo (☎ 800/448–0707) is the name given by a partnership of public and private entities to a 20,000-acre chunk of Green Mountain National Forest land (along with several private inholdings) just northeast of Brandon. More than 60 mi of trails take hikers, mountain bikers, and cross-country skiers through some of Vermont's most gorgeous mountain terrain. Attractions include Branbury State Park, on the shores of Lake Dunmore; secluded Silver Lake, a trout-fishing mecca; and sections of both the Long Trail and Catamount Trail (the latter is a Massachusetts-to-Québec ski trail). Both the Blueberry Hill Inn (☞ Dining and Lodging, *above*) and Churchill House Inn (☎ 802/247–3078) offer direct public access to trails.

GOLF

Neshobe Golf Club (⊠ Rte. 73, east of Brandon, ☎ 802/247–3611) has 18 holes of par-72 golf on a bent-grass course totaling nearly 6,500 yards. The Green Mountain views are terrific. Several local inns offer golf packages.

HIKING

About 8 mi east of Brandon on Route 73, a trail that takes an hour to hike starts at Brandon Gap and climbs steeply up **Mt. Horrid.** South of Lake Dunmore on Route 53, a large turnout marks a trail (a hike of about two hours) to the **Falls of Lana.** Four other trails—two short ones of less than a mile each and two longer ones—lead to the old abandoned Revolutionary War fortifications at **Mt. Independence**; to reach them, take the first left turn off Route 73 west of Orwell and go right at the fork. The road will turn to gravel and once again will fork; take a sharp left-hand turn toward a small marina. The parking lot is on the left at the top of the hill.

Shopping

The **Warren Kimble Gallery & Studio** (⊠ Off Rte. 73 E, ☎ 802/247–3026) is the workplace, gallery, and gift shop of the nationally renowned folk artist.

Middlebury

★ ㉔ *17 mi north of Brandon, 34 mi south of Burlington.*

In the late 1800s Middlebury was the largest Vermont community west of the Green Mountains: an industrial center of river-powered wool, grain, and marble mills. This is Robert Frost country; Vermont's late poet laureate spent 23 summers at a farm east of Middlebury. Otter Creek, the state's longest river, traverses the town center. Still a cultural and economic hub amid the Champlain Valley's serene pastoral patchwork, the town and countryside invite a day of exploration.

Smack in the middle of town, **Middlebury College** (☎ 802/443–5000), founded in 1800, was conceived as a more godly alternative to the worldly University of Vermont. The college has no religious affiliation today, however. The early 19th-century stone buildings contrast provocatively with the postmodern architecture of the Center for the Arts and the sports center. Music, theater, and dance performances take place throughout the year at the **Wright Memorial Theatre** and **Center for the Arts**.

The **Middlebury College Museum of Art** has a permanent collection of paintings, photography, works on paper, and sculpture. ⊠ *Center for* *the Arts, Rte. 30,* ☎ *802/443–5007.* ⌨ *Free.* ☉ *Tues.–Fri. 10–5, week-ends noon–5. Closed college holidays and last 2 weeks of Aug. and Dec.*

The **Vermont Folklife Center** has exhibits of photography, antiques, folk paintings, manuscripts, and other artifacts and contemporary works that examine facets of Vermont life. The center is in the basement of the restored 1801 home of Gamaliel Painter, the founder of Middle-bury College. ⌧ *2 Court St.,* ☎ *802/388–4964.* ⌨ *Donations accepted.* ☉ *Nov.–Apr., weekdays 9–5; May–Oct., weekdays 9–5, Sat. noon–4.*

The **Sheldon Museum,** an 1829 marble merchant's house, is the old-est community museum in the country. The period rooms contain Ver-mont-made textiles, furniture, toys, clothes, kitchen tools, and paintings. ⌧ *1 Park St.,* ☎ *802/388–2117.* ⌨ *$2; guided tour $4.* ☉ *June–Oct., Mon.–Sat. 10–5; Nov.–May, weekdays 10–5 (but call to make sure mu-seum is open).*

More than a crafts store, the **Vermont State Craft Center at Frog Hol-low** displays the work of more than 300 Vermont artisans. The cen-ter sponsors classes taught by some of those artists. There are other centers in Burlington and Manchester. ⌧ *1 Mill St.,* ☎ *802/388–3177.* ☉ *Call for hrs.*

☾ The Morgan horse—the official state animal—has an even temper, good stamina, and slightly truncated legs in proportion to its body. The Uni-versity of Vermont's **Morgan Horse Farm,** about 2½ mi west of Mid-dlebury, is a breeding and training center where in summer you can tour the stables and paddocks. ⌧ *74 Battell Dr. off Horse Farm Rd (follow signs off Rte. 23), Weybridge,* ☎ *802/388–2011.* ⌨ *$4.* ☉ *May–Oct., daily 9–5: last tour at 4:30.*

About 10 mi east of town on Route 125 (1 mi west of Middlebury Col-lege's Breadloaf campus), the easy ¾-mi **Robert Frost Interpretive Trail** winds through quiet woodland. Plaques along the way bear quotations from Frost's poems. A picnic area is across the road from the trailhead.

OFF THE
BEATEN PATH

LAKE CHAMPLAIN MARITIME MUSEUM – A replica of Benedict Arnold's Revolutionary War gunboat is part of this museum, which documents centuries of activity on the historically significant lake. The museum com-memorates the days when steamships sailed along the coast of northern Vermont carrying logs, livestock, and merchandise bound for New York City. Among the 11 exhibit buildings is a blacksmith's shop. A one-room stone schoolhouse built in the late 1810s houses historic maps, nautical prints, and maritime objects. Also on site are a nautical archaeology center and a conservation laboratory. ⌧ *Basin Harbor Rd., Basin Har-bor (14 mi west of Bristol, 7 mi west of Vergennes),* ☎ *802/475–2022.* ⌨ *$7.* ☉ *Early May–late Oct., daily 10–5.*

Dining and Lodging

$$–$$$ ✕ **Fire & Ice.** A 55-item salad bar (with peel-and-eat shrimp), prime rib, steak, fish, and a house specialty—homemade mashed potatoes—are all choices at a family-friendly spot that just celebrated its 25th an-niversary. Although large, the space is divided into several rooms (each with a different theme) as well as numerous intimate nooks and cran-nies for diners who wish privacy. Families with small children may want to request a table next to the "children's corner," which is outfitted with cushions and a VCR. Sunday dinner begins at 1 and includes crab legs and soup or the salad bar. ⌧ *26 Seymour St.,* ☎ *802/388–7166 or 800/367–7166. AE, D, DC, MC, V. No lunch Mon.*

$$–$$$ ✕ **Roland's Place.** Chef Roland Gaujac prepares classic French and ★ American dishes, elegantly served on Villeroy & Boch china, in a house

built in 1796. He opened his restaurant overlooking the Adirondacks after working as a chef in various parts of the world, including the French dining room in Los Angeles's Four Seasons Hotel. Some dishes use locally raised lamb, turkey, and venison; shrimp with chipotle and roasted garlic vinaigrette on fried ravioli is one entrée. A prix-fixe menu is available, and a special menu served daily from 5 to 6 lists numerous à la carte dishes for just $9. The restaurant has three guest rooms upstairs that are moderately priced and include a full breakfast. ⊠ *U.S. 7, New Haven,* ☎ *802/453–6309. AE, DC, MC, V. Closed Mon. No dinner Sun. Nov.–Apr.*

$$–$$$ ✕ **Woody's.** In addition to cool jazz, diner-deco light fixtures, and abstract paintings, Woody's has a view of Otter Creek below. Seafood and Vermont lamb are the restaurant's specialties—some folks say the Caesar salad is the best in the state. ⊠ *5 Bakery La.,* ☎ *802/388–4182. AE, MC, V. Closed Tues.*

$$$–$$$$ ✕▦ **Swift House Inn.** The main building at Swift House, the Georgian
★ home of a 19th-century governor and his philanthropist daughter, contains white-panel wainscoting, elaborately carved mahogany and marble fireplaces, and cherry paneling in the dining room. The rooms—most with Oriental rugs and nine with fireplaces—have period reproductions such as canopy beds, curtains with swags, and claw-foot tubs. Some bathrooms have double whirlpool tubs. Rooms in the gatehouse suffer from street noise but are charming; a carriage house holds six luxury accommodations. The dining room ($$$) offers entrées like herb-crusted rack of lamb with rosemary and Madeira sauce and creamy risotto with seasonal vegetables and maple syrup. A vegetarian menu is also available. ⊠ *25 Stewart La., 05753,* ☎ *802/388–9925,* FAX *802/388–9927. 21 rooms. Restaurant, pub, sauna, steam room. Continental breakfast. AE, D, DC, MC, V.*

$$–$$$$ ▦ **Middlebury Inn.** Gracious New England–style hospitality is served up along with traditional Yankee fare in this three-story, brick Georgian building, which has been an inn since 1827. The property now encompasses a contemporary motel (decorated, like the rooms in the inn, with Early American–style furnishings) and the Victorian-era Porter House Mansion. Rooms have phones, TVs, and hair dryers; those facing the lovely town green are subject to the noise of passing traffic. Plan to arrive between 3 and 4 for the inn's complimentary afternoon tea, served daily except holidays. In nice weather, you can eat lunch on the wicker-furnished porch. ⊠ *14 Courthouse Sq., 05753,* ☎ *802/ 388–4961 or 800/842–4666,* FAX *802/388–4563. 80 rooms. Two restaurants. Continental breakfast; MAP available. AE, D, MC, V.*

$–$$ ▦ **Lemon Fair.** This tidy, unfussy bed-and-breakfast occupies a building dating from 1796; it was tiny Bridport's first church before it was moved to its present location overlooking the town green in 1819. Furnishings are Early American in style, the grounds are spacious, and the entire establishment is kid-friendly. The B&B is just 8 mi from downtown Middlebury and 4 mi from Lake Champlain. The owners live next door and will rent out the entire house. ⊠ *Crown Point Rd., Bridport 05734,* ☎ *802/758–9238,* FAX *802/758–2135. 3 rooms without bath, 1 suite. Full breakfast. No credit cards.*

Outdoor Activities and Sports

The **Bike and Ski Touring Center** (⊠ 74 Main St., ☎ 802/388–6666) offers rentals and repairs.

BOATING

Chipman Point Marina (⊠ Rte. 73A, Orwell, ☎ 802/948–2288), where there is dockage for 60 boats, rents houseboats, sailboats, and pontoon fishing boats.

HIKING

On Route 116, about 5½ mi north of East Middlebury, a U.S. Forest Service sign marks a dirt road that forks to the right and leads to the start of the hike (about two to three hours) to **Abbey Pond,** which has a fantastic beaver lodge and dam in addition to a view of Robert Frost Mountain.

Shopping

Historic Marble Works (⊠ Maple St., ☎ 802/388–3701), a renovated marble manufacturing facility, is a collection of unique shops set amid quarrying equipment and factory buildings. One shop, De Pasquale's (☎ 802/388–3385), prepares subs and fresh fried fish platters for take-out and sells imported Italian groceries and wines. **Holy Cow** (⊠ 44 Main St., ☎ 802/388–6737) is where Woody Jackson creates and sells his Holstein cattle–inspired T-shirts, memorabilia, and paintings.

Bristol

㉕ *13 mi north of Middlebury*

At the northeastern threshold of the Green Mountain National Forest, where the rolling farmlands of the Champlain Valley meet the foothills of Vermont's main mountain chain, Bristol has a redbrick 19th-century Main Street that reflects the town's prosperous heyday as the center of a number of wood-products industries. Almost overshadowing the still-busy little downtown are the brooding heights of the Bristol Cliffs Wilderness Area, a section of national forest that has been assured permanent status as a primitive, roadless tract.

Dining and Lodging

$-$$ ✕☷ **Mary's at Baldwin Creek.** This restaurant ($$–$$$) and B&B in a 1790 farmhouse provides a truly inspired culinary experience. The "summer kitchen" has a fireplace and rough-hewn barn-board walls, and the main dining room is done in pastels. The innovative fare includes a superb garlic soup, Vermont rack of lamb with a rosemary-mustard sauce, and duck cassis smoked over applewood. Farmhouse dinners on Tuesdays in summer highlight Vermont products; Sunday brunch is a local ritual. Guests rooms, right above the restaurant, have simple, comfortable furnishings. ⊠ *Rte. 116, 05443,* ☎ *802/453–2432 or 877/453–2432,* ℻ *802/453–4825. 5 rooms without bath. Full breakfast. AE, MC, V. Closed Mon. in winter. No lunch.*

Outdoor Activities and Sports

A challenging 32-mi bicycle ride starts in Bristol: Take North Street from the traffic light in town and continue north to Monkton Ridge and on to Hinesburg. To return, follow Route 116 south through Starksboro and back to Bristol.

Shopping

Folkheart (⊠ 18 Main St., ☎ 802/453–4101) carries unusual jewelry, toys, and crafts from around the world.

En Route   From Bristol, Route 17 winds eastward up and over the **Appalachian Gap,** one of Vermont's most panoramic mountain passes. The views from the top and on the way down the other side toward the ski town of Waitsfield are a just reward for the challenging drive.

Waitsfield

㉖ *20 mi east of Bristol, 55 mi north of Rutland, 32 mi northeast of Middlebury, 19 mi southwest of Montpelier.*

Although in close proximity to Sugarbush and Mad River Glen ski areas, the Mad River valley towns of Waitsfield and Warren have maintained a decidedly low-key atmosphere. The gently carved ridges cradling the valley and the swell of pastures and fields lining the river seem to keep further notions of ski-resort sprawl at bay. With a map from the Sugarbush Chamber of Commerce you can investigate back roads off Route 100 that have exhilarating valley views.

Dining and Lodging

$$–$$$ ✕ **American Flatbread.** For ideologically and gastronomically sound pizza, you won't find a better place in the Green Mountains than this modest haven on the grounds of the Lareau Farm Country Inn between Waitsfield and Warren. Organic flour and produce fuel mind and body, and Vermont hardwood fuels the earth-and-stone oven. The "punctuated equilibrium flatbread," made with olive-pepper goat cheese and rosemary, is a dream, as are more traditional pizzas. This place is open Monday–Thursday 7:30 AM–8 PM for takeout, and Friday and Saturday for dinner as well. ⊠ *Rte. 100,* ☎ *802/496–8856. Reservations not accepted. MC, V. Closed Sun.*

$$–$$$ ✕ **Chez Henri.** Tucked in the shadows of Sugarbush ski area, this romantic slopeside bistro has garnered a year-round following with traditional French dishes: onion soup, cheese fondue, rabbit in red-wine sauce, and rack of lamb with rosemary-garlic sauce. Locals frequent the congenial bar and dine alfresco next to a stream. ⊠ *Sugarbush Village,* ☎ *802/583–2600. AE, MC, V.*

$$$$ ✕▥ **Pitcher Inn.** In 1997, four years after burning to the ground, this
★ Mad River Valley institution was reborn in an incarnation of *haute luxe*. Designed by architect David E. Sellers, each guest room has its own motif: In the Mallard, a curved ceiling gives the illusion of a duck blind, and the windows are etched and frosted in the likeness of the banks of a marsh. The Mountain Suite has a mountain mural, and a unique slate and mirror combination renders the effect of a waterfall. Rooms have stereos and a TV/VCR; most have fireplaces. The formal dining room, under the direction of chef Tom Bivins, focuses on locally grown produce and wild game. The inn has one of the state's finest wine cellars. ⊠ *Box 347, 275 Main St., Warren 05674,* ☎ *802/496–6350 or 888/867–4824,* FAX *802/496–6354. 8 rooms, 2 2-bedroom suites. 2 restaurants, in-room data ports. Full breakfast. AE, MC, V*

$$ ✕▥ **Tucker Hill Lodge.** Pine paneling and otherwise simple furnishings suffice at this 1940s lodge—most guests are more interested in skiing all day than enjoying in Victorian frills. Giorgio's Café occupies two dining rooms: one upstairs, with red tablecloths and a deep blue ceiling; and one downstairs, with a bar, open stone oven, and fireplace. Both have a warm Mediterranean feel. *Pettini a la Veneziana* (stone-seared scallops with raisins and pine nuts), and saltimbocca *alla Valdostana* (roulades of beef with fontina cheese and prosciutto) are two specialties. ⊠ *Rte. 17, 05673,* ☎ *802/496–3983 or 800/543–7841,* FAX *802/496–3203. 21 rooms, 15 with bath. Restaurant, bar, pool, tennis court, hiking, game room. Full breakfast; MAP available. AE, MC, V.*

$$–$$$$ ▥ **Inn at the Round Barn Farm.** Art exhibits have replaced cows in the big round barn here (one of only eight in the state), but the Shaker-style building still dominates the farm's 85 acres. The inn's guest rooms are in the 1806 farmhouse, where books line the walls of the cream-color library. The rooms are sumptuous, with eyelet-trimmed sheets, elaborate four-poster beds, rich-colored wallpapers, and brass wall lamps for easy bedtime reading. Six have fireplaces, three have whirlpool tubs, and four have steam showers. ⊠ *Box 247, E. Warren Rd., R.R. 1, 05673,* ☎ *802/496–2276,* FAX *802/496–8832. 11 rooms. Indoor pool, cross-country skiing, recreation room. Full breakfast. AE, D, MC, V.*

$$ ★ ⚅ **Beaver Pond Farm Inn.** This small 1840 farmhouse less than a mile from Sugarbush overlooks rolling meadows, a golf course, and cross-country ski trails. Guest rooms are decorated simply, and bathrooms are ample; the inn's focal point is the huge deck. The full breakfast might include orange-yogurt pancakes. The four-course dinner (served with MAP) features entrées such as rack of lamb or pork à l'orange; vegetarian meals will be served on request. Dinner is open to nonguests by reservation only. The inn has a limited practice driving range and is next door to the Sugarbush Golf Course. The innkeeper is building a reputation as a fly-fishing guide. ⊠ *Box 306, Golf Course Rd., 05674,* ☎ *802/583–2861,* 𝔽𝔸𝕏 *802/583–2860. 5 rooms (1 can sleep up to 4). Dining room, cross-country skiing. Full breakfast; MAP available Tues., Thurs., Sat. MC, V. Closed Jan.–mid-May.*

Nightlife and the Arts

The **Back Room at Chez Henri** (⊠ Sugarbush Village, ☎ 802/583–2600) has a pool table and is popular with the après-ski and late-night dance crowd. Local bands play danceable music at **Gallaghers** (⊠ Rtes. 100 and 17, ☎ 802/496–8800). **Giorgio's Café** (Tucker Hill Lodge, ☞ Dining and Lodging, *above*) is a cozy spot to warm yourself by the fire to the sounds of soft folk and jazz on weekends.

The **Green Mountain Cultural Center** (⊠ Inn at the Round Barn, E. Warren Rd., ☎ 802/496–7722), a nonprofit organization, brings concerts and art exhibits, as well as educational workshops, to the Mad River valley. The **Valley Players** (⊠ Rte. 100, ☎ 802/496–9612) present musicals, dramas, follies, and holiday shows.

Outdoor Activities and Sports

BIKING

The popular 14-mi Waitsfield–Warren loop begins when you cross the covered bridge in Waitsfield. Keep right on East Warren Road to the four-way intersection in East Warren; continue straight, then bear right, riding down Brook Road to the village of Warren; return by turning right (north) on Route 100 back toward Waitsfield.

GOLF

Great views and challenging play are the trademarks of the Robert Trent Jones–designed 18-hole, par-72 course at **Sugarbush Resort** (⊠ Golf Course Rd., ☎ 802/583–6727). The greens fee runs from $32 to $52; a cart (sometimes mandatory) costs $17.

ICE-SKATING

At the **Skadium** (⊠ Rte. 100, ☎ 802/496–8845 rink; 802/496–9199 recorded message), an outdoor rink, you can ice-skate in the winter and rollerblade or skateboard in warmer weather.

SLEIGH RIDES

The 100-year-old sleigh of the **Lareau Farm Country Inn** (⊠ Rte. 100, ☎ 802/496–4949) cruises along the banks of the Mad River.

Shopping

ART AND ANTIQUES

Luminosity Stained Glass Studios (⊠ Rte. 100, ☎ 802/496–2231), inside a converted church, specializes in stained glass, custom lighting, and art glass.

CRAFTS

All Things Bright and Beautiful (⊠ Bridge St., ☎ 802/496–3997) is a 12-room Victorian house jammed to the rafters with stuffed animals of all shapes, sizes, and colors as well as folk art, prints, and collectibles. **Warren Village Pottery** (⊠ Main St., Warren, ☎ 802/496–4162) sells handcrafted wares from its retail shop and specializes in functional stoneware pottery.

Skiing and Snow Sports

MAD RIVER GLEN

In 1995, Mad River Glen became the first ski area to be owned by a cooperative formed by the skiing community. The hundreds of shareholders are dedicated, knowledgeable skiers devoted to keeping skiing what it used to be—a pristine alpine experience. Mad River's unkempt aura attracts rugged individualists looking for less-polished terrain: The area was developed in the late 1940s and has changed relatively little since then. The single chairlift may be the only lift of its vintage still carrying skiers. Most of Mad River's trails (85%) are covered only by natural snow. ⊠ *Rte. 17, 05673,* ☎ *802/496–3551; 800/ 850–6742 for cooperative office; 802/496–2001 for snow conditions.*

Downhill. Mad River is steep, with natural slopes that follow the contours of the mountain. The terrain changes constantly on the 44 interconnected trails, of which 30% are beginner, 30% are intermediate, and 40% are expert. Intermediate and novice terrain is regularly groomed. Four chairs service the mountain's 2,037-ft vertical drop. There is no snowboarding on the mountain, but telemarkers will find many compatriots. Mad River sponsors the North American Telemark Festival in early March.

Child care. The **nursery** (☎ 802/496–2123) takes children from ages 6 weeks to 6 years. The ski school has classes for children from ages 4 to 12. Junior racing is available weekends and during holidays.

SUGARBUSH

In the Warren-Waitsfield ski world, Sugarbush is Mad River Glen's alter ego. Sugarbush's current owner, the American Skiing Company, has spent $28 million to keep the resort on the cutting edge. The new Slide Brook Express quad connects the two mountains, Sugarbush South and Sugarbush North. A computer-controlled system for snowmaking has increased coverage to nearly 70%. At the base of the mountain is a village with condominiums, restaurants, shops, bars, and a sports center. ⊠ *Box 350, Sugarbush Access Rd., accessible from Rte. 100 or Rte. 17, Warren 05674,* ☎ *802/583–2381; 800/537–8427 for lodging; 802/583–7669 for snow conditions.*

Downhill. Sugarbush is two distinct, connected mountain complexes. The Sugarbush South area is what old-timers recall as Sugarbush Mountain: With a vertical of 2,400 ft, it is known for formidable steeps toward the top and in front of the main base lodge. Sugarbush North offers what South has in short supply—beginner runs. North also has steep fall-line pitches and intermediate cruisers off its 2,600 vertical ft. There are 112 trails in all: 23% beginner, 48% intermediate, 29% expert. The resort has 18 lifts: seven quads (including four high-speed versions), three triples, four doubles, and four surface lifts.

Other activities. The **Sugarbush Health and Racquet Club** (☎ 802/583–6700), near the ski lifts, has Nautilus and Universal equipment; tennis, squash, and racquetball courts; a whirlpool, a sauna, and steam rooms; one indoor pool; and a 30-ft-high climbing wall.

Child care. The Sugarbush Day School accepts children from ages 6 weeks to 6 years; older children have indoor play areas and can go on outdoor excursions. There's half- and full-day instruction available for children from ages 4 to 11. Kids have their own Magic Carpet lift. Sugarbear Forest, a terrain garden, has fun bumps and jumps.

CROSS-COUNTRY SKIING

Blueberry Lake cross-country ski area (⌧ Plunkton Rd., Warren, ☎ 802/496–6687) has 30 km (18 mi) of groomed trails through thickly wooded glades. **Ole's** (⌧ Airport Rd., Warren, ☎ 802/496–3145) runs a cross-country center and small restaurant out of the tiny Warren airport; it has 60 km (37 mi) of groomed European-style trails that span out into the surrounding woods from the landing strips.

Brookfield

㉗ *15 mi south of Montpelier.*

The residents of secluded Brookfield have voted several times to keep its roads unpaved and even turned down an offered I–89 exit when the interstate highway was being built in the '60s. Crossing the nation's only **floating bridge** (⌧ Rte. 65 between Rtes. 12 and 14) still afloat feels like driving on water. The bridge, supported by nearly 400 barrels, sits at water level. It's the scene of the annual ice-harvest festival in January. The bridge is closed in winter.

Dining and Lodging

$$ ✕⊞ **Autumn Harvest Inn.** You'll be tempted to spend the whole day on the porch that graces the front of this casual inn, which was built in 1790. The inn, atop a knoll, has views of a 46-acre workhorse farm and the surrounding valley. Rooms in the older part of the house have more character; all have phones and TVs with VCRs. Prime rib and veal dishes are among the highlights of the seasonal country menu at the restaurant ($–$$; no lunch). ⌧ *R.F.D. 1, Box 1540, Clark Rd., Williamstown 05679,* ☎ *802/433–1355,* 🆗 *802/433–5501. 18 rooms. Restaurant, bar, pond, horseback riding, cross-country skiing. MAP and B&B plan available. AE, MC, V.*

$$ ⊞ **Green Trails Inn.** The enormous fieldstone fireplace that dominates
★ the living and dining area at Green Trails is symbolic of the stalwart hospitality of the innkeepers. Antique clocks fill the common areas, and the comfortably elegant rooms have antiques and Oriental rugs. One two-room suite has a fireplace, and two rooms have whirlpool tubs. Vegetarians are happily accommodated. This is a tranquil place for a walk down a tree-shaded country road. ⌧ *Main St., 05036,* ☎ *802/276–3412 or 800/243–3412. 14 rooms, 8 with bath. Cross-country skiing, snowshoeing, ski shop, sleigh rides. Full breakfast; MAP available in winter. D, MC, V.*

Central Vermont A to Z

Arriving and Departing
See Vermont A to Z, *below.*

Getting Around

BY BUS

Vermont Transit (☎ 802/864–6811; 800/451–3292; 800/642–3133 in VT) links Rutland, White River Junction, Burlington, and many smaller towns.

BY CAR

The major east–west road is U.S. 4, which stretches from White River Junction in the east to Fair Haven in the west. Route 125 connects Middlebury on U.S. 7 with Hancock on Route 100; Route 100 splits the region in half along the eastern edge of the Green Mountains. Route 17 travels east–west from Waitsfield over the Appalachian Gap through Bristol and down to the shores of Lake Champlain. I–91 and the parallel U.S. 5 follow the eastern border; U.S. 7 and Route 30 are the north–

south highways in the west. I–89 links White River Junction with Montpelier to the north.

Contacts and Resources

EMERGENCIES
Porter Hospital (✉ South St., Middlebury, ☎ 802/388–7901). **Rutland Medical Center** (✉ 160 Allen St., Rutland, ☎ 802/775–7111 or 800/649–2187 in Vermont).

GUIDED TOURS
Country Inns Along the Trail (✉ R.R. 3, Box 3115, Brandon 05733, ☎ 802/247–3300 or 800/838–3301) leads skiing, hiking, and biking trips from inn to inn in Vermont. The **Vermont Icelandic Horse Farm** (✉ N. Fayston Rd., Waitsfield 05673, ☎ 802/496–7141) conducts year-round guided riding expeditions on easy-to-ride Icelandic horses. Full-day, half-day, and hourly rides, weekend tours, and inn-to-inn treks are available.

LODGING REFERRAL SERVICES
Sugarbush Reservations (☎ 800/537–8427) and the **Woodstock Area Chamber of Commerce** (☎ 802/457–3555 or 888/496–6378) provide lodging referral services.

VISITOR INFORMATION
Addison County Chamber of Commerce (✉ 2 Court St., Middlebury 05753, ☎ 802/388–7951 or 800/733–8376). **Quechee Chamber of Commerce** (✉ Box 106, 15 Main St., Quechee 05059, ☎ 802/295–7900 or 800/295–5451). **Rutland Region Chamber of Commerce** (✉ 256 N. Main St., Rutland 05701, ☎ 802/773–2747). **Sugarbush Chamber of Commerce** (✉ Box 173, Rte. 100, Waitsfield 05673, ☎ 802/496–3409 or 800/828–4748). **Woodstock Area Chamber of Commerce** (✉ Box 486, 4 Central St., Woodstock 05091, ☎ 802/457–3555 or 888/496–6378).

NORTHERN VERMONT

Vermont's northernmost tier reveals the state's greatest array of contrasts. To the west, along Lake Champlain, Burlington and its Chittenden County suburbs have grown so rapidly that rural wags now say that Burlington's greatest advantage is that it's "close to Vermont." The north country also harbors Vermont's tiny capital, Montpelier, and its highest mountain, Mt. Mansfield, site of the famous Stowe ski slopes. To the northeast of Burlington and Montpelier spreads a sparsely populated and heavily wooded territory, the domain of loggers as much as farmers, where French spills out of the radio and the last snows melt toward the first of June.

You'll find plenty to do in the region's cities (Burlington, Montpelier, St. Johnsbury, and Barre), in the bustling resort area of Stowe, in the Lake Champlain Islands, and—if you like the outdoors—in the wilds of the Northeast Kingdom.

The coverage of towns in this area begins in the state capital, Montpelier; moves west towards Waterbury, Stowe, and Burlington; then north through the Lake Champlain Islands; east along the boundary with Canada toward Jay Peak and Newport; and south into the heart of the Northeast Kingdom before completing the circle in Barre.

Montpelier

28 *38 mi east of Burlington, 115 mi north of Brattleboro.*

With only about 8,000 residents, Montpelier is the country's least populous state capital. The intersection of State and Main streets is the city hub, bustling with the activity of state and city workers during the day. It's a pleasant place to spend an afternoon shopping and browsing; in true small-town Vermont fashion, though, the streets become deserted at night.

The **Vermont State House**—with a gleaming gold dome and granite columns 6 ft in diameter (plucked from the ground in nearby Barre)—is impressive for a city this size. The goddess of agriculture tops the dome. The Greek Revival building dates to 1836, although it was rebuilt after a fire in 1859; the latter year's Victorian style was adhered to in a lavish 1994 restoration. Interior paintings and exhibits make much of Vermont's sterling Civil War record. ⊠ *115 State St.,* ☎ *802/ 828–2228.* ☞ *Free.* ☉ *Weekdays 8–4; tours July–mid-Oct. weekdays every ½ hr 10–3:30, also Sat. 11–3.*

Perhaps you're wondering what the last panther shot in Vermont looked like? Why New England bridges are covered? What a niddy-noddy is? Or what Christmas was like for a Bethel boy in 1879? ("I skated on my new skates. In the morning Papa and I set up a stove for Gramper.") The **Vermont Museum,** on the ground floor of the Vermont Historical Society offices in Montpelier, satisfies the curious with intriguing and informative exhibits. ⊠ *109 State St.,* ☎ *802/828–2291.* ☞ *$3.* ☉ *Tues.–Fri. 9–4:30, Sat. 9–4, Sun. noon–4.*

Dining and Lodging

$$–$$$ ✕ **Chef's Table.** Nearly everyone working here is a student at the New
★   England Culinary Institute. Although this is a training ground, the quality and inventiveness are anything but beginner's luck. The menu changes daily. The atmosphere is more formal than that of the sister operation downstairs, the Main Street Bar and Grill (open daily). A 15% gratuity is added to the bill. ⊠ *118 Main St.,* ☎ *802/229–9202; 802/ 223–3188 for Grill. AE, D, MC, V. Closed Sun. No lunch weekends.*

$$–$$$ ✕ **Sarducci's.** Legislative lunches have been a lot more leisurely ever since Sarducci's came along to fill the trattoria void in Vermont's capital. These bright, cheerful rooms alongside the Winooksi River are a great spot for pizza fresh from wood-fired ovens, wonderfully textured homemade Italian breads, and imaginative pasta dishes such as pasta pugliese, which marries penne with basil, black olives, roasted eggplant, Portobello mushrooms, and sun-dried tomatoes. ⊠ *3 Main St.,* ☎ *802/ 223–0229. Reservations not accepted. AE, MC, V. No lunch Sun.*

$–$$ ✕ **Horn of the Moon.** The bulletin board plastered with notices of local events and political gatherings hints at Vermont's prominent progressive contingent. This vegetarian restaurant's cuisine includes a little Mexican, a little Italian, a lot of flavor, and not too much tofu. ⊠ *8 Langdon St.,* ☎ *802/223–2895. No credit cards. Closed Mon.*

$$–$$$ ⊞ **Inn at Montpelier.** This inn built in the early 1800s was renovated with the business traveler in mind, but the architectural detailing, antique four-poster beds, Windsor chairs, and the classical guitar on the stereo attract the leisure trade as well. The formal sitting room has a Federal feel to it, and the wide wraparound Colonial Revival porch is perfect for reading a good book or watching the townsfolk stroll by. The rooms in the annex are equally spiffy. ⊠ *147 Main St., 05602,* ☎ *802/223–2727,* ℻ *802/223–0722. 19 rooms. Meeting rooms. Continental breakfast. AE, D, DC, MC, V.*

Waterbury

   ㉙   *12 mi northwest of Montpelier.*

Waterbury's compact downtown consists of several brick business blocks, a state office complex that formerly served as a hospital, and

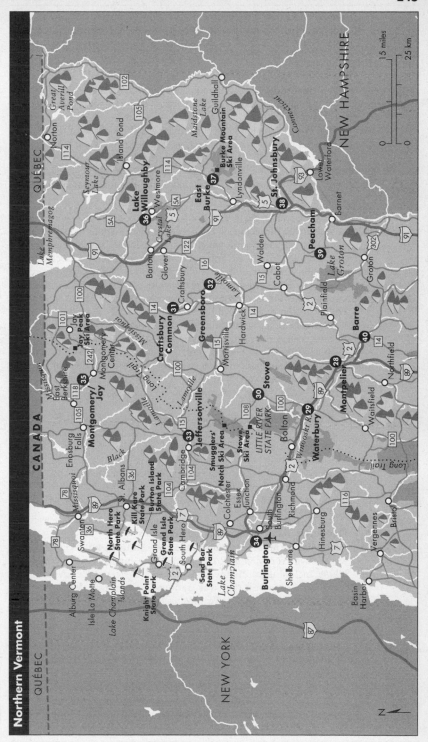

Northern Vermont

a little train station that comes to life only when Amtrak's *Vermonter* stops in town, once a day in each direction. The principal draws for visitors are north of I–89, along Route 100.

Waterbury holds one of Vermont's best-loved attractions: **Ben & Jerry's Ice Cream Factory,** the mecca, nirvana, and Valhalla for ice cream lovers. Ben and Jerry began selling ice cream from a renovated gas station in Burlington in the 1970s. Famous for their social and environmental consciousness, the boys do good works while living off the butterfat of the land. The tour only skims the surface of the behind-the-scenes goings-on at the plant—a flaw forgiven when the free samples are offered. ⊠ *Rte. 100, 1 mi north of I–89,* ☎ *802/244–8687.* 🎟 *Tour $2.* ☉ *June, daily 9–5; July–Aug., daily 9–8; Sept.–Oct., daily 9–6; Nov.–May, daily 10–5. Tours every ½ hr in winter, more frequently in summer.*

Dining and Lodging

$$$–$$$$ ✕🏨 **Thatcher Brook Inn.** There were once two sawmills across the street from this 1899 mansion, which was the residence for the sawyers and their families. Today the hub of activity is Ben & Jerry's ice cream factory, almost right next door. Twin gazebos are poised on either end of the front porch, and stands of giant white pines bolster the inn, defining its space on busy Route 100. Comfortable guest rooms have modern bathroom fixtures and Laura Ashley–style floral wallpaper; some have fireplaces and whirlpool tubs. Pine paneling, a fireplace, framed *Life* magazine covers, and tables painted with backgammon boards make the pub a popular socializing spot. Classic French cuisine, which might include pheasant, rack of lamb, or seafood, is served in the dining room. ⊠ *Rte. 100, 05676,* ☎ *802/244–5911 or 800/292–5911,* ℻ *802/244–1294. 24 rooms. Restaurant, pub. Full breakfast; MAP available. AE, D, DC, MC, V.*

$$–$$$ ✕🏨 **Black Bear Inn.** Teddy bears in all shapes and sizes decorate this mountaintop inn overlooking the Green Mountains. Many of the rooms have glass-door woodstoves and balconies, and Rooms 10R and 16R have private hot tubs and fireplaces. Grilled Atlantic salmon with a maple–Dijon mustard glaze is a typical dish at the inn's restaurant. ⊠ *Bolton Access Rd., Bolton 05477,* ☎ *802/434–2126 or 800/395–6335,* ℻ *802/434–5161. 24 rooms. Restaurant, pool, outdoor hot tub. Full breakfast. MC, V.*

Outdoor Activities and Sports

Mt. Mansfield State Forest and Little River State Park (⊠ U.S. 2, 1½ mi west of Waterbury, ☎ 802/244–7103) have extensive trail systems for hiking, including one that reaches the headquarters of the Civilian Conservation Corps unit that was stationed here in the 1930s. At Little River State Park, there are campsites, boat rentals, and trails leading to Mt. Mansfield and Camel's Hump.

Shopping

Green Mountain Chocolate Complex (⊠ Rte. 100, 2½ mi north of I–89, ☎ 802/244–1139) houses several gourmet and specialty shops including the Cabot Cheese Annex Store (☎ 802/244–6334) and Shimmering Glass Studio and Gallery (☎ 802/244–8134). **Cold Hollow Cider Mill** (⊠ Rte. 100, 3 mi north of I–89, ☎ 802/244–8771 or 800/327–7537) sells cider, baked goods, Vermont produce, and specialty foods. Tastes of fresh-pressed cider are offered while you watch how it is made.

Stowe

★ ③⓪   *8 mi north of Waterbury, 22 mi northwest of Montpelier, 36 mi northeast of Burlington.*

To many, Stowe rings a bell as the place where the von Trapp family, of *Sound of Music* fame, chose to settle after fleeing Austria. Set amid acres of pastures that fall away and allow for wide-angle panoramas of the mountains beyond, the **Trapp Family Lodge** (⊠ Luce Hill Rd., ☎ 802/253–8511 or 800/826–7000) is the site of a popular outdoor music series in summer and an extensive cross-country ski-trail network in winter.

For more than a century the history of Stowe has been determined by the town's proximity to **Mt. Mansfield,** at 4,393 ft the highest elevation in the state. As early as 1858, visitors were trooping to the area to view the mountain, which has a shape that suggests the profile of the face of a man lying on his back. If hiking to the top isn't your idea of a good time, in summer you can take the 4½-mi **toll road** to the top for a short scenic walk and a magnificent view. ⊠ *Mountain Rd., 7 mi from Rte. 100,* ☎ *802/253–3000.* 🖼 *Toll road $12.* ☉ *Late May–late Oct., daily 10–5.*

Mt. Mansfield's upper reaches are accessible by the eight-seat **gondola** that shuttles continuously up to the area of "the Chin" and the **Cliff House Restaurant** (☎ 802/253–3665; reservations essential). ⊠ *Mountain Rd., 8 mi from Rte. 100,* ☎ *802/253–3000.* 🖼 *$10.* ☉ *Mid-June–mid-Oct., daily 10–5; early Dec.–late Apr., daily 8–4 for skiers.*

When you tire of shopping on Stowe's Main Street and on Mountain Road, head for the **recreational path** that begins behind the Community Church in the center of town and meanders for 5⅓ mi along the river valley. There are many entry points along the way; whether you're on foot, skis, bike, or in-line skates, it's a tranquil means of enjoying the outdoors.

Dining and Lodging

$$–$$$ ✕ **Foxfire Inn.** A restored Colonial building might seem an unusual place to find Italian delicacies like veal rollatini, steak saltimbocca, and *tartufo* (vanilla and chocolate gelato in a chocolate cup with a raspberry center). Nonetheless, this old farmhouse just north of Stowe proper blends the two well. ⊠ *Rte. 100,* ☎ *802/253–4887. AE, D, MC, V. Closed Nov. No lunch.*

$$–$$$ ✕ **Villa Tragara.** Romance reigns in this intimate and creative north-
★ ern Italian restaurant, which consistently wins recognition as one of the state's best dining spots. Besides entrées such as *risotto con quaglie* (roast quail stuffed with toasted bread, prosciutto, sun-dried tomatoes, sage, and Asiago cheese and topped with a sauce of sherry and dried mixed fruit), the owner-chef prepares a five-course tasting menu for $40. The newest treat is the Italian tapas—smaller portions of many of the Villa's most popular offerings, moderately priced to allow patrons to pick and share dishes. (There's a $12 minimum charge per person for the tapas.) The restaurant has live entertainment Friday evenings and a popular dinner theater several Monday evenings throughout the year. ⊠ *Rte. 100, south of Stowe,* ☎ *802/244–5288. AE, MC, V. Restaurant closed Mon. No lunch.*

$–$$ ✕ **Miguel's Stowe Away.** In a little café just the other side of the border . . . actually, just the other side of Smugglers' Notch, Miguel's serves up all the Tex-Mex standards along with tasty surprises such as coconut-fried shrimp, Cajun lamb fajitas, and a Yankee-flavored maple flan. Steaks and burgers round out the gringo menu. The cozy front room has a pool table (no quarters required) and a bar stocked with frosty Corona beer. Miguel's has an outpost on the Sugarbush Access Road in Warren ☎ (802/583–3858). ⊠ *3148 Mountain Rd.,* ☎ *802/ 253–7574 or 800/245–1240. AE, D, MC, V. No lunch spring and fall.*

$$$$ ✕🏠 **Edson Hill Manor.** This French-Canadian–style manor built in 1940 sits atop 225 acres of rolling hills. Oriental rugs accent the dark wide-board floors, and a tapestry complements the burgundy-patterned sofas that face the huge stone fireplace in the living room. The guest rooms are pine paneled and have fireplaces, canopy beds, and down comforters. The dining room ($$$; no lunch; closed from Sunday to Thursday in April and May) is really the heart of the place: The walls of windows allowing contemplation of the inspiring view compete for your attention with wildflower paintings and vines climbing to the ceiling. The highly designed, sculpted food might include rack of lamb or pan-seared salmon. ✉ *1500 Edson Hill Rd., 05672,* ☎ *802/ 253–7371 or 800/621–0284,* FAX *802/253–4036. 25 rooms. Restaurant, pool, hiking, horseback riding, cross-country skiing, sleigh rides. Full breakfast; MAP available. AE, D, MC, V.*

$$$$ ✕🏠 **Topnotch at Stowe Resort and Spa.** This resort on 120 acres overlooking Mt. Mansfield, and just 3 mi from the base of the mountain, is one of the state's poshest. Floor-to-ceiling windows, a freestanding circular stone fireplace, and cathedral ceilings make the lobby an imposing setting. Rooms have thick carpeting, a small shelf of books, and accents such as painted barn-board walls or Italian prints. The minimum stay is two nights on weekends. The large European spa offers 20 massage-treatment rooms and a fitness program. Maxwell's restaurant serves Continental cuisine. ✉ *Mountain Rd., 05672,* ☎ *802/ 253–8585 or 800/451–8686,* FAX *802/253–9263. 77 rooms, 13 suites, 20 1- to 3-bedroom town homes. 2 restaurants, bar, 1 indoor and 1 outdoor pool, 14 tennis courts (4 indoor), health club, horseback riding, cross-country skiing, sleigh rides. Full breakfast; MAP available. AE, D, DC, MC, V.*

$$–$$$$ 🏠 **Inn at the Brass Lantern.** Home-baked cookies in the afternoon, a basket of logs by your fireplace, and stenciled hearts along the wainscoting reflect the care taken in turning this 18th-century farmhouse into a place of welcome. All rooms have country antiques and locally made quilts; most are oversize and some have fireplaces and whirlpool tubs. This B&B is next door to a Grand Union supermarket, but its breakfast room has a terrific view of Mt. Mansfield, a sight some guest rooms share. ✉ *Rte. 100, ½ mi north of Stowe, 05672,* ☎ *802/ 253–2229 or 800/729–2980,* FAX *802/253–7425. 9 rooms. Breakfast room. Full breakfast. AE, MC, V.*

$–$$ 🏠 **Sunset Motor Inn.** Strategically located among northern Vermont's big-three ski areas, this family-owned, family-friendly motel has clean and comfortable accommodations. Rooms numbered 70–87 in the newer section are larger and have whirlpool baths and refrigerators; the best are the ones facing the back of the motel. There's a restaurant next door. ✉ *Junction of Rtes. 15 and 100, Morrisville 05661,* ☎ *802/ 888–4956 or 800/544–2347,* FAX *802/888–3698. 55 rooms. Pool. AE, D, MC, V.*

Nightlife and the Arts

The **Matterhorn Night Club** (✉ Mountain Rd., ☎ 802/253–8198) has live music and dancing on weekends, DJs during the week. Live weekend entertainment takes place at **Stoweflake Inn** (✉ Mountain Rd., ☎ 802/253–7355). Entertainers perform at the **Topnotch at Stowe** (☞ Dining and Lodging, *above*) lounge on weekends.

Stowe Performing Arts (☎ 802/253–7792) sponsors a series of classical and jazz concerts during July in the Trapp Family Concert meadow. **Stowe Theater Guild** (✉ Town Hall Theater, Main St., ☎ 802/253– 3961 summer only) performs musicals in July and August.

Outdoor Activities and Sports

BIKING

The junction of Routes 100 and 108 is the start of a 21-mi tour with scenic views of Mt. Mansfield; the course takes you along Route 100 to Stagecoach Road, to Morristown, over to Morrisville, and south on Randolph Road. The **Mountain Bike Shop** (⊠ Mountain Rd., ☎ 802/253–7919) supplies equipment and rents bicycles.

CANOEING

Umiak Outdoor Outfitters (⊠ 849 S. Main St./Rte. 100, just south of Stowe Village, ☎ 802/253–2317) specializes in canoes and kayaks, rents them for day trips, and leads guided overnight excursions. The store also operates a rental outpost at Waterbury State Park, just off Route 100.

FISHING

The **Fly Rod Shop** (⊠ Rte. 100, 3 mi south of Stowe, ☎ 802/253–7346 or 800/535–9763) provides a guiding service; gives fly-tying, casting, and rod-building classes in winter; rents fly tackle; and sells equipment, including classic and collectible firearms.

HIKING

For the two-hour climb to **Stowe Pinnacle,** go 1½ mi south of Stowe on Route 100 and turn east on Gold Brook Road opposite the Nichols Farm Lodge; turn left at the first intersection, continue straight at an intersection by a covered bridge, turn right after 1.8 mi, and travel 2.3 mi to a parking lot on the left. The trail crosses an abandoned pasture and takes a short, steep climb to views of the Green Mountains and Stowe Valley.

ICE-SKATING

Jackson Arena (⊠ Park St., ☎ 802/253–6148) is a public ice-skating rink that rents skates.

SLEIGH RIDES

Charlie Horse Sleigh and Carriage Rides (⊠ Mountain Rd., ☎ 802/253–2215) operates rides daily from 11 to 7; reservations are suggested for evening rides.

TENNIS

Topnotch at Stowe Resort and Spa (☞ Dining and Lodging, *above*) has 10 outdoor and 4 indoor courts. Public courts are located at Stowe's elementary school.

Shopping

The **Mountain Road** is lined with shops from town up toward the ski area.

Skiing and Snow Sports

STOWE MOUNTAIN RESORT

To be precise, the name of the village is Stowe and the name of the mountain is Mt. Mansfield, but to generations of skiers, the area, the complex, and the region are just plain Stowe. The resort is a classic that dates from the 1930s. Even today the area's mystique attracts as many serious skiers as social skiers. In recent years, on-mountain lodging, improved snowmaking, new lifts, and free shuttle buses that gather skiers from lodges, inns, and motels along the Mountain Road have added convenience to the Stowe experience. Yet the traditions remain: the Winter Carnival in January, the Sugar Slalom in April, ski weeks all winter. Three base lodges provide the essentials, including two on-mountain restaurants. ⊠ *5781 Mountain Rd., 05672, ☎ 802/253–3000; 800/253–4754 for lodging; 802/253–3600 for snow conditions.*

Downhill. Mt. Mansfield, with a vertical drop of 2,360 ft, is one of the giants among Eastern ski mountains and the highest in Vermont. It was the only area in the East featured in Warren Miller's 1995 film, *Endless Winter.* The mountain's symmetrical shape allows skiers of all abilities long, satisfying runs from the summit. The famous Front Four runs (National, Liftline, Starr, and Goat) are the intimidating centerpieces for tough, expert runs, yet there is plenty of mellow intermediate skiing and one long beginner trail from the top that ends at the Toll House, where there is easier terrain. Mansfield's satellite sector is a network of intermediate and one expert trail off a basin served by a gondola. Spruce Peak, separate from the main mountain, is a teaching hill and a pleasant experience for intermediates and beginners; it also has a mountaintop trail that connects with slopes at neighboring resort Smugglers' Notch. In addition to the high-speed, eight-passenger gondola, Stowe has one quad, one triple, and six double chairlifts, plus one handle tow and poma, to service its 47 trails. Night-skiing trails are accessed by the gondola. The resort has 73% snowmaking coverage. Snowboard facilities include a halfpipe, quarterpipe, and two terrain parks—one for beginners, at the base of Spruce Peak, and one for experts on the Mt. Mansfield side.

Cross-country. The resort has 35 km (22 mi) of groomed cross-country trails and 40 km (24 mi) of backcountry trails. There are four interconnecting cross-country ski areas with more than 150 km (90 mi) of groomed trails within the town of Stowe.

Child care. The child-care center takes children from ages 6 weeks to 6 years, with kids' ski-school programs for ages 6 to 12. A center on Spruce Peak is headquarters for programs for children from ages 3 to 12, and there's another program for teenagers 13 to 17.

En Route Northwest of Stowe, an exciting and scenic if indirect route leads to Burlington: **Smugglers' Notch,** the narrow pass between Mt. Mansfield and Madonna Peak that is said to have sheltered 18th-century outlaws in its rugged, bouldered terrain. Weaving around the huge stones that shoulder the road, you'd hardly know you're on state highway Route 108. There are parking spots and picnic tables at the top. The notch road is closed in winter.

Craftsbury Common

③ *27 mi northeast of Stowe.*

The three villages of Craftsbury—Craftsbury Common, Craftsbury, and East Craftsbury—are among Vermont's finest and oldest towns. Handsome white houses and barns, the requisite common, a classic general store, and the Craftsbury Outdoor Center make them well worth the drive. The rolling farmland hints at the way Vermont used to be: The area's sheer distance from civilization and its rugged weather have kept most of the state's development farther south.

Lodging

$$$$ 🏠 **Inn on the Common.** Craftsbury Common is a perfect hamlet amid remote countryside, and the three white Federal-style buildings of this inn aptly represent the town's civility. All rooms contain antique reproductions and contemporary furnishings; deluxe rooms have generous seating areas and fireplaces. Cocktails and hors d'oeuvres are offered in one house's cozy library. Five-course dinners ($$$; open to nonguests by reservation) are served at a communal table in the dining room, which overlooks the inn's gardens. Guests have access to the facilities at the Craftsbury Sports Center and Albany's Wellness Barn, which has a lap pool, aerobic machines, a sauna, and a whirlpool. ✉ *On the common, 05827,* ☎ *802/586–9619 or 800/521–2233,* ℻ *802/ 586–2249. 15 rooms, 1 suite. Dining room, lounge, pool, tennis court. MAP. AE, MC, V.*

$$–$$$ ⊡ **Craftsbury Outdoor Center.** Outside of town and surrounded by lakes and hills, this outdoor enthusiasts' haven has standard accommodations and sporting packages. Because of a long season of snowcover— it's white here when the rest of Vermont is green—the cross-country skiing is terrific on the 160 km (99 mi) of trails (96 km/60 mi groomed) on the property and through local farmland. During the rest of the year, sculling and running camps are held; among the other activities are mountain biking and canoeing. Nonguests can ski, mountain bike, and canoe at day-use rates; equipment rental is available. The buffet-style meals include soups, stews, and homemade breads and desserts. ⊠ *Box 31, Lost Nation Rd., 05827,* ☎ *802/586–7767 or 800/729–7751,* ℻ *802/586–7768. 29 rooms, 3 with bath; 3 cottages; 2 efficiencies. Dining room, boating, mountain bikes, cross-country skiing. AP. MC, V.*

Greensboro

㉜ *10 mi southeast of Craftsbury Common.*

Greensboro is an idyllic small town with a long history as a vacation destination. **Willey's Store** (⊠ Main St., ☎ 802/533–2621), with wooden floors and tin ceilings, warrants exploration. You never know what you'll find—foodstuffs, baskets, candy, kitchen paraphernalia— in this packed-to-the-rafters emporium.

Dining and Lodging

$$$$ ✕⊡ **Highland Lodge.** Tranquillity defined: an 1860 house that overlooks a pristine lake, with 120 acres of rambling woods and pastures laced with hiking and skiing trails (ski rentals available). Widely known for its great front porch, this quiet family resort is part refined elegance and part casual country of the summer-camp sort. The comfortable guest rooms have Early American furnishings. Most rooms have views of the lake; the one- to three-bedroom cottages are more private (four with gas stoves stay open in winter). The traditional dinner menu, which incorporates Vermont foods, might include entrées such as roasted leg of lamb and grilled Black Angus sirloin. ⊠ *E. Craftsbury Rd., 05841,* ☎ *802/533–2647,* ℻ *802/533–7494. 11 rooms, 11 1- to 3-bedroom cottages. Restaurant, lake, tennis court, hiking, boating, cross-country skiing, recreation room, children's programs. MAP. D, MC, V. Closed mid-Mar.–late May and mid-Oct.–mid-Dec.*

$–$$ ⊡ **Brick House Guests and Perennial Pleasures Nursery.** Out of a handsome brick home flows an abundance of homespun entrepreneurship. British-born proprietor Judith Kane runs an eclectic B&B with large, antiques-filled bedrooms and a cozy library complete with fireplace, sherry, and books on everything from crystal healing to architectural history. The breakfasts, served on charmingly mismatched china, are sumptuous. Judith's daughter Rachel runs the nursery (closed on Monday and from mid-September to April), which specializes in heirloom plants and herbs. In summer you can sit for a spell in the gardens and enjoy traditional English cream tea (reservations advised). ⊠ *Box 128, 2 Brick House Rd., East Hardwick 05836,* ☎ *802/472–5512. 3 rooms, 1 with bath. Full breakfast. MC, V.*

Jeffersonville

㉝ *18 mi north of Stowe, 28 mi northeast of Burlington.*

Mt. Mansfield and Madonna Peak tower over Jeffersonville, whose activities are closely linked with those of Smugglers' Notch Ski Resort.

Boyden Valley Winery (⊠ Junction of Rtes. 15 and 104, Cambridge, ☎ 802/644–8151) conducts tours of its micro-winery and also showcases an excellent selection of Vermont specialty products and local handicrafts, including fine furniture. The winery is closed Monday.

Lodging

$$$$ 🏨 **Smugglers' Notch Resort.** Most of the condos at this large year-round resort (☞ Skiing and Snow Sports, *below*) have fireplaces and decks. The resort is known for its many family programs. Rates include lift tickets and ski lessons in season. ⊠ *Rte. 108, 05464,* ☎ *802/644–8851 or 800/451–8752,* FAX *802/644–1230. 375 condos. 3 restaurants, bar, indoor pool, hot tub, sauna, 10 tennis courts (2 indoors), exercise room, ice-skating, recreation room, baby-sitting, children's programs, nursery, playground. AE, DC, MC, V.*

$–$$ 🏨 **Highlander Motel.** The rooms are clean and tidy and just 2½ mi from Smugglers' Village. You can enjoy breakfast (the only meal the restaurant serves) by the fire. Pets are welcome. ⊠ *Rte. 108 S, 05464,* ☎ *802/644–2725 or 800/367–6471,* FAX *802/644–2725. 12 rooms. Restaurant, pool, recreation room. MC, V.*

Nightlife and the Arts

Most après-ski action in the Smugglers' Notch area revolves around the afternoon bonfires and nightly live entertainment in the **Meeting House** (⊠ The Village, Rte. 108, ☎ 802/644–8851).

Outdoor Activities and Sports

Smugglers' Notch State Park (⊠ Rte. 108, 10 mi north of Mt. Mansfield, ☎ 802/253–4014) is good for picnicking and hiking on wild terrain among large boulders.

Northern Vermont Llamas (⊠ 766 Lapland Rd., Waterville, ☎ 802/644–2257) offers half- and full-day treks from May through October along the cross-country ski trails of Smugglers' Notch. The llamas carry everything, including snacks and lunches.

Vermont Horse Park (⊠ Rte. 108 ☎ 802/644–5347) conducts rides on authentic horse-drawn sleighs. Indoors are tennis courts, a pool, and a hot tub.

Shopping

ANTIQUES

The **Buggy Man** (⊠ Rte. 15, 7 mi east of Jeffersonville, ☎ 802/635–2100) and **Mel Siegel** (⊠ Rte. 15, 7 mi east of Jeffersonville, ☎ 802/635–7838) stock affordable, quality antiques.

CLOTHING

Johnson Woolen Mills (⊠ Main St., Johnson, 9 mi east of Jeffersonville, ☎ 802/635–2271) is an authentic factory store with deals on woolen blankets, yard goods, and the famous Johnson outerwear.

CRAFTS

Vermont Rug Makers (⊠ Rte. 100C, East Johnson, 10 mi east of Jeffersonville, ☎ 802/635–2434) weaves imaginative rugs and tapestries from fabrics, wools, and exotic materials. Its International Gallery displays rugs and tapestries from countries throughout the world. The shop has a branch on Main Street in Stowe.

Skiing and Snow Sports

SMUGGLERS' NOTCH RESORT

This sprawling resort complex consistently wins accolades for its family programs: Its children's ski school is one of the best in the country—and possibly *the* best. But skiers of all levels come here (in 1996, Smugglers' became the first ski area in the East to designate a triple-black-diamond run—the Black Hole). All the essentials are available at the base of the lifts. The Family Snowmaking Learning Center demonstrates the processes of state-of-the-art computer-controlled snowmaking and teaches about weather and snow crystals. A new snowboard park was added in 1998. ⊠ *Rte. 108, 05464,* ☎ *802/644–8851 or 800/451–8752.*

Downhill. Smugglers' has three mountains. The highest, Madonna, with a vertical drop of 2,610 ft, is in the center and connects with a trail network to Sterling (1,500-ft vertical). The third mountain, Morse (1,150-ft vertical), is adjacent to Smugglers' "village" of shops, restaurants, and lodgings; it's connected to the other peaks by trails and a shuttle bus. The wild, craggy landscape lends a pristine, wilderness feel to the skiing experience on the two higher mountains. The tops of each of the mountains have expert terrain—a couple of double-black diamonds make Madonna memorable. Intermediate trails fill the lower sections. Morse has many beginner trails. Smugglers' 60 trails are served by five double chairlifts, including the Mogul Mouse Magic Lift, and three surface lifts. There is top-to-bottom snowmaking on all three mountains, allowing for 62% coverage.

Cross-country. The area has 37 km (23 mi) of groomed and tracked cross-country trails.

Other activities. The self-contained village has ice-skating, sleigh rides, and horseback riding.

Child care. The state-of-the-art, professional Child Care Center accepts children from ages 6 weeks to 12 years. Children from ages 3 to 17 can attend ski camps that have instruction, movies, games, and other activities.

Burlington

★ ㉞ *76 mi south of Montréal, 349 mi north of New York City, 223 mi northwest of Boston.*

The largest population center in Vermont, Burlington was named one of the country's "Dream Towns" by *Outside* magazine. The city, founded in 1763, is the center of a rapidly growing suburban area but has held its own against highway malls by cleverly positioning itself in the "festival marketplace" retail style, as well as by trading on its incomparable lakeside location. The city's eclectic population of 40,000 includes many transplants from larger urban areas as well as roughly 20,000 students from the area's five colleges. For years it was the only city in America with a socialist mayor—now the nation's sole socialist congressional representative.

The **Church Street Marketplace**—a pedestrian mall of intriguing boutiques, restaurants, sidewalk cafés, crafts vendors, and street performers—is an animated downtown focal point. Most people in central and northern Vermont come at least occasionally to the town center, if only to run errands or to see a show.

Crouched on the shores of Lake Champlain, which shimmers in the shadows of the Adirondacks to the west, Burlington's revitalized **waterfront** teems with outdoor enthusiasts who stroll along its recreation path and ply the waters in sailboats and motorcraft in summer. A 500-passenger, three-level cruise vessels, *The Spirit of Ethan Allen II,* takes people on narrated cruises on the lake and, in the evening, dinner and sunset sailings that drift by the Adirondacks and the Green Mountains. ⊠ *Burlington Boat House, College St. at Battery St.,* ☎ *802/862–8300.* ⌘ *$8.* ☉ *Cruises late May–mid-Oct., daily 10–9.*

Part of the waterfront's revitalization and still a work-in-progress, the
🐾 **Lake Champlain Basin Science Center** is in the perfect location to fulfill

its mission to educate the public about the ecology, history, and culture of the lake region. From looking at plankton through a "kidscope" to dragging a net off the University of Vermont research boat docked on the property, there are activities for the whole family. The university's Research Lab is scheduled to open at the Science Center in late 1999. ⊠ *One College St.,* ☎ *802/864–1848.* ▣ *$2.* ☉ *Mid-June–Labor Day, daily 11–5; fall and winter, weekends and school vacations 12:30–4:30.*

Crowning the hilltop above Burlington is the campus of the **University of Vermont** (☎ 802/656–3480), known simply as UVM for the abbreviation of its Latin name, Universitas Viridis Montis—the University of the Green Mountains. With more than 10,000 students, UVM is the state's principal institution of higher learning. The most architecturally interesting buildings face the **Green**, which contains some of the grandest surviving specimens of the elm trees that once shaded virtually every street in Burlington, as well as a statue of UVM founder Ira Allen, Ethan's brother. The **Robert Hull Fleming Art Museum** (⊠ Colchester Ave., ☎ 802/656–0750), just behind the Ira Allen Chapel, houses American portraits and landscapes, including works by Sargent, Homer, and Bierstadt; two Corots and a Fragonard; and an Egyptian mummy. Contemporary Vermont works are also exhibited.

Ethan Allen, Vermont's Revolutionary-era guerrilla fighter, remains a captivating figure. Exhibits at the visitor center at the **Ethan Allen Homestead** answer questions about his flamboyant life. The house contains frontier hallmarks like rough saw-cut boards and an open hearth for cooking. A re-created Colonial kitchen garden resembles the one the Allens would have had. After the tour, you can stretch your legs on scenic trails along the Winooski River. ⊠ *North Ave., off Rte. 127, north of Burlington,* ☎ *802/865–4556.* ▣ *$4.* ☉ *Mid-May–mid-June, daily 1–5; mid-June–mid-Oct., Mon.–Sat. 10–5, Sun. 1–5.*

A few miles south of Burlington, the Champlain Valley gives way to fertile farmland, affording stunning views of the rugged Adirondacks across the lake. You can trace much of New England's history simply
★ by wandering the 45 acres and 37 buildings of the **Shelburne Museum.** The outstanding 80,000-object collection of Americana consists of 18th- and 19th-century period homes and furniture, fine and folk art, farm tools, more than 200 carriages and sleighs, Audubon prints, an old-fashioned jail, even a private railroad car from the days of steam. The museum also has an assortment of duck decoys, an old stone cottage, and a display of early toys—as well as the *Ticonderoga,* an old side-wheel steamship, grounded amid lawn and trees. ⊠ *U.S. 7, Shelburne, 5 mi south of Burlington,* ☎ *802/985–3346.* ▣ *$17.50 for 2 consecutive days, $7 in winter for 1 day.* ☉ *Late May–late Oct., daily 10–5; call ahead for limited winter hrs.*

★ ⓒ **Shelburne Farms** has a history of improving the farmer's lot by developing new agricultural methods. Founded in the 1880s as a private estate, the 1,400-acre property is an educational and cultural resource center with, among other things, a working dairy farm, a Children's Farmyard, and a spot for watching the farm's famous cheddar cheese being made. Frederick Law Olmsted, co-creator of New York's Central Park, designed the magnificent grounds overlooking Lake Champlain. ⊠ *West of U.S. 7 at the junction of Harbor and Bay Rds., Shelburne, 6 mi south of Burlington,* ☎ *802/985–8686.* ▣ *Day pass $5, tour is an additional $4.* ☉ *Visitor center and shop daily 9–5; tours Memorial Day–mid-Oct., last tour at 3:30.*

ⓒ On the tour of the **Vermont Teddy Bear Company,** you'll hear more puns than you ever thought possible and learn how a few homemade bears, sold from a cart on Church Street, have turned into a multimillion-dollar business. A children's play tent is set up outdoors in summer, and you can wander the beautiful 57-acre property. ⊠ *2236 Shelburne Rd., Shelburne,* ☎ *802/985–3001.* ☜ *Tour $1.* ⊘ *Tours Mon.–Sat. 9:30–4, Sun. 10:30–4; store Mon.–Sat. 9–6, Sun. 10–5.*

At the 6-acre **Vermont Wildflower Farm,** the display along the flowering pathways changes constantly: violets in the spring, daisies and black-eyed Susans for summer, and fall colors that rival that of the trees' foliage. You can buy wildflower seeds, crafts, and books here. ⊠ *U.S. 7, Charlotte, 5 mi south of the Shelburne Museum,* ☎ *802/425–3500.* ☜ *$3.* ⊘ *Early May–late Oct., daily 10–5.*

OFF THE
BEATEN PATH

GREEN MOUNTAIN AUDUBON NATURE CENTER – Bursting with great things to do, see, and learn, this is a wonderful place to orient yourself to Vermont's outdoor wonders. The center's 300 acres of diverse habitats are a sanctuary for all things wild, and the 5 mi of trails provide an opportunity to explore and understand the workings of differing natural communities. Events at the center include dusk walks, wildflower and birding rambles, nature workshops, and educational activities for both kids and adults. The center is 18 mi southeast of Burlington. ⊠ *Huntington-Richmond Rd., Richmond,* ☎ *802/434–3068.* ☜ *Donations accepted.* ⊘ *Grounds dawn–dusk, center weekdays 9–4:30.*

LAKE CHAMPLAIN ISLANDS – When Vermonters talk about "the islands," chances are they're not referring to the Caribbean but to a place a lot closer to home—the Lake Champlain Islands, an elongated archipelago stretching southward from the Canadian border. The islands are a center of water recreation in summer and ice fishing in winter. One of the islands' more unusual claims to fame is the summer residence of the **Royal Lippizaner Stallions,** heirs to the celebrated Austrian dressage tradition; in July and August they perform in an outdoor arena just off U.S. 7 in North Hero (☎ *802/372–5683*). A preferred islands' lodging place is **Shore Acres Inn and Restaurant** (⊠ U.S. 2, North Hero, ☎ *802/372–8722*), with a lakeside location looking west toward the Green Mountains. North of Burlington, a scenic drive through the islands on U.S. 2 begins at I–89 and travels north through South Hero, Grand Isle, and Isle La Motte to Alburg Center, 5 mi from the Canadian border. Here Route 78 will take you east to the mainland.

MISSISQUOI NATIONAL WILDLIFE REFUGE – The 6,300 acres of federally protected wetlands, meadows, and woods provide a beautiful setting for bird-watching, canoeing, or walking nature trails. ⊠ *Swanton, 36 mi north of Burlington,* ☎ *802/868–4781.*

Dining and Lodging

$$–$$$ ✕ **Isabel's.** An old lumber mill on Lake Champlain houses this restaurant, which has high ceilings, exposed-brick walls, and knockout views. The menu is seasonal; past dishes, all presented with an artistic flair, have included Thai seafood pasta and vegetable Wellington. Lunch and weekend brunch are popular, and you can dine on the outdoor patio on warm days. ⊠ *112 Lake St.,* ☎ *802/865–2522. AE, D, DC, MC, V. No dinner Sun.– Mon. Nov.–Apr.*

$$–$$$ ✕ **Trattoria Delia.** Didn't manage to rent that villa in Umbria this year?
★ The next best thing, if your travels bring you to Burlington, is this superb Italian country eatery just around the corner from City Hall Park. Local game and produce are the stars, as in roast rabbit marinated in herbs, wine, and olive oil. The chef's passion for the truly homemade extends to wild boar sausage, salami, and fresh mozzarella. Wood-grilled

items are a specialty. ⊠ *152 St. Paul St.,* ☎ *802/864–5253. AE, D, DC, MC, V.*

$$ ✕ **NECI Commons.** The initials stand for New England Culinary Institute, the respected Montpelier academy whose students and teachers run this all-under-one-roof café, bakery, market, restaurant, and bar. The deli counter can get a little pricey—are you ready for garlic mashed potatoes at $4.99 a pound?—but everything is fresh and tasty. It's open daily for breakfast, lunch, and dinner. ⊠ *25 Church St.,* ☎ *802/862–6324. AE, D, MC, V.*

$$ ✕ **Sweet Tomatoes.** The dishes cooked in the wood-fired oven of this bright and boisterous trattoria send off a mouthwatering aroma. The menu includes pizzas and *caponata* (roasted eggplant with onions, capers, olives, parsley, celery, and tomatoes), and farfalle with sweet sausage, roasted red peppers, onions, tomatoes, black olives, and rosemary in a tomato basil sauce. In warm weather you can dine at outdoor tables abutting the bustling Church Street Marketplace. ⊠ *83 Church St.,* ☎ *802/660–9533. AE, MC, V.*

$–$$ ✕ **Libby's Blue Line Diner.** The menu here is diverse—a mix of classic diner cuisine and more upscale offerings such as eggplant burgers and brook trout. Portions are generous, and the prices are right. The only problem is this place's popularity: Reservations are not accepted and the lines can be long (Sunday breakfast is particularly popular). Try to go at an off time, between standard mealtimes. ⊠ *1 Roosevelt Hwy./U.S. 7, Colchester,* ☎ *802/655–0343. Reservations not accepted. AE, MC, V. No dinner Sun. in winter.*

$$$–$$$$ ✕▦ **Basin Harbor Club.** Owned by the Beach family since 1886, this
★ outstanding resort sprawls over 700 acres of prime real estate overlooking Lake Champlain. Luxurious accommodations, a full roster of activities including an 18-hole Geoffrey Cornish golf course, boating (including a 40-ft tour boat), and a day-long children's program make Basin Harbor a popular spot for families. Some rooms have fireplaces, decks, or porches. The restaurant menu is classic American, and the wine list excellent. Coats and ties are required in common areas after 6 PM. ⊠ *Basin Harbor Rd., Vergennes 05491,* ☎ *802/475–2311 or 800/622–4000,* ℻ *802/475–6545. 38 rooms in 3 guest houses, 77 cottages. 2 restaurants, pool, 18-hole golf course, 5 tennis courts, health club, bicycles, boating, children's programs (in summer and on fall weekends). MAP and AP available. MC, V. Closed mid-Oct.–mid-May.*

$$$–$$$$ ✕▦ **Inn at Essex.** About 10 mi from downtown Burlington, near Essex Outlet Fair, is a state-of-the-art inn and conference center dressed in country clothing. Rooms with flowered wallpaper and reproduction period desks lend the place some character, and many of the rooms have fireplaces. The two restaurants—the refined Butler's and the more casual Tavern—are run by the New England Culinary Institute. The sophisticated American cuisine at Butler's includes dishes such as sweet dumpling squash with ginger-garlic basmati rice, and lobster in yellow-corn sauce with spinach pasta. Five-onion soup, burgers, and daily flat-bread pizza specials are among the highlights at the Tavern. ⊠ *70 Essex Way, off Rte. 15, Essex Junction 05452,* ☎ *802/878–1100 or 800/288–7613,* ℻ *802/878–0063. 97 rooms. 2 restaurants, bar, pool, billiards, library. Continental breakfast. AE, D, DC, MC, V.*

$$–$$$$ ✕▦ **Inn at Shelburne Farms.** This is storybook land: Built at the turn
★ of the century as the home of William Seward and Lila Vanderbilt Webb, the Tudor-style inn perches on Saxton's Point overlooking Lake Champlain, the distant Adirondacks, and the sea of pastures that make up this 1,400-acre working farm. Each room is different, from the wallpaper to the period antiques. The two dining rooms ($$$–$$$$) define elegance, and the seasonal contemporary menu makes clever use of local ingredients. Sunday brunch (not served in May) is one of the

area's best. The inn's profits help support the farm's environmental education programs for local schools. ⊠ *Harbor Rd., Shelburne 05482,* ☎ *802/985–8498,* FAX *802/985–8123. 24 rooms, 17 with bath. Restaurant, lake, tennis court, hiking, boating, fishing, billiards, recreation room. AE, D, DC, MC, V. Closed mid-Oct.–mid-May.*

$$$ ✕⊞ **Radisson Hotel–Burlington.** This sleek corporate giant, which faces the lakefront, is the hotel closest to downtown shopping. Some rooms have incredible views of the Adirondack Mountains. The hotel's restaurant serves traditional but inspired Continental fare. ⊠ *60 Battery St., 05401,* ☎ *802/658–6500 or 800/333–3333,* FAX *802/658–4659. 255 rooms. 2 restaurants, bar, indoor pool, exercise room, airport shuttle. AE, D, DC, MC, V.*

$$–$$$$ ⊞ **Willard Street Inn.** High in the historic hill section of Burlington, this grand house with an exterior marble staircase and English gardens incorporates elements of Queen Anne and Colonial–Georgian Revival styles. The stately foyer, paneled in cherry, leads to a more formal sitting room with velvet drapes. The solarium is bright and sunny with marble floors, many plants, and big velvet couches to relax in while you contemplate views of Lake Champlain. All the rooms have down comforters and phones; some have lake views and canopied beds. Orange French toast is among the breakfast favorites. ⊠ *349 S. Willard St., 05401,* ☎ *802/651–8710 or 800/577–8712,* FAX *802/651–8714. 15 rooms, 12 with bath. Full breakfast. AE, D, DC, MC, V.*

Nightlife and the Arts

NIGHTLIFE

Name and local musicians come to **Higher Ground** (⊠ 1 Main St., Winooski, ☎ 802/654–8888). The music at the **Metronome** (⊠ 188 Main St., ☎ 802/865–4563) ranges from cutting-edge sounds to funk, blues, and reggae. The band Phish got its start at **Nectar's** (⊠ 188 Main St., ☎ 802/658–4771). This place is always jumping to the sounds of local bands and never charges a cover. **Vermont Pub and Brewery** (⊠ 144 College St., ☎ 802/865–0500) makes its own beer and fruit seltzers and is arguably the most popular spot in town. Folk musicians play here regularly.

THE ARTS

Burlington City Arts (☎ 802/865–7166; 802/865–9163 for 24-hr Artsline) has up-to-date arts-related information. **Flynn Theatre for the Performing Arts** (⊠ 153 Main St., ☎ 802/652–4500 for information; 802/863–5966 for tickets), a grandiose old structure, is the cultural heart of Burlington; it schedules the Vermont Symphony Orchestra, theater, dance, big-name musicians, and lectures. The **Lyric Theater** (☎ 802/658–1484) puts on musical productions in the fall and spring at the Flynn Theatre (☞ *above*). **St. Michael's Playhouse** (⊠ St. Michael's College, Rte. 15, Colchester, ☎ 802/654–2281 box office; 802/654–2617 administrative office) performs in the McCarthy Arts Center Theater. The **UVM Lane Series** (☎ 802/656–4455 for programs and times; 802/656–3085 for box office) sponsors classical as well as folk music concerts in the Flynn Theatre, Ira Allen Chapel, and the UVM Recital Hall.

Outdoor Activities and Sports

BEACHES

Some of the most scenic Lake Champlain beaches are on the Champlain Islands. **Knight Point State Park** (⊠ U.S. 2, North Hero, ☎ 802/372–8389) occupies a lovely spot in the Lake Champlain Islands, midway between mainland Vermont and New York State. **North Hero State Park** (⊠ Lakeview Dr. off U.S. 2, North Hero ☎ 802/372–8727) has a children's play area nearby. **Sand Bar State Park** (⊠ U.S. 2, Milton, ☎ 802/893–2825) has a great beach for small kids, with an extremely gentle drop-off. Arrive early to beat the summer crowds. Admission is $1; the park is open from mid-May to October.

The **North Beaches** are on the northern edge of Burlington: North Beach Park (⊠ Off North Ave., ☎ 802/864–0123), Bayside Beach (⊠ Rte. 127 near Malletts Bay), and Leddy Beach (⊠ Leddy Park Rd., off North Ave.), which is popular for sailboarding.

BIKING

A recreational path runs 9 mi along Burlington's waterfront. South of Burlington, a moderately easy 18½-mi trail begins at the blinker on U.S. 7 in Shelburne and follows Mt. Philo Road, Hinesburg Road, Route 116, and Irish Hill Road. **North Star Cyclery** (⊠ 100 Main St., ☎ 802/863–3832) and **Ski Rack** (⊠ 81 Main St., ☎ 802/658–3313) rent equipment and provide maps.

STATE PARKS

Grand Isle State Park (⊠ U.S. 2, 1 mi south of Grand Isle, ☎ 802/372–4300) has a fitness trail, hiking, and boat rentals. **Kill Kare State Park** (⊠ Rte. 36, on the mainland 4½ mi west of St. Albans Bay, then south on town road 3½ mi, ☎ 802/524–6021) is popular for camping, sailboarding, and hiking and also has boat rentals. There is ferry service from Kill Kare State Park to **Burton Island** (☎ 802/524–6353), a state park (with campsites) accessible only by water.

WATER SPORTS

Marina services are available north and south of Burlington. **Malletts Bay Marina** (⊠ 228 Lakeshore Dr., Colchester, ☎ 802/862–4072) and **Point Bay Marina** (⊠ 1401 Thompson's Point Rd., Charlotte, ☎ 802/425–2431) provide full service and repairs.

Burlington Community Boathouse (⊠ Foot of College St., Burlington Harbor, ☎ 802/865–3377) rents Jet Skis, sailboards, sailboats from 13 ft to 40 ft, and motorboats (some captained); the boathouse also gives lessons. **Marble Island Resort** (⊠ Colchester, ☎ 802/864–6800) has a marina and a nine-hole golf course.

Shopping

ANTIQUES

Architectural Salvage Warehouse (⊠ 212 Battery St., ☎ 802/658–5011) has claw-foot tubs, stained-glass windows, mantels, andirons, and the like. The large rhinoceros head bursting out of the **Conant Custom Brass** (⊠ 270 Pine St., ☎ 802/658–4482) storefront may tempt you in to see the custom work; the store specializes in decorative lighting and bathroom fixtures.

COUNTRY STORE

Shelburne Country Store (⊠ Village Green, off U.S. 7, Shelburne, ☎ 802/985–3657) offers a step back in time as you walk past the pot-bellied stove and take in the aroma emanating from the fudge neatly piled behind huge antique glass cases. Candles, weather vanes, glassware, and Vermont food products are its specialties.

CRAFTS

In addition to its popular pottery, **Bennington Potters North** (⊠ 127 College St., ☎ 802/863–2221) stocks interesting gifts, glassware, furniture, and other housewares. **Vermont State Craft Center** (⊠ 85 Church St., ☎ 802/863–6458) displays contemporary and traditional crafts by more than 200 Vermont artisans. **Yankee Pride** (⊠ Champlain Mill, E. Canal St., Winooski, ☎ 802/655–0500) has a large inventory of quilting fabrics and supplies as well as Vermont-made quilts.

MALLS AND MARKETPLACES

Burlington Square Mall (⊠ Church St., ☏ 802/658–2545) contains Porteous (the city's major department store, although at press time a new Filene's was set to open in fall 1999) and a few dozen shops. The **Champlain Mill** (⊠ U.S. 2/7, northeast of Burlington, ☏ 802/655–9477), a former woolen mill on the banks of the Winooski River, holds three floors of stores. **Church Street Marketplace** (⊠ Main St.–Pearl St., ☏ 802/863–1648), a pedestrian thoroughfare, is lined with boutiques, cafés, and street vendors. Built to resemble a ship, the **Wing Building** (⊠ Foot of King St., next to the ferry dock) houses boutiques, a café, and an art gallery.

En Route The top of the mountain pass on Route 242 in Montgomery Center and the Jay Peak area affords vast views of Canada to the north and of Vermont's rugged Northeast Kingdom to the east.

Montgomery/Jay

③⑤ *51 mi northeast of Burlington.*

Montgomery is a small village near the Canadian border and Jay Peak ski resort. Amid the surrounding countryside are seven historic covered bridges. **Kilgore's Store** (⊠ Main St., Montgomery Center, ☏ 802/326–3058), an old-time country store with an antique soda fountain, is a great place to stock up on picnic supplies or enjoy a hearty bowl of soup and an overstuffed sandwich.

Dining and Lodging

$$ ✕🏠 **Inn on Trout River.** The large stove is often the center of attention in the two-tier living and dining area of this 100-year-old inn, though the piano, the library, and the pub with a U-shape bar are also eye-catching. Guest rooms are decorated in either English country cottage style or country Victorian, and all have down quilts and flannel sheets in winter. The largest room has a Franklin potbellied stove, a dressing area, and a claw-foot tub. The back lawn rambles down to the river, and llama treks are available for groups. The restaurant ($$–$$$) specializes in American and Continental fare with a heart-healthy emphasis. ⊠ *Main St., Montgomery Center 05471,* ☏ *802/326–4391 or 800/338–7049,* 🗏 *802/326–3194. 10 rooms. Restaurant, pub, recreation room, library. Full breakfast; MAP available. AE, D, MC, V.*

$–$$ ✕🏠 **Black Lantern.** Built in 1803 as a hotel for mill workers, the inn has been providing bed and board ever since. Though the feeling is country, touches of sophistication abound: Provençal-print wallpaper in the dining room, a subtle rag-roll finish in the rooms in the renovated building next door. All the suites have whirlpools, and most have fireplaces. An outdoor hot tub, sheltered by a gazebo, overlooks the mountains. The restaurant menu ($$–$$$) includes pan-seared salmon with a red pepper sauce and grilled lamb Margarite. ⊠ *Rte. 118, Montgomery Village 05470,* ☏ *802/326–4507 or 800/255–8661,* 🗏 *802/326–4077. 10 rooms, 6 suites. Restaurant. Full breakfast. AE, D, MC, V.*

$$$ 🏠 **Hotel Jay & Jay Peak Condominiums.** Ski-lodge simplicity was the decorating goal at the hotel, with wood paneling in the rooms, built-in headboards, and vinyl wallpaper in the bathroom. Right at the lifts, the ski-in, ski-out hotel is convenient for skiers. Rooms on the southwest side have a view of Jay Peak, and those on the north overlook the valley; upper floors have balconies. The 120 condominiums (most slopeside) have fireplaces, one to three bedrooms, modern kitchens, and washers and dryers. In winter, a minimum two-night stay is required, and lift tickets and some meals are included in the rates. The summer rates are low. ⊠ *Rte. 242, 05859,* ☏ *802/988–2611 or 800/451–4449,* 🗏 *802/988–4049. 48 rooms, 120 condos. Restaurant, bar,* *pool, hot tub, sauna, 2 tennis courts, recreation room. MAP in winter, Continental breakfast in summer. AE, D, DC, MC, V.*

Skiing and Snow Sports

JAY PEAK

Sticking up out of the flat farmland, Jay averages 332 in of snowfall a year—more than any other Vermont ski area. Its proximity to Québec attracts Montréalers and discourages eastern seaboarders; hence, the prices are moderate and the lift lines generally shorter than at other resorts. The area offers tram rides to the summit from mid-June through mid-September ($8) and, in season, rents mountain bikes. ⌧ *Rte. 242, Jay 05859,* ☎ *802/988–2611; 800/451–4449 outside VT.*

Downhill. Jay Peak is in fact two mountains with 64 trails, the highest reaching nearly 4,000 ft with a vertical drop of 2,153 ft, served by a 60-passenger tram (the only one in Vermont). The area also has a quad, a triple, two double chairlifts, and two T-bars. An expansion scheduled to be completed for the 1999–2000 season will include the addition of a 7,700-ft-long, high-speed quad chairlift—the longest in eastern North America; it will also add snowmaking capability to three trails. The smaller mountain has more straight-fall-line, expert terrain, and the tram-side peak has many curving and meandering trails perfectly suited for intermediate and beginning skiers. Jay, highly rated for gladed skiing by major skiing publications, has 19 gladed trails. Every morning at 9 AM the ski school offers a free tour, from the tram down one trail. The area has 80% snowmaking coverage.

Cross-country. A touring center at the base of the mountain has 32 km (20 mi) of groomed cross-country trails. A network of 200 km (124 mi) of trails is in the vicinity.

Child care. The child care center for youngsters ages 2 and older is open from 9 to 9. Guests of the Hotel Jay or the Jay Peak Condominiums receive this nursery care free, as well as free skiing for children ages 6 and under, evening care, and supervised dining at the hotel. Children from ages 5 to 12 can participate in an all-day SKIwee program, which includes lunch.

CROSS-COUNTRY SKIING

Hazen's Notch Cross Country Ski Center and B & B (Rte. 58, ☎ 802/326–4708), delightfully remote at any time of the year, has 50 km (31 mi) of marked and groomed trails and rents equipment and snow shoes.

En Route   The descent from Jay Peak on Route 101 leads to Route 100, which can be the beginning of a scenic loop tour of Routes 14, 5, 58, and back to 100, or it can take you east to the city of **Newport** on Lake Memphremagog. Newport long neglected its waterfront but has recently constructed a handsome new marina and lakeside pavilion. Downtown, too, is on the rebound, with several new shops and factory outlets, including **Bogner Factory Outlet** (⌧ 48 Main St., ☎ 802/334–0135), which sells men's and ladies' ski-, golf-, and sportswear.

You will encounter some of the most unspoiled areas in all Vermont on the drive south from Newport on either U.S. 5 or I–91 (I–91 is faster, but U.S. 5 is prettier). This region, the Northeast Kingdom, is named for the remoteness and stalwart independence that have helped preserve its rural nature.

Lake Willoughby

❸❻ *30 mi east of Montgomery (summer route; 50 mi by winter route), 28 mi north of St. Johnsbury.*

Flanking the eastern and western shores of Lake Willoughby, the cliffs of surrounding Mts. Pisgah and Hor drop to water's edge, giving this glacially carved, 500-ft-deep lake a striking resemblance to a Norwegian fjord. Some also compare the landscape to Lucerne's or Scotland's. In any case, Lake Willoughby is stunning. The lake is popular for summer and winter recreation, and the trails to the top of Mt. Pisgah reward hikers with glorious views.

The **Bread and Puppet Museum** is a ramshackle barn that houses a surrealistic collection of props used in past performances by the world-renowned Bread and Puppet Theater. The troupe, whose members live communally on the surrounding farm, have been performing social and political commentary with the towering (they're supported by people on stilts), eerily expressive puppets for about 30 years. ⊠ *Rte. 122, Glover, 1 mi east of Rte. 16,* ☎ *802/525–3031.* 🖃 *Donations accepted.* ☉ *June–Oct., daily 9–5; other times by appointment.*

Lodging

$$–$$$$ 🖬 **WilloughVale Inn & Restaurant.** Few Vermont inns can claim a more spectacular location than this waterfront property at the northern end of Lake Willoughby. The main building, with its cozy dining room and wraparound veranda, has rooms with a water view and one spacious but unfortunately situated suite facing the rear of the building. An even better bet are the cottages on Willoughby's shore. They come with fully equipped kitchens, fireplaces, screened porches, and private docks. ⊠ *Rte. 5A, Westmore 05860,* ☎ *802/525–4123 or 800/594–9102,* 🖷 *802/ 525–4514. 7 rooms, 1 suite, 4 cottages. Boating. AE, MC, V.*

En Route   If it's a moose sighting you're after, head north on Route 114 toward **Island Pond.** A word of warning: Although the great beasts are fun to watch, they can be a deadly road hazard. When you see a "Moose" sign, cut your speed and watch the roadsides.

East Burke and West Burke

㊲   *17 mi south of Lake Willoughby.*

A jam-packed general store, a post office, and a couple of great places to eat are about all you'll find in the twin towns of East Burke and West Burke.

Dining and Lodging

$$–$$$ ✕ **River Garden Café.** You can eat outdoors on the enclosed porch or the patio and view the perennial gardens that rim the grounds; the café is bright and cheerful on the inside as well. The healthful fare includes roasted rack of lamb, warm artichoke dip, bruschetta, pastas, and fresh fish. ⊠ *Rte. 114, East Burke,* ☎ *802/626–3514. AE, D, MC, V. Closed Mon., Apr., and Nov.*

$$$ ✕🖬 **Wildflower Inn.** The hilltop views are great at this rambling com-
★   plex of old farm buildings on 500 acres. The rooms in the restored Federal-style main house and four other buildings are decorated simply with reproductions and contemporary furnishings. Rooms in the carriage house are somewhat dark and cramped; they have kitchenettes and bunk beds. In warm weather, the inn is family-oriented: There's a petting barn, planned children's activities, and a kid's swimming pool. At the restaurant ($–$$), homemade breads and vegetables grown in the garden accompany the country-style entrées. ⊠ *Darling Hill Rd., west of East Burke, Lyndonville 05851,* ☎ *802/626–8310 or 800/627– 8310,* 🖷 *802/626–3039. 12 rooms, 8 suites. Restaurant, pool, hot tub, sauna, tennis court, soccer, fishing, ice-skating, cross-country skiing, sleigh rides, sledding, recreation room. Full breakfast. MC, V. Closed Apr. and Nov.*

$ ✕⌂ **Old Cutter Inn.** A small converted farmhouse only ½ mi from the Burke Mountain base lodge offers quaint inn rooms in the main building, as well as comfortable if less charming accommodations in an annex. The restaurant ($$–$$$) serves fare that reflects the Swiss chef-owner's heritage, as well as superb Continental cuisine including osso buco and veal piccata. ⊠ *R.R. 1, Box 62, Old Pinkham Rd., East Burke 05832,* ☎ *802/626–5152 or 800/295–1943. 9 rooms, 5 with bath; 1 suite. Restaurant, bar, pool, hiking, biking, cross-country skiing. MAP available. D, MC, V. Closed Wed., Apr., and Nov.*

$$–$$$ ⌂ **Burke Mountain Resort.** The modern accommodations at this resort range from economical digs to luxurious slopeside town houses and condominiums with kitchens and TVs. Some rooms have fireplaces, and others have wood-burning stoves. A two-night minimum stay is required during winter months, and ski and lodging packages are available. ⊠ *Box 247, Burke Mountain Rd., East Burke 05832,* ☎ *802/626–3305 or 800/541–5480,* 𝖥𝖠𝖷 *802/626–3364. 150 condos. Restaurant. MC, V.*

Outdoor Activities and Sports

Village Sport Shop (⊠ 4 Broad St., Lyndonville, ☎ 802/626–8448) rents canoes, kayaks, bikes, rollerblades, paddleboats, snowshoes, and cross-country and downhill skis.

The **Wildflower Inn** (☞ Dining and Lodging, *above*) has 15-passenger sleighs drawn by Belgian draft horses.

Shopping

Bailey's Country Store (⊠ Rte. 114, East Burke, ☎ 802/626–3666), an institution, sells baked goods, wine, clothing, and sundries.

Skiing and Snow Sports

BURKE MOUNTAIN

This low-key, moderately priced resort draws many families from Massachusetts and Connecticut. There's plenty of terrain for beginners, but intermediate skiers, experts, racers, telemarkers, and snowboarders will find time-honored narrow New England trails. Many packages at Burke are significantly less expensive than those at other Vermont areas. Burke Mountain Academy has contributed a number of notable racers to the U.S. Ski Team. ⊠ *Mountain Rd., East Burke 05832,* ☎ *802/626–3305; 800/541–5480 for lodging; 800/922–2875 for snow conditions and special events.*

Downhill. With a 2,000-ft vertical drop, Burke is something of a sleeper among the larger Eastern ski areas. It has greatly increased its snowmaking capability (60%), which is enhanced by the mountain's northern location and exposure, assuring plenty of natural snow. In a recent expansion, a trail was developed on the east side of the mountain, and a snowboard park (with snowmaking capabilities) for all levels was created. Burke has one quad, one double chairlift, and two surface lifts. Lift lines, even on weekends and holidays, are light to nonexistent.

Cross-country. Burke Ski Touring Center has more than 95 km (57 mi) of trails (65 km/39 mi groomed); some lead to high points with scenic views. There's a snack bar at the center.

Child care. In the Children's Center, the nursery takes children from ages 6 months to 6 years. SKIwee and MINIriders lessons through the ski school are available to children from ages 4 to 16.

St. Johnsbury

③⑧   *16 mi south of East Burke, 39 mi east of Montpelier.*

St. Johnsbury is the southern gateway to the Northeast Kingdom.

Though the town was chartered in 1786, its identity was not firmly established until 1830, when Thaddeus Fairbanks invented the platform scale, a device that revolutionized weighing methods that had been in use since the beginning of recorded history. Because of the Fairbanks family's philanthropic bent, this city with a distinctly 19th-century industrial feel has a strong cultural and architectural imprint.

Opened in 1891, the **Fairbanks Museum and Planetarium** attests to the Fairbanks family's inquisitiveness about all things scientific. The redbrick building in the squat Romanesque Revival architectural style of H. H. Richardson houses Vermont plants and animals, as well as ethnographic and natural history collections from around the globe. There's also an intimate 50-seat planetarium and a hands-on exhibit room for kids. On the third Saturday in September, the museum sponsors the annual Festival of Traditional Crafts, with demonstrations of early American household and farm skills such as candle and soap making. ✉ *Main and Prospect Sts.*, ☎ *802/748–2372.* ☞ *$5.* ☉ *July–Aug., Mon.–Sat. 10–6, Sun. 1–5; Sept.–June, Mon.–Sat. 10–4, Sun. 1–5. Planetarium shows July–Aug., daily at 11 and 1:30; Sept.–June, weekends at 1:30.*

The **St. Johnsbury Athenaeum,** with its dark rich paneling, polished Victorian woodwork, and ornate circular staircases that rise to the gallery around the perimeter, is one of the oldest art galleries in the country. The gallery at the back of the building specializes in Hudson River School paintings and has the overwhelming *Domes of Yosemite* by Albert Bierstadt. ✉ *30 Main St.*, ☎ *802/748–8291.* ☞ *Free.* ☉ *Mon. and Wed. 10–8; Tues. and Thurs.–Fri. 10–5:30; Sat. 9:30–4.*

OFF THE
BEATEN PATH

CABOT CREAMERY – The biggest cheese producer in the state, a dairy cooperative, has a visitor center with an audiovisual presentation about the state's dairy and cheese industry. You can taste samples, purchase cheese, and tour the plant. The center is midway between Barre and St. Johnsbury. ✉ *2870 Main St./Rte. 215, 3 mi north of U.S 2, Cabot,* ☎ *802/563–2231; 800/639–4031 for orders only.* ☞ *$1.* ☉ *June–Oct., daily 9–5; Nov.–Dec. and mid-Feb.–May, Mon.–Sat. 9–4.*

Dining and Lodging

$$$$　✕☵ **Rabbit Hill Inn.** The rooms at Rabbit Hill are all different: The Loft, with an 8-ft Palladian window, a king canopy bed, a double whirlpool bath, and a corner fireplace, is one of the most requested. Rooms toward the front of the inn have views of the Connecticut River and New Hampshire's White Mountains. The low wooden beams of the Irish pub are a casual contrast to the rest of the inn. The low-ceiling dining room ($$$) serves regional cuisine, perhaps grilled sausage of Vermont pheasant with pistachios or smoked chicken and red lentil dumplings nestled in red-pepper linguine. Meat and fish are smoked on the premises, and the herbs and vegetables often come from gardens out back. A two-night minimum stay is required on weekends. ✉ *Rte. 18, Lower Waterford, 11 mi south of St. Johnsbury, 05848,* ☎ *802/748–5168 or 800/762–8669,* ☒ *802/748–8342. 16 rooms, 5 suites. Restaurant, pub, hiking, cross-country skiing. MAP. AE, MC, V. Closed 1st 3 wks of Apr., 1st 2 wks of Nov.*

Nightlife and the Arts

Catamount Arts (✉ 60 Eastern Ave., ☎ 802/748–2600) brings avantgarde theater and dance performances to the Northeast Kingdom as well as films and classical music.

Peacham

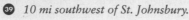 *10 mi southwest of St. Johnsbury.*

Tiny Peacham's stunning scenery and 18th-century charm have made it a favorite with urban refugees, artists seeking solitude and inspiration, and movie directors looking for the quintessential New England village. *Ethan Frome,* starring Liam Neeson, was filmed here.

Gourmet soups and hearty lamb and barley stew are among the seasonally changing take-out specialties at the **Peacham Store** (⊠ Main St., ☎ 802/592–3310). You can browse through the locally made crafts while waiting for your order. The store was a location for the filming of the 1996 movie *The Spitfire Grill.*

Barre

⓾ *7 mi east of Montpelier, 35 mi south of St. Johnsbury.*

Barre has been famous as the source of Vermont granite ever since two men began working the quarries in the early 1800s; the large number of immigrant laborers attracted to the industry made the city prominent in the early years of the American labor movement. Downtown, at the corner of Maple and North Main, look for the statue of a representative Italian stonecutter of a century ago. On Route 14, just north of Barre, stop at **Hope Cemetery** to see spectacular examples of carving.

You might recognize the sheer walls of the **Rock of Ages granite quarry** from *Batman and Robin,* the film starring George Clooney and Arnold Schwarzenegger. The attractions of the site range from the awe-inspiring (the quarry resembles the Grand Canyon in miniature) to the mildly ghoulish (you can consult a directory of tombstone dealers throughout the country). At the craft center, you can watch skilled artisans sculpt monuments; at the quarries themselves, 25-ton blocks of stone are cut from sheer 475-ft walls by workers who clearly earn their pay. ⊠ *Exit 6 off I–89, follow Rte. 63,* ☎ *802/476–3119.* 🎟 *Tour of active quarry $4, craftsman center and self-guided tour free.* ☉ *Visitor center daily May-Oct., except July 4; narrated tours every 45 mins 9:15–3 weekdays only June–mid-Oct.*

Dining

$–$$ ✕ **A Single Pebble.** Devotees of Chinese food have been making a pilgrimage to this restaurant since it opened in 1997. Chef and co-owner Steve Bogart has been cooking Asian dishes for more than 30 years, and he emphasizes authenticity as well as creativity. He prepares traditional clay pot dishes as well as wok specialties such as sesame catfish, Ants Climbing a Tree (a Szechuan dish of pork and cellophane noodles), and kung po chicken. The dry fried green beans (sautéed with flecks of pork, black beans, preserved vegetables, and garlic), mock eel (thinly sliced shiitake mushrooms), and Spicy Three River Soup are house specialties. All dishes can be made without meat. ⊠ *135 Barre-Montpelier Rd.,* ☎ *802/476–9700. D, MC, V. Closed Sun.–Mon. and Aug. No lunch.*

Nightlife and the Arts

Barre Opera House (⊠ City Hall, Main St., ☎ 802/476–8188) hosts music, opera, theater, and dance performances.

Northern Vermont A to Z

Arriving and Departing
See Vermont A to Z, *below.*

Getting Around

BY BUS

Vermont Transit (☎ 802/864–6811; 800/451–3292; 800/642–3133 in VT) links Burlington, Waterbury, Montpelier, St. Johnsbury, and Newport.

BY CAR

In north-central Vermont, I–89 heads west from Montpelier to Burlington and continues north to Canada. Interstate 91 is the principal north–south route in the east, and Route 100 runs north–south through the center of the state. North of I–89, Routes 104 and 15 provide a major east–west transverse. From Barton, U.S. 5 and Route 122 south are beautiful drives. Strip-mall drudge bogs down the section of U.S. 5 around Lyndonville.

BY FERRY

Lake Champlain Ferries (☎ 802/864–9804), in operation since 1826, operates three ferry crossings during the summer months and one— between Grand Isle and Plattsburgh, New York—in winter through thick lake ice. Ferries leave from the King Street Dock in Burlington, Charlotte, and Grand Isle. This is a convenient means of getting to and from New York, as well as a pleasant way to spend an afternoon.

BY TRAIN

The *Champlain Valley Weekender* runs between Middlebury and Burlington, with stops in Vergennes and Shelburne. The views from the coach cars, which date from the 1930s, are of Lake Champlain, the valley farmlands, and surrounding mountains. ☎ 802/463–3069 or 800/707–3530. ✉ $12 round-trip. ☼ July–early Sept., weekends, 2 trips per day.

Contacts and Resources

EMERGENCIES

Fletcher Allen Health Care (✉ 111 Colchester Ave., Burlington, ☎ 802/656–2345). For 24-hour medical health care information, call ☎ 802/656–2439.

GUIDED TOURS

P.O.M.G. Bike Tours of Vermont (✉ Richmond, ☎ 802/434–2270) leads weekend and five-day adult camping–bike tours.

True North Kayak Tours (✉ 53 Nash Pl., Burlington, ☎ 802/860–1910) operates a guided tour of Lake Champlain, a natural-history tour, and will arrange a custom multiday trip. The company also coordinates special trips for kids.

HIKING

The **Green Mountain Club** (✉ Rte. 100, Waterbury, ☎ 802/244–7037) maintains the Long Trail—the north–south border-to-border footpath that runs the length of the spine of the Green Mountains—as well as other trails nearby. The club headquarters sells maps and guides, and experts dispense advice.

LODGING REFERRAL SERVICE

The **Stowe Area Association** (☎ 800/247–8693) has a lodging referral service.

VISITOR INFORMATION

Lake Champlain Regional Chamber of Commerce (✉ 60 Main St., Suite 100, Burlington 05401, ☎ 802/863–3489). **Northeast Kingdom Chamber of Commerce** (✉ 30 Western Ave., St. Johnsbury 05819, ☎ 802/748–3678 or 800/639–6379). **Smugglers' Notch Area Chamber of Commerce** (✉ Box 364, Jeffersonville 05464, ☎ 802/644–2239).

The **Stowe Area Association** (✉ Main St., Box 1320, Stowe 05672, ☎ 802/253–7321 or 800/247–8693). **Vermont North Country Chamber of Commerce** (✉ The Causeway, Newport 05855, ☎ 802/334–7782 or 800/635–4643).

VERMONT A TO Z

Arriving and Departing

By Bus

Bonanza (☎ 800/556–3815) connects New York City and Providence with Bennington. **Vermont Transit** (☎ 802/864–6811 or 800/552–8737) connects Bennington, Brattleboro, Burlington, Rutland, and other Vermont cities and towns with Boston, Springfield, Albany, New York, Montréal, and cities in New Hampshire.

By Car

Interstate–91, which stretches from Connecticut and Massachusetts in the south to Québec in the north, reaches most points along Vermont's eastern border. I–89, from New Hampshire to the east and Québec to the north, crosses central Vermont from White River Junction to Burlington. Southwestern Vermont can be reached by U.S. 7 from Massachusetts and U.S. 4 from New York.

By Plane

Continental, Delta, United, and US Airways fly into **Burlington International Airport** (✉ Airport Dr., 4 mi east of Burlington off U.S. 2, ☎ 802/863–1889). **Rutland State Airport** (☎ 802/786–8881) has daily service to and from Boston on Colgan Air. West of Bennington and convenient to southern Vermont, **Albany–Schenectady County Airport** (☎ 518/869–3021) in New York State is served by 10 major U.S. carriers. *See* Air Travel *in* Smart Travel Tips A to Z for airline numbers.

By Train

Amtrak's (☎ 800/872–7245) *Vermonter* is a daytime service linking Washington, D.C., with Brattleboro, Bellows Falls, White River Junction, Montpelier, Waterbury, Essex Junction, and St. Albans. The *Adirondack,* which runs from Washington, D.C., to Montréal, serves Albany, Ft. Edward (near Glens Falls), Ft. Ticonderoga, and Plattsburgh, allowing relatively convenient access to western Vermont. The *Ethan Allen Express* connects New York City with Fair Haven and Rutland.

Getting Around

By Car

The official speed limit in Vermont is 50 mph, unless otherwise posted; on the interstates it's 65 mph. Right turns are permitted on a red light unless otherwise indicated. You can get a state map, which has mileage charts and enlarged maps of major downtown areas, free from the Vermont Travel Division. The *Vermont Atlas and Gazetteer,* sold in many bookstores, shows nearly every road in the state and is great for driving on the back roads.

By Plane

Aircraft charters are available at Burlington International Airport from **Valet Air Services** (☎ 802/863–3626 or 800/782–0773). **Mansfield Heliflight** (✉ Milton, ☎ 802/893–1003) provides helicopter transportation throughout New England.

Contacts and Resources

The Arts
Vermont Symphony Orchestra (☎ 802/864–5741) performs throughout Vermont.

B&B Reservation Agencies
American Country Collection of Bed and Breakfasts (✉ 1353 Union St., Schenectady, NY 12308, ☎ 518/370–4948 or 800/810–4948). You can also try calling the chambers of commerce in many ski areas.

Camping
Call Vermont's **Department of Forests, Parks, and Recreation** (☎ 802/241–3655) for a copy of the Vermont Campground Guide, which lists state parks and other public and private camping facilities.

For **camping reservations in state parks** in southeastern Vermont, call ☎ 802/885–8891 or 800/299–3071; in southwestern Vermont, ☎ 802/483–2001 or 800/658–1622; in northwestern Vermont, ☎ 802/879–5674 or 800/252–2363; in northeastern Vermont, ☎ 802/479–4280 or 800/658–6934. These numbers are used from the second Tuesday in January through May 1; after that, call the individual parks for reservations. Between Labor Day and January, no reservations are taken.

Emergencies
Ambulance, fire, police (☎ 911). **Medical Health Care Information Center** (☎ 802/864–0454). **Vermont State Police** (☎ 800/525–5555).

Fishing
For information about fishing, including licenses, call the **Vermont Department of Fish and Wildlife** (☎ 802/241–3700).

Foliage and Snow Hot Line
Call ☎ 802/828–3239 for tips on peak viewing locations and times and up-to-date snow conditions.

Guided Tours

BIKING
Bicycle Holidays (✉ Munger St., Middlebury, ☎ 802/388–2453 or 800/292–5388) creates custom-designed bike trips and will help you put together your own inn-to-inn tour by providing route directions and booking your accommodations. **Vermont Bicycle Touring** (✉ Monkton Rd., Bristol, ☎ 802/453–4811 or 800/245–3868) leads numerous tours throughout the state as well as throughout the rest of the country and in Europe.

CANOEING
Umiak Outdoor Outfitters (✉ 849 S. Main St., Stowe, ☎ 802/253–2317) has shuttles to nearby rivers for day excursions and customized overnight trips. **Vermont Canoe Trippers/Battenkill Canoe, Ltd.** (✉ River Rd., off Rte. 7A, Arlington, ☎ 802/362–2800) organizes canoe tours (some are inn-to-inn) and fishing trips.

FISHING
Strictly Trout (☎ 802/869–3116) will arrange a fly-fishing trip on any Vermont stream or river, including the Battenkill.

HIKING
New England Hiking Holidays (✉ North Conway, NH, ☎ 603/356–9696 or 800/869–0949) leads guided walks with lodging in country inns. **North Wind Hiking and Walking Tours** (✉ Waitsfield, ☎ 802/496–5771 or 800/496–5771) conducts guided walking tours through Vermont's countryside.

HORSEBACK RIDING

Kedron Valley Stables (✉ South Woodstock, ☎ 802/457–1480 or 800/ 225–6301) has one- to six-day riding tours with lodging in country inns.

Hiking

The **Green Mountain Club** (✉ Rte. 100, Waterbury Center, ☎ 802/244– 7037) publishes hiking maps and guides. The club also manages the Long Trail, the north–south trail that traverses the entire state.

Lodging Information

The **Vermont Chamber of Commerce** (☞ Visitor Information, *below*) publishes the *Vermont Travelers' Guidebook,* which is an extensive list of lodgings, and additional guides to country inns and vacation rentals. The **Vermont Travel Division** (☞ Visitor Information, *below*) has a brochure that lists lodgings at working farms.

State Parks

Vermont state parks open during the last week in May and close after the Labor Day or Columbus Day weekend, depending on location. Day-use charges are $2 per person for ages 14 and up, $1.50 for ages 4 to 13; children under 4 are free. Call individual parks or the **Department of Forests, Parks, and Recreation** (☎ 802/241–3655) for information.

Visitor Information

Forest Supervisor, Green Mountain National Forest (✉ 231 N. Main St., Rutland 05701, ☎ 802/747–6700). **Vermont Chamber of Commerce** (✉ Box 37, Montpelier 05601, ☎ 802/223–3443). **Vermont Travel Division** (✉ 134 State St., Montpelier 05602, ☎ 802/828–3237 or 800/ 837–6668). There are **state information centers** on the Massachusetts border at I–91, the New Hampshire border at I–89, the New York border at Route 4A, and the Canadian border at I–89.

4 MASSACHUSETTS

Only a half dozen states are smaller than Massachusetts, but few have influenced American life more profoundly. Generations of Bay State merchants, industrialists, and computer executives have charted the course of the country's economy; Massachusetts writers, artists, and academics have enriched American culture; and from the meeting house to the White House, the state's politicians, philosophers, and pundits have fueled national debates.

MASSACHUSETTS SEABOARD TOWNS—from New-buryport to Provincetown—were built before the Revolution, during the heyday of American shipping. These coastal villages evoke a bygone world of clipper ships, robust fishermen, and sturdy sailors bound for distant Cathay. In our own time, the high-tech firms of the greater Boston area helped to launch the information age, and the Massachusetts Institute of Technology (MIT) and Harvard supplied intellectual heft to deliver it to the wider world.

The Massachusetts town meeting set the tone for politics in the 13 original colonies. A century later, Boston was a hotbed of rebellion—Samuel Adams and James Otis, the "Sons of Liberty," started a war with words, inciting action against British colonial policies with patriotic pamphlets and fiery speeches at Faneuil Hall. Twentieth-century heirs to Adams include Boston's flashy midcentury mayor James Michael Curley; Thomas "Tip" O'Neill, the late Speaker of the House; and, of course, the Kennedys. In 1961, the young senator from the Boston suburb of Brookline, John Fitzgerald Kennedy, became president of the United States. JFK's service to Massachusetts was family tradition: In the years before World War I, Kennedy's grandfather John "Honey Fitz" Fitzgerald served in Congress and as mayor of Boston. But political families are nothing new here—Massachusetts is the only state that has sent both a father and a son (John Adams and John Quincy Adams) to the White House.

Massachusetts has an extensive system of parks, protected forests, beaches, and nature preserves. Like medieval pilgrims, readers of *Walden* come to Concord to visit the place where Henry David Thoreau wrote his prophetic essay. Thoreau's disciples can be found hiking to the top of the state's highest peak, Mt. Greylock; shopping for organic produce in an unpretentious college burg like Williamstown; or strolling the beaches of Cape Cod. For those who prefer the hills to the ocean, the rolling Berkshire terrain defines the landscape from North Adams to Great Barrington in the western part of the state. A favorite vacation spot since the 19th century, when eastern aristocrats built grand summer residences, the Berkshire Hills have been described as an inland Newport. This area attracts vacationers seeking superb scenery and food and an active cultural scene.

The list of Bay State writers, artists, and musicians who have shaped American culture is long indeed. The state has produced great poets in every generation: Anne Bradstreet, Phillis Wheatley, Emily Dickinson, Henry Wadsworth Longfellow, William Cullen Bryant, e.e. cummings, Robert Lowell, Elizabeth Bishop, Sylvia Plath, and Anne Sexton. Massachusetts writers include Louisa May Alcott, author of the enduring classic *Little Women*; Nathaniel Hawthorne, who re-created the Salem of his Puritan ancestors in *The Scarlet Letter*; Herman Melville, who wrote *Moby-Dick* in a house at the foot of Mt. Greylock; Eugene O'Neill, whose early plays were produced at a makeshift theater in Provincetown on Cape Cod; Lowell native Jack Kerouac, author of *On the Road*; and John Cheever, chronicler of suburban angst. Painters Winslow Homer and James McNeill Whistler both hailed from the Commonwealth. Norman Rockwell, the quintessential American illustrator, lived and worked in Stockbridge. Celebrated composer and Boston native Leonard Bernstein was the first American to conduct the New York Philharmonic. Joan Baez got her start singing in Harvard Square, and contemporary Boston singer-songwriter Tracy Chapman picked up the beat with folk songs for the new age.

Pleasures and Pastimes

Beaches
Massachusetts has many excellent beaches, especially on Cape Cod, where the waves are gentle and the water cool. Southside beaches, on Nantucket Sound, have rolling surf and are warmer. Open-ocean beaches on the Cape Cod National Seashore are cold and have serious surf. Parking lots fill up by 10 AM. Beaches not restricted to residents charge parking fees; for weekly or seasonal passes, contact the local town hall.

Bostonians head for wide sweeps of sand along the North Shore (beware of biting blackflies in late May and early June), among them Singing Beach in Manchester, Plum Island in Newburyport, and Crane Beach in Ipswich. Boston city beaches are not particularly attractive and definitely not for swimming, though the ongoing rehabilitation of Boston Harbor has made them somewhat cleaner.

Boating
Cape Cod and the North Shore are centers for ocean-going pleasure craft, with public mooring available in many towns—phone numbers for public marinas are listed under Contacts and Resources in the regional A to Z sections below, or you can contact local chambers of commerce (☞ Visitor Information in the A to Z sections). Sea kayaking is popular along the marshy coastline of the North Shore, where freshwater canoeing is also an option. Inland, the Connecticut River in the Pioneer Valley is navigable by all types of craft between the Turners Falls Dam, just north of Greenfield, and the Holyoke Dam. The large dams control the water level daily, so you will notice a tidal effect; if you have a large boat, beware of sandbanks. Canoes can also travel north of Turners Falls beyond the Vermont border; canoeing is also popular in the lakes and small rivers of the Berkshires.

Dining
Massachusetts invented the fried clam, which appears on many North Shore and Cape Cod menus. Creamy clam chowder is another specialty. Eating seafood "in the rough"—from paper plates in shacklike buildings—is a revered local custom.

Boston restaurants serve New England standards and cutting-edge cuisine. At country inns in the Berkshires and the Pioneer Valley you'll find traditional New England "dinners" strongly reminiscent of old England: double-cut pork chops, rack of lamb, game, Boston baked beans, Indian pudding, and the dubiously glorified "New England boiled dinner." On the Cape, ethnic specialties such as Portuguese kale soup and linguiça sausage appear on menus. The Cape's first-rate gourmet restaurants (with prices to match) include several in Brewster; on Nantucket and Martha's Vineyard, top-line establishments prepare traditional and innovative fare.

On the North Shore, Rockport is a "dry" town, though you can almost always take your own alcohol into restaurants; most places charge a nominal corking fee. This law leads to early closing hours—many Rockport dining establishments close by 9 PM.

Fishing
Deep-sea fishing trips depart from Boston, Cape Cod, and the South and North shores; surf casting is popular on the North Shore. The rivers, lakes, and streams of the Pioneer Valley and Berkshire County abound with fish—bass, pike, and perch, to name but a few. Stocked trout waters include the Hoosic River (south branch) near Cheshire; the Green River around Great Barrington; Notch Brook and the Hoosic River

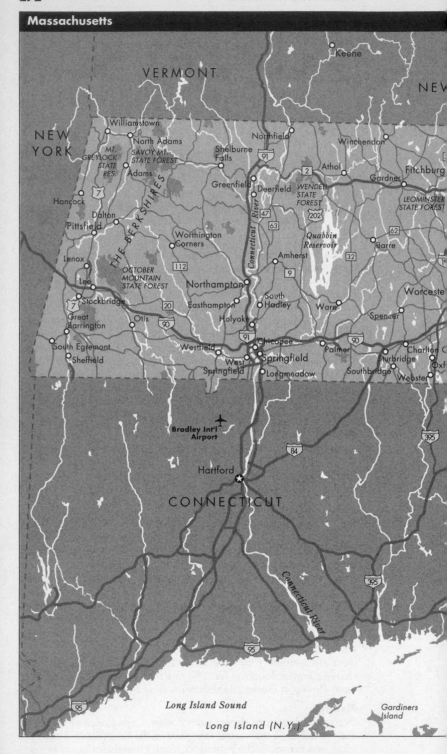

VERMONT

Keene

NEW

NEW
YORK

Williamstown

North Adams

SAVOY MT.
STATE FOREST

Shelburne
Falls

Northfield

Winchendon

Fitchburg

MT.
GREYLOCK
STATE
RES.

Adams

91

2

Athol

Gardner

Hancock

THE BERKSHIRES

Greenfield

Deerfield

WENDELL
STATE
FOREST

LEOMINSTER
STATE FOREST

Dalton

Pittsfield

Worthington
Corners

47

63

202

Quabbin
Reservoir

62

Barre

Lenox

OCTOBER
MOUNTAIN
STATE FOREST

112

Amherst

32

9

Worcester

Lee

7

Stockbridge

20

Northampton

Easthampton

South
Hadley

Ware

Spencer

Great
Barrington

Otis

90

Holyoke

91

Chicopee

Springfield

90

Palmer

Sturbridge

Charlton

Oxf

South Egremont

Sheffield

Westfield

West
Springfield

Longmeadow

Southbridge

Webster

Connecticut River

✈ Bradley Int'l
Airport

84

395

Hartford ★

CONNECTICUT

395

Connecticut River

95

95

Long Island Sound

Gardiners
Island

Long Island (N.Y.)

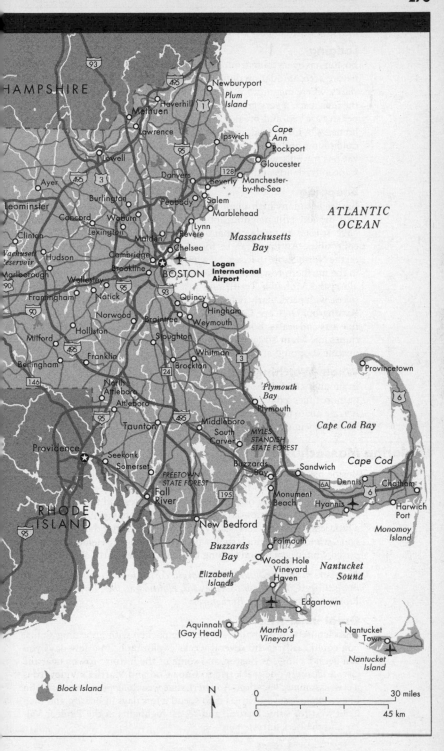

NEW HAMPSHIRE

Newburyport
Plum Island
Haverhill
Methuen
Lawrence
Ipswich
Cape Ann
Rockport
Lowell
Danvers
Gloucester
Ayer
Beverly
Manchester-by-the-Sea
Burlington
Peabody
Salem
Leominster
Concord
Woburn
Marblehead
Clinton
Lexington
Lynn
ATLANTIC OCEAN
Wachusett Reservoir
Hudson
Malden
Revere
Marlborough
Cambridge
Chelsea
Massachusetts Bay
Wellesley
Brookline
BOSTON
Logan International Airport
Framingham
Natick
Quincy
Norwood
Hingham
Holliston
Braintree
Weymouth
Milford
Stoughton
Bellingham
Franklin
Whitman
Brockton
North Attleboro
Attleboro
Plymouth Bay
Taunton
Middleboro
Plymouth
Providence
South Carver
MYLES STANDISH STATE FOREST
Cape Cod Bay
Seekonk
Somerset
FREETOWN STATE FOREST
Buzzards Bay
Sandwich
Cape Cod
Provincetown
RHODE ISLAND
Fall River
Monument Beach
Dennis
Chatham
New Bedford
Hyannis
Harwich Port
Falmouth
Monomoy Island
Buzzards Bay
Woods Hole
Vineyard Haven
Nantucket Sound
Elizabeth Islands
Edgartown
Nantucket Town
Aquinnah (Gay Head)
Martha's Vineyard
Nantucket Island
Block Island

N

0   30 miles
0   45 km

(north branch) near North Adams; Goose Pond and Hop Brook around Lee; and the Williams River around West Stockbridge.

Lodging

Boston has everything from luxury hotels to charming B&Bs. The signature accommodation outside Boston is the country inn; in the Berkshires, where magnificent mansions have been converted into lodgings, the inns reach a very grand scale indeed. Less extravagant and less expensive are bed-and-breakfast establishments, many of them in private homes. On Cape Cod, inns are plentiful, and rental homes and condominiums are available for long-term stays. Be sure to make reservations for inns well in advance during peak periods: summer on the Cape and islands and summer through winter in the Berkshires.

Shopping

Boston has many high-quality shops, especially in the Newbury Street and Beacon Hill neighborhoods, and most suburban communities have at least a couple of main-street stores selling old furniture and collectibles. Antiques can be found on the South Shore in Plymouth; on the North Shore in Essex, Newburyport, Marblehead, and elsewhere; in the northern towns of the Pioneer Valley (especially in Amherst or along the Mohawk Trail); and just about everywhere in the Berkshires, with particularly rich hunting grounds around Sheffield and Great Barrington. On Cape Cod, Provincetown and Wellfleet are centers for fine arts and crafts. Bookstores, gift shops, jewelers, and clothing boutiques line Main Street in Hyannis. Chatham's Main Street is a pretty, upscale shopping area.

Whale-Watching

In summer and fall, boats leave Boston, Cape Cod, and Cape Ann two or more times a day to observe the whales feeding a few miles offshore. It's rare not to have the extraordinary experience of seeing several whales, most of them extremely close up.

Exploring Massachusetts

Boston has the museums, the history, the shopping, and the traffic; Cape Cod and the North and South shores have beaches, more history, more shopping, and plenty of traffic. In the Berkshires and the Pioneer Valley you'll find centuries-old towns, antiques shopping, green hills, and a little less traffic. There's beauty to be discovered after the tourists have gone, wandering through snowy fields or braving the elements on a deserted winter beach, and sipping hot cider at the hearth of a local inn.

Numbers in the text and in the margin correspond to numbers on the maps: Cape Cod, Martha's Vineyard, Nantucket, the North Shore, the Pioneer Valley, and the Berkshires.

Great Itineraries

Massachusetts is a small state but one packed with appealing sights; you could easily spend several weeks exploring it. In a few days you can get a feeling for Boston and some of the historic towns near the city. A leisurely one-week trip to Cape Cod and Martha's Vineyard is a classic summer vacation. An alternative weeklong plan for those who like to explore several areas is to spend a few days in Boston and then head west for some historic and scenic highlights in the Pioneer Valley and the Berkshires.

IF YOU HAVE 3 DAYS

Spend two days touring 🖽 **Boston.** On the third day either swing west on Route 2 and tour **Lexington** and **Concord** or north on Route 1A and east on Route 129 to **Marblehead** ㉘. Explore Marblehead and have lunch there before heading west on Route 114 and north on Route 1A to **Salem** ㉙.

IF YOU HAVE 7 DAYS TO SPEND ON THE CAPE

Head south from Boston (take I–93 to Route 3 to U.S. 6). Stop in **Plymouth** and visit Plimoth Plantation. Have lunch in **Sandwich** ① and tour the town before continuing on U.S. 6 to 🎏 **Chatham** ⑪, where you'll stay the night (have dinner and stroll Main Street in the evening). The next day, drive to **Orleans** ⑫ and spend the day at Nauset Beach. On day three continue on U.S. 6 to 🎏 **Provincetown** ⑯, stopping briefly in **Wellfleet** ⑭ to tour the galleries and detouring east off U.S. 6 to Cahoon Hollow Beach. After dinner take a walk down Commercial Street. On morning four head to Race Point Beach, go on a whale-watching cruise, or take a dune-buggy tour. On day five take U.S. 6 to **Hyannis** ⑤, where you can catch the ferry to 🎏 **Martha's Vineyard** ⑰–㉓.

IF YOU HAVE 7 OR 8 DAYS

Follow the three-day itinerary above, and spend your third night in **Salem** ㉙. On day four take the Massachusetts Turnpike (I–90) out of Boston and make a half-day stop at **Old Sturbridge Village** ㊻. Afterward, continue west on I–90 and north on I–91, stopping briefly in **Northampton** ㊷ before heading to 🎏 **Deerfield** ㊵, where you'll spend the night and day five. On day six head to the Berkshires—from Deerfield head north on I–91 to Greenfield, where you'll take Route 2 west to 🎏 **Williamstown** ㊽. On the morning of day seven tour the Sterling and Francine Clark Art Institute in Williamstown. U.S. 7 south takes you through **Pittsfield** ㊿; detour west on U.S. 20 to **Hancock Shaker Village** before heading on to 🎏 **Lenox** ㉜, where you'll spend the night. On day eight, visit Edith Wharton's the Mount, in Lenox, and the Norman Rockwell Museum, in **Stockbridge** ㊴. If you're visiting in summer, take a picnic to an evening concert at Tanglewood.

When to Tour Massachusetts

Fall is the best time to visit western Massachusetts, and it's the perfect season to see Boston as well. Everyone else knows this, so make reservations well ahead. Summer is ideal for visits to the Cape and the beaches. Bostonians often find their city to be too hot and humid in July and August, but if you're visiting from points south, the cool evening coastal breezes might strike you as downright refreshing. Many towns save their best for Christmas—lobster boats parade around Gloucester harbor adorned with lights, inns open their doors for goodies and caroling, shops serve eggnog, and tree-lighting ceremonies are often magical moments. The off-season is the perfect time to try cross-country skiing, take a walk on a stormy beach, or spend a night by the fire, tucked under a quilt catching up on Hawthorne or Thoreau.

BOSTON

Updated by
Natalie Engler,
Carolyn Heller,
Robert Kahn,
Robert
Nadeau,
Lauren Paul,
and Anne
Stuart

New England's largest and most important city and the cradle of American independence, Boston is more than 360 years old, far older than the republic its residents helped to create. The city's most famous buildings are not merely civic landmarks but national icons; its local heroes are known to the nation: the Adamses, Reveres, and Hancocks, who live at the crossroads of history and myth.

At the same time, Boston is a contemporary center of high finance and higher technology, a place of granite and glass towers rising along what once were rutted village lanes. Its many students, artists, academics, and young professionals have made the town a haven for the arts, international cinema, late-night bookstores, Asian food, alternative music, and unconventional politics.

Best of all, Boston is meant for walking. Most of its historical and architectural attractions are in compact areas. Its varied and distinctive neighborhoods reveal their character to visitors who take the time to stroll through them. Should you need to make short or long hops between neighborhoods, the "T"—the safe, easy-to-ride trains of the Massachusetts Bay Transportation Authority (MBTA; ☞ Getting Around *in* Boston A to Z, *below,* for information)—covers the city.

Beacon Hill and Boston Common

Contender for the "Most Beautiful" award among the city's neighborhoods and the hallowed address of many literary lights, Beacon Hill is Boston at its most Bostonian. As if with a trip in a Wellsian time-machine, the redbrick elegance of its narrow, cobbled streets transports you back to the 19th century. From the gold-topped splendor of the State House to the neoclassical panache of its mansions, Beacon Hill exudes power, prestige, and a calm yet palpable undercurrent of history.

Beacon Hill is bounded by Cambridge Street to the north, Beacon Street to the south, the Charles River Esplanade to the west, and Bowdoin Street to the east. In contrast to Beacon Hill, the Boston Common, the country's oldest public park, has a far more egalitarian feel. Beginning with its use as public land for cattle grazing, the Common has always accommodated the needs and desires of Bostonians. The public hangings once held there, however, have gone the way of the Puritans.

Numbers in the text and in the margin correspond to numbers on the Boston map.

A Good Walk

Stock up on brochures at the **Visitor Information Center** on Tremont Street before heading into the **Boston Common** ① to see Frog Pond and the Central Burying Ground. Head back to **Beacon Street** near the corner of Park Street to reach Augustus Saint-Gaudens' Robert Gould Shaw Memorial, a commemoration of Boston's Civil War unit of free blacks. Walk past the **Park Street Church** ② and the **Granary Burying Ground** ③, the final resting place of some of Boston's most illustrious figures. Return to Beacon, turn left, and you'll arrive at the **Boston Athenaeum** ④. Retrace your steps to the neoclassical **State House** ⑤. Continue ahead two blocks to Arlington Street and, to your right, the footbridge that leads to the **Esplanade** ⑥. (The **Museum of Science** ⑦, best visited by car or T, is north of the Esplanade across the Charles River.) A pedestrian overpass (at the Charles/Massachusetts General Hospital T stop) connects the Esplanade with **Charles Street.** Head south on Charles, east on **Chestnut Street,** and north on Willow. This will land you at photogenic **Acorn Street.** Continue on Willow across **Mt. Vernon Street** to **Louisburg Square** ⑧. Turn east (to the right) on Pinckney Street and follow it to Joy Street: Two blocks north on Smith Court are the **African Meeting House** ⑨ and the **Museum of Afro American History and Abiel Smith School** ⑩. You can pick up a brochure here for the **Black Heritage Trail®** (you can also pick one up at the Shaw memorial).

TIMING

Allow yourself the better part of a day for this walk, particularly if you want to linger in the Common or in the antiques shops on Charles Street.

Sights to See

Acorn Street. Surely the most-photographed street in the city, Acorn is Ye Olde Colonial Boston at its best. Almost toylike row houses line one side, which 19th-century artisans once called home; on the other are the doors to Mt. Vernon Street's hidden gardens. The cobblestone street is rough going for some.

❾ African Meeting House. Built in 1806 and the centerpiece of the historic Smith Court African-American community, the African Meeting House is the oldest black church building in the United States. In 1832 the New England Anti-Slavery Society was formed here under the leadership of William Lloyd Garrison. A gallery on the first floor has changing exhibitions. At press time, the African Meeting House and the Museum of Afro American History (in the Abiel Smith School building) were closed because of renovations, due for completion in late 1999 and 2000. Call before visiting. In the meantime, the administrative offices have been relocated to suburban Brookline. The five residences on **Smith Court** are typical of black Bostonian homes of the 1800s, including No. 3, the 1799 clapboard house where William C. Nell, America's first published black historian, lived. ⊠ *Administrative offices during renovation: 138 Mountfort St., Brookline.* ⊠ *Permanent: 8 Smith Ct., off Joy St. between Cambridge and Myrtle Sts.,* ☎ *617/ 739–1200.* 🎟 *$5 donation suggested.* ⊙ *Memorial Day–Labor Day, daily 10–4; Labor Day–Memorial Day, weekdays 10–4. T stop: Park St., Charles/MGH.*

Beacon Street. One of the city's most famous thoroughfares, Beacon Street epitomizes Boston. From the magnificent ☞ **State House** to the stately patrician mansions, the street is lined with architectural treasures. The ☞ **Boston Athenaeum** is on this street, as are the **Appleton Mansions**, at Nos. 39 and 40. Only a few buildings have panes like those of the mansions: Sunlight on the imperfections in a shipment of glass sent to Boston around 1820 resulted in an amethystine mauve shade. The mansions are not open to the public. Farther along, you'll find some of the most important buildings of Charles Bulfinch—the ultimate designer of the Federal style in America—and dozens of elegant bowfront row houses.

Black Heritage Trail®. The mention of Beacon Hill conjures up images of wealthy Boston Brahmins; yet until the end of the 19th century, its north side was also home to many free blacks. The 1½-mi Black Heritage Trail celebrates that community, stitching together 14 Beacon Hill sites. Tours guided by National Park Service rangers meet at the Shaw Memorial on the Beacon Street side of the Boston Common. The ☞ **African Meeting House**, the Boston National Historical Park Visitor Center, and the ☞ **Visitor Information Center** have brochures with self-guided walking tours.

★ **❹ Boston Athenaeum.** Only 1,049 proprietary shares exist for membership in this cathedral of scholarship, and most have been passed down for generations. The public is permitted to walk through the first and second floors, to study the marble busts, the exquisite porcelain vases, lush oil paintings, and leather-bound books of this Brahmin institution. A second-floor gallery presents art shows, most with a literary bent. A guided tour affords one of the most marvelous sights in the world of Boston academe, the fifth-floor Reading Room. In the words of critic David McCord, it "combines the best elements of the Bodleian, Monticello, the frigate *Constitution,* a greenhouse, and an old New England sitting room." Among the Athenaeum's holdings are most of George Washington's private library and the King's Chapel Library sent from England by William and Mary in 1698. ⊠ *10½ Beacon St.,* ☎ *617/227–0270.* 🎟 *Free.* ⊙ *Weekdays 9–5:30; Sept.–May also Sat. 9– 4. Free guided tours Tues. and Thurs. at 3, by appointment 24 hrs ahead. T stop: Park St.*

❶ Boston Common. The oldest public park in the United States is the largest and undoubtedly the most famous of the town commons around which New England settlements were traditionally arranged. As old as the city

278

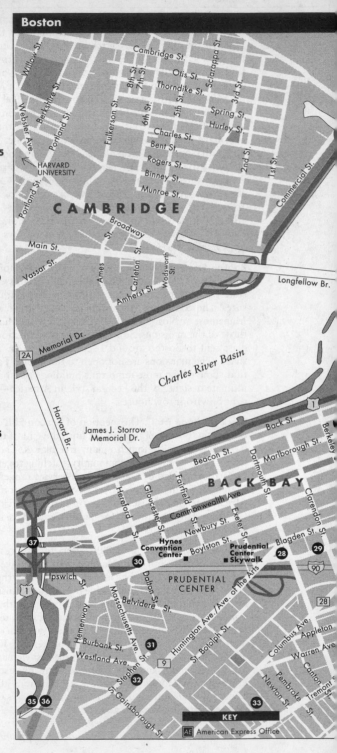

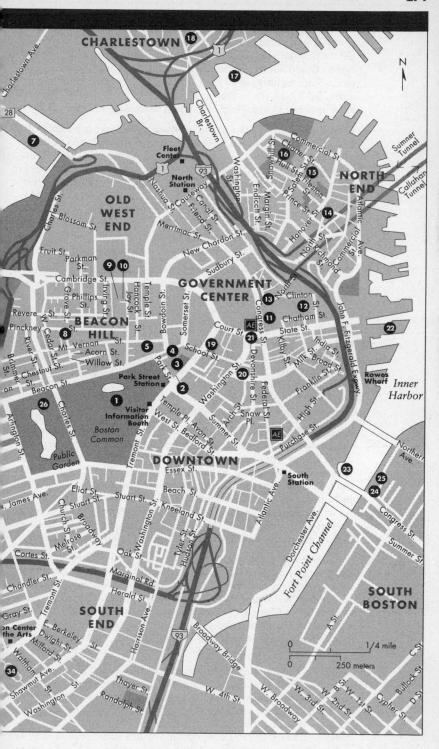

CHARLESTOWN

NORTH END

OLD WEST END

Fleet Center

North Station

BEACON HILL

GOVERNMENT CENTER

Park Street Station

Visitor Information Booth

Boston Common

Public Garden

DOWNTOWN

SOUTH END

South Station

Rowes Wharf

Inner Harbor

SOUTH BOSTON

Fort Point Channel

0   1/4 mile
0   250 meters

around it (it dates from 1634), the Common contains intriguing sights. The **Central Burying Ground** is the final resting place of Tories and Patriots, as well as many British casualties of the Battle of Bunker Hill. On the Beacon Street side of the Common sits the splendidly restored **Robert Gould Shaw Memorial**, executed in deep-relief bronze by Augustus Saint-Gaudens in 1897. It honors the 54th Massachusetts Regiment, led by the young Robert Gould Shaw, the first Civil War unit made up of free blacks. Their stirring saga inspired the 1989 movie *Glory.*

Charles Street. With few exceptions, Beacon Hill lacks commercial development, but the section of Charles Street north of Boston Common more than makes up for it. Antiques shops, bookstores, small restaurants, and flower shops vie for attention, but tastefully: Even the 7-Eleven storefront conforms to the prevailing Colonial aesthetic. The contemporary activity would present a curious sight to the elder Oliver Wendell Holmes, the publisher James T. Fields (of the famed Boston firm Ticknor & Fields), and many others who lived here when the neighborhood belonged to establishment literati. Charles Street sparkles at dusk from gas-fueled lamps, making it a romantic place for an evening stroll.

Chestnut Street. Delicacy and grace characterize virtually every structure along this street, from the fanlights above the entryways to the wrought-iron boot scrapers on the steps. The **Swan Houses**, at Nos. 13, 15, and 17, have Adam-style entrances, marble columnettes, and recessed arches commissioned from Charles Bulfinch.

⑥ Esplanade. At the northern end of Charles Street is one of several footbridges crossing Storrow Drive to the Esplanade, which stretches along the Charles River. The scenic patch of green is a great place to jog, picnic, and watch the sailboats along the river. For the almost nightly entertainment in the summer, hordes of Bostonians haul chairs and blankets to the lawn in front of the **Hatch Memorial Shell.**

Freedom Trail. A 2½-mi tour of the sites of the American Revolution, the Freedom Trail is a crash course in history. There are 16 sites beginning at the Boston Common and ending at the Bunker Hill Monument in Charlestown; depending on how many are visited in depth, the walk can take an aerobic 90 minutes or a leisurely full day. Trail walks led by National Park Service rangers take place from mid-April to November and begin at the Boston National Historical Park Visitor Center (☞ Downtown Boston, *below*); self-guided tour maps are available here and at the Visitor Information Center on Boston Common (☞ *below*).

③ Granary Burying Ground. "It is a fine thing to die in Boston," A. C. Lyons once remarked—alluding to Boston's cemeteries, among the most picturesque and historic in America. If you found a resting place here at the Old Granary (as it's affectionately called), just to the right of Park Street Church, chances are your headstone would have been eloquently ornamented and your neighbors would have been mighty eloquent, too: Samuel Adams, John Hancock, Paul Revere, and "Mother" Goose. ⊠ *Tremont St.* ۞ *Daily 8–4:30. T stop: Park St.*

★ ⑧ Louisburg Square. One of the most appealing corners in a neighborhood that epitomizes charm, Louisburg (pronounce the "s" as the locals do) Square is the very heart of Beacon Hill. Its houses—many built in the 1840s—have seen their share of famous tenants, including the Alcotts at No. 10 (Louisa May died here in 1888, on the day of her father's funeral). In 1852 the popular Swedish singer Jenny Lind was married in the parlor of No. 20, the residence of Samuel Ward, brother of Julia Ward Howe.

Mt. Vernon Street. Some of Beacon Hill's most distinguished addresses are on Mt. Vernon Street, whose houses rise tall from the pavement. The street even has a freestanding mansion, the Second Harrison Gray Otis House, at No. 85 (not open to the public). Henry James once wrote that this was "the only respectable street in America" (he lived with his brother William at No. 131 in the 1860s).

⑩ **Museum of Afro American History and Abiel Smith School.** Ever since Crispus Attucks became one of the famous victims of the Boston Massacre of 1770, the African-American community of Boston has played an important part in the city's history. Throughout the 19th century, abolition became the cause célèbre for Boston's intellectual elite, and during that time the black community thrived in neighborhoods like Smith Court and Joy Street. The museum was founded in 1964 to promote this history. Its headquarters occupy the 1830s Abiel Smith School, the first public grammar school for black children in Boston. At press time, the building was closed for renovations and due to reopen in 2000; call ahead. The renovations will create new space for the museum and for exhibits about the struggle for equal education in Boston. ✉ *Administrative offices during renovation: 138 Mountfort St., Brookline.* ✉ *Permanent: 46 Joy St.* ☎ *617/739–1200.* ⛫ *Donations suggested.* ⊙ *Weekdays 10–4. T stop: Park St., Charles/MGH.*

☕ ⑦ **Museum of Science.** With 15-ft lightning bolts in the Theater of Electricity and a 20-ft-high T-rex model, this is just the place to ignite any child's Jurassic spark. The museum, astride the Charles River Dam, has a restaurant, a gift shop, a planetarium, and a theater you can visit separately. The **Charles Hayden Planetarium,** with its sophisticated multi-image system, produces exciting programs on astronomical discoveries. The **Mugar Omni Theater** has a five-story domed screen (27,000 watts of power drive the 84 loudspeakers). ✉ *Science Park at the Charles River Dam,* ☎ *617/723–2500.* ⛫ *Museum $9, planetarium and theater $7.50 each; reduced-price combination tickets available for museum, planetarium, and Omni Theater.* ⊙ *Sat.–Thurs. 9–5, Fri. 9–9; extended hrs July 5–Labor Day. T stop: Science Park.*

② **Park Street Church.** If the Congregationalist Park Street Church, which was designed by Peter Banner and completed in 1810, could talk, what a joyful noise it would make. Samuel Smith's hymn "America" debuted here on July 4, 1831; two years earlier, William Lloyd Garrison began his long public campaign for the abolition of slavery. The church—called "the most impressive mass of brick and mortar in America" by Henry James—is earmarked by its steeple, considered by many critics to be the most beautiful in New England. ✉ *Zero Park St., at Tremont St.,* ☎ *617/523–3383.* ⊙ *Tours mid-June–Aug., Tues.–Sat. 9:30–3:30; Sun. services at 9, 10:45, and 5:30. T stop: Park St.*

⑤ **State House.** Charles Bulfinch's magnificent State House, one of the greatest works of classical architecture in America, is so striking that it hardly suffers for having been appendaged in three directions by bureaucrats and lesser architects. The neoclassical design is poised between Georgian and Federal; its finest features are the delicate Corinthian columns of the portico, the graceful pediment and window arches, and the vast yet visually weightless dome. The dome is sheathed in copper from the foundry of Paul Revere. ✉ *Beacon and Park Sts.,* ☎ *617/727–3676.* ⛫ *Free.* ⊙ *Tours Mon.–Sat. 10–4, last tour at 3:30. T stop: Park St.*

Visitor Information Center. You can pick up pamphlets, flyers, maps, and coupons at this kiosk between the Park Street and Boylston mass-transit stations. ✉ *Boston Common, Tremont St. near West St.,* ☎ *617/*

536–4100 or 888/733–2678 for recorded general information only. ☉
Daily 9–5.

Government Center and the North End

Government Center is the section of town Bostonians love to hate. Not only does it house that which they cannot fight—City Hall—but it also holds some of the bleakest architecture since the advent of poured concrete. The sweeping brick plaza aside City Hall and the twin towers of the John F. Kennedy Federal Office Building begins at the junction where Cambridge Street becomes Tremont Street.

Separating the Government Center area from the North End is the Fitzgerald Expressway, which will eventually be replaced with an underground highway in a massive construction project dubbed "the Big Dig" by locals. In the meantime, calling the area a mess is putting it mildly. Driver alert: The rerouting of traffic and constant reconfiguration of one-way streets have changed what was once a conquerable maze into a nearly impenetrable puzzle. Trust no maps.

Opposite the pedestrian tunnel beneath the Fitzgerald Expressway is the North End, the oldest neighborhood in Boston and one of the oldest in the New World. People walked these narrow byways when Shakespeare was not yet 20 years buried and Louis XIV was new to the throne of France. In the 17th century the North End *was* Boston—much of the rest of the peninsula was still underwater or had yet to be cleared.

Today's North End is almost entirely a creation of the late 19th century, when brick tenements began to fill up with European immigrants—first the Irish, then the Eastern European Jews, then the Portuguese, and finally the Italians. For more than 60 years the North End attracted an Italian population base. There are dozens of Italian restaurants here, along with Italian groceries, bakeries, churches, social clubs, and cafés.

Numbers in the text and in the margin correspond to numbers on the Boston map.

A Good Walk

The stark expanse of Boston's City Hall Plaza introduces visitors to the urban renewal age, but across Congress Street is **Faneuil Hall** ⑪, a site of political speechmaking since Revolutionary times. Just beyond that is **Quincy Market** ⑫, where shop-till-you-droppers can sample a profusion of international taste treats. For more Bostonian fare, walk back toward Congress Street to the **Blackstone Block** ⑬ and the city's oldest restaurant, the Union Oyster House, for some oysters and ale. Around the corner to the north on Blackstone Street are the open-air stalls of **Haymarket,** always aflutter with activity on Friday and Saturday. To sample Italian goodies, make your way through a pedestrian tunnel underneath the Fitzgerald Highway and enter the North End at Salem Street. Follow to Parmenter Street, turn right, and continue past Hanover Street, one of the North End's main thoroughfares; here Parmenter becomes Richmond Street. At North Street, turn left, following the Freedom Trail, to the **Paul Revere House** ⑭. Take Prince Street to Hanover Street, and then continue on Hanover to St. Stephen's, the only remaining church designed by Charles Bulfinch. Directly across the street is the Prado, or Paul Revere Mall, dominated by a statue of the patriot and hero. At the end of the mall is the **Old North Church** ⑮, of "One if by land, two if by sea" fame. Continue following the Freedom Trail to Hull Street and **Copp's Hill Burying Ground** ⑯, the resting place of many Revolutionary War heroes.

TIMING

You can explore Faneuil Hall and Quincy Market in about an hour, more if you linger in the food stalls or shop. Give yourself another two to three hours to stroll through the North End. Finish the day with an Italian meal or at least a cappuccino.

Sights to See

⑬ Blackstone Block. For decades the butcher trade dominated the city's oldest commercial block. Today, the block is Boston at its time-machine best, with more than three centuries of architecture on view. The centerpiece of the block is the **Union Oyster House** (☞ Dining, *below*), whose patrons have included Daniel Webster and John F. Kennedy.

⑯ Copp's Hill Burying Ground. An ancient and melancholy air hovers over this Colonial-era burial ground like a fine mist. Many headstones were chipped by practice shots fired by British soldiers during the occupation of Boston, and a number of musketball pockmarks can still be seen. ⊠ *Snowhill St.* ☉ *Apr.–Nov., daily 9–5; Dec.–Mar., daily 9–3. T stop: Haymarket, North Station.*

★ **⑪ Faneuil Hall.** Faneuil Hall was erected in 1742 to serve as a place for town meetings and a public market. Inside are the great mural *Webster's Reply to Hayne,* Gilbert Stuart's portrait of Washington at Dorchester Heights, and, on the top floors, the headquarters and museum of the Ancient and Honorable Artillery Company of Massachusetts, the oldest militia in the nation (1638). ⊠ *Faneuil Hall Sq.* 🎫 *Free.* ☉ *Daily 9–5. Closed Thanksgiving, Dec. 25, Jan. 1. T stop: Government Center, Aquarium.*

Haymarket. Centered on the relentlessly picturesque ☞ **Blackstone Block,** this exuberant maze of a marketplace is packed with loudly self-promoting vendors of fruit and vegetables who fill Marshall and Blackstone streets on Friday and Saturday from 7 AM until midafternoon.

★ **⑮ Old North Church.** The church is famous not only for its status as the oldest in Boston (1723) but for the two lanterns that glimmered from its steeple on the night of April 18, 1775. This is Christ Church, or the Old North, where a middle-aged silversmith named Paul Revere and a young sexton named Robert Newman managed that night to signal the departure by water to Lexington and Concord of the British regulars. (Longfellow's poem aside, the lanterns were not a signal *to* Revere but *from* him to the citizens of Charlestown across the harbor.) The church was designed by William Price from a study of Christopher Wren's London churches. ⊠ *193 Salem St.,* ☎ *617/523–6676.* ☉ *Daily 9–5; Sun. services at 9, 11, and 5. T stop: Haymarket, North Station.*

⑭ Paul Revere House. It is an interesting coincidence that the oldest house standing in one of the oldest sections of Boston should also have been the home of Paul Revere, patriot activist and silversmith. And it *is* a coincidence, since many homes of famous Bostonians have burned or been demolished over the years. It was saved from oblivion in 1902 and restored, lovingly though not quite authentically, to an approximation of its original 17th-century appearance. The house was built nearly a hundred years before Revere's 1775 midnight ride through Middlesex County. A few Revere furnishings are on display, and just gazing at Revere's silver creations brings the great man alive. Many special events are scheduled throughout the year for children. ⊠ *19 North Sq.,* ☎ *617/523–2338.* 🎫 *$2.50.* ☉ *Apr.–Oct., daily 9:30–5:15; Nov.–Dec., daily 9:30–4:15; Jan.–Mar., Tues.–Sun. 9:30–4:15. T stop: Haymarket, Aquarium.*

⑫ Quincy Market. Also known as Faneuil Hall Marketplace, this pioneer effort at urban recycling set the tone for many similar projects throughout America. The market consists of three block-long annexes: Quincy, North, and South markets, each 535 ft long, built to the 1826 design of Alexander Parris. Abundance and variety have been the watchwords of Quincy Market since its reopening in 1976. Some people consider it hopelessly commercial; in the peak summer season 50,000 or so visitors a day rather enjoy the extravaganza. At the east end of Quincy Market, **Marketplace Center** has tempting boutiques and food shops. ⊠ *Between Clinton and Chatham Sts.,* ☎ *617/338–2323.* ⊙ *Mon.– Sat. 10–9, Sun. noon–6. Restaurants and bars generally open daily 11 AM–2 AM; food stalls open earlier. T stop: Haymarket, Government Center, State St., Aquarium.*

Charlestown

Charlestown was a thriving settlement a year before Colonials headed across the Charles River to found Boston proper. The district lures visitors with two of the most visible—and vertical—monuments in Boston's history: the Bunker Hill Monument and the USS *Constitution*.

To get to Charlestown, you can take Bus 93 from Haymarket Square, Boston, which stops three blocks from the navy-yard entrance. A more interesting way to get here is to take the MBTA water shuttle from Long Wharf in downtown Boston, which runs every 15 or 30 minutes year-round.

Numbers in the text and in the margin correspond to numbers on the Boston map.

A Good Walk

Charlestown can be reached by foot via the Charlestown Bridge. From Copp's Hill Burial Ground, follow Hull Street to Commercial Street, and turn left to reach the bridge. The Charlestown Navy Yard will be on your right after you alight from the bridge. Ahead is the **USS Constitution** ⑰ museum and visitor center. From here, you can follow the red line of the Freedom Trail to the **Bunker Hill Monument** ⑱.

TIMING

Give yourself two or three hours for a Charlestown walk; the lengthy stroll across the bridge calls for endurance in cold weather. Many save Charlestown's stretch of the Freedom Trail for a second-day outing. You can avoid backtracking the historic route by taking the MBTA water shuttle that ferries back and forth between the navy yard and Long Wharf.

Sights to See

⑱ **Bunker Hill Monument.** British troops sustained heavy losses on June 17, 1775, at the Battle of Bunker Hill—one of the earliest major confrontations of the Revolutionary War. Most of the battle took place on Breed's Hill, which is where the monument, dedicated in 1843, stands. The famous war cry "Don't fire until you see the whites of their eyes" may not have been uttered by American colonel William Prescott or General Israel Putnam, but if either did shout it, he was quoting an old Prussian command that was necessary due to the inaccuracy of the musket. No matter. The Americans employed a deadly delayed-action strategy and proved themselves worthy fighters—though they lost the battle, the engagement made clear that the British could be challenged. The monument's zenith is reached by a flight of 294 steps. There is no elevator, but the views from the observatory are worth the arduous climb—for those in good condition. In the lodge at the base, dioramas tell the story of the battle; and ranger programs are conducted regularly. ⊠ *Main St. to Monument St., then straight uphill,* ☎ *617/242– 5641.* ⊡ *Free.* ⊙ *Lodge daily 9–5, monument daily 9–4:30. T stop: Community College.*

A multimedia presentation **"Whites of Their Eyes"** is shown in the Bunker Hill Pavilion near the navy-yard entrance. ✉ *55 Constitution Rd.,* ☎ *617/241–7576.* 🎫 *$3.* ☉ *Apr.–Nov., daily 9:30–5; shows every ½ hr, last at 4:30.*

☝ ⑰ **USS Constitution.** Better known as "Old Ironsides," the more than two-centuries-old USS *Constitution* is docked at the **Charlestown Navy Yard.** The oldest commissioned ship in the U.S. fleet, it is from the days of "wooden ships and iron men"—when she and her crew of 200 asserted the sovereignty of an improbable new nation. The ship's principal service was in the War of 1812. Of her 42 engagements, her record was 42–0. Once a year, on July 4, she is towed out into Boston Harbor. The adjacent **Constitution Museum** has artifacts and hands-on exhibits. ✉ *Charlestown Navy Yard, off Water St.,* ☎ *617/426–1812 museum; 617/242–5670 ship.* 🎫 *Constitution free; museum $4.* ☉ *Museum May–Oct., daily 9–6; Nov.–Apr., daily 10–5. Ship daily 9:30–sunset; 20-min tours, last at 3:30 PM. T stop: Haymarket; then MBTA Bus 92 or 93 to Charlestown City Sq. Or take the MBTA water shuttle from Long Wharf to Pier 4.*

Downtown Boston

The Financial District—what Bostonians usually refer to as "downtown"—may seem off the beaten track for people who are concentrating on following the Freedom Trail, yet there is much to see in a walk of an hour or two. There is little logic to the streets here; they were, after all, village lanes that only now happen to be lined with 40-story office towers. The area may be confusing, but it is mercifully small.

Downtown is home to some of Boston's most idiosyncratic neighborhoods. The old Leather District directly abuts Chinatown, which is also bordered by the Theater District (and the buildings of the Tufts New England Medical Center), farther west; to the south, the red light of the once brazen and now decaying Combat Zone flickers weakly.

Numbers in the text and in the margin correspond to numbers on the Boston map.

A Good Walk

After viewing the dramatic interior of **King's Chapel** ⑲ at the corner of Tremont (that's *Tre*-mont, not *Tree*-mont), visit the burying ground next door. Walk south on School Street, past the Globe Corner Bookstore, to Washington Street; turn right to see the **Old South Meeting House** ⑳, which seethed with revolutionary fervor in the 1770s. Retrace your steps on Washington and continue toward Court Street to get to the **Old State House** ㉑. In a traffic island in front is a circle of stones that marks the site of the Boston Massacre, a 1770 riot in which five townspeople were killed by British troops. Follow State Street east to the harbor and the **New England Aquarium** ㉒, on Central Wharf. From here you can walk south to **Rowes Wharf,** Boston's most glamorous waterfront development. Continue on Atlantic Avenue—most likely a solid wall of traffic due to the construction of an underground central artery highway nearby—to Congress Street, and then turn left onto the bridge to reach the *Beaver II* ㉓, a faithful re-creation of the hapless British ship that was carrying tea in 1773. Continue over the Congress Street Bridge to the **Children's Museum** ㉔ and **Computer Museum** ㉕, conveniently side by side. If you're starting to crave refreshment, cross back to Atlantic Avenue and continue south past South Station toward the distinctive gate marking **Chinatown.**

Boston MBTA (the "T")

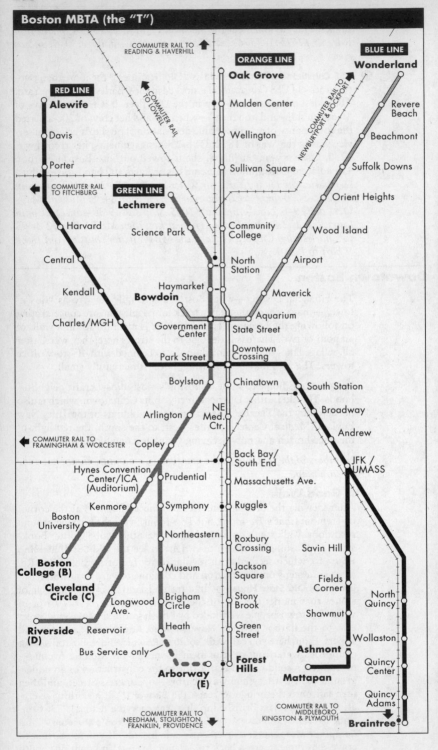

COMMUTER RAIL TO
READING & HAVERHILL

ORANGE LINE

BLUE LINE

Wonderland

RED LINE
Alewife

COMMUTER RAIL TO LOWELL

Oak Grove

Malden Center

Revere Beach

Davis

Wellington

Beachmont

Porter

Sullivan Square

COMMUTER RAIL TO NEWBURYPORT & ROCKPORT

Suffolk Downs

COMMUTER RAIL TO FITCHBURG

GREEN LINE
Lechmere

Orient Heights

Harvard

Science Park

Community College

Wood Island

Central

North Station

Airport

Kendall

Haymarket

Maverick

Bowdoin

Charles/MGH

Government Center

Aquarium

State Street

Park Street

Downtown Crossing

Boylston

Chinatown

South Station

Arlington

NE Med. Ctr.

Broadway

COMMUTER RAIL TO FRAMINGHAM & WORCESTER

Copley

Andrew

Back Bay/ South End

JFK / UMASS

Hynes Convention Center/ICA (Auditorium)

Prudential

Massachusetts Ave.

Kenmore

Symphony

Ruggles

Boston University

Northeastern

Roxbury Crossing

Savin Hill

Boston College (B)

Museum

Jackson Square

Fields Corner

North Quincy

Cleveland Circle (C)

Brigham Circle

Stony Brook

Shawmut

Longwood Ave.

Heath

Green Street

Ashmont

Wollaston

Riverside (D)

Reservoir

Bus Service only

Forest Hills

Mattapan

Quincy Center

Arborway (E)

Quincy Adams

COMMUTER RAIL TO NEEDHAM, STOUGHTON, FRANKLIN, PROVIDENCE

COMMUTER RAIL TO MIDDLEBORO, KINGSTON & PLYMOUTH

Braintree

TIMING

If you are traveling with small children, you may wish to limit this walk to the area around the New England Aquarium and the Computer and Children's museums. (In fact, you'll probably want to spend two or three hours just in the museums.) Otherwise budget about three hours for the walk, and be prepared for the often cool wind coming off the harbor.

Sights to See

㉓ **Beaver II.** A faithful replica of one of the ships forcibly boarded and unloaded the night Boston Harbor became a teapot bobs in the Fort Point Channel at the Congress Street Bridge. Visitors receive a complimentary cup of tea and may be pressed into donning feathers and war paint to reenact the tea drop. The site of the actual Boston Tea Party—a revolt over a tax on tea that the British had levied—is marked by a plaque on Atlantic Avenue. ⊠ *Congress St. Bridge,* ☎ *617/338–1773.* ⬛ *$8.* ☯ *Memorial Day–Labor Day, daily 9–6; Labor Day–Nov. and Mar.–Memorial Day, daily 9–5. T stop: South Station.*

Boston National Historical Park Visitor Center. National Park Service ranger–led tours of the Freedom Trail leave from the center, which stocks brochures about many attractions and walking tours and has rest rooms. ⊠ *15 State St., near the Old State House,* ☎ *617/242–5642.* ⬛ *Free.* ☯ *Daily 9–5. Tours mid-Apr.–late June and Labor Day–Nov., weekdays at 10 and 2, weekends at 10, 11, 1, and 2; late June–Labor Day, daily at 10, 11, 12, 1, 2, and 3.*

㉔ **Children's Museum.** Hands-on exhibits at this popular museum include computers, video cameras, and displays designed to help children understand cultural diversity, their own bodies, the nature of disabilities, and more. Don't miss Grandmother's Attic, where children can dress up in old clothing. ⊠ *Museum Wharf, 300 Congress St.,* ☎ *617/426–6500; 617/426–8855 for recorded information.* ⬛ *$7; $1 Fri. 5–9.* ☯ *Mid-June–Labor Day, daily 10–7, Fri. 10–9; Labor Day–mid-June, Tues.–Sun. 10–5, Fri. 10–9. T stop: South Station.*

Chinatown. Boston's Chinatown may be geographically small, but it is home to one of the larger concentrations of Chinese-Americans in the United States. Beginning in the 1870s, Chinese immigrants began to trickle in, many setting up tents in Ping On Alley. Immigration increased when restrictions were lifted after 1940. In recent years, Vietnamese, Korean-Japanese, Thai, and Malaysian eateries have popped up alongside the many Chinese restaurants—most along Beach and Tyler streets and Harrison Avenue. A three-story pagoda-style arch at the end of Beach Street welcomes visitors to the district. *T stop. Chinatown.*

㉕ **Computer Museum.** You can learn about the thinking machines running our lives in this user-friendly setting kids and adults enjoy. Conveniently next to the ☞ **Children's Museum,** the Computer Museum has more than 170 exhibits, including the two-story Walk-Through Computer™ and a software gallery with the newest games. ⊠ *300 Congress St.,* ☎ *617/426–2800; 617/423–6758 for talking computer.* ⬛ *$7; ½ price Sun. 3–5.* ☯ *Mid-June–Aug., daily 10–6; Sept.–mid-June, Tues.–Sun. 10–5. T stop: South Station.*

⑲ **King's Chapel.** Somber yet dramatic, King's Chapel looms over the corner of Tremont and School streets. The distinctive shape of the 1754 structure was not achieved entirely by design; for lack of funds it was never topped with the steeple that architect Peter Harrison had planned. The interior is a masterpiece of elegant proportion and Georgian calm. The chapel's bell is Paul Revere's largest and, in his judgment, his sweetest-sounding. Take the path to the right from the entrance of the **King's Chapel Burying Ground,** the oldest cemetery in the city. On the left is the gravestone (1704) of Elizabeth Pain, the model for Hester Prynne in Hawthorne's *The Scarlet Letter*. Elsewhere, you'll find the graves of the first Massachusetts governor, John Winthrop, and several generations of his descendants. ⊠ *58 Tremont St., at School St.,* ☎ *617/227–2155.* ☉ *Mid-June–Labor Day, Mon. and Thurs.– Fri., and Sat. 9:30–4, Sun. 1–3; Labor Day–mid-Oct., Mon. and Fri.–Sat. 9:30–3; mid-Oct.–mid-Apr., Sat. 9:30–3; mid-Apr.–mid-June, Mon. and Fri.– Sat. 10–2. Year-round music program Tues. 12:15–1. Services on Sun. at 11, Wed. at 12:15. T stop: Park St. or Government Center.*

☞ ㉒ **New England Aquarium.** This perennially popular attraction has added a 17,400-square-ft West Wing—with barking seals outside—to its already astounding main facility. Inside the main building are specimens of more than 2,000 species of marine life from penguins to jellyfish, many of which make their homes in a four-story ocean reef tank. Don't miss feeding time, a fascinating procedure that lasts nearly an hour. Educational programs, like the "Science at Sea" cruise, take place year-round. Sea lion shows are held aboard *Discovery*, a floating marine mammal pavilion; and whale-watch cruises ($24) leave from the aquarium's dock from April to October. ⊠ *Central Wharf, between Central and Milk Sts.,* ☎ *617/973–5200; 617/973–5277 for whale-watching information.* ▣ *$11, July 4–Labor Day $12.50.* ☉ *July–early Sept., Mon.–Tues. and Fri. 9–6, Wed.–Thurs. 9–8, weekends 9–7; early Sept.–June, weekdays 9–5, weekends 9–6. T Stop: Aquarium.*

㉒ **Old South Meeting House.** Some of the most fiery pre-Revolutionary town meetings were held at Old South, culminating in the tumultuous gathering of December 16, 1773, convened by Samuel Adams to address the question of dutiable tea that activists wanted returned to England. This was also the congregation of Phillis Wheately, the first published African-American poet. A permanent exhibition, "Voices of Protest," celebrates Old South as a forum for free speech from Revolutionary days to the present. ⊠ *310 Washington St.,* ☎ *617/482–6439.* ▣ *$3.* ☉ *Apr.–Oct., daily 9:30–5; Nov.–Mar., daily 10–4. T stop: State St., Downtown Crossing.*

㉑ **Old State House.** A brightly gilded lion and unicorn, symbols of British imperial power, adorn the State Street gable of this landmark structure. This was the seat of the Colonial government from 1713 until the Revolution, and after the evacuation of the British from Boston in 1776 it served the independent Commonwealth until its replacement on Beacon Hill was completed. The permanent collection traces Boston's Revolutionary War history. ⊠ *206 Washington St.,* ☎ *617/720–3290.* ▣ *$3.* ☉ *Daily 9–5. T stop: State St.*

Rowes Wharf. This 15-story Skidmore, Owings, and Merrill extravaganza is the site of the Boston Harbor Hotel and the Rowes Wharf Restaurant. Great views of Boston Harbor and the luxurious yachts parked in the marina can be had from under the complex's gateway six-story arch. Water shuttles pull up here from Logan Airport—the most spectacular way to enter the city. *T Stop: Aquarium.*

The Back Bay

In the folklore of American neighborhoods, the Back Bay stands with New York's Park Avenue and San Francisco's Nob Hill as a symbol of propriety and high social standing. The main east–west streets—Beacon Street, Marlborough Street, Commonwealth Avenue, Newbury Street, and Boylston Street—are bisected by eight streets named in alphabetical order from Arlington to Hereford. Note that Huntington Avenue has been renamed Avenue of the Arts, but you'll still hear locals use the old name.

Numbers in the text and in the margin correspond to numbers on the Boston map.

A Good Walk

A walk through the Back Bay properly begins with the **Public Garden** ㉖, the oldest botanical garden in the United States. Wander its paths to the corner of Commonwealth Avenue and Arlington Street. Walk up Arlington to Beacon Street and turn left to visit the **Gibson House** ㉗ museum. Follow Beacon to Berkeley and turn left to return to Commonwealth Avenue. Stroll the avenue to Clarendon, turn left, and head into **Copley Square** ㉘, where you will find **Trinity Church,** the Boston Public Library, and the **John Hancock Tower** ㉙. From Copley Square, you can walk north on Dartmouth to **Newbury Street** and its posh boutiques. For a dose of the avant-garde turn left on Hereford Street and right on Boylston and drop into the **Institute of Contemporary Art** ㉚. From there, proceed one block farther on Boylston Street to Massachusetts Avenue. Turn left to reach the **Christian Science Church** ㉛ and **Symphony Hall** ㉜.

TIMING

The Public Garden is such a delight in the spring and summer that you should give yourself at least a hour to explore it if this is when you're visiting. Distances between sights are a bit longer here than in other parts of the city, so allow one or two hours for a walk down Newbury Street. The Museum of Contemporary Art and the Christian Science Church can each be explored in an hour.

Sights to See

Boylston Street. This broad thoroughfare is the southern commercial spine of the Back Bay. It holds interesting shops and restaurants, the Hynes Convention Center, and an F.A.O. Schwarz store with a huge teddy bear sculpture on the sidewalk in front.

㉛ **Christian Science Church.** The world headquarters of the Christian Science faith has an Old World basilica and a sleek office complex designed by I. M. Pei. This church was established here by Mary Baker Eddy in 1879. Mrs. Eddy's original granite First Church of Christ, Scientist (1894), has since been enveloped by a domed Renaissance basilica, added to the site in 1906. In the publishing society's lobby is the fascinating **Mapparium,** a huge stained-glass globe that allows you to traverse its 30-ft diameter via a glass bridge. The Mapparium was closed for renovations in 1999 and was due to reopen early in 2000. Tours have been discontinued during the renovations. The 670-ft reflecting pool is a splendid sight on a hot summer day. ✉ *175 Ave. of the Arts,* ☎ *617/450–3790.* ☉ *Mother church Tues.–Sat. 10–4, Sun. 11:15–2; free 30-min tours. On Mon. only, original edifice open for tours. Sun. services at 10 AM and 7 PM. Mapparium Mon.–Sat. 10–4. T stop: Prudential.*

㉘ **Copley Square.** For thousands of folks in April, a glimpse of this square is a welcome sight; this is where Boston Marathon runners end their 26-mi race. The Boston Public Library, the Copley Plaza Hotel, and ☞ **Trinity Church** border the square. Copley Place, an upscale glass and brass urban mall, comprises two major hotels, shops, restaurants, and offices attractively grouped around bright, open indoor spaces. The ☞ **John Hancock Tower** looms over all. *T stop: Copley.*

㉗ **Gibson House.** One of the first Back Bay residences (1859), the Gibson House has been preserved with all its Victorian fixtures and furniture intact; a Gibson scion lived here until the 1950s and left things as they had always been. ✉ *137 Beacon St.,* ☎ *617/267–6338.* ✇ *$5.* ☉ *Tours May–Oct., Wed.–Sun. at 1, 2, and 3; Nov.–Apr., weekends at 1, 2, and 3. T stop: Arlington.*

㉚ **Institute of Contemporary Art.** Multimedia art, installations, film and video series, and other events take place in this cutting-edge institution inside a 19th-century police station and firehouse. ⊠ *955 Boylston St.,* ☎ *617/266–5152.* ☜ *$6; free Thurs. 5–9.* ⊙ *Wed.–Sun. noon–5, Thurs. noon–9. Tours weekends at 1 and 3. T stop: Hynes Convention Center.*

㉙ **John Hancock Tower.** The tallest building in New England is a stark and graceful reflective blue rhomboid tower designed by I. M. Pei. The 60th-floor observatory is one of the best vantage points in the city, and the "Boston 1775" exhibit shows what the city looked like before the great hill-leveling and landfill operations commenced in 1854. ⊠ *Observatory ticket office, Trinity Pl. and St. James Ave.,* ☎ *617/247–1977 or 617/572–6429.* ☜ *$5.* ⊙ *Apr.–Oct., daily 9 AM–10 PM; Nov.–Mar., Mon.–Sat. 9 AM–10 PM, Sun. 9–5. T stop: Copley.*

Newbury Street. The eight blocks of Newbury Street have been compared to New York's 5fth Avenue, and certainly this is Boston's poshest shopping mecca. But here the pricey boutiques are more intimate than grand, and people actually live above the trendy restaurants and hair salons. Toward the Massachusetts Avenue end, cafés proliferate and the stores get funkier.

Prudential Center Skywalk. The 50th-floor observatory atop the Prudential Center affords spectacular vistas of Boston, Cambridge, and the suburbs to the west and south—on clear days, you can even see Cape Cod. There are chairs for sitting and noisy interactive exhibits on Boston's history. ⊠ *800 Boylston St.,* ☎ *617/859–0648.* ☜ *$4.* ⊙ *Daily 10–10. T stop: Prudential.*

★ ☙ ㉖ **Public Garden.** The Public Garden is the oldest botanical garden in the United States. The park's pond has been famous since 1877 for its foot pedal–powered **swan boats,** which make leisurely cruises in warm months. They were invented by Robert Paget, who was inspired by the popularity of swan boats made fashionable by Wagner's opera *Lohengrin.* Paget descendants still run the boats. Follow the kids quack-quacking along the pathway between the pond and the park entrance at Charles and Beacon streets to the *Make Way for Ducklings* bronze statues. Jack, Kack, Lack, Mack, Nack, Ouack, Pack, and Quack compose Mrs. Mallard's pack—made famous in the 1941 classic children's story (set along Beacon Street and within the Public Garden). ☎ *617/635–4505.* ☜ *Swan boats $1.50.* ⊙ *Swan boats mid-Apr.–late Sept., daily 10–4. The garden gates do not close, but strolling is not recommended after dark. T stop: Arlington.*

㉜ **Symphony Hall.** The home of the Boston Symphony Orchestra since 1900, the hall was designed by the architectural firm McKim, Mead & White, but the acoustics, rather than the exterior design, make this a special place for performers and concertgoers. ⊠ *301 Massachusetts Ave.,* ☎ *617/266–1492 or 888/266–1200 box office.* ⊙ *Tours by appointment with volunteer office (call 1 wk ahead). T stop: Symphony.*

Trinity Church. In his 1877 masterpiece, architect Henry Hobson Richardson brought his Romanesque Revival style to maturity; all the aesthetic elements for which he was famous—bold masonry, careful arrangement of masses, sumptuously carved interior woodwork—come together magnificently. The church remains the centerpiece of Copley Square. ⊠ *Copley Sq.,* ☎ *617/536–0944.* ⊙ *Daily 8–6; Sun. services at 8, 9, 11, and 6. Mon.–Sat., services at 7:30, noon, and 5:30. T stop: Copley.*

The South End

History has come full circle in the South End. Once a fashionable neighborhood created with landfill in the mid-19th century, it was deserted by the well-to-do for the Back Bay toward the end of the century. Solidly back in fashion, today it is a polyglot of upscale eateries and ethnic enclaves of redbrick row houses in refurbished splendor or elegant decay. The Back Bay is French-inspired, but the South End's architectural roots are English, the houses continuing the pattern established on Beacon Hill (in a uniformly bowfront style), though aspiring to a much more florid standard of decoration.

There is a substantial Latino and black presence in the South End, particularly along Columbus Avenue and Massachusetts Avenue, which marks the beginning of the predominantly black neighborhood of Roxbury. Harrison Avenue and Washington Street at the north side of the South End lead to Chinatown, and consequently there is a growing Asian influence. Along East Berkeley Street, neighbors have created a lush community garden. Many lesbians and gay men live in the South End.

Numbers in the text and in the margin correspond to numbers on the Boston map.

A Good Walk

From the Back Bay, walk down Massachusetts Avenue to Columbus Avenue; turn left and follow it to **Rutland Square** ㉝ on your right. Cross to Tremont and continue on Tremont and turn right at **Union Park** ㉞. Walk south through the park to Shawmut Street, which holds a mixture of ethnic outlets and retail spaces. Walk east along Shawmut to East Berkeley Street, and then turn left (to the north) and head back to Tremont. On Tremont Street, near Clarendon Street, is the **Boston Center for the Arts.** After a break at one of the many trendy restaurants and shops along Tremont Street, retrace your steps on Tremont to Arlington and traverse the walkway over the Massachusetts Turnpike to reach **Bay Village,** on your right.

TIMING

You can walk through the South End in two to three hours. It's a good option on a pleasant day; go elsewhere in inclement weather, as most of what you'll see here is outdoors.

Sights to See

Bay Village. This neighborhood is a pocket of early 19th-century brick row houses that appears to be almost a toylike replication of Beacon Hill. Edgar Allan Poe once lived here. It seems improbable that so fine and serene a neighborhood can exist in the shadow of busy Park Square—a 1950s developer might easily have leveled these blocks in an afternoon—yet here it is, another Boston surprise. To get here, follow Columbus Avenue almost into Park Square, turn right on Arlington Street, then left onto one of the narrow streets of this neighborhood.

Boston Center for the Arts. Of Boston's multiple arts organizations, the city-sponsored arts and culture complex is the one that is closest "to the people." Here you can see the work of budding playwrights, view exhibits on Haitian folk art, or walk through an installation commemorating World AIDS Day. The BCA houses three small theaters, the Mills Gallery, and studio space for some 60 artists. ⊠ *539 Tremont St.,* ☎ *617/426–5000; 617/426–7700; 617/426–8835 Mills Galleries.* ▨ *Free.* ⊙ *Weekdays 9–5; Mills Galleries Wed. and Sun. 1–4, Thurs.–Sat. 1–4 and 7–10. T stop: Back Bay, South End.*

㉝ **Rutland Square.** Reflecting a time in which the South End was Boston's most prestigious address, this slice of a park is framed by lovely Italianate bowfront houses. ⊠ *Between Columbus Ave. and Tremont St.*

㉞ **Union Park.** Cast-iron fences, Victorian town houses, and a grassy knoll add up to a charming cityscape dating to the 1850s. ⊠ *Between Tremont St. and Shawmut Ave.*

The Fens

The marshland known as the Back Bay Fens gave this section of Boston its name, but two quirky institutions give it its character: Fenway Park, where hope for another World Series pennant springs eternal, and the Isabella Stewart Gardner Museum, the legacy of a bon vivant Brahmin. Kenmore Square, a favorite haunt for college students, adds a bit of funky flavor to the mix.

The Fens mark the beginning of Boston's Emerald Necklace, a loosely connected chain of parks designed by Frederick Law Olmsted that extends along the Fenway, Riverway, and Jamaicaway to Jamaica Pond, the Arnold Arboretum, and Franklin Park.

Numbers in the text and in the margin correspond to numbers on the Boston map.

A Good Tour

The attractions in the Fens are best visited separately. The **Museum of Fine Arts** ㉟, between Avenue of the Arts (the former Huntington Avenue) and the Fenway, and the **Isabella Stewart Gardner Museum** ㊱ are just around the corner from each other. **Kenmore Square** is at the west end of Commonwealth Avenue, not far from **Fenway Park** ㊲.

TIMING

The Green Line of the MBTA stops near the attractions on this tour. The Gardner is much smaller than the MFA, but each can take up an afternoon if you take a break at their cafés.

Sights to See

㊲ **Fenway Park.** Fenway may be one of the smallest parks in the major leagues (capacity 34,000), but it is one of the most loved. Since its construction in 1912, there has been no shortage of heroics: Babe Ruth pitched here when the place was new; Ted Williams and Carl Yastrzemski had epic careers here. ⊠ *4 Yawkey Way, between Van Ness and Lansdowne Sts.,* ☎ *617/267–8661 for recorded information; 617/267–1700 for tickets. T stop: Fenway.*

★ ㊱ **Isabella Stewart Gardner Museum.** A spirited young society woman named Isabella Stewart came from New York in 1860 to marry John Lowell Gardner. When it came time to create a permanent home for the Old Master paintings and Medici treasures she and her husband had acquired in Europe, she decided to build the Venetian palazzo of her dreams along Commonwealth Avenue. The complex stands as a monument to one woman's extraordinary taste.

Despite the loss of a few masterpieces in a daring 1990 robbery, there is much to see: a trove of spectacular paintings—including masterpieces like Titian's *Rape of Europa,* Giorgione's *Christ Bearing the Cross,* Piero della Francesca's *Hercules,* and John Singer Sargent's *El Jaleo*—as well as rooms bought outright from great European houses, Spanish leather panels, Renaissance hooded fireplaces, and Gothic tapestries. An intimate restaurant overlooks the courtyard, and in the spring and summer tables and chairs spill outside. To fully conjure up the spirit of days past, attend one of the concerts held September to May in the elegant Tapestry Room. ⊠ *280 The Fenway,* ☎ *617/566–1401; 617/566–1088 for café.* ⊡ *$10; $11 weekends. Concert and galleries $16; café and gift shop free.* ⊙ *Museum Tues.–Sun. 11–5; Sept.–May, weekend concerts at 1:30. T stop: Museum.*

Kenmore Square. Kenmore Square is home to fast-food parlors, rock-and-roll clubs, an abundance of university students, and an enormous sign advertising Citgo gasoline. The red, white, and blue neon sign put up in 1965 is so thoroughly identified with the area that historic preservationists have fought, successfully, to save it—proof that Bostonians are an open-minded lot who do not insist that their landmarks be identified with the American Revolution. ⊠ *Intersection of Commonwealth Ave., Brookline Ave., and Beacon St. T stop: Kenmore Sq.*

★ ㉟ **Museum of Fine Arts.** The MFA's holdings of American art surpass those of all but two or three U.S. museums. There are more than 50 works by John Singleton Copley, Colonial Boston's most celebrated portraitist, plus major paintings by Winslow Homer, John Singer Sargent, and Edward Hopper. Other artists represented include Mary Cassatt, Georgia O'Keeffe, and Berthe Morisot.

The museum also has a sublime collection of French Impressionists—38 Monets, the largest collection of his work outside France—plus renowned collections of Asian, Egyptian, and Nubian art. Three excellent galleries showcase the art of Africa, Oceania, and the Ancient Americas, expanding the MFA's emphasis on civilizations outside the Western tradition. The museum's West Wing presents changing exhibits of contemporary arts, prints, and photographs. The museum has a gift shop, a good restaurant, and a cafeteria; in the newly re-opened **Fraser Court,** a charming oasis of green trees and statuary, beverages are served on the terrace from April to October. On the Fenway Park side of the museum, the **Tenshin-En Garden,** the "Garden in the Heart of Heaven," allows visitors to experience landscape as a work of art (daily 10–4, except Monday from April to October). A combination of Japanese and American trees and shrubs fuses the concept of the Japanese garden with elements of the New England landscape. ⊠ *465 Ave. of the Arts,* ☎ *617/267–9300.* ⊡ *$10; voluntary admission Wed. 4–9:45, children under 17 with adult free.* ⊙ *Entire museum Mon.–Tues. 10–4:45, Wed.–Fri. 10–9:45, weekends 10–5:45. West Wing only Thurs.–Fri. 5–10 with admission reduced by $2. 1-hr tours available weekdays. T stop: Museum.*

Cambridge

Pronounced with either prideful satisfaction or a smirk, the nickname "the People's Republic of Cambridge" sums up this independent city of 95,000 west of Boston. Cambridge not only houses two of the country's greatest educational institutions—Harvard University and the Massachusetts Institute of Technology—it has a long history as a haven for freethinkers, writers, activists, and iconoclasts of every stamp. Once a center for publishing, Cambridge has become a high-tech mecca.

Cambridge is easily reached on the Red Line train. The Harvard Square area is notorious for limited parking. If you insist on driving into Cambridge, you may want to avoid the local circling ritual by pulling into a garage.

Numbers in the text and in the margin correspond to numbers on the Cambridge map.

A Good Walk

Begin your tour in **Harvard Square** ① near the T station entrance. Enter Harvard Yard for a look at one of the country's premier educational

Cambridge

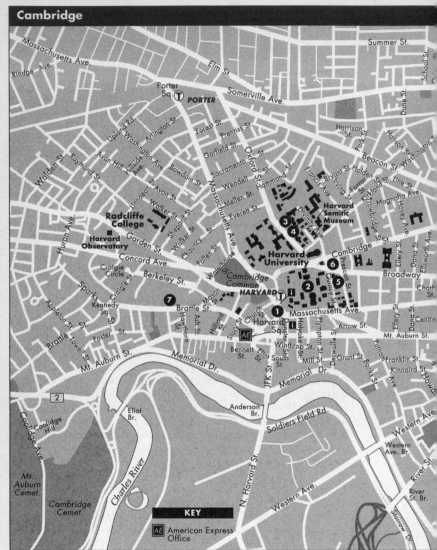

Arthur M. Sackler
Museum, **6**

Fogg Art Museum, **5**

Harvard Museum of
Natural History, **4**

Harvard Square, **1**

Harvard University, **2**

Longfellow National
Historic Site, **7**

Massachusetts
Institute of
Technology, **8**

Peabody Museum of
Archaeology and
Ethnology, **3**

institutions: **Harvard University** ②. Just past Memorial Hall (ask any student for directions) is Kirkland Street; turn right and follow it to Divinity Avenue and turn left. At 11 Divinity, you'll find an entrance to the complex of the **Peabody Museum** ③ and the **Harvard Museum of Natural History** ④. It's about a 15-minute walk to Harvard's **Fogg Art Museum** ⑤, on Quincy Street, and **Arthur M. Sackler Museum** ⑥, on Broadway. The **Longfellow National Historic Site** ⑦, which is closed for remodeling through 2000, is a 15-minute walk west of Harvard Square on Brattle Street.

In good weather, you can walk along Massachusetts Avenue through the bustle and ethnic diversity of urban Central Square and into the warehouse-like openness of the Kendall Square area, where the campus of the **Massachusetts Institute of Technology** ⑧ dominates the neighborhood. If the weather is poor, take the T Red Line heading inbound from Harvard Square two stops to Kendall Square.

TIMING

Budget at least two hours to explore Harvard Square, plus at least three more if you plan to go to either Harvard's cultural and history museums or the art museums. The walk down Massachusetts Avenue to MIT will take an additional 30 to 45 minutes, and you could easily spend an hour or two on the MIT campus admiring its architecture and visiting its museum or the List Visual Arts Center.

Sights to See

⑥ **Arthur M. Sackler Museum.** The richness of the East and artistic treasures of the ancient Greeks, Egyptians, and Romans fill three of the four floors of this modern structure. The changing exhibits are first-rate, but if time is limited, make a beeline for the Ancient and Asian art galleries on the fourth floor, where you can gaze at bronze relics from a Chinese dynasty, Buddhist sculptures, Greek friezes, or Roman marbles. The fee for the Sackler gains you entrance to the Fogg Art Museum (☞ *below*). ⊠ *485 Broadway,* ☎ *617/495–9400.* ⌨ *$5; free Wed., Sat. 10–noon, and after 4:30.* ☉ *Mon.–Sat. 10–5, Sun. 1–5.*

★ ⑤ **Fogg Art Museum.** Harvard's most famous art museum owns 80,000 works of art from every major period and from every corner of the world. The Fogg, behind Harvard Yard on Quincy Street, was founded in 1895; its collection focuses primarily on European, American, and Far Eastern works, with notable 19th-century French Impressionist and medieval Italian paintings. A ticket here is good for admission to the **Busch-Reisinger Museum** (☎ 617/495–9400), in the Werner Otto Hall, entered through the Fogg. From the serenity of the Fogg's Old Masters, you step into the jarring, mesmerizing world of German Expressionists and other 20th-century artists. ⊠ *32 Quincy St.,* ☎ *617/495–9400.* ⌨ *$5; free Wed., Sat. 10–noon.* ☉ *Mon.–Sat. 10–5, Sun. 1–5.*

④ **Harvard Museum of Natural History.** Many museums promise something for every member of the family; the Harvard museum complex actually delivers. There are three museums here; one fee admits you to all. The glass flowers in the **Botanical Museum** were created as teaching tools. The **Museum of Comparative Zoology** traces the evolution of animals (including dinosaurs) and humans. Oversize garnets and crystals are among the holdings of the **Mineralogical and Geological Museum**, which also has an extensive collection of meteorites. ⊠ *26 Oxford St.,* ☎ *617/495–3045* ⌨ *$5; free Sat. 9–noon.* ☉ *Mon.–Sat. 9–5, Sun. 1–5. T stop: Harvard Sq.*

① **Harvard Square.** Gaggles of students, street musicians, people hawking the paper *Spare Change* (as well as asking for some), end-of-the-world preachers, and political-cause proponents make for a nonstop pedestrian flow at this most celebrated of Cambridge crossroads. Harvard Square is where Massachusetts Avenue (locally, Mass Ave.), coming from Boston, turns and widens into a triangle broad enough to accommodate a brick peninsula (beneath which the MBTA station is located). Sharing the peninsula is the Out-of-Town newsstand, a local institution that occupies the restored 1928 kiosk that used to be the entrance to the MBTA station. Harvard Square is walled on two sides by banks, restaurants, and shops and on the third by Harvard University. The **Cambridge Visitor Information Booth** (☎ 617/497–1630), just outside the T station entrance, is a volunteer-staffed kiosk with maps and brochures. The booth is open from 9 to 5 (Sunday from 1 to 5) and has maps for historic and literary walking tours of the city, and an excellent guide to the bookstores in the square and beyond.

② **Harvard University.** In 1636 the Great and General Court of the Massachusetts Bay Colony established the country's first college here. Named in 1639 for John Harvard, a young Charlestown clergyman who died that year, leaving the college his entire library and half his estate, Harvard remained the only college in the New World until 1693, by which time it was firmly established as a respected center of learning. Students run the **Harvard University Events and Information Center,** which has maps of the university area. You can take a free hour-long walking tour of Harvard Yard. ✉ *Holyoke Center, 1350 Massachusetts Ave.,* ☎ *617/495–1573.* ☼ *Tours during the academic year, weekdays at 10 and 2, Sat. at 2; mid-June–Aug., Mon.–Sat. at 10, 11:15, 2, and 3:15, Sun. at 1:30 and 3. T stop: Harvard Sq.*

List Visual Arts Center. Founded by Albert and Vera List, pioneer collectors of modern art, this MIT center has three galleries showcasing exhibitions of cutting-edge art and mixed media. Stark works such as Thomas Hart Benton's painting *Fluid Catalytic Crackers* are in keeping with the center's mission to explore the cultural as well as scientific contexts that surround us. ✉ *Weisner Bldg., 20 Ames St.,* ☎ *617/253–4680.* ✇ *Free.* ☼ *Oct.–June, Tues.–Thurs. noon–6, Fri. noon–8, weekends noon–6. T stop: Kendall Sq.*

⑦ **Longfellow National Historic Site.** Once home to Henry Wadsworth Longfellow—the poet whose stirring "Miles Standish," "The Village Blacksmith," "Evangeline," "Hiawatha," and "Paul Revere's Midnight Ride" thrilled 19th-century America—this elegant mansion was a wedding gift for the poet in 1843. The National Park Service closed the house in 1998 for renovations that were expected to last through summer 2000. ✉ *105 Brattle St., ¼ mi from the Cambridge Information Booth,* ☎ *617/566–1689 for renovation information.*

⑧ **Massachusetts Institute of Technology.** MIT, at Kendall Square, occupies 135 acres 1½ mi southeast of Harvard, bordering the Charles River. The West Campus has some extraordinary buildings: The Kresge Auditorium, designed by Eero Saarinen with a curving roof and unusual thrust, rests on three, instead of four, points; the nondenominational MIT Chapel is a circular Saarinen design. Free campus tours leave from the **MIT Information Center** (✉ Building 7, 77 Massachusetts Ave., ☎ 617/253–4795) on weekdays at 10 and 2. The center is open weekdays from 9 to 5.

MIT Museum. A place where art and science meet, the MIT Museum showcases photos, paintings, and scientific instruments and memorabilia. A popular ongoing exhibit is the "Hall of Hacks," a look at the pranks MIT students have played over the years. Most notable here is a rare photo of Oliver Reed Smoot, Jr., a 1958 MIT Lambda Chi Alpha pledge. Smoot's future fraternity brothers used the diminutive freshman to measure the distance of the nearby Harvard Bridge, which spans the Charles. Every 5 ft or so became "One Smoot." To this day, the markings remain painted on the bridge. ⊠ *265 Massachusetts Ave.,* ☎ *617/253–4444.* ☞ *$3.* ⊘ *Tues.–Fri. 10–5, weekends noon–5. T stop: Kendall Sq.*

❸ **Peabody Museum of Archaeology and Ethnology.** The Peabody holds one of the world's most outstanding anthropological collections; exhibits focus on Native American and Central and South American cultures. The admission fee includes entrance to the Harvard Museum of Natural History (☞ *above*) as well. ⊠ *11 Divinity Ave.,* ☎ *617/495–2248.* ☞ *$5.* ⊘ *Mon.–Sat. 9–5, Sun. 1–5.*

Radcliffe College. Radcliffe continues to redefine its mission in a time of coeducation. Its lovely and serene yard is the heart of the college, founded in 1879 "to furnish instruction and the opportunities of collegiate life to women and to promote their higher education." An independent corporation within Harvard University, Radcliffe maintains its own physical plant, including the Agassiz Theater. The college also sponsors events, programs, and workshops devoted to women's issues. ⊠ *10 Garden St. T stop: Harvard Sq.*

Semitic Museum. This Harvard institution serves as an exhibit space for Egyptian, Mesopotamian, and ancient Near East artifacts and as a center for archaeological exploration. No stodginess here: A 1999 exhibit showcased 3,400-year-old cuneiform tablets from the Middle East that related the sexually charged tale of a head of government whose alleged philandering put him on public trial. ⊠ *6 Divinity Ave.,* ☎ *617/495–4631.* ☞ *Free.* ⊘ *Weekdays 10–4, Sun. 1–4.*

Dining

Back Bay/Beacon Hill
CONTEMPORARY

$$$$ ✕ **Ambrosia.** Chef Tony Ambrose likes his flavors vivid and his platters tall, from an ostrich meat appetizer to lobster salad with 22-karat-gold vinaigrette—you'll literally eat your money. Take down the French decorations, and the food is haute Yankee, based on native ingredients. The decor is designer-chic: burnished woods, floor-to-ceiling glass windows, an ever-changing arrangement of modern art on the walls. ⊠ *116 Ave. of the Arts,* ☎ *617/247–2400. Reservations essential. AE, MC, V. No lunch weekends.*

$$$–$$$$ ✕ **Biba.** Arguably Boston's best restaurant, and surely one of the most
★   original and high-casual restaurants in America, Biba is a place to see and to be seen. The menu encourages inventive combinations, unusual cuts and produce, and haute comfort food. Take your time, and don't settle for the "classic lobster pizza" if something like vanilla chicken with chestnut puree is available. The wine list is an adventure. ⊠ *272 Boylston St.,* ☎ *617/426–7878. Reservations essential. AE, D, DC, MC, V.*

$$–$$$ ✕ **Brew Moon.** Instead of the usual industrial decor of a brew pub, the flagships of this minichain look like California health-food palaces. The food often has ale as an ingredient and emphasizes salty and peppery elements that keep you ordering more. As often is the case at brewpubs, the darker and stronger ales are best. ⊠ *115 Stuart St., Back Bay,* ☎ *617/742–2739. Cambridge:* ⊠ *50 Church St., Harvard Square,* ☎ *617/499–2739. AE, DC, MC, V.*

$$–$$$ ✕ **Cena.** Red hot, Cena (pronounced like Latin, "*kay*-nah") captures the Symphony crowd with a bistro menu of world-beat flavors that quietly drops red meat and barely mentions chicken and cheese. Order the baked polenta with native wild mushrooms or the *udon* (Japanese noodles) bowl with sautéed local vegetables, and you'll never miss meat.

⊠ *14A Westland Ave.,* ☎ *617/262–1485. Reservations essential. AE, D, MC, V.*

$$–$$$ ✗ **Sonsie.** Café society blossoms along Newbury Street, particularly at the elegant Sonsie, where much of the clientele either sips coffee up front or angles for places at the bar. The restaurant, which opens at 7 AM, is famous for breakfasts that extend well into the afternoon. In warm weather, the entire front of Sonsie becomes an open-air café looking out on upper Newbury Street. The dishes on the menu are basic bistro with an American twist, such as sweet pumpkin tamales with spiced pumpkin flan. ⊠ *327 Newbury St.,* ☎ *617/351–2500. AE, DC, MC, V.*

CONTINENTAL

$$$–$$$$ ✗ **Ritz-Carlton Dining Room.** Traditional in the best sense of the word, the restaurant at the Ritz has a subtly modern menu that still includes classic rack of lamb, roast beef hash, broiled scrod, and seasonal Yankee favorites such as shad roe in May and June. The true glory of the Ritz is the service, aristocratic in its detail, democratically offered to all. Second-floor windows provide a commanding view of the Public Garden. ⊠ *15 Arlington St.,* ☎ *617/536–5700, ext. 6286. Reservations essential. Jacket and tie. AE, D, DC, MC, V.*

CUBAN

$$–$$$ ✗ **Mucho Gusto Café.** On a bohemian block full of jazz students from Berklee College sits this hospitable Cuban restaurant with an *I Love Lucy* decor (most of it for sale) and terrific food. The kitchen excels at black-bean soup, eggplant salad, french-fried onions, and *ropa vieja* (flank steak stewed until it shreds like "old clothes"). The coffee makes you want to get up and dance to the old mambos that are always playing. ⊠ *1124 Boylston St.,* ☎ *617/236–1020. Reservations not accepted for fewer than 5. AE, MC, V. No lunch Mon.–Wed.*

FRENCH

$$$$ ✗ **L'Espalier.** An elegantly modernized Victorian Back Bay town house
★ is the setting for one of the city's best restaurants. Chef-owner Frank McClelland creates an intoxicating blend of new French and newer American cuisine. You can simplify the opulent menu by choosing a prix-fixe tasting menu, such as the innovative vegetarian *dégustation.* ⊠ *30 Gloucester St.,* ☎ *617/262–3023. Reservations essential. Jacket and tie. AE, D, DC, MC, V. Closed Sun. No lunch.*

JAPANESE

$$–$$$ ✗ **Miyako.** A very competitive sushi bar amid many at this end of Back Bay, this little spot also offers estimable hot dishes, including *age shumai* (shrimp fritters), *hamachi teriyaki* (yellowtail teriyaki), and *agedashi dofu* (fried bean curd). Ask for one of the tatami rooms if you have a big party. ⊠ *279A Newbury St.,* ☎ *617/236–0222. AE, DC, MC, V.*

PERSIAN

$$$ ✗ **Lala Rokh.** This is one of the best restaurants of its kind in the United
★ States, a beautifully detailed and delicious fantasia upon Persian food and art, specifically from the Azerbaijani corner that is now northwest Iran. The food includes exotically flavored specialties and dishes as familiar (but superb here) as eggplant puree, pilaf, kebabs, *fesanjoon* (the classic pomegranate-walnut sauce), and lamb stews. ⊠ *97 Mt. Vernon St.,* ☎ *617/720–5511. AE, DC, MC, V. No lunch.*

SEAFOOD

$$$–$$$$ ✗ **Legal Sea Foods.** What began as a tiny restaurant upstairs over a
★ Cambridge fish market has grown to important regional status. The hallmark, as always, is extrafresh seafood. Once puritanically simple preparations have loosened up to include Chinese and French sauces, and wood-grilling is now the preparation of choice. The smoked blue-

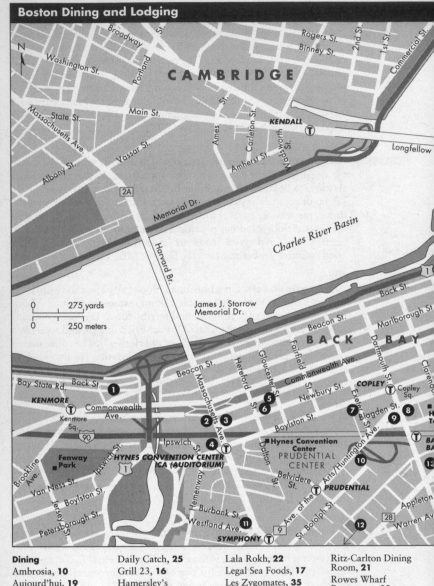

Boston Dining and Lodging

Dining

Ambrosia, **10**
Aujourd'hui, **19**
Baja Mexican Cantina, **13**
Biba, **20**
Brew Moon, **18**
Cena, **11**
Chau Chow, **36**

Daily Catch, **25**
Grill 23, **16**
Hamersley's Bistro, **14**
Jae's Café and Grill, **12**
Jimmy's Harborside, **34**
Julien, **31**
Jumbo Seafood, **37**

Lala Rokh, **22**
Legal Sea Foods, **17**
Les Zygomates, **35**
L'Espalier, **5**
Mamma Maria, **24**
Miyako, **6**
Mucho Gusto Café, **4**
Olives, **23**

Ritz-Carlton Dining Room, **21**
Rowes Wharf Restaurant, **32**
Sonsie, **3**
Tatsukichi-Boston, **29**
Turner Fisheries, **9**
Union Oyster House, **27**

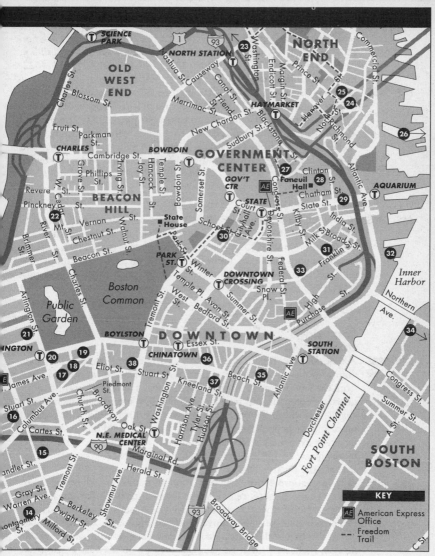

Lodging

Boston Harbor Hotel at Rowes Wharf, **32**

Chandler Inn, **15**

Eliot Hotel, **2**

Fairmont Copley Plaza, **8**

Four Seasons, **19**

Gryphon House, **1**

Hyatt Harborside at Boston International Logan Airport, **26**

Le Meridien Hotel, **33**

Lenox Hotel, **7**

Omni Parker House, **30**

Regal Bostonian, **28**

Ritz-Carlton, **21**

fish pâté is one of the finest appetizers anywhere. Dishes come to the table in whatever order they come out of the kitchen, as freshness is held to be more important than the order of courses. ✉ *26 Park Sq.,* ☎ *617/426–4444. Cambridge:* ✉ *5 Cambridge Center, Kendall Sq.,* ☎ *617/864–3400. Logan Airport:* ✉ *Terminal C,* ☎ *617/569–4622. Reservations not accepted. AE, D, DC, MC, V.*

$$$–$$$$ ✗ **Turner Fisheries of Boston.** On the first floor of the Westin Hotel in Copley Square, Turner Fisheries is second only to Legal Sea Foods (☞ *above*) in its traditional appeal and has outstripped it in trimmings and service. Turner broils, grills, bakes, fries, and steams everything in the ocean but also applies classic and modern sauces, vegetables, and pasta with panache. Any meal should begin with the creamy chowder. ✉ *10 Ave. of the Arts,* ☎ *617/424–7425. Reservations essential. AE, D, DC, MC, V.*

STEAK

$$$–$$$$ ✗ **Grill 23.** Dark paneling, comically oversize flatware, and waiters in white jackets lend this steak house a men's-club ambience. The rotisserie tenderloin with Roquefort mashed potatoes is a winner, as is the meat loaf with mashed potatoes and truffle oil. Seafood actually outsells beef by a narrow margin; grilled Maine salmon with winter root vegetable and truffle hash is one reason why. Break out your jacket and tie. ✉ *161 Berkeley St.,* ☎ *617/542–2255. Reservations essential. AE, D, DC, MC, V. No lunch.*

Cambridge

CONTEMPORARY

$$$–$$$$ ✗ **Salamander.** Take a deep breath as you enter the expansive main
     ★   dining room—it's enticingly filled with aromas of wood and spice from the wood-fired grills and ovens. Entrées are generous and appetizers are eccentric and flavorful, often Asian influenced (menu items change monthly). Favorites are the wood-grilled squid with coconut sauce and the pepper tenderloin over a ragout of wild mushrooms. The service is extremely well paced, and there's a great selection of wines by the glass. ✉ *1 Atheneum St.,* ☎ *617/225–2121. Reservations essential. AE, D, DC, MC, V. Closed Sun.*

$$$–$$$$ ✗ **Union Square Bistro.** This airy room, a floor above the ethnic mar-
     ★   kets of Union Square, remains true in spirit to the bistro ideal of offering warming foods to small, convivial groups. Former sous-chef Helidomar d'Oliveira has moved into the big toque, and the regulars are celebrating with his neat little Brazilian skewers and addictive *pao de aveijo* (cheese puffs). Brunch is served on Sunday. ✉ *16 Bow St., Union Sq., Somerville,* ☎ *617/628–3344. Reservations essential. AE, D, DC, MC, V.*

$$$ ✗ **Blue Room.** Hip, funky, and totally Cambridge, the Blue Room has brightly colored furnishings, a friendly staff, and counters where you can meet other diners while you eat. Convivial owner-chef Steve Johnson blends a whole world of ethnic cuisines, with an emphasis on Mediterranean and Latin American small plates. At peak hours the noise level can be high. ✉ *1 Kendall Sq.,* ☎ *617/494–9034. AE, D, DC, MC, V. No lunch Mon.–Sat.*

$$$ ✕ **East Coast Grill.** Owner-chef-author Chris Schlesinger built his na-
★ tional reputation on grilled foods and red-hot condiments but is now
angling to make his establishment one of the top fish restaurants in
town. Spices and condiments are more restrained, and Schlesinger has
compiled a selection of wines bold and flavorful enough to share a table
with the still highly spiced food. The dining space is completely informal.
Brunch is served on Sunday. ⊠ *1271 Cambridge St.,* ☎ *617/491–6568.
AE, D, MC, V. No lunch.*

$$$ ✕ **Green Street Grill.** Caribbean-born co-owner and chef John Levins
★ is one of the living masters of mixing hot spices with other distinctive
flavors. A recent example is beaten and boiled conch meat simmered
in a Scotch bonnet chili pepper, lime and thyme, green plantain, green
papaya, wild herb rum sauce. But expect an entirely different—and elaborate—preparation with Caribbean grouper or Muscovy duck. ⊠ *280
Green St.,* ☎ *617/876–1655. AE, DC, MC, V. No lunch.*

$$–$$$ ✕ **Cottonwood Café.** This is Tex-Mex pushed to the next dimension.
The atmosphere is Nuevo-Wave-o, with exotic architectural touches
and rustic southwestern details. Best of all is the Snake Bite appetizer:
deep-fried jalapeños stuffed with shrimp and cheese—impossible to resist yet nearly too spicy-hot to eat. ⊠ *1815 Massachusetts Ave.,* ☎ *617/
661–7440. Back Bay:* ⊠ *222 Berkeley St.,* ☎ *617/247–2225. Reservations essential. AE, D, DC, MC, V.*

ECLECTIC

$$$–$$$$ ✕ **Chez Henri.** French-Cuban cuisine may sound like a weird combi-
nation, but it works for this comfortable restaurant. The dinner menu
gets serious with duck tamale with ancho chili, a fancy paella, and truly
French desserts. Brunch is served on Sunday. Turnovers, fritters, and
grilled three-pork Cuban sandwiches are served in the bar. ⊠ *1 Shep-
ard St.,* ☎ *617/354–8980. Reservations not accepted. AE, DC, MC,
V. No lunch.*

FRENCH

$$$–$$$$ ✕ **Sandrine's Bistro.** Chef-owner Raymond Ost goes to his Alsatian
★ roots for flavors easy and intense, but this is a bistro only in the way
that little palace at Versailles was a country house. One hit is the *flam-
menkuche,* the Alsatian onion pizza, but much else is haute cuisine,
like trout Napoleon. ⊠ *8 Holyoke St.,* ☎ *617/497–5300. AE, MC, V.*

PORTUGUESE

$$ ✕ **Sunset Café.** Specialties at this lively café include kale soup thick-
★ ened with potatoes, *mariscada a chefe* (a great seafood combination
in a casserole with fine spices), and shrimp Ana María (panfried in
seafood stock). Among bargain-priced wines on the list are some of
the best Dão reds available outside Portugal. ⊠ *851 Cambridge St.,*
☎ *617/547–2938. AE, D, DC, MC, V.*

Charlestown

MEDITERRANEAN

$$$–$$$$ ✕ **Olives.** This bistro sets the local standard for grilled pizza, piled-on
★ platters of delicious things, "vertical food," and smart signature offer-
ings like the smoked beef short ribs. The crowded seating, noise, long
lines, and abrupt service only add to the legend. Come early or late—or
be prepared for an extended wait: Reservations are taken only for groups
of six or more at 5:30 or 8:30 PM, and there are few nearby alternatives.
⊠ *10 City Sq.,* ☎ *617/242–1999. AE, DC, MC, V. Closed Sun. No lunch.*

Chinatown

CHINESE

$–$$ ✕ **Chau Chow.** *Chau Chow* is the word for people from Swatow in
★ China's Fujian province, and they are known for their wonderful

Cambridge Dining and Lodging

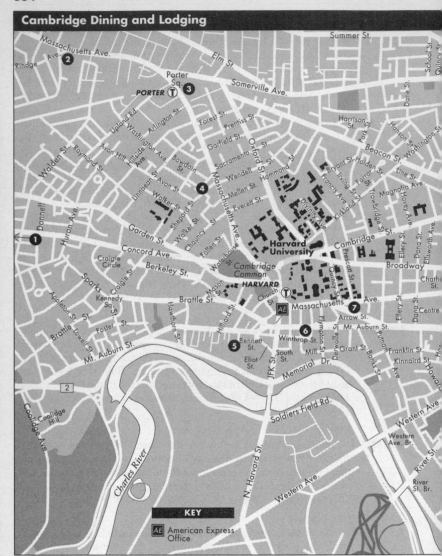

Dining

Blue Room, **11**

Chez Henri, **4**

Cottonwood Café, **3**

East Coast Grill, **9**

Green Street Grill, **14**

Salamander, **13**

Sandrine's Bistro, **6**

Sunset Café, **10**

Union Square
Bistro, **8**

Lodging

A Cambridge House
Bed and Breakfast, **2**

Charles Hotel, **5**

Inn at Harvard, **7**

Royal Sonesta
Hotel, **12**

Susse Chalet Inn, **1**

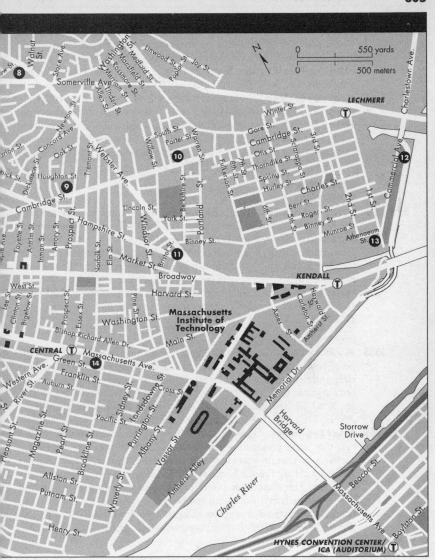

N

| 0 | | 550 yards |
| 0 | | 500 meters |

LECHMERE ⓣ

8

Walnut St.

Store Ave.

Somerville Ave.

Washington St.

Medford St.

Mansfield St.

Rossmore St.

W. Merriam St.

Linwood St.

Poplar St.

Joy St.

Linden St.

Allen St.

Newton Ave.

Concord Ave.

Oak St.

Dickinson St.

Houghton St.

Tremont St.

Webster Ave.

9

Cambridge St.

Fayette St.

Antrim St.

Amory St.

Inman St.

Prospect St.

Hampshire St.

Lincoln St.

Windsor St.

Market St.

Norfolk St.

Elm St.

Bristol St.

11

Broadway

Harvard St.

West St.

Prospect St.

Lee St.

Bigelow St.

Essex St.

Clinton St.

Washington St.

Bishop Richard Allen Dr.

Main St.

Massachusetts Institute of Technology

CENTRAL ⓣ Massachusetts Ave.

Green St.

Franklin St.

Western Ave.

River St.

Auburn St.

14

Magazine St.

Pearl St.

Brookline St.

Sidney St.

Pacific St.

Purrington St.

Albany St.

Landsdowne St.

Cross St.

Vassar St.

Pleasant St.

Allston St.

Putnam St.

Waverly St.

Henry St.

Amherst Alley

Charles River

South St.

Porter St.

Willow St.

Warren St.

10

Berkshire St.

York St.

Portland St.

Fulkerson St.

Binney St.

Winter St.

Gore St.

Cambridge St.

Otis St.

Thorndike St.

Spring St.

Hurley St.

7th St.

8th St.

6th St.

5th St.

Sciarappa St.

3rd St.

Charles St.

Bent St.

Roger St.

Binney St.

KENDALL ⓣ

Harvard St.

Carleton St.

Amherst St.

Ames St.

Munroe St.

Athenaeum St.

13

2nd St.

1st St.

Commercial Ave.

Charlestown Ave.

12

Memorial Dr.

Harvard Bridge

Storrow Drive

Beacon St.

Massachusetts Ave.

Boylston St.

HYNES CONVENTION CENTER/ ICA (AUDITORIUM) ⓣ

seafood. Try the clams in black bean sauce, steamed sea bass, gray sole with its fried fins, or any dish with their famous ginger sauce. Chau Chow has expanded to a larger storefront called Grand Chau Chow across the street and to the giant, three-floor Chau Chow City around two corners at 83 Essex Street. Seating at the original Chau Chow is very tight. ⊠ *50–52 Beach St.,* ☎ *617/292–5166. No credit cards.*

$–$$ ✕ **Jumbo Seafood.** It's not pretentious, but this is one of the best Can-
★   tonese restaurants east of Hong Kong, with live-tank fish and shrimp. Have a whole sea bass with ginger and scallions, and you'll understand the fuss. If you don't like seafood, there are outstanding and unusual vegetables like the stir-fried sugar-snap-pea tendrils. ⊠ *5–9 Hudson St.,* ☎ *617/542–2823. AE, MC, V.*

Downtown
CONTEMPORARY

$$$–$$$$ ✕ **Aujourd'hui.** The formula for Aujourd'hui's success has been to speak softly and attract a discreet crowd. The food reflects an inventive approach to regional ingredients and new American cuisine. Some entrées, such as rack of lamb with braised chard caponata and ragout of flageolet beans and pancetta, can be extremely rich, but the seasonal menu also offers "alternative cuisine" and vegetarian choices. Window tables overlook the Public Garden. ⊠ *Four Seasons Hotel, 200 Boylston St.,* ☎ *617/351–2071. Reservations essential. Jacket required. AE, D, DC, MC, V.*

FRENCH

$$$$ ✕ **Julien.** The handsomest dining room in the city serves some of the
★   best French food in Boston. Julien is a favorite of French business travelers and Boston Francophiles who enjoy the detail of a great Parisian restaurant in their own hometown. ⊠ *Hotel Meridien, 250 Franklin St.,* ☎ *617/451–1900, ext. 7120. Reservations essential. Jacket and tie. AE, D, DC, MC, V. Closed Sun. No lunch Sat.*

$$–$$$ ✕ **Les Zygomates.** *Zygomates,* in French, are the muscles on the human
★   face that make you smile—and this combination wine bar–bistro will certainly do that. In a world of culinary overstatement, Les Zygomates serves up classic French bistro fare that dares to be simple and simply delicious. The restaurant offers prix-fixe menus at both lunch and dinner. Pan-roasted tuna with red pepper coulis and grilled steak au bordelaise with roasted eggplant and garlic typify the taste. ⊠ *129 South St.,* ☎ *617/542–5108. Reservations essential. AE, D, DC, MC, V. No lunch weekends.*

JAPANESE

$$–$$$ ✕ **Tatsukichi-Boston.** Sushi and sashimi are specialties, as are pot-cooked dinners and *kushiagi* (deep-fried kabobs). Meals are served in a modern Japanese setting with Western or tatami-room seating. Upstairs is a karaoke lounge that's popular with Japanese business travelers and tourists. ⊠ *189 State St.,* ☎ *617/720–2468. AE, D, DC, MC, V. No lunch weekends.*

Faneuil Hall
AMERICAN

$$$–$$$$ ✕ **Union Oyster House.** At Boston's oldest continuing restaurant (it was established in 1826), it's best to have what Daniel Webster had—oysters on the half shell at the ground-floor raw bar, which is the oldest part of the restaurant and still the best. The rooms at the top of the narrow staircase are very Ye Olde New England. Uncomfortably small tables and chairs tend to undermine the simple, decent, but expensive food. There is valet parking after 5:30 PM. ⊠ *41 Union St.,* ☎ *617/ 227–2750. AE, D, DC, MC, V.*

North End

ITALIAN

$$$–$$$$ ✗ **Mamma Maria.** Despite the red-sauce name, Mamma Maria is one of the most elegant and romantic restaurants in the North End, from the smoked-seafood ravioli appetizer and the innovative sauces and entrées to the North End's best desserts. You can't go wrong with the tiramisu or specials like chocolate hazelnut cake. ⊠ *3 North Sq.,* ☎ *617/542–2823. AE, D, MC, V.*

SEAFOOD

$$ ✗ **Daily Catch.** Shoulder-crowding small, this storefront restaurant
★ specializes in calamari dishes, black squid-ink fettuccine, and linguine with clam sauce. You've just got to love this place—for the noise, the intimacy, and, above all, the food. ⊠ *323 Hanover St.,* ☎ *617/523–8567. Reservations not accepted. No credit cards.*

South End

CONTEMPORARY

$$$–$$$$ ✗ **Hamersley's Bistro.** Gordon Hamersley has earned renown for such
★ signature dishes as grilled mushroom-and-garlic sandwich, duck confit, and souffléed lemon custard. His place has a full bar, a café area with 10 tables for walk-ins, and a larger dining room that's a little more formal and decorative than the bar and café, though nowhere near stuffy. ⊠ *553 Tremont St.,* ☎ *617/423–2700. AE, D, DC, MC, V.*

MEXICAN

$$ ✗ **Baja Mexican Cantina.** Anything-but-traditional Mexican food is served in a postmodern Southwest decor. Start with a margarita made from your choice of premium tequilas. All the Cal-Mex food that follows is quite good, with lots of vegetarian options. If you're health-conscious, go for the salads, relatively low-fat burritos, or the lean hamburger served in a tortilla. ⊠ *111 Dartmouth St.,* ☎ *617/262–7575. AE, D, DC, MC, V.*

PAN-ASIAN

$$ ✗ **Jae's Café and Grill.** Jae's fusion cuisine attracts a young, happening crowd for sushi, dishes in hot stone pots, and rice noodles served with barely cooked vegetables. A big fish tank adorns the newly expanded main dining room. In the summer, there's lots of sidewalk seating. ⊠ *520 Columbus Ave.,* ☎ *617/421–9405. AE, DC, MC, V.*

Waterfront

CONTEMPORARY

$$$$ ✗ **Rowes Wharf Restaurant.** Chef Daniel Bruce creates scintillating mod-
★ ern menus between the field trips on which he takes his staff to hunt wild mushrooms—his personal passion. Sautéed local wild mushrooms over stone-ground polenta is his signature composition. Roasted Maine lobster with chorizo and sweet corn pudding is the latest thing in dry-heat seafood. The restaurant has Boston's most extensive list of American wines. ⊠ *70 Rowes Wharf,* ☎ *617/439–3995. Reservations essential. Jacket required. AE, D, DC, MC, V.*

SEAFOOD

$$–$$$ ✗ **Jimmy's Harborside.** The fish chowder here is fresh and bright-tasting, and seasonal fish specials simply broiled or fried are excellent. You will fish through a lot of cream sauce to find the traditional finnan haddie, however. The wine list is almost all American, with oversize bottles a specialty. ⊠ *242 Northern Ave.,* ☎ *617/423–1000. Reservations essential. AE, D, DC, MC, V. No lunch Sun.*

Lodging

If your biggest dilemma is deciding whether to spend $300 per night on old-fashioned elegance or extravagant modernity, you've come to the right city. The bulk of Boston's accommodations are not cheap; however, visitors with limited cash will find choices among the smaller, older establishments, the modern motels, or—perhaps the best option (if you can take early morning small talk)—the bed-and-breakfast inn.

Back Bay

$$$$ 🖬 **Eliot Hotel.** The luxurious suites at the Eliot have Italian marble bathrooms, two cable-equipped televisions, and tasteful pastel-hued decor. The airy restaurant, Clio, has been garnering rave reviews for its serene ambience and contemporary French-American cuisine. The Eliot is steps from Newbury Street and a short walk to Kenmore Square. ✉ *370 Commonwealth Ave., 02215,* ☎ *617/267–1607 or 800/443–5468,* 𝖥𝖠𝖷 *617/ 536–9114. 95 suites. Restaurant, in-room data ports, minibars, no-smoking rooms, room service, meeting rooms, baby-sitting, laundry service and dry cleaning, concierge, valet parking (fee). AE, D, DC, MC, V.*

$$$$ 🖬 **Fairmont Copley Plaza.** The public spaces of this 1912 landmark
★ are decidedly grand, with high gilded and painted ceilings, mosaic floors, marble pillars, and crystal chandeliers. Guest rooms have custom furniture from Italy, elegant marble bathrooms, and fax machines. One of the restaurants, called the Oak Room to match its mahogany-paneled twin in New York's Plaza Hotel, has a dance floor and a raw bar. Despite the imposing Victorian surroundings, the atmosphere is gracious and welcoming, thanks to the multilingual staff. ✉ *138 St. James Ave., 02116,* ☎ *617/267–5300 or 800/527–4727,* 𝖥𝖠𝖷 *617/247– 6681. 312 rooms, 67 suites. 2 restaurants, 2 bars, in-room data ports, minibars, no-smoking floors, room service, barbershop, beauty salon, exercise room, baby-sitting, laundry service and dry cleaning, concierge, business services, parking (fee). AE, D, DC, MC, V.*

$$$$ 🖬 **Four Seasons.** This stellar hotel, which overlooks the Public Garden, is famed for luxurious personal service of the sort demanded by
★ celebrities and heads of state. It has huge rooms with king-size beds and newly remodeled bathrooms with marble the color of cabernet and chocolate, and a fully equipped health club with whirlpool, sauna, and heated 51-ft swimming pool. The Bristol Lounge serves high tea daily at 3 PM. ✉ *200 Boylston St., 02116,* ☎ *617/338–4400 or 800/332– 3442,* 𝖥𝖠𝖷 *617/423–0154. 216 rooms, 72 suites. 2 restaurants, in-room data ports, in-room safes, minibars, no-smoking floors, room service, indoor pool, health club, baby-sitting, laundry service and dry cleaning, concierge, business services, parking (fee). AE, D, DC, MC, V.*

$$$$ 🖬 **Lenox Hotel.** The soundproof guest rooms at the Lenox contain custom-made traditional furnishings, spacious walk-in closets, and marble baths; some of the corner rooms have working fireplaces. The Samuel Adams Brew House and the popular bistro Anago are both worthy stops. ✉ *710 Boylston St., 02116,* ☎ *617/536–5300 or 800/225– 7676,* 𝖥𝖠𝖷 *617/236–0351. 209 rooms, 3 suites. 2 restaurants, bar, in-room data ports, no-smoking floor, room service, exercise room, baby-sitting, dry cleaning, concierge, parking (fee). AE, D, DC, MC, V.*

$$$$ 🖬 **Ritz-Carlton.** Despite the attractions of the upstart Four Seasons (☞
★ *above*), many visitors to Boston would never dream of staying anywhere but the Ritz, thanks to its unmatched location, dignified elegance, and fierce devotion to its guests' comfort and privacy. Suites in the older section have parlors with working fireplaces and wonderful views of the Public Garden. If you stay in the newer section, you'll trade the garden view for larger bathrooms with double sinks. Public rooms include the elegant café, the sedate bar, and the Lounge. ✉ *Arlington and Newbury Sts., 02117,* ☎ *617/536–5700 or 800/241–3333,* 𝖥𝖠𝖷 *617/*

536–1335. 233 rooms, 42 suites. Restaurant, bar, lobby lounge, in-room safes, no-smoking rooms, refrigerators, room service, beauty salon, exercise room, baby-sitting, laundry service, concierge, parking (fee). AE, D, DC, MC, V.

$ ⌶ **Chandler Inn.** This cozy hotel with economical rates and a friendly staff is one of the best bargains in the city. Close to an overpass near the Back Bay, at the end of one of the South End's prettiest streets, it's an easy walk to the T, the Amtrak station, Newbury Street's boutiques, or any of Tremont Street's trendy restaurants. Rooms are small but comfortable. The restaurant is open weekends only. ✉ *26 Chandler St., 02115,* ☎ *617/482–3450,* ℻ *617/542–3428. 56 rooms. Restaurant (weekends only), bar. Continental breakfast. AE, D, DC, MC, V.*

Cambridge

$$$$ ⌶ **Charles Hotel.** You can't stay much closer to the center of Harvard
★   Square than at this first-class hotel adjacent to the Kennedy School of Government. Guest rooms are equipped with terry robes, quilted down comforters, and Bose radios; suites have fireplaces. Both restaurants are excellent, and the Regattabar attracts world-class musicians. ✉ *1 Bennett St., 02138,* ☎ *617/864–1200 or 800/882–1818,* ℻ *617/864–5715. 296 rooms, 44 suites. 2 restaurants, 2 bars, in-room data ports, in-room safes, minibars, no-smoking rooms, room service, pool, spa, health club, nightclub, baby-sitting, laundry service and dry cleaning, concierge, business services, parking (fee). AE, DC, MC, V.*

$$$$ ⌶ **Royal Sonesta Hotel.** The views of Beacon Hill across the Charles
★   River are superb from this 10-floor building, which is near the Museum of Science and adjacent to the CambridgeSide Galleria. Impressive modern artworks are displayed throughout the hotel. Some suites have kitchenettes. The hotel offers great family excursion packages that include boat rides, ice cream, and bicycle rentals. ✉ *5 Cambridge Pkwy., 02142,* ☎ *617/806–4200 or 800/766–3782,* ℻ *617/806–4232. 374 rooms, 26 suites. 2 restaurants, 2 bars, in-room data ports, in-room safes, minibars, no-smoking rooms, room service, indoor-outdoor pool, spa, health club, bicycles, dry cleaning, business services, parking (fee). AE, D, DC, MC, V.*

$$$–$$$$ ⌶ **Inn at Harvard.** This hotel borders Harvard Yard, and its Georgian-
★   style brick exterior mirrors the design of Harvard's own buildings. Original 17th- and 18th-century sketches, on loan from the nearby Fogg Art Museum, and contemporary watercolors decorate the rooms, many of which have tiny balconies; most rooms have oversize windows with views of Harvard Square or Harvard Yard. Guests are granted access to the Cambridge YMCA in Central Square. ✉ *1201 Massachusetts Ave., 02138,* ☎ *617/491–2222 or 800/458–5886,* ℻ *617/491–6520. 109 rooms, 4 suites. Restaurant, in-room data ports, no-smoking floors, room service, dry cleaning, business services, parking (fee). AE, D, DC, MC, V.*

$$ $$$$ ⌶ **A Cambridge House Bed and Breakfast.** This Greek Revival Cambridge House home is on busy Massachusetts Avenue but set well back from the road. The no-smoking B&B is a haven of peace and otherworldliness, with richly carved cherry paneling, a grand mahogany fireplace, elegant Victorian antiques, and polished wood floors overlaid with Oriental rugs. Harvard Square is a distant walk, but public transportation is nearby. ✉ *2218 Massachusetts Ave., 02140,* ☎ *617/491–6300 or 800/232–9989,* ℻ *617/868–2848. 16 rooms, 12 with bath. Free parking. Full breakfast. MC, V.*

$ ⌶ **Susse Chalet Inn.** This is a typical Susse Chalet operation: clean, economical, and spare. A 10-minute drive from Harvard Square, it is isolated from most shopping and attractions but within walking distance of the Red Line terminus, offering T access to Boston and Cambridge sights. ✉ *211 Concord Turnpike, 02140,* ☎ *617/661–7800 or 800/524–2538,* FAX *617/868–8153. 78 rooms. In-room data ports, no-smoking rooms, coin laundry, dry cleaning, free parking. Continental breakfast. AE, D, DC, MC, V.*

Downtown

$$$$ 🏨 **Boston Harbor Hotel at Rowes Wharf.** Everything here is done on
★   a grand scale, starting with the dramatic entrance through an 80-ft arch-way. Guest rooms—decorated in shades of mauve, green, and soft yel-low—have either city or water views, and some have balconies. The Rowes Wharf Restaurant specializes in seafood and American cuisine and hosts a spectacular Sunday brunch. The hotel is within walking distance of Faneuil Hall, the North End, the New England Aquarium, and the Financial District. ✉ *70 Rowes Wharf, 02110,* ☎ *617/439–7000 or 800/752–7077* FAX *617/345–6799. 204 rooms, 26 suites. 2 restaurants, bar, outdoor café, no-smoking rooms, room service, in-door lap pool, beauty salons, spa, health club, concierge, business ser-vices, valet parking. AE, D, DC, MC, V.*

$$$$ 🏨 **Le Meridien Hotel.** Once the Federal Reserve Building, this 1922 Re-
★   naissance Revival landmark in the center of the Financial District still exudes an almost intimidating aura of money and power. Most rooms, including some bilevel, skylighted suites, have queen-size or king-size beds; all have a small sitting area. ✉ *250 Franklin St., 02110,* ☎ *617/451–1900 or 800/543–4300,* FAX *617/423–2844. 309 rooms, 17 suites. 2 restaurants, 2 bars, in-room data ports, minibars, no-smoking floors, room service, indoor pool, health club, laundry service and dry clean-ing, concierge, parking (fee). AE, D, DC, MC, V.*

$$$$ 🏨 **Regal Bostonian.** Old and new blend intriguingly at this small lux-
★   ury hotel: The Harkness Wing, built as a warehouse in 1824, has 42 rooms with working fireplaces and exposed beamed ceilings, while rooms in the newer wing are done in light woods, crackle finishes, and soft yellows and blues. The Bostonian is adjacent to Government Center and an underpass away from the Italian North End. Request a room facing away from the street if you'd rather not awaken to the bustle of Quincy Market at dawn. ✉ *Faneuil Hall Marketplace, 02109,* ☎ *617/523–3600 or 800/343–0922,* FAX *617/523–2454. 152 rooms, 11 suites. Restaurant, lobby lounge, in-room data ports, no-smoking rooms, room service, laundry service and dry cleaning, concierge, valet parking. AE, D, DC, MC, V.*

$$–$$$$ 🏨 **Omni Parker House.** The oldest continuously operating hotel in Amer-ica is known for two things: Parker House rolls and Boston cream pie, both of which were invented here. A 1998 renovation restored the orig-inal Colonial-style decor in both the lobby and guest rooms, and fur-niture was custom-built to accommodate the small size of the guest rooms. Appropriately, this historic hotel stands opposite old City Hall, near Government Center, right on the Freedom Trail. ✉ *60 School St., 02108,* ☎ *617/227–8600 or 800/843–6664,* FAX *617/742–5729. 552 rooms, 26 suites. Restaurant, lounge, in-room data ports, room ser-vice, baby-sitting, concierge, business services, valet parking (fee). AE, D, DC, MC, V.*

Kenmore Square

$$$–$$$$ 🏨 **Gryphon House.** Each suite in this four-story brownstone is the-
★   matically decorated; for instance, one evokes a Victorian parlor, another a medieval castle. Each is rich with amenities—gas fireplace, wet bar, refrigerator, TV/VCR, CD player—but nicest of all are the enormous bathrooms with oversize tubs and separate showers. Even the staircase is extraordinary: a 19th-century wallpaper mural, "El Dorado," wraps along the wall. (There is no elevator.) See if you can spot the recently commissioned faux marble work and trompe l'oeil paintings and mu-

rals by local artist Michael Ernest Kirk. ⊠ *9 Bay State Rd., 02215,* ☎ *617/375–9003,* FAX *617/425–0716. 8 suites. In-room data ports, no-smoking rooms, free parking. Continental breakfast. AE, D, DC, MC, V.*

Logan Airport

$$–$$$ 🏨 **Hyatt Harborside at Boston International Logan Airport.** It's easy to get anywhere from the Hyatt, which operates its own shuttle to all Logan Airport terminals and the Airport T stop; guests get a discount on the water shuttle that runs between the airport and downtown. All floors but one are nonsmoking, and all rooms are soundproofed. ⊠ *101 Harborside Dr., 02128,* ☎ *617/568–1234 or 800/233–1234,* FAX *617/567–8856. 270 rooms, 11 suites. Restaurant, bar, in-room data ports, room service, indoor pool, sauna, exercise room, laundry service and dry cleaning, concierge, business services, parking (fee). AE, D, DC, MC, V.*

Nightlife and the Arts

Nightlife

Good sources of information are the *Boston Globe* Calendar section and the weekly listings of the *Boston Phoenix* (both published on Thursday). The Friday "Music" and Sunday "Arts" sections in the *Boston Globe* also contain recommendations for the week's top events. *Boston* magazine's "On the Town" feature provides a somewhat less detailed but useful monthly overview. For clubs of all kinds, call to check cover charges, hours, and special theme nights.

BARS AND LOUNGES

Boston Beer Works (⊠ 61 Brookline Ave., Kenmore Square, ☎ 617/536–2337) serves up its own brews to students, young professionals, and baseball fans from nearby Fenway Park.

Bull & Finch Pub (⊠ 84 Beacon St., Beacon Hill, ☎ 617/227–9605), best known for inspiring the TV series *Cheers,* still often attracts long lines of tourists and students.

Cambridge Brewing Co., (⊠ 1 Kendall Sq., Bldg. 100, Cambridge, ☎ 617/494–1994) is a cheerful, noisy microbrewery that offers patio seating in warm weather. Despite the address, it's a long haul from the Kendall Square T-stop.

Club Café &Lounge (⊠ 209 Columbus Ave., Back Bay/South End, ☎ 617/536–0966) is among the smartest spots in town for gay men and lesbians, with a bar, lounge, and new American restaurant.

John Harvard's Brew House (⊠ 33 Dunster St., Harvard Sq., Cambridge, ☎ 617/868–3585), an English-style pub, dispenses a range of ales, lagers, pilsners, and stouts brewed on the premises.

Mercury Bar (⊠ 116 Boylston St., ☎ 617/482–7799), popular among well-heeled young professionals and theatergoers, has a sleek 100-ft bar facing a row of raised, semicircular booths and a separate dining room. Bar patrons can order from the extensive tapas menu.

Top of the Hub (⊠ Prudential Center, 800 Boylston St., ☎ 617/536–1775) has live jazz and fabulous views, making the steep drink prices worthwhile.

BLUES/R&B/FOLK CLUBS

Club Passim (⊠ 47 Palmer St., Harvard Sq., Cambridge, ☎ 617/492–7679) is one of the country's most famous venues for live folk music. The spare, light basement room has tables close together, with wait service, and a separate coffee bar–restaurant counter.

House of Blues (⊠ 96 Winthrop St., Harvard Sq., Cambridge, ☎ 617/491–2583) offers live blues nightly at 10; on Sunday there's a gospel brunch.

Marketplace Café (⊠ 300 Faneuil Hall, Quincy Market, ☎ 617/227–9660) is a "no cover" treasure in the North Market building, with jazz and blues nightly beginning at 9.

CAFÉS AND COFFEEHOUSES

Caffé Vittoria (⊠ 296 Hanover St., North End, ☎ 617/227–7606) is the biggest and the best of the Italian neighborhood's cafés. Stop in after dinner for coffee and tiramisu or cannoli.

Roasters (⊠ 85 Newbury St., ☎ 617/867–9967) has outdoor seating for sunny days. Inside, a huge bay window allows maximum people-watching while you nibble fresh pastry and sip coffee roasted on the premises.

Tealuxe (⊠ Zero Brattle St., Harvard Sq., Cambridge, ☎ 617/441–0077) is a tiny "tea bar" with more than 100 different herbal and traditional blends—and just one type of coffee.

1369 Coffee House (⊠ 757 Massachusetts Ave., Central Sq., Cambridge, ☎ 617/576–4600) serves fresh-brewed coffee in individual pots and provides outlets for portable computers.

COMEDY

Comedy Connection (⊠ Faneuil Hall Marketplace, ☎ 617/248–9700) books local and nationally known acts nightly.

Dick Doherty's Comedy Vault (⊠ Remington's, 124 Boylston St., ☎ 781/938–8088), tucked away in a former bank vault, offers sketch, stand-up, improv, and open-mike nights.

ImprovBoston (⊠ Back Alley Theater, 1253 Cambridge St., Cambridge, ☎ 617/576–1253) presents improv, including a Sunday family matinee.

DANCE CLUBS

Axis (⊠ 13 Lansdowne St., Kenmore Sq., ☎ 617/262–2424) has high-energy dancing for more than 1,000 people. Friday is "X Night," starring DJs from alternative radio station WFNX. On Sundays, Axis and next-door Avalon (☞ Rock Clubs, *below*) have a combined-admission "Gay Night."

International (⊠ 184 High St., ☎ 617/542–4747) is a strikingly elegant, multifaceted club in the generally staid Financial District. Theme nights include jazz, acid jazz, soul, and '70s dance hits.

Karma Club (⊠ 11 Lansdowne St., Kenmore Sq., ☎ 617/421–9678) is an exotic Asian-Indian fantasyland; drop in here for techno dance music, live pop, rock, and jazz concerts, or even a DJ lounge session featuring Sinatra, soul, or '80s funk.

M80 (⊠ 969 Commonwealth Ave., ☎ 617/562–8800), just off the Paradise (☞ Rock Club, *below*), is another Euro-club attracting hordes of Armani-clad real and wannabe jet-setters.

Man Ray (⊠ 21 Brookline St., Inman Sq., Cambridge, ☎ 617/864–0400) is the home of Boston's alternative and goth scene, with industrial, house, techno, disco, and trance music. Friday night is "Fetish Night." Wear black. The club is closed Monday and Tuesday.

The **Roxy** (⊠ 279 Tremont St.,, ☎ 617/338–7699) is Boston's biggest nightclub, renowned for theme events such as its reggae, salsa, swing, and Top 40 nights.

GAY AND LESBIAN CLUBS

For more on gay and lesbian nightlife, see the *Boston Phoenix* or *Bay Windows* newspaper.

Axis (☞ Dance Clubs, *above*).

Buzz Boston (⊠ 51–67 Stuart St., ☎ 617/267–8969), which stands just where the Theater District meets the South End, offers drinking and dancing for a 21-plus crowd.

Club Café and Lounge (☞ Bars and Lounges, *above*).

JAZZ

Regattabar (✉ Charles Hotel, Bennett and Eliot Sts., Cambridge, ☎ 617/864–1200; 617/876–7777 for tickets) headlines top names in jazz.
Ryles (✉ 212 Hampshire St., Cambridge, ☎ 617/876–9330) is one of the best places for new music and musicians, with a different group playing on each floor.
Scullers Jazz Club (✉ DoubleTree Guest Suites Hotel, 400 Soldiers Field Rd., ☎ 617/783–0811) presents two live jazz shows nightly Tuesday–Saturday. Reservations are advised.
Wally's Café (✉ 427 Massachusetts Ave., South End, ☎ 617/424–1408) has a loyal clientele hooked on jazz and blues. The performers are mostly locals.

ROCK CLUBS

Avalon (✉ 15 Lansdowne St., Kenmore Sq., ☎ 617/262–2424) hosts concerts by alternative, rock, and dance acts, then turns into a dance club. Themes include "Euro-night," Top 40, and techno; on Sundays, Avalon and next-door Axis (☞ Dance Clubs, *above*) have a combined-admission "Gay Night." **Ticketmaster** (☎ 617/931–2000) sells advance tickets.
Bill's Bar (✉ 5 Lansdowne St., Kenmore Sq., ☎ 617/421–9678) has live music nightly, including rock, reggae, alternative, and swing.
Lizard Lounge (✉ 1667 Massachusetts Ave., Cambridge, ☎ 617/547–0759), one of the area's hottest nightspots, presents national and lesser-known folk, rock, acid jazz and pop bands, a performance cabaret on Wednesdays, and a "poetry jam" on Sundays.
Mama Kin (✉ 36 Lansdowne St., Kenmore Sq., ☎ 617/536–2100), jointly owned by members of the Boston-based rock group Aerosmith and a local impresario, presents local and national bands.
Middle East Café (✉ 472 Massachusetts Ave., Central Sq., ☎ 617/497–0576) showcases live local and national acts as well as belly dancing, folk, jazz, and even the occasional country-tinged rock band.
Paradise Rock Club (✉ 967 Commonwealth Ave., ☎ 617/254–3939) is a small club known for having hosted big-name national and local rock, jazz, folk, blues, alternative, and country acts. Buy tickets at Ticketmaster (☞ *below*) or at the box office.

SINGLES

Trattoria Il Panino &Club (✉ 295 Franklin St., ☎ 617/338–1000) attracts mostly well-heeled professionals. The five-floor complex offers informal and formal dining, a jazz bar, and two dance floors. Go dressy.
Sonsie (☞ Back Bay/Beacon Hill *in* Dining, *above*) has no music except a stereo system that often gets drowned out by the conversation at this see-and-be-seen bistro. The bar crowd is full of trendy, cosmopolitan types and professionals.

The Arts

BosTix is Boston's official entertainment information center and the city's largest ticket agency. It is a full-price **Ticketmaster** outlet, and, beginning at 11 AM, it sells half-price tickets for same-day performances; the "menu board" in front of the booth announces the available events. Only cash and traveler's checks are accepted. People often begin lining up well before the agency opens. ✉ *Faneuil Hall Marketplace,* ☎ *617/723–5181 recorded message.* ☉ *Tues.–Sat. 10–6, Sun. 11–4.* ✉ *Copley Sq., near corner of Boylston and Dartmouth Sts.* ☉ *Mon.–Sat. 10–6, Sun. 11–4.* ✉ *Holyoke Arcade Bldg., Harvard Sq., Cambridge.* ☉ *Tues.–Sat. 10–6, Sun. 11–4.*

Ticketmaster (☎ 617/931–2000 or 617/931–2787) allows phone charges to major credit cards, weekdays 9 AM–10 PM, weekends 9–8.

There are no refunds or exchanges, and you pay a service charge. It also has outlets in local stores; call for nearest address.

NEXT Ticketing (☎ 617/423–6398), a Boston-based outlet, handles tickets for shows at the Harborlights outdoor performance center, the Orpheum Theatre, and Avalon and other nightclubs. The service, which uses a completely automated 24-hour ticket reservation system, also sells tickets online.

DANCE

Boston Ballet (✉ 19 Clarendon St., ☎ 617/695–6950), the city's premier dance company, performs classical and modern works, primarily at the Wang Center (☞ Theater, *below*). Its annual *Nutcracker* is a Boston holiday tradition. **Ballet Theatre of Boston** (✉ 186 Massachusetts Ave., ☎ 617/262–0961) offers a contemporary repertory, primarily at the Emerson Majestic Theatre (☞ Theater, *below*). **Dance Umbrella** (✉ 515 Washington St., ☎ 617/482–7570) performs contemporary and multicultural dance at the Emerson Majestic Theatre (☞ Theater, *below*).

FILM

The **Brattle Theatre** (✉ 40 Brattle St., Harvard Sq., Cambridge, ☎ 617/876–6837) is a small downstairs cinema catering to classic-movie buffs and fans of new foreign and independent films. **Harvard Film Archive** (✉ Carpenter Center for the Visual Arts, 24 Quincy St., Cambridge, ☎ 617/495–4700) screens the works of directors not usually shown at commercial cinemas.

MUSIC

Berklee Performance Center (✉ 136 Massachusetts Ave., ☎ 617/266–1400; 617/266–7455 for recorded information) is best known for its jazz programs. At press time **Harborlights** (✉ Boston Marine Industrial Park, ☎ 617/737–6100 or 617/443–0161), an outdoor concert venue on Boston Harbor, was set to move down the street from its former location. **Hatch Memorial Shell** (✉ off Storrow Dr. at Embankment, ☎ 617/727–9548) is a jewel of an acoustic shell where the Boston Pops perform free summer concerts. **Jordan Hall at the New England Conservatory** (✉ 30 Gainsborough St., ☎ 617/536–2412), ideal for everything from chamber music to a full orchestra, is home to the Boston Philharmonic. **Kresge Auditorium** (✉ 77 Massachusetts Ave., Cambridge, ☎ 617/253–2826 or 617/253–4003) is MIT's hall for pop and classical concerts. **Orpheum Theatre** (✉ 1 Hamilton Pl., off Tremont St., ☎ 617/482–0650) is a popular forum for national and local rock acts. **Pickman Recital Hall** (✉ 27 Garden St., Cambridge, ☎ 617/876–0956) is Longy School of Music's excellent acoustical setting for smaller ensembles and recitals. **Symphony Hall** (✉ 301 Massachusetts Ave., ☎ 617/266–1492 or 800/274–8499), one of the world's most perfect acoustical settings, is home to the Boston Symphony Orchestra and the Boston Pops.

OPERA

The **Boston Lyric Opera Company** (✉ 114 State St., ☎ 617/542–6772) presents three productions each season.

PERFORMANCE VENUES

Among the Theater District venues that present a variety of local and touring dance, drama, musical, and opera productions are the **Colonial Theatre** (✉ 106 Boylston St., ☎ 617/426–9366), **Shubert Theatre** (✉ 265 Tremont St., ☎ 617/426–9393), **Wang Center for the Performing Arts** (✉ 270 Tremont St., ☎ 617/482–9393), **Wilbur Theatre** (✉ 246 Tremont St., ☎ 618/423–7440).

THEATER

The **Boston Center for the Arts** (⊠ 539 Tremont St., ☎ 617/426–7700) houses more than a dozen quirky low-budget troupes in four spaces. **Charles Playhouse** (⊠ 74 Warrenton St., ☎ 617/426–6912), presents two long-running shows: the avant-garde *Blue Man Group,* and *Shear Madness* (☎ 617/426–5225), an audience-participation whodunit. **Emerson Majestic Theatre** (⊠ 219 Tremont St., ☎ 617/578–8727) hosts everything from dance to drama to classical concerts. The **Huntington Theatre Company** (⊠ 264 Ave. of the Arts, ☎ 617/266–0800), affiliated with Boston University, performs a mix of established 20th-century plays and classics. The **Loeb Drama Center** (⊠ 64 Brattle St., Harvard Sq., Cambridge, ☎ 617/495–2668) is home to the acclaimed American Repertory Theater, which produces classic and experimental works.

Outdoor Activities and Sports

Participant Sports

Most public recreational facilities, including the many skating rinks and tennis courts, are operated by the **Metropolitan District Commission** (⊠ 20 Somerset St., ☎ 617/727–5114 or ext. 555).

BIKING

The **Dr. Paul Dudley White Bikeway,** about 18 mi long, runs along both sides of the Charles River. The **Bicycle Workshop** (⊠ 259 Massachusetts Ave., Cambridge, ☎ 617/876–6555) rents bicycles, fixes flat tires (while you wait), and delivers bicycles to your hotel.

BILLIARDS

Flat Top Johnny's (⊠ 1 Kendall Square, Cambridge, ☎ 617/494–9565) is the hippest billiards hall around. Members of Boston's better local bands often hang out here on their nights off. **Jillian's Billiard Club** (⊠ 145 Ipswich St., ☎ 617/437–0300) is a semiposh joint near Fenway Park with the atmosphere of an English gentleman's library. The 56-table pool hall also has three bars, a café, darts, shuffleboard, table tennis, a motion simulator, and more than 200 high-tech games.

JOGGING

Both sides of the Charles River are popular with joggers. Many hotels have printed maps of nearby routes.

PHYSICAL FITNESS

The extensive facilities of the **Greater Boston YMCA** (⊠ 316 Ave. of the Arts, ☎ 617/536–7800) are open for $5 per day (for up to two weeks) to members of other YMCAs in the Boston area; if you have out-of-state YMCA membership, you can use the Boston Y free for up to a week. Nonmembers pay $10 per day or $65 for one month. The site has pools, squash, racquetball courts, cardiovascular equipment, free weights, aerobics, track, and sauna.

ROLLERBLADING

From May to October, **Memorial Drive** on the Cambridge side of the Charles River is closed to auto traffic on Sunday from 11 AM to 7 PM. On the Boston side of the river, the **Esplanade** area offers some excellent skating opportunities. **Beacon Hill Skate Shop** (⊠ 135 Charles St. S, off Tremont St., ☎ 617/482–7400) rents blades for $5 per hour or $15 per day (you need a credit card for deposit) year-round.

Spectator Sports

The **Boston Bruins** (☎ 617/624–1000; 617/931–2000 for Ticketmaster) of the National Hockey League hit the ice at the FleetCenter (⊠ Causeway St. at Haverhill St.). The **Boston Celtics** (☎ 617/624–1000;

617/931–2000 for Ticketmaster) of the National Basketball Association shoot their hoops at the FleetCenter. The **Boston Red Sox** (☎ 617/267–1700 for tickets) play American League baseball at Fenway Park (✉ 4 Yawkey Way). The **New England Patriots** (☎ 800/543–1776) of the National Football League play their games at Foxboro Stadium in Foxboro, 45 minutes south of the city.

Every Patriot's Day (the Monday closest to April 19), fans gather along the Hopkinton-to-Boston route of the **Boston Marathon** to cheer the more than 12,000 runners from all over the world. The race ends near Copley Square in the Back Bay. For information, call the Boston Athletic Association (☎ 617/236–1652).

Shopping

Boston's shops and stores are generally open from Monday to Saturday between 9:30 and 7. Some stores, particularly those in malls or tourist areas, are open on Sunday from noon until 5. The state sales tax of 5% does not apply to clothing or to food, except in restaurants. However, there is a 5% luxury tax on clothes priced over $175 per item; the tax is levied on the amount over $175. Boston's two daily newspapers, the *Globe* and the *Herald,* are the best places to learn about sales.

Shopping Districts

Most of Boston's stores and shops are in the area bounded by Quincy Market, the Back Bay, downtown, and Copley Square. There are few outlet stores in the area, but there are plenty of bargains, particularly in the world-famous Filene's Basement.

BOSTON

Charles Street in Beacon Hill attracts antiques and boutique lovers; some of the city's prettiest shops are here. (River Street, parallel to Charles and near the intersection with Chestnut, is also an excellent source for antiques.) **Copley Place** (✉ 100 Ave. of the Arts, ☎ 617/375–4400), an indoor shopping mall that connects the Westin and Marriott hotels in Back Bay, is a blend of the elegant, the glitzy, and the often overpriced. Prices in the shops on the second level tend to be a bit lower. **Downtown Crossing,** Boston's downtown shopping area, has a festival feeling year-round in its usually crowded pedestrian mall. The city's two largest department stores, Macy's and Filene's (with the famous Filene's Basement beneath it), are here. **Faneuil Hall Marketplace** (☎ 617/338–2323) continues to buzz despite its strong mall overtones and a surfeit of tourists. There are dozens of shops (mostly chains like Crate & Barrel and Victoria's Secret), pushcarts with a variety of wares, street performers, and one of the area's great food experiences, Quincy Market. Friday and Saturday are the days to walk through **Haymarket,** a jumble of outdoor fruit and vegetable vendors, meat markets, and fishmongers. **Newbury Street** in the Back Bay contains stylish clothing and jewelry boutiques and au courant art galleries. Toward Massachusetts Avenue, Newbury Street gets funkier with hip clothing stores, ice cream shops, music stores, bookstores, and Tower Music and Video.

CAMBRIDGE

CambridgeSide Galleria (✉ 100 CambridgeSide Pl., ☎ 617/621–8666) is a three-story mall in East Cambridge, accessible from the Green Line Lechmere T stop and a shuttle from the Kendall T stop. Filene's and Sears anchor the center. **Harvard Square** comprises just a few blocks but holds more than 150 stores selling clothes, books and records, furnishings, and a surprising range of specialty items.

Department Stores

Filene's (✉ 426 Washington St., ☎ 617/357–2100; ✉ CambridgeSide Galleria, Cambridge, ☎ 617/621–3800), a full-service department store, carries American name-brand and designer-label men's and women's formal, casual, and career clothing, including designers like Tommy Hilfiger, Calvin Klein, and Ralph Lauren. Jewelry, shoes, cosmetics, bedding, towels, and luggage are found at the Downtown Crossing store. **Filene's Basement** (✉ 426 Washington St., ☎ 617/542–2011) has spawned suburban outlets, but this is the only branch where items are automatically reduced in price according to the number of days they've been on the rack. **Macy's** (✉ 450 Washington St., ☎ 617/357–3000) carries men's and women's clothing, including top designers, as well as an extensive selection of housewares, furniture, and cosmetics. It has direct access to the Downtown Crossing T station. **Neiman Marcus** (✉ 5 Copley Pl., ☎ 617/536–3660), the flashy Texas retailer, has three levels of high fashion, Steuben glass, and gadgetry. **Saks Fifth Avenue** (✉ 1 Ring Rd., Prudential Center, ☎ 617/262–8500) offers top-of-the-line clothing, from more traditional styles to avant-garde apparel, plus accessories and cosmetics.

Specialty Stores

ANTIQUES

Autrefois Antiques (✉ 125 Newbury St., ☎ 617/424–8823) stocks ivory, silver, Chinese lamps and vases, and country-French and some Italian 18th- and 19th-century antiques and furniture. The dealers at the **Boston Antique Co-op** (✉ 119 Charles St., ☎ 617/227–9810 or 227–9811) sell everything from furniture to jewelry. **Cambridge Antique Market** (✉ 201 Msgr. O'Brien Hwy., Cambridge, ☎ 617/868–9655), off the beaten track, has four floors of dealers, some with reasonably priced items.

CLOTHING

Alan Bilzerian (✉ 34 Newbury St., ☎ 617/536–1001) is the place to go for the most avant-garde and au courant men's and women's clothing in Boston. **Jasmine** (✉ 329 Newbury St., ☎ 617/437–8466; ✉ 37A Brattle St., Cambridge, ☎ 617/354–6043) has the work of current designers from New York and Los Angeles. The Cambridge store includes the Sola and Sola Men shoe boutiques. **Louis, Boston** (✉ 234 Berkeley St., ☎ 617/262–6100) is the city's ultrapricey clothing store for men and women.

JEWELRY

Shreve, Crump & Low (✉ 330 Boylston St., ☎ 617/267–9100) sells the finest jewelry, china, crystal, and silver and has an extensive collection of clocks and watches.

Side Trip: Lexington and Concord

Lexington

To reach Lexington by car from Boston, take Memorial Drive in Cambridge to the Fresh Pond Parkway, then to Route 2 west. Exit Route 2 at Rtes. 4/225 and continue to Massachusetts Avenue if your first stop is the Museum of Our National Heritage. For Lexington center, take the Waltham St./Lexington exit from Route 2. Follow Waltham Street just under 2 mi to Massachusetts Ave.; you'll be just east of the Battle Green.

The **MBTA** (☎ 617/222–3200) operates buses to Lexington from Alewife station in Cambridge. Buses 62 and 76 make the trip in 25–30 minutes.

The events of the American Revolution are very much a part of present-day Lexington, a modern suburb that now sprawls out from the historic sights near the town center. On April 14–16, in honor of the 225th anniversary of the first day of the American Revolution, the town will re-create Paul Revere's ride, the retreat from Concord, and the skirmish at Lexington. More than 1,500 reenactors, as well as plenty of cannon fire and fifes and drums, will bring the events to life. Some 13 battles and ceremonies are scheduled along the original retreat route.

On April 19, 1775, Minuteman captain John Parker assembled his men out on **Battle Green,** a 2-acre, triangular piece of land, to await the arrival of the British, who were marching from Boston toward Concord to "teach rebels a lesson." Parker's role is commemorated in Henry Hudson Kitson's renowned sculpture, **The Minuteman** statue, which stands at the tip of the green, facing downtown Lexington. Because it's in a traffic island, it's a bit hard to pose for photos. A shot rang out from an unknown source—what Lexingtonians call "the shot heard 'round the world," although those in Concord claim the shot for their own.

The **visitor center** has a diorama of the 1775 clash on the green, plus a gift shop. ⊠ *1875 Massachusetts Ave.,* ☎ *781/862–1450.* ⊘ *Mid-Apr.–Oct., daily 9–5; Nov.–mid-Apr., generally weekdays 10–3, weekends 10–4.*

On the east side of the Green is **Buckman Tavern,** built in 1690, where the Minutemen gathered on the morning of April 19, 1775. A 35-minute tour takes in the tavern's seven rooms. ⊠ *1 Bedford St.,* ☎ *781/862–5598.* ⊡ *$4; combination ticket for the Buckman Tavern, Munroe Tavern, and Hancock-Clarke House $10.* ⊘ *Mid-Apr.–Oct., Mon.–Sat. 10–5, Sun. 1–5.*

As April 19 dragged on, British forces met far fiercer resistance in Concord. Dazed and demoralized after the battle at Old North Bridge (☞ Concord, *below*), the British backtracked and regrouped at the **Munroe Tavern** (built in 1695) while the Munroe family hid in nearby woods; then the troops retreated to Boston. The tavern is 1 mi east of Lexington Common. ⊠ *1332 Massachusetts Ave.,* ☎ *781/674–9238.* ⊡ *$4.* ⊘ *Mid-Apr.–Oct., Mon.–Sat. 10–5, Sun. 1–5.*

★ The **Museum of Our National Heritage** displays items and artifacts from all facets of American life, putting them in social and political context. The "Lexington Alarm'd" exhibit illustrates Revolutionary-era life through everyday household objects. ⊠ *33 Marrett Rd. (Rte. 2A at Massachusetts Ave.),* ☎ *781/861–6559.* ⊡ *Free; donation suggested.* ⊘ *Mon.–Sat. 10–5, Sun. noon–5.*

The **Minute Man National Historical Park Visitor Center** is part of the 800-acre Minute Man National Historical Park that extends into Lexington, Concord, and Lincoln. The center's exhibits and film focus on the Revolutionary War. ⊠ *Rte. 2A, ½ mi west of Rte. 128,* ☎ *781/862–7753.* ⊘ *May–Oct., daily 9–5; Nov.–Apr., daily 9–4.*

DINING

$ ✕ **Bertucci's.** Part of a popular chain, this Italian restaurant offers good food, reasonable prices, a large menu, and a family-friendly atmosphere. Specialties include ravioli, calzones, and a wide assortment of brick-oven-baked pizzas. ⊠ *1777 Massachusetts Ave.,* ☎ *781/860–9000.* AE, D, MC, V.

Concord

To reach Concord from Lexington, take Routes 4 and 225 through Bedford and Route 62 west to Concord; or from Massachusetts Avenue, pick up Route 2A west at the Museum of Our National Heritage or take Waltham Street south from Lexington Center to Route 2A. Following Route 2A is a longer but charming drive that takes you through parts of Minute Man National Historical Park. Stop off at the point where Revere's midnight ride ended with his capture by the British; it's marked with a boulder and plaque. Route 2A also takes you past the Minute Man National Historical Park Visitor Center. To reach Concord from Boston, follow Route 2 west, or take I–90 (the Massachusetts Turnpike) to I–95 north, and exit at Route 2, heading west.

While the initial Revolutionary War sorties were in Lexington, word of the American losses spread rapidly to surrounding towns: When the British marched into Concord, more than 400 Minutemen were waiting. A marker set in the stone wall along Liberty Street, behind the Old North Bridge Visitors Center, announces: "On this field the Minutemen and militia formed before marching down to the fight at the bridge."

At the **Old North Bridge** (⊠ Off Monument St., ½ mi from Concord center), the Concord Minutemen turned the tables on the British in the morning hours of April 19, 1775. The Americans did not fire first, but when two of their own fell dead from a redcoat volley, Major John Buttrick of Concord roared, "Fire, fellow soldiers, for God's sake, fire." The Minutemen released volley after volley, and the redcoats fled. Daniel Chester French's statue *The Minuteman* (1875) honors the country's first freedom fighters.

Of the confrontation, the essayist and poet Ralph Waldo Emerson wrote in 1837: "By the rude bridge that arched the flood/Their flag to April's breeze unfurled/Here once the embattled farmers stood/And fired the shot heard round the world." (The lines are inscribed at the foot of *The Minuteman.*) Hence, Concord claims the right to the "shot," believing that native son Emerson was, of course, referring to the North Bridge standoff. Park Service officials skirt the issue, saying the shot could refer to the battle on Lexington Green, when the very first shot rang out from an unknown source, or to Concord when Minutemen held back the redcoats in the revolution's first major battle, or even to the Boston Massacre. What's important is Emerson's vision that here began the modern world's first experiment in democracy.

The Reverend William Emerson, the grandfather of Ralph Waldo Emerson, watched rebels and redcoats battle from behind his home, the **Old Manse,** on Monument Street, within sight of the Old North Bridge. The house, built in 1770, was occupied by the family except for a period of 3½ years, when renter Nathaniel Hawthorne lived and wrote short stories here. The furnishings date from the late 18th century. ⊠ *269 Monument St.,* ☎ *978/369–3909.* ☎ *$5.50 for 40-min guided tour.* ☉ *Mid-Apr.–Oct., Mon.–Sat. 10–5, Sun. noon–5.*

The **Wright Tavern** (⊠ 2 Lexington Rd.), built in 1747, served as headquarters first for the Minutemen, then the British, then both on April 19. It is closed to the public.

The **Jonathan Ball House,** built in 1753, was a station on the underground railroad for runaway slaves during the Civil War. Ask to see the secret room. The house hosts art exhibits, and its garden and waterfall are refreshing sights. ⊠ *Art Association, 37 Lexington Rd.,* ☎ *978/369–2578.* ☎ *Free.* ☉ *Tues.–Sat. 10–4:30.*

Ralph Waldo Emerson lived in the Old Manse between 1834 and 1835 before moving to what is known as the **Ralph Waldo Emerson House,** where he resided until his death in 1882. Here he wrote the *Essays* ("To be great is to be misunderstood"; "A foolish consistency is the hobgoblin of little minds"). Except for items from Emerson's study, now at the nearby Concord Museum (☞ *below*), the Emerson House furnishings have been preserved as the writer left them, down to his hat resting on the newel post. ✉ *28 Cambridge Turnpike at Lexington Rd.,* ☎ *978/369–2236.* 🎫 *$4.50.* ☼ *Mid-Apr.–late Oct., Thurs.– Sat. 10–4:30, Sun. 2–4:30.*

The original contents of Emerson's private study are in the **Concord Museum,** just east of the town center. In a 1930 Colonial Revival structure, the museum houses 15 period rooms, ranging in decor from Colonial to Empire. It has the world's largest collection of Thoreau artifacts, including furnishings from the Walden Pond cabin, as well as a diorama of the Old North Bridge battle, Native American artifacts, and one of two lanterns hung at Boston's Old North Church on the night of April 18, 1775. ✉ *200 Lexington Rd. (entrance on Cambridge Tpke.),* ☎ *978/369–9763.* 🎫 *$6.* ☼ *Apr.–Dec., Mon.–Sat. 9– 5, Sun. noon–5; Jan.–Mar., Mon.–Sat. 11–4, Sun. 1–4.*

The dark brown exterior of Louisa May Alcott's family home, **Orchard House,** poses a sharp contrast to the light, wit, and energy so much in evidence inside. Named for the apple orchard that once surrounded it, Orchard House was home to the Alcott family from 1857 to 1877. Here Louisa wrote *Little Women,* based on her life with her three sisters. Many of the original furnishings remain in the house. Portraits and watercolors by May Alcott (the model for Amy) abound; in her room you can see where she sketched figures on the walls—the Alcotts encouraged such creativity. ✉ *399 Lexington Rd.,* ☎ *978/369–4118.* 🎫 *$5.50.* ☼ *Apr.–Oct., Mon.–Sat. 10–4:30, Sun. 1–4:30; Nov.–Dec. and mid-Jan.–Mar., weekdays 11–3, Sat. 10–4:30, Sun. 1–4:30.*

Nathaniel Hawthorne lived at the Old Manse (☞ *above*) from 1842 to 1845, working on stories and sketches; he then moved to Salem (where he wrote *The Scarlet Letter*) and later to Lenox (*The House of the Seven Gables*). In 1852 he returned to Concord, bought a rambling structure called **The Wayside,** and lived here until his death in 1864. The subsequent owner, Margaret Sidney (author of *Five Little Peppers and How They Grew*), kept Hawthorne's tower-study intact—to the fascination of visitors today. Prior to Hawthorne's ownership, the Alcotts lived here, from 1845 to 1848. ✉ *455 Lexington Rd.,* ☎ *978/369–6975.* 🎫 *$4.* ☼ *Mid-Apr.–Oct., daily except Wed., 10–5. Guided tours until 4:30.*

A Concord curiosity, the yard of the privately owned **Grapevine Cottage** has the original Concord grapevine, the grape that the Welch's jams and jellies company made famous. In 1983, Welch's moved its corporate headquarters from New York to Concord to bring the company "back to its roots." A plaque on the fence tells how Ephraim Wales Bull began cultivating the Concord grape. ✉ *491 Lexington Rd.* ☼ *Not open to the public.*

Each Memorial Day, Louisa May Alcott's grave in **Sleepy Hollow Cemetery** is decorated in commemoration of her death. Like Emerson, Thoreau, and Hawthorne, Alcott is buried in a section of the cemetery known as **Author's Ridge.** ✉ *Bedford St. (Rte. 62),* ☎ *978/318– 3233.* ☼ *Generally, daily 7 AM–dusk.*

A trip to Concord can also include a pilgrimage to **Walden Pond,** Henry David Thoreau's most famous residence. Here, in 1845, at age 28, Thoreau moved into a one-room cabin—built for $28.12½ cents— on the shore of this 100-ft-deep kettle hole, formed 12,000 years ago by the retreat of the New England glacier. Living alone over the next two years, Thoreau discovered the benefits of solitude and the beauties of nature. Thoreau later published *Walden* (1854), a collection of essays on observations he made while living here. The site of that first cabin is staked out in stone. A full-size, authentically furnished replica

In case you want to see the world.

At American Express, we're here to make your journey
a smooth one. So we have over 1,700 travel service locations in over 130 countries ready to help. What else
would you expect from the world's largest travel agency?

do more **Travel**

Call 1 800 AXP-3429 or visit
www.americanexpress.com/travel

In case you want to be welcomed there.

We're here to see that you're always welcomed at establishments everywhere. That's why millions of people carry the American Express® Card – for peace of mind, confidence, and security, around the world or just around the corner.

do more

Cards

In case you're running low.

We're here to help with more than 190,000 Express Cash locations around the world. In order to enroll, just call American Express at 1 800 CASH-NOW before you start your vacation.

do more AMERICAN EXPRESS

Express Cash

And in case you'd rather be safe than sorry.

We're here with American Express® Travelers Cheques. They're the safe way to carry money on your vacation, because if they're ever lost or stolen you can get a refund, practically anywhere or anytime. To find the nearest place to buy Travelers Cheques, call 1 800 495-1153. Another way we help you do more.

do more

Travelers Cheques

of the cabin stands about ½ mi from the original site, near the Walden Pond State Reservation parking lot. Even when the cabin is closed, you can peek through its windows. Now, as in Thoreau's time, the pond is a delightful summertime spot for swimming, fishing, and rowing, and there's hiking in the nearby woods. ⊠ *Rte. 126; from Concord take Main St. west from Monument Sq., turn left on Walden St., cross over Rte. 2 onto Rte. 126, and head south ½ mi to entrance (on left),* ☎ *978/369–3254.* ☎ *Free; parking across road from pond $2 per vehicle Memorial Day–Labor Day, free parking rest of yr.* ☉ *Daily until approximately ½ hr before sunset.*

DINING

$$–$$$ ✕ **Walden Grille.** Near the town center, Walden Grille prepares eclectic contemporary fare in an old brick firehouse turned upscale dining room. Lighter meals include salads (spinach and goat cheese with tomato-basil vinaigrette) or sandwiches (hummus and cucumber wrap), while heartier entrées may range from wild mushroom ravioli to grilled shrimp with risotto-polenta cakes. ⊠ *24 Walden St.* ☎ *978/371–2233. AE, D, DC, MC, V.*

Side Trip: Plymouth

If you have time to visit just one South Shore destination, make it Plymouth, a historic seaside town of narrow streets and clapboard mansions. Plymouth, 41 mi south of Boston, is known across the nation as "America's hometown" because of the 102 weary settlers who disembarked here in December 1620.

MBTA (☎ 617/222–3200) commuter rail service is available to Plymouth and nearby Kingston. **Plymouth & Brockton Street Railway** (☎ 508/746–0378) links Plymouth and the South Shore to Boston's South Station with frequent bus service. From the Plymouth-area train stations or bus depot, take the **Plymouth Area Link** buses (☎ 508/746–0378) to the town center or to Plimoth Plantation. To get to Plymouth by car, take the Southeast Expressway I–93 south to Route 3 toward Cape Cod; Exits 6 and 4 lead to downtown Plymouth and Plimoth Plantation, respectively.

★ ⓒ Over the entrance of the **Plimoth Plantation** is the caution: "You are now entering 1627." Believe it. Against the backdrop of the Atlantic Ocean, a Pilgrim village has been painstakingly re-created, from the thatched roofs, cramped quarters, and open fireplaces to the long-horned livestock. Throw away your preconception of white collars and funny hats; through ongoing research, the Plimoth staff has developed a portrait of the Pilgrims richer and more complex than that of the dour folk in elementary school textbooks. Listen to the quaint accents and mannerisms of the "residents," who never break out of character. Feel free to engage them in conversation about their life, but expect only curious looks if you ask about anything that happened later than 1627.

Elsewhere on the plantation is **Hobbamock's Homestead,** where descendants of the Wampanoag Indians re-create the life of a Native American who chose to live near the newcomers. In the **Carriage House Craft Center** you may see items created using the techniques of 17th-century English craftsmanship—that is, what the Pilgrims might have imported. (You can also buy samples.) At the **Nye Barn,** youngsters can see goats, cows, pigs, and chickens bred from 17th-century gene pools or bred to represent animals raised in the original plantation. The visitor center has gift shops, a cafeteria, and multimedia presentations. Dress for the weather, since most exhibits are outdoors. ⊠ *Warren Ave./Rte. 3A,* ☎ *508/746–1622.* ☎ *$18.50 (includes entry to Mayflower II); plantation only: $15.* ☉ *Apr.–Nov., daily 9–5.*

The ***Mayflower II,*** an exact replica of the 1620 *Mayflower,* is staffed
by Pilgrims and hearty mates in period dress. It is 2 mi down the road
from Plimoth Plantation (☞ *above*). ⊠ *State Pier,* ☎ *508/746–1622.*
▣ *$5.75 or as part of $18.50 Plimoth Plantation fee.* ◔ *Apr.–Nov.,
daily 9–5 (until 7 in July and Aug.).*

Plymouth Rock, a few dozen yards from the *Mayflower II,* is popularly
believed to have been the Pilgrims' stepping stone when they left the
ship. Given the stone's unimpressive appearance—many people are dis-
mayed that it's little more than a boulder—and dubious authenticity
(as explained on a nearby plaque), the grand canopy overhead seems
a trifle ostentatious. For a traditional view of the Pilgrims, visit the **Plymouth National Wax Museum,** on the top of Cole's Hill. It contains
26 scenes with 180 life-size models that tell the Pilgrims' story. ⊠ *16
Carver St.,* ☎ *508/746–6468.* ▣ *$5.* ◔ *Mar.–May and Nov., daily 9–
5; June and Sept.–Oct., daily 9–7; July–Aug., daily 9–9.*

A variety of historical houses are open for visits, including the 1640
Sparrow House, Plymouth's oldest structure. ⊠ *42 Summer St.,* ☎ *508/
747–1240.* ▣ *$2.* ◔ *Apr.–Dec., Thurs.–Tues. 10–5.*

The 1749 **Spooner House,** home to the same family for 200 years, has
guided tours, historic recipes, and a garden. ⊠ *27 North St.,* ☎ *508/
746–0012.* ▣ *By donation.* ◔ *June–Oct., Tues.–Thurs. 10–3:30 or 4.*

One of the country's oldest public museums, the **Pilgrim Hall Museum,**
established in 1824, transports visitors back to the time before the Pilgrims' landing, with items carried by those weary travelers to the New
World. Included are a carved chest, a remarkably well preserved wicker
cradle, Miles Standish's sword, John Alden's Bible, Native American
artifacts, and the remains of the *Sparrow-Hawk,* a 17th-century sailing ship that was wrecked in 1626. ⊠ *75 Court St./Rte. 3A,* ☎ *508/
746–1620.* ▣ *$5.* ◔ *Feb.–Dec., daily 9:30–4:30.*

It may be hard to imagine an entire museum devoted to a Thanksgiving side dish, but **Cranberry World,** operated by the Ocean Spray juice
company, is amazingly popular. After learning how the state's local crop
is grown, harvested, and processed, you can sip juices and sample products made from *Vaccinium macrocarpon* (the Latin name for cranberries).
In October, you can see harvesting techniques and attend local cranberry festivals. ⊠ *225 Water St.,* ☎ *508/747–2350.* ▣ *Free.* ◔ *Mid-
Apr.–Nov., daily 9:30–5.*

Dining

$$–$$$ ✕ **Bert's Cove.** This local landmark just off the entrance to Plymouth
Beach has great ocean views. The entrées include veal medallions, sirloin steak, risotto, and fresh seafood. ⊠ *140 Warren Ave., Rte. 3A,*
☎ *508/746–3330. AE, D, MC, V.*

Side Trip: New Bedford

New Bedford, 50 mi south of Boston, is home to the largest fishing
fleet on the East Coast. Although much of the town is industrial, the
restored historic district near the water is a delight. The town is the
setting for the beginning of Herman Melville's masterpiece, *Moby-Dick,*
a novel ostensibly about whaling. The city's whaling tradition is commemorated in the **New Bedford Whaling National Historical Park,** encompassing 13 blocks of the waterfront historic district. The park
visitor center, in an 1853 Greek Revival former bank, provides maps
and information about whaling-related sites. ⊠ *33 William St.,* ☎ *508/
991–6200.* ◔ *Daily 9–4.*

★ The **New Bedford Whaling Museum,** established in 1902, is the largest American museum devoted to the 200-year history of whaling. Scrimshaw, paintings, logbooks, and more bring the past to life. You can climb aboard an 89-ft, half-scale model of the 1826 whaling ship *Lagoda*—the world's largest ship model. A 22-minute film of an actual whaling chase is shown daily. In 1998, the museum acquired the bones of a 66-ft blue whale, and the skeleton will be displayed in an addition scheduled for completion in 2000. ⊠ *18 Johnny Cake Hill,* ☎ *508/997–0046.* ≊ *$4.50.* ☉ *Memorial Day–Labor Day, Fri.–Wed. 9–5, Thurs. 9–8; Labor Day–Memorial Day, daily 9–5.*

Seaman's Bethel, the small chapel described in *Moby-Dick,* was dedicated in 1832. Besides a ship's-bow pulpit it contains cenotaphs, tablets with the names of sailors lost at sea. ⊠ *15 Johnny Cake Hill,* ☎ *508/ 992–3295.* ≊ *Free.* ☉ *June–mid-Oct., Mon.–Sat. 10–4, Sun. 1–4.*

Dining

$-$$ ✗ **Antonio's.** If you'd like to sample the traditional fare of New Bedford's large Portuguese population, friendly, unadorned Antonio's serves up hearty portions of pork and shellfish stew, *bacalau* (salt cod), and grilled sardines, often on plates piled high with crispy fried potatoes and rice. ⊠ *267 Coggeshall St. (near the intersection of I–195 and Rte. 18),* ☎ *508/990–3636. No credit cards.*

Boston A to Z

Arriving and Departing

BY BUS

South Station (⊠ Atlantic Ave. and Summer St., ☎ 617/345–7451) is the depot for most of the major bus companies that serve Boston. For a list, *see* Massachusetts A to Z, *below.*

BY CAR

Interstate 95 (also called Route 128 in some parts) skirts the western edge of Boston. Interstate 93 connects Boston to the north and New Hampshire; the highway runs through the city as the Fitzgerald Expressway. This section of I–93 is scheduled to be turned into an underground highway as part of the massive Central Artery Project; expect construction and delays here well beyond 2000. Interstate 90 (a tollroad known as the Massachusetts Turnpike, or just "the Pike") enters the city from the west. Route 9, roughly parallel to I–90, passes through Newton and Brookline on its way into Boston from the west. Route 2 enters Cambridge from the northwest.

BY PLANE

Logan International Airport (⊠ I–93 N, Exit 24, ☎ 617/561–1800 or 800/235–6426 for 24-hr information about parking and the ground transportation options), across the harbor from downtown Boston, receives flights from most major domestic airlines and some carriers from outside the United States. *See* Air Travel *in* Smart Travel Tips A to Z for airline numbers. If you are driving from Logan to downtown, take the Sumner Tunnel; if that's not passable, try Route 1A north to Route 16, then to the Tobin Bridge and into Boston.

Cabs can be hired outside each terminal. Fares to and from downtown average about $15–$18 including tip, via the most-direct route, the Sumner Tunnel, assuming no major traffic jams. The **Ted Williams Tunnel** connects the airport to points south, but it is limited to taxis and commercial vehicles on weekdays. It opens to general traffic overnight, on weekends and holidays, and other times as indicated by lighted airport and highway signs. Toll is $2. Call **Massport** (☎ 617/561–1751) for taxi information.

The **Airport Water Shuttle** (☎ 800/235–6426) crosses Boston Harbor in about seven minutes, running between Logan Airport and Rowes Wharf (a free shuttle bus operates between the ferry dock and airline terminals). Adult fare is $10 one way. The **MBTA Blue Line** (617/222–3200 or 800/392–6100) subway to Airport station is one of the fastest ways to reach downtown from the airport. Shuttle bus 22 runs between Terminals A and B and the subway. Shuttle bus 33 goes to the subway from Terminals C, D, and E. **US Shuttle** (☎ 617/894–3100) provides door-to-door van service 24 hours a day between the airport and Boston, Cambridge, and many suburban destinations. Call and request a pickup when your flight arrives. To go to the airport, call for reservations 24 to 48 hours in advance. Sample one-way fares are $8 to downtown or the Back Bay, $15.50 to Cambridge.

BY TRAIN
Amtrak (☎ 617/482–3660 or 800/872–7245) Northeast Corridor trains from New York, Washington, D.C., and elsewhere stop at South Station, Back Bay Station, and the easy-to-access Route 128 station south of Boston. Some trains require reservations. New high-speed trains were scheduled to begin running between Boston and New York late in 1999. Amtrak's *Lake Shore Limited* travels daily from Boston to Chicago by way of Albany, Rochester, Buffalo, and Cleveland.

Getting Around
Massachusetts Bay Transportation Authority (MBTA; ☎ 617/222–3200 or 800/392–6100, TTY 617/722–5146) dispenses 24-hour information on bus, subway, and train routes; schedules; fares; and other matters, including wheelchair access. MBTA visitor passes are available for unlimited travel on city buses and subways for one-, three-, and seven-day periods (fares: $5, $9, and $18 respectively). Buy passes at the following MBTA stations: Airport, South Station, North Station, Back Bay, Government Center, and Harvard Square. Passes are also sold at the Boston Common Information Kiosk and at some hotels.

BY BUS
MBTA (☎ 617/222–3200) bus routes crisscross the metropolitan area and travel farther into suburbia than subway and trolley lines. Some suburban schedules are designed primarily for commuters. Current local fares are 60¢ for adults, 30¢ children from age 5 to 11; you must pay an extra fare for longer suburban trips. **Smart Traveler** (☎ 617/374–1234) provides service updates.

BY CAR
Boston is not an easy city to drive in because of the many one-way streets and the number of streets with the same name. It's important to have a map with you. If you must bring a car, keep to the main thoroughfares and park in lots—no matter how expensive—rather than on the street, which is a tricky business. Some neighborhoods have residents-only rules, with just a handful of two-hour visitor's spaces; others have meters (25¢ for 12–15 minutes, one or two hours maximum). Major public lots are at Government Center and Quincy Market, beneath Boston Common (entrance on Charles Street), beneath Post Office Square, at the Prudential Center, at Copley Place, and off Clarendon Street near the John Hancock Tower. Smaller lots are scattered throughout downtown. Most are expensive (expect to pay $10–$12 for an evening out; $18–$20 to park all day); the few city-run garages are a bargain at about $6 to $10 per day.

The **MBTA** (☞ *above*)—or "T," for short—operates subways, elevated trains, and trolleys along four different lines. Trains operate from about 5:30 AM to about 12:30 AM. Current T fares are 85¢ for adults, 40¢ for children from ages 5 to 11. An extra fare is required heading inbound from distant Green Line stops and in both directions for certain distant Red Line stops. The **Red Line** originates at Braintree and Mattapan to the south; the routes join near South Boston and proceed through downtown Boston (including South Station) to the western edge of Cambridge. The **Green Line,** a combined underground and elevated surface line, uses trolleys that operate underground in the central city. It originates at Cambridge's Lechmere, heads south, and divides into four routes; these end at Boston College (Commonwealth Avenue), Cleveland Circle (Beacon Street), Riverside, and Heath Street (Avenue of the Arts). Buses connect Heath Street to the old Arborway terminus. The **Blue Line** runs on weekdays from Bowdoin Square and on weeknights and weekends from Government Center to the Wonderland Racetrack in Revere, north of Boston. Logan Airport is among its stops. The **Orange Line** runs from Oak Grove in north suburban Malden to Forest Hills near the Arnold Arboretum. Park Street Station (on the Common) and State Street are the major downtown transfer points.

BY TAXI

Cabs are not easily hailed on the street; if you need to get somewhere in a hurry, use a hotel taxi stand or telephone for a cab. Taxis charge $2–$2.10 per mile; one-way streets often make circuitous routes necessary and increase your cost. Companies offering 24-hour service include **Boston Cab Association** (☎ 617/536–3200); **Checker** (☎ 617/536–7000); **Green Cab Association** (☎ 617/628–0600); **Independent Taxi Operators Association** (ITOA; ☎ 617/426–8700); **Town Taxi** (☎ 617/536–5000). In Cambridge, **Ambassador Brattle Cab** (☎ 617/492–1100); **Cambridge Checker Cab** (☎ 617/497–1500).

Contacts and Resources

B&B RESERVATION SERVICE

Bed and Breakfast Reservation Agency of Boston (✉ 47 Commercial Wharf, 02110, ☎ 617/720–3540, 800/248–9262, or 0800/895128 in the U.K.) can book a variety of accommodations ranging from historic B&Bs to modern condominiums.

EMERGENCIES

Ambulance, fire, police (☎ 911). **Massachusetts General Hospital** (☎ 617/726–2000). **Dental emergency** (☎ 508/651–3521). **Physician Referral Service** (☎ 617/726–5800). **Poison control** (☎ 617/232–2120).

GUIDED TOURS

ORIENTATION TOURS: The red **Beantown Trolleys** (✉ Transportation Bldg., 14 Charles St. S, ☎ 617/236–2148 or 800/343–1328) has 17 stops over two hours; cost is $18. Trolleys run every 20 minutes from 9 AM until 4 PM. From March to November **Brush Hill/Gray Line** (✉ Transportation Bldg., 14 Charles St. S, ☎ 617/236–2148 or 800/343–1328) picks up passengers from hotels for 3½-hour Boston–Cambridge tours. Other tours are available to Plymouth, Cape Cod, Salem and Marblehead, New Hampshire, and Newport. Reservations are required. The orange and green **Old Town Trolley** (✉ 329 W. 2nd St., South Boston, ☎ 617/269–7010) runs every 30 minutes from 9 AM to 3 or 4 PM; adult fares are $21. Cambridge tours are also available.

WALKING TOURS: The **Black Heritage Trail** (☎ 617/742–5415 or 617/739–2000), a self-guided walk, explores Boston's 19th-century black community, passing 14 sites. The 2½-mi **Freedom Trail** (☎ 617/242–5642) follows a red line past 16 of Boston's most important historic sites. For more information about the Black Heritage and Freedom trails, *see* Beacon Hill and Boston Common, *above.* The nonprofit **Historic Neighborhoods Foundation** (⊠ 99 Bedford St., ☎ 617/426–1885) covers the North End, Chinatown, Beacon Hill, the waterfront, and other urban areas on 90-minute guided walks from Wednesday to Saturday between April and November. Tours cost $5 and up. The **Society for the Preservation of New England Antiquities** (SPNEA; ⊠ 141 Cambridge St., ☎ 617/227–3956) conducts a walking tour of Beacon Hill that focuses on the neighborhood as it was in the early 1800s. Tours are given Saturdays May through October at 3 PM, with an added 10 AM tour in October, and cost $10. The **Women's Heritage Trail** (☎ 617/522–2872) celebrates more than 80 accomplished women on four self-guided walks. The Old State House (⊠ 206 Washington St.) and the Boston National Historic Park Service Visitor Center (⊠ 15 State St.) sell maps for $5.

The volunteers of **Boston by Foot** (⊠ 77 N. Washington St., ☎ 617/367–2345; 617/367–3766 for recorded information) conduct guided 90-minute walks daily from May to October. Most tours cost $8; no reservations are required.

WATER TOURS: Boston Harbor Cruises (⊠ 1 Long Wharf, ☎ 617/227–4321) runs harbor tours and other cruises (including whale-watching, sunset, and evening entertainment cruises; prices vary) from mid-April to October. The **Charles Riverboat Co.** (☎ 617/621–3001) offers a 55-minute narrated tour of the Charles River Basin. Tours depart from the CambridgeSide Galleria mall on the hour from noon to 5 daily from June to August and on weekends in April, May, and September; the fare is $8. **Massachusetts Bay Lines** (⊠ 60 Rowes Wharf, ☎ 617/542–8000) operates evening cruises with rock, blues, or reggae music and dancing, concessions, and cash bar, as well as daily harbor tours and sunset cruises.

Boston Duck Tours (⊠ 790 Boylston St., Plaza Level, ☎ 617/723–3825) uses World War II amphibious vehicles for 80-minute tours on the city's streets and the Charles River. Tours begin and end at the Avenue of the Arts entrance to the Prudential Center, at 101 Avenue of the Arts. From April to November, tours leave every half hour from 9 AM till dark; the fare is about $20. Tickets are sold inside the Prudential Center 9–8 Monday–Saturday and 9–6 on Sundays; weekend tours often sell out early.

LATE-NIGHT PHARMACIES

CVS (⊠ Porter Square Shopping Plaza, Massachusetts Ave., Cambridge, ☎ 617/876–5519). **CVS** (⊠ 155 Charles St., ☎ 617/227–0437). **CVS** (☎ 800/746–7287 for locations) has 24-hour stores in several suburbs.

VISITOR INFORMATION

The **Boston Common Information Kiosk** (⊠ Tremont St., where the Freedom Trail begins, ☎ 617/426–3115) is open from Monday to Saturday between 8:30 and 5 and on Sunday between 9 and 5. The **Boston Welcome Center** (⊠ 140 Tremont St., Boston 02111, ☎ 617/451–2227) is open from Sunday to Thursday between 9 and 5 and on Friday and Saturday between 9 and 6 for most of the year; it's open until 7 except Sunday during the summer. **Greater Boston Convention and Visitors Bureau** (⊠ 2 Copley Pl., Suite 105, Boston 02116, ☎ 617/536–4100 or 800/888–5515) has brochures and information.

CAPE COD

Updated by
Dorothy
Antczak and
Carolyn Heller

Dining
updated by
Seth Rolbein

A Patti Page song from the 1950s promises that "If you're fond of sand dunes and salty air, quaint little villages here and there, you're sure to fall in love with old Cape Cod." The tourism boom since the '50s has certainly proved her right. So popular has the Cape become that today parts of it have lost the charm that brought everyone here in the first place. Still, much of the area remains compellingly beautiful and unspoiled. Even at the height of the season, there won't be crowds at the less-traveled nature preserves and historic villages. Off-season, many beaches are dream material for solitary walkers, and life returns to a small-town hum.

Separated from the Massachusetts mainland by the 17½-mi Cape Cod Canal—at 480 ft, the world's widest sea-level canal—and linked to it by two heavily trafficked bridges, the Cape is always likened in shape to an outstretched arm bent at the elbow, its Provincetown fist turned back toward the mainland. The Cape "winds around to face itself" is how the writer Philip Hamburger has put it.

Each of the Cape's 15 towns is broken up into villages, which is where things can get complicated. The town of Barnstable, for example, consists of Barnstable, West Barnstable, Cotuit, Marstons Mills, Osterville, Centerville, and Hyannis. The terms Upper Cape and Lower Cape can also be confusing. **Upper Cape**—think upper arm, as in the shape of the Cape—refers to the towns of Bourne, Falmouth, Mashpee, and Sandwich. **Mid Cape** includes Barnstable, Yarmouth, and Dennis. Brewster, Harwich, Chatham, Orleans, Eastham, Wellfleet, Truro, and Provincetown make up the **Lower Cape.** The **Outer Cape,** as in outer reaches, is essentially synonymous with Lower Cape, though technically it includes only Wellfleet, Truro, and Provincetown.

There are three major roads on the Cape. U.S. 6 is the fastest way to get from the mainland to Orleans. Route 6A winds along the north shore through scenic towns; Route 28 dips south through the overdeveloped parts of the Cape. If you want to avoid malls, heavy traffic, and tacky motels, avoid Route 28 from Falmouth to Chatham. Past Orleans on the way out to Provincetown, the roadside clutter of much of Route 6 masks the beauty of what surrounds it.

Cape Cod is only about 70 mi from end to end—you can make a cursory circuit of it in about two days. But it is really a place for relaxing—for swimming and sunning; for fishing, boating, and playing golf or tennis; for attending the theater, hunting for antiques, and making the rounds of art galleries; for buying lobster and fish fresh from the boat; or for taking leisurely walks, bike rides, or drives along timeless country roads.

Sandwich

★ ❶ *3 mi east of the Sagamore Bridge, 11 mi west of Barnstable.*

The oldest town on Cape Cod, Sandwich was established in 1637 by some of the Plymouth Pilgrims and incorporated in 1638. Today it is a well-preserved, quintessential New England village with a white-columned town hall and streets lined with 18th- and 19th-century homes.

From 1825 until 1888, the main industry in Sandwich was the production of vividly colored glass, made in the Boston and Sandwich Glass Company's factory. The **Sandwich Glass Museum** contains relics of the town's early history, a diorama showing how the factory looked in its heyday, and examples of blown and pressed glass. Glassmaking demonstrations are held in the summer. ⊠ *129 Main St.,* ☎ *508/888–0251.* ☞ *$3.50.* ✆ *Apr.–Oct., daily 9:30–5; Nov.–Dec. and Feb.–Mar., Wed.–Sun. 9:30–4.*

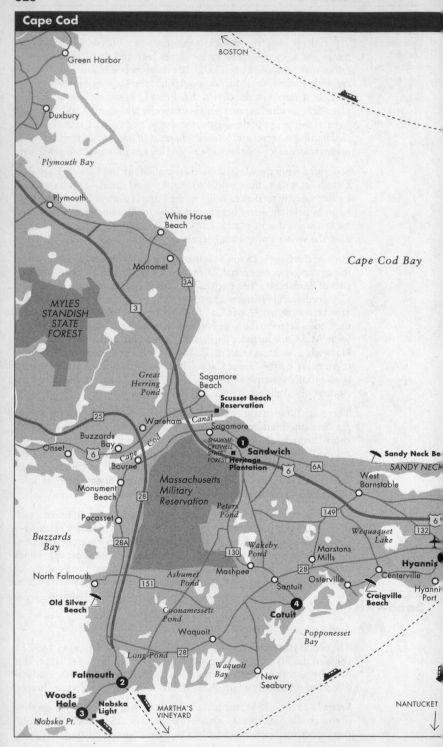

BOSTON

Green Harbor

Duxbury

Plymouth Bay

Plymouth

White Horse
Beach

Manomet

3A

Cape Cod Bay

3

MYLES
STANDISH
STATE
FOREST

*Great
Herring
Pond*

Sagamore
Beach

**Scusset Beach
Reservation**

25

Wareham

Canal

Sagamore

SHAWME-
CROWELL
STATE
FOREST

1 **Sandwich**

Buzzards
Bay

Onset

6

Bourne

Cape Cod

**Heritage
Plantation**

6A

6A

Sandy Neck Be

SANDY NECK

West
Barnstable

Monument
Beach

28

*Massachusetts
Military
Reservation*

*Peters
Pond*

149

*Wequaquet
Lake*

132

6

Pocasset

*Buzzards
Bay*

28A

130

*Wakeby
Pond*

Marstons
Mills

28

Hyannis

North Falmouth

151

*Ashumet
Pond*

Mashpee

Santuit

Osterville

Centerville

**Craigville
Beach**

Hyanni
Port

**Old Silver
Beach**

*Coonamessett
Pond*

4

Cotuit

*Popponesset
Bay*

Waquoit

Long Pond

28

*Waquoit
Bay*

New
Seabury

NANTUCKET

Falmouth

2

**Woods
Hole**

**Nobska
Light**

Nobska Pt.

MARTHA'S
VINEYARD

3

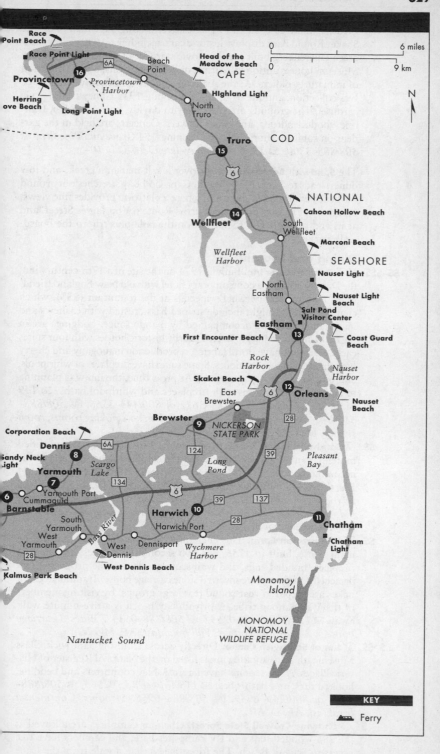

Race Point Beach

Race Point Light

Provincetown (16)

Herring Cove Beach

Long Point Light

Provincetown Harbor

6A

Beach Point

Head of the Meadow Beach

CAPE

Highland Light

North Truro

Truro (15)

6

COD

NATIONAL

Cahoon Hollow Beach

Wellfleet (14)

South Wellfleet

Marconi Beach

Wellfleet Harbor

SEASHORE

Nauset Light

North Eastham

Nauset Light Beach

Salt Pond Visitor Center

Eastham (13)

First Encounter Beach

Coast Guard Beach

Rock Harbor

Nauset Harbor

Skaket Beach

East Brewster

6 (12) Orleans

Nauset Beach

Brewster (9)

NICKERSON STATE PARK

28

Corporation Beach

Dennis (8)

6A

124

Long Pond

39

Pleasant Bay

Sandy Neck Light

Yarmouth (7)

Scargo Lake

134

6

39

Barnstable 6

Cummaquid

Yarmouth Port

South Yarmouth

West Yarmouth

Harwich (10)

Harwich Port

137

(11) Chatham

Chatham Light

28

West Dennis

Dennisport

Wychmere Harbor

West Dennis Beach

Kalmus Park Beach

Monomoy Island

Nantucket Sound

MONOMOY NATIONAL WILDLIFE REFUGE

KEY

Ferry

★ **Heritage Plantation,** an extraordinary complex of museum buildings, gardens, and a café, sits on 76 acres overlooking Shawme Pond. The Shaker Round Barn displays historic cars, including a 1930 yellow-and-green Duesenberg built for the movie star Gary Cooper. The Military Museum houses antique firearms, military uniforms, and a collection of miniature soldiers. At the Art Museum are an extensive Currier & Ives collection, antique toys, and a working 1912 Coney Island–style carousel. The grounds are planted with daylily, hosta, heather, fruit-tree, rhododendrons, and other flowers. Concerts are held in the gardens on summer afternoons and evenings. ⊠ *Grove and Pine Sts.,* ☎ *508/888–3300.* ⊡ *$9.* ☉ *Mid-May–late Oct., daily 10–5.*

The **Sandwich Boardwalk,** built over a salt marsh, a creek, and low dunes, leads to Town Neck Beach. Cape Cod Bay stretches out around the beach at the end of the walk, where a platform provides fine views, especially at sunset. From town cross Route 6A on Jarves Street, and at its end turn left and then right on the mile-plus trip to the board-walk parking lot.

Dining and Lodging

$$–$$$ ✕⌂ **Dan'l Webster Inn.** Built in 1971 on the site of a 17th-century inn, the Dan'l Webster is a contemporary hotel with old New England friendliness and hospitality. Chef's specials at the restaurant ($$$), which change monthly, might include striped bass crusted with cashews and macadamia nuts and accompanied by mango sauce. Lodgings are in the main inn and wings or in two nearby historic houses with four suites each. All rooms have floral fabrics, reproduction mahogany and cherry furnishings, and some antiques. Some suites have fireplaces or whirlpools, and one has a baby grand piano. At press time, the inn was planning to add 10 deluxe rooms with fireplaces and whirlpool baths. ⊠ *149 Main St., 02563,* ☎ *508/888–3622 or 800/444–3566,* ⅧⅩ *508/888–5156. 47 rooms, 9 suites. 2 restaurants, bar, no-smoking rooms, room service, pool. AE, D, DC, MC, V.*

$$ ⌂ **Sandwich Lodge & Resort.** Set amid 10 rolling acres, this glorified motel has suites and efficiencies with gleaming kitchens; some of the accommodations have two-person whirlpool tubs. ⊠ *Box 1038, 54 Rte. 6A, 02653,* ☎ *508/888–2275 or 800/282–5353,* ⅧⅩ *508/888–8102. 28 rooms, 36 suites, 3 efficiencies. Restaurant, bar, no-smoking rooms, indoor-outdoor pool, hot tub, shuffleboard, volleyball, recreation room. Continental breakfast. AE, D, MC, V.*

$$ ⌂ **Wingscorton Farm.** This enchanting oasis is a working farm. The main house, built in 1756, has two second-floor suites, each with a fireplace, braided rugs, and wainscoting. Also on the property are a detached cottage and a converted stone carriage house. Traditional clam-bakes are prepared year-round (for large groups) by visiting members of the Wampanoag tribe. A private bay beach is a five-minute walk away. ⊠ *11 Wing Blvd., 02537,* ☎ *508/888–0534. 2 suites, 1 carriage house, 1 2-bedroom cottage. Full breakfast. AE, MC, V.*

$–$$ ⌂ **Inn at Sandwich Center.** Directly across from the Sandwich Glass Museum, this no-smoking inn is listed on the National Register of Historic Places. All the rooms have Laura Ashley comforters and bedding, hooked rugs, and bathrobes. ⊠ *118 Tupper Rd., 02563,* ☎ *508/888–6958 or 800/249–6949,* ⅧⅩ *508/888–6958. 5 rooms. Continental breakfast. AE, D, MC, V.*

$ ⌂ **Shawme-Crowell State Forest.** Open-air campfires are allowed at the 285 wooded tent and RV campsites here, and campers have free access to Scusset Beach. The forest is less than a mile from the Cape Cod Canal. ⊠ *Rte. 130, 02563,* ☎ *508/888–0351.*

Nightlife and the Arts

Atmospheric **Bobby Byrne's Pub** (⊠ 65 Rte. 6A, ☎ 508/888–6088) is a good place to stop for a drink. **Town band concerts** (⊠ Henry T. Wing Elementary School, Rte. 130, ☎ 508/888–5144) are held on Thursday at 7:30 PM from late June to late August.

Outdoor Activities and Sports

The Cape Cod Canal is a good place to fish; the Army Corps of Engineers operates a **canal fishing hot line** (☎ 508/759–5991).

Shopping

The **Brown Jug** (⊠ 155 Main St., at Jarves St., ☎ 508/833–1088) specializes in antique glass and Staffordshire china. **Horsefeathers** (⊠ 454 Rte. 6A, E. Sandwich, ☎ 508/888–5298) sells antique linens, lace, and vintage baby and children's clothing. **Titcomb's Bookshop** (⊠ 432 Rte. 6A, E. Sandwich, ☎ 508/888–2331) stocks used, rare, and new books, including many Cape and nautical titles.

OFF THE BEATEN PATH

ROUTE 6A – If you're heading to Orleans and you're not in a hurry, take this lovely road that heads east from Sandwich, passing through the oldest settlements on the Cape. Part of the Old King's Highway historic district, this stretch is protected from development. Classic inns and enticing antiques shops alternate with traditional gray-shingled homes on this tree-lined route, and the woods periodically give way to broad vistas across the marshes. In autumn the foliage along the road is bright—maples with their feet wet in ponds and marshes put on a good display. Along 6A east of Sandwich center, you can stop to watch the harvesting of cranberries in flooded bogs.

Falmouth

❷ *15 mi south of the Bourne Bridge, 4 mi north of Woods Hole.*

Falmouth, the Cape's second-largest town, was settled in 1660. The **Falmouth Historical Society** conducts free walking tours in season and maintains two museums. The 1790 **Julia Wood House** retains wonderful architectural details—a widow's walk, wide-board floors, leaded-glass windows. The smaller **Conant House,** a 1724 half Cape next door, has military memorabilia, whaling items, sailors' valentines, and a genealogical and historical research library. ⊠ *Village Green, Palmer Ave.,* ☎ *508/548–4857.* ☞ *$3.* ☉ *Mid-June–mid-Sept., Wed.–Sun. 2–5.*

Old Silver Beach, a long crescent of white sand, is especially good for small children because a sandbar keeps it shallow at one end and creates tidal pools full of crabs and minnows. There are lifeguards, rest rooms, showers, and a snack bar. ⊠ *Off Quaker Rd., N. Falmouth.*

Dining and Lodging

$$$–$$$$ ✕ **Regatta of Falmouth-by-the-Sea.** The menu constantly evolves at this
★ restaurant with beautiful views of Nantucket Sound and Martha's Vineyard. Continental and Asian cuisines have been interacting lately, resulting in dishes such as the sautéed shellfish sampler: scallops, mussels, lobster, and shrimp with a sensational curried lobster sauce over Asian greens. ⊠ *217 Clinton Ave., Falmouth Harbor,* ☎ *508/548–5400. AE, MC, V. Closed Tues., also Oct.–Memorial Day. No lunch Sat.*

$–$$ ✕ **Quarterdeck Restaurant.** Part bar, part restaurant—but all Cape Cod—this spot is across the street from Falmouth's town hall, so the lunch talk tends to focus on local politics. The stained glass is not old and authentic, but the huge whaling harpoons are. Hearty sandwiches like Reubens and grilled chorizo are on the menu, along with nightly entrées that might include a swordfish kabob, skewered with mushrooms, onion, and green pepper and served over jasmine rice. ⊠ *164 Main St.,* ☎ *508/548–9900. AE, D, DC, MC, V.*

$$–$$$ ✕🏠 **Coonamessett Inn.** With plenty of art, wood, and hanging plants
★ all around, this is one of the best and oldest inn-restaurants on the Cape. One- or two-bedroom suites are in five buildings around a broad lawn that spills down to a wooded pond. Rooms are casually decorated, with bleached wood or pine paneling and New England antiques or reproductions. The menu in the lovely main dining room is traditional, maybe too much so for adventuresome palates. There are plenty of seafood choices, including mussels in a fennel and Pernod broth, and baked scrod. ⊠ *311 Gifford St., at Jones Rd., 02540,* ☎ *508/548–2300,* FAX *508/540–9831. 25 suites, 1 cottage. Restaurant, bar. Continental breakfast. AE, MC, V.*

$$–$$$ 🏠 **Wildflower Inn.** The innkeepers here call their decorating style "old
★ made new again:" Tables are constructed from early 1900s pedal sewing machine bases, and the living room's sideboard was a '20s electric stove. Guest rooms, two of which have whirlpool tubs, are also innovatively decorated. The five-course breakfast might include sunflower crepes, calendula corn muffins, or other delicious concoctions using the edible wildflowers grown out back. The inn is no-smoking. ⊠ *167 Palmer Ave., 02540,* ☎ FAX *508/548–9524 or 800/294–5459. 5 rooms, 1 cottage. Full breakfast. AE, MC, V.*

$$ 🏠 **Admiralty Inn.** Some rooms at this family-friendly motel outside Falmouth center have whirlpool tubs, and the town-house suites have cathedral ceilings, two baths, a loft, and a living room. There is beach access. Children under 12 stay free. ⊠ *51 Teaticket Hwy./Rte. 28, 02540,* ☎ *508/548–4240,* FAX *508/457–0535. 68 rooms, 30 suites. Restaurant, bar, indoor-outdoor pools, hot tub, children's programs, playground. AE, D, DC, MC, V.*

$$ 🏠 **Mostly Hall.** Looking very much like a private estate, this imposing
★ 1849 house has a wraparound porch and a dramatic widow's walk. Accommodations are in corner rooms, with reading areas, antiques and canopy beds, and leafy views through shuttered casement windows. Adirondack chairs are set around lush gardens in the backyard. No smoking is permitted. ⊠ *27 Main St., 02540,* ☎ *508/548–3786 or 800/ 682–0565,* FAX *508/457–1572. 6 rooms. Bicycles, library. Full breakfast. AE, D, MC, V. Closed Jan.*

Nightlife and the Arts

On Thursday evenings the **Nimrod Inn** (⊠ 100 Dillingham Ave., ☎ 508/ 540–4132) presents the Big Band and jazz sounds of the Stage Door Canteen Band. **Town band concerts** (⊠ Marina Park, Scranton Ave., ☎ 508/ 548–8500 or 800/526–8532) take place on summer Thursdays at 8 PM.

Outdoor Activities and Sports

BIKING

The **Shining Sea Trail** is an easy 3½-mi route between Locust Street in Falmouth and the Woods Hole ferry parking lot.

FISHING

Freshwater ponds are good for perch, pickerel, and trout; the required license is available at **Eastman's Sport & Tackle** (⊠ 150 Main St., ☎ 508/548–6900).

TENNIS

Falmouth Sports Center (⊠ 33 Highfield Dr., ☎ 508/548–7433) has three all-weather and six indoor tennis courts, plus racquetball courts and a health club.

Woods Hole

❸ *4 mi southwest of Falmouth, 19 mi south of the Bourne Bridge.*

Woods Hole is home to several major scientific institutions: the Woods Hole Oceanographic Institution (WHOI), the Marine Biological Laboratory (MBL), the National Marine Fisheries Service, and the U.S. Geological Survey's Branch of Marine Geology. The WHOI is the largest independent private oceanographic laboratory in the world. Its staff led the successful U.S.–French search for the *Titanic* (found about 400 mi off Newfoundland) in 1985. Although the Oceanographic Institution (✉ 86 Water St.) is not open to the public, you can learn about it at the small **WHOI Exhibit Center.** ✉ *15 School St.,* ☎ *508/289–2663.* ☞ *$2.* ☉ *Memorial Day–Labor Day, Mon.– Sat. 10–4:30, Sun. noon–4:30; Apr. and Nov.–Dec., Fri.–Sat. 10–4:30, Sun. noon–4:30; May and Sept.–Oct., Tues.–Sat. 10–4:30, Sun. noon–4:30.*

The **Marine Biological Laboratory** (✉ *7 MBL St.,* ☎ *508/289–7623* or *508/548–3705*) is closed to the public, but retired scientists conduct free 1½-hour tours during the summer. Make reservations one week ahead.

☼ The exhibition tanks at the **National Marine Fisheries Service Aquarium** contain regional fish and shellfish. You can see things up close through magnifying glasses. Several hands-on pools hold banded lobsters, crabs, snails, sea stars, and other creatures. The star attractions are two harbor seals, which can be seen in the outdoor pool near the entrance. The exhibits aren't high-tech, but they are definitely kid-friendly. ✉ *Albatross and Water Sts.,* ☎ *508/495–2267.* ☞ *Free.* ☉ *Late June–mid-Sept., daily 10–4; mid-Sept.–late June, weekdays 10–4.*

Dining

$–$$ ✕ **Fish Monger's Café.** The ambitious contemporary menu at this
★   restaurant on the Sound includes a light fried calamari appetizer with a hot-pepper sauce and many grilled seafood dishes with tropical fruit sauces—the mango and cilantro sauce over grilled salmon is particularly delectable. ✉ *25 Water St.,* ☎ *508/540–5376. Reservations not accepted. AE, MC, V. Closed Dec.–mid-Feb. and Tues. off-season.*

Cotuit

❹ *12 mi east of Falmouth.*

The center of this picturesque town is not much more than a crossroads with a coffee shop, pizza parlor, and general store, which all seem unchanged since the 1940s. Nearby Mashpee is one of two Massachusetts towns (the other is Aquinnah, formerly known as Gay Head, on Martha's Vineyard) that has municipally governed, as well as Native American–governed, areas. Mashpee also encompasses the resort community of New Seabury.

★ The **Cahoon Museum of American Art** is in a 1775 Georgian Colonial farmhouse that was once a tavern and an overnight way station for travelers on the Hyannis–Sandwich Stagecoach line. Its several rooms display American primitive paintings by Ralph and Martha Cahoon along with other 19th- and early 20th-century art. ✉ *4676 Rte. 28,* ☎ *508/428–7581.* ☞ *Free.* ☉ *Mar.–Jan., Tues.–Sat. 10–4.*

Dining and Lodging

$–$$ ✕ **The Flume.** Native American artifacts adorn the dining room of the Flume, owned for more than 25 years by author and Wampanoag elder Earl Mills. The menu concentrates on New England staples; the chowder is among the best on the Cape. ✉ *Lake Ave., off Rte. 130, Mash-*

pee, ☎ *508/477–1456. MC, V. Closed Thanksgiving–Easter. No lunch Columbus Day–Thanksgiving.*

$$$$ ✕🖼 **New Seabury Resort and Conference Center.** This self-contained
★ resort community on a 2,000-acre point surrounded by Nantucket Sound
contains furnished apartments—available for overnight stays or longer—
in some of its 13 villages. Among the amenities are fine waterfront din-
ing ($$–$$$), a restaurant overlooking the fairways ($$–$$$), and a
private beach. The resort's golf courses are open to the public from
September to May. ⊠ *Box 549, Rock Landing Rd., New Seabury 02649,*
☎ *508/477–9400 or 800/999–9033,* 🖷 *508/477–9790. 167 1- or 2-
bedroom units. 2 restaurants, 2 pools, 2 18-hole golf courses, minia-
ture golf, 16 tennis courts, health club, jogging, beach, windsurfing,
boating, jet skiing, bicycles, pro shops. AE, DC, MC, V.*

Hyannis

⑤ *11 mi east of Cotuit, 23 mi east of the Bourne Bridge.*

Perhaps best known for its association with the Kennedy clan, Hyan-
nis is the Cape's year-round commercial hub. The enlarged and annotated
photographs at the **John F. Kennedy Hyannis Museum** document JFK's
Cape years (1934–63). ⊠ *Old Town Hall, 397 Main St.,* ☎ *508/790–
3077.* 🎫 *$3.* ⊙ *Mon.–Sat. 10–4, Sun. 1–4.*

Hyannis Port, 1½ mi south of Hyannis, was a mecca for Americans
during the Kennedy presidency, when the **Kennedy Compound** became
the summer White House. The Kennedy mystique is such that tourists
still seek it out.

Kalmus Park Beach (⊠ South end, Ocean St., Hyannis Port) is a wide
beach with a section for windsurfers and a sheltered area for children.
It has a snack bar, rest rooms, showers, and lifeguards.

Dining and Lodging

$$$–$$$$ ✕ **The Paddock.** For 30 years, the Paddock has been synonymous with
★ excellent formal dining—in the authentically Victorian main dining
room or the breezy old-style-wicker summer porch. Steak au poivre with
five varieties of crushed peppercorns is but one of the many traditional
yet innovative preparations. The superb Pacific Rim chicken is a grilled
breast topped with oranges and mangoes, served on mixed greens and
Asian noodles. Manhattans are the drink of choice in the lounge, where
musicians perform in the evening. ⊠ *W. Main St. rotary, next to Melody
Tent,* ☎ *508/775–7677. AE, DC, MC, V. Closed mid-Nov.–Mar.*

$$–$$$ ✕ **Roadhouse Café.** Candlelight flickers off the white linen tablecloths
★ and dark wood wainscoting at this stylish café. The calamari appetizer
is a chef's favorite, and the codfish chowder is a hit with locals. In the
casual bistro and the handsome mahogany bar, you can order from a
lighter menu of pizzas and sandwiches. ⊠ *488 South St.,* ☎ *508/775–
2386. Reservations essential. AE, D, MC, V. No lunch.*

$–$$ ✕ **Baxter's Fish N' Chips.** The delicious fried clams here are served with
homemade tartar sauce. Picnic tables make it possible for you to lose
no time in the sun while you dine on lobster, burgers, or delicacies from
the excellent raw bar. ⊠ *Pleasant St.,* ☎ *508/775–4490. Reservations
not accepted. AE, MC, V. Closed weekdays Labor Day–Columbus Day
and entirely Columbus Day–Apr.*

$$–$$$$ 🖼 **Breakwaters.** If you were staying any closer to the water, you'd be
★ *in* the water—that's how close these charming weathered gray-shin-
gle cottages are to Nantucket Sound. The one-, two-, and three-bed-
room condos, rented by the day or week, offer all the comforts of home.
The units have one or two bathrooms; kitchens with microwaves, cof-
feemakers, refrigerators, toasters, and stoves; and a deck or patio with

a grill—and most have water views. An added plus: daily (except Sunday) maid service. ⊠ *Box 118, 432 Sea St., 02601,* ☎ FAX *508/775–6831. 18 cottages (weekly rentals only in season). Pool, beach, babysitting. No credit cards. Closed mid-Oct.–Apr.*

$–$$ ⊞ **Sea Breeze Inn.** The rooms at this cedar-shingle seaside B&B have antique or canopied beds and are decorated with well-chosen antiques. Innkeeper Patricia Gibney's breakfasts, served in the dining room or the gazebo, are worth rising early for. The nicest of the three detached cottages is the three-bedroom Rose Garden, which has two baths, a TV room, a fireplace, and a washer and dryer. ⊠ *397 Sea St., 02601,* ☎ *508/771–7213,* FAX *508/862–0663. 14 rooms, 3 cottages. No-smoking rooms. Continental breakfast. AE, D, MC, V.*

Nightlife and the Arts

The **Cape Cod Melody Tent** (⊠ 21 W. Main St., ☎ 508/775–9100) presents music and comedy shows. The **Prodigal Son** (⊠ 10 Ocean St., ☎ 508/771–1337) hosts live music most nights, with special events year-round, such as an acoustic folk music series on Sunday and spoken-word nights midweek. Weekends bring performances of up-and-coming rock, blues, and jazz bands. **Town band concerts** (⊠ Village Green, Main St., ☎ 508/362–5230 or 800/449–6647) take place at 7:30 PM on Wednesday in July and August.

Shopping

Cape Cod Mall (⊠ Between Rtes. 132 and 28, ☎ 508/771–0200) has 90 shops, a food court, and a movie complex.

Barnstable

❻ *16 mi east of Sandwich.*

Barnstable is the second-oldest town on the Cape (it was founded in 1639), and you'll get a feeling for its age in Barnstable Village, a lovely area of large old homes dominated by the Barnstable County Superior Courthouse.

★ Hovering above Barnstable Harbor and the 4,000-acre **Great Salt Marsh, Sandy Neck Beach** stretches 6 mi across a peninsula that ends at **Sandy Neck Light.** The beach is one of the Cape's most beautiful—dunes, sand, and sea spread east, west, and north. The lighthouse, a few feet from the eroding shoreline at the tip of the neck, has been out of commission since 1952. The main beach at Sandy Neck has lifeguards, a snack bar, rest rooms, and showers. ⊠ *Sandy Neck Rd. off Rte. 6A, W. Barnstable.* 🚘 *Parking $10 Memorial Day–Labor Day.* ☉ *Daily 9–9, but staffed only until 5.*

Lodging

$$–$$$ ⊞ **Beechwood Inn.** This yellow and pale-green 1853 Queen Anne is
★ trimmed with gingerbread, wrapped by a wide porch with a glider swing, and shaded by beech trees. The parlor is pure mahogany-and-red-velvet Victorian; the guest rooms are decorated with antiques in lighter, earlier Victorian styles. The inn is no-smoking. ⊠ *2839 Main St./Rte. 6A, 02630,* ☎ *508/362–6618 or 800/609–6618,* FAX *508/362–0298. 6 rooms. Refrigerators, bicycles. Full breakfast. AE, D, MC, V.*

$$ ⊞ **Acworth Inn.** The large rooms at this 1860 house on the National Register of Historic Places are decorated in pastels, designer linens, and hand-painted furniture. One breakfast specialty is the innkeeper's cranberry granola with homegrown fresh fruit or the creamy cinnamon rolls. The inn is no-smoking. ⊠ *Box 256, 4352 Main St./Rte. 6A, Cummaquid 02637 (1 mi east of Barnstable Village),* ☎ *508/362–3330 or 800/362–6363,* FAX *508/375–0304. 4 rooms, 1 suite. Bicycles. Full breakfast. AE, D, MC, V.*

Shopping

Black's Handweaving Shop (⊠ 597 Main St./Rte. 6A, W. Barnstable, ☎ 508/362–3955) is a barnlike shop with working looms.

Yarmouth and Yarmouth Port

❼ *21 mi east of the Sagamore Bridge, 4 mi west of Dennis.*

Yarmouth was settled in 1639 by farmers from the Plymouth Bay Colony. By 1829, when Yarmouth Port was incorporated as a separate village, the Cape had begun a thriving maritime industry. Many impressive sea captains' houses—some now B&Bs and museums—still line the streets, and Yarmouth Port has some real old-time stores.

For a peek into the past, stop at **Hallet's,** a country drugstore preserved as it was in 1889, when the current owner's grandfather Thatcher Hallet opened it. ⊠ *139 Main St./Rte. 6A, Yarmouth Port,* ☎ *508/362–3362.* 🎫 *Free.* 🕓 *Call for hrs.*

★ ℭ One of Yarmouth Port's most beautiful spots is Bass Hole, which stretches from Homer's Dock Road to the salt marsh. **Bass Hole Boardwalk** extends over a marshy creek. The 2½-mi **Callery-Darling nature trails** meander through salt marshes, vegetated wetlands, and upland woods. Gray's Beach is a little crescent of sand with calm waters. ⊠ *Trail entrance on Center St. near the Gray's Beach parking lot.*

ℭ An entertaining and educational stop for kids, **ZooQuarium** has sea lion shows, wandering peacocks, a petting zoo with native wildlife, pony rides in summer, aquariums, educational programs, and the Children's Discovery Center. ⊠ *674 Rte. 28, W. Yarmouth,* ☎ *508/775–8883.* 🎫 *$7.50.* 🕓 *Mid-Feb.–June and Sept.–late Nov., daily 9:30–5; July–Aug., daily 9:30–6.*

Dining and Lodging

$$–$$$ ★ ✕ **Inaho.** Yuji Watanabe's sushi and sashimi are artistically presented, and his tempura is fluffy and light. The authentic Japanese ambience (there's a traditional garden out back), the attention to detail, and the remarkably high quality of the ingredients may make you forget you're still on old Cape Cod. ⊠ *157 Main St./Rte. 6A, Yarmouth Port,* ☎ *508/362–5522. MC, V. Closed Mon. No lunch.*

$–$$ ✕ **Jack's Outback.** Tough to find, tough to forget, this eccentric little serve-yourself-pretty-much-anything-you-want joint goes by the motto "Good food, lousy service." Solid breakfasts give way to thick burgers and traditional favorites like Yankee pot roast. Jack's has no liquor license, and you can't BYOB. ⊠ *161 Main St., Yarmouth Port,* ☎ *508/362–6690. Reservations not accepted. No credit cards. No dinner Sun.–Mon.*

$$ ★ 🏨 **Wedgewood Inn.** This handsome 1812 Greek Revival building, white with black shutters and fan ornaments on the facade, is on the National Register of Historic Places. Inside, the sophisticated country decor is a mix of fine Colonial antiques, handcrafted cherry pencil-post beds, antique quilts, and maritime paintings. The inn is no smoking. ⊠ *83 Main St./ Rte. 6A, Yarmouth Port, 02675,* ☎ *508/362–5157 or 508/362–9178,* 🅵🅰🆇 *508/362–5851. 4 rooms, 5 suites. Full breakfast. AE, DC, MC, V.*

$–$$ 🏨 **Village Inn.** Many of the guests who stay here say it's just like staying at Grandmother's—provided, of course, that Grandmother maintains the kind of clean, snug rooms found in Esther Hickey's 1795 sea captain's house. The rooms, which have floors with wide pine planks, are lessons in history: The Provincetown Room, for instance, served as the house's schoolroom. Avoid the Wellfleet Room, which is as big as the oyster that bears its name. The Brewster, Truro, and Hyannis rooms connect to make one large space. The large first-floor Yarmouth Room has its own library, bathroom with fireplace, and private entrance. The common rooms have as many books as some public libraries. The inn is no-smoking. ⊠ *Box 1, 92 Main St./Rte. 6A, Yarmouth Port, 02675,* ☎ *508/362–3182. 10 rooms. Full breakfast. MC, V.*

$ **Americana Holiday Motel.** If you want (or need) the convenience of staying on Route 28, this family-owned motel is a good choice. Rooms in the rear Pine Grove section overlook serene sea pines. ⊠ *99 Main St./Rte. 28, W. Yarmouth 02673,* ☎ *508/775–5511 or 800/445–4497,* FAX *508/790–0597. 149 rooms, 4 suites. Coffee shop, refrigerators, 1 indoor and 2 outdoor pools, hot tub, sauna, putting green, shuffleboard, video games, playground. Continental breakfast (before July 4 and after Labor Day only). AE, D, DC, MC, V. Closed Nov.–Mar.*

Nightlife and the Arts

The 90-member **Cape Cod Symphony Orchestra** (☎ 508/362–1111) gives classical and children's concerts from October to May.

Shopping

Cummaquid Fine Arts (⊠ 4275 Rte. 6A, Cummaquid, ☎ 508/362–2593) has works by Cape Cod and New England artists, and decorative antiques. **Parnassus Book Service** (⊠ Rte. 6A, Yarmouth Port, ☎ 508/ 362–6420), in an 1840 former general store, specializes in Cape Cod, maritime, and antiquarian books. **Peach Tree Designs** (⊠ 173 Rte. 6A, Yarmouth Port, ☎ 508/362–8317) carries home furnishings and accessories made by local craftspeople.

Dennis

⑧ *4 mi east of Yarmouth, 7 mi west of Brewster.*

Hundreds of sea captains lived in Dennis when fishing, salt making, and shipbuilding were the main industries. The elegant houses they constructed still line the streets. The town has conservation areas, nature trails, and numerous ponds for swimming.

The holdings of the **Cape Museum of Fine Arts** include more than 850 works by Cape-associated artists. The museum hosts film festivals, lectures, and art classes. ⊠ *60 Hope La.,* ☎ *508/385–4477.* ⊡ *$5.* ☉ *Late-May–Nov., Mon.–Wed. and Fri.–Sat. 10–5, Thurs. 10–7:30, Sun. 1–5; Dec.–mid-May, Tues.–Sat. 10–5, Sun. 1–5.*

Corporation Beach (⊠ Corporation Rd.) on Dennis's bay side is a beautiful crescent of white sand backed by low dunes; there are lifeguards, showers, rest rooms, and a food stand. On the south shore, one of the best beaches is the long, wide **West Dennis Beach** (⊠ Davis Beach Rd., W. Dennis), which has bathhouses, lifeguards, a playground, and food concessions.

Dining and Lodging

$$–$$$ ✕ **Gina's by the Sea.** Some places are less than the sum of their parts; ★ Gina's is more. In a funky, often-crowded old building tucked into a sand dune, the aroma of fine northern Italian cooking blends with a fresh breeze off the bay. Look for lots of fresh pasta and seafood. ⊠ *134 Taunton Ave.,* ☎ *508/385–3213. Reservations not accepted. AE, MC, V. Closed Dec.–Mar. and Mon.–Wed. Oct.–Nov. No lunch Apr.– June and Sept.–Nov.*

$$–$$$ ✕ **Scargo Café.** Because the Cape Playhouse is right across the street, this café with a neocolonial feel is a favorite haunt before and after shows. Try the mussels Ferdinand, a plate of farm-raised mussels with a buttery Pernod sauce over pasta. ⊠ *799 Rte. 6A,* ☎ *508/385–8200. AE, D, MC, V.*

$–$$ 🏠 **Four Chimneys Inn.** This three-story, four-chimney 1881 Queen Anne
★   gem is a relaxing getaway in the heart of the Mid Cape. The eight rooms
    are tastefully furnished and have views of either Scargo Lake or of the
    surrounding woods and gardens. ⊠ *946 Main St./Rte. 6A, 02638,* ☎
    508/385–6317 or 800/874–5502, FAX *508/385–6285. 7 rooms, 1 suite.*
    Continental breakfast. AE, MC, V. Closed Dec.–mid-Feb.

$–$$ 🏠 **Isaiah Hall B&B Inn.** Lilacs and pink roses trail the white fence out-
★   side this 1857 Greek Revival farmhouse on a residential road on the
    bay side. Guest rooms are decorated with country antiques, floral-print
    wallpapers, and homey quilts. In the carriage house, rooms have sten-
    ciled white walls and knotty pine, and some have small balconies over-
    looking gardens. Smoking is not permitted. ⊠ *152 Whig St., 02638,*
    ☎ *508/385–9928 or 800/736–0160,* FAX *508/385–5879. 9 rooms, 1 suite.*
    Picnic area, badminton, croquet. Continental breakfast. AE, MC, V.
    Closed mid-Oct.–Mar.

Nightlife and the Arts

For Broadway-style shows and children's plays, attend a production
at the **Cape Playhouse** (⊠ Main St./Rte. 6A, ☎ 508/385–3911), one
of the most renowned summer theaters in the country. The **Reel Art
Cinema** (☎ 508/385–4477) at the Cape Museum of Fine Arts (☞
above) shows avant garde, classic, art, and independent films on weekends between October and April.

Outdoor Activities and Sports

See Cape Cod Rail Trail *in* Cape Cod A to Z, *below.*

Shopping

Scargo Pottery (⊠ 30 Dr. Lord's Rd. S, off Rte. 6A, ☎ 508/385–3894)
is in a pine forest, where potter Harry Holl's unusual wares sit on tree
stumps and hang from branches. Inside are the workshop and kiln, plus
work by Holl's four daughters.

Brewster

❾ *7 mi east of Dennis, 5 mi west of Orleans.*

Brewster is the perfect place to learn about the natural history of the
Cape: The area contains conservation lands, state parks, forests, freshwater ponds, and marshes.

For nature enthusiasts, a visit to the **Cape Cod Museum of Natural History** is a must. In the museum and on the grounds are a library, nature
and marine exhibits, and trails through 80 acres of forest and marshland rich in birds and wildlife. The exhibit hall upstairs has a display
of aerial photographs documenting the process by which the Chatham
sandbar split in two. The museum also offers guided canoe and kayak
trips from May through September, and several cruises that explore
different Cape waterways: Nantucket Sound, Pleasant Bay, and Nauset Marsh. ⊠ *869 Main St./Rte. 6A,* ☎ *508/896–3867; 800/479–
3867 in MA.* 🎫 *$5.* ☉ *Mon.–Sat. 9:30–4:30, Sun. 11–4:30.*

The **Brewster Store** (⊠ 1935 Main St./Rte. 6A, at Rte. 124, ☎ 508/
896–3744) is a local landmark. Built in 1852, this typical New England
general store provides such essentials as the daily papers, penny candy,
and benches out front for conversation.

The 1,961 acres of **Nickerson State Park** (⊠ Rte. 6A, ☎ 508/896–3491)
consist of oak, pitch pine, hemlock, and spruce forest dotted with freshwater kettle ponds formed by glacial action. Recreational opportunities include fishing, boating, biking along 8 mi of trails, cross-country
skiing, and bird-watching. **Flax Pond** has picnic areas, a bathhouse,
and water-sports rentals.

Dining and Lodging

$$$$ ✕ **Chillingsworth.** This crown jewel of Cape restaurants is extremely
★ formal, terribly pricey, and completely upscale. The classic French
menu and wine cellar continue to win award after award. The seven-
course table d'hôte menu ($40–$56) includes an assortment of appetizers, entrées—like super-rich risotto, roast lobster, or grilled
venison—and "amusements." At dinner, a modest bistro menu is served
in the Garden Room, a patio-like area in the front of the restaurant.
⊠ *2449 Main St./Rte. 6A,* ☎ *508/896–3640. Reservations essential.
AE, DC, MC, V. Closed Mon. mid-June–Thanksgiving; some weekdays Memorial Day–mid-June and mid-Oct.–Thanksgiving; and entirely
Thanksgiving–Memorial Day.*

$$$$ ✕ **High Brewster.** The restored Colonial farmhouse of this country inn
★ has low ceilings and exposed ceiling beams, and it overlooks a picture-
perfect landscape. The five-course prix-fixe regional American menu
changes frequently. Longtime dinner highlights include squash soup,
grilled duck breast with a black-currant reduction, and apple-rum ice
cream. ⊠ *964 Setucket Rd.,* ☎ *508/896–3636 and 800/203–2634.
Reservations essential. AE, MC, V. Closed 1st 2 wks in Jan.; call for
weekday hrs off-season. No lunch.*

$$$$ ⊞ **Ocean Edge.** This self-contained resort with superior sports facilities is almost like a town. Concerts, tournaments, clambakes, and
other activities are scheduled throughout the summer. The modern accommodations range from oversize hotel rooms to luxurious condominiums in the woods. ⊠ *2907 Main St./Rte. 6A, 02631,* ☎ *508/896–
9000 or 800/343–6074,* ℻ *508/896–9123. 90 rooms, 197 condominium units. 3 restaurants, pub, room service, 2 indoor and 4 outdoor pools, ponds, saunas, driving range, 18-hole golf course, putting
greens, 11 tennis courts, basketball, exercise room, beach, bicycles, children's programs, concierge. AE, D, DC, MC, V.*

$$–$$$$ ⊞ **Captain Freeman Inn.** The opulent details at this splendid 1866 Vic-
★ torian include a marble fireplace, herringbone-inlay flooring, ornate Ital-
ian ceiling medallions, and 12-ft ceilings. Guest rooms in the no-smoking
inn have hardwood floors, antiques, and eyelet spreads. The eight "lux-
ury rooms" are truly indulgent. ⊠ *15 Breakwater Rd., 02631,* ☎ *508/
896–7481 or 800/843–4664,* ℻ *508/896–5618. 12 rooms. Pool, bad-
minton, croquet, bicycles. Full breakfast. AE, MC, V.*

$–$$ ⊞ **Old Sea Pines Inn.** Fronted by a white-column portico, the Old Sea
Pines evokes the summer estates of an earlier time. A sweeping stair-
case leads to rooms decorated with framed old photographs and antique furnishings. Rooms in a newer building are sparsely but well
decorated. The rooms with shared baths are *very* small but a steal in
summer. ⊠ *Box 1070, 2553 Main St./Rte. 6A, 02631,* ☎ *508/896–
6114,* ℻ *508/896–7387. 25 rooms, 15 with bath; 5 suites. Restaurant.
Full breakfast. AE, D, DC, MC, V. Closed Jan.–Mar.*

$ ⚠ **Nickerson State Park.** Some of the popular sites at this 2,000- acre
park are right on the edges of ponds. The facilities include showers,
bathrooms, barbecue areas, and a store. ⊠ *3488 Main St./Rte. 6A, E.
Brewster 02631,* ☎ *508/896–3491; 508/896–4615 for reservations,*
℻ *508/896–3103. 418 sites. No credit cards.* ☉ *Open mid-Oct.–mid-
Apr. to self-contained campers only.*

Outdoor Activities and Sports

Captain's Golf Course (⊠ 1000 Freeman's Way, ☎ 508/896–5100) is a
great 18-hole, par-72 public course with a greens fee ranging from $20
to $45; rental carts are not available. The **Cape Cod Rail Trail Bikeway**
(☞ Cape Cod A to Z *below*) cuts through Brewster at Long Pond Road,
Underpass Road, Millstone Road, and other points. **Jack's Boat Rentals**
(⊠ Nickerson State Park, Flax Pond, Rte. 6A, ☎ 508/896–8556) rents

canoes, kayaks, Seacycles, Sunfish, pedal boats, and sailboards. **Ocean Edge Golf Course** (⊠ Villagers Dr./Rte. 6A, ☎ 508/896–5911), an 18-hole, par-72 course winding around five ponds, has a greens fee that ranges from $25 to $59. Carts, mandatory at certain times, cost $14.

Shopping

Kemp Pottery (⊠ 258 Main St./Rte. 6A, W. Brewster, ☎ 508/385–5782) has functional and decorative stoneware and porcelain. **Kingsland Manor** (⊠ 440 Main St./Rte. 6A, W. Brewster, ☎ 508/385–9741) sells everything "from tin to Tiffany." The **Spectrum** (⊠ 369 Main St./Rte. 6A, ☎ 508/385–3322) purveys American arts and crafts including art glass and pottery. **Sydenstricker Galleries** (⊠ 490 Main St./Rte. 6A, ☎ 508/385–3272) is a working glass studio.

Harwich

🔟 *3 mi east of Dennisport, 1 mi south of Brewster.*

Originally known as Setucket, Harwich separated from Brewster in 1694 and was renamed after the famous seaport in England. Like other townships on the Cape, Harwich is actually a cluster of seven small villages, including Harwich Port. Three naturally sheltered harbors make the town, like its English namesake, a popular spot for boaters. Wychmere Harbor is particularly beautiful. Each September Harwich holds a Cranberry Festival to celebrate the importance of this indigenous berry.

Once a private school, the pillared 1844 Greek Revival building of **Brooks Academy** now houses the museum of the **Harwich Historical Society.** In addition to a large photo-history collection and exhibits on artist Charles Cahoon (grandson of Alvin), the socio-technological history of the cranberry culture, and shoemaking, the museum displays antique clothing and textiles, china and glass, fans, toys, and much more. There is also an extensive genealogical collection for researchers. On the grounds is a powder house that was used to store gunpowder during the Revolutionary War, as well as a restored 1872 outhouse. ⊠ *80 Parallel St.,* ☎ *508/432–8089.* 🔳 *Donations accepted.* ☉ *June–mid-Oct., Wed.–Sun. 1–4.*

Dining and Lodging

$$ ✕ **Brax Landing.** In this local stalwart, perched alongside busy Saquatucket Harbor, you'll pass by tanks full of steamers and lobsters in the corridor leading to the dining room. The restaurant sprawls around a big bar that serves drinks like the "Moxie" (pink lemonade and vodka, "calm seas guaranteed"). The swordfish and the Chatham scrod are favorites, both served simply and well. There's a notable children's menu, and Sunday brunch, served from 10 to 2, is an institution. ⊠ *Rte. 28 at Saquatucket, Harwich Port,* ☎ *508/432–5515. Reservations not accepted. AE, DC, MC, V.*

$$–$$$ 🔳 **Augustus Snow House.** This grand Victorian epitomizes elegance. The
★   stately dining room is the setting for the three-course breakfast, with dishes like baked pears in a raspberry-cream sauce. Guest rooms, which all have fireplaces, are decorated with Victorian-print wallpapers, luxurious carpets, and fine antiques and reproduction furnishings. ⊠ *528 Main St., Harwich Port 02646,* ☎ *508/430–0528 or 800/320–0528,* 🖷 *508/432–7995. 5 rooms. Full breakfast. AE, D, MC, V.*

Nightlife and the Arts

Town band concerts in Harwich take place in summer on Tuesday at 7:30 PM in Brooks Park (⊠ Main St., ☎ 508/432–1600).

Outdoor Activities and Sports

Cape Water Sports (⊠ 337 Main St., Harwich Port, ☎ 508/432–7079) rents Sunfish, Hobie Cats, Lasers, powerboats, surfbikes, day sailers, and canoes. Fishing trips are operated from spring to fall on the *Golden Eagle* (⊠ Wychmere Harbor, Harwich Port, ☎ 508/432–5611).

Cranberry Valley Golf Course (⊠ 183 Oak St., ☎ 508/430–7560) has a championship 18-hole, par-72 layout. The greens fee is $45; an optional cart costs $20.

Chatham

⑪ *5 mi east of Harwich, 1 mi west of Orleans.*

At the bent elbow of the Cape, Chatham has all the charm of a quiet seaside resort, with relatively little commercialism. And it *is* charming: gray-shingled houses with tidy awnings and cheerful flower gardens, an attractive Main Street with crafts and antiques stores alongside homey coffee shops, and a five-and-ten. It's well-to-do without being ostentatious, casual and fun but refined, and never tacky.

The view from **Chatham Light** (⊠ Main St., ☎ 508/945–0719)—of the harbor, the offshore sandbars, and the ocean beyond—justifies the crowds that gather to share it. The lighthouse is especially dramatic on a foggy night, as the beacon's light pierces the mist. Coin-operated telescopes allow a close look at the famous Chatham Break, the result of a fierce 1987 nor'easter that blasted a channel through a barrier beach just off the coast.

Monomoy National Wildlife Refuge is a 2,750-acre preserve including the Monomoy Islands, a fragile, 9-mi-long barrier-beach area south of Chatham. A paradise for bird-watchers, the islands are an important stop along the North Atlantic Flyway for migratory waterfowl and shore birds. The Cape Cod Museum of Natural History (☞ Brewster, *above*)) and the Massachusetts Audubon Society in South Wellfleet (☞ Wellfleet, *below*) conduct island tours. The **Monomoy National Wildlife Refuge headquarters,** on Morris Island, has a visitor center (☎ 508/945–0594), open daily from 8 to 5, where you can pick up pamphlets. **Harding's Beach,** west of Chatham center, is open to the public and charges daily parking fees to nonresidents in season.

Dining and Lodging

$$$ ✕ **Christian's.** The influences at this landmark town establishment stem from two continents. Downstairs, an Old Cape–country-French motif prevails in the decor and on the menu: Boneless roast duck with raspberry sauce and flaky sautéed sole with lobster and lemon-butter sauce are typical entrées. Upstairs is casual and great for families, with a movie theme, a seafood-based menu (with some Mexican influences), and a mahogany-panel piano bar. ⊠ *443 Main St.,* ☎ *508/945–3362. AE, D, DC, MC, V. Closed weekdays Jan.–Mar.*

$$–$$$ ✕ **Vining's Bistro.** Chatham's restaurants tend to serve conservative fare,
★ but the cuisine at this bistro is among the most inventive in the area. The wood grill, where the chef employs zesty spices from all over the globe, is the center of attention. The exotic Bangkok fisherman's stew, the spit-roasted Jamaican chicken, and the Portobello mushroom sandwich are among the best dishes here. ⊠ *595 Main St.,* ☎ *508/945–5033. Reservations not accepted. AE, D, MC, V. Closed mid-Jan.–Apr.*

$$ ✕ **Chatham Squire.** What was a bar scene and not much more has evolved into an excellent dining experience. The fish served here is as good as it gets, and the kitchen continues to innovate without forgetting its Cape roots. The Squire is not as inexpensive as it was (or as its exterior implies), but it is much finer. ⊠ *487 Main St.,* ☎ *508/945–0945. Reservations not accepted. AE, D, MC, V.*

$$$$ ⊞ **Wequassett Inn.** This exquisite, traditional resort offers accommodations
★ in 20 Cape-style cottages along a bay and on 22 acres of woods. Luxurious dining, attentive service, evening entertainment, and plenty of sunning and sporting opportunities are among the draws. Decor is Early
American, with country pine furniture and such homey touches as handmade quilts and duck decoys. ⊠ *Rte. 28, Pleasant Bay, 02633,* ☎ *508/
432–5400 or 800/225–7125,* FAX *508/432–5032. 102 rooms, 2 suites.
Restaurant, grill, piano bar, room service, pool, 4 tennis courts, exercise
room, windsurfing, boating. AP. AE, D, DC, MC, V. Closed Nov.–Apr.*

$$$–$$$$ ⊞ **Queen Anne Inn.** Built in 1840 as a wedding present for the daugh-
ter of a famous clipper-ship captain, this grand structure has large rooms
furnished in a casual yet elegant style. Some have working fireplaces,
private balconies, and hot tubs. Lingering and lounging are encour-
aged—around the large pool, on the veranda, in front of the fireplace
in the sitting room, and in the plush parlor. ⊠ *70 Queen Anne Rd.,
02633,* ☎ *508/945–0394 or 800/545–4667,* FAX *508/945–4884. 31
rooms. Restaurant, bar, pool, spa, 3 tennis courts. AE, D, MC, V.*

$$–$$$$ ⊞ **Captain's House Inn.** Fine architectural details, superb taste in decorating, and a feeling of quiet comfort are part of what makes this no-
smoking inn one of the Cape's finest. The rooms, spread over four
buildings, have varied personalities—some are lacy and feminine,
others refined and elegant. The luxury suites are particularly spacious
and have every amenity imaginable. ⊠ *371 Old Harbor Rd., 02633,*
☎ *508/945–0127,* FAX *508/945–0866. 16 rooms, 3 suites. Croquet, bicycles. Full breakfast. AE, D, MC, V.*

$$–$$$ ⊞ **Moses Nickerson House.** Warm, thoughtful service and fine an-
★ tiques set the tone at this no-smoking B&B. Each room in the 1839
house has its own look: one has dark woods, leathers, Ralph Lauren
fabrics, and English hunting antiques; another has a high canopy bed
and a Nantucket hand-hooked rug. All rooms have queen-size beds and
wide-board pine flooring. Bathrooms, however, are small. ⊠ *364 Old
Harbor Rd., 02633,* ☎ *508/945–5859 or 800/628–6972,* FAX *508/
945–7087. 7 rooms. Full breakfast. AE, D, MC, V.*

Nightlife and the Arts

Monomoy Theatre (⊠ 776 Main St., ☎ 508/945–1589) presents summer productions by the Ohio University Players. Chatham's summer
town band concerts (⊠ Kate Gould Park, Main St., ☎ 508/945–5199)
begin at 8 PM on Friday and draw up to 6,000 people.

Shopping

Cape Cod Cooperage (⊠ 1150 Queen Anne Rd., at Rte. 137, ☎ 508/
432–0788) sells traditional woodenware made by an on-site cooper. At
Chatham Glass Co. (⊠ 758 Main St., W. Chatham, ☎ 508/945–5547)
you can watch glass being blown and buy it, too. **Fancy's Farm of
Chatham** (⊠ Rte. 28, W. Chatham, ☎ 508/945–1949) sells everything
you need for a beach picnic. **Yellow Umbrella Books** (⊠ 501 Main St.,
☎ 508/945–0144) has an excellent selection of new and used books.

Orleans

⑫ *6 mi north of Chatham, 35 mi east of the Sagamore Bridge.*

Incorporated in 1797, Orleans is part quiet seaside village and part
bustling commercial center. A walk along Rock Harbor Road, a winding street lined with gray-shingled houses, white picket fences, and neat
gardens, leads to the bay-side **Rock Harbor,** the base of a small commercial fishing fleet whose catch hits the counters at the fish market
here. Sunsets over the harbor are memorable.

Nauset Beach (✉ Beach Rd.)—not to be confused with Nauset Light Beach at Cape Cod National Seashore—is a 10-mi-long sweep of sandy ocean beach with low dunes and large waves good for bodysurfing or board surfing. There are lifeguards, rest rooms, showers, and a food concession.

Skaket Beach on Cape Cod Bay is a sandy stretch with calm warm water good for children. There are rest rooms, lifeguards, and a snack bar. ✉ *Skaket Beach Rd.*

Dining and Lodging

$$–$$$ ✕ **Kadee's Lobster & Clam Bar.** A summer landmark, Kadee's serves good clams and fish-and-chips that you can grab on the way to the beach from the take-out window. Or you can sit down in the dining room for steamers and mussels, pasta and seafood stews, or the Portuguese kale soup. There's a miniature golf course out back. Unfortunately, the prices seem to have gone through the roof. ✉ *212 Main St.,* ☎ *508/255–6184. Reservations not accepted. MC, V. Closed day after Labor Day–week before Memorial Day and weekdays in early June.*

$$–$$$ ✕ **Nauset Beach Club.** What was once the unsung local hero has be-
★ come widely known for its fine dining. You might feel as if you're eating in someone's former living room (you are), though the sophisticated, contemporary Italian cuisine is superior to that of the finest home cooks. *Zuppa di pesce* (Italian seafood stew) is one of many menu highlights. ✉ *222 Main St., E. Orleans,* ☎ *508/255–8547. AE, D, DC, MC, V. Reservations accepted only for parties of 6 or more. No lunch. No dinner Sun.–Mon. mid-Oct.–Memorial Day.*

$–$$ ✕ **Lobster Claw.** If you're over 6 ft tall, keep an eye out for the fishing nets hanging from the ceiling inside this goofy little spot. Tables are lacquered turquoise, portions are huge, and the lobster roll is one of the best. ✉ *Rte. 6A,* ☎ *508/255–1800. Reservations not accepted. AE, D, DC, MC, V.*

$$ 🏠 **Kadee's Gray Elephant.** A mile from Nauset Beach, this 200-year-
★ old house contains small vacation studio and one-bedroom apartments. Unique on the Cape, they are a cheerful riot of color, from wicker painted lavender or green to beds layered in quilts and comforters mixing plaids and florals. The kitchens are equipped with microwaves, attractive glassware, irons and boards—and even lobster crackers. ✉ *Box 86, 216 Main St., E. Orleans 02643,* ☎ *508/255–7608,* 𝔽𝔸𝕏 *508/240–2976. 8 apartments. Restaurant, miniature golf, gift shop. MC, V.*

Nightlife and the Arts

The **Academy Playhouse** (✉ 120 Main St., ☎ 508/255–1963) hosts a dozen or so productions year-round, including original works. The **Cape & Islands Chamber Music Festival** (☎ 508/255–9509) presents three weeks of top-caliber performances in August.

Outdoor Activities and Sports

Arey's Pond Boat Yard (✉ Off Rte. 28, S. Orleans, ☎ 508/255–0994) has a sailing school where individual and group lessons are taught. **Goose Hummock Shop** (✉ Rte. 6A off the Rte. 6 rotary, ☎ 508/255–0455) sells licenses, which are required for fishing in Orleans's freshwater ponds. **Rock Harbor Charter Boat Fleet** (✉ Rock Harbor, ☎ 508/255–9757 or 800/287–1771 in MA) goes for bass and blues in the bay from spring to fall. Walk-ons are welcome.

Shopping

Addison Holmes Gallery (✉ 43 Rte. 28, ☎ 508/255–6200), housed in four rooms of a brick-red Cape, represents area artists. **Hannah** (✉ 47 Main St., ☎ 508/255–8234) has unique women's fashions. **Tree's**

Place (⊠ Rte. 6A, at Rte. 28, ☎ 508/255–1330) displays the works of New England artists.

Eastham

⓭ *4 mi north of Orleans.*

Like many other Cape towns, Eastham (incorporated in 1651) started as a farming community, later turning to the sea and to salt making for its livelihood. A more atypical industry here was asparagus growing; from the late 1800s through the 1920s, Eastham was known as the "Asparagus Capital."

The park on busy U.S. 6 at Samoset Road has as its centerpiece the **Eastham Windmill,** the oldest windmill on Cape Cod. ⊠ *U.S 6.* ☜ *Free.* ☉ *Late June–Labor Day, Mon.–Sat. 10–5, Sun. 1–5.*

A great spot for watching sunsets over the bay, **First Encounter Beach** (⊠ Samoset Rd., off U.S. 6) is laden with history. Near the parking lot, a bronze marker commemorates the first encounter between local Indians and passengers from the *Mayflower,* who explored the area for five weeks in late 1620.

★ Along 40 mi of shoreline from Chatham to Provincetown, the 44,000-acre **Cape Cod National Seashore** encompasses superb ocean beaches, rolling dunes, wetlands, pitch pine and scrub oak forest, wildlife, and several historic structures. Self-guided nature, hiking, biking, and horse trails lace these landscapes. **Salt Pond Visitor Center** has a museum and offers guided tours, boat trips, and lectures, as well as evening beach walks and campfire talks in summer. ⊠ *Visitor center, off U.S. 6,* ☎ *508/255–3421.* ☜ *Free.* ☉ *Mar.–June and Sept.–Dec., daily 9–4:30; July–Aug., daily 9–5; Jan.–Feb., weekends 9–4:30.*

Roads and bicycle trails lead to Coast Guard and Nauset Light beaches, which begin an unbroken 30-mi stretch of barrier beach extending to Provincetown—the "Cape Cod Beach" of Thoreau's 1865 classic, *Cape Cod.* You can still walk its length, as Thoreau did. Tours of the much-photographed red and white **Nauset Light** (☎ 508/240–2612) are given on weekends in season.

Low grass and heathland backs the long **Coast Guard Beach.** It has no parking lot, so park at the Salt Pond Visitor Center and take the free shuttle or walk the 1¾-mi **Nauset Trail** to the beach.

Lodging

$$$–$$$$ 🏠 **Whalewalk Inn.** With windows galore, this 1830 whaling master's home on 3 acres of rolling lawns and gardens has an airy feeling. Wideboard pine floors, fireplaces, and 19th-century country antiques provide historical appeal. The spacious rooms at the no-smoking inn have floral fabrics and and antique or reproduction furniture. ⊠ *220 Bridge Rd., 02642,* ☎ *508/255–0617,* 𝖥𝖠𝖷 *508/240–0017. 11 rooms, 5 suites. Bicycles. Full breakfast. MC, V.*

$$–$$$ 🏠 **Penny House Inn.** Antiques and collectibles decorate the rooms, all with air-conditioning, in this rambling, no-smoking inn sheltered by a wave of privet hedge. Common areas include the Great Room, with a fireplace and lots of windows, a combination sunroom-library, and a garden patio set with umbrella tables. ⊠ *4885 County Rd./U.S. 6, 02642,* ☎ *508/255–6632 or 800/554–1751,* 𝖥𝖠𝖷 *508/255–4893. 11 rooms. Full breakfast. AE, D, MC, V.*

$ ⛺ **Atlantic Oaks Campground.** Primarily an RV camp, this campground forest is less than a mile north of the Salt Pond Visitor Center. RV hookups, including cable TV, cost $35 for two people; tent sites are $26 for two people. Showers are free. ⊠ *U.S. 6, 02642,* ☎ *508/*

255–1437 or 800/332–2267. 100 RV sites, 30 tent sites. Bicycles, playground, coin laundry. D, MC, V. Closed Nov.–Apr.

Wellfleet

⑭ *10 mi north of Eastham, 13 mi southeast of Provincetown.*

Less than 2 mi wide, tastefully developed Wellfleet attracts many artists and writers because of its fine restaurants, historic houses, and many art galleries.

★ The **Massachusetts Audubon Wellfleet Bay Sanctuary,** a 1,000-acre haven for more than 250 species of birds, is a superb place for walking, birding, and looking west over the salt marsh and bay at wondrous sunsets. The Audubon Society hosts naturalist-led wildlife tours year-round; phone reservations are required. ⊠ *Off U.S. 6, S. Wellfleet,* ☎ *508/349–2615.* ▣ *$3.* ☉ *Daily 8 AM–dusk.*

A good stroll around town would take in Commercial and Main streets and end at **Uncle Tim's Bridge.** The short walk across this arcing landmark—with its much-photographed view over marshland and a tidal creek—leads to a small wooded island.

For a **scenic loop** through a classic Cape landscape near Wellfleet's Atlantic beaches—with scrub and pines on the left, heathland meeting cliffs and the ocean below on the right—take LeCount Hollow Road north of the Marconi Station turnoff. Access to the first and last of four beaches on this stretch, **LeCount Hollow** and **Newcomb Hollow,** is restricted to residents in season. Between the two hollows, the spectacular dune-drop Atlantic beaches **White Crest** and **Cahoon Hollow,** open to the public, charge a $10 parking fee to nonresidents in season. Cahoon Hollow has lifeguards, rest rooms, and a restaurant and music club. Backtrack to Cahoon Hollow Road and turn west for the southernmost entrance to the town of Wellfleet proper, across U.S. 6.

Dining and Lodging

$$–$$$ ✕ **Aesop's Tables.** Inside this 1805 captain's house—a worthy choice
★ for a special dinner—are five dining rooms; aim for a table on the porch overlooking the town center. This is a great place to sample various preparations of local seafood; the signature dish is an exotic bouillabaisse with mounds of fresh-off-the-boat seafood. "Death by Chocolate" is a popular dessert. On some nights in summer, the tavern hosts jazz musicians. ⊠ *316 Main St.,* ☎ *508/349–6450. AE, DC, MC, V. Closed Columbus Day–Mother's Day. No lunch.*

$$–$$$ ✕ **Finely JP's.** The dining room is noisy, but the wonderful Italian-in-
★ fluenced fish and pasta dishes are worth it. The appetizers, among them the warm spinach and scallop salad and the blackened beef with charred-pepper relish, are especially good, and the Wellfleet paella draws raves. ⊠ *U.S. 6, S. Wellfleet,* ☎ *508/349–7500. Reservations not accepted. D, MC, V. Closed Mon.–Wed. Thanksgiving–Memorial Day; Mon.–Tues. Memorial Day–mid-June and Oct.–Thanksgiving; Tues. Labor Day–Oct.*

$–$$ ✕ **Bayside Lobster Hutt.** Diners at long tables break bread with strangers and often as not wind up as neighbors on the beach the next day. Though nothing fancy, the seafood is always fresh. ⊠ *91 Commercial St.,* ☎ *508/349–6333. Reservations not accepted. No credit cards. Closed mid-Sept.–Memorial Day.*

$$–$$$ ▥ **Surf Side Colony Cottages.** These one- to three-bedroom cottages
★ on the Atlantic shore of the Outer Cape have fireplaces, kitchens, and screened porches. The exteriors are retro-Florida, but the interiors are tastefully decorated. ⊠ *Box 937, Ocean View Dr., S. Wellfleet 02663,* ☎ *508/349–3959,* ℻ *508/349–3959. 18 cottages. Picnic areas, coin laundry. MC, V. 1- to 2-wk minimum in summer. Closed Nov.–Mar.*

$ 🛏 Holden Inn. If you're watching your budget and can deal with modest basics, try this old-time place just out of the town center. The lodge has shared baths, an outdoor shower, and a screened-in porch with a view of the bay. Rooms with private baths that have old porcelain sinks are available in adjacent 1840 and 1890 buildings. All rooms are clean and simple. ⊠ *140 Commercial St., 02667,* ☎ *508/349–3450. 27 rooms, 13 with bath. No credit cards. Closed mid-Oct.–mid-Apr.*

Nightlife and the Arts

The **Beachcomber** (⊠ Cahoon Hollow Beach, off U.S. 6, ☎ 508/349–6055) has a happy hour with live music and dancing in summer. The drive-in movie is alive and well at the **Wellfleet Drive-In Theater** (⊠ U.S. 6, ☎ 508/349–7176 or 508/255–9619). Art galleries host cocktail receptions during the **Wellfleet Gallery Crawl,** on Saturday evenings in July and August. The **Wellfleet Harbor Actors Theater** (⊠ Kendrick St., past E. Commercial St., ☎ 508/349–6835) stages American plays, satires, and farces mid-May–mid-October.

Outdoor Activities and Sports

Jack's Boat Rentals (⊠ Gull Pond, ☎ 508/349–7553) rents canoes, kayaks, sailboats, and sailboards.

Shopping

Blue Heron Gallery (⊠ 20 Bank St., ☎ 508/349–6724), one of the Cape's best galleries, carries contemporary works. **Karol Richardson** (⊠ 11 W. Main St., ☎ 508/349–6378) designs women's wear in luxurious fabrics. **Kendall Art Gallery** (⊠ 40 E. Main St., ☎ 508/349–2482) carries contemporary art and has a serene sculpture garden.

Truro

⑮ *3 mi north of Wellfleet, 7 mi southeast of Provincetown.*

Truro, a town of high dunes and rivers fringed by grasses, is a popular retreat for artists, writers, and politicos. Edward Hopper, who summered here from 1930 to 1967, found the Cape light ideal for his ℃ austere realism. At **Pamet Harbor,** off Depot Road, you can walk out on the flats at low tide and discover the creatures of the salt marsh.

Truly a breathtaking sight, **Highland Light,** also called Cape Cod Light, is the Cape's oldest lighthouse. Erosion threatened to cut the structure from its 117-ft perch and drop it into the sea, but local citizens raised funds in 1996 to move the lighthouse back 450 ft to safety. ⊠ *Off S. Highland Rd.* 🎫 *$3.* ☉ *Mid-June–Sept., daily 10–8.*

Head of the Meadow Beach, a relatively uncrowded part of the National Seashore off U.S. 6, has only temporary rest-room facilities available in summer and no showers. The **Head of the Meadow Trail** is 2 mi of easy cycling between dunes and salt marshes from the beach's parking lot to High Head Road, off Route 6A in North Truro. Bird-watchers love this area.

Lodging

$–$$ 🛏 Truro Vineyards of Cape Cod Inn. This elegant inn is decorated in a wine motif, not surprising since it's on the site of a working winery. Antique casks and presses stand in the corners, and deep greens and burgundies predominate. Rooms have four-poster beds and modern baths. Homegrown berries often garnish breakfast dishes, and a large sundeck has sweeping views of the vineyard. The inn is no-smoking. ⊠ *Rte. 6A, N. Truro 02652,* ☎ *508/487–6200,* 𝔽𝔸𝕏 *508/487–4248. 5 rooms. Full breakfast. MC, V.*

$ ⚏ **Hostelling International–Truro.** In a former Coast Guard station on the dunes, this handsome facility has 42 beds and kitchen facilities. ✉ *Box 402, N. Pamet Rd., 02666,* ☎ *508/349–3889. MC, V. Closed Labor Day–mid-June.*

Outdoor Activities and Sports

The **Highland Golf Links** (✉ Lighthouse Rd., N. Truro, ☎ 508/487–9201), a nine-hole, par-36 course on a cliff overlooking the Atlantic, has a greens fee of $16; an optional cart costs $13.

Provincetown

★ ⑯ *7 mi northwest of Truro, 27 mi north of Orleans, 62 mi from the Sagamore Bridge.*

Provincetown's shores form a curled fist at the very tip of the Cape. The town was for decades a bustling seaport, with fishing and whaling as its major industries. Fishing is still an important source of income for many Provincetown natives, although the town is a major whale-watching, rather than hunting, mecca.

One of the first of many historically important visitors to anchor in this hospitable natural harbor was Bartholomew Gosnold, who arrived in 1602 and named the area Cape Cod after the abundant codfish he found in the local waters. The Pilgrims arrived on Monday, November 21, 1620, when the *Mayflower* dropped anchor in Provincetown Harbor after a difficult 63-day voyage; while in the harbor they signed the Mayflower Compact, the first document to declare a democratic form of government in America. Ever practical, one of the first things the Pilgrims did was to come ashore to wash their clothes, thus initiating the age-old New England tradition of Monday washday. They stayed in the area for five weeks before moving on to Plymouth.

During the American Revolution, Provincetown Harbor was controlled by the British, who used it as a port from which to sail to Boston and launch attacks on Colonial and French vessels. In November 1778 the 64-gun British frigate *Somerset* ran aground and was wrecked off Provincetown's Race Point—every 60 years or so the shifting sands uncover her remains.

Provincetown is the nation's oldest continuous arts colony: Painters began coming here in 1899 for the unique Cape Cod light. Eugene O'Neill's first plays were written and produced here, and the Fine Arts Work Center continues to have in its ranks some of the most important writers of our time. In the busy downtown, Portuguese-American fishermen mix with painters, poets, writers, whale-watching families, cruise-ship passengers on brief stopovers, and many lesbian and gay residents and visitors, for whom P-town, as it's almost universally known, is one of the most popular East Coast seashore spots.

In summer, Commercial Street, the town's main thoroughfare, is packed with sightseers and shoppers browsing the treasures of the galleries and crafts shops. At night, raucous music and people spill out of bars, drag shows, and sing-along lounges. It's a fun, crazy place, with the extra dimension of the fishing fleet unloading their catch at MacMillan Wharf, in the center of the action. On the wharf are a large municipal parking facility and the Chamber of Commerce, so it's a sensible place to start a tour of town.

Driving from one end of 3-mi-long Commercial Street to the other could take forever in season—walking is definitely the way to go. Many architectural styles—Victorian, Second Empire, Gothic, and Greek Revival, to name a few—were used to build houses for sea captains and merchants. The Provincetown Historical Society publishes walking-tour pamphlets, available for about $1 at many shops in town. Free Provincetown gallery guides are also available.

The quiet East End of town is mostly residential, with some top galleries. The similarly quiet West End has a number of small inns with neat lawns and elaborate gardens.

The **Pilgrim Monument,** which stretches incongruously into the sky over the small town, commemorates the first landing of the Pilgrims in the New World and their signing of the Mayflower Compact, America's first rules of self-governance. Climb the 252-ft-high tower (116 steps and 60 ramps) for a panoramic view—dunes on one side, harbor on the other, and the entire bay side of Cape Cod beyond. At the base is a museum of Lower Cape and Provincetown history. ⊠ *High Pole Hill,* ☎ 508/487–1310. ⊠ $5. ⊙ *Apr.–June and Sept.– Nov., daily 9–5; July and Aug., daily 9–7; last admission 45 mins before closing.*

Founded in 1914 to collect and show the works of Provincetown-associated artists, the **Provincetown Art Association and Museum** (PAAM) houses a 1,650-piece permanent collection; exhibits here combine the works of up-and-comers with established artists of the 20th century. ⊠ *460 Commercial St.,* ☎ 508/487–1750. ⊠ $3. ⊙ *Nov.–Apr., weekends noon–4 and by appointment; Memorial Day–Labor Day, daily noon–5 and 8–10; May and Sept.–Oct., Fri.–Sun. noon–5.*

Near the Provincetown border, **massive dunes** meet the road in places, turning U.S. 6 into a sand-swept highway. Scattered among the dunes are primitive cottages, called dune shacks, built from flotsam and other found materials, that have provided atmospheric as well as cheap lodgings to artists and writers over the years—among them Eugene O'Neill, e. e. cummings, Jack Kerouac, and Norman Mailer.

The **Province Lands,** scattered with ponds, cranberry bogs, and scrub, begin at High Head in Truro and stretch to the tip of Provincetown. Bike and walking trails wind through forests of stunted pines, beech, and oak and across desertlike expanses of rolling dunes—these are the "wilds" of the Cape. ⊠ *Visitor center: Race Point Rd.,* ☎ *508/487– 1256.* ⊙ *Apr.–Nov., daily 9–5.*

All the **National Seashore beaches** have lifeguards, showers, and rest rooms. There is a daily parking fee; annual passes are more economical if you're staying longer than a week. Only **Herring Cove Beach,** off U.S. 6, has food.

Race Point Beach, at the end of U.S. 6, has a remote feeling, with a wide swath of sand stretching around the point and Coast Guard Station. Because it faces north, the beach gets sun all day long.

Dining and Lodging

$$$ ✕ **Café Edwige.** Delicious contemporary cuisine, friendly service, a
★ homey setting—Café Edwige delivers night after night. Two good starters are the Maine crab cake and the warm goat cheese on crostini; for an entrée try lobster and Wellfleet scallops over pasta with a wild mushroom and tomato broth. Don't pass on the wonderful desserts. ⊠ *333 Commercial St.,* ☎ *508/487–2008. AE, DC, MC, V. Closed Nov.–May.*

$$$ ✕ **The Mews.** This P-town favorite is still going strong. Downstairs, the main dining room opens onto magnificent harbor views. The menu focuses on seafood with a cross-cultural flair. One favorite is the rich and spicy Wellfleet scallops, shrimp, and crab mousse in a wonton over grilled filet mignon. Brunch is served daily in season. ⊠ *429 Commercial*

St., ☎ *508/487–1500. Reservations not accepted. AE, D, DC, MC, V. No lunch weekdays off-season or Sat. Columbus Day–Memorial Day.*

$$–$$$ ✕ **Bubala's by the Bay.** Personality abounds at this funky restaurant
★ inside a building painted bright yellow and adorned with campy carved birds. The kitchen serves three meals, with lots of local seafood, and the wine list is priced practically at retail. The bar scene picks up in the evening. ⊠ *183 Commercial St.,* ☎ *508/487–0773. AE, D, MC, V. Closed Halloween–Mar.*

$$–$$$ ✕ **Front Street.** Many consider this the best restaurant in town. Well
★ versed in classic Italian cooking, chef-owners Donna Aliperti and Kathleen Cotter also venture into other Mediterranean regions. Duck smoked in Chinese black tea is served with a different lusty sauce every day—one of the best is fresh tropical fruit with mixed peppercorns. The wine list is a winner. Call well ahead for a reservation. ⊠ *230 Commercial St.,* ☎ *508/487–9715. Reservations essential. AE, D, MC, V. Closed Jan.–mid-May.*

$$–$$$ ✕ **Lobster Pot.** Provincetown's Lobster Pot is fit to do battle with all the Lobster Pots anywhere on the Cape. As you enter you'll pass through one of the hardest-working kitchens on the Cape, which consistently turns out fresh New England classics and some of the best chowder around. ⊠ *321 Commercial St.,* ☎ *508/487–0842. Reservations not accepted. AE, D, DC, MC, V. Closed Jan.*

$$–$$$ ✕ **Napi's.** The zesty meals on Napi's internationally inspired menu in-
★ clude many vegetarian choices and Greco-Roman items like delicious shrimp feta (shrimp flambé in ouzo and Metaxa, served with a tomato, garlic, and onion sauce). Both the food and the whimsically tasteful interior share a penchant for unusual, striking juxtapositions. ⊠ *7 Freeman St.,* ☎ *508/487–1145. Reservations essential. AE, D, DC, MC, V. No lunch June–mid-Sept.*

$ ✕ **Mojo's.** At Provincetown's fast-food institution, the tiniest of kitchens
★ turns out everything from fresh-cut french fries to fried clams, tacos, and tofu burgers. How they crank it out so fast and so good is anybody's guess. ⊠ *5 Ryder St. Ext.,* ☎ *508/487–3140. Reservations not accepted. No credit cards. Closed at some times mid-Oct.–early May, depending on weather and crowds.*

$$$–$$$$ ⊞ **Brass Key.** Convenient to Commercial Street's restaurants, shops,
★ and nightlife, this gay-popular complex is fast becoming Provincetown's most luxurious resort. In season, complimentary cocktails are served in the courtyard; in winter, wine is served before a roaring fire in the common room. Rooms have antique furniture and decidedly modern amenities; all have Bose stereos, mini-refrigerators, and TV/VCRs (there's a videocassette library). Deluxe rooms have gas fireplaces and whirlpool baths. Smoking is not allowed. ⊠ *67 Bradford St., 02657,* ☎ *508/487–9005 or 800/842–9858,* FAX *508/487–9020. 33 rooms. In-room safes, pool, spa. Continental breakfast. AE, D, MC, V.*

$$–$$$$ ⊞ **Bayshore.** This apartment complex on the water, ½ mi from the town
★ center, is a great option for longer stays. Many of the units have fireplaces, decks, and large water-view windows; all have full kitchens, modern baths, and phones. Rentals are mostly by the week in season. Pets are welcome. ⊠ *493 Commercial St., 02657-2413,* ☎ FAX *508/487–9133. 19 apartments. Beach. AE, MC, V.*

$–$$$ ⊞ **Fairbanks Inn.** A block from Commercial Street, this comfortable inn includes a 1776 main house and auxiliary buildings. Many rooms have four-poster or canopy beds, fireplaces, Oriental rugs on wide-board floors, and antique furnishings. The wicker-filled sunporch and the garden are good places to take your afternoon cocktail. ⊠ *90 Bradford St., 02657,* ☎ *508/487–0386 or 800/324–7265. 13 rooms, 1 efficiency. Free parking. Continental breakfast. AE, MC, V.*

$–$$$ 🏠 **The Masthead.** Hidden away in the quiet west end of Commercial Street, the Masthead is a charming cluster of shingled houses that overlook a lush lawn, a 450-ft-long boardwalk, and a private beach. Spacious rooms, efficiencies, apartments, and cottages are among the lodging options. The cottages, which sleep four to seven, are ideal for families or larger groups and for longer stays. ✉ *Box 577, 31–41 Commercial St., 02657,* ☎ *508/ 487–0523 or 800/395–5095,* Ⅲ *508/487–9251. 7 apartments, 3 cottages, 2 efficiencies, 9 rooms. Beach, dock. AE, D, DC, MC, V.*

$ 🏠 **The Meadows.** At the far west end of Bradford Street, between the town center and the beach, the Meadows is a good value, especially for families. The motel-like rooms are bright and comfortable; all have TVs with HBO and mini-refrigerators. ✉ *122 Bradford St. Ext., 02657,* ☎ *508/487–0880 or 888/675–0880. 20 rooms. MC, V.*

Nightlife and the Arts

The **Cape Cod National Seashore** (☎ 508/487–1256) sponsors sunset beach walks, sing-alongs, and sunset campfire talks on Provincetown beaches.

The **Provincetown Playhouse Mews Series** (✉ Town Hall, 260 Commercial St., ☎ 508/487–0955) presents varied summer concerts. The **Provincetown Repertory Theatre** (☎ 508/487–0600) mounts productions of classic and modern drama in the summer. The **Provincetown Theatre Company** (☎ 508/487–8673) stages classics, modern drama, and new works by local authors year-round.

During the summer the **Boatslip Beach Club** (✉ 161 Commercial St., ☎ 508/487–1669) holds a mixed gay and lesbian tea dance daily from 3:30 to 6:30 on the outdoor deck. A pianist plays easy-listening tunes on weekends (nightly in season) at **Napi's** (☞ Dining and Lodging, *above*). The **Pied Piper** (✉ 193A Commercial St., ☎ 508/487–1527) draws hordes of gay men to its post–tea dance gathering. Later in the evening, the crowd is mostly, though not exclusively, women.

Outdoor Activities and Sports

BIKING

The **Province Lands Trail** is a fairly strenuous 5¼-mi loop off the Beech Forest parking lot on Race Point Road in Provincetown, with spurs to Herring Cove and Race Point beaches and to Bennett Pond.

FISHING

You can go for fluke, bluefish, and striped bass on a walk-on basis from spring to fall with **Cap'n Bill & Cee Jay** (✉ MacMillan Wharf, ☎ 508/ 487–4330 or 800/675–6723).

GUIDED TOUR

Art's Dune Tours are hour-long narrated auto tours through the National Seashore and the dunes around Provincetown. ☎ *508/487– 1950 or 508/487–1050; 800/894–1951 in MA only.* 🎟 *$10 daytime, $12 sunset.* ☉ *Mid-Apr.–late Oct.*

HORSEBACK RIDING

The **Province Lands Horse Trails** lead to the beaches through or past dunes, cranberry bogs, forests, and ponds. **Nelson's Riding Stable** (✉ 43 Race Point Rd., ☎ 508/487–1112) offers trail rides by reservation.

WHALE-WATCHING

One of the joys of Cape Cod is spotting whales while they're swimming in and around the feeding grounds at Stellwagen Bank, about 6 mi off the tip of Provincetown. Many people also come aboard for birding, especially during spring and fall migration. Several tour operators take whale-watchers out to sea for three- to four-hour morning, afternoon, or sunset trips.

Dolphin Fleet tours are accompanied by scientists from the Center for Coastal Studies in Provincetown who know many of the whales by name and tell you about their habits and histories. Reservations are essential. ⊠ *Tickets: MacMillan Wharf, Chamber of Commerce building,* ☎ *508/349–1900 or 800/826–9300.* 🎟 *$18 (seasonal variations).* ⊙ *Tours Apr.–Oct.*

The **Ranger V,** the largest whale-watching boat, sails with a naturalist on board. ⊠ *Tickets: Bradford and Standish Sts.,* ☎ *508/487–3322 or 800/992–9333.* 🎟 *$18.* ⊙ *Tours Apr.–mid-Oct.*

Shopping

Berta Walker Gallery (⊠ 208 Bradford St., ☎ 508/487–6411) represents Provincetown-affiliated artists working in various media. **Giardelli Antonelli** (⊠ 417 Commercial St., ☎ 508/487–3016) specializes in handmade clothing by local designers. **Northern Lights Leather** (⊠ 361 Commercial St., ☎ 508/487–9376) has clothing, boots, shoes, and accessories of soft leather, plus silk clothing. **Remembrances of Things Past** (⊠ 376 Commercial St., ☎ 508/487–9443) deals in articles from the 1920s to the 1960s. **West End Antiques** (⊠ 146 Commercial St., ☎ 508/487–6723) specializes in variety: $4 postcards, a $3,000 model ship, handmade dolls, and glassware.

Cape Cod A to Z

Arriving and Departing

BY BOAT

Bay State Cruise Company makes the three-hour trip between Commonwealth Pier in Boston and MacMillan Wharf in Provincetown daily from mid-June to Labor Day, and weekends only through the end of September. ☎ *617/457–1428 in Boston,* ☎ *508/487–9284 in Provincetown.* 🎟 *One-way/same-day round-trip: $18/$30, $5 additional for bicycles each way.*

BY BUS

Bonanza Bus Lines (☎ 508/548–7588 or 800/556–3815) operates direct service to Bourne, Falmouth, and Woods Hole from Boston and Providence. **Plymouth & Brockton Street Railway** (☎ 508/771–6191 or 508/746–0378) travels to Provincetown from Boston and Logan Airport, with stops in several Cape towns en route.

BY CAR

From Boston (60 mi), take Route I–93 South to Route 3 South, across the Sagamore Bridge, which becomes Route 6, the Cape's main artery. From western Massachusetts, northern Connecticut, and northeastern New York State, take I–84 East to the Massachusetts Turnpike (I–90 East) and take I–495 South and East to the Bourne Bridge. From New York City, and all other points south and west, take I–95 North toward Providence, where you'll pick up I–195 East (toward Fall River/New Bedford) to Route 25 East to the Bourne Bridge.

BY PLANE

Barnstable Municipal Airport (⊠ 480 Barnstable Rd., Rte. 28 rotary, Hyannis, ☎ 508/775–2020), the Cape's main air gateway, is served by Cape Air/Nantucket Airlines, Colgan Air, and US Airways Express. **Provincetown Municipal Airport** (⊠ Race Point Rd., ☎ 508/487–0241) has year-round Boston service through Cape Air/Nantucket Airlines. *See* Air Travel *in* Smart Travel Tips A to Z for airline phone numbers.

Getting Around

BY BICYCLE

The Cape's premier bike path, the **Cape Cod Rail Trail,** follows the paved right-of-way of the old Penn Central Railroad. About 30 mi long, the easy-to-moderate trail passes salt marshes, cranberry bogs, ponds, and Nickerson State Park. The trail starts at the parking lot off Route 134 south of U.S. 6, near Theophilus Smith Road in South Dennis, and it ends at the post office in South Wellfleet. If you want to cover only a segment, there are parking lots in Harwich (across from Pleasant Lake Store on Pleasant Lake Avenue) and in Brewster (at Nickerson State Park).

For bike rentals, try **Bert & Carol's Lawnmower & Bicycle Shop** (⊠ 347 Orleans Rd./Rte. 28, N. Chatham, ☎ 508/945–0137); **Corner Cycle** (⊠ 115 Palmer Ave., Falmouth, ☎ 508/540–4195); **Little Capistrano Bike Shop** (⊠ U.S. 6, Eastham, ☎ 508/255–6515); the **Rail Trail Bike Shop** (⊠ 302 Underpass Rd., Brewster, ☎ 508/896–8200).

BY BUS
The **Cape Cod Regional Transit Authority** (☎ 508/385–8326; 800/352–7155 in Massachusetts) operates its SeaLine service along Route 28 daily except Sunday between Hyannis and Woods Hole and connects in Hyannis with the Plymouth & Brockton line. The driver will stop when signaled along the route. The "b-bus" is a fleet of minivans that transports passengers daily door-to-door anywhere on the Cape. Make reservations, which are essential, no later than 11 AM on the day before you want to depart. The H2O Line operates scheduled service several times daily, year-round, between Hyannis and Orleans along Route 28.

BY CAR
From the Bourne Bridge, you can take Route 28 south to Falmouth and Woods Hole (about 15 mi), or go around the rotary, following the signs to U.S. 6; this will take you to the Lower Cape and central towns more quickly. On summer weekends, avoid arriving in the late afternoon. U.S. 6, Route 6A, and Route 28 are heavily congested eastbound on Friday evening and westbound on Sunday afternoon. When approaching one of the Cape's numerous rotaries (traffic circles), keep in mind that vehicles already in the rotary have the right of way.

BY TAXI
All Village Taxi (Falmouth, ☎ 508/540–7200). **Cape Cab** (Provincetown, ☎ 508/487–2222). **Eldredge Taxi** (Chatham, ☎ 508/945–0068). **Hyannis Taxi** (☎ 508/775–0400 or 800/773–0600).

Contacts and Resources
B&B RESERVATION AGENCIES
Bed and Breakfast Cape Cod (⊠ Box 1312, Orleans 02653, ☎ 508/255–3824 or 800/541–6226, FAX 508/240–0599).

CAMPING
The **Cape Cod Chamber of Commerce** (☞ Visitor Information, *below*) maintains a list of private campgrounds.

CAR RENTALS
Budget (☎ 508/771–2744 or 800/527–0700) rents cars at the Barnstable and Provincetown airports.

EMERGENCIES
Cape Cod Hospital (⊠ 27 Park St., Hyannis, ☎ 508/771–1800). **Falmouth Hospital** (⊠ 100 Ter Heun Dr., Falmouth, ☎ 508/548–5300).

GUIDED TOURS
Cape Cod Tours travels the main streets and back roads of the Mid Cape and gives a good overview of the history of Hyannis and the surrounding areas. Hotel pick-up service is available. ☎ 508/362–1117. ▦ *$12; purchase ticket ½ hr before departure.*

Patriot Boats operates charters and two-hour day and sunset cruises between Falmouth and the Elizabeth Islands on the 68-ft schooner *Liberté*. ⊠ *227 Clinton Ave., Falmouth,* ☎ *508/548–2626; 800/734–0088 in MA.* 🚢 *$20.*

HOUSE RENTALS

Commonwealth Associates (⊠ 551 Main St., Harwich Port 02646, ☎ 508/432–2618) can assist in finding rentals in the Harwiches, Brewster, and Chatham. **Donahue Real Estate** (⊠ 850 Main St., Falmouth 02540, ☎ 508/548–5412) lists apartments and houses on the Upper Cape. **Roslyn Garfield Associates** (⊠ 115 Bradford St., Provincetown 02657, ☎ 508/487–1308) lists rentals for Wellfleet, Truro, and Provincetown.

LATE-NIGHT PHARMACIES

CVS (⊠ 64 Davis Straits, Falmouth, ☎ 508/540–4307). **CVS** (⊠ Patriot Square Mall, Rte. 134, Dennis, ☎ 508/398–0724).

OUTDOOR ACTIVITIES AND SPORTS

The Cape Cod Chamber of Commerce's *Sportsman's Guide* describes fishing regulations and surf-fishing access locations and contains a map of boat-launching facilities. The Division of Fisheries and Wildlife has a book of maps of Cape ponds. Freshwater fishing licenses are available for a nominal fee at bait and tackle shops.

VISITOR INFORMATION

Army Corps of Engineers 24-hour recreation hot line (☎ 508/759–5991). **Cape Cod Chamber of Commerce** (⊠ U.S. 6 and Rte. 132, Hyannis, ☎ 508/362–3225 or 888/332–2732). **Tide, marine, and weather forecast hot line** (☎ 508/771–5522).

MARTHA'S VINEYARD

Updated by
Karl Luntta and
Carolyn Heller

Dining
updated by
Seth Rolbein

Far less developed than Cape Cod yet more cosmopolitan than Nantucket, Martha's Vineyard is an island with a double life. From Memorial Day through Labor Day the quieter, some might say real, Vineyard quickens into a vibrant, star-studded frenzy. The busy main port, Vineyard Haven, welcomes day-trippers fresh off a ferry or private yacht. Oak Bluffs, where pizza and ice cream emporiums reign supreme, has the air of a boardwalk. Edgartown is flooded with seekers of chic who wander tiny streets that hold boutiques, stately whaling captains' homes, and charming inns. Summer regulars include a host of celebrities, among them William Styron, Walter Cronkite, and Sharon Stone. If you're planning to stay overnight, especially on a weekend, be sure to make reservations well in advance; spring is not too early. Things begin to slow down in mid-September, though, and in many ways the Vineyard's off-season persona is even more appealing than its summer self. There's more time to linger over pastoral and ocean vistas, free from the throng of cars, bicycles, and mopeds.

The island is roughly triangular, with maximum distances of about 20 mi east to west and 10 mi north to south. The Down-Island end comprises Vineyard Haven, Oak Bluffs, and Edgartown, the most popular and most populated towns; ferry docks, shops, and centuries-old houses and churches line the main streets. Up-Island, the west end of the Vineyard, is more rural. In Chilmark, West Tisbury, and Aquinnah (formerly called Gay Head), country roads meander through woods and tranquil farmland.

The Vineyard, except for Oak Bluffs and Edgartown, is dry: There are no liquor stores, and restaurants don't serve liquor. Most restaurants in "dry" towns allow you to bring your own beer or wine.

Vineyard Haven (Tisbury)

⑰ *3.3 mi west of Oak Bluffs, 8 mi northwest of Edgartown by the inland route.*

The past and the present blend with a touch of the bohemian in Vineyard Haven (officially named Tisbury), the island's busiest year-round community. **William Street,** one block west of commercial Main, is a quiet stretch of white picket fences and Greek Revival houses. Part of a National Historic District, the street recalls the town's 19th-century past.

Beautiful and green, exclusive **West Chop,** about 2 mi north of Vineyard Haven along Main Street, claims some of the island's most distinguished residents. The 52-ft white-and-black brick **West Chop Lighthouse** (⊠ W. Chop Rd.) was built in 1838. On the point beyond the lighthouse is a landscaped scenic overlook with benches.

Lake Tashmoo Town Beach, at the end of Herring Creek Road, has swimming in a warm, relatively shallow lake or in the cooler Vineyard Sound. There is parking, and lifeguards are on duty. **Owen Park Beach,** a small harbor beach off Main Street, has a children's play area and lifeguards.

Dining and Lodging

$$$–$$$$ ✕ **Black Dog Tavern.** This island landmark (widely known for its T-shirts and other merchandise) serves all the usual suspects, such as codfish and pasta; the food (if that still matters) is just fine at breakfast, lunch, or dinner. Waiting for a table is something of a tradition, although locals have generally adopted Yogi Berra's line: It's so crowded, no one goes there anymore. ⊠ *Beach St. Ext.,* ☎ *508/693–9223. Reservations not accepted. AE, D, MC, V. BYOB.*

$$$–$$$$ ✕ **Le Grenier.** Calling a restaurant French in a dry town is a stretch, but the cuisine here is authentic and expert. For frogs' legs, sweetbreads, tournedos, and calves' brains, Le Grenier is the clear choice. ⊠ *Upper Main St.,* ☎ *508/693–4906. AE, MC, V. BYOB. No lunch.*

$$ ✕ **Cafe Moxie.** They've hit the right combination here: great food and a stylish ambience. Fancy pizzas and salads make up most of the lunch choices, but at night the menu includes dishes such as seared codfish with mustard and sourdough crust or half-jerk chicken with arugula and avocado salad. ⊠ *Main St. at Centre St.,* ☎ *508/693–1484. D, MC, V. Closed Mon.*

$$$–$$$$ ⌂ **Thorncroft Inn.** About a mile from the ferry on 3½ acres of woods, ★ the somewhat formal main inn, a 1918 Craftsman bungalow, is adorned with fine Colonial and Renaissance Revival antiques and tasteful reproductions. Ten rooms have working fireplaces; some rooms have whirlpool baths or canopy beds. The inn is no-smoking. ⊠ *Box 1022, 460 Main St., 02568,* ☎ *508/693–3333 or 800/332–1236,* ℻ *508/693–5419. 14 rooms. Full breakfast. AE, D, DC, MC, V.*

$$–$$$ ⌂ **Hanover House.** This charming inn within walking distance of the ferry has spotless rooms decorated in casual country style with a combination of antiques and reproduction furniture. Some rooms have private entrances that open onto spacious sundecks. The three suites in the carriage house are roomy, with private decks or patios. Homemade breads and muffins and a special house cereal are served each morning on the sunporch. ⊠ *Box 2107, 28 Edgartown Rd., 02568,* ☎ *508/ 693–1066 or 800/339–1066,* ℻ *508/696–6099. 12 rooms, 3 suites. Continental breakfast. AE, D, MC, V. Closed Dec.–Mar.*

$ ⚘ **Martha's Vineyard Family Campground.** Wooded sites, recreational ★ facilities, a camp store, bicycle rentals, and electrical and water hookups are among the amenities at this campground, which also holds eight

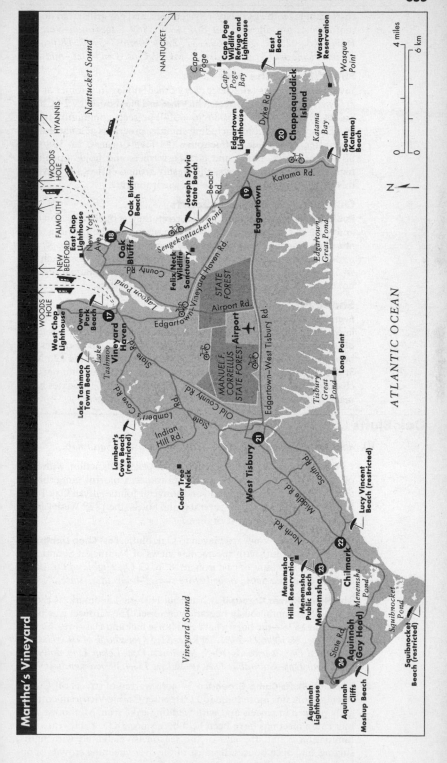

Martha's Vineyard

rustic cabins (with electricity, refrigerators, and gas grills). No dogs or motorcycles are allowed. ⊠ *Box 1557, 569 Edgartown–Vineyard Haven Rd., 02568,* ☎ *508/693–3772,* FAX *508/693–5767. 180 sites, 8 cabins. Picnic area, coin laundry. D, MC, V. Closed mid-Oct.–mid-May.*

Nightlife and the Arts

Town band concerts take place every other Sunday in summer at 8 PM at Owen Park off Main Street. The **Vineyard Playhouse** (⊠ 24 Church St., ☎ 508/693–6450 or 508/696–6300) presents community theater and Equity productions, including summer programs at a natural amphitheater. **Wintertide Coffeehouse** (⊠ Five Corners, ☎ 508/693–8830) hosts folk, blues, and jazz performers and holds open-mike nights. Light meals, desserts, and freshly ground coffees are served in this homey alcohol- and smoke-free environment.

Outdoor Activities and Sports

Public tennis courts are on Church Street; they're open in season only, and a fee is charged (reserve with the attendant the previous day). **Martha's Vineyard Scooter and Bike Rental** (⊠ 24 Union St., ☎ 508/693–0782) rents scooters and bicycles. **Wind's Up!** (⊠ 199 Beach Rd., ☎ 508/693–4252 or 508/693–4340) rents day sailers, catamarans, surfboards, sea kayaks, canoes, Sunfish, and windsurfers.

Shopping

Bramhall & Dunn (⊠ 19 Main St., ☎ 508/693–6437) carries crafts, linens, hand-knit sweaters, and fine antique country-pine furniture. **Bunch of Grapes Bookstore** (⊠ 68 Main St., ☎ 508/693–2291) carries new books and sponsors book signings. **C. B. Stark Jewelers** (⊠ 126 Main St., ☎ 508/693–2284) creates one-of-a-kind pieces, including island charms. **Paper Tiger** (⊠ 29 Main St., ☎ 508/693–8970) carries handmade paper and gift items, plus works by local artists.

Oak Bluffs

⓲ *4 mi east of Vineyard Haven, 22 mi northeast of Aquinnah.*

Circuit Avenue is the bustling center of the Oak Bluffs action, with most of the town's shops, bars, and restaurants. Colorful gingerbread-trimmed guest houses and food and souvenir joints enliven Oak Bluffs Harbor, once the setting for several grand hotels (the 1879 Wesley Hotel on Lake Avenue is the last of them).

On the way from Vineyard Haven to Oak Bluffs, **East Chop Lighthouse** stands atop a bluff with spectacular views of Nantucket Sound. The 40-ft tower was built of cast iron in 1876. ⊠ *Off Highland Dr.* ☞ *$2.* ☉ *Late June–late Sept., hour before sunset–hour after sunset.*

☾ The **Flying Horses Carousel,** a National Historic Landmark, is the nation's oldest continuously operating carousel. The carousel was handcrafted in 1876—the horses have real horse hair and glass eyes. ⊠ *Oak Bluffs Ave.,* ☎ *508/693–9481.* ☞ *Rides $1; $8 for a book of 10.* ☉ *Easter–Memorial Day, weekends 10–5; Memorial Day–Labor Day, daily 10–10; Labor Day–Columbus Day, weekdays 11–4:30, weekends 10–5.*

★ The **Oak Bluffs Camp Ground,** a 34-acre warren of streets off Circuit Avenue, contains more than 300 Carpenter Gothic Victorian cottages gaily painted in pastels and with wedding-cake trim. Methodist summer camp meetings have been held here since 1835. Each year on Illumination Night, the end of the season is celebrated with lights, singing, and open houses. Because of the overwhelming crowds of onlookers, the date is not announced until the week before the event.

Joseph A. Sylvia State Beach (⊠ Off Beach Rd.), between Oak Bluffs and Edgartown, is a 6-mi-long beach with calm water and a view of Cape Cod. Vendors sell food here, and there's parking.

Dining and Lodging

$$$ ✕ **Brasserie 162.** In this warmly sophisticated restaurant, draped white fabric breaks up the room into airy but intimate spaces. Thai and Cuban influences appear in dishes like "fire and ice" (tuna ceviche with fresh lime, ginger, coconut, and chilies) or a spring roll of soft-shell crab and mango. The eclectic menu ranges from halibut roasted in a banana leaf to spicy duck in a corn tamale, plus sushi and tapas. ⊠ *162 Circuit Ave.,* ☎ *508/696–6336. AE, D, MC, V. Mid-Oct.–mid-May.*

$$$ ✕ **Smoke 'n Bones.** This is the island's only rib joint, with a smoker out back and hickory, apple, oak, and mesquite wood stacked around the lot. The place has a cookie-cutter, prefab feeling, but it's fun, with details kids can really enjoy, like a hole in each tabletop for a bucket to hold discarded ribs. As the menu says, Bone appetit. ⊠ *Siloam Rd., about 7 blocks from Oak Bluffs,* ☎ *508/696–7427. Reservations not accepted. No credit cards.*

$$$ ✕ **Sweet Life Café.** An island favorite, this café has a interior that's so
★ subdued you may feel like you've entered someone's home. A baked goat-cheese tart is an excellent beginning, while the main courses include Angus sirloin with a marrow crust. Desserts remain superb, especially a mixed berry *crostata* (tart). ⊠ *63 Upper Circuit Ave.,* ☎ *508/ 696–0200. Reservations essential. AE, D, MC, V. Closed Jan.–Mar.*

$–$$ ✕ **Linda Jean's.** Tired of the gourmet world and looking for good diner food, comfortable booths, and friendly waitresses? No problem. Except one: You may have to wait. ⊠ *34 Circuit Ave.,* ☎ *508/693–4093. Reservations not accepted. No credit cards.*

$$$ ⬚ **Oak House.** The wraparound veranda of this pastel-painted 1872
★ Victorian looks across a busy street to the beach. The well-preserved wood of the inn's name provides a solid backdrop (in ceilings and wainscoting) for the choice antique furniture and nautical-theme accessories. An elegant afternoon tea is served in a glassed-in sunporch, with cakes and cookies baked by innkeeper Betsi Luce, a Cordon Bleu–trained pastry chef. The inn is no-smoking. ⊠ *Box 299, Sea View Ave., 02557,* ☎ *508/693–4187,* ⅎ̶ⅈ̶ *508/696–7385. 8 rooms, 2 suites. Continental breakfast. AE, D, MC, V. Closed mid-Oct.–mid-May.*

$$–$$$ ⬚ **Sea Spray Inn.** This porch-wrapped Victorian is on an open park
★ that borders an ocean beach; public tennis and golf are within walking distance. Some of the simply adorned rooms have king-size, four-poster feather beds; a garden-side room opens to a private enclosed porch. Smoking is not permitted. ⊠ *Box 2355, 2 Nashawena Park, 02557,* ☎ *508/693–9388,* ⅎ̶ⅈ̶ *508/696–7765. 6 rooms, 1 suite. Continental breakfast. MC, V. Closed mid-Nov.–mid-Apr.*

$$ ⬚ **Martha's Vineyard Surfside Motel.** These two buildings are right in the thick of things. Rooms are spacious, bright, and well maintained, with typical motel furnishings. ⊠ *Box 2507, Oak Bluffs Ave., 02557,* ☎ *508/693–2500 or 800/537–3007,* ⅎ̶ⅈ̶ *508/693–7343. 34 rooms, 4 suites. Hot tub. AE, D, MC, V.*

$ ⬙ **Webb's Camping Area.** This campground on 84 acres is woodsy and private, with some water-view sites and a store. Swimming is permitted in Lagoon Pond, and there are bathrooms, showers, laundry facilities, playgrounds, and RV hookups. ⊠ *R.F.D. 3, Box 100, Barnes Rd., 02568,* ☎ *508/693–0233. No pets. MC, V. Closed day after Labor Day–mid-May.*

Nightlife and the Arts

Atlantic Connection (⊠ 124 Circuit Ave., ☎ 508/693–7129) hosts reggae, R&B, funk, and blues performers and has a strobe-lit dance floor.

Town band concerts take place every other Sunday in summer at 8 PM at the gazebo in Ocean Park on Beach Road.

Outdoor Activities and Sports

BIKING

DeBettencourt's (⊠ Circuit Ave. Ext., ☎ 508/693–0011) rents bikes, mopeds, scooters, and Jeeps.

BOATING AND FISHING

Dick's Bait and Tackle (⊠ New York Ave., ☎ 508/693–7669) rents gear, sells bait, and has a current list of fishing regulations. The party boat **Skipper** (☎ 508/693–1238) leaves for deep-sea fishing trips out of Oak Bluffs Harbor in summer. **Vineyard Boat Rentals** (⊠ Dockside Marketplace, Oak Bluffs Harbor, ☎ 508/693–8476) rents Boston Whalers, Bayliners, and Jet Skis.

GOLF

Farm Neck Golf Club (⊠ Farm Neck Way, ☎ 508/693–3057), a semiprivate club, has 18 holes in a par-72 championship layout. The greens fee ranges from $36 to $80; a cart (required at certain times) costs $25. Reservations are required at least 48 hours in advance.

TENNIS

Niantic Park in Oak Bluffs has courts that cost a small fee to use.

Shopping

Book Den East (⊠ New York Ave., ☎ 508/693–3946) stocks 20,000 out-of-print, antiquarian, and paperback books. **Laughing Bear** (⊠ 138 Circuit Ave., ☎ 508/693–9342) carries fun children's and women's wear made of Balinese or Indian batiks plus jewelry and accessories from around the world.

Edgartown and Chappaquiddick Island

9½ mi southeast of Vineyard Haven via Beach Rd., 8½ mi east of West Tisbury.

⑲ Once a well-to-do whaling town, **Edgartown** has preserved some of its elegant past. Sea captains' houses from the 17th and 18th centuries, ensconced in well-manicured gardens and lawns, line the streets, and the many shops here attract see-and-be-seen crowds. The **Old Whaling Church** (⊠ 89 Main St., ☎ 508/627–8619 for tour), built in 1843 as a Methodist church and now a performing-arts center, has a six-column portico, unusual triple-sash windows, and a 92-ft clock tower. The stylish 1840 **Dr. Daniel Fisher House** (⊠ 99 Main St.) has a wraparound roof walk, a small front portico with fluted Corinthian columns, and a side portico with thin fluted columns.

Martha's Vineyard Historical Society administers a complex of buildings and lawn exhibits that constitute the Vineyard Museum and Oral History Center. The **Francis Foster Museum** houses the Gale Huntington Reference Library and 19th-century miniature photographs of 110 Edgartown whaling masters. The **Capt. Francis Pease House**, an 1850s Greek Revival structure, exhibits Native American, prehistoric, pre-Columbian, and more recent artifacts. ⊠ *School St.,* ☎ *508/627–4441.* ⊡ *$6.* ☉ *July–Labor Day, daily 10–4:30; Labor Day–June, Wed.–Fri. 1–4, Sat. 10–4.*

★ ☾ The 350-acre **Felix Neck Wildlife Sanctuary,** a Massachusetts Audubon Society preserve 3 mi out of Edgartown toward Oak Bluffs and Vineyard Haven, has 6 mi of hiking trails traversing marshland, fields, woods, seashore, and waterfowl and reptile ponds. Naturalist-led events include sunset hikes, stargazing, snake or bird walks, and canoeing. ⊠

Off Edgartown–Vineyard Haven Rd., ☎ 508/627–4850. ⌦ $3. ☉ Center mid-June–mid-Sept., daily 8–4; mid-Sept.–mid-June, Tues.–Sun. 9–4. Trails daily sunrise–7 PM.

South Beach (⊠ Katama Rd.), also called Katama Beach, is the island's largest, a 3-mi ribbon of sand on the Atlantic with strong surf and occasional riptides. Check with the lifeguards before swimming here. Parking is limited.

⓴ **Chappaquiddick Island,** a sparsely populated area with many nature preserves, makes for a pleasant day trip or bike ride on a sunny day. The island is actually connected to the Vineyard by a long sand spit that begins in South Beach in Katama. It's a spectacular 2¾-mi walk, or you can take the On Time ferry, which departs about every five minutes from 7 AM to midnight in season.

★ The 200-acre **Wasque Reservation** (pronounced *wayce*-kwee) connects Chappaquiddick Island with the Vineyard and forms Katama Bay. **Wasque Beach** is accessed by a flat boardwalk with benches overlooking the west end of Swan Pond. Beyond that are beach, sky, and boat-dotted sea. From the grove, a long boardwalk leads down amid the grasses to **Wasque Point.** There's plenty of wide beach here to sun on, but swimming is dangerous because of strong currents. *East end of Wasque Rd., 5 mi from Chappaquiddick ferry landing, ☎ 508/627–7260. ⌦ $3 cars, plus $3 per adult, Memorial Day–mid-Sept.; free rest of year. ☉ Property 24 hrs; gatehouse Memorial Day–Columbus Day, daily 9–5. Rest rooms, drinking water.*

At the end of Dyke Road is the **Dyke's Bridge,** infamous as the scene of the 1969 accident in which a young woman died in a car driven by Senator Edward M. Kennedy. The **Cape Poge Wildlife Refuge,** across Dyke's Bridge, is more than 6 mi of wilderness—dunes, woods, cedar thickets, moors, salt marshes, ponds, tidal flats, and barrier beach. The best way to get to the refuge is as part of a naturalist-led Jeep drive (☎ 508/627–3599). Permits for four-wheel-drive vehicles (the cost ranges from $70 to $110) are available on-site or through Coop's Bait and Tackle (☞ Outdoor Activities and Sports, *below*). *East end of Dyke Rd., 3 mi from the Chappaquiddick ferry landing.*

East Beach on Chappaquiddick Island, one of the area's best beaches, is accessible only by boat or Jeep from the Wasque Reservation. The relatively isolated strand, a good place to bird-watch, has heavy surf.

Dining and Lodging

$$$$ ✕ **L'étoile.** Both the stunning setting—a glass-enclosed dining room in
★ the Charlotte Inn (☞ *below*)—and the classic yet creative food have preserved L'étoile's reputation as perhaps the Vineyard's finest traditional restaurant. Not to be missed are a terrine of grilled vegetable appetizer, roasted ivory king salmon with a horseradish and scallion crust, and Black Angus sirloin with zinfandel and oyster sauce. The Californian and European wines in L'etoile's cellar are well selected, if a little pricey. The outdoor patio is ideal for brunch ($24 prix fixe). ⊠ *27 S. Summer St., ☎ 508/627–5187. Reservations essential. AE, MC, V. Closed Jan.–mid-Feb. and weekdays Oct.–Dec. and late Feb.–Apr. No lunch.*

$$$$ ✕ **Savoir Fare.** Drawing everyone from Walter Cronkite to President
★ Clinton, Savoir Fare has carved out a reputation as the Vineyard's celebrity favorite. They come for the food: crisp, grilled flattened quail, cornmeal-dusted softshell crabs, and scallops, all presented with an attention to detail. ⊠ *14 Church St., in courtyard opposite town hall, ☎ 508/627–9864. AE, MC, V. Closed Nov.–Apr. No lunch.*

$–$$ ✕ **The Sand Bar.** More bar than sand, the Sand Bar is a watering hole for fans of the New England Patriots football team. The food is secondary to the sports on the tube out back, or the breeze on the front porch. The same owners run the downstairs CJ's and send up their award-winning clam chowder. ✉ *Main St.,* ☎ *508/627–9027. Reservations not accepted. AE, D, MC, V.*

$$$$ ⊞ **Charlotte Inn.** As you approach the Scottish barrister's desk at
★   check-in, you enter a tasteful and elegant bygone era. No computers here; guests are hand-written into the register by the dignified, attentive staff. Beautiful antique furnishings and paintings fill the property—your bed could be a hand-carved four-poster. Come to the inn for an Edwardian fantasy, an utterly tranquil winter holiday, or a sumptuous meal at L'étoile (☞ *above*). ✉ *27 S. Summer St., 02539,* ☎ *508/627–4751,* ℻ *508/627–4652. 23 rooms and 2 suites in 5 buildings. Restaurant. Continental breakfast. AE, MC, V.*

$$$$ ⊞ **Harbor View Hotel.** This historic hotel, centered in an 1891 gray-shingle main building with wraparound veranda and a gazebo, is part of a complex in a residential neighborhood a few minutes from town. Town houses have cathedral ceilings, decks, kitchens, and large living areas with sofa beds. Rooms in other buildings, however, resemble upscale motel rooms. A good beach for walking stretches ¾ mi from the hotel's dock, from which there's good fishing. ✉ *131 N. Water St., 02539,* ☎ *508/627–7000 or 800/225–6005,* ℻ *508/627–8417. 124 units. Restaurant, bar, room service, pool, 2 tennis courts, laundry service, concierge. AE, DC, MC, V.*

$$$$ ⊞ **Mattakesett.** This community of individually owned three- and four-bedroom homes and condominiums is within walking distance of South Beach. All units are spacious, sleep six to eight, and have phones, full kitchens with dishwashers, washer/dryers, and decks. Usually there's a one-week minimum stay. It's best to book for summer by January 15. ✉ *Katama Rd., 02539,* ☎ *508/627–8920,* ℻ *508/627–7015. ✉ Reservations c/o Stanmar Corp., 130 Boston Post Rd., Sudbury, MA 01776,* ☎ *978/443–1733,* ℻ *978/443–0479. 92 units. Pool, 8 tennis courts, aerobics, bicycles, children's programs. No credit cards. Closed Columbus Day–Memorial Day.*

$$–$$$ ⊞ **Daggett House.** The flower-bordered lawn that separates the main house
★   from the harbor makes a great retreat after a day of exploring town, a minute away. All four no-smoking inn buildings—the main 1660 Colonial house, the Captain Warren house across the street, the Henry Lyman Thomas house around the corner, and a three-room cottage between the main house and the water—are decorated with fine wallpapers, antiques, and reproductions. Breakfast and dinner are served in the 1750 tavern. ✉ *Box 1333, 59 N. Water St., 02539,* ☎ *508/627–4600 or 800/ 946–3400,* ℻ *508/627–4611. 27 rooms, 4 suites. AE, D, MC, V.*

Outdoor Activities and Sports

Big Eye Charters (☎ 508/627–3649) operates fishing charters that leave from Edgartown Harbor. **Coop's Bait and Tackle** (✉ 147 W. Tisbury Rd., ☎ 508/627–3909) sells accessories and bait, rents fishing gear, and has a list of fishing regulations. **Wheelhappy** (✉ 8 S. Water St., ☎ 508/627–5928) rents bicycles and will deliver them to you.

Shopping

Bickerton & Ripley Books (✉ Main St., ☎ 508/627–8463) carries current and island-related titles. **Edgartown Scrimshaw Gallery** (✉ 17 N. Water St., ☎ 508/627–9439) stocks some antique pieces, as well as Nantucket lightship baskets and nautical paintings. The **Gallery Shop** (✉ 20 S. Summer St., ☎ 508/627–8508) sells 19th- and 20th-century oils and watercolors, plus small English antiques. **Optional Art** (✉ 35 Winter St., ☎ 508/627–5373) carries handcrafted fine jewelry.

West Tisbury

㉑ *9 mi west of Edgartown.*

Very much the small New England village, complete with a white steepled church, West Tisbury has a vibrant agricultural life, with several active horse and produce farms. The weekly **West Tisbury Farmers' Market**—Massachusetts's largest—is held on Wednesday and Saturday from 9 to noon mid-June to mid-October at the 1859 **Agricultural Hall** (⊠ South Rd., ☎ 508/693–9549) near the town hall.

Winery at Chicama Vineyards was started in 1971 by George and Cathy Mathiesen and their six children. From 3 acres of trees and rocks, they created a winery that today produces nearly 100,000 bottles a year from chardonnay, cabernet, and other European grapes. ⊠ *Stoney Hill Rd.,* ☎ *508/693–0309.* 🎫 *Free.* ☉ *Memorial Day–Columbus Day, Mon.– Sat. 11–5, Sun. 1–5; call for off-season hrs and tastings.*

Long Point, a 633-acre preserve, is an open area of grassland and heath bounded on the east by the freshwater Homer's Pond, on the west by the saltwater West Tisbury Great Pond, and on the south by a mile of fantastic South Beach on the Atlantic Ocean. Arrive early on summer days if you're coming by car—the lot fills quickly. *Mid-June–mid-Sept., turn left onto the unmarked dirt road (Waldron's Bottom Rd., look for mailboxes) ³⁄₁₀ mi west of airport on Edgartown–W. Tisbury Rd., at end, follow signs to Long Point parking lot. Mid-Sept.–mid-June, follow unpaved Deep Bottom Rd. (1 mi west of airport) 2 mi to lot.* ☎ *508/693–3678.* 🎫 *Mid-June–mid-Sept., $7 per vehicle, $3 per adult; free rest of year.* ☉ *Daily 9–6.*

Lambert's Cove Beach (⊠ Lambert's Cove Rd.) has fine sand and very clear water. On the Vineyard Sound side, it has calm waters and views of the Elizabeth Islands. In season the beach is restricted to residents and those staying in West Tisbury.

★ At the center of the island, the **Manuel F. Correllus State Forest** is a 2,000-acre pine and scrub-oak forest crisscrossed with hiking trails and circled by a paved but rough bike trail (mopeds are prohibited). There's a 2-mi nature trail, a 2-mi par course, and horse trails. *Headquarters on Barnes Rd. by the airport,* ☎ *508/693–2540.* 🎫 *Free.* ☉ *Daily dawn– dusk.*

Dining and Lodging

$$$$ ✕ **Red Cat.** When compared to the town offerings, this restaurant seems
★ like the culinary equivalent of a lovely, less-touristed beach. The atmosphere is casual, and the cooking has a decidedly island lilt to it, including "Bleu on Blue," a signature dish of fresh bluefish baked with creamy blue cheese. ⊠ *688 State Rd., near North Rd.,* ☎ *508/693– 9599. Reservations essential in season. MC, V. BYOB. Closed Mon. No lunch. Call for off-season hrs.*

$$–$$$ ✕🏨 **Lambert's Cove Country Inn.** A narrow road winds through pine woods to this secluded inn surrounded by gardens and old stone walls. Rooms in the 1790 farmhouse have light floral wallpapers and a country feel. Those in outbuildings have screened porches or decks. The soft candlelight and excellent Continental cooking make the restaurant ($$$; reservations essential; BYOB) a destination for a special occasion. The chef's delicate creations rely on local produce and seafood. Especially good are the crisp-baked soft-shell crab appetizer and the grilled Muscovy duck breast on caramelized onions. ⊠ *Off Lambert's Cove Rd., W. Tisbury;* ⊠ *mailing address: R.R. 1, Box 422, Vineyard Haven 02568,* ☎ *508/693–2298,* 📠 *508/693–7890. 15 rooms. Restaurant, tennis court. Full breakfast. AE, MC, V.*

$ 🖼 **Hostelling International–Martha's Vineyard.** The only budget alternative in season, this hostel is one of the country's best. You'll catch up on local events from the bulletin board, and there is a large common kitchen. Doing morning chores is required in summer. ⊠ *Box 158, Edgartown–W. Tisbury Rd., 02575,* ☎ *508/693–2665 or 800/909–4776, ext. 27. 78 dorm-style beds. Barbecue grills, volleyball, coin laundry. MC, V. Closed daytime 10–5 and completely Nov.–Apr. 11 PM curfew June–Aug.*

Nightlife and the Arts
Hot Tin Roof (⊠ Martha's Vineyard Airport, ☎ 508/693–1137), owned by Carly Simon, is the island's hottest club, with big-name artists.

Outdoor Activities and Sports
Stop at the grammar school on Old County Road to reserve one of its hard-surface **tennis courts. Misty Meadows Horse Farm** (⊠ Old County Rd., ☎ 508/693–1870) conducts trail rides.

Shopping
Granary Gallery (⊠ Red Barn Emporium, Old County Rd., ☎ 508/ 693–0455 or 800/472–6279) showcases sculptures and mostly representational paintings by island and international artists, including the photographs of the late Alfred Eisenstaedt.

Chilmark

㉒ *5½ mi southwest of West Tisbury, 12 mi southwest of Vineyard Haven.*

Chilmark is a rural village whose ocean-view roads, rustic woodlands, and lack of crowds have drawn chic summer visitors and resulted in stratospheric real estate prices. Laced with rough roads and winding stone fences that once separated fields and pastures, Chilmark reminds people of what the Vineyard was like in an earlier time, before developers took over.

A dirt road leads off South Road to beautiful **Lucy Vincent Beach,** which in summer is open only to Chilmark residents and those staying in town.

Dining and Lodging
$$$–$$$$ ✕ **Feast of Chilmark.** Civilized and calming, the Feast is a welcome break
★ from the Vineyard's busier joints. The seafood entrées, light appetizers, and fresh salads play up summer tastes and flavors, and the whole menu takes advantage of local produce. ⊠ *Beetlebung Corner,* ☎ *508/645–3553. AE, MC, V. BYOB. No lunch.*

$$$$ ✕🖼 **Inn at Blueberry Hill.** Exclusive and secluded, this unique property comprising 56 acres of former farmland puts you in the heart of the rural Vineyard. The restaurant ($$$–$$$$) is relaxed and elegant, and the fresh, innovative, and health-conscious food is superb. Guest rooms are simply and sparsely decorated with Shaker-inspired island-made furniture, handmade mattresses with all-cotton sheets and duvets. Some of the less expensive rooms are on the small side; a number of rooms can be combined to create larger units. Though the restaurant serves only dinner, the cooks will prepare box lunches for guests. ⊠ *R.R. 1, Box 309, 74 North Rd., 02535,* ☎ *508/645–3322 or 800/ 356–3322,* 📠 *508/645–3799. 21 rooms, 4 suites. Restaurant, lap pool, beauty salon, massage, tennis court, exercise room, meeting room, airport shuttle. Full breakfast. AE, MC, V. Closed Nov.–Apr.*

Menemsha

★ ㉓ *1½ mi northwest of Chilmark.*

Unspoiled by the "progress" of the 20th century, Menemsha is a jumble of weathered fishing shacks, fishing and pleasure boats, drying nets, and lobster pots. **Menemsha Public Beach,** adjacent to Dutcher's Dock, is a pebbly beach with gentle surf on Vineyard Sound. The views to the west make it a great place to catch the sunset. There are rest rooms, food concessions, lifeguards, and parking spaces.

Dining and Lodging

$–$$ ✕ **The Bite.** Fried everything—clams, fish-and-chips, you name it—is on the menu at this roadside shack, where two outdoor picnic tables are the only seating options. The Bite closes at 3 PM on weekdays and 7 PM on weekends. ⊠ *Basin Rd.,* ☎ *no phone. No credit cards.*

$–$$ ✕ **Larson's.** Basically a retail fish store, with reasonable prices and su-
★ perb quality, Larson's will open oysters, stuff quahogs, and cook a lobster to order. The best deal is a dozen littlenecks or cherrystones for
$7. They taste especially good with a bottle of your own wine, sitting
at an outdoor picnic tables or on a blue bench. Larson's closes at 6 PM
on weekdays and at 7 PM on weekends. ⊠ *Dutcher's Dock,* ☎ *508/
645–2680. MC, V. No seating. BYOB. Closed mid-Oct.–mid-May.*

$$$$ ✕▥ **Beach Plum Inn.** A woodland setting, a panoramic view of the water,
and a romantic restaurant (reservations essential; BYOB) where the chef
serves up fresh catch of the day, sea bass, and lobster are among the
attractions of this 10-acre retreat. The inn's cottages are decorated in
casual beach style. Inn rooms—some with private decks with great
views—have modern furnishings. No smoking is permitted. ⊠ *Beach
Plum La., 02552,* ☎ *508/645–9454,* 䕎 *508/645–2801. 5 rooms, 4
cottages. Restaurant, tennis court, croquet. Full breakfast. AE, D,
MC, V. Closed mid-Oct.–mid-May.*

$$ ▥ **Menemsha Inn and Cottages.** All with screened porches, fireplaces,
★ and full kitchens, the cottages here are spaced on 10 acres; some have
more privacy and better water views than others. You can also stay in
the 1989 inn building or the pleasant Carriage House, both of which
have white walls, plush blue or sea-green carpeting, and Appalachian-
pine reproduction furniture. All rooms and suites have private decks,
most with fine sunset views. ⊠ *Box 38, North Rd., 02552,* ☎ *508/
645–2521. 9 rooms, 6 suites, 12 cottages. Continental breakfast (inn
and Carriage House only). No credit cards. Closed Nov.–Apr.*

Aquinnah (Gay Head)

㉔ *4 mi west of Menemsha, 12 mi southwest of West Tisbury.*

Aquinnah, formerly called Gay Head, is an official Native American
township. The Wampanoag tribe is the guardian of the 420 acres that
constitute the Aquinnah Native American Reservation. In 1997, the
town voted to change Gay Head back to its original Native American
name, Aquinnah (pronounced a-*kwih*-nah), which is Wampanoag for
"land under the hill." Also in Aquinnah is the 380-acre estate of the
late Jacqueline Onassis.

Quitsa Pond Lookout (⊠ State Rd.) has a good view of the adjoining
Menemsha and Nashaquitsa ponds, the woods, and the ocean beyond.

From a roadside iron pipe, **Aquinnah spring** (⊠ State Rd.) gushes
water cold enough to slake a cyclist's thirst on the hottest day. Feel free
to fill a canteen. Locals come from all over the island to fill jugs. The
spring is just over the town line.

★ The spectacular **Aquinnah Cliffs** (⊠ State Rd.), a National Historic Land-
mark, are part of the Wampanoag reservation land. These dramatically
striated walls of red clay are the island's major attraction, as evidenced
by the tour bus–filled parking lot. Native American crafts and food

shops line the short approach to the overlook, from which you can see the Elizabeth Islands to the northeast across Vineyard Sound and Noman's Land Island—part wildlife preserve, part military bombing-practice site—3 mi off the Vineyard's southern coast.

Adjacent to the cliffs overlook, the redbrick **Aquinnah Lighthouse** is precariously stationed atop the rapidly eroding cliffs. The lighthouse is open to the public on summer weekends at sunset, weather permitting; private tours can also be arranged. ☎ 508/645–2211. ☜ $2.

Striking **Moshup Beach** provides access to the Aquinnah Cliffs. Come early in the day to ensure a quieter experience and a parking spot. Climbing the cliffs is against the law—they're eroding much too quickly on their own. It's also illegal to take any of the clay with you. ⊠ Parking lot: State Rd. and Moshup Trail ☜ Parking $15 Memorial Day–Labor Day.

Dining and Lodging

$$$$ ✕🗟 **Outermost Inn.** Standing alone on acres of moorland, the inn is
★ wrapped with windows revealing breathtaking views of sea and sky. The restaurant (reservations required; BYOB; no lunch) seats twice for dinner, at 6 and 8 PM four to six nights a week from spring to fall. Dinners ($58) are prix fixe. The overall decor of the inn is clean and contemporary, with white walls, local art, and polished light-wood floors. Each room has a phone, and one has a whirlpool tub. ⊠ R.R. 1, Box 171, Lighthouse Rd., 02535, ☎ 508/645–3511, ℻ 508/645–3514. 7 rooms. Restaurant. Full breakfast. AE, D, MC, V. Closed Nov.–May.

Martha's Vineyard A to Z

Arriving and Departing

BY BUS

Bonanza Bus Lines (☎ 508/548–7588 or 800/556–3815) travels to the Woods Hole ferry port from Rhode Island, Connecticut, and New York year-round.

BY FERRY

Car-and-passenger ferries travel to Vineyard Haven from Woods Hole on Cape Cod year-round. In season, passenger ferries from Falmouth and Hyannis on Cape Cod, and from New Bedford, serve Vineyard Haven and Oak Bluffs. All provide parking where you can leave your car overnight—the fees range from $6 to $10 a night.

FROM FALMOUTH: The *Island Queen* makes the 35-minute trip to Oak Bluffs from late May to Columbus Day. ⊠ Falmouth Harbor, ☎ 508/ 548–4800. ☜ Round-trip $10, $6 bicycles. One-way $6, $3 bicycles.

Patriot Boats (☎ 508/548–2626) allows passengers on its daily Falmouth Harbor–Oak Bluffs mail runs ($5 one-way) and operates a year-round 24-hour water taxi. You can also charter a boat for about $300.

FROM HYANNIS: Hy-Line makes the 1¾-hour run to Oak Bluffs between May and October. From June to mid-September, the "Around the Sound" cruise makes a one-day round-trip from Hyannis with stops at Nantucket and Martha's Vineyard ($31). Call to reserve a space in summer because the parking lot often fills up. ⊠ Ocean St. dock, ☎ 508/778–2600; 508/778–2602 for reservations; 508/693–0112 in Oak Bluffs. ☜ One-way $11, $5 bicycles.

FROM NANTUCKET: Hy-Line makes 2¼-hour runs to and from Oak Bluffs from early June to mid-September—the only inter-island passenger service. (To get a car from Nantucket to the Vineyard, you must return to the mainland and drive from Hyannis to Woods Hole.) ☎ *508/778–2600 in Hyannis; 508/693–0112 in Oak Bluffs; 508/228–3949 in Nantucket.* 🖃 *One-way $11, $5 additional for bicycles.*

FROM NEW BEDFORD: The *Schamonchi* travels between Billy Woods Wharf and Vineyard Haven from mid-May to mid-October. The 600-passenger ferry makes the 1½-hour trip at least once a day, several times in high season, allowing you to avoid Cape traffic. Note that round-trip fares apply only for same-day travel; overnight stays require the purchase of two one-way tickets. ☎ *508/997–1688 (New Bedford); Martha's Vineyard ticket office:* ⊠ *Beach Rd., Vineyard Haven,* ☎ *508/693–2088.* 🖃 *Round-trip $17 adults, $5 bicycles. One-way $9.50, $2.50 bicycles.*

FROM WOODS HOLE: The **Steamship Authority** runs the only car ferries, which make the 45-minute trip to Vineyard Haven year-round and to Oak Bluffs from late May through September. If you plan to take a car, you'll definitely need a reservation in summer or on weekends in the fall (passenger reservations are not necessary). ☎ *508/477–8600 for information and car reservations; 508/693–9130 on the Vineyard; 508/540–1394 TTY.* 🖃 *Passengers one-way year-round, $5; bicycles $3 additional. Cars one-way in season (mid-May–mid-Oct.) $47 per car, call for off-season rates.*

BY PLANE

Martha's Vineyard Airport (☎ 508/693–7022) is in West Tisbury, about 5 mi west of Edgartown. **Cape Air/Nantucket Airlines** connects the Vineyard year-round with Boston (including an hourly summer shuttle), Hyannis, Nantucket, and New Bedford. It offers joint fares and ticketing and baggage agreements with several major carriers. **Direct Flight** (☎ 508/693–6688) is a year-round charter service based on the Vineyard. **US Airways Express** has service to the Vineyard out of Boston and New York City's LaGuardia Airport, as well as to Hyannis and Nantucket, and seasonal service from Washington, D.C. For airline telephone numbers, *see* Air Travel *in* Smart Travel Tips A to Z.

TOWN HARBOR FACILITIES

Edgartown (☎ 508/627–4746). **Menemsha** (☎ 508/645–2846). **Oak Bluffs** (☎ 508/693–4355). **Vineyard Haven** (☎ 508/696–4249).

Getting Around
BY CAR

Driving on the island is fairly simple (though the few main roads can be crowded in summer). You can book rentals by using the free phone at the Woods Hole ferry terminal.

BY FERRY

The three-car **On Time** ferry makes the five-minute run to Chappaquiddick Island. ⊠ *Dock St., Edgartown,* ☎ *508/627–9427.* 🖃 *Round-trip $1 individual, $5 car and driver, $3 bicycle and rider, $4 moped or motorcycle and rider.* ☼ *Memorial Day–mid-October, about every five mins, daily 7 AM–midnight, less frequently off-season.*

BY FOUR-WHEEL-DRIVE

Four-wheel-drive vehicles are allowed from Katama Beach to Wasque Reservation with $70 annual permits ($110 for vehicles not registered on the island) sold on the beach in summer, or anytime at the **Dukes County Courthouse** (⊠ Treasurer's Office, Main St., Edgartown 02539, ☎ 508/627–4250). **Wasque Reservation** (☎ 508/627–7260) has a separate mandatory permit and requires that vehicles carry certain equipment, such as a shovel, tow chains, and rope; call the rangers before setting out.

BY LIMOUSINE
Muzik's Limousine Service (☎ 508/693–2212) provides limousine service on- and off-island.

BY MINIBUS IN EDGARTOWN

The **Martha's Vineyard Transit Authority** (☎ 508/627–9663 or 508/627–7448) has three shuttle bus routes, two in Edgartown and one in Tisbury. One-way fares are $1.50 or less; weekly, monthly, or seasonal passes are available.

BY SHUTTLE BUS

From late June to early September, shuttles operate between Vineyard Haven, Oak Bluffs, and Edgartown. Buses from the Down-Island towns to Aquinnah—stopping at the airport, West Tisbury, Chilmark, and on demand wherever it's safe to do so—run every couple of hours in July and August. For the current bus schedule, call the **shuttle hot line** (☎ 508/693–1589 or 508/693–0058).

BY TAXI

All Island Taxi (☎ 508/693–3705 or 800/693–8294). **Martha's Vineyard Taxi** (☎ 508/693–8660).

Contacts and Resources

B&B RESERVATION AGENCIES

DestINNations (✉ 572 Rte. 28, Suite 3, W. Yarmouth 02673, ☎ 508/428–5600 or 800/333–4667). **Martha's Vineyard and Nantucket Reservations** (✉ Box 1322, Lagoon Pond Rd., Vineyard Haven 02568, ☎ 508/693–7200; 800/649–5671 in MA).

CAR RENTALS

Budget (☎ 508/693–1911), **Hertz** (☎ 508/693–2402), and **All Island** (☎ 508/693–6868) arrange rentals from their airport desks.

EMERGENCIES

Martha's Vineyard Hospital (✉ Linton La., Oak Bluffs, ☎ 508/693–0410). **Vineyard Medical Services** (✉ State Rd., Vineyard Haven, ☎ 508/693–6399) provides walk-in care; call for days and hours.

GUIDED TOURS

The 50-ft sailing catamaran **Arabella** (☎ 508/645–3511) makes day and sunset sails out of Menemsha to Cuttyhunk and the Elizabeth Islands. The teakwood sailing yacht **Ayuthia** (☎ 508/693–7245) sails to Nantucket or the Elizabeth Islands out of Coastwise Wharf in Vineyard Haven. **Liz Villard** (☎ 508/627–8619) leads walking tours of Edgartown's "history, architecture, ghosts, and gossip."

HOUSE RENTALS

Martha's Vineyard Vacation Rentals (✉ Box 1207, 107 Beach Rd., Vineyard Haven 02568, ☎ 508/693–7711). **Sandcastle Realty** (✉ Box 2488, 256 Vineyard Haven Rd., Edgartown 02539, ☎ 508/627–5665).

LATE-NIGHT PHARMACIES

Leslie's Drug Store (✉ 65 Main St., Vineyard Haven, ☎ 508/693–1010) is open daily and has a pharmacist on 24-hour call for emergencies.

VISITOR INFORMATION

Martha's Vineyard Chamber of Commerce is two blocks from the Vineyard Haven ferry. There are town information booths by the Vineyard Haven Steamship terminal, on Circuit Avenue in Oak Bluffs, and on Church Street in Edgartown; these are generally open daily in season. ✉ *Beach Rd., Vineyard Haven 02568,* ☎ *508/693–0085.* ☺ *Weekdays 9–5.*

NANTUCKET

Updated by
Dorothy
Antczak and
Carolyn Heller

Dining
updated by
Seth Rolbein

At the height of its prosperity in the early to mid-19th century, the little island of Nantucket was the foremost whaling port in the world. Its harbor bustled with whaling ships and merchant vessels. Ship's chandleries, cooperages, and other shops stood cheek by jowl along the wharves. Barrels of whale oil were off-loaded from ships onto wagons, then wheeled along cobblestone streets to refineries and candle factories. Strong sea breezes carried the smoke and smells of booming industry through town as its inhabitants eagerly took care of business. Shipowners and sea captains built elegant mansions that today remain remarkably unchanged, thanks to a very strict code regulating any changes to structures within the town of Nantucket, an official National Historic District.

People on a day trip usually enjoy the architecture and historical museums, dine at one of the many fine restaurants, and browse in the art galleries, crafts shops, and boutiques downtown. One signature item is the now-expensive ($400 and up) Nantucket lightship basket, woven of oak or cane. Those who stay longer will have time to explore more of the island. Its moors—swept with fresh salt breezes and scented with bayberry, wild roses, and cranberries—and its miles of white-sand beaches make Nantucket a respite from the rush and regimentation of life elsewhere. Most shops stay open until Christmas. If you do plan to linger, however, make reservations well in advance; for summer weekends, early spring would not be too early.

Nantucket Town

㉕ *30 mi southeast of Hyannis, 107 mi southeast of Boston.*

Nantucket Town has one of the country's finest historical districts, with beautiful 18th- and 19th-century architecture and a museum of whaling history. The **Nantucket Historical Association** (☎ 508/228–1894) operates 14 historic properties along Nantucket Town's streets as museums. At any of them you can purchase an NHA Visitor Pass ($10), which entitles you to entry at all 14 museums, or you can pay single admission at each (prices vary). Most NHA properties are open daily from Memorial Day to Columbus Day; hours vary from year to year, so call ahead.

The **Peter Foulger Museum and Nantucket Historical Association Research Center** provide a glimpse into Nantucket's genealogical past. The museum displays portraits, textiles, porcelains, silver, and furniture. The Research Center is open only to researchers. ✉ *Broad St.,* ☎ *508/228–1655.* ⊠ *$4 or NHA pass. Research permit $10 (2 days).* ☉ *Weekdays 10–4.*

★ An 1846 factory built for refining spermaceti and making candles houses the excellent **Whaling Museum.** The exhibits here include a fully rigged whaleboat, harpoons and other implements, portraits of sea captains, a large scrimshaw collection, and the skeleton of a 43-ft finback whale. Lectures on whaling history are given daily. ✉ *Broad St.,* ☎ *508/228–1894.* ⊠ *$5 or NHA pass. Museum closes in early Dec. and reopens on weekends in Apr.*

Built in 1818, the **Pacific National Bank,** at the corner of Main and Fair streets, is a monument to the Nantucket whaling ships it once financed. Above the old-style teller cages, murals show the town as it was in its whaling heyday. At 93–97 Upper Main Street are the **"Three Bricks,"** identical redbrick mansions with columned Greek Revival porches at their front entrances. They were built between 1836 and 1838 by a whaling merchant for his three sons.

Two white porticoed Greek Revival mansions built in 1845–46 stand across the street from the "Three Bricks." One of the buildings, called the **Hadwen House,** is a museum that surveys Nantucket's affluent whaling era. A guided tour points out the grand circular staircase, fine plasterwork, carved Italian marble fireplace mantels, and Victorian gas chandeliers and furnishings. ⊠ *96 Main St.,* ⊠ *$3 or NHA pass.* ⊘ *Mid-June–Labor Day, daily 10–5; spring and fall hrs vary.*

The shingles of the 1805 **Old Gaol,** which held prisoners until 1933, mask the building's massive square timbers. Walls, ceilings, and floors are bolted with iron. ⊠ *15R Vestal St.* ⊠ *Free.* ⊘ *Mid-June–Labor Day, daily 10–5; Labor Day–Columbus Day, daily 11–3.*

Several windmills sat on Nantucket hills in the 1700s, but only the **Old Mill,** a 1746 Dutch-style octagonal structure made of lumber from shipwrecks, remains. When the wind is strong enough, corn is ground into meal that is sold here. ⊠ *50 Prospect St., at S. Mill St.,* ☎ *508/228–1894.* ⊠ *$2 or NHA pass.* ⊘ *Mid-June–Labor Day, daily 10–5; Memorial Day–mid-June and Labor Day–Columbus Day, daily 11–3. Call for hrs rest of yr.*

★ The tower of the **First Congregational Church** provides the best view of Nantucket—for those who climb the 92 steps. Rising 120 ft, the tower is capped by a weather vane that depicts a whale catch. Peek in at the church's 1850 trompe l'oeil ceiling. ⊠ *62 Centre St.,* ☎ *508/228–0950.* ⊠ *$3.* ⊘ *Mid-June–mid-Oct., Mon.–Sat. 10–4.*

The **Oldest House,** a 1686 saltbox also called the Jethro Coffin House, really is the oldest house on the island. The structure's most noteworthy element is the massive central brick chimney with a giant brick horseshoe adornment. Leaded-glass windows and enormous hearths are among the elements of note in the sparsely furnished interior. Cutaway panels reveal 17th-century construction techniques. ⊠ *Sunset Hill,* ☎ *508/228–1894.* ⊠ *$3 or NHA pass.* ⊘ *Mid-June–Labor Day, daily 10–5; call for spring hrs.*

Small, white-painted **Brant Point Light** (⊠ Easton St.) sits on Brant Point, which has superb views of the harbor and town. The beach here is not large, but it's a great place to watch boats coming and going. The point was the site of the second-oldest lighthouse in the country (1746), though the present light was built in the 19th century. Tradition says that if you throw two pennies overboard as you round Brant Point, you are sure to return to Nantucket.

Ⓒ **Maria Mitchell Aquarium** presents local marine life in salt- and freshwater tanks. Family marine ecology trips are conducted four times weekly in season. ⊠ *28 Washington St., near Commercial Wharf,* ☎ *508/228–5387.* ⊠ *$1.* ⊘ *Mid-June–Aug., Tues.–Sat. 10–4.*

Children's Beach (⊠ S. Beach St.), a calm harbor beach suited to small children, is an easy walk from town. It has a park and playground, a lifeguard, food service, and rest rooms. Six miles west of town and accessible only by foot, **Eel Point** (⊠ Eel Point Rd.) has one of the island's most beautiful and interesting beaches—a sandbar extends out 100 yards, keeping the water shallow, clear, and calm. There are no services, just lots of birds, wild berries and bushes, and solitude.

Jetties Beach (⊠ Hulbert Ave.), a short bike or shuttle ride from town, is the most popular beach for families because of its calm surf, lifeguards, bathhouse, snack bar, water-sports rentals, and tennis. Known for great sunsets and surf, **Madaket Beach** is reached by shuttle bus or by the Madaket bike path (5.6 mi) off Cliff Road. Lifeguards are on

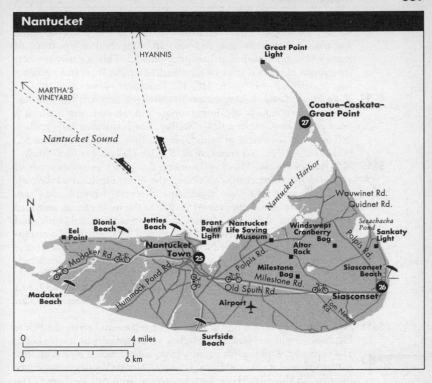

Nantucket

duty, and there are rest rooms. **Surfside** (⌧ Surfside Rd.) is the premier surf beach, with lifeguards, rest rooms, a snack bar, and a wide
strand. About 2 mi south of the center of town, the beach attracts college students and families and is great for kite-flying and surf casting.

Dining and Lodging

$$$$ ✕ **India House.** A short stroll from downtown brings you to a handsome old inn with a kitchen known for its whimsy. Try the three-course
"Floribbean flight" dinner—shrimp *rémoulade* (a seasoned sauce made
with mayonnaise), black grouper, and caramelized bananas—or the
"drunken" shrimp and lobster sautée. Starting on the Fourth of July,
an excellent brunch includes three-berry French toast and poached eggs
with smoked salmon and caviar. ⌧ *37 India St.,* ☎ *508/228–9043.
Reservations not accepted for brunch. AE, D, MC, V. Closed Jan.–Mar.
No lunch.*

$$$$ ✕ **21 Federal.** The epitome of sophisticated, gentrified island dining,
★ 21 Federal serves some of the island's best new and traditional American cuisine. Entrées have luxurious touches, such as sautéed halibut
with saffron risotto, morels, and osetra caviar. ⌧ *21 Federal St.,* ☎
508/228–2121. AE, MC, V. Closed Jan–Mar.

$$$–$$$$ ✕ **American Seasons.** The culinary context here is geographic: From the
★ four corners of the continental United States, chef and owner Michael
Getter gathers specialties. You can mix and match, taking Nantucket lob-
ster for an appetizer and then an excellent green peppercorn–crusted sir-
loin from the "wild west" for the main course. ⌧ *80 Centre St.,* ☎ *508/
228–7111. AE, MC, V. Closed mid-Dec.–early Apr. No lunch.*

$$$–$$$$ ✕ **Atlantic Cafe.** The Atlantic has been the island's belly-up-to-the-bar
hangout since 1978. Two salty codfish cakes with plenty of slaw and
fries help the beer go down. "Mary and the Boys" is a Bloody Mary with
six shrimp. ⌧ *15 S. Water St.,* ☎ *508/228–0570. AE, DC, MC, V.*

$$$–$$$$ ✗ **Obadiah's Native Seafood.** Bluefish, scallops, lobster, swordfish, scrod—fish has been Obadiah's stock in trade for more than 20 years. The patio is especially nice, and you can order children's portions of many of the main dishes at half price plus $2. This is easily the best straight-ahead seafood value on the island. ⊠ *2 India St., at Independence La.,* ☎ *508/228–4430. AE, MC, V. Closed Sept.–June.*

$–$$ ✗ **Sushi by Yoshi.** It may be pocket-sized—a tiny kitchen and just about a dozen seats in the dining room—but this restaurant, which is open year-round, packs a flavor wallop. The Nantucket roll (scallion and avocado with tuna or salmon) is excellent. ⊠ *2 E. Chestnut St.,* ☎ *508/228–1801. No credit cards. BYOB. Call for hrs Oct.–May.*

$$$$ ✗⊞ **Harbor House.** This family-oriented complex provides scads of
★ amenities like its more upscale sibling, the White Elephant (☞ *below*), at a lower price. The 1886 main inn and several "town houses" are set on a flower-filled quadrangle very near the town center. Standard rooms are done in English-country style, with bright floral fabrics and queen-size beds. All rooms have phones and TVs. The hotel's restaurant ($$–$$$) serves simple New England fare—there's a three-course early-bird special between 5 and 6:30 and a lavish Sunday brunch buffet (reservations essential). ⊠ *Box 1139, S. Beach St., 02554,* ☎ *508/228–1500 or 800/475–2637 for reservations,* FAX *508/228–7639. 113 rooms. Restaurant, lounge, room service, concierge, business services. AE, D, DC, MC, V. Closed mid-Dec.–mid-Apr.*

$$$$ ✗⊞ **White Elephant.** Long a hallmark of service and style, the White Elephant is right on Nantucket Harbor, separated only by a wide lawn. The rooms have an English country look, with stenciled pine armoires, sponge-painted walls, and floral fabrics. A similar decor characterizes the one- to three-bedroom cottages (some with full kitchens). The main hotel has a formal restaurant with a waterside outdoor café, a lounge with entertainment, and a large harborside pool. ⊠ *Box 1139, 50 Easton St., 02554,* ☎ *508/228–2500 or 800/475–2637 for room reservations,* FAX *508/325–1195. 48 rooms, 32 cottages. Restaurant, lounge, room service, pool, croquet, concierge, meeting rooms. AE, D, DC, MC, V. Closed late Oct.–early May.*

$$$–$$$$ ⊞ **Westmoor Inn.** The many common areas in this yellow Federal-style
★ mansion include a wide lawn set with Adirondack chairs, a garden patio secluded behind 11-ft hedges, and a wicker-filled sunroom. The guest rooms are decorated in country-French style; most have soft florals and stenciled walls. One first-floor suite has a giant bath with a whirlpool tub and French doors opening onto the lawn. The inn is no-smoking. ⊠ *Cliff Rd., 02554,* ☎ *508/228–0877 or 888/236–7310,* FAX *508/ 228–5763. 14 rooms. Bicycles. Continental breakfast. AE, MC, V. Closed early Dec.–mid-Apr.*

$$$ ⊞ **Centerboard Guest House.** White walls, blond-wood floors, and nat-
★ ural woodwork create a dreamy atmosphere at this no-smoking inn a few blocks from the center of town. Stained-glass lamps, antique quilts, and fresh flowers adorn the rooms; the first-floor suite is stunning, with 11-ft ceilings, a Victorian living room with fireplace and bar, inlaid parquet floors, and a green-marble bath with whirlpool tub. ⊠ *Box 456, 8 Chester St., 02554,* ☎ *508/228–9696. 6 rooms, 1 suite. Continental breakfast. AE, MC, V.*

$$ ⊞ **76 Main Street.** This 1883 B&B blends antiques and reproductions,
★ Oriental rugs, handmade quilts, and lots of fine woods. Room 3 has wonderful woodwork, a carved-wood armoire, and twin four-posters; Room 1 has large windows, massive redwood pocket doors, and an eyelet-dressed canopy bed. The motel-like annex rooms have low ceilings, but they are spacious enough for families. No smoking is permitted. ⊠ *76 Main St., 02554,* ☎ *508/228–2533. 18 rooms. Continental breakfast. AE, D, MC, V. Closed Jan.–Mar.*

$ 🏨 **Nesbitt Inn.** This family-run guest house in the center of town has comfortable, shared-bath rooms (including inexpensive singles) done in Victorian style, with lace curtains, some marble-top and brass antiques, and a sink in each room. Some beds are not as firm as they should be, but the Nesbitt is a very good buy in this town. Ask for a room away from the popular bar-restaurant next door. ⊠ *Box 1019, 21 Broad St., 02554,* ☎ *508/228–0156 or 508/228–2446. 13 rooms without bath. Grill, no-smoking rooms, refrigerator. Continental breakfast. No pets. MC, V.*

Nightlife and the Arts
NIGHTLIFE
A piano-vocal duo or a solo pianist plays most nights at the formal, harbor-view **Brant Point Grill at the White Elephant** (⊠ Easton St., ☎ 508/228–2500) from Memorial Day to mid-September. The **Brotherhood of Thieves** (⊠ 23 Broad St., ☎ no phone) presents folk musicians and has a well-stocked bar. **Hearth at the Harbor House** (⊠ S. Beach St., ☎ 508/228–1500) hosts dancing to live music (from country to folk) on weekends year-round. Folks of all ages dance at the **Muse** (⊠ 44 Surfside Rd., ☎ 508/228–6873) to rock, reggae, and other music, live or recorded.

THE ARTS
Actors Theatre of Nantucket (⊠ Methodist Church, 2 Centre St., at Main St., ☎ 508/228–6325) presents Broadway-style plays between Memorial Day and Columbus Day, children's post-beach matinees in July and August, comedy nights, and other events. **Band concerts** (☎ 508/228–7213) are held at 6 PM Thursdays and Sundays, July 4–Labor Day, at Children's Beach. The **Nantucket Musical Arts Society** (☎ 508/228–1287) presents Tuesday-evening concerts in July and August at the First Congregational Church (⊠ 62 Centre St.). **Theatre Workshop of Nantucket** (⊠ Bennett Hall, 62 Centre St., ☎ 508/228–4305), a community theater, stages plays, musicals, and readings.

Outdoor Activities and Sports
BIRD-WATCHING
The **Maria Mitchell Association** (⊠ 2 Vestal St., ☎ 508/228–9198) organizes wildflower and bird walks from June to Labor Day.

BOATING
Nantucket Harbor Sail (⊠ Swain's Wharf, ☎ 508/228–0424) rents sailboats.

FISHING
Barry Thurston's Fishing Tackle (⊠ Harbor Sq., ☎ 508/228–9595) dispenses fishing tips and rents gear. The *Herbert T.* (⊠ Slip 14, ☎ 508/228–6655) and other boats are available for seasonal charter from Straight Wharf.

ROLLERBLADING
Nantucket Sports Locker (⊠ 14 Cambridge St., ☎ 508/228–6610) rents skates and protective gear.

WHALE-WATCHING
Nantucket Whalewatch (⊠ Hy-Line dock, Straight Wharf, ☎ 978/283–0313 or 800/942–5464) operates naturalist-led full-day excursions ($75; reservations essential) on Tuesday from mid-July through August.

Shopping
ANTIQUES
Forager House Collection (⊠ 20 Centre St., ☎ 508/228–5977) specializes in folk art and Americana. **Janis Aldridge** (⊠ 50 Main St., ☎ 508/228–6673) carries home furnishings and beautifully framed antique engravings. **Nina Hellman Antiques** (⊠ 48 Centre St., ☎ 508/228–4677) carries scrimshaw, ship models, nautical instruments, and other marine

antiques, plus folk art and Nantucket memorabilia. **Paul La Paglia** (⊠ 38 Centre St., ☎ 508/228–8760) has moderately priced antique prints.

The stock at **Mitchell's Book Corner** (⊠ 54 Main St., ☎ 508/228–1080) includes books on Nantucket and whaling and ocean-related children's titles. **Nantucket Bookworks** (⊠ 25 Broad St., ☎ 508/228–4000) carries hardcover and paperback books, with an emphasis on children's books and literary works.

Cordillera Imports (⊠ 18 Broad St., ☎ 508/228–6140) sells jewelry, affordable clothing in natural fibers, and crafts from Latin America, Asia, and elsewhere. **Murray's Toggery Shop** (⊠ 62 Main St., ☎ 508/228–0437) stocks traditional footwear and clothing—including the famous Nantucket Reds (cotton pants that fade to pink with washing)—for men, women, and children. An outlet store (⊠ 7 New St., ☎ 508/228–3584) has discounts of up to 50%.

Four Winds Craft Guild (⊠ 6 Ray's Ct., ☎ 508/228–9623) carries antique and new scrimshaw and lightship baskets, as well as ship models, duck decoys, and a kit for making your own lightship basket.

The **Museum Shop** (⊠ 1 Broad St. next to the Whaling Museum, ☎ 508/228–5785) has island-related books, antique whaling tools, reproduction furniture, and toys. **Robert Wilson Galleries** (⊠ 34 Main St., ☎ 508/228–6246 or 508/228–2096) carries contemporary American marine, impressionist, and other art. **Seven Seas Gifts** (⊠ 46 Centre St., ☎ 508/228–0958) stocks inexpensive gift and souvenir items, including shells, baskets, toys, and Nantucket jigsaw puzzles.

Siasconset

★ ❷ *7 mi east of Nantucket Town.*

First a whaling town and then an artist's colony, Siasconset (or 'Sconset, as locals call their town) is a charming village of streets with tiny rose-covered cottages and driveways of crushed white shells. At the central square are the post office, a liquor store, a bookstore, a market, and two restaurants. **Siasconset Beach,** at the end of a 7-mi bike path, has golden sand, moderate to heavy surf, a lifeguard, showers, rest rooms, and a playground. Restaurants are nearby.

★ The **Milestone Bog** (⊠ Off Milestone Rd.), more than 200 acres of working cranberry bogs surrounded by conservation land, is always a beautiful sight to behold, especially during the fall harvest, which begins in September and continues for six weeks. At any time of year, the bog and the moors have a remarkable quiet beauty that's well worth experiencing.

A good spot for bird-watching, **Sesachacha Pond** (pronounced seh-*sah*-kah-cha or, more often, just *sah*-kah-cha) is circled by a walking path that leads to an Audubon wildlife area. It's off Polpis Road.

★ An unmarked dirt track off Polpis Road between Wauwinet and Siasconset leads to **Altar Rock,** from which the view is spectacular. The rock sits on a high spot amid open moor and bog land—technically called lowland heath—which is very rare in the United States. The entire area, of which the Milestone Bog (☞ *above*) is a part, is laced with paths leading in every direction. Keep track of the trails you travel so you'll be able to find your way back.

Dining and Lodging

$$$$ ✕ **Chanticleer.** For more than 20 years, Anne and Jean-Charles Berruet
★ have been serving superb French food in a formal country setting. Some
people have come to feel that the food and ambience have become heavy
and overbearing. Still, for many a Nantucket trip would not be complete without getting dressed up and making the trip here, where dining is a commitment to a classic form of elegance. ⊠ *9 New St.,* ☎
508/257–6231. Jacket required. AE, MC, V. Closed Mon. and mid-Oct.–early May.

$$$–$$$$ ✕ **'Sconset Café.** If you stop by this café and there is no table (as is
★ often the case), someone will give you a beeper, send you down to the
beach or over to the nearby Summer House for a drink, and beep you
when your table is ready. On the dinner menu are local fish and a few
other items like duck; for lunch are reasonably priced sandwiches and
salads. ⊠ *Post Office Sq.,* ☎ *508/257–4008. No credit cards. BYOB
(liquor store next door). Closed 1st wk of Oct.—mid-May.*

$$$$ ✕🏠 **Summer House.** Clustered around a flower-filled lawn across from
'Sconset Beach, these one- and two-bedroom rose-covered cottages are
furnished in romantic English country style: trompe-l'oeil-bordered
white walls, white eyelet spreads, and stripped English-pine antique furnishings. Some find the service at the restaurant ($$$–$$$$; reservations essential for dinner) overly fussy, but most patrons enjoy the
'Sconset bluff ocean views and live piano music. The seafood specials
are often the highlights of the menu. ⊠ *Box 800, Ocean Ave., 02564,*
☎ *508/228–6609,* 🖷 *508/228–1878. 8 cottages. 2 restaurants, bar, piano
bar, pool. Continental breakfast. AE, MC, V. Closed Nov.–late Apr.*

$$$$ 🏠 **Wade Cottages.** On a bluff overlooking the ocean, this complex of
guest rooms, apartments, and cottages in 'Sconset couldn't be better located for beach lovers: The buildings are arranged around a central lawn
with a great ocean view. Most inn rooms and cottages have sea views,
and all have phones. Furnishings are generally in somewhat worn beach
style, with some antique pieces. ⊠ *Box 211, Shell St., 02564,* ☎ *508/
257–6308;* ☎ *212/989–6423 off-season;* 🖷 *508/257–4602. 8 rooms
(3-night minimum), 4 with bath; 6 apartments (1-wk minimum); 3 cottages (2-wk minimum). Badminton, Ping-Pong, beach, coin laundry. Continental breakfast. AE, MC, V. Closed mid-Oct.–late May.*

Outdoor Activities and Sports

BIKING

The 8-mi **Polpis Bike Path,** a long trail with gentle hills, winds alongside Polpis Road past the moors, the cranberry bogs, and Sesachacha
Pond almost into Siasconset. The 6½ mi **'Sconset Bike Path** starts at
the rotary east of town and parallels Milestone Road, ending in the
village. It is mostly level, with some gentle hills and benches and drinking fountains at strategic locations along the way.

NATURE TOURS

The Trustees of Reservations sponsor naturalist-led **Great Point Natural History Tours** (☎ 508/228–6799) from June to October.

En Route A scenic drive along Polpis Road takes you past the precariously
perched **Sankaty Light,** built in 1849, and large areas of open moorland. The entrance to the 205-acre **Windswept Cranberry Bog,** open
to walkers and bike riders, is also on Polpis, between Quidnet and
Wauwinet roads.

Coatue–Coskata–Great Point

㉗ *12¾ mi from Nantucket Town to Great Point, 11 mi from 'Sconset.*

Wauwinet Road leads to the gateway of Coatue–Coskata–Great Point, an unpopulated spit of sand comprising three cooperatively managed wildlife refuges that can be entered only on foot or by four-wheel-drive over-sand vehicle (☎ 508/228–2884 for information). The area's beaches, dunes, salt marshes, and stands of oak and cedar provide a major habitat for marsh hawks, oystercatchers, terns, herring gulls, and other birds. Because of frequent dangerous currents and riptides and the lack of lifeguards, swimming is strongly discouraged, especially around the Great Point Light.

The **Nantucket Life Saving Museum,** on the road back to town from Great Point, is housed in a re-creation of an 1874 Life Saving Service station. Exhibits include original rescue equipment and boats, artifacts recovered from the wreck *Andrea Doria,* and photos and accounts of daring rescues. ⊠ *Fulling Hill Rd., off Polpis Rd.,* ☎ *508/228–1885.* 🎫 *$3.* ⊙ *Mid-June–Columbus Day, Tues.–Sun. 9:30–4.*

Dining and Lodging

$$$$ ✕🏨 **Wauwinet.** Some people would say that this historic 19th-century
★ hotel is the only place to stay on Nantucket. The tasteful Topper's restaurant ($$$–$$$$; dinner reservations essential) serves alluring dishes like pan-seared sea scallops with lobster risotto and roasted rack of cervena (venison from a farm-raised New Zealand deer) with creamy polenta and forest-mushroom glaze. The rooms and cottages are decorated in country-beach style, with pine antiques; some have water views. There are also boat shuttles to Coatue beach across the harbor, and the innkeeper runs a Land Rover tour of the Great Point reserve—all of which are included in the room rate. Jitney service to and from town 8 mi away, plus Steamship pickup, make the hotel a convenient place to stay if you don't have a car. ⊠ *Box 2580, Wauwinet Rd., Nantucket 02584,* ☎ *508/228–0145 or 800/426–8718,* 🆚 *508/228–7135. 25 rooms, 5 cottages. Restaurant, bar, room service, 2 tennis courts, croquet, boating, mountain bikes, library, concierge, business services. Full breakfast. AE, DC, MC, V. Closed Nov.–Apr.*

Nantucket A to Z

Arriving and Departing

BY FERRY

Year-round service is available from Hyannis only. Hy-Line has two boats, one of which runs between Nantucket and Martha's Vineyard in summer only. The only way to get a car to Nantucket is on the Steamship Authority. To get a car from the Vineyard to Nantucket, you would have to return to Woods Hole, drive to Hyannis, and take the ferry from there.

The **Steamship Authority** (☎ 508/228–3274 on Nantucket; 508/477–8600 on the Cape) runs car-and-passenger ferries to the island from Hyannis year-round. The trip takes 2¼ hours. A newer, faster passenger ferry takes just an hour. 🎫 *One-way $11; bicycles $5; cars $110 mid-May–mid-Oct., $80 mid-Oct.–mid-May. High-speed passenger ferry $20 one-way, $5 bicycles.*

Hy-Line (☎ 508/228–3949 on Nantucket; 508/778–2600 in Hyannis) departs from Hyannis from early May through October. The trip takes from 1¾ to 2 hours. The cost one-way is $11, plus $5 for bicycles. There is also service from Oak Bluffs on Martha's Vineyard (☎ 508/693–0112) from early June to mid-September; that trip takes 2¼ hours and costs the same.

Hy-Line's high-end, high-speed boat, *The Grey Lady,* ferries passengers from Hyannis and back year-round. The trip takes just over an hour.

That speed has its downside in rough seas—lots of bouncing and lurching that some find nauseating. ⊠ *Ocean St. dock,* ☎ *508/778–0404 or 800/492–8082.* 🚢 *One-way $29, bicycles $4.50.*

BY PLANE

Nantucket Memorial Airport (☎ 508/325–5300) is about 3½ mi southeast of town via Old South Road; cars and four-wheel-drive vehicles can be rented at the airport. **Business Express/Delta Connection** flies from Boston year-round and from New York (LaGuardia) in season.

Cape Air/Nantucket Air flies from Hyannis year-round and runs charters. For airline telephone numbers, *see* Air Travel *in* Smart Travel Tips A to Z.

Getting Around

BY BICYCLE AND MOPED

Nantucket Bike Shop (⊠ Steamboat Wharf and Straight Wharf, ☎ 508/228–1999), open between April and October, rents bicycles and mopeds and provides an excellent touring map. Daily rentals typically cost from $18 to $30 for a bicycle and from $45 to $65 for a moped, though half-, full-, and multiple-day rates are available.

BY BUS

From mid-June to Labor Day, **Barrett's Tours** (⊠ 20 Federal St., ☎ 508/228–0174 or 800/773–0174), across from the Information Bureau in Nantucket Town, runs beach shuttles to 'Sconset ($5 round-trip, $3 one-way), Surfside ($3 round-trip, $2 one-way), and Jetties ($1 one-way) several times daily. Children pay half fare to 'Sconset and Surfside. The **Nantucket Regional Transit Authority** (☎ 508/228–7025; TDD 508/325–0788) runs shuttle buses around the island between June and September. Most service begins at 7 AM and ends at 11 PM. Fares are 50¢ in town, $1 to 'Sconset and Madaket, $10 for a three-day pass, $15 for a seven-day pass, and $30 for a one-month pass. Seasonal passes are also available.

BY TAXI

A-1 Taxi (☎ 508/228–3330 or 508/228–4084). **All Points Taxi** (☎ 508/228–5779). **BG's Taxi** (☎ 508/228–4146).

Contacts and Resources

CAR RENTALS

Budget (☎ 508/228–5666 or 888/228–5666). **Hertz** (☎ 508/228–9421 or 800/654–3131). **Nantucket Windmill** (☎ 508/228–1227 or 800/228–1227).

EMERGENCIES

Nantucket Cottage Hospital (⊠ 57 Prospect St., ☎ 508/228–1200).

GUIDED TOURS

The third-generation Nantucketers at **Barrett's Tours** (⊠ 20 Federal St., ☎ 508/228–0174 or 800/773–0174) conduct 1½-hour bus tours of the island. **Carried Away** (☎ 508/228–0218) takes people on narrated carriage rides through the Nantucket's historic district in season. Sixth-generation Nantucketer Gail Johnson of **Gail's Tours** (☎ 508/257–6557) narrates a lively 1½-hour van tour of island highlights. **Nantucket Whalewatch** (⊠ Straight Wharf, Hy-Line dock, ☎ 978/283–0313 or 800/942–5464) runs excursions in season.

HARBOR FACILITIES

The **Boat Basin** (☎ 508/325–1350 or 800/626–2628) operates harbor facilities year-round, with shower and laundry facilities, electric power, cable TV, phone hookups, a fuel dock, and summer concierge service.

HOUSE RENTALS

Congdon & Coleman (⊠ 57 Main St., Nantucket 02554, ☎ 508/325–

5000, FAX 508/325–5025). **'Sconset Real Estate** (⊠ Box 122, Siasconset 02564, ☎ 508/257–6335; 508/228–1815 in winter).

Nantucket Pharmacy (⊠ 45 Main St., ☎ 508/228–0180) stays open until 10 from Memorial Day to Labor Day.

DestINNations (⊠ 572 Rte. 28, Suite 3, W. Yarmouth 02673, ☎ 800/ 333–4667). **Martha's Vineyard and Nantucket Reservations** (⊠ Box 1322, 73 Lagoon Pond Rd., Vineyard Haven, 02568, ☎ 508/693–7200; 800/649–5671 in Massachusetts).

The **Nantucket Information Bureau** (⊠ 25 Federal St., ☎ 508/228–0925) monitors room availability in season and at holidays for last-minute bookings. At night, check the board outside for available rooms.

The **Chamber of Commerce** (⊠ 48 Main St., Nantucket 02554, ☎ 508/ 228–1700). **Nantucket Visitors Service and Information Bureau** (⊠ 25 Federal St., ☎ 508/228–0925).

THE NORTH SHORE

Updated by
Carolyn Heller

The slice of Massachusetts's Atlantic coast known as the North Shore extends past grimy docklands and through Boston's well-to-do northern suburbs to the picturesque Cape Ann region, and beyond Cape Ann to Newburyport, just south of New Hampshire. In addition to miles of fine beaches, the North Shore encompasses Marblehead, a quintessential New England sea town; Salem, which thrives on a history of witches, millionaires, and the maritime trades; Gloucester, the oldest seaport in America; quaint Rockport, crammed with crafts shops and artists' studios; and Newburyport, with its redbrick center and rows of clapboard Federal mansions. Bright and busy in the short summer season, the North Shore is calmer between November and June.

Marblehead

28 *15 mi north of Boston.*

Marblehead's narrow, winding streets and old clapboard houses retain much of the character of the village founded in 1629 by fishermen from Cornwall and the Channel Islands. The proud spirit of the ambitious merchant sailors who made Marblehead prosper in the 18th century can still be felt in many of the impressive Georgian mansions that line downtown streets. It's a sign of the times that today's fishing fleet is small compared to the armada of pleasure craft in the harbor. This is one of New England's premier sailing capitals, and Race Week (usually the last week of July) draws boats from all along the eastern seaboard. Parking in town can be difficult; try the 30-car public lot at the end of Front Street, the lot on State Street by the Landing restaurant, or the metered areas on the street. The Marblehead Chamber of Commerce (☞ Visitor Information *in* North Shore A to Z, *below*) has a complete visitor guide with a walking tour of the city.

Downtown **Crocker Park** (⊠ Front St.) is a lovely place for a walk or picnic with a view of Marblehead harbor.

Plaques on homes tell the date of construction and the original owner. A few mansions are owned and operated by the town historical society and are open to the public. One exquisite example of Marblehead's high society of yore can be seen in the **Jeremiah Lee Mansion.** Colonel Lee was one of the wealthiest people in the colonies in 1768, and although

The North Shore

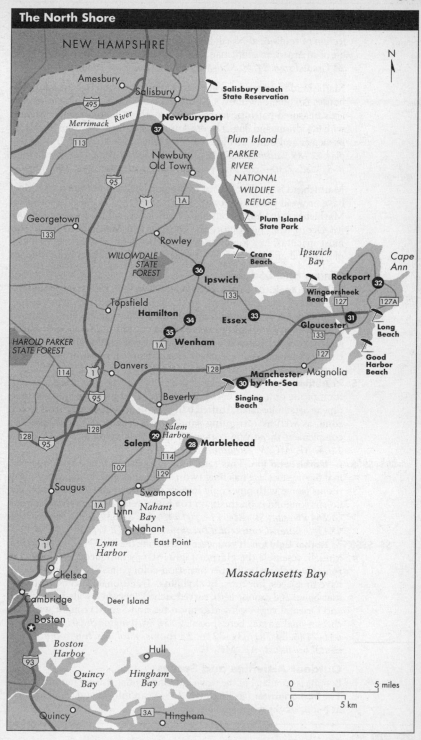

NEW HAMPSHIRE

Amesbury

Salisbury

Salisbury Beach
State Reservation

495

Newburyport

Merrimack River

113

37

Newbury
Old Town

Plum Island

PARKER
RIVER
NATIONAL
WILDLIFE
REFUGE

95

1

1A

Plum Island
State Park

Georgetown

133

Rowley

WILLOWDALE
STATE
FOREST

Crane
Beach

Ipswich
Bay

Cape
Ann

36

Ipswich

Wingaersheek
Beach

Rockport

32

133

127

127A

Topsfield

Hamilton

34

Essex

33

Gloucester

31

Long
Beach

HAROLD PARKER
STATE FOREST

35

Wenham

1A

133

127

Good
Harbor
Beach

114

1

Danvers

128

Magnolia

95

Beverly

Manchester-
by-the-Sea

30

Singing
Beach

128

128

Salem
Harbor

95

29

Salem

28

Marblehead

107

114

129

Saugus

Swampscott

1A

Lynn

Nahant
Bay

Nahant

Lynn
Harbor

East Point

Massachusetts Bay

1

Chelsea

Cambridge

Deer Island

Boston

Boston
Harbor

Hull

93

Quincy
Bay

Hingham
Bay

0   5 miles

0   5 km

Quincy

3A

Hingham

few furnishings original to the house remain, the mahogany paneling, hand-painted wallpaper, and other appointments, as well as a fine collection of traditional North Shore furniture, provide a glimpse into the life of an American gentleman. ⊠ *161 Washington St.,* ☎ *781/631–1069.* 🎟 *Guided tour $4.* ⊘ *Mid-May–Oct., Mon.–Sat. 10–4, Sun. 1–4.*

Marblehead's Victorian-era municipal building, **Abbott Hall,** built in 1876, houses Archibald Willard's painting *The Spirit of '76.* One of America's treasured patriotic icons, it depicts three Revolutionary veterans with fife, drum, and flag. The deed used to buy the town from the Nanapashemet and other artifacts of Marblehead's history are also on display. ⊠ *188 Washington St.,* ☎ *781/631–0528.* ⊘ *Mon.–Tues. and Thurs. 8–5, Wed. 7:30–7:30, Fri. 8–1; May–Oct., also Sat. 9–6, Sun. 11–6.*

Marblehead is not known for sprawling beaches, but the ones it does have are well maintained and mostly used by "'headers" (natives of Marblehead) for family outings or quick ocean dips. **Deveraux Beach** (⊠ Ocean Ave., just before the causeway to Marblehead Neck), the most spacious, has some sandy and some pebbled areas, as well as a playground and a good lobster shack. Parking is $5 for nonresidents.

Dining and Lodging

$–$$ ✕ **King's Rook.** At this cozy café and wine bar, the crisp single-serving pizzas include one with goat cheese, roasted red peppers, and caramelized onions, and another loaded with veggies. The restaurant also serves elegant sandwiches like the curried egg salad with raisins and the overstuffed turkey. The signature dessert, lemonberry-jazz, layers lemon cream, Maine blueberries, and lemon mousse on a shortbread crust. ⊠ *12 State St.,* ☎ *781/631–9838. MC, V. No dinner Mon.*

$ ✕ **Truffles.** This gourmet café–take-out shop has everything you need for a picnic or a quick coffee break. Prepared items include Mediterranean artichoke salad, stuffed baby eggplant, and smoked-turkey calzone, as well as intriguing sandwiches. The house-made pastries complement the strong coffee. ⊠ *114 Washington St.,* ☎ *781/639– 1104. AE, MC, V. No dinner.*

$$$–$$$$ 🏨 **Marblehead Inn.** This rambling Victorian mansion with a carved mahogany staircase has nine two-room suites with living rooms, bedrooms (some with pineapple four-poster beds), and kitchenettes. The no-smoking inn is on the main road between Salem and Marblehead. ⊠ *264 Pleasant St. (Rte. 114), 01945,* ☎ *781/639–9999 or 800/399– 5843. 9 suites. Continental breakfast. AE, MC, V.*

$$–$$$$ 🏨 **Harbor Light Inn.** If you were to describe the ideal New England inn, ★ it might resemble the Harbor Light. Stately antiques are arranged in rooms with floral wallpaper or period-color paint. Several guest rooms have fireplaces, hot tubs, or skylights. Traditional touches, including four-poster and canopy beds, carved arched doorways, wide-board floors, and Oriental rugs—plus afternoon tea and Saturday-night wine and cheese—make a stay here special. ⊠ *58 Washington St., 01945,* ☎ *781/ 631–2186,* 𝔽𝔸𝕏 *781/631–2216. 21 rooms. Pool, meeting room. Continental breakfast. AE, MC, V.*

Outdoor Activities and Sports

Boating is popular, but the town has long waiting lists for mooring space. The **harbormaster** (☎ 781/631–2386) can inform you of nightly fees at public docks when space is available.

Salem

★ ㉙ *4 mi east of Marblehead, 15 mi north of Boston.*

Salem unabashedly calls itself "Witch City." During the town's wildly popular October "Haunted Happenings," museums and businesses are converted into haunted houses, graveyards, or dungeons, as the town celebrates its spooky past. Year-round, witches astride broomsticks decorate the police cars; numerous witch-related attractions and shops, as well current-day resident witchcraft practitioners, recall the city's infamous connection with the witchcraft hysteria and trials of 1692. That witchcraft mania began in January 1692 when several Salem-area girls fell ill, and William Griggs, the village physician, declared that the girls were bewitched. More than 150 men and women were charged with practicing witchcraft, a crime punishable by death. After the resulting trials later that year, 19 innocent people were hanged.

Witchcraft aside, Salem's charms include compelling museums, trendy waterfront stores and restaurants, and a wide common with a children's playground. Settled in 1626, the town has a rich maritime tradition; frigates out of Salem opened the Far East trade routes and generated the wealth that created America's first millionaires. Among Salem's native sons were writer Nathaniel Hawthorne, navigator Nathaniel Bowditch, and architect Samuel McIntire.

A good place to start your Salem tour is the large **National Park Service Visitor Center,** which has a wide variety of booklets and pamphlets, including a "Maritime Trail" and "Early Settlement Trail" for Essex County, as well as a free 27-minute film. ⊠ *2 New Liberty St.,* ☎ *978/ 740–1650.* ☉ *Daily 9–5.*

One way to explore Salem is to follow the 1½-mi Heritage Trail (painted in red on the sidewalk) around town. For those who prefer to ride rather than walk, the **Salem Trolley** leaves every hour for a guided tour from near the National Park Visitor Center. You may get off and back on the trolley en route. *Trolley Depot, 191 Essex St.,* ☎ *978/744–5469.* ▣ *$9.* ☉ *Apr.–Oct., daily 10–5, with extended hrs July–Oct.; Nov. and Mar., weekends 10–4.*

★ Tour highlights at the **House of the Seven Gables,** which was immortalized in the classic 1851 novel by Nathaniel Hawthorne, include the period furnishings, a secret staircase, and a garret containing an antique scale model of the house. The complex of 17th-century buildings includes the small house where Hawthorne was born in 1804; it was moved from its original location elsewhere in Salem. ⊠ *54 Turner St. (off Derby St.),* ☎ *978/744–0991.* ▣ *Guided tours $7.* ☉ *May–Nov., daily 10– 5; Dec.–Apr., daily 10–5, Sun. noon–5; closed first 2 wks in Jan.*

The **Salem Maritime National Historic Site,** run by the National Park Service, focuses on Salem's heritage as a major seaport with a thriving overseas trade. The park site includes the 1762 home of Elias Derby, America's first millionaire; the 1819 Customs House, made famous in Nathaniel Hawthorne's *The Scarlet Letter;* several sites relating to sea trade; and a replica of *The Friendship,* a 171-ft, three-masted 1797 trader merchant vessel. ⊠ *174 Derby St.,* ☎ *978/740–1660.* ▣ *Guided tours $3, grounds free.* ☉ *Daily 9–5.*

★ Salem's vast, dazzling maritime riches are the focal point of the **Peabody and Essex Museum,** which celebrated its 200th anniversary in 1999. The East India Hall Galleries on Liberty Street are filled with maritime art and history and the spoils of the Asian export trade—ranging from 16th-century Chinese blue porcelain to Indian colonial silver. Galleries in **Plummer Hall** on Essex Street house New England portraits, Revere silver, scrimshaw, a whale's jaw, and boat models that illustrate Salem's seafaring past. ⊠ *East India Sq.,* ☎ *978/745–9500 or 800/ 745–4054.* ▣ *$8.50; good for 2 consecutive days.* ☉ *Memorial Day– Oct., Mon.–Sat. 10–5, Sun. noon–5; Nov.–Memorial Day, Tues.–Sat. 10–5, Sun. noon–5.*

For an informative if somewhat hokey introduction to the 1692 witchcraft hysteria, visit the **Salem Witch Museum,** which stages a half-hour multisensory re-creation of the 1692 events, using 13 sets, life-size models, and a taped narration. The museum also sells an interesting pamphlet detailing the events that led to the witch trials. ⊠ *19½ Washington Sq. N,* ☎ *978/744–1692.* ⊡ *$4.50.* ⊙ *Daily 10–5 (until 7 July–Aug.).*

The figures at the **Salem Wax Museum of Witches and Seafarers** tell the town's story, detailing its rich maritime tradition and the witch-related hysterics of 1692. ⊠ *282–288 Derby St.,* ☎ *978/740–2929.* ⊡ *$4.50, or $7.95 for a combination ticket with the Salem Witch Village (☞ below).* ⊙ *Nov.–Apr., daily 9–5; May–June and Sept., daily 9–6; July–Aug. and Oct., daily 9–7.*

At the **Salem Witch Village,** you can learn about historic and modern witchcraft's spiritual and religious practices. ⊠ *282–288 Derby St.,* ☎ *978/740–2929.* ⊡ *$4.50, or $7.95 for a combination ticket with the Salem Wax Museum (☞ above).* ⊙ *Nov.–Apr., daily 9–5; May–June and Sept., daily 9–6; July–Aug. and Oct., daily 9–7.*

The **Witch Dungeon Museum** features a guided tour of dungeons where accused witches were kept and a live reenactment of one trial, as adapted from 1692 transcripts. ⊠ *16 Lynde St.,* ☎ *978/741–3570.* ⊡ *$4.50.* ⊙ *Apr.–Nov., daily 10–5; evening hrs around Halloween.*

No witch ever lived at **Witch House,** but more than 200 accused witches were questioned here. It's the only remaining structure with direct ties to the 1692 trials; the decor remains authentic to the period. ⊠ *310½ Essex St.,* ☎ *978/744–0180.* ⊡ *$5.* ⊙ *Mid-Mar.–Nov., daily 10–4:30 (until 6 July–Aug.).*

Ⓒ Children will enjoy the **Salem 1630 Pioneer Village,** where costumed "interpreters" help re-create the Salem of the early 17th century, when it was a fishing village and the Commonwealth's first capital. Replicas of thatched-roof cottages, period gardens, and wigwams have been constructed at the site. ⊠ *Forest River Park (follow Rte. 114 east, then turn left onto West Ave.),* ☎ *978/744–0991.* ⊡ *$5.* ⊙ *Apr.–Nov., Mon.–Sat. 10–5, Sun. noon–5.*

Ⓒ **Salem Willows Park,** at the eastern end of Derby Street, has picnic grounds, beaches, food stands, amusements, games, boat rentals, and fishing bait.

Although Salem became famous as the witch-trials city, it is Danvers (formerly Salem Village)—several miles northwest of present-day Salem—that has the real relics of the witchcraft episode. The **Rebecca Nurse Homestead** was the home of aged, pious Rebecca, a devout churchgoer accused of being a witch. The charge caused shock waves in the community. Her trial was a mockery (she was first pronounced innocent, but the jury was urged to change its verdict), and she was hanged in 1692. Her family secretly buried her body somewhere on the grounds of this house, which has period furnishings and 17th-century vegetable and herb gardens. ⊠ *149 Pine St., Danvers,* ☎ *978/774–8799.* ⊡ *$3.50.* ⊙ *May–Labor Day, Tues.–Sun. 1–4:30; Labor Day–Oct., weekends 1–4:30 or by appointment; May–mid-June, by appointment.*

Dining and Lodging

$$–$$$ ✕ **Chase House.** This restaurant on Pickering Wharf overlooking the harbor is extremely busy in summer. The menu emphasizes steaks, seafood, and pasta. A house specialty is the baked lobster stuffed with still more lobster and, for the abstemious, the "heart-healthy" scrod. ⊠ *Pickering Wharf,* ☎ *978/744–0000. AE, D, DC, MC, V.*

$$-$$$ ✕ **The Grapevine.** An inviting upscale bistro opposite Pickering Wharf, the Grapevine serves contemporary northern Italian fare. The lunch menu include pastas and risottos. Among the changing dinner offerings are lamb scallopini sautéed with green peppercorns, shrimp and roasted garlic ravioli, and balsamic-glazed pork chops with Vidalia-onion home fries, as well as vegetarian selections. ✉ *26 Congress St.,* ☎ *978/745–9335. AE, MC, V.*

$$$ ✕🏨 **Hawthorne Hotel.** An imposing redbrick structure, this hotel stands on the green, just a short walk from the commercial center, the waterfront, and other attractions. Guest rooms are appointed with reproduction 18th-century antiques, armchairs, and desks. The hotel's formal, chandelier-bedecked restaurant, Nathaniel's, is one of the more elegant eateries in Salem; the ambitious menu includes lobster, swordfish in mustard cream, prime rib, and poached sole on spinach with a champagne sauce. ✉ *18 Washington Sq. W, 01970,* ☎ *978/744–4080 or 800/729–7829,* FAX *978/745–9842. 83 rooms, 6 suites. Restaurant, bar, lounge, exercise room, meeting rooms. AE, D, DC, MC, V.*

$$-$$$ 🏨 **Inn at Seven Winter St.** Built in 1871, this inn has been authentically restored to re-create the Victorian era. Rooms are spacious and well furnished, with heavy mahogany and walnut antiques. Some open to a deck, some have whirlpool tubs, and some have marble fireplaces. The one-room studio has a microwave and refrigerator; the suites have kitchens. The no-smoking inn is better suited to couples than families. ✉ *7 Winter St., 01970,* ☎ *978/745–9520 or 800/932–5547,* FAX *978/745–0523. 7 rooms, 2 suites, 1 studio. Breakfast room. Continental breakfast. AE, MC, V.*

$-$$ 🏨 **Amelia Payson Guest House.** This elegantly restored 1845 Greek Revival house has been converted into a bright, airy bed-and-breakfast; it is near all historic attractions. The pretty rooms, which have nonworking marble fireplaces, are decorated with floral-print wallpaper, brass and canopy beds, and white wicker furnishings. The downstairs parlor has a grand piano. Smoking is not allowed. ✉ *16 Winter St., 01970,* ☎ *978/744–8304. 3 rooms, 1 studio. Breakfast room. Continental breakfast. AE, MC, V.*

Shopping

The **Broom Closet** (✉ 3 Central St., ☎ 978/741–3669) stocks dried herbs, aromatic oils, candles, tarot cards, and New Age music. **Crow Haven Corner** (✉ 125 Essex St., ☎ 978/745–8763) is the former haunt of Laurie Cabot, once dubbed Salem's "official" witch. Her daughter, Jody, now presides over crystal balls, herbs, tarot decks, healing stones, and books about witchcraft. **Pyramid Books** (✉ 214 Derby St., ☎ 978/745–7171) stocks New Age and metaphysical books.

The **Pickering Wharf Antique Gallery** (☎ 978/741–3113) has five rooms with about 30 dealers.

Manchester-by-the-Sea

30 *9 miles northeast of Salem, 28 mi northeast of Boston.*

Incorporated in 1645, Manchester became a fashionable summer community for well-to-do urbanites in the mid-19th century. Today it is a small seaside commuter suburb built around a picturesque harbor. Bostonians visit the town for its lovely, long **Singing Beach** (✉ Off Rte. 127), so called because of the noise your feet make against the white sand. The beach has lifeguards, food stands, and rest rooms, but no parking; either take the commuter train from Boston or park in the private pay lot ($15 per day for nonresidents) by the railroad station—a ½-mi walk to the beach.

Lodging

$–$$ 🏠 **Old Corner Inn.** Built in 1865 and once used as the summer residence of the Danish Embassy, the Old Corner Inn has bedrooms with bird's-eye maple floors, four-poster beds, brass gaslight-era fixtures, featherbeds, and claw-foot tubs. Some rooms have working fireplaces. Although the country location is attractive, it's a mile walk from the village center and about 1½ miles from the beach. An apartment with bedroom, sitting room, private bath, and kitchenette is available. ✉ *2 Harbor St., 01944,* ☎ *978/526–4996. 8 rooms, 5 with bath; 1 apartment. Continental breakfast. AE, MC, V.*

Gloucester

❸❶ *8 mi east of Manchester, 36 mi northeast of Boston.*

On Gloucester's fine seaside promenade is a famous statue of a man steering a ship's wheel, his eyes searching the horizon. The statue, which honors those "who go down to the sea in ships," was commissioned by the town citizens in 1923 in celebration of Gloucester's 300th anniversary. The oldest seaport in the nation, this is a workaday town and still a major fishing port. One portrait of Gloucester's fishing community can be found in Sebastian Junger's 1997 book, *A Perfect Storm,* about a Gloucester fishing boat caught in "the storm of the century" in October 1991.

The creative side of the town's personality is illuminated by the **Rocky Neck** neighborhood, the first-settled artists' colony in the United States. Its alumni include Winslow Homer, Maurice Prendergast, Jane Peter, and Cecilia Beaux. Today Rocky Neck remains home to many artists; its galleries are usually open daily 10 AM to 10 PM during the busy summer months. To get here, follow East Main Street from downtown toward Eastern Point.

Gloucester has some of the best beaches on the North Shore. Parking for the beaches costs about $10 on weekdays and about $15 on weekends, when the lots often fill by 10 AM. **Wingaersheek Beach** (✉ Exit 13 off Rte. 128) is a well-protected cove of white sand and dunes, with the white Annisquam lighthouse in the bay. **Good Harbor Beach** (✉ Signposted from Rte. 127A) is a dune-backed beach with a rocky islet just offshore. **Long Beach** (✉ Off Rte. 127A on Gloucester-Rockport town line) is another excellent place for sunbathing; parking is $5.

Hammond Castle Museum, a stone "medieval" castle built in 1926 by the inventor John Hays Hammond, Jr., contains medieval-style furnishings and paintings. The Great Hall houses an organ impressive for its 8,200 pipes. From the castle you can also see "Norman's Woe Rock," made famous by Longfellow in his poem *The Wreck of the Hesperus.* ✉ *80 Hesperus Ave. (on the south side of Gloucester off Rte. 127),* ☎ *978/283–2080 or 978/283–7673.* 🎫 *$6.* ☉ *Memorial Day–Labor Day, daily 9–6; Labor Day–mid-Oct., weekends 10–4; Nov. 1–Memorial Day, weekends 10–4. The museum often closes to host weddings or special events; call ahead to check hrs.*

Dining and Lodging

$$$ ✕ **White Rainbow.** The dining room in this excellent restaurant is in
★   the basement of a downtown store, and candlelight provides a romantic atmosphere. The Continental and new American specialties include Maui onion soup, grilled filet mignon, lobster, and fresh fish of the day. ✉ *65 Main St.,* ☎ *978/281–0017. AE, D, DC, MC, V.*

$$–$$$ ✕ **Evie's Rudder.** Quaint and quirky, this Rocky Neck restaurant has been dishing up good food and entertainment in a century-old former fish-packing plant for more than 40 years. You can sit in the dimly lighted

dining room or outside on a wharf-side deck to feast on seafood, chicken, steak, and New England clam chowder. ⊠ *73 Rocky Neck Ave.,* ☎ *978/283–7967. D, MC, V. Closed Nov.–Mar.; Apr. and Oct. reduced hrs.*

$–$$ ⌕ **Cape Ann Motor Inn.** This wood-shingle, three-story motel is as close to the sand as they come, right on Long Beach on the Gloucester-Rockport line. Half the smallish rooms have kitchenettes, and all have balconies and superb views over beach, sea, and the twin lights of Thatcher's Island. ⊠ *33 Rockport Rd., 01930,* ☎ *978/281–2900 or 800/464–8439,* FAX *978/281–1359. 30 rooms, 1 suite. Continental breakfast. AE, D, MC, V.*

$–$$ ⌕ **Cape Ann's Marina Resort.** This year-round hostelry less than a mile from Gloucester really comes alive in summer, when a full-service restaurant, a whale-watch boat, and deep-sea fishing excursions operate on and from the premises. The rooms, with views of the water, have color TVs, balconies, and air-conditioning, should the Atlantic breezes be insufficient. ⊠ *75 Essex Ave., 01930,* ☎ *978/283–2116 or 800/626–7660,* FAX *978/281–4905. 52 rooms. Restaurant (mid-Apr.– mid-Nov.), indoor pool. AE, D, MC, V.*

$–$$ ⌕ **Vista Motel.** The name is apt, because every room in this motel perched atop a small, steep hill overlooks the sea and Good Harbor Beach, just a few minutes' walk away. Some rooms have decks, all have refrigerators, and 20 also have a two-burner stove and cooking equipment. ⊠ *22 Thatcher Rd., 01930,* ☎ *978/281–3410. 40 rooms (30 in winter). Pool. AE, MC, V.*

Nightlife and the Arts

The **Rhumb Line** (⊠ 40 Railroad Ave., ☎ 978/283–9732) has good food and live entertainment every night but Tuesday, with rock-and-roll on Friday and Saturday and jazz on Sunday.

The **Gloucester Stage Company** (⊠ 267 E. Main St., ☎ 978/281–4099) is a nonprofit professional group that stages new plays and revivals. The **Hammond Castle Museum** (⊠ 80 Hesperus Ave., ☎ 978/283–2080) has a summer chamber-music concert series.

Outdoor Activities

BOATING

You can sail along the harbor and coast aboard the 65-ft schooner *Thomas E. Lannon,* crafted in Essex in 1996 and modeled after the great boats built a century ago. There are two-hour and half-day sails, as well as sunset and Sunday brunch cruises. ⊠ *37 Rogers St., Seven Seas Wharf,* ☎ *978/281–6634.*

FISHING

Captain Bill's Deep Sea Fishing/Whale Watch (⊠ 33 Harbor Loop, ☎ 978/283–6995 or 800/339–4253) operates full- and half-day excursions from May to October. **Coastal Fishing Charters,** under the same ownership as Cape Ann Whale Watch (⊠ Rose's Wharf, 415 Main St., ☎ 978/283–5113), operates day and evening fishing trips, kids' trips in Gloucester harbor, and island trips. The **Yankee Fishing Fleet** (⊠ 75 Essex Ave., ☎ 978/283–0313 or 800/942–5464) conducts deep-sea fishing trips.

WHALE-WATCHING

The most popular special-interest tours on the North Shore are whale-sighting excursions, which are generally offered from May through October. Reputable operations include **Cape Ann Whale Watch** (⊠ 415 Main St., ☎ 978/283–5110 or 800/877–5110); **Captain Bill's Whale Watch** (☞ Fishing, *above*); and **Yankee Whale Watch** (⊠ 75 Essex Ave., ☎ 978/283–0313 or 800/942–5464).

Rockport

③ *4 mi north of Gloucester, 40 mi north of Boston.*

Rockport, at the very tip of Cape Ann, derives its name from its granite formations. Many Boston-area structures are made of stone from the town's long-gone quarries. Rockport is a mecca for summer tourists attracted by its hilly rows of colorful clapboard houses, historic inns, artists' studios, and small bathing beaches. (It's also very accessible to Boston—the commuter rail stops in town.) Though it's a tourist haunt, Rockport has not gone overboard on T-shirt shacks and the other accoutrements of a summer economy: Shops sell crafts, folk and fine art, clothing, and cameras, and restaurants serve quiche, seafood, or homebaked cookies rather than fast food.

You can walk out to the end of **Bearskin Neck** for an impressive view of the open Atlantic. The nearby lobster shack in view is known as "Motif No. 1" because of its popularity as a subject for artists and amateur painters. The **Rockport Art Association Gallery** (⊠ 12 Main St., ☎ 978/546–6604), open all year, displays the best work of local artists.

Dining and Lodging

$$$ ✕ **My Place by the Sea.** This restaurant is perched right at the tip of Bearskin Neck, with a lower deck on rocks over the ocean. The menu offers New England seafood specialties such as lobster, plus steaks, pasta, salads, and sandwiches. ⊠ *Bearskin Neck,* ☎ *978/546–9667. AE, D, DC, MC, V. BYOB. Closed Nov.–Mar.*

$$–$$$ ✕ **Brackett's Oceanview Restaurant.** The big bay window of this homey restaurant has an excellent view across the beach. The menu includes scallop casserole, fish cakes, and other seafood dishes. ⊠ *27 Main St.,* ☎ *978/546–2797. AE, D, DC, MC, V. BYOB. Closed Nov.–late-Mar.*

$$–$$$ ✕ **The Greenery.** For lunch at this airy café try a sproutwich, which is loaded with cheese, mushrooms, sunflower seeds, and sprouts, or an entrée like crab-salad quiche or steamers. Pan-seared citrus salmon, lobster, and grilled swordfish with lime and Dijon mustard are among the seafood offerings at dinner, but you can also order steaks, burgers, and a chef's salad. ⊠ *15 Dock Square,* ☎ *978/546–9593. AE, MC, V. Closed Jan.–Apr. and Mon.–Tues. Nov.–Dec.*

$–$$ ✕ **Portside Chowder House.** This great little hole-in-the-wall is one of the few restaurants in Rockport open year-round. Chowder is the house specialty; also served are lobster and crab plates, salads, burgers, and sandwiches. ⊠ *Bearskin Neck,* ☎ *978/546–7045. No credit cards. Reduced hrs during winter; call ahead.*

$$–$$$$ ✕🗹 **Yankee Clipper Inn.** The imposing Georgian mansion, built as a
★ private home, that forms the main part of this perfectly located inn sits surrounded by gardens on a rocky point jutting into the sea. Guest rooms vary somewhat in size, but most are spacious. Furnished with antiques, they contain four-poster or canopy beds, and all but one have an ocean view. In the Quarterdeck, a newer building across the lawn, the rooms have fabulous sea views; the decor here is more modern, and rooms are good-size. The Bullfinch House across the street is an 1840 Greek Revival house, appointed with antique furnishings but with less-grand views. In the attached Veranda restaurant, diners sit on the glass-enclosed porch overlooking the water or in the cozy dining room off the parlor. Among the entrées are garlic-roasted duck, pumpkin ravioli in cream sauce with prosciutto, and Veranda sole, layered with cheese, crab meat, and fresh herbs and poached in a white wine sauce. ⊠ *96 Granite St., 01966,* ☎ *978/546–3407 or 800/545–3699,* FAX *978/546–9730. 26 rooms, 6 suites. Restaurant, pool. Full breakfast; MAP available. AE, D, MC, V. Closed mid-Dec.–Mar.*

$$–$$$ ⊡ **Addison Choate Inn.** This historic inn sits inconspicuously among
★ private homes, just a minute's walk from the center of Rockport. The
spacious rooms, with large tile bathrooms, are beautifully decorated;
the navy-and-white captain's room contains a canopy bed, handmade
quilts, and Oriental rugs. Other rooms—all with polished pine floors—
have their share of antiques and local seascape paintings. In the third-
floor suite, huge windows look out over the rooftops to the sea. The
two comfortably appointed duplex stable-house apartments have skylights, cathedral ceilings, and exposed wood beams. ⊠ *49 Broadway,
01966,* ☎ *978/546–7543 or 800/245–7543,* ℻ *978/546–7638. 5
rooms, 1 suite, 2 apartments. Pool. Continental breakfast. D, MC, V.*

$$–$$$ ⊡ **Seacrest Manor.** Surrounded by large gardens, this distinctive 1911
clapboard mansion sits atop a hill overlooking the sea; the inn's motto
is "Decidedly small, intentionally quiet." Two elegant sitting rooms are
furnished with antiques and leather chairs; one has a huge looking glass
salvaged from the old Philadelphia Opera House. The hall and staircase are hung with paintings—some depicting the inn—done by local
artists. Guest rooms vary in size and character and combine simple traditional and antique furnishings; some have large, private decks. ⊠ *99
Marmion Way, 01966,* ☎ *978/546–2211. 8 rooms, 6 with bath. Full
breakfast, afternoon tea. No credit cards. Closed Dec.–Mar.*

$–$$ ⊡ **Sally Webster Inn.** Sally Webster was a member of Hannah Jumper's
★ so-called hatchet gang, which smashed up the town's liquor stores in
1856 and turned Rockport into the dry town it remains today. Sally
lived in this house for much of her life, and the guest rooms are named
for members of her family. They contain rocking chairs; nonworking
brick fireplaces; pineapple four-poster, brass, canopy, or spool beds;
and wide-board pine floors covered with Oriental rugs. ⊠ *34 Mt. Pleasant St., 01966,* ☎ *978/546–9251 or 877/546–9251. 8 rooms. Continental breakfast. D, MC, V. Closed late Dec.–Jan.*

Nightlife and the Arts

During the **Rockport Chamber Music Festival** (☎ 978/546–7391),
mid-June to mid-July, musicians and music lovers gather for classical
concerts.

Shopping

An artist's colony, Rockport has a tremendous concentration of studios and galleries selling the work of local artists. Most of these are
on Main Street near the harbor and on Bearskin Neck. The *Rockport
Fine Arts Gallery Guide,* available from the Rockport Chamber of Commerce (☞ Visitor Information *in* North Shore A to Z, *below*), lists some
30 reputable galleries in town.

Essex

⑬ *12 mi west of Rockport, 31 mi north of Boston.*

The small, picturesque town of Essex, once an important shipbuilding center, is surrounded by salt marshes and is filled with antiques stores
and seafood restaurants.

The **Essex Shipbuilding Museum,** which is still a working shipyard, has
exhibits on 19th-century shipbuilding, including displays of period tools
and ship models. ⊠ *66 Main St. (Rte. 133),* ☎ *978/768–7541.* ☞ *$4.*
☉ *Late May–late Oct., Mon.–Sat. 10–5, Sun. 1–5; late Oct.–late May,
weekends 1–4.*

From April through October, you can explore the area's salt marshes,
rivers, and local wildlife during a 1½-hour narrated cruise on the *Essex
River Queen,* run by **Essex River Cruises** (⊠ Essex Marina, 35 Dodge
St., ☎ 978/768–6981 or 800/748–3706).

Dining

$$–$$$ ✕ **Jerry Pelonzi's Hearthside.** This 250-year-old converted farmhouse is the epitome of coziness. Four small dining rooms have open fireplaces and exposed beams: The first is low-ceilinged with stencils on the walls; the others have cathedral ceilings with rough-panel walls and small windows. Traditional entrées include baked stuffed haddock, seafood casserole, sirloin steak, lobster, and chicken. ⊠ *109 Eastern Ave./Rte. 133,* ☎ *978/768–6002 or 978/768–6003. AE, MC, V.*

$–$$ ✕ **Woodman's of Essex.** Back in 1916, Lawrence "Chubby" Wood-
★ man dipped a shucked clam in batter and threw it into the french fryer as a kind of joke, apparently creating the first fried clam in town. Today this large wooden shack with unpretentious booths is *the* place for seafood in the rough. The menu includes lobster, a raw bar, clam chowder, and, of course, fried clams. ⊠ *121 Main St. (Rte. 133),* ☎ *978/768–6451 or 800/649–1773. No credit cards.*

Shopping

Essex is a popular antiquing destination. Most of the shops are along Route 133 (Main St.). Here's a sampling: the **White Elephant** (⊠ 32 Main St., ☎ 978/768–6901); **Chebacco Antiques** (⊠ 38 Main St., ☎ 978/768–7371); **Howard's Flying Dragon Antiques** (⊠ 136 Main St., ☎ 978/768–7282).

Hamilton

㉞ *3 mi south of Ipswich, 33 mi north of Boston.*

Settled in 1638, incorporated in 1793, and named after Alexander Hamilton, the town of Hamilton is said to have the highest horse-to-person ratio in the Northeast. Most of the property in this small town is owned by a few families who are dedicated to keeping the landscape rural and undeveloped—there are miles of wooded trails.

The one spectator sport of note in horse-loving Hamilton is polo. The very grand **Myopia Hunt Club** (☎ 978/468–4433 or 978/468–7956 for polo schedules in season)—one of the most exclusive clubs in America—stages polo matches (open to the public) on weekends Memorial Day through October at its grounds along Route 1A.

Dining and Lodging

$$$ ✕ **The Black Cow.** A young professional crowd hangs out at this comfortable tap and grill. The food is similar to what you'd find at an upscale bar in Boston: smoked-chicken ravioli; grilled tuna steak with potatoes, oven-dried tomatoes, roasted onions, and capers; New York strip steak; and seared duck breast with pecan rice. ⊠ *16 Bay Rd./Rte. 1A,* ☎ *978/468–1166. AE, MC, V.*

$$–$$$$ ⌷ **Miles River Country Inn.** Staying in this sprawling Colonial home
★ amid acres of lawns and gardens is like being a guest at a private country estate. The guest rooms, living room, and sunporch are all comfortably appointed with country-style antiques. In winter you can cross-country ski for miles in fields and woods, right from the front door; in milder weather, you can wander the fields and gardens. Breakfast often includes eggs from the hens of the gracious innkeepers, Gretel and Peter Clark, and honey from Gretel's beehives. ⊠ *823 Bay Rd./Rte. 1A, 01936,* ☎ *978/468–7206. 8 rooms, 6 with bath. Cross-country skiing. AE, MC, V.*

Wenham

㉟ *2 mi south of Hamilton.*

Settled in 1635, Wenham is now a residential community with rolling fields, giant elms, and rows of maple trees. The lovely **Sedgwick Gar-**

dens at Long Hill surround the former summer home of Ellery Sedgwick, editor of the *Atlantic Monthly* from 1909 to 1938. The 114-acre property includes numerous gardens, a lotus pool, Chinese pagoda, and a woodland path lined with unusual plants. The gardens are on the town line with Beverly. ⊠ *Essex St./Rte. 22 (Exit 18 from Rte. 128), Beverly,* ☎ *978/921–1944.* ▨ *By donation.* ⊙ *Daily 8 AM–dusk.*

Ⅽ At the **Wenham Museum** kids can look at the extensive antique doll collection and the large room full of model trains. ⊠ *132 Main St. (Rte. 1A),* ☎ *978/468–2377.* ▨ *$4.* ⊙ *Tues.–Sun. 10–4, also some Mon. holidays.*

Ipswich

❸❻ *6 mi northwest of Essex, 36 mi north of Boston.*

Quiet little Ipswich, settled in 1633 and famous for its clams, is said to have more 17th-century houses standing and occupied than any other place in America; more than 40 were built before 1725. Among the noteworthy homes are the circa-1650 **John Whipple House** (⊠ 1 South Village Green), with large fireplaces and wide-board floors, and the **John Heard House** (⊠ 54 S. Main St.), a 1795 Federal-style house. Information and a booklet with a suggested walking tour are available at the **Visitor Information Center.** ⊠ *20 S. Main St., next to Town Hall,* ☎ *978/356–8540.* ⊙ *Summer and fall, daily 10–4.*

★ **Crane Beach,** one of the North Shore's most beautiful beaches, is 4 mi long and sandy, backed by dunes and a nature trail. Nearby, Castle Hill (☞ Nightlife and the Arts, *below*), a 59-room Stuart-style mansion built in 1927, is open for tours and summer concerts. ⊠ *290 Argilla Rd.,* ☎ *978/356–4354.* ▨ *Apr.–Labor Day, parking $10 weekdays, $15 weekends; Labor Day–Mar., parking $5.* ⊙ *Daily 8–sunset.*

Several small islands can be explored by taking a two-hour **Crane Island Tour** (☎ 978/356–4351) across the Castle Neck river. You can tour Hog Island, view sets from the 1996 film *The Crucible* (filmed here and in nearby Essex), and admire the many birds and wildlife protected at this refuge.

Ⅽ At **Goodale Orchards,** a short drive from the beach, you can pick-your-own of whatever fruit is in season or buy apples and other produce, while the kids feed the barnyard animals. A small winery produces hard cider and fruit wines. You can watch the regular cider being made with wood presses in the back of the barn. ⊠ *123 Argilla Rd.,* ☎ *978/356–5366.* ⊙ *May–Dec.*

Ⅽ **New England Alive** is a petting farm and nature study center with New England wild animals as well as farm animals and some reptiles. ⊠ *189 High St. (Rtes. 1A and 133),* ☎ *978/356–7013.* ▨ *$6.* ⊙ *May–Nov., weekdays 10–5, weekends 9:30–6.*

Dining

$ ✕ **Clam Box.** No visit to Ipswich is complete without a sampling of the town's famous clams, and where better than at a restaurant shaped like a box of fried clams? Since 1932, locals and tourists have come to this casual spot for excellent clams and the accompanying fries and onion rings. ⊠ *246 High St./Rte. 1A,* ☎ *978/356–9707. No credit cards.*

Nightlife and the Arts

Castle Hill (⊠ Argilla Rd., ☎ 978/356–7774) holds an annual summer festival of pop, folk, and classical music, plus a jazz ball and winter-holiday concert.

Outdoor Activities and Sports

The Massachusetts Audubon Society's **Ipswich River Wildlife Sanctuary** (⊠ 87 Perkins Row, Topsfield, ☎ 978/887–9264) contains trails through marshland hills with remains of early Colonial settlements as well as abundant wildlife. You can pick up a self-guiding trail map from the office, but note that the office and trails are closed Mondays. The sanctuary is southwest of Ipswich, 1 mi off Route 97.

Newburyport

③⑦ *12 mi north of Ipswich, 38 mi north of Boston.*

Newburyport's High Street is lined with some of the finest examples of Federal-era (1790–1810) mansions in New England. The city was once a leading port and shipbuilding center, and the houses were built for prosperous sea captains. An energetic downtown renewal program has brought new life to the town's brick-front center. Renovated buildings house restaurants, taverns, and shops that sell everything from nautical brasses to antique Oriental rugs. The civic improvements have been matched by private restorations of the town's housing stock, much of which dates from the 18th century, with a scattering of 17th-century homes in some neighborhoods.

Newburyport is a good walking city, and there is all-day free parking down by the water. A stroll through the **Waterfront Park and Promenade** yields a good view of the harbor and the fishing and pleasure boats that moor here. The **Custom House Maritime Museum,** built in 1835 in Classical Revival style, contains ship models, tools, paintings, and exhibits on maritime history. ⊠ *25 Water St.,* ☎ *978/462–8681.* ☞ *$3.* ☉ *Apr.–Dec., Mon.–Sat. 10–4, Sun. 1–4.*

A causeway leads from Newburyport to the narrow spit of land known as **Plum Island,** which harbors a summer colony (rapidly becoming year-round) at one end. **Parker River National Wildlife Refuge,** on Plum Island, comprises 4,662 acres of salt marsh, freshwater marsh, beaches, and dunes. Bird-watching, surf fishing, plum and cranberry picking, swimming, and hiking are among the exhilarating pastimes here. The 2-mi Hellcat Swamp Trail cuts through the marshes and sand dunes, taking in the best of the sanctuary. Trail maps are available at the office. The refuge is so popular in summer, especially on weekends, that cars begin to line up at the gate before 7 AM. Only a limited number of cars are let in, though there's no restriction on the number of people using the beach. ⊠ *Sunset Dr., about ½ mi south of bridge to Plum Island,* ☎ *978/465–5753.* ☞ *$5 per car; $2 for bicycles and walk-ins.* ☉ *Daily dawn–dusk. Beach sometimes closed during endangered-species nesting season in spring and early summer. No pets.*

Dining and Lodging

$$$ ✕ **Scandia.** This restaurant is well known locally for its fine cuisine;
★   among the house specialties are Caesar salad prepared table-side and a veal and lobster sauté. The narrow 15-table dining room is lighted with candles on the tables and chandeliers with candle bulbs. The Sunday brunch has hot entrées, cold salads, crepes, waffles, and omelets. ⊠ *25 State St.,* ☎ *978/462–6271. AE, D, DC, MC, V.*

$$–$$$ ☗ **Clark Currier Inn.** This 1803 Federal mansion has been restored with
★   care, taste, and imagination, making it one of the best inns on the North Shore. Guest rooms are spacious and furnished with antiques, including one with a glorious sleigh bed dating from the late 19th century. ⊠ *45 Green St., 01950,* ☎ *978/465–8363. 8 rooms. Continental breakfast. AE, D, MC, V.*

Nightlife and the Arts

The **Grog Shop** (⊠ 13 Middle St., ☎ 978/465–8008) hosts blues and rock bands several nights weekly.

Outdoor Activities and Sports

Surf casting is popular—bluefish, pollock, and striped bass can be taken from the ocean shores of Plum Island; permits to remain on the beach after dark are free for anyone entering Parker River National Wildlife Refuge (☞ *above*) with fishing equipment in the daylight. You don't need a permit to fish from the public beach at Plum Island. The best spot is around the mouth of the Merrimack River.

Newburyport Whale Watch (⊠ 54 Merrimac St., ☎ 978/465–9885 or 800/848–1111) operates deep-sea fishing charters and whale-watching and dinner cruises.

The North Shore A to Z

Arriving and Departing

BY BOAT

A boat leaves Boston for Gloucester daily between Memorial Day and Labor Day at 10 AM; the return boat leaves Gloucester at 3 PM. For information, contact **A. C. Cruise Lines** (⊠ 290 Northern Ave., Boston, ☎ 617/261–6633 or 800/422–8419).

BY BUS

The **Coach Company** bus line (☎ 800/874–3377) runs an express commuter bus between Boston and Newburyport on weekdays. **Massachusetts Bay Transportation Authority (MBTA)** buses (☎ 617/222–3200 for schedules) leave daily from Boston's Haymarket Station for Marblehead and Salem. Travel time is about 1 to 1¼ hours.

BY CAR

See Getting Around, *below.*

BY TRAIN

MBTA (☎ 617/222–3200 for schedules) trains travel from Boston's North Station to Salem (25–30 minutes), Manchester (40–50 minutes), Gloucester (55–60 minutes), Rockport (70 minutes), Ipswich (50–55 minutes), and Newburyport (60–65 minutes).

Getting Around

BY BUS

The **Cape Ann Transportation Authority** (CATA, ☎ 978/283–7916) covers the Gloucester, Rockport, and Essex region with buses and water shuttles.

BY CAR

The primary link between Boston and the North Shore is Route 128, which breaks off from I–95 and follows the coast northeast to Gloucester. To pick up Route 128 from Boston, take I–93 north to I–95 north to Route 128. If you stay on I–95, you'll reach Newburyport. A less direct route, but a scenic one north of Lynn, is Route 1A, which leaves Boston via the Callahan Tunnel. Beyond Beverly, Route 1A travels inland toward Ipswich and Essex; at this point, Route 127 follows the coast to Gloucester and Rockport.

From Boston to Salem or Marblehead, follow Route 128 to Route 114 into Salem and on to Marblehead. An alternate route to Marblehead: follow Route 1A north, then pick up Route 129 north along the shore through Swampscott and into Marblehead.

Contacts and Resources

Beverly Hospital (⊠ 85 Herrick St., Beverly, ☎ 978/922–3000).

CVS Pharmacy (⊠ 53 Dodge St., Beverly, ☎ 978/927–3291) is open 24 hours a day. **Walgreen's** (⊠ 201 Main St., Gloucester, ☎ 978/283–7361) is open until 10 on weeknights and until 6 on weekends.

Marblehead Chamber of Commerce (⊠ Box 76, 62 Pleasant St., Marblehead, 01945, ☎ 781/631–2868). **National Park Service Visitor Information** (⊠ 2 New Liberty St., Salem 02642, ☎ 978/740–1650). **North of Boston Visitors and Convention Bureau** (⊠ 17 Peabody Sq., Peabody, 01960, ☎ 978/977–7760 or 800/742–5306). **Rockport Chamber of Commerce** (⊠ Box 67, 3 Main St., Rockport, 01966, ☎ 978/546–6575).

THE PIONEER VALLEY

Updated by
Kay and Bill
Scheller

The Pioneer Valley, a string of historic settlements along the Connecticut River from Springfield in the south up to the Vermont border, formed the western frontier of New England from the early 1600s until the late 18th century. The river and its fertile banks first attracted farmers and traders, and the Connecticut later became a source of power and transport for the earliest industrial cities in America. The northern regions of the Pioneer Valley remain rural and tranquil; farms and small towns have typical New England architecture. Farther south, the cities of Holyoke and Springfield are more industrial. Educational pioneers came to this region as well—to form Mount Holyoke College, America's first college for women, and four other major colleges, as well as several well-known prep schools.

Northfield

😁 *97 mi northwest of Boston.*

Just south of the Vermont border, this country town is known mainly as a center for hikers, campers, and other lovers of the outdoors.

The **Northfield Mountain Recreation and Environmental Center** has 29 mi of hiking trails, and you can rent canoes and kayaks at the large campground at Barton Cove. From here you can paddle to the Munn's Ferry campground, accessible only by canoe. The center also runs 1½-hour sightseeing tours of the Pioneer Valley, along a 12-mi stretch of the Connecticut River between Northfield and Gill, on the *Quinnetukut II* riverboat. Bus tours head up the mountain, where you can see a large underground power station at work. In winter, the center rents cross-country skis and snowshoes and offers lessons. ⊠ 99 *Miller's Falls Rd.,* ☎ 413/659–3714. 🎫 *Bus tour free; riverboat tour $7.* ☉ *Wed.–Sun. 9–5. Bus tour Sept.–Oct., Wed.–Fri. noon–3, weekends 10–3; riverboat tour June–early Oct., Tues.–Sun. 11–3.*

Lodging

$–$$ 🏨 **Northfield Country House.** This big, lovely English manor house sits
★ on 16 acres of land amid thick woodlands. A wide staircase leads to the bedrooms; the three largest have fireplaces. Rooms are decorated with antiques, and several have brass beds. The two rooms that were once servants' quarters can be rented together as a suite. The owner has considerably renovated this century-old house and has planted hundreds of tulip and daffodil bulbs in the gardens. ⊠ 181 *School St., 01360,* ☎ 413/498–2692 or 800/498–2692. 7 rooms. Pool. Full breakfast. MC, V.

The Pioneer Valley

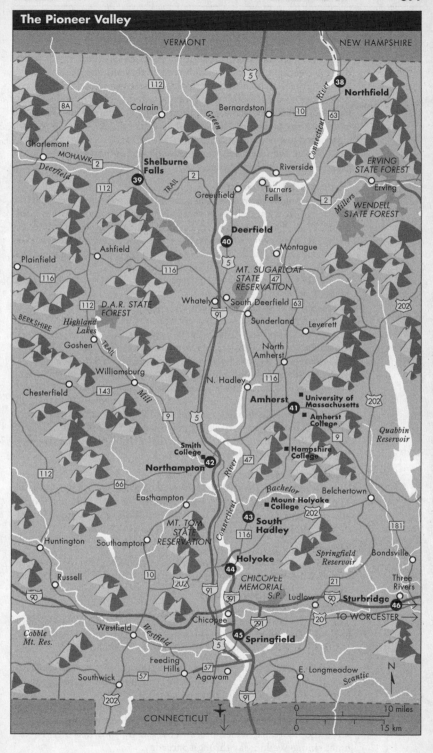

VERMONT

NEW HAMPSHIRE

112

5

8A

Colrain

Bernardston

38 **Northfield**

10

63

Charlemont

MOHAWK 2

Deerfield

Shelburne Falls

39

TRAIL

2

Greenfield

Turners Falls

Riverside

Connecticut River

Green River

Miller

ERVING STATE FOREST

Erving

2

WENDELL STATE FOREST

Ashfield

116

Deerfield

40

5

Montague

Plainfield

112

D.A.R. STATE FOREST

BERKSHIRE

Highland Lakes

TRAIL

Goshen

Whately

South Deerfield

MT. SUGARLOAF STATE RESERVATION

47

91

63

Sunderland

Leverett

202

Williamsburg

Mill

North Amherst

Chesterfield

143

9

5

N. Hadley

116

Amherst

41

University of Massachusetts

Amherst College

202

112

66

Northampton

42

Smith College

Connecticut River

47

9

Hampshire College

Quabbin Reservoir

Easthampton

Bachelor

Mount Holyoke College

Belchertown

Huntington

Southampton

MT. TOM STATE RESERVATION

116

43 **South Hadley**

202

Springfield Reservoir

181

Bondsville

Russell

10

202

91

Holyoke

44

CHICOPEE MEMORIAL S.P.

21

Three Rivers

90

391

Ludlow

90

Sturbridge

46

Cobble Mt. Res.

Westfield

Chicopee

291

20

TO WORCESTER

Westfield River

45 **Springfield**

5

Southwick

57

Feeding Hills

57

Agawam

E. Longmeadow

Scantic

202

91

N

CONNECTICUT

0   10 miles

0   15 km

Shelburne Falls

39 *106 mi northwest of Boston.*

A near-perfect example of small-town America, Shelburne Falls straddles the Deerfield River. A sprinkling of quality antiques shops and the Copper Angel Restaurant overlooking the river make the village a good place to spend a half day. From May to October an arched, 400-ft abandoned trolley bridge is transformed by Shelburne Falls' Women's Club into the **Bridge of Flowers** (⊠ at Water St., ☎ 413/625–2544), a gardened promenade bursting with colors. In the riverbed just downstream from the town are 50 immense **glacial potholes** ground out of granite during the last ice age.

Dining and Lodging

$$–$$$ ✕ **Copper Angel Restaurant.** This restaurant between the Deerfield River and State Street specializes in vegetarian cuisine but also serves poultry and fish. The organic produce–based menu includes lentil cutlets with vegetarian gravy, a tofu stir-fry with peanut sauce, stuffed chicken breast with garlic mashed potatoes, and orange-pepper shrimp. A deck over the water is pleasant for summer dining. ⊠ *2 State St., ☎ 413/625–2727. Reservations not accepted. MC, V. Closed Mon.–Tues. Nov.–Mar.*

$ ✕ **Shelburne Falls Coffee Roasters.** A good pit stop inside an old farmhouse, this coffeehouse, which opens at 6 AM (and closes at 6 PM), serves coffees, teas, espresso drinks, soups, and focaccia. For dessert try the shortbread or chocolate-chip cookies. ⊠ *Rte. 2, 4 mi east of Shelburne Falls village, ☎ 413/625–0116. No credit cards. No dinner.*

$$ 🏠 **Penfrydd Farm.** In the middle of a 160-acre working farm, this serene B&B occupies a rejuvenated farmhouse and has exposed beams, skylights, and a big whirlpool tub. The ideal place to get away from it all, Penfrydd Farm has fabulous fall foliage and plenty of snow for snowshoeing and cross-country skiing in winter. ⊠ *Box 100A, R.R. 1, 105 Hillman Rd., Colrain 01340, ☎ 413/624–5516. 4 rooms. Cross-country skiing. Continental breakfast. MC, V.*

Outdoor Activities and Sports

You can raft along the Deerfield River at Charlemont, on the Mohawk Trail. From April to October **Zoar Outdoor** (☎ 413/339–4010) operates one-day raft tours over 10 mi of Class II–III rapids daily. The outfit also conducts canoe and kayak tours and rock climbs.

Shopping

The **Salmon Falls Artisans Showroom** (⊠ Ashfield St., ☎ 413/625–9833) carries sculpture, pottery, glass, and furniture by 175 local artisans.

Skiing and Snow Sports

BERKSHIRE EAST

This ski area attracts a mostly regional college crowd and loyal families and youngsters interested in the area's racing program. ⊠ *Box 727, South River Rd., Charlemont 01339, ☎ 413/339–6617.*

Downhill. The 1,200-ft vertical was once considered more difficult than that of neighboring ski areas. Blasting, widening, and sculpting tamed many of the steeper trails, but you can still find steep pitches toward the top. Wide, cruisable intermediate slopes are plentiful, as is beginner terrain. One triple and three double chairlifts and one surface lift serve the 36 trails, which are all covered by snowmaking. There's night skiing Wednesday through Saturday.

Child care. The nursery takes infants and children up to 8 years old on weekends; children under 6 ski free. Older children can take classes at the ski school. Aspiring racers from age 5 to 18 can train on weekends.

Deerfield

⑩ *10 mi southeast of Shelburne Falls.*

Deerfield is the perfect New England village, though not without a past darkened by tragedy. A horse pulling a carriage clip-clops past perfectly maintained 18th-century homes, neighbors leave their doors unlocked and tip their hats to strangers, kids play ball in fields by the river, and the bell of the impossibly beautiful brick church peals from a white steeple. Settled by Native Americans more than 8,000 years ago, Deerfield was originally a Pocumtuck village—deserted after deadly epidemics and a war with the Mohawks that all but wiped out the tribe. English pioneers eagerly settled into this frontier outpost in the 1660s and 1670s, but two bloody massacres at the hands of the Indians and the French caused the village to be abandoned until 1707, when construction began on the buildings that remain today.

★ Although it has a turbulent past, **Historic Deerfield** now basks in a genteel aura. **The Street**, a tree-lined avenue of 18th- and 19th-century houses, is protected and maintained as a museum site, with 14 of the preserved buildings open to the public year-round. Some homes contain antique furnishings and decorative arts; other buildings exhibit textiles, silver, pewter, or ceramics. The well-trained guides are able to converse knowledgeably about the exhibits and Deerfield's history. With 52 buildings on 93 acres, this village provides an impressive glimpse into 18th- and 19th-century American life. Start your visit at the information center in Hall Tavern and don't miss the **Wells-Thorn House**, whose rooms depict life as it changed from 1725 to 1850. You could spend several days in Historic Deerfield, but plan on at least one full day. Purchase of an all-house admission ticket includes access to the new **Flynt Center of Early New England Life** (⊠ 37D Old Main St.), which houses two exhibit galleries. One of the galleries holds 2,500 decorative objects from 1600 to the present. ⊠ *The Street,* ☎ *413/774-5581.* 🖪 *1-wk admission to all houses $12; single-house admission $6.* ☉ *Daily 9:30–4:30.*

🄲 The massive store at the **Yankee Candle Company and Car Museum** in South Deerfield holds millions of candles, Christmas decorations, and foodstuffs. The Bavarian Christmas Village provides an imaginative shopping experience; kids love the Dip-Your-Own Candle station. The outdoor patio at Chandler's Tavern Restaurant is a delightful spot for lunch. The car museum exhibits more than 70 American and European cars, including Lamborghinis, antique classics, and novelty dragsters. ⊠ *U.S. 5/Rte. 10, S. Deerfield,* ☎ *413/665-2929.* 🖪 *Store free; museum $5.* ☉ *Daily 9:30–6; call for holiday hrs.*

Dining and Lodging

$$$ ✕ **Sienna.** The atmosphere at Sienna is soothing and the service well
★ mannered, but the food is what really shines. Choices from the ever-changing menu might include tuna loin on a light stir-fry of zucchini, fennel, and gnocchi with a mustard sauce. After an irresistible dessert, your evening ends with the personal touch of a handwritten check on stationery. ⊠ *6 Elm St., S. Deerfield,* ☎ *413/665-0215. Reservations essential. MC, V. Closed Mon.–Tues. No lunch.*

$$$-$$$$ ✕🏨 **Deerfield Inn.** Period wallpapers decorate the rooms in the main
★ inn, which was built in 1884; the rooms in an outbuilding have identical papers but are newer (1981) and closer to the parking lot. All rooms have antiques and replicas, sofas, and bureaus, and some have four-poster or canopy beds. The restaurant's menu ($$$), which showcases American cuisine, changes monthly, but two house specialties—duck and Indian pudding—are always available. The inn is no-smoking. ⊠

81 Old Main St., 01342, ☎ *413/774–5587 or 800/926–3865,* FAX *413/ 773–8712. 23 rooms. Restaurant, bar, coffee shop. Full breakfast. AE, DC, MC, V.*

$ ✕☷ **Whately Inn.** Antiques and four-poster beds slope gently on old-wood floors at the Whately. The dining room ($–$$) has a fireplace and exposed beams, tables on a raised stage at one end, and some booths; it's dimly lighted, with candles on the tables. Prime Angus steaks, baked lobster with shrimp stuffing, rack of lamb, and other entrées come with salad, appetizer, dessert, and coffee. The restaurant is very busy on weekends; Sunday dinner begins at 1 PM. The full menu is also served in the more casual lounge. ⊠ *Chestnut Plain Rd., Whately Center 01093,* ☎ *413/665–3044 or 800/942–8359. 4 rooms. Restaurant. AE, D, DC, MC, V.*

$$–$$$ ☷ **Brandt House Country Inn.** The owner of this 16-room, turn-of-the-
★ century Colonial Revival mansion set on 3½ manicured acres is an interior decorator, and her touch is evident throughout. The sun-lit, spacious common rooms are filled with plants, plump easy chairs, and handsome contemporary furnishings; the elegantly appointed guest rooms have feather beds. Still, the emphasis is on comfort and hominess, and kids and well-behaved dogs are welcome. Breakfast is served on the porch in nice weather, or in bed on request. Room 8, with a full kitchen and sleeping loft, sleeps up to five. The inn is 7 mi north of Deerfield. ⊠ *29 Highland Ave., Greenfield 01301,* ☎ *413/774–3329 or 800/235–3329,* FAX *413/772–2908. 10 rooms, 8 with bath; 1 suite. Billiard room, tennis court. Continental breakfast weekdays, full breakfast weekends. MC, V.*

$–$$ ☷ **Yellow Gabled House.** Edna Stahelek has often been told she reminds guests of their mother or favorite aunt. Her home, built circa 1800, is sunny and gracious, with an elegant dining room and a living room with a grandfather clock and other antiques. The upstairs guest rooms include a suite with a private bath and sitting room. The no-smoking B&B is just off I–91, 4 mi from Historic Deerfield. ⊠ *111 N. Main St., South Deerfield 01373,* ☎ *413/665–4922. 2 rooms share bath, 1 suite. Full breakfast. No credit cards.*

$ ☷ **Sunnyside Farm Bed and Breakfast.** Maple antiques and family heirlooms decorate this inn's country-style rooms, all of which are hung with fine-art reproductions and have views across the fields. A full country breakfast, often including strawberries from the farm next door, is served family-style in the dining room. The farm is about 8 mi south of Deerfield, convenient to cross-country skiing, mountain biking, and hiking. ⊠ *21 River Rd., Whately 01093,* ☎ *413/665–3113. 5 rooms without bath. Pool. Full breakfast. No credit cards.*

Amherst

❹ *14 mi south of Deerfield.*

Three of the Pioneer Valley's five major colleges—the University of Massachusetts (UMass), Amherst College, and Hampshire College—are in small but lively Amherst, which has a large village green. Its bookstores, bars, and cafés reflect the area's youthful orientation.

The poet Emily Dickinson (1830–86) was born and died in the **Emily Dickinson Homestead.** The house contains some of the poet's belongings, but most of her manuscripts are elsewhere. Guided tours are the only way to visit the house, and reservations are advisable. ⊠ *280 Main St.,* ☎ *413/542–8161.* ☜ *$4.* ☉ *Wed.–Sat.; call for hrs.*

The **Amherst History Museum at the Strong House,** built in the mid-1700s, has an extensive collection of household tools, furniture, china, and clothing that reflects changing styles of interior decoration. Most items are Amherst originals, dating from the 18th to the mid-20th century. ⊠ *67 Amity St.,* ☎ *413/256–0678.* ⛉ *$3.* ⊙ *May–mid-Oct., Wed.–Sat. 12:30–4; mid-Oct.–May, Fri.–Sat. 12:30–4.*

The effort to save Yiddish books and preserve Jewish culture has become a major movement, and the **National Yiddish Book Center** is its core. The center is housed in a thatched-roof building that resembles a cluster of structures typical of a shtetl, or traditional Eastern European Jewish village. Inside, a contemporary space contains more than 1.3 million books, a fireside reading area, a kosher dining area, and a visitor center with exhibits. The work here is performed out in the open: Hundreds of books pour in daily, and workers come across everything from family keepsakes to rare manuscripts. ⊠ *Harry and Jeanette Weinberg Building, Hampshire College, Rte. 116,* ☎ *800/535–3595.* ⛉ *Free.* ⊙ *Sun.–Fri. 10–3:30.*

Dining and Lodging

$–$$ ✕ **Judie's.** For 20 years students have crowded around small tables on the glassed-in porch at Judie's, ordering burgers, salads, sandwiches, fancy pastas, and delicious desserts. The atmosphere is casual and artsy—a painting on canvas covers each tabletop. ⊠ *51 N. Pleasant St.,* ☎ *413/253–3491. Reservations not accepted. AE, D, MC, V.*

$ ✕ **Black Sheep.** Newspapers and books are strewn about the tables at this student-oriented counter-service café, which typifies Amherst dining. A half dozen coffee selections complement excellent desserts and creative, high-quality sandwiches that include the C'est la brie (a baguette smothered with brie, roasted peppers, spinach, and raspberry mustard) and the French Kiss (truffle pâté, Dijon mustard, and red onion on a baguette). The Black Sheep opens daily at 7 AM. ⊠ *79 Main St.,* ☎ *413/253–3442. MC, V.*

$$–$$$ ✕⊡ **Lord Jeffery Inn.** This gabled brick inn sits on the green between the town center and the Amherst College campus. Many bedrooms have a light floral decor; others have stencils and pastel woodwork. The formal dining room, where traditional dishes are served, is collegiate and Colonial, with old wood panels, heavy drapery, and a large fireplace. Burgers, salads, and the like are served at Boltwood's Tavern, which has a small bar and a wraparound porch. ⊠ *30 Boltwood Ave., 01002,* ☎ *413/253–2576 or 800/742–0358,* ℻ *413/256–6152. 40 rooms, 8 suites. Restaurant, bar. AE, DC, MC, V.*

$–$$$ ⊡ **Allen House Victorian Inn.** A rare find, this inn built in 1886 has
★ been restored with precision: It's a glorious reproduction of the Aesthetic period of the Victorian era. Busy, colorful wallcoverings reach to the high ceilings. Antiques include a burled walnut headboard and dresser set, wicker "steamship" chairs, screens, and carved golden-oak beds. Lace curtains grace the windows in the rooms, whose supremely comfortable beds have goose-down comforters. Allen House is a short walk from the center of Amherst. ⊠ *599 Main St., 01002,* ☎ *413/253–5000. 7 rooms. Full breakfast. No credit cards.*

$–$$ ⊡ **Campus Center Hotel.** Atop the UMass campus and convenient to all of Amherst, this modern hotel has spacious rooms with large windows that allow excellent views over campus and countryside. The walls are exposed cinderblock, and the rooms have simple furnishings. Guests can use university exercise facilities with prior reservation, and because the hotel is at a college, no tax is charged for accommodations. ⊠ *University of Massachusetts, Murray D. Lincoln Tower, 01003,* ☎ *413/549–6000,* ℻ *413/545–1210. 116 rooms, 2 suites. Restaurant, 2 indoor pools, 3 tennis courts. AE, D, DC, MC, V.*

Nightlife and the Arts

Major ballet and modern dance companies appear in season at the **UMass**

Fine Arts Center (⊠ Haigis Hall, ☏ 413/545–2511). The **William D. Mullens Memorial Center** (⊠ University Dr., University of Massachusetts, ☏ 413/545–0505) hosts concerts, theatrical productions, and other entertainment.

Outdoor Activities and Sports

BIKING

Valley Bicycles (⊠ 319 Main St., ☏ 413/256–0880) rents bikes and dispenses cycling advice.

FISHING

The Connecticut River sustains shad, salmon, and several dozen other fish species. At **BioShelters** (⊠ 500 Sunderland Rd., ☏ 413/549–3558) you pay $2.50 ($6 for a family of four) to drop your line, plus an amount that varies depending on what fish you catch and the size.

Shopping

The **Leverett Crafts and Arts Center** (⊠ Montague Rd., Leverett, ☏ 413/548–9070) houses 20 resident artists who create jewelry, ceramics, glass, and textiles.

Atkins Farms Country Market (⊠ Rte. 116, South Amherst, ☏ 413/253–9528), surrounded by a sea of apple orchards and gorgeous views of the Holyoke Ridge, is an institution in the Pioneer Valley. Hay rides take place in the fall, and there are children's events year-round. The farm sells many varieties of apples and other fresh produce, along with delicious cider doughnuts.

OFF THE
BEATEN PATH

QUABBIN RESERVOIR – This reservoir, which provides drinking water for the greater Boston area, was created in 1939 by flooding the Swift River valley, including four towns. Today the Quabbin is a quiet retreat with facilities for fishing, hiking, and picnicking. The two great dams that hold back 400 billion gallons of water can be viewed at the south end, near the visitor center. The center displays pictures of the drowned villages. No fire, alcohol, or dogs are permitted. ⊠ *485 Ware Rd., off Rte. 9, 15 mi southeast of Amherst, Belchertown,* ☏ *413/323–7221.* ▣ *Free.* ☉ *Visitor center daily 9–4:30; grounds daily dawn–dusk.*

Northampton

42 *8 mi northeast of Amherst.*

The small, bustling college town of Northampton is listed on the National Register of Historic Places. Tracy Kidder's 1999 nonfiction book *Home Town* describes how the community has successfully absorbed an influx of new residents over the past few decades. Packed with restaurants and activists, the town, first settled in 1654, is most famous as the site of **Smith College,** the nation's largest liberal arts college for women. The redbrick quadrangles of this institution founded in 1871 resemble the layouts of the women's colleges at Cambridge University, England, which were built around the same period. Worth visiting are the **Lyman Plant House** and the **botanic gardens.** The College Art Museum (⊠ Elm St., ☏ 413/584–2700), which holds more than 24,000 objects and works in a variety of media, is open in the afternoon from Tuesday to Sunday.

Historic Northampton maintains three houses that are open for tours: Parsons House (1730), Shepherd House (1798), and Damon House (1813). ⊠ *Headquarters, 46 Bridge St.,* ☏ *413/584–6011.* ▣ *Houses $3.* ☉ *Tours Mar.–Dec., Thurs.–Sun. noon–4.*

The folks who concocted the Teenage Mutant Ninja Turtles cartoon ☺ characters in the 1980s operate the **Words and Pictures Museum,** a repository of sequential art where you can see the latest comic books and graphic novels and create your own. ⊠ *140 Main St.,* ☎ *413/586–8545.* ▨ *$3.* ☉ *Sun. and Tues.–Thurs. noon–5, Fri. noon–8, Sat. 10–8.*

Northampton was the Massachusetts home of the 30th U.S. president, Calvin Coolidge. He practiced law here and served as mayor from 1910 to 1911. The **Coolidge Room** at the **Forbes Library** (⊠ 20 West St., ☎ 413/587–1011) contains a collection of his papers and memorabilia.

☺ Within **Look Memorial Park** (⊠ 300 N. Main St., Florence, ☎ 413/ 584–5457) are a small zoo, a wading pool, and children's playgrounds.

Dining and Lodging

$$ ✗ **Eastside Grill.** One of the dining rooms here is a glassed-in porch, and the other is wood-paneled with comfortable wood-and-leather booths. The menu includes a large selection of appetizers, great if you've just stopped by for a drink, and entrées such as blackened fish of the day and oysters on the half shell. ⊠ *19 Strong Ave.,* ☎ *413/ 586–3347. AE, D, DC, MC, V. No lunch.*

$–$$ ✗ **Hunan Gourmet.** In a college town that knows its Chinese food, the Gourmet has been favored by discerning locals for years. The prices are low enough to appeal to students, and there are plenty of red-star items to satisfy hot-and-spicy fans. Among the house specialties are Hunan Triple Crown (jumbo shrimp, chicken, and roast pork with fresh vegetables in a spicy sauce) and Tsing Tao duck (shredded Beijing duck sautéed with shredded vegetables in a special sauce). ⊠ *261 King St.,* ☎ *413/585–0202. AE, MC, V.*

$–$$ ✗ **Northampton Brewery.** This microbrewery serves quality pub food— burgers, pizza, porterhouse steak—and exotic home brews. You can sup in warm weather on the roof deck, which also has a bar. ⊠ *11 Brewster Ct.,* ☎ *413/584–9903. AE, D, MC, V.*

$–$$ ✗ **Paul and Elizabeth's.** Plants fill this high-ceiling natural-foods restaurant. Among the seasonal dishes are butternut-squash soup, a large salad platter, Japanese tempura, and innovative fish entrées. ⊠ *150 Main St.,* ☎ *413/584–4832. AE, MC, V.*

$ ✗ **Sylvester's Restaurant.** Few people have heard of Dr. Sylvester Graham, a 19th-century Northampton resident, but most Americans are familiar with the graham cracker, which was named after him. Graham believed in eating healthful foods and exercising, unpopular ideas in the 1830s: Emerson called him "the poet of bran bread and pumpkins." His former home has been converted into a restaurant that serves homemade breads and healthy soups. Breakfast is served all day, and brunch—served weekends until 3—can be a crowded event. ⊠ *111 Pleasant St.,* ☎ *413/586–5343. MC, V. No dinner.*

$$–$$$ ✗▥ **Hotel Northampton.** You can pull up a wicker chair on the porch of this downtown hotel and watch Northampton go by. Room furnishings include Colonial reproductions and heavy curtains. Some rooms have four-poster beds, balconies overlooking a busy street or the parking lot, whirlpool tubs, and heated towel racks. Extensive renovations and a new wing are welcome changes. The Wiggins Tavern (no lunch) serves hearty American fare and an elaborate Sunday brunch; the Coolidge Park Café serves burgers and sandwiches. ⊠ *36 King St., 01060,* ☎ *413/584–3100 or 800/547–3529,* ☒ *413/584–9455. 99 rooms, 6 suites, 2 efficiency units. 2 restaurants, bar, no-smoking rooms. Continental breakfast. AE, D, DC, MC, V.*

$$ ▥ **Inn at Northampton.** Country French prints hang on the walls of this inn's large and tastefully furnished rooms, many of which overlook the parking lot. The more expensive rooms face the indoor pool and solarium and have sliding glass doors that open onto a balcony or a patio. Montana's Steak House (no lunch) serves steak, chicken, and seafood in an Old Victorian West atmosphere. ⊠ *1 Atwood Dr., 01060,* ☎ *413/586–1211 or 800/582–2929. 122 rooms, 2 suites. Restaurant, bar, 1 indoor and 1 outdoor pool, hot tub, 2 tennis courts, meeting rooms. Continental breakfast weekdays only. AE, D, DC, MC, V.*

$ 🏠 **Twin Maples Bed and Breakfast.** Fields and woods surround this 200-year-old farmhouse, which is 7 mi northwest of Northampton near the village of Williamsburg. Colonial-style antiques and reproductions furnish the small rooms, which have restored brass beds. ⊠ *106 South St., Williamsburg 01096,* ☎ *413/268–7925 or 413/268–7244,* FAX *413/268–7243. 3 rooms without bath. Full breakfast. AE, MC, V.*

Nightlife and the Arts
Much of Northampton's live music scene (☎ 413/584–0610 for information) centers on the Iron Horse, the Pearl Street Nightclub, and the Calvin Theatre.

The **Northampton Center for the Arts** (⊠ 17 New South St., ☎ 413/584–7327 or 413/586–8282) hosts theater, dance, and musical events and houses two galleries for the visual arts. Some of the ongoing classes—tai chi and swing dance are two of many offerings—are open to walk-ins.

Outdoor Activities and Sports
The **Norwottuck Rail Trail** is a paved 9-mi path that links Northampton with Belchertown. Great for pedaling, rollerblading, jogging, and cross-country skiing, it runs along the old Boston & Maine Railroad bed.

At the wide place in the Connecticut River known as the Oxbow is the Massachusetts Audubon Society's **Arcadia Nature Center and Wildlife Sanctuary,** where you can try the hiking and nature trails and scheduled canoe trips. ⊠ *127 Combs Rd., Easthampton (3 mi from Northampton),* ☎ *413/584–3009.* ⊡ *$3 (free for Massachusetts Audubon members).* ☉ *Tues.–Sun. dawn–dusk; office 9–3.*

Shopping
The 8,000-square-ft **Antique Center of Northampton** (⊠ 9½ Market St., ☎ 413/584–3600) houses 60 dealers. The **Ferrin Gallery at Pinch Pottery** (⊠ 179 Main St., ☎ 413/586–4509) sells contemporary ceramics, jewelry, and glass. **Thorne's Marketplace** (⊠ 150 Main St., ☎ 413/584–5582) is a funky four-floor indoor mall in a former department store.

South Hadley
❹❸   *10 mi south of Amherst.*

Although it remained a farming community well into the 20th century, South Hadley has long been known primarily as a college town. **Mount Holyoke College,** founded in 1837, was the first women's college in the United States. Among the college's alumnae are Emily Dickinson and playwright Wendy Wasserstein. The handsome wooded campus, encompassing two lakes and lovely walking or riding trails, was landscaped by Frederick Law Olmsted. ⊠ *Rte. 116,* ☎ *413/538–2245.*

Mount Holyoke's **College Art Museum** has exhibits of Asian, Egyptian, and classical art. ⊠ *Rte. 116,* ☎ *413/538–2245.* ⊡ *Free.* ☉ *Tues.–Fri. 11–5, weekends 1–5.*

Lodging
$$–$$$ 🏠 **Clark Tavern Inn.** Early customers at this 1742 inn included Min-
★   utemen on their way to fight in Concord and Lexington. Two centuries

later, when the planned route for I–91 ran right through the property, two dedicated preservationists saved the house by moving it to its new site and at that time installed modern plumbing and heating. Braided rugs, canopy beds, and stencils create a Colonial atmosphere. Fires warm two large but cozy common rooms; in summer, you can nap in the garden hammock or take a dip in the pool. Breakfast can be served fireside, on the screened-in porch, or in your room. ⊠ *98 Bay Rd., Hadley 01035,* ☎ *413/586–1900,* 𝔽𝔸𝕏 *413/587–9788. 3 rooms. Pool. Full breakfast. AE, D, DC, MC, V.*

Outdoor Activities and Sports

Sportsman's Marina Boat Rental Company (⊠ Rte. 9, Hadley, ☎ 413/586–2426) rents canoes and boats during summer and early fall.

Shopping

The **Hadley Antique Center** (⊠ 227 Russell St./Rte. 9, ☎ 413/586–4093) contains more than 70 different stores.

The **Village Commons** (⊠ College St.), across from Mount Holyoke College, is an outdoor mall with a movie theater, several restaurants, and shops with everything from handmade picture frames to lingerie. **Mona's Lace Place** (⊠ Village Commons, 19 College St., ☎ 413/535–2523) stocks gifts, curtains, boxes, Christmas ornaments, bridal accessories, and more. The **Odyssey Bookstore** (⊠ Village Commons, 9 College St., ☎ 413/534–7307) has gifts, cards, and more than 50,000 titles. Drop into **Tailgate Picnic** (⊠ Village Commons, 7 College St., ☎ 413/532–7597) for specialty bagels, sandwiches, cold pastas, wine, and crackers; you can order the prepared foods to go.

Holyoke

⓸ *5 mi south of South Hadley.*

A downtrodden town of crumbling redbrick factories and murky canals, Holyoke has little to interest the visitor apart from an imaginatively restored industrial city center and a children's museum.

✆ The **Heritage State Park** tells the story of this papermaking community, the nation's first planned industrial city. The park is the starting point for the **Heritage Park Railroad.** Its antique steam train runs sporadically, depending on financing and demand. A merry-go-round operates on weekends from 12 to 4. ⊠ *221 Appleton St.,* ☎ *413/534–1723.* ☞ *Park free; charge for railroad.* ☉ *Tues.–Sun. noon–4:30.*

✆ The **Children's Museum,** beside Heritage State Park in a converted mill by a canal, is packed with hands-on games and educational toys. Within the museum are a state-of-the-art TV station, a multitiered interactive exhibit on the body, a giant bubblemaker, and a sand pendulum. ⊠ *444 Dwight St.,* ☎ *413/536–5437.* ☞ *$4.* ☉ *Tues.–Sat. 9:30–4:30, Sun. noon–5.*

A 3½-mi round-trip hike at the **Mt. Tom State Reservation** (⊠ U.S 5, ☎ 413/536–0416) leads to the summit, whose sheer basalt cliffs were formed by volcanic activity 200 million years ago. At the top are excellent views over the Pioneer Valley and the Berkshires.

Dining and Lodging

$$$ ✕ **Delaney House.** Eating here always feels like an event, in part because of the elegantly set tables and tasteful Victorian decor in the several dining rooms in the hundred-plus-year-old portion of the building. It's also because of the live music that flows out of the comfortable lounge. The biggest plus is the food, tasty and beautifully presented in ample portions. Most choices are standard American: prime rib, baked sea scallops, and rack of lamb. Among the more ambitious offerings are chicken Portobello, grilled salmon pesto, and lobster regale—a 2½-pound lobster with mussels, clams, shrimp, and scallops. On Sunday, the restaurant opens at 1 for dinner. ⊠ *U.S. 5 at Smith's Ferry,* ☎ *413/532–1799. AE, D, DC, MC, V. No lunch.*

$$–$$$ ✕⌆ **Yankee Pedlar Inn.** This sprawling inn stands at a busy crossroads near I–91. Antiques and four-poster or canopy beds furnish the charming rooms. The elaborate Victorian bridal suite is heavy on lace and curtains; the beamed carriage house has rustic appointments and simple canopy beds. Duck au poivre and filet mignon are among the dishes served in the Grill Room, which is painted burgundy and accented with stained glass. The Oyster Bar serves more casual fare and hosts local musicians Thursday through Saturday evenings. ⊠ *1866 Northampton St., 01040,* ☎ *413/532–9494,* ☒ *413/536–8877. 28 rooms, 11 suites. Restaurant, bar, nightclub, meeting rooms. Continental breakfast. AE, D, DC, MC, V.*

Shopping

Holyoke Mall at Ingleside (⊠ Holyoke St., Exit 15 off I–91, ☎ 413/536–1440) has nearly 200 stores and restaurants, including Christmas Tree Shops, Sears, Filene's, and Lord & Taylor. Ruby Tuesday's serves a great burger and has a terrific salad bar.

Springfield

④⑤ *8 mi south of Holyoke, 101 mi southwest of Boston.*

The late children's book author Theodore Geisel, also known as Dr. Seuss, was born here. Springfield is the largest city in the Pioneer Valley, an industrial town where modern skyscrapers rise between grand historic buildings. Too often overlooked by travelers hesitant to add an apparent rust-belt destination to their itineraries, Springfield does have several rewarding museums and historic sites.

Springfield Armory, the country's first arsenal, was established in 1779 and closed in 1968. The armory, which made small arms for the U.S. military, contains an extensive firearms collection. ⊠ *1 Armory Sq., off State St.,* ☎ *413/734–8551.* ⌂ *Free.* ☉ *Wed.–Sun. 10–4:30.*

Dr. James Naismith invented basketball in Springfield in 1891. The **Naismith Memorial Basketball Hall of Fame** has a cinema, a two-story basketball fountain, and a moving walkway from which you can shoot baskets into 20 different-size hoops. ⊠ *W. Columbus Ave. at Union St.,* ☎ *413/781–6500.* ⌂ *$8.* ☉ *Daily 9–6.*

Four museums have set up shop at the **museum quadrangle** near downtown. There's a Dr. Seuss exhibit at the **Connecticut Valley Historical Museum** (☎ 413/263–6895), which commemorates the history of the Pioneer Valley. The **George Walter Vincent Smith Art Museum** (☎ 413/263–6894) contains a private collection of Japanese armor, ceramics, and textiles and a gallery of American paintings. The **Museum of Fine Arts** (☎ 413/263–6800) has paintings by Gauguin, Renoir, Degas, and Monet, as well as 18th-century American paintings and contemporary works. The **Springfield Science Museum** (☎ 413/263–6875) has an "Exploration Center" of touchable displays, a planetarium, a kid-focused eco-center, and dinosaur exhibits. ⊠ *State and Chestnut Sts.* ⌂ *$4 pass valid for all museums.* ☉ *Wed.–Sun. noon–4.*

☾ **Forest Park,** Springfield's leafy, 735-acre retreat, is an ideal urban green space. There are hiking paths, paddleboats on Porter Lake, tennis courts, picnic groves, and a wonderful pond filled with hungry ducks. The **Zoo in Forest Park,** one of the highlights for children, is home to nearly 200 domestic and exotic animals. ⊠ *Rte. 83/Sumner Ave.,* ☎ *413/787–6461; 413/733–2251 for zoo.* ⊡ *Park $1 per car weekdays, $2 per car on weekends; zoo $3.50.* ⊘ *Park daily; zoo mid-Apr.–mid-Nov., daily 10–5.*

⨀ **Riverside Park,** New England's largest superpark and waterpark, has added many new rides, attractions, and improvements since 1997. Among the more than 130 rides and shows are the Mind Eraser (roller coaster) and Shipwreck Falls. ⊠ *1623 Main St./Rte. 159 (south from Rte. 57 west of Springfield), Agawam,* ☎ *413/786–9300 or 800/370–7488.* ⊡ *$28.* ⊘ *Memorial Day–Labor Day, Sun.–Thurs. 11–6, weekends 11–11; Apr.–Memorial Day and Labor Day–Oct., weekends 11–11.*

Dining and Lodging

$$–$$$ ✕ **Student Prince and Fort Restaurant.** Named after a 1930s operetta, this downtown restaurant established in 1935 is known for its rendition of classic German food—bratwurst, schnitzel, and sauerbraten—and steaks, chops, and seafood. ⊠ *8 Fort St.,* ☎ *413/734–7475.* D, DC, MC, V.

$$ ✕ **Theodore's.** Here you can dine saloon style in booths near the bar or in a small adjacent dining room. The decor is yard-sale eclectic, with framed old-time advertisements lending a whimsical air. Burgers, sandwiches, chicken, and seafood are on the menu. ⊠ *201 Worthington St.,* ☎ *413/736–6000.* AE, MC, V. *No lunch weekends.*

$$ ✕ **Wild Apple Cafe.** Choose a table in the tiny mall courtyard or in the more formal, intimate back room, which is set with linens at night. House specialties such as chicken pot pie and meatloaf share the billing with more ambitious offerings like pan-seared salmon fillet with fresh julienne vegetables and smoked chicken, broccoli, and red pepper crepes. Lunch includes a large selection of hearty sandwiches and salads. All items are available for take-out. ⊠ *Eastmeadow Shops, 60 Shaker Rd., East Longmeadow,* ☎ *413/525–4444.* AE, D, MC, V. *Closed Sun.*

$–$$ ⌂ **Hill House.** The area's newest B&B is an elegant 1923 brick Georgian Revival home. The living room, centered on a baby grand piano, has a marble fireplace. A grand mahogany staircase leads to the tidy, comfortable guest rooms, which all have air-conditioning. An expanded Continental breakfast is served in the lovely paneled dining room. The only drawback here is the noise: The house is close to I-91, and guests have to sleep with windows closed and air-conditioner on in warm weather. ⊠ *418 Longhill St., 01108,* ☎ *413/739–5328. 4 rooms. Continental breakfast.* MC, V.

Nightlife and the Arts

The **Springfield Symphony Orchestra** (☎ 413/733–2291) performs from October to May at Symphony Hall (⊠ 75 Market Pl.) and mounts a summer program of concerts in the Springfield area. **Theodore's** (☞ Dining and Lodging, *above*) hosts blues bands on weekend evenings.

Sturbridge

㊻   *31 mi east of Springfield, 55 mi southwest of Boston.*

Sturbridge is best known as the home of an outstanding open-air museum. **Old Sturbridge Village,** one of the country's finest period restorations and the star attraction of central Massachusetts, is just east of the Pioneer Valley. The village is a model of an early 1800s New England town, with more than 40 historic buildings (moved here from other towns) on a 200-acre site. Some of the village houses are furnished with canopy beds and elaborate decoration; in the simpler, single-story cottages, interpreters wearing period costumes demonstrate home-based crafts like spinning, weaving, shoe-making, and cooking.

Also here are several mills, including a saw mill. On the informative short boat ride along the Quinebaug River, you can learn about river life in 19th-century New England and catch a glimpse of ducks, geese, turtles, and other local wildlife. The village store contains an amazing variety of goods necessary for everyday life in the 19th century. ⊠ *1 Old Sturbridge Village Rd., ☎ 508/347–3362 or 800/733–1830. ☜ $16, valid for 2 consecutive days. ☉ Apr.–Oct., daily 9–5; mid-Feb.– Mar. and Nov.–Dec., daily 10–4; Jan.–mid-Feb., call for hrs.*

Dining and Lodging

$–$$ ✕ **Rom's.** This 700-seat restaurant is something of a local institution. The six dining rooms have an Early American decor, with wood paneling and beam ceilings. Rom's, which serves Italian and American cuisine from pizza to roast beef, attracts crowds with a classic formula: good food at low prices. The veal Parmesan is very popular, as is the Thursday lunch buffet. ⊠ *Rte. 131, ☎ 508/347–3349. AE, DC, MC, V.*

$$$ ✕🏨 **Sturbridge Host.** Across the street from Old Sturbridge Village on Cedar Lake, this hotel has luxuriously appointed bedrooms with Colonial decor and reproduction furnishings. Some rooms have fireplaces, balconies, or patios. Dinner is served nightly in Portobella's Italian Restaurant ($$–$$$), and a less formal pub menu with club sandwiches and burgers is offered daily at lunch and dinner in the Ox Head Tavern. ⊠ *U.S. 20, 01566, ☎ 508/347–7393 or 800/582–3232, ☎ 508/ 347–3944. 237 rooms, 9 suites. 2 restaurants, bar, indoor pool, miniature golf, tennis court, sauna, basketball, health club, racquetball, boating, fishing, meeting rooms. AE, D, DC, MC, V.*

$$ ✕🏨 **Publick House Historic Inn Complex.** Each of the three inns and
★   the motel in this complex has its own character. The 17 rooms in the Publick House, which dates to 1771, are Colonial in design, with uneven wide-board floors; some have canopy beds. The neighboring Chamberlain House consists of larger suites, and the Country Motor Lodge has more modern rooms. The Crafts Inn, about a mile away, has a library, lounge, pool, and eight rooms with four-poster beds and painted wood paneling. The big and bustling restaurant at the Publick House is very busy on weekends. The fare is traditional Yankee—lobster pies, double-thick lamb chops, Indian pudding, and pecan bread pudding. ⊠ *Rte. 131, On-the-Common, 01566, ☎ 508/347–3313 or 800/782–5425, ☎ 508/347–5073. 118 rooms, 12 suites. Restaurant, bar, pool, tennis court, jogging, shuffleboard, playground, meeting rooms. Continental breakfast at Crafts Inn. AE, DC, MC, V.*

$$ ✕🏨 **Sturbridge Country Inn.** The atmosphere at this onetime farmhouse on Sturbridge's busy Main Street is between that of an inn and a plush business hotel. Guest rooms—all with working gas fireplaces and whirlpool tubs—have reproduction antiques. The best is the top-floor suite; avoid the first-floor rooms, which are comparably priced but small and noisy. The casual Field Stone Tavern ($–$$; closed November to May; no lunch weekdays) serves sandwiches, salads, prime rib, and seafood entrées. The barn adjoining the inn has been converted into a theater where performances are staged year-round. ⊠ *Box 60, 530 Main St., 01566, ☎ 508/347–5503; 508/347–7603 for restaurant; ☎ 508/ 347–5319. 6 rooms, 3 suites. Restaurant, bar, hot tub. Continental breakfast. AE, D, MC, V.*

The Pioneer Valley A to Z

Arriving and Departing

Peter Pan Bus Lines (☎ 413/781–2900 or 800/237–8747) links Boston, Springfield, Holyoke, Northampton, Amherst, and South Hadley.

BY CAR

Interstate 91 runs north–south through the valley, from Greenfield to Springfield. Interstate 90 links Springfield to Boston. Route 2 connects Boston with Greenfield.

BY PLANE

Bradley International Airport (⊠ Rte. 20; take Exit 40 off I–91, ☎ 860/292–2000) in Windsor Locks, Connecticut, is the most convenient airport for flying into the Pioneer Valley. American, Continental, Delta, Midway, Northwest, TWA, United, and US Airways serve Bradley. *See* Air Travel *in* Smart Travel Tips A to Z for airline phone numbers.

BY TRAIN

Amtrak (☎ 800/872–7245) serves Springfield from New York City, stopping in New Haven. The *Lake Shore Limited* between Boston and Chicago calls at Springfield once daily in each direction, and three more trains run between Boston and Springfield every day.

Getting Around

BY BUS

Local bus companies with regular service are the **Pioneer Valley Transit Authority** (☎ 413/781–7882) and **Greenfield Montague Transportation Area** (☎ 413/773–9478).

BY CAR

Interstate 91 passes through or near Springfield, Holyoke, Northampton, Hadley, Deerfield, and Greenfield. Northfield is east (via Route 10) of I–91 on Route 63. Route 2 heads west from Greenfield to Shelburne Falls. Amherst is east of Northampton on Route 9. Sturbridge is east of Springfield, I–90 to I–84.

Contacts and Resources

ANTIQUES

For a list of members of the **Pioneer Valley Antique Dealers Association** write to Maggie Herbert (⊠ 201 N. Elm St., Northampton 01060).

EMERGENCIES

Baystate Medical Center (⊠ 759 Chestnut St., Springfield, ☎ 413/784–0000). **Cooley Dickenson Hospital** (⊠ 30 Locust St., Northampton, ☎ 413/582–2000). **Holyoke Hospital** (⊠ 575 Beech St., Holyoke, ☎ 413/534–2500).

RESERVATION SERVICE

Berkshire Bed-and-Breakfast Service (☎ 413/268–7244 or 800/762–2751, FAX 413/268–7243) provides information and takes reservations for B&B and other Pioneer Valley accommodations.

VISITOR INFORMATION

Amherst Area Chamber of Commerce (⊠ 11 Spring St., 01002, ☎ 413/253–0700). **Greater Northampton Chamber of Commerce** (⊠ 62 State St., 01060, ☎ 413/584–1900). The **Greater Springfield Convention and Visitors Bureau** (⊠ 1441 Main St., Springfield 01115, ☎ 413/787–1548).

THE BERKSHIRES

Updated by
Kay and Bill
Scheller

More than a century ago, wealthy families from New York and Boston built "summer cottages" in western Massachusetts's Berkshire Hills—great country estates that earned Berkshire County the nickname "inland Newport." Most of those grand houses have been converted into schools or hotels. Occupying the entire far western end of the state, the area is only about a 2½-hour drive directly west from Boston or north from New York City, yet it lives up to the storybook image of rural New England with wooded hills, narrow winding roads, and compact charming villages. Many cultural events take place in summer, among them the renowned Tanglewood classical music festival in Lenox. The foliage blazes brilliantly in fall, skiing is popular in winter, and spring is the time for maple sugaring. The scenic Mohawk Trail runs east to west across the northern section of the region.

North Adams

47 *130 mi northwest of Boston.*

Once a railroad boomtown and a thriving industrial city, North Adams is still industrial but no longer thriving. It's worth a stop if you're intrigued by the ghosts of the Industrial Revolution or are a railway buff.

Exhibits at the restored freight yard that now is the **Western Gateway Heritage State Park** outline the town's past successes, including the construction of the Hoosac tunnel between 1850 and 1875. ⊠ *9 Furnace St., Bldg. 4,* ☎ *413/663–6312.* ☜ *$1 suggested donation.* ☉ *Daily 10–5.*

The only natural bridge in North America caused by water erosion is the marble arch at **Natural Bridge State Park.** The bridge crosses a narrow 500-ft chasm containing numerous faults and fractures. ⊠ *Rte. 8 N,* ☎ *413/663–6392.* ☜ *$2 per car.* ☉ *Memorial Day–Columbus Day, weekdays 8:30–4:30, weekends 10–6.*

One sign that things may be on the upswing in North Adams is the new **Massachusetts Museum of Contemporary Arts,** or Mass MoCA, one of the nation's largest centers for contemporary performing and visual arts. On 13 acres and consisting of 27 buildings (6 renovated), the vast complex contains galleries, studios, performance venues, cafés, and shops. Exhibits and performances will include everything from art exhibitions to dance and music concerts and film presentations. ⊠ *87 Marshall St.,* ☎ *413/664–4481.* ☜ *$8.* ☉ *June–Oct., Sun.–Thurs. 10–5, Fri.–Sat. 10–7; Nov.–May, Tues.–Sun. 10–5.*

Picnic tables at the **Mohawk Trail State Forest** (⊠ Rte. 2, Charlemont, ☎ 413/339–5504) are set up under large evergreen trees. A few well-maintained hiking trails of a mile or so lead to a scenic lookout. A camping area and a few log cabins, which can be rented for under $10 a night, are available.

Lodging

$$ 🏠 **Blackington Manor B&B.** Dan and Betsy Epstein's meticulously re-
★ stored 1849 Italianate mansion is furnished with antiques and filled with music. The Epsteins are both professional musicians, and the couple hosts concerts and chamber music workshops throughout the year. Several of the elegantly appointed guest rooms have pianos. The mansion, built by a wealthy textile manufacturer, is notable for its intricate wrought-iron balconies, floor-to-ceiling windows, a spacious bay window, and decorative corbels. A kosher kitchen is available for stays of 1 week or longer. ⊠ *1391 Massachusetts Ave., 01247,* ☎ *413/663–5795 or 800/795–8613, 413/663–3121. 4 rooms. Pool. Full breakfast. MC, V.*

En Route   Many people approach the Berkshires along Route 2 from Boston and the East Coast. The **Mohawk Trail,** a more than 50-mi stretch from Orange to Williamstown that is lovely in fall, follows the path blazed long ago by Native Americans that ran along the Deerfield River through the Connecticut Valley to the Berkshire Hills. Just beyond the town of Charlemont stands *Hail to the Sunrise,* a 900-pound bronze statue of an Indian facing east, with arms uplifted, dedicated to the five Native American nations that lived along the Mohawk Trail. Some mostly tacky "Indian trading posts" on the highway carry out the Mohawk theme. Also along the road are antiques stores, flea markets, and several places to pull off the road, picnic, and take photos.

Bypassing the entrance to the **Hoosac railway tunnel** (which took 24 years to build and at 4½ mi was the longest in the nation when it was completed in 1875), Route 2 begins a steep ascent to Whitcomb Summit, then continues to the spectacular Western Summit, with excellent views, before dropping through a series of hairpin turns into North Adams.

Williamstown

48 *10 mi west of North Adams.*

When Colonel Ephraim Williams left money to found a free school in what was then known as West Hoosuck, he stipulated that the name be changed to Williamstown. Williams College opened in 1793, and even today life in this placid town revolves around it. Graceful campus buildings like the Gothic cathedral, built in 1904, line wide Main Street. The collection and exhibits at the **Williams College Museum of Art** focus on American and 20th-century art. ☒ *Main St.,* ☎ *413/597–2429.* ▨ *Free.* ☼ *Tues.–Sat. 10–5, Sun. 1–5.*

★ The **Sterling and Francine Clark Art Institute** is one of the nation's notable small art museums. Its famous works include more than 30 paintings by Renoir, as well as canvases by Monet, Pisarro, and Degas. ☒ *225 South St.,* ☎ *413/458–9545.* ▨ *$5.* ☼ *Tues.–Sun. 10–5.*

The **Chapin Library of Rare Books and Manuscripts** at Williams College contains original copies of the Four Founding Documents of the United States—the Declaration of Independence, the Articles of Confederation, the Constitution, and the Bill of Rights—and 35,000 books, manuscripts, and illustrations dating from as far back as the 9th century. ☒ *Stetson Hall, Main St.,* ☎ *413/597–2462.* ▨ *Free.* ☼ *Weekdays 10–noon and 1–5.*

Dining and Lodging

$$$ ✕ **Main Street Cafe.** Owner-chef Jeff Bendavid and his wife, Peggy Apple,
★ moved their restaurant from North Bennington, Vermont, to be closer to the majority of their patrons. Bendavid continues to serve up northern Italian treats that have earned the restaurant rave reviews in publications nationwide. The appetizer sampler includes fresh grilled eggplant stuffed with marinated grilled chicken and fontina cheese, topped with a tomato-horseradish dijonnaise sauce, and crab cakes with a citrus tomato sauce. Among the entrées are veal Marsala and a risotto of the day. Brick-oven pizza and a light salad menu are available in the bistro after 9 PM. ☒ *16 Water St.,* ☎ *413/458–3210. MC, V. No lunch.*

$$–$$$ ✕ **Mezze Bistro.** Live entertainment, cabarets, and seasonal parties set the tone for one of Williamstown's most popular spots. Like the entertainment, the menu changes often, featuring entrées such as veal sweetbreads with artichoke hearts and radicchio, sautéed pork with roasted shallots, prosciutto over soft polenta, and oven-roasted fennel gazpacho. If you're hankering for a taste of late-night SoHo, drop by for a martini or coffee. ☒ *84 Water St.,* ☎ *413/458–0123. AE, MC, V. Closed Mon. Sept.–May. No lunch.*

$$–$$$ ✕ **Wild Amber Grill.** The White Amber's simple decor belies the ambitiousness of its menu. The owner-chef changes his contemporary American menu frequently, but the menu always lists beef, poultry, and a meatless option. The moderately priced wine list has been shrewdly selected. On some weekends, musicians perform next to the fireplace in the lounge. Sunday brunch is served from 11 to 2. ☒ *101 North St.,* ☎ *413/458–4000. AE, MC, V. Closed Tues. No lunch.*

The Berkshires

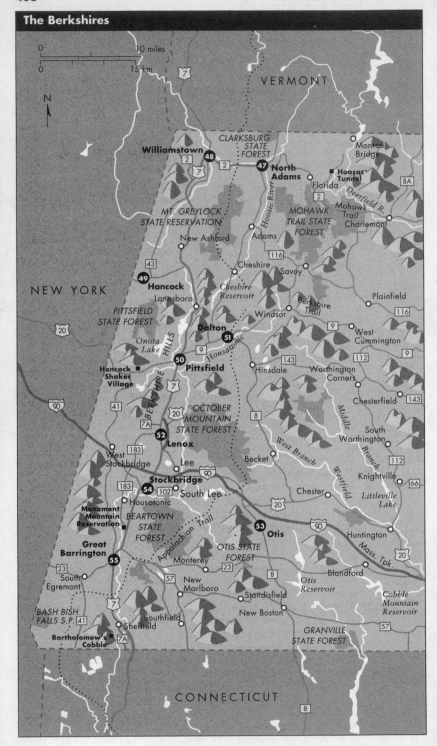

0   10 miles

0   15 km

N

VERMONT

NEW YORK

CONNECTICUT

CLARKSBURG STATE FOREST

Williamstown 48
2
7
47 **North Adams**
Monroe Bridge
■ Hoosac Tunnel
Florida
2
8A
Deerfield R.
Mohawk Trail
Charlemont
MT. GREYLOCK STATE RESERVATION
MOHAWK TRAIL STATE FOREST
New Ashford
Adams
Hoosic River
43
49 **Hancock**
Lanesboro
Cheshire
116
Savoy
Cheshire Reservoir
Plainfield
Berkshire Trail
116
PITTSFIELD STATE FOREST
20
Onota Lake
Dalton 51
Windsor
9
West Cummington
112
9
50 **Pittsfield**
9
Housatonic
143
Hinsdale
Worthington Corners
Chesterfield
143
Hancock Shaker Village ■
Middle Branch
41
7
OCTOBER MOUNTAIN STATE FOREST
8
South Worthington
112
90
20
7A
52 **Lenox**
West Branch
Knightville
66
112
West Stockbridge
183
Lee
Becket
Littleville Lake
Chester
Stockbridge
54 102
183
South Lee
20
Westfield
Housatonic
90
Huntington
20
Monument Mountain Reservation ■
BEARTOWN STATE FOREST
53 **Otis**
Mass. Tpk.
90
Appalachian Trail
OTIS STATE FOREST
Great Barrington 55
Monterey
23
Otis Reservoir
Blandford
Cobble Mountain Reservoir
23
South Egremont
57
New Marlboro
8
7
BASH BISH FALLS S.P. 41
Southfield
Standisfield
New Boston
GRANVILLE STATE FOREST
57
Sheffield
7A
Bartholomew's Cobble ■

CONNECTICUT

8

$ ✕ **Cozy Corner.** Fish-and-chips is the house specialty, but the Greek-Italian-American menu also highlights gyros, pasta, pizza, and treats such as shrimp Santorini (prepared with feta cheese and Greek wine). The restaurant is immaculate, the ambience minimal, the portions ample, and the value excellent. ✉ *850 Simonds Rd.,* ☎ *413/458–3854. AE, MC, V.*

$$$–$$$$ ▦ **The Orchards.** Although it's right on Route 2 and surrounded by parking lots, this hotel compensates for these shortcomings with a beautiful central courtyard with fruit trees and a pond stocked with koi. English antiques furnish most of the spacious accommodations. The inner rooms, which have one-way windows looking onto the courtyard, are best for summer stays. The outer rooms have less-distinguished views, but their fireplaces add appeal for winter visits. The restaurant, Jasmine, serves three meals a day. Morning coffee and afternoon tea are complimentary. ✉ *222 Adams Rd., 01267,* ☎ *413/458–9611 or 800/225–1517,* 𝔽𝔸𝕏 *413/458–3273. 47 rooms, 2 suites. Restaurant, bar, pool, hot tub, sauna, exercise room, meeting rooms. AE, DC, MC, V.*

$$–$$$ ▦ **Williams Inn.** The large rooms in this modern hotel have good-quality American furnishings and floral-print drapes and bedspreads. The atmosphere is collegiate in the comfortable lounge, which has an open fireplace. ✉ *On-the-Green, 01267,* ☎ *413/458–9371 or 800/828–0133,* 𝔽𝔸𝕏 *413/458–2767. 103 rooms. Restaurant, bar, coffee shop, dining room, indoor pool, hot tub, sauna. AE, D, DC, MC, V.*

$$ ▦ **Field Farm Guest House.** Built in 1948 on 296 acres, this house re-
★ sembles a modern museum. It was donated as part of a land trust by the former owners and is now run as a B&B by a nonprofit organization. The large windows in the guest rooms have expansive views of the grounds. Three rooms have private decks; two rooms have working fireplaces with tiles depicting animals, birds, and butterflies. Guests can prepare simple meals in the pantry area. The grounds, open to the public, include a pond, sculptures, a nature center, and 4 mi of trails. ✉ *554 Sloan Rd., off Rte. 43, 01267,* ☎ *413/458–3135. 5 rooms. Pool, tennis court, fishing. D, MC, V. Full breakfast.*

$$ ▦ **River Bend Farm.** One of the founders of Williamstown built this farmhouse, now restored with complete authenticity. The kitchen, through which guests enter, contains an open-range stove and an oven hung with dried herbs. Some bedrooms have wide-plank walls, curtains of unbleached muslin, and four-poster beds with canopies or rope beds (yes, they really are comfortable). All rooms are sprinkled with antique pieces—chamberpots, washstands, wing chairs, and spinning wheels. ✉ *643 Simonds Rd., 01267,* ☎ *413/458–5504. 4 rooms without bath. Continental breakfast. No credit cards.*

$–$$ ▦ **Berkshire Hills Motel.** All the rooms at this two-story brick-and-clapboard motel about 3 mi south of Williamstown are furnished in Colonial style. The lounge has a fireplace, and guests can use the barbecue on the deck. Although the motel is close to the road, the spacious grounds in back encompass a brook, woodlands, landscaped gardens, and an outdoor heated pool. ✉ *U.S. 7, 01267,* ☎ *413/458–3950 or 800/388–9677. 21 rooms. Pool. Continental breakfast. AE, D, MC, V.*

Nightlife and the Arts

Jazz and blues musicians perform on weekends at the tavern in the **Williams Inn** (☞ Dining and Lodging, *above*). The **Williamstown Theatre Festival** (✉ Williams College, Adams Memorial Theatre, ☎ 413/597–3400), which runs from late June to August, presents well-known theatrical works with famous performers on the Main Stage and contemporary works on the Other Stage.

Outdoor Activities and Sports

BIKING

The gently rolling Berkshire Hills are excellent cycling terrain. Mountain bike trails can be found at the Mt. Greylock State Reservation (☞ *below*). You can rent a bike from **Mountain Goat Bicycle Shop** (⊠ 130 Water St., ☎ 413/458–8445), which is about 7 mi west of Mt. Greylock.

GOLF

Waubeeka Golf Links (⊠ U.S. 7, ☎ 413/458–5869), an 18-hole, par-72 course, is open to the public and rents golf clubs.

En Route   The centerpiece of the 10,327-acre **Mt. Greylock State Reservation** (⊠ Rockwell Rd., Lanesboro, ☎ 413/499–4262 or 413/499–4263) is 3,491-ft-high Mt. Greylock, the highest point in Massachusetts. The reservation, south of Williamstown, has facilities for cycling, fishing, horseback riding, camping, and snowmobiling. Many treks—including a portion of the Appalachian Trail—start from the parking lot at the summit, an 8-mi drive from the base of the mountain. **Baskin Lodge** (☎ 413/743–1591 or 443–0011), also at the summit, provides overnight accommodations, snacks, and souvenirs from May to October. A visitor center at the base of the mountain is open daily, year-round. The Sperry Road turn-off leads to a camping-picnic area; there's a modest charge.

Hancock

❹❾ *15 mi south of Williamstown.*

Hancock, the closest village to the Jiminy Peak resort, comes into its own during ski season. For summer guests, the resort has an alpine slide, a putting course, tennis courts, swimming facilities, and trout fishing.

Dining and Lodging

$$ ✕🏠 **Hancock Inn.** This inn, which dates from the late 1700s, provides
★ cozy Old World accommodations a mile from Jiminy Peak. Two small dining rooms ($$$–$$$$) have fireplaces, stained-glass windows, and candles on the tables. The menu changes weekly but might list duckling in port wine with grapes, honey-mustard lamb chops, and veal and shrimp Dijon. ⊠ *Rte. 43, 01237,* ☎ *413/738–5873. 6 rooms. Restaurant. Full breakfast. AE, MC, V. No lunch.*

$$$$ 🏠 **Country Inn at Jiminy Peak.** The massive stone fireplaces in its lobby and lounge lend this hotel a ski-lodge atmosphere. The modern condo-style suites accommodate up to four people and have kitchenettes separated from the living area by a bar and high stools; the suites at the rear of the building overlook the slopes. The inn offers lodging-skiing packages. ⊠ *Corey Rd., 01237,* ☎ *413/738–5500 or 800/882–8859 outside MA,* ℻ *413/738–5513. 96 suites. Restaurant, bar, pool, 2 hot tubs, 2 saunas, miniature golf, 5 tennis courts, exercise room, meeting rooms. AE, D, DC, MC, V.*

Nightlife and the Arts

In winter, the **Blarney Room** (☎ 413/443–4752), on the top floor of the main lodge at the Brodie ski area (☞ *below*), has entertainment nightly and live music on weekends and Sunday afternoon. **Ruby's** (⊠ Rte. 8/Cheshire Rd., Lanesboro, ☎ 413/499–3993) has dancing to Top 40 hits spun by a DJ on Thursday, Friday, and Saturday.

Shopping

Amber Springs Antiques (⊠ 29 S. Main St./U.S. 7, Lanesboro, ☎ 413/442–1237), in a shop behind an old white-clapboard house, stocks eclectic American furnishings from the 19th to mid-20th century. Tools, pottery, and country-store items are the house specialties.

Skiing and Snow Sports

BRODIE

The snow can be green, the beer is often green, and the decor is *always* green here. Yet it's more than the Irish ambience that attracts crowds for weekend and night skiing: The base lodge has a restaurant and bar with live entertainment, lodging (not fancy) is within walking distance of the lifts, and RV trailers can be accommodated. There's express bus service from New York City on weekends. ⊠ *U.S. 7, New Ashford 01237,* ☎ *413/443–4752; 413/443–4751 for snow conditions.*

Downhill. Almost all the 40 trails at Brodie are beginner and intermediate despite the black diamonds, which designate steeper (but not expert) runs; the vertical is 1,250 ft. Four double chairlifts and two surface lifts serve the trails.

Cross-country. The area's cross-country skiing covers 25 km (16 mi) of trails, half of which are groomed daily.

Other activities. A sports center, **Brodie Racquet Club** (☎ 413/458–4677), 1 mi from the ski area, has five indoor courts for tennis and five for racquetball, an exercise room, and a snack bar.

Child care. The nursery takes infants through age 8 by the hour, half day, or full day. There are afternoon, weekend, and holiday ski-instruction programs for children.

JIMINY PEAK

This area, 2½ hours from New York City and three hours from Boston, has all the amenities of a major mountain resort. Condominiums and an all-suites country inn are within walking distance of the ski lifts; more condominium complexes are nearby; and two restaurants and bars are at the slopes. Rentals are available on a nightly or weekly basis. ⊠ *Corey Rd., 01237,* ☎ *413/738–5500; 888/454–6469; 413/738–7325 for snow conditions.*

Downhill. With a vertical of 1,140 ft and nine lifts, Jiminy has near big-time status. It is mostly a cruising mountain—trails are groomed daily, and only on some are small moguls left to build up along the side of the slope. The steepest black-diamond runs are on the upper headwalls; longer outer runs make for good intermediate terrain. A quad chair—dubbed Q1 because it was the first in Massachusetts—serves Jiminy's shorter left-side slopes. A longer triple chair is on the right. A 1998 expansion added another mountain, Widow's White Peak, and 30% more skiable terrain to the area. There's skiing nightly in season.

Other activities. Jiminy has a snowboard park and an old-fashioned ice rink.

Child care. The nursery takes children from 6 months. Children from age 4 to 12 can take daily SKIwee lessons; those from 6 to 15 can take a series of eight weekends of instruction with the same teacher. The kids' ski area has its own lift.

Pittsfield

🛈 *22 mi south of Williamstown.*

Fast-food chains and run-down storefronts dominate downtown Pittsfield, the county seat and geographic center of the Berkshires. But not every town in the region can be relentlessly quaint, and Pittsfield does have an engaging small-town atmosphere.

🖰 A local repository with a bit of everything, the **Berkshire Museum** contains animal exhibits, an aquarium, phosphorescent rocks, historical

relics, and works of art. ⊠ *39 South St.,* ☏ *413/443–7171.* ☞ *$6.* ☉
Tues.–Sat. 10–5, Sun. 1–5.

The **Herman Melville Memorial Room** at the Berkshire Athenaeum
houses books, letters, and memorabilia of the author of *Moby-Dick.*
⊠ *Berkshire Public Library, 1 Wendell Ave.,* ☏ *413/499–9486.* ☞ *Free,
but request admission at the Local History Department.* ☉ *Call for hrs.*

Arrowhead, the house Herman Melville purchased in 1850, is just outside Pittsfield; the underwhelming tour includes the study in which *Moby-
Dick* was written. ⊠ *780 Holmes Rd.,* ☏ *413/442–1793.* ☞ *$5.* ☉
*Memorial Day–Oct., daily 10–5, with guided tours on the hr; Nov.–
late May, weekdays by appointment.*

★ **Hancock Shaker Village** was founded in the 1790s, the third Shaker
community in America. At its peak in the 1840s, the village had almost 300 inhabitants who made their living farming, selling seeds and
herbs, making medicines, and producing crafts. The religious community
officially closed in 1960, its 170-year life span a small miracle considering
its population's vows of celibacy (they took in orphans to maintain their
constituency). Many examples of Shaker ingenuity are visible at Hancock today: The **Round Stone Barn** and the **Laundry and Machine Shop**
are two of the most interesting buildings. Also on site are a farm, some
period gardens, a museum shop with reproduction Shaker furniture,
a picnic area, and a café. ⊠ *U.S. 20, 6 mi west of Pittsfield,* ☏ *413/
443–0188.* ☞ *$10 for guided tour (ticket good for 2 consecutive days);
$13.50 for self-guided tour (ticket good for 10 consecutive days)).* ☉
*Apr.–mid-May and late Oct.–Nov., daily 10–3 (guided tours only, on
the hr); mid-May–late Oct., daily 9:30–5 (self-guided season); Dec.–
Mar., guided tours by appointment.*

Dining and Lodging
$$–$$$ ✕ **Dakota.** Moose and elk heads watch over diners, and the motto is
"Steak, Seafood, and Smiles" at this large, highly acclaimed restaurant
decorated like a rustic hunting lodge. Meals cooked on the mesquite
grill include salmon steaks, shrimp, and trout. A hearty brunch buffet
is served on Sunday. ⊠ *U.S. 7 and 20,* ☏ *413/499–7900. AE, D, DC,
MC, V. No lunch Mon.–Sat.*

$$$–$$$$ ▣ **Crowne Plaza Pittsfield.** Two tiers of rooms surround the large, glass-
dome swimming pool at this freshly renovated downtown hotel. Some
rooms have a view of the mountains. ⊠ *Berkshire Common, South
St., 01201,* ☏ *413/499–2000,* FAX *413/442–0449. 173 rooms. 3 restau-
rants, bar, indoor pool, hot tub, sauna, exercise room, nightclub, meet-
ing rooms. AE, D, DC, MC, V.*

Nightlife and the Arts
The **Berkshire Ballet** (⊠ Koussevitzky Arts Center, Berkshire Community
College, West St., ☏ 413/445–5382) performs classical and contem-
porary works year-round, including *The Nutcracker* at Christmas-
time. On weekends in winter a DJ at the **Tamarack Lounge** (⊠ Dan
Fox Dr., ☏ 413/442–8316), in the Bousquet ski area's base lodge, spins
dance tunes.

Outdoor Activities and Sports
The **Housatonic River** flows south from Pittsfield between the Berkshire
Hills and the Taconic Range toward Connecticut. You can rent canoes,
rowboats, paddleboats, small motorboats, and even pontoon party-
boats from the **Onota Boat Livery** (⊠ 463 Pecks Rd., ☏ 413/442–1724),
which also provides dock space on Onota Lake and sells fishing tackle
and bait.

Skiing and Snow Sports

BOUSQUET SKI AREA

Other areas have entered an era of glamour and high prices, but Bousquet remains an economical, no-nonsense place to ski. The inexpensive lift tickets are the same price every day, and there's night skiing except Sunday. You can go tubing when conditions allow. ⊠ *Dan Fox Dr., 01201, ☎ 413/442–8316; 413/442–2436 for snow conditions.*

Downhill. Bousquet, with a 750-ft vertical drop, has 21 trails, but only if you count every change in steepness and every merging slope. Though this is a generous figure, you will find some good beginner and intermediate runs, with a few steeper pitches. There are three double chairlifts and two surface lifts.

Other activities. The facilities at the **Berkshire West Athletic Club** (⊠ Dan Fox Dr., ☎ 413/494–4600), across the street from Bousquet, include four handball courts, six indoor tennis courts, a sauna and steam room, an indoor pool, a whirlpool, and free weights. Aerobics classes are conducted.

Child care. Bous-Care Nursery watches children age 6 months and up by the hour; reservations are suggested. Ski instruction classes are offered twice daily on weekends and holidays for children age 5 and up.

Dalton

🟠 *3 mi northeast of Pittsfield.*

The paper manufacturer Crane and Co., started by Zenas Crane in 1801, is the major employer in working-class Dalton. Exhibits at the **Crane Museum of Paper Making,** in the handsomely restored Old Stone Mill (1844), trace the history of American papermaking from Revolutionary times to the present. ⊠ *E. Housatonic St., off Rte. 9, ☎ 413/684–2600. ☜ Free. ☉ June–mid-Oct., weekdays 2–5.*

Lodging

$–$$ 🏨 **Dalton House.** Guests in the main house share a split-level sitting room and a sunny breakfast room. The average-size bedrooms are cheerful, with floral-print wallpaper and white wicker chairs. Two suites in the carriage house have sitting areas, exposed beams, period furnishings, and quilts. ⊠ *955 Main St., 01226, ☎ 413/684–3854. 9 rooms, 2 suites. Pool. Continental breakfast. AE, MC, V.*

Lenox

🟢 *8 miles south of Dalton, 5 mi south of Pittsfield, 146 mi west of Boston.*

In the thick of the "summer cottage" region, rich with old inns and majestic buildings, the sophisticated village of Lenox epitomizes the Berkshires. The outstanding Tanglewood music festival (☞ Nightlife and the Arts, *below*) takes place here.

★ **The Mount,** a Classical Revival mansion built in 1902, was the former summer home of novelist Edith Wharton. The house and grounds were designed by Wharton, who is considered by many to have set the standard for 20th-century interior decoration. In designing the Mount, she followed the principles set forth in her book *The Decoration of Houses* (1897), creating a calm and well-ordered home. A "Women of Achievement" lecture series takes place here on Mondays in July and August. ⊠ *Plunkett St., ☎ 413/637–1899. ☜ $6. ☉ May, weekends 9–3; June–Oct., daily 9–3.*

☾ The **Railway Museum,** in a restored 1902 railroad station in central Lenox, contains period exhibits and a large working model railway.

It's the starting point for the **Berkshire Scenic Railway,** which travels over a portion of the historic New Haven Railway's Housatonic Valley Line. ✉ *Willow Creek Rd.,* ☎ *413/637–2210.* 🎫 *$2.* ☉ *Memorial Day weekend–Oct., weekends 10–4.*

Dining and Lodging

$$$ ✗ **Café Lucia.** *Bistecca alla fiorentina* (porterhouse steak grilled with olive oil, garlic, and rosemary) and *ravioli basilico e pomodoro* (homemade ravioli with fresh tomatoes, garlic and basil) are among the dishes that change seasonally at this upbeat northern Italian restaurant. The sleek decor includes track lighting and photographs of the owners' Italian ancestors. ✉ *90 Church St.,* ☎ *413/637–2640. Reservations essential up to 1 month ahead during Tanglewood. AE, DC, MC, V. Closed Mon. July–Oct. and Sun.–Mon. Nov.–June. No lunch.*

$$$ ✗ **Church St. Café.** Original art covers the walls, the tables are surrounded by ficus trees, and classical music wafts through the air at Church St. Café. The menu, which changes with the seasons, might include roast duck with thyme and Madeira sauce, rack of pork with wild mushrooms, and crab cakes. ✉ *69 Church St.,* ☎ *413/637–2745. DC, MC, V. Closed Sun.–Mon. Nov.–Apr.*

$$–$$$ ✗ **Trattoria Il Vesuvio.** *Proprietaria* Anna Arace, a native of Pompeii,
 ★ is on hand nightly to assure that every dish meets her exacting standards. Among the house specialties are *arrosto di vitello,* roast breast of veal stuffed with sliced prosciutto and spinach, cooked in a brick oven and served with red wine sauce; *linguini con vongole,* baby clams sautéed in virgin olive oil, white wine, garlic, and parsley, served over pasta; and *lasagna di verdura,* homemade pasta layered with eggplant, sweet red onions, braised spinach, cheeses, and marinara sauce. Save room for Anna's homemade tiramisu. ✉ *242 Pittsfield Rd.,* ☎ *413/ 637–4904. AE, D, MC, V. Closed Tues. Sept.–June. No lunch.*

$$$$ ✗🏨 **Blantyre.** Modeled after a castle in Scotland, this suprememly el-
 ★ egant manor house, a member of Relais & Châteaux, sits amid 100 acres of manicured lawns and woodlands. Lavishly decorated rooms in the main house have hand-carved four-poster beds, overstuffed chaise longues, chintz-covered chairs, walk-in closets, and Victorian bathrooms. The rooms in the carriage house are well-appointed but can't compete with the formal grandeur of the main house. The outstanding restaurant (reservations essential; jacket and tie) serves "refined Country House cuisine"—no cream or heavy sauces, light on the butter. Imaginative dishes on the $75 prix-fixe menu may include loin of Texas antelope with white leeks and pink peppercorns. After dinner coffee and cognac are served in the music room, where a harpist plays. ✉ *16 Blantyre Rd., off U.S. 20, 01240,* ☎ *413/637–3556,* 🖷 *413/637–4282. 13 rooms, 10 suites. Restaurant, pool, hot tub, sauna, tennis court, croquet, hiking. Continental breakfast. AE, DC, MC, V. Closed Nov.–May.*

$$$$ ✗🏨 **Wheatleigh.** Wheatleigh was built in 1893, a wedding present for an American heiress who married a Spanish count. Set amid 22 wooded acres, the mellow brick building, based on a 16th-century Florentine palazzo, has rooms with high ceilings, intricate plaster moldings, English antiques, and some modern furnishings. The rarefied environment makes this not the best place to bring young children. The main restaurant, a huge room with marble fireplaces and cut-glass chandeliers, has an excellent reputation for its "contemporary classical" cuisine; the $75 prix-fixe menus include roast antelope, pheasant, rabbit, and lobster. The Grill Room serves full meals in a more casual setting. ✉ *Hawthorne Rd., 02140,* ☎ *413/637–0610,* 🖷 *413/637–4507. 19 rooms. 2 restaurants, bar, pool, tennis court, exercise room, meeting rooms. AE, DC, MC, V.*

$$–$$$$ ✗🏨 **The Village Inn.** The oldest inn in Lenox has been welcoming guests since 1775. Several of the rooms have fireplaces or whirlpool tubs; all have antique furnishings. English tea is served daily in summer and on weekends in the off-season. Breakfast (open to the public) is not included in the room rates during summer; a complimentary Continental breakfast is served off-season. The restaurant serves traditional fare—corn chowder, pecan-breaded breast of chicken, Yankee pot roast, and pan-seared swordfish with a cucumber-yogurt sauce. ⊠ *16 Church St., 01240, ☎ 413/637–0527 or 800/253–0917, FAX 413/637–9756. 32 rooms. Restaurant, bar. Continental breakfast Nov.–Apr. AE, D, DC, MC, V.*

$$$$ ⊞ **Eastover.** An antidote to the posh atmosphere prevailing in most of Lenox, this resort was opened by an ex-circus roustabout. Noisy fun and informality are the order of the day here. The functional rooms range from dormitory- to motel-style; though the period wallpapers are stylish, the rooms with four or more beds resemble hospital wards. A herd of buffalo lives on the huge grounds. The facilities are extensive, and rates include all meals and activities. The inn houses one of the country's largest privately held collections of Civil War artifacts. ⊠ *Box 2160, 430 East St., off U.S. 20 and 7, 01240, ☎ 413/637–0625 or 800/822–2386, FAX 413/637–4939. 195 rooms, 120 with bath. Dining room, 1 indoor and 1 outdoor pool, sauna, driving range, 5 tennis courts, badminton, exercise room, horseback riding, volleyball, mountain biking, cross-country skiing, downhill skiing, tobogganing. AP. AE, D, MC, V.*

$$$–$$$$ ⊞ **Cranwell Resort and Hotel.** The best rooms in this complex are in the century-old Tudor mansion; they're furnished with antiques and have marble bathrooms. Two smaller buildings have 20 rooms each, and there are several small cottages, each with a kitchen. Most of the facilities are open to the public, as are the resort's restaurants, where you can dine formally or informally. ⊠ *55 Lee Rd., 02140, ☎ 413/ 637–1364 or 800/272–6935, FAX 413/637–4364. 95 rooms. 3 restaurants, pool, exercise room, driving range, 18-hole golf course, 2 tennis courts, bicycles, cross-country skiing. Continental breakfast. AE, D, DC, MC, V.*

$$–$$$$ ⊞ **Cliffwood Inn.** Six of the seven guest rooms in this Colonial Revival building have fireplaces, and four more fireplaces glow in the common areas. Much of the inn's furniture comes from Europe; most guest rooms have canopy beds. The patio and pool area are well designed; indoors there's a counter-current pool. ⊠ *25 Cliffwood St., 01240, ☎ 413/637– 3330 or 800/789–3331, FAX 413/637–0221. 7 rooms. Indoor pool, outdoor pool, hot tub. Continental breakfast. No credit cards.*

$$–$$$$ ⊞ **Garden Gables.** On 5 acres of wooded grounds a two-minute walk from the center of Lenox, this 250-year-old "summer cottage" has been an inn since 1947. The three common parlors have fireplaces, and one long, narrow room has a unique five-legged Steinway piano. Rooms come in various shapes, sizes, and colors; some have brass beds, and others have pencil four-posters. Some rooms have sloping ceilings, fireplaces, whirlpool baths, or woodland views. Three have private decks. Breakfast is served buffet-style in the airy dining room. ⊠ *Box 52, 135 Main St., 01240, ☎ 413/637–0193, FAX 413/637–4554. 18 rooms. Pool. Full breakfast. AE, D, MC, V.*

$$–$$$$ ⊞ **Whistler's Inn.** The antiques decorating the parlor of this English
★ Tudor mansion are ornate, with a touch of the exotic. The library, formal parlor, music room, and grand dining room all impress. Designer drapes and bedspreads adorn the rooms, three of which have working fireplaces. The carriage house is only open May through October; one room in it has an African decor, and another is done in southwestern style. Some rooms have air-conditioning. ⊠ *5 Greenwood St., 01240, ☎ 413/637–0975, FAX 413/637–2190. 14 rooms. Badminton, croquet, library. Full breakfast. AE, D, MC, V.*

$$–$$$ ☒ **Apple Tree Inn.** Location, location, location: This inn stands across from Tanglewood's main gate. The parlor has a grand piano, velvet couches, and hanging plants. Some guest rooms in the main inn have working fireplaces. Avoid Room 5, which is above the kitchen. The motor-lodge annex has less character. ☒ *334 West St., 01240,* ☎ *413/ 637–1477. 32 rooms, 30 with bath; 2 suites. Restaurant, bar, pool, tennis court. Continental breakfast. AE, D, MC, V.*

Nightlife and the Arts

The **Berkshire Performing Arts Theater** (☒ 70 Kemble St., ☎ 413/637– 1800), on the campus of the National Music Center, attracts top-name artists in jazz, folk, opera, rock, and blues and presents children's shows. **Shakespeare and Company** (☒ Plunkett St., ☎ 413/637–1199) performs the works of Shakespeare and Edith Wharton from May to October at the Mount. The tavern at the **Village Inn** (☒ 16 Church St., ☎ 413/637–0527) is a good, dark place to have a drink.

Tanglewood (☒ West St., off Rte. 183, ☎ 413/637–5165 or 617/266– 1492; 617/266–1200 to order tickets from Symphony Charge), the summer home of the Boston Symphony Orchestra, is just outside Lenox. The 200-acre estate attracts thousands every year to concerts by world-famous performers from mid-June to Labor Day. The 5,000-seat main shed hosts larger concerts; the Seiji Ozawa Hall (named for the BSO conductor) seats around 1,200 and is used for recitals, chamber music, and more intimate performances by summer program students and soloists. One of the most rewarding ways to experience Tanglewood is to purchase lawn tickets, arrive early with blankets or lawn chairs, and have a picnic.

Outdoor Activities and Sports

Undermountain Farm (☒ 400 Undermountain Rd., ☎ 413/637–3365) gives horseback-riding lessons and conducts guided trail rides year-round, weather permitting.

Shopping

The **Hand of Man–Craft Gallery** (☒ 5 Walker St., ☎ 413/637–0631) handles the work of several hundred artists. **Stone's Throw Antiques** (☒ 51 Church St., ☎ 413/637–2733) carries fine antiques. The **Ute Stubich Gallery** (☒ 69 Church St., ☎ 413/637–3566) sells folk and contemporary art.

Perfect Picnics (☒ 72 Church St., ☎ 413/637–3015) prepares gourmet picnic baskets and delivers them free of charge (including to Tanglewood).

Skiing and Snow Sports

CROSS-COUNTRY

Cranwell Resort and Hotel (☒ 55 Lee Rd., ☎ 413/637–1364 or 800/ 272–6935) has miles of skiable golf course and trails. **Kennedy Park** (☒ Main St., just past the Church on the Hill) has 22 mi of walking trails that are great for skiing, especially if you enjoy some hills.

Otis

53 *21 mi southeast of Lenox.*

A more rustic alternative to the polish of Stockbridge and Lenox, Otis, with a ski area and 20 lakes and ponds, supplies plenty of what made the Berkshires desirable in the first place—the great outdoors. The dining options here are slim; your best bet is to pack a picnic of goodies from a Lenox gourmet shop.

Deer Run Maples (☒ Ed Jones Rd., ☎ 413/269–7588) is one of several sugar houses where you can spend the morning tasting freshly tapped maple syrup that's been drizzled onto a dish of snow. Sugaring season varies with the weather; it can be anytime between late February and early April.

Nightlife and the Arts

Jacob's Pillow Dance Festival (✉ George Cantor Rd. at Rte. 20, Becket, ☎ 413/637–1322; 413/243–0745 for box office mid-May through August), the oldest in the nation, happens over 10 weeks each summer. The participants range from well-known contemporary classical ballet companies to Native American dance groups. Before the main events, showings of works-in-progress and even of some of the final productions are staged outdoors, often free of charge. You can picnic on the grounds or eat at the Pillow Café.

Dining and Lodging

$–$$ ✕ **Dream Away Lodge.** When the Dream Away reopened in 1998, folk-music fans hailed the revival of the comfortably-worn-around-the-edges, "middle of nowhere" roadhouse once run by the late "Mama" Maria Fresca, a musician, cook, and spirited hostess who befriended many performers (scenes from Bob Dylan's road-show movie *Renaldo and Clara* were filmed here). Wednesday is music night, with acoustic folk, blues, and other traditional sounds. Bar-menu Wednesdays features burgers, pastas, and spicy fries; four-course prix-fixe offerings other nights might include roast cilantro chicken or salmon fillet in puff pastry, and homemade desserts. ✉ *County Rd., Becket,* ☎ *413/623–8725. No credit cards. Closed Mon.–Tues. No lunch.*

$$ ☒ **Maplewood 1850 House.** This no-nonsense B&B in an old farmhouse is steps from the Farmington River and across a meadow from the ski ridge. The decor of the well-maintained rooms is functional. Hank, the host, knows the Otis area well and is happy to provide tips about outdoor recreation and activities. ✉ *Main St., 01253,* ☎ *413/269–7351,* FAX *413/269–7276. 6 rooms without bath, 2 suites. MC, V.*

Outdoor Activities and Sports

The **Otis Reservoir** (✉ Off Rte. 8, ☎ 413/269–6002), the largest body of fresh water in Massachusetts used exclusively for recreation, has facilities for swimming, boating, and fishing. **J & D Marina** (✉ 1367 Reservoir Rd., East Otis, ☎ 413/269–4839) rents boats and has a small restaurant.

You can hike, bike, or cross-country ski at the 3,800-acre **Otis State Forest** (✉ Rte. 23). The 8,000-acre **Tolland State Forest** (✉ Rte. 8, ☎ 413/269–6002) allows swimming in the Otis Reservoir and camping.

Skiing and Show Sports

Otis Ridge Ski Area (✉ Rte. 23, ☎ 413/269–4444), a family-style ski area with mostly mild terrain, has reasonable rates and night-skiing facilities.

Stockbridge

❺❹ *7 mi south of Lenox, 149 mi west of Boston.*

Stockbridge, a major tourist destination, has the look of small-town New England down pat. Its artistic and literary inhabitants have included sculptor Daniel Chester French, writers Norman Mailer and Robert Sherwood, and, fittingly enough, that champion of small-town America, painter Norman Rockwell, who lived here from 1953 until his death in 1978.

The **Norman Rockwell Museum** displays the largest collection of Rockwell originals in the world. The museum also mounts exhibits by other artists. You can stroll along the river walk or picnic on the vast grounds. ✉ *Rte. 183 (2 mi from Stockbridge),* ☎ *413/298–4100.* ☒ *$9.* ☉ *Daily 10–5.*

Chesterwood was for 33 years the summer home of the sculptor Daniel Chester French, who created *The Minuteman* in Concord and the Lincoln Memorial in Washington, D.C. Tours are given of the house, which is maintained in the style of the 1920s, and of the studio, where you can view the casts and models French used to create the Lincoln Memorial. ⊠ *Williamsville Rd. off Rte. 183,* ☎ *413/298–3579.* ⊠ *$6.50.* ☉ *May–Oct., daily 10–5.*

The 15-acre **Berkshire Botanical Gardens** contain greenhouses, ponds, nature trails, and perennial, rose, and herb gardens. Picnicking is encouraged. In July, the garden is the site of a well-attended antiques show. ⊠ *Rtes. 102 and 183,* ☎ *413/298–3926.* ⊠ *$5.* ☉ *May–mid-Oct., daily 10–5.*

Naumkeag, a Berkshire cottage once owned by Joseph Choate, an ambassador during the administration of U.S. president William McKinley and a successful New York lawyer, provides a glimpse into the gracious living of the "gilded era" of the Berkshires. The 26-room gabled mansion, designed by Stanford White in 1886, sits atop Prospect Hill. It is decorated with many original furnishings and art that spans three centuries; the collection of Chinese export porcelain is also noteworthy. The meticulously kept 8 acres of formal gardens are themselves worth a visit. ⊠ *South Prospect Hill,* ☎ *413/298–3239.* ⊠ *$7.* ☉ *Memorial Day–Columbus Day, daily 10–4:15.*

Dining and Lodging

$$ ✕ **Once Upon a Table.** The atmosphere is casual yet vaguely romantic at this little restaurant in an alley off Stockbridge's main street. The Continental and new American cuisine includes seasonal dishes, with appetizers such as escargots, and potpie entrées. ⊠ *36 Main St.* ☎ *413/ 298–3870. Reservations essential. AE, MC, V. No lunch Mon.–Tues. Call for winter hrs.*

$$$ ✕🏨 **Williamsville Inn.** A couple of miles south of West Stockbridge, ★ this inn re-creates the late 1700s, when it was built. The rooms have wide-board floors, embroidered chairs, and four-poster or canopy beds. Several have country furnishings, two have working fireplaces, and four rooms in the converted barn have wood-burning stoves. One of the dining rooms ($$$–$$$$) is a cozy library; the other one has a fireplace made of unpolished, locally hewn marble. Entrées include roasted breast of duck with blackberry sauce and potatoes, spicy roasted loin of pork with black-bean chili and corn bread, and vegetarian options. ⊠ *Rte. 41, 01266,* ☎ *413/274–6118,* 📠 *413/274–3539. 15 rooms, 1 suite. Restaurant, bar, pool, tennis court, croquet, horseshoes. Full breakfast. AE, MC, V.*

$$–$$$ ✕🏨 **Red Lion Inn.** An inn since 1773, the Red Lion has a large main building and seven annexes, each of which is different (one is a converted fire station). Many rooms are small; the ones in the annex houses tend to be more appealing. All the rooms are furnished with antiques and reproductions and hung with Rockwell prints; some have Oriental rugs. The same menu—with an emphasis on New England specialties—is served in both of the dining rooms and (in season) in the garden. Jackets and ties (no jeans) are required in the formal dining room. Evenings, there's live entertainment in the Lion's Den. ⊠ *Main St., 02162,* ☎ *413/298–5545,* 📠 *413/298–5130. 111 rooms, 96 with bath; 26 suites. 2 restaurants, bar, pool, massage, exercise room, meeting rooms. AE, D, DC, MC, V.*

$$–$$$$ 🏨 **Inn at Stockbridge.** Antiques and feather comforters are among the accents in the rooms of this inn run by the attentive Alice and Len Schiller. The two serve breakfast in their elegant dining room, and every evening they provide wine and cheese while guests study an extensive notebook

of area restaurants. Each of the four rooms in the adjacent building has a decorative theme such as Kashmir, St. Andrews, and Provence. ⊠ *Box 618, U.S. 7, 02162,* ☎ *413/298–3337 or 888/466–7865,* 𝕱𝕬𝕏 *413/298–3406. 12 rooms. Pool. Full breakfast. AE, D, MC, V.*

$$-$$$ ⭐ ⊡ **Historic Merrell Inn.** This inn, built more than 200 years ago as a private residence (it was later a stagecoach stopover), has some good-size rooms, several with working fireplaces. Meticulously maintained, the Merrell has an unfussy yet authentic style, with polished wide-board floors, painted walls, and wood antiques. The sitting room has an open fireplace and contains the only intact "bird cage" Colonial bar—a semi-circular bar surrounded by wooden slats—in the country. Breakfast is cooked to order. ⊠ *1565 Pleasant St./Rte. 102, South Lee 01260,* ☎ *413/243–1794 or 800/243–1794,* 𝕱𝕬𝕏 *413/243–2669. 9 rooms, 1 suite. Full breakfast. MC, V.*

Nightlife and the Arts

The **Berkshire Theatre Festival** (☎ 413/298–5536; 413/298–5576 for box office) stages nightly performances during summer in Stockbridge. Plays written by local schoolchildren are performed occasionally during the summer. The **Red Lion's Lion's Den** (☞ Dining and Lodging, *above*) presents live jazz, folk, or blues nightly. **Robbins-Zust Family Marionettes** (⊠ East Rd., Richmond, ☎ 413/698–2591) mounts a varied program that always includes Punch and Judy and classic fairy-tale stories and performs year-round throughout the Berkshires.

Shopping

Downtown Stockbridge's many "country stores" sell New England kitsch at premium prices—you're better off heading out of town to the smaller, less-crowded shops. **Sawyer Antiques** (⊠ Depot St., West Stockbridge, ☎ 413/232–7062) sells Early American furniture and accessories in a spare clapboard structure that was a Shaker mill.

Great Barrington

55 *7 mi south of Stockbridge.*

The largest town in the southern Berkshires was the first place to free slaves under due process of law and was also the birthplace of W. E. B. Du Bois, the civil rights leader, author, and educator. The many ex–New Yorkers who live in Great Barrington expect great food and service, and the restaurants here deliver complex, tasteful fare. The town is also a mecca for antiques hunters, as are the nearby villages of South Egremont and Sheffield.

Bartholomew's Cobble, south of Great Barrington, is a natural rock garden beside the Housatonic River (the Native American name means "river beyond the mountains"). The 277-acre site is filled with trees, ferns, wildflowers, and hiking trails. The visitor center has a museum. ⊠ *Rte. 7A,* ☎ *413/229–8600.* 🎫 *$3.* ☉ *Daily dawn–dusk; museum Wed.–Sun. 9–4:30 in summer, weekdays 9–4:30 rest of yr.*

Mt. Washington State Forest (⊠ Rte. 23, ☎ 413/528–0330) is 16 mi southwest of Great Barrington on the New York State border. The free primitive camping area is open year-round, but there's a catch—you have to hike 1½ mi from the parking lot. The forest's Bash Bish Brook (say that 10 times, fast) flows through a gorge and over a 50-ft waterfall into a clear natural pool.

Dining and Lodging

$$$ ✕ **Helsinki Tea Company.** The last theater project Deborah McDowell was involved in before opening a restaurant was *The Lost World,* and this cozy spot suggests a lost world of Old European elegance. It's a hodgepodge of colorful cushions, fringed draperies, and objets d'art that meld to give the feeling of an intimate café. The emphasis is on Finnish, Russian, and Jewish cuisines, prepared with lots of spices and served in big portions. It doesn't get much cozier than sitting by a roaring fire, tucking into an order of Midnight Train to Moscow (chicken-apple bratwurst, hot cabbage slaw, and potato latkes), and then lingering over one of the numerous tea offerings (or something stronger—the restaurant has a full liquor license). Music and poetry readings are a Monday-night feature. ⊠ *284 Main St.,* ☎ *413/528–3394. MC, V.*

$$–$$$ ✕⌂ **Egremont Inn.** The public rooms in this 1780 inn are enormous, and each has a fireplace. Bedrooms are on the small side but have four-poster beds, claw-foot baths, and, like the rest of the inn, unpretentious furnishings. Windows sweep around two sides of the stylish restaurant ($$$; reservations essential on weekends in season), where flames flicker in a huge fireplace. The menu changes frequently but always includes salmon or another fresh fish, a homemade pasta, and a hearty meat dish like rib-eye steak with caramelized onions. There's a three-night minimum in season. ⊠ *10 Old Sheffield Rd., South Egremont 01258,* ☎ *413/528–2111 or 800/859–1780,* ℻ *413/528–3284. 19 rooms, 1 suite. Restaurant, bar, pool, tennis court. Continental breakfast. AE, D, MC, V.*

$$–$$$ ✕⌂ **Stagecoach Hill Inn.** Built in 1765, this handsome redbrick inn has been welcoming travelers since 1829. An eclectic mix of family heirlooms, antiques, and period reproductions furnishes the rooms in both the main building and the cottage. The dinner menu is as varied as the furnishings: house-cured gravlax, Cuban black bean soup, veal piccata, baked shrimp Provençale, and potato-and-basil-encrusted salmon fillet. A pub menu is served in the tavern, which has a fireplace. ⊠ *854 S. Undermountain Rd., Sheffield 01257,* ☎ *413/229–8585. 16 rooms, 12 with bath. 2 restaurants, pool. Continental breakfast. AE, MC, V.*

$$–$$$$ ⌂ **Weathervane Inn.** Originally a farmhouse, this 1785 inn on 10 landscaped acres has period-appointed guest rooms and comfortable sitting rooms. Home-baked cookies and cakes are served at afternoon tea, and the Lornes will prepare gourmet boxed picnic dinners. Golf courses and tennis courts are nearby. ⊠ *Box 388, Rte. 23, South Egremont 01258,* ☎ *413/528–9580 or 800/528–9580,* ℻ *413/528–1713. 13 rooms. Bar, pool. Full breakfast. AE, MC, V, AE.*

$–$$$ ⌂ **Barrington Court Motel.** This motel is set back from U.S. 7, and each room is nicely furnished and has cable TV and air-conditioning. Rooms on the second floor have sitting areas. ⊠ *400 Stockbridge Rd., 01230,* ☎ *413/528–2340. 21 rooms, 3 efficiency units. Pool, playground. AE, D, MC, V.*

$$ ⌂ **Mountain View Motel.** This motel 1 mi west of Butternut Basin ski area has pleasant accommodations with coffeemakers; Norman Rockwell prints hang on the walls. ⊠ *304 State Rd./Rte. 23E, 01230,* ☎ *413/528–0250,* ℻ *413/528–0137. 16 rooms, 1 suite, 1 efficiency. AE, MC, V.*

$$ ⌂ **Turning Point Inn.** In 1995, the O'Rourke family purchased this 200-year-old inn, which once served as a stagecoach stop. Because they are chefs, the O'Rourkes place as much emphasis on food as on accommodations. The six second-floor bedrooms are cozy and simply decorated. The two-bedroom cottage has a living-room kitchen and heated sun porch. Dinners, served on weekends only, are prix fixe and beautifully prepared and presented. The breakfast menu changes daily. ⊠ *3 Lake Buel Rd., 01230,* ☎ *413/528–4777. 6 rooms, 4 with bath; 1 cottage. Full breakfast. AE, MC, V.*

$–$$ ⌂ **Ivanhoe Country House.** The Appalachian Trail runs right across the property of this 1780 house. The antiques-furnished rooms are generally spacious; four have working fireplaces, several have private porches or balconies, and all have excellent views. The large sitting room has antique desks, a piano, a fireplace, and comfortable couches. The owners have several golden retrievers; dogs are welcome. A Continental breakfast is brought to your door each morning. ⌧ *254 S. Undermountain Rd./Rte. 41, Sheffield, 01257,* ☎ *413/229–2143. 9 rooms, 2 suites. Refrigerators, pool. Continental breakfast. No credit cards.*

Nightlife and the Arts

Jazz musicians perform at the **Egremont Inn** (☞ Dining and Lodging, *above*) on Friday and Saturday.

The **Berkshire Opera Company** (⌧ 314 Main St., ☎ 413/528–4420) performs two operas in Great Barrington in July and August—one a classic, the other a 20th-century work in English.

Outdoor Activities and Sports

Three miles north of Great Barrington, you can leave your car in a parking lot beside U.S. 7 and climb Squaw Peak on **Monument Mountain.** The 2½-mi circular hike (a trail map is displayed in the parking lot) takes you up 900 ft, past glistening white quartzite cliffs from which Native Americans are said to have leapt to their deaths to placate the gods. The view of the surrounding mountains from the peak is superb.

North of Great Barrington is the large and untamed **Beartown State Forest,** which has miles of hiking trails and a small campground where the fee for a site is $4 a night (first come, first served). ⌧ *Blue Hill Rd., Monterey,* ☎ *413/528–0904.*

Shopping

The Great Barrington area, including the small towns of Sheffield and South Egremont, has the greatest concentration of antiques stores in the Berkshires. Some shops are open sporadically, and many are closed on Tuesday. For a list of storekeepers, send a self-addressed, stamped envelope to the **Berkshire County Antiques Dealers Association** (⌧ R.D. 1, Box 1, Sheffield 01257, ☎ 413/528–4252). The 100-plus dealers in the three-story **Coffman's Country Antiques Market** (⌧ Jennifer House Commons, U.S. 7, ☎ 413/528–9282) sell furniture, quilts, baskets, and silverware. **Corashire Antiques** (⌧ Rte. 23 and U.S. 7 at Belcher Sq., ☎ 413/528–0014), a shop in a red barn, carries American country furniture and accessories (mostly painted, nothing formal), including the occasional Shaker piece. **Mullin-Jones Antiquities** (⌧ 525 S. Main St./U.S. 7, ☎ 413/528–4871) has 18th- and 19th-century country-French antiques: armoires, buffets, tables, chairs, and gilded mirrors.

Red Barn Antiques (⌧ Rte. 23, South Egremont, ☎ 413/528–3230) carries antique lamps and 19th-century American furniture, glass, and accessories. The **Splendid Peasant** (⌧ Rte. 23 and Sheffield Rd., South Egremont, ☎ 413/528–5755) houses an extensive collection of museum-quality 18th- and 19th-century American folk art, including weather vanes, game boards, decoys, and painted furniture.

Bradford Galleries (⌧ U.S. 7, Sheffield, ☎ 413/229–6667) holds monthly auctions of furniture, paintings and prints, china, glass, silver, and Oriental rugs. A tag sale of household items occurs daily. **Darr Antiques and Interiors** (⌧ 28 S. Main St./U.S. 7, Sheffield, ☎ 413/229–7773) displays elegant 18th- and 19th-century American, English, Continental, and Asian furniture and accessories in an impressive Colonial house. A second building houses another 1,600 square ft of antiques. **Dovetail Antiques** (⌧ U.S. 7, Sheffield, ☎ 413/229–2628) shows American clocks, pottery, and country furniture. Some of the pottery on display at **Great Barrington Pottery** (⌧ Rte. 41, Housatonic, ☎ 413/274–6259) is crafted on site; there are gallery-style showrooms, European and Japanese gardens, and a tea room.

Antiques at the Buggy Whip Factory (✉ Main St./Rte. 272, Southfield, ☎ 413/229–3576) provides space for 95 dealers selling jewelry, glass, china, sterling, books, formal and country furniture, and 19th-century fabrics.

Skiing and Snow Sports

BUTTERNUT BASIN

This friendly resort has good base facilities, pleasant skiing, 100% snow-making capabilities, and a decent eatery in the base lodge. Skiers from New York's Long Island and Westchester County and Connecticut's Fairfield County flock to the area. There are three snow parks for snowboarders; ski and snowboard lessons are available for kids and adults. Kids six and under ski free if accompanied by a paying adult. ✉ *Rte. 23, 01230,* ☎ *413/528–2000, ext. 112; 413/528–4433 for ski school; 800/438–7669 for snow conditions.*

Downhill. Only a steep chute or two interrupt the mellow intermediate terrain on 22 trails. There are slopes for beginners and something for everyone off the area's 1,000-ft vertical. One quad, one triple, and four double chairlifts, plus two surface lifts, keep skier traffic spread out.

Cross-country. Butternut Basin has 8 km (4 mi) of groomed cross-country trails.

Child care. The nursery takes children from age 2½ to age 6, and younger toddlers or infants by appointment. The ski school's SKIwee program is for children from 4 to 12 years old.

The Berkshires A to Z

Arriving and Departing

BY BUS

Bonanza Bus Lines (☎ 800/556–3815) connects points throughout the Berkshires with Albany, New York City, and Providence. **Peter Pan Bus Lines** (☎ 413/442–4451 or 800/237–8747) serves Lee and Pittsfield from Boston and Albany.

BY CAR

The Massachusetts Turnpike (I–90) connects Boston with Lee and Stockbridge and continues into New York, where it becomes the New York State Thruway. To reach the Berkshires from New York City take either I–87 or the Taconic State Parkway.

Abbott's Limousine and Livery Service, Inc. (☎ 413/243–1645) provides transportation to and from airports throughout the region, including New York, Boston, and Hartford. It requires 24-hour notice.

BY TRAIN

Amtrak (☎ 800/872–7245) runs the *Lake Shore Limited,* which stops at Pittsfield once daily in each direction on its route between Boston and Chicago.

Getting Around

BY CAR

The main north–south road within the Berkshires is U.S. 7. Route 2 runs from the northern Berkshires to Greenfield at the head of the Pioneer Valley and continues across Massachusetts into Boston. The scenic section of Route 2 known as the Mohawk Trail runs from Williamstown to Orange.

Contacts and Resources

ARTS LISTINGS

The daily *Berkshire Eagle* covers the area's arts festivals; from June to Columbus Day the *Eagle* publishes *Berkshires Week,* the summer bible for events information. The *Williamstown Advocate* prints general arts listings. The Thursday edition of the *Boston Globe* publishes news of major concerts.

CANOEING

Pleasant **canoe trips** in the Berkshires include Lenox–Dalton (19 mi), Lenox–Stockbridge (12 mi), Stockbridge–Great Barrington (13 mi), and, for experts, Great Barrington–Falls Village (25 mi). Information about these and other trips can be found in *The AMC River Guide to Massachusetts, Rhode Island, and Connecticut* (⊠ Appalachian Mountain Club, 5 Joy St., Boston 02198).

EMERGENCIES

Fairview Hospital (⊠ 29 Lewis Ave., Great Barrington, ☎ 413/528–0790). **Hillcrest Hospital** (⊠ 165 Tor Ct., Pittsfield, ☎ 413/443–4761). **North Adams Regional Hospital** (⊠ Hospital Ave., North Adams, ☎ 413/663–3701).

HIKING

Berkshire Region Headquarters (⊠ 740 South St., Pittsfield, ☎ 413/442–8928) has information about trails and hiking.

New England Hiking Holidays (☎ 603/356–9696 or 800/869–0949) of North Conway, New Hampshire, organizes guided hiking vacations through the Berkshires, with overnight stays at country inns. Hikes cover from 5 to 9 mi per day.

LODGING REFERRALS

Lenox Chamber of Commerce (☎ 413/637–3646 or 800/255–3669). **Southern Berkshires Chamber of Commerce** (☎ 413/528–4006).

VISITOR INFORMATION

Berkshire Visitors Bureau (⊠ Berkshire Common, Pittsfield 01201, ☎ 413/443–9186 or 800/237–5747). **Lenox Chamber of Commerce** (⊠ Lenox Academy Building, 75 Main St., 01240, ☎ 413/637–3646). **Mohawk Trail Association** (⊠ Box 2031, Charlemont 01339, ☎ 413/664–6256).

MASSACHUSETTS A TO Z

Arriving and Departing

By Bus

Bonanza (☎ 800/556–3815) serves Boston, Cape Cod, and the eastern part of the state from Providence, with connecting service to New York. **Greyhound** (☎ 800/231–2222) buses connect Boston with all major cities in North America. **Peter Pan Bus Lines** (☎ 617/426–7838 or 800/237–8747) connects Boston with cities elsewhere in Massachusetts and in Connecticut, New Hampshire, and New York. **Plymouth & Brockton Buses** (☎ 508/746–0378) link Boston with the South Shore and Cape Cod. The Boston depot for the bus companies is **South Station** (⊠ Atlantic Ave. and Summer St., ☎ 617/345–7451).

By Car

Boston is the traffic hub of New England, with interstate highways approaching it from every direction. New England's chief coastal highway, I–95, skirts Boston; I–90 leads west to the Great Lakes and Chicago. Interstate–91 brings visitors to the Pioneer Valley in western Massachusetts from Vermont and Canada to the north and Connecticut and New York to the south.

By Plane

Boston's **Logan International Airport** (☞ Arriving and Departing *in* Boston A to Z, *above*) has scheduled flights by most major domestic and foreign carriers. **Bradley International Airport** (☞ Arriving and Departing *in* The Pioneer Valley A to Z, *above*) in Windsor Locks, Connecticut, 18 mi south of Springfield on I–91, has scheduled flights by major U.S. airlines.

By Train

The Northeast Corridor service of **Amtrak** (☎ 800/872–7245) links Boston with the principal cities between it and Washington, D.C. The *Lake Shore Limited,* which stops at Springfield and the Berkshires, carries passengers from Chicago to Boston.

Getting Around

See Arriving and Departing, *above,* or the regional A to Z sections, *above.*

By Car

The speed limit on interstate highways is 65 mph; 55 mph may be posted near urban areas. Other highways are 50 mph, except as indicated in settled areas. Rights turns on red are permitted unless otherwise posted.

Contacts and Resources

Camping

A list of private campgrounds throughout Massachusetts can be obtained free from the **Massachusetts Office of Travel and Tourism** (☞ *below*).

Emergencies

Ambulance, fire, police (☎ 911).

Visitor Information

Massachusetts Office of Travel and Tourism (✉ 100 Cambridge St., Boston 02202, ☎ 617/727–3201 or 800/447–6277).

5 RHODE ISLAND

From the coast of Block Island, you can
view much of southern Rhode Island. To the
northwest lie the delicate barrier beaches of
South County. The glimmer on the
northeastern horizon is Newport, a city of
mansions and Colonial homes. From
Newport Harbor it's a 25-mile trip up
Narragansett Bay to the Ocean State's lively
capital, Providence; 20 miles farther north is
the Blackstone Valley, birthplace of the
American Industrial Revolution. Its easily
accessible history and natural beauty make
Rhode Island an appealing New England
destination.

WITH PROPER PLANNING, a traveler in Rhode Island can pick apples in the morning in the Blackstone Valley, ice-skate in downtown Providence by noon, walk a South County beach after a delicious lunch, and end the day with a sunset sail in Newport. Besides possessing such recreational offerings, the smallest state in the nation—just 1,500 square mi (500 of that being water)—is packed with American history: The state holds 20% of the country's National Historic Landmarks and has more restored Colonial and Victorian buildings than anywhere else in the United States.

Revised and
updated by
K. D. Weaver

In May 1776, before the Declaration of Independence was issued, Rhode Island and Providence Plantations—the state's official name—passed an act removing the king's name from all state documents. This action was typical of the independent-thinking colony. A steadfast insistence upon separation of church and state made Rhode Island attractive to Jews and Quakers, who in the 17th and 18th centuries fled puritanical Massachusetts for Newport and Providence. The first public school was established in forward-thinking Newport in 1664. (Rhode Island continues to be a force in education, with 70,000 students at 10 colleges and universities.) In the 19th century the state flourished, as its entrepreneurial leaders constructed some of the nation's earliest cotton mills, textile mills, and foundries for jewelry. Industry attracted workers from French Canada, Italy, Ireland, England and Eastern Europe, descendants of whom have retained much of their heritage in numerous ethnic enclaves all across the state.

Diversity from community to community makes the Ocean State a favorite test market for new products. The same economic diversity has also produced some less attractive elements: crowded state highways with potholes, massive military facilities, abandoned factories, and a reputation for political corruption. At the close of the 20th century, tourism has emerged as the state's biggest money maker. Neighborhoods, remote townships, even rough-hewn cities like Pawtucket and Woonsocket are now constructing bike paths, historic walkways, and visitor centers. Leading the way is the capital city of Providence, where leaders are aggressively reshaping the city in what has been termed a renaissance. Statewide, roads are being fixed, and the body politic has generally been purged of corruption.

Rhode Island's 39 towns and cities—none more than 50 mi apart—all hold architectural gems and historic sights. You can tour a gilded-age mansion in Newport and, an hour later, be inside the 1786 John Brown House in Providence, once considered the finest home in North America. Natural attractions such as Narragansett Bay—the second-largest bay on the East Coast and a mecca for world-class sailors—and the barrier beaches of South County round out Rhode Island's list of attractions; inspired culinary artistry and fine accommodations complement the mix. With so many offerings in such a compact space, it's easy to explore the Rhode Island that fits your interests.

Pleasures and Pastimes

Beaches

Rhode Island has 400 mi of shoreline with more than 100 salt- and freshwater beaches. Almost all the ocean beaches around the resort communities of Narragansett, Watch Hill, Newport, and Block Island are open to the public. Deep sands blanket most Rhode Island beaches,

Rhode Island

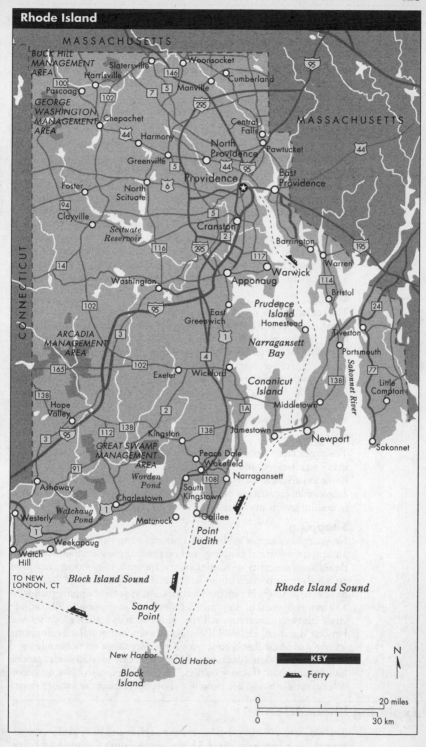

MASSACHUSETTS

BUCK HILL MANAGEMENT AREA

Slatersville
Woonsocket
Harrisville
146
Cumberland
100
Pascoag
102
Manville
7
5
GEORGE WASHINGTON MANAGEMENT AREA
Chepachet
295
44
Harmony
Central Falls
MASSACHUSETTS
Greenville
5
North Providence
44
Pawtucket
44
5
44
95
Providence
East Providence
Foster
North Scituate
6
94
Clayville
5
Scituate Reservoir
Cranston
2
116
Barrington
295
117
Warren
195
Washington
Warwick
114
Apponaug
Bristol
102
95
East Greenwich
Prudence Island
24
Homestead
Tiverton
CONNECTICUT
ARCADIA MANAGEMENT AREA
3
1
Narragansett Bay
Portsmouth
165
4
77
102
Exeter
Wickford
Conanicut Island
Little Compton
138
1A
Middletown
138
Hope Valley
2
Sakonnet River
3
95
112
138
Kingston
138
Jamestown
Newport
91
GREAT SWAMP MANAGEMENT AREA
Peace Dale
Wakefield
Sakonnet
Ashaway
Worden Pond
108
Narragansett
Charlestown
South Kingstown
1
Westerly
Watchaug Pond
Matunuck
Galilee
1
Weekapaug
Point Judith
Watch Hill

TO NEW LONDON, CT
Block Island Sound

Rhode Island Sound

Sandy Point

New Harbor
Old Harbor
Block Island

KEY
🚢 Ferry

N

0   20 miles

0   30 km

and their waters are clear and clean—in some places, the water takes on the turquoise color of the Caribbean Sea. There's a beautiful view of Newport's harbor from the beach at Fort Adams State Park; nearby Middletown has a long beach adjacent to a bird sanctuary; and Jamestown's Mackerel Cove Beach is sheltered from heavy surf. With naturally occurring white sands and a rock reef to the north that's ideal for snorkeling, Mansion Beach on Block Island is one of the most splendid coastal stretches in New England.

Boating

It should come as no surprise that a place nicknamed the Ocean State would attract a multitude of boaters. Colonial Newport prospered from shipbuilding and overseas trading, and even today boating is the city's second-largest industry after tourism. Point Judith Pond, close to deep Atlantic waters, harbors New England's largest commercial fishing fleet and nearly four dozen sportfishing charter boats. Block Island's Great Salt Pond is New England's busiest summertime harbor, hosting more than 1,700 boats on weekends. At the head of the Narragansett Bay, an impressive riverfront park, Waterplace, is a destination for small powerboats, canoes, and kayaks. Many tidal rivers and salt ponds in South County are ideal for kayaking and canoeing.

Dining

The regional fare prepared in Rhode Island includes johnnycakes, a corn-cake–like affair cooked on a griddle, and the native clam, the quahog (pronounced *ko*-hog), which is served raw, stuffed, fried, and in chowder. "Shore dinners" consist of clam chowder, steamed soft-shell clams, clam cakes, sausage, corn-on-the-cob, lobster, watermelon, and Indian pudding (a steamed pudding made with cornmeal and molasses). The Federal Hill neighborhood in Providence holds superlative Italian restaurants, and several dozen other restaurants in the city rival many of Boston's finest eateries.

Lodging

The major chain hotels are represented in Rhode Island, but the state's many smaller bed-and-breakfasts and other inns offer a more downhome experience. Rates are very much seasonal; in Newport, for example, winter rates are often half those of summer. Many inns located in coastal towns are closed in winter.

Shopping

Newport is a shopper's—but not a bargain hunter's—city. You can find antiques, traditional clothing, and marine supplies in abundance. Antiques are a specialty of South County; more than 30 stores are within an hour's drive of each other. Towns such as Wickford and Watch Hill have unique shops in postcard settings. An upscale shopping mall with 150 stores opened in downtown Providence in August 1999, and the city's ethnic communities sell specialties such as Italian groceries and Hmong (Laotian) clothing. Providence's student population supports a variety of secondhand boutiques and funky shops on Wickenden and Thayer streets. The Blackstone Valley contains myriad outlet stores; unlike suburban "factory outlets," these places, often low on decor, offer great deals and are usually a short walk from the factory floor.

Exploring Rhode Island

The Blackstone Valley region and the capital city of Providence compose the northern portion of Rhode Island. South County to the west and Newport County to the east, make up the southern portion of the state. The museums and country roads of the Blackstone Valley make it a good family destination; Providence has history, intellectual and cultural vitality, and great food. Both southerly regions have beaches, boating, and historical sights, with Newport being more historically significant, more upscale, and more crowded.

Numbers in the text and in the margin correspond to numbers on the maps: Central Providence, the Blackstone Valley, South County and Newport County, Block Island, Downtown Newport, and Greater Newport.

Great Itineraries

By car it's less than an hour from any one place in Rhode Island to another. Though the distances are short, the state is densely populated, and getting around its cities and towns can be confusing; it's best to map out your route in advance. In five days, you can visit all four regions of the state, as well as Block Island. On a shorter visit of several days, you can still take in two regions, such as Providence and Newport. Most of the sights in Providence can be seen in one day. The Blackstone Valley will also occupy one day, but during fall foliage season, you will want to spend more time here. Newport has many facets and will require two busy days. South County, with its superb beaches, is generally a relaxing two-day destination.

In Rhode Island, however, just one day can be an unforgettable adventure. A day-long drive from Watch Hill to Newport can include a beach hike at Napatree Point or go-cart rides in Misquamicut, a fishing trip out of Galilee, a tour of a Newport mansion, and dinner at an exquisite French restaurant.

IF YOU HAVE 3 DAYS

Spend a day and a half in the historic waterfront city of ▦ **Newport** ㊵–㋕, and then make the 40-minute drive north to ▦ **Providence** ①–⑰. Though this city's attractions are less packaged than Newport's, they include sophisticated restaurants, historic districts, two large city parks, and a new outdoor skating rink.

IF YOU HAVE 5 DAYS

Spend your first three days in ▦ **Newport** ㊵–㋕ and ▦ **Providence** ①–⑰; then take two days to explore South County. With pristine beaches and no shortage of restaurants and inns, South County encourages a take-it-as-it-goes attitude that's just right for summer and fall touring. Shop and soak up the turn-of-the-century elegance of ▦ **Watch Hill** ㉓, and then spend a day on the beach in **Charlestown** ㉕ or **South Kingstown** ㉖ (try **Misquamicut** ㉔ if you prefer beaches with a carnival atmosphere). ▦ **Narragansett** ㉗, which has great beaches and numerous B&Bs, is one option for a second South County night. A day trip to **Block Island** ㉙–㉜ allows enough time to see some of its treasures, though many people could linger for a week.

When to Tour Rhode Island

The best time to visit Rhode Island is between May and October. Newport hosts several high-profile music festivals in summer; Providence is at its prettiest; and Block Island and the beach towns of South County are in full swing (though not nearly as crowded as Newport). Because of the light traffic and the often gorgeous weather, October is a great time to come to Rhode Island. The colorful fall foliage of the Blackstone Valley is as bright and varied as any in New England.

PROVIDENCE

The November 1998 inauguration of an outdoor ice rink in formerly unremarkable Kennedy Plaza amounted to a debutante ball for Providence, with marching bands, fireworks, and speeches. Long considered an awkward stepchild of greater Boston (50 mi to the north) by even its own residents, Providence is beginning to shrug off its apparent inferiority complex.

The decline of Providence's two main industries, textiles and jewelry, precipitated a population exodus in the 1940s and '50s. In the '60s and '70s, major Rhode Island naval installations were phased out, and the 1990s began with a statewide banking crisis. But the bad news has ended, and New England's third-largest city (behind Boston and Worcester) is poised to start the new millennium as a renaissance city. In the past five years, rivers have been rerouted and railroad tracks have been put underground. Dilapidated neighborhoods are being rejuvenated. A convention center and a riverfront park have opened, and an upscale shopping mall was set to open in fall 1999. Many travelers now prefer the revamped T. F. Green State Airport over Boston's Logan Airport.

Behind renascent Providence is its personable mayor of 15 years, Vincent "Buddy" Cianci, who markets his own pasta sauce and has become a sought-after authority on rejuvenating American cities. Cianci recently forged a cultural exchange program with Florence, Italy, that promises to bring Italian artwork and artisans to Providence. Time spent courting Hollywood dealmakers has resulted in a string of movies being filmed in the city, including *Something About Mary* and *Outside Providence*, and an NBC dramatic show entitled *Providence*. The city, home to the Johnson and Wales University Culinary Institute, has also emerged as a gastronomical hotbed, with more restaurants per capita than any other major city in America.

Roger Williams founded Providence in October 1635 as a refuge for freethinkers and religious dissenters escaping the dictates of the Puritans of Massachusetts Bay Colony. It remains a community willing to embrace independent thinking in business, the arts, and academia. Brown University, the Rhode Island School of Design (RISD), and Trinity Square Repertory Company are major forces in New England's intellectual and cultural life. Playing to that strength, Providence is striving to have its once-abandoned downtown (now called Downcity, to erase the connotations of the old downtown) populated by artists and art studios. A state referendum has exempted such artists from income taxes. Such statewide support is not surprising, because improvements here are typically a boon to the rest of the state. Because it is so integral to the rest of the state, Providence is sometimes called the city-state of Rhode Island.

A Good Walk and Tour

Begin at the **Rhode Island State House** ①, where the south portico looks down over the city of Providence and the farthest reach of Narragansett Bay. After touring the capitol, proceed to Smith Street, at the north end of the State House grounds. Follow the road east to **Roger Williams National Memorial** ②. **Benefit Street** ③ is one block east (up the hill). Walk south on the historic street to the **Museum of Art, Rhode Island School of Design** ④, and the **Providence Athenaeum** ⑤.

Head east (away from the Providence River) on College Street and north (to the left) on Prospect Street to reach the **John Hay Library** ⑥. The **Brown University** ⑦ campus is across the street. Walk east on Waterman Street; you can enter the grounds at Brown Street. After you've toured the campus, exit from the gate at George Street (to the south) and turn right, which will take you back to Benefit Street. Walk south for one block, where you'll see the handsome **First Unitarian Church of Providence** ⑧. The magnificent **John Brown House** ⑨ is two blocks south of here. From the Brown house, walk one block downhill on Power Street and turn right on South Main Street. Proceed north until you reach the **Market House** ⑩ and, one block farther north, the **First Baptist Church in America** ⑪. Turn left at Steeple Street (also called Thomas Street), and you will shortly reach **Waterplace Park and Riverwalk** ⑫.

The **Rhode Island Black Heritage Society** ⑬, the Italian neighborhood of **Federal Hill** ⑭, and **Wickenden Street** ⑮ are best visited via car or taxi. The stately **Governor Henry Lippit House Museum** ⑯ and the **Museum of Rhode Island History at Aldrich House** ⑰ are four blocks apart in the eastern end of Providence; you'll need a car or taxi to visit them.

TIMING

The timing of the walk from the State House to Waterplace Park will vary greatly depending on how much time you spend at each sight. If you stop for a half hour at most sights and an hour at the RISD Museum of Art, the tour will take about six hours. To see the rest of the sights, add in several additional hours.

Sights to See

❸ **Benefit Street.** The centerpiece of any visit to Providence is the "Mile of History," where a bumpy cobblestone sidewalk passes a row of early Federal and 19th-century candy-color houses crammed shoulder-to-shoulder on a steep hill overlooking downtown. Romantic Benefit Street is a reminder of the wealth brought to Colonial Rhode Island through the triangular trade of slaves, rum, and molasses. Much of Providence beyond Benefit Street was brought back into fashion in the 1980s by Bostonians looking for cheaper real estate, even though the investment meant enduring an hour-long commute. The **Providence Preservation Society** (✉ 21 Meeting St., at Benefit St., ☎ 401/831–7440) offers maps and pamphlets with self-guided tours.

❼ **Brown University.** The nation's seventh-oldest college, founded in 1764, is an Ivy League institution with more than 40 academic departments, including a school of medicine. Gothic and Beaux Arts structures dominate the campus, which has been designated a National Historic Landmark. University tours leave daily at 10, 11, 1, 3, and 4 from the admissions office, in the Corliss-Brackett House. Thayer Street is the campus's principal commercial thoroughfare. ✉ *Corliss-Brackett House, 45 Prospect St., ☎ 401/863–2378 or 401/863–2703 for tour information.*

⑭ **Federal Hill.** You're as likely to hear Italian as English in this neighborhood that is vital to Providence's culture and sense of self. The stripe down the middle of Atwells Avenue is repainted each year in red, white, and green, and a huge *pigna* (pinecone), an Italian symbol of abundance and quality, hangs on an arch soaring over the street. Hardware shops sell boccie sets and the corner store sells china statues of saints, but the "Avenue," as locals call it, isn't cutesy. The Columbus Weekend Festival (held on the Sunday of that weekend), with music, food stands, and parades, is not to be missed.

⑪ **First Baptist Church in America.** This historic house of worship was built in 1775 for a congregation established in 1638 by Roger Williams and his fellow Puritan dissenters. The church, one of the finest examples of Georgian architecture in the United States, has a carved wood interior, a Waterford crystal chandelier, and graceful but austere Ionic columns. ✉ *75 N. Main St., ☎ 401/751–2266.* 🎟 *Free; donations appreciated.* ☉ *Mon.–Thurs. 9:30–3, Fri. 9:30–1; call ahead on Sat. Tours are guided Memorial Day–Columbus Day; self-guided the rest of the year. Sun. service at 11, guided tour at 12:15; July–Aug., Sun. service at 10, guided tour at 11:15.*

Central Providence

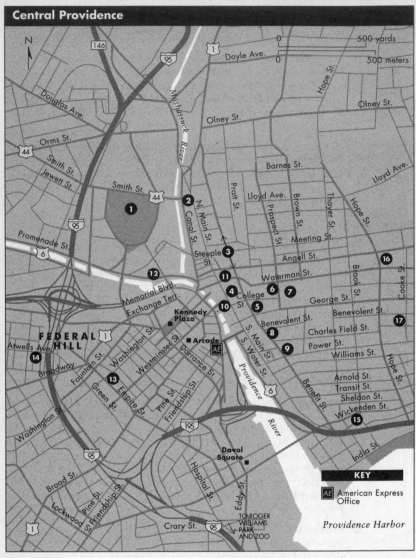

8 **First Unitarian Church of Providence.** This Romanesque house of worship made of Rhode Island granite was built in 1816. Its steeple houses a 2,500-pound bell, the largest ever cast in Paul Revere's foundry. ✉ *1 Benevolent St. (corner of Benefit St.),* ☎ *401/421–7970.* ☎ *Free.* ⊙ *Guided tours by appointment; Sun. service at 10:30.*

16 **Governor Henry Lippit House Museum.** The two-term Rhode Island governor made his fortune selling textiles to both armies during the Civil War, and he spared no expense in building his home, an immaculate Renaissance Revival mansion, in 1863. The floor of the billiard room is made with nine types of inlaid wood; the ceilings are intricately hand-painted (some look convincingly like tiger maple), and the neoclassical chandeliers are cast in bronze. The home was fitted with central heating and electricity, quite an extravagance at the time. ✉ *199 Hope St.,* ☎ *401/453–0688,* FAX *401/453–8221.* ☎ *$6.* ⊙ *Apr.–Dec., Tues.–Fri. 11–3; Jan.–Mar. and weekends by appointment only. Phone ahead, as the museum sometimes closes for private functions.*

★ **9** **John Brown House.** John Quincy Adams called this house "the most magnificent and elegant private mansion that I have ever seen on this continent." George Washington and other historical figures also visited the house. Designed by Joseph Brown for his brother in 1786, the three-story Georgian mansion has elaborate woodwork and is filled with decorative art, furniture, silver, and items from the China trade, which is how John Brown made his fortune. In addition to opening trade with China, John Brown is famous for his role in the burning of the British customs ship *Gaspee.* He was also a slave trader: His abolitionist brother, Moses, brought charges against him for illegally engaging in the buying and selling of human lives. Across the street and open to the public only on Friday from 1 to 4 is the Nightingale House, built by Brown's chief rival in the China trade. ✉ *52 Power St.,* ☎ *401/331–8575.* ☎ *$6.* ⊙ *Mar.–Dec., Tues.–Sat. 10–5, Sun. noon–4; Jan.–Feb., Mon.–Thurs. by appointment, Fri.–Sat. 10–5, Sun. noon–4.*

6 **John Hay Library.** Built in 1910 and named for Abraham Lincoln's secretary, "the Hay" houses 11,000 items related to the 16th president. The noncirculating research library, part of ☞ **Brown University,** also stores American drama and poetry collections, 500,000 pieces of American sheet music, the Webster Knight Stamp Collection, the letters of horror and science-fiction writer H. P. Lovecraft, military prints, and a world-class collection of toy soldiers. ✉ *20 Prospect St.,* ☎ *401/863–2146.* ☎ *Free.* ⊙ *Weekdays 9–5.*

10 **Market House.** Designed by Joseph Brown and owned by the Rhode Island School of Design, this brick structure was central to Colonial Providence's trading economy. Tea was burned here in March 1775, and the upper floors were used as barracks for French soldiers during the Revolutionary War. From 1832 to 1878, Market House served as the seat of city government. A plaque shows the height reached by floodwaters during the Great Hurricane of 1938. The building is not open to the public. ✉ *Market Sq., S. Main St.*

★ **4** **Museum of Art, Rhode Island School of Design.** This small college museum is amazingly comprehensive. Many of the exhibitions, which change annually, are of textiles, a long-standing Rhode Island industry. The museum's permanent holdings include the Abby Aldrich Rockefeller collection of Japanese prints, Paul Revere silver, 18th-century porcelain, and French Impressionist paintings. Popular with children are the 10-ft statue of Buddha and the Egyptian mummy from the Ptolemaic period (circa 300 BC). Admission includes the adjoining **Pendleton**

House, a replica of an early 19th-century Providence house. ⊠ *224 Benefit St.,* ☎ *401/454–6500.* 🎫 *$5.* ⊙ *Wed.–Sun. 10–5, Fri. 10–8.*

⑰ Museum of Rhode Island History at Aldrich House. The Federal-style Aldrich House, built in 1822, was given to the Rhode Island Historical Society in 1974 by the heirs of New York financier Winthrop W. Aldrich. The first comprehensive museum about Rhode Island history, it presents rotating exhibits. ⊠ *110 Benevolent St.,* ☎ *401/331–8575.* 🎫 *$2.* ⊙ *Tues.–Fri. 9–5, Sun. noon–4; until 9 PM 3rd Thurs. of each month.*

★ ⑤ Providence Athenaeum. Established in 1753 and housed in a granite 1838 Greek Revival structure, this is among the oldest lending libraries in the world. The Athenaeum was the center of the intellectual life of old Providence. Here Edgar Allan Poe, visiting Providence to lecture at Brown, met and courted Sarah Helen Whitman, who was said to be the inspiration for his poem "Annabel Lee." The library holds Rhode Island art and artifacts, an original set of elephant folio *Birds of America* prints by John J. Audubon, and one of the world's best collections of travel literature. Changing exhibits showcase parts of the collection. ⊠ *251 Benefit St.,* ☎ *401/421–6970.* 🎫 *Free.* ⊙ *June–Labor Day, Mon.–Thurs. 10–8, Fri. 10–5; Labor Day–May, Mon.–Thurs. 10–8, Fri.–Sat. 10–5, Sun. 1–5.*

⑬ Rhode Island Black Heritage Society. The historical photographs, taped interviews, and other artifacts at this museum chronicle the contributions of African-Americans to Rhode Island life, beginning with the days of slave trading (until its abolition in 1774, slavery was a key element in Rhode Island's economy). Also examined is the present-day experience—education, political integration, and new immigration from Africa, the Caribbean, and elsewhere. ⊠ *202 Washington St., 2nd floor,* ☎ *401/751–3490 or 800/335–3490.* 🎫 *Donation requested.* ⊙ *Weekdays 10–4:30, Sat. by appointment.*

❶ Rhode Island State House. Rhode Island's awe-inspiring capitol, erected in 1900, has the first unsupported marble dome in the United States (and the fourth largest in the world), which was modeled on St. Peter's Basilica in Rome. The gilded statue *Independent Man* tops the ornate white Georgia marble exterior. Engraved on the south portico is a passage from the Royal Charter of 1663: "To hold forth a lively experiment that a most flourishing civil state may stand and best be maintained with full liberty in religious concernments." The interior's focal point is a full-length portrait of George Washington by Rhode Islander Gilbert Stuart, the same artist who created the likeness on the $1 bill. You'll also see the original parchment charter granted by King Charles to the colony of Rhode Island in 1663 and military accoutrements of Nathaniel Greene, Washington's second-in-command during the Revolutionary War. In Room 220, booklets are available for self-guided tours. A gift shop is on the basement level. ⊠ *82 Smith St.,* ☎ *401/ 222–2357.* ⊙ *Weekdays 8:30–4:30; guided tours 9–11.*

❷ Roger Williams National Memorial. Roger Williams contributed so significantly to the development of the concepts that underpin the Declaration of Independence and the Constitution that the National Park Service dedicated a 4½-acre park to his memory. Displays offer a quick course in the life and times of Rhode Island's founder, who wrote the first-ever book on the language of the native people of North America. ⊠ *282 N. Main St.,* ☎ *401/521–7266.* 🎫 *Free.* ⊙ *Daily 9–4:30.*

OFF THE BEATEN PATH   **ROGER WILLIAMS PARK AND ZOO** – This beautiful 430-acre Victorian park is immensely popular. You can picnic, feed the ducks in the lakes, ride a pony, or rent a paddleboat or miniature speedboat. At Carousel

Village, kids can ride the vintage carousel or a miniature train. There's also the Museum of Natural History and the Cormack Planetarium, and the Tennis Center has Rhode Island's only public clay courts. More than 900 animals of 150 different species live at the zoo. Among the attractions are the Tropical Rainforest Pavilion, the African Plains exhibit, and an open-air aviary. To get here from downtown, take I–95 south to U.S. 1 south (Elmwood Avenue); the park entrance will be the first left turn. ⊠ *Elmwood Ave.,* ☎ *401/785–3510 for zoo; 401/785–9457 for museum; 401/785–9450 for park.* ☎ *$3.50.* ☉ *Zoo daily 9–5 (until 4 in winter), museum daily 10–5.*

⑫ **Waterplace Park and Riverwalk.** A key component of Providence's revitalization effort, Waterplace Park was completed in 1997. The 4-acre tract with Venetian-style footbridges, cobblestone walkways, and an amphitheater encircling a tidal pond has won national and international design awards. The Riverwalk passes the junction of three rivers—the Woonasquatucket, Providence, and Moshassuck—a nexus of the shipping trade during the city's early years. On sunny summer days the park draws pedestrians, boaters, artists, and performers. The amphitheater hosts free concerts and plays. Inquire about upcoming events at the visitor information center, in the clock tower. ⊠ *Boat House Clock Tower, 2 American Express Way,* ☎ *401/751–1177.* ☉ *Daily 10–4.*

⑮ **Wickenden Street.** The main artery in the Fox Point district, a working-class Portuguese neighborhood that is undergoing gentrification, Wickenden Street is chockablock with antiques stores, galleries, and trendy cafés. Professors, artists, and students are among the newer residents here. Many of the houses along Wickenden, Transit, Gano, and nearby streets are still painted the pastel colors of Portuguese homes.

Dining

American/Casual

$$ ✗ **Union Station Brewery.** The historic brick building that houses this brew pub was once the freight house for the Providence Train Station. You can wash down a tasty chipotle-glazed pork quesadilla, an old-fashioned chicken potpie, or ale-batter fish-and-chips with a pint of Providence cream ale or one of several other fine beers brewed here. ⊠ *36 Exchange Terr.,* ☎ *401/274–2739. AE, D, DC, MC, V.*

Contemporary

$$$$ ✗ **The Gatehouse.** A redbrick cottage houses this much-praised restau-
★ rant, where the views of the Seekonk River and the classy decor (which includes works from owner Henry Kate's art collection) complement the New Orleans–influenced New England cuisine. Chef Steven Marsella, who trained under Louisiana's Frank Brigtsen and Emeril Lagasse, prepares dishes that might include slow-roasted duck with sautéed vegetables, served with spiced pumpkin gravy and accompanied by cranberry wild rice, butternut squash puree, and spaghetti squash. ⊠ *4 Richmond Sq.,* ☎ *401/521–9229. Reservations essential on weekends. AE, DC, MC, V. No lunch Sat.*

$$$ ✗ **Al Forno.** The owners of Al Forno, George Germon and Johanne
★ Killeen, wrote *Cucina Simpatica,* an acclaimed book on the art of food, and their restaurant cemented the city's reputation as a culinary center in New England. Try a wood-grilled pizza as an appetizer, followed by roasted clams and spicy sausage in a tomato broth or charcoal-seared tournedos of beef with mashed potatoes (called "dirty steak" by regulars) and onion rings. Your dessert could be crepes with apricot puree or a fresh cranberry tart. Meals are served both upstairs, in the rustic dining room, and downstairs, in a room with white mar-

ble flooring. ⊠ *577 S. Main St.,* ☎ *401/273–9760. Reservations not accepted. AE, DC, MC, V. Closed Sun.–Mon. No lunch.*

$$$ ✕ **Rue de l'Espoir.** At this homey, longtime Providence favorite, dishes are designed to be fun. A few of the many eclectic offerings are a lobster Madeira crepe, Szechuan duck quesadillas, and Caribbean-spiced grilled pork porterhouse chops. Wide-plank pine floors, an ornate tin ceiling, and wooden booths set the mood in the dining room. The spacious barroom, where many locals prefer to dine, has a mural in bright pastels and a fine selection of jazz CDs. Breakfast is served on weekdays, brunch on weekends. ⊠ *99 Hope St.,* ☎ *401/751–8890. AE, D, DC, MC, V. Closed Mon.*

French

$$$ ✕ **Pot au Feu.** As night falls, business-driven downtown Providence
★ clears out, and this bastion of French country cuisine lights up. For a quarter century the chefs here have worked to perfect the basics, like pâté du foie gras, beef bourguignon, and potatoes au gratin. Such classically rendered dishes—and a distinctive list of French wines—have inspired a devoted corps of regulars. The dining experience is more casual at the downstairs Bistro than at the upstairs Salon. ⊠ *44 Custom House St.,* ☎ *401/273–8953. AE, DC, MC, V. Salon closed Sun.–Mon.*

Indian

$ ✕ **India.** Mango chicken curry and swordfish kabobs are two of the entrées at this downtown restaurant filled with Oriental rugs, colorful paintings, and plants. India is known for its freshly made breads, including *paratha,* wheat bread cooked on a grill and stuffed with various fillings. ⊠ *123 Dorrance St.,* ☎ *401/278–2000. AE, MC, V.*

Italian

$$$ ✕ **Camille's Roman Garden.** Perhaps the most classic of the Italian eateries on Federal Hill, the second-oldest family-run restaurant in the United States serves traditional fare like veal scallopini and shrimp scampi. Black-tie service and reproductions of early Renaissance murals in the massive dining room (which was a speakeasy in the 1920s) impart an air of sophistication. ⊠ *71 Bradford St.,* ☎ *401/751–4812. AE, DC, MC, V. Closed Sun. July–Aug.*

$$$ ✕ **L'Epicureo.** One of Providence's most refined restaurants was founded as half of a Federal Hill butcher shop called Joe's Quality. Joe's daughter Rozann and son-in-law Tom Buckner transformed the former market into an Italian bistro that has won high marks for its wood-grilled steaks, veal chops, and pasta dishes like fettuccine tossed with arugula, garlic, and lemon. ⊠ *238 Atwells Ave.,* ☎ *401/454–8430. AE, D, DC, MC, V. Closed Sun.–Mon. No lunch.*

$ ✕ **Angelo's Civita Farnese.** On Federal Hill in the heart of Little Italy, lively (even boisterous) Angelo's is a family-run place with Old World charm. Locals come here for good-size portions of fresh and simply prepared pasta. ⊠ *141 Atwells Ave.,* ☎ *401/621–8171. Reservations not accepted. No credit cards.*

Japanese

$–$$ ✕ **Tokyo Restaurant.** New carpeting and a fresh coat of paint may be in order at Tokyo, but the Japanese cuisine served here is the best in the state. Choose traditional or American seating—or take a stool at the sushi bar, where local fish like tuna, mackerel, and eel are prepared alongside red snapper and fish from points beyond. The designer rolls include beef, squid, duck, and seaweed. ⊠ *123 Wickenden St.,* ☎ *401/ 331–5330. AE, D, MC, V.*

Steak

$$$$ ✕ **Capital Grille.** Dry-aged beef is the star, but lobster and fish are also on the menu at the cavernous Capital Grille. The mashed potatoes, cottage fries, and Caesar salads are served in portions that will sate even the heartiest appetite. Leather, brass, mahogany, oil portraits, a mounted wooden canoe, and Bloomberg News ticking away in the barroom lend this establishment the feel of an opulent men's club. ⊠ *1 Cookson Pl.,* ☎ *401/521–5600. AE, D, DC, MC, V. No lunch weekends.*

Lodging

$$–$$$$ ⊞ **Marriott Hotel.** The Marriott may lack the old-fashioned grandeur of a property like the Providence Biltmore (☞ *below*), but the hotel has all the modern conveniences. Tones of mauve and green grace the good-size rooms. The Blue Fin Grille restaurant specializes in local seafood prepared with a French flair. ⊠ *Charles and Orms Sts. near Exit 23 off I-95, 02904,* ☎ *401/272–2400 or 800/937–7768,* ℻ *401/ 273–2686. 345 rooms, 6 suites. Restaurant, 1 indoor and 1 outdoor pool, sauna, health club, meeting rooms. AE, D, DC, MC, V.*

$$$ ⊞ **Providence Biltmore.** The Biltmore, completed in 1922, has a sleek
★ Art Deco exterior, an external glass elevator with delightful views of Providence, and a grand ballroom. The personal attentiveness of its staff (there is a European-style concierge system), the downtown location, and modern amenities make this hotel one of the city's best. ⊠ *Kennedy Plaza, Dorrance and Washington Sts., 02903,* ☎ *401/421– 0700 or 800/294–7209,* ℻ *401/455–3040. 87 rooms, 157 suites. Restaurant, café, health club, meeting rooms. AE, D, DC, MC, V.*

$$$ ⊞ **Westin Hotel.** The multiturreted 25-story Westin towers over Providence's compact downtown, connected by a skywalk to the city's gleaming convention center. Its good-size rooms have reproduction period furniture, and half have king-size beds; many have good views of the city. The redbrick hotel's Agora restaurant has an award-winning wine cellar. ⊠ *1 W. Exchange St., 02903,* ☎ *401/598–8000 or 800/ 937–8461,* ℻ *401/598–8200. 341 rooms, 23 suites. 2 restaurants, 2 bars, pool, hot tub, health club, meeting rooms. AE, D, DC, MC, V.*

$$–$$$ ⊞ **Old Court Bed & Breakfast.** This three-story Italianate inn on historic Benefit Street was built in 1863 as a rectory. Antique furniture, richly colored wallpaper, and memorabilia throughout the house reflect the best of 19th-century style. The comfortable, spacious rooms have high ceilings and chandeliers; most have nonworking marble fireplaces and some have views of the state house and downtown. ⊠ *144 Benefit St., 02903,* ☎ *401/751–2002,* ℻ *401/272–4830. 10 rooms, 1 suite. Full breakfast. AE, D, MC, V.*

$$ ⊞ **State House Inn.** The beautifully restored rooms of this classy inn
★ convenient to the state house are furnished with Shaker- or Colonial-style pieces, and a few have working fireplaces. Some rooms in the 1880s Colonial Revival home are on the small side, but that's the only drawback to this inviting B&B. The inn is no-smoking. ⊠ *43 Jewett St., 02903,* ☎ *401/351–6111,* ℻ *401/351–4261. 10 rooms. Full breakfast. AE, D, MC, V.*

$–$$ ⊞ **C. C. Ledbetter's.** The unmarked somber green exterior of innkeeper C. C. Ledbetter's mansard-roof 1770 home gives few hints of the vibrant interior. Lively art, photographs, quilts, and a shrewd blend of contemporary furnishings and antiques fill the place. The rooms at this B&B across from the John Brown House are priced well below the competition, making it a favorite of the parents of Brown University students. ⊠ *326 Benefit St., 02903,* ☎ ℻ *401/351–4699. 5 rooms, 1 with bath. Continental breakfast. D, MC, V.*

Nightlife and the Arts

For events listings, consult the daily *Providence Journal* and the weekly *Providence Phoenix* (free in restaurants and bookstores). Brown University and the Rhode Island School of Design often present free lectures and performances.

Nightlife

BARS

The **Custom House Tavern** (⊠ 36 Weybosset St., ☎ 401/751–3630) is a friendly downtown gathering place. At the fashionable **Hot Club** (⊠ 575 S. Water St., ☎ 401/861–9007) you may develop a sense of déjà vu; waterside scenes from the movie *Something About Mary* were shot here. **Oliver's** (⊠ 83 Benevolent St., ☎ 401/272–8795), a popular hangout for Brown students that serves good pub food, has three pool tables. **Snookers** (⊠ 145 Clifford St., ☎ 401/351–7665) is a stylish billiard hall in the Jewelry District; through a double doorway at the rear of the billiard room is a '50s-style lounge where food is served.

MUSIC CLUBS

AS220 (⊠ 111 Empire St., ☎ 401/831–9327) is a gallery and performance space; the musical styles run the gamut from techno-pop, hiphop, and jazz to traditional Hmong folk music and dance. The **Call** (⊠ 15 Elbow St., ☎ 401/751–2255), a large blues bar, hosts top local groups like Roomful of Blues. In the same building and under the same management as The Call (☞ *above*) is the **Century Lounge,** which hosts a variety of progressive bands. Proclaiming itself "Rhode Island's number-one reason to party," the **Complex** (⊠ 180 Pine St., ☎ 401/751–4263) is home to four different clubs, the most popular being a mecca for swing dancers. **Gerardo's** (⊠ 1 Franklin Sq., ☎ 401/274–5560) is a popular gay and lesbian disco. The **Living Room** (⊠ 23 Rathbone St., ☎ 401/521–5200) presents live entertainment nightly, often by prominent local blues musicians. **Lupo's Heartbreak Hotel** (⊠ 239 Westminster St., ☎ 401/272–5876), a roadhouse-style nightclub, books local and international talents.

The Arts

FILM

The **Cable Car Cinema** (⊠ 204 S. Main St., ☎ 401/272–3970) is on the musty side, but the theater books a fine slate of alternative and foreign flicks. There are couches rather than seats, and street performers entertain prior to most shows. The new **Providence Place Mall** (⊠ 1 Providence Pl.), near the Westin, has a 16-screen cinema complex and an IMAX theater; at press time no telephone was available.

MUSIC

Rock bands and country acts occasionally perform at the 14,500-seat **Providence Civic Center** (⊠ 1 LaSalle Sq., ☎ 401/331–6700). The **Providence Performing Arts Center** (⊠ 220 Weybosset St., ☎ 401/421–2787), a 3,200-seat theater and concert hall that opened in 1928, hosts touring Broadway shows, concerts, and other large-scale happenings. Its lavish interior contains painted frescoes, Art Deco chandeliers, bronze moldings, and marble floors. The **Rhode Island Philharmonic** (☎ 401/831–3123) presents 18 concerts at Veterans Memorial Auditorium (☞ *below*) between October and May. **Veterans Memorial Auditorium** (⊠ 69 Brownell St., ☎ 401/222–3150) hosts concerts, plays, children's theater, and ballet.

THEATER

Alias Stage (⊠ 31 Elbow St., ☎ 401/831–2919), an ambitious offshoot of Trinity Square Repertory (☞ *below*), presents original works. **Brown University** (⊠ Leeds Theatre, 77 Waterman St., ☎ 401/863–2838) mounts productions of contemporary, sometimes avant-garde, works as well as classics. **New Gate Theatre** (⊠ 134 Mathewson St., ☎ 401/421–9680) specializes in new plays but also stages Broadway musicals and a popular Christmas cabaret. **Trinity Square Repertory Company** (⊠ 201 Washington St., ☎ 401/351–4242), one of New England's best theater companies, presents plays in the renovated Majestic movie house. The varied season generally includes classics, foreign plays, and new works. Plays are also offered at the **Providence Performing Arts Center** and **Veterans Memorial Auditorium** (☞ Music, *above*).

Outdoor Activities and Sports

Basketball

The **Providence College Friars** play Big East basketball at the Providence Civic Center (⊠ 1 LaSalle Sq., ☎ 401/331–6700 for event information; 401/331–2211 for tickets).

Biking

The best biking in the Providence area is along the 14½-mi **East Bay Bicycle Path,** which hugs the Narragansett Bay shore from India Point Park through four towns before it ends in Independence Park in Bristol. **Esta's Too** (⊠ 257 Thayer St., ☎ 401/831–2651), which rents bicycles, is near the East Bay Bicycle Path.

Boating

Prime boating areas include the Providence River, the Seekonk River, and Narragansett Bay. **Baer's River Workshop** (⊠ 222 S. Water St., ☎ 401/453–1633) rents canoes and kayaks from April to October and conducts guided tours of Providence's waterfront. The **Narragansett Boat Club** (⊠ River Rd., ☎ 401/272–1838) has information about local boating.

Football

The **Brown Bears** (☎ 401/863–2773) of Brown University play at Brown Stadium (⊠ Elmgrove and Sessions Sts.).

Golf

The 18-hole, par-72 **Triggs Memorial Golf Course** (⊠ 1533 Chalkstone Ave., ☎ 401/521–8460) has lengthy fairways. The greens fee ranges from $25 to $30; an optional cart costs $24.

Hockey

The **Providence Bruins** (☎ 401/331–6700), a farm team of the Boston Bruins, play at the Civic Center. The **Brown Bears** (☎ 401/863–2773) play high-energy hockey at Meehan Auditorium (⊠ 235 Hope St.).

Ice-skating

A new outdoor ice rink downtown, **Fleet Skating Center** (⊠ Kennedy Plaza, ☎ 401/331–5544) has become a popular destination. It's open October through April, daily 10–8. Skates are available for rent.

Jogging

Three-mile-long, tree-lined **Blackstone Boulevard** is a good place to run.

Shopping

Antiques

Wickenden Street contains many antiques stores and several art galleries. The **Cat's Pajamas** (⊠ 227 Wickenden St., ☎ 401/751–8440) specializes in 20th-century jewelry, linens, housewares, accessories, and small furnishings. **CAV** (⊠ 14 Imperial Pl., ☎ 401/751–9164) is a large restaurant, bar, and coffeehouse (with music Friday and Saturday nights) in a revamped factory space. It sells fine rugs, tapestries, prints, portraits, and antiques. **Tilden-Thurber** (⊠ 292 Westminster St., ☎ 401/272–3200) carries high-end Colonial- and Victorian-era furniture, antiques, and estate jewelry.

Art

The **Alaimo Gallery** (⊠ 301 Wickenden St., ☎ 401/421–5360) specializes in hand-colored engravings, magazine and playbill covers, political cartoons, antique prints, book plates, antique posters, and box labels. **JRS Fine Art** (⊠ 218 Wickenden St., ☎ 401/331–4380) sells works by national, regional, and Rhode Island artists. The **Peaceable Kingdom** (⊠ 116 Ives St., ☎ 401/351–3472) stocks folk art. The store's strengths include Native American jewelry and crafts, Haitian paintings, Oriental rugs, and kilims. Hmong story cloths (from Laos) are another specialty.

Foods

Roma Gourmet Foods (⊠ 310 Atwells Ave., ☎ 401/331–8620) on Federal Hill sells homemade pasta, bread, pizza, pastries, and meats and cheeses. **Tony's Colonial** (⊠ 311 Atwells Ave., ☎ 401/621–86750), a superb Italian grocery and deli, stocks freshly prepared foods.

Malls

America's first shopping mall is the **Arcade** (⊠ 65 Weybosset St., ☎ 401/598–1199), built in 1828. A National Historic Landmark, this graceful Greek Revival building has three tiers of shops and restaurants. Expect the unusual at **Copacetic Rudely Elegant Jewelry** (⊠ The Arcade, 65 Weybosset St., ☎ 401/273–0470), which sells the work of more than 130 diverse artists. The **Game Keeper** (⊠ The Arcade, 65 Weybosset St., ☎ 401/351–0362) sells board games, puzzles, and gadgets.

The new downtown **Providence Place Mall** (⊠ 1 Providence Pl., Francis and Hayes Sts., ☎ 401/270–1000) is anchored by Filene's, Lord & Taylor, and Nordstrom; a movie complex and 150 other shops and restaurants will complete the mix.

Maps

The **Map Center** (⊠ 671 N. Main St., ☎ 401/421–2184) carries maps of all types and nautical charts.

Providence A to Z

Arriving and Departing

See Arriving and Departing *in* Rhode Island A to Z, *below.*

Getting Around

BY BUS

RIPTA (Rhode Island Public Transportation Authority; ☎ 401/781–9400; 800/244–0444 in RI) buses run around town and to T. F. Green State Airport; the main terminal is in Kennedy Plaza (⊠ Washington and Dorrance Sts.). The fares range from $1 to $3.

BY CAR

Overnight parking is not allowed on Providence streets, and during the day it can be difficult to find curbside parking, especially downtown and on Federal and College hills. The Westin Hotel (☞ Lodging, *above*) downtown has a large parking garage. To get from T. F. Green Airport to downtown Providence, take I–95 north to Exit 22.

BY TAXI

Fares are $2 at the flag drop, then $2 per mi. The ride from the airport to downtown takes about 15 minutes and costs about $20. Try **Airport Taxi** (☎ 401/737–2868), **Checker Cab** (☎ 401/273–2222), **Economy Cab** (☎ 401/944–6700), or **Yellow Cab** (☎ 401/941–1122).

Contacts and Resources

EMERGENCIES

Rhode Island Hospital (⊠ 593 Eddy St., ☎ 401/444–4000).

GUIDED TOURS

Peter Pan Pirate Ship operates a six-wheeled, amphibious Alvis Stalwart (a military surplus vehicle) that tours Providence daily from April to November (⊠ Departs from Kennedy Plaza, ☎ 800/237–8747); the cost is $14.95. **Providence Preservation Society** (⊠ 21 Meeting St., ☎ 401/831–7440) publishes a walking-tour guidebook ($2.50) to historic Benefit Street and leads house tours on the second weekend in June.

24-HOUR PHARMACY

Brooks Pharmacy (⊠ 1200 N. Main St., ☎ 401/272–3048).

VISITOR INFORMATION

Greater Providence Convention and Visitors Bureau (⊠ 1 W. Exchange St., 02903, ☎ 401/274–1636).

THE BLACKSTONE VALLEY

The 45-mi-long Blackstone River, a federally designated American Heritage River, runs from Worcester, Massachusetts, to Pawtucket, Rhode Island, where its power was first harnessed in 1790, setting off America's Industrial Revolution. Along the river and its tributaries are many old mill villages and towns separated by woods and farmland. Pawtucket and Woonsocket grew into large cities in the 1800s when a system of canals, and later railroads, became distribution channels for local industry, which attracted a steady flow of French, Irish, and Eastern European immigrants.

This area in the northern portion of the state is named for William Blackstone, who in 1628 became the first European to settle in Boston. In 1635, having grown weary of the ways of the Puritan settlers who had become his neighbors, this Anglican clergyman built a new home in what was wilderness and is now called Rhode Island. Called "the sage of the wilderness," Blackstone was known for traveling atop a docile white bull. His cabin and his writings were destroyed in 1675, during the year-long King Philip's War, a devastating conflict between European settlers and Native Americans.

In 1986 the National Park Service designated the Blackstone Valley a National Heritage Corridor. A planned bike path will run from Worcester to the Narragansett Bay, and a prominent new museum in Woonsocket relates the region's history through multimedia exhibits. The valley is emerging as a significant destination for visitors, but much work remains to be done; signage is lacking, and accommodations can be difficult to find. Luckily, the hotels and inns of Providence are a short drive away, making the Blackstone Valley an excellent day trip.

Pawtucket

⑱ *5 mi north of Providence.*

In Algonquian, "petuket" (similar to standard Rhode Island pronunciation of the city's name, accent on the second syllable) means "water falls." A small village was established at the falls in 1670 by Joseph Jenks, Jr., who considered the area a prime spot for an iron forge. When Samuel Slater arrived 120 years later, he was delighted to find a corps of skilled mechanics ready to assist him in his dream of organizing America's first factory system. Many of Pawtucket's older buildings were torn down as part of urban renewal projects in the 1970s, but significant portions of the city's history have been preserved and are worth a visit.

In 1793, Samuel Slater and two Providence merchants built the first factory in America to produce cotton yarn from water-powered machines. The yellow clapboard **Slater Mill Historic Site** houses classrooms, a theater, and machinery illustrating the conversion of raw cotton to finished cloth. A 16,000-pound waterwheel powers an operational 19th-century machine shop; it and the adjacent 1758 Sylvanus Brown House are open to the public. ⊠ *67 Roosevelt Ave.,* ☎ *401/725–8638.* ⬜ *$6.50.* ☉ *June–Nov., Mon.–Sat. 10–5, Sun. 1–5; Mar.–May, weekends 1–5; Dec.–Feb., weekends, 1 PM tour only. Guided tours given daily; call for times.*

Slater Memorial Park stretches along Ten Mile River. Within this stately park are picnic tables, tennis courts, playgrounds, a river walk, and two historic sites. Eight generations of Daggetts lived in the **Daggett House,** Pawtucket's oldest home, which was built in 1685. Among the 17th-century antiques on display are bedspreads owned by Samuel Slater. The **Loof Carousel,** built by Charles I. D. Loof, has 42 horses, three dogs, and a lion, camel, and giraffe that are the earliest examples of the Danish immigrant's work. ⊠ *Newport Ave./Rte. 1A,* ☎ *401/728–0500 for park information.* ⬜ *Park and carousel free; Daggett House $2.* ☉ *Park daily dawn–dusk; Daggett House June–Sept., weekends 2–5; carousel July–Labor Day, daily 10–5, late-Apr.–June and Labor Day–Columbus Day, weekends 10–5.*

Dining

$-$$ ✕ **Modern Diner.** This 1941 Sterling Streamline eatery—a classic from the heyday of the stainless steel diner—was the first diner to be listed on the National Register of Historic Places. The Modern serves standard diner fare and some specialty items, including lobster Benedict and French toast with custard sauce and berries. ⊠ *364 East Ave.,* ☎ *401/726–8390. No credit cards. No dinner.*

Outdoor Activities and Sports

The **Pawtucket Red Sox,** the Triple-A farm team of baseball's Boston Red Sox, play at McCoy Stadium (⊠ 1 Columbus Ave., ☎ 401/724–7300).

Woonsocket

⑲ *10 mi north of Pawtucket, 15 mi north of Providence.*

Rhode Island's sixth-largest city (population 40,000) was settled in the late 17th century, home to a sawmill and Quaker farmers for its first 100 years. A steep hill on the northern end of the city looks down on the Blackstone River, which makes a dozen turns in its 5-mi course through Woonsocket. The river's flow spawned textile mills that made Woonsocket a thriving community in the 19th and early 20th centuries; today a museum is dedicated to this industrial heritage. Manufacturing plants remain the city's leading employers.

Multimedia and more traditional exhibits at the **Museum of Work and Culture** examine the lives of American factory workers and owners during the Industrial Revolution. The genesis of the textile workers' union is described, as are the events that led to the National Textile Strike of 1934. A model of the triple decker (a three-family tenement building) demonstrates the practicality behind what was once the region's preeminent style of home. Youngsters may be interested in presentations about child labor. ⊠ *42 S. Main St.,* ☎ *401/769–9675.* ⬜ *$5.* ☉ *Weekdays 9:30–4, Sat. 10–5, Sun. 1–5.*

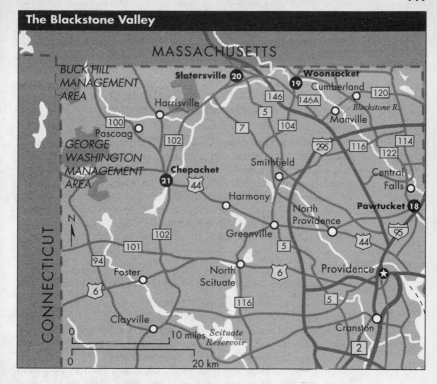

The Blackstone Valley

Dining and Lodging

$ ✗ **Ye Olde English Fish & Chips.** Fresh fried fish and potatoes have been served at this statewide institution for eons. The decor is simple—wood paneling and booths—so it must be the inexpensive and consistently excellent food, served in red plastic baskets, that has kept folks returning to this joint since 1922. ⊠ *Market Sq., S. Main St.,* ☎ *401/762–3637. No credit cards. Closed Sun.–Mon.*

$–$$ ⊞ **The Pilsbury House.** Stately Prospect Street stretches along the crest of the ridge north of the Blackstone River; its mansions, like the mansard-roof Pilsbury House, were built by mill owners in the late 1800s. The common room has a baby grand piano, a parquet floor, and a fireplace with a maple hearth. The two guest rooms on the second floor are furnished in Victorian style, with antiques, plants, high beds, and fringed lamp shades. The third-floor suite has a more rustic-country decor. ⊠ *341 Prospect St., 02895,* ☎ *401/766–7983 or 800/205–4112. 2 rooms, 1 suite. Full breakfast. AE, D, DC, MC, V.*

Nightlife and the Arts

The impressive entertainment lineup at **Chan's Fine Oriental Dining** (⊠ 267 Main St., ☎ 401/765–1900) includes blues, jazz, and folk performers. Reservations are required; ticket prices range from $10 to $24.

Shopping

Storefront renovations and public improvement of the road and sidewalks have made for much better shopping along Main Street in Woonsocket. **Main Street Antiques** (⊠ 32 Main St., ☎ 401/762–0805) is a good place to start your browsing.

Slatersville

➋⓿ *3 mi west of Woonsocket.*

Samuel Slater's brother, John, purchased a small sawmill and blacksmith shop along the Branch River and turned the area, now part of North Smithfield township, into America's first company town, Slatersville. With their factory well removed from population centers, Slater and his partners built homes, a town green, a Congregational church, and a general store for their workers. The village, west of the junction of Routes 102 and 146, has been well preserved, and though it doesn't have many amenities for visitors, it is a fine place for for an afternoon stroll.

Dining

$ ✕ **Wright's Farm Restaurant.** Chicken family style (all-you-can-eat bread, salad, roast chicken, pasta, and potatoes), a northern Rhode Island tradition, was born of a Woonsocket social club's need to feed many people as efficiently as possible. More than a dozen restaurants in the Blackstone Valley serve this food combo; Wright's Farm, the largest, dishes up 300 tons of chicken each year. Excluding drinks, the meals cost $8 per person. ⌧ *84 Inman Rd., 2 mi west of Slatersville off Rte. 102, Burrillville,* ☎ *401/769–2856. No credit cards. Closed Mon.–Tues. No lunch.*

Chepachet

㉑ *12 mi south of Slatersville, 20 mi northwest of Providence.*

Antiques shops and other businesses line Main Street in the village of Chepachet, at the intersection of Routes 44 and 102 in the township of Glocester. The setting feels so much out of a storybook that you might find it jolting to see paved roads and automobiles upon exiting emporiums like the **Brown & Hopkins Country Store** (⌧ 79 Main St., ☎ 401/568–4830). Established in 1809, B&H has been in operation longer than any other country store in America. Crafts, penny candy, a deli, antiques, and a potbellied stove await you.

Snowhurst Farm (⌧ 421 Chopmist Hill Rd., ☎ 401/568–8900) grows 16 varieties of apples that you pick yourself for 55¢ per pound, from late August until about Columbus Day. This working farm has cattle, horses, and sheep. From Chepachet, drive 2 mi south on U.S. 44 to Route 102; the farm is 2 mi south of the intersection.

Dining

$$ ✕ **Stagecoach Tavern.** Formerly a stagecoach stop between Providence and Hartford, this establishment serves hearty meat dishes and pastas at reasonable prices. Locals hang out at the casual bar. ⌧ *1157 Main St.,* ☎ *401/568–2275. AE, D, MC, V.*

Shopping

Old Chepachet Village (⌧ 11 Money Hill Rd., ☎ 401/567–0200) houses 30 crafts and antiques stores in a 10,000-square-ft building.

OFF THE   **BUCK HILL MANAGEMENT AREA –** Tucked away in the remote northwest
BEATEN PATH corner of the state, 7 mi northwest of Chepachet, this area supports waterfowl, songbirds, deer, pheasant, owls, foxes, and wild turkeys. Hiking trails traverse the preserve and cross into Connecticut and Massachusetts. ⌧ *Buck Hill Rd. off Rte. 100 (Wallum Lake Rd.),* ☎ *401/789–0281.* ⌫ *Free.* ☉ *Daily, from ½ hr before sunrise to ½ hr after sunset.*

Blackstone Valley A to Z

Arriving and Departing

BY BUS
Rhode Island Public Transit Authority (☎ 401/781–9400; 800/244–0444 in RI) buses travel from Providence's Kennedy Plaza (⌧ Washington and Dorrance Sts.) to towns in the Blackstone Valley.

BY CAR

Pawtucket is north of Providence on I–95. To reach Woonsocket, take Route 146 northwest from Providence and head north at Route 99; from Woonsocket, take Route 146A west to Route 102 to get to Slatersville. Chepachet is southwest of Slatersville on Route 102 and west of Providence on U.S. 44.

Getting Around

See Arriving and Departing, *above.*

BY CAR

The easiest way to explore the Blackstone Valley is by car, though a good map is needed because signage satisfying visitors' needs is not yet in place. Call the **Blackstone Valley Tourism Council** (☞ Visitor Information *in* Contacts and Resources, *below*) for a map or pick up *Street Atlas Rhode Island,* available at most gas stations.

Contacts and Resources

EMERGENCIES

Landmark Medical Center (⊠ 115 Cass Ave., Woonsocket, ☎ 401/769–4100).

GUIDED TOURS

Blackstone Valley Explorer (⊠ 171 Main St., Pawtucket, ☎ 401/725–1500 or 800/619–2628) is a 49-passenger, canopied riverboat offering various tours of the Blackstone River. Tours are given from April to October and depart from a number of landings along the river.

VISITOR INFORMATION

The **Blackstone Valley Tourism Council** (⊠ 171 Main St., Pawtucket 02860, ☎ 401/724–2200 or 800/454–2882), a good first stop, has a slide show that introduces the region, as well as staff who can help with information and itineraries. A complete list of factory stores is also available. **Northern Rhode Island Chamber of Commerce** (⊠ 6 Blackstone Valley Pl., Suite 105, Lincoln 02865, ☎ 401/334–1000).

SOUTH COUNTY

When the principal interstate traffic shifted from U.S. 1 to I–95, coastal Rhode Island—known within the state as South County—largely escaped the advance of malls and tract-housing developments that overtook other, more accessible areas. With 19 preserves and state parks encompassing beaches, forests, and swamps, South County is a region that respects the concept of wilderness.

Westerly

㉒ *50 mi southwest of Providence, 100 mi southwest of Boston, 140 mi northeast of New York City.*

The village of Westerly is a busy little railway town that grew up in the late 19th century around a major station on what is now the New York–Boston Amtrak corridor. The 30-square-mi community of 15 villages has since sprawled out along U.S. 1. Victorian and Greek Revival mansions line many streets off the town center, which borders Connecticut and the Pawcatuck River. During the Industrial Revolution and into the 1950s, Westerly was distinguished for its flawless blue granite, from which monuments throughout the country were made.

Watch Hill and Misquamicut (☞ *below* for both) are summer communities recognized without mention of their township, Westerly. Casinos in Uncasville and Ledyard, Connecticut, are slowly changing Westerly's economic climate. Many residents work in the Mohegan Sun and Foxwoods casinos, and vacationers are discovering that Westerly's B&Bs provide pleasant alternatives to casino hotels.

Wilcox Park (⊠ 71½ High St., ☎ 401/596–8590), designed in 1898 by Warren Manning, an associate of Frederick Law Olmsted and Calvert Vaux, is an 18-acre park in the heart of town with a garden designed so that people with visual and other impairments can identify—by taste, touch, and smell—such plants as chives and thyme.

Dining and Lodging

$$$$ ✕🏨 **Weekapaug Inn.** Weekapaug is a picturesque coastal village 6 mi
★   southeast of Westerly center and 3 mi from Misquamicut Beach. This inn, with a peaked roof and huge wraparound porch, sits on a peninsula surrounded on three sides by salty Quonochontaug Pond. The rooms are cheerful, if not particularly remarkable; most are big and bright, with wide windows that have impressive views. The standards at the restaurant, which has a full-time baker, are high: Each new daily menu emphasizes seafood and lists four to six entrées. ⊠ *25 Spring Ave., Weekapaug 02891,* ☎ *401/322–0301,* ℻ *401/322–1016. 55 rooms. Restaurant. MAP available. No credit cards. Closed Nov.–June.*

$$–$$$ ✕🏨 **Shelter Harbor Inn.** This inn, about 6 mi east of downtown in a
★   quiet rural setting not far from the beach, has many rooms with fireplaces and decks. The rooms are furnished with a combination of Victorian antiques and reproduction pieces; bedspreads and curtains are in muted floral patterns. The frequently changing menu at the excellent restaurant might include smoked scallops and cappellini or pecan-crusted duck breast. Breakfast is good every day, but Sunday brunch is legendary. ⊠ *10 Wagner Rd., off U.S. 1, 02891,* ☎ *401/322–8883 or 800/468–8883,* ℻ *401/322–7907. 23 rooms. Restaurant, hot tub, croquet, paddle tennis. Full breakfast. AE, D, DC, MC, V.*

$$ 🏨 **Grandview Bed and Breakfast.** Relaxed and affordable, this B&B on a rise above Route 1A has comfortable, if nondescript, rooms (the front ones have ocean views). The common room has a TV with VCR. Breakfast is served on the porch year-round. ⊠ *212 Shore Rd., Dunn's Corners (between Misquamicut and Weekapaug), 02891,* ☎ *401/596–6384 or 800/447–6384,* ℻ *401/596–6384. 9 rooms, 5 with bath. Continental breakfast. AE, MC, V.*

Watch Hill

★ ㉓ *5 mi south of downtown Westerly.*

Watch Hill, a Victorian-era resort village, contains miles of beautiful beaches. Most of its well-kept summer houses are owned by wealthy families who have passed ownership down through generations. Sailing and socializing are the top activities for Watch Hill residents. Visitors come to tour the attractive streets, shop, and hit the beaches. A **statue of Ninigret** stands watch over Bay Street. Long before the first Europeans showed up, southern Rhode Island was inhabited by the Narragansetts, a powerful Native American tribe. The Niantics, ruled by Chief Ninigret in the 1630s, were one branch of the tribe.

☼ **Flying Horse Carousel,** at the beach end of Bay Street, is the oldest merry-go-round in America. It was built by the Charles W. F. Dare Co. of New York in about 1867. The horses, suspended from above, swing out when in motion. Each is hand-carved from a single piece of wood. Adults are not permitted to ride the carousel. ⊠ *Bay St.* 🎫 *50¢.* ☉ *Mid-June–Labor Day, weekdays 1–9, weekends 11–9.*

The immensity of the **Ocean House** (⊠ 2 Bluff Ave., ☎ 401/348–8161; ☞ Dining and Lodging, *below*), a yellow-clapboard Victorian building, will just about take your breath away. Built by George Nash in

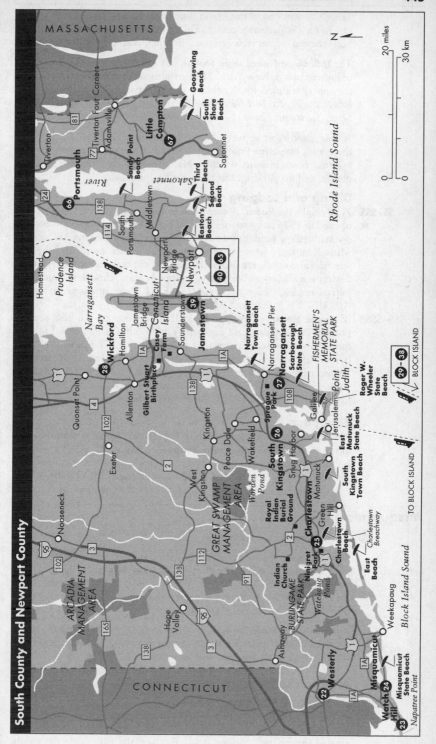

South County and Newport County

MASSACHUSETTS

Goosewing Beach

South Shore Beach

Little Compton **57**

Tiverton Four Corners
Adamsville
81
Tiverton
77 Sandy Point Beach
Portsmouth
Sakonnet
24
66
138
Third Beach
Second Beach
South Portsmouth
114
Easton's Beach

Middletown

Sakonnet River

Newport Bridge
Newport
40–**65**

Homestead
Prudence Island
Narragansett Bay

Rhode Island Sound

Jamestown
Conanicut Island
39
Jamestown Bridge
Saunderstown

Wickford
28
Hamilton
Casey Farm
Gilbert Stuart Birthplace
1A

Quonset Point
11
Allenton
4
138
11
Narragansett Town Beach
Narragansett Pier
27 Narragansett
Scarborough State Beach

102

Exeter
West Kingston
Kingston
Peace Dale
Wakefield
26
South Kingstown
Snug Harbor
108
Sprague Park
Galilee
FISHERMEN'S MEMORIAL STATE PARK
Point Judith
Roger W. Wheeler State Beach

29–**38**
BLOCK ISLAND

Jerusalem
East Matunuck State Beach

Nooseneck
95
102
3
GREAT SWAMP MANAGEMENT AREA
Worden Pond
2
South Mahunuck
South Kingstown Town Beach

Green Hill

ARCADIA MANAGEMENT AREA
165
133
112
91
Royal Indian Burial Ground
Charlestown
25
Charlestown Beach
Charlestown Breachway
TO BLOCK ISLAND

138
Hope Valley
95
3
Indian Church
BURLINGAME STATE PARK
Ninigret Park
Watchaug Pond
1
East Beach

Ashaway

Block Island Sound

Weekapaug
11
Misquamicut
Misquamicut State Beach

CONNECTICUT
22 Westerly
1A
Watch Hill **23**
Napatree Point

N
20 miles
30 km

1868, this was one of the grand hotels that helped earn Watch Hill its fame as a 19th-century resort. Though the place is a bit down at the heels these days, its views of the Atlantic Ocean remain unparalleled.

The **U.S. Coast Guard Light Station** has great views of the ocean and of Fishers Island, New York. The tiny museum contains exhibits about the light. Parking is for the elderly only; everyone else must walk from lots at the beach. ⊠ *Lighthouse Rd.,* ☎ *no phone.* ⌸ *Free.* ☉ *May–Sept., Tues. and Thurs. 1–3.*

A long, sandy spit between Watch Hill's Little Narragansett Bay and the ocean, **Napatree Point** is a protected conservation area (great for a stroll) teeming with wildlife. Napatree has no admission fee, no phone, and no parking, but there's a fee lot nearby.

Dining and Lodging

$$–$$$ ✗ **Olympia Tea Room.** A step back in time, this small restaurant that
★   opened in 1916 has varnished wood booths and a soda fountain—try a marshmallow sundae or an orangeade—behind a long marble counter. Mussels steamed in white wine are on the dinner menu, and the lobster rolls and salads are delicious. The "world-famous Avondale swan" dessert is a fantasy of ice cream, whipped cream, chocolate sauce, and puff pastry. ⊠ *30 Bay St.,* ☎ *401/348–8211. Reservations not accepted. AE, MC, V. Closed Nov.–Mar.*

$$$–$$$$ 🏨 **Ocean House.** This grand old lady has one of the best seaside porches in New England and a private beach. Casual, relaxing, and quiet, the inn has a reassuring if faded elegance. The furniture could best be described as maple eclectic. Ask for a room with an ocean view. Splintery stairs lead to an excellent private beach. ⊠ *2 Bluff Ave., 02891,* ☎ *401/348–8161. 59 rooms. Restaurant, lounge, beach. Full breakfast; MAP available. MC, V. Closed Sept.–June.*

Shopping

Bay Street is a good place to shop for jewelry, summer clothing, and antiques. The **Book and Tackle Shop** (⊠ 7 Bay St., ☎ 401/596–0700) buys, sells, and appraises old and rare books, prints, autographs, and photographs. **Puffins of Watch Hill** (⊠ 60 Bay St., ☎ 401/596–1770) carries fine American crafts, collectibles, pottery, jewelry, and gifts.

Misquamicut

㉔ *2 mi east of Watch Hill.*

Strip motels jostle for attention in Misquamicut, where a giant water slide, a carousel, miniature golf, a game arcade, children's rides, batting cages, and fast-food stands attract visitors by the thousands. The mile-long beach is accessible year-round, but the amusements are open only between Memorial Day and Labor Day.

Atlantic Beach Park (⊠ 337 Atlantic Ave., ☎ 401/322–9298) offers more games and rides for the kids than any other Misquamicut facility. Two-mile-long **Misquamicut State Beach** (⊠ Atlantic Ave., ☎ 401/596–9097), open to the public, has parking, shower facilities, and a snack bar located at the state-run beach pavilion.

Dining and Lodging

$$ ✗ **Paddy's Seafood Restaurant.** The food is good and the portions are generous at this no-frills, family-style beachside restaurant. Lobster, scrod, stuffed shrimp, grilled tuna, and other seafood plates rule the menu, but you can also order pastas and salads. ⊠ *159 Atlantic Ave.,* ☎ *401/596–2610. AE, D, MC, V. Closed Oct.–Apr.*

$$–$$$ ⚏ **Breezeway Motel.** The Bellone family takes great pride in its business and offers a variety of accommodations: villas with fireplaces and hot tubs, suites, efficiencies, and standard rooms. The grounds hold a swing set, shuffleboard, and floodlighted fountains. ⊠ *Box 1368, 70 Winnapaug Rd., 02891,* ☏ *401/348–8953 or 800/462–8872,* FAX *401/ 596–3207. 47 rooms, 9 suites, 2 villas. Refrigerators, pool, recreation room. Continental breakfast. AE, D, DC, MC, V. Closed Nov.–May.*

Nightlife and the Arts

The **Windjammer** (⊠ 337 Atlantic Ave., ☏ 401/322–9298), open Memorial Day to Labor Day, hosts dancing to rock bands in a room that holds 1,500.

Charlestown

㉕ *10 mi east of Misquamicut.*

Charlestown stretches along the Old Post Road (Route 1A). The 37-square-mi township contains parks, the largest saltwater marsh in the state, 4 mi of pristine beaches, and many oceanfront motels, summer chalets, and cabins.

The 2,100-acre **Burlingame State Park** (⊠ 75 Burlingame Park Rd., ☏ 401/322–7337 or 401/322–7994) has nature trails, picnic and swimming areas, and campgrounds, as well as boating and fishing on Watchaug Pond. **Ninigret Park** (⊠ Park La. off Rte. 1A, ☏ 401/364–1222) is a 172-acre park with picnic grounds, ball fields, a bike path, tennis courts, nature trails, and a spring-fed pond; also here is the **Frosty Drew Observatory and Nature Center** (☏ 401/364–9508), which presents nature and astronomy programs on Friday evening.

Ninigret National Wildlife Refuge consists of two stretches of beachlands and marshes, plus the abandoned naval air station on Ninigret Pond. Nine miles of trails cross 400 acres of diverse upland and wetland habitats—including grasslands, shrublands, wooded swamps, and freshwater ponds. ⊠ *Rte. 1A,* ☏ *401/364–9124.* ⚏ *Free.* ☉ *Daily dawn to dusk.*

Many Narragansetts still live in the Charlestown area, but their historic sites are unmarked and easy to miss. The **Royal Indian Burial Ground,** on the left side of Narrow Lane north of U.S. 1, is the resting place of sachems (chiefs). You'll recognize it by the tall fences, but there's no sign. It's not open for visits except during the annual Narragansett meeting, usually the second Sunday in August, when tribal members from around the nation convene for costumed dancing and rituals.

The two beaches in Charlestown have calm, warm waters that make them popular with families. Both beaches have parking, a snack bar, and rest rooms. **Charlestown Town Beach** (⊠ Charlestown Beach Rd.) ends at a breachway that is part of Ninigret National Wildlife Refuge (☞ *above*). Glorious **East Beach** (⊠ East Beach Rd.), composed of 3½ mi of dunes backed by the crystal-clear waters of Ninigret Pond, is a 2-mi hike from the breachway at Charlestown Town Beach. Parking is available at the end of East Beach Road.

Dining and Lodging

$$ ✕⚏ **The General Stanton Inn.** For helping pay the ransom of a native princess in 1655, the Narragansetts rewarded Thomas Stanton with the land where this inn stands. Stanton, a trader from England, first ran it as a schoolhouse for African-American and Native American children. Since the 18th century, it has provided dining and lodging in a Colonial atmosphere. The rooms have low ceilings, uneven floorboards, small windows, and period antiques and wallpapers. The din-

ing rooms in the restaurant have brick fireplaces, beams, and wooden floors. Traditional New England fare—steaks, lobster, scrod, rack of lamb—is prepared. ⊠ *Old Post Rd. (Rte. 1A), 02813,* ☎ *401/364–0100,* ⅀ *401/364–5021. 16 rooms. Restaurant, bar. Full breakfast. AE, MC, V. Restaurant closed Nov.–Apr.*

Outdoor Activities and Sports

Narragansett Kayak Co. (⊠ 2144 Matunuck Schoolhouse Rd., ☎ 401/364–2000) rents canoes and kayaks. **Ocean House Marina** (⊠ 60 Town Dock Rd., ☎ 401/364–6040), at the Cross Mills Exit off U.S. 1, is a full-service marina with boat rentals and fishing supplies.

Shopping

Artists Guild and Gallery (⊠ 5429 Post Rd., off U.S. 1, ☎ 401/322–0506) exhibits 19th- and 20th-century art. **Fox Run Country Antiques** (⊠ Intersection of Rtes. 1 and 2, Crossland Park complex, ☎ 401/364–3160; 401/377–2581 for appointments) sells jewelry, lighting devices, Orientalia, antiques, china, and glassware.

The **Fantastic Umbrella Factory** (⊠ 4920 Old Post Rd., off U.S. 1, ☎ 401/364–6616) comprises four rustic shops and a barn built around a wild garden. For sale are hardy perennials and unusual daylilies, greeting cards, kites, crafts, tapestries, and incense. There is also an art gallery, a greenhouse, and a café that serves organic foods.

South Kingstown

26 *2 mi east of Charlestown, 6 mi west of Point Judith Pond.*

In summer months, the 55-square-mi town of South Kingstown—encompassing Wakefield, Snug Harbor, Matunuck, Green Hill, Kingston, and 10 other villages—offers a wealth of history, outdoor recreation, and entertainment. At the old **Washington County Jail,** built in 1792 in Wakefield, the largest South Kingstown village, you can view jail cells, rooms from the Colonial period, a Colonial garden, and changing exhibits about South County life. ⊠ *1348 Kingstown Rd.,* ☎ *401/783–1328.* ⅀ *Free.* ☉ *May–Oct., Tues., Thurs., and Sat. 1–4.*

Crabs, mussels, and starfish populate the rock reef that extends to the right of **Matunuck Beach** (⊠ Succotash Rd). Southward, the reef gives way to a sandy bottom. When the ocean is calm, you can walk on the reef and explore its tidal pools. **East Matunuck State Beach** (⊠ Succotash Rd.) is popular with the college crowd for its white sand and picnic areas. **Roy Carpenter's Beach** (⊠ Matunuck Beach Rd.) is part of a cottage-colony of seasonal renters but is open to the public for a fee. **South Kingstown Town Beach** (⊠ Matunuck Beach Rd.) draws many families.

Dining and Lodging

$$ ✕ **Mews Tavern.** The food at this cheery tavern is consistently excellent. Rhode Islanders consider it the best place in the state to get a hamburger (buy one, get one free on Thursday night), but you can also order seafood. Beer is also popular here; 69 varieties are on tap. ⊠ *465 Main St.,* ☎ *401/783–9370. Reservations not accepted. AE, D, MC, V.*

$$ ✕⬚ **Larchwood Inn.** This 168-year-old country inn with a Scottish flavor is set in a grove of larch trees. The dining room ($–$$) is open for three meals daily; the halibut stuffed with scallops is delicious. Ask for a table near the fireplace in winter or a patio spot under the trees in summer. Rooms range from suites with grand views to smaller, back-of-the-house affairs. ⊠ *521 Main St., Wakefield 02879,* ☎ *401/783–5454,* ⅀ *401/783–1800. 18 rooms. Restaurant. AE, D, DC, MC, V.*

$$ ⬚ **Admiral Dewey Inn.** Victorian antiques furnish the rooms of this inn, which was built in 1898 as a seaside hotel—it's across the road

from Matunuck Beach—and is now on the National Register of Historic Places. Some rooms have views of the ocean; others are tucked cozily under the eaves. Smoking is permitted only on the wraparound veranda, which is filled with old-fashioned rocking chairs. ⊠ *668 Matunuck Beach Rd., 02881,* ☎ *401/783–2090. 10 rooms, 8 with bath. Continental breakfast. MC, V.*

Nightlife and the Arts

Ocean Mist (⊠ 145 Matunuck Beach Rd., ☎ 401/782–3740) is a distinctive beachfront barroom with music nightly in summer and on weekends off-season. The hard-drinking crowd at this hangout of South County's younger generation can be as rough-hewn as the building. The barn-style **Theatre-by-the-Sea** (⊠ Cards Pond Rd., off U.S. 1, ☎ 401/782–8587), built in 1933 and listed on the National Register of Historic Places, presents musicals and plays in summer.

Outdoor Activities and Sports

FISHING

Gil's Custom Tackle (⊠ 101 Main St., Wakefield, ☎ 401/783–1370) sells recreational fishing gear. **Snug Harbor Marina** (⊠ 410 Gooseberry Rd., Wakefield, ☎ 401/783–7766) sells bait, rents kayaks, and arranges fishing charters. At Snug Harbor it is not uncommon to see on the docks giant tuna and sharks weighing more than 300 pounds.

HIKING

Great Swamp (⊠ Great Neck Rd. near West Kingston, ☎ 401/789–0281), a temporary home to migrating waterfowl, has a network of hiking trails.

WATER SPORTS

The **Watershed** (⊠ 396 Main St., Wakefield, ☎ 401/789–3399) rents surfboards, Windsurfers, body boards, and wet suits. Owner Peter Pan gives lessons at nearby Narragansett Town Beach.

Shopping

Dove and Distaff Antiques (⊠ 365 Main St., Wakefield, ☎ 401/783–5714) is a good spot for Early American furniture. **Peter Pots Authentic Americana** (⊠ 494 Glen Rock Rd., West Kingston, ☎ 401/783–2350) sells stoneware, period furniture, and collectibles.

Hera Gallery (⊠ 327 Main St., Wakefield, ☎ 401/789–1488), a women's art cooperative, exhibits the work of emerging local artists. It's open Wednesday–Friday 1–5, Saturday 10–4.

Narragansett

㉗ *2 mi east of South Kingstown.*

The popular beach town of Narragansett is on the peninsula east of Point Judith Pond and the Pettaquamscutt River. Its 16 villages include Galilee, Bonnett Shores, and Narragansett Pier.

Narragansett Pier, the beach community often called simply the Pier, was named for an amusement wharf that no longer exists. The Pier, now populated by summertime "cottagers," college students, and commuting professionals, was in the late 1800s a posh resort linked by rail to New York and Boston. Many summer visitors headed for the Narragansett Pier Casino, which had a bowling alley, billiard tables, tennis courts, a rifle gallery, a theater, and a ballroom. The grand edifice burned to the ground in 1900. Only the **Towers** (⊠ Rte. 1A, ☎ 401/783–7121), the grand stone entrance to the former casino, remain. Most of the mansions built during Narragansett's golden age are along Ocean Road, from Point Judith to Narragansett Pier.

The village of **Galilee** is a busy, workaday fishing port from which whale-watching excursions, fishing trips, and the **Block Island Ferry** (✉ Galilee State Pier, ☎ 401/783–4613) depart. The occasionally pungent smell of seafood and bait will lead you to the area's fine restaurants and markets. From the port of Galilee it's a short drive to the **Point Judith Lighthouse** (✉ 1460 Ocean Rd., ☎ 401/789–0444) and a beautiful ocean view. The lighthouse is open from dawn to dusk.

The highlight of **Sprague Park** (✉ Kingstown Rd. and Strathmore St.) is the **Narragansett Indian Monument.** Sculptor Peter Toth created the 5-ton, 23-ft monument from the trunk of a giant Douglas fir, working with hammer and chisel 12 hours a day for two months.

☾ **Adventureland in Narragansett** has bumper boats, miniature golf, batting cages, and a go-cart track. ✉ *Rte. 108,* ☎ *401/789–0030.* ⊡ *Combination tickets $1.50–$9.50.* ☯ *Mid-June–Labor Day, daily 10–10; Labor Day–Oct. and mid-Apr.–mid-June, weekends 10–10.*

☾ The seven buildings of the **South County Museum** house 20,000 artifacts dating from 1800 to 1933. Exhibits include a country kitchen, a carpentry shop, a cobbler's shop, a tack shop, a working print shop, and an antique carriage collection. ✉ *Canonchet Farm, Anne Hoxie La. off Rte. 1A,* ☎ *401/783–5400.* ⊡ *$3.50.* ☯ *May–June and Sept.–Oct., Wed.–Sun. 11–4; July–Aug., Wed.–Mon. 10–4.*

Popular **Narragansett Town Beach** (✉ Rte. 1A) is within walking distance of many hotels and guest houses. Its pavilion has changing rooms, showers, and concessions. **Roger W. Wheeler State Beach** (✉ Sand Hill Cove Rd., Galilee) has a new pavilion; the beach, sheltered from ocean swells, has picnic areas and a playground. **Scarborough State Beach** (✉ Ocean Rd.), considered by many the jewel of the Ocean State's beaches, has a pavilion with showers and concessions. On weekends, teenagers and college students blanket the sands.

Dining and Lodging

$$$ ✕ **Basil's.** French and Continental cuisine are served in an intimate set-
★ ting within walking distance of Narragansett Town Beach. Dark floral wallpaper and fresh flowers decorate the small dining room. The specialty is veal topped with a light cream-and-mushroom sauce; among the other dishes are fish and duck à l'orange. ✉ *22 Kingstown Rd.,* ☎ *401/789–3743. AE, DC, MC, V. Closed Mon., and Oct.–June Tues. No lunch.*

$$$ ✕ **Coast Guard House.** This restaurant, housed in an 1888 building that served as a lifesaving station for 50 years, displays interesting photos of Narragansett Pier and the Casino. Candles light the tables, and picture windows on three sides allow views of the ocean. The fare is American—seafood, pasta, veal, steak, and lamb. The upstairs lounge hosts entertainers and has a DJ on Friday and Saturday night. ✉ *40 Ocean Rd.,* ☎ *401/789–0700. AE, D, DC, MC, V.*

$$$ ✕ **Spain Restaurant.** South County's only true Spanish restaurant is appropriately dark and atmospheric. The appetizers include shrimp in garlic sauce, stuffed mushrooms, and Spanish sausages; lobster, steak, and paella are some of the main courses. ✉ *1144 Ocean Rd.,* ☎ *401/783–9770. AE, D, DC, MC, V.*

$$ ✕ **Aunt Carrie's.** This popular family-owned restaurant has been serving up Rhode Island shore dinners, clam cakes and chowder, and fried seafood for nearly 80 years. At the height of the season the lines can be long; one alternative is to order from the take-out window and picnic on the grounds of the nearby lighthouse. ✉ *Rte. 108 and Ocean Rd., Point Judith,* ☎ *401/783–7930. Reservations not accepted. MC, V. Closed Oct.–Mar. and Mon.–Thurs. in Apr., May, and Sept.*

$$ ✕ **George's of Galilee.** This restaurant at the mouth of the Point Judith harbor has been a "must" for tourists since 1948. The "stuffies" (baked stuffed quahogs) are some of the best in the state. The menu offers a variety of fried and broiled seafood, chicken, steak and pasta. Its proximity to the beach and its large outside bar on the second floor make George's a very busy place all summer. ✉ *Sand Hill Cove Rd., Port of Galilee,* ☎ *401/783–2306. Reservations not accepted. AE, D, MC, V. Closed Dec. and weekdays Nov. and Jan.*

$$–$$$ 🏨 **Stone Lea.** McKim, Mead & White, the architectural firm responsible for the State House and other Rhode Island landmarks, designed this dignified shingle-covered house, which has views across Narragansett Bay to Newport, Jamestown, Tiverton, and Block Island. This B&B, in a section of private homes called Millionaire's Mile, has details such as bay windows, carved wood paneling, and a grand staircase that rises from the parquet floor of the foyer. The Block Island room and the three other large rooms are worth the extra cost. Breakfast is almost as substantial as the home, which is built on a foundation of Rhode Island granite. ✉ *40 Newton Ave., 02882,* ☎ *401/783–8237,* 🅵🅰🆇 *401/ 783–9546. 7 rooms. Full breakfast. AE, MC, V.*

$–$$ 🏨 **The Richards.** Imposing and magnificent, this mansion has a broodingly Gothic mystique that is quite different from the spirit of the typical summer house. French windows in the wood-panel common rooms downstairs open up to views of a lush landscape, and a grand swamp oak is the centerpiece of the garden. A fire crackles in the library fireplace on chilly afternoons. Some rooms have 19th-century English antiques, floral-upholstered furniture, and fireplaces. Breakfast consists of main courses like eggs Florentine, oven pancakes, and fresh fruit and baked goods. ✉ *144 Gibson Ave., 02882,* ☎ *401/789–7746. 4 rooms, 2 with bath; 1 2-bedroom suite. Full breakfast. No credit cards.*

Outdoor Activities and Sports

FISHING

The **Frances Fleet** (✉ 2 State St., ☎ 401/783–4988 or 800/662–2824) operates day and overnight fishing trips. Narragansett-based charter boats include the *Persuader* (☎ 401/783–5644), *Prowler* (☎ 401/ 783–8487), and *Seven B's V* (☎ 401/789–9250). **Maridee Canvas–Bait & Tackle** (✉ 120 Knowlesway Ext., ☎ 401/789–5190) stocks supplies and provides helpful advice.

WHALE-WATCHING

Whale-watching excursions aboard the *Lady Frances* (✉ Frances Fleet, 2 State St., Point Judith, ☎ 401/783–4988 or 800/662–2824) depart at 1 PM and return at 6 PM. The fare is $30. The trips operate Monday through Saturday from July to Labor Day.

En Route Off Route 1A between Narragansett and Wickford are two historic sights in beautiful locations. The **Silas Casey Farm** still functions much as it has since the 18th century. The farmhouse contains original furniture, prints, paintings, and 300 years of political and military documents. Nearly 30 mi of stone walls surround the 360-acre farmstead. ✉ *Boston Neck Rd., Saunderstown,* ☎ *401/295–1030.* 🎟 *$3.* ☉ *June–mid-Oct., Tues., Thurs., and Sat. 1–5.*

Built in 1751, the **Gilbert Stuart Birthplace** was the home of America's foremost portraitist of George Washington. It lies on a country road and along little Mattatuxet River. The adjacent 18th-century snuff mill was the first in America. ✉ *815 Gilbert Stuart Rd., Saunderstown,* ☎ *401/294–3001.* 🎟 *$3.* ☉ *Apr.–Oct., Thurs.–Mon. 11–4:30.*

Wickford

★ ㉘ *10 mi north of Narragansett Pier, 15 mi south of Providence.*

The Colonial village of Wickford has a little harbor, dozens of 18th-
and 19th-century homes, and antiques and curiosity shops. This bay-
side spot is the kind of almost-too-perfect, salty New England period
piece that is usually conjured up only in books and movies. In fact,
Wickford was John Updike's model for the New England of his novel
The Witches of Eastwick.

Old Narragansett Church, now called St. Paul's, was built in 1707. It's
one of the oldest Episcopal churches in America. ⊠ *55 Main St.,* ☎
401/294–4357. ☉ *July–Labor Day, Fri.– Sat., Sun. 11–4 (services at
8 and 9:30).*

Smith's Castle, built in 1678 by Richard Smith, Jr., is a beautifully preserved saltbox plantation house on the quiet shore of an arm of Narragansett Bay. It was the site of many orations by Roger Williams, from
whom Smith bought the surrounding property. The grounds have one
of the first military burial grounds (open during daylight hours) in the
country: Interred in a marked mass grave are 40 colonists killed in the
Great Swamp battle of 1675. The Narrangansetts were nearly anni-
hilated, ending King Philip's War in Rhode Island. ⊠ *55 Richard
Smith Dr., 1 mi north of Wickford,* ☎ *401/294–3521.* ☜ *$3.* ☉ *May
and Sept., Fri.–Sun. noon–4; June–Aug., Thurs.–Mon. noon–4. Castle tours by appointment Oct.–Apr.*

Shopping

ANTIQUES

Mentor Antiques (⊠ 7512 Post Rd., ☎ 401/294–9412) receives monthly
shipments of antique English furniture—mahogany, pine, and oak. **Wickford Antiques Center I** (⊠ 16 Main St., ☎ 401/295–2966) sells wooden
kitchen utensils, country furniture, china, glass, linens, and jewelry. **Wickford Antiques Center II** (⊠ 93 Brown St., ☎ 401/295–2966) carries antique furniture from many periods and fine art.

CRAFTS

Needlepoint pillows, Florentine leather books, lamps, and woven
throws are a few of the gifts and home furnishings at **Askham & Tel-
ham Inc.** (⊠ 12 Main St., ☎ 401/295–0891).

South County A to Z

Arriving and Departing

BY BUS

RIPTA (Rhode Island Public Transportation Authority; ☎ 401/781–9400
or 800/244–0444 in RI) provides service from Providence and Warwick to Kingston, Wakefield, Narragansett, and Galilee.

BY CAR

Interstate 95 passes 10 mi north of Westerly before heading inland toward
Providence. U.S. 1 and Route 1A follow the coastline along Narragansett
Bay and are the primary routes through the South County resort towns.

BY PLANE

The closest major airport is in Warwick, south of Providence (☞ Arriving and Departing *in* Rhode Island A to Z, *below*). **Westerly Airport** (⊠ Airport Rd., 2 mi south of Westerly off U.S. 1, ☎ 401/596–
2460) is served by New England Airlines (☎ 401/596–2460 or 800/
243–2460), which flies from Westerly to Block Island and operates charter flights.

BY TRAIN
Amtrak (☎ 800/872–7245) trains stop in Westerly and Kingston.

Getting Around
See Arriving and Departing, *above.*

Contacts and Resources
EMERGENCIES
South County Hospital (✉ 100 Kenyon Ave., Wakefield, ☎ 401/782–8000). **Westerly Hospital** (✉ 25 Wells St., Westerly, ☎ 401/596–6000).

24-HOUR PHARMACY
CVS Pharmacy (✉ Granite Shopping Center, 114 Granite St., Westerly, ☎ 401/596–0306).

VISITOR INFORMATION
The state operates a visitor information center off I–95 at the Connecticut border. **Charlestown Chamber of Commerce** (✉ 4945 Old Post Rd., 02813, ☎ 401/364–3878). **Greater Westerly Chamber of Commerce** (✉ 74 Post Rd., Westerly 02891, ☎ 401/596–7761 or 800/732–7636). **Narragansett Chamber of Commerce** (✉ The Towers, Rte. 1A, 02882, ☎ 401/783–7121). **South County Tourism Council** (✉ 4808 Tower Hill Rd., Wakefield 02879, ☎ 401/789–4422 or 800/548–4662).

BLOCK ISLAND

Visitors have been seeking out Block Island, 12 mi off Rhode Island's southern coast, since the 19th century. Despite the many people who come here each summer, and thanks to the efforts of local conservationists, the island's beauty has been preserved; its 365 freshwater ponds support more than 150 species of migrating birds.

The original inhabitants of the island were Native Americans who called it Manisses, or "Isle of the Little God." Since the eloquent Native American name was abandoned, the island has had many names. In 1524, the explorer Giovanni da Verrazano named it Louisa, after the mother of King Francis I of France; however, the king's wife, Claudia, died soon after Verrazano's return, and the island was renamed Claudia's. Following a visit in 1614 by the Dutch explorer Adrian Block, the island was given the name Adrian's Eyelant, and later Block Island. In 1661 the island was settled by farmers and fishermen from Massachusetts Bay Colony. They gave Block Island its second official name, the Town of New Shoreham, when it became part of the colony of Rhode Island in 1672.

Block Island is a laid-back community. Phone numbers are exchanged by the last four digits (466 is the prefix), and you can dine at any of the island's establishments in shorts and a T-shirt. The heaviest visitor activity takes place between May and Columbus Day—at other times, most restaurants, inns, stores, and visitor services close down. If you plan to stay overnight in summer, make reservations well in advance (for weekends in July and August, March is not too early).

Block Island has two harbors, Old Harbor and New Harbor. Approaching Block Island by sea from New London (Connecticut), Newport, or Point Judith, you'll see Old Harbor and its group of Victorian hotels. The Old Harbor area is the island's only village. Most of the inns, shops, and restaurants are here, and it's a short walk from the ferry landing to any hotel and to most of the interesting sights.

With the exception of a short strip called Moped Alley (actually Weldon's Way), where visitors test-drive mopeds, there's not a bad walk on all of Block Island. The West Side loop is gorgeous.

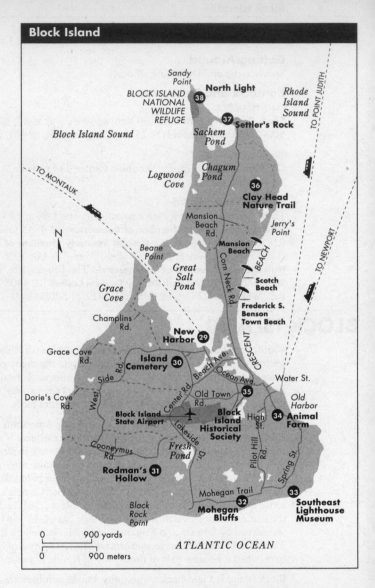

Block Island

Sandy Point

BLOCK ISLAND NATIONAL WILDLIFE REFUGE

North Light **38**

Rhode Island Sound

TO POINT JUDITH

Settler's Rock **37**

Sachem Pond

Block Island Sound

Chagum Pond

Logwood Cove

TO MONTAUK

Clay Head Nature Trail **36**

Mansion Beach Rd.

Jerry's Point

Beane Point

Mansion Beach

Great Salt Pond

Corn Neck Rd.

Scotch Beach

BEACH

Grace Cove

Frederick S. Benson Town Beach

Champlins Rd.

New Harbor **29**

Grace Cove Rd.

Island Cemetery **30**

West Side Rd.

Beach Ave.

Ocean Ave.

Water St.

CRESCENT

TO NEWPORT

Dorie's Cove Rd.

Center Rd.

Old Town Rd.

35

Old Harbor

Block Island State Airport

Block Island Historical Society

High St.

Animal Farm **34**

Lakeside Dr.

Cooneymus Rd.

Fresh Pond

Pilot Hill Rd.

Spring St.

Rodman's Hollow **31**

Mohegan Trail

Southeast Lighthouse Museum **33**

Black Rock Point

Mohegan Bluffs **32**

N

0 900 yards

0 900 meters

ATLANTIC OCEAN

29 Three docks, two hotels, and four restaurants huddled in the southeast corner of the Great Salt Pond make up the **New Harbor** commercial area. The harbor itself—also called Great Salt Pond—shelters as many as 1,700 boats on busy weekends, hosts sail races and fishing tournaments, and is the landing point for two ferries that run from Montauk on Long Island (New York) to Block Island.

30 The **Island Cemetery,** ½ mi west on West Side Road from New Harbor, has held the remains of island residents since the 1700s. At this well-maintained graveyard you can spot the names of long-standing Block Island families (Ball, Rose, Champlin) and take in fine views of the Great Salt Pond, the North Light, and the Rhode Island coast; on a clear day, the Jamestown–Newport Bridge will be visible to the east.

To explore the island's **west side,** continue past Island Cemetery; you will pass a horse farm and some small ponds. You get to the beach by turning right on Dorie's Cove Road or Cooneymus Beach Road; both dead-end at the island's tranquil west shore. One mile down, peaceful

West Side Road jogs left and turns into Cooneymus Road. On your right ½ mi farther is a deep ravine.

★ ③① **Rodman's Hollow** (⊠ off Cooneymus Rd.) is a fine example of a glacial outwash basin. This was the first piece of property purchased in the island's quarter-century-long tradition of land conservation, an effort that has succeeded in saving 25% of the island from development. At Rodman's you can descend along winding paths to the ocean, where you can hike the coastline, lie on beaches at the foot of sand and clay cliffs, or swim, if the waters are calm.

③② The 200-ft cliffs along Mohegan Trail, the island's southernmost road, are called **Mohegan Bluffs**—so named for an Indian battle in which the local Manisses pinned down an attacking band of Mohegans at the base of the cliffs. From **Payne Overlook**, west of the Southeast Lighthouse Museum (☞ *below*), you can see to Montauk Point, New York, and beyond. An intimidating set of stairs leads down to the beach.

③③ **Southeast Lighthouse Museum** is a "rescued" 1873 redbrick beacon with gingerbread detail. For 120 years, erosion ate away at the bluffs, until the lighthouse sat precariously close to the edge of a 200-ft drop-off. An inspired grassroots movement raised the funds necessary to move the structure away from the precipice in 1993. The lighthouse, a National Historic Landmark, has a small museum. ⊠ *Mohegan Trail,* ☎ *401/466–5009.* ⊞ *$5.* ☉ *Memorial Day–Labor Day, daily 10–4.*

☺ ③④ The owners of the 1661 Inn and Hotel Manisses (☞ Dining and Lodging, *below*) run a small **Animal Farm** with a collection of llamas, emus, sheep, goats, and ducks. The animals happily coexist in a meadow next to the hotel. ⊠ *Off Spring or High St.,* ☎ *401/466–2063.* ⊞ *Free.* ☉ *Daily dawn–dusk.*

③⑤ Exhibits at the **Block Island Historical Society** describe the island's farming and maritime pasts. Many original pieces furnish the society's headquarters, an 1850 mansard-roof home that's well worth a visit. ⊠ *Old Town Rd.,* ☎ *401/466–2481 or 401/466–5009.* ⊞ *$2.* ☉ *July–Aug., daily 10–4; June and Sept., weekends 10–4.*

★ ③⑥ *Outside* magazine hailed the **Clay Head Nature Trail** as Rhode Island's best hike. It's about a mile, but other trails lead off of it. The trail meanders past Clay Head Swamp and along 150-ft-high oceanside cliffs. Songbirds chirp and flowers bloom along the paths that lead into the interior—an area called the Maze. The trailhead is at the end of a dirt road that begins at Corn Neck Road, just past Mansion Beach Road; it is recognizable by a simple white-post marker. Trail maps are available at the **Nature Conservancy** (⊠ Ocean Ave., ☎ 401/466–2129).

③⑦ **Settler's Rock,** on the spit of land between Sachem Pond and Cow Beach, is a monument that lists the names of the original settlers and marks the spot where they landed in 1661. A 1-mi hike over sandy terrain will get you to the somber North Light (☞ *below*).

★ ③⑧ **North Light,** a granite lighthouse on the northernmost tip of the Block Island National Wildlife Refuge, was built in 1867. In 1993, it was restored and reopened as a maritime museum. The protected area is a temporary home to American oystercatchers, piping plovers, and other rare migrating birds. From a parking lot at the end of Corn Neck Road, it's a mile-long hike over sand to the lighthouse. ⊠ *Corn Neck Rd.,* ☎ *401/466–3200.* ⊞ *$2.* ☉ *Mid-June–Labor Day, daily 10–4, weather permitting.*

The east side of the island has a number of beaches. The 2½-mi **Crescent Beach** runs from Old Harbor to Jerry's Point. **Frederick J. Benson Town Beach,** a family beach less than 1 mi down Corn Neck Road from Old Harbor, has a beach pavilion, parking, showers, and lifeguards. Young summer workers congregate ½ mi north of Town Beach at **Scotch Beach** to play volleyball, to surf, and to sun themselves. **Mansion Beach,** off Mansion Beach Road south of Jerry's Point, has deep white sand and is easily one of New England's most beautiful beaches. In the morning, you may spot deer on the dunes.

Dining and Lodging

$$$ ✕ **Eli's.** In summer there's always a wait at Block Island's favorite restau-
★   rant, but the food is worth your patience. Pastas are the menu's main-
         stays, but the kitchen makes extensive excursions into local seafood,
         Asian dishes, and steaks like the Carpetbagger, a 12-ounce filet mignon
         filled with lobster, mozzarella, and sun-dried tomatoes, topped with a
         béarnaise sauce. ✉ *Chapel St.,* ☎ *401/466–5230. Reservations not ac-
         cepted. MC, V. Closed Jan.–Feb., and Sun.–Wed. Mar.–May.*

$$–$$$ ✕ **Finn's.** A Block Island institution, Finn's serves reliable fried and
         broiled seafood and prepares a wonderful smoked bluefish pâté. For
         lunch try the Workman's Special platter—a burger, coleslaw, and french
         fries. You can eat inside or out on the deck, or get food to go. Finn's
         raw bar is on an upstairs deck that overlooks Old Harbor. ✉ *Ferry
         Landing,* ☎ *401/466–2473. Reservations not accepted. AE, MC, V.
         Closed mid-Oct.–May.*

$ ✕ **The BeacHead.** The food at the BeacHead—especially the Rhode Is-
         land clam chowder—is very good, the price is right, and you won't feel
         like a tourist at this locals' hangout. Play pool, catch up on town gos-
         sip, or sit at the bar and stare out at the sea. The menu and service are
         unpretentious; burgers are served on paper plates with potato chips
         and pickles. ✉ *Corn Neck Rd.,* ☎ *401/466–2249. Reservations not
         accepted. No credit cards.*

$$$–$$$$ ✕⊡ **Atlantic Inn.** Bravely facing the elements on a hill above the ocean,
★   this long, white, classic Victorian resort has big windows, high ceil-
         ings, and a sweeping staircase. Most of the oak and maple furnishings
         in the rooms are original to the building. And then there are the views:
         Isolated from the hubbub of the Old Harbor area, you can perch on
         a hillside, look out over the harbor, and contemplate the shape of the
         island. Each morning the inn's pastry chef prepares a buffet breakfast
         with fresh-baked goods. The restaurant ($$$$; reservations essential;
         no lunch; closed from November to April) serves four-course, prix-fixe
         meals. The inn welcomes children. ✉ *Box 1788, High St., 02807,* ☎
         401/466–5883 or 800/224–7422, FAX *401/466–5678. 21 rooms. Restau-
         rant, 2 tennis courts, croquet, playground, meeting rooms. Continen-
         tal breakfast. D, MC, V. Closed Nov.–Easter.*

$$$–$$$$ ✕⊡ **Hotel Manisses.** The chef at the island's premier restaurant (closed
         November–April) for American cuisine uses herbs and vegetables from
         the hotel's garden and locally caught seafood to prepare superb dishes
         such as littleneck clams Dijonnaise. Period furnishings and knick-
         knacks fill the rooms in the 1872 mansion, some of which were named
         after shipwrecks; because of the antiques, the hotel is not suitable for
         children. The extras here include picnic baskets, an animal farm, is-
         land tours, afternoon wine and hors d'oeuvres in a parlor overlook-
         ing the garden, and many rooms with whirlpool baths. ✉ *1 Spring St.,
         02807,* ☎ *401/466–2421 or 800/626–4773,* FAX *401/466–3162. 17
         rooms. Restaurant, fans. Full breakfast. MC, V.*

$$$–$$$$ ⊡ **Blue Dory Inn.** This Old Harbor district inn has been a guest house
★   since its construction in 1898. Thanks to Ann Loedy, the dynamic owner-
         manager, things in the main building and the three small shingle-and-
         clapboard outbuildings run efficiently. Though not large, the rooms
         are tastefully appointed, and each has either an ocean or a harbor view.

Couples looking for a romantic hideaway often enjoy the Tea House, which has a porch overlooking Crescent Beach. ⊠ *Box 488, Dodge St., 02807,* ☎ *401/466–2254 or 800/992–7290. 12 rooms, 4 cottages, 3 suites. Full breakfast. AE, D, MC, V.*

$$$–$$$$ ⊞ **1661 Inn and Guest House.** If your island vacation fantasy includes
★ lounging in bed while gazing at swans in the marshes that overlook the blue Atlantic, come to the 1661. Even if your room doesn't face the water, you can loll on the inn's expansive deck or curl up in a chair on the lawn; from both spots you'll enjoy the panorama of the water below. The room decor reflects the innkeepers' attention to detail: Floral wallpaper in one room matches the colors of the hand-painted tiles atop its antique bureau, and another room has a collection of wooden model ships. The ample breakfast buffet might consist of fresh bluefish, corned-beef hash, sausage, Belgian waffles, roast potatoes, French toast, scrambled eggs, hot and cold cereal, fruit juices, and fresh muffins. ⊠ *Spring St., 02807,* ☎ *401/466–2421 or 800/626–4773,* ℻ *401/466–2858. 21 rooms, 19 with bath. Playground. Full breakfast. AE, MC, V. Closed mid-Nov.–mid-Apr.*

$$–$$$ ⊞ **Barrington Inn.** When a former Welcome Wagon hostess decides to open a B&B, you can bet she'll do things right. Owners Howard and Joan Ballard run a tidy, inviting place. They enjoy helping you plan your days; the breakfast table is known as "command central." The inn, meticulously clean, precisely arranged, and thoroughly soundproofed, has unusual views of Trims Pond, Great Salt Pond, and Crescent Beach. It is not recommended for families with children. Three rooms have private decks; there's also a large common deck. ⊠ *Box 397, Beach Ave., 02807,* ☎ *401/466–5510,* ℻ *401/466–5880. 6 rooms, 2 apartments. Continental breakfast. D, MC, V.*

$$–$$$ ⊞ **Surf Hotel.** A stone's throw from the ferry dock, in the heart of the Old Harbor area and near Crescent Beach, the Surf seems to have changed little over the years; in fact, it's not hard to imagine what the hotel must have been like when it first opened in 1876. Dimly lighted hallways take you to small rooms furnished with a jumble of antique furniture and odds and ends. The rooms have sinks but share toilets and baths, but the many return guests don't seem to mind sharing. ⊠ *Box C, Dodge St., 02807,* ☎ *401/466–2241. 38 rooms, 3 with bath. Breakfast room. Continental breakfast. MC, V. Closed mid-Oct.–Apr.*

Nightlife and the Arts

Many regular visitors consider Block Island's nightlife its best offering, and you'll find a good number of places to get a drink. Check the *Block Island Times* for band listings. **Captain Nick's Rock and Roll Bar** (⊠ 34 Ocean Ave., ☎ 401/466–5670), a fortress of summertime debauchery, has four bars and two decks on two floors. In season, bands play nightly. A 360-degree mural that depicts Block Island in the 1940s covers the walls at atmospheric **Club Soda** (⊠ 35 Connecticut Ave., ☎ 401/466–5397). **McGovern's Yellow Kittens Tavern** (⊠ Corn Neck Rd., ☎ 401/466–5855) hosts reggae, rock, and R&B bands every night in season.

Outdoor Activities and Sports

Boating

Block Island Boat Basin (⊠ West Side Rd., New Harbor, ☎ 401/466–2631) is the island's best-stocked ship's store. **New Harbor Kayak** (⊠ Ocean Ave., New Harbor, ☎ 401/466–2890) rents kayaks. **Oceans & Ponds** (⊠ Ocean and Connecticut Aves., ☎ 401/466–5131) rents kayaks and books charter-boat trips.

Fishing

Most of Rhode Island's record fish have been caught on Block Island. From almost any beach, skilled anglers can land tautog and bass. Bonito and fluke are often hooked in the New Harbor channel. Shell-fishing licenses may be obtained at the town hall, on Old Town Road. **Oceans & Ponds** (☞ *above*) sells tackle and fishing gear, operates charter trips, and provides guide services. **Twin Maples** (⊠ Beach Ave., ☎ 401/466–5547) is the island's only bait shop.

Hiking

The **Greenway,** a well-maintained trail system, meanders across the island, but some of the best hikes are along the beaches. You can hike around the entire island in about eight hours. Trail maps for the Greenway are available at the **Chamber of Commerce** (⊠ Water St., ☎ 401/466–2982) and the **Nature Conservancy** (⊠ Ocean Ave. near Payne's Dock, ☎ 401/466–2129). The Nature Conservancy conducts nature walks; call for times or check the local papers.

Water Sports

Island Outfitters (⊠ Ocean Ave., ☎ 401/466–5502) rents wet suits, spear-guns, and scuba gear. PADI-certification diving courses are available, and beach gear and bathing suits are for sale. **Para-sailing on Block Island** (⊠ Old Harbor Basin, ☎ 401/466–2474) also rents jet boats.

Shopping

Red Herring (⊠ The Shoreline, Water St., 2nd floor, ☎ 401/466–2540) sells distinctive folk art and crafts—pottery, jewelry, home furnishings. **Scarlet Begonia** (⊠ Dodge St., ☎ 401/466–5024) carries unusual jewelry and crafts, including place mats and handmade quilts. **Spring Street Gallery** (⊠ Spring St., ☎ 401/466–5374) shows and sells paintings, photographs, stained glass, serigraphs, and other work by island artists and artisans.

Block Island A to Z

Arriving and Departing

BY CAR AND FERRY

Interstate Navigation Co. (⊠ Galilee State Pier, Narragansett, ☎ 401/783–4613) operates ferry service from Galilee, a one-hour trip, for $16.30 round-trip; there are six or seven trips a day. Make auto reservations well ahead. Foot passengers cannot make reservations; you should arrive 45 minutes ahead in high season—the boats do fill up. Ferries run daily from Memorial Day to October from Providence's India Street Pier to Newport's Fort Adams State Park, and to Block Island, and then return along the same route in the afternoon. The company also has summer service from New London, Connecticut. A new high-speed ferry may be added in 2000.

Nelseco Navigation (⊠ 2 Ferry Rd., New London, CT, ☎ 860/442–7891) operates an auto ferry from New London, Connecticut, in summer. Reservations are advised for the two-hour trip. One-way fares from New London are $15 per adult and $28 per vehicle.

Viking Ferry Lines (☎ 516/668–5709) operates passenger and bicycle service from Montauk, Long Island (New York), from mid-May to mid-October. The trip, which takes 1¾ hours, costs $16 each way, plus $3 per bicycle.

BY PLANE

Block Island Airport (⊠ Center Rd., ☎ 401/466–5511) is served by a few small airlines. **Action Air** (☎ 203/448–1646 or 800/243–8623) flies in from Groton, Connecticut, between June and October. **New England**

Airlines (☎ 401/466–5881 or 800/243–2460) flies from Westerly to Block Island and operates charter flights.

Getting Around

BY BICYCLE AND MOPED

The best way to explore the island is by bicycle (about $15 a day to rent) or moped (about $40). Most of the rental places that follow are open through October and have child seats for bikes: **Block Island Boat Basin** (☎ 401/466–2631); **Esta's at Old Harbor** (☎ 401/466–2651); **Moped Man** (☎ 401/466–5011); **Old Harbor Bike Shop** (☎ 401/466–2029); and **Sea Crest Inn** (☎ 401/466–2882), bikes only.

BY CAR

Corn Neck Road runs north to Settler's Rock from Old Harbor. West Side Road loops west from New Harbor; to return to the Old Harbor area, take Cooneymus Road east and Lakeside Drive, Center Road, and Ocean Avenue north. If you need to rent a car, try **Block Island Car Rental** (☎ 401/466–2297).

BY TAXI

Taxis are plentiful at the Old Harbor and New Harbor ferry landings. The island's dispatch services include **Minuteman Taxi** (☎ 401/466–3131) and **Wolfie's Taxi** (☎ 401/466–5550). **O.J.'s Taxi** operates year-round (☎ 401/741–0500).

Contacts and Resources

HOME RENTALS

Inns and hotels on Block Island are booked well in advance for weekends in July and August. Many visitors rent homes for a week or more. Many houses, however, are booked solid by April. **Block Island Realty** (✉ Chapel St., 02807, ☎ 401/466–54260) and **Sullivan Real Estate** (✉ Water St., 02807, ☎ 401/466–5521) handle rentals.

VISITOR INFORMATION

Block Island Chamber of Commerce (✉ Drawer D, Water St., 02807, ☎ 401/466–2982).

NEWPORT COUNTY

Perched gloriously on the southern tip of Aquidneck Island and bounded on three sides by water, Newport is one of the great sailing cities of the world and the host to world-class jazz, blues, folk, and classical music festivals. Colonial houses and gilded-age mansions grace the city. Newport County encompasses all of Newport, plus Conanicut Island, also known as Jamestown, and the portion of Rhode Island east of Newport that abuts Massachusetts. The most-visited town in the area east of Newport is Little Compton.

Jamestown

39 *25 mi south of Providence, 3 mi west of Newport.*

The east and west passages of Narragansett Bay encompass the 9-mi-long, 1-mi-wide landmass that goes by the names Jamestown and Conanicut Island. Valuable as a military outpost in days gone by, the island was once considered an impediment to commercial cross-bay shipping.

In 1940 the Jamestown Bridge linked the island to western Rhode Island, and in 1969 the Newport Bridge completed the cross-bay route, connecting Newport to the entire South County area. Summer residents have come to Jamestown since the 1880s, but never to the same extent as in Watch Hill, Narragansett, or Newport. The locals' "We're not a T-shirt town" attitude has resulted in a relatively low number of visitors, even in July and August, making this a peaceful alternative to the hustle and bustle of nearby Newport and South County.

The conditions range from tranquil to harrowing at **Beavertail State Park,** which straddles the southern tip of Conanicut Island. The currents and surf here are famously deadly during rough seas and high winds; but on a clear, calm day, the park's craggy shoreline seems intended for sunning, hiking, and climbing. The **Beavertail Lighthouse Museum,** in what was the lighthouse keeper's quarters, has displays about Rhode Island's lighthouses. ⊠ *Beavertail Rd.,* ☎ *401/423–3270.* 🖾 *Free.* ☉ *Museum June–Labor Day, daily 10–4. Park daily.*

Thomas Carr Watson's family had worked the **Watson Farm** for 190 years before he bequeathed it to Society for the Preservation of New England Antiquities when he died in 1979. The 285-acre spread, whose mission includes educating the public about agrarian history, has 2 mi of trails along Jamestown's southwestern shore with amazing views of Narragansett Bay and North Kingstown. If you're lucky, you'll spot a coyote among the many critters on land. ⊠ *455 North Rd.,* ☎ *401/423–0005.* 🖾 *$3.* ☉ *June–mid-Oct., Tues., Thurs., and Sun. 1–5.*

The English-designed **Jamestown Windmill,** built in 1789, ground corn for nearly 100 years—and it still works. Mills like this one were once common in Rhode Island. ⊠ *North Rd., east of Watson Farm,* ☎ *no phone.* 🖾 *Free.* ☉ *Mid-June–Sept., weekends 1–4.*

A working 1859 hand tub and a horse-drawn steam pump are among the holdings of the **Jamestown Fire Department Memorial Museum,** an informal display of firefighting equipment in a garage that once housed the fire company. ⊠ *50 Narrangansett Ave.,* ☎ *401/423–0062.* 🖾 *Free.* ☉ *Daily 7–3; inquire next door at Fire Department if door is locked.*

Fort Wetherill State Park, an outcropping of stone cliffs at the tip of the southeastern peninsula, has been a picnic destination since the 1800s. There's great swimming at the small cove here. ⊠ *Ocean St.,* ☎ *401/423–1771.* 🖾 *Free.* ☉ *Daily dawn–dusk.*

Sandy **Mackerel Cove Beach** (⊠ Beavertail Rd.) is sheltered from the currents of Narragansett Bay. Parking costs $10 for nonresidents.

The **Jamestown and Newport Ferry Co.** stops in Newport at Bowen's Landing and Long Wharf and will stop on request at Fort Adams or Goat Island. The 26-ft passenger ferry departs on its half-hour voyage from Ferry Wharf about every 1½ hours, from 9 AM to 10 PM (11:30 PM on weekends). The last run leaves from Newport at 10:30 PM (midnight on weekends). The ferry operates from Memorial Day to mid-October. ⊠ *Ferry Wharf,* ☎ *401/423–9900.* 🖾 *About $6.*

Dining and Lodging

$$$–$$$$ ✕ **Trattoria Simpatico.** A jazz trio plays on sunny weekends at Jamestown's signature restaurant, while patrons dine alfresco under a 275-year-old copper beech tree. An herb garden, fieldstone walls, and white linen complete the picture. You can munch splendid salads, taste pasta dishes cooked northern Italian style, or try meats prepared with a Continental flair. One memorable appetizer is crispy-skin duck confit with deep-fried fettuccine, savoy cabbage, and onion marmalade. ⊠ *13 Narragansett Ave.,* ☎ *401/423–3731. Reservations essential on summer weekends. AE, D, MC, V. No lunch weekdays Labor Day–Memorial Day, no lunch weekends Memorial Day–Labor Day.*

$$$ ✕ **Jamestown Oyster Bar.** Whether you're ordering clam chowder and a dollar draft or grilled swordfish and a martini, you'll feel right at home here. Oysters are kept on ice behind the bar, where tenders pour fine microbrews and wines. The burgers are locally renowned,

but for something more delicate, try one of the seafood specials listed on the chalkboard. ⊠ *22 Narragansett Ave.,* ☏ *401/423–3380. Reservations not accepted. AE, MC, V. No lunch weekdays.*

$ ✕ **East Ferry Market and Deli.** Year-rounders and summer residents frequent this standby, which is open daily from 6 AM to 5 PM for coffee, salads, and specialty sandwiches. Grab a table on the patio if you can. ⊠ *47 Conanicus Ave.,* ☏ *401/423–1592. No credit cards.*

$$$$ ⊡ **Bay Voyage.** In 1889 this Victorian inn was shipped to its current location from Newport and named in honor of its trip. The inn's one-bedroom suites, furnished in floral prints and pastels, have been sold as time shares, which makes availability tight in summer months. The view and the facilities make staying here a memorable experience; the restaurant is known for its Sunday brunch. ⊠ *150 Conanicus Ave., 02835,* ☏ *401/ 423–2100,* FAX *401/423–3209. 32 suites. Restaurant, bar, kitchenettes, pool, indoor hot tub, sauna, exercise room. AE, D, DC, MC, V.*

$ ⊡ **East Bay B&B.** If Karen Montoya's three rooms aren't booked, you can get a great deal at her humble B&B. The circa-1896 Victorian is peaceful day and night, even though it's a block from Jamestown's two main streets and bustling wharf. The original trim and bullnose molding are all in great shape, as is the formal living room, which has a fireplace and Oriental rugs. ⊠ *14 Union St., 02835,* ☏ *401/423–2715. 3 rooms, 1 with bath. Continental breakfast. No credit cards.*

Outdoor Activities and Sports

DIVING AND KAYAKING

Ocean State Scuba (⊠ 79 N. Main Rd., ☏ 401/423–1662 or 800/933–3483) rents kayaks and diving equipment.

GOLF

Jamestown Country Club (⊠ 245 Conanicus Ave., ☏ 401/423–9930) has a crisp nine-hole course, where for $10 you can play all day.

Newport

30 mi from Providence, 80 mi from Boston.

The island city of Newport preserves Colonial industry and gilded-aAge splendor as no other place in the country does. The golden age of Newport ran from roughly 1720 to the 1770s, when products like cheese, clocks, and furniture as well as livestock and the slave trade put the city on a par with Charleston, South Carolina; the two cities trailed only Boston as centers of New World maritime commerce. In the mid-1700s, Newport was home to the best shipbuilders in North America. Their small, swift, and reliable slave ships were the stars of the triangle trade (rum to Africa for slaves; slaves to the West Indies for molasses; molasses and slaves back to America, where the molasses was made into rum). This unsavory scheme guaranteed investors a 20% return on their money and earned Newport the dubious distinction of being the largest slave-trading port in the North. In 1774, progressive Rhode Island became the first colony to outlaw trading in slaves.

In the 19th century, Newport became a summer playground for the wealthy. These riches were not made in Rhode Island but imported by the titans of the gilded age and translated into the fabulous "cottages" overlooking the Atlantic. Newport's mansions served as proving grounds for the country's best young architects. Richard Upjohn, Richard Morris Hunt, and firms like McKim, Mead, & White have left a legacy of remarkable homes, many now open to the public.

Recreational sailing, a huge industry in Newport today, convincingly melds the attributes of two eras: the conspicuous consumption of the gilded age and the nautical expertise of the Colonial era. Tanned young sailors often fill Newport bars and restaurants, where they talk of wind, waves, and expensive yachts. For those not arriving by water, a sailboat tour of the harbor is a great way to get your feet wet.

Newport in summer can be exasperating, its streets jammed with visitors, the traffic slowed by sightseeing buses (3½ million people visit the city each year). Yet the quality of Newport's sights and its arts festivals persuade many people to brave the crowds. In fall and spring, you can explore the city without having to stand in long lines.

Downtown Newport

More than 200 pre-Revolutionary buildings (mostly private residences) remain in Newport, more than in any other city in the country. Most of these national treasures are in the neighborhood known as the Point.

A GOOD WALK

The ideal first sight in a walking tour is the Colonial-era **Hunter House** ④⓪. Walk north from Hunter House on Washington Street. At Van Zandt Avenue, turn right and proceed to the **Common Burial Ground** ④①. Aptly named Farewell Street crosses the cemetery, then heads southeast. At the Marlborough Street intersection you'll pass the country's oldest bar and restaurant, the **White Horse Tavern** ④②. Across Farewell Street stands **Friends Meeting House** ④③. To the east, Marlborough intersects Spring Street and Broadway; ahead on your right you'll see the **Wanton-Lyman-Hazard House** ④④, the oldest home in Newport. Follow Spring Street three short blocks south to Washington Street, which heads west into Washington Square. Over your left shoulder is the imposing **Colony House** ④⑤. At the bottom of Washington Square is the **Museum of Newport History at the Brick Market** ④⑥.

Walk two blocks east on Touro Street (on the south side of the square); **Touro Synagogue** ④⑦ will be on your left. Next door is the **Newport Historical Society** ④⑧. Cross the road and follow High Street one block; then turn right on Church Street to see the immaculate **Trinity Church** ④⑨. Proceed east on Church Street. Across Bellevue Avenue are the four pillars of **Redwood Library** ⑤⓪. The **Newport Art Museum and Art Association** ⑤① is one block south. You can continue south on Bellevue Avenue and cross Memorial Boulevard to visit Newport's gilded-age mansions (☞ Greater Newport, *below*), if you have the energy.

TIMING: This walk covers 2½ mi. If you spend time inside each building, it should take about 4½ hours to reach Bellevue Avenue. It's best to do this walk one day and the mansions of Bellevue Avenue (☞ Greater Newport, *below*) another. If you have only one day, you will have to limit the number of sights you visit.

SIGHTS TO SEE

④⑤ **Colony House.** This redbrick structure above downtown Washington Square was where, on May 4, 1776, Rhode Island and Providence Plantations signed an act that removed King George's name from all state documents. The same year, from the balcony of this building, the Declaration of Independence was read to Newporters. In 1781, George Washington met here with French commander Count Rochambeau to plan the Battle of Yorktown, which led to the end of the Revolutionary War. ⊠ *Washington Sq.,* ☎ *401/846–2980.* ☺ *Tours by appointment.*

④① **Common Burial Ground.** Farewell Street is lined with historic cemeteries; the many tombstones at this 17th-century graveyard are fine examples of Colonial stone carving, much of it the work of John Stevens.

④③ **Friends Meeting House.** Built in 1699, this is the oldest Quaker meeting house in the country. With its wide-plank floors, simple benches, balcony, and beam ceiling (considered lofty by Colonial standards), this

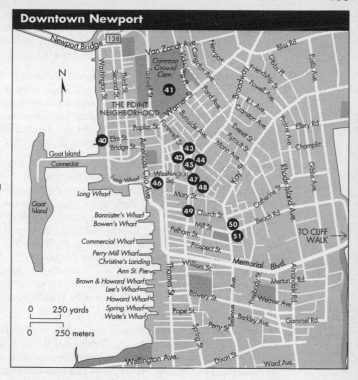

Downtown Newport

two-story shingle structure reflects the quiet reserve and steadfast faith of Colonial Quakers. ⊠ *29 Farewell St.,* ☎ *401/846–0813.* ⊡ *$5.* ⊙ *Tours by appointment.*

★ ④⓪ **Hunter House.** The French admiral Charles Louis d'Arsac de Ternay used this lovely 1748 home as his Revolutionary War headquarters. The carved pineapple over the doorway was a symbol of welcome throughout Colonial America; a fresh pineapple placed out front signaled an invitation to neighbors to visit a returned seaman or to look over a shop's new stock. The elliptical arch in the central hall is a typical Newport detail. Pieces made by Newport artisans Townsend and Goddard furnish much of the house. ⊠ *54 Washington St.,* ☎ *401/ 847–7516.* ⊡ *$8.* ⊙ *May–Sept, daily 10–5; Oct., weekends 10–5.*

④⑥ **Museum of Newport History at the Brick Market.** This restored building once used for slave trading houses a city museum. Multimedia exhibits explore the Newport's social and economic influences, and antiques like the printing press of James Franklin (Ben's brother) inspire the imagination. Built in 1760 and designed by Peter Harrison, who was also responsible for the Touro Synagogue and the Redwood Library, the building served as a theater and a town hall. The museum and the Gateway Information Center (☞ Visitor Information *in* Newport County A to Z, *below*) are departure points for walking tours of Newport; call for times. ⊠ *127 Thames St.,* ☎ *401/841–8770.* ⊡ *$5.* ⊙ *May–Nov., Mon. and Wed.–Sat. 10–5, Sun. 1–5; Dec.–Apr., Fri.– Sat. 10–4, Sun. 1–5.*

⑤① **Newport Art Museum and Art Association.** Richard Morris Hunt designed the Stick-style Victorian building that houses this community-supported center for the arts. The galleries exhibit contemporary works by New England artists. ⊠ *76 Bellevue Ave.,* ☎ *401/848–8200.* ⊡ *$4.* ⊙ *Memorial Day–Labor Day, daily 10–5; Labor Day–Memorial Day, Mon.–Tues. and Thurs.–Sat. 10–4, Sun. 12–4.*

48 **Newport Historical Society.** The headquarters of the historical society has a library and a small exhibit with Newport memorabilia, furniture, and maritime items. ⊠ *82 Touro St.,* ☎ *401/846–0813.* 🎫 *Free.* ⊙ *Tues.–Fri. 9:30–4:30, Sat. 9:30–noon (to 4:30 mid-June–Aug.).*

50 **Redwood Library.** Peter Harrison designed the nation's oldest library (chartered in 1747) in continuous use, a magnificent structure that, though made of wood, mimics the look of a Roman temple—the original exterior paint was mixed with sand to resemble stone. The library's paintings include works by Gilbert Stuart and Rembrandt Peale. ⊠ *50 Bellevue Ave.,* ☎ *401/847–0292.* 🎫 *Free.* ⊙ *Mon.–Sat. 9:30–5:30.*

47 **Touro Synagogue.** Jews, like Quakers and Baptists, were attracted by Rhode Island's religious tolerance; they arrived from Amsterdam and Lisbon as early as 1658. The oldest surviving synagogue in the United States was dedicated in 1763. Although simple on the outside, the Georgian building, designed by Peter Harrison, has an elaborate interior. Its classical style influenced Thomas Jefferson in the building of Monticello and the University of Virginia. ⊠ *85 Touro St.,* ☎ *401/847–4794.* 🎫 *Free.* ⊙ *July 4 weekend–Labor Day, Sun.–Fri. 10–5; Memorial Day weekend–July 4 weekend and Labor Day–Columbus Day, Sun. 11–3 and weekdays 1–3; Columbus Day–Memorial Day weekend, Sun. 1–3 and weekdays for 2 PM tour only. Guided tours begin on the ½ hr. Services Fri. 6 or 7 PM, Sat. 8:45 AM; call to confirm.*

49 **Trinity Church.** This Colonial beauty was built in 1724 and modeled after London churches designed by Sir Christopher Wren. A special feature of the interior is the three-tier wineglass pulpit, the only one of its kind in America. The lighting, woodwork, and palpable feeling of history make attending services here an unforgettable experience. ⊠ *Queen Anne Sq.,* ☎ *401/846–0660.* 🎫 *Free.* ⊙ *June–Oct., daily 10–4; Nov.–May, by appointment. Services Sun. at 8 and 10; off-season at 8 and 10:30.*

44 **Wanton-Lyman-Hazard House.** Newport's oldest residence dates from the mid-17th century. The dark-red building was site of the city's Stamp Act riot of 1765; after the British Parliament levied a tax on most printed material, the Sons of Liberty stormed the house, which was occupied by the English stamp master. The home was later a center of social life for 5,000 French troops who moved into the city when an occupying British army left for New York City in 1779. The house contains period artifacts, and there's a period garden. ⊠ *17 Broadway,* ☎ *401/846–0813.* 🎫 *$4.* ⊙ *By appointment.*

42 **White Horse Tavern.** William Mayes, the father of a successful and notorious pirate, received a tavern license in 1687, which makes this building, built in 1673, the oldest tavern in America. Its gambrel roof, low dark-beam ceilings, cavernous fireplace, and uneven plank floors epitomize Newport's Colonial charm (☞ Dining and Lodging, *below*). ⊠ *Marlborough and Farewell Sts.,* ☎ *401/849–3600.*

Greater Newport

The gilded-age mansions of Bellevue Avenue are what many people associate most with Newport. These late 19th century homes are almost obscenely grand, laden with ornate rococo detail and designed with a determined one-upmanship. Also in this area are some museums and the childhood home of Jacqueline Onassis.

The **Preservation Society of Newport County** (☎ 401/847–1000) maintains 12 mansions, some of which are described below. Guided tours are given of each; you can purchase a combination ticket at any of the properties for a substantial discount. The hours and days the houses are open during the off-season are subject to change, so it's wise to call ahead. Chateau-sur-Mer, the Elms, and, in some years, the Marble House or the Breakers are decorated for Christmas and usually open for tours daily from Thanksgiving Day to Christmas Day.

A GOOD TOUR

At the corner of Memorial Boulevard and Bellevue Avenue is the **International Tennis Hall of Fame Museum at the Newport Casino** ⑫, birthplace of the U.S. Open. Before you visit the mansions (or stop by when you're done), you can walk south on Bellevue Avenue, make a right on Bowery Street, and turn left at Thames Street to visit the **International Yacht Restoration School** ⑬. Back on Bellevue Avenue, catercorner from Newport Casino is **Kingscote** ⑭, the first "cottage" along this walking tour. The **Elms** ⑮ is two blocks south. Three blocks farther is **Chateau-sur-Mer** ⑯, and **Rosecliff** ⑰ is four more blocks in the same direction. **Astors' Beechwood** ⑱ and the **Marble House** ⑲ are on the same side of this lengthy block of palaces. Farther down, on the corner of Lakeview and Bellevue, is **Belcourt Castle** ⑳. Beyond this mansion, Bellevue Avenue turns 90 degrees west and dead-ends at what most consider the end of the **Cliff Walk** ㉑. From here you can stroll along the Rhode Island Sound to Newport's most renowned mansion, the **Breakers** ㉒, which can be reached from the Cliff Walk by heading west on Ruggles Avenue and north on Ochre Point Avenue.

You can walk the first part of this tour, but you'll need a car to visit three sights. The **Museum of Yachting** ㉓ is at Fort Adams State Park. From downtown Newport, drive south on Thames Street to Wellington Avenue. Turn right and follow Wellington to the bend where Wellington becomes Halidon Avenue. Turn right on Harrison Avenue. One mile to the right is the entrance to the park; the museum is at the end of Fort Adams Road. To reach **Hammersmith Farm** ㉔, turn right as you exit the park; the entrance is 300 yards down on the right. To get back to town, you can follow Ocean Drive to Bellevue Avenue. To reach the **Naval War College Museum** ㉕, at the intersection with Memorial Boulevard, turn left; Memorial becomes America's Cup Avenue. At the cemetery, turn left on Farewell Street. Farewell runs into Bridge Access Road, where you will veer left to reach the Connell Highway traffic circle. Exit at the west end of the circle on Training Station Road. A small bridge will take you to Coasters Harbor Island. Park at the naval base entrance and walk two blocks along the same road to the museum, which is on a hill to your right.

TIMING: If you have one day, it's best to tour two or three mansions and see the others only from the outside. To avoid long lines in summer, go early or choose the less-popular but still amazing mansions—the Elms, Kingscote, and Belcourt Castle. It's under 2 mi from Kingscote to Belcourt—the first and last mansions on Bellevue Avenue. Plan on spending one hour at each mansion you visit. The full Cliff Walk is 3½ mi long. Seeing the Tennis Hall of Fame, three mansions, walking the length of Bellevue Avenue, and returning via the Cliff Walk takes five or six hours. The driving portion of the tour is about 11 mi long. You could easily spend an hour at each sight on the drive.

Greater Newport

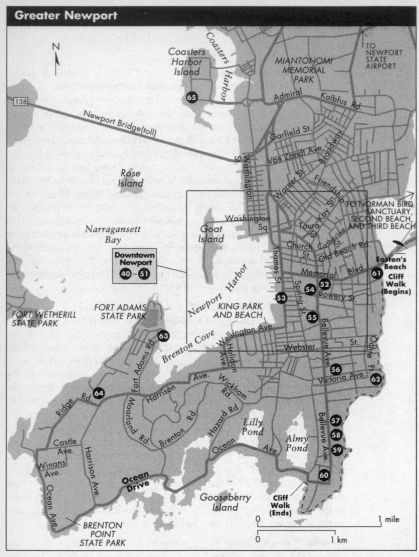

N

138
Newport Bridge (toll)

Coasters Harbor
Coasters Harbor Island

MIANTONOMI MEMORIAL PARK

TO NEWPORT STATE AIRPORT

65

Admiral
Kalbfus Rd.

Garfield St.

St. Washington

Van Zandt Ave.
Broadway

Warner St.
Friendship St.

Rose Island

Washington Sq.

Goat Island

Narragansett Bay

Touro St.
Kay St.
Catherine St.

TO NORMAN BIRD SANCTUARY, SECOND BEACH, AND THIRD BEACH

Church St.
Old Beach Rd.

Downtown Newport
40 – 51

Newport Harbor

Thames St.

Memorial Blvd.

Easton's Beach
Cliff Walk (Begins)
61

52
54
Bowery St.

53
Spring St.

FORT WETHERILL STATE PARK

FORT ADAMS STATE PARK

KING PARK AND BEACH

55

Wellington Ave.

Webster St.

Odhe Pl.

63

Brenton Cove

Holiday Ave.

Fort Adams Rd.

56
Victoria Ave.
62

64

Ridge Rd.

Harrison Ave.

Wickham Rd.

Moorland Rd.

Brenton Rd.

Hazard Rd.

Lilly Pond

Almy Pond

Belvue Ave.

57
58
59

Castle Ave.

Ocean Ave.

60

Winans Ave.

Harrison Ave.

Ocean Drive

Gooseberry Island

Cliff Walk (Ends)

Ocean Ave.

BRENTON POINT STATE PARK

0 _____ 1 mile
0 _____ 1 km

Astors'
Beechwood, **58**
Belcourt Castle, **60**
The Breakers, **62**
Chateau-sur-Mer, **56**
Cliff Walk, **61**

The Elms, **55**
Hammersmith
Farm, **64**
International Tennis
Hall of Fame
Museum at the
Newport Casino, **52**

International Yacht
Restoration
School, **53**
Kingscote, **54**
Marble House, **59**
Museum of
Yachting, **63**

Naval War College
Museum, **65**
Rosecliff, **57**

SIGHTS TO SEE

⑤⑧ Astors' Beechwood. The original mistress of this oceanfront mansion, Caroline Schermerhorn Astor, was the queen of American society in the late 19th century; her list of "the Four Hundred" was the first social register. Her husband, William Backhouse Astor, was a reserved businessman and a member of one of the wealthiest families in the nation (much of the Astors' fortune came from real estate, the China trade, and fur trading in North America). As they guide visitors through the 1857 mansion, actors in period costume play the family, their servants, and their household guests. ⊠ *580 Bellevue Ave.,* ☎ *401/846–3772.* ⊡ *$8.75.* ⊙ *Mid-May–Oct., daily 10–5; Nov.–Dec., Wed.–Sun. 10–4; Feb.–mid-May, weekends 10–4; call about Christmas hrs and events.*

⑥⓪ Belcourt Castle. Richard Morris Hunt based this 1894 Gothic Revival mansion, built for banking heir Oliver H. P. Belmont, on Louis XIII's hunting lodge. The house is so filled with European and Asian treasures that locals have dubbed it the Metropolitan Museum of Newport. Sip tea and admire the stained glass and carved wood, and don't miss the Golden Coronation Coach. ⊠ *657 Bellevue Ave.,* ☎ *401/846–0669 or 401/849–1566.* ⊡ *$8.* ⊙ *Apr.–Memorial Day, daily 10–5; Memorial Day–Columbus Day, daily 9–5; mid-Oct.–Dec., daily 10–4; Mar., weekends 10–4.*

★ **⑥② The Breakers.** It's easy to understand why it took 2,500 workers in the early 1890s two years to build the most magnificent Newport palace, the 70-room home of railroad heir Cornelius Vanderbilt II. A few of the marvels within the four-story Italian Renaissance–style palace are a gold-ceiling music room, a blue marble fireplace, rose alabaster pillars in the dining room, and a porch with a mosaic ceiling that took Italian artisans six months, lying on their backs, to install. To build the Breakers today would cost $400 million. ⊠ *Ochre Point Ave.,* ☎ *401/847–6544.* ⊡ *$10.* ⊙ *Mid-Mar.–Oct., daily 10–5; Nov., weekends 10–4; open Dec. some years (call).*

⑤⑥ Chateau-sur-Mer. Bellevue Avenue's first stone mansion was built in the Victorian Gothic style in 1852 for William S. Wetmore, a tycoon involved in the China trade, and enlarged in the 1870s by Richard Morris Hunt. The Gold Room by Leon Marcotte and the Renaissance Revival–style dining room and library by the Florentine sculptor Luigi Frullini are sterling examples of the work of leading 19th-century designers. Upstairs, the bedrooms are decorated in the English Aesthetic style with wallpaper by Arts and Crafts designers William Morris and William Burges. In December, the house is decorated for a Victorian Christmas. ⊠ *Bellevue Ave. at Shepard Ave.,* ☎ *401/847–1000.* ⊡ *$8.* ⊙ *May–Sept., daily 10–5; Oct.–mid-Nov., weekends 10–4; Thanksgiving–Dec. 23, daily 10–4; Jan.–Mar., weekends 10–4; Apr., weekends 10–5.*

Chepstow. This Italianate villa with a mansard roof is not as grand as other Newport mansions, but it houses a remarkable collection of art and furniture gathered by the Morris family of New York City. Built in 1861, the home was designed by Newport architect George Champlin Mason and is the latest addition to the list of homes owned by the Preservation Society of Newport County. ⊠ *120 Narragansett Ave.,* ☎ *401/847–1000.* ⊡ *$9.* ⊙ *May–Oct., Fri.–Sat. 10–5.*

★ **⑥① Cliff Walk.** Easton's Beach (also called First Beach) is the beginning of this spectacular 3½-mi path that runs south along Newport's cliffs to Bailey's Beach. The promenade has views of sumptuous mansions on one side and the rocky coastline on the other; walking any section of it is worth the effort. The Cliff Walk can be accessed from any road running east off Bellevue Avenue. The unpaved sections can be difficult for small children or people with mobility problems.

⑤⑤ The Elms. In designing this graceful 48-room French neoclassical mansion, architect Horace Trumbauer paid homage to the style, fountains, broad lawn, and formal gardens of the Château d'Asnières near Paris. The Elms was built for Edward Julius Berwind, a bituminous-coal baron, in 1899. The trees throughout the 12-acre backyard are labeled, providing an exemplary botany lesson. ✉ *Bellevue Ave.,* ☎ *401/842–0546.* 🎫 *$8.* ☉ *May–Oct., daily 10–5; 1st 2 wks of Nov. and Thanksgiving Day–Dec. 23, daily 10–4; Jan.–Apr., weekends 10–4.*

★ ⑥④ Hammersmith Farm. This elaborate country estate was the childhood summer home of Jacqueline Bouvier Kennedy Onassis, the site of her wedding to John F. Kennedy, and a summer White House during the Kennedy Administration. It is the only working farm in Newport. Loaded with Bouvier and Kennedy memorabilia, the house is so comfortable that it seems as though its owners have temporarily stepped out of its rooms. The gardens, with breathtaking views of Narragansett Bay, were designed by Frederick Law Olmsted. ✉ *Ocean Dr. near Ft. Adams,* ☎ *401/846–7346.* 🎫 *$8.50.* ☉ *Memorial Day–Labor Day, daily 10–5; Mar.–Memorial Day and Labor Day–mid-Nov., daily 10–5; special openings around Christmas.*

⑤② International Tennis Hall of Fame Museum at the Newport Casino. The photographs, memorabilia, and multimedia exhibits at the Hall of Fame provide a definitive chronicle of the game's greatest moments and characters. Newport Casino is an ideal location for the museum. The magnificent shingle-style social club was designed by Stanford White and built in 1880 for publisher James Gordon Bennett, Jr., who quit the nearby men's club, the Newport Reading Room, after a polo player—at Bennett's behest—rode a horse into the building and was subsequently banned. Bennett further retaliated by commissioning the Casino, which has 13 grass courts and one court-tennis facility (court tennis is the 13th-century precursor to modern tennis). The Casino quickly became the social and recreational hot spot of the gilded age. ✉ *194 Bellevue Ave.,* ☎ *401/849–3990.* 🎫 *$8; tennis courts $35 per person per hour.* ☉ *Daily 9:30–5.*

⑤③ International Yacht Restoration School. This school, off Thames Street in a former power plant, lets you watch shipwrights and students as they overhaul historically significant sailboats and power boats. Placards recount each boat's past. The 1885 racing schooner *Coronet* and the original "cigarette boat" are two standouts. ✉ *449 Thames St.,* ☎ *401/848–5777.* 🎫 *Free.* ☉ *Apr.–Nov., daily 9–5; Dec.–Mar., Mon.–Sat. 10–5.*

Isaac Bell House. Considered one of the finest examples of American shingle-style architecture, this Bellevue Avenue home currently being restored is open to the public as a work inprogress. The exterior has been completed; inside, a short film documents the effort to revitalize the McKim, Mead & White design, and you are given a tour of various rooms. Bell, who built the home in 1883, was a wealthy cotton broker. ✉ *Bellevue Ave., at Perry St.,* ☎ *401/847–1000.* 🎫 *$9.* ☉ *May–Oct., Fri.–Sat. 10–5.*

⑤④ Kingscote. This Victorian mansion completed in 1841 was designed by Richard Upjohn for George Noble Jones, a Savannah, Georgia, plantation owner. (Newport was popular with Southerners before the Civil War.) Decorated with antique furniture, glass, and Asian art, it contains a number of Tiffany windows. ✉ *Bowery St., off Bellevue Ave,* ☎ *401/847–1000.* 🎫 *$8.* ☉ *May–Sept., daily 10–5; Apr. and Oct., weekends 10–4.*

⑤⑨ Marble House. Perhaps the most opulent Newport mansion, the Marble House, with its extravagant gold ballroom, was the gift of William

Vanderbilt to his wife, Alva, in 1892. Alva divorced William in 1895 and married Oliver Perry Belmont, becoming the lady of Belcourt Castle. When Oliver died in 1908, she returned to Marble House. Mrs. Belmont was involved with the suffragist movement and spent much of her time campaigning for women's rights. The Chinese teahouse behind the estate was built in 1913. ⊠ *Bellevue Ave., near Ruggles St.,* ☎ *401/847–1000.* 🎫 *$6.* ☉ *Apr.–Oct., daily 10–5; Jan.–Mar., weekends 10–4; open Dec. some years (call).*

㊻ Museum of Yachting. The museum has four galleries: Mansions and Yachts, Small Craft, America's Cup, and the Hall of Fame for Single-handed Sailors. In summer, eight wooden yachts constitute a floating exhibition. ⊠ *Ft. Adams Park, Ocean Dr.,* ☎ *401/847–1018.* 🎫 *$3.* ☉ *May–Oct., daily 10–5; Nov.–May, by appointment.*

㊺ Naval War College Museum. The Naval War College, the oldest school of its kind in the world, represents the pinnacle of education in the U.S. Navy. The museum's exhibits analyze the history of naval warfare and tactics and trace the history of the navy in Narragansett Bay. ⊠ *Founders Hall, Gate 1, Naval Education and Training Center, Cushing Rd.,* ☎ *401/841–4052.* 🎫 *Free.* ☉ *Daily 10–4.*

OFF THE
BEATEN PATH

NORMAN BIRD SANCTUARY – The 450-acre preserve has nature trails, guided tours, and a small natural history museum. From Bellevue Avenue, turn east on Memorial Boulevard (Route 138A), pass First Beach, then turn right on Purgatory Road. Make another right on Hanging Rock Road. ⊠ *583 Third Beach Rd., Middletown,* ☎ *401/846–2577.* 🎫 *$4.* ☉ *Labor Day–Memorial Day, Tues.–Sun. 9–5; Memorial Day–Labor Day, daily 9–5.*

㊸ Rosecliff. Newport's most romantic mansion was built for Mrs. Hermann Oelrichs in 1902; her father had amassed a fortune from Nevada silver mines. Stanford White modeled the palace after the Grand Trianon at Versailles. Rosecliff has 40 rooms, including the Court of Love and a grand ballroom, and a heart-shape staircase. ⊠ *Bellevue Ave., at Marine Ave.,* ☎ *401/847–5793.* 🎫 *$8.* ☉ *May–Oct., daily 10–5.*

Beaches

Easton's Beach (⊠ Memorial Blvd.), also known as First Beach, is popular for its carousel. **Fort Adams State Park** (⊠ Ocean Dr.), a small beach with a picnic area and lifeguards in summer, has views of Newport Harbor. **Sachuest Beach,** or Second Beach, east of First Beach in the Sachuest Point area of Middletown, is a beautiful sandy area adjacent to the Norman Bird Sanctuary (☞ Greater Newport, *above*). Dunes and a campground make it popular with young travelers and surfers. **Third Beach,** in the Sachuest Point area of Middletown, is on the Sakonnet River. It has a boat ramp and is a favorite of windsurfers.

Dining and Lodging

$$$$ ✕ **The Black Pearl.** Visitors and yachters flock to this dignified converted dock shanty, where award-winning clam chowder is sold by the quart. Dining is in the casual tavern or the formal Commodore's Room. The latter serves an appetizer of black-and-blue tuna with red-pepper sauce. The French and American entrées include duck breast with green peppercorn sauce and swordfish with Dutch pepper butter. ⊠ *Bannister's Wharf,* ☎ *401/846–5264. Commodore Room: Reservations essential. Jacket required. AE, MC, V.*

$$$–$$$$ ✕ **Asterix & Obelix.** Danish chef John Bach-Sorensen makes fine din-
★ ing as fun and colorful as the madcap French cartoon strip after which this eatery was named. An auto repair garage before Sorensen took it over, the restaurant has a concrete floor painted to look like it's been

covered with expensive tiling. The garage doors can be opened or closed depending on the weather. Asian twists enliven the French-influenced Mediterranean fare, and there is a carefully selected menu of wines, brandies, and aperitifs. Sunday brunch is served year-round. ☒ *599 Thames St.,* ☎ *401/841–8833. AE, D, DC, MC, V. No lunch.*

$$$–$$$$ ✕ **Clarke Cooke House.** Waiters in tuxedos and the richly patterned cushions on wood chairs and booths underscore this restaurant's luxurious Colonial atmosphere. Formal dining is on the upper level, in a room with a timber-beam ceiling, green latticework, and water views; there's open-air dining in warm weather. The refined Mediterranean menu incorporates local seafood; game dishes often appear as specials. ☒ *Bannister's Wharf,* ☎ *401/849–2900. Reservations essential on summer weekends. Jacket required upstairs. AE, D, DC, MC, V.*

$$$–$$$$ ✕ **La Petite Auberge.** The colorful owner-chef, who once worked for General Charles de Gaulle, prepares delicacies like trout with almonds, duck flambé with orange sauce, and medallions of beef with goose-liver pâté. The setting for his exquisite cooking is a series of intimate rooms inside a Colonial house. In summer, dinner is served in the courtyard. ☒ *19 Charles St.,* ☎ *401/849–6669. AE, MC, V.*

$$$–$$$$ ✕ **Restaurant Bouchard.** There are regional takes on French cuisine at this upscale yet homey restaurant. Sautéed local cod, for instance, is topped with fresh Maine crab and asparagus, then finished with a light beurre blanc. ☒ *505 Thames St.,* ☎ *401/846–0123. AE, D, MC, V.*

$$$–$$$$ ✕ **White Horse Tavern.** The nation's oldest operating tavern, once a meeting house for Colonial Rhode Island's General Assembly, offers intimate dining with black-tie service, a top-notch wine cellar, and consistently excellent food. The tavern serves suave American cuisine, including local seafood and beef Wellington, along with more exotic entrées such as cashew-encrusted venison tenderloin topped with an apple-cider *demi-glace* (sauce). ☒ *Marlborough and Farewell Sts.,* ☎ *401/849–3600. Reservations essential. Jacket required. AE, D, DC, MC, V. No lunch Mon.–Wed.*

$$–$$$ ✕ **The Mooring.** The seafood chowder at this family-oriented restaurant won the local cook-off so many times the contest's officials removed it from further competition. In fine weather you can dine on the enclosed patio overlooking the yachts in the harbor; on chilly winter evenings, take advantage of the open fire in the sunken interior room. The prices are fairly reasonable, and there's plenty of parking. ☒ *Sayer's Wharf,* ☎ *401/846–2260. AE, D, DC, MC, V.*

$$–$$$ ✕ **Pronto.** Jazz and new Italian cuisine prepared with a European flair lure people to cozy, funky, chandelier-bedecked Pronto. The beef carpaccio appetizer is the best in town; rack of lamb and farfalle pasta with shiitake mushrooms, kalamata olives, and chèvre are among the entrées. ☒ *464 Thames St.,* ☎ *401/847–5251. AE, MC, V.*

$$–$$$ ✕ **Scales & Shells.** Busy, sometimes noisy, but always excellent, this ★ restaurant serves as many as 15 types of superbly fresh wood-grilled fish. The cooks occasionally send your waitperson to your table with your future dinner so you'll know exactly how fresh the fish is. Similar offerings are available in a more formal setting upstairs at Upscales. ☒ *527 Thames St.,* ☎ *401/848–9378. Reservations not accepted downstairs. No credit cards.*

$$ ✕ **Puerini's.** The aroma of garlic and basil greets you as soon as you enter this laid-back neighborhood restaurant. Lace curtains hang in the windows, and black-and-white photographs of Italy cover the soft-pink walls. The long and intriguing menu includes green noodles with chicken in marsala wine sauce, tortellini with seafood, and cavatelli with four cheeses. ☒ *24 Memorial Blvd.,* ☎ *401/847–5506. Reservations not accepted. MC, V. Closed Mon. in winter. No lunch.*

$ ✕ **Ocean Coffee Roasters.** Known to locals as Wave Café, this nonchalant diner draws locals aplenty for fresh-roasted coffee and fresh-baked muffins as well as bagels, salads, and homemade Italian soups. Breakfast is served until 2 PM. ✉ *22 Washington Sq.,* ☎ *401/846–6060. Reservations not accepted. MC, V.*

$$$$ ✕▥ **Vanderbilt Hall.** A former YMCA building (originally a Vander-
★ bilt home) donated to Newport by the Vanderbilt family in 1909 has been converted into the city's most sophisticated inn and restaurant. A butler greets arriving guests, a musician solos nightly at the grand piano in the center of the home, and there's a classy billiard room. Room 35 has a king-size bed and three windows with views of Newport Harbor and Trinity Church; suites have office space and sitting rooms. All the rooms have bathrobes and are decorated with antiques. The butler serves canapés and cocktails in the common room while patrons peruse the options for dinner: classic Continental cuisine served on Wedgwood china at tables set with silver. ✉ *41 Mary St., 02840,* ☎ *401/ 846–6200,* ℻ *401/846–0701. 40 rooms, 10 suites. Dining room, pool, spa, billiards. Continental breakfast available. AE, DC, MC, V.*

$$$$ ▥ **Cliffside Inn.** Grandeur and comfort come in equal supply at this
★ swank Victorian home on a tree-lined street near the Cliff Walk. The wide front porch has a view of the lawn, and the rooms—all with Victorian antiques, some with bay windows—are light and airy. The Governor's Suite (named for Governor Thomas Swann, of Maryland, who built the home in 1880) has a two-sided fireplace, a whirlpool bath, a four-poster king-size bed, and a brass birdcage shower. Seven other rooms also have whirlpool baths; 10 have working fireplaces. ✉ *2 Seaview Ave., 02840,* ☎ *401/847–1811 or 800/845–1811. 15 rooms. Air-conditioning. Full breakfast. AE, D, DC, MC, V.*

$$$$ ▥ **Elm Tree Cottage.** William Ralph Emerson (Ralph Waldo's cousin) designed the Elm Tree, a shingle-style house. This 1882 architectural treasure has massive guest rooms (most with fireplaces) furnished with English antiques and decorated by owner Priscilla Malone, an interior designer. Guests rave about her creative breakfasts, served on linen-bedecked tables. The inn is no-smoking; there's a two-night minimum weekends, three on holiday weekends. ✉ *336 Gibbs Ave., 02840,* ☎ *401/849–1610 or 800/882–3356,* ℻ *401/849–2084. 5 rooms, 1 suite. Lounge. Full breakfast. AE, MC, V.*

$$$$ ▥ **Francis Malbone House.** The design of this stately painted-brick house
★ is attributed to Peter Harrison, the architect responsible for the Touro Synagogue and the Redwood Library. A lavish inn with period reproduction furnishings, the 1760 structure was tastefully doubled in size in the mid-1990s. All new rooms have whirlpool tubs and fireplaces. The rooms in the main house are all in corners (with two windows) and look out over the courtyard, which has a fountain, or across the street to the harbor. Fifteen rooms have working fireplaces. One suite, the Counting House, has its own entrances from Thames Street and the garden. ✉ *392 Thames St., 02840,* ☎ *401/846–0392 or 800/846–0392. 16 rooms, 2 suites. Full breakfast. AE, MC, V.*

$$$–$$$$ ▥ **Castle Hill Inn and Resort.** Much of the furniture at this inn is orig-
★ inal to the structure, a summer home built in 1874 on a cliff at the mouth of the Narragansett Bay. Views over the bay are enthralling, and the public areas have tremendous charm. The inn, 3 mi from the center of Newport, is famous for its Sunday brunches. On Sunday afternoons, the lawn is crowded with people enjoying cocktails. ✉ *Ocean Dr., 02840,* ☎ *401/849–3800. 38 rooms, 35 with bath. Restaurant, 3 beaches. Full breakfast. AE, D, MC, V.*

$$$–$$$$ ▥ **Inntowne.** This small town-house hotel is in the center of Newport, 1½ blocks from the harbor. The neatly appointed rooms are decorated in a floral motif. Light sleepers may prefer rooms on the upper floors, which let in less traffic noise. The staff members are on hand throughout the day to give sightseeing advice. ⊠ *6 Mary St., 02840,* ☎ *401/ 846–9200 or 800/457–7803,* FAX *401/846–1534. 26 rooms. Air-conditioning. Continental breakfast. AE, MC, V.*

$$$–$$$$ 🏨 **Newport Islander Doubletree Hotel.** On Goat Island across from the Colonial Point District, the Doubletree has great views of the harbor and the Newport Bridge. Most rooms have water views. There's free parking, and although the hotel is a 15-minute walk to Newport's center, bike and moped rentals are nearby. All rooms have oak furnishings and multicolor jewel-tone fabrics. ⊠ *Goat Island, 02840,* ☎ *401/ 849–2600,* FAX *401/846–8342. 269 rooms. Restaurant, indoor pool, saltwater pool, beauty salon, sauna, tennis court, health club, racquetball, boating, meeting rooms. AE, D, DC, MC, V.*

$$–$$$$ 🏨 **Newport Marriott.** This luxury hotel on the harbor at Long Wharf has an atrium lobby with marble floors and a gazebo. Rooms that don't border the atrium overlook the city or the waterfront. Fifth-floor rooms facing the harbor have sliding French windows that open onto large decks. Rates vary greatly according to season and location (harbor-view rooms cost more). ⊠ *25 America's Cup Ave., 02840,* ☎ *401/ 849–1000 or 800/228–9290,* FAX *401/849–3422. 307 rooms, 10 suites. Restaurant, bar, indoor pool, hot tub, sauna, health club, racquetball, meeting rooms. AE, D, DC, MC, V.*

$$$ 🏨 **Ivy Lodge.** The only B&B in the mansion district, this grand (though
★ small by Newport's standards) Victorian has gables and a Gothic turret. Designed by Stanford White, the home has 11 fireplaces, large and lovely rooms, a spacious dining room, window seats, and two common rooms. The defining feature is a Gothic-style 33-ft-high oak entryway with a three-story turned baluster staircase and a dangling wrought-iron chandelier. Summer guests congregate on the wraparound front porch, which has wicker chairs. ⊠ *12 Clay St., 02840,* ☎ *401/ 849–6865. 8 rooms. Full breakfast. AE, MC, V.*

$$–$$$ 🏨 **Admiral Benbow Inn.** Listed on the National Register of Historic Places, this tidy 1855 Victorian is ideally situated on Newport's tranquil Historic Hill, between Bellevue Avenue and Thames Street. Maple and pine trees shade the front yard. Period antiques decorate the rooms, each of which has either an antique brass or hand-carved wood bed. Two rooms have fireplaces, and one has a private deck with a harbor view. Kitchen facilities are available. ⊠ *93 Pelham St., 02840,* ☎ *401/846–4256. 15 rooms. Continental breakfast. AE, D, MC, V.*

$–$$ 🏨 **Harbor Base Pineapple Inn.** This basic motel is the least expensive lodging in Newport. All rooms contain two double beds; some also have kitchenettes. Close to the naval base and jai alai, it's a five-minute drive from downtown. ⊠ *372 Coddington Hwy., 02840,* ☎ *401/847– 2600. 48 rooms. AE, D, DC, MC, V.*

Nightlife and the Arts

Detailed events calendars can also be found in *Newport This Week* and the *Newport Daily News.*

NIGHTLIFE

For a sampling of Newport's lively nightlife, you need only stroll down **Thames Street** after dark. The **Candy Store** (⊠ Bannister's Wharf, ☎ 401/849–2900) in the Clarke Cooke House restaurant (☞ Dining and Lodging, *above*) is a snazzy place for a drink. **Newport Blues Café** (⊠ 286 Thames St., ☎ 401/841–5510) hosts great blues performers. **One Pelham East** (⊠ 270 Thames St., ☎ 401/847–9460) draws a young crowd for progressive rock, reggae, and R&B. **Great American Pub at Thames Street Station** (⊠ 337 America's Cup Ave., ☎ 401/849–9480) plays high-energy dance music and videos and books rock bands from Thursday to Monday in summer.

Murder-mystery plays are performed on Thursday evening from June to October at 8 PM at the **Astors' Beechwood** (⊠ 580 Bellevue Ave., ☎ 401/846–3772). **Newport Children's Theatre** (⊠ Box 144, ☎ 401/848–0266) mounts several productions each year. **Newport Playhouse & Cabaret** (⊠ 102 Connell Hwy., ☎ 401/848–7529) stages comedies and musicals; dinner packages are available.

Outdoor Activities and Sports

BASEBALL

Sunset League Baseball (⊠ America's Cup Ave. and Marlborough St., ☎ 401/847–5609), an amateur league, has played at Cardines Field since 1908. The ticket price is $1, and the talent level is impressive.

BIKING

Ten Speed Spokes (⊠ 18 Elm St., ☎ 401/847–5609) rents bikes for $25 per day. The 12-mi swing down Bellevue Avenue, along Ocean Drive and back, is a great route to ride your rented wheels.

BOATING

Adventure Sports Rentals (⊠ The Inn at Long Wharf, America's Cup Ave., ☎ 401/849–4820) rents sailboats, kayaks, and canoes. **Newport Yacht Services Worldwide** (⊠ 580 Thames St., ☎ 401/846–7720) charters yachts. **Oldport Marine Services** (⊠ Sayer's Wharf, ☎ 401/847–9109) operates harbor tours and daily and weekly crewed yacht charters, rents moorings, and provides launch services. **Sail Newport** (⊠ Ft. Adams State Park, ☎ 401/846–1983) rents sailboats by the hour.

DIVING

Newport Diving Center (⊠ 550 Thames St., ☎ 401/847–9293) operates charter dive trips, refills Nitrox, conducts PADI training and certification, and offers rentals, sales, and service.

FISHING

Beachfront Bait Shop (⊠ 103 Wellington Ave., ☎ 401/849–4665) stocks gear and tackle. **Fishin' Off** (⊠ American Shipyard, Goat Island Causeway, ☎ 401/849–9642) runs charter fishing trips on a 36-ft Trojan. The **Saltwater Edge** (⊠ 561 Thames St., ☎ 401/842–0062) sells fly-fishing tackle, gives lessons, and conducts guided trips.

JAI ALAI

Newport Jai Alai (⊠ 150 Admiral Kalbfus Rd., ☎ 401/849–5000) has its season from March to mid-September.

Shopping

Many of Newport's arts and antiques shops are on Thames Street; others are on Spring Street, Franklin Street, and at Bowen's and Bannister's wharves. The Brick Market area—between Thames Street and America's Cup Avenue—has more than 40 shops.

ANTIQUES

Aardvark Antiques (⊠ 475 Thames St., ☎ 401/849–7233) carries architectural pieces such as mantels, doors, and stained glass; the nearby yard sells unique fountains and garden statuary. The 125 dealers at the **Armory** (⊠ 365 Thames St., ☎ 401/848–2398), a vast 19th-century structure, carry antiques, china, and estate jewelry. **John Gidley House** (⊠ 22 Franklin St., ☎ 401/846–8303) sells Continental furnishings from the 18th and 19th centuries. The **Nautical Nook** (⊠ 86 Spring St., ☎ 401/846–6810) stocks nautical-theme antiques and collectibles: maps, navigational instruments, model boats, and ships in bottles.

ART AND CRAFTS

ARTifacts (⊠ 192 Thames St., ☎ 401/848–2222) sells hand-painted wood, glass, and faux marble. **Kelly & Gillis** (⊠ 29 America's Cup Ave., ☎ 401/849–7380) carries offbeat and artsy American crafts. **MacDowell Pottery** (⊠ 140 Spring St., ☎ 401/846–6313) showcases the wares of many New England potters. The delicate and dramatic blown-glass gifts at **Thames Glass** (⊠ 688 Thames St., ☎ 401/846–0576) are designed by Matthew Buechner and created in the adjacent studio. **William Vareika Fine Arts** (⊠ 212 Bellevue Ave., ☎ 401/849–6149) exhibits and sells American paintings and prints from the 18th to the 20th century.

BOOKS

The **Armchair Sailor** (⊠ 543 Thames St., ☎ 401/847–4252) stocks marine and travel books, charts, and maps.

CLOTHING

Explorer's Club (⊠ 104 Spring St., ☎ 401/846–8465) specializes in quality outdoor sportswear with British and American labels. **JT's Ship Chandlery** (⊠ 364 Thames St., ☎ 401/846–7256) is a major supplier of clothing, marine hardware, and equipment. **Michael Hayes** (⊠ 204 Bellevue Ave., ☎ 401/846–3090) sells upscale clothing for men, women, and children. **Tropical Gangsters** (⊠ 375 Thames St., ☎ 401/847–9113) stocks hip clothes for men and women.

Portsmouth

66   *4 mi north of Newport.*

Portsmouth is now mainly a bedroom community for professionals who work in other parts of Rhode Island and Massachusetts, but it has a number of attractions such as a topiary garden and a beach. Its most significant resident was Anne Hutchinson. A religious dissident and one of the country's first feminists, she led a group of settlers to the area in 1638 after being banished from the Massachusetts Bay Colony.

Half the fun of a trip to Portsmouth is a ride on the **Old Colony & Newport Railway,** which follows an 8-mi route along Narragansett Bay from Newport to Portsmouth's Green Animals Topiary Gardens (☞ *below*). The vintage diesel train and two century-old coaches make three-hour round-trips, with a 1¼-hour stop at the gardens. ⊠ *19 America's Cup Ave.,* ☎ *401/624–6951.* ☑ *$6.* ☉ *May–mid-Nov.*

Green Animals is a large topiary garden on a Victorian estate. More than 100 years old, the garden contains sculpted shrubs, flower gardens, winding pathways and a variety of trees. Most notable are the animal-shape plants: an elephant, a camel, a giraffe, and even a teddy bear. Also on the grounds are a remarkable Victorian toy collection and a plant shop. ⊠ *Cory La. off Rte. 114,* ☎ *401/847–1000.* ☑ *$6.50.* ☉ *May–Oct., daily 10–5.*

Portsmouth's **Sandy Point Beach** (⊠ Sandy Point Ave.) is a choice spot for families and beginning windsurfers because of the calm surf along the Sakonnet River.

En Route   Route 77, the main thoroughfare to Little Compton, passes through **Tiverton Four Corners,** a great place to stretch your legs and catch your first breath of East Bay air. **Provender** (⊠ 3883 Main Rd., ☎ 401/624–8096), in a former general store and post office, is a gourmet foods store, coffee shop, and bakery. Also within walking distance are a half dozen galleries and gift shops. The delicious **Gray's Ice Cream** (⊠ Intersection of Rtes. 77 and 179, ☎ 401/624–4500), across the street fronting Provender, is produced and sold in this stout building.

Little Compton

⑥⑦ *19 mi from southeast of Portsmouth.*

The rolling estates, lovely homes, farmlands, woods, and gentle western shoreline make Little Compton one of the Ocean State's prettiest areas. Little Compton and Tiverton were part of Massachusetts until 1747—to this day, residents here often have more roots in Massachusetts than in Rhode Island. "Keep Little Compton little" is a popular sentiment, but considering the town's remoteness and its steep land prices, there may not be all that much to worry about.

Little Compton Commons (✉ Meetinghouse La.) is the epitome of a New England town square. As white as the clouds above, the spire of the Georgian-style United Congregational Church rises over the tops of adjacent oak trees. Within the triangular lawn is a cemetery with Colonial headstones, among them that of Elizabeth Padobie, said to be the first white girl born in New England. Surrounding the green is a rock wall and all the elements of a small community: town hall, a community center, the police station, and the school. You will find town squares only in a few northern Rhode Island towns, ones that were once a part of the Massachusetts Bay Colony; Rhode Islanders, adamant about separating church and state, did not favor this layout.

A neatly kept timepiece of Rhode Island living, the 1680 **Wilbur House** was occupied by eight generations of Wilburs—the first of which included 11 children born between 1690 and 1712. The Common Room is 17th century; the bedrooms 18th and 19th; the kitchen 19th; and the living room 18th. The barn museum holds a one-horse shay, an oxcart, and a buggy and coach. ✉ *548 W. Main Rd.,* ☎ *401/635–4559.* ▣ *$4.* ☉ *Mid-June–mid-Sept., Tues.–Sat. 2–5; mid-Sept.–early Oct., weekends 2–5.*

Sakonnet Point, a surreal spit of land, reaches out toward three tiny islands. The point begins where Route 77 ends. The ½-mi hike to the tip of Sakonnet Point passes tidal pools, a beach composed of tiny stone, and outcroppings that recall the surface of the moon. Parking is sometimes available in the lot adjacent to Sakonnet Harbor.

Tours and tastings are free of charge at **Sakonnet Vineyard,** New England's largest winery. A few of its brands are well known, including Eye of the Storm, which was born of compromise: A power outage caused by a hurricane forced the wine makers to blend finished wine with what was in the vats. ✉ *162 W. Main Rd.,* ☎ *401/635–8486.* ▣ *Free.* ☉ *Oct.–May, daily 11–5, tours on the hr noon–4; June–Sept., daily 10–6, tours on the hr 11–5.*

Dining and Lodging

$$–$$$ ✕ **Abraham Manchester's.** Little Compton's former general store houses a restaurant with a basic menu of chicken, steak, seafood, and pasta. Antiques adorn the walls of the bar and dining room, enhancing the feel of history. Take time to cross the street and look for the Rhode Island Red Monument (actually a plaque in the ground)—this community developed the famous Rhode Island Red breed of chicken. ✉ *Main Rd.,* ☎ *401/635–2700. MC, V.*

$$ ✕ **Commons Lunch.** Across from the church on the town square, this unpretentious old-Yankee restaurant opens daily at 5 AM. The food may not be spectacular, but it's reliable and priced to move. The menu is greasy-spoon standard, with Rhode Island favorites like cabinets (milk shakes). ✉ *South of Commons Rd.,* ☎ *401/635–4388. No credit cards. No dinner.*

$$ ▣ **The Roost.** A former farmhouse amid the fields of Sakonnet Vineyards is an intimate B&B that's remote yet accessible to rural pleasures like hiking, biking, and main-street shopping. Rooms are smartly furnished. Call well ahead for stays on summer weekends. ⊠ *170 W. Main Rd., 02837,* ☎ *401/635–8486,* FAX *401/635–2101. 3 rooms. Continental breakfast. AE, MC, V.*

Outdoor Activities and Sports

FISHING

The 38-ft boat *Oceaneer* (⊠ Sakonnet Point Marina, ☎ 401/635–4292) can accommodate up to six people on chartered fishing trips.

HIKING

Wilbur Woods (⊠ Swamp Rd.), a 30-acre hollow with picnic tables and a waterfall, is a good place for a casual hike. A trail winds along and over Dundery Brook.

Newport County A to Z

Arriving and Departing

BY BUS

RIPTA (Rhode Island Public Transportation Authority; ☎ 401/847–0209; 800/244–0444 in RI) buses leave from Providence for Newport and also serve the city from other Rhode Island destinations.

BY CAR

From Providence take I–95 east into Massachusetts and head south on Route 24. From South County, take U.S. 1 north to Route 138 east. From Boston take I–93 south to Route 24 south.

BY FERRY

Interstate Navigation Co. (⊠ Fort Adams State Park, ☎ 401/783–4613) operates passenger ferry service (passengers and bicycles only) from Providence and Block Island to Newport from mid-June to Labor Day. The one daily round-trip leaves Providence in the morning and returns in the early evening; sailing time is about two hours.

BY PLANE

Newport State Airport (☎ 401/846–2200) is 3 mi northeast of Newport. Charters fly from here to T. F. Green State Airport in Warwick, south of Providence. **Cozy Cab** (☎ 401/846–2500) runs a shuttle service ($15) between the airport and Newport's visitor's bureau.

Getting Around

BY BUS

See Arriving and Departing, *above.*

BY CAR

With the exception of Ocean Drive, Newport is a walker's city. In summer, traffic thickens, and the narrow one-way streets can constitute an unbearable maze. It's worth parking in a pay lot and leaving your car behind while you visit in-town sights; one lot is at the **Gateway Information Center** (⊠ 23 America's Cup Ave.).

BY FERRY AND WATER TAXI

The **Jamestown and Newport Ferry Co.** (☎ 401/423–9900) runs a passenger ferry about every 1½ hours from Newport's Bowen's Landing and Long Wharf (and, on request, Fort Adams and Goat Island) to Jamestown's Ferry Wharf. The ferry operates from Memorial Day to mid-October. **Old Port Marine Company** (☎ 401/847–9109)) operates a water-taxi service for boaters in Newport Harbor.

Contacts and Resources

EMERGENCIES

Newport Hospital (⊠ Friendship St., ☎ 401/846–6400).

GUIDED TOURS

More than a dozen yacht companies operate tours of Narragansett Bay and Newport Harbor. Outings usually last just two hours and cost about $25 per person. *Flyer* (☎ 401/848–2100), a 57-ft catamaran, departs from Long Wharf. *Madeline* (☎ 401/847–0298), a 72-ft schooner, departs from Bannister's Wharf. *RumRunner II* (☎ 401/847–0299), a vintage 1929 motor yacht, once carried "hooch"; it leaves from Bannister's Wharf. *The Spirit of Newport* (☎ 401/849–3575), a 200-passenger multideck ship, departs for tours of Narragansett Bay and Newport Harbor from the Newport Harbor Hotel, on America's Cup Avenue, from May to mid-October.

Viking Bus and Boat Tours of Newport (⊠ Gateway Information Center, 23 America's Cup Ave., ☎ 401/847–6921) conducts Newport tours in buses from April to October. One-hour boat tours of Narragansett Bay operate from mid-May to Columbus Day weekend.

Newport on Foot (☎ 401/846–5391), led by guide extraordinaire Anita Raphael, organizes 1- to 2-mi walks through Colonial Newport. The **Newport Historical Society** (⊠ 82 Touro St., ☎ 401/846–0813) sponsors walking tours on Saturday from May to November.

24-HOUR PHARMACY

Brooks Pharmacy (⊠ 268 Bellevue Ave., ☎ 401/849–4600).

VISITOR INFORMATION

Newport County Convention and Visitors Bureau (⊠ Gateway Information Center, 23 America's Cup Ave., ☎ 401/849–8048 or 800/326–6030) has parking, rest rooms, and a gift shop. This spacious visitor center shows an orientation film and provides maps and advice.

RHODE ISLAND A TO Z

Arriving and Departing

By Bus

Bonanza Bus Lines (☎ 800/556–3815), **Greyhound Lines** (☎ 800/231–2222), and **Peter Pan Bus Lines** (☎ 800/237–8747) serve the Providence Bus Terminal. A shuttle service connects the **Providence Bus Terminal** (⊠ Bonanza Way, off Exit 25 from I–95, ☎ 401/751–8800) with Kennedy Plaza (⊠ Washington and Dorrance Sts.) in downtown Providence, where you can board the local public transit buses. **Bonanza** (☞ *above*) runs a bus from Boston's Logan Airport to Providence.

By Car

Interstate 95, which cuts diagonally across the state, is the fastest route to Providence from Boston, coastal Connecticut, and New York City. Interstate 195 links Providence with New Bedford and Cape Cod. Route 146 links Providence with Worcester and I–90. U.S. 1 follows much of the Rhode Island coast east from Connecticut before turning north to Providence. The detailed *Street Atlas Rhode Island,* published by Arrow Map, Inc., is available at many bookstores.

By Plane

T. F. Green State Airport (⊠ U.S. 1, Warwick, ☎ 401/737–4000), 10 mi south of Providence, has scheduled daily flights by several major airlines, including American, Continental/Northwest, Southwest, United, and US Airways, with additional service by regional carriers.

For airline numbers, *see* Air Travel *in* Smart Travel Tips A to Z. The main regional airports in Rhode Island are in Westerly (☞ South County A to Z, *above*), Newport (☞ Newport County A to Z, *above*), and Block Island (☞ Block Island A to Z, *above*).

By Train
Amtrak (☎ 800/872–7245) service between New York City and Boston makes stops at Westerly, Kingston, and Providence. **Providence Station** (✉ 100 Gaspee St., ☎ 401/727–7379) is the city's main station. The **MBTA commuter rail service** (☎ 617/722–3200) connects Boston and Providence during weekday morning and evening rush hours for about half the cost of an Amtrak ride.

Getting Around

By Bus
RIPTA (Rhode Island Public Transportation Authority; ☎ 401/781–9400; 800/244–0444 in RI) buses crisscross the state.

By Car
Interstate 95 is the fastest route to the cities in southern and eastern Rhode Island. U.S. 1 travels more or less parallel to I–95, though closer to the coast. Route 146 passes through the northeastern portion of the Blackstone Valley. U.S. 44 travels west from Providence toward Connecticut. Route 138 heads east from Route 1 to Jamestown, Newport, and Tiverton in easternmost Rhode Island.

The speed limit on interstate highways is 65 mph; state routes vary, with 55 mph the top speed. Right turns are permitted on red lights after stopping. Free state maps are available at all chambers of commerce and at visitor information centers in Providence and Newport and at T. F. Green State Airport.

Contacts and Resources

Emergencies
Ambulance, fire, police (☎ 911).

Fishing
For information on pricing and where to buy licenses for freshwater fishing, contact the Department of Environmental Management's **Division of Licensing** (☎ 401/333–3576 or 401/222–3075). No license is needed for saltwater fishing.

B&B Reservation Service
Bed and Breakfast of Rhode Island, Inc. (✉ Box 3291, Newport 02840, ☎ 401/849–1298).

Guided Tours
Stumpf Balloons (☎ 401/253–0111) offers aerial sight-seeing tours by balloon from May to November. Fall foliage trips are popular.

Hiking
One of the best trail guides for the region is the *AMC Massachusetts and Rhode Island Trail Guide,* available at local outdoors shops or from the **Appalachian Mountain Club** (✉ 5 Joy St., Boston, MA 02114, ☎ 617/523–0636). The **Rhode Island Audubon Society** (✉ 12 Sanderson Rd., Smithfield 02917, ☎ 401/949–5454) leads interesting hikes and field expeditions around the state.

Visitor Information
Rhode Island Department of Economic Development, Tourism Division (✉ 1 W. Exchange St., Providence 02903, ☎ 401/222–2601 [ask to be transferred to Tourism Divison] or 800/556–2484).

6 CONNECTICUT

The southern gateway to New England is a small state with plenty of variety. Southwestern Connecticut is home to commuters, celebrities, and others who enjoy its sophisticated atmosphere and convenience to New York City. The Connecticut River valley has a stretch of river villages punctuated by a few small cities and Hartford. The northwest's Litchfield Hills have grand inns and rolling farmlands. Along the southeastern coast are New Haven, home to Yale and some fine museums, and quiet shoreline villages. The sparsely populated towns in the northeast's Quiet Corner are known for their antiquing potential.

Updated by
J. Amanda
Nielsen

Introduction by
Michelle
Bodak Acri

CONNECTICUT MAY BE the third smallest state in the nation, but it is among the hardest to define. Indeed, you can travel from any point in the Nutmeg State, as it is known, to any other in less than two hours, yet the land you travel—fewer than 60 mi top to bottom and 100 mi across—is as varied as a drive across the country. There are Connecticut's 253 mi of shoreline and the salty sea air that blows over beach communities like Old Lyme and Stonington. The state has patchwork hills and peaked mountains in its northwestern corner, along with once-upon-a-time mill towns built along rivers such as the Housatonic. Finally, Connecticut has seemingly endless farmland in the northeast, where cows just might outnumber people (and definitely outnumber the traffic lights), as well as chic bedroom communities of New York City such as Greenwich and New Canaan, where boutique shopping bags seem to be the dominant species. Each section of the state is unique; each defines Connecticut.

Just as diverse as the landscape are the state's residents, who numbered more than 3¼ million at last count. There really is no such thing as the definitive Connecticut Yankee, however. Yes, families can trace their roots back to the 1600s, when Connecticut was founded as one of the 13 original colonies, but the state motto is also "He who transplanted still sustains." And so the face of the Nutmegger is that of the family from Naples who tend the pizza ovens in New Haven and the farmer in Norfolk whose land dates back five generations, the grandmother from New Britain who makes the state's best pierogi and the ladies who lunch from Westport, not to mention the celebrity nestled in the Litchfield Hills and the Bridgeport entrepreneur working to close the gap between Connecticut's struggling cities and its affluent suburbs.

A unifying characteristic of the Connecticut Yankee, however, is his or her propensity for inventiveness. You might say that Nutmeggers have been setting trends for centuries. They are historically known for both their intellectual abilities and their desire to have a little fun. As evidence of the former, consider that the nation's first public library was opened in New Haven in 1656 and its first statehouse built in Hartford in 1776, Tapping Reeve opened the first law school in Litchfield in 1784, and West Hartford's Noah Webster published the first dictionary in 1806. As proof of the latter, note that Lake Compounce in Bristol was the country's first amusement park, Bethel's P. T. Barnum staged the first three-ring circus, and the hamburger, the lollipop, the Frisbee, and the Erector set were all invented within the state's 5,009 square miles.

Not surprisingly, Nutmeggers have a healthy respect for their history. For decades, the Mystic Seaport museum, which traces the state's rich maritime past through living history exhibits, has been the premier tourist attraction. Today, however, slot machines in casinos in the southeastern woods of Connecticut are giving the sailing ships a run for their money. Foxwoods Casino near Ledyard, opened in 1992 and run by the Mashantucket Pequots, is the world's largest casino—it draws more than 55,000 visitors per day—and the Mohegan Sun Casino in nearby Uncasville is working hard to catch up. Thanks in large part to the lure of these casinos, not to mention the state's rich cultural attractions, cutting-edge restaurants, shopping outlets, first-rate lodgings, and abundance of natural beauty (including 93 state parks and 32 state forests), tourism is now the second leading industry in the state. Anyone who has explored even part of Connecticut will discover that a small state can have big diversity—and appeal.

Pleasures and Pastimes

Antiquing

Although you'll find everything from chic boutiques to vast outlet malls in Connecticut, the state is an antiquer's paradise. The Litchfield Hills region, in the state's northwest corner, is the heart of antiques country. In the Quiet Corner, east of the Connecticut River, are several hundred dealers and complexes. Mystic, Old Saybrook, and other towns along the coast are filled with markets, galleries, and shops, many specializing in antique prints, maps, books, and collectibles.

Dining

Call it the fennel factor or the arugula influx. However you wish to characterize it, southern New England has witnessed a gastronomic revolution in recent years. Preparation and ingredients now reflect the culinary trends of nearby Manhattan and Boston. Although a few traditional favorites remain, such as New England clam chowder, Yankee pot roast, and grilled haddock, Grand Marnier is now favored on ice cream over hot fudge sauce, sliced duck is wrapped in phyllo and served with a ginger-plum sauce (the orange glaze decidedly absent), and everything from lavender to fresh figs is used to season and complement dishes. Dining in the cities is international: Indian, Vietnamese, Thai, Malaysian, and Japanese restaurants, even Spanish tapas bars. The locals are also going a tad decadent; designer martinis are quite the rage, brew pubs have popped up all around the state—heck, even caviar is making a comeback. The one drawback of this turn toward sophistication is that finding an under–$10 dinner entrée is proving increasingly difficult.

Fishing

Connecticut teems with possibilities for anglers, from deep-sea fishing in coastal waters to fly-fishing in the state's many streams. Try the Litchfield Hills region for freshwater fish: If you're just a beginner, don't fret—you'll be catching trout or bass in the Housatonic River in no time. Southeastern Connecticut is the charter- and party-boat capital of New England. Charter fishing boats take passengers out on Long Island Sound for half-day, full-day, and overnight trips.

Lodging

Connecticut has plenty of business-oriented chain hotels and low-budget motels, but the state's unusual inns, resorts, bed-and-breakfasts, and country hotels are far more atmospheric. You'll pay dearly for rooms in summer on the coast and in autumn in the hills, where thousands peek at the peaking foliage. Rates are lowest in winter, but so are the temperatures, making spring the best time for bargain seekers to visit.

State Parks

Sixty percent of Connecticut is forest land, some of it under the jurisdiction of the state parks division, which also manages several beaches on the southern shoreline. Many parks have campgrounds. Trails meander through most of the parks—the hiking is especially spectacular around the cool, clear water at Lake Waramaug State Park and the 200-ft-high waterfall at Kent Falls State Park. At Gillette Castle State Park in East Haddam there are several trails, some on former railroad beds. Some state parks have no entrance fees year-round. At others the fee varies ($5–$10), depending on the time of year, day of the week, and whether or not your car bears a Connecticut license plate.

Exploring Connecticut

Southwestern Connecticut contains the wealthy coastal communities. Moving east along the coast (in most states you usually travel north or south along the coast, but in Connecticut you actually travel east or west), you'll come to New Haven and the southeastern coast, which is broken by many small bays and inlets. The Quiet Corner in the northeast, bordered by Rhode Island to the east and Massachusetts to the north, contains rolling hills and tranquil countryside. To the west are the fertile farmland of the Connecticut River valley and the state's capital, Hartford. In the northwestern part of the state is the Litchfield Hills area, covered with miles of forests, lakes, and rivers.

Numbers in the text and in the margin correspond to numbers on the maps: Southwestern Connecticut, Connecticut River Valley, Downtown Hartford, Litchfield Hills, Downtown New Haven, Southeastern Connecticut, and the Quiet Corner.

Great Itineraries

The Nutmeg State is a confluence of different worlds, where farm country meets country homes, and fans of the New York Yankees meet downeastern Yankees. To get the best sense of this variety, especially if you have only a few days, start in the scenic Litchfield Hills, where you can see historic town greens and trendy cafés juxtaposed in a way that's uniquely Connecticut. If you have a bit more time, head south for the wealthy southwestern corner of the state and then over to New Haven, with its cultural pleasures. If you have five days or a week (the minimum time needed to truly sample the state's myriad flavors), take in the capital city of Hartford and the surrounding towns of the Connecticut River valley and head down to the southeastern shoreline. If you have kids or an interest in the sea, Mystic alone could occupy a few days.

IF YOU HAVE 1 DAY

Begin a day in the Litchfield Hills in **New Preston** ㉟ and then head for Lake Waramaug. In **West Cornwall** ㊳ have a look at the state's largest covered bridge. Working your way north, stop in **Lakeville** ㊵ and **Salisbury** ㊶ (a good place to stop for lunch). Turning south, spend a couple of hours in **Litchfield** ㊼, where you can tour historic houses before continuing south via **Bethlehem** ㊾ to **Woodbury** 51 to visit the town's churches and antiques shops.

IF YOU HAVE 3 DAYS

Greenwich ①, a wealthy community with grand homes and great restaurants, makes a good starting point for a several-day tour that begins near New York. From here head to **Stamford** ②, where you can visit the Whitney Museum of American Art at Champion or hit the mall across the street. East along the coast is **Norwalk** ③, whose SoNo commercial district and Maritime Aquarium are popular attractions. Have dinner in **Westport** ⑩, and end your first day in **Ridgefield** ⑥. After touring Ridgefield the next morning, head for **New Preston** ㉟ and the Litchfield Hills. From here drive north via **West Cornwall** ㊳ to **Norfolk** ㊸. Then it's on to **Litchfield** ㊼, where you may want to conclude your day. If not, travel a little farther south to charming **Washington** ㊿. Begin day three in **Woodbury** 51 and then head to **New Haven** 54–61. Near the Yale University campus are many great museums, shops, and restaurants.

IF YOU HAVE 5 DAYS

With five days you can explore some of the state's cities as well as its historic interior towns and coastal villages. Spend the morning of your first day in **Hartford** ㉒–㉙ and the early part of the afternoon in **West Hartford** ㉚ before heading to **Farmington** ㉛, which has two excellent house museums, and **Simsbury** ㉜, where you can visit Massacoh Plantation. Spend the night in either town. On your second day, head west to **Woodbury** 51, stopping in **Litchfield** ㊼ and **Kent** ㊱. Stay the night in **Washington** ㊿ or **Ridgefield** ⑥. Begin your third day in south-

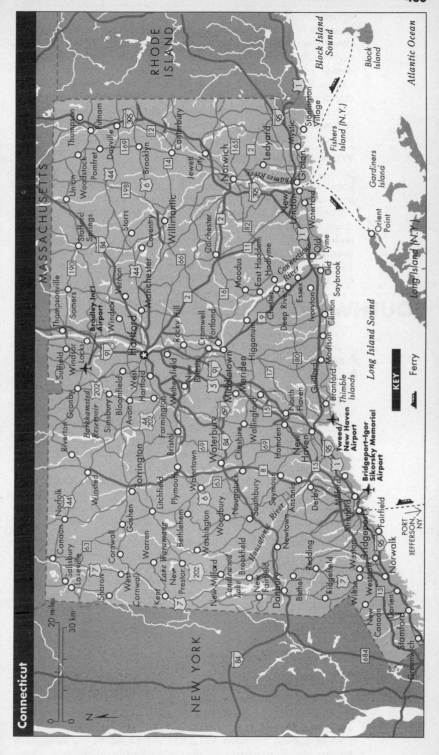

KEY

Ferry

western Connecticut in **Greenwich** ①, followed by stops in **Stamford** ②, **Westport** ⑩, and **Bridgeport** ⑫. Spend the remainder of your day in 🔄 **New Haven** ㊴–�. Start your fourth day in **Essex** ⑭ and visit the Connecticut River Museum. At Gillette Castle State Park in **East Haddam** ⑰ you can tour the hilltop estate built by the actor William Gillette. From here, backtrack to the coastal town of **Old Saybrook** ㉕ and then cross the river to 🔄 **Old Lyme** ㉖, a former art colony. On the fifth day, continue touring the coast, starting in either **New London** ㉘ or **Groton** ㉚ and heading east toward **Mystic** ㉛. Take time to visit Mystic Seaport before heading to the little village of **Stonington** ㉜.

When to Tour Connecticut

Connecticut is lovely year-round, but fall and spring are particularly appealing times to visit. A drive in fall along the rolling hills of the state's back roads or the Merritt Parkway (a National Scenic Byway) is a memorable experience. Leaves of yellow, orange, and red color the fall landscape, but the state blooms in springtime, too—town greens are painted with daffodils and tulips, and blooming trees punctuate the rich green countryside. The scent of flower blossoms is in the air, especially in Fairfield, which holds an annual Dogwood Festival. Many attractions that are closed in winter reopen in March or April.

SOUTHWESTERN CONNECTICUT

One to two hours away by car or train from midtown Manhattan, southwestern Connecticut is a rich swirl of old New England and new New York. Encompassing all of Fairfield County, this region consistently reports the highest cost of living and most expensive homes of any area in the country. Its bedroom towns are home primarily to white-collar executives; some still make the nearly two-hour dash to and from Gotham, but most enjoy a more civilized morning drive to Stamford, which is reputed to have more corporate headquarters per square mile than any other U.S. city. Strict zoning has preserved a certain privacy and rusticity uncommon in other such densely populated areas, and numerous celebrities—Paul Newman, David Letterman, Michael Bolton, Diana Ross, and Mel Gibson, among them—live in Fairfield County. The combination of drivers, winding roads, and heavily wooded countryside has resulted in at least one major problem: According to a survey in central Fairfield County, nearly 50% of area drivers have struck a deer.

Venture away from the wealthy communities, and you'll discover cities in different stages of urban renewal: Stamford, Norwalk, Bridgeport, and Danbury. These four have some of the region's best cultural and shopping opportunities, but the economic disparity between Connecticut's upscale towns and troubled cities is perhaps nowhere more visible than in Fairfield County.

Greenwich

① *28 mi northeast of New York City, 64 mi southwest of Hartford.*

You'll have no trouble believing that Greenwich is one of the wealthiest towns in the United States when you drive along U.S. 1 (called Route 1 by the locals, and which goes by the names West Putnam Avenue, East Putnam Avenue, and the Post Road, among others), where the streets are lined with ritzy car dealers, Euro-chic clothing shops, and other posh businesses. The town has a few historic sights, too. **Greenwich Avenue,** which runs perpendicular to the Post Road and ends, under a different name, at a viewpoint where people often drop a line into Long Island Sound, has a heavy concentration of swanky boutiques as well as the requisite Gap and Pier 1.

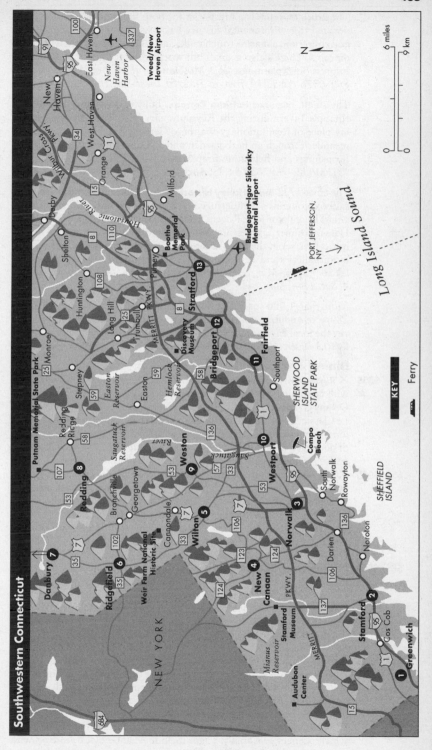

Southwestern Connecticut

KEY

▬▬▬ Ferry

Long Island Sound

Tweed/New Haven Airport

New Haven Harbor

Bridgeport-Igor Sikorsky Memorial Airport

PORT JEFFERSON, NY

SHEFFIELD ISLAND

SHERWOOD ISLAND STATE PARK

Compo Beach

Boothe Memorial Park

Discovery Museum

Putnam Memorial State Park

Weir Farm National Historic Site

Audubon Center

Stamford Museum

Mianus Reservoir

Hemlock Reservoir

Easton Reservoir

Saugatuck Reservoir

Housatonic River

Saugatuck River

NEW YORK

New Haven
East Haven
West Haven
Orange
Milford
Derby
Shelton
Huntington
Long Hill
Monroe
Stepney
Trumbull
Redding Ridge
Easton
Stratford
Bridgeport
Fairfield
Southport
Penny
Redding
Georgetown
Branchville
Weston
Westport
Danbury
Ridgefield
Canondale
Wilton
New Canaan
Norwalk
South Norwalk
Rowayton
Darien
Noroton
Stamford
Cos Cob
Greenwich

Wilbur Cross Pkwy
Merritt Pkwy
Merritt Pkwy

N ← 6 miles / 6 km

100 · 91 · 95 · 34 · 11 · 15 · 337 · 8 · 110 · 108 · 25 · 59 · 58 · 107 · 53 · 35 · 7 · 102 · 33 · 7 · 106 · 123 · 124 · 137 · 136 · 1 · 57 · 136 · 684

1 · 2 · 3 · 4 · 5 · 6 · 7 · 8 · 9 · 10 · 11 · 12 · 13

The **Bruce Museum** is a must-visit for both kids and adults. A section devoted to environmental history has a wigwam, a spectacular mineral collection, a marine touch tank, and a 16th-century-era woodland diorama. There's also a small but worthwhile collection of American Impressionist paintings. ⊠ *1 Museum Dr. (Exit 3 off I–95),* ☎ *203/ 869–0376.* 🎟 *$3.50, free on Tues.* ☉ *Tues.–Sat. 10–5, Sun. 1–5.*

The small, barn-red **Putnam Cottage,** built in 1690 and operated as Knapp's Tavern during the Revolutionary War, was a frequent meeting place of Revolutionary War hero General Israel Putnam. You can meander through an herb garden and examine the cottage's Colonial furnishings and fieldstone fireplaces. ⊠ *243 E. Putnam Ave./U.S. 1,* ☎ *203/869–9697.* 🎟 *$4.* ☉ *Apr.–Dec., Wed., Fri., and Sun. 1–4.*

The circa-1732 **Bush–Holley Historic Site,** a handsome central-chimney saltbox, contains a wonderful collection of 19th- and 20th-century artworks by sculptor John Rogers, potter Leon Volkmar, and painters Childe Hassam, Elmer Livingstone MacRae, and John Twachtman. The visitor center, set in the historic site's circa-1805 storehouse, holds exhibition galleries and a gift shop. ⊠ *39 Strickland Rd.,* ☎ *203/869–6899.* 🎟 *$6.* ☉ *Jan.–Mar., Sat. 11–4, Sun. 1–4; Apr.–Dec., Wed.–Fri. noon– 4, Sat. 11–4, Sun. 1–4.*

More than 1,000 species of flora and fauna have been recorded at the 280-acre **Audubon Center** in northern Greenwich, where exhibits survey the local environment and 8 mi of trails traverse woods and fields. ⊠ *613 Riversville Rd.,* ☎ *203/869–5272.* 🎟 *$3.* ☉ *Mon.–Sun. 9–5.*

Dining and Lodging

$$$$ ★ **✕ Restaurant Jean-Louis.** Roses, Limoges china, and white tablecloths with lace underskirts complement this restaurant's world-class cuisine. On any given night, the five-course Celebration Menu or the four-course Le Classic Menu might include diced vegetables cooked in saffron bouillon with mussels and scallops, served with a parsley coulis, or roast breast of duck on a bed of wilted spinach. ⊠ *61 Lewis St.,* ☎ *203/622–8450. Jacket required. AE, D, DC, MC, V. No lunch Mon.–Thurs.*

$$$–$$$$ **✕ The Ivy.** The chef at this restaurant describes the cuisine as Continental Italian, with a French twist. Among the appetizers are a potato pancake topped with goat cheese and meaty slices of Portobello mushroom; for an entrée try the risotto of the day, flavored with anything from rabbit to salmon, or the chicken roulade stuffed with spinach and fontina cheese. ⊠ *554 Old Post Rd., No. 3,* ☎ *203/661–3200. AE, D, DC, MC, V. No lunch weekends.*

$$$–$$$$ **✕ 64 Greenwich Avenue.** With a country-yet-contemporary American decor and superbly presented contemporary American cuisine, 64 Greenwich has flair to spare. A tasty small plate (as appetizers are called here) of baked goat cheese with crispy shrimp may be followed by New York Black Angus sirloin or perhaps shrimp fricassee. Don't miss the desserts, especially the crème brûlée. ⊠ *64 Greenwich Ave.,* ☎ *203/ 861–6400. AE, DC, MC, V.*

$$$–$$$$ ★ **✕🏠 Homestead Inn.** Not far from the water, this enormous Italianate wood-frame house has a belvedere, ornate bracketed eaves, and an enclosed wraparound Victorian porch. Rooms are decorated with antiques and period reproductions. For all its architectural appeal, though, the Homestead is becoming better known for the up-to-the-minute fine French cuisine prepared by master chef Thomas Henkelmann. The menu, which changes seasonally, might include Atlantic black sea bass with a veal-based black truffle sauce. Reservations are essential for dinner, for which a jacket is required. ⊠ *420 Field Point Rd., 06830,* ☎ *203/ 869–7500,* 📠 *203/869–7502. 17 rooms, 6 suites. Restaurant, meeting rooms. AE, MC, V.*

$$$–$$$$ 🏨 **Hyatt Regency Greenwich.** The Hyatt's vast but comfortable atrium contains a flourishing lawn and abundant flora. The rooms are spacious, with modern furnishings and many amenities. The pleasant Winfield's restaurant serves interesting renditions of classic dishes. ⊠ *1800 E. Putnam Ave., 06870,* ☎ *203/637–1234,* 𝔽𝔸𝕏 *203/637–2940. 374 rooms, 1 suite. Restaurant, bar, in-room data ports, indoor pool, sauna, health club, business services, meeting rooms. AE, D, DC, MC, V.*

$$$ 🏨 **Greenwich Harbor Inn.** Rooms at this informal harbor-side inn have soft colors, floral bedspreads, and reproductions of 18th-century antiques. More like an upscale chain property than an inn, the hotel is within walking distance of the railroad station and the Greenwich Avenue boutiques. ⊠ *500 Steamboat Rd., 06830,* ☎ *203/661–9800,* 𝔽𝔸𝕏 *203/629–4431. 96 rooms, 2 suites. Restaurant, pub, dock. AE, DC, MC, V.*

$$–$$$ 🏨 **Stanton House Inn.** The original structure of this Federal-style mansion, within walking distance of downtown, was built in 1840. In 1899, under architect Stanford White's supervision, the house was enlarged. The interior has been carefully decorated with a mixture of antiques and reproductions; two rooms have fireplaces. ⊠ *76 Maple Ave., 06830,* ☎ *203/869–2110,* 𝔽𝔸𝕏 *203/629–2116. 24 rooms, 22 with bath. Pool. Continental breakfast. AE, D, DC, MC, V. No smoking.*

Stamford

② *6 mi northeast of Greenwich, 38 mi southwest of New Haven, 33 mi northeast of New York City.*

Glitzy office buildings, chain hotels, and major department stores are among the new landmarks in revitalized Stamford, the most dynamic city on the southwestern shore. Restaurants, nightclubs, and shops line Atlantic and lower Summer streets, poised to harness the region's affluence and satisfy the desire of suburbanites to spend an exciting night on the town without having to travel to New York City.

The primary focus of the **Whitney Museum of American Art at Champion,** a facility affiliated with the Whitney Museum in New York City, is 20th-century American painting and photography. Past exhibitions (there is no permanent collection) have included works by Edward Hopper, Alexander Calder, and Georgia O'Keeffe. Free gallery talks are held on Tuesday, Thursday, and Saturday at 12:30. ⊠ *Atlantic St. and Tresser Blvd.,* ☎ *203/358–7630.* 🎟 *Free.* ⊙ *Tues.–Sat. 11–5. Closed Sun.–Mon.*

🐾 Oxen, sheep, pigs, and other animals roam the **Stamford Museum and Nature Center,** a New England–style farmstead with many nature trails for visitors to explore. Exhibits survey natural history, art, Americana, and Native American life. Two enjoyable times to visit are spring harvest and maple-sugaring season—call for exact dates. ⊠ *39 Scofieldtown Rd./Rte. 137,* ☎ *203/322–1646.* 🎟 *Grounds $5, planetarium an additional $2, observatory $3 (but no grounds fee).* ⊙ *Grounds Mon.–Sat. 9–5, Sun. 1–5; farm daily 9–5; planetarium shows Sun. 3 PM; observatory Fri. 8–10 PM.*

The 64-acre **Bartlett Arboretum,** owned by the University of Connecticut, holds natural woodlands, cultivated gardens, marked ecology trails, a swamp walk, and a pond. The wildflower garden is stunning in the spring. ⊠ *151 Brookdale Rd., off High Ridge Rd. (Exit 35 off Merritt Pkwy.),* ☎ *203/322–6971.* 🎟 *Free.* ⊙ *Grounds daily 8:30–dusk; visitor center weekdays 8:30–4.*

Dining and Lodging

$$$–$$$$ ✕ **Amadeus.** One of a dozen great restaurants along Stamford's stretch of Summer Street, Amadeus leads the pack. The dining room overflows with lush flower arrangements, and lavishly framed prints dot the walls. The fare is Continental with a Viennese flair: Try the Mediterranean fish and shellfish soup, followed by the trademark Vienna schnitzel, served with golden pan-fried potatoes. ⊠ *201 Summer St.,* ☎ *203/348–7775. AE, D, DC, MC, V. No lunch weekends.*

$$–$$$ ✕ **Kathleen's.** Behind a striking facade of black with cornflower-blue trim is a wonderful, quiet little eatery that serves hearty interpretations of regional American cuisine: pan-seared yellowfin tuna with white- and black-bean sauces, veal with country ham stuffing, and many pastas. Save room for the apple pie or Kathleen's famous chocolate cake. For fine takeout, you can stop next door at Katie's. ⊠ *25 Bank St.,* ☎ *203/323–7785. AE, D, DC, MC, V. No lunch weekends.*

$$–$$$ ✕ **La Hacienda.** The decor of this restaurant is more upscale Mexican
  ★   than Americanized south-of-the-border—there are no streamers here. The imaginative and authentic cuisine includes chicken mole and *tacos píbil,* a Yucatán specialty consisting of shredded pork marinated in a delicious roasted-tomato salsa. ⊠ *222 Summer St.,* ☎ *203/324–0577. AE, DC, MC, V. No lunch Sun.*

$$$–$$$$ ▦ **Westin Stamford.** The ultramodern entrance of this downtown luxury hotel should prepare you for the dramatic atrium lobby, which has a brass-and-glass-enclosed gazebo. The attractive rooms are understated and elegant, with subdued colors and comfortable wing chairs; bathrooms are spacious. ⊠ *1 First Stamford Pl., 06902,* ☎ *203/967–2222,* FAX *203/967–3475. 451 rooms, 23 suites. Restaurant, indoor pool, 2 tennis courts, health club, meeting rooms. AE, D, DC, MC, V.*

$$–$$$$ ▦ **Stamford Marriott Hotel.** The Marriott stands out for its up-to-date facilities and convenience to trains and airport buses. Furnishings are modern and comfortable, if unmemorable. ⊠ *2 Stamford Forum, 06901,* ☎ *203/357–9555,* FAX *203/358–0157. 500 rooms, 6 suites. Restaurant, bar, coffee shop, indoor-outdoor pool, barbershop, beauty salon, health club, jogging, racquetball, car rental. AE, D, DC, MC, V.*

Nightlife and the Arts

NIGHTLIFE

For alternative dance music try the **Art Bar** (⊠ 84 W. Park Pl., ☎ 203/973–0300), which draws a collegiate crowd and is gay and lesbian on Sunday night. At the **Terrace Club** (⊠ 1938 W. Main St., ☎ 203/961–9770) you can dance to everything from ballroom and country western to Top 40 and disco on weekends. **Tigin Pub** (⊠ 175 Bedford St., ☎ 203/353–8444) has the feel of an Irish pub.

THE ARTS

The **Stamford Center for the Arts** (☎ 203/325–4466) presents everything from one-act plays and comedy shows to musicals and film festivals. Performances are held at the Rich Forum (⊠ 307 Atlantic St.) and the Palace Theatre (⊠ 61 Atlantic St.). The **Stamford Symphony Orchestra** (☎ 203/325–1407) and the **Connecticut Grand Opera and Orchestra** (☎ 203/327–2867) perform at the Palace Theatre.

Outdoor Activities and Sports

The greens fee at the 18-hole, par-72 **Sterling Farms Golf Course** (⊠ 1349 Newfield Ave., ☎ 203/461–9090) ranges from $28 to $35; an optional cart costs $20.

Shopping

The **Stamford Town Center** (⊠ 100 Greyrock Pl., ☎ 203/356–9700) houses 130 chiefly upscale shops, including Saks Fifth Avenue, Talbot's, a Pottery Barn Design & Superstore, and Tommy Hilfiger. Northern Stamford's **United House Wrecking** (⊠ 535 Hope St., ☎ 203/348–5371) sells acres of architectural artifacts, decorative accessories, antiques, nautical items, and lawn and garden furnishings.

Norwalk

③ *14 mi northeast of Stamford, 47 mi northeast of New York City, 16 mi southwest of Bridgeport.*

In the 19th century, Norwalk became a major New England port and manufactured pottery, clocks, watches, shingle nails, and paper. It later fell into a state of neglect, in which it has remained for much of this century. During the past decade, however, Norwalk's coastal business district has been the focus of a major redevelopment project.

Art galleries, restaurants, and trendy boutiques have blossomed on and around Washington Street; the stretch is now known as the SoNo (short for South Norwalk) commercial district.

Norwalk is the home of Yankee Doodle Dandies: In 1756, Colonel Thomas Fitch threw together a motley crew of Norwalk soldiers and led them off to fight at Fort Crailo, near Albany, New York. Supposedly, Norwalk's women gathered feathers for the men to wear as plumes in their caps in an effort to give them some appearance of military decorum. Upon the arrival of these foppish warriors, one of the British officers sarcastically dubbed them "macaronis"—slang for dandies. The saying caught on, and so did the song.

★ ℃ The cornerstone of the SoNo district is the **Maritime Aquarium at Norwalk,** a 5-acre waterfront center that explores the ecology and history of Long Island Sound. Besides the huge aquarium, there are marine-mammal cruises aboard the *Oceanic,* and an IMAX theater. Although not as popular as Mystic Seaport (☞ New Haven and the Southeastern Coast, *below*), the aquarium is one of the state's most worthwhile attractions—especially for families. ⊠ *10 N. Water St.,* ☎ *203/852–0700.* ⌨ *Aquarium $7.75, IMAX theater $6.50, combined $12.* ☉ *Labor Day–June, daily 10–5; July–Labor Day, daily 10–6.*

Restoration continues at the **Lockwood-Mathews Mansion Museum,** an ornate tribute to Victorian decorating that was the summer home of LeGrand Lockwood in the late 19th century. It's hard not to be impressed by the octagonal rotunda and 50 rooms of gilt, frescoes, marble, woodwork, and etched glass. ⊠ *295 West Ave.,* ☎ *203/838–9799.* ⌨ *$5.* ☉ *Apr.–early-Jan., Tues.–Fri. 11–3, Sun. 1–4, Sat. 1–4 for special exhibitions; Jan.–Mar. by appointment.*

The 3-acre park at the **Sheffield Island Lighthouse** is a prime spot for a picnic. The 1868 lighthouse has four levels and 10 rooms to explore. *Ferry service from Hope Dock (corner of Washington and North Sts.),* ☎ *203/838–9444 for ferry and lighthouse.* ⌨ *Round-trip ferry service and lighthouse tour $12; tour only $4.* ☉ *Ferry Memorial Day–mid-June, weekends 10, 12:30, and 3; mid-June–Labor Day, daily 9:30 and 1:30, weekends 10, 12:30, and 3. Lighthouse open when ferry is docked.*

Dining and Lodging

$$$ ✕ **Côte d'Azur.** Dining is by candlelight at this neighborhood bistro with rustic furnishings and yellow walls. Past delicacies on the seasonally changing menu have included marinated braised rabbit, red snapper with roasted fennel, black olives and a spicy tomato sauce, or a Provençal fish soup. ⊠ *86 Washington St.,* ☎ *203/855–8900. MC, V. Closed Sun.–Mon.*

$$$ ✕ **Meson Galicia.** The inventive tapas served in this restored trolley barn in downtown Norwalk electrify the taste buds. Ingredients may include sweetbreads, capers, asparagus, chorizo . . . the list goes on. Come with an empty stomach and an open mind, and let the enthusiastic staff spoil you. Those in the know ask for the superior paella, even though it's not on the menu. ⊠ *10 Wall St.,* ☎ *203/866–8800. AE, D, DC, MC, V. Closed Mon. No lunch weekends.*

$$ ✕🏠 **Silvermine Tavern.** The cozy rooms at this inn, one of the state's best values, are furnished with hooked rugs and antiques along with some modern touches. The large, low-ceiling dining rooms ($$$; closed on Tuesday) are romantic, with an eclectic Colonial decor; many tables overlook a millpond. Traditional New England favorites receive modern accents—roast duckling, for instance, is served with maple mashed sweet potatoes and a peach reduction. Sunday brunch here is a local tradition. ⊠ *194 Perry Ave., 06850,* ☎ *203/847–4558,* 🆑 *203/847–9171. 10 rooms, 1 suite. Restaurant. Continental breakfast. AE, DC, MC, V.*

Nightlife and the Arts
Some good bars can be found in the SoNo district of South Norwalk. **Barcelona** (⊠ 63 N. Main St., ☎ 203/899–0088), a wine bar, is a hot spot for Spanish tapas. Brewing memorabilia adorns the **Brewhouse** (⊠ 13 Marshall St., ☎ 203/853–9110).

The **Fairfield Orchestra** (☎ 203/831–6020) performs at the Norwalk Concert Hall (⊠ 125 East Ave.). Its offshoot, the Orchestra of the Old Fairfield Academy, performs Baroque music on antique or reproduction period instruments.

Shopping
Stew Leonard's (⊠ 100 Westport Ave., ☎ 203/847–7213), the self-proclaimed "Disneyland of Supermarkets," has a petting zoo, animated characters lining the aisles, scrumptious chocolate chip cookies, and great soft ice cream. Along **Washington Street** in South Norwalk (SoNo) are some excellent galleries and crafts dealers.

New Canaan

④ *5 mi northwest of Norwalk, 33 mi southwest of New Haven.*

So rich and elegant is the landscape in New Canaan that you may want to pick up a local street map and spend the afternoon driving around the estate-studded countryside. Or you might prefer lingering on **Main Street,** which is loaded with upscale shops.

The **New Canaan Nature Center** comprises more than 40 acres of woods and habitats. You can take part in the hands-on natural science exhibits at the Discovery Center in the main building or walk along the many nature trails. Demonstrations take place in fall at the cider house and in spring at the maple sugar shed (reservations required). ⊠ *144 Oenoke Ridge,* ☎ *203/966–9577.* 🆑 *Donation suggested for museum.* ☉ *Grounds daily dawn–dusk, museum Mon.–Sat. 9–4.*

Lodging
$$–$$$ 🏠 **Maples Inn.** This yellow clapboard structure a short drive from downtown has 13 gables, most of which are veiled by a canopy of aged maples. Bedrooms are furnished with antiques and queen-size canopy beds. Mahogany chests, gilt frames, and brass lamps gleam from energetic polishing. The Mural Room, whose walls are painted with images of New Canaan in each of the four seasons, is an ideal setting for breakfast. ⊠ *179 Oenoke Ridge, 06840,* ☎ *203/966–2927,* 🆑 *203/966–5003. 10 rooms, 3 suites, 10 apartments. Continental breakfast. AE, MC, V.*

Wilton

⑤ *6 mi northeast of New Canaan, 27 mi southwest of New Haven.*

Quiet and unassuming, this lovely, tree-shaded town with graceful turn-of-the-century houses is one of Fairfield County's many bedroom communities.

★ **Weir Farm National Historic Site** is dedicated to the legacy of painter J. Alden Weir (1852–1919), one of the earliest American Impressionists. The property's 60 wooded acres include hiking paths, picnic areas, and a restored rose and perennial garden. Tours of Weir's studio and sculptor Mahonri Young's studio are given, and you can take a self-guided walk past Weir's painting sites. ✉ *735 Nod Hill Rd.,* ☎ *203/ 834–1896.* ⌨ *Free.* ☉ *Grounds daily dawn–dusk, visitor center Wed.– Sun. 8:30–5.*

The forest and wetlands of 146-acre **Woodcock Nature Center** (✉ 56 Deer Run Rd., ☎ 203/762–7280) are the site of botany walks, birding and geology lectures, and hikes.

Dining

$$$ ✗ **Mediterranean Grill.** The owners of Norwalk's Meson Galicia (☞ *above*) run this stylish dining room in an otherwise dull shopping center. The Mediterranean is a tribute to things Spanish—trendy Spanish, that is. Appetizers range from a sweet-onion tart with wild mushrooms to grilled baby squid with a bell-pepper vinaigrette. Expertly prepared dishes from other Mediterranean lands include examples from Morocco, Greece, and Italy. ✉ *Wilton Center, 5 River Rd.,* ☎ *203/762–8484. AE, D, DC, MC, V. Closed Mon. No lunch weekends.*

Nightlife and the Arts

The **Wilton Playshop** (✉ Lovers La., ☎ 203/762–7629) presents five major productions a year, from musicals to mysteries.

Shopping

Antiques sheds and boutiques can be found along and off U.S. 7. **Cannondale Village** (✉ Off U.S. 7, ☎ 203/762–2233), a pre–Civil War farm village, holds a complex of antiques shops and boutiques.

Ridgefield

❻ *8 mi north of Wilton, 43 mi west of New Haven.*

In Ridgefield, you'll find a rustic Connecticut atmosphere within an hour of Manhattan. The town center, which you approach from Wilton on Route 33, is a largely residential sweep of lawns and majestic homes.

The **Aldrich Museum of Contemporary Art** presents changing exhibitions of cutting-edge work rivaling that of any small collection in New York and has an outstanding 2-acre sculpture garden. ✉ *258 Main St.,* ☎ *203/ 438–4519.* ⌨ *$5.* ☉ *Tues.–Thurs. and weekends noon–5, Fri. noon–8.*

A British cannonball is lodged in a corner of the **Keeler Tavern Museum,** a historic inn and the former home of the noted architect Cass Gilbert (1859–1934). Furniture and Revolutionary War memorabilia fill the museum, where guides dressed in Colonial costumes conduct tours. The sunken garden is particularly lovely in the spring. ✉ *132 Main St.,* ☎ *203/438–5485.* ⌨ *$4.* ☉ *Feb.–Dec., Wed. and weekends 1–4.*

Dining and Lodging

$$–$$$$ ✗🗔 **Stonehenge Inn & Restaurant.** The manicured lawns and bright white-clapboard buildings of Stonehenge are visible just off U.S. 7. The inn's tasteful rooms are a mix of Waverly and Schumacher fabrics; the gem of a restaurant ($$$–$$$$) is run by Bruno Crosnier. The Maryland crab cakes with asparagus sauce is a fine starter. Among the entrées are medallions of venison with dauphine potatoes (fried croquettes) laced with garlic and sweet green peppercorns, and simple and elegant Dover sole. ✉ *Stonehenge Rd. off U.S. 7, 06877,* ☎ *203/438–6511,* 🖷 *203/438–2478. 12 rooms, 4 suites. Restaurant. Continental breakfast. AE, MC, V.*

$$$ ✕⊠ **The Elms Inn.** The best rooms at this inn are in the frame house built by a Colonial cabinetmaker in 1760; antiques and reproductions furnish all the rooms. Chef Brendan Walsh presents fine new American cuisine in the restaurant ($$$–$$$$)—pan-roasted Maryland crab cakes with three-pepper relish, maple-thyme grilled loin of venison, and the like. ⊠ *500 Main St., 06877,* ☎ FAX *203/438–2541. 20 rooms, 4 suites. Restaurant, pub. Continental breakfast. AE, DC, MC, V.*

Shopping

The **Hay Day Market** (⊠ 21 Governor St., ☎ 203/431–4400) stocks hard-to-find fresh produce, jams, cheeses, sauces, baked goods, flowers, and much more. Other locations are in Greenwich (☎ 203/637–7600) and Westport (☎ 203/254–5200).

Danbury

7 *9 mi north of Ridgefield, 20 mi northwest of Bridgeport.*

A middle-class slice of suburbia, Danbury was the hat capital of America for nearly 200 years—until the mid-1950s. Rumors persist that the term "mad as a hatter" originated here. Hat makers suffered widely from the injurious effects of mercury poisoning, a fact that is said to explain the resultant "madness" of veteran hatters.

The **Military Museum of Southern New England** exhibits an impressive collection of U.S. and allied forces memorabilia from World War II, plus 19 tanks dating from that war to the present. A computer program allows access to the names on the Vietnam Veterans Memorial in Washington. ⊠ *125 Park Ave.,* ☎ *203/790–9277.* ⊡ *$4.* ⊙ *Tues.– Sat. 10–5, Sun. noon–5.*

⊙ A station built in 1903 for the New Haven Railroad houses the **Danbury Railway Museum.** In the train yard are 20 or so examples of freight and passenger railroad stock, including a restored 1944 caboose, a 1948 Alco locomotive, and an operating locomotive turntable. Museum exhibits include vintage American Flyer model trains. ⊠ *White St. and Patriot Dr.,* ☎ *203/778–8337.* ⊡ *$3.* ⊙ *Wed.–Sat. 10–4, Sun. noon– 4, and by appointment.*

Dining

$$$$ ✕ **Ondine.** Drifts of flowers, soft lighting, hand-written menus, and waiters in white jackets make every meal at Ondine feel like a celebration. The five-course prix-fixe traditional French menu, updated once a week, might include medallions of venison with a hunter's sauce made of blackberries or fresh salmon with a horseradish crust served with parsley sauce. The Grand Marnier soufflé is the signature dessert. ⊠ *69 Pembroke Rd./Rte. 37,* ☎ *203/746–4900. AE, D, DC, MC, V. Closed Mon. No lunch.*

Outdoor Activities and Sports

Golf Digest has rated the 18-hole, par-72 **Richter Park Golf Course** (⊠ 100 Aunt Hack Rd., ☎ 203/792–2550) one of the country's top 25 public courses. The greens fee is $44; an optional cart costs $23.

Shopping

The **Danbury Fair Mall** (⊠ U.S. 7 and I–84, ☎ 203/743–3247) has more than 225 shops as well as a huge working carousel in the food court. **Stew Leonard's** (⊠ 99 Federal Rd., ☎ 203/790–8030), with a petting zoo, animated characters in the aisles, and great soft ice cream, is an experience as much as a supermarket.

Redding

⑧ *11 mi east of Danbury*

Redding was the home of Mark Twain's estate, Stormfield. Little has changed since Twain described the area as "one of the loveliest spots in America."

In the winter of 1778–79, three brigades of Continental Army soldiers under the command of General Israel Putnam made their winter encampment at the site of **Putnam Memorial State Park,** known as "Connecticut's Valley Forge." Superb for hiking, picnicking, and cross-country skiing, the park has a small history museum. ⊠ *Rtes. 58 and 107, West Redding,* ☎ *203/938–2285.* ▣ *Donation suggested.* ☉ *Grounds 8 AM–dusk; museum Memorial Day–Nov., Mon–Wed. and Fri.–Sat. 10–5.*

En Route From Redding to Weston, take Route 53 south along the picturesque **Saugatuck Reservoir.**

Weston

⑨ *6 mi south of Redding, 36 mi southwest of New Haven.*

Erica Jong, Keith Richards, Christopher Plummer, and other artists and entertainers have homes in heavily wooded Weston.

The 1,746 acres of woodlands, wetlands, and rock ledges at the **Nature Conservancy's Devil's Den Preserve** (⊠ 33 Pent Rd., ☎ 203/226–4991) include 20 mi of hiking trails. Trail maps are available in the parking-lot registration area, and guided walks take place year-round. There are no rest rooms, and pets and bikes are not allowed.

Dining

$$$–$$$$ ✕ **Cobb's Mill Inn.** It's hard to take your eyes off the ducks and swans frolicking in the waterfall outside this former mill and inn, which is now a charming restaurant. Still, the Continental cuisine also warrants your attention. The pheasant pistachio pâté is a good starter. The menu is heavy on red meat dishes, but lighter fare includes grilled swordfish and shrimp *l'Arlesienne* (shrimp sautéed in garlic butter with cherry tomatoes, leeks, white wine, and Pernod). The Sunday brunch (entrées cost $10 to $16) is a good deal. ⊠ *12 Old Mill Rd., off Rte. 57,* ☎ *203/227–7221. AE, D, DC, MC, V. No lunch Mon. or Sat.*

Westport

⑩ *7 mi south of Weston, 47 mi northeast of New York City.*

Westport, an artists' mecca since the turn of the century, continues to attract creative types. Despite commuters and corporations, the town remains more arty and cultured than its neighbors: If the rest of Fairfield County is stylistically five years behind Manhattan, Westport lags by just five months. Paul Newman and Joanne Woodward have their main residence here, as does America's homemaking and entertaining guru, Martha Stewart.

Summer visitors to Westport congregate at **Sherwood Island State Park,** which has a 1½-mi sweep of sandy beach, two water's-edge picnic groves, an environmental-protection museum with artifacts from the parks and forestry divisions, and several food concessions. The museum and concessions are open seasonally. ⊠ *I–95, Exit 18,* ☎ *203/226–6983.* ▣ *$5–$12.* ☉ *Daily 8 AM–dusk.*

Dining and Lodging

$$$–$$$$ ✕ **Splash.** Cutting-edge Pacific Rim cuisine at a white-clapboard country club? That's right. The funky made-for-sharing dishes include "Baang" chicken salad with shreds of white meat tossed with Asian vegetables and sesame oil; wok-seared salmon; and hibachi-grilled Shanghai beef with cilantro oil and matchstick potatoes. ⊠ *The Inn at Longshore, 260 Compo Rd. S,* ☎ *203/454–7798. AE, D, MC, V. Closed Mon.*

$$$–$$$$
★
✕ **Tavern on Main.** This intimate restaurant takes the tavern concept to a new level—fresh flowers and soft music included. In winter the glow of fireplaces reaches every table, and in summer a terrace with an awning beckons. The sophisticated comfort food includes starters like wild mushroom ravioli and a roasted walnut and endive salad. Among the notable entrées are the potato-wrapped sea bass on a bed of Swiss chard, and the lamb chops with an herb crust and minted couscous. All the desserts are made in-house; the French apple tart is a blue-ribbon winner. ⊠ *146 Main St.,* ☎ *203/221–7222. AE, DC, MC, V.*

$$$$
★
✕▦ **Inn at National Hall.** Each whimsically exotic room at this towering Italianate redbrick inn is a study in innovative restoration, wall-stenciling, and decorative painting (including magnificent hand-painted trompe l'oeil designs). The furniture collection, with antique and new pieces, is exceptional. The rooms and suites are magnificent—some have sleeping lofts and 18-ft windows overlooking the Saugatuck River. At Miramar, Todd English, a Boston superstar, creates such dishes as grilled sirloin over Tuscan bruschetta and tortelli of butternut squash with brown butter and sage; his lunch pizzas are wonderful. ⊠ *2 Post Rd. W, 06880,* ☎ *203/221–1351 or 800/628–4255; 203/222–2267 for restaurant;* ℻ *203/221–0276. 8 rooms, 7 suites. Restaurant, refrigerators, in-room VCRs, meeting room. Continental breakfast. AE, D, DC, MC, V.*

$–$$$
✕▦ **Westport Inn.** Bedrooms in this upscale motor lodge have attractive contemporary furniture. Rooms surrounding the large indoor pool are set back nicely and are slightly larger than the rest. The delightful Christina's ($$–$$$) has an ever-changing menu of American-Mediterranean cuisine that always lists seafood and pasta dishes. For lighter fare, try the Grill Room. ⊠ *1595 Post Rd. E, 06880,* ☎ *203/259–5236 or 800/446–8997; 203/255–8889 for restaurant;* ℻ *203/254–8439. 114 rooms, 2 suites. Restaurant, bar, indoor pool, hot tub, sauna, health club. AE, D, DC, MC, V.*

Nightlife and the Arts

The **Levitt Pavilion for the Performing Arts** (⊠ Jesup Rd., ☎ 203/221–4422) sponsors an excellent series of summer concerts, most of them free, that range from jazz to classical, folk-rock to blues. The **Westport Country Playhouse** (⊠ 25 Powers Ct., ☎ 203/227–4177) presents six productions each summer in a converted barn.

Shopping

J. Crew, Ann Taylor, Coach, Laura Ashley, Brooks Brothers, and other fashionable shops have made **Main Street** in Westport the outdoor equivalent of upscale malls such as Stamford Town Center.

Fairfield

⑪ *9 mi east of Westport, 33 mi south of Waterbury.*

Fairfield still has many old Dutch and English Colonials on a network of quaint, winding roads north of U.S. 1. Each May the Greenfield Hill Congregational Church hosts the annual **Dogwood Festival** (☎ 203/259–5596), which has been going strong for more than six decades. The **Quick Center for the Arts** (⊠ Fairfield University, N. Benson Rd., ☎ 203/254–4010) hosts musical and theatrical performances, children's shows, and a lecture series with international speakers.

The **Connecticut Audubon Center of Fairfield** (⊠ 2325 Burr St., ☎ 203/259–6305) maintains a 160-acre wildlife sanctuary that includes 6 mi of rugged hiking trails and special walks for people with visual impairments and mobility problems.

The **Connecticut Audubon Birdcraft Museum** (✉ 314 Unquowa Rd., ☎ 203/259–0416), operated by the Connecticut Audubon Society, has a children's activity corner, 6 acres with trails, and a pond that attracts waterfowl during their spring and fall migrations.

Dining

$ ✕ **Rawley's Hot Dogs.** The hot dogs at this drive-in are deep-fried in vegetable oil, then grilled for a few seconds—a recipe the stand has been following since it opened in 1946. Martha "It's a good thing" Stewart is among the regulars. Her favorite? A cheesedog with the works. ✉ *1886 Post Rd.,* ☎ *203/259–9023. No credit cards. Closed Sun.*

Bridgeport

⑫ *5 mi east of Fairfield, 28 mi south of Waterbury, 63 mi west of New London.*

Bridgeport, a city that has endured some economic hard times, is working hard to overcome its negative image. Recent improvements by civic leaders, as well as a number of unique attractions, make it a worthwhile stop.

☾ Exhibits at the **Barnum Museum,** associated with past resident and former mayor P. T. Barnum, depict the life and times of the great showman, who presented performers like General Tom Thumb and Jenny Lind, the Swedish Nightingale. You can tour a scaled-down model of Barnum's legendary five-ring circus. ✉ *820 Main St.,* ☎ *203/331–1104.* ⌨ *$5.* ⊙ *Tues.–Sat. 10–4:30, Sun. noon–4:30.*

The indoor walk-through South American rain forest at the 30-acre **Beardsley Park and Zoological Gardens** itself justifies a visit. Also in the park, which is north of downtown Bridgeport, are a carousel museum, a working carousel, and a New England farmyard. ✉ *1875 Noble Ave.,* ☎ *203/394–6565.* ⌨ *$5.* ⊙ *Park daily 9–4; rain forest daily 10–3:30.*

Captain's Cove on historic Black Rock Harbor is the home port of the HMS *Rose*—a replica of a Revolutionary War frigate and one of the largest wooden tall ships in action today—and the Lightship #112 *Nantucket.* Band concerts take place on Sunday afternoon in summer. The boardwalk holds two dozen shops and a casual restaurant. ✉ *1 Bostwick Ave. (I–95, Exit 26),* ☎ *203/335–1433.* ⌨ *Cove free, lightship tour $2, frigate tour (when it's in port) $5.* ⊙ *Tours on the hr Memorial Day–Labor Day, weekends noon–4.*

☾ The draws at the **Discovery Museum and Wonder Workshop** include a planetarium, several hands-on science exhibits, a computer-art exhibit, Hoop Smarts (a virtual basketball game), the *Challenger* learning center (which has a simulated space flight), and a children's museum. The Wonder Workshop schedules storytelling, arts-and-crafts, science, and other programs. ✉ *4450 Park Ave.,* ☎ *203/372–3521.* ⌨ *$7.* ⊙ *Tues.–Sat. 10–5, Sun. noon–5.*

Outdoor Activities and Sports

The **Bridgeport Bluefish** (✉ Harbor Yard, 500 Main St., off I–95, ☎ 203/333–1608) is a team in the Atlantic League of Professional Baseball.

Stratford

⑬ *3 mi east of Bridgeport, 15 mi southwest of New Haven.*

Stratford, named after the English town Stratford-upon-Avon, has more than 150 historic homes, many of which are on Long Island Sound. The Academy Hill neighborhood, near the intersection of Main (Route 113) and Academy Hill streets, is a good area to stroll.

Boothe Memorial Park & Museum, a 32-acre complex with several unusual buildings, includes a blacksmith shop, carriage and tool barns, and a museum that traces the history of the trolley. Also on the grounds are a beautiful rose garden and a children's playground. The site is 3 mi north of Stratford. ⊠ *Main St., Putney,* ☎ *203/381–2046.* ⊡ *Free.* ☉ *Park daily dawn–dusk. Museum June–Oct., Tues.–Fri. 11–1, weekends 1–4.*

Southwestern Connecticut A to Z

Arriving and Departing
BY BUS

Bonanza Bus Lines (☎ 800/556–3815) provides service to Danbury from Hartford, New York, and Providence. **Peter Pan Bus Lines** (☎ 800/343–9999) stops in Bridgeport en route from Hartford, Boston, Providence, and New York.

BY CAR

The main routes into southwestern Connecticut are Route 15 (called the Merritt Parkway in this area) and I–95 (also known as the Connecticut Turnpike).

BY PLANE

Bridgeport–Igor Sikorsky Memorial Airport (⊠ 1000 Great Meadow Rd., Exit 30 off I–95, ☎ 203/576–7498 or 203/377–0331), 4 mi south of Stratford, is served by US Airways Express (☎ 800/428–4322).

BY TRAIN

Amtrak (☎ 800/872–7245) stops in Stamford and Bridgeport. **Metro-North Railroad** (☎ 800/638–7646; 212/532–4900 from New York City) trains stop in Greenwich, Stamford, Norwalk, New Canaan, Wilton, Danbury, Redding, Westport, Fairfield, Bridgeport, and Stratford.

Getting Around
BY BUS

Connecticut Transit buses (☎ 203/327–7433) stop in Greenwich, Stamford, and Norwalk. The Greater Bridgeport Transit District's **People Movers** (☎ 203/333–3031) provide bus transportation in Bridgeport, Stratford, and Fairfield. **Norwalk Transit** provides bus service in Norwalk (☎ 203/852–0000) and Westport (☎ 203/226–0422).

BY CAR

The Merritt Parkway and I–95 are the main arteries; both can have harrowing rush-hour snarls. Greenwich, Stamford, Norwalk, Westport, Fairfield, Bridgeport, and Stratford are on or just off I–95. From I–95 or the Merritt Parkway take Route 124 north to New Canaan; U.S. 7 north to Wilton or Danbury; U.S. 7 and Route 33 north to Ridgefield; Route 53 north to Weston; and Route 58 north to Redding.

Contacts and Resources
EMERGENCIES

Norwalk Hospital (⊠ 34 Maple St., Norwalk, ☎ 203/852–2000). **St. Vincent's Hospital** (⊠ 2800 Main St., Bridgeport, ☎ 203/576–6000).

24–HOUR PHARMACY

CVS Pharmacy (⊠ 235 Main St., Norwalk, ☎ 203/847–6057).

VISITOR INFORMATION

Coastal Fairfield County Convention and Visitors Bureau (⊠ The Gate Lodge–Mathews Park, 297 West Ave., Norwalk 06850, ☎ 203/899–

2799 or 800/866–7925). **Housatonic Valley Tourism District** (⊠ 30 Main St., Danbury 06810, ☎ 203/743–0546 or 800/841–4488).

HARTFORD AND THE CONNECTICUT RIVER VALLEY

Westward expansion in the New World began along the meandering Connecticut River. Dutch explorer Adrian Block first explored the area in 1614, and in 1633 a trading post was set up in what is now Hartford. Within five years, throngs of restive Massachusetts Bay colonists had settled in this fertile valley. What followed was more than three centuries of shipbuilding, shad hauling, and river trading with ports as far away as the West Indies and the Mediterranean.

Less touristy than the coast and northwest hills, the Connecticut River valley is a swath of small villages and uncrowded state parks punctuated by a few small cities and a large one: the capital city of Hartford. To the south of Hartford, with the exception of industrial Middletown, genuinely quaint hamlets vie for a share of Connecticut's tourist crop with antiques shops, scenic drives, and trendy restaurants.

Essex Area

⑭ *29 mi east of New Haven.*

Essex looks much as it did in the mid-19th century, at the height of its shipbuilding prosperity. So important to a young America was Essex's boat manufacturing that the British burned more than 40 ships here during the War of 1812. Gone are the days of steady trade with the West Indies, when the aroma of imported rum, molasses, and spices hung in the air. Whitewashed houses—many the former roosts of sea captains—line Main Street, which has shops that sell clothing, antiques, paintings and prints, and sweets.

In addition to pre-Colonial artifacts and displays, the **Connecticut River Museum** has a full-size reproduction of the world's first submarine, the *American Turtle*; the original was built by David Bushnell in 1775. ⊠ *Steamboat Dock, 67 Main St.,* ☎ *860/767–8269.* ☜ *$4.* ☉ *Tues.–Sun. 10–5.*

The **Essex Steam Train and Riverboat** travels alongside the Connecticut River and through the lower valley; if you wish to continue, a riverboat can take you up the river. The train trip lasts an hour; the riverboat ride, 90 minutes. ⊠ *Exit 3 off Rte. 9,* ☎ *860/767–0103.* ☜ *Train fare $10; combined train-boat fare $15.* ☉ *May–Oct.; call for schedule.*

Dining and Lodging

$$–$$$ ✕ **Steve's Centerbrook Café.** Latticework and gingerbread trim are among the architectural accents of the Victorian house that holds this bright café. The culinary accents lean toward the ornate as well, especially in the few classic French dishes. Although the menu changes regularly, you can usually find rack of lamb or grilled salmon. Save room for the *marjolaine,* a hazelnut torte covered with chocolate. ⊠ *78 Main St., Centerbrook,* ☎ *860/767–1277. AE, MC, V. Closed Mon. No lunch.*

$$–$$$ ✕▥ **Griswold Inn.** Two-plus centuries of catering to changing tastes at what's billed as America's oldest continuously operating inn has resulted in a kaleidoscope of decor—some Colonial, a touch of Federal, a little Victorian, and just as many modern touches as are necessary to meet present-day expectations. The chefs at the restaurant ($$–$$$) prepare country-style and more sophisticated dishes—try the famous

1776 sausages, which come with sauerkraut and German potato salad, or the risotto croquettes. The Tap Room, built in 1738 as a school-house, is ideal for after-dinner drinks. The English Hunt Breakfast, a feast of muffins, eggs, fresh cod, creamed chipped beef, and smoked bacon, is a Sunday event. ⊠ *36 Main St., 06426,* ☎ *860/767–1776,* ﷼ *860/767–0481. 31 rooms, 4 suites. Restaurant, bar. Continental breakfast. AE, MC, V.*

$$–$$$ ⊞ **Riverwind.** All the guest rooms at this splendid inn have antique fur-nishings, collectibles, and touches of stenciling. One room has a coun-try-pine bed and a painted headboard; another holds a carved oak bed; a third contains an 18th-century bird's-eye maple four-poster with a canopy. Co-owner Barbara Barlow serves a hearty country breakfast of Smithfield ham, her own baked goods, and several casseroles. Freshly brewed tea and coffee and home-baked cookies are always on hand. ⊠ *209 Main St., Deep River 06417,* ☎ *860/526–2014. 7 rooms, 1 suite. Full breakfast. AE, MC, V. 2-night minimum weekends mid–Apr.–Dec.*

Ivoryton

⑮   *4 mi west of Essex.*

Ivoryton was named for its steady import of elephant tusks from Kenya and Zanzibar during the 19th century—piano keys were Ivory-ton's leading export during this time. At one time, the Comstock-Ch-eney piano manufacturers processed so much ivory that Japan regularly purchased Ivoryton's surplus, using the scraps to make souvenirs. The depression closed the lid on Ivoryton's pianos, and what remains is a sleepy, shady hamlet.

The **Museum of Fife and Drum,** said to be the only one of its kind in the world, contains martial sheet music, instruments, and uniforms chron-icling America's history of parades, from the Revolutionary War to the present. Performances take place on Tuesday night in summer. ⊠ *62 N. Main St.,* ☎ *860/767–2237 or 860/399–6519.* ▦ *$2.* ☉ *June–Sept., weekends 1–5 or by appointment. Closed 3rd weekend in July and 4th weekend in Aug.*

Dining and Lodging

$$–$$$$ ✕⊞ **Copper Beech Inn.** A magnificent copper beech tree shades the im-posing main building of this Victorian inn, set on 7 wooded acres. The four rooms in the main house have an old-fashioned feel, right down to the claw-foot tubs; the nine rooms in the Carriage House are more modern and have decks. The distinctive country-French menu in the romantic dining room ($$$–$$$$; reservations essential; jacket and tie; no lunch) changes seasonally. Specials might include the inn's renowned bouillabaisse or lamb with an herb crust. Dinner starts at 1 PM on Sun-day. ⊠ *46 Main St., 06442,* ☎ *860/767–0330 or 888/809–2056. 13 rooms. Restaurant. Continental breakfast. AE, DC, MC, V.*

Chester

⑯   *5 mi north of Ivoryton, 24 mi northwest of New London.*

Arty Chester has a quaint Main Street lined with tony antiques shops and boutiques—shopping is a favorite pastime in this upscale town.

Dining

$$$–$$$$ ✕ **Restaurant du Village.** A black wrought-iron gate beckons you away from the antiques stores of Chester's Main Street, and an off-white awning draws you through the door of this classic little Colonial storefront, painted in historic Newport blue and adorned with flower boxes. Here you can sample exquisite classic French cuisine—escargots in puff pas-

Connecticut River Valley

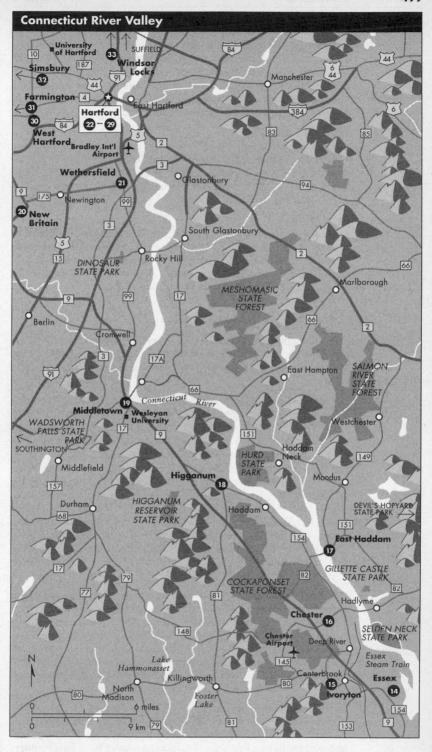

University of Hartford

Simsbury **33** **SUFFIELD**
32 **Windsor Locks**
187 91

Farmington **44**
31 4
30 84 **East Hartford**
West Hartford **Hartford**
Bradley Int'l Airport **22 — 29** 5

Wethersfield 2

21 3
1/5 **Glastonbury** 94
Newington 99
20 New Britain 3 **South Glastonbury** 2 66

5
15 **Rocky Hill** **Marlborough**
DINOSAUR STATE PARK 99 17 MESHOMASIC STATE FOREST 66 2

Berlin 9
Cromwell 3 66
91 17A **East Hampton** SALMON RIVER STATE FOREST

19 *Connecticut River*
Middletown 406 Westchester
WADSWORTH FALLS STATE PARK Wesleyan University 17 9 151 149
SOUTHINGTON Haddam Neck
Middlefield HURD STATE PARK Moodus
157 **Higganum** **18**
Durham HIGGANUM RESERVOIR STATE PARK Haddam DEVIL'S HOPYARD STATE PARK
68 151
154 **East Haddam**
17 79 **17** GILLETTE CASTLE STATE PARK
77 82 82
81 Hadlyme
148 **Chester** **16** SELDEN NECK STATE PARK
COCKAPONSET STATE FOREST
N Chester Airport Deep River Essex Steam Train
Lake Hammonasset 145 Centerbrook **Essex**
Killingworth 80 **15** **14**
80 North Madison Foster Lake **Ivoryton**
6 miles 153 154
9 km 79 81 9

try, filet mignon—while recapping the day's shopping coups. ⊠ *59 Main St.,* ☎ *860/526–5301. AE, MC, V. Closed Mon. No lunch.*

$$$ ✕ **Fiddler's.** The specialties at this fine fish house are the rich bouill-abaisse and the lobster with a sauce of peaches, peach brandy, shallots, mushrooms, and cream. Blond bentwood chairs, lacy stenciling on the walls, prints of famous schooners, and the amber glow of oil lamps lend the place a gentrified air. ⊠ *4 Water St.,* ☎ *860/526–3210. DC, MC, V. Closed Mon. No lunch Sun.*

Nightlife and the Arts

Goodspeed at Chester presents new works or works in progress at the Norma Terris Theatre (⊠ N. Main St./Rte. 82, ☎ 860/873–8668) from April to December. The **National Theatre of the Deaf** (⊠ 5 W. Main St., ☎ 860/526–4971) performs in sign language and the spoken word from September through December.

Shopping

Ceramica (⊠ 36 Main St., ☎ 800/782–1238) carries hand-painted Italian tableware and decorative accessories. The **Connecticut River Artisans** (⊠ 69 Main St., ☎ 860/526–5575), a crafts cooperative, sells one-of-a-kind works, including pottery, jewelry, and folk art.

East Haddam

⑰ *7 mi north of Chester, 28 mi southeast of Hartford.*

Fishing, shipping, and musket-making were the chief enterprises at East Haddam, the only town in the state that occupies both banks of the Connecticut River. This lovely town retains much of its old-fashioned charm.

★ **Gillette Castle State Park** holds the outrageous 24-room oak-and-field-stone hilltop castle built by the eccentric actor and dramatist William Gillette between 1914 and 1919; he modeled it after the medieval castles of the Rhineland. You can tour the castle and hike on trails near the remains of the 3-mi private railroad that chugged about the property until the owner's death in 1937. Gillette, who was born in Hartford, wrote two famous Civil War plays and was beloved for his play *Sherlock Holmes* (he performed the title role). In his will, Gillette demanded that the castle not fall into the hands of "some blithering saphead who has no conception of where he is or with what surrounded." To that end, the castle and 200-acre grounds were designated a state park that's an excellent spot for hiking and picnicking. ⊠ *67 River Rd., off Rte. 82,* ☎ *860/526–2336.* 🎫 *Castle $4; grounds free.* ☉ *Hours were in flux at press time; call ahead.*

★ The upper floors of the 1876 Victorian gingerbread **Goodspeed Opera House** have served as a venue for theatrical performances for more than 100 years. In the 1960s the Goodspeed underwent a restoration that included the stage area, the Victorian bar, the sitting room, and the drinking parlor. More than 14 Goodspeed productions have gone on to Broadway, including *Annie.* The performance season runs from April to December. ⊠ *Rte. 82,* ☎ *860/873–8668.* 🎫 *Tour $2.* ☉ *Tours Memorial Day–Columbus Day; call for times.*

St. Stephen's Church is listed in the *Guinness Book of Records* as having the oldest bell in the United States. Crafted in Spain in the year 815, the bell is believed to have been taken from a monastery by Napoléon and used for ballast in a ship. A Captain Andrews from East Haddam discovered it in Florida and brought it back to his hometown, where it now sits in the belfry of St. Stephen's, a small stone Episcopal church with cedar shingles. The church was built in 1794 and was moved to its present site in 1890. ⊠ *Main St./Rte. 149,* ☎ *860/873–9547.* ⊙ *Call for hrs.*

Sixty-foot cascades flow down Chapman Falls at the 860-acre **Devil's Hopyard State Park.** The park's campground is near the falls. ⊠ *366 Hopyard Rd., 3 mi north of junction of Rtes. 82 and 156,* ☎ *860/873–8566. 21 sites.* 🍴 *Day use free; campsites $9.* ⊙ *Park daily 8 AM–dusk. Campground daily Memorial Day–Labor Day and weekends mid-Apr.–Memorial Day.*

Lodging

$$–$$$ 🖼 **Bishopsgate Inn.** Around the bend from the landmark Goodspeed Opera House (☞ *above*), this 1818 Federal-style inn contains cozy and inviting rooms furnished with period reproductions, a smattering of antiques, and fluffy featherbeds. Four rooms have fireplaces, and one has a sauna. You can order elaborate candlelight dinners served in your room. ⊠ *Box 290, 7 Norwich Rd./Rte. 82, 06423,* ☎ *860/873–1677,* FAX *860/873–3898. 5 rooms, 1 suite. Full breakfast. MC, V.*

Higganum

⑱ *15 mi north of East Haddam.*

Higganum's name is a variation on the Native American word *higganumpus* (fishing place). Indeed, it was the home for many years to several important shad fisheries. Today Higganum is a well-wooded town with sleepy, narrow streets and small, quaint homes.

The three formal herb gardens—a knot garden of interlocking hedges, a typical 18th-century geometric garden with central sundial, and a topiary garden—at the **Sundial Herb Garden** surround an 18th-century farmhouse. An 18th-century barn serves as a formal tearoom and a shop where you'll find herbs, books, and rare and fine teas. Sunday afternoon teas and special programs take place throughout the year. ⊠ *59 Hidden Lake Rd. (6 mi from Higganum Center; head south on Rte. 81, turn right on Brault Hill Rd., and right again when road ends),* ☎ *860/345–4290.* 🍴 *$1.* ⊙ *Jan.–late-Nov., weekends 10–5 (except last 2 weekends of Oct.); late Nov.–Dec. 24, daily 10–5.*

Lodging

$ 🏕 **Nelson's Family Campground.** A 2-acre pond, a pool, a playground, a recreation hall, boccie, tennis, volleyball, and planned activities keep the folks at this camping area's wooded and field sites busy. ⊠ *71 Mott Hill Rd., East Hampton,* ☎ *860/267–4561 or 860/267–5300.* 🍴 *$27. 315 sites. Coin laundry, electric hook-ups, fire rings, flush toilets, showers, water. Closed Columbus Day–mid-Apr.*

Middletown

⑲ *14 mi north of Higganum, 24 mi northeast of New Haven.*

Middletown, once a bustling river city, was named for its location halfway between Hartford and Long Island Sound (it's also halfway between New York City and Boston). It is home to Wesleyan University. The wealthiest town in the state from about 1750 to 1800, Middletown had been in decline for more than a century before being chosen to take part in the National Trust for Historic Preservation's "Main Street Program." A multiyear rehabilitation project aims to revitalize the downtown area.

The imposing campus of Wesleyan University, founded here in 1831, is traversed by **High Street,** which Charles Dickens once called "the loveliest Main Street in America"—even though Middletown's actual Main

Street runs parallel to it a few blocks east. High Street is an architecturally eclectic thoroughfare. Note the massive, fluted Corinthian columns of the Greek Revival Russell House (circa 1828) at the corner of Washington Street, across from the pink Mediterranean-style Davison Arts Center, built just 15 years later; farther on are gingerbreads, towering brownstones, Tudors, and Queen Annes. A few hundred yards up on Church Street, which intersects High Street, is the Olin Library. The 1928 structure, Wesleyan University's library, was designed by Henry Bacon, the architect of the Lincoln Memorial.

The Federal **General Mansfield House** has 18th- and 19th-century decorative arts, Civil War memorabilia and firearms, and local artifacts. ⊠ *151 Main St.,* ☎ *860/346–0746.* ⬚ *$2.* ☉ *Sun. 2–4:30, Mon. 1–4, and by appointment.*

Dinosaurs once roamed the area around **Dinosaur State Park,** north of Middletown. Tracks dating from the Jurassic period, 200 million years ago, are preserved here under a giant geodesic dome. From May to October you can make plaster casts of tracks on a special area of the property. (Call ahead to learn what materials you will need.) An exhibit center with interactive displays interprets the dinosaurs, geology, and paleontology of the Connecticut River valley region. A great place for hiking, the park has nature trails that run through woods, along a ridge, and through swamps on a boardwalk. ⊠ *West St., east of I–91 Exit 23, Rocky Hill,* ☎ *860/529–8423.* ⬚ *$2.* ☉ *Exhibits Tues.–Sun. 9–4:30; trails daily 9–4.*

You can pick your own fruits and vegetables at **Lyman Orchards** (⊠ Rtes. 147 and 157, Middlefield, ☎ 860/349–3673), just south of Middletown, from June to October—berries, peaches, pears, apples, and even pumpkins. It's also the site of the state's largest indoor farmers' market.

Dining

$ ✕ **O'Rourke's Diner.** For a university town, Middletown has surprisingly few worthy eateries. The food at this stainless-steel-and-glass-brick diner is a cut above that at any of the "real" restaurants. You'll find the expected diner fare, along with a tasty Irish stew, corned-beef hash, and regional delicacies like steamed cheeseburgers (not served on weekends); it's all unusually good. The weekend breakfast menu is extensive. The diner opens at 4:30 AM. ⊠ *728 Main St.,* ☎ *860/346–6101. No credit cards. No dinner.*

Nightlife and the Arts

Wesleyan University's **Center for the Arts** (⊠ Between Washington Terr. and Wyllys Ave., ☎ 860/685–3355) frequently hosts concerts, theater, films, and art exhibits.

At last count, **Eli Cannon's** (⊠ 695 Main St., ☎ 860/347–3547) had 28 beers on tap and more than 100 bottled selections.

Outdoor Activities and Sports

Called by some "a public course with a private feel," the **Lyman Orchards Golf Club** (⊠ Rte. 157, Middlefield, ☎ 860/349–8055) has two 18–hole championship courses. The greens fee at both the par-72 course designed by Robert Trent Jones and par-71 course designed by Gary Player ranges between $35 and $49. Carts ($11) are mandatory.

Shopping

Tours of the **Wesleyan Potters** (⊠ 350 S. Main St., ☎ 860/347–5925) pottery and weaving studios can be arranged in advance. Jewelry, clothing, baskets, pottery, weavings, and more are for sale.

Skiing and Snow Sports

POWDER RIDGE

The trails here drop straight down from the 500-ft-high ridge for which this ski area is named. Half the 15 trails are designed for intermediate skiers, with the others split between beginner trails and expert Black Diamonds; all of the trails are lighted for night skiing. One quad lift, two doubles, and a handle tow cover the mountain. Special features include a snowtubing area, a snowboard park, an alpine park, a full-service restaurant, and ski instruction for children ages 4 and up. ✉ *99 Powder Hill Rd., Middlefield 06455,* ☎ *860/349–3454.*

New Britain

⑳ *13 mi northwest of Middletown, 10 mi southwest of Hartford.*

New Britain got its start as a manufacturing center producing sleigh bells. From these modest beginnings, it soon became known as "Hardware City," distributing builders' tools, ball bearings, locks, and other such items. No longer a factory town, New Britain is home to the Central Connecticut State College campus and a thriving performing arts community.

The **New Britain Museum of American Art,** in a turn-of-the-century house that holds 19 galleries and more than 4,000 works of art, surveys the entire history of American art. Though the collection includes luminaries such as Thomas Cole, Georgia O'Keeffe, and Thomas Hart Benton, the selection of Impressionist artists deserves special note— Mary Cassatt, William Merritt Chase, Childe Hassam, and John Henry Twachtman, among others. ✉ *56 Lexington St.,* ☎ *860/229–0257.* 🖭 *$3; free Sat. 10–noon.* ☉ *Tues.–Fri. 1–5, Sat. 10–5, Sun. noon–5.*

Outdoor Activities and Sports

The **New Britain Rock Cats,** the Double-A affiliate of baseball's Minnesota Twins, play at New Britain Stadium (✉ Willow Brook Park, S. Main St., ☎ 860/224–8383) from April to September.

Wethersfield

㉑ *7 mi northeast of New Britain, 32 mi northeast of New Haven.*

Wethersfield, a vast Hartford suburb, dates from 1634. As was the case throughout early Connecticut, the Native Americans indigenous to these lands fought the arriving English with a vengeance; here their struggles culminated in the 1637 Wethersfield Massacre, when Pequot Indians killed nine settlers. Three years later, the citizens held a public election, America's first defiance of British rule, for which they were fined five British pounds.

The Joseph Webb House, Silas Deane House, and Isaac Stevens House, all built in the mid- to late 1700s, form one of the state's best historic-house museums, the **Webb-Deane-Stevens Museum.** The structures, well-preserved examples of Georgian architecture, reflect their owners' lifestyles as, respectively, a merchant, a diplomat, and a tradesman. The Webb House, a registered National Historic Landmark, was the site of the strategy conference between George Washington and the French general Jean-Baptiste Rochambeau that led to the British defeat at Yorktown. ✉ *211 Main St. (Exit 26 off I–91),* ☎ *860/529–0612.* 🖭 *$8.* ☉ *May–Oct., Wed.–Mon. 10–4; Nov.–Apr., weekends 10–4.*

Comstock Ferre & Co. (✉ 263 Main St., ☎ 860/571–6590), founded in 1820, is the country's oldest continuously operating seed company. In a chestnut post-and-beam building, a National Historic Landmark that dates to the late 1700s, Comstock Ferre sells more than 800 varieties of seeds and 3,000 varieties of perennials.

Dining

$$$ ✕ **Ruth's Chris Steak House.** Every steak at this branch of the national chain is served sizzling hot and dripping with flavorful butter. Heat from an 1,800° oven seals in the juices. ⊠ *2513 Berlin Turnpike, Newington,* ☎ *860/666–2202. AE, D, DC, MC, V. No lunch.*

Hartford

4 mi north of Wethersfield, 45 mi northwest of New London, 81 mi northeast of Stamford.

Formerly one of the nation's most powerful cities, Connecticut's capital seems past its prime. The decline of the insurance and defense industries in the past two decades has left the once-lovely city in some disrepair, although it offers some notable sights for visitors. Some ambitious programs for downtown renewal are in the works, too. America's insurance industry was born here in the early 19th century—largely in an effort to protect the Connecticut River valley's tremendously important shipping interests. Throughout the 19th century, insurance companies expanded their coverage to include fires, accidents, life, and (in 1898) automobiles. Through the years, Hartford industries have included the inspection and packing of tobacco (a once prominent industry in the northern river valley) and the manufacture of everything from bedsprings to artificial limbs, pool tables, and coffins. Hartford's distinctive office towers make what is actually an ever-expanding suburban development seem more urban.

㉒ The Federal **Old State House,** a building with an elaborate cupola and roof balustrade, was designed in the early 1700s by Charles Bulfinch, architect of the U.S. Capitol. The Great Senate Room, where everyone from Abraham Lincoln to George Bush has spoken, contains a Gilbert Stuart portrait of George Washington that remains in its commissioned location. For a chance to see a two-headed calf, drop by the small but distinctive museum of oddities upstairs. And at 12:15 every Tuesday, the trial of the Africans who mutinied on the *Amistad* in 1839–an event depicted in Stephen Spielberg's 1997 film of the same name—is re-enacted in the very courtroom where it was first held. ⊠ *800 Main St.,* ☎ *860/522–6766.* ⊡ *Free.* ☉ *Weekdays 10–4, Sat. 11–4.*

★ **㉓** With more than 50,000 artworks and artifacts spanning 5,000 years, the **Wadsworth Atheneum** is the second largest public art museum in New England and the oldest in the nation, predating the Metropolitan Museum of Art by 35 years. Among notable items to look for are five wall drawings by Connecticut's own Sol LeWitt, the well-known conceptual artist, as well as the first American acquisitions of works by Salvador Dalí and the Italian artist Caravaggio. Particularly impressive are the museum's collections of Baroque, Impressionist, and Hudson River School artists—including pieces by Frederic Church and Thomas Cole—as well as what some consider the world's finest collection of Pilgrim-era furnishings. The Museum Café, though a bit pricey, is a lovely spot for lunch. ⊠ *600 Main St.,* ☎ *860/278–2670.* ⊡ *$7; free Sat. 11–noon and Thurs.* ☉ *Tues.–Sun. 11–5 (1st Thurs. of most months until 8).*

㉔ The **Center Church,** built in 1807, is patterned after London's Church of St. Martin-in-the-Fields. The parish itself dates from 1632 and was started by Puritan clergyman Thomas Hooker (1586–1647), one of the chief founders of Hartford. Five of the stained-glass windows were created by Louis Tiffany. The Ancient Burying Ground, in the churchyard, is filled with granite and brownstone headstones, some dating from

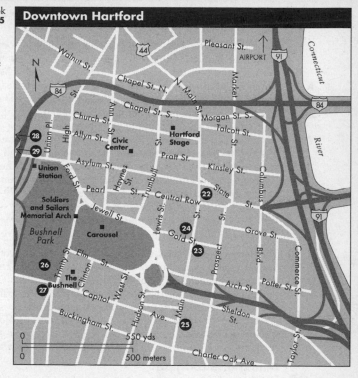

Downtown Hartford

the 1600s. ✉ *675 Main St.,* ☎ *860/249–5631.* 🎟 *Free.* ☻ *Mid-Apr.–mid-Dec., Wed. and Fri. 11–2 and by appointment.*

㉕ The **Butler-McCook Homestead** was built in 1782 and occupied continuously by the same family until 1971. Its furnishings show the evolution of American taste over time. There's an extensive collection of Japanese armor and Asian bronzes, Victorian-era toys, and a restored Victorian garden, originally designed by Jacob Weidenmann in 1865. ✉ *396 Main St.,* ☎ *860/522–1806 or 860/247–8996.* 🎟 *$4.* ☻ *Mid-May–mid-Oct., Tues., Thurs., and Sun. noon–4.*

Bushnell Park, which fans out from the State Capitol building (☞ *below*), was the first public space in the country with natural landscaping instead of a traditional village-green configuration. The park was created by the firm of Frederick Law Olmsted, the Hartford-born landscape architect who, with Calvert Vaux, designed New York City's Central Park. Amid Bushnell's 40 acres are 150 varieties of trees as well as landmarks like a 1914 Stein & Goldstein carousel and the 100-ft-tall, 30-ft-wide medieval-style Soldiers and Sailors Memorial Arch, dedicated to Civil War soldiers.

㉖ Rising above Bushnell Park and visible citywide is the grandiose **State Capitol,** a colossal edifice composed of wholly disparate architectural elements. Built in 1879 of marble and granite—to a tune of $2.5 million—this gilt-dome wonder is replete with crockets, finials, and pointed arches. It houses the governor's office and legislative chambers and displays historic statuary, flags, and furnishings. ✉ *210 Capitol Ave.,* ☎ *860/240–0222.* 🎟 *Free.* ☻ *Weekdays 9–3; tours weekdays 9:15–1:15 on the hr year-round and Sat. 10:15–2:15 on the hr Apr.–Oct.*

㉗ The **Museum of Connecticut History** exhibits artifacts of Connecticut military, industrial, and political history, including the state's original Colonial charter. It holds a vast assemblage of Samuel Colt firearms; the so-called Arm of Law and Order was manufactured in Hartford. ✉ *231 Capitol Ave.,* ☎ *860/566–3056.* ☑ *Free.* ⊙ *Weekdays 9:30–4.*

Nook Farm, a late-19th-century neighborhood, was home to several prominent families. Samuel Langhorne Clemens, better known as Mark Twain, built his Stick-style Victorian mansion here in 1874.

★ ㉘ During his residency at the **Mark Twain House,** he published seven major novels, including *Tom Sawyer, Huckleberry Finn,* and *The Prince and the Pauper.* Personal memorabilia and original furnishings are on display. One-hour guided tours of the house discuss its spectacular architecture and interior and Twain's family life. Renovations in 1998 restored the master bedroom and the drawing room and also opened to the public for the first time the rooms of the family butler, George Griffin, a prominent member of Hartford's African-American community. ✉ *351 Farmington Ave., at Forest St.,* ☎ *860/493–6411, ext. 23.* ☑ *$9.* ⊙ *Memorial Day–mid-Oct. and Dec., Mon.–Sat. 9:30–5, Sun. 11–5, last tour at 4; mid-Oct.–Nov. and Jan.–Memorial Day Mon. and Wed.–Sat. 9:30–5, Sun. noon–5, last tour at 4.*

㉙ The **Harriet Beecher Stowe House,** a Victorian Gothic cottage erected in 1871, stands as a tribute to the author of one of 19th-century America's most popular and influential novels, *Uncle Tom's Cabin.* Inside are her personal writing table and effects, several of her paintings, a period pinewood kitchen, and a terrarium of native ferns, mosses, and wildflowers. ✉ *71 Forest St.,* ☎ *860/525–9317.* ☑ *$6.50.* ⊙ *Memorial Day–Columbus Day and Dec., Mon.–Sat. 9:30–4, Sun. noon–4; mid-Oct.–Nov. and Jan.–Memorial Day, Tues.–Sat. 9:30–4, Sun. noon–4.*

Dining and Lodging

$$$$ ✗ **Cavey's.** It takes 20 minutes to get here from Hartford, but the drive is worth it. Downstairs is a formal French restaurant decorated with priceless antiques; the cuisine is classic all the way. Upstairs is a casual Italian dining room with Palladian windows, rush-seated wooden chairs, and contemporary art. Although both menus change seasonally, Cavey's French restaurant can be counted on for exemplary rack of lamb. Veal marsala is a perennial star upstairs. ✉ *45 E. Center St., Manchester,* ☎ *860/643–2751. AE, MC, V. Closed Sun.–Mon. No lunch downstairs.*

$$$–$$$$ ✗ **Max Downtown.** The latest of restaurateur Richard Rosenthal's
★ culinary creations, upscale Max Downtown serves cuisine from around the world—everything from Portobello mushroom napoleon and steamed miso-sake–glazed Chilean sea bass to aged New York strip steak and grilled veal loin chop. A separate cigar bar serves classic port and single-malt liquor. ✉ *CityPlace, 185 Asylum St.,* ☎ *860/522–2530. Reservations essential. AE, DC, MC, V. No lunch weekends.*

$$$–$$$$ ✗ **The Savannah.** The dining experience at this chic eatery is truly eclec-
★ tic: Dishes combine French, Spanish, Asian, and southern influences. Favorites include an appetizer of ravioli filled with a puree of sweet potato and topped with chive butter sauce and a touch of nutmeg, and an entrée of tuna crusted with sesame seeds and served with risotto and jícama-ginger salsa. ✉ *391 Main St.,* ☎ *860/278–2020. AE, DC, MC, V. Closed Sun.–Mon. No lunch Sat.*

$$$ ✗ **Civic Café.** Spacious, hip, and smartly designed, Civic Café recalls restaurants in New York and San Francisco. Sashimi-style tuna with seaweed and wasabi, and Black Angus steak with a mixed greens and Roquefort cheese salad are two choices on the fusion menu. The eatery also has a cappuccino bar and a Wednesday-night Martini Club. Care for a banana-nut-flavored "Monkey" martini? ✉ *150 Trumbull St.,* ☎ *860/493–7412. AE, D, DC, MC, V. Closed Sun. No lunch Sat.*

$$ ✗ **First and Last Tavern.** What looks to be a simple neighborhood joint south of downtown is actually one of the state's most hallowed pizza

parlors. The long, old-fashioned wooden bar in one room is jammed most evenings with suburbia-bound daily-grinders shaking off their suits. The main dining room is just as noisy, its brick outer wall covered with the requisite array of celebrity photos. ⊠ *939 Maple Ave.,* ☎ *860/956–6000. Reservations not accepted. AE, D, DC, MC, V. No lunch Sun.*

$$–$$$$ 🏠 **Goodwin Hotel.** Connecticut's only truly grand city hotel looks a
★ little odd in the downtown business district—the Civic Center dwarfs the ornate dark red structure, a registered historic landmark built in 1881. Despite the hotel's stately exterior, its rooms are nondescript but are large and tastefully done in Colonial style and have Italian marble baths. The clubby, mahogany-panel Pierpont's Restaurant serves passable new American fare. ⊠ *1 Haynes St., 06103,* ☎ *860/246–7500 or 800/922–5006, FAX 860/247–4576. 124 rooms, 11 suites. Restaurant, exercise room, meeting rooms. AE, D, DC, MC, V.*

$$–$$$ 🏠 **Hilton Hartford Hotel.** At 15 stories, this is the city's largest hotel. It's not sumptuous, but there are touches of elegance, such as the street-level lobby abloom with fresh flowers. Connected to the Civic Center by an enclosed bridge, the Hilton is within walking distance of the downtown area. ⊠ *315 Trumbull St. (at the Civic Center Plaza), 06103,* ☎ *860/728–5151, FAX 860/240–7247. 389 rooms, 8 suites. Restaurant, bar, indoor pool, health club. AE, D, DC, MC, V.*

$ 🏠 **Ramada Inn Capitol Hill.** Adjacent to Bushnell Park, the Ramada has an unobstructed view of the State Capitol. Ask for a room in front—the ones facing the rear overlook the train station around the corner, a parking lot, and a busy highway. The restaurant serves steaks, hamburgers, and other traditional American fare. ⊠ *440 Asylum St., 06103,* ☎ *860/246–6591, FAX 860/728–1382. 96 rooms. Restaurant. Continental breakfast weekdays. AE, D, DC, MC, V.*

Nightlife and the Arts

NIGHTLIFE

The **Arch Street Tavern** (⊠ 85 Arch St., ☎ 860/246–7610) hosts local rock bands. For barbecue and blues head to **Black-Eyed Sally's** (⊠ 350 Asylum St., ☎ 860/278–7427). Arch Ale and Bacchus Ale are two popular beers that you might find among the 40 at the **Hartford Brewery** (⊠ 35 Pearl St., ☎ 860/246–2337). **Mozzicato–De Pasquale's Bakery, Pastry Shop & Caffe** (⊠ 329 Franklin Ave., ☎ 860/296–0426) serves up late-night Italian pastries in the bakery and espresso, cappuccino, and gelato in the café, which has a full bar.

THE ARTS

The Tony Award–winning **Hartford Stage Company** (⊠ 50 Church St., ☎ 860/527–5151) turns out future Broadway hits, innovative productions of the classics, and new plays. **Theatreworks** (⊠ 233 Pearl St., ☎ 860/527–7838), the Hartford equivalent of Off-Broadway, presents experimental new dramas.

The **Bushnell** (⊠ 166 Capitol Ave., ☎ 860/246–6807) hosts the Hartford Ballet (☎ 860/525–9396), the Hartford Symphony (☎ 860/244–2999), and tours of major musicals. The **Hartford Conservatory** (⊠ 834 Asylum Ave., ☎ 860/246–2588) presents musical performances, with an emphasis on traditional works. The mammoth **Meadows Music Theater** (⊠ 63 Savitt Way, ☎ 860/548–7370) hosts nationally known acts. **Real Art Ways** (⊠ 56 Arbor St., ☎ 860/232–1006) presents modern and experimental musical compositions in addition to avant-garde and foreign films.

Outdoor Activities and Sports

The **Hartford Wolf Pack** (☎ 860/246–7825) of the American Hockey League plays at the 16,500-seat Civic Center (⊠ 1 Civic Center Plaza).

Skiing and Snow Sports

MT. SOUTHINGTON

This mountain, an easy half-hour drive southwest of Hartford, has 14 trails off the 425 ft of vertical range split equally among basic beginner, intermediate, and advanced. All trails are lighted for night skiing and are serviced by one triple chairlift, one double, two T-bars, 1 J-bar, and a handle tow. There are also a halfpipe and terrain park for snowboarders. The ski school (with 150 instructors) includes a popular SKIwee program for kids from 4 to 12 years old. The Mountain Room provides respite for skiers and snowboarders alike. ⊠ *396 Mount Vernon Rd., Southington 06489,* ☎ *860/628–0954; 860/628–7669 for conditions.*

West Hartford

③⓪ *5 mi west of Hartford, 33 mi northeast of Woodbury.*

More metropolitan than many of its suburban neighbors, West Hartford is alive with a sense of community. Gourmet food and ethnic grocery stores abound, as do unusual boutiques and shops. A stroll around West Hartford Center (Exit 42 off I–84) will reveal well-groomed streets busy with pedestrians and lined with coffee shops.

★ ☼ A life-size walk-through replica of a 60-ft sperm whale greets patrons of the **Science Center of Connecticut,** whose attractions include a wildlife sanctuary and planetarium. The Kids Factory teaches about magnetics, motion, optics, sound, and light through colorful hands-on exhibits. Some "Mathmagical" toys in the lower exhibit hall are a giant bubble maker, a hands-on weather station, and "Kaleidovision"—a 30-ft by 9-ft walk-in kaleidoscope. ⊠ *950 Trout Brook Dr.,* ☎ *860/231–2824.* ▣ *Science Center $6; laser and planetarium shows $3.* ☻ *Sept.–June, Tues.–Wed. and Fri.–Sat. 10–5, Thurs. 10–8, Sun. noon–5; July–Aug., Mon.–Wed. and Fri.–Sat. 10–5, Thurs. 10–8, Sun. noon–5.*

The **Noah Webster House and Museum** is the birthplace of the famed author (1758–1843) of the *American Dictionary.* The 18th-century farmhouse contains Webster memorabilia and period furnishings. ⊠ *227 S. Main St.,* ☎ *860/521–5362.* ▣ *$5.* ☻ *Sept.–June, daily 1–4; July–Aug., Mon.–Tues. and Thurs.–Fri. 10–4, weekends 1–4.*

The **Museum of American Political Life** houses rare political materials and memorabilia—buttons, posters, bumper stickers, and pamphlets—from the campaigns of U.S. presidents from George Washington to the present. A small section is devoted to memorabilia from the women's rights and temperance movements. ⊠ *University of Hartford, 200 Bloomfield Ave.,* ☎ *860/768–4090.* ▣ *Donation suggested.* ☻ *Sept.–May, Tues.–Fri. 11–4, weekends noon–4. Closed Sun. June–Aug.*

Dining

$$–$$$ ✕ **Butterfly Chinese Restaurant.** The piano entertainment suggests that this is not your ordinary order-by-number Chinese restaurant; indeed, the food is authentic, the staff outgoing. Among the 140 mostly Cantonese (some Szechuan) entrées are Peking duck and shrimp with walnuts. ⊠ *831 Farmington Ave.,* ☎ *860/236–2816. AE, MC, V.*

Farmington

③① *5 mi southwest of West Hartford*

Busy Farmington, incorporated in 1645, is a classic river town with lovely estates, a perfectly preserved main street, and the prestigious **Miss Porter's School** (⊠ 60 Main St.), the late Jacqueline Kennedy Onassis's alma mater. Antiques shops can be found near the intersection of Routes 4 and 10, along with some excellent house museums.

★ The **Hill-Stead Museum** was converted from a private home into a museum by its unusual owner, Theodate Pope, a turn-of-the-century architect. She also designed the elaborate sunken garden, now the elegant stage for poetry readings by nationally known writers every other week in summer. A Colonial Revival farmhouse, it contains a superb collection of Impressionist art. Paintings of haystacks by Monet hang at each end of the drawing room, and Manet's *The Guitar Player* hangs in the middle. ⊠ *35 Mountain Rd.,* ☎ *860/677–4787.* ⚏ *$6.* ☉ *May–Oct., Tues.–Sun. 10–5; Nov.–Apr., Tues.–Sun. 11–4.*

A museum since the 1930s, the **Stanley-Whitman House** was built in 1720 and has a massive central chimney, an overhanging second story, and superlative 18th-century furnishings. ⊠ *37 High St.,* ☎ *860/677–9222.* ⚏ *$5.* ☉ *Nov.–Apr., Sun. noon–4 and by appointment; May–Oct., Wed.–Sun. noon–4.*

Dining and Lodging

$$$–$$$$ ✕ **Ann Howard's Apricots.** A white Colonial with dozens of windows looking out over gardens and the Farmington River holds the area's best eatery. Fine new American cuisine—like the grilled filet mignon with crispy fried Bermuda onions and a shiitake *demi-glace* (a rich brown sauce) or the duck with cashew wild rice—is presented in the quiet, cozy formal dining room; less expensive fare is available in the convivial pub. ⊠ *1593 Farmington Ave.,* ☎ *860/673–5903. AE, DC, MC, V.*

$$–$$$ 🏨 **Farmington Inn.** This modern alternative to the Barney House (☞ *below*) has an ill-chosen white-painted brick exterior, but the rooms are generous in size and appointed tastefully with antiques and reproductions. Much nicer than a chain hotel, it's very close to Miss Porter's and area museums. ⊠ *827 Farmington Ave., 06032,* ☎ *860/677–2821 or 800/648–9804,* 𝖥𝖠𝖷 *860/677–8332. 59 rooms, 13 suites. Business services, meeting rooms. Continental breakfast. AE, D, DC, MC, V.*

$$ 🏨 **Barney House.** This 1832 mansion on a quiet street is set amid 4½ acres of formal gardens. Owned and operated by the University of Connecticut Foundation as a conference center, Barney House accepts overnight guests by reservation. Many antiques furnish the large rooms, all of which have ornately papered walls, lead-glass bookcases, fetching bed quilts, and substantial bathrooms with modern plumbing. Smoking is not allowed. ⊠ *11 Mountain Spring Rd., 06032,* ☎ *860/674–2796,* 𝖥𝖠𝖷 *860/677–7259. 7 rooms. Tennis court, Continental breakfast. AE, MC, V.*

Shopping

The upscale 140-shop **Westfarms Mall** (⊠ I–84, Exit 40, ☎ 860/561–3024) includes Nordstrom, April Cornell, Williams-Sonoma, and Restoration Hardware.

Simsbury

③② *12 mi north of Farmington via Rte. 10.*

With its Colonial-style shopping centers, smattering of antiques shops, and proliferation of insurance-industry executives, Simsbury closely resembles the chic bedroom communities of Fairfield County (☞ Southwestern Connecticut, *above*).

At the Simsbury Historical Society's **Massacoh Plantation** you'll learn about the 300-year, largely agrarian history of Simsbury, which was settled in 1640 and incorporated in 1670. On the property are a Victorian carriage house (circa 1880), a 1795 cottage and herb garden, a

1740 schoolhouse, and the highlight, the period-furnished 1771 Colonial home of sea captain Elijah Phelps. You can view the houses only on a tour, but the highly strollable grounds are accessible all the time. ✉ *800 Hopmeadow St.,* ☎ *860/658–2500.* 🎫 *$6.* ☉ *Tours May–Oct., daily 1–4 (last tour at 2:30).*

A 1½-mi climb from the parking lot at the southern section of **Talcott Mountain State Park** to the 165-ft Heublein Tower, a former private home, rewards you with views of four states. ✉ *Rte. 185,* ☎ *860/242–1158.* 🎫 *Free.* ☉ *Park daily 8 AM–sunset. Tower late Apr.–Labor Day, Thurs.–Sun. 10–5; Labor Day–late Oct., daily 10–5.*

The **Old New-Gate Prison and Copper Mine,** 7 mi north of Simsbury, was the country's first chartered copper mine (in 1707) and later (in 1773) Connecticut's first Colonial prison. Tours of the underground mine (where temperatures rarely top 55°) are a great way to chill out in summer. There are hiking trails and a picnic area. ✉ *Newgate Rd., East Granby,* ☎ *860/653–3563 or 860/566–3005.* 🎫 *$3.* ☉ *Mid-May–Oct., Wed.–Sun. 10–4:30.*

Lodging

$$$-$$$$ 🏨 **Simsbury 1820 House.** The rooms at this inn perched on a hillside contain a judicious mix of antiques and modern furnishings. Each of the rooms and suites in the main house has a special feature—a decorative fireplace or balcony, a patio, a wet bar, a dormer with a cozy window seat. Under the porte cochere and across the parking lot is a former carriage house with 10 rooms; the split-level Executive Suite here has a private patio, entrance, and hot tub. ✉ *731 Hopmeadow St., 06070,* ☎ *860/658–7658 or 800/879–1820,* 📠 *860/651–0724. 29 rooms, 3 suites. Continental breakfast. AE, D, DC, MC, V.*

$$-$$$ 🏨 **Avon Old Farms Hotel.** This 20-acre compound of redbrick Colonial-style buildings is set into the Avon countryside at the foot of Talcott Mountain, about midway between Farmington and Simsbury. An immense place that caters largely to business travelers, it has quietly elegant rooms. ✉ *Rte. 10 and U.S. 44, Avon 06001,* ☎ *860/677–1651,* 📠 *860/677–0364. 160 rooms. Restaurant, pub, pool, meeting rooms. AE, D, DC, MC, V.*

Shopping

Arts Exclusive Gallery (✉ 690 Hopmeadow St., ☎ 860/651–5824) represents 35 contemporary artists. The **Farmington Valley Arts Center** (✉ 25 Arts Center La., Avon, ☎ 860/678–1867) shows the works of nationally known artists.

Windsor Locks

③③ *13 mi northeast of Simsbury, 94 mi northeast of Greenwich, 48 mi northeast of New Haven, 56 mi northwest of New London.*

Windsor Locks was named for the locks of a canal built to bypass falls in the Connecticut River in 1833; in 1844 the canal closed to make way for a railroad line. You'll see long, low tobacco barns in the area. The town has the largest airport near Hartford.

★ The more than 70 aircraft at the **New England Air Museum** include flying machines that date from 1870. A World War II–era P-47 Thunderbolt and B-29 Superfortress are on display, along with other vintage fighters and bombers. *Next to Bradley International Airport, off Rte. 75,* ☎ *860/623–3305.* 🎫 *$6.50.* ☉ *Daily 10–5.*

The **Hatheway House,** 7 mi north of Windsor Locks, is one of the finest architectural specimens in New England. The walls of its neoclassical north wing (1794) still wear their original 18th-century French hand-blocked wallpaper. The double-front doors and gambrel roof of the main house (1761) were typical accoutrements of Connecticut River valley homes. An ornate picket fence fronts the property. ⊠ *55 S. Main St. (take Rte. 75 north from Windsor Locks), Suffield,* ☎ *860/668–0055 or 860/247–8996.* 🎦 *$4.* 🕓 *Mid-May–June and Sept.–mid-Oct., Wed. and weekends 1–4; July–Aug., Wed.–Sun. 1–4.*

Hartford and the Connecticut River Valley A to Z

Arriving and Departing

BY BUS AND TRAIN

Hartford's renovated **Union Station** (⊠ 1 Union Pl.) is the main terminus for Amtrak (☎ 800/872–7245) trains and Greyhound (☎ 800/231–2222 or 800/237–8747) and Peter Pan Bus Lines (☎ 800/231–2222 or 800/237–8747) buses. Bus and train service are available to most major northeastern cities.

BY CAR

Interstates 84 and 91, Route 2, Route 202, and U.S. 44 intersect in Hartford. The junction of I–84 and I–91 in downtown Hartford is notorious for near-gridlock conditions during rush hour.

BY PLANE

Bradley International Airport (⊠ Rte. 20, Windsor Locks; take Exit 40 off I–91, ☎ 860/627–3000), 12 mi north of Hartford, is served by American, Continental, Delta, Midway, Northwest, TWA, United, and US Airways. *See* Air Travel *in* Smart Travel Tips A to Z for airline phone numbers.

Getting Around

BY BUS

Connecticut Transit (☎ 860/525–9181) provides bus service throughout the greater Hartford area. The fare varies according to destination.

BY CAR

The major road through the valley is Route 9, which extends from south of Hartford at I–91 to I–95 at Old Saybrook. Essex, Ivoryton, Chester, Higganum, Middletown, and New Britain are all on or near Route 9; Wethersfield is east of Route 9 on Route 175. From just below Deep River to just above Higganum, Route 154 loops east of Route 9; head east from Route 154 on Route 151 to reach East Haddam. Farmington is west of Hartford on Route 4. To reach Simsbury head west from Hartford on U.S. 202/44 and north on U.S. 202. To reach Windsor Locks, take I–91 north from Hartford and head north on Route 159.

Contacts and Resources

EMERGENCIES

Hartford Hospital (⊠ 80 Seymour St., ☎ 860/545–5000). **Middlesex Hospital** (⊠ 28 Crescent St., Middletown, ☎ 860/344–6000).

LATE-NIGHT PHARMACIES

CVS (⊠ 1099 New Britain Ave., West Hartford, ☎ 860/236–6181). **Community Pharmacy** (⊠ 197 Main St., Deep River, ☎ 860/526–5379).

VISITOR INFORMATION

Connecticut River Valley and Shoreline Visitors Council (⊠ 393 Main St., Middletown 06457, ☎ 860/347–0028 or 800/486–3346). **Greater Hartford Tourism District** (⊠ 234 Murphy Rd., Hartford 06114, ☎ 860/244–8181 or 800/793–4480). **Central Connecticut Tourism District** (⊠ 1 Grove St., Suite 310, New Britain 06053, ☎ 860/225–3901). **Connecticut's North Central Tourism Bureau** (⊠ 111 Hazard Ave., Enfield 06082, ☎ 860/763-2578 or 800/248–8283).

THE LITCHFIELD HILLS

Two scenic highways, I–84 and Route 8, form the southern and eastern boundaries of the Litchfield Hills region. New York, to the west, and Massachusetts, to the north, complete the rectangle. Here in the foothills of the Berkshires is some of the most spectacular and unspoiled scenery in Connecticut. Grand old inns are plentiful, as are sophisticated eateries. Rolling farmlands abut thick forests, and trails—including a section of the Appalachian Trail—traverse the state parks and forests. Two rivers, the Housatonic and the Farmington, attract anglers and canoeing enthusiasts, and the state's three largest natural lakes, Waramaug, Bantam, and Twin, are here. Sweeping town greens and stately homes anchor Litchfield, New Milford, and Sharon. Kent, New Preston, and Woodbury draw avid antiquers, and Washington, Salisbury, and Norfolk provide a glimpse into New England village life as it might have existed two centuries ago.

Favorite roads for admiring fall foliage are U.S. 7, from New Milford through Kent and West Cornwall to Canaan; Routes 41 to 4 from Salisbury through Lakeville, Sharon, Cornwall Bridge, and Goshen to Torrington; and Route 47 to U.S. 202 to Route 341 from Woodbury through Washington, New Preston, and Warren to Kent.

New Milford

㉞ *28 mi west of Waterbury.*

If you're approaching the Litchfield Hills from the south, New Milford is a practical starting point to begin a visit. It was also a starting point for a young cobbler named Roger Sherman, who, in 1743, opened his shop where Main and Church streets meet. A Declaration of Independence signatory, Sherman also helped draft the Articles of Confederation and the Constitution.

Up to its junction with Route 67, the combined U.S. 7/202 is a dull stretch of shopping centers. But where the road crosses the Housatonic River, you'll find old shops, galleries, and eateries all within a short stroll of New Milford green—one of the longest in New England.

OFF THE
BEATEN PATH   **THE SILO –** New Yorkers who miss Zabar's and Balducci's feel right at home in this silo and barn packed with objets de cookery, crafts, and an array of goodies and sauces. The founder and music director of the New York Pops, Skitch Henderson, and his wife, Ruth, own and operate this bazaar, where culinary superstars give a variety of cooking classes between March and December. ✉ *44 Upland Rd., 4 mi north of the New Milford town green on U.S. 202,* ☎ *860/355–0300.* ☉ *Apr.–Dec., daily 10–5; Jan.–Mar., Tues.–Sun. 10–5.*

Dining and Lodging

$$–$$$ ✗ **Bistro Café.** Copper pots and vintage black-and-white photos adorn the walls of this café in a redbrick corner building. The well-crafted regional American dishes change monthly—tender grilled swordfish with whipped potatoes, veggies, and a chive aioli one month, oven-roasted duck with pecans and cranberry coulis the next. You can sample buffalo, moose, antelope, kangaroo, alligator, or northern black bear—they're all farm-raised and low in cholesterol. Upstairs is a taproom where you can relax with a bottle of wine or feast from the same menu as downstairs. ✉ *31 Bank St.,* ☎ *860/355–3266. AE, MC, V.*

$$ 🏨 **Homestead Inn.** The Homestead, high on a hill overlooking New Milford's town green, was built in 1853 and opened as an inn in 1928. Life is casual here, and the owners, Rolf and Peggy Hammer, are al-

ways game for a leisurely chat. Breakfast is served in a cheery living room, where you can sit by the fire. The eight rooms in the main house have more personality than those in the motel-style structure next door. ⊠ *5 Elm St., 06776,* ☎ *860/354–4080,* FAX *860/354–7046. 14 rooms. Continental breakfast. AE, D, DC, MC, V.*

New Preston

③⑤ *4 mi north of New Milford.*

The crossroads village of New Preston, perched above a 40-ft waterfall on the Aspetuck River, has a little town center that's packed with antiques shops specializing in everything from 18th-century furnishings to out-of-print books.

Lake Waramaug, north of New Preston on Route 45, is an area that reminds many of Austria and Switzerland. If you drive the 8-mi perimeter of the lake, named for Chief Waramaug, one of the most revered figures in Connecticut's Native American history, you'll see beautiful inns—many of which serve delicious food—and homes. **Lake Waramaug State Park** (⊠ 30 Lake Waramaug Rd., ☎ 860/868–0220 or 860/868–2592), at the northwest tip of the lake, is an idyllic 75-acre spread, great for picnicking and lakeside camping.

The popular **Hopkins Vineyard,** overlooking Lake Waramaug, produces more than 13 varieties of wine, from sparkling to dessert. A weathered red barn houses a gift shop and a tasting room, and there's a picnic area. The wine bar serves a fine cheese-and-pâté board. ⊠ *Hopkins Rd.,* ☎ *860/868–7954.* 🖼 *Free.* ☉ *Jan.–Feb., Fri.–Sat. 10–5, Sun. 11–5; Mar.–Apr., Thurs.–Sat. 10–5, Sun. 11–5; May–Dec., Mon.–Sat. 10–5, Sun. 11–5.*

Dining and Lodging

$ ★ ✕ **Black Bear Coffee Roasters.** Bright and airy, with plank flooring and iron café tables, Black Bear sells delicious coffee roasted on the premises and creative soups, salads, sandwiches, and wraps, like the Black Forest—smoked ham, spinach, sprouts, and Brie wrapped in a soft garlic tortilla. Scones and crumb cakes are don't-miss desserts. ⊠ *239 New Milford Turnpike/U.S. 202, Marble Dale (1 mi west of New Preston),* ☎ *860/868–1446. MC, V. Closed Tues. No dinner.*

$$$$ ★ ✕🖼 **Boulders Inn.** The most idyllic and prestigious of the inns along Lake Waramaug opened in 1940 but still looks like the private home it was a century ago. Apart from the main house, a carriage house and several guest houses command panoramic views of the countryside and the lake. The rooms, four with double whirlpool baths, contain Victorian antiques and wood-burning fireplaces. The exquisite menu at the window-lined, stone-wall dining room ($$$) changes seasonally but might include sesame-crusted sushi tuna or chipotle-marinated venison. ⊠ *E. Shore Rd./Rte. 45, 06777,* ☎ *860/868–0541 or 800/552–6853,* FAX *860/868–1925. 15 rooms, 2 suites. Restaurant, lake, tennis court, boating. MAP. AE, MC, V.*

$$$–$$$$ ★ ✕🖼 **Birches Inn.** One of the area's poshest inns, the Birches is something of a Lake Waramaug institution. Antiques and reproductions decorate the rooms; three on the waterfront have private decks. Executive chef Frederic Faveau presides over the lakeview dining room ($$$; closed Tuesday and Wednesday; no lunch). Among his signature dishes are grilled marinated leg of lamb with Parmesan polenta, sautéed mustard greens, and a roasted garlic sauce. ⊠ *233 West Shore Rd., 06777,* ☎ *860/868–1735,* FAX *860/868–1815. 8 rooms. Restaurant. Full breakfast. AE, MC, V.*

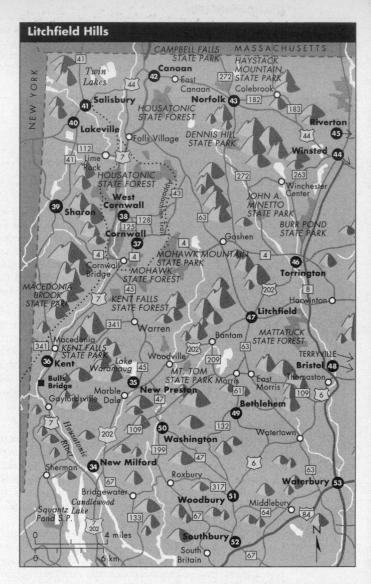

Litchfield Hills

$–$$
★ ✕🏠 **Hopkins Inn.** A grand 1847 Victorian that sits on a hill overlooking Lake Waramaug, the Hopkins is one of the best bargains in the Hills. Most rooms have plain white bedspreads, simple antiques, and pastel floral wallpaper. In winter, the inn smells of burning firewood; year-round, it is redolent with the aromas from the rambling dining rooms ($$$; closed January through late March), which serve outstanding Swiss and Austrian dishes—calves' brains in black butter, sweetbreads Viennese. When the weather is kind, you can dine on the terrace and view the lake. ✉ *22 Hopkins Rd. (1 mi off Rte. 45), 06777,* ☎ *860/868–7295,* FAX *860/868–7464. 8 rooms with bath, 2 rooms share bath, 1 room with hall bath, 2 apartments. Restaurant. Full breakfast. AE, MC, V.*

Shopping

More than a dozen shops with art, antiques, and related items can be found within walking distance of downtown New Preston. **Ray Boas, Bookseller** (✉ 6 Church St., ☎ 860/868–9596) stocks thousands of antiquarian and out-of-print books. The **Trumpeteer** (✉ 5 Main St.,

☎ 860/868–9090) specializes in English antiques and eccentricities with a masculine touch.

Kent

 12 mi northwest of New Preston; reached from New Milford on U.S. 7 or from New Preston on Rte. 341.

Kent has the area's greatest concentration of art galleries, some nationally renowned. Home to a prep school of the same name, Kent once held many ironworks. The Schaghticoke Indian Reservation is also here. During the Revolutionary War, 100 Schaghticokes helped defend the Colonies: They transmitted messages of army intelligence from the Litchfield Hills to Long Island Sound, along the hilltops, by way of shouts and drum beats. **Bulls Bridge** (⊠ U.S. 7, south of Kent), one of three covered bridges in Connecticut, is open to cars.

Hardware-store buffs and vintage-tool aficionados will feel at home at the **Sloane-Stanley Museum.** Artist and author Eric Sloane (1905–1985) was fascinated by Early American woodworking tools, and his collection (on display) ranges from the 17th to the 19th century. The museum, a re-creation of Sloane's last studio, also encompasses the ruins of a 19th-century iron furnace. Sloane's books and prints, which celebrate vanishing aspects of American heritage such as barns and covered bridges, are on sale here. ⊠ U.S. 7, ☎ 860/927–3849 or 860/566–3005. ☑ $3. ☉ Mid-May–Oct., Wed.–Sun. 10–4.

Outdoor Activities and Sports

The **Appalachian Trail's** longest riverwalk, off Route 341, is the almost 8-mi hike from Kent to Cornwall Bridge along the Housatonic River. The early-season trout fishing is superb at 2,300-acre **Macedonia Brook State Park** (⊠ Macedonia Brook Rd. off Rte. 341, ☎ 860/927–3238), where you can also hike and cross-country ski.

Shopping

The **Bachelier-Cardonsky Gallery** (⊠ Main St., ☎ 860/927–3129), one of the foremost galleries in the Northeast, exhibits contemporary works. The **Paris–New York–Kent Gallery** (⊠ Kent Station, off U.S. 7, ☎ 860/927–4152) shows contemporary works by local and world-famous artists. **Pauline's Place** (⊠ 79 N. Main St., ☎ 860/927–4475) specializes in Victorian, Georgian, Art Deco, Edwardian, and contemporary jewelry.

En Route Heading north from Kent toward Cornwall, you'll pass the entrance to 295-acre **Kent Falls State Park** (⊠ Rte. 7, ☎ 860/927–3238), where you can hike a short way to one of the most impressive waterfalls in the state and picnic in the lush hemlock grove above the falls. Admission is free.

Cornwall

 12 mi north of Kent.

Among the virgin pines and thick forest in Cornwall, fleeting pockets of civilization came and went throughout the 18th and 19th centuries. Starvation and cold took the lives of most who settled here in the eerily named communities of Mast Swamp, Wildcat, Great Hollow, and Ballyhack. Today small farms and old houses are nestled in the steep, rocky mountains, separated by dark woods.

Mohawk Mountain State Park (⊠ 1 mi south of Cornwall off Rte. 4, ☎ 860/927–3238) is a great spot for a picnic. The view at the top of 1,683-ft Mohawk Mountain is breathtaking, especially during foliage season; the hike up is 2½ mi.

Skiing and Snow Sports

MOHAWK MOUNTAIN

Mohawk's 23 trails, ranging down 640 vertical ft, include plenty of intermediate terrain, with a few trails for beginners and a few steeper sections toward the top of the mountain. A small section is devoted to snowboarders. Trails are serviced by one triple lift and four doubles and are lit for night skiing except on Sunday. The base lodge has munchies and a retail shop, and the Pine Lodge, halfway up the slope, has an outdoor patio. Mohawk's SKIwee program is for kids from age 5 to 12. There are facilities for ice-skating. ⊠ *46 Great Hollow Rd., off Rte. 4, 06753,* ☎ *860/672–6100; 860/672–6464 for conditions.*

West Cornwall

③⑧ *3 mi northwest of Cornwall.*

Connecticut's most romantic covered bridge, the wooden, barn-red, one-lane **Cornwall Bridge,** is not in the town of the same name but several miles up U.S. 7 on Route 128 in West Cornwall. The Cornwall Bridge was built in 1841 and has since carried travelers into West Cornwall, now the site of a few notable crafts shops and restaurants. The bridge, which won national recognition for its superb restoration, incorporates strut techniques that were copied by bridge builders around the country.

Lodging

$ ⚠ **Housatonic Meadows State Park.** Tall pine trees near the Housatonic River shade the campsites here. Fly-fishers consider this 2-mi stretch of the river among the best places in New England to test their skills against trout and bass. ⊠ *U.S. 7, Cornwall Bridge,* ☎ *860/672–6772 or 860/927–3238.* ⊡ *$10. 102 sites. Flush toilets, water (hand pump). No credit cards. Campground closed Jan.–mid-Apr.*

Outdoor Activities and Sports

Clarke Outdoors (⊠ U.S. 7, ☎ 860/672–6365) rents canoes and kayaks and operates 10-mi trips from Falls Village to Housatonic Meadows State Park. **Housatonic Anglers** (⊠ U.S. 7, ☎ 860/672–4457), which operates half- and full-day tours, provides fly-fishing instruction for trout and bass on the Housatonic and its tributaries. **Housatonic River Outfitters** (⊠ Rte. 128, ☎ 860/672–1010) operates a full-service fly shop and gives guided trips of the region; offers classes in fly fishing, fly tying, and casting; and sells vintage and antique gear.

Shopping

Cornwall Bridge Pottery Store (⊠ Rte. 128, ☎ 860/672–6545) sells its own pottery, glass by Simon Pearce, and Shaker-style furniture. **Ian Ingersoll Cabinetmakers** (⊠ Main St. by the Cornwall Bridge, ☎ 860/ 672–6334) stocks reproduction Shaker-style furniture.

Sharon

③⑨ *10 mi west of Cornwall, 24 mi northwest of Litchfield.*

The well-preserved Colonial town of Sharon was a manufacturing center during Colonial times. Munitions, oxbows, wooden mousetraps—all sorts of things were made here. An attempt in later years to introduce the silkworm failed because of New England's unwelcoming climate, but the mulberry trees that were planted as part of the experiment still line Main Street. Perhaps the strangest sight in town is the elaborate **Hotchkiss Clock Tower,** which looms above the intersection of Routes 4 and 41. It was built in 1885 of native gray granite as a memorial to town son Benjamin Berkeley Hotchkiss, the inventor of the Hotchkiss explosive shell.

With many trails and nature walks, the **Sharon Audubon Center,** a 758-acre sanctuary with a wide variety of birds, is one of the best places to hike in Connecticut. On-site are an exhibit center, a gift shop, and a library. ⊠ *325 Cornwall Bridge Rd.,* ☎ *860/364-0520.* ⌘ *$3.* ⊙ *Mon.–Sat. 9–5, Sun. 1–5; trails dawn–dusk.*

Lakeville

 9 mi north of Sharon.

You can usually spot an original Colonial home in handsome Lakeville by looking for the grapevine design cut into the frieze above the front door. It's the apparent trademark of the builder of the town's first homes. The lake of Lakeville is **Lake Wononscopomuc.** As you drive along U.S. 44 or Rte. 41, you'll glimpse the lake–the closest you're likely to get because most of its shoreline is private property.

The holdings of the **Holley House Museum,** which chronicle 18th- and 19th-century life, include a 1768 ironmaster's home with an 1808 Classical Revival wing that contains family furnishings, Colonial portraits, and a Holley Manufacturing Co. pocketknife exhibit. "From Corsets to Freedom" is a popular hands-on exhibit, set in the 1870s, demonstrating the debate between women's rights versus "women's sphere" in the home. Tours are conducted. Admission also includes the on-site **Salisbury Cannon Museum,** where hands-on exhibits and activities survey the contributions of area residents and the local iron industry to the American Revolution. ⊠ *15 Millerton Rd.,* ☎ *860/435-2878.* ⌘ *$3.* ⊙ *Mid-June–mid-Oct., weekends noon–5 and by appointment.*

From mid-June to mid-September, **Music Mountain** (⊠ Falls Village, ☎ 860/824–7126) presents chamber music concerts on Sunday afternoon and jazz concerts on Saturday night.

Outdoor Activities and Sports

Auto racing at renowned **Lime Rock Park** (⊠ Rte. 112, ☎ 860/435–5000 or 800/722–3577) takes place on occasional Saturday and holiday Mondays from late April to mid-October; amphitheater-style lawn seating allows for great views all around. **Rustling Wind Stables** (⊠ Mountain Rd., Falls Village, ☎ 860/824–7634) gives lessons, takes riders along the beautiful trails of Canaan Mountain, and operates pony rides for the kids by appointment.

Salisbury

 6 mi north of Lakeville.

Salisbury, were it not for the obsolescence of its ironworks, might today be the largest city in Connecticut. Instead, it settles for having both the state's highest mountain, Bear Mountain (2,355 ft), and its highest point, the shoulder of Mt. Frissel (2,380 ft)—whose peak is in Massachusetts. There's a spot on Mt. Frissel where if the urge strikes you (as it does many) you can stretch your limbs across the Connecticut, Massachusetts, and New York borders. Not yet yuppified, Salisbury is New England the way it used to be, with beautiful old houses waiting to be restored.

Iron was discovered here in 1732, and for the next century, the slopes of Salisbury's Mt. Riga produced the finest iron in America. Swiss and Russian immigrants, and later Hessian deserters from the British army, worked the great furnaces. These people inbred and lived in tiny hillside cabins in these parts until well into the 20th century, long after the last forge cast a glow in 1847. "Raggies," as they were known, are cloaked in a legend of black magic and suspicion and are believed to be responsible for various mishaps and ghostly sightings. As for the ironworks, the spread of rail transport opened up better and more accessible sources of ore, the region's lumber supply was depleted, and the introduction of the Bessemer process of steel manufacturing—partially invented by Salisbury native Alexander Holley—reduced the demand for iron products. Most signs of cinder heaps and slag dumps are long gone, replaced by grand summer homes and gardens.

Harney & Sons Fine Teas supplies its high-quality Darjeeling, Earl Grey, Keemun, and other blends to some of the world's best hotels and restaurants. At the tasting room you can sample some of the 100 varieties, and there's a gift shop. If you call ahead you might even be able to schedule a tour, led by founder John Harney himself, of the factory where the tea is blended and packaged. ⊠ *11 Brook St., ☎ 860/435–5050. ⌸ Free. ☉ Mon.–Sat. 10–5.*

Dining and Lodging

$$$$ ✕⊞ **Under Mountain Inn.** The nearest neighbors of this white-clapboard farmhouse are the horses grazing in the field across the road. Antiques, knickknacks, and objets d'art fill every space; chess and checkers games are set up by the fireplace. The hospitality has a pronounced British flavor (there's a British video lounge and "The Pub"—a replica of an English taproom); dinner, too, recalls Britain with dishes such as hearty steak-and-kidney pie. You can work off some of those calories with a hike on the nearby Appalachian Trail. The restaurant ($$–$$$; reservations essential) is open to the public on Friday and Saturday. ⊠ *482 Under Mountain Rd./Rte. 41, 06068, ☎ 860/435–0242, ℻ 860/435–2379. 7 rooms. Restaurant, pub, hiking. MAP. MC, V.*

$$–$$$$ ✕⊞ **White Hart Inn.** With its white paint and broad front porch, the
★ White Hart, which has welcomed travelers since the 1860s, stands out on Salisbury's village green. The rooms and suites have excellent Colonial-reproduction furniture, good reading lamps, and modern bathrooms. A few steps away in the 1815 Gideon Smith House, similar rooms and suites are available on two levels. Dining in any of the White Hart's three restaurants—the bright and sunny Garden Room, the tavernlike Tap Room, or the elegant American Grill—is a pleasure. Duck is served with apricots, black cherries, and mango chutney. ⊠ *The Village Green, 06068, ☎ 860/435–0030, ℻ 860/435–0040. 23 rooms, 3 suites. 3 restaurants, meeting rooms. AE, DC, MC, V.*

Shopping

The **Salisbury Antiques Center** (⊠ 46 Library St., off U.S. 44, ☎ 860/435–0424) carries a varied selection of American and English pieces. The **Village Store** (⊠ Main St./U.S. 44, ☎ 860/435–9459) stocks high-quality sportswear, bikes, cross-country skis, hiking boots, and maps; you can rent cross-country skis, snowshoes, and bikes here.

Canaan

㊷ *10 mi northeast of Salisbury, 84 mi northeast of Stamford, 42 mi northwest of Hartford.*

Canaan is one of the more developed towns in the Litchfield region: It has a McDonald's. Canaan was the site of some important late-18th-century industry, including a gun-barrel factory and a paper mill, and was also the home of Captain Gershom Hewitt, who is credited with securing the plans of Fort Ticonderoga for Ethan Allen.

Canaan Union Station (⊠ Main St., junction U.S. 44 and U.S. 7) was built in 1871 as a train station and now houses a pub-style restaurant and a few shops.

Dining and Lodging

$$$ ✕ **Cannery Café.** The eggshell-color walls of this storefront American
★ bistro are painted with a pattern of gleaming gold stars; elegant brass
fixtures reflect the muted lighting. All is crisp and clean, the service
chatty but refined. Pistachio-crusted salmon and grilled lamb headline
the menu. Sunday brunch is a favorite with locals. ⊠ *85 Main St. (U.S.
44 and 7),* ☎ *860/824–7333. AE, MC, V. No lunch.*

$ ✕ **Collin's Diner.** There's no denying that this 1942 O'Mahony diner,
★ inspired by the jazzy railroad dining cars of the '20s and '30s, is a clas-
sic beauty. Although locals count on Collin's for traditional diner fare,
the specials are the biggest draw—on Friday there's baked stuffed
shrimp, on Saturday a meaty 2-inch cut of prime rib. ⊠ *U.S. 44,* ☎
860/824–7040. No credit cards. ☉ *Thurs.–Tues. 5:30–5, Wed. 5:30–
1. Call for extended summer hrs.*

$ ⚠ **Lone Oak Campsites.** This family campground has two pools, a hot
tub, a store-deli, and a lounge with a full bar. Throughout July and
August, and on weekends for the rest of the summer, the place hops
with live entertainment and planned activities. ⊠ *Rte. 44, East Canaan
06024,* ☎ *860/824–7051. 500 sites, 1 cabin, 6 trailers. Coin laundry,
electric and sewer hook-ups, fire rings, flush toilets, showers, water.
Closed mid-Oct.–mid-Apr. 2-night minimum stay for trailers and
cabin; 3-night minimum stay on holidays.*

Shopping

The **Connecticut Woodcarvers Gallery** (⊠ U.S. 44, East Canaan, ☎ 860/
824–0883) sells the work of woodcarver Joseph Cieslowski, whose
unique relief carvings embellish clocks, mirrors, and decorative pan-
els. Carved pieces by other artists are also for sale.

Norfolk

㊸ *7 mi east of Canaan, 59 mi north of New Haven.*

Norfolk, thanks to its severe climate and terrain, is one of the best-
preserved villages in the Northeast. Notable industrialists have been
summering here for two centuries, and many enormous homesteads
still exist. The striking town green is at the junction of Route 272 and
U.S. 44. At its southern corner is a fountain—designed by Augustus
Saint-Gaudens and executed by Stanford White—a memorial to Joseph
Battell, who turned Norfolk into a major trading center.

You can purchase most of what you see at **Hillside Gardens,** one of the
foremost nurseries and perennial gardens in the Northeast. The 5 acres
of gardens, surrounded by stone walls, glow from May to September
with daffodils, lilies, foxgloves, chrysanthemums, and ornamental
grasses. ⊠ *515 Litchfield Rd./Rte. 272, 2½ mi south of town green,*
☎ *860/542–5345.* ⊠ *Free.* ☉ *May–mid-Sept., daily 9–5.*

Dr. Frederick Shepard Dennis lavishly entertained guests, among them
President Howard Taft and several Connecticut governors, in the stone
pavilion at the summit of what is now **Dennis Hill State Park.** From its
1,627-ft height, you can see Haystack Mountain, New Hampshire, and,
on a clear day, New Haven harbor, all the way across the state. You
can picnic on the park's 240-acre grounds, which are adjacent to Hill-
side Gardens (☞ *above*), or hike. ⊠ *Rte. 272,* ☎ *860/482–1817.* ⊠
Free. ☉ *Daily 8 AM–dusk.*

Dining and Lodging

$$–$$$ ✕ **The Pub.** Bottles of trendy beers line the shelves of this down-to-earth
★ restaurant on the ground floor of a redbrick Victorian near the town
green. Burgers and other pub fare are on the menu alongside strip steak

and lamb curry. This place is a real melting pot. ⊠ *U.S. 44,* ☎ *860/ 542–5716. AE, MC, V. Closed Mon.*

$$$$
★
🛏 **Greenwoods Gate.** Every room in this romantic hideaway holds amenities from chocolates and cognac to soaps and fresh flowers; champagne or a deep massage is available with notice. Starched white linens cover the beds of the suites (the Levi Thompson, with three levels and a whirlpool for two, is the most requested). A spread of muffins and fruit is followed by a hot breakfast, and wine and cheese are available in the afternoon. The inn is no-smoking and has a two-night minimum on weekends. ⊠ *105 Greenwoods Rd. E/U.S. 44, 06058,* ☎ *860/ 542–5439,* 🖷 *860/542–5897. 4 suites. Full breakfast. No credit cards.*

$$$–$$$$
★
🛏 **Manor House.** Among this 1898 Bavarian Tudor's remarkable features are its bibelots, mirrors, carpets, antique beds, and prints—not to mention the 20 stained-glass windows designed by Louis Tiffany. The vast Spofford Room has windows on three sides, a king-size canopy bed with a cheery fireplace opposite, and a balcony. The Morgan Room has the most remarkable feature—a private wood-panel elevator (added in 1939). It also has a private deck. This inn is not suitable for young children. ⊠ *Box 447, Maple Ave., 06058,* ☎ 🖷 *860/542– 5690. 7 rooms, 1 suite. Full breakfast. AE, D, DC, MC, V.*

Nightlife and the Arts

The **Norfolk Chamber Music Festival** (☎ 860/542–3000), at the Music Shed on the Ellen Battell Stoeckel Estate at the northwest corner of the Norfolk green, presents world-renowned artists and ensembles on Friday and Saturday summer evenings and on Sunday afternoons. Students from the Yale School of Music perform on Thursday evening and Saturday morning. The festival also sponsors the Indian Summer series in October and November. Early arrivals can stroll or picnic on the 70-acre grounds or visit the art gallery.

Outdoor Activities and Sports

One of the most spectacular views in the state can be seen from **Haystack Mountain State Park** (⊠ Rte. 272, ☎ 860/482–1817), with a challenging trail to the top for the brave and a road halfway up for the rest of us. **Loon Meadow Farm** (⊠ Loon Meadow Dr., ☎ 860/542– 6085) operates horse-drawn sleigh, hay, and carriage rides.

Shopping

Norfolk Artisans Guild (⊠ Greenwoods Rd. E, ☎ 860/542–5487) carries works by more than 60 local artisans—from hand-painted pillows to hand-crafted baskets.

Winsted

44 *9 mi southeast of Norfolk, 28 mi north of Waterbury, 25 mi northwest of Hartford.*

With its rows of old homes and businesses seemingly untouched since the 1940s, Winsted still looks a bit like the set of a Frank Capra movie. Though it's far less fashionable than nearby Norfolk, the town, which was devastated by a major flood in 1955, is still worth a brief stop. You can drive around the hills and alongside the reservoirs, hoping to glimpse the notorious "Winsted Wild Man," who has been described during sightings that span several centuries as possessing everything from cloven feet to a hairy, 8-ft, 300-pound frame. Authorities explain away these stories as black bear sightings.

Most of the several hundred hanging and standing lamps at the **Kerosene Lamp Museum,** which occupies a former country store, date from 1852 to 1880. ⊠ *100 Old Waterbury Turnpike/Rte. 263, Winchester Center (4 mi west of Winsted),* ☎ *860/379–2612.* 🎟 *Free.* ☉ *Daily 9:30–4.*

Nightlife and the Arts

The **Gilson Café and Cinema** (✉ 354 Main St., ☎ 860/379–6069), a refurbished Art Deco movie house, serves food and drinks unobtrusively during movies, every evening except Monday. You must be 21 or older for shows on the weekend.

Outdoor Activities and Sports

Main Stream Canoe and Kayaks (✉ U.S. 44, New Hartford, ☎ 860/693–6791, ℻ 860/693–1649) rents and sells canoes and kayaks, conducts day trips on the Farmington River, and offers lessons. Moonlight trips take place on summer evenings. **North American Canoe Tours** (✉ Satan's Kingdom State Recreation Area, U.S. 44, New Hartford, ☎ 860/739–0791) rents tubes and flotation devices for exhilarating self-guided tours along the Farmington River. The company is open for business on weekends from Memorial Day to June and daily from June to Labor Day.

Shopping

Folkcraft Instruments (✉ Corner of High and Wheeler Sts., ☎ 860/379–9857) crafts harps and psalteries on the premises.

Skiing and Snow Sports

SKI SUNDOWN

This area has some neat touches—a sundeck on the top of the mountain and a Senior Spree social club for skiers 55 and older—as well as excellent facilities and equipment. The vertical drop is 625 ft. Of the 15 trails, 8 are for beginners, 4 for intermediates, and 3 for advanced skiers. All are lighted at night and serviced by three triple chairs and one double. Terrain features are set up on the mountain; lessons are available for ages 4 and up. ✉ *Ratlum Rd., New Hartford, 06057,* ☎ *860/379–9851; 860/379–7669 for conditions.*

Riverton

45 *6 mi north of Winsted.*

Almost every New Englander has sat in a Hitchcock chair. Riverton, formerly Hitchcockville, is where Lambert Hitchcock built the first one, in 1826. The Farmington and Still rivers meet in this tiny hamlet. It's in one of the more unspoiled regions in the Hills, great for hiking and driving.

The **Hitchcock Museum,** showcasing beautiful examples of 18th- and 19th-century furniture, is in the gray granite Union Church. The nearby Hitchcock Factory Store, which sells first-quality merchandise at outlet prices and also has a seconds department, is open year-round. ✉ *Rte. 20,* ☎ *860/379–4826.* 🎫 *Donation suggested.* ⊙ *By appointment only.*

Lodging

$$ 🏨 **Old Riverton Inn.** This historic inn, built in 1796 and overlooking the west branch of the Farmington River and the Hitchcock Chair Factory, is a peaceful weekend retreat. Rooms are small—except for the fireplace suite—and the decorating, which includes Hitchcock furnishings, is for the most part ordinary, but the inn always delivers warm hospitality. The inviting dining room serves traditional New England fare—the stuffed pork chops are local favorites. ✉ *Rte. 20, 06065,* ☎ *860/379–8678 or 800/378–1796,* ℻ *860/379–1006. 11 rooms, 1 suite. Restaurant. AE, D, DC, MC, V.*

Outdoor Activities and Sports

American Legion and People's State Forests (☎ 860/379–2469) border the west bank and the east bank, respectively, of the West Branch of the Farmington River—a designated National Wild and Scenic River. You can picnic beneath the 200-year-old pines along the riverbank, and the hiking, fishing, tubing, and canoeing here are superb.

Torrington

 14 mi south of Riverton.

Torrington was the birthplace of abolitionist John Brown. Also born here was Gail Borden, who developed the first successful method for the production of evaporated milk. Torrington's pines were for years used for shipbuilding, and its factories produced brass kettles, needles, pins, and bicycle spokes. This old town has a few hidden charms for those willing to overlook its rougher sections.

The **Hotchkiss-Fyler House,** a 16-room century-old Queen Anne structure with a slate and brick exterior, is one of the better house museums in Connecticut. The design high points include hand-stenciled walls and intricate mahogany woodwork and ornamental plaster. European porcelains, American and British glass, and paintings by Winfield S. Clime are on display. If you plan to arrive around noon on a weekday, call ahead; the house sometimes closes briefly at lunchtime. ⊠ *192 Main St.,* ☎ *860/482–8260.* ▨ *$2.* ☺ *Tours Apr.–Oct. and last 2 wks of Dec., Tues.–Fri. 10–4, weekends noon–4.*

Nightlife and the Arts

The **Warner Theatre** (⊠ 68 Main St., ☎ 860/489–7180), an Art Deco former movie palace, presents live Broadway musicals, ballet, and concerts by touring pop, classical, and country musicians.

Outdoor Activities and Sports

The lures at 436-acre **Burr Pond State Park** (⊠ Burr Mountain Rd./Rte. 8, ☎ 860/482–1817) are canoe rentals, a crystal-clear pond, hiking paths, and wheelchair-accessible picnic grounds.

Litchfield

 5 mi south of Torrington, 48 mi north of Bridgeport, 34 mi west of Hartford.

Everything in Litchfield, the wealthiest and most noteworthy town in the Litchfield Hills, seems to exist on a larger scale than in neighboring burgs, especially the impressive **Litchfield Green** and the white Colonials that line the broad elm-shaded streets. Harriet Beecher Stowe, author of *Uncle Tom's Cabin,* and Henry Ward Stowe were born and raised in Litchfield, and many famous Americans earned their law degrees at the Litchfield Law School. Today lovely but exceptionally expensive boutiques and hot-spot restaurants line the downtown, attracting celebrities and the town's monied citizens.

In 1773, Judge Tapping Reeve enrolled his first student, Aaron Burr, in what was to become the first law school in the country. (Before Judge Reeve, students studied the law as apprentices, not in formal classes.)

★ The **Tapping Reeve House and Litchfield Law School** is dedicated to Reeve's remarkable achievement and to the notable students who passed through its halls: Oliver Wolcott, Jr., John C. Calhoun, Horace Mann, 3 U.S. Supreme Court justices, and 15 governors, not to mention senators, congressmen, and ambassadors. Renovations in 1998 made the museum into one of the state's most worthy attractions, with interactive multimedia exhibits, an excellent introductory film, and beautifully restored facilities. ⊠ *82 South St.,* ☎ *860/567–4501.* ▨ *$3 (includes Litchfield Historical Society Museum;* ☞ *below).* ☺ *Tues.–Sat. 11–5, Sun. 1–5.*

The well-organized galleries at the **Litchfield Historical Society Museum** display decorative arts, paintings, and antique furnishings. The extensive reference library has information about the town's historic buildings, including the Sheldon Tavern (where George Washington slept on several occasions) and the Litchfield Female Academy, where in the late 1700s Sarah Pierce taught girls not just sewing and deportment but also mathematics and history. ⊠ *7 South St., at Rtes. 63 and 118, ☎ 860/ 567–4501.* ⊠ *$5 (includes Tapping Reeve House and Litchfield Law School; ☞ above).* ⊙ *Mid-Apr.–mid-Nov., Tues.–Sat. 11–5, Sun. 1–5.*

A stroll through the landscaped grounds of **White Flower Farm** is nearly always a pleasure, and gardeners will find many ideas here. The farm is the home base of a mail-order operation that sells perennials and bulbs to gardeners throughout the United States. ⊠ *Rte. 63 (3 mi south of Litchfield), ☎ 860/567–8789.* ⊠ *Free.* ⊙ *Nov.–Mar., daily 10–5; Apr.–Oct., daily 9–6.*

Haight Vineyard and Winery flourishes despite the area's severe climate. Stop in for vineyard walks, winery tours, and tastings. ⊠ *29 Chestnut Hill Rd./Rte. 118 (1 mi east of Litchfield), ☎ 860/567–4045.* ⊠ *Free.* ⊙ *Mon.–Sat. 10:30–5, Sun. noon–5.*

The **White Memorial Conservation Center** is Connecticut's largest nature center and wildlife sanctuary. The 4,000-acre sanctuary contains fishing areas, bird-watching platforms, two self-guided nature trails, several boardwalks, and 35 mi of hiking, cross-country skiing, and horseback-riding trails. The main conservation center houses natural-history exhibits and a gift shop. ⊠ *U.S. 202 (2 mi west of village green), ☎ 860/567–0857.* ⊠ *Grounds free; conservation center $4.* ⊙ *Grounds 24 hrs; conservation center Mon.–Sat. 9–5, Sun. noon–5.*

The chief attractions at **Topsmead State Forest** are a Tudor-style cottage built by architect Henry Dana, Jr., and a 40-acre wildflower preserve. The forest holds picnic grounds, hiking trails, and cross-country skiing areas. ⊠ *Buell Rd. off E. Litchfield Rd., ☎ 860/567–5694.* ⊠ *Free.* ⊙ *Forest daily 8 AM–dusk; house tours June–Oct., 2nd and 4th weekends of the month.*

Dining and Lodging

$$$–$$$$
★ ✕ **West Street Grill.** This sophisticated dining room on the town green is *the* place to see and be seen, both for patrons and for the state's up-and-coming chefs, many of whom have gotten their start here. Imaginative grilled fish, steak, poultry, and lamb dishes are served with fresh vegetables and pasta or risotto. Regulars favor JJ's scallops, served with an orange and brown butter sauce, wilted watercress, and a shredded-potato-and-shallot cake. The ice cream and sorbets, made by the restaurant, are worth every calorie. ⊠ *43 West St./U.S 202, ☎ 860/ 567–3885. AE, MC, V.*

$$–$$$ ✕ **Village Restaurant.** The folks who run this storefront eatery in a red-brick town house serve food as tasty as any in town—inexpensive pub grub in one room, updated New England cuisine in the other. Whether you order burgers or homemade ravioli, you'll get plenty to eat. ⊠ *25 West St., ☎ 860/567–8307. AE, MC, V.*

$$–$$$ ✕⊟ **Tollgate Hill Inn and Restaurant.** The Tollgate, formerly a stage-coach stop, retains a romantic tavern atmosphere. The seasonal menu, however, is contemporary: The walnut-crusted roast rack of lamb with apple-dried cherry chutney is one good choice. Vibrant Colonial prints and comfortable period furnishings decorate the guest rooms, which are in the main building, a nearby schoolhouse, and a modern building; many have working fireplaces. ⊠ *U.S. 202, 06759 (2½ mi east of Litchfield Center), ☎ 860/567–4545, ℻ 860/567–8397. 15 rooms, 5 suites. Restaurant. Continental breakfast. AE, D, DC, MC, V.*

Outdoor Activities and Sports

Lee's Riding Stables (⊠ 57 E. Litchfield Rd., ☎ 860/567–0785) conducts trail and pony rides. At **Mt. Tom State Park** (⊠ U.S. 202, ☎ 860/

868–2592), you can boat, hike, swim, and fish in summer and ice-skate in winter. The view from atop the mountain is outstanding.

Shopping

Black Swan Antiques (✉ 17 Litchfield Commons, U.S. 202, ☎ 860/ 567–4429) carries 17th- and 18th-century English and Continental country furniture. **Carretta Glass Studio** (✉ 513 Maple St., ☎ 860/567– 4851), open by appointment, sells remarkable glass sculptures and works that are made on the premises. The **P.S. Gallery** (✉ 41 West St., ☎ 860/567–1059) is an excellent fine-arts gallery. **Susan Wakeen Dolls** (✉ 425 Bantam Rd., ☎ 860/567–0007) creates stunning limited-edition and play dolls.

Bristol

48 *17 mi southeast of Litchfield.*

There were some 275 clock makers in and around Bristol during the late 1800s—it is said that by the end of the 19th century just about every household in America told time to a Connecticut clock. Eli Terry (for whom nearby Terryville is named) first mass-produced clocks in the mid-19th century. Seth Thomas (for whom nearby Thomaston is named) learned under Terry and carried on the tradition.

Lake Compounce, which opened in 1846, is the oldest amusement park in the country. The rides and attractions at the 325-acre facility include an antique carousel, a classic wooden roller coaster, and a whitewater raft ride. The park also has picnic areas, a beach, and a water playground with slides, spray fountains, and a wave pool. The Sky Coaster and Zoomerang offer hair-raising rides. ✉ *Rte. 229 N, I–84 Exit 31,* ☎ *860/583–3631.* ☑ *$19.95 rides and general admission; $4.95 general admission.* ⊙ *Memorial Day–late Sept., call for hrs.*

★ The **Carousel Museum of New England** displays carousel art, much of it full-size pieces, in the Coney Island, Country Fair, and Philadelphia styles. Miniature carousels are also on display, and volunteers occasionally demonstrate the craft at the antique carving shop. ✉ *95 Riverside Ave.,* ☎ *860/585–5411.* ☑ *$4.* ⊙ *Apr.–Nov., Mon.–Sat. 10–5, Sun. noon–5; Dec.–Mar., Thurs.–Sat. 10–5, Sun. noon–5.*

Lodging

$$–$$$ **Chimney Crest Manor.** All the rooms in this impressive circa-1930 Tudor mansion have spectacular views of the Farmington Valley. The 40-ft-long Garden Suite, in what was the mansion's ballroom, has gleaming hardwood floors, a fireplace, a queen-size canopy bed, its own kitchen, and tile walls with a dazzling sunflower motif. Breakfast, which might include yogurt pancakes, is served on fine china in the formal dining room or, more casually, on the grand fieldstone patio. Among the handsome public spaces are a library, sunroom, and salon. ✉ *5 Founders Dr., 06010,* ☎ *860/582–4219,* FAX *860/584–5903. 2 rooms, 4 suites. Full breakfast. MC, V.*

Bethlehem

49 *16 mi west of Bristol.*

Come Christmas, Bethlehem is the most popular town in Connecticut. Cynics say that towns such as Canaan, Goshen, and Bethlehem were named primarily with the hope of attracting prospective residents and not truly out of religious deference. In any case, the local post office has its hands full postmarking the 220,000 pieces of holiday greetings mailed from Bethlehem every December.

The **Bethlehem Christmas Town Festival** (☎ 203/266–5557), which takes place in early December, draws quite a crowd. Year-round, the **Christmas Shop** (✉ 18 East St., ☎ 203/266–7048) hawks the trimmings and trappings that help set the holiday mood.

The Benedictine nuns at the **Abbey of Regina Laudis,** who were made famous by their best-selling album *Women in Chant,* make and sell fine handcrafts, honey, cheese, herbs, beauty products, and more. An 18th-century Neapolitan crèche with 80 hand-painted Baroque porcelain figures is on view from March to December. ✉ *Flanders Rd.,* ☎ *203/266–7637.* ⊙ *Mon.–Tues. and Thurs.–Sun. 10–4.*

Washington

⑤⓪ *11 mi west of Bethlehem.*

The beautiful buildings of the Gunnery prep school mingle with stately Colonials and churches in Washington, one of the best-preserved Colonial towns in Connecticut. The Mayflower Inn, south of the Gunnery on Route 47, attracts an exclusive clientele. Washington, which was settled in 1734, became in 1779 the first town in the United States to be named for George Washington.

Dining and Lodging

$$$$ ★ ✕🏨 **Mayflower Inn.** Though the most expensive suites at this inn cost more than $700 a night, the Mayflower is always booked months in advance—and with good reason. Running streams, rambling stone walls, and rare specimen trees fill the inn's 28 impeccably groomed acres. Each of the rooms is an individual work of art with fine antiques, 18th- and 19th-century art, and four-poster canopy beds. The colossal baths have mahogany wainscoting, much marble, and handsome Belgian tapestries on the floors. At the restaurant ($$$–$$$$), chef Thomas Moran offers an ever-changing menu with entrées such as roast Muscovy duck breast on a barley, wheatberry, and vegetable risotto. ✉ *118 Woodbury Rd./Rte. 47, 06793,* ☎ *860/868–9466,* 🖷 *860/868–1497. 17 rooms, 8 suites. Restaurant, pool, tennis court, health club, meeting rooms. AE, MC, V.*

En Route The **Institute for American Indian Studies,** between Roxbury and Washington, is an excellent and thoughtfully arranged collection of exhibits and displays that details the history of Northeastern Woodland Native Americans. Highlights include a replicated longhouse and nature trails. The Institute is at the end of a forested residential road (just follow the signs from Route 199). ✉ *Curtis Rd. off Rte. 199,* ☎ *860/868–0518.* 🖙 *$4.* ⊙ *Jan.–Mar., Wed.–Sat. 10–5, Sun. noon–5; Apr.–Dec., Mon.–Sat. 10–5, Sun. noon–5.*

Woodbury

⑤① *8 mi southeast of Bridgewater.*

There may very well be more antiques shops in the quickly growing town of Woodbury than in all the towns in the rest of the Litchfield Hills combined. Five magnificent **churches** and the Greek Revival **King Solomon's Temple,** formerly a Masonic lodge, line Route 6; they represent some of the finest-preserved examples of Colonial religious architecture in New England.

The **Glebe House** is the large gambrel-roofed Colonial in which Dr. Samuel Seabury was elected America's first Episcopal bishop in 1783. It holds an excellent collection of antiques. British horticulturist Gertrude Jekyll designed the historic garden. ✉ *Hollow Rd.,* ☎ *203/263–2855.* 🖙 *$5.* ⊙ *Apr.–Nov., Wed.–Sun. 1–4, Dec.–Mar. by appointment.*

Dining and Lodging

$$–$$$$ ✕ **Good News Café.** Carole Peck is a kitchenhold name in these parts,
★ and her decision to open a restaurant in Woodbury was met with cheers.
The emphasis is on healthful, innovative fare: venison filet mignon with
a horseradish crust, wok-seared shrimp with new potatoes, grilled green
beans, and a garlic aioli. You can drop by for cappuccino and munchies
in a separate room decorated with fascinating vintage radios. ⊠ *694 Main
St. S,* ☎ *203/266–4663. AE, MC, V. Closed Tues.*

$–$$ ✕ **Charcoal Chef.** Sprung straight from the 1950s, this eatery with knotty-
pine paneling is the real thing. Feast on charcoal-broiled halibut,
chicken, steaks, or burgers served with a baked potato or fries and
coleslaw. The bartender pours generous drinks. ⊠ *670 Main St. N (Rte.
6 on the way to Watertown),* ☎ *203/263–2538. No credit cards.*

$$–$$$ ⊞ **Tucker Hill Inn.** Susan Cebelenski runs this B&B in her 1923 Colo-
nial-style clapboard home, which has spacious rooms with cable TV
and VCRs and country-style furnishings. The location is great—about
40 minutes from both New Haven and Hartford. ⊠ *96 Tucker Hill
Rd., Middlebury 06762,* ☎ *203/758–8334,* FAX *203/598–0652. 4 rooms,
2 with bath. Full breakfast. AE, MC, V.*

$–$$ ⊞ **Curtis House.** Connecticut's oldest inn (1754), at the foot of Wood-
bury's antiques row, may also be its cheapest; some rooms are even
under $50. The inn has seen dozens of alterations and renovations over
the years, but the floorboards still creak like friendly ghosts, and the
TVs in some rooms look to be from the Ed Sullivan era. A fireplace
roars downstairs, where the restaurant serves filling dishes in the steak-
and-potato genre. ⊠ *506 Main St./Rte. 6, 06798,* ☎ *203/263–2101.
18 rooms, 12 with bath. Restaurant. D, MC, V.*

Shopping

British Country Antiques (⊠ 50 Main St. N, ☎ 203/263–5100) imports
polished pine and country furniture from England and France. **Country
Loft Antiques** (⊠ 557 Main St. S, ☎ 203/266–4500) sells 18th- and 19th-
century French antiques. **David Dunton** (⊠ Rte. 132 off Rte. 47, ☎ 203/
263–5355) is a respected dealer of formal American Federal furniture.
Mill House Antiques (⊠ 1068 Main St. N, ☎ 203/263–3446) carries formal and country English and French furniture and has the state's largest
collection of Welsh dressers. The **Woodbury Pewterers** (⊠ 860 Main St.
S., ☎ 203/263–2668) factory store offers discounts on fine reproductions of Early American tankards, Revere bowls, candlesticks, and more.

Skiing and Snow Sports

WOODBURY SKI AREA

This ski area with a 300-ft vertical drop has 18 downhill trails of varying difficulty that are serviced by a double chairlift, three rope tows,
a handle tow, and a T-bar. About half of the 15 km (9 mi) of cross-
country trails are groomed, and 2 km (1 mi) are lighted and covered
by snowmaking when necessary. There's an extensive snowboard and
alpine park, a skateboard and in-line skating park, and a special area
for sledding and tubing serviced by two lifts and three tows. Snow biking and snowshoeing are other options. Ski parties are held on Friday
and Saturday nights in the base lodge; lessons are given for adults and
for children ages 2 and up. ⊠ *Rte. 47, 06798,* ☎ *203/263–2203.*

Southbury

52 *6 mi south of Woodbury, 36 mi south of Winsted, 18 mi northwest of
New Haven.*

Southbury, a former agricultural community with well-preserved Colonial homes and many antiques shops, has been heavily developed.
Like New Milford to the west, the town acts as the bridge between

southern Connecticut's modern suburbia and the Litchfield Hills' pre-20th-century charm.

Lodging

$$$ ⊞ **Heritage Inn.** Renovations completed in 1998 have given this large resort a much-needed face-lift, including a new Colonial look and improved facilities. Drop by the pub Schadrack's for light fare ($$) or a drink after a day on the greens. ⊠ *522 Heritage Rd., 06488,* ☎ *203/ 264–8200 or 800/932–3466,* FAX *203/264–5035. 160 rooms, 3 suites. Restaurant, bar, 18-hole and 9-hole golf course, 3 tennis courts, health club. AE, D, DC, MC, V.*

Outdoor Activities and Sports

G.E.M. Morgans (⊠ 75 N. Poverty Rd., ☎ 203/264–6196) conducts hay and carriage rides using registered Morgan horses.

Waterbury

🚳 *15 mi northeast of Southbury, 28 mi southwest of Hartford, 28 mi north of Bridgeport.*

Waterbury may well be one of America's gloomiest cities, with a somewhat dingy downtown, but civic leaders have plans to remedy that. Many of the several dozen important buildings in the historic downtown date back to the days when the city was the cradle of the brass industry in the United States. The dramatic 240-ft **Clock Tower** (⊠ 389 Meadow St.) was modeled after the city hall tower in Siena, Italy.

Stop by the **Waterbury Region Convention and Visitors Bureau** (⊠ 21 Church St., ☎ 203/597–9527) to pick up literature that contains a detailed and fascinating self-guided walking tour of the downtown area.

The **Mattatuck Museum** has a fine collection of 19th- and 20th-century Connecticut art and memorabilia documenting the state's industrial history. ⊠ *144 W. Main St.,* ☎ *203/753–0381.* ⊡ *Free.* ⊙ *Tues.– Sat. 10–5.*

Dining and Lodging

$$$–$$$$ ✕ **Diorio Restaurant and Bar.** The dining room at Diorio, a Waterbury
★ tradition for more than a half-century, retains its original mahogany bankers' booth, marble brass bar, high tin ceilings, exposed brick, and white-tile floors. The dishes here are expertly prepared, from the juicy shrimp scampi to the dozens of pasta, chicken, veal, steak, and seafood plates. ⊠ *231 Bank St.,* ☎ *203/754–5111. AE, D, DC, MC, V. Closed Sun. No lunch Sat.*

$$$ ✕ **Carmen Anthony Steak House.** A worthy re-creation of the steak
★ houses of old, Carmen Anthony has rich wood paneling, handsome oil paintings on the walls, and white linen on the tables. You can order Delmonico, filet mignon, porterhouse, and other steaks; the popular "Italian" steaks are served on a bed of rotini pasta. ⊠ *496 Chase Ave.,* ☎ *203/757–3040. AE, D, DC, MC, V. No lunch.*

$$–$$$ ⊞ **House on the Hill.** Owner-innkeeper Marianne Vandenburgh's fanciful B&B is surrounded by lush gardens in a historic hillside neighborhood. The three-story 1888 Victorian has a glorious exterior color scheme of teal, sage-green, red, and ivory. The accommodations here are furnished in a welcoming blend of antiques and nostalgia. ⊠ *92 Woodbury Terr., 06710,* ☎ *203/757–9901. 4 suites. Full breakfast. No credit cards. Closed Dec. 15–Jan. 15.*

Nightlife and the Arts

Seven Angels Theatre (⊠ Hamilton Park Pavilion, Plank Rd., ☎ 203/ 757–4676) presents top-rate plays, musicals, children's theater, cabaret concerts, and youth programs.

Shopping

Howland-Hughes (⊠ 120 Bank St., ☎ 203/753–4121) is stocked entirely with items made in Connecticut, from Wiffle balls to Pez candies, fine pottery to glassware.

Litchfield Hills A to Z

Arriving and Departing

BY BUS

Bonanza Bus Lines (☎ 800/556–3815) operates daily buses between New York City's Port Authority terminal and Southbury.

BY CAR

U.S. 44 west and U.S. 6 south are the most direct routes from Hartford to the Litchfield Hills. To get here from New York, take I–684 to I–84, from which the roads off Exits 7 to 18 head northward into the Hills.

BY PLANE

The airport nearest to the Litchfield Hills region is Hartford's **Bradley International Airport** (☞ Connecticut River Valley A to Z, *above*).

Getting Around

BY BUS

There is no local bus service in the Litchfield Hills.

BY CAR

U.S. 7 winds from New Milford through Kent, Cornwall Bridge, Cornwall, and West Cornwall to Canaan. Sharon is west of U.S. 7 on Route 4; continue north from Sharon on Route 41 to get to Lakeville and Salisbury. U.S. 44 heading east from Salisbury passes through Canaan, Norfolk, and Winsted. Route 63 travels southeast from South Canaan through Litchfield to Waterbury; at Watertown head west from Route 63 on U.S. 6 and north on Route 61 to get to Bethlehem. Southbury is at the junction of U.S. 6 and I–84. Route 8, the main north–south road through the eastern part of the Litchfield Hills, passes through Winsted, Torrington, and Waterbury; Bristol is east of Route 8 off Route 6, and Riverton is east of Route 8 on Route 20.

Contacts and Resources

EMERGENCIES

New Milford Hospital (⊠ 21 Elm St., ☎ 860/355–2611). **Sharon Hospital** (⊠ 50 Hospital Hill Rd., ☎ 860/364–4141).

24-HOUR PHARMACY

CVS (⊠ 627 Farmington Ave., Bristol, ☎ 860/582–8167).

VISITOR INFORMATION

Litchfield Hills Travel Council (⊠ Box 968, Litchfield 06759, ☎ 860/567–4506).

NEW HAVEN AND THE SOUTHEASTERN COAST

As you drive northeast along I–95, culturally rich New Haven is the final urban obstacle between southwestern Connecticut's overdeveloped coast and southeastern Connecticut's quieter shoreline villages. The remainder of the jagged coast, which stretches all the way to the Rhode Island border, consists of small coastal villages, quiet hamlets, and undisturbed beaches. The only interruptions along this mostly undeveloped seashore are the industry and piers of New London and Groton. Mystic, Stonington, Old Saybrook, and Guilford are havens for fans of antiques and boutiques. North of Groton, near the town of Ledyard, the Mashantucket Pequot Reservation owns and operates Foxwoods Casino and the Mashantucket Pequot Museum & Research Center. The Mohegan Indians run the Mohegan Sun casino in Uncasville.

Some call southeastern Connecticut the charter- and party-boat capital of New England. Charter fishing boats take passengers for half-day, full-day, and some overnight trips at fees from $20 to $35 per person; tuna-fishing trips may cost as much as $100 a day.

New Haven

46 mi northeast of Greenwich, 36 mi south of Hartford.

New Haven's history goes back to the 17th century, when its squares, including a lovely central green for the public, were laid out. The city, a cultural center, is home to Yale University. The historic district surrounding Yale and the shops, museums, theaters, and restaurants on nearby **Chapel Street** are handsome and prosperous. Visitors should be careful about exploring areas away from the campus and city common at night.

54 Bordered on one side by the Yale campus, the **New Haven Green** (✉ Between Church and College Sts.) is a fine example of early urban planning. As early as 1638, village elders set aside the 16-acre plot as a town common. Three early 19th-century churches—the Gothic-style **Trinity Episcopal Church,** the Georgian-style **Center Congregational Church,** and the predominantly Federal **United Church**—contribute to its present appeal. Sculptor Ed Hamilton's three sided, 14-ft-high *Amistad* memorial in front of City Hall (✉ 165 Church St.) shows key incidents in the life of Joseph Cinque, one of the Africans kidnapped from Sierra Leone in 1839. Part of the Africans' battle for freedom took place in New Haven.

55 A historic example of New Haven's innovation is the **Grove Street Cemetery** (✉ 227 Grove St.), the first planned public cemetery in the nation. Walk under the imposing Egyptian Revival arch, circa 1845, and you can see the final resting place of Connecticut greats like Noah Webster, Eli Whitney, and Charles Goodyear.

New Haven is a manufacturing center dating from the 19th century, but the city owes its fame to Elihu Yale. In 1718, Yale's contributions enabled the Collegiate School, founded in 1701, to settle in New ★ Haven, where it changed its name to **Yale University,** for which honor he never donated another dime to the school. This is one of the nation's great universities, and its campus holds some handsome neo-Gothic buildings and a number of noteworthy museums. The university's knowledgeable guides conduct one-hour walking tours that include Connecticut Hall in the Old Campus, which counts Nathan Hale, William Howard Taft, and Noah Webster among its past residents. ✉ *Yale Visitors Center, 149 Elm St.,* ☎ *203/432–2300.* ☉ *Tours weekdays at 10:30 and 2, weekends at 1:30. Tours start from 149 Elm St. on north side of New Haven Green.*

James Gamble Rogers, an American architect, designed many build-**56** ings for Yale, his alma mater, including the **Sterling Memorial Library** (✉ 120 High St., ☎ 203/432–2798), which he built to be "a cathedral of knowledge and a temple of learning." This is evident in the major interior area, which resembles a Gothic cathedral. The collec-**57** tions at Yale's **Beinecke Rare Book and Manuscript Library** (✉ 121 Wall St., ☎ 203/432–2977) include a Gutenberg Bible, illuminated manuscripts, and original Audubon bird prints, but the building is almost as much of an attraction—the walls are made of marble cut so thinly that the light shines through, making the interior a breathtaking sight on sunny days.

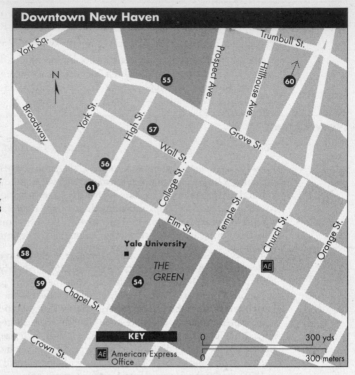

Downtown New Haven

KEY

AE American Express Office

0   300 yds
0   300 meters

⑤⑧ Since its founding in 1832, the **Yale University Art Gallery** has amassed more than 100,000 objects from around the world, dating from ancient Egypt to the present day. Highlights include works by Van Gogh, Manet, Monet, Picasso, Winslow Homer, and Thomas Eakins, as well as Etruscan and Greek vases, Chinese ceramics and bronzes, and early Italian paintings. The gallery's collection of American decorative arts is considered one of the finest in the world. Be certain not to miss the re-creation of a Mithraic shrine downstairs. ⊠ *1111 Chapel St.,* ☎ *203/432–0600.* ☞ *Free.* ◷ *Tues.–Sat. 10–5, Sun. 1–6.*

⑤⑨ The **Yale Center for British Art** has the most comprehensive collection of British art outside of Britain. The center's skylighted galleries, designed by Louis I. Kahn, contain works by Constable, Hogarth, Gainsborough, Reynolds, and Turner, to name but a few. You'll also find rare books and paintings documenting English history. Renovations in 1998 gave the museum new carpets and wall hangings and spruced-up permanent exhibits. ⊠ *1080 Chapel St.,* ☎ *203/432–2800.* ☞ *Free.* ◷ *Tues.–Sat. 10–5, Sun. noon–5.*

☙ ⑥⓪ Yale's **Peabody Museum of Natural History** opened in 1876; with more than 9 million specimens, it's one of the largest natural history museums in the nation. In addition to exhibits on Andean, Mesoamerican, and Pacific cultures, the venerable museum has an excellent collection of birds, including a stuffed dodo and passenger pigeon. But the main attractions for children and amateur paleontologists alike are some of the world's earliest reconstructions of dinosaur skeletons. ⊠ *170 Whitney Ave.,* ☎ *203/432–5050.* ☞ *$5.* ◷ *Mon.–Sat. 10–4:45, Sun. noon–4:45.*

The most notable example of the Yale campus's neo-Gothic architecture is the **Harkness Tower** (⊠ High St.), built between 1917 and ⑥① 1921, which was modeled on St. Botolph's Tower in Boston, England. The university's famous motto, inscribed on Memorial Gate near the tower, is sometimes described as the world's greatest anticlimax: "For God, for country, and for Yale."

Dining and Lodging

$$$ ✕ **Union League Café.** Creative twists enliven this café's changing country-French menu. Typical selections are the walnut-crusted sea bass with saffron, leeks, and potatoes, and roast duck breast with celeriac mousse and sautéed apple slices. The menu is prix-fixe on Sunday. ⊠ *1032 Chapel St., ☏ 203/562–4299. AE, MC, V. No lunch weekends.*

$$–$$$ ✕ **Caffé Adulis.** High ceilings and exposed brick lend this trendy Ethiopian restaurant a comfortable, contemporary feel. The house specialty is shrimp *barka* (shrimp in a tomato-basil sauce with unsweetened coconut, dates, Parmesan cheese, and light cream). Another worthy northeast African entrée is *tibsies*, a fajita-like affair. There are several vegetarian dishes, including fragrant stews. ⊠ *228 College St., ☏ 203/777–5081. Reservations not accepted. AE, MC, V. No lunch.*

$$–$$$ ✕ **Pika Tapas Café.** Chic and colorful, this cosmopolitan café serves
★ delicate Spanish hors d'oeuvres meant for sharing; each region in Spain is well represented on the menu. *Gambas al ajilo* (shrimp sautéed in a pungent, good-to-the-last-drop garlic sauce) and baked goat cheese on parsley toast are among the popular tapas. A few salads and entrées—the paella is a standout—are also prepared. ⊠ *39 High St., ☏ 203/ 865–1933. AE, MC, V. No lunch Sun.*

$ ✕ **Frank Pepe's.** Does this place serve the best pizza in the world, as
★ some reviewers claim? If it doesn't, it comes close. Pizza is the only thing prepared here—try the famous white-clam pie, and you won't be disappointed. Expect to wait an hour or more for a table—or, on weekend evenings, come after 10. The Spot (☏ 203/865–7602), right behind the restaurant, is owned by Pepe's and is usually open when Pepe's is not. ⊠ *157 Wooster St., ☏ 203/865–5762. Reservations not accepted. No credit cards. Closed Tues. No lunch Mon. and Wed.–Thurs.*

$ ✕ **Louis' Lunch.** This all-American luncheonette on the National Register of Historic Places claims to be the birthplace of the hamburger in America. The first-rate burgers are cooked in an old-fashioned, upright broiler and served with either a slice of tomato or cheese on two slices of toast. (Don't even think about asking for ketchup.) ⊠ *263 Crown St., ☏ 203/562–5507. No credit cards. Closed Sun.–Mon. No dinner.*

$$$ ⊞ **Three Chimneys Inn.** This 1870 Victorian mansion is one of the classi-
★ est small inns in the state. Rooms have posh Georgian furnishings: mahogany four-poster beds, oversize armoires, Chippendale desks, and Oriental rugs. The sitting room and library have working fireplaces. ⊠ *1201 Chapel St., 06511, ☏ 203/789–1201, FAX 203/776–7363. 10 rooms. Business services, meeting rooms. Full breakfast. AE, MC, V.*

$$–$$$ ⊞ **Omni New Haven Hotel at Yale.** The new kid on the block, the 19-floor Omni, opened in 1998 and is the only large hotel in the city. With modern amenities and a view of the green, it's comfortable and convenient to the heart of New Haven. The rooftop restaurant is named Galileo's for its lofty height, though the menu is somewhat more down to earth, with traditional hotel fare like salmon or filet mignon at reasonable prices. ⊠ *155 Temple St., 06511, ☏ 203/772–6664, FAX 203/ 974–6777. 299 rooms, 7 suites. Restaurant, lounge, health club, business services, meeting rooms. Continental breakfast. AE, MC, V.*

$$ ⊞ **New Haven Hotel.** A quiet spot in the heart of the city, the New Haven has the feel of a small, exclusive hotel. But the amenities are those of a large facility. The Queen Anne–style rooms are comfortable and modern, and the restaurant, Templeton's, serves innovative American cuisine. ⊠ *229 George St., 06510, ☏ 203/498–3100, FAX 203/498–3190. 92 rooms. Restaurant, bar, indoor lap pool, hot tub, business services, meeting rooms. AE, D, DC, MC, V.*

Nightlife and the Arts

NIGHTLIFE

BAR (⊠ Crown St. at College St., ☎ 203/495–1111) is a cross between a nightclub, a brick-oven pizzeria, and a brew pub. **Richter's** (⊠ 990 Chapel St., ☎ 203/777–0400) is famous for its half-yard glasses of beer. Alternative and traditional rock bands play at **Toad's Place** (⊠ 300 York St., ☎ 203/624–8263).

THE ARTS

The **Long Wharf Theatre** (⊠ 222 Sargent Dr., ☎ 203/787–4282) presents works by new writers and imaginative revivals of neglected classics. The **Shubert Performing Arts Center** (⊠ 247 College St., ☎ 203/562–5666 or 800/228–6622) hosts musicals and dramas, usually following their run in the Big Apple, and also opera. The **Yale Cabaret** (⊠ 217 Park St., ☎ 203/432–1566) can be counted on for unusual plays and good food at great prices during the school year. The highly professional **Yale Repertory Theatre** (⊠ Chapel and York Sts., ☎ 203/432–1234) mounts world premieres and is known for its fresh interpretations of the classics.

The century-old **New Haven Symphony Orchestra** (☎ 203/865–0831) plays at Yale University's Woolsey Hall (⊠ College and Grove Sts.). The orchestra's Young People's Concerts series—the country's leading music program for children—is in its seventh decade. The **SNET Oakdale Theatre** (⊠ 95 S. Turnpike Rd./Rte. 150, ☎ 203/265–1501) in Wallingford, 18 mi north of New Haven, presents nationally known theatrical and musical performances. **Yale School of Music** (☎ 203/432–4157) presents an impressive roster of performers, from classical to jazz; most events take place in the Morse Recital Hall in Sprague Memorial Hall (⊠ College and Wall Sts.).

Outdoor Activities and Sports

A public beach, nature trails, and a stunning antique carousel in a century-old beach pavilion are attractions of the 88-acre **Lighthouse Point Park** (⊠ Lighthouse Rd. off Rte. 337, ☎ 203/946–8005), in southeastern New Haven.

The **New Haven Ravens** (☎ 800/728–3671), the Double-A affiliate of baseball's Seattle Mariners, play home games at Yale Field (⊠ 252 Derby Ave./Rte. 34, West Haven) from April to September.

The **Beast of New Haven** (☎ 203/777–7878), an American Hockey League team, plays at the New Haven Coliseum (⊠ S. Orange St. at George St., ☎ 203/772–4200).

Shopping

Chapel Street, near the town green, has a pleasing assortment of shops and eateries. **Arethusa Book Shop** (⊠ 87 Audubon St., ☎ 203/624–1848) carries a huge selection of out-of-print and used books, including first editions. **Atticus Bookstore & Café** (⊠ 1082 Chapel St., ☎ 203/776–4040), in the heart of Yale University, was one of the first stores to combine books and food; it's been a favorite among museum groupies and theatergoers for years.

En Route The oldest rapid-transit car and the world's first electric freight locomotive are among classic trolleys on display at the **Shoreline Trolley Museum.** Admission includes a 3-mi round-trip ride aboard a vintage trolley. ⊠ *17 River St., East Haven (midway between New Haven and Branford),* ☎ *203/467–6927.* ⬗ *$5.* ☉ *Memorial Day–Labor Day, daily 11–5; May, Sept.–Oct., and Dec., weekends 11–5; Apr. and Nov., Sun. 11–5.*

Branford

⑥² *8 mi east of New Haven.*

Founded in 1644, Branford was a prosperous port and the site of a salt-works that during the Revolutionary War provided salt to preserve food for the Continental Army. Today it is a charming seaside town with a close-knit community of artists and craftspeople. The summer cottages are shoulder to shoulder, with tiny, well-kept yards and colorful gardens.

The small Branford village of Stony Creek, with a few tackle shops, a general store, and a marina, is the departure point for cruises around the **Thimble Islands.** This group of 365 tiny islands was named for its abundance of thimbleberries, which are similar to gooseberries. Legend has it that Captain Kidd buried pirate gold on one island. Two sight-seeing vessels vie for your patronage, the *Volsunga IV* (☎ 203/481–3345 or 203/488–9978) and the *Sea Mist II* (☎ 203/488–8905). Both depart from Stony Creek Dock, at the end of Thimble Island Road, from May to Columbus Day.

Dining

$$ ✕ **Le Petit Café.** The prix-fixe menu at this small café focuses on coun-
★ try dishes from southern France. Chef Roy Ip, the former sous chef at Raoul's in Manhattan, serves up a veritable feast, including fresh bread and pâté, a tray of five or six appetizers (perhaps grilled leeks or sea-weed salad), soup, a choice of six entrées (such as steak au poivre or pan-roasted salmon), and a dessert. ⊠ *225 Montowese St.,* ☎ *203/483–9791. Reservations essential. MC, V. Closed Mon.–Tues. No lunch.*

Shopping

Branford Craft Village (⊠ 779 E. Main St., ☎ 203/488–4689), on the 150-year-old, 85-acre Bittersweet Farm, contains a dozen crafts shops and studios, an herb garden, a barnyard petting zoo, an antiques shop, and a small café. The village is closed Monday.

Guilford

⑥³ *885 mi east of Stony Creek, 37 mi west of New London.*

Another of the state's sleepy shoreline towns, Guilford has its heart in the neon-lit Americana of U.S. 1, but its soul lies in the quiet stretches of slightly rocky beaches.

The **Henry Whitfield State Museum** is the oldest house in the state and the oldest stone house in New England. It was built by the Reverend Henry Whitfield, an English minister, in 1639. The furnishings in the medieval-style building were made between the 17th and 19th centuries. The visitor center contains two exhibition galleries and a gift shop. ⊠ *248 Old Whitfield St.,* ☎ *203/453–2457.* ☞ *$3.* ☉ *Feb.–mid-Dec., Wed.–Sun. 10–4:30; mid-Dec.–Jan. by appointment.*

Dining

$$–$$$ ✕ **Quattro's.** The two owner-chefs here are Ecuadoran but are trained
★ in the Italian style of cooking. Although their menu includes traditional pasta dishes, these pros really cut loose with the daily specials. Look for delicacies like the smoky bacon-wrapped scallops served over a bed of lobster sauce and the filet mignon topped with fresh spinach, sautéed shrimp, and cognac sauce. ⊠ *1300 Boston Post Rd.,* ☎ *203/453–6575. Reservations essential. AE, DC, MC, V.*

Shopping

The **Guilford Handcrafts Center** (⊠ 411 Church St., ☎ 203/453–5947) sponsors three major crafts exhibitions a year and has an excellent shop.

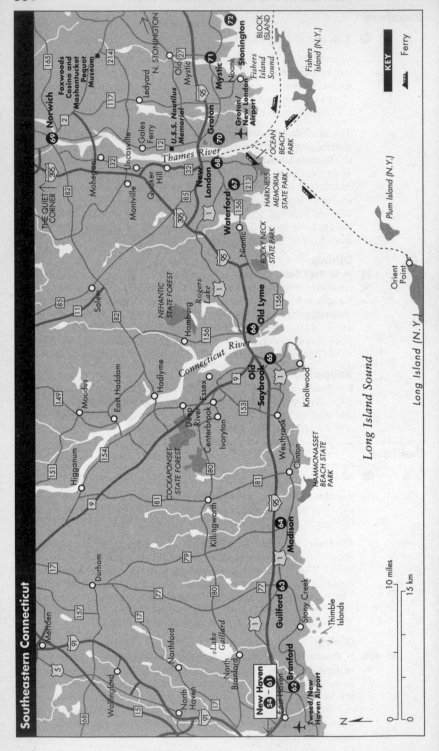

Southeastern Connecticut

Madison

64   *5 mi east of Guilford, 62 mi northeast of Greenwich.*

Coastal Madison has an understated charm. Ice cream parlors, antiques stores, and quirky gift boutiques prosper along U.S. 1, the town's main street.

Hammonasset Beach State Park, the largest of the state's shoreline sanctuaries, has 2 mi of white sandy beaches and a popular 541-site campground. ⊠ *I–95, Exit 62,* ☎ *203/245–2785 for park, 203/245–1817 for campground.* ⊐ *Park $5–$12 Apr.–Sept., free Oct.–Mar. Campground $12 year-round.* ☉ *Park daily 8 AM–dusk.*

Dining and Lodging

$$$$ ✕⊡ **Inn at Lafayette.** Skylights, painted murals, and handcrafted woodwork are among the design accents at this airy hostelry in a converted 1830s church. The rooms may be small for the price, but the decoration is immaculate, with beautiful fabrics and reproduction 17th- and 18th-century antique furniture. The modern marble baths have telephones. Look for fresh food and flawless service at Café Allegre ($$–$$$), the inn's popular restaurant. The menu is largely southern Italian, with a dash of French. ⊠ *725 Boston Post Rd., 06443,* ☎ *203/245–7773,* 𝔽𝔸𝕏 *203/245–6256. 5 rooms. Restaurant, bar, business services. Continental breakfast. AE, DC, MC, V.*

Shopping

The **Clayhouse** (⊠ 749 Boston Post Rd., ☎ 203/318–0399) is a fine paint-your-own ceramic studio. **R. J. Julia Booksellers** (⊠ 768 Boston Post Rd., ☎ 203/245–3959) is an excellent independent bookstore.

En Route   Among the 70 discount stores at **Clinton Crossing Premium Outlets** (⊠ I–95, Exit 63, ☎ 860/664–0700), you can find Off 5th–Saks Fifth Avenue, Donna Karan, and Lenox. Represented at **Westbrook Factory Stores** (⊠ I–95, Exit 65, ☎ 860/399–8656) are Carter's, Springmaid/Wamsutta, Oneida, J. Crew, and Clifford & Wills.

Old Saybrook

65   *9 mi east of Madison, 29 mi east of New Haven.*

Old Saybrook, once a lively shipbuilding and fishing town, bustles with summer vacationers and antiques shoppers.

Dining and Lodging

$$ $$$ ✕ **Aleia's.** This restaurant is as light, bright, and bountiful as the Italian countryside. Raffia, silk flowers, and hand-painted plates from Capri
★   decorate the walls, and trompe l'oeil fruits, vegetables, and herbs adorn the tabletops. Chef-owner Kimberly Snow adds nouvelle touches to her mother's tried-and-true recipes, like the Maine crab cakes with *rémoulade* (a seasoned sauce made with mayonnaise), shaved carrots, hearts of palm and jícama, or the veal scallopini and rock shrimp in garlic and white wine, served with diced red potatoes. ⊠ *1687 Boston Post Rd.,* ☎ *860/399–5050. AE, MC, V. Closed Mon. No lunch.*

$$ ✕ **Café Routier.** Duck-leg ragout in a rich red-wine sauce, fried oys-
★   ters with a chipotle rémoulade, and steak au poivre with potatoes Dauphinois are among the dishes served at this classy café. White tablecloths and candlelight provide a fitting atmosphere in which to enjoy the snappy French and American cuisine. Some of France's finest vintages are served from the copper wine bar. ⊠ *1080 Boston Post Rd.,* ☎ *860/388–6270. AE, D, DC, MC, V. Closed Sun.–Mon. No lunch.*

$ ✕ **Pat's Kountry Kitchen.** Upbeat service and traditional New England fare have made this home-style restaurant a local institution. Best sellers are the fresh clam hash, pork chops, and apple-cranberry-raisin pie. ⊠ *U.S. 1,* ☎ *860/388–4784. AE, MC, V.*

$$$$ ✕⛨ **Saybrook Point Inn & Spa.** Rooms at the Saybrook are furnished mainly in 18th-century style, with reproductions of British furniture and Impressionist art. The health club and pools overlook the inn's marina and the Connecticut River. The Terra Mar Grille, overlooking the river and Long Island Sound, serves stylish Continental cuisine, including papillote of cod with mussels, oven-steamed in paper with fish broth and julienne vegetables. ⊠ *2 Bridge St., 06475,* ☎ *860/395–2000,* FAX *860/388–1504. 55 rooms, 7 suites. Restaurant, 1 indoor and 1 outdoor pool, spa, health club, meeting rooms. AE, D, DC, MC, V.*

$$$$ ⛨ **Water's Edge Inn & Resort.** With its spectacular setting on Long Is-
★ land Sound, this traditional weathered gray-shingle compound in West-
brook is one of the Connecticut shore's premier resorts. The main building has warm and bright public rooms furnished with antiques and reproductions, and its upstairs bedrooms, with wall-to-wall carpeting and clean, modern bathrooms, afford priceless views of the sound. Suites in the surrounding outbuildings are not as nicely kept and lack the fine views. ⊠ *1525 Boston Post Rd., Westbrook, 06498,* ☎ *860/ 399–5901 or 800/222–5901,* FAX *860/399–6172. 163 rooms and suites. Restaurant, bar, 1 indoor and 1 outdoor pool, spa, health club, 2 tennis courts, volleyball, beach, meeting rooms. AE, D, DC, MC, V.*

Outdoor Activities and Sports

Colvin Yachts (⊠ Hammock Rd. S, Westbrook–Old Saybrook, ☎ 860/ 399–9300) rents and charters boats (sailboat rentals start at about $150 per day). **Deep River Navigation Company** (⊠ Saybrook Point, ☎ 860/ 526–4954) runs narrated cruises up the Connecticut River, along the shoreline or out into Long Island Sound. Deep-sea fishing and private charter boats, whose rentals range from $425 for a half day to $525 and up for a full day, are available at **Sea Sprite Charters** (⊠ 113 Harbor Pkwy., Clinton, ☎ 860/669–9613). Charters leave from Old Saybrook Point.

Shopping

More than 120 dealers operate out of the **Essex-Saybrook Antiques Village** (⊠ 345 Middlesex Turnpike, ☎ 860/388–0689). **North Cove Outfitters** (⊠ 75 Main St., ☎ 860/388–6585) is Connecticut's version of L.L. Bean. **Saybrook Country Barn** (⊠ 2 Main St., ☎ 860/388–0891) has everything country, from tiger-maple dining-room tables to hand-painted pottery.

Old Lyme

66 *4 mi east of Old Saybrook, 40 mi south of Hartford.*

Old Lyme, on the other side of the Connecticut River from Old Saybrook, is renowned among art lovers for its history as America's foremost Impressionist art colony. Artists continue to be attracted to the area for its lovely countryside and shoreline. The town also has handsome old houses, many built for sea captains.

Central to Old Lyme's artistic reputation is the **Florence Griswold Museum,** a former boarding house that hosted members of the Old Lyme art colony, including Willard Metcalfe, Clark Voorhees, Childe Hassam, and Henry Ward Ranger, in the early 20th century. Griswold, the descendant of a well-known family, offered artistic encouragement as well as housing. The artists painted for their hostess the double row of panels in the dining room that now serve as the museum's centerpiece. Many of their other works are on display in revolving exhibits, along with 19th-century furnishings and decorative items. The landscaped 11-acre estate is a perfect setting for the 1817 late-Georgian mansion. The museum is part of the Connecticut Impressionist Art Trail, a self-guided tour of 12 sites (*see* Connecticut A to Z, *below,* for information about the trail). ☒ *96 Lyme St.,* ☏ *860/434–5542.* ☞ *$4.* ☉ *Jan.–May, Wed.–Sun. 1–5; June–Dec., Tues.–Sat. 10–5, Sun. 1–5.*

The **Lyme Academy of Fine Arts,** in a Federal home built in 1817, has a popular gallery with works by contemporary artists, including the academy's students and faculty. ☒ *84 Lyme St.,* ☏ *860/434–5232.* ☞ *$2 donation suggested.* ☉ *Tues.–Sat. 10–4, Sun. 1–4.*

Dining and Lodging

$$–$$$ ✕⊞ **Bee & Thistle Inn.** Behind a weathered stone wall in the Old Lyme
★ historic district is a three-story 1756 Colonial house with 5½ acres of broad lawns, towering trees, blooming flowers in a formal garden, and herbaceous borders. The scale of rooms throughout is small and inviting, with fireplaces in the downstairs parlors and dining rooms and light and airy curtains in the multipaned guest-room windows. Most rooms have canopy or four-poster beds with old quilts and afghans. Breakfast (not included in the price) can be brought to your room before or after a morning soak in an herbal bath (scented soap provided). Fireplaces and candlelight create a romantic atmosphere in the excellent restaurant ($$$–$$$$; closed on Tuesday and the first three weeks in January), where classic American cuisine—like grilled free-range chicken, filet mignon, crab cakes—is served with style. ☒ *100 Lyme St., 06371,* ☏ *860/434–1667 or 800/622–4946,* 𝖥𝖠𝖷 *860/434–3402. 11 rooms, 1 cottage. Restaurant. AE, D, DC, MC, V.*

$$–$$$ ✕⊞ **Old Lyme Inn.** A white clapboard 1850s farmhouse with blue shutters is the centerpiece of this dining and lodging establishment in the heart of Old Lyme's historic district. Behind the ornate iron fence, tree-shaded lawn, and banister front porch are spacious guest rooms impeccably decorated with antiques and contemporary furnishings. When she isn't busy working for the local art academy or the Connecticut River Museum, innkeeper Diana Field Atwood-Johnson is lifting pot lids in the kitchen for whiffs of the creative American dishes prepared by her chef for the always-busy dining rooms. Diana collects local art, some of which is displayed in the cozy ground-floor common rooms. ☒ *85 Lyme St., 06371 (just north of I–95)* ☏ *860/434–2600 or 800/ 434–5352,* 𝖥𝖠𝖷 *860/434–5352. 13 rooms. Restaurant. Continental breakfast. AE, D, DC, MC, V.*

Waterford and Niantic

㉗ *13 mi east of Old Lyme (Waterford).*

Less cutesy than Mystic and less military than Groton, Waterford and Niantic are working shoreline towns, but not without their down-to-earth charms.

Harkness Memorial State Park, the former summer estate of Edward Stephen Harkness, a silent partner in Standard Oil, encompasses formal gardens, picnic areas, a beach for strolling and fishing (but not swimming), and the 42-room Italian villa–style mansion, Eolia. Classical, pop, and jazz talents perform at the **Summer Music at Harkness** (☏ 800/969–3400) festival in July and August. ☒ *275 Great Neck Rd./Rte. 213, Waterford,* ☏ *860/443–5725.* ☞ *Memorial Day–Labor Day $4–$8; free rest of year.* ☉ *Daily 8 AM–dusk.*

Among the attributes of **Rocky Neck State Park** are its picnic facilities, saltwater fishing, and historic stone and wood pavilion, which was built in the 1930s. The park's mile-long crescent-shape strand is one of the finest beaches on Long Island Sound. ☒ *Rte. 156, I–95, Exit 72, Ni-*

antic, ☎ *860/739–5471.* 🎫 *Apr.–Sept. $5–$12; free Oct.–Mar.* ◉ *Daily 8 AM–dusk.*

☯ The **Children's Museum of Southeastern Connecticut,** about a mile from Waterford, is an excellent facility that uses a hands-on approach to engage kids in the fields of science, math, and current events. ✉ *409 Main St., Niantic,* ☎ *860/691–1255.* 🎫 *$3.50.* ◉ *Tues.–Sat. 9:30–4:30, Fri. 9:30–8, Sun. noon–4.*

New London

🔟 *3 mi east of Waterford, 46 mi east of New Haven.*

The state's maritime heritage is very evident in this small city on the Thames, which blends modern attributes and history. New London is home to the **U.S. Coast Guard Academy,** whose 100-acre cluster of red-brick buildings includes a museum and visitors' pavilion with a gift shop. The three-masted training bark, the USCGC *Eagle,* may be boarded when in port. ✉ *15 Mohegan Ave.,* ☎ *860/444–8270.* 🎫 *Free.* ◉ *Academy daily 9–5; museum weekdays 9–4:30, Sat. 10–4:30, Sun. noon–5.*

The **Lyman Allyn Art Museum,** at the southern end of the Connecticut College campus, was named by founder Harriet U. Allyn after her father, a whaling merchant. Housed in a neoclassical building designed by Charles Platt are collections of American fine arts from the country's earliest years through today. The galleries of Connecticut's decorative arts and American Impressionist paintings are noteworthy. ✉ *625 Williams St.,* ☎ *860/443–2545.* 🎫 *$4.* ◉ *Tues.–Sat. 10–5, Sun. 1–5.*

☯ It's a toss-up who will enjoy **Lyman Allyn Dolls & Toys** more, children or their parents, who can find the toys of their youth at this museum. A lovingly refurbished Victorian dollhouse, a hall of dolls, a construction site with classic toys, and a Lego playstation are just a few of the attractions. Many galleries include interactive "playzones" where children (and adults) can play. ✉ *Harris Place, 165 State St.,* ☎ *860/437–1947.* 🎫 *$4.* ◉ *Tues.–Sat. 11–5.*

The **Monte Cristo Cottage,** the boyhood home of Nobel Prize–winning playwright Eugene O'Neill, was named for the literary count, his actor-father's greatest role. The setting figures in two of O'Neill's landmark plays, *Ah, Wilderness!* and *Long Day's Journey into Night.* ✉ *325 Pequot Ave.,* ☎ *860/443–0051.* 🎫 *$4.* ◉ *Memorial Day–Oct., Tues.–Sat. 10–5, Sun. 1–5.*

The beach at **Ocean Beach Park** (✉ 1225 Ocean Ave., ☎ 860/447–3031) is ½-mi long. Also here are an Olympic-size outdoor pool (with a triple water slide), a miniature golf course, a video arcade, a board-walk, and a picnic area.

Dining and Lodging

$ ✕ **Recovery Room.** It's a favorite game of Connecticut pizza parlors to declare "We're as good as Pepe's"—a reference to the famed New Haven eatery. But this white Colonial storefront eatery, presided over by the friendly Cash family, lives up to its claim. Plenty of "boutique" toppings are available, but don't ruin a great pizza with too many flavors. Perfection is realized by the three-cheese 'za with grated Parmesan, Romano, and Gorgonzola. ✉ *445 Ocean Ave.,* ☎ *860/443–2619. MC, V. No lunch weekends.*

$$$ 🏨 **Radisson Hotel.** The rooms have nondescript furnishings but are quiet and spacious at this downtown property convenient to State Street, I-95, and the Amtrak station. ✉ *35 Gov. Winthrop Blvd., 06320,* ☎ *860/443–7000,* ᖴᗩ᙭ *860/443–1239. 116 rooms, 4 suites. Restaurant, bar, indoor pool. AE, D, DC, MC, V.*

Nightlife and the Arts

The **El 'n' Gee Club** (⊠ 86 Golden St., ☎ 860/437–3800) presents heavy metal, reggae, and other local and national bands. The **Garde Arts Center** (⊠ 325 State St., ☎ 860/444–6766) hosts the Eastern Connecticut Symphony Orchestra, a theater series, innovative dance programs, and other events. Connecticut College's **Palmer Auditorium** (⊠ Mohegan Ave., ☎ 860/439–2787) presents dance and theater programs.

Norwich Area

⑥⑨ *15 mi north of New London, 37 mi southeast of Hartford.*

Outstanding Georgian and Victorian structures surround the triangular town green in Norwich, and more can be found downtown by the Thames River. The Connecticut Trust for Historic Preservation and the state Department of Economic Development are renovating this former mill town—here's hoping for a prosperous rebound.

The **Slater Memorial Museum & Converse Art Gallery** on the grounds of the Norwich Free Academy has the largest plaster-cast collection of classical statues in the country, including *Winged Victory, Venus de Milo,* and Michelangelo's *Pietà.* ⊠ *108 Crescent St.,* ☎ *860/887–2505 or 860/887–2506.* ☞ *$2.* ☉ *Sept.–June, Tues.–Fri. 9–4, weekends 1–4; July–Aug., Tues.–Sun. 1–4.*

Foxwoods Casino, on the Mashantucket Pequot Indian Reservation, 15 mi from Norwich near Ledyard, is the world's largest gambling operation and a major draw for many visitors. The skylit compound draws more than 55,000 visitors daily to its 5,750 slot machines, 3,500-seat high-stakes bingo parlor, poker rooms, keno station, smoke-free gaming area, theater, and Race Book room. This complex includes the Grand Pequot Tower, the Great Cedar Hotel, and Two Trees Inn, which have more than 1,400 rooms combined, as well as a retail concourse, a food court, and 25 restaurants. A large game room and arcade and a movie theater in-the-round keep the kids entertained, along with Turbo Ride, which has specially engineered seats that simulate takeoffs and G-force pressure. ⊠ *Rte. 2, Mashantucket,* ☎ *860/312–3000 or 800/752–9244.* ☉ *Daily 24 hrs.*

★ Opened in 1998, the **Mashantucket Pequot Museum & Research Center,** a large complex across from Foxwoods Casino, explores the history and culture of Northeastern Woodland tribes in general and the Pequots in particular with exquisitely researched detail. Some highlights include a glacial crevasse, a caribou hunt from 11,000 years ago, a 17th-century fort, and a sprawling "immersion environment"—a re-creation of a 16th-century village with life-size figures and real smells and sounds. The research center, open to scholars and schoolchildren free of charge, holds thousands of books and artifacts. Native American cuisine is available at the restaurant, and the shop sells contemporary Native American arts and crafts. ⊠ *110 Pequot Trail, Mashantucket,* ☎ *860/396–6800.* ☞ *$10.* ☉ *Daily 10–7.*

The Mohegan Indians, known as the Wolf People, operate the **Mohegan Sun,** which has more than 3,000 slot machines, 180 gaming tables, bingo, a theater, "Kids Quest" family entertainment complex, and, among 20 food-and-beverage suppliers, three fine-dining restaurants. For betting on the ponies or even on greyhounds, you'll find Race Book, a Simulcast theater with New York Racing Association broadcasts. Free entertainment, including nationally known acts, is presented nightly in the Wolf Den. ⊠ *Mohegan Sun Blvd. off I–395, Uncasville,* ☎ *888/226–7711.*

Lodging

$$$$ ⊞ **Grand Pequot Tower.** Foxwoods' newest hotel is an imposing 17 stories. Mere steps from the gaming floors, the expansive showpiece contains deluxe rooms and suites. ⊠ *Box 3777, Rte. 2, Mashantucket 06339,* ☎ *800/369–9663. 750 rooms, 75 suites. 4 restaurants, 2 bars, indoor pool, beauty salon, health club, meeting rooms. AE, D, DC, MC, V.*

$$$–$$$$ ⊞ **Norwich Inn and Spa.** This posh Georgian-style inn is on 42 rolling acres on right by the Thames River. The spa provides an entire spectrum of fitness classes, massages, and beauty treatments. You'll find four-poster beds, wood-burning fireplaces and a complete galley kitchen in the posh villas, and comfy country decor in the guest rooms. Jack Flaws, chef at the fine Prince of Wales Restaurant, serves up luscious dishes like caramelized Chilean sea bass as well as lighter spa fare. Don't miss the classic French toast for breakfast. ⊠ *607 W. Thames St./Rte. 32, 06360,* ☎ *860/886–2401 or 800/275–4772,* ℻ *860/886–4492. 65 rooms, 70 villas. Restaurant, indoor pool, spa. AE, DC, MC, V.*

Outdoor Activities and Sports

The **Norwich Navigators** (☎ 800/644–2867), the Double-A affiliate of baseball's New York Yankees, play at Senator Thomas J. Dodd Stadium (⊠ 14 Stott Rd.).

Groton

⑦ *15 mi south of Norwich, 6 mi south of Ledyard.*

Groton is a town tied to the sea. The world's first nuclear-powered submarine, the *Historic Ship Nautilus,* launched from Groton in 1954, is permanently berthed at the **Submarine Force Museum**; you're welcome to climb aboard and imagine yourself as a crew member during the boat's trip under the North Pole more than 40 years ago. The adjacent museum charts submarine history with memorabilia, artifacts, and displays, including working periscopes and controls. The museum is outside the entrance to the submarine base. ⊠ *Crystal Lake Rd.,* ☎ *860/449–3174 or 860/449–3558.* ☎ *Free.* ☉ *Mid-May–mid-Oct., Wed.–Mon. 9–5, Tues. 1–5; late Oct.–early May, Wed.–Mon. 9–4.*

Fort Griswold Battlefield State Park contains the remnants of a Revolutionary War fort. Historic displays at the museum here mark the site of the massacre of American defenders by Benedict Arnold's British troops in 1781. A sweeping view of the shoreline can be had from the top of the Groton monument. ⊠ *Monument St. and Park Ave.,* ☎ *860/ 445–1729.* ☉ *Park daily 8 AM–dusk. Museum and monument Memorial Day–Labor Day, daily 10–5.*

Outdoor Activities and Sports

Captain John's Dock (☎ 860/443–7259) operates lighthouse cruises, as well as sightseeing tours in search of whales, seals, or eagles aboard the 100-ft-long *Sunbeam Express.* Naturalists from Mystic Aquarium (☞ *below*) accompany the boat.

Mystic

⑦ *8 mi east of Groton.*

The town of Mystic has tried with dedication (if also with excessive commercialism) to recapture the seafaring spirit of the 18th and 19th centuries. This is where some of the nation's fastest clipper ships were built in the mid-19th century. Downtown Mystic has an interesting collection of boutiques and galleries.

★ ☉ **Mystic Seaport,** the largest marine museum in the world, encompasses 17 acres of indoor and outdoor exhibits that provide a fascinating look at the area's rich maritime heritage. In the narrow streets and historic homes and buildings, craftspeople give demonstrations of open-hearth cooking, weaving, and other skills of yesteryear. With more than 480 vessels, Mystic Seaport has the largest collection of ships and boats in the world, including the *Charles W. Morgan,* the last remaining wooden whaling ship afloat, and the 1882 training ship *Joseph Conrad.* You can climb aboard for a look or for sail-setting demonstrations and reenactments of whale hunts. The shipyard here is building a replica of the 129-foot "freedom schooner" *Amistad,* which will serve as a floating classroom after its planned July 1999 launch. In 1839, captured Africans aboard the *Amistad* mutinied and won their freedom. Among the other attractions are dozens of spectacular ship's figureheads, the world's largest collection of maritime art, 19th-century cruises on 19th-century vessels, thousands of manuscripts and maps, and a period tavern. The museum can be very crowded in summer and early fall; if possible, plan to visit between October and May. ⊠ *75 Greenmanville Ave.,* ☎ *860/572–0711.* ⊡ *$16.* ☉ *May–Oct., daily 9–5; Nov.–Apr., daily 9–4.*

☖ Sea lions and dolphins and whales—oh, my! The **Mystic Aquarium and Institute for Exploration,** with more than 6,000 specimens and 24 exhibits of sea life, includes Seal Island, a 2½-acre outdoor exhibit that shows off seals and sea lions from around the world; the Marine Theater, where Atlantic bottlenose dolphins perform; and the beloved Penguin Pavilion. The aquarium completed a major expansion in spring 1999, adding new exhibits such as a re-creation of the Alaska coastline, with the world's largest (750,000-gallon) outdoor beluga whale habitat. World-renowned ocean explorer Dr. Robert Ballard uses high-tech exhibits to take a simulated dive 3,000 ft below the ocean surface. ⊠ *55 Coogan Blvd.,* ☎ *860/572–5955.* ⊡ *$13.* ☉ *July–Aug., daily 9–6; Sept.–June, daily 9–5.*

Dining and Lodging

$$–$$$ ✕ **Go Fish.** In this town by the sea, it's only right to dine on seafood,
★ and this sophisticated restaurant captures all the tastes—and colors— of the ocean. The black granite sushi bar, with its myriad tiny, briny morsels, is worth the trip in itself. The glossy blue tables in the two large dining rooms are the perfect setting for the signature bouillabaisse, with aioli, fennel toast, and saffron-scented broth. The menu offers options for vegetarians and carnivores as well, but the lobster ravioli in a light cream sauce is a must-try. ⊠ *Olde Mistick Village, I–95, Exit 90,* ☎ *860/536–2662. AE, MC, V. No lunch Sun.*

$–$$$ ✕ **Abbott's Lobster in the Rough.** If you want some of the state's best
★ lobsters, mussels, crabs, or clams on the half shell, grab a bottle of wine and slip down to this unassuming seaside lobster shack in sleepy Noank, a few miles southwest of Mystic. Seating is outdoors or on the dock, where the views are magnificent. ⊠ *117 Pearl St., Noank,* ☎ *860/536–7719. AE, MC, V. BYOB. Closed Columbus Day–1st Fri. in May and weekdays Labor Day–Columbus Day.*

$–$$ ✕ **Mystic Pizza.** It's hard to say who benefited most from the success of the 1988 sleeper film *Mystic Pizza:* then-budding actress Julia Roberts or the pizza parlor on which the film is based (though no scenes were filmed here). This joint, which is often teeming with customers in summer, does serve other dishes but is best known for its inexpensive pizza, garlic bread, and grinders. ⊠ *56 W. Main St.,* ☎ *860/536–3700 or 860/536–3737. D, MC, V.*

$$$–$$$$ ✕▨ **Inn at Mystic.** The highlight of this inn, which sprawls over 15 hill-
★ top acres and overlooks picturesque Pequotsepos Cove, is the five-bedroom Georgian Colonial mansion in which Lauren Bacall and Humphrey Bogart honeymooned. Almost as impressive are the rambling four-bedroom gatehouse and the unusually attractive motor lodge. The convivial, sun-filled Floodtide Restaurant specializes in New England fare. Brunch

fans flock here on Sunday. ⊠ *U.S. 1 and Rte. 27, 06355,* ☎ *860/536–9604 or 800/237–2415,* 𝔽𝔸𝕏 *860/572–1635. 67 rooms. Restaurant, pool, tennis court, dock, boating. AE, D, DC, MC, V.*

$$–$$$$ ✕🖼 **Whaler's Inn and Motor Court.** A perfect compromise between a chain motel and a country inn, this complex with public rooms that contain lovely antiques is one block from the Mystic River and downtown. Guest rooms are decorated in a Victorian style with quilts and reproduction four-poster beds. The restaurant, Bravo Bravo, serves nouvelle Italian food: The fettuccine comes with grilled scallops, roasted apples, sun-dried tomatoes, and a Gorgonzola cream sauce. The bagel shop here is terrific. ⊠ *20 E. Main St., 06355,* ☎ *860/536–1506 or 800/243–2588,* 𝔽𝔸𝕏 *860/572–1250. 41 rooms. 2 restaurants, outdoor café, meeting rooms. AE, MC, V.*

$$$$ 🖼 **Steamboat Inn.** The rooms at this inn are named after famous Mystic schooners, but it's hardly a creaky old establishment—many of the rooms look as though they've been arranged for the cover shot of *House Beautiful.* Six have wood-burning fireplaces, all have whirlpool baths, and most have dramatic river views. Despite the inn's busy downtown location (within earshot of the eerie hoot of the Bascule Drawbridge and the chatter of tourists), the rooms are the most luxurious and romantic in town. ⊠ *73 Steamboat Wharf, off W. Main St., 06355,* ☎ *860/536–8300,* 𝔽𝔸𝕏 *860/536–9528. 10 rooms. Continental breakfast. AE, D, MC, V.*

Outdoor Activities and Sports

Private charter boats depart from **Noank Village Boatyard** (⊠ 38 Bayside Ave., ☎ 860/536–1770). **Shaffer's Boat Livery** (⊠ 106 Mason's Island Rd., ☎ 860/536–8713) rents small outboard skiffs.

Shopping

Finer Line Gallery (⊠ 48 W. Main St., ☎ 860/536–8339) exhibits nautical and other prints. At the **Mystic Factory Outlets** (⊠ Coogan Blvd.), nearly two dozen stores discount famous-name clothing and other merchandise. **Olde Mistick Village** (⊠ I–95, Exit 90, ☎ 860/536–1641), a re-creation of what an American village might have looked like in the early 1700s, is at once hokey and picturesque. The stores here sell crafts, clothing, souvenirs, and food. **Tradewinds Gallery** (⊠ 20 W. Main St., ☎ 860/536–0119) represents some New England artists but specializes in antique maps and prints.

Stonington

72 *7 mi east of Mystic, 57 mi east of New Haven.*

The pretty village of Stonington pokes into Fishers Island Sound. Today a quiet fishing community clustered around white-spired churches, Stonington is far less commercial than Mystic. In the 19th century, though, this was a bustling whaling, sealing, and transportation center. Historic buildings line the town green and border both sides of Water Street up to the imposing Old Lighthouse Museum. You can tour the **home of Captain Nat Palmer** (⊠ 40 Palmer St., between N. Water and N. Main Sts., ☎ 860/535–8445), who discovered Antarctica in 1821.

The **Old Lighthouse Museum** has six rooms of exhibits depicting life in a coastal town circa 1649, shipping, and whaling. It occupies a lighthouse built in 1823 and moved to higher ground 17 years later. Climb to the top of the tower for a spectacular view of Long Island Sound and three states. ⊠ *7 Water St.,* ☎ *860/535–1440.* 🎫 *$4.* ☉ *July–Aug., daily 10–5; May–June and Sept.–Oct., Tues.–Sun. 10–5, or by appointment.*

The **Stonington Vineyards,** a small coastal winery, has grown premium vinifera, including chardonnay and French hybrid grape varieties, since 1987. You can browse through the works of local artists in the small gallery or take a picnic lunch on the grounds. ⊠ *523 Taug-wonk Rd.,* ☎ *860/535–1222.* 🎟 *Free.* ☉ *Daily 11–5; tours at 2.*

Dining and Lodging

$$–$$$ ✕🏠 **Randall's Ordinary.** The waiters dress in Colonial garb at this inn
★ famed for its open-hearth cooking. Arrive by 7 PM and watch the
preparations before sitting down at rustic wood tables. The prix-fixe
menu ($$$; reservations essential for dinner) changes daily; choices
might include out-of-this-world Nantucket scallops or loin of pork. The
17th-century John Randall House provides simple accommodations,
but all rooms have modern baths with whirlpool tubs and showers.
The barn houses irregular-shape guest rooms, all with authentic early
Colonial decor. ⊠ *Box 243, Rte. 2, North Stonington, 7 mi north of
Stonington, 06359,* ☎ *860/599–4540,* 🖷 *860/599–3308. 14 rooms,
1 suite. Restaurant. Continental breakfast. AE, MC, V.*

$$$–$$$$ 🏠 **Antiques & Accommodations.** The British influence is evident in the
★ Georgian formality of this Victorian country home, built about 1861.
Exquisite furniture and accessories, some of them for sale, decorate the
rooms. An 1820 house has similarly furnished suites. Aromatic can-
dles and fresh flowers create an inviting atmosphere. Breakfast is a grand
four-course affair served by candlelight on fine china, sterling silver,
and crystal. ⊠ *32 Main St., North Stonington, 7 mi north of Stonington,
06359,* ☎ *860/535–1736 or 800/554–7829. 3 rooms, 2 suites. Full
breakfast. MC, V.*

New Haven and the Southeastern Coast A to Z

Arriving and Departing

BY BUS

Peter Pan (☎ 800/237–8747) buses service New Haven from Boston,
Hartford, and New York. **Prime Time Shuttle** (☎ 800/733–8267) pro-
vides shuttle service between New Haven and LaGuardia and John F.
Kennedy airports in New York City.

BY CAR

Interstate 95 and U.S. 1, which run mostly parallel but sometimes inter-
twine, are the main routes to and through southeastern Connecticut; the
two roads intersect with I–91 (coming south from Hartford) in New Haven.

BY FERRY

From New London, **Cross Sound Ferry** (☎ 860/443–5281) operates year-
round passenger and car service to and from Orient Point, Long Island,
New York. The high-speed ferry can make the trip in 90 minutes. **Fish-
ers Island Ferry** (☎ 860/443–6851) has passenger and car service to and
from Fishers Island, New York, from New London. **Interstate Naviga-
tion** (☎ 401/783–4613) operates passenger and car service from New Lon-
don to and from Block Island, Rhode Island, from June to early September.

BY PLANE

Tweed/New Haven Airport (⊠ Burr St. off I–95, ☎ 203/466–8833),
5 mi southeast of the city, is served by US Airways Express (☎ 800/
428–4322).

BY TRAIN

Amtrak (☎ 800/872–7245) trains make stops in New Haven, New Lon-
don, and Mystic. **Metro-North Railroad** (☎ 800/638–7646; 212/532–
4900 in New York City) stops in New Haven.

Getting Around

BY BUS

Connecticut Transit (☎ 203/624–0151) provides local bus service in New
Haven and surrounding towns; there is also service to and from
Tweed/New Haven Airport.

BY CAR

Most of the southeastern Connecticut towns described above are on or just off I–95 and U.S. 1, and a car is the easiest way to explore much of the area. Interstate 395 branches north from I–95 to Norwich.

BY TAXI

Metro Taxi (☎ 203/777–7777) serves New Haven and environs.

BY TRAIN

The Connecticut Department of Transportation's **Shore Line East** (☎ 800/255–7433 in Connecticut) operates commuter rail service (weekdays, westbound in the morning, eastbound in the evening) connecting New Haven, Branford, Guilford, Madison, Clinton, Westbrook, Old Saybrook, and New London.

Contacts and Resources

EMERGENCIES

Lawrence & Memorial Hospital (✉ 365 Montauk Ave., New London, ☎ 860/442–0711). **Yale–New Haven Hospital** (✉ 20 York St., ☎ 203/688–4242).

LATE-NIGHT PHARMACY

CVS (✉ 1168 Whalley Ave., New Haven, ☎ 203/389–4714) is open until 10 on weeknights, 9 on weekends.

VISITOR INFORMATION

Connecticut River Valley and Shoreline Visitors Council (✉ 393 Main St., Middletown 06457, ☎ 860/347–0028 or 800/486–3346). **Connecticut's Mystic and More** (✉ Box 89, 470 Bank St., New London 06320, ☎ 860/444–2206 or 800/863–6569). **Greater New Haven Convention and Visitors District** (✉ 59 Elm St., Suite 100, New Haven 06511, ☎ 203/777–8550 or 800/332–7829).

THE QUIET CORNER

Few visitors to Connecticut experience the old-fashioned ways of the state's "Quiet Corner," a vast patch of sparsely populated towns that looks today much as Litchfield County did in 1980. The Quiet Corner has a reclusive allure: People used to leave New York City for the Litchfield Hills; now many are leaving for northeastern Connecticut, where the stretch of Route 169 from Brooklyn past Woodstock has been named a National Scenic Byway.

The cultural capital of the Quiet Corner is Putnam, a small mill city on the Quinebaug River whose formerly industrial town center has been transformed into a year-round antiques mart. Smaller jewels in and around the Putnam area are Brooklyn, Pomfret, Thompson, and Woodstock—four towns where authentic Colonial homesteads still seem to outnumber the contemporary, charmless clones that are springing up all too rapidly across the state.

Brooklyn

⑦ *45 mi east of Hartford.*

The village of Brooklyn bears no resemblance to the more famous borough of New York City that carries the same name. White picket fences and beautifully restored Colonial homes are the norm here.

The **New England Center for Contemporary Art** is a four-story pre-Revolutionary barn that hosts exhibitions of 20th-century art. ✉ *Rte. 169,* ☎ *860/774–8899.* *Free.* ☉ *April–Nov., Tues.–Sun. 1–5.*

Dining

$$$$ ✕ **Golden Lamb Buttery.** Connecticut's most unusual and magical din-
★   ing experience has achieved almost legendary status. Eating here is far
more than a chance to enjoy good food: It's a social and gastronomical event. There is one seating each for lunch and dinner in this converted barn. Owners Bob and Virginia "Jimmie" Booth have a vintage
Jaguar roadster and a hay wagon that guests can ride in before dinner
(a musician accompanies you). Choose from one of three daily soups
and four entrées, which might include duck à l'orange or pan-fried beef
tenderloin. ⊠ *Wolf Den and Bush Hill Rds. (off Rte. 169),* ☎ *860/
774–4423. Reservations essential. No credit cards. Closed Jan.–late May
and Sun.–Mon. No dinner Tues.–Thurs.*

Pomfret

74 *6 mi north of Brooklyn.*

Pomfret, one of the grandest towns in the region, was once known as
the inland Newport. The hilltop campus of the Pomfret School offers
some of Connecticut's loveliest views.

Sharpe Hill Vineyard, one of the state's newer wineries, is centered on
an 18th-century-style barn in the hills of Pomfret. Tours and tastings
are given, and from May to October you can nibble on smoked salmon
and fruit and cheese in the European-style wine garden. ⊠ *108 Wade
Rd.,* ☎ *860/974–3549.* 🎫 *Free.* 🕐 *Fri.–Sun. 11–5.*

Dining and Lodging

$–$$ ✕ **Vanilla Bean Café.** A perfect stop for lunch, this tan Colonial-style
barn serves salads and hearty sandwiches in an informal dining room.
Dinner entrées such as lobster ravioli and roast pork with winter vegetables are served until 8. From May to October, fare from the outside grill is served on the patio until 9; the indoor grill is fired up for
burgers year-round. The cheesecake gets rave reviews. Breakfast is
served on weekends. ⊠ *450 Deerfield Rd. (U.S. 44, Rte. 97, and Rte.
169),* ☎ *860/928–1562. No credit cards. No dinner Mon.–Tues.*

$$ 🏠 **Karinn Bed and Breakfast.** Grand Victorian furnishings and a hos-
pitable manager, Karen Schirack, make this 100-year-old inn near
Pomfret's town center the nicest of the area's many moderately priced
B&Bs. The antiques-filled rooms were once part of Miss Vinton's
School for Girls. Smoked-ham quiche and Belgian waffles are two
dishes on the breakfast menu. ⊠ *330 Pomfret St., 06258,* ☎ *860/928–
5492,* 𝖥𝖠𝖷 *860/928–6026. 5 rooms. Full breakfast. No credit cards.*

Shopping

Majilly (⊠ 56 Babbitt Hill Rd., ☎ 860/974–3714), an upscale line of
hand-painted ceramic pottery crafted in Italy, is based in a 150-year-
old barn. Open from April to December (Thursday through Saturday
10–5 and by appointment), the outlet sells still-gorgeous seconds at 50%
to 70% off the retail prices. **Martha's Herbary** (⊠ 589 Pomfret St./Rte.
169, ☎ 860/928–0009), set in a 1780 home, is an herb-theme gift shop
and garden. Classes in the demonstration kitchen cover everything from
cooking with herbs to making herbal facial masks.

Putnam

75 *5 mi northeast of Pomfret.*

Ambitious antiques dealers have reinvented Putnam, a mill town 30
mi west of Providence that became neglected after the depression. Put-
nam's downtown, with more than 10 antiques shops, is the heart of
the Quiet Corner's antiques trade. The first weekend in November is

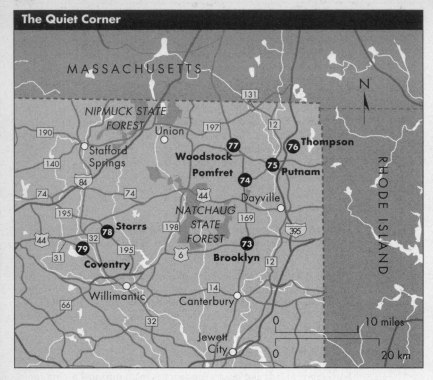

The Quiet Corner

Antiquing Weekend, when nearly two dozen area shops offer discounts and give workshops.

Dining

$$–$$$ ✕ **Vine Bistro.** This stylish trattoria-bistro is *the* place to go for a break from antiquing. Don't miss the eggplant rollatini (thinly sliced eggplant rolled with ricotta, mozzarella, Parmesan, and sun-dried tomatoes with a marinara sauce), a starter; you can follow with the house special: Pasta D'Vine (sautéed chicken breast with artichoke hearts, tomatoes, black olives, mushrooms, and homemade angel-hair pasta). ⊠ *85 Main St.,* ☎ *860/928–1660. Reservations essential. AE, MC, V. Closed Mon.*

Shopping

The three-level, 20,000-square-ft **Antiques Marketplace** (⊠ 109 Main St., ☎ 860/928–0442) houses nearly 200 dealers. The 30,000-square-ft **Putnam Antique Exchange** (⊠ 75–83 Main St., ☎ 860/928–1905) stocks 18th-century to Art Deco–era paintings, stained glass, architectural elements, and fine furnishings.

Thompson

76 *4 mi north of Putnam, 50 mi north of Groton.*

Thompson, like Pomfret, has 19th-century estates and restored Colonial homes. One particularly impressive stretch is along Route 200, from Thompson Center to where it crosses I–395.

Dining and Lodging

$$$ ✕ **White Horse at Vernon Stiles Inn.** The restaurant inside this rambling white Colonial will give you an inkling of what such places in New England were like 150 years ago. The food spans generations, though, with traditional favorites like the New York sirloin with a peppercorn-cognac cream sauce and tender New Zealand lamb with rosemary, garlic, and lemon. ⊠ *351 Thompson Rd. (Rtes. 193 and 200),* ☎ *860/923–9571. AE, D, DC, MC, V. Closed Mon.*

$$–$$$ 🔲 **Lord Thompson Manor.** You may feel like you've landed in En-
★ gland's Devonshire countryside when you reach the end of the ½ mi
winding driveway that leads to this stunning B&B. The 30-room man-
sion has African marble fireplaces and parquet floors; Frederick Law
Olmsted laid out the sprawling grounds. ⊠ *Box 428, Rte. 200, 06277,*
☎ *860/923–3886,* FAX *860/923–9310. 3 rooms, 4 suites. Meeting
rooms. Full breakfast. AE, D, DC, MC, V.*

Woodstock

🟠 *10 mi west of Thompson.*

The landscape of this enchanting town is splendid in every season—
the gently rolling hills seem to stretch for miles. **Roseland Cottage,** prob-
ably the region's most notable historic home, is a pink board-and-batten
Gothic Revival home built in 1846 by New York publisher and mer-
chant Henry Bowen. The pride of its grounds is an 1850s boxwood
parterre garden that four presidents—Ulysses S. Grant, Rutherford B.
Hayes, Benjamin Harrison, and William McKinley—have visited. An
hour-long stroll around the grounds is one of several dozen walks held
during the Quiet Corner's **Walking Weekend** offered each Columbus
Day weekend. ⊠ *556 Rte. 169,* ☎ *860/928–4074.* 🎫 *$4.* ☉ *June–mid-
Oct., Wed.–Sun. 11–5. Tours on the hr, last one at 4.*

Dining and Lodging

$$–$$$ ✕🔲 **Inn at Woodstock Hill.** This inn on a hill overlooking the coun-
tryside has sumptuous rooms with antiques, four-poster beds, fireplaces,
pitched ceilings, and timber beams. The restaurant ($$$; reservations
essential) next door serves excellent Continental and American shrimp,
veal, and chicken dishes. ⊠ *94 Plaine Hill Rd., South Woodstock
06267,* ☎ *860/928–0528,* FAX *860/928–3236. 22 rooms. Restaurant,
meeting rooms. D, MC, V.*

Shopping

The **Christmas Barn** (⊠ 835 Rte. 169, ☎ 860/928–7652) has 12 rooms
of country and Christmas goods. **Scranton's Shops** (⊠ 300 Rte. 169,
☎ 860/928–3738) sells antiques and the wares of 90 local artisans. **Windy
Acres Florist** (⊠ Rte. 171, ☎ 860/928–0554) overflows with fresh and
dried floral arrangements, baskets, pottery, and other collectibles.

Storrs

🟠 *25 mi southwest of Woodstock.*

The majority of the rolling hillside and farmland of Storrs is occupied
by the 4,400 acres and 12,000 students of the main campus of the **University of Connecticut** (UConn). Many cultural programs, sporting
events, and other happenings take place here. University Parking Services and the Student Union supply campus maps.

Hand puppets, rod puppets, body puppets, shadow puppets, mari-
⊙ onettes—the **Ballard Institute and Museum of Puppetry** has more than
2,000 puppets in its extraordinary collection. Half were created by Frank
Ballard, a master of puppetry who established the country's first complete undergraduate and graduate degree program in puppetry at
UConn more than three decades ago. Exhibits change seasonally. If you're
lucky you might even catch Oscar the Grouch from *Sesame Street* on
display. ⊠ *Univ. of Connecticut Depot Campus, 6 Bourn Place, U-212,*
☎ *860/486–4605.* 🎫 *$2.* ☉ *Hours vary; call ahead.*

The permanent collection of the **William Benton Museum of Art** includes European and American paintings, drawings, prints, and sculptures from the 16th century to the present. ⊠ *Univ. of Connecticut, 245 Glenbrook Rd.,* ☎ *860/486–4520.* ⊠ *Free.* ⊙ *Tues.–Fri. 10–4:30, weekends 1–4:30. Closed between exhibitions.*

Talk about diversity! The **University of Connecticut Greenhouses** are internationally acclaimed for their more than 3,000 different kinds of plants, from 900 varieties of exotic orchids to banana plants and a redwood tree. Organized tours are given weekends in March and April. ⊠ *Univ. of Connecticut, 75 N. Eagleville Rd.,* ☎ *860/486–4052.* ⊠ *Free.* ⊙ *Weekdays 8–4.*

Nightlife and the Arts

The **Jorgenson Auditorium** (⊠ Univ. of Connecticut, 2132 Hillside Rd., ☎ 860/486–4226) presents music, dance, and theater programs. In the Harriet S. Jorgensen Theatre (aka "Baby Jorgensen") downstairs in the Jorgenson Auditorium (☞ *above*), the **Connecticut Repertory Theatre** (⊠ ☎ 860/486–3969) produces musicals, Shakespeare, and modern dramas. **Mansfield Drive-In** (⊠ Rtes. 31 and 32, Mansfield, ☎ 860/423–4441), with three big screens, is one of the state's few remaining drive-in theaters.

Shopping

The **Eastern Connecticut Flea Market** (⊠ Mansfield Drive-In, Rtes. 31 and 32, Mansfield, ☎ 860/456–2578), with more than 150 vendors selling everything from T-shirts to toys and jewelry, unfolds on Sunday from the first weekend of spring until Thanksgiving weekend.

Coventry

 5 mi southwest of Storrs.

Coventry is the birthplace of the Revolutionary War hero Captain Nathan Hale, who was hanged as a spy by the British in 1776. It was Hale who spoke the immortal last words, "I only regret that I have but one life to lose for my country."

The **Nathan Hale Homestead** was rebuilt by Deacon Richard Hale, Nathan's father, in 1776. Ten Hale children, six of whom served in the Revolutionary War, were raised here. Family artifacts are on exhibit in the completely furnished house. The grounds include a corncrib and an 18th-century barn. ⊠ *2299 South St.,* ☎ *860/742–6917.* ⊠ *$4.* ⊙ *Mid-May–mid-Oct., daily 1–5.*

Coventry's **Caprilands Herb Farm** (⊠ 534 Silver Street, ☎ 860/742–7244) draws thousands of visitors annually to 38 gardens with more than 300 varieties of herbs, which you can purchase. There's a noon luncheon lecture program, and tea is held on the weekends (phone for reservations).

The Quiet Corner A to Z

Arriving and Departing

BY CAR

You'll need a car to reach and to explore the Quiet Corner. Many Nutmeggers live their entire lives without even noticing I–395, let alone driving on it, but this is the main highway connecting Worcester, Massachusetts, with New London—and it passes right through the Quiet Corner. From Hartford take I–84 east to U.S. 44 east, and from Providence, Rhode Island, take either U.S. 44 or 6 west.

Getting Around

BY CAR

All the towns in the Quiet Corner are on or near historic Route 169.

Contacts and Resources

EMERGENCIES

Rockville General Hospital (✉ 31 Union St., Vernon, ☎ 860/872–5292). **Windham Community Memorial Hospital** (✉ 112 Mansfield Ave., Willimantic, ☎ 860/456–6715).

LATE-NIGHT PHARMACY

CVS (✉ Mansfield Shopping Plaza, Storrs, ☎ 860/487–0223) is open until 9 Monday through Saturday and until 6 on Sunday.

VISITOR INFORMATION

Northeast Connecticut Visitors District (✉ Box 598, Putnam 06260, ☎ 860/928–1228).

CONNECTICUT A TO Z

Arriving and Departing

By Bus

Bonanza Bus Lines (☎ 800/556–3815) connects Hartford, Farmington, Southbury, Waterbury, Manchester, and Danbury with Boston and New York. **Greyhound** (☎ 800/231–2222) links Connecticut with most major cities in the United States. **Peter Pan Bus Lines** (☎ 800/237–8747) serves the eastern seaboard, including many New England cities.

By Car

From New York City head north on I–95, which hugs the Connecticut shoreline into Rhode Island or, to reach the Litchfield Hills and Hartford, head north on I–684, then east on I–84. From Springfield, Massachusetts go south on I–91, which bisects I–84 in Hartford and I–95 in New Haven. From Boston take I–95 south through Providence or take the Massachusetts Turnpike west to I–84. Interstate 395 runs north–south from southeastern Connecticut to Massachusetts.

By Plane

Many people visiting Connecticut fly into New York City's **John F. Kennedy International Airport** (☎ 718/244–4444) or **LaGuardia Airport** (☎ 718/533–3400), both of which are served by many major carriers. Another option is **Bradley International Airport** (☞ Connecticut River Valley A to Z, *above*), north of Hartford.

AIRPORT TRANSFERS

The **Airport Connection** (☎ 860/627–3400) has scheduled service from Bradley to Hartford's Union Station, as well as door-to-door service. **Connecticut Limo** (☎ 800/472–5466) operates bus and van service between Connecticut and the New York airports and to and from Bradley International Airport. **Prime Time Shuttle** (☎ 800/733–8267) serves New Haven and Fairfield counties and the greater Danbury area with service to and from both New York airports.

By Train

Amtrak (☎ 800/872–7245) runs from New York to Boston, stopping in Stamford, Bridgeport, and New Haven before heading either north to Hartford or east to Mystic. **Metro-North Railroad** (☎ 800/638–7646; 212/532–4900 from New York City) stops locally between Greenwich and New Haven, and a few trains head inland to New Canaan, Danbury, and Waterbury.

Getting Around

By Bus

See By Bus *in* the regional A to Z sections, *above,* for intrastate bus information.

By Car

The interstates are the quickest routes between many points in Connecticut, but they are busy and ugly. The speed limits on Connecticut's interstates change, sometimes going from 65 mph to 45 mph and back quite quickly through the cities. Be certain to check for posted speed limits. Right turns on red are legal unless posted otherwise.

If time allows, skip the interstates in favor of the historic Merritt Parkway (Route 15), which winds between Greenwich and Middletown; U.S. 7 and Route 8, extending between I–95 and the Litchfield Hills; Route 9, which heads south from Hartford through the Connecticut River valley to Old Saybrook; and scenic Route 169, which meanders through the Quiet Corner. Maps are available free from the **Connecticut Office of Tourism** (☞ Visitor Information, *below*).

Contacts and Resources

B&B Reservation Services

B&B, Ltd. (☎ 203/469–3260). **B&B of Mystic** (☎ 860/892–5006). **Covered Bridge B&B Reservation Service** (☎ 860/542–5944). **Nutmeg B&B Agency** (☎ 860/236–6698).

Emergencies

Ambulance, fire, police (☎ 911).

Fishing

For information about fishing licenses and regulations, call the **Department of Environmental Protection** (☎ 860/424–3000).

Guided Tours

The **Connecticut Impressionist Art Trail** (✉ Box 793, Old Lyme 06371) is a self-guided tour of a dozen museums important to the 19th-century American Impressionist movement. Write to the above address for a map.

Visitor Information

Connecticut Office of Tourism (✉ 505 Hudson St., Hartford 06106, ☎ 800/282–6863 for brochure). **State Parks Division Bureau of Outdoor Recreation** (✉ 79 Elm St., Hartford 06106, ☎ 860/424–3200). **Antiquarian and Landmarks Society** (✉ 394 Main St., Hartford 06103, ☎ 860/247–8996).

Connecticut Campground Owners Association (✉ 14 Rumford St., West Hartford 06107, ☎ 860/521–4704). **Connecticut State Golf Association** (✉ 35 Cold Spring Rd., Rocky Hill 06067, ☎ 860/257–4171).

State welcome centers, in Darien on I–95 northbound, North Stonington on I–95 southbound, Danbury on I–84 eastbound and Willington on I–84 westbound, have visitor information.

7 BACKGROUND AND ESSENTIALS

Portraits of New England

Books and Videos

Smart Travel Tips A to Z

A NEW ENGLAND PAUL REVERE WOULD RECOGNIZE

Just 20 years after the Declaration of Independence, the Reverend Timothy Dwight, President of Yale College and grandson of the fiery Puritan preacher Jonathan Edwards, set out on the first of a series of annual rambles through his native New England. In his journal, Dwight declared, "A succession of New England villages, composed of neat houses, surrounding neat schoolhouses and churches, adorned with gardens, meadows, and orchards, and exhibiting the universally easy circumstances of the inhabitants, is . . . one of the most delightful prospects which this world can afford." More than two hundred years after Dwight's first tour, the graceful small towns he described remain intact: Clapboard farmhouses, weather-beaten barns, lovely old churches, and some of the nation's best schools still line the rural routes in all six New England states.

The difference from Dwight's day to our own is that a whole world of cities and suburbs has grown up around these rural villages. New England's first cities—Portland, Boston, Providence, Newport, New London, New Haven—began as harbor towns. In the 17th century, English Puritans, fleeing religious persecution and civil war, were the first Europeans to make their fortunes in these harbors. Merchants, fishers, and shipbuilders from all over the world thrived here in the years before the American Revolution.

Even as their cities expanded, New Englanders protected their natural resources. The most famous pioneer of conservation and outdoor recreation is poet and naturalist Henry David Thoreau, who led the way in the 1840s with his famous pilgrimages to Walden Pond in Massachusetts and Mount Katahdin in Maine. In the years after the Civil War, New Englanders flocked to the mountains and the seashore seeking relief from the pressures of city life. Nature lovers and amateur mountaineers cut hiking trails and built rustic shelters in the White Mountains of New Hampshire; Massachusetts families camped and tramped in the rolling Berkshire hills; in Maine, Harvard president Charles W. Eliot and his fellow "rusticators" conserved craggy cliffs, rocky beaches, and pine forests for future generations by donating land to establish Acadia National Park. By 1910, Vermont hikers had begun work on the 265-mi "Long Trail," which connects the Green Mountain summits from Canada to the Massachusetts border. During the Great Depression, conservationists rescued the trail from highway planners who would have paved this favorite mountain footpath.

New England's tangle of turnpikes and highways originated with the area's first inhabitants. The Pocumtucks, Nehantics, Nipmucks, Wampanoags, Pequots, Mohegans, Kennebecs, Penobscots, and Narragansetts created footpaths with skills that modern engineers might envy. This vast trail network extended over rolling hills, through dense woodlands, along riverbanks and the Atlantic coast. The Mohawk Trail—Route 2 on your Massachusetts road map—ran east to west through the Deerfield and Connecticut River valleys to the Hudson River. Seasonal feasts and athletic competitions were held along this route for hundreds of years.

Like well-worn Native American byways, the familiar ingredients of the New England diet have been around since before the *Mayflower*: clams, cranberries, pumpkins, corn, squash, beans, blueberries, cod, and lobster. Clambakes and baked beans were also Native American specialties.

Another New England specialty is education: There are 65 institutions of higher learning in the greater Boston area alone. Dedication to the life of the mind is fostered at Harvard, Yale, and hundreds of excellent secondary schools, colleges, and universities throughout the region.

When it comes to weather, variety is New England's great virtue: All four seasons get full play here. September and October are dazzling as the dying leaves turn color. Foliage enthusiasts take to the rural roads and country inns to observe the way in which warm sunny days and cool autumn nights work together to paint the treetops crimson and gold. Winter usually brings plenty of snow, but if Mother Nature fails to satisfy skiers, resort owners rely on high-tech Yankee know-how (in the form of snowmaking devices) to make up the difference. Spring brings crocuses, muddy boots, and maple syrup—sugaring begins when the days are warm and the nights are still below freezing. Summer is the season to enjoy New England's lakes, beaches, and ocean resorts, from Cape Cod to Bar Harbor. Although they may not agree on matters of state, both George Bush and Bill Clinton concede that New England is a great place for a summer vacation: President Clinton is a regular guest on Martha's Vineyard and former president Bush is a longtime summer resident of Kennebunkport, Maine.

The streets of Boston, New England's largest city, provide a crash course in the early political history of the United States. The red line of the Freedom Trail begins at Boston Common, America's oldest public park, and winds past a dozen Revolutionary-era memorials, including the Granary Burial Ground where the victims of the Boston Massacre were laid to rest; Faneuil Hall, the meeting house and marketplace that earned the name "the Cradle of Liberty"; Old North Church, immortalized in Longfellow's poem "Paul Revere's Ride"; and the obelisk commemorating the Battle of Bunker Hill. Monuments to 18th-century glory stand alongside glass office towers in the busy financial district; and in the North End, the house where midnight rider Paul Revere lived is just around the corner from some of the best Italian restaurants in town.

The story of the preservation of Boston's most elegant neighborhood gives us clues about the New England character that we know incompletely from novels, films, and history books. The Boston Brahmin, the ingenious Yankee, the doom-laden Puritan, and the straitlaced reformer have contributed as much to our sense of the place as have New England's snug harbors, salty sea air, stone walls, and pine forests. In 1947, Beacon Hill matrons, dressed in felt hats and furs, conducted a sit-in to save the brick sidewalks of this historic neighborhood, whose noteworthy architectural elements include its gaslights, cast-iron fences, and sturdy brownstones. With true New England spirit, these earnest women let their opinions be known. Such a polished group of protesters was impossible to resist. Tradition was properly preserved.

These days prominent people with roots in New England are a diverse crowd. The traditional monikers—Yankee, Puritan, and Brahmin—no longer quite fit. New England luminaries include culinary icon Julia Child; actors and philanthropists Paul Newman and Joanne Woodward; actresses Glenn Close, Meg Ryan, and Geena Davis; actor James Spader; disco diva Donna Summer; rockers Aerosmith and Talking Heads; *Star Trek*'s Mr. Spock, Leonard Nimoy; media exec Sumner Redstone; Supreme Court Justice David Souter; conservative pundit John McLaughlin; novelist John Irving; and talk show host Conan O'Brien.

Despite two hundred years of growth and change—and several large cities notwithstanding—the Reverend Dwight would still recognize his beloved New England. And he'd be delighted you've decided to visit.

— Laura E. Cronin

A SOLO SOJOURN ON CAPE COD'S BEACHES

When you ride a motorcycle slowly across the Newport Bridge on a fair, windless Saturday morning in early May, it comes as a bit of a shock to realize that there are seagulls at your elbows. They glide without moving their wings, a few feet from the handlebars. Several hundred yards below, the sea is a silent blue-green diamond field, full of sparkling whitecap flaws. If you are on your way north, to the outer dunes of Cape Cod, the gulls will stay there, like feather guides, wild and discrete, nearby, in the bright droning of the north Atlantic surf.

I am spending the better part of a week walking the lower Cape, from Chatham to Provincetown, staying the night at different inns in different towns along the way, relishing the clean sheets and hot showers, setting off again early the next morning. A small rucksack reduces my worldly possessions to about seven pounds. The landscape is the journey's rationale: forest, wetlands, ponds, and ocean a movable spa. I want to swim in the surf and the kettle holes, eat seafood caught nearby, hang my shabby body out in the wind to dry, like a threadbare rug after a long winter.

Even during the late spring or early fall, when mild breezes and empty beaches make walking a delight, spending a week outdoors in New England invites a tormented relationship with the weather, and so I plan on constantly changing plans. If long stretches of beach walking become too grueling, I'm prepared to find a road that winds along the coast; a storm could restrict me to the same town for three days; head winds might send me into the forest for shelter. I will rely on that fascinating state of mind we tend to abandon as we fumble through middle age: serendipity.

Henry David Thoreau made three trips to Cape Cod in the middle of the 19th century and published his journal descriptions in book form in 1865.

In a piece called "Walking," originally published in *The Atlantic* in 1862, he remarks: "I have met with but one or two persons in the course of my life who understood the art of Walking, that is, of taking walks—who had a genius, so to speak, for *sauntering*: which word is beautifully derived 'from idle people who roved about the country, in the middle Ages . . . under pretense of going *à la Sainte Terre*,' to the Holy Land, till the children exclaimed, 'There goes a *Sainte-Terrer*,' a Saunterer, a Holy-Lander . . . Some . . . would derive the word from *sans terre*, without land or home, which . . . will mean, having no particular home, but equally at home everywhere. For this is the secret of successful sauntering . . . no more vagrant than the meandering river, which is all the while sedulously seeking the shortest course to the sea."

Thoreau is known for his eccentricities: living as a hermit in a cabin at Walden Pond, paddling down Concord rivers in a rowboat, or exploring the remote forests of northern Maine in the company of Native American guides. But in fact, he was as sane, and almost as suburban, as anyone. He taught in a secondary school, he worked as a surveyor, and he took an active interest in his family's pencil-manufacturing business. One legacy of Thoreau's life and work is his understanding that there can be no appreciation of solitude without society's presence; there can be no healthy arrangement of human affairs without the surrounding energies of the natural world.

The year's first contact with the ocean is always startling. In the fading afternoon light the water shines more brightly than the sky, in Caribbean shades, with lime-green shallows and blue depths offshore, as if lit by an underwater sun: The sand is free of people, but there are a dozen terns out fishing. They lift off and fly upstream, land, settle their feathers, and drift gently past again.

At low tide, a beach walk is a pleasant stroll on hard sand, with playful surf cooling your ankles. At high tide, the same walk becomes a grueling trudge through ankle-deep, shifting grains. T. E. Lawrence knew. Tide is everything. It is a short climb up to the summit of the Chatham Bar itself. Turning back, I can see the shingled homes and white steeples, the New England Thoreau knew.

Ten yards down the beach's outer slope, every trace of human presence disappears. It is not being on the beach by myself that is so exhilarating; it is being in the company of the shorebirds, the horseshoe crabs, and the striped bass swimming in schools offshore. The spring waves crumble and boom. Long hollow green-and-yellow tunnels rise, slide, tower, and fall along the scalloped ridges at the bottom of the tier of dunes. The sky is cloudless and blue, without any trace of high summer's humid haze. It is low tide and the gulls are fishing.

Every mile or so I stop to remove a piece of clothing. Long pants, sweater, T-shirt, socks, and sneakers all end up in the rucksack, and, after a three-hour walk up the Nauset beaches, I arrive at the green lawn, the oasis of the Nauset Knoll, with a sunburn on the back of my knees.

I sit watching the light easing, the cool gray mists rolling in. I fall asleep when my breathing synchronizes with the waves arriving from the ocean, the water snoring.

I study the wrinkled map. A route runs through Orleans to the old Cape Cod railroad bed, which the astute citizens have transformed into a bike trail. It leads quietly through an enormous marsh, through a pine wood, and past freshwater kettle ponds with beautiful names.

As I walk out into the marsh, the wind begins veering from the north. A mackerel sky appears. Everything seethes: water and grasses, even last year's unraked oak leaves. The railroad bed passes straight through the marsh in a way a road never would. I head out onto the cattail territory, the nesting red-winged blackbirds watching me go. Turtles are basking, but as the clouds send shadows like wind gusts across the water, I watch them one by one plop and swim down. As I reach the edge of the black kettle pond, a marsh hawk begins to wheel and cry. Something about the bird screaming and the haunting impression made by the visible sky is simultaneously startling and reassuring; a brief experience of the world, a Zen telephone call.

Hours pass. As the features of the world glide by, I can identify them on the map. This is satisfying; just reading off the names tells a traveler what the inhabitants thought about the place he's in: Ireland Land, Mean Tide Way, Winterberry Road.

Out here the boundaries dissolve: bird/human, man/nature, mudflat/bay. This is "land" because there are acres and acres of cattails waving, but it is sea as well, because the water fumes a few feet from the trail. And the misty atmosphere clings to the fibers of your sweater, drips gently from your eyebrows, mingling with the sweat above your eyes.

After a 3-mile crossing of the marsh, in the shelter of the first woods on the northern side, I notice a tiny sand crescent at the edge of Herring Pond. I settle under a young maple and spread a cloth for a picnic lunch. Testing the shallow, transparent water, I think, why not, and quickly wade in. Standing waist deep, just about to plunge, I notice a fur head paddling a few yards offshore: A muskrat is diving and reappearing after long fishing trips to the bottom. The raw wind and the May chill of the pond quickly transform my idea of a leisurely swim into a quick splash and a sprint back to shore for a towel.

After I cross the lowlands and have my picnic and my swim, I stop briefly in an ancient cemetery and browse among the gravestones the way you'd wander the aisles of a bookstore, looking for titles, other lives. Bright orange and yellow lichen stand out on the wet black tilted graves. Some of the stones are so old the writing has been worn to an illegible carved wrinkle, haiku epitaphs faded like the bones they identify.

Cold water and the shadows of the pine trees on the gold needles at their feet make me think of the first Pilgrim expeditions to this territory. By walking through a landscape and stopping to swim the waters, a traveler can sense the world in a way earlier generations did. I can trace the roots of our current ecological crises back to the First Encounter Beach, a mile from where I am hiking along and musing. That "first encounter" between European and native civilizations was an exchange of weapons fire. The European conception of land as property displaced a native understanding of the natural realm as common bounty. If you cannot own an ocean, or a cloud, or the sunlight, how can you own a hill, a meadow, a salt marsh, a beach?

In the imagination of everyone who grew up in New England, there is a kind of Ur-Town, and I was convinced that no such place remained. Wellfleet changes my mind. There is a forested bay and an estuary ringed by the hardwoods and the quiet town. The white steeple leans away into the changing clouds. The few streets wind among the watermen's houses, and the children still run barefoot in the picket fence backyards. A dog yelps, a slow car putters by, the ships in the harbor ride their algae moorings, and a walker sidles effortlessly in.

I eat a plate of pasta with oyster sauce and drink a glass of wine at a place called Aesop's Tables, and for the only time in my week outdoors the sky pours, and just as the world grows absolutely black, the lightning bolts of the passing squall make the candles on every table tremble and fade. Ancient Taoist philosophers in China said that hunger makes the best sauce; it's also true that a thunderstorm makes a room cozy and a dinner by a ship captain's hearth even more delightful.

The next morning, after an hour spent winding among small hardwood thickets and low watery ferns, for the first time out of earshot of the sea, I get that little uh-oh feeling that usually means, "You are completely lost."

The world and the map no longer coincide. I choose the world. I make the week's most valuable mistake, turning left at an unsigned intersection. The road gives way to a sandy trail, and I find myself in one of those beautiful lost valleys where the wealthy hide. A woman mowing in a pasture explains a different route to the water, and in half an hour I reach a dune paradise— long, deep, surging ridges, grassy bowls, sheltered valleys entirely without footprints. It is only the swarm of hungry mosquitoes that starts me sprinting toward the coast, where the onshore wind will keep them away. The bay is a different body of water altogether; it is pacific, with transparent green and blue gradations, quite shallow, with visible stones and randomly strewn kelp drawings on the bottom. I wade in and swim. The ocean here is warmer and as quiet as a pond. No matter how hot I am, the cool is instant, total, and as I sit eating my market picnic, alone in all directions, even my thoughts are clean.

The next few miles of walking are effortless. Here along Ryder Beach the heather rolls up toward the forest and the land itself begins to swell. It is bare without being barren, somewhat wistfully austere. Edward Hopper built himself a house in Truro in the 1930s, and the clear light he gave his life to is still here. Up in the warm meadows, there is toe-soft loam producing flowers, twitching gently in the early afternoon; coiled streams and estuaries are set in beside the land. I'm trying not to exaggerate, but you can't tell if what you're seeing is a painting or a dream.

The morning of the final day, I wake to a room full of chilly fog. Having left both windows open, I am literally wrapped in weather. On the Highland Road to the Cape Cod Lighthouse for the final leg, my footsteps have a new reluctance.

One of the most remarkable aspects of this week outdoors is the experience of the ocean on its own terms; what seems recreational and tame among the tilted umbrellas and radios and Frisbee-chasing dogs becomes altogether unfamiliar after a few hours alone. Water rises and falls, wrapping an entire globe as it rockets through outer space, centrifugally whirling as it goes. The water speaks in tongues, and after several days you begin to listen.

My hands are actually cold, my knuckles frozen. I'm playing Guess the Season. In a world of sand and water and wind, there are fewer clues. The wind booms, the ocean's humming, and the loud waves build and fall and shake the gravel I'm on as the last wave hisses and recedes into the next.

After several days of steady traveling up the coast, walking and thinking fuse, the ordinary divisions of mind and body lose their boundaries. The easygoing motion of my limbs seems to belong to the Cape dunes and riverbeds, the way the ebbing and flooding tides, the piled clouds, the crying birds do. Toward the end of his life Thoreau made an unobtrusive entry in his journal: "All I can say is that I live and breathe and have my thoughts." Out here that short list of attributes seems plenty.

The harbor side streets are empty as I go searching for a room. It is strange to have touched a long stretch of geography with your feet. You feel a friendship toward the roaming world out there; contact has given you calm.

A lighthouse blinks every four seconds. A white lobster boat is mooring in the last light. I find a room in a house by the water. As New England weather will, the sky changes while I'm at the front desk checking in. Up on the third floor, I can look off into the sunset's afterglow. The sky clears, turning cheddar gold.

— Anthony Chase

WHAT TO READ & WATCH BEFORE YOU GO

New England has been home to some of America's classic authors, among them Herman Melville, Edith Wharton, Mark Twain, Robert Frost, Ralph Waldo Emerson, Henry Wadsworth Longfellow, and Emily Dickinson. Henry David Thoreau wrote about New England in *Cape Cod, The Maine Woods,* and his masterpiece, *Walden.* Modern New England literary voices have included writers as disparate as the Beat Generation's Jack Kerouac, many of whose early works were set in his native Lowell, Massachusetts; and Stephen King, the horrormeister of Bangor, Maine.

Fiction and film offer insight into aspects of New England's character. Melville's *Moby-Dick,* set on a 19th-century Nantucket whaler, captures the spirit of the whaling era; Gregory Peck starred in the 1956 screen version under John Huston's direction. Nathaniel Hawthorne portrayed early New England life in his novels *The Scarlet Letter* (the poorly received 1995 movie stars Demi Moore) and *The House of the Seven Gables* (the actual house, in Salem, Massachusetts, is open to the public). Although he was born in New York, Henry James grew up in and around Boston, whose mid-19th-century polite society he dissected with his usual deftness and delicacy in *The Bostonians* (the 1984 film starred Christopher Reeve and Vanessa Redgrave). The beautiful 1994 screen adaptation of Louisa May Alcott's classic, *Little Women,* casts Winona Ryder as Jo and Susan Sarandon as Marmee. Visitors are welcome at Alcott's house (look for shots of it in the movie) in Concord, Massachusetts. Some scenes were also filmed at Historic Deerfield in the Pioneer Valley. A specially constructed 17th-century village on Hog Island, near Essex, Massachusetts, was a 1995 location for the filming of *The Crucible,* Arthur Miller's 1953 play about the Salem witch trials. The movie stars Daniel Day-Lewis and Winona Ryder.

Two books, one fiction and the other social history, provide a fascinating look at that storied creature, the Boston Brahmin. *The Late George Apley,* the classic novel by Newburyport, Massachusetts, native John P. Marquand, follows a Beacon Hill denizen from cradle to grave; Cleveland Amory's *The Proper Bostonians* takes a look at Apley's real-life milieu. Turning to a vastly different Boston social realm, Edwin O'Connor's novel *The Last Hurrah* focuses on the Hub's Irish-American politicians, in particular a central character based on legendary Boston mayor James Michael Curley. John Ford directed an excellent 1958 film adaptation starring Spencer Tracy. For a taste of the Boston demimonde, complete with plenty of inside references and local color, there are always George V. Higgins's crime novels, such as *The Friends of Eddie Coyle,* and the *Spenser* private eye series, written by Robert Parker.

Social chronicler Tracy Kidder examines modern-day Northampton, Massachusetts, in *Home Town,* published in 1999. His book explores how that peaceful college town in the Pioneer Valley has kept itself a community in the face of changing times and an influx of new residents.

Next to Thoreau's *Cape Cod,* perhaps the best nonfiction account of life on the Cape before the postwar resort revolution is Henry Beston's 1928 *The Outermost House,* a description of the author's solitary sojourn in a dwelling on the Great Beach, near Chatham. Sadly, Beston's hideaway was destroyed several decades ago, in a ferocious storm.

The Cape's bohemian mecca of Provincetown figured prominently in the career of playwright Eugene O'Neill, whose early works were performed at the Provincetown Playhouse. It was O'Neill (his boyhood home is preserved in New London, Connecticut) who created one of the most vivid portrayals of the dark side of the New England persona in his 1926 play *Desire under the Elms,* although some readers might give the Calvinist gloom award to Edith Wharton for her novel *Ethan Frome,* filmed on location in Vermont in 1993 with Liam Neeson in the title role. (Wharton's grand residence, the Mount, is in Lenox, Massachusetts, and offers a much cheerier atmosphere.)

Among books written about the Maine islands are Philip Conkling's *Islands in Time,* Bill Caldwell's *Islands of Maine,* and Charlotte Fardelmann's *Islands Down East.* Kenneth Roberts set a series of historical novels, beginning with *Arundel,* in the coastal Kennebunk region during the Revolutionary War and also wrote *Trending into Maine,* a book of essays on traditional but rapidly changing Down East ways of life. Sarah Orne Jewett's 1896 novel, *The Country of the Pointed Firs,* describes the heart of small-town life with sympathy. Ruth Moore's *Candalmas Bay, Speak to the Winds,* and *The Weir* and Elisabeth Ogilvie's "Tide Trilogy" books capture both the romanticism and hardships of coastal life. Carolyn Chute's 1985 best-seller, *The Beans of Egypt, Maine,* offers a fictional glimpse of the hardships of contemporary rural life. The 1994 movie version of the book, starring Martha Plimpton, is in video stores with the title *Forbidden Choices.*

Charles Morrissey's *Vermont: A History* delivers just what the title promises; it's part of a series of bicentennial histories, all published by Norton, in which the other five New England states are also represented. *Without a Farmhouse Near,* by Deborah Rawson, describes the impact of change on small Vermont communities, as does Joe Sherman's *Fast Lane on a Dirt Road. Real Vermonters Don't Milk Goats,* by Frank Bryan and Bill Mares, looks at the lighter side of life in the Green Mountain

state. Howard Frank Mosher, long a resident of Vermont's sparsely populated, bleakly beautiful Northeast Kingdom, has written works of fiction including *A Stranger in the Kingdom, Northern Borders,* and *Where the Rivers Flow North,* all dealing with the hard lives and bristly independence of the region's natives. *Where the Rivers Flow North* was made into an acclaimed independent film in 1993, with stars Rip Torn and Michael J. Fox. Another video with a Vermont locale—although in a vastly different, comic vein—is John O'Brien's 1996 *Man with a Plan,* about a retired dairy farmer who decides to run for Congress.

Visitors to New Hampshire may enjoy the classic 19th-century history-cum-travel guide *The White Mountains: Their Legends, Landscape, and Poetry,* by Thomas Starr King, and *The Great Stone Face and Other Tales of the White Mountains,* by Nathaniel Hawthorne. New Hampshire was also blessed with the poet Robert Frost, whose first books, *A Boy's Way* and *North of Boston,* are set here, as is his long poem *New Hampshire.* It's commonly accepted that the Grover's Corners of Thornton Wilder's play *Our Town* is the real-life Peterborough. The 1981 movie *On Golden Pond* was partially filmed on Squam Lake.

Other books and video capture different sides of New England life. Sloan Wilson's novel *The Man in the Gray Flannel Suit* renders the life of a Connecticut commuter (Gregory Peck in the movie version) in the 1950s. In *Theophilus North* (1973), Thornton Wilder portrays Newport, Rhode Island, in 1929, its social heyday. Julia Roberts's first movie, the charming *Mystic Pizza,* focuses on a group of young Mystic, Connecticut, women and their romances.

Anyone traveling with young children should check out Robert McCloskey's classic picture books, which can get anyone in the mood for a trip to the area. These include *Make Way for Ducklings* (set in Boston) and *Blueberries for Sal* and *Morning in Maine* (both set in Maine).

Also published by Fodor's, *New England's Best Bed & Breakfasts* has more than 300 reviews of places to stay and things to do in the region; *National Parks and Seashores of the East* covers many New England destinations; and *Where Should We Take the Kids? The Northeast* provides ideas on what to do with the little ones while in New England. Fodor's Compass American Guides, handsomely illustrated with color photographs, provide topical and cultural essays and historical background. Look for *Southern New England,* by Anna Mundow, covering Connecticut, Rhode Island, and Massachusetts; *Vermont,* by Don Mitchell; *Maine,* by Charles Calhoun; and *Boston,* by Patricia Dixon, David Lyon, Joe Sartore, and Patricia Harris.

SMART TRAVEL TIPS A TO Z

Smart Travel Tips A to Z

AIR TRAVEL

BOOKING YOUR FLIGHT

Price is just one factor to consider when booking a flight: Frequency of service and even a carrier's safety record are often just as important. Major airlines offer the greatest number of departures. Smaller airlines—including regional and no-frills airlines—usually have a limited number of flights daily. On the other hand, so-called low-cost airlines usually are cheaper, and their fares impose fewer restrictions, such as advance-purchase requirements. Safety-wise, low-cost carriers as a group have a good history—about equal to that of major carriers.

When you book, **look for nonstop flights** and **remember that "direct" flights stop at least once.** Try to **avoid connecting flights,** which require a change of plane. Two airlines may jointly operate a connecting flight, so ask if your airline operates every segment—you may find that your preferred carrier flies you only part of the way.

Ask your airline if it offers electronic ticketing, which eliminates all paperwork. There's no ticket to pick up or misplace. You go directly to the gate and give the agent your confirmation number—a real blessing if you've lost your ticket or made last-minute changes in travel plans. There's no worry about waiting in line at the airport while precious minutes tick by.

CARRIERS

➤ MAJOR AIRLINES: **American** (☎ 800/433–7300). **Continental** (☎ 800/525–0280). **Delta** (☎ 800/221–1212). **Northwest** (☎ 800/225–2525). **Southwest** (☎ 800/435–9792). **TWA** (☎ 800/221–2000). **United** (☎ 800/241–6522). **US Airways** (☎ 800/428–4322).

➤ REGIONAL AIRLINES: **Business Express** (☎ 800/345–3400). **Cape Air/Nantucket Airlines** (☎ 508/790–3122 or 888/352–0714). **Colgan Air** (☎ 800/206–1800). **Midway** (☎ 800/446–4392).

➤ FROM THE U.K.: **American** (☎ 0345/789–789). **British Airways** (☎ 0345/222–111). **Virgin Atlantic** (☎ 01293/747–747).

CHECK-IN & BOARDING

Assuming that not everyone with a ticket will show up, airlines routinely overbook planes. When that happens, airlines ask for volunteers to give up their seats. In return these volunteers usually get a certificate for a free flight and are rebooked on the next flight out. If there are not enough volunteers, the airline must choose who will be denied boarding. The first to get bumped are passengers who checked in late and those flying on discounted tickets, so **get to the gate and check in as early as possible,** especially during peak periods.

Always **bring a government-issued photo ID to the airport,** even for domestic flights. You may be asked to show it before you are allowed to check in

CUTTING COSTS

The least-expensive airfares to New England must usually be purchased in advance and are non-refundable. It's smart to **call a number of airlines, and when you are quoted a good price, book it on the spot**—the same fare may not be available the next day. Always **check different routings** and look into using different airports. Travel agents, especially low-fare specialists (☞ Discounts & Deals, *below*), are helpful.

Consolidators are another good source. They buy tickets for scheduled international flights at reduced rates from the airlines, then sell them at prices that beat the best fare available directly from the airlines, usually without restrictions. Sometimes you can even get your money back if you need to return the ticket. Carefully read the fine print detailing penalties for changes and cancellations, and **confirm your consolidator reservation with the airline.**

When you **fly as a courier** you trade your checked-luggage space for a ticket deeply subsidized by a courier service. There are restrictions on when you can book and how long you can stay.

➤ CONSOLIDATORS: **Cheap Tickets** (☎ 800/377–1000). **Up & Away Travel** (☎ 212/889–2345). **Discount Airline Ticket Service** (☎ 800/576–1600). **Unitravel** (☎ 800/325–2222). **World Travel Network** (☎ 800/409–6753).

ENJOYING THE FLIGHT

For more legroom **request an emergency-aisle seat.** Don't sit in the row in front of the emergency aisle or in front of a bulkhead, where seats may not recline. If you have dietary concerns, **ask for special meals when booking.** These can be vegetarian, low-cholesterol, or kosher, for example. On long flights, try to maintain a normal routine, to help fight jetlag. At night **get some sleep.** By day **eat lightly, drink water** (not alcohol), and **move around the cabin** to stretch your legs.

FLYING TIMES

Flying time to Boston is 1 hour from New York, 2 hours and 15 minutes from Chicago, 6 hours from Los Angeles, 4 hours from Dallas, and 8 hours from London.

HOW TO COMPLAIN

If your baggage goes astray or your flight goes awry, complain right away. Most carriers require that you **file a claim immediately.**

➤ AIRLINE COMPLAINTS: U.S. Department of Transportation **Aviation Consumer Protection Division** (✉ C-75, Room 4107, Washington, DC 20590, ☎ 202/366–2220). **Federal Aviation Administration Consumer Hotline** (☎ 800/322–7873).

AIRPORTS

A major gateway to New England is Boston's Logan International Airport, the largest airport in New England. Bradley International Airport, in Windsor Locks, Connecticut, 12 mi north of Hartford, is convenient to western Massachusetts and all of Connecticut. T. F. Green State Airport, just outside Providence, Rhode Island, is another major airport. Additional New England airports served by major carriers include those in Manchester, New Hampshire (which is growing rapidly and is a lower-cost alternative to Boston); Portland and Bangor, Maine; Burlington, Vermont; and Hyannis and Worcester, Massachusetts (☞ regional and state A to Z sections *in* corresponding chapters for information).

➤ AIRPORT INFORMATION: **Logan International Airport** (Exit 24 off I–93 N, East Boston, MA, ☎ 800/235–6426). **Bradley International Airport** (Rte. 20; take Exit 40 off I–91, Windsor Locks, CT, ☎ 860/292–2000). **T. F. Green State Airport** (U.S. 1, or Exit 22 off I–95, Warwick, RI, ☎ 401/737–4000).

BIKE TRAVEL

BIKES IN FLIGHT

Most airlines accommodate bikes as luggage, provided they are dismantled and boxed. For bike boxes, often free at bike shops, you'll pay about $5 (at least $100 for bike bags) from airlines. International travelers can sometimes substitute a bike for a piece of checked luggage at no charge; otherwise, the cost is about $100. Domestic and Canadian airlines charge $25–$50.

BOAT & FERRY TRAVEL

See the A to Z sections at the end of Chapters 1 through 6.

BUS TRAVEL

All New England states have bus service; fares are cheap and buses normally run on schedule, although service can be infrequent and travel time can be long due to traffic and frequent stops.

FARES & SCHEDULES

➤ BUS INFORMATION: Bonanza (☎
800/556–3815). Concord Trailways
(☎ 800/639–3317). Greyhound Lines
(☎ 800/231–2222). Peter Pan Trailways (☎ 800/343–9999). Vermont
Transit (☎ 802/864–6811 or 800/
451–3292).

BUSINESS HOURS

Banks in New England are generally
open weekdays from 9 AM until 3 PM,
post offices weekdays between 8 AM
and 5 PM; many branches operate
Saturday morning hours. Business
hours tend to be weekdays from 9 to
5. Many stores may not open until 10
or 11, but they remain open until 6 or
7; most carry on brisk business on
Saturday as well. Stores in tourist
areas may be open on Sundays, too.
Suburban shopping malls are generally open seven days a week, with
evening hours every day except Sunday. All across New England, so-
called convenience stores sell food
and sundries until about 11 PM.
Along the highways and in major
cities you can usually find all-night
diners, supermarkets, drugstores, and
convenience stores.

CAMERAS & PHOTOGRAPHY

➤ PHOTO HELP: Kodak Information
Center (☎ 800/242–2424). *Kodak
Guide to Shooting Great Travel
Pictures,* available in bookstores or
from Fodor's Travel Publications
(☎ 800/533–6478; $16.50 plus $4
shipping).

EQUIPMENT PRECAUTIONS

Always **keep your film and tape out
of the sun.** Carry an extra supply of
batteries, and **be prepared to turn on
your camera or camcorder** to prove to
security personnel that the device is
real. Always **ask for hand inspection
of film,** which becomes clouded after
successive exposures to airport X-ray
machines, and **keep videotapes away
from metal detectors.**

CAR RENTAL

Rates in Boston begin at $41 a day
and $200 a week for an economy car
with air-conditioning, an automatic
transmission, and unlimited mileage.
This does not include tax on car
rentals, which is 5%.

➤ MAJOR AGENCIES: **Alamo** (☎ 800/
327–9633; 0181/759–6200 in the
U.K.). **Avis** (☎ 800/331–1212; 800/
879–2847 in Canada; 02/9353–9000
in Australia; 09/525–1982 in New
Zealand). **Budget** (☎ 800/527–0700;
0144/227–6266 in the U.K.). **Dollar**
(☎ 800/800–4000; 0181/897–0811
in the U.K., where it is known as
Eurodollar; 02/9223–1444 in Australia). **Hertz** (☎ 800/654–3131; 800/
263–0600 in Canada; 0181/897–
2072 in the U.K.; 02/9669–2444 in
Australia; 03/358–6777 in New
Zealand). **National InterRent** (☎
800/227–7368; 0345/222525 in the
U.K., where it is known as Europcar
InterRent).

CUTTING COSTS

To get the best deal **book through a
travel agent who will shop around.**
Also **price local car-rental companies,**
although the service and maintenance
may not be as good as those of a
major player. Remember to ask about
required deposits, cancellation penalties, and drop-off charges if you're
planning to pick up the car in one city
and leave it in another. If you're
traveling during a holiday period,
also make sure that a confirmed
reservation guarantees you a car.

INSURANCE

When driving a rented car you are
generally responsible for any damage
to or loss of the vehicle as well as for
any property damage or personal
injury that you may cause. Before you
rent, see what coverage your personal
auto-insurance policy and credit cards
already provide.

For about $15 to $20 per day, rental
companies sell protection, known as a
collision- or loss-damage waiver
(CDW or LDW), that eliminates your
liability for damage to the car. In
Massachusetts the car-rental company
must pay for damage to third parties
up to a preset legal limit, beyond
which your own liability insurance
kicks in. However, **make sure you
have enough coverage to pay for the
car.** If you do not have auto insurance
or an umbrella policy that covers
damage to third parties, purchasing
liability insurance and a CDW or
LDW is highly recommended.

REQUIREMENTS & RESTRICTIONS

In New England you must be 21 to rent a car, and rates may be higher if you're under 25. You'll pay extra for child seats (about $3 per day), which are compulsory for children under five, and for additional drivers (about $2 per day). Non-U.S. residents will need a reservation voucher, a passport, a driver's license, and a travel policy that covers each driver, in order to pick up a car.

SURCHARGES

Before you pick up a car in one city and leave it in another **ask about drop-off charges or one-way service fees,** which can be substantial. Note, too, that some rental agencies charge extra if you return the car before the time specified in your contract. To avoid a hefty refueling fee **fill the tank just before you turn in the car,** but be aware that gas stations near the rental outlet may overcharge.

CAR TRAVEL

Because public transportation is spotty or completely lacking in the outer reaches of New England, a car is the most convenient means of transportation.

AUTO CLUBS

➤ In Australia: **Australian Automobile Association** (☎ 02/6247–7311).

➤ In Canada: **Canadian Automobile Association** (CAA, ☎ 613/247–0117).

➤ In New Zealand: **New Zealand Automobile Association** (☎ 09/377–4660).

➤ In the U.K.: **Automobile Association** (AA, ☎ 0990/500–600). **Royal Automobile Club** (RAC, ☎ 0990/722–722 for membership; 0345/121–345 for insurance).

➤ In the U.S.: **American Automobile Association** (☎ 800/564–6222).

GASOLINE

Self-service gas stations are the norm in New England, though in some of the less populated regions you'll find stations with one or two pumps and a friendly attendant who provides full service (pumping your gas, checking your tires and oil, washing your windows). At press time, rates for unleaded regular gas at self-service stations in New England were about $1.09 per gallon (somewhat higher in Connecticut); rates at full-service stations ranged from 10¢ to 30¢ more.

ROAD MAPS

Each of the states in New England makes available a map that has directories, mileage, and other useful information—contact the state offices of tourism (☞ Visitor Information, *below*). Jimapco produces detailed maps of Massachusetts. Hagstrom sells maps of Connecticut. Rand McNally prints a detailed map of Rhode Island. Delorme publishes topographical atlases of Connecticut/Rhode Island, Maine, New Hampshire, and Vermont that include most back roads and many outdoor recreation sites. The maps are widely available in the state.

RULES OF THE ROAD

The speed limit in much of New England is 65 mph on interstate and some limited-access highways (55 mph in densely populated areas), and 50 mph on most other roads (25–30 mph in towns and cities). In New England, drivers can turn right at a red light (unless signs indicate otherwise) providing they come to a full stop and check to see that the intersection is clear first.

CHILDREN IN NEW ENGLAND

In New England, there's no shortage of things to do with children. Major museums have children's sections, and there are children's museums in cities large and small. Children love the roadside attractions found in many tourist areas, and miniature golf courses are easy to come by. Attractions such as beaches and boat rides, parks and planetariums, lighthouses and llama treks are fun for youngsters as are special events, such as crafts fairs and food festivals.

Be sure to plan ahead and **involve your youngsters** as you outline your trip. When packing, include things to keep them busy en route. On sightseeing days try to schedule activities of special interest to your children. If you are renting a car don't forget to **arrange for a car seat** when you reserve.

➤ LOCAL INFORMATION: Consult Fodor's lively by-parents, for-parents *Where Should We Take the Kids? Northeast* (available in bookstores, or ☎ 800/533–6478; $16).

FLYING

If your children are two or older **ask about children's airfares.** As a general rule, infants under two not occupying a seat fly at greatly reduced fares or even for free. Experts agree that it's a good idea to use safety seats aloft for children weighing less than 40 pounds. Airlines set their own policies: U.S. carriers usually require that the child be ticketed, even if he or she is young enough to ride free, since the seats must be strapped into regular seats. Do **check your airline's policy about using safety seats during take-off and landing.** And since safety seats are not allowed just everywhere in the plane, get your seat assignments early.

When reserving, **request children's meals or a freestanding bassinet** if you need them. But note that bulk head seats, where you must sit to use the bassinet may lack an overhead bin or storage space on the floor.

LODGING

Chain hotels and motels welcome children, and New England has many family-oriented resorts with lively children's programs. You'll also find farms that accept guests and that are lots of fun for children; the Vermont Travel Division (☞ Visitor Information, *below*) publishes a directory. Rental houses and apartments abound, particularly around ski areas; off-season, these can be economical as well as comfortable touring bases. Some country inns, especially those with a quiet, romantic atmosphere and those furnished with antiques, are less enthusiastic about little ones, so **be up front about your traveling companions** when you reserve.

Most hotels allow children under a certain age to stay in their parents' room at no extra charge; others charge them as extra adults; be sure to **find out the cutoff age for children's discounts.**

SIGHTS & ATTRACTIONS

Places that are especially good for children are indicated by a rubber duckie icon in the margin.

COMPUTERS ON THE ROAD

Checking your e-mail or surfing the Web can sometimes be done in the business centers of major hotels, which usually charge an hourly rate. Web access is also available at many fax and copy centers, many of which are open 24 hours and on weekends. In major cities look for cyber cafés, where tabletop computers allow you to log on while sipping coffee and listening to live jazz. Whether you have e-mail at home or not, you can **arrange to have a free temporary e-mail address** from several services, including one available at www.hotmail.com (the site explains how to apply for an address).

CONSUMER PROTECTION

Whenever shopping or buying travel services in New England, **pay with a major credit card** so you can cancel payment or get reimbursed if there's a problem. If you're doing business with a particular company for the first time, **contact your local Better Business Bureau and the attorney general's offices** in your state and the company's home state, as well. Have any complaints been filed? Finally, if you're buying a package or tour, always **consider travel insurance** that includes default coverage (☞ Insurance, *below*).

➤ LOCAL BBBs: Council of Better Business Bureaus (✉ 4200 Wilson Blvd., Suite 800, Arlington, VA 22203, ☎ 703/276–0100, FAX 703/525–8277).

CUSTOMS & DUTIES

When shopping, **keep receipts** for all purchases. Upon reentering the country, **be ready to show customs officials what you've bought.** If you feel a duty is incorrect or object to the way your clearance was handled, note the inspector's badge number and ask to see a supervisor. If the problem isn't resolved, write to the appropriate authorities, beginning with the port director at your point of entry.

IN AUSTRALIA

Australia residents who are 18 or older may bring home $A400 worth of souvenirs and gifts (including jewelry), 250 cigarettes or 250 grams of tobacco, and 1,125 ml of alcohol (including wine, beer, and spirits). Residents under 18 may bring back $A200 worth of goods. Prohibited items include meat products. Seeds, plants, and fruits need to be declared upon arrival.

➤ INFORMATION: **Australian Customs Service** (Regional Director, ✉ Box 8, Sydney, NSW 2001, ☎ 02/9213–2000, FAX 02/9213–4000).

IN CANADA

Canadian residents who have been out of Canada for at least 7 days may bring home C$500 worth of goods duty-free. If you've been away less than 7 days but more than 48 hours, the duty-free allowance drops to C$200; if your trip lasts 24–48 hours, the allowance is C$50. You may not pool allowances with family members. Goods claimed under the C$500 exemption may follow you by mail; those claimed under the lesser exemptions must accompany you. Alcohol and tobacco products may be included in the 7-day and 48-hour exemptions but not in the 24-hour exemption. If you meet the age requirements of the province or territory through which you reenter Canada, you may bring in, duty-free, 1.14 liters (40 imperial ounces) of wine or liquor *or* 24 12-ounce cans or bottles of beer or ale. If you are 16 or older you may bring in, duty-free, 200 cigarettes and 50 cigars. Check ahead of time with Revenue Canada or the Department of Agriculture for policies regarding meat products, seeds, plants, and fruits.

You may send an unlimited number of gifts worth up to C$60 each duty-free to Canada. Label the package UNSOLICITED GIFT—VALUE UNDER $60. Alcohol and tobacco are excluded.

➤ INFORMATION: **Revenue Canada** (✉ 2265 St. Laurent Blvd. S, Ottawa, Ontario K1G 4K3, ☎ 613/993–0534; 800/461–9999 in Canada).

IN NEW ZEALAND

Homeward-bound residents 17 or older may bring back $700 worth of souvenirs and gifts. Your duty-free allowance also includes 4.5 liters of wine or beer; one 1,125-ml bottle of spirits; and either 200 cigarettes, 250 grams of tobacco, 50 cigars, or a combination of the three up to 250 grams. Prohibited items include meat products, seeds, plants, and fruits.

➤ INFORMATION: **New Zealand Customs** (Custom House, ✉ 50 Anzac Ave., Box 29, Auckland, New Zealand, ☎ 09/359–6655, FAX 09/359–6732).

IN THE U.K.

From countries outside the EU, including the United States, you may bring home, duty-free, 200 cigarettes or 50 cigars; 1 liter of spirits or 2 liters of fortified or sparkling wine or liqueurs; 2 liters of still table wine; 60 milliliters of perfume; 250 milliliters of toilet water; plus £136 worth of other goods, including gifts and souvenirs. If returning from outside the EU, prohibited items include meat products, seeds, plants, and fruits.

➤ INFORMATION: **HM Customs and Excise** (✉ Dorset House, Stamford St., Bromley Kent BR1 1XX, ☎ 0171/202–4227).

IN THE U.S.

Non-U.S. residents ages 21 and older may import into the United States 200 cigarettes or 50 cigars or 2 kilograms of tobacco, 1 liter of alcohol, and gifts worth $100. Meat products, seeds, plants, and fruits are prohibited.

➤ INFORMATION: **U.S. Customs Service** (inquiries, ✉ 1300 Pennsylvania Ave. NW, Washington, DC 20229, ☎ 202/927–6724; complaints, ✉ Office of Regulations and Rulings, 1300 Pennsylvania Ave. NW, Washington, DC 20229; registration of equipment, ✉ Resource Management, 1300 Pennsylvania Ave. NW, Washington, DC 20229, ☎ 202/927–0540).

DINING

Seafood is king throughout New England. Clams, quahogs, lobster, and scrod are prepared here in an infinite number of ways, some fancy and expensive, others simple and moderately priced. One of the best ways to enjoy seafood is in the rough—off paper plates on a picnic table at a clam boil or clambake—or at one of the many shacklike eating places along the coast, where you can smell the salt air.

Among the quintessentially New England dishes served at inland resorts and inns are Indian pudding, clam chowder, fried clams, and cranberry anything. You can also find multicultural variations on themes, such as Portuguese *chouriço* (a spicy red sausage that transforms a clam boil into something heavenly) and the mincemeat pie made with pork in the tradition of the French Canadians who populate the northern regions.

The restaurants we list are the cream of the crop in each price category. Properties indicated by an ✕🍴 are lodging establishments whose restaurant warrants a special trip. Following is the price chart used in this book; note that prices do not include tax, which is 6% in Connecticut, 7% in Maine, 5% in Massachusetts, 8% in New Hampshire, 7% in Rhode Island, and 9% in Vermont.

CATEGORY	COST*
$$$$	over $40
$$$	$25–$40
$$	$15–$25
$	under $15

*cost of a three-course dinner, per person, excluding drinks, taxes, and tip

RESERVATIONS & DRESS

Reservations are always a good idea: we mention them only when they're essential or are not accepted. Book as far ahead as you can, and reconfirm as soon as you arrive. We mention dress only when men are required to wear a jacket or a jacket and tie.

DISABILITIES & ACCESSIBILITY

In Boston, many sidewalks are brick or cobblestone and may be uneven or sloping; many have curbs cut at one end and not the other. To make matters worse, Boston drivers are notorious for running yellow lights and ignoring pedestrians. Back Bay has flat, well-paved streets; older Beacon Hill is steep and difficult; Quincy Market's cobblestone and brick malls are crisscrossed with smooth, tarred paths. The downtown financial district and Chinatown are accessible, while areas such as the South End and the Italian North End may prove more problematic for people who use wheelchairs. In Cape Cod, a number of towns such as Wellfleet, Hyannis, and Chatham have wide streets with curb cuts; and the Cape Cod National Seashore has several accessible trails. In Kennebunkport, as in many of Maine's coastal towns south of Portland, travelers with mobility impairments will have to cope with crowds as well as with narrow, uneven steps and sporadic curb cuts. L.L. Bean's outlet in Freeport is fully accessible, and Acadia National Park has some 50 accessible mi of carriage roads that are closed to motor vehicles. In New Hampshire, many of Franconia Notch's natural attractions are accessible.

➤ LOCAL RESOURCES: **Massachusetts Bay Transportation Authority** (MBTA, Office for Transportation Access, 10 Boylston Pl., Boston 02116, ☎ 617/222–5123, TTY 617/222–5415) has a brochure, "MBTA: Access," that outlines Boston's transportation options. **Cape Cod Chamber of Commerce** (U.S. 6 and Rte. 132, Hyannis 02601, ☎ 508/362–3225 or 888/332–2732) has two publications with accessibility ratings: "Visitor's Guide" and "Accommodations Directory." The **Cape Cod National Seashore** (South Wellfleet 02663, ☎ 508/349–3785) publishes "Cape Cod National Seashore Accessibility." The **New Hampshire Office of Vacation Travel** (☎ 603/271–2343) puts out "New Hampshire Guide Book," which includes accessibility ratings for lodgings and restaurants.

LODGING

When discussing accessibility with an operator or reservations agent **ask hard questions.** Are there any stairs, inside *or* out? Are there grab bars next to the toilet *and* in the shower/tub? How wide is the doorway to the room? To the bathroom? For the most extensive facilities meeting the latest legal specifications **opt for newer accommodations.**

➤ COMPLAINTS: **Disability Rights Section** (✉ U.S. Department of Justice, Civil Rights Division, Box 66738, Washington, DC 20035-6738,

☎ 202/514–0301; 800/514–0301; 202/514–0301 TTY; 800/514–0301 TTY, ℻ 202/307–1198) for general complaints. **Aviation Consumer Protection Division** (☞ Air Travel, *above*) for airline-related problems. **Civil Rights Office** (✉ U.S. Department of Transportation, Departmental Office of Civil Rights, S-30, 400 7th St. SW, Room 10215, Washington, DC 20590, ☎ 202/366–4648, ℻ 202/366–9371) for problems with surface transportation.

TRAVEL AGENCIES

In the United States, although the Americans with Disabilities Act requires that travel firms serve the needs of all travelers, some agencies specialize in working with people with disabilities.

➤ TRAVELERS WITH MOBILITY PROBLEMS: **Access Adventures** (✉ 206 Chestnut Ridge Rd., Rochester, NY 14624, ☎ 716/889–9096), run by a former physical-rehabilitation counselor. **CareVacations** (✉ 5-5110 50th Ave., Leduc, Alberta, Canada T9E 6V4, ☎ 780/986–6404 or 780/986–8332) has group tours and is especially helpful with cruise vacations. **Flying Wheels Travel** (✉ 143 W. Bridge St., Box 382, Owatonna, MN 55060, ☎ 507/451–5005 or 800/535–6790, ℻ 507/451–1685). **Hinsdale Travel Service** (✉ 201 E. Ogden Ave., Suite 100, Hinsdale, IL 60521, ☎ 630/325–1335).

➤ TRAVELERS WITH DEVELOPMENTAL DISABILITIES: **Sprout** (✉ 893 Amsterdam Ave., New York, NY 10025, ☎ 212/222–9575 or 888/222–9575, ℻ 212/222–9768).

DISCOUNTS & DEALS

Be a smart shopper and **compare all your options** before making decisions. A plane ticket bought with a promotional coupon from travel clubs, coupon books, and direct-mail offers may not be cheaper than the least expensive fare from a discount ticket agency. And always keep in mind that what you get is just as important as what you save.

DISCOUNT RESERVATIONS

To save money **look into discount-reservations services** with toll-free

numbers, which use their buying power to get a better price on hotels, airline tickets, even car rentals. When booking a room, always **call the hotel's local toll-free number** (if one is available) rather than the central reservations number—you'll often get a better price. Always ask about special packages or corporate rates.

➤ AIRLINE TICKETS: ☎ **800/FLY–4–LESS.**

➤ HOTEL ROOMS: **Central Reservation Service (CRS)** (☎ 800/548–3311). **RMC Travel** (☎ 800/245–5738). **Steigenberger Reservation Service** (☎ 800/223–5652).

PACKAGE DEALS

Don't confuse packages and guided tours. When you buy a package, you travel on your own, just as though you had planned the trip yourself. Fly/drive packages, which combine airfare and car rental, are often a good deal.

ELECTRICITY

Overseas visitors will need to bring adapters to convert their personal appliances to the U.S. standard: AC, 110 volts/60 cycles, with a plug of two flat pins set parallel to one another.

GAY & LESBIAN TRAVEL

➤ RESOURCE: *Fodor's Gay Guide to the USA, 2nd edition,* provides information on travel in Boston and Provincetown, Massachusetts, and in Ogunquit, Maine (available in bookstores, or from Fodor's at ☎ 800/533–6478; $20 plus shipping).

➤ GAY- AND LESBIAN-FRIENDLY TRAVEL AGENCIES: **Different Roads Travel** (✉ 8383 Wilshire Blvd., Suite 902, Beverly Hills, CA 90211, ☎ 323/651–5557 or 800/429–8747, ℻ 323/651–3678). **Kennedy Travel** (✉ 314 Jericho Turnpike, Floral Park, NY 11001, ☎ 516/352–4888 or 800/237–7433, ℻ 516/354–8849). **Now Voyager** (✉ 4406 18th St., San Francisco, CA 94114, ☎ 415/626–1169 or 800/255–6951, ℻ 415/626–8626). **Yellowbrick Road** (✉ 1500 W. Balmoral Ave., Chicago, IL 60640, ☎ 773/561–1800 or 800/642–2488, ℻ 773/561–4497). **Skylink Travel and Tour** (✉ 1006 Mendocino Ave., Santa Rosa, CA 95401, ☎ 707/546–

9888 or 800/225–5759, FAX 707/546–9891), serving lesbian travelers.

HEALTH

MEDICAL PLANS

No one plans to get sick while traveling, but it happens, so **consider signing up with a medical-assistance company.** Members get doctor referrals, emergency evacuation or repatriation, 24-hour telephone hot lines for medical consultation, cash for emergencies, and other personal assistance. Coverage varies by plan, so **review the benefits of each carefully.**

➤ MEDICAL-ASSISTANCE COMPANIES: **International SOS Assistance** (8 Neshaminy Interplex, Suite 207, Trevose, PA 19053, ☎ 215/245–4707 or 800/523–6586, FAX 215/244–9617; 12 Chemin Riantbosson, 1217 Meyrin 1, Geneva, Switzerland, ☎ 4122/785–6464, FAX 4122/785–6424; 10 Anson Rd., 14-07/08 International Plaza, Singapore, 079903, ☎ 65/226–3936, FAX 65/226–3937).

LYME DISEASE

Lyme disease, so named for its having been first reported in the town of Lyme, Connecticut, is a potentially debilitating disease carried by deer ticks, which thrive in dry, brush-covered areas. **Use insect repellent;** outbreaks of Lyme disease all over the East Coast make it imperative (even in urban areas) that you protect yourself from ticks from early spring through summer. To prevent bites, **wear light-colored clothing and tuck pant legs into socks.** Look for black ticks about the size of a pin head around hairlines and the warmest parts of the body. If you have been bitten, **consult a physician, especially if you see the telltale bull's-eye bite pattern.** Influenza-like symptoms often accompany a Lyme infection. Early treatment is imperative. Also **ask your physician about Lymerix, the new Lyme disease vaccine;** it takes three shots and 12 months to be 80% effective but is worth considering.

HOLIDAYS

Major national holidays include New Year's Day (Jan. 1); Martin Luther King, Jr., Day (3rd Mon. in Jan.); President's Day (3rd Mon. in Feb.); Memorial Day (last Mon. in May); Independence Day (July 4); Labor Day (1st Mon. in Sept.); Thanksgiving Day (4th Thurs. in Nov.); Christmas Eve and Christmas Day (Dec. 24 and 25); and New Year's Eve (Dec. 31). Patriot's Day (3rd Mon. in Apr.) is a Massachusetts state holiday.

INSURANCE

The most useful travel insurance plan is a comprehensive policy that includes coverage for trip cancellation and interruption, default, trip delay, and medical expenses (with a waiver for preexisting conditions).

Without insurance you will lose all or most of your money if you cancel your trip, regardless of the reason. Default insurance covers you if your tour operator, airline, or cruise line goes out of business. Trip-delay covers expenses that arise because of bad weather or mechanical delays. Study the fine print when comparing policies.

British and Australian citizens need extra medical coverage when traveling overseas. Always **buy travel policies directly from the insurance company;** if you buy it from a cruise line, airline, or tour operator that goes out of business you probably will not be covered for the agency or operator's default, a major risk. Before you make any purchase **review your existing health and homeowner's policies** to find what they cover away from home.

➤ TRAVEL INSURERS: In the U.S. **Access America** (✉ 6600 W. Broad St., Richmond, VA 23230, ☎ 804/285–3300 or 800/284–8300), **Travel Guard International** (✉ 1145 Clark St., Stevens Point, WI 54481, ☎ 715/345–0505 or 800/826–1300). In Canada **Voyager Insurance** (✉ 44 Peel Center Dr., Brampton, Ontario, Canada L6T 4M8, ☎ 905/791–8700; 800/668–4342 in Canada).

➤ INSURANCE INFORMATION: In the U.K. the **Association of British Insurers** (✉ 51–55 Gresham St., London EC2V 7HQ, ☎ 0171/600–3333, FAX 0171/696–8999). In Australia the **Insurance Council of Australia** (☎ 03/9614–1077, FAX 03/9614–7924).

LODGING

Hotel and motel chains provide standard rooms and amenities in major cities and at or near traditional vacation destinations. At small inns, where each room is different and amenities vary in number and quality, price isn't always a reliable indicator; fortunately, when you call to make reservations, most hosts will be happy to give all manner of details about their properties, down to the color scheme of the handmade quilts—so **ask all your questions before you book.** Also **ask if the property has a Web site**; sites can have helpful information and pictures, although it's always wise to confirm how up-to-date the information is. At small inns, **don't expect a telephone, TV, or honor bar in your room**; you may even have to share a bathroom. The rooms in the lodgings reviewed here have private baths unless otherwise indicated.

The lodgings we list are the cream of the crop in each price category. We always list the facilities that are available—but we don't specify whether they cost extra: When pricing accommodations, always ask what's included and what costs extra. Properties indicated by an ✕⌗ are lodging establishments whose restaurant warrants a special trip. Following is the price chart used in this book; note that prices do not include tax, which is 12% in Connecticut, 7% in Maine, 5.7% state tax plus up to 10% local tax in Massachusetts, 8% in New Hampshire, 12% in Rhode Island, and 9% in Vermont.

CATEGORY	BOSTON, THE CAPE, AND THE ISLANDS*	OTHER AREAS*
$$$$	over $220	over $180
$$$	$160–$220	$130–$180
$$	$110–$160	$80–$130
$	under $110	under $80

All prices are for a standard double room during peak season and do not include tax or gratuities. Some inns add a 15% service charge.

Assume that hotels operate on the European Plan (EP, with no meals) unless we specify that they use the Continental Plan (CP, with a Continental breakfast daily) or serve a full breakfast daily (indicated in the italicized service information at the end of the review). If more than breakfast is served, we specify whether the lodging operates on the Modified American Plan (MAP, with breakfast and dinner daily), or the American Plan (AP, with all meals).

APARTMENT & VILLA RENTALS

If you want a home base that's roomy enough for a family and comes with cooking facilities **consider a furnished rental.** These can save you money, especially if you're traveling with a group. Home-exchange directories sometimes list rentals as well as exchanges.

➤ INTERNATIONAL AGENTS: **Rent-a-Home International** (✉ 7200 34th Ave. NW, Seattle, WA 98117, ☎ 206/789–9377, FAX 206/789–9379).

B&BS

The bed-and-breakfasts and small inns of New England offer some of the region's most distinctive lodging experiences. Some are homey and casual, others provide a stay in a historic property in a city or out in the country, and still others are modern and luxurious. Most inns offer breakfast—hence the name bed-and-breakfast—yet this formula varies, too; at one B&B you may be served muffins and coffee, at another a multicourse feast with fresh flowers on the table. Many inns prohibit smoking, which is a fire hazard in older buildings, and some of the inns with antiques or other expensive furnishings do not allow children. Almost all say no to pets. Always be sure to **ask about any restrictions** when you're making a reservation.

➤ RESERVATION SERVICES: *See* Contacts and Resources *in* the A to Z sections at the end of Chapters 1 through 6.

CAMPING

The state offices of tourism (☞ Visitor Information, *below*) supply information about privately operated campgrounds and ones in parks run by state agencies and the federal government.

HOME EXCHANGES

If you would like to exchange your home for someone else's **join a home-exchange organization,** which will send you its updated listings of available exchanges for a year and will include your own listing in at least one of them. It's up to you to make specific arrangements.

➤ EXCHANGE CLUBS: **HomeLink International** (⊠ Box 650, Key West, FL 33041, ☎ 305/294–7766 or 800/638–3841, FAX 305/294–1448; $88 per year). **Intervac U.S.** (⊠ Box 590504, San Francisco, CA 94159, ☎ 800/756–4663, FAX 415/435–7440; $83 per year).

HOSTELS

No matter what your age you can **save on lodging costs by staying at hostels.** In some 5,000 locations in more than 70 countries around the world, Hostelling International (HI), the umbrella group for a number of national youth-hostel associations, offers single-sex, dorm-style beds and, at many hostels, couples rooms and family accommodations. Membership in any HI national hostel association, open to travelers of all ages, allows you to stay in HI-affiliated hostels at member rates (one-year membership is about $25 for adults; hostels run about $10–$25 per night). Members also have priority if the hostel is full; they're eligible for discounts around the world, even on rail and bus travel in some countries.

➤ ORGANIZATIONS: **Hostelling International—American Youth Hostels** (⊠ 733 15th St. NW, Suite 840, Washington, DC 20005, ☎ 202/783–6161, FAX 202/783–6171). **Hostelling International—Canada** (⊠ 400–205 Catherine St., Ottawa, Ontario K2P 1C3, ☎ 613/237–7884, FAX 613/237–7868). **Youth Hostel Association of England and Wales** (⊠ Trevelyan House, 8 St. Stephen's Hill, St. Albans, Hertfordshire AL1 2DY, ☎ 01727/855215 or 01727/845047, FAX 01727/844126). **Australian Youth Hostel Association** (⊠ 10 Mallett St., Camperdown, NSW 2050, ☎ 02/9565–1699, FAX 02/9565–1325). **Youth Hostels Association of New Zealand** (⊠ Box 436, Christchurch, New Zealand, ☎ 03/379–9970, FAX 03/365–4476). Membership in the U.S. $25, in Canada C$26.75, in the U.K. £9.30, in Australia $44, in New Zealand $24.

HOTELS

Hotel chains are amply represented in New England. Some of the large chains, such as Holiday Inn, Hilton, Hyatt, Marriott, and Ramada, operate all-suites, budget, business-oriented, or luxury resorts, often variations on the parent corporation's name (Courtyard by Marriott, for example). Though some chain hotels may have a standardized look to them, this "cookie-cutter" approach also means that you can rely on the same level of comfort and efficiency at all properties in a well-managed chain, and at a chain's premier properties—its so-called flagship hotels—the decor and services may be outstanding.

Most hotels will hold your reservation until 6 PM; **call ahead if you plan to arrive late.** Some will hold a late reservation for you if you reserve with a credit-card number.

When you call to make a reservation, **ask all the necessary questions up front.** If you are arriving with a car, ask if the hotel has a parking lot or covered garage and whether there is an extra fee for parking. If you like to eat your meals in, ask if the hotel has a restaurant or whether it has room service (most do, but not necessarily 24 hours a day—and be forewarned that it can be expensive). Most hotels and motels have in-room TVs, often with cable movies, but verify this if you like to watch TV. If you want an in-room crib for your child, there will probably be an additional charge.

All hotels listed have private bath unless otherwise noted.

➤ TOLL-FREE NUMBERS: **Adam's Mark** (☎ 800/444/2326). **Baymont Inns** (☎ 800/428–3438). **Best Western** (☎ 800/528–1234). **Choice** (☎ 800/221–2222). **Clarion** (☎ 800/252–7466). **Colony** (☎ 800/777–1700). **Comfort** (☎ 800/228–5150). **Days Inn** (☎ 800/325–2525). **Doubletree and Red Lion Hotels** (☎ 800/222–8733). **Embassy Suites** (☎ 800/362–2779). **Fairfield Inn** (☎ 800/228–2800). **Forte** (☎ 800/225–5843). **Four Seasons** (☎ 800/332–3442). **Hilton** (☎ 800/445–8667). **Holiday Inn** (☎ 800/465–4329). **Howard Johnson** (☎ 800/654–4656). **Hyatt Hotels & Resorts** (☎

800/233–1234). **Inter-Continental** (☎ 800/327–0200). **La Quinta** (☎ 800/531–5900). **Marriott** (☎ 800/228–9290). **Le Meridien** (☎ 800/543–4300). **Nikko Hotels International** (☎ 800/645–5687). **Omni** (☎ 800/843–6664). **Quality Inn** (☎ 800/228–5151). **Radisson** (☎ 800/333–3333). **Ramada** (☎ 800/228–2828). **Renaissance Hotels & Resorts** (☎ 800/468–3571). **Ritz-Carlton** (☎ 800/341–3333). **ITT Sheraton** (☎ 800/325–3535). **Sleep Inn** (☎ 800/221–2222). **Westin Hotels & Resorts** (☎ 800/228–3000). **Wyndham Hotels & Resorts** (☎ 800/822-4200).

MONEY MATTERS

Prices throughout this guide are given for adults. Substantially reduced fees are almost always available for children, students, and senior citizens. For information on taxes, *see* Taxes, *below.*

ATMS

Automatic teller machines (ATMs) are a useful way to obtain cash. A debit card, also known as a check card, deducts funds directly from your checking account and helps you stay within your budget. When you want to rent a car, though, you may still need an old-fashioned credit card. Although you can always *pay* for your car with a debit card, some agencies will not allow you to *reserve* a car with a debit card.

➤ ATM LOCATIONS: **Cirrus** (☎ 800/424–7787). **Plus** (☎ 800/843–7587) for locations in the U.S. and Canada, or visit your local bank.

BANKS

In general, U.S. banks will not cash a personal check for you unless you have an account at that bank (it doesn't have to be at that branch). Only in major cities are large bank branches equipped to exchange foreign currencies. Therefore, it's best to rely on credit cards, cash machines, and traveler's checks to handle expenses while you're traveling.

CREDIT CARDS

Using a credit card on the road allows you to delay payment and gives you certain rights as a consumer (☞ Consumer Protection, *above*).

Throughout this guide, the following abbreviations are used: **AE,** American Express; **D,** Discover; **DC,** Diner's Club; **MC,** Master Card; and **V,** Visa.

➤ REPORTING LOST CARDS: To report lost or stolen credit cards, call the following toll-free numbers: **American Express** (☎ 800/327–2177); **Discover Card** (☎ 800/347–2683); **Diners Club** (☎ 800/234–6377); **Master Card** (☎ 800/307–7309); and **Visa** (☎ 800/847–2911).

CURRENCY

The basic unit of U.S. currency is the dollar, which is subdivided into 100 cents. Coins are the copper penny (1¢) and four silver coins: the nickel (5¢), the dime (10¢), the quarter (25¢), and the fairly rare half-dollar (50¢). Silver $1 coins are rarely seen in circulation. Paper money comes in denominations of $1, $5, $10, $20, $50, and $100. All these bills are the same size and green in color; they are distinguishable only by the dollar amount indicated on them and by pictures of various famous American people and monuments. Bills were redesigned in 1998, and you'll see both old and new designs in circulation; the main differences in appearance are larger numbers for the denominations and larger pictures of the people and monuments.

At press time (summer 1999), the exchange rate was $1.62 to the pound sterling, 60¢ to the Canadian dollar, and 66¢ to the Australian dollar.

CURRENCY EXCHANGE

In the United States, it is not as easy to find places to exchange currency as it is in European cities. In major international cities, such as Boston, currency may be exchanged at some bank branches, as well as at currency-exchange booths in airports and at foreign-currency offices such as American Express Travel Service and Thomas Cook (check local directories for addresses and phone numbers). The best strategy is to **buy traveler's checks in U.S. dollars** before you come to the United States; although the rates may not be as good abroad, the time saved by not having to search constantly for exchange facilities far outweighs any financial loss.

For the most favorable rates, **change money through banks.** Although fees charged for ATM transactions may be higher abroad than at home, Cirrus and Plus exchange rates are excellent, because they are based on wholesale rates offered only by major banks. You won't do as well at exchange booths in airports or rail and bus stations, in hotels, in restaurants, or in stores, although you may find their hours more convenient. To avoid lines at airport exchange booths, **get a bit of local currency before you leave home.**

➤ EXCHANGE SERVICES: **International Currency Express** (☎ 888/842–0880). **Thomas Cook Currency Services** (☎ 800/287–7362 for telephone orders and retail locations).

TRAVELER'S CHECKS

Do you need traveler's checks? It depends on where you're headed. If you're going to rural areas and small towns, go with cash; traveler's checks are best used in cities. Lost or stolen checks can usually be replaced within 24 hours. To ensure a speedy refund, buy your own traveler's checks— don't let someone else pay for them: irregularities like this can cause delays. The person who bought the checks should make the call to request a refund.

NATIONAL AND STATE PARKS AND FORESTS

National and state parks offer a broad range of visitor facilities, including campgrounds, picnic grounds, hiking trails, boating, and ranger programs. State forests are usually somewhat less developed. For more information on any of these, contact the state tourism offices or parks departments (☞ Contacts and Resources, at the end of Chapters 1 through 6).

CONNECTICUT

The Litchfield Hills have a strong concentration of wilderness areas, of which the best include Kent Falls State Park, Mt. Tom, Dennis Hill, Haystack Mountain, Campbell Falls, Housatonic Meadows, and Burr Pond. A 53-mile swath of the Appalachian Trail, which is part of the national park system, also cuts through Litchfield County. Elsewhere in the state, Rocky Neck State Park in Niantic has one of the finest beaches on Long Island Sound; Wadsworth Falls, near Wesleyan University, has a beautiful waterfall and 285 acres of forest; and Dinosaur State Park, north of Middletown in Rocky Hill, has dinosaur tracks dating from the Jurassic period. There's excellent hiking and picnicking at Gillette Castle State Park, an outrageous hilltop castle on 117 acres.

MASSACHUSETTS

Cape Cod National Seashore, a 40-mi stretch of the Cape between Chatham and Provincetown, offers excellent swimming, biking, bird-watching, and nature walks. Parks in Lowell, Gardner, North Adams, Holyoke, Lawrence, Lynn, Roxbury, and Fall River, which commemorate the Industrial Revolution, have been created as part of the Urban Heritage State Park Program for Economic Revitalization.

MAINE

Acadia National Park, which preserves fine stretches of shoreline and high mountains, covers much of Mount Desert Island and more than half of Isle au Haut and Schoodic Point on the mainland. Baxter State Park comprises more than 200,000 acres of wilderness surrounding Katahdin, Maine's highest mountain. Hiking and moose-watching are major activities. The Allagash Wilderness Waterway is a 92-mi corridor of lakes and rivers surrounded by vast commercial forest property.

NEW HAMPSHIRE

The White Mountain National Forest covers 770,000 acres of northern New Hampshire. New Hampshire parklands vary widely, even within a region. Major recreation parks are at Franconia Notch, Crawford Notch, and Mt. Sunapee. Rhododendron State Park near Fitzwilliam in the Monadnock region has a singular collection of wild rhododendrons; Mt. Washington Park (White Mountains) is on top of the highest mountain in the Northeast.

RHODE ISLAND

With 19 preserves, state parks, beaches, and forest areas, including Charlestown's Burlingame State Park and Ninigret National Wildlife Refuge, South County is a region that respects the concept of wilderness. Fifteen state parks in Rhode Island permit camping.

VERMONT

The 275,000-acre Green Mountain National Forest extends south from the center of the state to the Massachusetts border. Hikers treasure the miles of trails; canoeists work its white waters; and campers and anglers find plenty to keep them happy. Among the most popular spots are the Falls of Lana and Silver Lake near Middlebury; Hapgood Pond between Manchester and Peru; and Chittenden Brook near Rochester.

NATIONAL PARK PASSES

Look into discount passes to save money on national park entrance fees. The Golden Eagle Pass ($50) gets you and your companions free admission to all parks for one year. (Camping and parking are extra). Both the Golden Age Passport ($10), for those 62 and older, and the Golden Access Passport (free), for travelers with disabilities, entitle holders to free entry to all national parks, plus 50% off fees for the use of many park facilities and services. You must show proof of age and of U.S. citizenship or permanent residency (such as a U.S. passport, driver's license, or birth certificate) and, if requesting Golden Access, proof of disability. All three passes are available at all national park entrances where entrance fees are charged. Golden Eagle and Golden Access passes are also available by mail.

➤ PASSES BY MAIL: **National Park Service** (✉ National Capitol Area Office, 1100 Ohio Dr. SW, Washington, DC 20242, ☎ 202/208–4747).

OUTDOOR ACTIVITIES & SPORTS

Biking, fishing, and hiking are popular in New England. Biking trails are plentiful; freshwater-lake fishing, surfcasting, deep-sea fishing, angling, and trout fishing are available; and for hikers, New England has many miles of the famous Appalachian Trail. Ask state information offices (☞ Visitor Information, *below*) about sporting opportunities. For information abous

skiing, one of the region's most popular sports, *see* Skiing, *below.*

BEACHES

Long, wide beaches edge the New England coast from southern Maine to southern Connecticut; the most popular are on Cape Cod, Martha's Vineyard, Nantucket, and the shore areas north and south of Boston; on Maine's York County coast; Block Island Sound in Rhode Island; and the coastal region of New Hampshire. Many are maintained by state and local governments and have lifeguards on duty; they may have picnic facilities, rest rooms, changing facilities, and concession stands. Depending on the locale, you may need a parking sticker to use the lot. The waters are at their warmest in August, though they're cold even at the height of summer along much of the Maine coast. Inland, there are small lake beaches, most notably in New Hampshire and Vermont.

BIKING

Cape Cod, in Massachusetts, has miles of bike trails, some paralleling the National Seashore, most on level terrain. On either side of the Cape Cod Canal is an easy 7-mi straight trail with views of the canal traffic. Other favorite areas for bicycling are the Massachusetts Berkshires, the New Hampshire lakes region, and Vermont's Northeast Kingdom. Nantucket, Martha's Vineyard, and Block Island can be thoroughly explored by bicycle. Biking in Maine is especially scenic in and around Kennebunkport, Camden, Deer Isle, and the Schoodic Peninsula. The carriage paths in Acadia National Park are ideal. Sunday River Ski Resort operates a mountain bike park during the summer months.

➤ BIKING: **Maine Sport Outdoor School** (U.S. 1, Rockport, 04856, ☎ 207/236–8797 or 800/722–0826). **Vermont Bicycle Touring** (Box 711, Bristol, 05443, ☎ 802/453–4811 or 800/245–3868).

BOATING

In most lakeside and coastal resorts, sailboats and powerboats can be rented at a local marina. Newport, Rhode Island, and Maine's Penobscot

Bay are famous sailing areas. Lakes in New Hampshire and Vermont are splendid for all kinds of boating. The Connecticut River in the Pioneer Valley and the Housatonic River in the Berkshires are popular for canoeing. In Massachusetts, Gloucester and Newburyport are traditional fishing ports, and Essex is known for saltwater and freshwater canoeing.

FISHING

Anglers will find sport aplenty throughout the region—surf-casting along the shore, deep-sea fishing in the Atlantic on party and charter boats, fishing for trout in rivers, and angling for bass, landlocked salmon, and other fish in freshwater lakes. Maine's Moosehead and Rangeley Lakes regions are draws for serious anglers. Sporting goods stores and bait-and-tackle shops are reliable sources for licenses—necessary in fresh waters—and for leads to the nearest hot spots.

➤ FISHING: **Connecticut's Department of Environmental Protection** (Fisheries Division, 79 Elm St., Hartford 06106, ☎ 860/424–3474). **Maine Department of Inland Fisheries and Wildlife** (284 State St., State House Station 41, Augusta, ME 04333, ☎ 207/287–8000). **Massachusetts Division of Fisheries and Wildlife** (100 Cambridge St., Room 1902, Boston, MA 02202, ☎ 617/727–3151). **New Hampshire Fish and Game Department,** Information and Education Division (2 Hazen Dr., Concord, NH 03301, ☎ 603/271–3211). Rhode Island's **Department of Environmental Management, Division of Fish and Wildlife** (4808 Tower Hill Rd., Wakefield, RI 02879, ☎ 401/789–3094). **Vermont Fish and Wildlife Department** (103 S. Main St., Waterbury, VT 05676, ☎ 802/241–3700).

HIKING

Probably the most famous trails are the 255-mi Long Trail, which runs north–south through the center of Vermont, and the Maine-to-Georgia Appalachian Trail, which runs through New England on both private and public land. You'll find good hiking in many state parks throughout the region.

➤ HIKING: **Green Mountain Club** (Box 650, Rte. 100, Waterbury, VT 05677, ☎ 802/244–7037). **Appalachian Mountain Club** (Box 298, Gorham, NH 03581, ☎ 603/466–2725). **White Mountains National Forest** (719 North Main St., Laconia, NH 03246, ☎ 603/528–8721). **Audubon Society of New Hampshire** (3 Silk Farm Rd., Concord, NH 03301, ☎ 603/224–9909).

PACKING

The principal rule on weather in New England is that there are no rules. A cold, foggy morning in spring can and often does become a bright, 60-degree afternoon. A summer breeze can suddenly turn chilly, and rain often appears with little warning. Thus, the best advice on how to dress is to **layer your clothing** so that you can peel off or add garments as needed for comfort. Showers are frequent, so **pack a raincoat and umbrella.** Even in summer you should bring long pants, a sweater or two, and a waterproof windbreaker, for evenings are often chilly and sea spray can make things cool.

Casual sportswear—walking shoes and jeans—will take you almost everywhere, but swimsuits and bare feet will not: Shirts and shoes are required attire at even the most casual venues. Dress in restaurants is generally casual, except at some of the distinguished restaurants of Boston, Newport, Maine coast towns such as Kennebunkport, a number of inns in the Berkshires, and in Litchfield and Fairfield counties in Connecticut.

In summer, **bring a hat and sunscreen.** Remember also to **pack insect repellent**; to prevent Lyme disease you'll need to guard against ticks from early spring through the summer (☞ Health, *above*).

In your carry-on luggage **bring an extra pair of eyeglasses or contact lenses** and **enough of any medication you take** to last the entire trip. You may also want your doctor to write a spare prescription using the drug's generic name, since brand names may vary from country to country. In luggage to be checked, **never pack prescription drugs or valuables.** To avoid customs delays, carry medications in their original packaging. And don't forget to copy down and carry addresses of offices that handle refunds of lost traveler's checks.

CHECKING LUGGAGE

How many carry-on bags you can bring with you is up to the airline. Most allow two, but not always, so **make sure that everything you carry aboard will fit under your seat, and get to the gate early.** Note that if you have a seat at the back of the plane, you'll probably board first, while the overhead bins are still empty.

If you are flying internationally, note that baggage allowances may be determined not by piece but by weight—generally 88 pounds (40 kilograms) in first class, 66 pounds (30 kilograms) in business class, and 44 pounds (20 kilograms) in economy.

Airline liability for baggage is limited to $1,250 per person on flights within the United States. On international flights it amounts to $9.07 per pound or $20 per kilogram for checked baggage (roughly $640 per 70-pound bag) and $400 per passenger for unchecked baggage. You can buy additional coverage at check-in for about $10 per $1,000 of coverage, but it excludes a rather extensive list of items, shown on your airline ticket.

Before departure **itemize your bags' contents** and their worth, and label the bags with your name, address, and phone number. (If you use your home address, cover it so that potential thieves can't see it readily.) Inside each bag **pack a copy of your itinerary.** At check-in **make sure that each bag is correctly tagged** with the destination airport's three-letter code. If your bags arrive damaged or fail to arrive at all, file a written report with the airline before leaving the airport.

PASSPORTS & VISAS

When traveling internationally **carry a passport even if you don't need one** (it's always the best form of ID), and **make two photocopies of the data page** (one for someone at home and another for you, carried separately from your passport). If you lose your passport promptly call the nearest embassy or consulate and the local police.

➤ U.K. CITIZENS: **U.S. Embassy Visa Information Line** (☎ 01891/200–290; calls cost 49p per minute, 39p per minute cheap rate) for U.S. visa information. **U.S. Embassy Visa Branch** (✉ 5 Upper Grosvenor Sq., London W1A 1AE) for U.S. visa information; send a self-addressed, stamped envelope. Write the **U.S. Consulate General** (✉ Queen's House, Queen St., Belfast BTI 6EO) if you live in Northern Ireland. Write the **Office of Australia Affairs** (✉ 59th fl., MLC Centre, 19-29 Martin Pl., Sydney NSW 2000) if you live in Australia. Write the **Office of New Zealand Affairs** (✉ 29 Fitzherbert Terr., Thorndon, Wellington) if you live in New Zealand.

PASSPORT OFFICES

The best time to apply for a passport or to renew is during the fall and winter. Before any trip, check your passport's expiration date, and, if necessary, renew it as soon as possible.

➤ AUSTRALIAN CITIZENS: **Australian Passport Office** (☎ 131–232).

➤ CANADIAN CITIZENS: **Canadian Passport Office** (☎ 819/994–3500 or 800/567–6868).

➤ NEW ZEALAND CITIZENS: **New Zealand Passport Office** (☎ 04/494–0700 for information on how to apply; 04/474–8000 or 0800/225–050 in New Zealand for information on applications already submitted).

➤ U.K. CITIZENS: **London Passport Office** (☎ 0990/210–410) for fees and documentation requirements and to request an emergency passport.

SENIOR-CITIZEN TRAVEL

To qualify for age-related discounts **mention your senior-citizen status up front** when booking hotel reservations (not when checking out) and before you're seated in restaurants (not when paying the bill). When renting a car ask about promotional car-rental discounts, which can be cheaper than senior-citizen rates.

➤ EDUCATIONAL PROGRAMS: **Elderhostel** (✉ 75 Federal St., 3rd fl., Boston, MA 02110, ☎ 877/426–8056, FAX 877/426–2166).

SHOPPING

Antiques, crafts, maple syrup and sugar, fresh produce, and clothing and housewares lure shoppers to New England's factory outlet stores, flea markets, shopping malls, bazaars, yard sales, country stores, and farmers' markets.

KEY DESTINATIONS

Best bets for antiquing in Connecticut include U.S. 7 (in Wilton and Ridgefield, and also in western Litchfield County), New Preston, Putnam and Woodstock, Woodbury and Litchfield, and the area of West Cornwall just east of the covered bridge. Antiques stores are plentiful in Newport but are a specialty of Rhode Island's South County: The best places to browse are Wickford, Charlestown, and Watch Hill. In Massachusetts, there's a large concentration of antiques stores on the North Shore around Essex, but there are also plenty in Salem and Cape Ann. Also try the Berkshires around Great Barrington, South Egremont, and Sheffield. Particularly in the Monadnock region of New Hampshire, dealers abound in barns and home stores strung along back roads—along Route 119, from Fitzwilliam to Hinsdale; Route 101, from Marlborough to Wilton; and in the towns of Hopkinton, Hollis, and Amherst. In the Seacoast region, the stretch of Route 4 between Barrington and Concord is another mecca. In Maine, antiques shops are clustered in Wiscasset and Searsport and along Route 1 between Kittery and Scarborough.

For crafts, try Washington Street in South Norwalk, Connecticut, and in Massachusetts, Boston, Cape Cod, and the Berkshires. In Vermont, Burlington and Putney are crafts centers. On Maine's Deer Isle, Haystack Mountain School of Crafts attracts internationally renowned craftspeople to its summer institute. The Schoodic Peninsula is home to many skilled artisans. Passamaquoddy baskets can be found in Eastport.

For outlet stores, in Connecticut, try Clinton, Westbrook, and Mystic; in Massachusetts, the area around New Bedford and Fall River; in Maine, shop along the coast in Kittery, Freeport, and Ellsworth; in New Hampshire, North Conway; and in Vermont, Manchester. In Rhode Island's Blackstone Valley, dozens of clothing and manufacturing outlets are actually inside factory walls.

Opportunities abound for obtaining fresh farm produce from the source; some farms allow you to pick your own strawberries, raspberries, blueberries, and apples. October in Maine is prime time for pumpkins and potatoes. There are maple-syrup producers who demonstrate the process to visitors, most noticeably in Vermont. Maple syrup is available in different grades; light amber is the most refined; many Vermonters prefer grade C, the richest in flavor and the one most often used in cooking. A sugarhouse can be the most or the least expensive place to shop, depending on how tourist-oriented it is. Small grocery stores are often a good source of less-expensive syrup.

SKIING

The softly rounded peaks of New England have been attracting skiers for a full century.

LIFT TICKETS

A good bet is that the bigger and more famous the resort, the higher the price of a lift ticket. A single-day, weekend-holiday adult lift ticket always has the highest price; astute skiers look for off-site purchase locations, senior discounts and junior pricing, and package rates, multiple days, stretch weekends (a weekend that usually includes a Monday or Friday), frequent-skier programs, and season-ticket plans to save their skiing dollars. Some independently owned areas are bona fide bargains for skiers who don't require the glamour and glitz of the high-profile resorts.

LODGING

Most ski areas described in this book have a variety of accommodations—lodges, condominiums, hotels, motels, inns, bed-and-breakfasts—close to or at a short distance from the action. For stays of three days or more, a package rate may be the best way to go. Packages vary in composition, price, and availability throughout the season; their components may include a room, meals, lift tickets, ski lessons, rental equipment, transfers to the mountain, parties, races, and use of a sports center, tips, and taxes.

TRAIL RATING

Ski areas have devised standards for rating and marking trails and slopes that offer fairly accurate guides. Trails are rated Easier (green circle), More Difficult (blue square), Most Difficult (black diamond), and Expert (double diamond). Keep in mind that trail difficulty is measured relative to that of other trails *at the same ski area,* not to those of an area down the road, in another state, or in another part of the country; a black-diamond trail at one area may rate only a blue square at a neighboring area. Yet the trail-marking system throughout New England is remarkably consistent and reliable.

EQUIPMENT RENTAL AND LESSONS

Rental equipment is available at all ski areas, at ski shops around resorts, and even in cities far from ski areas. Shop personnel will advise customers on the appropriate equipment and how to operate it. Within the United States, the Professional Ski Instructors of America (PSIA) have devised a progressive teaching system that is used with relatively little variation at many schools (though not the ones at the New England resorts run by the American Skiing Company). This allows skiers to have more fulfilling lessons at ski schools in different ski areas. Some ski schools have adopted the PSIA teaching system for children, and many also use SKIwee, which awards progress cards and applies other standardized teaching approaches.

CHILD CARE

Nurseries can be found at virtually all ski areas and often accept children from ages six weeks to six years. Parents must usually supply formula and diapers for infants; reservations are advised.

STUDENTS IN NEW ENGLAND

➤ STUDENT I.D.s & SERVICES: **Council on International Educational Exchange** (CIEE, ✉ 205 E. 42nd St., 14th fl., New York, NY 10017, ☎ 212/822–2600 or 888/268–6245, ☒ 212/822–2699) for mail orders only, in the U.S. **Travel Cuts** (✉ 187 Col-

lege St., Toronto, Ontario M5T 1P7, ☎ 416/979–2406 or 800/667–2887) in Canada.

TAXES

SALES TAX

Sales taxes in New England are as follows: Connecticut 6%; Maine 6%; Massachusetts 5%; Rhode Island 7%; Vermont 5%. No sales tax is charged in New Hampshire. Some states and municipalities levy an additional tax (from 1% to 10%) on lodging or restaurant meals.

TELEPHONES

COUNTRY CODES

The country code for the United States is 1.

DIRECTORY & OPERATOR INFORMATION

To reach an operator in New England, dial 0. To reach directory assistance information, dial 1, then the area code and 555–1212. Within immediate local calling areas, dial 411.

INTERNATIONAL CALLS

From the United States, dial 011, followed by the country code, the city code, and the phone number. To have an operator assist you, dial 0 and ask for the overseas operator. The country code for Australia is 61; New Zealand, 64; and the United Kingdom, 44. To reach Canada, dial 1+ area code + number.

LONG-DISTANCE CALLS

Competitive long-distance carriers make calling within the United States relatively convenient and let you avoid hotel surcharges. By dialing an 800 number, you can get connected to the long-distance company of your choice.

➤ LONG-DISTANCE CARRIERS: **AT&T** (☎ 800/225–5288). **MCI** (☎ 800/888–8000). **Sprint** (☎ 800/366–2255).

PUBLIC TELEPHONES

Instructions for pay telephones should be posted on the phone, but generally you insert your coins—anywhere from 25¢ to 35¢ for a local call in New England—in a slot and wait for the steady hum of a dial tone before dialing the number you wish to reach. If you dial a long-distance number, the operator will come on the line and tell you how much more money you must insert for your call to go through.

TIME

New England is in the Eastern time zone.

TIPPING

At restaurants, a 15% tip is standard for waiters; up to 20% is expected at more expensive establishments. The same goes for taxi drivers, bartenders, and hairdressers. Coat-check operators usually expect $1; bellhops and porters should get 50¢ to $1 per bag; hotel maids in hotels should get about $1.50 per day of your stay. On package tours, conductors and drivers usually get $10 per day from the group as a whole; check whether this has already been figured into your cost. For local sightseeing tours, you may individually tip the driver-guide $1–$5, depending on the length of the tour and the number of people in your party, if he or she has been helpful or informative. Ushers in theaters do not expect tips.

TOURS & PACKAGES

On a prepackaged tour or independent vacation everything is prearranged so you'll spend less time planning—and often get it all at a good price.

BOOKING WITH AN AGENT

Travel agents are excellent resources. But it's a good idea to collect brochures from several agencies because some agents' suggestions may be influenced by relationships with tour and package firms that reward them for volume sales. If you have a special interest **find an agent with expertise in that area**; ASTA (☞ Travel Agencies, *below*) has a database of specialists worldwide.

Make sure your travel agent knows the accommodations and other services of the place they're recommending. Ask about the hotel's location, room size, beds, and whether it has a pool, room service, or programs for children, if you care about these. Has your agent been there in person or sent others whom you can contact?

Do some homework on your own, too: Local tourism boards can provide information about lesser-known and small-niche operators, some of which may sell only direct.

BUYER BEWARE

Each year consumers are stranded or lose their money when tour operators—even large ones with excellent reputations—go out of business. So **check out the operator.** Ask several travel agents about its reputation, and try to **book with a company that has a consumer-protection program.** (Look for information in the company's brochure). In the United States, members of the National Tour Association and United States Tour Operators Association are required to set aside funds to cover your payments and travel arrangements in case the company defaults. It's also a good idea to choose a company that participates in the American Society of Travel Agent's Tour Operator Program (TOP); ASTA will act as mediator in any disputes between you and your tour operator.

Remember that the more your package or tour includes the better you can predict the ultimate cost of your vacation. Make sure you know exactly what is covered, and **beware of hidden costs.** Are taxes, tips, and transfers included? Entertainment and excursions? These can add up.

➤ TOUR-OPERATOR RECOMMENDATIONS: **American Society of Travel Agents** (☞ Travel Agencies, *below*). **National Tour Association** (NTA, ✉ 546 E. Main St., Lexington, KY 40508, ☎ 606/226–4444 or 800/ 682–8886). **United States Tour Operators Association** (USTOA, ✉ 342 Madison Ave., Suite 1522, New York, NY 10173, ☎ 212/599–6599 or 800/ 468–7862, FAX 212/599–6744).

TRAIN TRAVEL

State-run, national, and international train service are options in New England: Massachusetts's MBTA connects Boston with outlying areas on the north and south shores of the state; Amtrak offers frequent daily service along its Northeast Corridor route from Washington and New York to Boston and Vermont. Amtrak plans to introduce high-speed service along the Boston–Washington corridor by 2000.

➤ TRAIN INFORMATION: **Amtrak** (☎ 800/872–7245). **Massachusetts Bay Transportation Authority** (☎ 617/ 722–5000).

TRAVEL AGENCIES

A good travel agent puts your needs first. Look for an agency that has been in business at least five years, emphasizes customer service, and has someone on staff who specializes in your destination. In addition, **make sure the agency belongs to a professional trade organization.** The American Society of Travel Agents (ASTA), with 27,000 agents in some 170 countries, is the largest and most influential in the field. Operating under the motto ìIntegrity in Travel,î it maintains and enforces a strict code of ethics and will step in to help mediate any agent-client disputes if necessary. ASTA also maintains a website that includes a directory of agents. (Note that if a travel agency is also acting as your tour operator, see Buyer Beware in Tour Operators, above.)

➤ LOCAL AGENT REFERRALS: **American Society of Travel Agents** (ASTA, ☎ 800/965–2782 24-hr hot line, FAX 703/684–8319, www.astanet.com). **Association of Canadian Travel Agents** (✉ 1729 Bank St., Suite 201, Ottawa, Ontario K1V 7Z5, ☎ 613/521–0474, FAX 613/521–0805). **Association of British Travel Agents** (✉ 55–57 Newman St., London W1P 4AH, ☎ 0171/637–2444, FAX 0171/637–0713). **Australian Federation of Travel Agents** (✉ Level 3, 309 Pitt St., Sydney 2000, ☎ 02/9264–3299, FAX 02/9264–1085). **Travel Agents' Association of New Zealand** (✉ Box 1888, Wellington 10033, ☎ 04/499–0104, FAX 04/499–0786).

VISITOR INFORMATION

➤ TOURIST INFORMATION: **Connecticut Office of Tourism** (505 Hudson St., Hartford, CT 06106, ☎ 860/270–8081 or 800/282–6863). **Maine Tourism Association** (325-B Water St., Box 2300, Hallowell, ME 04347, ☎ 207/623–0363 or 800/533–9595 for brochures). **Massachusetts Office of Travel and Tourism** (100 Cambridge St., Boston, MA 02202, ☎ 617/727–3201 or 800/447–6277 for brochures). **New Hampshire Office of Travel and Tourism Development** (Box 1856, Concord, NH 03302, ☎ 603/271–2343, 800/258–3608 for seasonal events, 800/386–4664 for brochures). **Rhode Island Department of Eco-** nomic Development, Tourism Division (1 West Exchange St., Providence, RI 02903, ☎ 401/222–2601 or 800/556–2484 for brochures). **Vermont Department of Tourism and Marketing** (134 State St., Montpelier, VT 05602, ☎ 802/828–3237 or 800/837–6668 for brochures). **Vermont Chamber of Commerce, Department of Travel and Tourism** (Box 37, Montpelier, VT 05601, ☎ 802/223–3443).

➤ IN THE U.K.: **Discover New England** (Admail 4 International, Greatness La., Sevenoaks TN14 5BQ, ☎ 01732/742777).

WEB SITES

Do **check out the World Wide** when you're planning. You'll find everything from up-to-date weather forecasts to virtual tours of famous cities. Fodor's Web site, www.fodors.com, is a great place to start your travels. For more information specifically on New England, take a look at the sites listed below. Besides material on sights and lodgings, most have a calendar of events and other special features, some of which are noted.

CONNECTICUT

The site of the Connecticut State Tourism Office (www.tourism.state.ct.us) is easy to navigate; from the home page you can access a vacation planner, an events calendar, and links to lodging, transport, outdoors, and regional-tourism sites.

MAINE

The comprehensive Maine State Government site (www.state.me.us) has two notable links: "Tourism Office" brings you to www.visitmaine.com, which has an events calendar, links to local and regional chambers of commerce, and sightseeing, lodging, and dining information; "Maine's State Parks" provides details about park fees, facilities, and regulations.

MASSACHUSETTS

The site of the Massachusetts Office of Travel and Tourism (www.mass-vacation.com) is a good trip-planning resource, with a calendar of events and seasonal information about fall foliage. "What to See and Do" has a useful beach finder and in the fall a weekly foliage report. Boston.com (www.boston.com), home of the *Boston Globe* online, has news and feature articles, ample travel information, and links to towns throughout Massachusetts via "Your Town." The site for Boston's arts and entertainment weekly, the *Boston Phoenix* (www.bostonphoenix.com), has nightlife, movie, restaurant, and fine and performing arts listings. There are links to the *Providence Phoenix* and the *Worcester Phoenix* sites. The frequently updated site of the Cape Cod Information Center (www.all-capecod.com) carries events information and has useful town directories with weather, sightseeing, lodging, and dining entries.

NEW HAMPSHIRE

The resources on the New Hampshire Office of Travel and Tourism Development site (www.visitnh.gov) can be explored by region or activity. Regional sections have links to local chamber of commerce web sites.

RHODE ISLAND

The official site of the Rhode Island Tourism Division (www.visitrhodeisland.com) is attractive (if slow because of the heavy graphics), and has a vacation planner and events calendars. There are useful links to sites via "Attractions" in the trip planner.

VERMONT

The newly redesigned Vermont Department of Travel and Tourism (www.1-800-vermont.com) site can help you find just about any kind of information with links from the home page.

GENERAL INTEREST

A must-visit for anyone interested in the greener side of travel, the Great Outdoor Recreation Page (www.gorp.com) is arranged into three easily navigated categories: attractions, activities, and locations; within most of the "locations" are links to the state parks office. Another helpful resource is the National Park Service site (www.nps.gov), which lists all the national parks and has extensive historical, cultural, and environmental information.

➤ CONNECTICUT

www.state.ct.us/tourism

➤ MAINE

www.state.me.us

➤ MASSACHUSETTS

www.mass-vacation.com; www.boston.com; www.bostonphoenix.com; www.allcapecod.com

➤ NEW HAMPSHIRE

www.visitnh.gov

➤ RHODE ISLAND

www.visitrhodeisland.com

➤ VERMONT

www.travel-vermont.com

➤ GENERAL INTEREST

www.gorp.com; www.nps.gov

WHEN TO GO

All six New England states are largely year-round destinations. But you might want to **stay away from rural areas during mud season in April and black-fly season in the last two weeks of May.** Many smaller museums and attractions are open only from Memorial Day to mid-October, at other times by appointment only.

Memorial Day is the start of the migration to the beaches and the mountains, and summer begins in earnest on July 4. Those who are driving to Cape Cod in July or August should know that Friday and Sunday are the days weekenders clog the overburdened Route 6; a better time to visit the beach areas and the islands may be after Labor Day.

Fall is the most colorful season in New England, a time when many inns and hotels are booked months in advance by foliage-viewing visitors. New England's dense hardwood forests explode in color as the diminishing hours of autumn daylight signal trees to stop producing chlorophyll. As green is stripped away from the leaves of maples, oaks, birches, beeches, and other deciduous species, a rainbow of reds, oranges, yellows, purples, and other vivid hues is revealed. The first scarlet and gold colors emerge in mid-September in northern areas; "peak" color occurs at different times from year to year. Generally, it's best to **visit the northern reaches in late September and early October and move southward as the month progresses.**

All leaves are off the trees by Halloween, and hotel rates fall as the leaves do, dropping significantly until ski season begins. November and early December are hunting season in much of New England; those who venture into the woods then should wear bright orange clothing.

Winter is the time for downhill and cross-country skiing. New England's major ski resorts, having seen dark days in years when snowfall was meager, now have snowmaking equipment.

In spring, despite mud season, maple sugaring goes on in Maine, New Hampshire, and Vermont, and the fragrant scent of lilacs is never far behind.

CLIMATE

HARTFORD, CT

Jan.	36F	2C	May	70F	21C	Sept.	74F	23C
	20	− 7		47	8		52	11
Feb.	38F	3C	June	81F	27C	Oct.	65F	18C
	20	− 7		56	13		43	6
Mar.	45F	7C	July	85F	29C	Nov.	52F	11C
	27	− 3		63	17		32	0
Apr.	59F	15C	Aug.	83F	28C	Dec.	38F	3C
	38	3		61	16		22	− 6

BOSTON, MA

Jan.	36F	2C	May	67F	19C	Sept.	72F	22C
	20	− 7		49	9		56	13
Feb.	38F	3C	June	76F	24C	Oct.	63F	17C
	22	− 6		58	14		47	8
Mar.	43F	6C	July	81F	27C	Nov.	49F	9C
	29	− 2		63	17		36	2
Apr.	54F	12C	Aug.	79F	26C	Dec.	40F	4C
	38	3		63	17		25	− 4

BURLINGTON, VT

Jan.	29F	− 2C	May	67F	19C	Sept.	74F	23C
	11	−12		45	7		50	10
Feb.	31F	− 1C	June	77F	25C	Oct.	59F	15C
	11	−12		56	13		40	4
Mar.	40F	4C	July	83F	28C	Nov.	45F	7C
	22	− 6		59	15		31	− 1
Apr.	54F	12C	Aug.	79F	26C	Dec.	31F	− 1C
	34	1		58	14		16	− 9

PORTLAND, ME

Jan.	31F	− 1C	May	61F	16C	Sept.	68F	20C
	16	− 9		47	8		52	11
Feb.	32F	0C	June	72F	22C	Oct.	58F	14C
	16	− 9		54	15		43	6
Mar.	40F	4C	July	76F	24C	Nov.	45F	7C
	27	− 3		61	16		32	0
Apr.	50F	10C	Aug.	74F	23C	Dec.	34F	1C
	36	2		59	15		22	− 6

➤ FORECASTS: **Weather Channel Connection** (☎ 900/932–8437), 95¢ per minute from a Touch-Tone phone.

FESTIVALS AND SEASONAL EVENTS

➤ DECEMBER: The **reenactment of the Boston Tea Party** takes place on the *Beaver II* in Boston Harbor. Christmas celebrations are plentiful throughout New England: In **Nantucket** (MA), the first weekend of the month sees an early Christmas celebration with elaborate decorations, costumed carolers, theatrical performances, art exhibits, and a tour of historic homes. In **Newport** (RI), several Bellevue Avenue mansions open for the holidays, and there are candlelight tours of Colonial homes throughout the month. At **Mystic Seaport** (CT), costumed guides escort visitors to holiday activities including lantern-light tours. **Old Saybrook** (CT) has a Christmas Torchlight Parade and Muster of Ancient Fife and Drum Corps, which ends with a carol sing at the Church Green. The little town of **Bethlehem** (CT) is the site a large Christmas festival each December. More than 200 spectacularly decorated trees and wreaths grace the halls of the Wadsworth Atheneum in Hartford (CT) during its annual **Festival of Trees.** Historic **Strawbery Banke** (NH) has a Christmas Stroll, with carolers, through nine historic homes decorated for the season. **Christmas Prelude** in Kennebunkport (ME) celebrates winter with concerts, caroling, and special events. The final day of the year is observed with festivals, entertainment, and food in many locations during **First Night Celebrations.** Some of the major cities hosting First Nights are Portland (ME); Burlington, Montpelier, and St. Johnsbury (all in VT); Providence (RI); Boston; and, in Connecticut, Danbury, Hartford, and Norwalk.

➤ JANUARY: The Bethel (ME) **Winter Festival** has snowshoe and cross-country races, sleigh rides, fireworks, ice-skating, and a snowman contest. Stowe's (VT) **Winter Carnival** heats up around mid-month; it's among the country's oldest such celebrations. Brookfield (VT) holds its **Ice Harvest Festival,** one of New England's largest. The weeklong **Winter Carnival** in Jackson (NH) includes ski races, ice sculptures, and parades. **Daffodil Days** at Blithewolde Gardens presents

55,000 flowering bulbs on a 33-acre seaside estate in Bristol (RI). The University of Vermont **Lane Series,** in Burlington, showcases internationally known performers in music, dance, and theater this month and throughout the winter.

➤ FEBRUARY: The Camden Snow Bowl in Camden (ME) is the site of the U.S. National Toboggan Championships. On tap at the **Brattleboro Winter Carnival,** held during the last week of the month, are jazz concerts and an ice fishing derby. The **Mad River Valley Winter Carnival** (VT) is a week of winter festivities, including dogsled races and ski races and fireworks; Burlington's **Vermont Mozart Festival** showcases the Winter Chamber Music Series. The **New England Boat Show** is held in Boston's Bayside Expo Center.

➤ MARCH: This is the season for **maple-sugaring festivals and events:** Throughout the month and into April, the sugarhouses of Connecticut, Maine, New Hampshire, Massachusetts, and Vermont demonstrate procedures from maple-tree tapping to sap boiling. During **Maine Maple Sunday** Maine sugarhouses open for tours and tastings. Maine's Moosehead Lake has a renowned **Ice-Fishing Derby,** and Rangeley's **New England Sled Dog Races** attract more than 100 teams from throughout the Northeast and Canada. Devotees of chocolate head to Portland (ME) in late March for the **Chocolate Lovers' Fling.** Stratton Mountain (VT) hosts the **U.S. Open Snowboarding Championships.** March 17 is traditionally a major event in Boston: Its **St. Patrick's Day Parade** is one of the nation's largest.

➤ APRIL: During **Reggae Weekend** at Sugarloaf/USA (ME), Caribbean reggae bands play outdoors and inside throughout the weekend. During Sunday River's (ME) annual **Bust 'n' Burn Mogul Competition,** professional and amateur bump skiers test their mettle on the notorious White Heat trail's man-eating moguls. Early blooms are the draw of Bristol's (RI) **Annual Spring Bulb Display,** which takes place at Blithewolde Gardens and Arboretum, and of Nantucket's **Daffodil Festival,** which

CANADA   QUÉBEC

Stratton

Rangeley

Mooselookmeguntic
Lake

Newport

Colebrook

Enosburg
Falls

Wilton

St. Albans

Orleans

Barton

Island
Pond

North
Stratford

Errol

Groveton

Rumford

Newry

Morrisville

Hardwick

Lyndonville

Lancaster

Berlin

Bethel

Lake
Champlain

Burlington

Stowe

St. Johnsbury

Littleton

Gorham

S. Paris

Mechanic Falls

Montpelier

Barre

Twin Mtn.

Bartlett

Bridgton

Fryeburg

Auburn

Vergennes

Woodsville
Lincoln

North Conway
Conway

Sebago
Lake

Middlebury

Tamworth

Sebago Lake

Randolph

VERMONT

Brandon

Ossipee

Westbrook

Meredith

Lake
Winnipesaukee

Portland

Rutland

Woodstock

Lebanon

Bristol

Biddeford

Poultney

Wallingford

Ludlow

Claremont

Laconia

Stratford

Springfield

Manchester

NEW HAMPSHIRE

Rochester

Arlington

Concord

Dover

Bennington

Keene

Manchester

Portsmouth

Wilmington

Brattleboro

Milford

Nashua

Amesbury

Haverhill

Newburyport

Williamstown

Athol

Fitchburg

Lawrence

Lowell

Gloucester

Greenfield

Gardner

Leominster

Concord

Danvers

Beverly

Salem

Pittsfield

Lexington

Cambridge

Northampton

Marlborough

Boston

Stockbridge

MASSACHUSETTS

Worcester

Braintree

Sandisfield

Chicopee

Springfield

Brockton

Winsted

Putnam

Bridgewater

Plymouth

Torrington

Windsor
Locks

Manchester

Willimantic

Providence

Taunton

Sandwich

New Britain

Bristol

Waterbury

Meriden

Hartford

Warwick

Fall River

Hyannis

Middletown

Norwich

CONNECTICUT

RHODE
ISLAND

New Bedford

Newport

Falmouth

Wallingford

Danbury

New
London

Westerly

Wakefield

Oak Bluffs

Martha's
Vineyard

New Haven

Bridgeport

Long
Island Sound

Block
Island Sound

Block
Island

Norwalk

Long Island (N.Y.)

NEW
YORK

Connecticut River

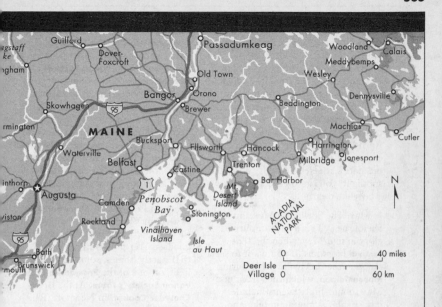

N

ATLANTIC OCEAN

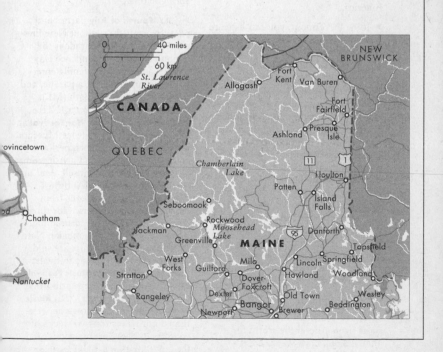

celebrates spring with a flower show, elaborate shop-window displays, and a procession of antique cars along roadsides bursting with daffodils. You can gorge on sea grub at Boothbay Harbor's (ME) **Fishermen's Festival,** held on the third weekend in April. Dedicated runners draw huge crowds to the **Boston Marathon,** run each year on Patriot's Day (the Monday nearest April 19). At the **Maple Festival,** held early each April in St. Albans (VT), the state's sweetest specialty takes the spotlight; you can try Sugar on Snow, a taffylike treat.

➤ MAY: The Shelburne Museum in Shelburne (VT) is awash in purple glory in mid-May, when the **Lilac Festival** blossoms. If you want to see a moose, visit Greenville (ME) during **MooseMainea,** which runs from mid-May to mid-June. Events include moose safaris, mountain bike and canoe races, a parade and a family fun day. **Lobsterfest** kicks off Mystic Seaport's (CT) summer of festivities with live entertainment and plenty of good food. Holyoke's (MA) **Shad Fishing Derby** is said to be the largest freshwater fishing derby in North America.

➤ JUNE: In Vermont, you can listen to jazz at Burlington's **Discover Jazz Festival** or folk at Warren's **Ben & Jerry's One World One Heart Festival,** which is held at Sugarbush. **Jacob's Pillow Dance Festival** at Becket (MA) in the Berkshires hosts performers of various dance traditions from June to September. The spring thaw calls for a number of boating celebrations, including the **Vermont Canoe and Kayak Festival** in Stowe; the **Yale–Harvard Regatta** along New London's (CT) Thames River, the oldest intercollegiate athletic event in the country; the **Boothbay Harbor Windjammer Days,** which starts the high season for Maine's boating set; and the **Blessing of the Fleet** in Provincetown (MA), which culminates a weekend of festivities—a quahog feed, a public dance, a crafts show, a parade. Mystic Seaport in Mystic (CT) invites small-boat enthusiasts from around the world for its annual **Small Craft Weekend;** it's followed by the **Sea Music Festival,** a celebration of New England's quintessential folk music. Young ones are the stars of Somersworth's (NH) **International Children's Festival,** where games, activities, and crafts keep everybody busy. **A Taste of Hartford** lets you eat your way through Connecticut's capital city while enjoying outdoor music, dance, comedy, and magic. New Haven becomes the center of the arts world for the weeklong **International Festival of Arts and Ideas,** showcasing music, dance, theater, film, visual arts, literature, and thoughtful debate. Nothing is sweeter than a fresh Maine strawberry, and during the **Strawberry Festival** in Wiscasset you can get your fill of strawberry shortcake and other goodies. You can visit Providence's (RI) stately homes, some by candlelight, on one of the **Providence Preservation Society's tours.** At the **Great Chowder Cookoff** in Newport (RI), dozens of restaurants compete for the distinction of having the best chowder in New England. Portsmouth (RI) hosts the **Newport International Polo Series** in early June and in late September. Major **crafts and antiques fairs** are held in Farmington (CT) and Springfield (MA).

➤ JULY: **Fourth of July** parties and parades occur throughout New England; Bristol's (RI) parade is the nation's senior Independence Day parade; and concerts, family entertainment, an art show, a parade, and fireworks are held in Bath (ME). Later in the month, Exeter (NH) holds a **Revolutionary War Festival** at the American Independence Museum with battle reenactments, period crafts and antiques, and a visit from George Washington himself. And the **Mashpee Powwow** (MA) brings together Native Americans from North and South America for three days of dance contests, drumming, a fireball game, and a clambake; Native American food and crafts are sold. Some of the better music festivals include the **Marlboro Music Festival** of classical music, held at Marlboro College (VT); Newport's (RI) **Music Festival,** which brings together celebrated musicians for two weeks of concerts in Newport mansions, and the city's **Rhythm & Blues Festival;** the **Bar Harbor Festival** (ME), which hosts classical, jazz, and popular music concerts into August; the **Bowdoin Summer Music Festival** (ME), a six-week series of chamber music concerts; and the **Tanglewood Music Festival** at Lenox (MA), which shifts into high gear with performances by the Boston Symphony Orchestra and a slew of major entertainers. Glorious outdoor concert sites and sumptuous picnics are sidelights to fine music at the **Vermont Mozart Festival**, held throughout northern Vermont in July and August. Shoppers can rummage through major **antiques fairs** in Wolfeboro (NH) and Dorset (VT), or simply admire the furnishings of homes during **Open House Tours** in Litchfield (CT) and Camden (ME). Boaters and the men and women who love them flock to the **Sail Festival** at the City Pier in New London (CT) to watch sail races, outdoor concerts, fireworks, and the Ugliest Dog Contest. In nearby Mystic, vintage powerboats and sailboats are on view at the **Antique and Classic Boat Rendezvous.** The **Yarmouth Clam Festival** (ME) is more than a seafood celebration—expect fireworks, a parade, continuous entertainment, and a crafts show throughout the three-day event. Two of the region's most popular **country fairs** are held in Bangor (ME) and on Cape Cod in Barnstable (MA).

➤ AUGUST: The **music festivals** continue—in Newport (RI) with **Ben & Jerry's Newport Folk Festival** and JVC's Jazz Festival and in Essex (CT) with the **Great Connecticut Traditional Jazz Festival.** Stowe (VT) hosts a popular **Antique and Classic Car Rally.** Popular arts, crafts, and antiques festivals include the **Southern Vermont Crafts Fair** in Manchester (VT), the **Outdoor Arts Festival** in Mystic (CT), the **Maine Antiques Festival** in Union, and the **Fair of the League of New Hampshire Craftsmen** at Mt. Sunapee State Park in Newbury. There's a **Lobster Festival** in Rockland (ME) and a **Blueberry Festival** in Rangeley Lake (ME). Rhode Islanders honor their favorite shellfish at the **International Quahog Festival** in Wickford. Most summers find a **major air show** with precision teams, acrobat and stunt pilots, and military planes both flying and on display at the Brunswick (ME) Naval Air Station. Brunswick's **Maine Festi-**

val, a four-day celebration of Maine arts. The **SoNo Arts Festival** in South Norwalk (CT) celebrates the waterfront and the arts with special events, parades, art shows. A few general summer fairs include the **Woodstock Fair** (CT), which has livestock shows, Colonial crafts, puppet shows, and food, and the **Martha's Vineyard Agricultural Fair** (MA), which includes contests, animal shows, a carnival, and evening entertainment.

➤ SEPTEMBER: New England's dozens of Labor Day fairs include the **Vermont State Fair** in Rutland, with agricultural exhibits and entertainment; the **Providence Waterfront Festival** (RI), a weekend of arts, crafts, ethnic foods, musical entertainment, and boat races; the **International Seaplane Fly-In Weekend,** which sets Moosehead Lake (ME) buzzing; and the **Champlain Valley Exposition,** a Burlington (VT) event with all the features of a large county fair. Foot stomping and guitar strumming are the activities of choice at several musical events: the **Rhythm and Roots** festival of Cajun food, music, and dancing at Stepping Stone Ranch in Escoheag (RI), the **National Traditional Old-Time Fiddler's Contest** in Barre (VT), the **Bluegrass Festival** in Brunswick (ME), and the **Rockport Folk Festival** in Rockport (ME). In Stratton (VT), artists and performers gather for the **Stratton Arts Festival.** One of the best and oldest **antiques shows** in New England occurs in New Haven (CT). Providence (RI) shows off its diversity during its **Annual Heritage Festival.** Agricultural fairs not to be missed are the **Common Ground Country Fair** in Unity (ME), an organic farmer's delight; the **Deerfield Fair** (NH), one of New England's oldest; and the **Eastern States Exposition** in Springfield (MA), New England's largest. The six small Vermont towns of Walden, Cabot, Plainfield, Peacham, Barnet, and Groton host the weeklong **Northeast Kingdom Fall Foliage Festival** (VT). Crafts, entertainment, and buckets of fried scallops are served up at the **Bourne Scallopfest** in Buzzards Bay (MA). For the **Martha's Vineyard Striped Bass and Bluefish Derby,** from mid-September to mid-October, locals drop everything to cast their lines in search

588

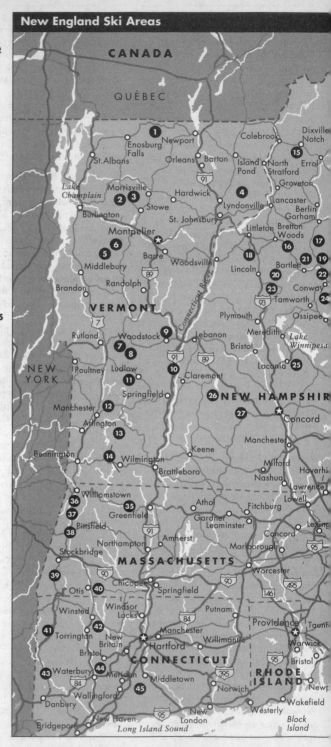

New England Ski Areas

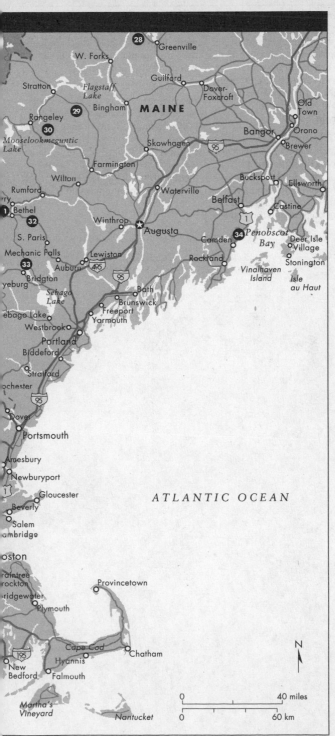

of a prize-winning whopper. The weekend-long **Eastport Salmon Festival** (ME) hosts entertainers and crafts artists. At the **Annual Seafood Festival** in Hampton Beach (NH), you can sample the seafood specialties of more than 50 local restaurants, dance to live bands, and watch fireworks explode over the ocean.

➤ OCTOBER: The **Fryeburg Fair** (ME) presents agricultural exhibits, harness racing, an iron-skillet-throwing contest, and a pig scramble. The **Nantucket Cranberry Harvest** in Massachusetts is a three-day celebration including bog and inn tours and a crafts fair. Connecticut's Quiet Corner holds a **Walking Weekend,** with 50 guided scenic walks through the towns, along rivers, and in the woods of this rural area.

➤ NOVEMBER: In Vermont there are two major events in this otherwise quiet month: The **International Film Festival** presents films dealing with environmental, human rights, and political issues for a week in Burlington, and the **Bradford Wild Game Supper** draws thousands to taste large and small game animals and birds.

INDEX

NOTES

FODOR'S NEW ENGLAND

EDITOR: Linda Cabasin

Editorial Contributors: Michelle Bodak Acri, Dorothy Antczak, Natalie Engler, Paula J. Flanders, Carolyn Heller, Robert Kahn, Karl Luntta, Robert Nadeau, Hilary M. Nangle, J. Amanda Nielsen, Lauren Paul, Seth Rolbein, Bill Scheller, Kay Scheller, Anne Stuart, K. D. Weaver

Editorial Production: Melissa Klurman

Maps: David Lindroth, *cartographer;* Steven Amsterdam and Bob Blake, *map editors*

Design: Fabrizio La Rocca, *creative director;* Guido Caroti, *associate art director;* Jolie Novak, *photo editor;* Melanie Marin, *photo researcher*

Production/Manufacturing: Rebecca Zeiler

PHOTOGRAPHY

Kevin Galvin, cover (Warwick, MA.).

Attitash Bear Peak: Sharon McNeil, p. 12E.

Balsams Grand Resort Hotel, p.10B.

Biba, p. 30E.

The Golden Lamb Buttery, p. 30G.

Blaine Harrington, p. 15B.

Historic Merrell Inn, p. 30C.

Robert Holmes, p. 10A.

The Image Bank: Alan Becker, p. 15C. *Walter Bibikow,* p. 7D, 21H. *Bullaty/Lomeo,* p. 12F. *Andy Caulfield,* p. 21J. *Joe Devenney,* p. 7C, 9F, 16D. *Steve Dunwell,* p. 1, 3 bottom right, 11C, 13H, 13I, 17F, 23B, 23C, 25C, 25D, 25E. *Brett Froomer,* p. 24 center. *David W. Hamilton,* p. 19B. *Patti McConville,* p. 9E, 17 bottom right. *Paul McCormick,* p. 6 top. *Michael Melford,* p. 2 bottom left, 4-5, 7B, 8, 9 center, 15 bottom right, 16E, 18 top, 24A, 32. *Derek Redfearn,* p. 3 top left. *Alvis Upitis,* p. 6A. *Pete Turner,* p. 11D. *Stephen Wilkes,* p. 18A.

Inn at Shelburne Farms, p. 2 top left, 30D.

William H. Johnson/Johnson's Photography, p. 13G.

James Lemass, p. 22A.

The Lodge at Moosehead Lake: Macduff Everton, p. 2 top right.

Mad River Glen: T.J. Greenwood, p. 14A.

The Manor on Golden Pond: George W. Gardner, p. 30B.

Manor House: Randy O'Rourke, p. 30J.

The Maritime Aquarium of Norwalk: Norma Mondazzi, p. 24B.

Massachusetts Office of Travel & Tourism: Kindra Clineff, p. 2 bottom center, p. 3 center, 19D, 20E, 20F, 20G, 21I, 30H, 27 bottom.

The Mount Washington Hotel & Resort, p. 27 top.

Nantucket Island Chamber of Commerce: Thomas P. Benincas, Jr., p.19C.

Random House Photo Library, p. 28, 29 top, 29 bottom.

Rhode Island Tourism Division: p. 3 top right. Chuck Browning, p. 23 bottom.

Smugglers' Notch Resort, p. 30I.

State of Vermont Department of Tourism, p. 2 bottom right.

Sugarloaf/USA: p. 30A. Gary Pearl, p.3 bottom left.

Ullikana Bar Harbor, p. 30F.

Vermont Travel & Tourism, p. 17G.

COPYRIGHT

ISBN 0–679–00320–7

ISSN 0192–3412

IMPORTANT TIP

Although all prices, opening times, and other details in this book are based on information supplied to us at press time, changes occur all the time in the travel world, and Fodor's cannot accept responsibility for facts that become outdated or for inadvertent errors or omissions. So always **confirm information when it matters,** especially if you're making a detour to visit a specific place.

SPECIAL SALES

Fodor's Travel Publications are available at special discounts for bulk purchases for sales promotions or premiums. Special editions, including personalized covers, excerpts of existing guides, and corporate imprints, can be created in large quantities for special needs. For more information, contact your local bookseller or write to Special Markets, Fodor's Travel Publications, 201 East 50th Street, New York, NY 10022. Inquiries from Canada should be directed to your local Canadian bookseller or sent to Random House of Canada, Ltd., Marketing Department, 2775 Matheson Boulevard East, Mississauga, Ontario L4W 4P7. Inquiries from the United Kingdom should be sent to Fodor's Travel Publications, 20 Vauxhall Bridge Road, London SW1V 2SA, England.

PRINTED IN THE UNITED STATES OF AMERICA

10 9 8 7 6 5 4 3 2 1

ABOUT OUR WRITERS

Every Y2K trip is a significant trip. So if there was ever a time you needed excellent travel information, it's now. Acutely aware of that fact, we've pulled out all stops in preparing Fodor's *New England 2000*. To help you zero in on what to see in New England, we've gathered some great color photos of the key sights in every state. To show you how to put it all together, we've created great itineraries and neighborhood walks. And to direct you to the places that are truly worth your time and money in this important year, we've rallied the team of endearingly picky know-it-alls we're pleased to call our writers. Having seen all corners of the regions they cover for us, they're real experts. If you knew them, you'd poll them for tips yourself.

Michelle Bodak Acri, who wrote a new introduction to Connecticut, has lived in the Nutmeg State for 30 years, the last eight of them working as an editor for *Connecticut* magazine.

J. Amanda Nielsen, updater of the Connecticut chapter, lived in the state for 15 years before moving near Boston in 1999. She graduated from the University of Connecticut and worked for two years as an editor for *Connecticut* magazine.

Hilary M. Nangle, formerly travel editor for a daily newspaper in Maine, is now a freelancer based in the state's scenic midcoast. She writes regularly about travel, food, and skiing for publications in the United States and Canada.

Originally from Maine but now an 18-year-resident of New Hampshire, **Paula J. Flanders** writes travel features for newspapers and magazines around the country. New Hampshire, her Fodor's territory, remains one of her favorite subjects.

A number of talented writers worked on the Massachusetts chapter. Boston lodging updater **Natalie Engler** is a senior editor at *Information Week*. **Carolyn Heller,** a Cambridge-based travel writer, provided the latest updates on Boston Side Trips, the North Shore, Cape Cod, Martha's Vineyard, and Nantucket. **Robert Kahn,** who writes headlines for the *Boston Sun-* *day Herald,* checked out the latest developments in Cambridge. **Robert Nadeau** writes a dining column for the *Boston Phoenix* and updates Boston dining for Fodor's. Boston exploring updater **Lauren Paul** loves to stroll along Newbury Street; in her more productive mode, she covers technology, business, and parenting issues. Boston nightlife and the arts scout **Anne Stuart** has written for *The Washington Post, The Boston Globe,* and *Boston* magazine, among others.

Rhode Island updater **K. D. Weaver,** a transplant to the state from Maine, is the editor of the weekly *Block Island Times* and a stringer for the Associated Press. Following the renaissance of Providence has been a particular interest.

Kay and Bill Scheller, who revised the Vermont chapter as well as the Berkshires and Pioneer Valley sections of Massachusetts, have a total of more than 30 years' experience as contributors to Fodor's guides. They are the authors of several books on travel in New England and the Northeast. The Schellers live in northern Vermont.

Fodor's editor **Linda Cabasin** has hiked Newport's Cliff Walk on a crisp October weekend and walked Boston's Freedom Trail on a warm July 4. She loves introducing her son to favorite New England places, from Cape Cod to Mystic Seaport in Connecticut.

Don't Forget to Write

We love feedback—positive and negative—and follow up on all suggestions. So contact the New England editor at editors@fodors.com or c/o Fodor's, 201 East 50th Street, New York, New York 10022. Have a wonderful trip!

Karen Cure
Editorial Director